1950	1951	1952	1953	1954	1955	1956	1957	1958	1959	1960	1961	1962	1963	1964
192.1	208.1	219.1	232.6	239.8	257.9	270.6	285.3	294.6	316.3	330.7	341.1	361.9	381.7	409.3
55.1	60.5	53.5	54.9	54.1	69.7	72.7	71.1	63.6	80.2	78.2	77.1	87.6	93.1	99.6
38.8	60.4	75.8	82.8	76.0	75.3	79.7	87.3	95.4	97.9	100.6	108.4	118.2	123.8	130.0
2.2	4.5	3.2	1.3	2.6	3.0	5.3	7.3	3.3	1.5	5.9	7.2	6.9	8.2	10.9
288.3	333.4	351.6	371.6	372.5	405.9	428.2	451.0	456.8	495.8	515.3	533.8	574.6	606.9	649.8
23.6	27.2	29.2	30.9	32.5	34.4	38.1	41.1	42.8	44.6	46.4	47.8	49.4	51.4	53.9
264.4	306.2	322.5	340.7	340.0	371.5	390.1	409.9	414.0	451.2	468.9	486.1	525.2	555.5	595.9
24.6	28.9	30.9	34.1	33.7	35.2	33.8	37.1	39.0	42.0	44.0	47.1	51.9	55.2	58.3
239.8	277.3	291.6	306.6	306.3	336.3	356.3	372.8	375.0	409.2	424.9	439.0	473.3	500.3	537.6
7.4	8.8	9.3	9.6	10.6	12.0	13.5	15.5	15.9	18.8	21.9	22.9	25.4	28.5	30.1
17.9	22.6	19.4	20.3	17.6	22.0	22.0	21.4	19.0	23.6	22.7	22.8	24.0	26.2	28.0
8.2	8.8	9.6	8.6	9.9	14.8	12.6	12.4	10.0	15.6	13.9	14.2	19.9	21.9	25.4
21.8	19.4	20.5	22.4	24.8	26.7	29.0	32.8	37.0	39.5	43.0	46.9	49.2	52.6	56.1
228.1	256.5	273.8	290.5	293.0	314.2	337.2	356.3	367.1	390.7	409.4	426.0	453.2	476.3	510.2
20.6	28.9	34.0	35.5	32.5	35.4	39.7	42.4	42.2	46.1	50.5	52.2	57.0	60.5	58.8
207.5	227.6	239.8	255.1	260.5	278.8	297.5	313.9	324.9	344.6	358.9	373.8	396.2	415.8	451.4
1,203.7	1,328.2	1,328.2	1,435.3	1,416.2	1,494.9	1,525.6	1,551.1	1,539.2	1,629.1	1,665.3	1,708.7	1,799.4	1,873.3	1,973.3
8.5	10.3	3.9	4.0	−1.3	5.6	2.1	1.7	−.8	5.8	2.2	2.6	5.3	4.1	5.3
791.8	819.0	844.3	880.0	894.0	944.5	989.4	1,012.1	1,028.8	1,067.2	1,091.1	1,123.2	1,170.2	1,207.3	1,291.0

1950	1951	1952	1953	1954	1955	1956	1957	1958	1959	1960	1961	1962	1963	1964
24.1	26.0	26.5	26.7	26.9	26.8	27.2	28.1	28.9	29.1	29.6	29.9	30.2	30.6	31.0
1.3	7.9	1.9	.8	.7	−.4	1.5	3.3	2.8	.7	1.7	1.0	1.0	1.3	1.3
33.1	35.9	37.2	40.4	38.2	43.0	44.9	45.5	42.6	47.7	48.8	49.1	53.2	56.3	60.1
114.1	119.2	125.2	128.3	130.3	134.5	136.0	136.8	138.4	141.0	141.8	146.5	149.2	154.7	161.9
152.3	154.9	157.6	160.2	163.0	165.9	168.9	172.0	174.9	177.8	180.7	183.7	186.5	189.2	191.9
62.2	62.0	62.1	63.0	63.6	65.0	66.6	66.9	67.6	68.4	69.6	70.5	70.6	71.8	73.1
3.3	2.1	1.9	1.8	3.5	2.9	2.8	2.9	4.6	3.7	3.9	4.7	3.9	4.1	3.8
5.3	3.3	3.0	2.9	5.5	4.4	4.1	4.3	6.8	5.5	5.5	6.7	5.5	5.7	5.2
51.7	53.8	55.4	57.5	58.4	60.1	60.9	62.5	64.4	66.5	67.6	70.0	72.5	75.4	78.7
8.3	4.0	3.1	3.6	1.6	3.0	1.3	2.6	3.0	3.3	1.7	3.5	3.6	4.0	4.3

(Continued on back cover)

ECONOMICS

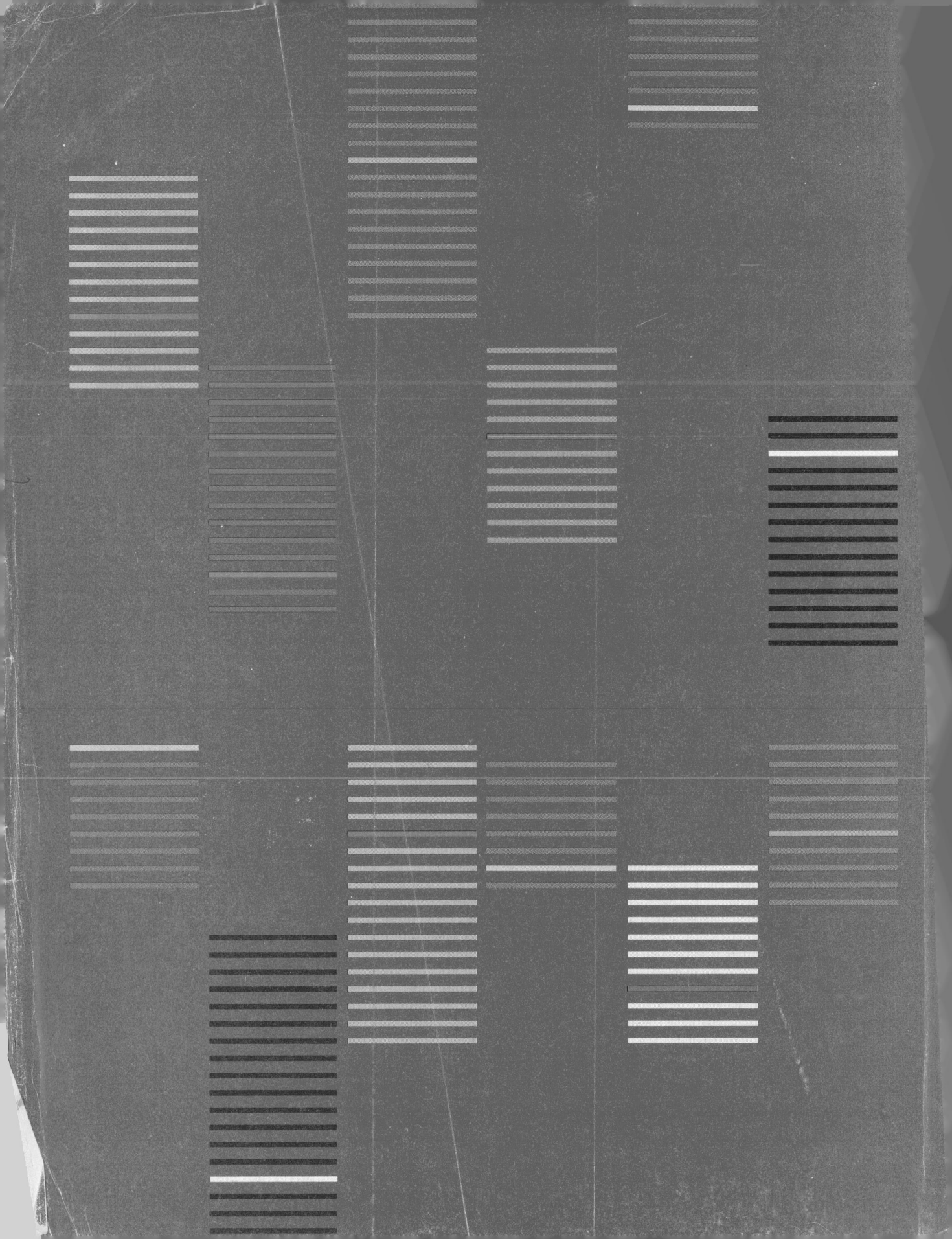

ECONOMICS

PRINCIPLES, PROBLEMS, AND POLICIES

ELEVENTH EDITION

CAMPBELL R. McCONNELL

Professor of Economics, University of Nebraska—Lincoln

STANLEY L. BRUE

Professor of Economics, Pacific Lutheran University

McGraw-Hill Publishing Company

New York   St. Louis   San Francisco   Auckland   Bogotá   Caracas   Hamburg   Lisbon   London   Madrid   Mexico
Milan   Montreal   New Delhi   Oklahoma City   Paris   San Juan   São Paulo   Singapore   Sydney   Tokyo   Toronto

Economics: Principles, Problems, and Policies

1 2 3 4 5 6 7 8 9 0 VNH VNH 8 9 4 3 2 1 0 9

ISBN 0-07-044967-8

This book was set in Baskerville by York Graphic Services, Inc.

The editors were Scott D. Stratford, Michael R. Elia, and Edwin Hanson;

the production supervisor was Salvador Gonzales.

The design was done by Binns & Lubin.

The drawings were done by J & R Services, Inc.

Von Hoffmann Press, Inc., was printer and binder.

Library of Congress Cataloging-in-Publication Data

McConnell, Campbell R.
   Economics: principles, problems, and policies /
Campbell R. McConnell, Stanley L. Brue.—11th ed.
     p.   cm.
   Includes index.
   ISBN 0-07-044967-8
   1. Economics.   I. Brue, Stanley L., (date).
   II. Title.
HB171.5.M47   1990
   330—dc20   89-12570

About the authors

Campbell R. McConnell earned his Ph.D. from the University of Iowa after receiving degrees from Cornell College and the University of Illinois. He is currently Carl Adolph Happold Professor of Economics at the University of Nebraska—Lincoln, where he has taught since 1953. He is also coauthor of *Contemporary Labor Economics,* 2d ed. (McGraw-Hill) and has edited readers for the principles and labor economics courses. He is a contributor to the recently published volume *The Principles of Economics Course: A Handbook for Instructors* (McGraw-Hill). He is a recipient of the University of Nebraska Distinguished Teaching Award and is past-president of the Midwest Economics Association. His primary areas of interest are labor economics and economic education. He has an extensive collection of jazz recordings and enjoys reading jazz history.

Stanley L. Brue did his undergraduate work at Augustana College (S.D.) and received his Ph.D from the University of Nebraska—Lincoln. He teaches at Pacific Lutheran University, where he has been honored as a recipient of the Burlington Northern Faculty Achievement Award for classroom excellence and professional accomplishment. He teaches courses in principles of economics, labor economics, industrial organization, and the history of economic thought. Professor Brue is coauthor of *Economic Scenes: Theory in Today's World,* 4th ed. (Prentice-Hall); *The Evolution of Economic Thought,* 4th ed. (Harcourt Brace Jovanovich); and *Contemporary Labor Economics,* 2d ed. (McGraw-Hill). For relaxation, he enjoys boating on Puget Sound, salmon fishing, and skiing trips with his family.

To Mem
and to Terri and Craig

Contents in brief

Contents

Note: The global symbol 🌐 appears below in all chapter sections with substantial global content.

Part I
An introduction to economics and the economy

Part 2
National income, employment, and fiscal policy

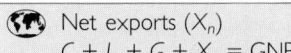

Part 3
Money, banking, and monetary policy

Part 4
Problems and controversies in macroeconomics

Part 5
The economics of the firm and resource allocation

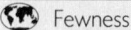

Part 6
Current economic problems

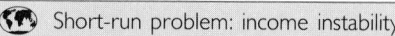

Part 7
International economics and the world economy

Preface

This eleventh edition is the most extensive revision since *Economics* was first published in 1960. The sweeping character of this revision reflects a number of mutually reinforcing considerations. Most importantly, a coauthor has joined *Economics,* bringing with him an abundance of new ideas relating to content, organization, and pedagogy.

OVERVIEW OF THE REVISION

Deferring a detailed discussion of this revision for a moment, let us first note that four major objectives have permeated our revision efforts.

Internationalization We have been very aware of the need to internationalize our presentation. Examples, applications, and, more importantly, analysis and policy have all been substantially reconceived to reflect the globalization of the American economy. The chapter-by-chapter synopsis of specific changes later in this preface will make clear the extensiveness of our efforts in pursuing this goal. To identify at a glance each section where our coverage has been globalized, we have inserted this symbol (🌐) in the Contents.

Macroeconomics Perhaps the most pervasive controversies in economics over the past decade or so have been in macroeconomics. Hence, a great amount of our energy was devoted to rewriting and restructuring the chapters comprising macroeconomics. Briefly, the main changes in the approach to macro are as follows:
- The aggregate demand–aggregate supply model has been extensively reworked to stress the difference between the determinants of the shapes of the aggregate demand and aggregate supply curves and the various curve shifters or non-price-level determinants of the curves.
- We more fully integrate the aggregate demand–aggregate supply model throughout the text.
- We have emphasized the strong intellectual ties

of monetarism and rational expectations theory to classical economics.
- The differences in the competing macro paradigms have been brought into much sharper focus. These include differences in assumptions, analytical conclusions, and policy proscriptions.
- The locations of the various macro chapters have been significantly altered. In particular, the chapters on the inflation-unemployment tradeoff and the public debt (Chapters 19 and 20) now follow Part 3 on money and monetary policy. We feel that this reorganization will substantially enhance student understanding of Chapters 19 and 20.

Modern topics We have made a special effort to add modern topics throughout the book. This will become apparent in our detailed description of changes in the edition. Just a few examples are state lotteries, economics of crime, the Coase theorem, current eclectic Federal Reserve policy, the median voter model, the U.S.—Canadian Free-Trade pact, antidumping duties in foreign trade, Gorbachev's reform program, intervention on exchange markets by the Group of Seven (G-7) nations, capital flight from the less developed countries, the impacts of airline deregulation, rent-seeking activity, the newly revised index of economic indicators, "real" business cycle theory, "*P*-star" as a monetary tool, and the savings and loan crisis. In short, we have endeavored to make the new edition a book for the 1990s.

Pedagogy In this revision we have been especially alert for opportunities to improve pedagogy. For example:
- All diagrams have been redrawn. A number of new diagrams and tables have been added to make it easier for the student to visualize the interrelation of concepts involved in some of the more complicated discussions. Tables 17-3, 19-1, and 23-3 and Figures 14-3, 16-2, 17-1, and 36-1 are illustrative.

- Many examples have been recast to enhance the interest of today's teachers and students. Long-time adopters will find, for example, that bread and drill presses have given way to pizzas and industrial robots.
- We have carefully pruned and consolidated material where it was possible to do so without losing the sense or style of the writing.
- The Last Word minireadings have been relocated to enhance their visibility and use.
- End-of-chapter questions have been carefully revised and updated.
- *Test Bank I* has been revitalized with the addition of 860 new multiple-choice questions. Furthermore, in both test banks questions are now grouped by topic or concept, are sequenced to match the outline of each chapter, and are designated by type of question (definitional, conceptual, graphical, etc.). This reordering of questions will facilitate their usefulness in test construction.
- The revised *Instructor's Resource Manual* now contains suggested answers to *all* the text's end-of-chapter questions.
- Chapter 1 contains a new appendix on the construction and interpretation of graphs.
- For the first time in this new revision individual paperback volumes on *Microeconomics* and *Macroeconomics* are available to more fully meet the needs of instructors and students.
- New state-of-the-art computerized materials have been generated for student use.
- Other pedagogical improvements permeate the eleventh edition package as will be noted in the ensuing discussion of the details of the revision.

Previous users of *Economics* will immediately note that the text is two chapters shorter than in the previous edition. This was accomplished as follows. The chapter on radical economics (Chapter 40 in the tenth edition) was deleted. The two chapters on economic growth (Chapter 21 and 22 in the previous edition) were reconceived as one chapter. The material on international economic issues in Chapter 43 of the tenth edition was either integrated into other chapters or deleted. As a partial offset to this three-chapter reduction, an essentially new chapter on government and economic policy, Chapter 33, has been added as an introduction to Part 6's series of chapters on economic problems and issues.

THE REVISION PROCESS

We undertook the most ambitious revision efforts in the book's history to ensure that the eleventh edition will continue to meet the needs of the modern principles course.

To a significant extent, this revision represents the results of two detailed questionnaires prepared by the publisher. One was rather broad and intended to survey in general teachers of principles of economics; the other was specifically intended to survey instructors who recently taught from the tenth edition of *Economics*. The general survey produced approximately 500 responses, comprising nearly a one-third response rate, from instructors who indicated what they desired in a principles textbook for the 1990s. The specific survey elicited seventy-five responses from adopters who indicated their preferences, their priorities in covering various topics, their evaluations of the pedagogical aids, and their suggestions, identifying in detail the changes they felt should be made in this new edition.

This revision also reflects the results of detailed reviews obtained from more than fifty economists—some current users of the text, some not. Many provided complete reviews of the tenth edition; others provided complete reviews of the manuscript representing the entire eleventh edition as it developed; some did both. And a number of reviewers who concentrate their teaching and writing in particular areas, such as macroeconomics, money and banking, and international economics, examined our treatment of these topics. In a few cases, these specialist reviewers sent us "back to square one" causing us to rework a section or rethink the organization of material and resubmit it to them once again for further assessment. This process continued until the reviewers were satisfied we treated "their" topics properly and sufficiently within the scope of a principles course, and we were satisfied we were treating that material soundly and at a level which a principles student can understand.

To further assure clarity, a senior editor at McGraw-Hill undertook the task of reading the most heavily revised chapters, examining them in detail from the perspective of an average student and suggesting changes in both organization and presentation that would make the material easier to read and understand.

We trust that the outcome of this detailed revision is a text which is clearly superior to its predecessor.

Although the eleventh edition bears only a modest resemblance to the first, the basic purpose remains the same—to introduce the beginning economics student to those principles essential to an understanding of the fundamental economic problems and the policy alternatives society may utilize to contend with these problems. It is hoped that the ability to reason accurately and objectively about economic matters and the development of a lasting interest in economics will be two valuable byproducts of this basic objective. Our intention remains to present the principles and problems of economics in a straightforward, logical fashion. To this end, great stress continues to be put upon clarity of presentation and organization.

THE REVISION IN DETAIL

What's new in this eleventh edition and what makes it different from the previous edition?

Part I Introduction *Chapter 1* on methodology has been thoroughly reworked and reorganized. The roles of inductive and deductive reasoning are clarified and treated earlier in the chapter as is the difference between micro- and macroeconomics. The differences between positive and normative economics are made explicit and illustrated. The chapter now ends with a new section on "the economic perspective" wherein the roles of rational behavior and cost-benefit comparisons are introduced. A new Last Word provides a factual profile of the American economy. A new appendix on the understanding of graphic analysis has been added.

Chapter 2 has been tightened by deferring treatment of the "five fundamental questions" to Chapter 5. A new application of the production possibilities curve focuses upon international specialization and our recent trade deficits. A new Last Word discusses the reallocation of resources implicit in the Gorbachev reforms.

Several modest changes are incorporated in *Chapter 3*. For example, a distinction is made between self-interest and selfishness; the definition of

a market is made more explicit; and several international examples have been added. The new Last Word deals with specialization based upon comparative advantage.

In *Chapter 4* on individual markets, the discussions of the determinants of demand and supply have been carefully reworked and illustrations have been updated and extended. A new capstone section at the end of the chapter considers the foreign exchange market as a prelude to the internationalization of Parts 2, 3, and 4. A new Last Word explores the supply and demand for physician services.

Chapter 5 now begins with an introduction to the five fundamental questions prior to outlining how a competitive market system functions. This chapter's final section on big business has been extensively rewritten.

Chapter 6 has been substantially condensed in that it now focuses exclusively on the basic economic functions of government. Material concerned with the evaluation of government's role and public choice theory has been shifted to the new Chapter 33. In addition, the graphical analysis of externalities has been recast for greater clarity and the circular flow model has been reconceived to provide a better perception of how government affects the economy. The chapter summary has been reworked and expanded as have the end-of-chapter questions.

In *Chapter 7* the sections on the household and business sectors have been judiciously trimmed to make room for a new section on the international sector. Here we indicate the quantitative importance of world trade, show the relationship of world trade to finance, and point out several of the more salient economic implications of trade.

In *Chapter 8* the material on the personal income tax has been rewritten and shortened to reflect the new tax legislation. The section on the overall tax structure has also been rewritten and the concluding section now stresses two issues: the relationship of the tax structure to reindustrialization and tax changes designed to reduce the Federal budget deficit. The new Last Word discusses state lotteries and the controversy surrounding them.

Part 2 Macroeconomics In *Chapter 9* an important new section on measuring the price level has been added prior to the discussion of nominal and real GNP. Other changes include a reworking of the chapter introduction, pedagogical improvements in the value-added table, the addition of exports and imports to the circular flow diagram, and an updating of the discussion of the underground economy. The Last Word on the CPI has been revised and updated.

Chapter 10 features a new table and brief discussion which present international comparisons of unemployment and inflation rates. The section on cost-push inflation has been reworked for greater clarity and to stress the self-limiting character of such inflation. Other changes include clarifications in the sections on frictional and cyclical unemployment; the addition of specific data on part-time and discouraged workers; and a comparison of disaggregated unemployment rates for the 1982 recession year and the 1988 full employment year. The new Last Word is concerned with the potential impact of changes in stock prices upon the economy.

The purpose of *Chapter 11* has been altered. Rather than an overview of macroeconomics, it is now designed as a springboard for the macro theory which follows. Hence, much of the material in this chapter is new to the eleventh edition. A new opening section stresses the importance of a macro model and the ensuing discussions of aggregate demand and aggregate supply elaborate non-price-level determinants, that is, the factors which shift the aggregate demand and supply curves. Tenth edition material on stabilization policies has been excised and repositioned in later chapters.

The aggregate demand–aggregate supply comparison of classical and Keynesian economics has been reviewed in *Chapter 12* in the interest of greater clarity and to emphasize that classical economists envisioned that, with a stable money supply, aggregate demand would also be stable. Other changes include the addition of a second panel to the classical interest rate diagram to further demonstrate why a rightward shift of the saving curve allegedly would not result in a surplus of savings. Students are also reminded that a price level change can cause a change in investment through the interest rate effect

The tenth edition's appendix material on international trade and equilibrium output has been simplified and integrated into the body of *Chapter*

13. The section in which the aggregate demand curve is derived from the Keynesian expenditures model now incorporates discussions of the wealth, interest-rate, and foreign-purchases effects.

Chapter 14 on fiscal policy contains several notable revisions. Exports and imports are now included in the discussion of discretionary policy and an entire new section on fiscal policy in an open economy has been introduced. The distinction between cyclical and structural deficits is now included in the full-employment budget material and the discussion of the automatic stabilizers has been restated and condensed. A new Last Word introduces and discusses the newly revised index of leading economic indicators.

Part 3 Money   Chapters 15, 16, and 17 in this edition appeared as Chapters 17, 18, and 19 in the tenth edition.

In *Chapter 15* the discussion of money market equilibrium has been expanded and clarified by incorporating the relationship between interest rates and bond prices. The tenth edition's Last Word on the Monetary Control Act of 1980 has been dropped, but some of its more important provisions are now presented in the body of the chapter. The chapter now features a fascinating Last Word on the widespread use of beer as money in Angola.

Instructors will find two visible changes in *Chapter 16*. First, we have added a diagram showing the relationship between an initial new deposit in the banking system and the resulting multiple-deposit expansion of the money supply. Second, there is a new Last Word on bank and thrift failures.

The introductory material in *Chapter 17* has been tightened so that the discussion moves quickly into how the Fed controls the money supply. In this regard, a new diagram has been added to help students better understand open-market operations. In particular, the diagram clarifies the distinction between the Fed's purchase of securities from a commercial bank and from the general public. Discussion of the Keynesian cause-effect chain of monetary policy is deferred to the section on "Monetary policy, equilibrium NNP, and the price level." The presentation of easy and tight money policies included in this section has been improved and Table 17-3 has been added to provide a recapitulation. The section dealing with the shortcomings of monetary policy has been condensed and recent policies are discussed. An important section on the linkages of monetary policy to the international economy has been included. Similarly, net exports have been added to Figure 17-3's summary of Keynesian theory.

Part 4 Macro issues In this eleventh edition *Chapter 18* on monetarism and rational expectations theory (RET) has been regrouped with three other chapters to constitute a unit on problems and controversies in macroeconomics.

Chapter 18 has undergone a thorough revision which includes a restatement of the monetarist transmission mechanism; the use of aggregate demand–aggregate supply analysis to explain the monetary rule and the Keynesian criticism thereof; and a linking of RET to the general rationality assumptions which underlie economics. The decline in money velocity which has occurred since 1982 is also noted. The new Last Word deals with the Federal Reserve's experimental "*P*-star" tool for forecasting long-term inflation.

Chapter 19 on the inflation-unemployment relationship also embodies fundamental changes. Its new location after the money and banking chapters and the chapter on monetarism and RET allows students to more easily grasp the issues and policies examined therein. In terms of content the introductory discussion of the Phillips Curve has been shortened and the simple graphics of demand-pull and cost-push inflation has been deleted. New material on the decline of inflation during the 1980s has been inserted. The "accelerationist" view of the Phillips Curve is now recast as the natural rate theory and the discussion is rewritten to distinguish between short-run and long-run Phillips Curves. The model is now used to explain disinflation as well as inflation. Material on the new classical distinction between short- and long-run aggregate supply curves is introduced and demand-pull and cost-push inflation are now considered in this context. The model itself is treated as an outgrowth of the natural rate criticisms of Keynesianism. The discussion of policy options for combatting stagflation has been greatly condensed. A new table (Table 19-1) summarizes and contrasts the views of Keynesians, monetarists, rational expectationists, and supply siders. The new

classical "real" business cycle theory is the topic of the new Last Word.

Revisions in *Chapter 20* on budget deficits and the public debt include new material on the deficit's relationship to the United States' debtor nation status; a brief discussion of the new classical view of deficits; an updating of the Gramm-Rudman-Hollings law; and a discussion of the line item veto as a means of reducing deficits. The new Last Word presents the provocative view that higher taxes may *increase* the budget deficit.

Chapter 21 on economic growth is a consolidation of the tenth edition's Chapters 21 and 22. Much of the material on growth theory has been omitted and the treatment of the growth controversy has been greatly condensed. The discussion of the productivity slowdown has been revised and centers upon new data (Table 21-4). A new Last Word explores the possibility that our poor productivity performance in recent years is attributable largely to inadequate public investment in the economy's infrastructure.

Part 5 Microeconomics In *Chapter 22* the discussion of the total revenue test for elasticity has been modestly extended for greater clarity and a second panel has been added to Figure 22-3 to reinforce the total revenue-price elasticity relationship. The section on legal prices contains a new segment on the expected economic effects of interest rate ceilings on credit cards. A new study of commuter rail transportation is summarized to illustrate the impact of time upon price elasticity of demand and to apply the total revenue test. The material on excise tax incidence has been shifted to Chapter 33.

The major changes in *Chapter 23* on consumer behavior are pedagogical. A new table (Table 23-3) explains the utility-maximizing rule by sequence of purchase and a new end-of-chapter question ties the rule to a downsloping demand curve. A new Last Word deals with the diamond-water paradox.

In *Chapter 24* the discussion of diminishing returns has been carefully rewritten for greater clarity and a short section has been added to explain shifts in the average cost curves. The material on diseconomies of scale has been reworked and updated as has the Last Word on scale economies and industry concentration.

The changes in *Chapter 25* are mostly pedagogical in nature. For example, students are reminded of the factors which shift the short-run supply curve; the discussion of the exodus of firms from a competitive industry has been slightly extended; and Figure 25-6 which identifies the marginal cost curve as the firm's short-run supply curve has been redrawn for greater clarity.

Chapter 26 on monopoly embodies several notable changes. The material on entry barriers has been reorganized and slightly expanded. A new diagram elaborates the price-marginal revenue relationship. The discussion of price discrimination has been reorganized and the diagram illustrating regulated monopoly has been reconceived. An extended end-of-chapter problem explores the relationships between price elasticity, total revenue, and marginal revenue.

The section on product differentiation in *Chapter 27* has been redone to explicitly sort out the various aspects of differentiation and to add new examples. The material on advertising includes new empirical evidence and brings the pro- and anticompetitive views of advertising into sharper focus. A new Last Word employs the "prisoners' dilemma" to explain why firms might spend too much on advertising.

In *Chapter 28* the discussion of obstacles to oligopolistic collusion is now followed by a section which relates these obstacles to OPEC. The case study of the automobile industry has been substantially rewritten and updated. A revised Last Word explores the oligopolistic structure of the beer industry.

The changes in *Chapter 29* on resource demand are primarily pedagogical. For example, new examples of changes in resource demand are included; the section on the profit-maximizing combination of inputs has been simplified; and a new quantitative end-of-chapter problem has been added.

Chapter 30 on wage determination features a large number of modest changes. For example, the characteristics of purely competitive and monopolistic labor markets are made more explicit; rising opportunity costs are stressed in explaining upsloping labor supply curves; and the discussions of inclusive unionism and the minimum wage have both been slightly extended.

In *Chapter 31* the discussion of Henry George's single tax has been condensed and simplified and Table 31-1 has been added to emphasize the wide range of interest rates which exist. New material on the loanable funds theory of interest has been written for the microeconomic paperback volume.

Chapter 32 on general equilibrium has been extensively revised and shortened. In particular, the tenth edition's illustration of the automobile industry has been replaced with an extended discussion of both the domestic and international ramifications of the OPEC oil price increases. The discussion of the welfare implications of the competitive market system has been sharply pruned.

Part 6 Current problems Aside from materials shifted from the tenth edition's Chapters 6, 24, and 37, the contents of *Chapter 33* on government and public policy are new. This chapter examines important aspects of public finance and the theory of public choice. Specifically, it includes discussions of the optimal output of a public good; the Coase theorem; the excess burden of an excise tax; and the revealing of preferences through majority voting. The new Last Word on Pentagon coal purchases presents an interesting example of the special-interest effect (rent-seeking activity). We feel this chapter provides a useful prelude to the more topical chapters of Part 6 which follow.

Chapter 34 on antitrust and regulation includes a number of changes. A new brief section on the "superior product" defense of business monopoly has been added; the IBM case is mentioned to illustrate the resurgence of the "rule of reason"; material on the Reagan administration's interpretation of antitrust has been condensed; and the sections on airline deregulation and social regulation have been extensively rewritten and updated.

Chapter 35 on the farm problem has also been changed significantly. The section outlining the history of the farm problem had been extended through the 1970s and 1980s. The material on the rationale for farm policies has been tightened and the discussion of farm policy now focuses primarily upon price supports and considers their international implications. The new Last Word is an internationally oriented analysis of the sugar program.

The treatment of urban economics in *Chapter 36* features the following changes: a new figure (Figure 36-1) is the focal point for an entirely rewritten discussion of internal and external economies of scale; the "black underclass" hypothesis is outlined in the discussion of central-city poverty;

new material on mass-transit pricing is included; and the discussion of pollution is considerably condensed in lieu of its treatment in Chapter 33.

In *Chapter 37* on income inequality and poverty the tenth edition's material on discrimination has been moved to Chapter 38. The discussion of income distribution by quintiles has been elaborated to include the recent trend toward greater inequality. Our discussion of the effect of taxes and government benefits on the distribution of income has been upgraded through the inclusion of the findings from an important new Census Bureau study. New material and a graph on the poverty rate appear as does a concluding section on the "workfare" approach to poverty reduction. The new Last Word follows up on this discussion with a detailed look at the new welfare reform law.

Chapter 38 on labor market issues addresses three topics which can be treated individually, as a group, or not at all. The primary topic—unionism and its economic implications—has been accorded some rewrite and updating. The second topic is labor market discrimination which is relocated from Chapter 37. Immigration, the final topic, has been relocated from the tenth edition's Chapter 43. A new Last Word on the Immigration Reform and Control Act of 1986 concludes the chapter.

Part 7 World economy *Chapter 39* on comparative advantage and protectionism includes the following changes: a section on the "antidumping" argument for protection has been added; the agenda of the Uruguay Round of GATT negotiations is presented; the U.S.-Canadian free-trade agreement is discussed; the relationship between U.S. trade deficits and protectionist pressures is analyzed; and new data on the costs of protection are included.

Chapter 40 on exchange rates and the balance of payments now includes a thorough discussion of the causes, consequences, and possible solutions to the U.S. trade imbalance. The chapter ends with a new Last Word on how the rise in the value of the yen has affected the dollar prices of goods and services in Tokyo.

In *Chapter 41* on the less developed countries the descriptive material which introduces the chapter has been condensed; a more diverse classification of nations is presented; the discussions of unemployment and labor productivity have been reworked; the "capital flight" problem is intro-

duced; the treatment of the role of government in development has been extended and reconceived for a more balanced presentation; and the section on the LDC debt crisis has been entirely rewritten and augmented with a new diagram (Figure 41-2) and table (Table 41-4).

Chapter 42 on the Soviet economy has also been subjected to a major overhaul. The material on the Soviet economic performance has been reworked and a new table (Table 42-1) compares U.S. and U.S.S.R. growth records. More importantly, the tenth edition's "general evaluation" and "U.S.S.R. in crisis?" sections have been deleted in favor of an extended discussion of the Gorbachev reforms. The new Last Word provides interesting insights as to what *perestroika* means for a Soviet tractor factory.

"Last word" minireadings Our survey indicated that many instructors appreciate the "Last Word" minireadings which appear toward the conclusion of each chapter. These selections serve several purposes: some provide meaningful real-world applications of economic concepts; others reveal "human interest" aspects of economic problems; and still others extend or challenge the concepts and interpretations of mainstream economics. Twenty-three of the forty-two Last Words are new to the eleventh edition; a number of others have been extensively revised and updated.

PRODUCT DIFFERENTIATION

We feel this text embraces a number of departures in content and organization which perhaps distinguish it from other books in the field.

1 The principles course sometimes fails to provide students with a comprehensive and meaningful definition of economics. To avoid this shortcoming, one complete chapter (Chapter 2) is devoted to a careful statement and development of the economizing problem and an exploration of its implications. The foundation thereby provided should be helpful in putting the many particular subject areas of economics into proper perspective.

2 For better or worse, government is an integral component of modern capitalism. Its economic role, therefore, should not be treated piecemeal or as an afterthought. This text introduces the economic functions of government early and accords

them systematic treatment, in Chapters 6 and 8. Chapter 33 examines salient facets of public finance and public choice theory, serving as a prelude to a group of problem- and policy-oriented chapters.

3 This volume continues to put considerable emphasis upon economic growth. Chapter 2 employs the production possibilities curve to lay bare the basic ingredients of growth. Chapter 21 discusses the rate and causes of American growth, in addition to some of the controversies surrounding growth. Chapter 41 focuses upon the less developed countries and the growth obstacles which confront them. An important segment of Chapter 42 concerns the Soviet Union's growth record. Beyond this it will be found that the chapters on price theory pay special attention to the implications that the various market structures have for technological progress.

4 It is understandable that the elusiveness of general equilibrium analysis eminently qualifies this topic for omission at the principles level. The result, however, is a grievous shortcoming of most introductory courses. A sincere effort is made in this book to remedy this deficiency. Specifically, an entire chapter (Chapter 5) is devoted to the notion of the market system, and another chapter (Chapter 32) explicitly outlines in rather sophisticated terms the nature and significance of general equilibrium analysis.

5 We have purposely given considerable attention to microeconomics in general and to the theory of the firm in particular. There are two reasons for this emphasis. In the first place, the concepts of microeconomics are difficult for most beginning students. Short expositions usually compound these difficulties by raising more questions than they answer. Second, we have coupled analysis of the various market structures with a discussion of the social implications of each. The impact of each market arrangement upon price and output levels, resource allocation, and the rate of technological advance is carefully assessed.

6 Part 6 provides a broad spectrum of chapters on current socioeconomic problems. As most students see it, this is where the action is. We have sought to guide the action along logical lines through the application of appropriate analytical tools. Our bias in Part 6 is in favor of inclusiveness; each instructor can effectively counter this bias by omitting those chapters felt to be less relevant for a particular group of students.

ORGANIZATION AND CONTENT

In terms of organization, this book has been written with the conviction that the basic prerequisite of an understandable economics text is the logical arrangement and clear exposition of subject matter. This concern with organization is perhaps most evident in Part 1, which centers upon the step-by-step development of a comprehensive and realistic picture of American capitalism. This coherent group of introductory chapters is substituted for the traditional smattering of more or less unrelated background topics that frequently introduce the student to the study of economics.

Throughout this volume the exposition of each particular topic and concept is directly related to the level of difficulty which in our experience the average student is likely to encounter. It is for this reason that microeconomics and employment theory are purposely accorded comprehensive and careful treatments. Simplicity in these instances is correlated with comprehensiveness, not brevity. Furthermore, our experience suggests that in the treatment of each basic topic—employment theory, money, and banking, international economics, and so forth—it is highly desirable to couple analysis and policy. A three-step development of basic analytical tools is employed: (1) verbal description and illustration, (2) numerical examples, and (3) graphic presentation based upon these numerical illustrations.

As noted in the summary of major eleventh edition changes, the material is organized around seven basic topics: (1) an introduction to economics and the American economy; (2) macro theory and fiscal policy; (3) money and monetary policy; (4) macroeconomic problems and issues; (5) economics of the firm and resource allocation; (6) current microeconomic problems; and (7) international economics and the world economy.

Part 1 is designed to introduce the method and subject matter of economics and to develop the ideological framework and the factual characteristics of American capitalism. This group of chapters develops in an orderly fashion the overall picture of how our economy operates. After an introduction to the methodology of economics in Chapter 1, an entire chapter is devoted to defining and explaining the economic problem. Chapters 3 to 5 develop the capitalistic ideology and the notion of the most fundamental institution of capitalism—the market system. Early emphasis upon the market system is designed to provide the necessary orientation for the detailed treatment of pricing found in Part 5 and to contribute to an understanding of macroeconomics in Part 2 and, more specifically, the topics of inflation and deflation. Chapter 6 introduces government as a basic economic component of modern capitalism; this short chapter stresses the redistributional, allocative, and stabilization functions of government. Upon this superstructure of a mixed public-private economy, Chapters 7 and 8 add the factual information concerning the private and public sectors of the economy, thereby making our mixed capitalism model much more realistic. However, instructors who wish to minimize institutional-descriptive material may choose to omit Chapters 7 and 8. Those instructors who are especially anxious to embroil their students in macro theory and policy may choose to assign only Chapters 2, 3, and 4 from Part 1.

Part 2 treats macro theory and fiscal policy. Chapter 9 embodies systematic discussions of the national income accounts; measurement of the price level; and the use of price indices to adjust nominal GNP. Some instructors may choose to truncate this discussion by omitting or deemphasizing the income approach to GNP which is less relevant to the ensuing theory chapters than is the expenditures approach. Chapter 10 treats the characteristics, causes, and consequences of cyclical fluctuations. Chapter 11 introduces the aggregate demand–aggregate supply model and the next three chapters are devoted to classical and neo-Keynesian employment theory and to fiscal policy.

Part 3 emphasizes the balance sheet approach to money and banking. This approach seems most in accord with the goal of providing the student with an analytical tool needed in reasoning through, as opposed to memorizing, the economic impact of the various basic banking transactions. Just as fiscal policy is linked directly to income theory in Part 2, monetary policy immediately follows the discussion of money and banking,

The first half of the book is completed with Part 4, consisting of four chapters on current macroeco-

nomic problems and controversies. In Chapter 18 monetarism and rational expectations theory are presented and compared with Keynesianism. Chapter 19 focuses upon how the various macro paradigms view the problem of simultaneous inflation and unemployment. The issues surrounding large budget deficits and the public debt are explored in Chapter 20. Finally, Chapter 21 deals with economic growth and the problems and controversies related thereto.

For reasons already noted, the treatment of pricing and resource allocation in Part 5 is purposely detailed. After Chapter 22's fairly rigorous review of supply and demand and price elasticity, consumer behavior is analyzed in Chapter 23. Then in Chapter 24 we switch to the supply side of the product market and examine short-run and long-run costs. Throughout Chapters 25 to 28 emphasis is placed upon the social implications of the various market structures. What is the significance of each market structure for price and output levels, resource allocation, and technological progress? Emphasis in the discussion of distribution—Chapters 29 to 31—is generally in accord with the relative quantitative importance of the various market shares in our economy. Labor markets are accorded rather extended discussion, but we have not belabored the analysis of rent, interest, and profits. Chapter 32 provides a capstone discussion of general equilibrium, including an introduction to input-output analysis.

Part 6 deals largely with domestic issues: the monopoly problem, the farm problem, the problems of the cities, the economics of inequality and poverty, and several labor market issues. As a prelude to this group of problem- and policy-oriented chapters, Chapter 33 examines some salient aspects of the public sector and public choice theory. In each of the ensuing five chapters an attempt has been made to (1) describe the historical and factual background of the problem, (2) analyze its causes and effects, (3) explore government policy, and (4) offer a thought-provoking discussion of public policy alternatives. As noted, instructors may choose to use the chapters of Part 6 selectively.

Part 7 deals with international economics and the world economy. Although a number of topics explored in Chapters 39 and 40 have been introduced earlier—for example, specialization, exchange rates, and international trade deficits and surpluses—we feel it important to survey international trade and finance systematically and with some rigor. Chapter 41 presents an ov erview of the problems and prospects of the less developed countries. Finally, Chapter 42 offers a fairly comprehensive discussion of the Soviet economy with emphasis upon the Gorbachev reforms.

ORGANIZATIONAL ALTERNATIVES

Though economics instructors are in general agreement as to the basic content of a principles of economics course, there are considerable differences of opinion as to what particular arrangement of material is best. The structure of this book is designed to provide considerable organizational flexibility. And we are happy to report that users of prior editions have informed us that they accomplished substantial rearrangements of chapters with little sacrifice of continuity. Though we have chosen to move from macro- to microeconomics, there is no reason why the introductory material of Part 1 cannot be followed immediately by the microanalysis of Part 5. Similarly, in our judgment money and banking can best be taught after, rather than before, macroeconomics. Those who disagree will encounter no special problems by preceding Chapter 9 with Chapters 15, 16, and 17. Furthermore, some instructors will prefer to intersperse the microeconomics of Part 5 with the problems chapters of Part 6. This is easily accomplished. Chapter 35 on the farm problem may follow Chapter 25 on pure competition; Chapter 34 on antitrust and regulation may follow Chapters 26 to 28 on imperfect competition. Chapter 38 on labor market issues may either precede or follow Chapter 30 on wages, and Chapter 37 on income inequality may follow Chapters 30 and 31 on the distributive shares of national income.

Those who teach the typical two-semester course and who feel comfortable with the book's organization will find that, by putting the first four parts in the first semester and Parts 5 through 7 in the second, the material is divided both logically in terms of content and quite satisfactorily in terms of quantity and level of difficulty between the two semesters. For those instructors who choose to put more emphasis upon international economics, it is suggested that Parts 1, 2, 3, and 7 be treated the first semester and Parts 4, 5, and 6 the second. For a course based on three quarters of work we would suggest Chapters 1 through 14 for the first quarter, 15 through 32 for the second, and 33 through 42 for the third. Finally, those interested in the one-semester course will be able to discern several possible groups of chapters that will be appropriate to such a course. Tentative outlines for three one-semester courses, emphasizing macroeconomics, microeconomics, or a survey of micro and macro theory, follow this preface on page xlii. Also included are several one-quarter course options.

STUDENT FRIENDLY: STUDY AIDS

As in its previous ten editions, *Economics* is highly student oriented.

1 Students who are comfortable with graphic analysis and a few related quantitative concepts are in an advantageous position to understand principles of economics. To help students in this regard, a new appendix to Chapter 1 carefully reviews graphing, line slopes, and linear equations.

2 The introductory paragraphs of each chapter state objectives, present an organizational overview of the chapter, and relate the chapter to what has been covered before and what will follow.

3 Given that a significant portion of any introductory course is devoted to terminology, terms are accorded special emphasis. In particular, each important term is in **boldface type** where it first appears in each chapter. We have tried to make all definitions clear and succinct. At the end of each chapter all new terms are listed in the "Terms and Concepts" section. Finally, at the end of the book a comprehensive glossary of almost 1000 terms is found. This glossary also is contained in the *Study Guide*.

4 We have taken great care to write the legends which accompany all diagrams in such a way that they are self-contained analyses of the relevant concepts depicted therein. We feel this is a strategic means of reinforcing student comprehension.

5 Much thought has gone into the end-of-chapter questions. Though purposely intermixed, the questions are of three general types. Some are designed to highlight the main points of each chapter. Others are "open-end" discussion, debate, or thought questions. Wherever pertinent, numerical prob-

lems which require the student to derive and manipulate key concepts and relationships are employed. Numerical problems are stressed in those chapters which deal with analytical material. In this eleventh edition we have made a special effort to provide more quantitative questions on the assumption that active student involvement is critical to understanding. Some optional "advanced analysis" questions accompany certain theory chapters. These problems usually involve the stating and manipulation of certain basic concepts in equation form.

Answers to *all* end-of-chapter questions—both quantitative and essay—are provided in the *Instructor's Resource Manual*.

Many of the end-of-chapter questions deal with subject matter that is reinforced by the excellent computerized tutorial accompanying the text. A "Floppy-disk" symbol (▯) appears in conjunction with questions whose underlying content correlates to a lesson in the tutorial program.

In addition to its considerable aesthetic merit, the multicolor format of the eleventh edition stresses the use of color to enable students more quickly and easily to "get the picture," that is, to perceive the ideas expressed in each diagram and chart.

INSTRUCTOR FRIENDLY: THE SUPPLEMENTS

The eleventh edition is accompanied by a myriad of supplements which we feel equals or surpasses competing texts in terms of both quantity and quality.

Study guide Professor William Walstad has prepared the eleventh edition of the *Study Guide* which many students find to be an indispensable aid. It contains for each chapter an introductory statement, a checklist of behavioral objectives, an outline, a list of important terms, fill-in questions, problems and projects, objective questions, and discussion questions. The glossary found at the end of *Economics* also appears in the *Study Guide*. The *Guide* comprises, in our opinion, a superb "portable tutor" for the principles student. Separate *Study Guides* have been prepared to correspond with the individual macro and micro paperback editions of the text.

Economic concepts *Economic Concepts* provides carefully designed programmed materials for all the key analytical areas of the principles course. Revised by Professor W. H. Pope for use with the eleventh edition of *Economics,* it can be used as an effective supplement with any mainstream text.

Instructor's resource manual Professor Joyce Gleason of the University of Nebraska—Lincoln, working with William Walstad, has assumed primary responsibility for revising and updating the *Instructor's Resource Manual*. It comprises chapter summaries, teaching tips and suggestions, learning objectives, chapter outlines, data and visual aid sources with suggestions for classroom use, and questions and problems. As noted, answers to all the text's end-of-chapter questions are also found in the *Manual*. We trust instructors—both those who have used previous editions of *Economics* and those adopting it for the first time—will find this *Manual* to be useful and timesaving.

New to this edition is a computerized version of the *Manual,* suitable for use with IBM-PC computers, IBM-PC compatibles, and MacIntosh computers. The version for IBM-PCs and compatibles is available in both $5\frac{1}{4}$-inch and $3\frac{1}{2}$-inch formats. Users of *Economics* can now print out portions of the *Manual's* contents, complete with their own additions or alterations, for use as student handouts or in whatever ways they might wish.

As with the *Study Guide,* separate editions of the *Instructor's Resource Manual* have been prepared to correspond with the individual macro and micro paperback editions of the text. Users of one or both of these volumes will find that the material in the accompanying *Manual* correlates to the chapter sequencing in the text.

Dual test banks The new edition of *Economics* is supplemented by two test banks of objective, predominantly multiple-choice, questions. *Test Bank I* now comprises some 3600 questions, all written by the text authors; approximately 2750 are carried over from the previous edition and 860 have been prepared by the authors for the new edition. *Test Bank II,* revised by Professor Walstad, contains approximately 3100 questions. For all test items in both test banks, the nature of each question is identified (e.g., G, graphical; C, conceptual, etc.) as are the pages in the text containing the material which is the basis for each question. Adoptors of the text will be able to use this sizable number of questions, organized into two parallel test banks of equal quality, with maximum flexibility. We believe that the fact that the text authors and *Study Guide* authors have prepared all the test items will assure the fullest possible correlation with the content of the text.

As with the *Study Guide* and *Instructor's Resource Manual,* separate versions of both test banks have been prepared to correspond with the individual macro and micro editions of the text.

Computerized testing   Both test banks are available in a variety of computerized versions. One version, the MICROEXAMINER system, is among the simplest and most user-friendly test-generation systems available. It is provided for IBM-PC computers and compatibles, the Apple II Family of personal computers, and MacIntosh computers.

Another version, the DIPLOMA system, from Brownstone Research Group, provides considerable flexibility and options to users, particularly for instructors who wish to modify existing questions or combine their own questions with those provided with the text. It is available for IBM-PCs and compatibles. Additional items available from Brownstone include the popular GRADEBOOK classroom management software and a unique self-testing program, PROCTOR, for testing individual students.

Finally, MACROTEST II from Chariot Software will be available to support MacIntosh computers.

All these systems feature the ability to generate multiple tests, with versions "scrambled" to be distinctive, and have other useful features. They will meet the various needs of the widest spectrum of computer users.

Color transparencies   Some 200 new full-color transparencies for overhead projectors have been prepared especially for the eleventh edition. These encompass all the figures which appear in *Economics* and are available upon request to adoptors.

Student software   For users of IBM-PCs and compatibles, the new student software package prepared by Professor William Gunther of the University of Alabama provides a full range of carefully

prepared computer applications. Twenty core topics in the principles course receive full tutorial programs, with graphics-based coverage in all appropriate areas.

In addition, students can quiz themselves with a self-testing program accompanying each test chapter. The package also features simulation games, in both macroeconomics and in microeconomics. Unlike other simulation packages, significant portions of each game can be used after students have learned only part of the material in the course. In this way, students can learn from them prior to the hectic final weeks of a term. Parts of each simulation, both in macroeconomics and microeconomics, involve a global economy in keeping with the globalization of the course and the eleventh edition.

End-of-chapter questions throughout the text that relate to the content of one of the tutorial programs are highlighted by a floppy disk symbol ( ). The questions themselves are not necessarily contained within the tutorial program, but the tutorial does contain material that relates directly to the concepts underlying the highlighted questions.

For users of MacIntosh computers, there is an exciting new tutorial program, *VizEcon*. Developed by Professor William A. Phillips of the University of Southern Maine, this innovative package uses Apple's HYPERCARD programming environment to produce an extremely interactive learning experience. Dynamic shifts of curves, screen animation, sound effects, and simple-to-use command keys are features of this program. Its development was underwritten by grant funds and consultation from Apple Computer Inc.

Videos   New to this edition are videotapes on topics of interest to economic students. Your local McGraw-Hill representative can provide details on these videos.

DEBTS

The publication of this eleventh edition will extend the life of *Economics* into its fourth decade. The acceptance of *Economics,* which was generous from the outset, has expanded with each edition. This gracious reception has no doubt been fostered by the many teachers and students who have been kind enough to provide the benefit of their suggestions and criticisms.

Our colleagues at the University of Nebraska—Lincoln and Pacific Lutheran University have generously shared knowledge of their specialties with us and have provided encouragement. We are especially indebted to professors Harish Gupta, Jerry Petr, and Norris Peterson who have been most helpful in offsetting our comparative ignorance in their areas of specialty. Merlin Erickson has rendered considerable assistance in locating data.

The eleventh edition has benefited from a number of perceptive reviews. In both quantity and quality, they provided the richest possible source of suggestions for this revision. The contributors, to whom we are especially grateful, are listed at the conclusion of this Preface.

Professor W. H. Pope of Ryerson Polytechnical Institute in his role as coauthor of the Canadian edition of ECONOMICS has provided both general guidance and innumerable suggestions for improvement. He has also been responsible for the revision of *Economic Concepts* and, with the assistance of Professor Mark Lovewell, undertook the arduous task of providing suggested answers to all the nonquantitative end-of-chapter questions which appear in the *Instructor's Resource Manual*. Thanks also goes to Professor Ernest Ankrim of Pacific Lutheran University who coded each *Test Bank* item by type of question and identified the corresponding text page number.

We are greatly indebted to the many professionals at McGraw-Hill—and in particular Scott Stratford, Mel Haber, Sal Gonzales, and Clay Stone—for their expertise in the production and distribution of the book. Binns & Lubin has given the book another of their unique designs. Our greatest debts are to Edwin Hanson and Mike Elia for their direct supervision of this revision. Their patience and many positive contributions are gratefully acknowledged.

Given this myriad of assistance, we see no compelling reason why the authors should assume full responsibility for errors of omission or commission. But we bow to tradition.

Campbell R. McConnell

Stanley L. Brue

A NOTE FROM THE SENIOR AUTHOR

As mentioned earlier in this Preface, Stan Brue joins this edition as my new co-author. It has benefited enormously from the expertise, energy, and meticulous care he has brought to the project. Our ongoing collaboration is a highly satisfying relationship for me.

C. R. M.

ACKNOWLEDGMENTS

Reviewers for the Eleventh Edition

Roger L. Adkins
Marshall University

Mahmoud Arya
Edison Community College

Lawrence J. Belcher
University of North Carolina

J. Lloyd Blackwell III
University of North Dakota

Robert B. Catlett
Emporia State University

Steven L. Cobb
North Texas State University

Ross P. Daniel III
Louisiana State University

Edward J. Deak
Fairfield University

Donald H. Dutkowsky
Syracuse University

Joseph F. Flubacher
LaSalle University

Ralph R. Frasca
University of Dayton

Rhona Free
Eastern Connecticut State University

Gary A. Gigliotti
Rutgers University

Martin Giesbrecht
Northern Kentucky University

Nicholas Grunt
Tarrant County Junior College

Robert W. Haseltine
State University of New York College—Geneseo

Dennis W. Jansen
Texas A & M University

Walter L. Johnson
University of Missouri—Columbia

Leonard Lardaro
University of Rhode Island—Kingston

Woo Bong Lee
Bloomsburg University

Stephen E. Lile
Western Kentucky University

Eng Seng Loh
Kent State University

Gerald Lynch
Purdue University

H. Richard Moss
Ricks College

K. R. Nair
West Virginia Wesleyan College

Rollie C. Nye
Wytheville Community College

A. Maureen O'Brien
University of Minnesota

Michael Peddle
College of the Holy Cross

Arthur Peterson
Middlesex Community College

Andrew Policano
University of Iowa

Henry J. Raimondo
University of Massachusetts—Boston

Chris C. Rhoden
Solano Community College

Teresa Riley
Youngstown State University

Dolores K. Roman
Parks College of St. Louis University

David Rosenbaum
University of Nebraska—Lincoln

Peter Rupert
West Virginia University

Dan G. Rupp
Fort Hays State University

Mark E. Schaefer
Georgia State University

xi

James R. Seldon
University of Wisconsin—LaCrosse

Zena A. Seldon
University of Wisconsin—LaCrosse

David Shorow
Richland College

John R. Sinton
Community College of Finger Lakes

Kim Sosin
University of Nebraska—Omaha

Mitchell Stengel
University of Michigan

Herbert F. Thomson
Muskingum College

Ike Van de Wetering
Iowa State University

David D. VanHoose
Indiana State University—Bloomington

Percy O. Vera
Sinclair Community College

Mark S. Walbert
Illinois State University

Stanton A. Warren
Niagara University

Arthur L. Welsh
Pennsylvania State University

SUGGESTED ONE-SEMESTER AND ONE-QUARTER COURSE OUTLINES
(Core chapters are indicated by "c"; optional chapters by "o")

Chapter	One-semester course			One-quarter course	
	Macro emphasis	Micro emphasis	Macro-micro survey	Macro emphasis	Micro emphasis
1	c	c	c	c	c
2	c	c	c	c	c
3	c	c	c	c	c
4	c	c	c	c	c
5	c	c		c	c
6	c	c		c	c
7	o	o			
8	o	o			
9	c		c	c	
10	c		c	c	
11	c		c	c	
12	c		c	c	
13	c		c	c	
14	c		c	c	
15	c		c	c	
16	c		c	c	
17	c		c	c	
18	c		c	o	
19	c		o	o	
20	c		o		
21	c		o		
22		c	c		c
23		o			
24		c	c		c
25		c	c		c
26		c	c		c
27		c	o		c
28		c	o		c
29		c			c
30		c			c
31		c			c
32		o			o
33		o			
34		o[1]			
35		o[2]			
36		o			
37		o[3]			
38		o[4]			
39	o	o			
40	o	o			
41	o				
42	o				

[1] If used, Chapter 34 may follow Chapter 28.
[2] If used, Chapter 35 may follow Chapter 25.
[3] If used, Chapter 37 may follow Chapter 30 or 31.
[4] If used, Chapter 38 may follow Chapter 30.

ECONOMICS

PART I

CONSUMER GOODS
CONSUMER GOODS
CONSUMER GOODS
CONSUMER GOODS
CONSUMER GOODS
CONSUMER GOODS
CONSUMER GOODS
CONSUMER GOODS
CONSUMER GOODS
CONSUMER GOODS

PROGRESSIVE TAX
PROGRESSIVE TAX
PROGRESSIVE TAX
PROGRESSIVE TAX
PROGRESSIVE TAX
PROGRESSIVE TAX
PROGRESSIVE TAX
PROGRESSIVE TAX
PROGRESSIVE TAX
PROGRESSIVE TAX
PROGRESSIVE TAX
PROGRESSIVE TAX
PROGRESSIVE TAX

ECONOMIC GOALS
ECONOMIC GOALS
ECONOMIC GOALS
ECONOMIC GOALS
ECONOMIC GOALS
ECONOMIC GOALS
ECONOMIC GOALS
ECONOMIC GOALS
ECONOMIC GOALS
ECONOMIC GOALS
ECONOMIC GOALS
ECONOMIC GOALS
ECONOMIC GOALS

MICROECONOMICS

An
Introduction
to Economics and
the Economy

DEMAND CURVE
DEMAND CURVE
DEMAND CURVE
DEMAND CURVE
DEMAND CURVE
DEMAND CURVE
DEMAND CURVE
DEMAND CURVE
DEMAND CURVE

CIRCULAR FLOW MODEL
CIRCULAR FLOW MODEL
CIRCULAR FLOW MODEL
CIRCULAR FLOW MODEL
CIRCULAR FLOW MODEL
CIRCULAR FLOW MODEL
CIRCULAR FLOW MODEL
CIRCULAR FLOW MODEL
CIRCULAR FLOW MODEL
CIRCULAR FLOW MODEL
CIRCULAR FLOW MODEL
CIRCULAR FLOW MODEL

VALUE-ADDED TAX
VALUE-ADDED TAX
VALUE-ADDED TAX
VALUE-ADDED TAX
VALUE-ADDED TAX
VALUE-ADDED TAX
VALUE-ADDED TAX
VALUE-ADDED TAX
VALUE-ADDED TAX
VALUE-ADDED TAX
VALUE-ADDED TAX

FIVE FUNDAMENTAL QUESTIONS
FIVE FUNDAMENTAL QUESTIONS
FIVE FUNDAMENTAL QUESTIONS
FIVE FUNDAMENTAL QUESTIONS
FIVE FUNDAMENTAL QUESTIONS
FIVE FUNDAMENTAL QUESTIONS
FIVE FUNDAMENTAL QUESTIONS
FIVE FUNDAMENTAL QUESTIONS
FIVE FUNDAMENTAL QUESTIONS
FIVE FUNDAMENTAL QUESTIONS
FIVE FUNDAMENTAL QUESTIONS
FIVE FUNDAMENTAL QUESTIONS

COMPETITION
COMPETITION
COMPETITION
COMPETITION
COMPETITION
COMPETITION
COMPETITION
COMPETITION
COMPETITION
COMPETITION
COMPETITION
COMPETITION
COMPETITION

OPPORTUNITY COSTS
OPPORTUNITY COSTS
OPPORTUNITY COSTS
OPPORTUNITY COSTS
OPPORTUNITY COSTS
OPPORTUNITY COSTS
OPPORTUNITY COSTS
OPPORTUNITY COSTS
OPPORTUNITY COSTS
OPPORTUNITY COSTS
OPPORTUNITY COSTS
OPPORTUNITY COSTS
OPPORTUNITY COSTS

LAW OF SUPPLY
LAW OF SUPPLY
LAW OF SUPPLY
LAW OF SUPPLY
LAW OF SUPPLY
LAW OF SUPPLY
LAW OF SUPPLY
LAW OF SUPPLY
LAW OF SUPPLY
LAW OF SUPPLY
LAW OF SUPPLY
LAW OF SUPPLY
LAW OF SUPPLY

CORPORATION
CORPORATION
CORPORATION
CORPORATION
CORPORATION
CORPORATION
CORPORATION
CORPORATION
CORPORATION
CORPORATION
CORPORATION
CORPORATION
CORPORATION

CAPITALISM
CAPITALISM
CAPITALISM
CAPITALISM
CAPITALISM
CAPITALISM
CAPITALISM
CAPITALISM
CAPITALISM
CAPITALISM
CAPITALISM
CAPITALISM

measure by the great economists of the past—for example, Adam Smith, David Ricardo, John Stuart Mill, Karl Marx, and John Maynard Keynes.[1] And it is currently commonplace for world leaders to receive and invoke the advice and policy prescriptions of economists; "the political economist is now a fixture in the high councils of government."[2] To illustrate: The President of the United States benefits from the ongoing counsel of his Council of Economic Advisers. The broad spectrum of economic issues with which political leaders must contend, and on which they must assume some reasonable posture, is suggested by the contents of the annual *Economic Report of the President,* which covers issues such as unemployment and inflation, economic growth and productivity, taxation and public expenditures, poverty and income maintenance, the balance of payments and the international monetary system, labor-management relations, pollution, discrimination, immigration, and competition and antitrust, to enumerate only a few of the areas covered.

ported by the news media? What of the depressing stories of homeless "street people"? Why did the stock market "crash" on October 19, 1987? Of what economic significance was that dramatic decline in stock values? Is it desirable that corporate raiders be allowed to achieve hostile takeovers of corporations? Why is inflation undesirable? What can be done to reduce unemployment? Are existing welfare programs effective and justifiable? Should we continue to subsidize farmers? Do we need further reform of our tax system? Does America need to "reindustrialize" to reassert its dominant position in world trade and finance? Has the deregulation of the airlines, trucking, and banking industries been a boon or a bane to society? Should the legal minimum wage be increased? Since the responses to such questions are determined in large measure by our elected officials, intelligence at the polls requires that we have a basic working knowledge of economics. Needless to say, a sound grasp of economics is more than helpful to politicians themselves!

ECONOMICS FOR CITIZENSHIP

These comments correctly imply that a basic understanding of economics is essential if we are to be well-informed citizens. Most of the specific problems of the day have important economic aspects, and as voters we can influence the decisions of our political leaders in coping with these problems. What are the causes and consequences of the "twin deficits"—the Federal budget deficit and the international trade deficit—that are constantly re-

[1] Any of the following three volumes—Robert Heilbroner, *The Worldly Philosophers,* 6th ed. (New York: Simon and Schuster, Inc., 1986); Daniel R. Fusfeld, *The Age of the Economist,* 5th ed. (Chicago: Scott, Foresman and Company, 1986); or E. Ray Canterbery, *The Making of Economics,* 3d ed. (Belmont, Calif.: Wadsworth Publishing Company, 1987)—will provide the reader with a fascinating introduction to the historical development of economic ideas.

[2] Walter W. Heller, *New Dimensions of Political Economy* (New York: W. W. Norton & Company, Inc., 1967), p. 14. This is not to imply that political leaders are always pleased with the advice they receive. "Sound economics" and "good politics" are not necessarily synonymous.

PERSONAL APPLICATIONS

Economics is also a vital discipline for somewhat more mundane and immediate reasons. Economics is of practical value in business. An understanding of the overall operation of the economic system puts the business executive in a better position to formulate policies. The executive who understands the causes and consequences of inflation is better equipped during inflationary periods to make more intelligent business decisions than otherwise. Indeed, more and more economists are appearing on the payrolls of large corporations. Their job? To gather and interpret economic information upon which rational business decisions can be made. Also economics gives the individual as a consumer and worker some insights as to how to make wiser buying and employment decisions. How should one decide what to buy and in which amounts? How can one "hedge" against the reduction in the purchasing power of the dollar which accompanies inflation? Which occupations pay well; which are most immune to unemployment? Similarly, an individual who understands, for example, the relationship between budget and trade deficits, on the one hand, and security (stock and bond) values, on the other, will be able to make more enlightened personal investment decisions.

In spite of its practical benefits, however, the reader must be forewarned that economics is mainly an academic, not a vocational, subject. Unlike accounting, advertising, corporation finance, and marketing, economics is not primarily a how-to-make-money area of study.[3] A knowledge of economics will be helpful in running a business or in managing one's personal finances, but this is not its primary objective. In economics, problems are usually examined from the *social*, rather than from the *personal*, point of view. The production, exchange, and consumption of goods and services are discussed from the viewpoint of society as a whole, rather than from the standpoint of one's own bankbook.

Methodology

What do economists do? What are their goals? What procedures do they employ? The title of this volume—*Economics: Principles, Problems, and Policies*—contains a thumbnail answer to the first two questions. Economists formulate economic *principles* which are useful in the establishment of *policies* designed to solve economic *problems*. The procedures employed by the economist are summarized in Figure 1-1. The economist ascertains and gathers facts which are relevant to consideration of a specific economic problem. This task is sometimes called **descriptive** or **empirical economics** (box 1). The economist also states economic principles, that is, generalizes about the way individuals and institutions actually behave. Deriving principles is called **economic theory** or "economic analysis" (box 2).

As we see in Figure 1-1, economists are as likely to move from theory to facts in studying economic behavior as they are to move from facts to theory. Stated more formally, economists use both deductive and inductive methods. **Induction** involves the distilling or creating of principles from facts. Here we begin with an accumulation of facts which

[3] An economist has been defined as an individual with a Phi Beta Kappa key on one end of a watch chain and with no watch on the other.

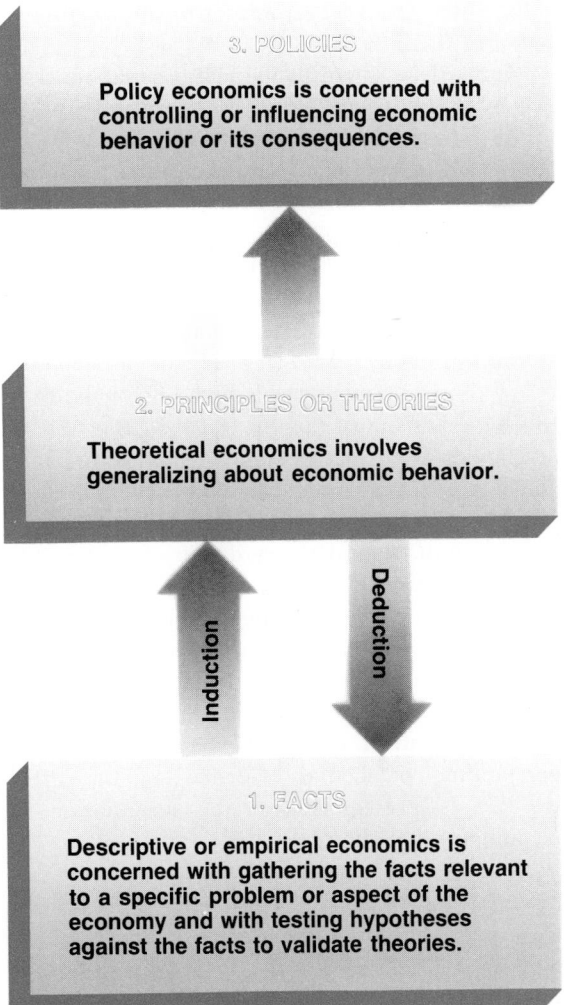

FIGURE 1-1

The relationship between facts, principles, and policies in economics

In analyzing problems or aspects of the economy, economists may use the inductive method whereby they gather, systematically arrange, and generalize upon facts. Alternatively, the deductive method entails the development of hypotheses which are then tested against facts. Generalizations derived from either method of inquiry are useful not only in explaining economic behavior, but also as a basis for formulating economic policies.

is then arranged systematically and analyzed so as to permit the derivation of a generalization or principle. Induction moves from facts to theory, from the particular to the general. The inductive method is suggested by the left upward arrow from box 1 to box 2 in the figure.

Similarly, economists frequently set about their task by beginning at the level of theory and proceed to the verification or rejection of this theory by an appeal to the facts. This is **deduction** or the hypothetical method. Thus, economists may draw upon casual observation, insight, logic, or intuition to frame a tentative, untested principle called an **hypothesis.** For example, they may conjecture, on the basis of "armchair logic," that it is rational for consumers to buy more of a product when its price is low than when its price is high. The validity of this hypothesis must then be tested by the systematic and repeated examination of relevant facts. The deductive method goes from the general to the particular, from theory to facts. This method is implicit in the right downward arrow from box 2 to box 1 in Figure 1-1.

Deduction and induction are complementary, rather than opposing, techniques of investigation. Hypotheses formulated by deduction provide guidelines for the economist in gathering and systematizing empirical data. Conversely, some understanding of factual evidence—of the "real world"—is prerequisite to the formulation of meaningful hypotheses.

Finally, the general knowledge of economic behavior which economic principles provides can then be used in formulating policies, that is, remedies or solutions, for correcting or avoiding the problem under scrutiny. This final aspect of the field is sometimes called "applied economics" or **policy economics** (box 3).

Continuing to use Figure 1-1 as a point of reference, let us now examine the economist's methodology in more detail.

DESCRIPTIVE ECONOMICS

All sciences are empirical. That means all sciences are based upon facts, that is, upon observable and verifiable behavior of certain data or subject matter. In the physical sciences the factual data are inorganic. As a social science, economics is concerned with the behavior of individuals and institutions engaged in the production, exchange, and consumption of goods and services.

The gathering of facts can be an infinitely complex task. Because the world of reality is cluttered with a myriad of interrelated facts, the economist must use discretion in gathering them. One must distinguish economic from noneconomic facts and then determine which economic facts are relevant and which are irrelevant for the particular problem under consideration. But even when this sorting process has been completed, the relevant economic facts may appear diverse and unrelated.

ECONOMIC THEORY

The task of economic theory or analysis is to systematically arrange, interpret, and generalize upon facts. Principles and theories—the end result of economic analysis—bring order and meaning to a number of facts by tying these facts together, putting them in correct relationship to one another, and generalizing upon them. "Theories without facts may be barren, but facts without theories are meaningless."[4]

Principles and theories are meaningful statements drawn from facts, but facts, in turn, serve as a constant check on the validity of principles already established. Facts—how individuals and institutions actually behave in producing, exchanging, and consuming goods and services—change with time. This makes it essential that economists continuously check existing principles and theories against the changing economic environment. The history of economic ideas is strewn with once-valid generalizations about economic behavior which were rendered obsolete by the changing course of events.

Terminology   A word on terminology is essential at this juncture. Economists talk about "laws," "principles," "theories," and "models." These terms all mean essentially the same thing: generalizations, or statements of regularity, concerning the economic behavior of individuals and institutions. The term "economic law" is a bit misleading because it implies a high degree of exactness, universal application, and even moral rightness. So, to a lesser degree, does the term **principle.** And some people incorrectly associate the term "theory" with idle pipe dreams and ivory-tower hallucinations,

[4] Kenneth E. Boulding, *Economic Analysis: Microeconomics,* 4th ed. (New York: Harper & Row, Publishers, Incorporated, 1966), p. 5.

divorced from the facts and realities of the world. The term "model" has much to commend it. A model is a simplified picture of reality, an abstract generalization of how the relevant data actually behave. In this book these four terms will be used synonymously. The choice of terms in labeling any particular generalization will be governed by custom or convenience. Hence, the relationship between the price of a product and the quantity consumers purchase will be called the "law" of demand, rather than the theory or principle of demand, because this is the customary designation.

Several other points regarding the character and derivation of economic principles are in order.

Generalizations Economic principles are **generalizations** and, as the term implies, characterized by somewhat imprecise quantitative statement. Economic facts are usually diverse; some individuals and institutions act one way and some another way. Economic principles are therefore frequently stated in terms of averages or statistical probabilities. For example, when economists say that the average household earned an income of about $32,000 in 1988, they are generalizing. It is recognized that some households earned much more and a good many others much less. Yet this generalization, properly handled and interpreted, can be very meaningful and useful.

Similarly, economic generalizations are often stated in terms of probabilities. A researcher may tell us that there is a 95 percent probability that every $1.00 reduction in personal income taxes will result in a $.92 increase in consumer spending.

"Other things equal" assumption Like other scientists, economists make use of the *ceteris paribus* or **other things being equal assumption** in constructing their generalizations. That is, they assume all other variables except those under immediate consideration are held constant. This technique simplifies the reasoning process by isolating the relationship under consideration. To illustrate: In considering the relationship between the price of product X and the amount of X purchased, it is most helpful to assume that, of all the factors which might influence the amount of X purchased (for example, the price of X, the prices of other goods, consumer incomes and tastes), only the price of X varies. The economist is then able to focus upon the "price of X–purchases of X" rela-

tionship without reasoning being blurred or confused by the intrusion of other variables.

In the natural sciences controlled experiments usually can be performed where "all other things" are in fact held constant or virtually so. Thus, scientists can test the assumed relationship between two variables with great precision. But economics is not a laboratory science. The economist's process of empirical verification is based upon "real-world" data generated by the actual operation of the economy. In this rather bewildering environment "other things" *do* change. Despite the development of rather complex statistical techniques designed to hold other things equal, such controls are less than perfect. As a result, economic principles are less certain and less precise in application than those of the laboratory sciences.

Abstractions Economic principles, or theories, are necessarily abstractions. They do not embody the full bloom of reality. The very process of sorting out noneconomic and irrelevant facts in the fact-gathering process involves abstracting from reality. Unfortunately, the abstractness of economic theory prompts the uninformed to identify theory as something which is impractical and unrealistic. This is nonsense! As a matter of fact, economic theories are practical for the simple reason that they are abstractions. The level of reality is too complex and bewildering to be very meaningful. Economists theorize in order to give meaning to a maze of facts which would otherwise be confusing and useless and to put facts into a more usable, practical form. Thus, to generalize is to abstract or purposely simplify; generalization for this purpose is practical, and therefore so is abstraction. An economic theory is a model—a simplified picture or map—of some segment of the economy. This model enables us to understand reality better *because* it avoids the confusing details of reality. Finally, theories—*good* theories—are grounded on facts and therefore are realistic. Theories which do not fit the facts are simply not good theories.

Macro and micro There are two essentially different levels of analysis at which the economist may derive laws concerning economic behavior. The level of **macroeconomics** is concerned either with the economy as a whole or with the basic subdivisions or aggregates—such as the government, household, and business sectors—which make up the economy. An aggregate is a collection of specific economic units which are treated *as if* they were one unit. Thus, we might find it convenient to lump together the almost eighteen million businesses in our economy and treat them as if they were one huge unit. In dealing with aggregates, macroeconomics is concerned with obtaining an overview, or general outline, of the structure of the economy and the relationships among the major aggregates which constitute the economy. No attention is given to the specific units which make up the various aggregates. It is not surprising, then, to find that macroeconomics entails discussions of such magnitudes as *total* output, the *total* level of employment, *total* income, *total* expenditures, the *general* level of prices, and so forth, in analyzing various economic problems. In short, macroeconomics examines the forest, not the trees. It gives us a bird's-eye view of the economy.

On the other hand, **microeconomics** is concerned with *specific* economic units and a *detailed* consideration of the behavior of these individual units. When operating at this level of analysis, the economist figuratively puts an economic unit, or very small segment of the economy, under the microscope to observe the details of its operation. Here we talk in terms of an individual industry, firm, or household, and concentrate upon such magnitudes as the output or price of a *specific* product, the number of workers employed by a single firm, the revenue or income of a particular firm or household, the expenditures of a given firm or family, and so forth. In microeconomics we examine the trees, not the forest. Microeconomics is useful in achieving a worm's-eye view of some very specific component of our economic system.

The macro–micro distinction is not to imply that the subject matter of economics is so highly compartmentalized that each and every topic can be readily labeled as "macro" or "micro"; many topics and subdivisions of economics are rooted in both. Indeed, there has been a convergence of macro- and microeconomics in important areas in recent years. For example, while the problem of unemployment was treated primarily as a macroeconomic topic some fifteen or twenty years ago ("unemployment depends on *aggregate* spending"), economists now recognize that decisions made by *individual* workers in searching for jobs and the manner in which specific product and labor markets function are also critical in determining the unemployment rate.

Graphic expression Many of the economic models or principles presented in this book will be expressed graphically. Those readers who want to refresh themselves on graphing and some other relevant quantitative relationships are strongly urged to read the appendix to this chapter.

POLICY ECONOMICS: POSITIVE AND NORMATIVE

As we move from the fact and principles levels (boxes 1 and 2) of Figure 1-1 to the policy level (box 3) we are making a critical leap from positive to normative economics.

Positive economics deals with facts (once removed at the level of theory) and is devoid of value judgments. Positive economics attempts to set forth scientific statements about economic behavior. **Normative economics,** in contrast, embodies someone's value judgments about what the economy should be like or what particular policy action should be recommended on the basis of some given economic generalization or relationship.

Put very simply, positive economics is concerned with *what is,* while normative economics embodies subjective feelings about *what ought to be*. Positive economics is concerned with what the economy is actually like; normative economics has to do with whether certain conditions or aspects of the economy are desirable or not. Consider this example: Positive statement: "Unemployment is 7 percent of the labor force." Normative statement: "Unemployment ought to be reduced." Second positive, factual statement: 'Other things being the same, if tuition is increased, enrollment at Gigantic State University will fall." Related normative statement: "Tuition should be lowered at GSU so that more students can obtain an education." Indeed, whenever such words as "ought" or "should" appear in a sentence, there is a strong chance you are dealing with a normative statement.

It should be stressed that most of the apparent disagreement among economists involves normative, value-based policy questions. To be sure, we will find later on that various economists present and support different theories or models of the economy and its component parts. But by far most economic controversy reflects differing opinions or value judgments as to what our society should be like. For example, there is greater agreement about the actual distribution of income in our society than there is about how income should be distributed. The important point to be reemphasized is that value judgments or normative statements come into play at the level of policy economics.

As noted earlier, successful policy economics draws heavily upon economic principles. For example, one almost universally accepted economic principle indicates that, within certain limits, there is a direct relationship between total spending and the level of employment in the economy. "If total spending increases, the volume of employment will rise. Conversely, if total spending decreases, the volume of employment will fall." This principle can be invaluable to government in determining its economic policies. For example, if government economists note that available statistics indicate an actual slackening of total expenditures, the principle will permit them to predict the undesirable consequence of unemployment. Aware of this anticipated result, public officials are now in a position to set in motion certain government policies designed to bolster total spending and head off or reduce expected unemployment. In short, we must be able to predict in order to effectively control. Economic principles help make prediction possible and are the basis for sound economic policy.

Economic goals It is important at this point that we note, and reflect upon, a number of **economic goals** or value judgments which are widely, though not universally, accepted in our society and, indeed, in many other societies. These goals may be briefly listed as follows:

I ECONOMIC GROWTH The production of more and better goods and services, or, more simply stated, a higher standard of living, is desired.

2 FULL EMPLOYMENT Suitable jobs should be available for all who are willing and able to work.

3 ECONOMIC EFFICIENCY We want to get the maximum benefits at the minimum cost from the limited productive resources which are available.

4 PRICE LEVEL STABILITY Sizable upswings or downswings in the general price level, that is, inflation and deflation, should be avoided.

5 ECONOMIC FREEDOM Business executives, workers, and consumers should enjoy a high degree of freedom in their economic activities.

6 AN EQUITABLE DISTRIBUTION OF INCOME No group of citizens should face stark poverty while other citizens enjoy extreme luxury.

7 ECONOMIC SECURITY Provision should be made for those who are chronically ill, disabled, handicapped, aged, or otherwise dependent.

8 BALANCE OF TRADE We seek a reasonable balance in our international trade and financial transactions.

This list of widely accepted goals[5] provides the basis for several significant points. First, note that this or any other statement of basic economic goals inevitably entails problems of interpretation. What are "sizable" changes in the price level? What is a "high degree" of economic freedom? What is an "equitable" distribution of income? Although most of us might accept the above goals as generally stated, we might also disagree very substantially as to their specific meanings and hence as to the types of policies needed to attain these goals. It is noteworthy that, although goals 1 to 4 and 8 are subject to reasonably accurate measurements, the inability to quantify goals 5 to 7 undoubtedly contributes to controversy over their precise meaning.

Second, certain of these goals are complementary in that to the extent one goal is achieved, some other goal or goals will also tend to be realized. For example, the achieving of full employment (goal 2) obviously means the elimination of unemployment, a basic cause of low incomes (goal 6) and economic insecurity (goal 7). Furthermore, considering goals 1 and 6, it is generally agreed that the sociopolitical tensions which may accompany a highly unequal distribution of income are tempered to the extent

[5] There are other goals which might be added. For example, improving the physical environment is a widely held goal.

that most incomes rise absolutely as a result of economic growth.

Third, some goals may be conflicting or mutually exclusive. Some economists argue that those forces which further the attainment of economic growth and full employment may be the very same forces which cause inflation. In fact, the apparent conflict between goals 2 and 4 has been at the forefront of economic research and debate in recent years. Goals 1 and 6 may also be in conflict. Some economists point out that efforts to achieve greater equality in the distribution of income may weaken incentives to work, invest, innovate, and take business risks, that is, to do the things that promote rapid economic growth. They argue that government tends to equalize the distribution of income by taxing high-income people quite heavily and transferring those tax revenues to low-income people. The incentives of a high-income individual will be diminished because taxation reduces one's income rewards. Similarly, a low-income person will be less motivated to work and engage in other productive activities when government stands ready to subsidize that individual. In Chapter 37 we will encounter a more sophisticated statement of this conflict. International example: Through central planning the Soviet Union has been able to virtually eliminate unemployment with the result that this source of worker insecurity has almost disappeared. However, with little fear of losing one's job, Soviet workers are quite cavalier regarding work effort and therefore productivity and efficiency in the Soviet Union are quite low (Chapter 42). Here we have a conflict between goal 7, economic security, and goal 1, the growth of worker productivity.

This leads us to a fourth point: When basic goals do conflict, society is forced to develop a system of priorities for the objectives it seeks. To illustrate: If full employment and price stability are to some extent mutually exclusive, that is, if full employment is accompanied by some inflation *and* price stability entails some unemployment, society must decide upon the relative importance of these two goals. Suppose the relevant choice is between, say, a 7 percent annual increase in the price level accompanied by full employment on the one hand, and a perfectly stable price level with 8 percent of the labor force unemployed on the other. Which is the better choice? Or how about a compromise goal

in the form of, say, a 4 percent increase in the price level each year with 6 percent of the labor force out of work? There is clearly ample room for disagreement here.

Formulating economic policy The creation of specific policies designed to achieve the broad economic goals of our society is no simple matter. A brief examination of the basic steps in policy formulation is in order.

1 The first step is to make a clear statement of goals. If we say that we have "full employment," do we mean that everyone between, say, 16 and 65 years of age has a job? Or do we mean that everyone who wants to work has a job? Should we allow for some "normal" unemployment caused by workers' voluntarily changing jobs?

2 Next, we must state and recognize the possible effects of alternative policies designed to achieve the goal. This entails a clear-cut understanding of the economic impact, benefits, costs, and political feasibility of alternative programs. Thus, for example, economists currently debate the relative merits and demerits of fiscal policy (which has to do with changing government spending and taxes) and monetary policy (which entails altering the supply of money) as alternative means of achieving and maintaining full employment (Chapter 18).

3 We are obligated to both ourselves and future generations to look back upon our experiences with chosen policies and evaluate their effectiveness; it is only through this type of evaluation that we can hope to improve policy applications. Did a given change in taxes or the supply of money alter the level of employment to the extent originally predicted? Did deregulation of a particular industry (for example, the airlines) yield the predicted beneficial results? If not, why not?

Pitfalls to straight thinking

Our discussion of the economist's procedure has, up to this point, skirted some of the specific problems and pitfalls frequently encountered in attempting to think straight about economic problems. Consider the following impediments to valid economic reasoning.

BIAS

In contrast to a neophyte physicist or chemist, the budding economist ordinarily brings into economics a bundle of biases and preconceptions about the field. For example, one might be suspicious of business profits or feel that deficit spending is invariably evil. Needless to say, biases may cloud our thinking and interfere with objective analysis. The beginning economics student must be willing to shed biases and preconceptions which are simply not warranted by facts.

LOADED TERMINOLOGY

The economic terminology to which we are exposed in newspapers and popular magazines is sometimes emotionally loaded. The writer—or more frequently the particular interest group he or she represents—may have a cause to further or an ax to grind, and terms will be slanted to solicit the support of the reader. Hence, we may find a governmental flood-control project in the Great Plains region called "creeping socialism" by its opponents and "intelligent democratic planning" by its proponents. We must be prepared, therefore, to discount such terminology in achieving objectivity in the understanding of important economic issues.

DEFINITIONS

No scientist is obligated to use popularized or immediately understandable definitions of his or her terms. The economist may find it convenient and essential to define terms in such a way that they are clearly at odds with the definitions held by most people in everyday speech. So long as the economist is explicit and consistent in these definitions, he or she is on safe ground. A typical example: The term "investment" to the average citizen is associated with the buying of bonds and stocks in the securities market. How often have we heard someone talk of "investing" in General Motors stock or government bonds? But to the economist, "investment" means the purchase of real capital assets such as machinery and equipment, or the construc-tion of a new factory building, not the purely financial transaction of swapping cash or part of a bank balance for a neatly engraved piece of paper.

FALLACY OF COMPOSITION

Another pitfall in economic thinking is to assume that "what is true for the individual or part of a group is necessarily also true for the group or whole." This is a logical **fallacy of composition;** it is *not* correct. The validity of a particular generalization for an individual or part does *not* necessarily ensure its accuracy for the group or whole.

A noneconomic example may help: You are watching a football game on a sunny autumn afternoon. The home team executes an outstanding play. In the general excitement, you leap to your feet to get a better view. Generalization: "If you, *an individual,* stand, then your view of the game is improved." But does this also hold true for the group—for everyone watching the game? Certainly not! If everyone stands to watch the play, everyone—including you—will probably have the same or even a worse view than when seated!

Consider an example or two from economics: A wage increase for Smith is desirable because, given constant product prices, it increases Smith's purchasing power and standard of living. But if everyone realizes a wage increase, product prices will likely rise, that is, inflation will occur. Therefore, Smith's standard of living may be unchanged as higher prices offset her larger salary. Second illustration: An *individual* farmer who is fortunate enough to reap a bumper crop is likely to realize a resulting income that is larger than usual. This is a correct generalization. Does it apply to farmers as a *group?* Possibly not, for the simple reason that to the individual farmer, crop prices will not be influenced (reduced) by this bumper crop, because each farmer is producing a negligible fraction of the total farm output. But to farmers as a group, prices vary inversely with total output.[6] Thus, as *all* farmers realize bumper crops, the total output of farm products rises, thereby depressing prices. If price

---

[6] This assumes there are no government programs which fix farm prices.

declines are relatively greater than the increased output, farm incomes will *fall.*

Recalling our earlier distinction between macroeconomics and microeconomics, the fallacy of composition reminds us that *generalizations which are valid at one of these levels of analysis may or may not be valid at the other.*

CAUSE AND EFFECT: POST HOC FALLACY

Still another hazard in economic thinking is to assume that simply because one event precedes another, the first is necessarily the cause of the second. This kind of faulty reasoning is known as the **post hoc, ergo propter hoc,** or **after this, therefore because of this, fallacy.**

A classic example clearly indicates the fallacy inherent in such reasoning. Suppose that early each spring the medicine man of a tribe performs his ritual by cavorting around the village in a green costume. A week or so later the trees and grass turn green. Can we safely conclude that event A, the medicine man's gyrations, has caused event B, the landscape's turning green? Obviously not. The rooster crows before dawn, but this doesn't mean the rooster is responsible for the sunrise!

It is especially important in analyzing various sets of empirical data *not* to confuse **correlation** with **causation.** *Correlation* is a technical term which indicates that two sets of data are associated in some systematic and dependable way; for example, we may find that when X increases, Y also increases. But this does not necessarily mean that X is the cause of Y. The relationship could be purely coincidental or determined by some other factor, Z, not included in the analysis. Example: Economists have found a positive correlation between education and income. In general, people with more education earn higher incomes than do people with less education. Common sense prompts us to label education as the cause and higher incomes as the effect; more education suggests a more productive worker and such workers receive larger monetary rewards. But, on second thought, might not causation run the other way? That is, do people with higher incomes buy more education, just as they buy more automobiles and more steaks? Or is the relationship explainable in terms of still other factors? Are education and in-

LAST WORD

The American economy: a factual profile

As a prelude to studying the functioning of our economy, it is interesting and informative to be aware of some salient facts.

1 *Output and income* In 1988 the United States produced $4862 billion of goods and services, an amount far greater than any other nation. Output per capita was $17,480 as compared to $12,840 for Japan, $8,870 for Great Britain, $1,860 for Mexico, and $120 for Ethiopia. However, based on Federal government definitions, over 13 percent of all Americans live in poverty.

2 *Price level* Historically, the price level has both risen (inflation) and fallen (deflation). However, with the exception of a year or two, the United States has experienced varying degrees of inflation since World War II. By 1988 the price level was almost $3\frac{1}{3}$ times as high as it was in 1967.

3 *Employment and unemployment* In the post-World War II period, employment in the United States has increased from 57 million in 1947 to 115 million in 1988. Our job growth over the 1947–1988 period has doubled that of Japan; Great Brit-

come positively correlated because the bundle of characteristics—ability, motivation, personal habits—required to succeed in education are the same characteristics required to be a productive and highly paid worker? Upon reflection, seemingly simple cause-effect relationships—"more education results in more income"—may prove to

ain, West Germany, and Italy have experienced virtually no job growth. In the past decade our unemployment rate has averaged 7.3 percent per year. The unemployment rate for blacks is over twice that of whites.

4 *Businesses* Of the 17.6 million business firms in the United States, approximately 82 percent are relatively small unincorporated businesses (proprietorships and partnerships). The 18 percent which are corporations account for about 90 percent of total business sales. If our largest corporation, General Motors, were a nation, its annual output would exceed that of all but about 22 or 24 nations of the world. There were 61,622 business failures in 1987 and 685,600 new businesses were incorporated in that same year.

5 *Government* Governments—Federal, state, and local combined—account for about 20 percent of our national output. Approximately one-third of government's output is for national defense. One out of six workers is a government employee. The national debt is currently $2600 billion, or about $10,568 per person.

6 *International trade* The United States exported $251 billion and imported $410 billion worth of goods and services in 1987. Exports are 11 percent and imports are 13 percent of our national output. Most of our trade is with other industrially-advanced nations; Canada, not Japan, is our major trading partner.

The statistical table found inside the covers of this book is designed as a readily accessible source of information about important trends in the American economy.

be suspect or perhaps flatly incorrect.

In short, cause-and-effect relationships are typically not self-evident in economics; the economist must look carefully before leaping to the conclusion that event A caused event B. Certainly the simple fact that A preceded B is not sufficient to warrant any such conclusion.

The economic perspective

The methodology used by economists is common to all of the natural and social sciences. Similarly, all scholars are aware of the reasoning errors which we have just discussed. Hence, economists do *not* think in a special way. But they *do* think about things from a special perspective. Economists have developed a keen alertness to certain aspects of everyday conduct and situations. More specifically, they look for *rationality* or *purposefulness* in human actions and economic institutions. This purposefulness implies that people, individually and collectively, make choices by comparing costs and benefits. It therefore might be said that the **economic perspective** is a *cost-benefit perspective*.

Because people make economic choices from a wide array of alternatives, all choices entail sacrifices or costs. To buy a new VCR may mean not being able to afford a new personal computer. Taking a course in economics may preclude taking a course in accounting, political science, or computer science. A decision by government to provide improved health care for the elderly may mean deteriorating health care for children in poverty. Alas, costs are everywhere! Naturally, people are most directly aware of personal monetary costs; that is, expenses incurred when paying tuition, buying hamburgers, hiring babysitters, renting apartments, or attending concerts. But we shall find in Chapter 2 that costs occur in *all* situations in which incomes or resources are scarce relative to wants.

Economic actions of workers, producers, and consumers, of course, also produce personal economic benefits. For example, workers receive wages, producers garner profits, and consumers obtain satisfaction. People *compare* these benefits with costs in deciding how to spend their time, which products to buy, whether or not to work, which goods to produce and sell, and so forth. If the added benefits associated with a given course of action exceed the added costs, then it is rational to take that action. But if added costs are greater than added benefits, that action is not rational and should not be undertaken. Furthermore, when costs or benefits *change,* people *alter* their behavior accordingly. Economists look carefully at costs and benefits to understand the everyday activities of people and institutions in the economy. This economic perspective will become increasingly evident as you advance through this book.

CHAPTER SUMMARY

1 Economics is concerned with the efficient use of scarce resources in the production of goods and services to satisfy material wants.

2 Economics is studied for several reasons: **a** It provides valuable knowledge concerning our social environment and behavior; **b** it equips a democratic citizenry to render fundamental decisions intelligently; **c** although not chiefly a vocational discipline, economics may provide the business executive or consumer with valuable information.

3 The tasks of descriptive or empirical economics are **a** the gathering of those economic facts which are relevant to a particular problem or specific segment of the economy, and **b** the testing of hypotheses against facts to validate theories.

4 The generalizations stated by economists are called "principles," "theories," "laws," or "models." The derivation of these principles is the task of economic theory.

5 Induction entails the distilling of theories from facts; deduction involves stating a hypothesis and then gathering facts to determine whether the hypothesis is valid.

6 Some economic principles are concerned with macroeconomics (the economy as a whole or major aggregates), while others pertain to microeconomics (specific economic units or institutions).

7 Economic principles are particularly valuable as predictive devices; they are the bases for the formulation of economic policy designed to solve problems and control undesirable events.

8 Positive statements embody facts ("what is"), while normative statements encompass value judgments ("what ought to be").

9 Economic growth, full employment, economic efficiency, price level stability, economic freedom, equity in the distribution of income, economic security, and reasonable balance in our international trade and finance are all widely accepted economic goals in our society. Some of these goals are complementary; others are mutually exclusive.

10 In studying economics there are numerous pitfalls which the beginner may encounter. Some of the more important chuckholes strewn along the road to economic understanding are **a** biases and preconceptions, **b** terminological difficulties, **c** the fallacy of composition, and **d** the difficulty of establishing clear cause-effect relationships.

11 The economic perspective envisions individuals and institutions making rational decisions based upon costs and benefits.

TERMS AND CONCEPTS

economics

descriptive or empirical economics

economic theory

induction and deduction

hypothesis

policy economics

principles or generalizations

ceteris paribus or "other things being equal" assumption

macroeconomics and microeconomics

positive and normative economics

economic goals

fallacy of composition

post hoc, ergo propter hoc or "after this, therefore because of this" fallacy

correlation and causation

economic perspective

QUESTIONS AND STUDY SUGGESTIONS

1 Explain in detail the interrelationships between economic facts, theory, and policy. Critically evaluate: "The trouble with economics is that it is not practical. It has too much to say about theory and not enough to say about facts."

2 Analyze and explain the following quotation:[7]

Facts are seldom simple and usually complicated; theoretical analysis is needed to unravel the complications and interpret the facts before we can understand them . . . the opposition of facts and theory is a false one; the true relationship is complementary. We cannot in practice consider a fact without relating it to other facts, and the relation is a theory. Facts by themselves are dumb; before they will tell us anything we have to arrange them, and the arrangement is a theory. Theory is simply the unavoidable arrangement and interpretation of facts, which gives us generalizations on which we can argue and act, in the place of a mass of disjointed particulars.

3 Of what significance is the fact that economics is not a laboratory science? What problems may be involved in deriving and applying economic principles?

[7] Henry Clay, *Economics for the General Reader* (New York: The Macmillan Company, 1925), pp. 10–11.

4 Explain each of the following statements:
a "Like all scientific laws, economic laws are established in order to make successful prediction of the outcome of human actions."[8]
b "Abstraction . . . is the inevitable price of generality . . . indeed abstraction and generality are virtually synonyms."[9]
c "Numbers serve to discipline rhetoric."[10]

5 Indicate whether each of the following statements pertains to microeconomics or macroeconomics:
a The unemployment rate in the United States was 7 percent in 1986.
b The Alpo dogfood plant in Bowser, Iowa, laid off 15 workers last month.
c An unexpected freeze in central Florida reduced the citrus crop and caused the price of oranges to rise.
d Our national output, adjusted for inflation, grew by 2.5 percent in 1986.
e Last week Manhattan Chemical Bank lowered its interest rate on business loans by one-half of 1 percentage point.
f The consumer price index rose by more than 12 percent in 1980.

6 Identify each of the following as either a positive or a normative statement:

a The high temperature today was 89 degrees.
b It was too hot today.
c The general price level rose by 4.4 percent last year.
d Inflation greatly eroded living standards last year and should be reduced by government policies.

7 To what extent would you accept the eight economic goals stated and described in this chapter? What priorities would you assign to them? It has been said that we seek simply four goals: progress, stability, justice, and freedom. Is this list of goals compatible with that given in the chapter?

8 Analyze each of the following specific goals in terms of the eight general goals stated on page 7, and note points of conflict and compatibility: **a** The lessening of environmental pollution; **b** increasing leisure; and **c** protection of American producers from foreign competition. Indicate which of these specific goals you favor and justify your position.

9 Interpret the curve in Figure 19-2 on page 370, indicating the nature of the public policy dilemma it illustrates. Which of the choices posed by the curve do you prefer? Why?

10 Explain and give an illustration of **a** the fallacy of composition, and **b** the "after this, therefore because of this" fallacy. Why are cause-and-effect relationships difficult to isolate in the social sciences?

11 "Economists should never be popular; men who afflict the comfortable serve equally those who comfort the afflicted and one cannot suppose that American capitalism would long prosper without the critics its leaders find such a profound source of annoyance."[11] Interpret and evaluate.

[8] Oskar Lange, "The Scope and Method of Economics," *Review of Economic Studies,* vol. 13, 1945–1946, p. 20.

[9] George J. Stigler, *The Theory of Price* (New York: The Macmillan Company, 1947), p. 10.

[10] Victor R. Fuchs, *How We Live* (Cambridge, Mass.: Harvard University Press, 1983), p. 5.

[11] John Kenneth Galbraith, *American Capitalism,* rev. ed. (Boston: Houghton Mifflin Company, 1956), p. 49.

Graphs and their meaning

If you glance quickly through the pages of this text, you will find a large number of graphs. Some will appear to be relatively simple, while others appear more formidable. Contrary to student folklore, graphs are *not* designed by economists to confuse students! On the contrary, graphs are employed to help students visualize and understand important economic relationships. Graphs are a means by which economists express their theories or models. The physicist and chemist sometimes illustrate their theories by building Tinker-Toy arrangements of multicolored wooden balls that represent protons, neutrons, and so forth, held in proper relation to one another by wires or sticks. Economists often use graphs to illustrate their models, and by understanding these "pictures" students can more readily comprehend what economists are saying.

Most of the principles or models we shall encounter will explain the relationship between just two sets of economic facts; therefore, simple two-dimensional graphs are a convenient way of visualizing and manipulating these relationships.

CONSTRUCTING A GRAPH

A graph is merely a visual representation of the relationship between two variables. Table 1 provides us with a simple hypothetical illustration which shows the relationship between income and consumption. Without ever having studied economics, one would expect intuitively that high-income people would consume more than low-income people. Thus we are not surprised to find in Table 1 that consumption increases as income increases.

How can the information in Table 1 be expressed graphically? Glance at the graph shown in Figure 1. Now look back at the information in

Table 1 and we will explain how to represent that information in a meaningful way by constructing the graph you just examined.

What we are trying to show visually, or graphically, is how consumption changes as income changes. Since income is the determining factor, we represent it on the horizontal axis of the graph as is customary. And, because consumption is dependent upon income, we represent it on the vertical axis of the graph as is also customary. Actually, what we are doing is representing the independent variable on the horizontal axis and the dependent variable on the vertical axis.

Now we simply have to arrange the vertical and horizontal scales of the graph so that they conveniently reflect the range of values of consumption and income, as well as to mark the steps in convenient graphic increments. As you can see, the ranges in the graph cover the ranges of values in Table 1. Similarly, as it so happens in this example, the increments on both scales are $100 for approximately each half-inch.

Next, we have to locate for each consumption value and the income value that it depends upon a single point which reflects the same information graphically. Our five income–consumption combinations are plotted by drawing perpendiculars from the appropriate points on the **vertical** and

TABLE 1 **The relationship between income and consumption**

Income (per week)	Consumption (per week)	Point
$ 0	$ 50	A
100	100	B
200	150	C
300	200	D
400	250	E

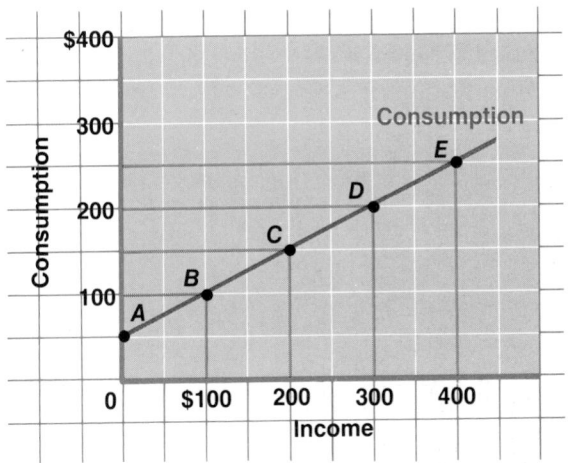

FIGURE I

Graphing the direct relationship between consumption and income

Two sets of data which are positively or directly related, such as consumption and income, graph as an upsloping line. In this case the vertical intercept is $50 and the slope of the line is $+\frac{1}{2}$.

horizontal axes. For example, in plotting point *C*—the $200 income–$150 consumption point—perpendiculars must be drawn up from the horizontal (income) axis at $200 and across from the vertical (consumption) axis at $150. These perpendiculars intersect at point *C*, which locates this particular income–consumption combination. You should verify that the other income–consumption combinations shown in Table 1 are properly located in Figure 1. By assuming that the same general relationship between income and consumption prevails at all other points between the five points graphed, a line or curve can be drawn to connect these points.

Using Figure 1 as a benchmark, we can now make a number of additional important comments.

DIRECT AND INVERSE RELATIONSHIPS

In this instance our upsloping line tells us that there is a direct relationship between income and consumption. By a positive or **direct relationship** we mean that the two variables—in this case consumption and income—change in the *same* direction. An increase in consumption is associated with an increase in income; conversely, a decrease in consumption is associated with a decrease in income. When two sets of data are positively or directly related, they will always graph as an *upsloping* line as in Figure 1.

In contrast, two sets of data may be inversely related. Consider Table 2, which shows the relationship between the price of basketball tickets and game attendance at Gigantic State University. We observe a negative or **inverse relationship** between ticket prices and attendance; these two variables change in *opposite* directions. When ticket prices decrease, attendance increases. Conversely, when ticket prices increase, attendance decreases. In Figure 2 we have plotted the six data points of Table 2 following the same procedure outlined above. We find that an inverse relationship will always graph as a *downsloping* line.

DEPENDENT AND INDEPENDENT VARIABLES

Although the task is sometimes formidable, economists seek to determine which variable is "cause" and which is "effect." Or, more formally, we want to ascertain the independent and the dependent variable. By definition, the **dependent variable** is the "effect" or outcome; it is the variable which

TABLE 2 **The relationship between ticket prices and attendance**

Ticket price	Attendance (thousands)	Point
$25	0	A
20	4	B
15	8	C
10	12	D
5	16	E
0	20	F

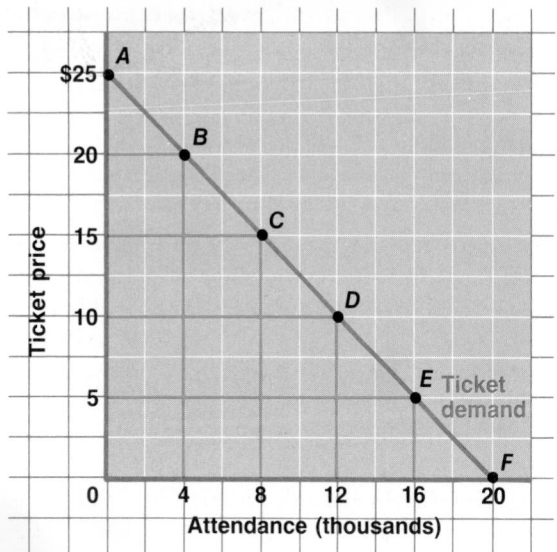

FIGURE 2

Graphing the inverse relationship between ticket prices and game attendance

Two sets of data which are negatively or inversely related, such as ticket price and the attendance at basketball games, graph as a downsloping line. The slope of this line is $-1\frac{1}{4}$.

changes as a consequence of a change in some other (independent) variable. Similarly, the **independent variable** is the "cause"; it is the variable which causes the change in the dependent variable. As noted earlier, in our income–consumption example it is generally agreed that income is the independent variable and consumption is the dependent variable. It is correct to say that income causes consumption to be what it is rather than the other way around. Similarly, ticket prices determine attendance at GSU basketball games; attendance does not determine ticket prices. Ticket price is the independent variable and the quantity purchased is the dependent variable.

You may recall from your high school courses that mathematicians always put the independent variable (cause) on the horizontal axis and the dependent variable (effect) on the vertical axis. Economists are less tidy; their graphing of independent and dependent variables is more arbitrary. Thus, their conventional graphing of the income–consumption relationship is consistent with mathematical presentation. But economists put price and cost data on the vertical axis. Hence, the economist's graphing of GSU's ticket price–attendance data conflicts with mathematical procedure.

OTHER VARIABLES HELD CONSTANT

You have probably sensed that our simple two-variable graphs ignore a variety of other factors which might affect the amount of consumption which occurs at each income level or the number of people who attend GSU basketball games at each possible ticket price. When economists plot the relationship between any two variables, they invoke the *ceteris paribus* or "other things being equal" assumption discussed in the body of the chapter. Thus, in Figure 1 all other factors (that is, all factors other than income) which might affect the amount of consumption are presumed to be constant or unchanged. Similarly, in Figure 2 all factors other than ticket price which might influence attendance at GSU basketball games are assumed constant. In reality, we know that "other things" often change, and when they do, the specific relationships presented in our two tables and graphs will change. Specifically, we would expect the lines we have plotted to shift to new locations.

For example, what might happen to the income–consumption relationship if there occurred a stock market "crash" such as that of October 1987? The expected impact of this dramatic fall in the value of stocks would be to make people feel less wealthy and therefore less willing to consume at each income level. In short, we would anticipate a downward shift of the consumption line in Figure 1. You should plot a new consumption line based on the assumption that consumption is, say, $20 less at each income level. Note that the relationship remains direct, but the line has merely shifted to reflect less consumer spending at each level of income.

Similarly, a variety of factors other than ticket prices might affect GSU game attendance. For example, if the government were to abandon its program of student loans, GSU enrollment and hence attendance at games might be less at each ticket price. You are urged to redraw Figure 2 on the assumption that 2000 fewer students attend GSU games at each ticket price. Question 2 at the end of this appendix introduces other variables which might cause the relationship shown in Figure 2 to shift to another position.

SLOPE OF A LINE

Lines can be described in terms of their slopes. The **slope of a straight line** between any two points is defined as the ratio of the vertical change (the rise or fall) to the horizontal change (the run) involved in moving between those points. For example, moving from point **B** to point **C** in Figure 1 we find that the rise or vertical change (the change in consumption) is +$50 and the run or horizontal change (the change in income) is +$100. Therefore:

$$\text{Slope} = \frac{\text{vertical change}}{\text{horizontal change}} = \frac{+50}{+100} = +\frac{1}{2}$$

Note that our slope of 1/2 is positive because consumption and income change in the same direction, that is, consumption and income are directly or positively related.

What does this slope of +1/2 indicate? It tells us that there will be a $1 increase in consumption for every $2 increase in income. Similarly, it indicates that for every $2 decrease in income there will be a $1 decrease in consumption.

For our ticket price–attendance data the relationship is negative or inverse with the result that the slope of Figure 2's line is negative. In particular, the vertical change or fall is 5 and the horizontal change or run is 4. Therefore:

$$\text{Slope} = \frac{\text{vertical change}}{\text{horizontal change}} = \frac{-5}{+4} = -1\tfrac{1}{4}$$

What does this slope of −5/+4 or −1¼ tell us? It means that lowering the price of a ticket by $5 will increase attendance by 4000 people. Or, alternatively stated, it implies that a $1 price reduction will increase attendance by 800 persons.

In addition to its slope, the only other bit of information needed in locating a line is the vertical intercept. By definition, the **vertical intercept** is the point at which the line meets the vertical axis. For Figure 1 the intercept is $50. This means that, if current income was somehow zero, consumers would still spend $50. How might they manage to consume when they have no current income? Answer: By borrowing or by selling off some of their assets. Similarly, the vertical intercept in Figure 2 tells us that at a $25 ticket price GSU's basketball team would be playing their games in an empty auditorium.

Given the intercept and the slope, our consumption line can be very succinctly described in equation form. In general, a linear equation is written as $y = a + bx$, where y is the dependent variable, a is the vertical intercept, b is the slope of the line, and x is the independent variable. For our income–consumption example, if we let C represent consumption (the dependent variable) and Y represent income (the independent variable), we can write $C = a + bY$. By substituting the values of the intercept and the slope for our specific data, we have $C = 50 + .5Y$. This equation allows us to determine consumption at **any** level of income. For example, at the $300 income level (point **D** in Figure 1), our equation predicts that consumption will be $200 [= $50 + (.5 × $300)]. You should confirm that at the $250 income level consumption will be $175.

When economists reverse mathematical convention by putting the independent variable on the vertical axis and the dependent variable on the horizontal axis, in a sense the standard linear equation solves for the independent, rather than the dependent, variable. We noted earlier that this case is relevant for our GSU ticket price–attendance data. If we let P represent the ticket price and A represent attendance, our relevant equation is $P = 25 − 1.25A$, where the vertical intercept is 25 and the negative slope is −1¼ or −1.25. But knowing the value for P enables us to solve for A, which is actually our dependent variable. For example, if $P = 15$, then the values in our equation become: $15 = 25 − 1.25(A)$, or $1.25A = 10$, or $A = 8$. You are urged to check this answer against Figure 2 and also to use this equation to predict GSU ticket sales when price is $7.50.

SLOPE OF A NONLINEAR CURVE

Let us now move from the simple world of linear relationships (straight lines) to the slightly more complex world of nonlinear relationships (curves). By definition, the slope of a straight line is constant throughout. In contrast, the slope of a curve changes as we move from one point to another on the curve. For example, consider the upsloping curve *AA* in Figure 3a. Although its slope is positive throughout, we observe that the slope diminishes or flattens as we move northeast along the curve. Given that the slope is constantly changing, we can only measure the slope at some particular point on the curve.

How is this done? We begin by drawing a straight line which is tangent to the curve at that point where we want to measure its slope. By definition, a line is **tangent** at that point where it touches, but does not intersect, the curve. Thus, line *aa* is tangent to curve *AA* at point *P* in Figure 3a. Having done this, we can measure the slope of *AA* at point *P* simply by measuring the

slope of the straight tangent line *aa*. Specifically, in Figure 3a we see that, when the vertical change (rise) in *aa* is +10, the horizontal change (run) is also +10. Thus, the slope of the tangent *aa* line is 10/10 or +1 and therefore the slope of *AA* at *P* is also +1.

Now consider the downsloping curve *BB* in Figure 3b. In this case we note that the slope of *BB* is negative and that the slope diminishes as we move southeast along the curve. What is the slope at point *P*? Again, we draw line *bb* which is tangent to curve *BB* at *P*. In this case we see that when the vertical change (fall) in *bb* is −10, the horizontal change is only +5. Thus, the slope of *BB* at point *P* is −10/+5 or −2. Question 6 at the end of this appendix is relevant.

APPENDIX SUMMARY

I Graphs are a convenient and revealing means of presenting economic relationships or principles.

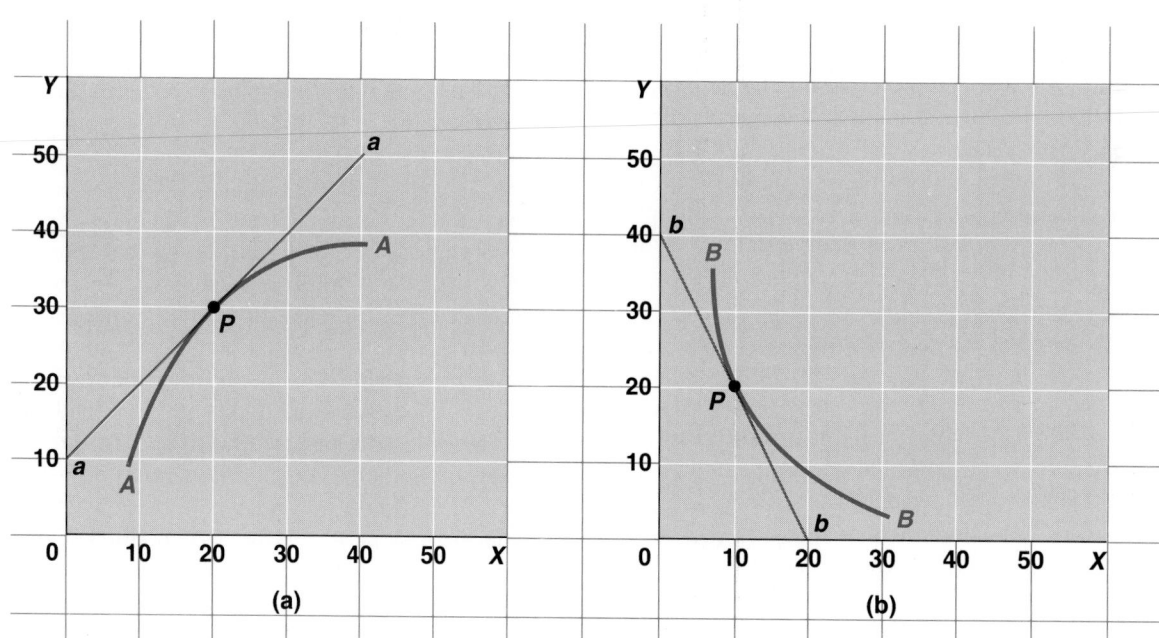

FIGURE 3

Determining the slopes of curves

The slope of a nonlinear curve changes as one moves from point to point on the curve. The slope at any point can be determined by drawing a straight line tangent to that point and calculating the slope of that line.

2 Two variables are positively or directly related when their values change in the same direction. Two variables which are directly related will plot as an upsloping line on a graph.

3 Two variables are negatively or inversely related when their values change in opposite directions. Two variables which are inversely related will graph as a downsloping line.

4 The value of the dependent variable ("effect") is determined by the value of the independent variable ("cause").

5 When "other factors" which might affect a two-variable relationship are allowed to change, we can expect the plotted relationship to shift to a new location.

6 The slope of a straight line is the ratio of the vertical change to the horizontal change in moving between any two points. The slope of an upsloping line is positive, while that of a downsloping line is negative.

7 The vertical (or horizontal) intercept and the slope of a line establish its location and are used in expressing the relationship between two variables as an equation.

8 The slope of a curve at any point is determined by calculating the slope of a straight line drawn tangent to that point.

APPENDIX TERMS AND CONCEPTS

vertical and horizontal axes

direct and inverse relationships

dependent and independent variables

slope of a straight line

vertical intercept

tangent

APPENDIX QUESTIONS AND STUDY SUGGESTIONS

1 Briefly explain the use of graphs as a means of presenting economic principles. What is an inverse relationship? How does it graph? What is a direct relationship? How does it graph? Graph and explain the relationships one would expect to find between **a** the number of inches of rainfall per month and the sale of umbrellas, **b** the amount of tuition and the level of enrollment at a university, and **c** the size of a university's athletic scholarships and the number of games won by its football team. In each case cite and explain how considerations other than those specifically mentioned might upset the expected relationship. Is your second generalization consistent with the fact that, historically, enrollments and tuition have both increased? If not, explain any difference.

2 Indicate how each of the following might affect the data shown in Table 2 and Figure 2 of this appendix:

  a GSU's athletic director schedules higher-quality opponents.

  b GSU's fighting aardvarks experience three losing seasons.

  c GSU contracts to have all of its home games televised.

3 The following table contains data on the relationship between saving and income. Rearrange these data as required and graph the data on the accompanying grid. What is the slope of the line? The vertical intercept? Interpret the meaning of both the slope and the intercept. Write the equation which represents this line. What would you predict saving to be at the $12,500 level of income?

Income (per year)	Saving (per year)
$15,000	$1,000
0	−500
10,000	500
5,000	0
20,000	1,500

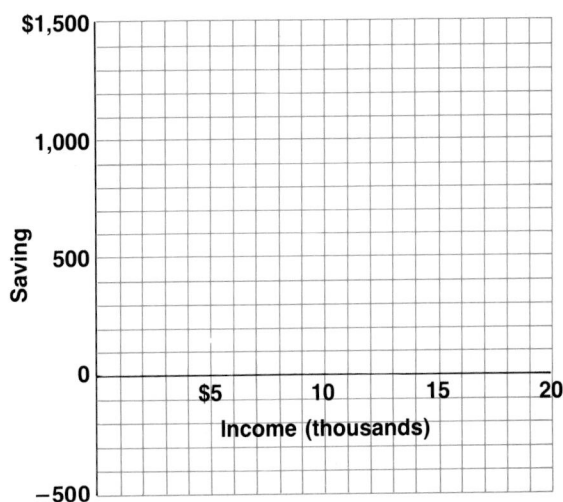

4 Construct a table from the following data shown on the accompanying graph. Which is the dependent and which the independent variable? Summarize the data in equation form.

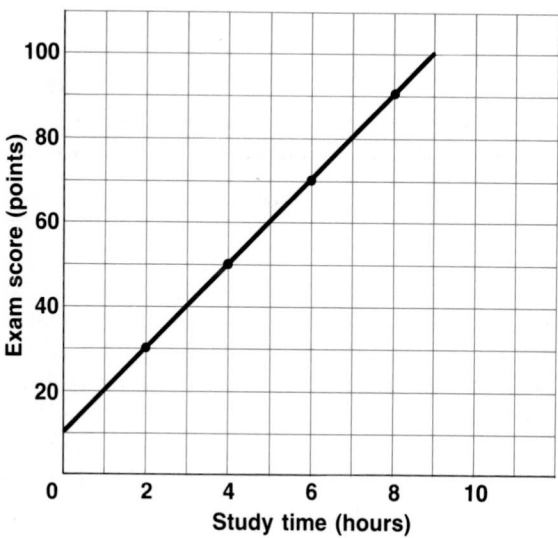

5 Suppose that when the interest rate which must be paid to borrow funds is 16 percent, businesses find it unprofitable to invest in machinery and equipment. However, when the interest rate is 14 percent, $5 billion worth of investment is profitable. At 12 percent, a total of $10 billion of investment is profitable. Similarly, total investment increases by $5 billion for each successive 2 percentage point decline in the interest rate. Indicate the relevant relationship between the interest rate and investment verbally, tabularly, graphically, and as an equation. Put the interest rate on the vertical axis and investment on the horizontal axis and in your equation use the form $i = a - bI$, where i is the interest rate, a is the vertical intercept, b is the slope of the line, and I is the level of investment. Comment upon the advantages and disadvantages of verbal, tabular, graphic, and equation forms of presentation.

Note to the reader: You undoubtedly have observed that a floppy disk symbol precedes each of the questions in this appendix. This icon is used throughout the text to indicate that a particular question relates to the content of one of the tutorial programs in the student software which accompanies this book. Please refer to the Preface for more detail about this software.

6 The accompanying diagram shows curve **XX** and three tangents at points **A**, **B**, and **C**. Calculate the slope of the curve at these three points.

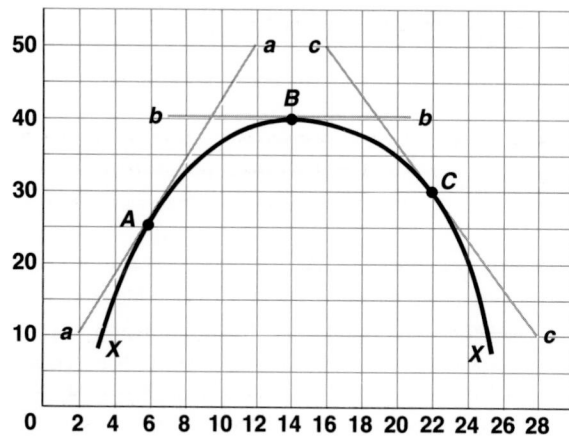

7 In the accompanying diagram, is the slope of curve **AA'** positive or negative? Does the slope increase or decrease as we move from **A** to **A'**? Answer the same two questions for curve **BB'**.

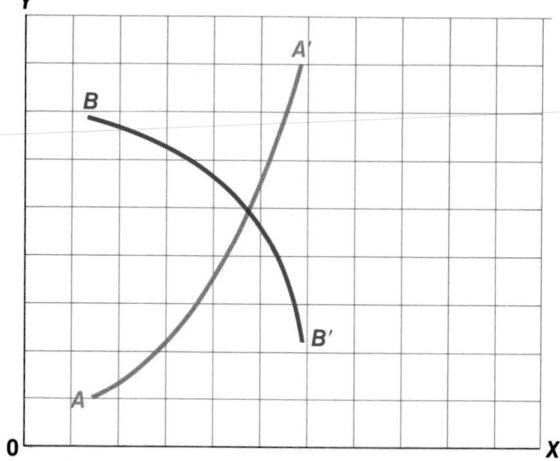

CHAPTER 2

An introduction to the economizing problem

The primary objective of this chapter is to introduce and explore certain fundamental considerations which constitute the foundation of economic science. Basically, we want to expand upon the definition of economics introduced in Chapter 1 and explore the essence of the economizing problem. To this end, we shall illustrate, extend, and modify our definition of economics by the use of so-called production possibilities tables and curves. Finally, we shall survey briefly the different ways in which institutionally and ideologically diverse economies go about "solving" or responding to the economizing problem.

The foundation of economics

Two fundamental facts provide a foundation for the field of economics and, in fact, comprise the **economizing problem.** It is imperative that we carefully state and fully understand these two facts, because everything that follows in our study of economics depends directly or indirectly upon them. The first fact is this: *Society's material wants, that is, the material wants of its citizens and institutions, are virtually unlimited or insatiable.* Second: *Economic resources—the means of producing goods and services—are limited or scarce.*

UNLIMITED WANTS

Let us systematically examine and explain these two facts in the order stated. In the first statement, precisely what do we mean by "material wants"? We mean, first, the desires of consumers to obtain and use various *goods* and *services* which provide **utility,** the economist's term for pleasure or satisfaction.[1] An amazingly wide range of products fills the bill in this respect: houses, automobiles, toothpaste, compact-disc players, pizzas, sweaters, and the like. In short, innumerable products which we sometimes classify as *necessities* (food, shelter, clothing) and *luxuries* (perfumes, yachts, mink coats) are all capable of satisfying human wants. Needless to say, what is a luxury to Smith may be a necessity to Jones, and what is a commonplace necessity today may have been a luxury a few short years ago.

But services satisfy our wants as much as do tangible products. A repair job on our car, the removal of our appendix, a haircut, and legal advice

[1] This definition leaves a variety of wants—recognition, status, love, and so forth—for the other social sciences to worry about.

have in common with goods the fact that they satisfy human wants. On reflection, we realize that we indeed buy many goods, for example, automobiles and washing machines, for the services they render. The differences between goods and services are often less than they seem to be at first.

Material wants also include those which businesses and units of government seek to satisfy. Businesses want factory buildings, machinery, trucks, warehouses, communications systems, and other things that assist them in realizing their production goals. Government, reflecting the collective wants of its citizenry or goals of its own, seeks highways, schools, hospitals, and military hardware.

As a group, these material wants are, for practical purposes, *insatiable,* or *unlimited,* which means that material wants for goods and services are incapable of being completely satisfied.[2] A simple experiment will help to verify this point: Suppose we are asked to list those goods and services we want but do not now possess. If we take time to ponder our unfilled material wants, chances are our list will be impressive. And over a period of time, wants multiply so that, as we fill some of the wants on the list, at the same time we add new ones. Material wants, like rabbits, have a high reproduction rate. The rapid introduction of new products whets our appetites, and extensive advertising tries to persuade us that we need countless items we might not otherwise consider buying. Not too many years ago, the desire for personal computers, light beer, video recorders, digital watches, and microwave ovens was nonexistent. Furthermore, we often cannot stop with simple satisfaction: The acquisition of an Escort or Chevette has been known to whet the appetite for a Porsche or Mercedes.

In summary, we may say that at any given time the individuals and institutions which constitute

society have innumerable unfulfilled material wants. Some of these wants—food, clothing, shelter—have biological roots. But some are also influenced by the conventions and customs of society: The specific kinds of food, clothing, and shelter we seek are frequently determined by the general social and cultural environment in which we live. Over time, wants change and multiply, abetted by the development of new products and by extensive advertising and sales promotion.

Finally, let us emphatically add that the overall end or objective of all economic activity is the attempt to satisfy these diverse material wants.

SCARCE RESOURCES

Consider now the second fundamental fact: *Economic resources are limited or scarce.* What do we mean by "economic resources"? In general, we are referring to all the natural, human, and manufactured resources that go into the production of goods and services. This clearly covers a lot of ground: factory and farm buildings and all sorts of equipment, tools, and machinery used in the production of manufactured goods and agricultural products; a variety of transportation and communication facilities; innumerable types of labor; and, last but not least, land and mineral resources of all kinds. There is an apparent need for a simplified classification of such resources, which we shall meet with the following categories: (1) *property* resources—land or raw materials and capital; (2) *human* resources—labor and entrepreneurial ability.

Resource categories   Let us examine these various resource categories.

LAND   What does the economist mean by **land?** Much more than do most people. Land refers to all natural resources—all "gifts of nature"—which are usable in the productive process. Such resources as arable land, forests, mineral and oil deposits, and water resources come under this general classification.

CAPITAL   What about **capital?** Capital, or investment goods, refers to all manufactured aids to production, that is, all tools, machinery, equipment,

---

[2] It should be mentioned in passing that the fallacy of composition is relevant here. Our wants for a *particular* good or service can be satisfied; that is, over a short period of time we can get sufficient amounts of toothpaste or beer. Certainly one appendicitis operation is par for the course. But goods *in general* are another story. Here we do not, and presumably cannot, get enough. We shall say more about the satisfying of wants for specific goods in Chapter 23.

and factory, storage, transportation, and distribution facilities used in producing goods and services and getting them to the ultimate consumer. The process of producing and accumulating capital goods is known as **investment.**

Two other points are pertinent. First, *capital goods* ("tools") differ from *consumer goods* in that the latter satisfy wants directly, whereas the former do so indirectly by facilitating the production of consumable goods. Second, the term "capital" as here defined does *not* refer to money. True, business executives and economists often talk of "money capital," meaning money which is available for use in the purchase of machinery, equipment, and other productive facilities. But money, as such, produces nothing; hence, it is not to be considered as an economic resource. *Real capital*—tools, machinery, and other productive equipment—is an economic resource; *money* or *financial capital* is not.

LABOR **Labor** is a broad term which the economist uses in referring to all of the physical and mental talents of men and women which are usable in producing goods and services (with the exception of a special set of human talents—entrepreneurial ability—which, because of their special significance in a capitalistic economy, we choose to consider separately). Thus the services of a logger, retail clerk, machinist, teacher, professional football player, and nuclear physicist all fall under the general heading of labor.

ENTREPRENEURIAL ABILITY Finally, what can be said about this special human resource which we label **entrepreneurial ability,** or, more simply, *enterprise?* We shall give the term a specific meaning by assigning four related functions to the entrepreneur.

1 The entrepreneur takes the initiative in combining the resources of land, capital, and labor in the production of a good or service. Both a sparkplug and a catalyst, the entrepreneur is at once the driving force behind production and the agent who combines the other resources in what is hoped will be a profitable venture.

2 The entrepreneur undertakes the chore of making basic business-policy decisions, that is, those nonroutine decisions which set the course of a business enterprise.

3 The entrepreneur is an innovator—the person who attempts to introduce on a commercial basis new products, new productive techniques, or even new forms of business organization.

4 The entrepreneur is a risk bearer. This is apparent from a close examination of the other three entrepreneurial functions. The entrepreneur in a capitalistic system has no guarantee of profit. The reward for his or her time, efforts, and abilities may be attractive profits *or* losses and eventual bankruptcy. In short, the entrepreneur risks not only time, effort, and business reputation, but his or her invested funds and those of associates or stockholders.

Resource payments We shall see shortly how these resources are provided to business institutions in exchange for money income. The income received from supplying property resources—raw materials and capital equipment—is called *rental* and *interest income.* The income accruing to those who supply labor is called *wages* and includes salaries and various wage and salary supplements in the form of bonuses, commissions, royalties, and so forth. Entrepreneurial income is called *profits,* which, of course, may be a negative figure—that is, losses.

These four broad categories of economic resources, or *factors of production* as they are often called, leave room for debate when it comes to classifying specific resources. For example, suppose you receive a dividend on some Exxon stock which you may own. Is this an interest return for the capital equipment which the company was able to buy with the money you provided in buying Exxon stock? Or is this return a profit which compensates you for the risks involved in purchasing corporate stock? What about the earnings of a one-person general store where the owner is both the entrepreneur and the labor force? Are the owner's earnings to be considered as wages or profit income? The answer to both queries is "some of each." The important point is this: Although we might quibble about classifying a given flow of income as wages, rent, interest, or profits, all income can be listed without too much arbitrariness under one of these general headings.

Relative scarcity All economic resources, or factors of production, have one fundamental characteristic in common: *They are scarce or limited in supply.* Our "spaceship earth" contains only limited amounts of resources which can be put to use in the production of goods and services. Quantities of arable land, mineral deposits, capital equipment, and labor (time) are all limited; that is, they are available only in finite amounts. Because of the scarcity of productive resources and the constraint this scarcity puts upon productive activity, output will necessarily be limited. Society will *not* be able to produce and consume all the goods and services it might want. Thus, in the United States—one of the most affluent nations—output per person was limited to $19,755 in 1988. As a glance ahead at Table 41-1 indicates, in the poorest nations annual output per person may be as low as $200 or $300!

Economics and efficiency

We have arrived once again at the basic definition of economics first stated at the beginning of Chapter 1. *Economics is the social science concerned with the problem of using or administering scarce resources (the means of producing) so as to attain the greatest or maximum fulfillment of society's unlimited wants (the goal of producing).* Economics is concerned with "doing the best with what we have." If our wants are virtually unlimited and our resources are scarce, we cannot satisfy all society's material wants. The next best thing is to achieve the greatest possible satisfaction of these wants. Economics is a science of efficiency—efficiency in the use of scarce resources.

Precisely what is meant by *efficiency* as economists use the term? It means something similar to the term "efficiency" as used in engineering. The mechanical engineer tells us that a steam locomotive is only "10 percent efficient" because a large part—some 90 percent—of the energy in its fuel is not transformed into useful power but is wasted through friction and heat loss. The maximum output of usable power is not derived from the inputs of fuel.

Economic efficiency is also concerned with *inputs* and *outputs*. Specifically, it is concerned with the relationship between the units of scarce resources which are put into the process of production and the resulting output of some wanted product. More output from a given quantity of inputs designates an increase in efficiency. Less output from a given bundle of inputs indicates a decline in efficiency.

FULL EMPLOYMENT AND FULL PRODUCTION

Society wants to use its scarce resources efficiently; that is, it wants to get the maximum amount of useful goods and services produced with its limited resources. To achieve this it must realize both full employment and full production.

By **full employment** we mean that all available resources should be employed. No workers should be involuntarily out of work; the economy should provide employment for all who are willing and able to work. Nor should capital equipment or arable land sit idle. Note we say all *available* resources should be employed. Each society has certain customs and practices which determine what particular resources are available for employment. For example, legislation and custom provide that children and the very aged should not be employed. Similarly, it is desirable for productivity to allow farmland to lie fallow periodically.

By **full production** we simply mean that resources should be allocated efficiently; that is, employed resources should be utilized so as to make the most valuable contribution to total output. We should avoid allocating astrophysicists to farming and experienced farmers to our space research centers! Nor do we want Iowa's farmland planted to cotton and Alabama's to corn when experience indicates that the opposite assignment would provide the nation substantially more of both products from the same amount of land. Full production also implies that the best-available technologies are employed. We don't want our farmers harvesting wheat with scythes or picking corn by hand. Nor do we want to produce autos with the primitive assembly-line techniques Henry Ford introduced in the 1920s.

PRODUCTION POSSIBILITIES TABLE

The nature of the economizing problem can be brought into even clearer focus by the use of a production possibilities table.[3] This device reveals the core of the economizing problem: *Because resources are scarce, a full-employment, full-production economy cannot have an unlimited output of goods and services. Furthermore, choices must be made on which goods and services to produce and which to forgo.*

Assumptions We make several specific assumptions to set the stage for our illustration.

1 EFFICIENCY The economy is operating at full employment and achieving full production.

2 FIXED RESOURCES The available supplies of the factors of production are fixed in both quantity and quality. But, of course, they can be shifted or reallocated, within limits, among different uses; for example, a relatively unskilled laborer can work on a farm, at a fast-food restaurant, or in a gas station.

3 FIXED TECHNOLOGY The state of the technological arts is constant; this is, technology does not change during the course of our analysis. The second and third assumptions are another way of saying that we are looking at our economy at some specific point in time, or over a very short period of time. Over a relatively long period it would be unrealistic to rule out technological advances and the possibility that resource supplies might vary.

4 TWO PRODUCTS To simplify our illustration further, suppose our economy is producing just two products—industrial robots and pizza—instead of the innumerable goods and services actually produced. Pizza is symbolic of **consumer goods,** that is, those goods which directly satisfy our wants; industrial robots are symbolic of **capital goods,** that is, those goods which satisfy our wants *indirectly* by permitting more efficient production of consumer goods.

Necessity of choice Now, is it not evident from our assumptions that a choice must be made among alternatives? The available resources are limited.

[3] Paul A. Samuelson and William D. Nordhaus, *Economics,* 13th ed. (New York: McGraw-Hill Book Company, 1989), pp. 26–29.

Thus the total amounts of robots and pizza that our economy is capable of producing are limited. *Limited resources mean a limited output.* Since resources are limited in supply and fully employed, any increase in the production of robots will necessitate the shifting of resources away from the production of pizza. And the reverse holds true: If we choose to step up the production of pizza, needed resources must come at the expense of robot production. *Society cannot have its cake and eat it, too.* Facetiously put, there's no such thing as a "free lunch." This is the essence of the economizing problem.

Let us generalize by noting in Table 2-1 some alternative combinations of robots and pizza which our economy might conceivably choose. Though the data in this and the following tables are hypothetical, the points illustrated are of tremendous practical significance. At alternative A, our economy would be devoting all its resources to the production of robots, that is, capital goods. At alternative E, all available resources would be devoted to the production of pizza, that is, consumer goods. Both these alternatives are clearly unrealistic extremes; any economy typically strikes a balance in dividing its total output between capital and consumer goods. As we move from alternative A to E, we step up the production of consumer goods (pizza). How? By shifting resources away from capital goods production. When we remember that consumer goods directly satisfy our wants, any movement toward alternative E looks tempting. In making this move, society increases the current satisfaction of its wants. But there is a cost involved. This shift of resources catches up with society over

TABLE 2-1 **Production possibilities of pizza and robots with full employment, 1990 (hypothetical data)**

Type of product	Production alternatives				
	A	B	C	D	E
Pizza (in hundred thousands)	0	1	2	3	4
Robots (in thousands)	10	9	7	4	0

time as its stock of capital goods dwindles—or at least ceases to expand at the current rate—with the result that the potential for greater future production is impaired. In short, in moving from alternative A toward E, society is in effect choosing "more now" at the expense of "much more later." In moving from E toward A, society is choosing to forgo current consumption. This sacrifice of current consumption frees resources which can now be used to increase the production of capital goods. By building up its stock of capital in this way, society can anticipate greater production and, therefore, greater consumption in the future.

The critical idea is this: *At any point in time, a full-employment, full-production economy must sacrifice some of product X to obtain more of product Y.* The basic fact that economic resources are scarce prohibits such an economy from having more of both X and Y.

PRODUCTION POSSIBILITIES CURVE

To ensure our understanding of the **production possibilities table,** let us view these data graphically. We employ a simple two-dimensional graph, arbitrarily putting the output of robots (capital goods) on the vertical axis and the output of pizza (consumer goods) on the horizontal axis, as in Figure 2-1. Following the plotting procedure discussed in the appendix to Chapter 1, we can locate the "production possibilities" or "transformation"[4] curve, as shown in Figure 2-1.

Each point on the production possibilities curve represents some maximum output of the two products. Thus the curve is, in effect, a frontier. To realize the various combinations of pizza and robots which fall on the production possibilities curve, society must achieve full employment and full production. All combinations of pizza and robots *on* the curve represent maximum quantities attainable only as the result of the most efficient use of all available resources. Points lying *outside* the production possibilities curve, like point *W*, would be

[4] Why "transformation"? Because in moving from one alternative to another, say, from B to C, we are in effect transforming robots into pizza by shifting resources from the production of the former to the production of the latter.

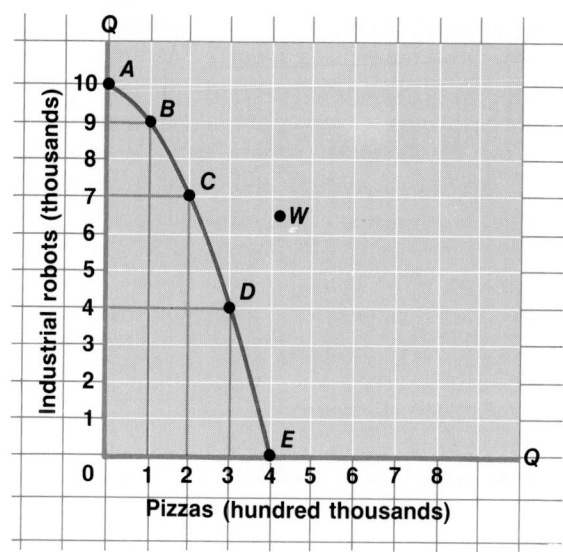

FIGURE 2-1

The production possibilities curve

Each point on the production possibilities curve represents some maximum output of any two products. Society must choose which product-mix it desires: more robots mean less pizza, and vice versa. Limited supplies of human and property resources make any combination of robots and pizza lying outside the production possibilities curve, such as *W*, unattainable.

superior to any point on the curve; but such points are unobtainable, given the current supplies of resources and technology. The production barrier of limited resources prohibits the production of any combination of capital and consumer goods lying outside the production possibilities curve.

OPTIMAL PRODUCT-MIX

If all outputs on the production possibilities curve reflect full employment and full production, which combination will society prefer? Consider, for example, points *B* and *D* in Figure 2-1. Which output-mix is superior or "best"? This is a nonscientific or normative matter; it reflects the values of society as expressed by its control group—the dictatorship, the party, the electorate, the citizenry, the individual institutions, or some combination thereof. What the economist can say is that if a society's production possibilities are as in Table 2-1 *and* if that society seeks the product-mix indicated by, say, alternative B, it is *not* using its resources efficiently if it realizes a total output comprised only of $8\frac{7}{8}$ units of robots and $\frac{9}{10}$ unit of pizza. And the economist can also say that the society cannot hope to achieve a national output of $9\frac{1}{2}$ units of robots and $1\frac{3}{8}$ units of pizza with its available resources. These are quantitative, objective, positive statements. But, although he or she may have opinions as an individual, the economist as a social scientist cannot say that combination B is "better" or "worse" than combination D. This is purely a qualitative or normative matter.

LAW OF INCREASING OPPORTUNITY COSTS

We have stressed that resources are scarce relative to the virtually unlimited wants which these resources can be used to satisfy. As a result, choices among alternatives must be made. Specifically, more of X (pizza) means less of Y (robots). *The amount of other products which must be forgone or sacrificed to obtain some amount of any given product is called the opportunity cost of that good.* In our case the amount of Y (robots) which must be forgone or given up to get another unit of X (pizza) is the *opportunity cost,* or simply the *cost,* of that unit of X. In moving from possibility A to B in Table 2-1, we find that the cost of 1 unit of pizza is 1 unit of robots. But, as we now pursue the concept of cost through the additional production possibilities—B to C, C to D, and so forth—an important economic principle is revealed to us. In moving from alternative A to alternative E, the sacrifice or cost of robots involved in getting each additional unit of pizza *increases.* In moving from A to B, just 1 unit of robots is sacrificed for 1 more unit of pizza; but going from B to C involves the sacrifice of 2 units of robots for 1 more of pizza; then 3 of robots for 1 of pizza; and finally 4 for 1. Conversely, you should confirm that in moving from E to A the cost of an additional robot is $\frac{1}{4}$, $\frac{1}{3}$, $\frac{1}{2}$, and 1 unit of pizza respectively for each of the four shifts.[5]

---

[5] A distinction between the opportunity cost of an *added* unit of a good and the *total,* or cumulative, opportunity cost is evident here. For example, the opportunity cost of the third unit of pizza in Table 2-1 is 3 units of robots $(= 7 - 4)$. But the total opportunity cost of 3 units of pizza is 6 units of robots $(= 10 - 4$ or $1 + 2 + 3)$.

Concavity Graphically, the **law of increasing opportunity costs** is reflected in the shape of the production possibilities curve. Specifically, the curve is *concave* or bowed out from the origin. Why? Because, as verified by the gray lines in Figure 2-1, when the economy moves from *A* toward *E*, it must give up successively larger amounts of robots (1, 2, 3, 4) as shown on the vertical axis to acquire equal increments of pizza (1, 1, 1, 1) as shown on the horizontal axis. Technically, this means that the slope of the production possibilities curve becomes steeper as we move from *A* to *E* and such a curve, by definition, is concave as viewed from the origin.

Rationale What is the economic rationale for the law of increasing opportunity costs? *Why* does the sacrifice of robots increase as we get more pizza? The answer to this query is rather complex. But, simply stated, it amounts to this: *Economic resources are not completely adaptable to alternative uses.* As we attempt to step up pizza production, resources which are less and less adaptable to this use must be induced, or "pushed," into this line of production. If we start at *A* and move to *B*, we can first pick resources whose productivity of pizza is greatest in relation to their productivity of robots. But as we move from *B* to *C*, *C* to *D*, and so on, those resources which are highly productive of pizza become increasingly scarce. To get more pizza, resources whose productivity in robots is great in relation to their productivity in pizza will be needed. It will obviously take more and more of such resources—and hence an increasingly great sacrifice of robots—to achieve a given increase of 1 unit in the production of pizza. This lack of perfect flexibility, or interchangeability, on the part of resources and the resulting increase in the sacrifice of one good that must be made in the acquisition of more and more units of another good is the rationale for the law of increasing opportunity costs, costs in this case being stated as sacrifices of goods and not in terms of dollars and cents.

The reader should verify that (1) under the unrealistic assumption of perfect adaptability of resources the production possibilities would be a straight line, implying *constant* opportunity costs; and (2) the law of increasing costs holds true in moving up the curve from alternative E to alternative A.

Reprise It is worth pausing to reemphasize that the production possibilities curve illustrates four basic concepts. First, the *scarcity* of resources is implicit in that all combinations of output lying outside the production possibilities curve are unobtainable. Second, *choice* is reflected in the need for society to select among the various attainable combinations of goods lying on (or within) the curve. Third, the downward slope of the curve implies the notion of *opportunity cost*. Finally, the concavity of the curve reveals *increasing opportunity costs*.

Unemployment, growth, and the future

It is important to understand what happens when the first three assumptions underlying the production possibilities curve are released.

UNEMPLOYMENT AND UNDEREMPLOYMENT

The first assumption was that our economy is characterized by full employment and full production. How would our analysis and conclusions be altered if idle resources were available (unemployment) or if employed resources were used inefficiently (underemployment)? With full employment and full production, our five alternatives represent a series of maximum outputs; that is, they illustrate what combinations of robots and pizzas might be produced when the economy is operating at its full capacity. With *un*employment or *under*employment, the economy would be producing less than each alternative shown in Table 2-1.

Graphically, a situation of unemployment or underemployment can be illustrated by a point *inside* the original production possibilities curve, which has been reproduced in Figure 2-2. Point *U* is such a point. Here we find the economy is falling short of the various maximum combinations of pizza and robots reflected by all the points *on* the production possibilities curve. The gray arrows in Figure 2-2 indicate three of the possible paths back to full employment and full production. A movement toward full employment and full production will entail a greater output of one or both products.

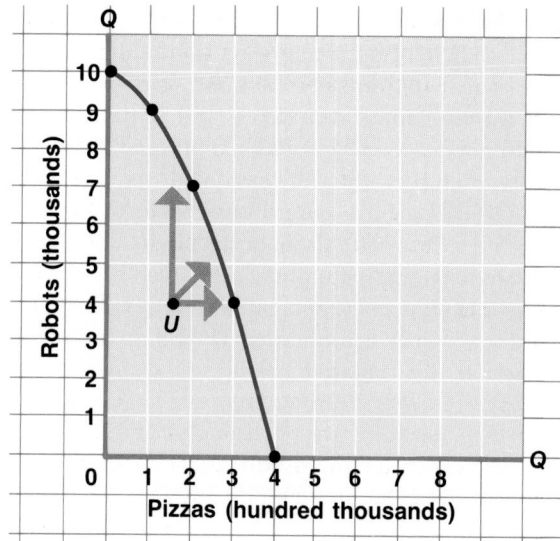

FIGURE 2-2

Unemployment and the production possibilities curve

Any point inside the production possibilities curve, such as *U*, indicates unemployment or underemployment. By moving toward full employment and full production, the economy can produce more of either or both of the two products, as the arrows indicate.

A GROWING ECONOMY

What happens to the production possibilities curve when we drop the remaining assumptions that the quantity and quality of resources and technology are fixed? The answer is: The production possibilities curve will shift position; that is, the potential total output of the economy will change.

Expanding resource supplies Let us now abandon the simplifying assumption that our total supplies of land, labor, capital, and entrepreneurial ability are fixed in both quantity and quality. Common sense tells us that over a period of time a nation's growing population will bring about increases in the supplies of labor and entrepreneurial ability.[6]

---

[6] This is not to say that population growth as such is always desirable. In Chapter 41 we shall discover that overpopulation can be a constant drag upon the living standards of many less developed countries. In advanced countries overpopulation can have adverse effects upon the environment and the quality of life.

Also, the quality of labor usually improves over time. For example, the percentage of the labor force with a high school education rose from 30 percent in 1960 to 40 percent in 1987. Historically, our stock of capital has increased at a significant, though unsteady, rate. And although we are depleting some of our energy and mineral resources, new sources are constantly being discovered. The drainage of swamps and the development of irrigation programs add to our supply of arable land. Assuming continuous full employment and full production, the net result of these increased supplies of the factors of production will be the ability to produce more of both robots and pizza. Thus, in, say, the year 2010, the production possibilities of Table 2-1 for 1990 may be obsolete, having given way to those shown in Table 2-2. Observe that the greater abundance of resources results in a greater potential output of one or both products at each alternative; economic growth, in the sense of an expanded potential output, has occurred.

But note this important point: Such a favorable shift in the production possibilities curve does not guarantee that the economy will actually operate at a point on that new curve. The economy might fail to realize fully its new potentialities. Some 120 million jobs will give us full employment at the present time, but ten or twenty years from now our labor force, because of a growing population, will be larger, and 120 million jobs will not be sufficient for full employment. In short, the production possibilities curve may shift, but the economy may fail to produce at a point on that new curve.

Technological advance Our other simplifying assumption is a constant or unchanging technology.

TABLE 2-2 **Production possibilities of pizza and robots with full employment, 2010 (hypothetical data)**

Type of product	Production alternatives				
	A′	B′	C′	D′	E′
Pizza (in hundred thousands)	0	2	4	6	8
Robots (in thousands)	14	12	9	5	0

Observation tells us that technology has progressed remarkably over a long period. What does an advancing technology entail? New and better goods *and* improved ways of producing these goods. For the moment, let us think of technological advance as entailing merely improvements in capital facilities—more efficient machinery and equipment. How does such technological advance alter our earlier discussion of the economizing problem? In this way: Technological advance, by improving productive efficiency, allows society to produce more goods with a fixed amount of resources. As with increases in resource supplies, technological advance permits the production of more robots *and* more pizza.

What happens to the production possibilities curve of Figure 2-2 when the supplies of resources increase or an improvement in technology occurs? The curve shifts outward and to the right, as illustrated by the dark blue curve in Figure 2-3. **Economic growth**—*the ability to produce a larger total output—is reflected in a rightward shift of the production possibilities curve; it is the result of increases in resource supplies and technological progress.* The consequence of growth is that our full-employment economy can enjoy a greater output of *both* robots and pizza. While a static, no-growth economy must sacrifice some of X to get more of Y, a dynamic, growing economy can have larger quantities of both X and Y.

Economic growth does *not* typically entail proportionate increases in a nation's capacity to produce various products. Note in Figure 2-3 that, while the economy is able to produce twice as much pizza, the increase in robot production is only 40 percent. On Figure 2-3 the student should pencil in two new production possibilities curves: one to show the situation where a better technique for producing robots has been developed, the technology for producing pizza being unchanged, and the other to illustrate an improved technology for pizza, the technology for producing robots being constant.

A sober postscript is necessary: In modern industrial societies we are inclined to take economic growth—more-or-less continuous rightward shifts of the production possibilities curve—for granted. But, as the recent catastrophic famine in Ethiopia, Chad, the Sudan, and other African nations indicates, in some circumstances the production possi-

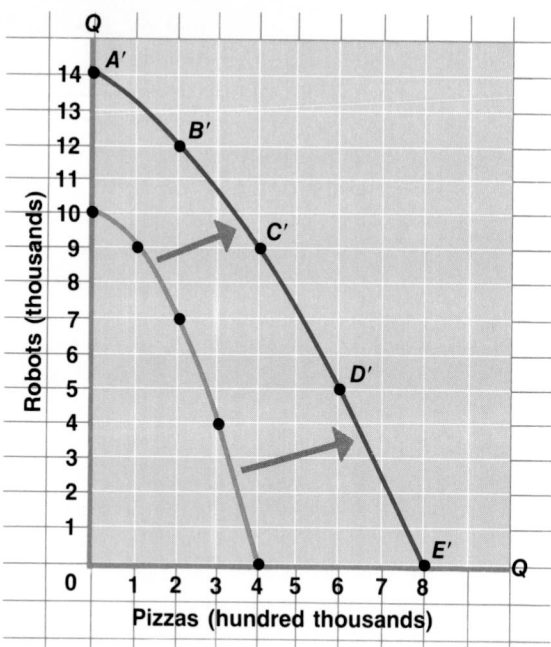

FIGURE 2-3

Economic growth and the production possibilities curve

The expanding resource supplies and technological advances which characterize a growing economy move the production possibilities curve outward and to the right. This permits the economy to enjoy larger quantities of both types of goods.

bilities curve may shift leftward. An important cause of the African famine is ecological degradation or, more simply, poor land-use practices. Land has been deforested, overfarmed, and overgrazed, causing the production possibilities of these highly agriculturally oriented countries to diminish. Combined with rapid population growth, the leftward-shifting production possibilities curves have resulted in malnourishment and famine. Chapter 41's Last Word explores this topic in some detail.

PRESENT CHOICES AND FUTURE POSSIBILITIES

You may have anticipated this important point in the foregoing paragraphs: *An economy's current choice of position on its production possibilities curve is a basic determinant of the future location of that curve.* To illustrate this notion, let us designate the two axes of the production possibilities curve as "goods for the future" and "goods for the present," as in Figures 2-4a and b. By "goods for the future" we refer to such things as capital goods, research and education, and preventive medicine, which obviously tend to increase the quantity and quality of property resources, enlarge the stock of technological information, and improve the quality of human resources. It is, as we have already seen, "goods for the future" which are the ingredients of economic growth. By "goods for the present" we mean pure consumer goods in the form of foodstuffs, clothing, "boom boxes," automobiles, power mowers, and so forth.

Now suppose there are two economies, Alphania and Betania, which at the moment are identical in every respect except that Alphania's current (1990) choice of position on its production possibilities curve strongly favors "present goods" as opposed to "future goods." The dot in Figure 2-4a indicates this choice. Betania, on the other hand, renders a current (1990) choice which stresses large amounts of "future goods" and lesser amounts of "present goods" (Figure 2-4b). Now, all other things being the same, we can expect the future (2010) production possibilities curve of Betania to be farther to the right than that of Alphania. That is, by currently choosing an output which is more conducive to technological advance and to increases in the quantity and quality of property and human resources, Betania will tend to achieve greater economic growth than will Alphania, whose current choice of output places less emphasis upon those goods and services which cause the production possibilities curve to shift rightward. Thinking solely in terms of capital goods, Betania is choosing to make larger current additions to its "national factory"—that is, to invest more of its current output—than is Alphania. The payoff or benefit from this choice is more rapid growth—greater future productive capacity—for Betania. The cost, of course, is fewer consumer goods in the present.

REAL-WORLD APPLICATIONS

Let us consider several of many possible applications of the production possibilities curve.

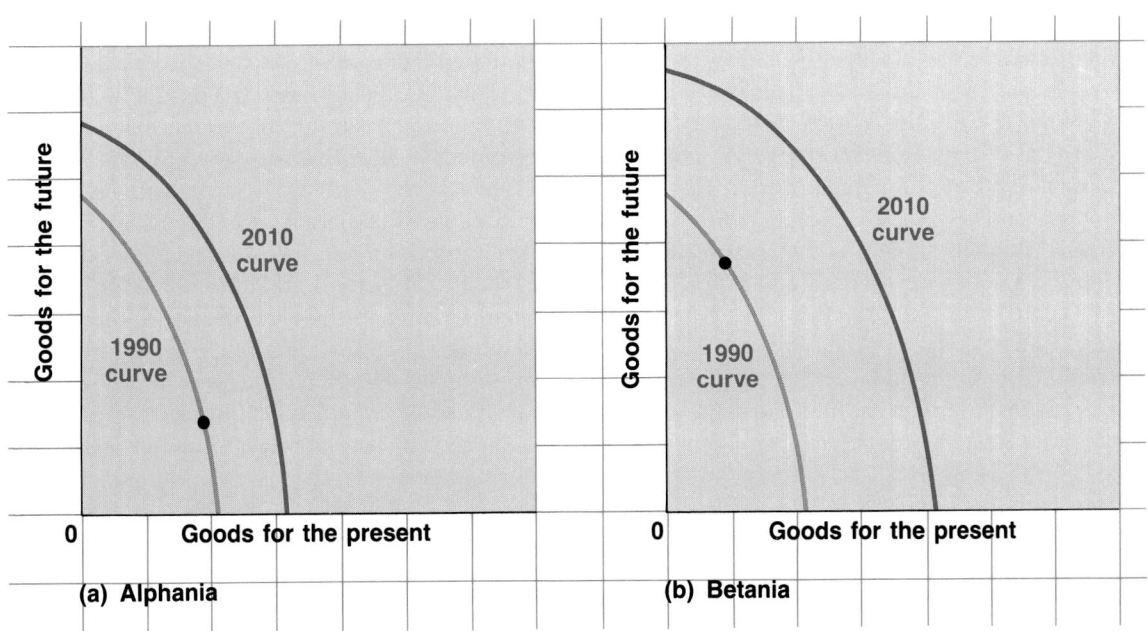

FIGURE 2-4

An economy's present choice of position on its production possibilities curve helps determine the curve's future location

A current choice favoring "present goods," as rendered by Alphania in (a), will cause a modest rightward shift of the curve. A current choice favoring "future goods," as rendered by Betania in (b), will result in a greater rightward shift of the curve.

I Microeconomic budgeting While our discussion is in macroeconomic terms—that is, in terms of the output of the entire economy—the concepts of scarcity, choice, and opportunity cost also apply at the microeconomic level. Hence, individuals have limited money incomes because they provide limited amounts of resources to the productive process. A limited budget means one must engage in choices or tradeoffs in buying goods and services (Chapter 23). The purchase of a pair of blue jeans may entail the opportunity cost of dinner and a rock concert. Similarly, many students are faced with the problem of allocating a fixed amount of time between studying and working to finance their education. The implied production possibilities type of tradeoff is that more hours spent working will mean more income, but also indicate less study time and a lower grade average.

2 Going to war An historical illustration: In beginning to produce war goods for World War II (1941–

1946), the United States found itself with considerable unemployment. Hence, our economy was able to accomplish the production of an almost unbelievably large quantity of war goods and at the same time increase the volume of consumer goods output (Figure 2-2).[7] The Soviet Union, on the other hand, entered World War II at almost capacity production; that is, the Soviet economy was operating close to full employment. Therefore, its military preparations entailed a considerable shifting of resources from the production of civilian goods and a concomitant drop in the standard of living.

Curiously, the United States found its position during the Vietnam War to be similar to that of the Soviet Union during World War II. Our economy was at full employment in the mid-1960s and the Johnson administration accelerated military

---

[7] There did occur, however, rather acute shortages of specific types of consumer goods.

spending for Vietnam while simultaneously increasing expenditures on domestic "war on poverty" programs. This attempt to achieve simultaneously more pizza and more robots—or, more accurately, more guns and more butter—in a full-employment economy was doomed to failure. The attempt to spend beyond our capacity to produce—to realize a point like *W* in Figure 2-1—contributed significantly to the double-digit inflation of the 1970s.

3 Discrimination Discrimination based on race, sex, age, or ethnic background is an obstacle to the efficient allocation or employment of human resources and thereby keeps the economy operating at some point inside the production possibilities curve. Simply put, discrimination prevents blacks, women, and others from obtaining jobs wherein society can utilize efficiently the skills and talents which they possess. The elimination of discrimination would therefore help to move the economy from some point inside the production possibilities curve toward a point on the curve. Rough estimates suggest that the elimination of racial discrimination alone would allow the production of a 4 percent larger national output with the same amount of labor inputs![8]

4 Productivity slowdown Since the mid-1960s the United States has experienced a rather alarming decline in the rate of growth of labor productivity; that is, the growth of output per worker-hour has diminished (Chapter 21). Some economists feel a major cause of this decline is that the rate of increase in the mechanization of labor has slowed because of insufficient investment. The proposed remedy is to increase investment as compared to consumption. That is, a *D* to *C* type of shift in Figure 2-1 is recommended. Special tax incentives to make business investment more profitable are an appropriate policy to facilitate this shift. The expectation is that the restoration of a more rapid rate of productivity growth will accelerate the growth of the economy (that is, the rightward shift of the production possibilities curve) through time.

[8] Joint Economic Committee, *The Cost of Racial Discrimination* (Washington, 1980), pp. 2–5.

5 International trade aspects The simple message of the production possibilities curve is that a nation cannot live beyond its means or production potential. When the possibility of international trade is taken into account, this statement must be modified in two ways.

First, we will discover in later chapters that through international specialization and trade a nation can circumvent the output constraint imposed by its domestic production possibilities curve. That is, we shall find that international specialization and trade have the same impact as having more and better resources or discovering improved production techniques. Both have the effect of increasing the quantities of both capital and consumer goods available to society. International specialization and trade are the equivalent of economic growth.

Second, within the context of international trade, a nation can achieve a combination of goods outside of its domestic production possibilities curve (such as point *W* in Figure 2-1) by incurring a *trade deficit,* that is, by buying and receiving an amount of imported goods from the rest of the world which exceeds the amount of goods exported to the rest of the world. As a matter of fact, the United States has been doing just that in recent years. In 1987, for example, the United States had a trade deficit of approximately $160 billion or, in other words, we imported $160 billion more worth of goods than we exported. The net result was that in 1987 the United States enjoyed some $160 billion of output in excess of what it produced domestically.

This looks like a very favorable state of affairs. Unfortunately, there is a catch. To finance its deficit—to pay for its excess of imports over exports—the United States must go into debt to its international trading partners *or* it must give up ownership of some of its assets to those other nations. Analogy: How can you live beyond your current income? Answer: Borrow from your parents, the sellers of goods, or a financial institution. Or, alternatively, sell some of your real assets (your car or stereo) or financial assets (stocks or bonds) which you own. This is what the United States has been doing. We find that a major consequence of our large and persistent trade deficits is that foreign nationals hold larger portions of American private and public debt and own larger amounts of our business corporations, agricultural land, and real estate. To pay our debts and to repurchase those assets we must in the future live well *within* our means. We must settle for some combination of goods within our production possibilities curve so that we can export more than we import—that is, incur a *trade surplus*—as a means of paying off our world debts and reacquiring ownership of those assets.

6 Gorbachev's choices This chapter's Last Word, concerning the constraints which the production possibilities curve imposes upon Mikhail Gorbachev's program to revitalize the Soviet economy, is relevant reading at this point.

The "isms"

We must now recognize that a variety of different institutional arrangements and coordinating mechanisms may be used by a society in responding to the economizing problem. Generally speaking, the industrially advanced economies of the world differ essentially on two grounds: (1) the ownership of the means of production, and (2) the method by which economic activity is coordinated and directed. Let us briefly examine the main characteristics of the two "polar" types of economic systems.

PURE CAPITALISM

Pure, or **laissez faire, capitalism** is characterized by the private ownership of resources and the use of a system of markets and prices to coordinate and direct economic activity. In such a system each participant is motivated by his or her own self-interests; each economic unit seeks to maximize its income through individual decision making. The market system functions as a mechanism through which individual decisions and preferences are communicated and coordinated. The fact that goods and services are produced and resources are supplied under competitive conditions means there are many independently acting buyers and sellers of each product and resource. As a result, economic power is widely dispersed. Advocates of pure capitalism argue that such an economy is conducive to

efficiency in the use of resources, output and employment stability, and rapid economic growth. Hence, there is little or no need for government planning, control, or intervention. Indeed, the term *laissez faire* roughly translates as "let it be," that is, keep the government from interfering with the economy. The reason is that such interference will disturb the efficiency with which the market system functions. Government's role is therefore limited to the protection of private property and establishing an appropriate legal framework to facilitate the functioning of free markets (Chapter 5).

THE COMMAND ECONOMY

The polar alternative to pure capitalism is the **command economy** or **communism,** characterized by public ownership of virtually all property resources and collective determination of economic decisions through central economic planning. All major decisions concerning the level of resource use, the composition and distribution of output, and the organization of production are determined by a central planning board. Business firms are governmentally owned and produce according to state directives. That is, production targets are determined by the planning board for each enterprise and the plan specifies the amounts of resources to be allocated to each enterprise so that it might realize its production goals. Workers are assigned to occupations and perhaps even allocated geographically by the plan. The division of output between capital and consumer goods is centrally decided as is the allocation of consumer goods among the citizenry. Capital goods are allocated among industries in terms of the central planning board's long-term priorities.

MIXED SYSTEMS

Real-world economies are arrayed between the extremes of pure capitalism and the command economy. The United States economy leans toward pure capitalism, but with important differences. As we shall find in Chapter 6, government plays an active role in our economy in promoting economic stability and growth, in providing certain goods and services which would be underproduced or not produced at all by the market system, in modifying the distribution of income, and so forth. In contrast to the wide dispersion of economic power among many small units which characterizes pure capitalism, American capitalism has spawned powerful economic organizations in the form of large corporations and strong labor unions. The ability of these power blocs to manipulate and distort the functioning of the market system to their advantage provides a further reason for governmental involvement in the economy. While the Soviet Union approximates the command economy, it relies to some extent upon market-determined prices and has some vestiges of private ownership.

But it must be emphasized that private ownership and reliance on the market system do not always go together, nor do public ownership and central planning. For example, the *fascism* of Hitler's Nazi Germany has been dubbed **authoritarian capitalism** because the economy was subject to a high degree of governmental control and direction, but property was privately owned. In contrast, the Yugoslavian economy of **market socialism** is characterized by public ownership of resources coupled with increasing reliance upon free markets to organize and coordinate economic activity. The Swedish economy is also a hybrid system. Although over 90 percent of business activity is in private hands, government is deeply involved in achieving economic stability and in redistributing income. Similarly, the capitalistic Japanese economy entails a great deal of planning and "coordination" between government and the business sector. Table 2-3 summarizes the various ways economic systems can be categorized on the basis of the two criteria we are using. Keep in mind that the real-world examples we have plugged into this framework are no more than rough approximations.

THE TRADITIONAL ECONOMY

Table 2-3 is couched in terms of industrially advanced or at least semideveloped economies. Many of the less developed countries of the world have **traditional** or **customary economies** (Chapter 41). Production methods, exchange, and the distribution of income are all sanctioned by custom. Heredity and caste circumscribe the economic

LAST WORD

Gorbachev's choices

The scarce resources—unlimited wants dilemma underscores the difficult choices now being made in the Soviet economy.

Since coming to power in 1985, Soviet leader Mikhail Gorbachev has moved vigorously to revitalize a lagging economy. The Soviet economy has fared badly in the past fifteen years or so. Economic growth has declined, production methods have become increasingly obsolete in comparison to other industrialized nations, and manufactured goods are shoddy by western standards.

A basic feature of Gorbachev's program of "restructuring" or reforming the economy is to invest heavily in technologically advanced machinery and equipment to update the Soviet Union's "national factory." How might this be done? From what alternative uses might the needed resources be obtained?

The most obvious option is to reduce consumption. But consumption levels are already low in the Soviet Union. Per capita consumption is only about one-third that of the United States and many basic consumer goods are in chronic short supply. Indeed, a basic objective of reform is to provide the Soviet population with long-promised increases in their standard of living.

Another option is to reallocate resources from the military sector to investment. It is estimated that Soviet military spending is about equal to that of the United States. Given that the Soviet national output is only about one-half that of the United States, their military burden is roughly twice as great as ours. It is reasonable to assume that recent arms agreements with the United States and its allies, the withdrawal of Soviet troops from Afghanistan, and announced plans to reduce the size of the Red Army are motivated by a desire to reallocate resources from the military to investment and consumption uses.

Another option is to increase efficiency. That is, instead of freeing up resources from alternative uses, can existing resources somehow be made capable of producing more output? One means of doing this is to enhance the incentives of workers and managers to produce. The Gorbachev reforms include modest steps to permit for-profit production outside of the central planning system and farmers are now permitted to lease land from the government to produce crops for profits. Another way of increasing productivity is to obtain the superior technologies and managerial skills of other industrialized nations. Thus we find the Gorbachev regime showing a greater interest in joint ventures in which American, German, and Japanese firms construct and help manage plants in the Soviet Union.

The extent to which the Gorbachev reforms will be successful in rejuvinating the Soviet economy remains unclear at this time. It is clear that the scarce resources–unlimited wants problem is very much in evidence in the overall character of those reforms.

TABLE 2-3 **Comparative economic systems**

		Coordinating mechanism	
		Market system	Central planning
Ownership of resources	Private	United States	Nazi Germany
	Public	Yugoslavia	Soviet Union

roles of individuals and socioeconomic immobility is pronounced. Technological change and innovation are closely constrained because they clash with tradition and threaten the social fabric. Economic activity is secondary to religious and cultural values and society's desire to perpetuate the status quo. In making the decision to pursue economic development, traditional economies must face the question as to which model in Table 2-3 will result in growth and simultaneously be the least incompatible with other economic and noneconomic goals valued by that society.

The basic point to be emphasized is that there is no unique or universally accepted way to respond to the economizing problem. Various societies, having different cultural and historical backgrounds, different mores and customs, and contrasting ideological frameworks—not to mention resources which differ both quantitatively and qualitatively—use different institutions in dealing with the reality of relative scarcity. The Soviet Union, the United States, and Great Britain, for example, are all—in terms of their accepted goals, ideology, technologies, resources, and culture—attempting to achieve efficiency in the use of their respective resources. The best method for responding to the unlimited wants–scarce resources dilemma in one economy may be inappropriate for another economic system.

CHAPTER SUMMARY

I The science of economics centers upon two basic facts: first, human material wants are virtually unlimited; second, economic resources are scarce.

2 Economic resources may be classified as property resources—raw materials and capital—or as human resources—labor and entrepreneurial ability.

3 Economics is concerned with the problem of administering scarce resources in the production of goods and services for the fulfillment of the material wants of society. Both the full employment and the full production of available resources are essential if this administration is to be efficient.

4 At any point in time a full-employment, full-production economy must sacrifice the output of some types of goods and services to achieve increased production of others. Because resources are not equally productive in all possible uses, the shifting of resources from one use to another gives rise to the law of increasing opportunity costs; that is, the production of additional units of product X entails the sacrifice of increasing amounts of product Y.

5 Over time, technological advance and increases in the quantity and quality of human and property resources permit the economy to produce more of all goods and services. Society's choice as to the composition of current output is a determinant of the future location of the production possibilities curve.

6 The various economic systems of the world differ in their ideologies and also in their responses to the economizing problem. Critical differences center upon **a** private versus public ownership of resources, and **b** the use of the market system versus central planning as a coordinating mechanism.

TERMS AND CONCEPTS

utility	law of increasing opportunity costs
economizing problem	
land, capital labor, and entrepreneurial ability	economic growth
investment	pure or laissez faire capitalism
full employment	command economy or communism
full production	
consumer goods	authoritarian capitalism
capital goods	market socialism
production possibilities table (curve)	traditional or customary economies

QUESTIONS AND STUDY SUGGESTIONS

1 "Economics is the study of the principles governing the allocation of scarce means among competing ends when the objective of the allocation is to maximize the attainment of the ends."[9] Explain. Why is the problem of unemployment a part of the subject matter of economics?

2 "Wants aren't insatiable. I can prove it. I get all the coffee I want to drink every morning at breakfast." Critically analyze. Explain: "Goods and services are scarce because resources are scarce." Analyze: "It is the nature of all economic problems that absolute solutions are denied us."

3 What are economic resources? What are the major functions of the entrepreneur? "Economics is . . . neither capitalist nor socialist: it applies to every society. Economics would disappear only in a world so rich that no wants were unfulfilled for lack of resources. Such a world is not imminent and may be impossible, for time is always limited."[10] Carefully evaluate and explain these statements. Do you agree that time is an economic resource?

4 Comment on the following statement from a newspaper article: "Our junior high school serves a splendid hot meal for $1 without costing the taxpayers anything, thanks in part to a government subsidy."

5 The following is a production possibilities table for war goods and civilian goods:

Type of production	Production alternatives				
	A	B	C	D	E
Automobiles (in millions)	0	2	4	6	8
Guided missiles (in thousands)	30	27	21	12	0

a Show these production possibilities data graphically. What do the points on the curve indicate? How does the curve reflect the law of increasing opportunity costs? Explain. If the economy is currently at point *C*,

[9] George J. Stigler, *The Theory of Price* (New York: The Macmillan Company, 1947), p. 12.

[10] Joseph P. McKenna, *Intermediate Economic Theory* (New York: Holt, Rinehart and Winston, Inc., 1958), p. 2.

what is the cost of 1 million more automobiles? Of 1000 more guided missiles?

b Label point *G* inside the curve. What does it indicate? Label point *H* outside the curve. What does this point indicate? What must occur before the economy can attain the level of production indicated by point *H*?

c Upon what specific assumptions is the production possibilities curve based? What happens when each of these assumptions is released?

d Suppose improvement occurs in the technology of producing guided missiles but not in the production of automobiles. Draw the new production possibilities curve. Now assume that a technological advance occurs in producing automobiles but not in producing guided missiles. Draw the new production possibilities curve. Finally, draw a production possibilities curve which reflects technological improvement in the production of both products.

6 What is the opportunity cost of attending college?

7 "The present choice of position on the production possibilities curve is a major factor in economic growth." Explain.

8 Contrast the means by which pure capitalism, market socialism, and a command economy attempt to cope with economic scarcity.

9 Explain how an international trade deficit may permit an economy to acquire a combination of goods in excess of its domestic production potential. Explain why nations try to avoid having trade deficits.

10 The British coal-mining industry was virtually shut down for a year during 1984 to 1985 because of a strike. Can you speculate as to how this might have affected **a** the location of Britain's production possibilities curve, and **b** the economy's actual point of operation relative to the curve?

CHAPTER 3

Pure capitalism and the circular flow

The task of the present chapter is to describe the capitalist ideology and to explain how pure, or laissez faire, capitalism would function.

Strictly speaking, pure capitalism has never existed and probably never will. Why, then, do we bother to consider the operation of such an economy? Because it gives us a very rough *first approximation* of how the United States economy functions. And approximations or models, when properly handled, can be very useful. In other words, pure capitalism constitutes a simplified model which we shall then modify and adjust in later chapters to correspond more closely to the reality of American capitalism.

In explaining the operation of pure capitalism, we shall discuss: (1) the institutional framework and basic assumptions which make up the capitalist ideology; (2) certain institutions and practices common to all modern economies; (3) capitalism and the circular flow of income; (4) how product and resource prices are determined; and (5) the market system and the allocating of economic resources. The first three topics constitute the present chapter; the latter two will be the subject matter of Chapters 4 and 5.

Capitalist ideology

Unfortunately, there is no neat and universally accepted definition of capitalism. We are therefore required to examine in some detail the basic tenets of pure capitalism to acquire a comprehensive understanding of what it entails. In short, the framework of capitalism embodies the following institutions and assumptions: (1) private property, (2) freedom of enterprise and choice, (3) self-interest as the dominant motive, (4) competition, (5) reliance upon the price or market system, and (6) a limited role for government.

PRIVATE PROPERTY

Under a capitalistic system, property resources are owned by private individuals and private institutions rather than by government. **Private property,** coupled with the freedom to negotiate binding legal contracts, permits private persons or businesses to obtain, control, employ, and dispose of property resources as they see fit. The institution of private property is sustained over time by the *right to bequeath,* that is, by the right of a property owner to designate the recipient of this property at the time of death.

Needless to say, there are broad legal limits to this right of private ownership. For example, the use of one's resources for the production of illicit drugs is prohibited. Nor is public ownership nonexistent. Even in pure capitalism, recognition is given to the fact that public ownership of certain "natural monopolies" may be essential to the achievement of efficiency in the use of resources.

FREEDOM OF ENTERPRISE AND CHOICE

Closely related to private ownership of property is freedom of enterprise and choice. Capitalism charges its component economic units with the responsibility of making certain choices, which are registered and made effective through the free markets of the economy.

Freedom of enterprise means that under pure capitalism, private business enterprises are free to obtain economic resources, to organize these resources in the production of a good or service of the firm's own choosing, and to sell it in the markets of their choice. No artificial obstacles or restrictions imposed by government or other producers block an entrepreneur's choice to enter or leave a particular industry.

Freedom of choice means that owners of property resources and money capital can employ or dispose of these resources as they see fit. It also means that laborers are free to enter any of those lines of work for which they are qualified. Finally, it means that consumers are at liberty, within the limits of their money incomes, to buy that collection of goods and services which they feel is most appropriate in satisfying their wants. Freedom of consumer choice may well be the most profound of these freedoms. The consumer is in a particularly strategic position in a capitalistic economy; in a sense, the consumer is sovereign. The range of free choices for suppliers of human and property resources is circumscribed by the choices of consumers. The consumer ultimately decides what the capitalistic economy should produce, and resource suppliers must make their free choices within the constraints thereby delineated. Resource suppliers and businesses are not really "free" to produce goods and services consumers do not desire.

Again, broad legal limitations prevail in the expression of all these free choices.

ROLE OF SELF-INTEREST

Because capitalism is an individualistic system, it is not surprising to find that the primary driving force of such an economy is the promotion of one's **self-interest;** each economic unit attempts to do what is best for itself. Hence, entrepreneurs aim at the maximization of their firms' profits or, as the case might be, the minimization of losses. And, other things being equal, owners of property resources attempt to achieve the highest price obtainable from the rent or sale of these resources. Given the amount and irksomeness of the effort involved,

those who supply human resources will also attempt to obtain the highest possible incomes from their employment. Consumers, in purchasing a given product, will seek to obtain it at the lowest price. In short, capitalism presumes self-interest as the fundamental *modus operandi* for the various economic units as they express their free choices. The motive of self-interest gives direction and consistency to what might otherwise be an extremely chaotic economy.

It is worth noting that the pursuit of economic self-interest should not be confused with selfishness. The stockholder who receives corporate dividends may contribute a portion to the United Way or leave bequests to grandchildren. Similarly, a local church official will carefully compare price and quality among various brands in buying new pews for the church.

COMPETITION

Freedom of choice exercised in terms of promoting one's own monetary returns provides the basis for **competition,** or economic rivalry, as a fundamental feature of capitalism. Competition, as economists see it, entails:

1 The presence of large numbers of independently acting buyers and sellers operating in the market for any particular product or resource.

2 The freedom of buyers and sellers to enter or leave particular markets.

Let us briefly explore these two related aspects of competition.

Large numbers The essence of competition is the widespread diffusion of economic power within the two major aggregates—businesses and households—which comprise the economy. When a large number of buyers and sellers are present in a particular market, no one buyer or seller will be able to demand or offer a quantity of the product sufficiently large to noticeably influence its price. Let us examine this statement in terms of the selling or supply side of the product market.

We have all observed that when a product becomes unusually scarce, its price will rise. For example, an unseasonable frost in Florida may seriously curtail the output of citrus crops and sharply increase the price of oranges. Similarly, *if* a single producer, or a small group of producers acting together, can somehow control or restrict the total supply of a product, then price can be raised to the seller's advantage. By controlling supply, the producer can "rig the market" on his or her own behalf. Now the essence of competition is that there are so many sellers that each, *because he or she is contributing an almost negligible fraction of the total supply,* has virtually no influence over the supply or, therefore, over product price.

For example, suppose there are 10,000 farmers, each of whom is supplying 100 bushels of corn in the Kansas City grain market at some particular time when the price of corn happens to be $4 per bushel. Could a single farmer who feels dissatisfied with the existing price cause an artificial scarcity of corn and thereby boost the price above $4? The answer clearly is "No." Farmer Jones, by restricting output from 100 to 75 bushels, exerts virtually no effect upon the total supply of corn. In fact, the total amount supplied is reduced only from 1,000,000 to 999,975 bushels. This obviously is not much of a shortage! Supply is virtually unchanged, and, therefore, the $4 price persists. In brief, competition means that each seller is providing a drop in the bucket of total supply. Individual sellers can make no noticeable dent in total supply; hence, a seller cannot *as an individual producer*[1] manipulate product price. This is what is meant when it is pointed out that an individual competitive seller is "at the mercy of the market." The same rationale applies to the demand side of the market. Buyers are plentiful and act independently. Thus single buyers cannot manipulate the market to their advantage.

The important point is this: *The widespread diffusion of economic power underlying competition controls the use and limits the potential abuse of that power.* Economic rivalry prevents economic units from wreaking havoc upon one another as they attempt to further their self-interests. Competition imposes limits upon expressions of self-interest by buyers and sellers. Competition is a basic regulatory force in capitalism.

---

[1] Of course, if a number of farmers simultaneously restricted their production, the resulting change in total supply could no longer be ignored, and price would rise. Competition (a large number of sellers) implies the impossibility of such collusion.

Entry and exit   Competition also assumes that it is a simple matter for producers to enter or leave a particular industry; there are no artificial legal or institutional obstacles to prohibit the expansion or contraction of specific industries. This aspect of competition is prerequisite to the flexibility which is essential if an economy is to remain efficient over time. Freedom of entry is necessary if the economy is to adjust appropriately to changes in consumer tastes, technology, or resource supplies. This matter will receive detailed treatment in Chapter 5.

MARKETS AND PRICES

The basic coordinating mechanism of a capitalist economy is the market or price system. *Capitalism is a market economy.* The decisions rendered by the buyers and sellers of products and resources are made effective through a system of markets. Indeed, by definition, a **market** is simply a mechanism or arrangement which brings the buyers or "demanders" and the sellers or "suppliers" of a good or service into contact with one another. A McDonald's, a gas station, a grocery supermarket, a Sotheby's art auction, the New York Stock exchange, and worldwide foreign exchange markets are but a few of innumerable illustrations. The preferences of sellers and buyers are registered on the supply and demand sides of various markets, and the outcome of these choices is a system of product and resource prices. These prices are guideposts upon which resource owners, entrepreneurs, and consumers make and revise their free choices in furthering their self-interests. Just as competition is the controlling mechanism, so a system of markets and prices is a basic organizing force. The market system is an elaborate communication system through which innumerable individual free choices are recorded, summarized, and balanced against one another. Those who obey the dictates of the market system are rewarded; those who ignore them are penalized by the system. Through this communication system, society renders its decisions concerning what the economy should produce, how production can be efficiently organized, and how the fruits of productive endeavor are to be distributed among the individual economic units which make up capitalism.

Not only is the market system the mechanism

through which society renders decisions concerning how it allocates its resources and distributes the resulting output, but it is through the market system that these decisions are carried out. However, a word of caution: Economic systems based upon the ideologies of socialism and communism also depend upon market systems, but not to the same degree or in the same way as does pure capitalism. Socialistic and communistic societies use markets and prices primarily to implement the decisions made wholly or in part by a central planning authority. In capitalism, the market system functions both as a device for registering innumerable choices of free individuals and businesses *and* as a mechanism for carrying out these decisions.

In Chapters 4 and 5 we shall analyze the mechanics and the operation of the market system.

LIMITED GOVERNMENT

A competitive capitalist economy is thought to be conducive to a high degree of efficiency in the use or allocation of its resources. Hence, there is allegedly little real need for governmental intervention in the operation of such an economy beyond its aforementioned role of imposing broad legal limits upon the exercise of individual choices and the use of private property. The concept of pure capitalism as a self-regulating and self-adjusting type of economy precludes any significant economic role for government. However, as we shall find in Chapter 6, a number of limitations and potentially undesirable outcomes associated with capitalism and the market system have resulted in an active economic role for government.

Other characteristics

Private property, freedom of enterprise and choice, self-interest as a motivating force, competition, and reliance on a market system are all institutions and assumptions which are more or less exclusively associated with pure capitalism. In addition, there are certain institutions and practices which are characteristic of all modern economies. They are (1) the use of an advanced technology and large amounts of capital goods, (2) specialization, and

(3) the use of money. Specialization and an advanced technology are prerequisites to the efficient employment of any economy's resources. The use of money is a permissive characteristic which allows society more easily to practice and reap the benefits of specialization and of the employment of advanced productive techniques.

EXTENSIVE USE OF CAPITAL GOODS

All modern economies—whether they approximate the capitalist, socialist, or communist ideology—are based upon an advanced technology and the extensive use of capital goods. Under pure capitalism it is competition, coupled with freedom of choice and the desire to further one's self-interest, which provides the means for achieving technological advance. The capitalistic framework is felt to be highly effective in harnessing incentives to develop new products and improved techniques of production. Why? Because the monetary rewards derived therefrom accrue directly to the innovator. Pure capitalism therefore presupposes the extensive use and relatively rapid development of complex capital goods: tools, machinery, large-scale factories, and facilities for storage, transportation, and marketing.

Why are the existence of an advanced technology and the extensive use of capital goods important? Because the most direct method of producing a product is usually the least efficient.[2] Even Robinson Crusoe avoided the inefficiencies of direct production in favor of **roundabout production.** It would be ridiculous for a farmer—even a backyard farmer—to go at production with bare hands. Obviously, it pays huge dividends in terms of more efficient production and, therefore, a more abundant output, to fashion tools of production, that is, capital equipment, to aid in the productive process. There is a better way of getting water out of a well than to dive in after it!

But there is a catch involved. As we recall our discussion of the production possibilities curve and the basic nature of the economizing problem, it is

---

[2] Remember that consumer goods satisfy wants directly, while capital goods do so indirectly through the more efficient future production of consumer goods.

evident that, with full employment and full production, resources must be diverted from the production of consumer goods in order to be used in the production of capital goods. We must currently tighten our belts as consumers in order to free resources for the production of capital goods which will increase productive efficiency and permit us to have a greater output of consumer goods at some future date.

SPECIALIZATION

The extent to which society relies upon **specialization** is astounding. The vast majority of consumers produce virtually none of the goods and services they consume and, conversely, consume little or nothing of what they produce. The hammer-shop laborer who spends a lifetime stamping out parts for jet engines may never "consume" an airplane trip. The assembly-line worker who devotes 8 hours a day to the installation of windows in Camaros may own a Honda. Few households seriously consider any extensive production of their own food, shelter, and clothing. Many farmers sell their milk to the local dairy and then buy margarine at the Podunk general store. Society learned long ago that self-sufficiency breeds inefficiency. The jack-of-all-trades may be a very colorful individual, but is certainly lacking in efficiency.

Specialization and efficiency   In what specific ways might human specialization—**the division of labor**—enhance productive efficiency? First, specialization permits individuals to take advantage of existing differences in their abilities and skills. If caveman A is strong, swift afoot, and accurate with a spear, and caveman B is weak and slow, but patient, this distribution of talents can be most efficiently utilized by making A a hunter and B a fisherman. Second, even if the abilities of A and B are identical, specialization may prove to be advantageous. Why? Because by devoting all one's time to a single task, the doer is more likely to develop the appropriate skills and to discover improved techniques than when apportioning time among a number of diverse tasks. One learns to be a good hunter by hunting! Finally, specialization—devoting all one's time to, say, a single task—obviously avoids the loss of time which is entailed

in shifting from one job to another. For all these reasons the division of labor results in greater productive efficiency in the use of human resources.

Specialization also is desirable on a regional and international basis. Oranges could be grown in Nebraska, but because of the unsuitability of the land, rainfall, and temperature, the costs involved would be exceedingly high. Florida could achieve some success in the production of wheat, but for similar reasons such production would be a relatively costly business. As a result, Nebraskans produce those products—wheat in particular—for which their resources are best adapted, and Floridians do the same, producing oranges and other citrus fruits. In so doing, both produce surpluses of their specialties. Then, very sensibly, Nebraskans and Floridians swap some of their surpluses. Specialization permits each area to turn out those goods which its resources can most efficiently produce. In this way both Nebraska and Florida can enjoy a larger amount of both wheat and oranges than would otherwise be the case. Similarly, on an international basis we find the United States specializing in such items as commercial aircraft and computers which it sells abroad in exchange for video recorders from Japan, bananas from Honduras, shoes from Italy, and woven baskets from Thailand. In short, human and geographical specialization are both essential in achieving efficiency in the use of resources. This chapter's Last Word examines specialization at a somewhat more sophisticated level.

Disadvantages   Despite these advantages, specialization does entail certain drawbacks. For example, the potential monotony and drudgery of specialized work are well known. Imagine the boredom of our previously mentioned assembly-line worker who is still putting windows in Camaros. Second, specialization and mutual interdependence vary directly with one another. The less each of us produces for oneself, the more we are dependent upon the output of others. A dockworkers' or truckers' strike may very quickly result in product shortages. A third problem centers upon the exchanging of the surpluses which specialization entails. An examination of this problem leads us into a discussion of the use of money in the domestic and world economies.

USE OF MONEY

Virtually all economies, advanced or primitive, are money-using. Money performs a variety of functions (see Chapter 15), but first and foremost it is a **medium of exchange.**

In our Nebraska–Florida example, it is necessary for Nebraskans to trade or exchange wheat for Florida's oranges if both states are to share in the benefits of specialization. If trade was highly inconvenient or prohibited for some reason, gains from specializing would be lost to society. Why? Because consumers want a wide variety of products and, in the absence of trade, would tend to devote their human and material resources to many diverse types of production. If exchange could not occur or was very inconvenient to transact, Nebraska and Florida would be forced to be more self-sufficient, and the advantages of specialization would not be realized. *In short, a convenient means of exchanging goods is a prerequisite of specialization.*

Now exchange can, and sometimes does, occur on the basis of **bartering,** that is, swapping goods for goods. But bartering as a means of exchange can pose serious problems for the economy. Specifically, exchange by barter requires a *coincidence of wants* between the two transactors. In our example, we assumed that Nebraskans had excess wheat to trade and that they wanted to obtain oranges. And we assumed Floridians had excess oranges to swap and that they wanted to acquire wheat. So exchange occurred. But if this coincidence of wants did not exist, trade would be stymied. Let us pose such a problem.

Suppose Nebraska does not want any of Florida's oranges but is interested in buying potatoes from Idaho. Ironically enough, Idaho wants Florida's oranges but not Nebraska's wheat. And, to complicate matters, suppose that Florida wants some of Nebraska's wheat but none of Idaho's potatoes. The situation is summarized in Figure 3-1.

In no case do we find a coincidence of wants. Trade by barter clearly would be difficult. To overcome such a stalemate, modern economies use *money,* which is simply a convenient social invention for facilitating the exchange of goods and services. Historically, cattle, cigarettes, shells, stones, pieces of metal, and many other diverse commodities have been used, with varying degrees of suc-

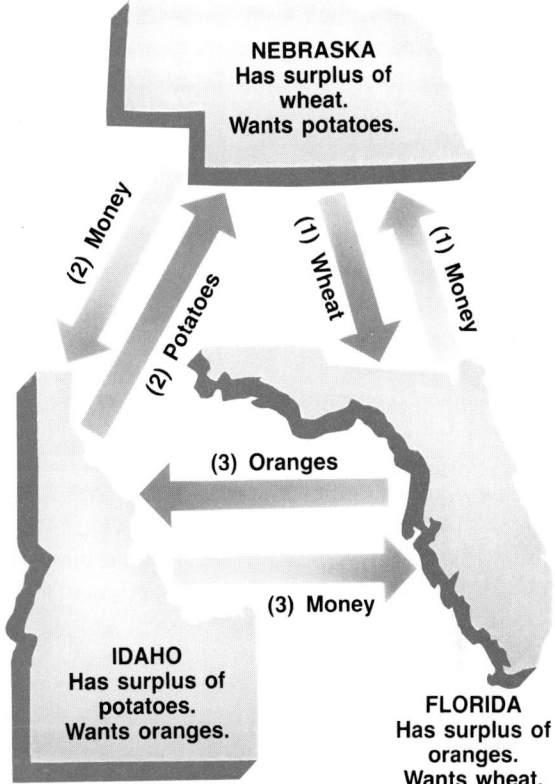

FIGURE 3-1

Money facilitates trade where wants do not coincide

By the use of money as a medium of exchange, trade can be accomplished, as indicated by the arrows, despite a noncoincidence of wants. By facilitating exchange, the use of money permits an economy to realize the efficiencies of specialization.

cess, as a medium for facilitating exchange. But to be money, an item needs to pass only one test: *It must be generally acceptable by buyers and sellers in exchange.* Money is socially defined; whatever society accepts as a medium of exchange *is* money. Most modern economies, for reasons made clear in Chapter 15, find it convenient to use pieces of paper as money. We shall assume that this is the case with the Nebraska–Florida–Idaho economy; they use pieces of paper which they call "dollars" as money. Can the use of paper dollars as a medium of exchange overcome the stalemate we have posed?

Indeed it can, with trade occurring as shown in Figure 3-1:

1 Floridians can exchange money for some of Nebraska's wheat.

2 Nebraskans can take the money realized from the sale of wheat and exchange it for some of Idaho's potatoes.

3 Idahoans can then exchange the money received from the sale of potatoes for some of Florida's surplus oranges.

The willingness to accept paper money (or any other kind of money, for that matter) as a medium of exchange has permitted a three-way trade which allows each state to specialize in one product and obtain the other product(s) its residents desire, despite the absence of a coincidence of wants between any two of the parties. Barter, resting as it does upon a coincidence of wants, would have impeded this exchange and in so doing would have induced the three states not to specialize. Of course, the efficiencies of specialization would then have been lost to those states. Strange as it may first seem, two exchanges—surplus product for money and then money for a wanted product—are simpler than the single product-for-product exchange which bartering entails. Indeed, in this example, product-for-product exchange would not be likely to occur at all.

On a global basis the fact that different nations have different currencies complicates international specialization and exchange. However, the existence of foreign exchange markets permits, for example, Americans, Japanese, Germans, Britons, and Mexicans to exchange dollars, yen, marks, pounds, and pesos for one another in order to complete the desired international exchanges of goods and services.

A final example: Imagine a Detroit laborer producing crankshafts for Oldsmobiles. At the end of the week, instead of receiving a brightly colored piece of paper endorsed by the company comptroller, or a few pieces of paper neatly engraved in green and black, the laborer receives from the company paymaster four Oldsmobile crankshafts. Inconvenient as this is, and with no desire to hoard crankshafts, the laborer ventures into the Detroit business district, intent upon spending this hardearned income on, say, a bag of groceries, a pair of jeans, and a movie. Obviously, the worker is faced with some inconvenient and time-consuming trad-

ing, and may not be able to negotiate any exchanges at all. Finding a clothier who has jeans and who happens to be in the market for an Oldsmobile crankshaft can be a formidable task. And, if the jeans do not trade evenly for crankshafts, how do the transactors "make change"? Examples such as this demonstrate that money is one of the great social inventions of civilization.

To recapitulate: The use of technologically advanced capital goods, a high degree of specialization in production, and the use of money are basic institutional characteristics of all modern economies.

The circular flow model

Our discussion of specialization and the related need for a monetary system to facilitate exchange puts us in a position to reemphasize the role of markets and prices in a capitalistic economy. The remainder of this chapter is devoted to a general overview of the market system for the purpose of pinpointing the two basic types of markets of pure capitalism and noting the character of the transactions which occur therein.

RESOURCE AND PRODUCT MARKETS

Figure 3-2 provides the simple overview we seek. The upper half of the diagram portrays the **resource market.** Here, households, which directly or indirectly (through their ownership of business corporations) own all economic resources, *supply* these resources to businesses.[3] Businesses, of course, will *demand* resources because they are the means by which firms produce goods and services. The interaction of demand and supply for the immense variety of human and property resources establishes the price of each. The payments which businesses make in obtaining resources are costs to

---

[3] For present purposes think of businesses simply as organizational charts, that is, institutions on paper apart from the capital, raw materials, labor, and entrepreneurial ability which breathe life into them and make them "going concerns."

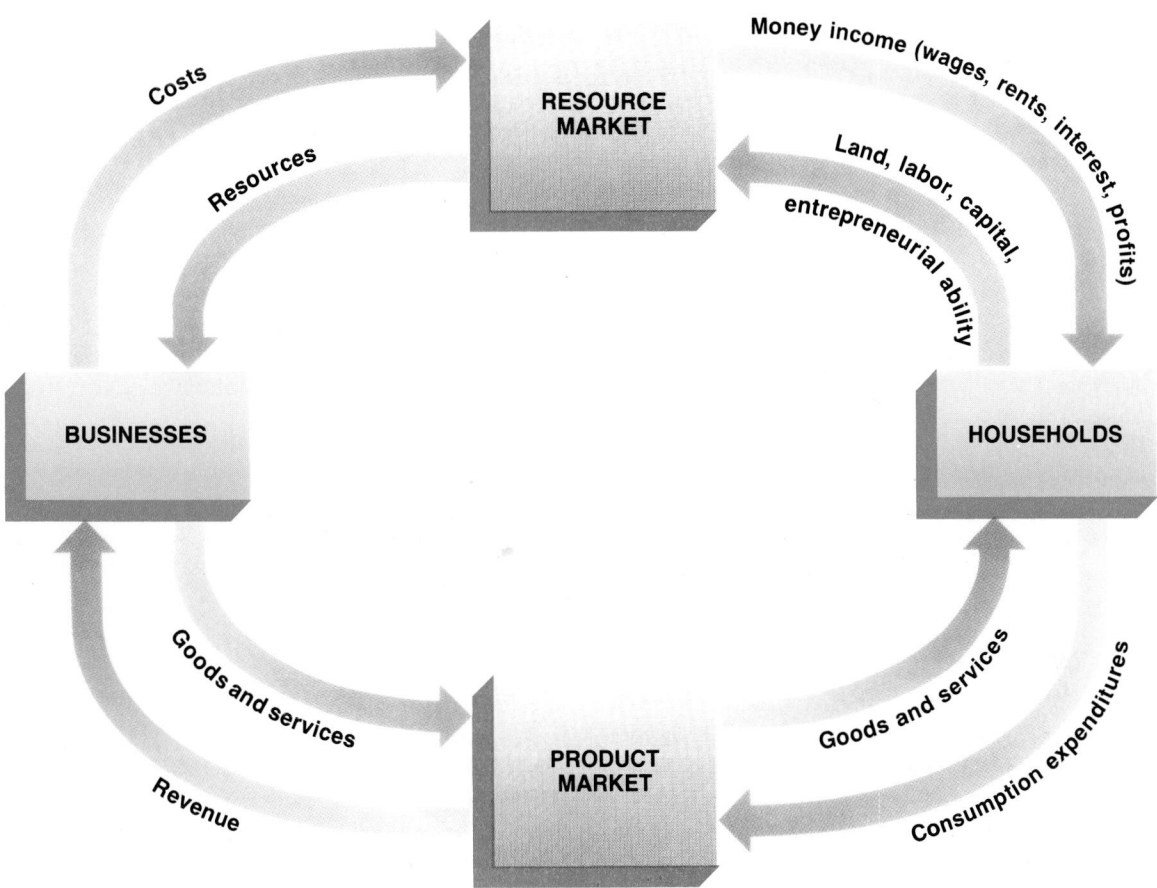

FIGURE 3-2

The circular flow of output and income

The prices paid for the use of land, labor, capital, and entrepreneurial ability are determined in the resource market shown in the upper loop. Businesses are on the demand side and households on the supply side of this market. The prices of finished goods and services are determined in the product market located in the lower loop. Households are on the demand side and businesses on the supply side of this market.

businesses, but simultaneously constitute flows of wage, rent, interest, and profit income to the households supplying these resources.

Now consider the **product market** shown in the bottom half of the diagram. The money income received by households from the sale of resources does not, as such, have real value. Consumers cannot eat or wear coins and paper money. Hence, through the expenditure of money income, households express their *demand* for a vast array of goods and services. Simultaneously, businesses combine the resources they have obtained to produce and *supply* goods and services in these same markets. The interaction of these demand and supply deci-

sions determines product prices (Chapter 4). Note, too, that the flow of consumer expenditures for goods and services constitutes sales revenues or receipts from the viewpoint of businesses.

The **circular flow model** implies a complex, interrelated web of decision making and economic activity. Note that households and businesses participate in both basic markets, but on different sides of each. Businesses are on the buying or demand side of the resource markets, and households, as resource owners and suppliers, are on the selling or supply side. In the product market, these positions are reversed; households, as consumers, are on the buying or demand side, and businesses are on the selling or supply side. Each group of economic units both buys and sells.

Furthermore, the specter of scarcity haunts these transactions. Because households have only limited amounts of resources to supply to businesses, the money incomes of consumers will be limited. This means that each consumer's income will go only so far. A limited number of dollars clearly will not permit the purchase of all the goods and services which the consumer might like to buy. Similarly, because resources are scarce, the output of finished goods and services is also necessarily limited. Scarcity and choice permeate our entire discussion.

To summarize: In a monetary economy, households, as resource owners, sell their resources to businesses and, as consumers, spend the money income received therefrom in buying goods and services. Businesses must buy resources in order to produce goods and services; their finished products are then sold to households in exchange for consumption expenditures or, as businesses view it, revenues. The net result is a counterclockwise *real* flow of economic resources and finished goods and services, and a clockwise *money* flow of income and consumption expenditures. These flows are simultaneous and repetitive.

LIMITATIONS

There are certain noteworthy shortcomings and omissions inherent in the circular flow overview of the workings of pure capitalism:

1 The circular flow model does not reflect the myriad facts and details relevant to specific households, specific businesses, and specific resource and product markets. Nor does it show transactions *within* the business and household sectors. Indeed, the main virtue of the circular flow model is that it lays bare the fundamental operations of pure capitalism without ensnaring the viewer in a maze of details. We seek here a view of the whole forest; the examination of specific trees will come later.

2 The circular flow model makes no mention of the economic role of government. The reason? The institutions of pure capitalism would allegedly give rise to a self-contained, self-regulating economy in which government's role would be minor. In Chap-

LAST WORD

Accounting or painting?

If I am a better accountant than you are and, conversely, you are a better house painter than I am, then it is intuitively correct and not surprising that it is efficient for me to specialize in accounting and you in painting houses. But the concept of *comparative advantage* indicates that specialization will enhance efficiency even if you are *both* a better accountant *and* a better house painter than I am. The following illustration reveals why this is true.

Consider the case of a certified public accountant (CPA) who, we shall assume, is also a skilled house painter. Let us suppose the CPA needs his house painted and can paint it in fewer hours than can the professional painter he is thinking of hiring. Should the CPA take time off from his accounting to paint his own house or should he specialize in accounting and hire a painter? The answer to this question depends upon how much income the CPA must give up to paint the house relative to what it would cost him to hire a house painter to do the job. Suppose the CPA can earn $50 per hour doing accounting and must pay the painter $15 per hour for his services. Also suppose that it will take the accountant 30 hours to paint his house compared to 40 hours needed by the house painter. Finally, let us assume that the CPA receives no special pleasure from painting.

We can conclude from this information that the CPA should hire the house painter. The reason is that his opportunity cost of painting the house is $1,500 (= 30 hours × $50 per hour of sacrificed income), while his cost of hiring the painter to do the job is only $600 (= 40 hours × $15 per hour paid to the painter). Although the CPA is better than the house painter at both accounting and house painting, the CPA's relative or comparative advantage lies in accounting. He therefore will lower his cost of getting his house painted by specializing in accounting and using some of the proceeds to hire the house painter.

Similarly, the house painter may be able to reduce his cost of obtaining accounting services by specializing in painting and using some of his income to hire the CPA. For example, suppose the painter would require 10 hours to prepare his income tax return whereas the CPA could prepare the painter's return in 2 hours. The house painter therefore would sacrifice $150 of income (= 10 hours × $15 per hour of sacrificed income) to accomplish a task which he could get done for $100 (= 2 hours × $50 per hour of the CPA's time). Under this set of assumptions, the painter has a relative or comparative advantage in painting houses and therefore should specialize in house painting. By hiring the CPA to prepare his tax return, the painter lowers his cost of getting his tax return completed.

What is true for our hypothetical CPA and house painter is also true for two regions of a country or two nations of the world. Regions and nations can also reduce their cost of obtaining products they want by specializing on the basis of their relative or comparative advantage.

ter 6 the circular flow will be modified to reflect the economic functions of government in the mixed capitalism which now characterizes the United States economy.

3 Our model at this point excludes international markets. Just as we must later consider the government or public sector, we must also add a "rest of the world" sector.

4 This model assumes that households spend exactly all their money income and that, therefore, the flows of income and expenditure are constant in volume. In real terms this means that the levels of output and employment are constant. Macroeconomics is concerned with the causes and effects of fluctuations in income and output flows.

5 The circular flow model should *not* be viewed as a perpetual motion machine. The economic processes described by the model exhaust human energies and absorb physical resources. Furthermore, much-publicized problems of environmental pollution stem from the fact that most inputs in the production and consumption processes are eventually returned to the system as some form of waste.

6 Our discussion of the circular flow does not explain how resource and market prices are actually determined. This is the task to which we turn in the ensuing chapter: How are resource and market prices determined in a purely capitalistic economy?

CHAPTER SUMMARY

1 The capitalistic system is characterized by private ownership of resources and the freedom of individuals to engage in the economic activities of their choice as a means for advancing their material well-being. Self-interest is the driving force of such an economy, and competition functions as a regulatory or control mechanism. Capitalistic production is not organized in terms of a government plan, but rather features the market system as a means of organizing and making effective the myriad individual decisions which determine what is produced, the methods of production, and the sharing of output. The capitalist ideology envisions government playing a minor and relatively passive economic role.

2 Specialization and an advanced technology based on the extensive use of capital goods are features common to all modern economies. Functioning as a medium of exchange, money circumvents problems entailed in barter-

ing and thereby permits greater specialization both domestically and internationally.

3 An overview of the operation of the capitalistic system can be gained through the circular flow of income. This simplified model locates the product and resource markets and presents the major income-expenditure flows and resources-output flows which constitute the lifeblood of the capitalistic economy.

TERMS AND CONCEPTS

private property	specialization and division of labor
freedom of enterprise	
freedom of choice	medium of exchange
self-interest	bartering
competition	circular flow model
market	resource and product markets
roundabout production	

QUESTIONS AND STUDY SUGGESTIONS

1 "Capitalism may be characterized as an automatic self-regulating system motivated by the self-interest of individuals and regulated by competition."[4] Explain and evaluate.

2 Explain how the market system is a means of communicating and implementing decisions concerning allocation of the economy's resources.

3 What advantages result from "roundabout" production? What problem is involved in increasing a full-employment, full-production economy's stock of capital goods? Illustrate this problem in terms of the production possibilities curve. Does an economy with unemployed resources face the same problem?

4 What are the advantages of specialization in the use of human and material resources? The disadvantages? Explain: "Exchange is the necessary consequence of specialization."

5 What problems does barter entail? Indicate the economic significance of money as a medium of exchange. "Money is the only commodity that is good for nothing but to be gotten rid of. It will not feed you, clothe you, shelter you, or amuse you unless you spend or invest it. It imparts value only in parting."[5] Explain this statement.

6 Describe the operation of pure capitalism as portrayed by the circular flow model. Locate resource and product markets and emphasize the fact of scarcity throughout your discussion. Specify the limitations of the circular flow model.

[4] Howard R. Bowen, *Toward Social Economy* (New York: Holt, Rinehart and Winston, Inc., 1948), p. 249.

[5] Federal Reserve Bank of Philadelphia, "Creeping Inflation," *Business Review,* August 1957, p. 3.

CHAPTER 4

Understanding individual markets: demand and supply

Teach a parrot to say, "Demand and supply," and you have an economist! There is a strong element of truth in this quip because, in fact, the simple tools of demand and supply can take one far in understanding not only specific economic issues, but also the operation of the entire economic system.

The overriding goal of this chapter is to understand the nature of markets and how prices and outputs are determined. Our circular flow model of Chapter 3 got us on the right track by delineating the participants in both product and resource markets. But we assumed there that product and resource prices were "given"; no attempt was made to explain how prices are "set" or determined. Let us build on the circular flow model by discussing more fully the concept of a market.

Markets defined

A **market** is defined as *an institution or mechanism which brings together buyers ("demanders") and sellers ("suppliers") of particular goods and services.* Markets assume a wide variety of forms. The corner gas station, the fast-food outlet, the local record shop, a farmer's roadside stand—all are familiar markets. The New York Stock Exchange and the Chicago Board of Trade are highly sophisticated markets where buyers and sellers of stocks and bonds and farm commodities, respectively, from all over the world are brought into contact with one another. Similarly, auctioneers bring together potential buyers and sellers of art, livestock, used farm equipment, and sometimes real estate. The all-American quarterback and his agent bargain with the owner of an NFL team. A graduating chemistry major interviews with Union Carbide and du Pont at the university placement office. All these situations which link potential buyers with potential sellers constitute markets. As our examples imply, some markets are local while others are national or international in scope. Some are highly personal, involving face-to-face contact between demander and supplier; others are impersonal in that buyer and seller never see or know one another.

Our concern in this chapter is with the functioning of *perfectly competitive markets*. You may remember from Chapter 3 that such markets presume large numbers of independently acting buyers and sellers interested in exchanging a standardized product. More precisely, the kind of market we have in mind is not the record shop or corner gas station where products have price tags on them, but such competitive markets as a central grain exchange, a stock market, or a market for foreign currencies where the equilibrium price is

49

"discovered" by the interacting decisions of buyers and sellers. Similarly, we seek to find how prices are established in resource markets by the demand decisions of competing businesses and the supply decisions of competing households (Figure 3-2). We shall concentrate on the *product market,* then shift our attention later in the chapter to the *resource market.* The task is to explain the mechanics of prices.

Demand

The term "demand" has a very specific meaning to the economist. **Demand** is defined as *a schedule which shows the various amounts of a product which consumers are willing and able to purchase at each specific price in a series of possible prices during some specified period of time.*[1] Demand simply portrays a series of alternative possibilities which can be set down in tabular form. It shows the quantities of a product which will be demanded at various prices, all other things being equal. As our definition indicates, we usually view demand from the vantage point of price; that is, we read demand as showing the amounts consumers will buy at various possible prices. It is equally correct and sometimes more useful to view demand from the reference point of quantity. That is, instead of asking what quantities can be sold at various prices, we can ask what prices can be gotten from consumers for various quantities of a good. Table 4-1 is a hypothetical **demand schedule** for a single consumer who is purchasing bushels of corn.

This tabular portrayal of demand reflects the relationship between the price of corn and the quantity that our mythical consumer would be willing and able to purchase at each of these prices. Note that we say willing and *able,* because willingness alone is not effective in the market. I may be willing to buy a Porsche, but if this willingness is not backed by the ability to buy, that is, by the necessary dollars, it will not be effective and, therefore, not reflected in the market. In Table 4-1, if the

[1] In adjusting this definition to the resource market, merely substitute the word "resources" for "product" and "businesses" for "consumers."

TABLE 4-1 **An individual buyer's demand for corn** *(hypothetical data)*

Price per bushel	Quantity demanded per week
$5	10
4	20
3	35
2	55
1	80

price of corn in the market happened to be $5 per bushel, our consumer would be willing and able to buy 10 bushels per week; if it were $4, the consumer would be willing and able to buy 20 bushels per week; and so forth.

The demand schedule in and of itself does not tell us which of the five possible prices will actually exist in the corn market. As we have already said, this depends on demand *and supply.* Demand, then, is simply a tabular statement of a buyer's plans, or intentions, with respect to the purchase of a product.

Note that, to be meaningful, the quantities demanded at each price must relate to some specific time period—a day, a week, a month, and so forth. To say that "a consumer will buy 10 bushels of corn at $5 per bushel" is vague and meaningless. To say that "a consumer will buy 10 bushels of corn *per week* at $5 per bushel" is clear and very meaningful.

LAW OF DEMAND

A fundamental characteristic of demand is this: All else being constant, as price falls, the corresponding quantity demanded rises. Or, alternatively, other things being equal, as price increases, the corresponding quantity demanded falls. In short, there is a negative or *inverse* relationship between price and quantity demanded. Economists have labeled this inverse relationship the **law of demand.** Upon what foundation does this law rest? There are several levels of sophistication upon which to argue the case.

1 Common sense and simple observation are consistent with a downsloping demand curve. People ordinarily *do* buy more of a given product at a low price than they do at a high price. To consumers, price is an obstacle which deters them from buying. The higher this obstacle, the less of a product they will buy; the lower the price obstacle, the more they will buy. In other words, a high price discourages consumers from buying, and a low price encourages them to buy. The plain fact that businesses have "sales" is concrete evidence of their belief in the law of demand. "Bargain days" are based on the law of demand. Businesses reduce their inventories by lowering prices, not by raising them.

2 In any given time period each buyer of a product will derive less satisfaction or benefit or utility from each successive unit of a product. For example, the second "Big Mac" will yield less satisfaction to the consumer than the first; the third still less added benefit or utility than the second; and so forth. Hence, because consumption is subject to **diminishing marginal utility**—successive units of a given product yield less and less extra satisfaction—consumers will only buy additional units if price is reduced.

3 At a slightly more sophisticated level the law of demand can be explained in terms of income and substitution effects. The **income effect** indicates that, at a lower price, one can afford more of the good without giving up any alternative goods. In other words, a decline in the price of a product will increase the purchasing power of one's money income; hence, you are able to buy more of the product than before. A higher price will have the opposite effect. The **substitution effect** suggests that, at a lower price, one has the incentive to substitute the cheaper good for similar goods which are now relatively more expensive. Consumers tend to substitute cheap products for dear products. To illustrate: A decline in the price of beef will increase the purchasing power of consumer incomes, enabling them to buy more beef (the income effect). At a lower price, beef is relatively more attractive and it is substituted for pork, mutton, chicken, and fish (the substitution effect). The income and substitution effects combine to make consumers able and willing to buy more of a product at a low price than at a high price.

THE DEMAND CURVE

This inverse relationship between product price and quantity demanded can be presented on a simple two-dimensional graph measuring quantity demanded on the horizontal axis and price on the vertical axis.[2] The process involved is that of locating on the graph those five price-quantity possibilities shown in Table 4-1. We do this by drawing perpendiculars from the appropriate points on the two axes. Thus, for example, in plotting the "$5-price–10-quantity-demanded" possibility, we must draw a perpendicular from the horizontal (quantity) axis at 10 to meet a perpendicular drawn from the vertical (price) axis at $5. If this is done for all five possibilities, the result is a series of points as shown in Figure 4-1. Each of these points represents a specific price and the corresponding quantity which the consumer will choose to purchase at that price. Now, assuming the same inverse relationship between price and quantity demanded at all points between the ones graphed, we can generalize on the inverse relationship between price and quantity demanded by drawing a curve to represent *all* price–quantity-demanded possibilities within the limits shown on the graph. The resulting curve is called a **demand curve** and is labeled *DD* in Figure 4-1. It slopes downward and to the right because the relationship it portrays between price and quantity demanded is negative or inverse. The law of demand—people buy more at a low price than they do at a high price—is reflected in the downward slope of the demand curve.

What is the advantage of graphing our demand schedule? After all, Table 4-1 and Figure 4-1 contain exactly the same data and reflect the same relationship between price and quantity demanded. The advantage of graphing is that it permits us to represent clearly a given relationship—in this case the law of demand—in a much simpler way than we could if we were forced to rely upon verbal and

[2] Putting price on the vertical axis and quantity demanded on the horizontal axis is a matter of economic tradition. A mathematician would place price on the horizontal axis and quantity demanded on the vertical axis, because price is the independent variable and quantity is the dependent variable (see appendix to Chapter 1).

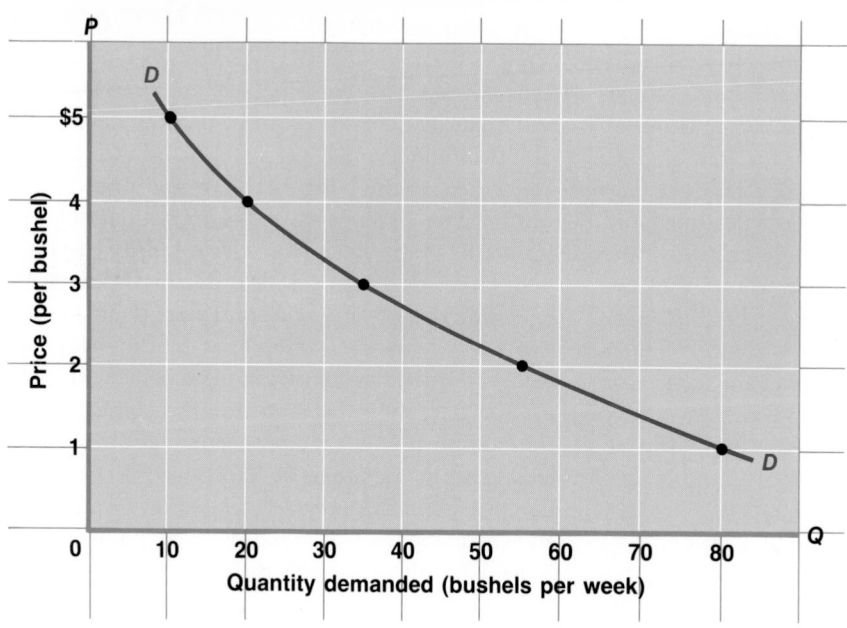

FIGURE 4-1

An individual buyer's demand curve for corn

An individual's demand schedule graphs as a downsloping curve such as *DD*, because price and quantity demanded are inversely related. Specifically, the law of demand generalizes that consumers will buy more of a product as its price declines.

tabular presentation. A single curve on a graph, if understood, is simpler to state *and to manipulate* than tables and lengthy verbal presentations would be. Graphs are invaluable tools in economic analysis. They permit clear expression and handling of sometimes complex relationships.

INDIVIDUAL AND MARKET DEMAND

Until now we have been dealing in terms of just one consumer. The assumption of competition obligates us to consider a situation in which many buyers are in the market. The transition from an *individual* to a *market* demand schedule can be accomplished easily by the process of summing the quantities demanded by each consumer at the various possible prices. If there were just three buyers in the market, as is shown in Table 4-2, it would be an easy chore to determine the total quantities demanded at each price. Figure 4-2 shows the same summing procedure graphically, using only the $3 price to illustrate the adding-up process. Note that we are simply summing the three individual demand curves *horizontally* to derive the total demand curve.

TABLE 4-2 **Market demand for corn, three buyers (hypothetical data)**

Price per bushel	Quantity demanded			Total quantity demanded per week
	First buyer	Second buyer	Third buyer	
$5	10	+ 12	+ 8	= 30
4	20	+ 23	+ 17	= 60
3	35	+ 39	+ 26	= 100
2	55	+ 60	+ 39	= 154
1	80	+ 87	+ 54	= 221

Competition, of course, entails many more than three buyers of a product. So—to avoid a lengthy addition process—let us suppose there are 200 buyers of corn in the market, each of whom chooses to buy the same amount at each of the various prices as our original consumer does. Thus, we can determine total or market demand by multiplying the quantity-demanded data of Table 4-1 by 200, as in Table 4-3. Curve D_1 in Figure 4-3 indicates this market demand curve for the 200 buyers.

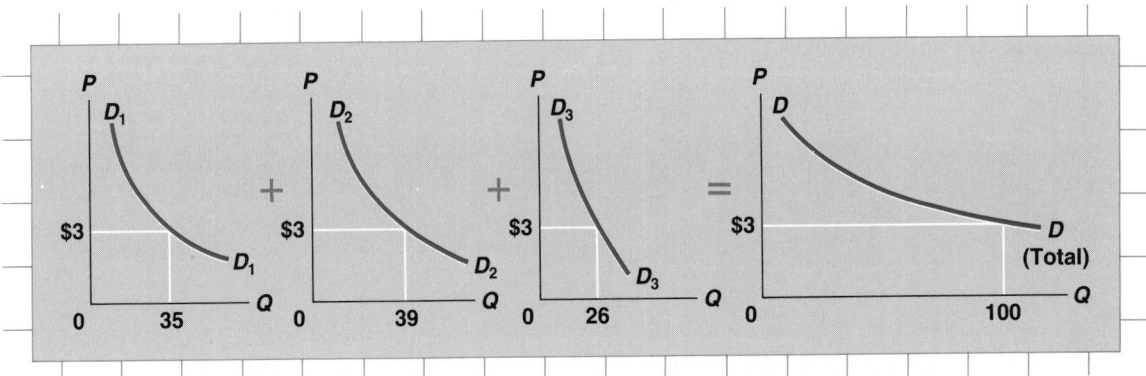

FIGURE 4-2

The market demand curve is the sum of the individual demand curves

Graphically the market demand curve (**D** total) is found by summing horizontally the individual demand curves (**D₁**, **D₂**, and **D₃**) of all consumers in the market.

DETERMINANTS OF DEMAND

When the economist constructs a demand curve such as D_1 in Figure 4-3, the assumption is made that price is the most important determinant of the amount of any product purchased. But the economist is aware that factors other than price can and do affect purchases. Thus, in locating a given demand curve such as D_1, it must also be assumed that "other things are equal"; that is, other *nonprice determinants*[3] of the amount demanded are conveniently assumed to be constant. When these nonprice determinants of demand do in fact change, the location of the demand curve will shift to some new position to the right or left of D_1. For this reason these determinants are also referred to as *demand shifters.*

What are the major nonprice determinants of market demand? The basic ones are (1) the tastes or preferences of consumers, (2) the number of consumers in the market, (3) the money incomes of consumers, (4) the prices of related goods, and (5) consumer expectations with respect to future prices and incomes.

[3] By nonprice determinants we mean factors other than the price of the specific product under consideration. We shall find that changes in the prices of *other* goods may affect the demand for the specific product.

CHANGES IN DEMAND

What happens if one or more of the determinants of demand should change? We know the answer: A change in one or more of the determinants will change the demand schedule data in Table 4-3 and therefore the location of the demand curve in Figure 4-3. Such a change in the demand schedule data, or, graphically, a shift in the location of the demand curve, is designated as a *change in demand.*

TABLE 4-3 **Market demand for corn, 200 buyers (hypothetical data)**

(1) Price per bushel	(2) Quantity demanded per week, single buyer		(3) Number of buyers in the market		(4) Total quantity demanded per week
$5	10	×	200	=	2,000
4	20	×	200	=	4,000
3	35	×	200	=	7,000
2	55	×	200	=	11,000
1	80	×	200	=	16,000

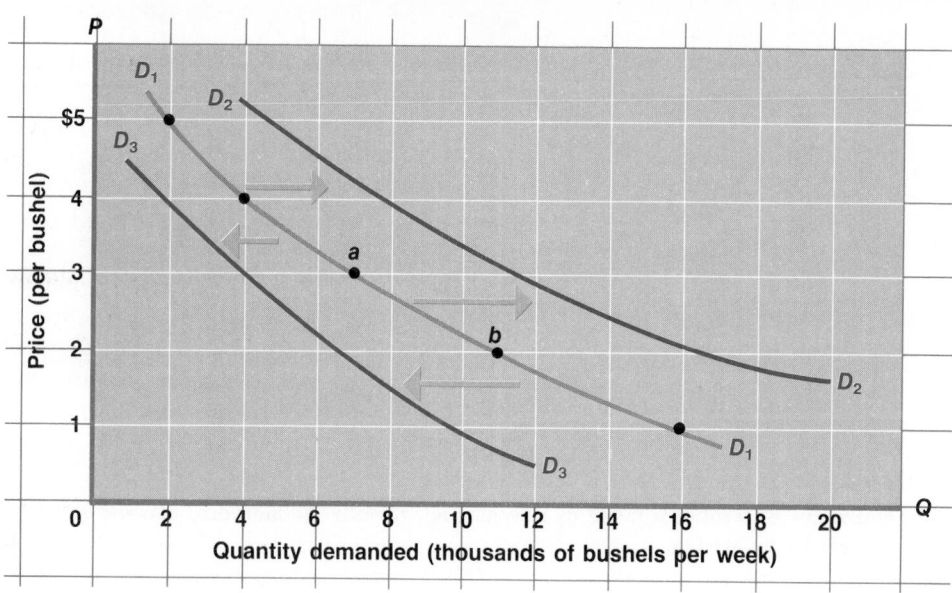

FIGURE 4-3

Changes in the demand for corn

A change in one or more of the determinants of demand—consumer tastes, the number of buyers in the market, money incomes, the prices of other goods, or consumer expectations—will cause a change in demand. An increase in demand shifts the demand curve to the right, as from D_1 to D_2. A decrease in demand shifts the demand curve to the left, as from D_1 to D_3. A change in the quantity demanded involves a movement, caused by a change in the price of the product under consideration, from one point to another—as from a to b—on a fixed demand curve.

More specifically, if consumers become willing and able to buy more of this particular good at each possible price than is reflected in column 4 of Table 4-3, an *increase in demand* has occurred. In Figure 4-3, this increase in demand is reflected in a shift of the demand curve to the *right,* for example, from D_1 to D_2. Conversely, a *decrease in demand* occurs when, because of a change in one or more of the determinants, consumers buy less of the product at each possible price than is indicated in column 4 of Table 4-3. Graphically, a decrease in demand entails a shift of the demand curve to the *left,* for example, from D_1 to D_3 in Figure 4-3.

Let us now examine the effect upon demand of changes in each of the aforementioned nonprice determinants.

l Tastes A change in consumer tastes or preferences favorable to this product—possibly prompted by advertising or fashion changes—will mean that more will be demanded at each price; that is, demand will increase. An unfavorable change in consumer preferences will cause demand to decrease, shifting the curve to the left. It is worth noting that technological change in the form of a new product may prompt a revision of consumer tastes. For example, the development and consumer acceptance of the hand calculator virtually eliminated the demand for slide rules. Similarly, the introduction of compact discs has tended to decrease the demand for long-playing records.

2 Number of buyers It is equally obvious that an increase in the number of consumers in a market will constitute an increase in demand. Fewer consumers will be reflected by a decrease in demand. Examples: Dramatic improvements in communications have made financial markets international in scope, tending to increase the demand for stocks, bonds, and other financial instruments. The "baby boom" of the post-World War II period increased the demand for diapers, baby lotion, and services of obstetricians. Increasing life expectancy has increased the demands for medical care, retirement communities, and nursing homes. American trade negotiators are trying to reduce foreign trade barriers to American farm products in order to increase the demands for those products.

3 Income The impact of changes in money income upon demand is a bit more complex. For most commodities, a rise in income will cause an increase in demand. Consumers typically buy more steaks, stereos, and Scotch as their incomes increase. Conversely, the demand for such products will decline in response to a fall in incomes. Commodities whose demand varies *directly* with money income are called **superior,** or **normal, goods.**

Although most products are normal goods, there are a few exceptions. Examples: As incomes increase beyond some point, the amounts of bread or potatoes or cabbages purchased at each price may diminish because the higher incomes now allow consumers to buy more high-protein foods, such as dairy products and meat. Rising incomes may also tend to decrease demands for used clothing and third-hand automobiles. Similarly, rising incomes may cause the demands for hamburger and margarine to decline as wealthier consumers switch to T-bones and butter. Goods whose demand varies *inversely* with a change in money income are called **inferior goods.**

4 Prices of related goods Whether a given change in the price of a related good will increase or decrease the demand for the product under consideration will depend upon whether the related good is a substitute for, or a complement to, it. For example, butter and margarine are **substitute goods.** When the price of butter rises, consumers will purchase a smaller amount of butter, and this will cause the demand for margarine to increase.[4] Con-

versely, as the price of butter falls, consumers will buy larger quantities of butter, causing the demand for margarine to decrease. To generalize: When two products are substitutes, the price of one good and the demand for the other are *directly* related. So it is with Millers and Budweiser, sugar and Nutrasweet, Toyotas and Hondas, tea and coffee, and so forth.

But other pairs of products are **complementary goods;** they "go together" in that they are jointly demanded. If the price of gasoline falls and, as a result, you drive your car more, this extra driving will increase your demand for motor oil. Conversely, an increase in the price of gasoline will diminish the demand for motor oil.[5] Thus gas and oil are jointly demanded; they are complements. And so it is with ham and eggs, tuition and textbooks, VCRs and video cassettes, golf clubs and golf balls, cameras and rolls of film, and so forth. When two commodities are complements, the price of one good and the demand for the other are *inversely* related.

Many pairs of goods, of course, are not related at all—they are *independent* goods. For such pairs of commodities as, for example, butter and golf balls, potatoes and automobiles, bananas and wristwatches, we should expect that a change in the price of one would have little or no impact upon the demand for the other.

5 Expectations Consumer expectations about such things as future product prices, product availability, and future income can shift demand. Consumer expectations of higher future prices may prompt them to buy now in order to "beat" the anticipated price rises, and, similarly, the expectation of rising incomes may induce consumers to be less tightfisted in their current spending. Conversely, expectations of falling prices and income will tend to decrease the current demand for products. First example: If freezing weather destroys a substantial portion of Florida's citrus crop, consumers may reason that forthcoming shortages of frozen orange juice will escalate its price. Hence,

---

[4] Note that the consumer is moving up a stable demand curve for butter. But the demand curve for margarine shifts to the right (increases). Given the supply of margarine, this rightward shift in demand means more margarine will be purchased and that its price will also rise.

[5] Again note that, while the buyer is moving up a stable demand curve for gasoline, the demand for motor oil shifts to the left (decreases). Given the supply of motor oil, this decline in demand for motor oil will reduce both the amount purchased and its price.

they "stock up" on orange juice by purchasing extraordinarily large quantities now. Second example: Several years ago Johnny Carson jokingly predicted a toilet paper shortage. Many of his TV fans took his comment seriously and within a few days toilet paper was not to be found on the shelves of many supermarkets. Third example: A first-round NFL draft choice might splurge for a new Mercedes in anticipation of a lucrative professional football contract.

We might summarize by saying that an increase in the demand for product X—the decision of consumers to buy more of X at each possible price—can be caused by (1) a favorable change in consumer tastes, (2) an increase in the number of buyers in the market, (3) a rise in income if X is a normal good *or* a fall in income if X is an inferior good, (4) an increase in the price of related good Y if Y is a substitute for X *or* a decrease in price of related good Y if Y is a complement to X, and (5) expectations of future increases in prices and incomes. Conversely, a decrease in the demand for X can be associated with (1) an unfavorable change in tastes, (2) a decrease in the number of buyers in the market, (3) a rise in income if X is an inferior good *or* a fall in income if X is a normal good, (4) an increase in the price of related good Y if Y is complementary to X *or* a decrease in the price of related good Y if Y is a substitute for X, and (5) expectations of future price and income declines. Table 4-4 provides a convenient listing of the determinants of demand along with additional illustrations.

CHANGES IN QUANTITY DEMANDED

A "change in demand" must not be confused with a "change in the quantity demanded." We have noted that a **change in demand** refers to a shift in the entire demand curve either to the right (an increase in demand) or to the left (a decrease in demand). The consumer's state of mind concerning purchases of this product has been altered. The cause: a change in one or more of the determinants of demand. As used by economists, the term "demand" refers to a schedule or curve; therefore, a "change in demand" must mean that the entire

TABLE 4-4 Determinants of demand: factors that shift the demand curve

1 Change in buyer tastes Example: Physical fitness increases in popularity, increasing demand for jogging shoes and bicycles

2 Change in number of buyers Examples: Japanese reduce import quotas on American telecommunications equipment, thereby increasing the demand for such equipment; a decline in the birthrate reduces the demand for education

3 Change in income Examples: An increase in incomes increases the demand for such normal goods as butter, lobster, and filet mignon, while reducing the demand for such inferior goods as cabbage, turnips, retreaded tires, and used clothing

4 Change in the prices of related goods Examples: A reduction in air fares reduces the demand for bus transportation (substitute goods); a decline in the price of video cassette recorders increases the demand for video cassettes (complementary goods)

5 Change in expectations Example: Inclement weather in South America causes the expectation of higher future coffee prices, thereby increasing the current demand for coffee

schedule has changed and that graphically the curve has shifted its position.

In contrast, a **change in the quantity demanded** designates the movement from one point to another point—from one price-quantity combination to another—on a fixed demand curve. The cause of a change in the quantity demanded is a change in the price of the product under consideration. In Table 4-3 a decline in the price asked by suppliers of corn from $5 to $4 will increase the quantity of corn demanded from 2000 to 4000 bushels.

Figure 4-3 is helpful in making the distinction between a change in demand and a change in the quantity demanded. The shift of the demand curve D_1 to either D_2 or D_3 entails a "change in demand." But the movement from point a to point b on curve D_1 is a "change in the quantity demanded."

The reader should decide whether a change in demand or a change in the quantity demanded is involved in each of the following illustrations:

1 Consumer incomes rise, with the result that more jewelry is purchased.

2 A barber raises the price of haircuts and experiences a decline in volume of business.

3 The price of Toyotas goes up, and, as a consequence, the sales of Chevrolets increase.

Supply

Supply may be defined as *a schedule which shows the various amounts of a product which a producer is willing and able to produce and make available for sale in the market at each specific price in a series of possible prices during some specified time period.*[6] This **supply schedule** portrays a series of alternative possibilities, such as those shown in Table 4-5 for a single producer. Supply tells us the quantities of a product which will be supplied at various prices, all other factors being held constant. Let us suppose, in this case, that our producer is a farmer producing corn, the demand for which we have just considered. Our definition of supply indicates that supply is usually viewed from the vantage point of price. That is, we read supply as showing the amounts producers will offer at various possible prices. It is equally correct and more useful in some instances to view supply from the reference point of quantity. Instead of asking what quantities will be offered at various prices, we can ask what prices will be required to induce producers to offer various quantities of a good.

LAW OF SUPPLY

It will be immediately noted that Table 4-5 shows a positive or *direct* relationship between price and quantity supplied. As price rises, the corresponding quantity supplied rises; as price falls, the quantity supplied also falls. This particular relationship is called the **law of supply.** It simply tells us that

[6] In talking of the resource market, our definition of supply reads: a schedule which shows the various amounts of a resource which its owners are willing to supply in the market at each possible price in a series of prices during some specified time.

producers are willing to produce and offer for sale more of their product at a high price than they are at a low price. Why? This again is basically a commonsense matter.

Price, we recall, is a deterrent from the consumer's standpoint. The obstacle of a high price means that the consumer, being on the paying end of this price, will buy a relatively small amount of the product; the lower the price obstacle, the more the consumer will buy. The supplier, on the other hand, is on the receiving end of the product's price. To a supplier, price is revenue per unit and therefore is an inducement or incentive to produce and sell a product. The higher the price of the product, the greater the incentive to produce and offer it in the market.

Consider a farmer whose resources are shiftable within limits among alternative products. As price moves up in Table 4-5, the farmer will find it profitable to take land out of wheat, oats, and soybean production and put it into corn. Furthermore, higher corn prices will make it possible for the farmer to cover the costs associated with more intensive cultivation and the use of larger quantities of fertilizers and pesticides. All these efforts result in more output of corn. Consider a manufacturing concern. Beyond some point manufacturers usually encounter increasing production costs per unit of output. Therefore, a higher product price is necessary to cover these rising costs. But why do costs rise? They rise because certain productive resources—in particular, the firm's plant and machinery—cannot be expanded in a short period of time. Hence, as the firm increases the amounts of more readily variable resources such as labor, materials, and component parts, the fixed plant will at

TABLE 4-5 **An individual producer's supply of corn (hypothetical data)**

Price per bushel	Quantity supplied per week
$5	60
4	50
3	35
2	20
1	5

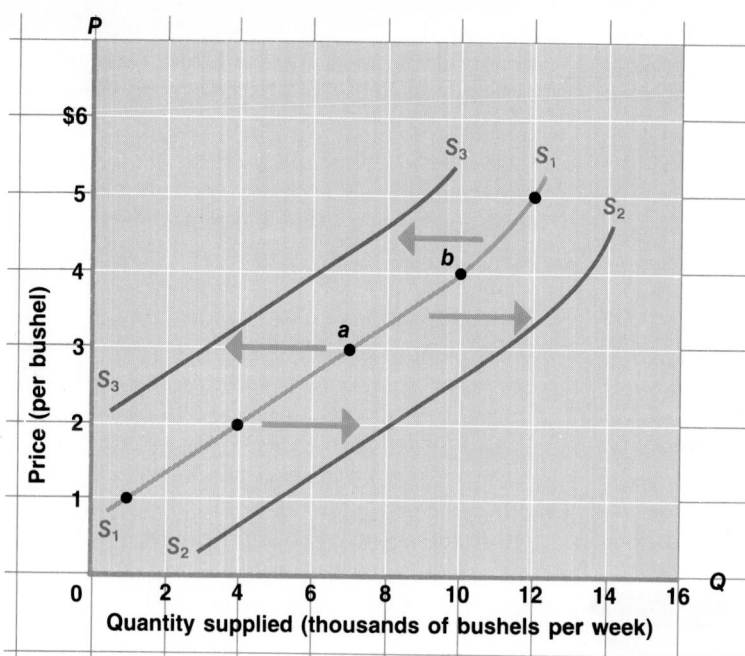

FIGURE 4-4

Changes in the supply of corn

A change in one or more of the determinants of supply—resource prices, productive techniques, the prices of other goods, taxes and subsidies, price expectations, or the number of sellers in the market—will cause a change in supply. An increase in supply shifts the supply curve to the right, as from S_1 to S_2. A decrease in supply is shown graphically as a movement of the curve to the left, as from S_1 to S_3. A change in the quantity supplied involves a movement caused by a change in the price of the product under consideration, from one point to another—as from a to b—on a fixed supply curve.

some point become crowded or congested with the result that productive efficiency declines and the cost of successive units of output increases. Producers must receive a higher price to produce these more costly units.[7] Price and quantity supplied are directly related.

THE SUPPLY CURVE

As in the case of demand, it is convenient to present graphically the concept of supply. Our axes in Figure 4-4 are the same as those in Figure 4-3, except for the change of "quantity demanded" to "quantity supplied." The graphing procedure is the same as that previously explained, but of course the quantity data and relationship involved are different. The market supply data graphed in Figure 4-4 as S_1 are shown in Table 4-6, which assumes there are 200 suppliers in the market having the same supply schedules as the producer previously portrayed in Table 4-5.

[7] Chapters 24 and 25 provide a more sophisticated explanation of the relationship between costs and supply.

TABLE 4-6 Market supply of corn, 200 producers *(hypothetical data)*

(1) Price per bushel	(2) Quantity supplied per week, single producer		(3) Number of sellers in the market		(4) Total quantity supplied per week
$5	60	×	200	=	12,000
4	50	×	200	=	10,000
3	35	×	200	=	7,000
2	20	×	200	=	4,000
1	5	×	200	=	1,000

DETERMINANTS OF SUPPLY

In constructing a supply curve, the economist assumes that price is the most significant determinant of the quantity supplied of any product. But, as with the demand curve, the supply curve is anchored on the "other things are equal" assumption. That is, the supply curve is drawn on the supposition that certain nonprice determinants of the amount supplied are given and do not change. If any of these nonprice determinants of supply do in fact change, the location of the supply curve will be altered.

The basic nonprice determinants of supply are (1) resource prices, (2) the technique of production, (3) taxes and subsidies, (4) prices of other goods, (5) price expectations, and (6) the number of sellers in the market. To repeat: A change in any one or more of these determinants or *supply shifters* will cause the supply curve for a product to move either to the right or the left. A shift to the *right,* from S_1 to S_2 in Figure 4-4, designates an *increase in supply:* Producers are now supplying larger quantities of the product at each possible price. A shift to the *left,* S_1 to S_3 in Figure 4-4, indicates a *decrease in supply:* Suppliers are offering less at each price.

CHANGES IN SUPPLY

Let us consider the effect of changes in each of these determinants upon supply.

1 Resource prices As indicated in our explanation of the law of supply, the relationship between production costs and supply is an intimate one. A firm's supply curve is based upon production costs; a firm must receive higher prices for additional units of output because those extra units are more costly to produce. It follows that a decrease in resource prices will lower production costs and increase supply, that is, shift the supply curve to the right. Example: If the prices of seed and fertilizer decrease, we can expect the supply of corn to increase. Conversely, an increase in input prices will raise production costs and reduce supply, that is, shift the supply curve to the left. Example: Increases in the prices of iron ore and coke will increase the cost of producing steel and tend to reduce its supply.

2 Technology A technological improvement means that the discovery of new knowledge permits us to produce a unit of output more efficiently, that is, with fewer resources. Given the prices of these resources, this will lower production costs and increase supply. Example: Recent dramatic breakthroughs in the area of superconductivity portend the possibility of transporting electric power with little or no loss. Currently, about 30 percent of electric power is lost when transmitted by copper cable. Consequence? Significant cost reductions and supply increases in a wide range of products where energy is an important input.

3 Taxes and subsidies Businesses treat most taxes as costs. Therefore, an increase in, say, sales or property taxes will increase costs and reduce supply. Conversely, subsidies are "taxes in reverse." If government subsidizes the production of some good, it in effect lowers costs and increases supply. In Chapter 6 we will see how government might tax or subsidize certain products to alter their supply for the purpose of improving the allocation of resources.

4 Prices of other goods Changes in the prices of other goods can also shift the supply curve for a product. A decline in the price of wheat may cause a farmer to produce and offer more corn at each possible price. Conversely, a rise in the price of wheat may make farmers less willing to produce and offer corn in the market. A firm manufacturing athletic equipment might reduce its supply of basketballs in response to a rise in the price of soccer balls.

5 Expectations Expectations concerning the future price of a product can also affect a producer's current willingness to supply that product. It is difficult, however, to generalize concerning the way the expectation of, say, higher prices will affect the present supply curve of a product. Farmers might withhold some of their current corn harvest from the market, anticipating a higher corn price in the future. This will cause a decrease in the current supply of corn. Similarly, if the price of IBM stock is expected to rise significantly in the near future, the supply offered today for sale might decrease. On the other hand, in many types of manufacturing, expected price increases may induce firms to expand their production facilities, causing supply to increase.

6 Number of sellers Given the scale of operations of each firm, the larger the number of suppliers, the

TABLE 4-7 Determinants of supply: factors that shift the supply curve

1 **Change in resource prices** Examples: A decline in the price of fertilizer increases the supply of wheat; an increase in the price of irrigation equipment reduces the supply of corn

2 **Change in technology** Example: The development of a more effective insecticide for corn rootworm increases the supply of corn

3 **Changes in taxes and subsidies** Examples: An increase in the excise tax on cigarettes reduces the supply of cigarettes; a decline in subsidies to state universities reduces the supply of higher education

4 **Change in prices of other goods** Example: A decline in the prices of mutton and pork increases the supply of beef

5 **Change in expectations** Example: Expectations of substantial declines in future oil prices cause oil companies to increase current supply

6 **Change in number of suppliers** Example: An increase in the number of firms producing personal computers increases the supply of personal computers; formation of a new professional football league increases the supply of professional football games

greater will be market supply. As more firms enter an industry, the supply curve will shift to the right. The smaller the number of firms in an industry, the less the market supply will be. This means that as firms leave an industry, the supply curve will shift to the left. Table 4-7 provides a checklist of the determinants of supply; the accompanying illustrations deserve careful study.

CHANGES IN QUANTITY SUPPLIED

The distinction between a "change in supply" and a "change in the quantity supplied" parallels that between a change in demand and a change in the quantity demanded. A **change in supply** is involved when the entire supply curve shifts. An increase in supply shifts the curve to the right; a decrease in supply shifts it to the left. The cause of a change in supply is a change in one or more of the determinants of supply. The term "supply" is used by economists to refer to a schedule or curve. A "change in supply" therefore must mean that the entire schedule has changed and that the curve has shifted.

A **change in the quantity supplied,** on the other hand, refers to the movement from one point to another point on a stable supply curve. The cause of such a movement is a change in the price of the specific product under consideration. In Table 4-6 a decline in the price of corn from $5 to $4 decreases the quantity of corn supplied from 12,000 to 10,000 bushels.

Shifting the supply curve from S_1 to S_2 or S_3 in Figure 4-4 entails "changes in supply." The movement from point a to point b on S_1, however, is merely a "change in the quantity supplied."

The reader should determine which of the following involves a change in supply and which entails a change in the quantity supplied:

1 Because production costs decline, producers sell more automobiles.
2 The price of wheat declines, causing the number of bushels of corn sold per month to increase.
3 Fewer oranges are offered for sale because their price has decreased in retail markets.
4 The Federal government doubles its excise tax on liquor.

Supply and demand: market equilibrium

We may now bring the concepts of supply and demand together to see how the interaction of the buying decisions of households and the selling decisions of producers will determine the price of a product and the quantity which is actually bought and sold in the market. In Table 4-8, columns 1 and 2 reproduce the market supply schedule for corn (from Table 4-6), and columns 2 and 3, the market demand schedule for corn (from Table 4-3). Note that in column 2 we are using a common set of prices. We assume competition—the presence of a larger number of buyers and sellers.

Now the question to be faced is this: Of the five[8] possible prices at which corn might sell in this mar-

[8] Of course, there are many possible prices; our example shows only five of them.

TABLE 4-8 **Market supply and demand for corn (hypothetical data)**

(1) Total quantity supplied per week	(2) Price per bushel	(3) Total quantity demanded per week	(4) Surplus (+) or shortage (−) (arrows indicate effect on price)
12,000	$5	2,000	+10,000 ↓
10,000	4	4,000	+ 6,000 ↓
7,000	3	7,000	0
4,000	2	11,000	− 7,000 ↑
1,000	1	16,000	−15,000 ↑

ket, which will actually prevail as the market price for corn? Let us derive our answer through the simple process of trial and error. For no particular reason, we shall start with an examination of $5. Could this be the prevailing market price for corn? The answer is "No," for the simple reason that producers are willing to produce and offer in the market some 12,000 bushels of corn at this price while buyers, on the other hand, are willing to take only 2000 bushels off the market at this price. In other words, the relatively high price of $5 encourages farmers to produce a great deal of corn, but that same high price discourages consumers from taking the product off the market. Other products appear as "better buys" when corn is high-priced. The result in this case is a 10,000-bushel **surplus** or *excess supply* of corn in the market. This surplus, shown in column 4, is the excess of quantity supplied over quantity demanded at the price of $5. Practically put, corn farmers would find themselves with unwanted inventories of output.

Could a price of $5—even if it existed temporarily in the corn market—persist over a period of time? Certainly not. The very large surplus of corn would prompt competing sellers to bid down the price to encourage buyers to take this surplus off their hands. Suppose price gravitates down to $4. Now the situation has changed considerably. The lower price has encouraged buyers to take more of this product off the market and, at the same time, has induced farmers to use a smaller amount of resources in producing corn. The surplus, as a re-

sult, has diminished to 6000 bushels. However, a surplus or excess supply still exists and competition among sellers will once again bid down the price of corn. We can conclude, then, that prices of $5 and $4 will be unstable because they are "too high." The market price for corn must be something less than $4.

To avoid letting the cat out of the bag before we fully appreciate how supply and demand determine product price, let us now jump to the other end of our price column and examine $1 as the possible market price for corn. It is evident from column 4 that at this price, quantity demanded is in excess of quantity supplied by 15,000 units. This relatively low price discourages farmers from devoting their resources to corn production; the same low price encourages consumers to attempt to buy more corn than would otherwise be the case. Corn is a "good buy" when its price is relatively low. In short, there is a 15,000-bushel **shortage** of, or *excess demand* for, corn. Can this price of $1 persist as the market price? No. Competition among buyers will bid up the price to something greater than $1. In other words, at a price of $1, many consumers who are willing and able to buy at this price will be left out in the cold. Many potential consumers, in order to ensure that they will not have to do without, will express a willingness to pay a price in excess of $1 to ensure getting some of the available corn. Suppose this competitive bidding up of price by buyers boosts the price of corn to $2. This higher price has reduced, but not eliminated, the shortage of corn. For $2, farmers are willing to devote more resources to corn production, and some buyers who were willing to pay $1 for a bushel of corn will choose not to buy corn at a price of $2, deciding to use their incomes to buy other products or maybe to save more of their incomes. But a shortage of 7000 bushels still exists at a price of $2. We can conclude that competitive bidding among buyers will push market price to some figure greater than $2.

By trial and error we have eliminated every price but $3. So let us now examine it. At a price of $3, *and only at this price,* the quantity which farmers are willing to produce and supply in the market is identical with the amount consumers are willing and able to buy. As a result, there is neither a shortage nor a surplus of corn at this price. We have already seen that a surplus causes price to decline and a shortage causes price to rise. With neither a shortage nor a surplus at $3, there is no reason for the actual price of corn to move away from this price. The economist calls this price the *market-clearing* or **equilibrium price,** equilibrium meaning "in balance" or "at rest." At $3, quantity supplied and quantity demanded are in balance; that is, **equilibrium quantity** is 7000 bushels. Hence $3 is the only stable price of corn under the supply and demand conditions shown in Table 4-8. Or, stated differently, the price of corn will be established where the supply decisions of producers and the demand decisions of buyers are mutually consistent. Such decisions are consistent with one another only at a price of $3. At any higher price, suppliers want to sell more than consumers want to buy and a surplus will result; at any lower price, consumers want to buy more than producers are willing to offer for sale, as is evidenced by the consequent shortage. Discrepancies between supply and demand intentions of sellers and buyers, re-

spectively, will prompt price changes which subsequently will bring these two sets of plans into accord with one another.

A graphic analysis of supply and demand should yield the same conclusions. Figure 4-5 puts the market supply and market demand curves for corn on the same graph, the horizontal axis now measuring both quantity demanded and quantity supplied. A close examination of this diagram clearly indicates that at any price above the equilibrium price of $3, quantity supplied will exceed quantity demanded. This surplus will cause a competitive bidding down of price by sellers eager to relieve themselves of their surplus. The falling price will cause less corn to be offered and will simultaneously encourage consumers to buy more. Any price below the equilibrium price will entail a shortage; that is, quantity demanded will exceed quantity supplied. Competitive bidding by buyers will push the price up toward the equilibrium level. And this rising price will simultaneously cause pro-

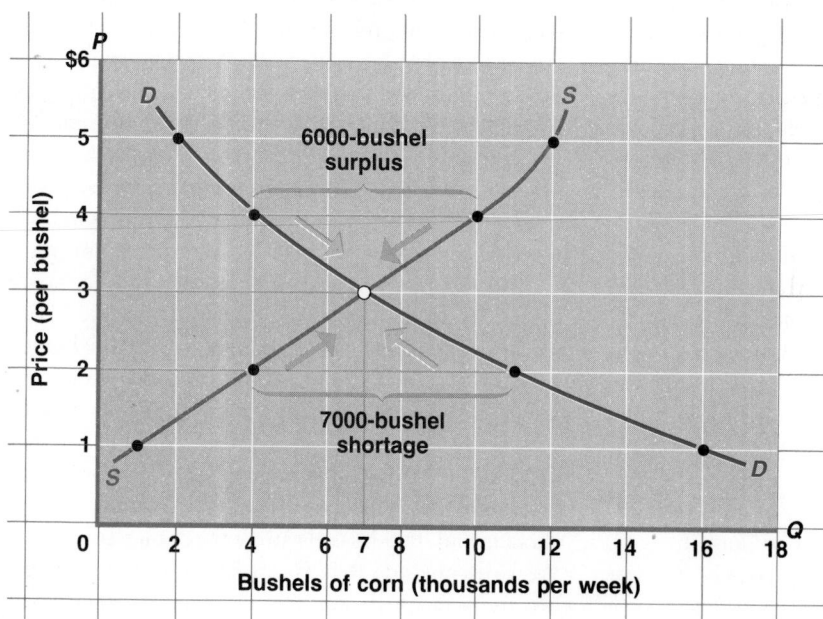

FIGURE 4-5

The equilibrium price and quantity for corn as determined by market demand and supply

The intersection of the downsloping demand curve **D** and the upsloping supply curve **S** indicates the equilibrium price and quantity, $3 and 7000 bushels in this instance. The shortages of corn which would exist at below-equilibrium prices, for example, 7000 bushels at $2, drive price up, and in so doing, increase the quantity supplied and reduce the quantity demanded until equilibrium is achieved. The surpluses which above-equilibrium prices would entail, for example, 6000 bushels at $4, push price down and thereby increase the quantity demanded and reduce the quantity supplied until equilibrium is achieved.

ducers to increase the quantity supplied and ration buyers out of the market, thereby causing the shortage to vanish. *Graphically, the intersection of the supply curve and the demand curve for the product will indicate the equilibrium point.* In this case equilibrium price and quantity are $3 and 7000 bushels.

RATIONING FUNCTION OF PRICES

The ability of the competitive forces of supply and demand to establish a price where selling and buying decisions are synchronized is called the **rationing function of prices.** In this case, the equilibrium price of $3 clears the market, leaving no burdensome surplus for sellers and no inconvenient shortage for potential buyers. The composite of freely made individual buying and selling decisions sets this price which clears the market. In effect, the market mechanism of supply and demand says this: Any buyer who is willing and able to pay $3 for a bushel of corn will be able to acquire one; those who are not, will not. Similarly, any seller who is willing and able to produce bushels of corn and offer them for sale at a price of $3 will be able to do so successfully; those who are not, will not. As we will see shortly, were it not that competitive prices automatically bring supply and demand decisions into consistency with one another, some type of administrative control by government would be necessary to avoid or control the shortages or surpluses which might otherwise occur.

CHANGES IN SUPPLY AND DEMAND

It was noted earlier that demand might change because of fluctuations in consumer tastes or incomes, changes in consumer expectations, or variations in the prices of related goods. On the other hand, supply might vary in response to changes in technology, resource prices, or taxes. Our analysis would be incomplete if we did not stop to consider the effect of changes in supply and demand upon equilibrium price.

Changing demand Let us first analyze the effects of a change in demand, assuming that supply is conveniently constant. Suppose that demand in-

creases, as shown in Figure 4-6a. What is the effect upon price? Noting that the new intersection of the supply and demand curves is at a higher point on both the price and quantity axes, we can conclude that an increase in demand, other things (supply) being equal, will have a *price-increasing effect* and a *quantity-increasing effect.* (The value of graphic analysis now begins to become apparent; we need not fumble with columns of figures in determining the effect on price and quantity but only compare the new with the old point of intersection on the graph.) A decrease in demand, as illustrated in Figure 4-6b, reveals both *price-decreasing* and *quantity-decreasing effects.* Price falls, and quantity also declines. *In brief, we find a direct relationship between a change in demand and the resulting changes in both equilibrium price and quantity.*

Changing supply Let us reverse the procedure and analyze the effect of a change in supply on price, assuming that demand is constant. If supply increases, as in Figure 4-6c, the new intersection of supply and demand is located at a lower equilibrium price. Equilibrium quantity, however, increases. If supply decreases, on the other hand, this will tend to increase product price. Figure 4-6d illustrates this situation. Here, price increases but quantity declines. In short, an increase in supply has a *price-decreasing* and a *quantity-increasing effect.* A decrease in supply has a *price-increasing* and a *quantity-decreasing effect. There is an inverse relationship between a change in supply and the resulting change in equilibrium price, but the relationship between a change in supply and the resulting change in equilibrium quantity is direct.*

Complex cases Obviously, a host of more complex cases might arise, involving changes in both supply and demand. Two cases are possible when it is supposed that supply and demand change in *opposite directions.* Assume first that supply increases and demand decreases. What effect does this have upon equilibrium price? This example couples two price-decreasing effects, and the net result will be a price fall greater than that which would result from either change taken in isolation. How about equilibrium quantity? Here the effects of the changes in supply and demand are opposed: The increase in supply tends to increase equilibrium quantity, but the decrease in demand tends to reduce the equilib-

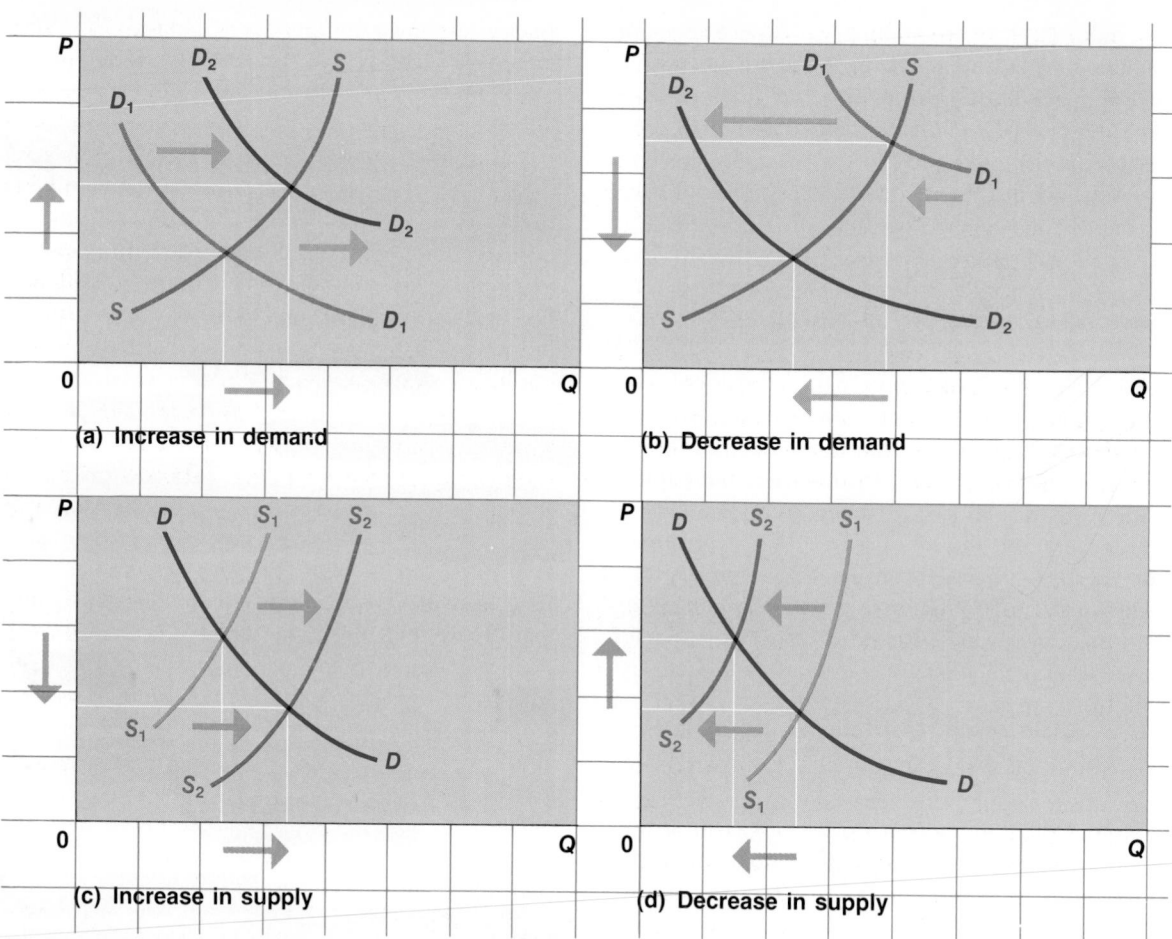

FIGURE 4-6

Changes in demand and supply and the effects on price and quantity

The increase in demand of (a) and the decrease in demand of (b) indicate a direct relationship between a change in demand and the resulting changes in equilibrium price and quantity. The increase in supply of (c) and the decrease in supply of (d) show an inverse relationship between a change in supply and the resulting change in equilibrium price, but a direct relationship between a change in supply and the accompanying change in equilibrium quantity.

rium quantity. The direction of the change in quantity depends upon the relative sizes of the changes in supply and demand. The second possibility is for supply to decrease and demand to increase. Two price-increasing effects are involved here. We can predict an increase in equilibrium price greater than that caused by either change taken separately. The effect upon equilibrium quantity is again indeterminate, depending upon the relative size of the changes in supply and demand. If the decrease in supply is relatively larger

than the increase in demand, the equilibrium quantity will be less than it is initially. But if the decrease in supply is relatively smaller than the increase in demand, the equilibrium quantity will increase as a result of these changes. The reader should trace through these two cases graphically to verify the conclusions we have outlined.

What if supply and demand change in the *same direction?* Suppose first that supply and demand both increase. What is the effect upon equilibrium price? It depends. Here we must compare two conflicting effects on price—the price-decreasing effect of the increase in supply and the price-increasing effect of the increase in demand. If the increase in supply is of greater magnitude than the increase in demand, the net effect will be for equilibrium price to decrease. If the opposite holds true, equilibrium price will increase. The effect upon equilibrium quantity is certain: Increases in supply and in demand both have quantity-increasing effects. This means that equilibrium quantity will increase by an amount greater than that which either change would have entailed in isolation. Second, a decrease in both supply and demand can be subjected to similar analysis. If the decrease in supply is greater than the decrease in demand, equilibrium price will rise. If the reverse holds true, equilibrium price will fall. Because decreases in supply and demand both have quantity-decreasing effects, it can be predicted with certainty that equilibrium quantity will be less than that which prevailed initially.

Incidentally, the possibility that supply and demand will both change in a given period of time is not unlikely. As a matter of fact, a single event might simultaneously affect both supply and demand. For example, a technological improvement in cheese production might lower both the supply of, and the demand for, fluid milk.

Needless to say, special cases might arise where a decrease in demand and a decrease in supply, on the one hand, and an increase in demand and an increase in supply, on the other, exactly cancel out. In both these cases, the net effect upon equilibrium price will be zero; price will not change. The reader should again work out these more complex cases in terms of supply and demand curves to verify all these results.

THE RESOURCE MARKET

What about the shape of the supply and demand curves in the resource market? As in the product market, resource supply curves are typically upsloping, and resource demand curves are downsloping. Why?

Resource supply curves generally slope upward; that is, they reflect a *direct* relationship between resource price and quantity supplied, because it is in the interest of resource owners

themselves to supply more of a particular resource at a high price than at a low price. High income payments in a particular occupation or industry encourage households to supply more of their human and property resources. Low-income payments discourage resource owners from supplying resources in this particular occupation or industry and, as a matter of fact, encourage them to supply their resources elsewhere. There is strong evidence, incidentally, that most college students choose their major (their occupation) on the basis of prospective financial rewards.

On the demand side, businesses tend to buy less of a given resource as its price rises, and they tend to substitute other relatively low-priced resources for it. Entrepreneurs will find it profitable to substitute low- for high-priced resources. More of a particular resource will be demanded at a low price than at a high price. The result? A downsloping demand curve for the various resources.

In short, just as the supply decisions of businesses and the demand decisions of consumers determine prices in the product market, so the supply decisions of households and demand decisions of businesses set prices in the resource market.

"OTHER THINGS EQUAL" REVISITED

Recall from Chapter 1 that as a substitute for their inability to conduct controlled experiments, economists invoke the "other things being equal" assumption in their analyses. We have seen in the present chapter that a number of forces bear upon both supply and demand. Hence, in locating specific supply and demand curves, such as D_1 and S in Figure 4-6a, economists are isolating the impact of what they judge to be the most important determinant of the amounts supplied and demanded—that is, the price of the specific product under consideration. In thus representing the laws of demand and supply by downsloping and upsloping curves respectively, the economist assumes that all the nonprice determinants of demand (incomes, tastes, and so forth) and supply (resource prices, technology, and other factors) are constant or unchanging. That is, price and quantity demanded are inversely related, *other things being equal*. And price and quantity supplied are directly related, *other things being equal.*

By failing to remember that the "other things equal" assumption is requisite to the laws of demand and supply, one can encounter confusing situations which *seem* to be in conflict with these laws. For example: Suppose Ford sells 200,000 Escorts in 1989 at an average price of $8000; 300,000 at an average price of $8500 in 1990; and 400,000 in 1991 at an average price of $9000. Price and the number purchased vary *directly,* and these real-world data seem to be at odds with the law of demand. But is there really a conflict here? The answer, of course, is "No." These data do *not* refute the law of demand. The catch is that the law of demand's "other things equal" assumption has been violated with the passage of time. Specifically, because of, for example, growing incomes, population growth, and relatively high gasoline prices which increase the attractiveness of compact cars, the demand curve for Escorts has increased over the years—shifted to the right as from D_1 to D_2 in Figure 4-6a—causing price to rise and, simultaneously, a larger quantity to be purchased.

Conversely, consider Figure 4-6d. Comparing the original S_1D and the new S_2D equilibrium positions, we note that *less* of the product is being sold or supplied at a higher price; that is, price and quantity supplied seem to be *inversely* related, rather than *directly* related as the law of supply indicates. The catch again is that the "other things equal" assumption underlying the upsloping supply curve has been violated. Perhaps production costs have gone up or a specific tax has been levied on this product, shifting the supply curve from S_1 to S_2. These examples also emphasize the importance of our earlier distinction between a "change in the quantity demanded (or supplied)" and a "change in demand (supply)."

Application: the foreign exchange market[9]

Let us close this chapter by applying our understanding of demand and supply to the **foreign exchange market,** that is, to the market wherein various national currencies are exchanged for one another. At the outset two points merit emphasis. On the one hand, real-world foreign exchange markets conform closely to the kinds of markets we have studied in this chapter. These are competitive markets characterized by large numbers of buyers and sellers dealing in a standardized "product" such as the American dollar, the German mark, the British pound, or the Japanese yen. On the other hand, the price or exchange value of a nation's currency is an unusual price in that it links **all** domestic (United States) prices with **all** foreign (say, Japanese or German) prices. As a consequence, a change in exchange rates can have very important implications for a nation's levels of domestic production and employment.

THE DOLLAR–YEN MARKET

Skirting technical details, let us examine how the foreign exchange market for, say, dollars and yen might function. To begin with, when nations trade there arises a need to exchange their currencies. For example, American exporters who sell to Japan want to be paid in dollars, not yen; but Japanese importers of American goods possess yen, not dollars. This problem is resolved by Japanese offering or supplying yen in exchange for dollars. Conversely, American importers need to pay Japanese exporters with yen, not dollars. To do so they go to the foreign exchange market as demanders of yen. In short, we can think of Japanese importers as suppliers of yen and American importers as demanders of yen. The interaction of the demand for, and the supply of, yen will establish the dollar price of yen. Suppose the equilibrium dollar price of yen—or, in other words, the dollar–yen exchange rate—is $1 = ¥100. That is, a dollar will buy 100 yen (the "dollar price" of 1 yen is 1 cent) and therefore 100 yen worth of Japanese goods. Conversely, 100 yen will buy $1 worth of American goods.

CHANGING RATES: DEPRECIATION AND APPRECIATION

What might cause this exchange rate to change? The nonprice determinants of the demand for and the supply of yen are quite similar to those we have already discussed. From the vantage point of the

---

[9] Some instructors may choose to skip this section.

United States, a number of things might occur to increase the demand for—and therefore the dollar price—of yen. For example, incomes might rise in the United States, causing Americans to buy not only more domestic goods, but also more Sony televisions, more Nikon cameras, and more Nissan automobiles from Japan. To do this Americans need to obtain more yen, so the demand for yen increases. Or there may occur a change in American tastes which enhances our preferences for Japanese goods. For instance, when gasoline prices soared in the 1970s, many American auto buyers shifted their demands from large, gas-guzzling domestic cars to gas-efficient Japanese compact cars. In so doing the demand for yen increased. The critical point is that an increase in the American demand for Japanese goods will increase the demand for yen and raise the dollar price of yen. Let us suppose the dollar price of yen rises from $1 = ¥100 (or 1¢ = ¥1) to $2 = ¥100 (or 2¢ = ¥1). When the dollar price of yen *increases,* we say there has been a **depreciation** of the dollar relative to the yen. This means that it now takes more dollars (pennies in this case) to buy a single unit of a foreign currency (the yen). A dollar is now worth less in that it will now buy fewer yen and therefore a smaller quantity of Japanese goods.

If events opposite to those we have presumed had occurred—that is, if incomes rose in Japan and Japanese preferences for American goods strengthened—then the *supply* of yen in foreign exchange markets would increase. This increase in the supply of yen relative to demand would cause the equilibrium dollar price of yen to *decrease.* For example, supply might increase to the extent that the dollar price of yen declines from the original $1 = ¥100, or 1¢ = ¥1, to $.50 = ¥100 or ½¢ = ¥1. This *decrease* in the dollar price of yen means there has been an **appreciation** of the dollar relative to the yen. It now takes fewer dollars (pennies) to buy a single yen than previously. The dollar is worth more because it is now capable of purchasing more yen and therefore more Japanese goods.

ECONOMIC CONSEQUENCES

The rather profound consequences of changes in exchange rates are quite easily perceived. Suppose

the dollar depreciates, that is, the dollar price of yen rises from 1¢ = ¥1 to 2¢ = ¥1. This clearly means that the yen and therefore **all** Japanese goods are now more expensive to Americans. So what happens? American consumers shift their expenditures from Japanese to American goods. For example, the Chevy Corsica is now relatively more attractive than the Honda Accord to American consumers. In general terms, this means that American industries are stimulated by the indicated shift in expenditures and their production and employment both rise. Conversely, Japanese export industries find the sales of their products diminishing, so output and employment both tend to decline. The depreciation of the dollar has caused America to become more prosperous and Japan less so. You are urged to confirm that an appreciation of the dollar's value relative to the yen will tend to depress the American economy and stimulate the Japanese economy.

With the economic stakes so high, it is easy to understand why governments often interfere with otherwise "free" foreign exchange markets. Thus, the United States government might attempt to depreciate the dollar when our economy is in recession. The problem, however, is that the consequent shift in American expenditures from foreign goods to domestic goods will lower Japanese exports and tend to depress *their* economy. The Japanese government may well be interested in offsetting the depreciation of the dollar which the Americans desire. Both the economic and political implications of exchange rates are great. We will return to such considerations in later chapters.

CHAPTER SUMMARY

1 A market is any institution or arrangement which brings buyers and sellers of some product or service together.

2 Demand refers to a schedule which summarizes the willingness of buyers to purchase a given product during a specific time period at each of the various prices at which it might be sold. According to the law of demand, consumers will ordinarily buy more of a product at a low price than they will at a high price. Therefore, other things being equal, the relationship between price and quantity demanded is negative or inverse and demand graphs as a downsloping curve.

3 Changes in one or more of the basic determinants of demand—consumer tastes, the number of buyers in the market, the money incomes of consumers, the prices of related goods, and consumer expectations—will cause the market demand curve to shift. A shift to the right is an increase in demand; a shift to the left, a decrease in demand. A "change in demand" is to be distinguished from a "change in the quantity demanded," the latter involving the movement from one point to another point on a fixed demand curve because of a change in the price of the product under consideration.

4 Supply is a schedule showing the amounts of a product which producers would be willing to offer in the market during a given time period at each possible price at which the commodity might be sold. The law of supply says that, other things being equal, producers will offer more of a product at a high price than they will at a low price. As a result, the relationship between price and quantity supplied is a direct one, and the supply curve is upsloping.

5 A change in resource prices, production techniques, taxes or subsidies, the prices of other goods, price expectations, or the number of sellers in the market will cause the supply curve of a product to shift. A shift to the right is an increase in supply; a shift to the left, a decrease in supply. In contrast, a change in the price of the product under consideration will result in a change in the quantity supplied, that is, a movement from one point to another on a given supply curve.

6 Under competition, the interaction of market demand and market supply will adjust price to that point at which the quantity demanded and the quantity supplied are equal. This is the equilibrium price. The corresponding quantity is the equilibrium quantity.

7 The ability of market forces to synchronize selling and buying decisions so as to eliminate potential surpluses or shortages is termed the "rationing function" of prices.

8 A change in either demand or supply will cause equilibrium price and quantity to change. There is a positive or direct relationship between a change in demand and the resulting changes in equilibrium price and quantity. Though the relationship between a change in supply and the resulting change in equilibrium price is inverse, the relationship between a change in supply and equilibrium quantity is direct.

9 The concepts of supply and demand also apply to the resource market.

10 The foreign exchange market is an important application of demand and supply analysis. Foreign importers are suppliers of their currencies and American importers are demanders of foreign currencies. The resulting equilibrium exchange rates link the price levels of all nations.

LAST WORD

The supply and demand for physician services

Economists and health policy makers have attempted to determine the possible impact of recent increases in the supply of physicians upon the equilibrium price of the physicians' services.

The basic supply and demand model predicts that an increase in supply of any given product or service will reduce the equilibrium price and increase equilibrium quantity. Over the past two decades, the physician-to-population ratio in the United States has risen sharply. Have physicians' fees fallen relative to other prices in response to the growing competition among the rapidly expanding numbers of physicians?

Other things being equal, increases in the supply of physician services should reduce medical fees and increase the quantity of medical services provided. But other things have *not* been constant. Several of the determinants of the demand for physician services have complicated the picture by dramatically changing over the last two decades. People have experienced rising levels of take-home income, the population itself is aging, the number of people qualifying for government programs which provide health care for the poor and the aged has risen, and an increasing number of workers have gained health-care coverage under employer-provided medical insurance plans. Each of these factors has tended to increase the demand for physician services.

Another factor may be at work on the demand side. Economic theory assumes that the supply of and the demand for any given product are independent of one another. That is, factors which cause supply to shift are distinct from factors which shift the demand curve. But in the area of physician services a number of researchers have put forth a "demand-shifting hypothesis" which suggests that physicians have the ability through their diagnoses and recommendations to increase the demand for their services. Specifically, it is argued that an increase in the supply of medical doctors will bring about an increase in the demand for medical services.

A recent empirical test of this hypothesis as applied to surgeons has provided support for it. The overall conclusion of the study is that:

Where surgeons are more numerous, the demand for operations increases. Other things being equal, a 10 percent higher surgeon/population ratio results in about a 3 percent increase in the number of operations and an *increase* in price.[1]

Note that an increase in the supply of surgeons in a given geographic area could give rise to an increase in the price of surgical services only if demand had increased.

Will the demand-increasing factors—rising income, greater insurance coverage, and physician-induced demand—continue to swamp increases in physician supply, further boosting the equilibrium price of physician services? Can we expect the average level of earnings of physicians to rise over the next decade? Emerging evidence indicates that the answer may be "No" to both questions. Price competition and fee discounts recently have become common as a greater number of physicians compete for patients. Many physicians have abandoned private practice and opted to become either paid employees of for-profit corporations providing medical care or for health maintenance organizations (HMOs). In fact, a recent study has concluded that rising competition among a rapidly growing number of physicians since 1965 has *decreased* the average real income of physicians by 19 to 45 percent over that period.

Conclusion: The factors which increase the demand for physician services, including the alleged physician-induced demand, may *not* enable physicians to offset in total the future supply impact of their growing numbers.

[1] Victor R. Fuchs, *The Health Economy* (Cambridge, Mass: Harvard University Press, 1986, p. 147.

Depreciation of the dollar reduces our imports and stimulates our domestic economy; appreciation of the dollar increases our imports and depresses our domestic economy.

TERMS AND CONCEPTS

market	surplus
demand	shortage
demand schedule (curve)	supply
law of demand	law of supply
diminishing marginal utility	supply schedule (curve)
income and substitution effects	equilibrium price and quantity
normal (superior) good	rationing function of prices
inferior good	foreign exchange market
substitute goods	depreciation and appreciation of the dollar
complementary goods	
change in demand (supply) versus change in the quantity demanded (supplied)	

QUESTIONS AND STUDY SUGGESTIONS

1 Explain the law of demand. Why does a demand curve slope downward? What are the determinants of demand? What happens to the demand curve when each of these determinants changes? Distinguish between a change in demand and a change in the quantity demanded, noting the cause(s) of each.

2 Critically evaluate: "In comparing the two equilibrium positions in Figure 4-6a, I note that a larger amount is actually purchased at a higher price. This refutes the law of demand."

3 Explain the law of supply. Why does the supply curve slope upward? What are the determinants of supply? What happens to the supply curve when each of these determinants changes? Distinguish between a change in supply and a change in the quantity supplied, noting the cause(s) of each.

4 Explain the following news dispatch from Hull, England: "The fish market here slumped today to what local commentators called 'a disastrous level'—all because of a shortage of potatoes. The potatoes are one of the main

CHAPTER 5

The market system and the five fundamental questions

We saw in Chapter 3 that the capitalist ideology makes clear the importance of freedom of enterprise and choice. Consumers are at liberty to buy what they choose; businesses, to produce and sell what they choose; and resource suppliers, to make their property and human resources available in whatever occupations they choose. Upon reflection, we might wonder why such an economy does not collapse in complete chaos. If consumers want breakfast cereal, businesses choose to produce aerobic shoes, and resource suppliers want to offer their services in manufacturing computer software, production would seem to be deadlocked because of the apparent inconsistency of these free choices.

Fortunately, two other features of capitalism —a system of markets and prices and the force of competition—provide the coordinating and organizing mechanisms which overcome the potential chaos posed by freedom of enterprise and choice. The competitive market system is a mechanism both for communicating the decisions of consumers, producers, and resource suppliers to one another and for synchronizing those decisions toward consistent production objectives.

Armed with an understanding of individual markets and prices gained from Chapter 4, we are now in a position to analyze the operation of the market system. More specifically, in this chapter we first want to understand how the market system operates as a mechanism for communicating and coordinating individual free choices. We also seek to evaluate the operation of a market economy.

The five fundamental questions

To understand the functioning of a market economy we must first recognize that there are **Five Fundamental Questions** to which *every* economy must respond. These questions are:

1 *How much* is to be produced? At what level—to what degree— should available resources be employed or utilized in the production process?

2 *What* is to be produced? What collection of goods and services will best satisfy society's material wants?

3 *How* is that output to be produced? How should production be organized? What firms should do the producing and what productive techniques should they utilize?

4 *Who* is to receive the output? In particular, how should the output of the economy be shared by individual consumers?

5 Can the system *adapt* to change? Can the system negotiate appropriate adjustments in response to changes in consumer wants, resource supplies, and technology?

Two points are relevant at the outset. First, we will defer the "how much" question for the moment. Macroeconomics deals in detail with the complex question of the level of resource employment. Second, the Five Fundamental Questions are merely an elaboration of the choices which underlie Chapter 2's production possibilities curve. Stated differently, the Five Fundamental Questions would be irrelevant were it not for the unlimited wants–scarce resources dilemma portrayed by the production possibilities curve.

Operation of the market system

The setting for our discussion is provided by Chapter 3's circular flow diagram (Figure 3-2). In examining how the market system answers the Fundamental Questions, we must add demand and supply diagrams as developed in Chapter 4 to represent the various product and resource markets embodied in the circular flow model.

DETERMINING WHAT IS TO BE PRODUCED

Given the product and resource prices established by competing buyers and sellers in both the product and resource markets, how would a purely capitalistic economy decide the types and quantities of goods to be produced? Remembering that businesses are motivated to seek profits and avoid losses, we can generalize that those goods and services which can be produced at a profit will be produced and those whose production entails a loss will not. And what determines profits or the lack of them? Two things:

1 The total revenue which a firm gets from selling a product.
2 The total costs of producing it.

Both total revenue and total costs are price-times-quantity figures. Total revenue is found by multiplying product price by the quantity of the product sold. Total costs are found by multiplying the price of each resource used by the amount employed and summing the costs of each.

Economic costs and profits   To say that those products which can be produced profitably will be produced and those which cannot will not is only an accurate generalization if the meaning of **economic costs** is clearly understood. In order to grasp the full meaning of costs, let us once again think of businesses as simply organizational charts, that is, businesses "on paper," distinct and apart from the capital, raw materials, labor, and entrepreneurial ability which make them going concerns. To become actual producing firms, these "on paper" businesses must secure all four types of resources. *Economic costs are the payments which must be made to secure and retain the needed amounts of these resources.* The per unit size of these costs—that is, resource prices—will be determined by supply and demand conditions in the resource market. The point to emphasize is that—like land, labor, and capital—entrepreneurial ability is a scarce resource and consequently has a price tag on

it. Costs therefore must include not only wage and salary payments to labor and interest and rental payments for capital and land, but also payments to the entrepreneur for the functions he or she performs in organizing and combining the other resources in the production of some commodity. The cost payment for these contributions by the entrepreneur is called a **normal profit.** Hence, a product will be produced only when total revenue is large enough to pay wage, interest, rental, *and* normal profit costs. Now if total revenues from the sale of a product exceed all production costs, including a normal profit, the remainder will accrue to the entrepreneur as the risk taker and organizing force in the going concern. This return above all costs is called a **pure,** or **economic, profit.** It is *not* an economic cost, because it need not be realized for the business to acquire and retain entrepreneurial ability.

Profits and expanding industries   A few hypothetical examples will explain more concretely how the market system determines what is to be produced. Suppose that the most favorable relationship between total revenue and total cost in producing product X occurs when the firm's output is 15 units. Assume, too, that the best combination of resources to use in producing 15 units of X entails 2 units of labor, 3 units of land, 1 of capital, and 1 of entrepreneurial ability, selling at prices of $2, $1, $3, and $3, respectively. Finally, suppose that the 15 units of X which these resources produce can be sold for $1 per unit. Will firms enter into the production of product X? Yes, they will. A firm producing product X under these conditions will be able to pay wage, rent, interest, and normal profit costs of $13 [= (2 × $2) + (3 × $1) + (1 × $3) + (1 × $3)]. The difference between total revenue of $15 and total costs of $13 will be an economic profit of $2.

This economic profit is evidence that industry X is a prosperous one. Such an industry will tend to become an **expanding industry** as new firms, attracted by these above-normal profits, are created or shift from less profitable industries. But the entry of new firms will be a self-limiting process. As new firms enter industry X, the market supply of X will increase relative to the market demand. This will lower the market price of X (Figure 4-6c) to the end that economic profits will in time disappear; that is, profits will be competed away. The market supply and demand situation prevailing when economic profits become zero will determine the total amount of X produced. At this point the industry will have achieved its "equilibrium size," at least until a further change in market demand or supply upsets that equilibrium.

Losses and declining industries But what if the initial market situation for product X were less favorable? Suppose conditions in the product market initially were such that the firm could sell the 15 units of X at a price of just 75 cents per unit. Total revenue, would be $11.25 (= 15 × 75 cents). After paying wage, rental, and interest costs of $10, the firm would yield a below-normal profit of $1.25. In other words, *losses* of $1.75 (= $11.25 − $13) would be incurred. Certainly, firms would not be attracted to this unprosperous **declining industry.** On the contrary, if these losses persisted, entrepreneurs would seek the normal profits or possibly even the economic profits offered by more prosperous industries. This means that, in time, existing firms in industry X would go out of business entirely or migrate to other industries where normal or better profits prevail. However, as this happens, the market supply of X will fall relative to the market demand, thereby raising product price (Figure 4-6d) to the end that losses will eventually disappear. Industry X will then stabilize itself in size. The market supply and demand situation that prevails at that point where economic profits are zero will determine the total output of product X. Again, the industry for the moment will have reached its equilibrium size.

"Dollar votes" The important role of consumer demand in determining the types and quantities of goods produced must be emphasized. Consumers, unrestrained by government and possessing money incomes from the sale of resources, spend their dollars upon those goods which they are most willing and able to buy. These expenditures are in effect **dollar votes** by which consumers register their wants through the demand side of the product market. If these votes are great enough to provide a normal profit, businesses will produce that product. An increase in consumer demand, that is, an increase in the dollar votes cast for a product, will mean economic profits for the industry producing

it. As we have just seen, these profits will signal the expansion of that industry and increases in the output of the product. Conversely, a decrease in consumer demand, that is, fewer votes cast for the product, will result in losses and, in time, contraction of the adversely affected industry. As firms leave the industry, the output of the product declines. Indeed, the industry may cease to exist. In short, the dollar votes of consumers play a key role in determining what products profit-seeking businesses will produce. As noted in Chapter 3, the capitalistic system is sometimes said to be characterized by **consumer sovereignty** because of the strategic role of consumers in determining the types and quantities of goods produced.

A much-publicized illustration of consumer sovereignty occurred a few years ago when a substantial number of consumers rejected the "new" Coca-Cola. Despite elaborate market surveys and extensive advertising, many Coke drinkers judged the new product to be inferior and engaged in organized protests until the manufacturer responded by once again making the original "classic" Coke available.

Market restraints on freedom From the viewpoint of businesses, we now see that firms are not really "free" to produce what they wish. The demand decisions of consumers, by making the production of some products profitable and others not, restrict the choice of businesses in deciding what to produce. Businesses must synchronize their production choices with consumer choices or face the penalty of losses and eventual bankruptcy.

Much the same holds true with respect to resource suppliers. The demand for resources is a **derived demand**—derived, that is, from the demand for the goods and services which the resources help produce. There is a demand for autoworkers only because there is a demand for automobiles. More generally, in seeking to maximize the returns from the sale of their human and property resources, resource suppliers are prompted by the market system to make their choices in accord with consumer demands. If only those firms which produce goods wanted by consumers can operate profitably, only those firms will demand resources. Resource suppliers will not be "free" to allocate their resources to the production of goods which consumers do not value highly. The reason? There will be no firms producing such products, because consumer demand is not sufficient to make it profitable. In short, consumers register their preferences on the demand side of the product market, and producers and resource suppliers respond appropriately in seeking to further their own self-interests. The market system communicates the wants of consumers to businesses and resource suppliers and elicits appropriate responses.

ORGANIZING PRODUCTION

How is production to be organized in a market economy? This Fundamental Question is composed of three subquestions:

1 How should resources be allocated among specific industries?

2 What specific firms should do the producing in each industry?

3 What combinations of resources—what technology—should each firm employ?

Production and profits The preceding section has answered the first subquestion. The market system steers resources to those industries whose products consumers want badly enough to make their production profitable. It simultaneously deprives unprofitable industries of scarce resources. If all firms had sufficient time to enter prosperous industries and to leave unprosperous industries, the output of each industry would be large enough for the firms to make just normal profits. If total industry output at this point happens to be 1500 units and the most profitable output for each firm is 15 units, as in our previous example, the industry will be made up of 100 competing firms.

The second and third subquestions are closely intertwined. In a competitive market economy, the firms which do the producing are those which are willing and able to employ the economically most efficient technique of production. And what determines the most efficient technique? Economic efficiency depends upon:

1 Available technology, that is, the alternative combinations of resources or inputs which will produce the desired output.

2 The prices at which the needed resources can be obtained.

Least-cost production The combination of resources which is most efficient economically depends not only upon the physical or engineering data provided by available technology but also upon the relative worth of the required resources as measured by their market prices. Thus, a technique which requires just a few physical inputs of resources to produce a given output may be highly *in*efficient economically *if* the required resources are valued very highly in the market. In other words, *economic efficiency entails getting a given output of product with the smallest input of scarce resources, when both output and resource inputs are measured in dollars-and-cents terms.* In short, that combination of resources which will produce, say, $15 worth of product X at the lowest possible money cost is the most efficient.

Table 5-1 will help illustrate these points. Suppose there are three different techniques by which the desired $15 worth of product X can be produced. The quantity of each resource required by each production technology and the prices of the required resources are shown in Table 5-1. By multiplying the quantities of the various resources required by the resource prices in each of the three techniques, the total cost of producing $15 worth of X by each technique can be determined. Technique No. 2 is economically the most efficient of the three techniques, for the simple reason that it is the least costly way of producing $15 worth of X. Technique No. 2 permits society to obtain $15 worth of output by using up a smaller amount of resources— $13 worth in this instance—than the $15 worth which would be used up by the two alternative techniques.

But what guarantee is there that technique No. 2 will actually be used? The answer is that firms will want to use the most efficient technique because it yields the greatest profit.

We must emphasize that a change in *either* technology *or* resource prices may cause the firm to shift from the technology now employed. For example, if the price of labor falls to 50 cents, technique No. 1 will now be superior to technique No. 2. That is, businesses will find that they can lower their costs by shifting to a technology which involves the use of more of that resource whose price has fallen. The reader also should verify that a new technique involving 1 unit of labor, 4 of land, 1 of capital, and 1 of entrepreneurial ability will be

TABLE 5-1 **Techniques for producing $15 worth of product X (hypothetical data)**

Resource	Price per unit of resource	Technique No. 1	Technique No. 2	Technique No. 3
Labor	$2	4	2	1
Land	1	1	3	4
Capital	3	1	1	2
Entrepreneurial ability	3	1	1	1
Total cost of $15 worth of X		$15	$13	$15

preferable to all three techniques listed in Table 5-1, assuming the resource prices given there.[1]

DISTRIBUTING TOTAL OUTPUT

The market system enters the picture in two ways in solving the problem of distributing total output. Generally speaking, any given product will be distributed to consumers on the basis of their ability and willingness to pay the existing market price for it. If the price of X is $1 per unit, those buyers who are able and willing to pay that price will get a unit of this product; those who are not, will not. This, we recall from Chapter 4, is the rationing function of equilibrium prices.

What determines a consumer's ability to pay the equilibrium price for X and other available products? The size of one's money income. And money income in turn depends upon the quantities of the various property and human resources which the income receiver supplies and the prices which they command in the resource market. Thus, resource prices play a key role in determining the size of each household's income claim against the total output of society. Within the limits of a consumer's money income, his or her willingness to pay the equilibrium price for X determines whether or not

[1] There is a geographic or locational aspect to the question of organizing production which we ignore at this point. The question *"Where* to produce?" will be considered in detail in Chapter 36.

some of this product is distributed to that person. And this willingness to buy X will depend upon one's preference for X in comparison with available close substitutes for X and their relative prices. Thus, product prices play a key role in determining the expenditure patterns of consumers.

We should emphasize that there is nothing particularly ethical about the market system as a mechanism for distributing output. Those households which manage to accumulate large amounts of property resources by inheritance, through hard work and frugality, through business acumen, or by crook will receive large incomes and thus command large shares of the economy's total output. Others, offering unskilled and relatively unproductive labor resources which elicit low wages, will receive meager money incomes and small portions of total output.

ACCOMMODATING CHANGE

Industrial societies are dynamic: Consumer preferences, technology, and resource supplies all change. This correctly implies that the particular allocation of resources which is *now* the most efficient for a *given* pattern of consumer tastes, for a *given* range of technological alternatives, and for *given* supplies of resources can be expected to become obsolete and inefficient as consumer preferences change, new techniques of production are discovered, and resource supplies alter over time. Can the market economy negotiate adjustments in resource uses appropriate to such inevitable changes and thereby remain efficient?

Guiding function of prices   Let us suppose a change occurs in consumer tastes. Specifically, let us say that, because of greater health consciousness, consumers decide they want more exercise bikes and fewer cigarettes than the economy is currently providing. Will the market system communicate this change to businesses and resource suppliers and prompt appropriate adjustments?

The assumed change in consumers' taste will be communicated to producers through an increase in the demand for bikes and a decline in the demand for cigarettes. This means that bike prices will rise and cigarette prices will fall. Now, assuming firms in both industries are enjoying precisely normal profits prior to these changes in consumer demand, higher exercise bike prices mean economic profits for the bike industry, and lower cigarette prices will entail losses for the cigarette industry. Self-interest induces new competitors to enter the prosperous bike industry. Losses will in time force firms to leave the depressed cigarette industry.

But these adjustments, we recall, are both self-limiting. The expansion of the bike industry will continue only to the point at which the resulting increase in the market supply of bikes brings bike prices back down to a level at which normal profits again prevail. Similarly, contraction in the cigarette industry will persist until the accompanying decline in the market supply of cigarettes brings cigarette prices up to a level at which the remaining firms can receive a normal profit. Or, in the extreme, the cigarette industry may cease to exist. The crucial point to note is that these adjustments in the business sector are completely appropriate to the assumed changes in consumer tastes. Society—meaning consumers—wants more exercise bikes and fewer cigarettes, and that is precisely what it is getting as the bike industry expands and the cigarette industry contracts. These adjustments, incidentally, portray the concept of consumer sovereignty at work.

This analysis proceeds on the assumption that resource suppliers are agreeable to these adjustments. Will the market system prompt resource suppliers to reallocate their human and property resources from the cigarette to the bike industry,

thereby permitting the output of bikes to expand at the expense of cigarette production? The answer is "Yes."

The economic profits which initially follow the increase in demand for bikes will not only provide that industry with the inducement to expand but will also give it the added receipts with which to obtain the resources essential to its growth. Higher bike prices will permit firms in that industry to pay higher prices for resources, thereby drawing resources from what are now less urgent alternative employments. Willingness and ability to employ more resources in the exercise bike industry will be communicated back into the resource market through an increase in the demand for resources. Substantially the reverse occurs in the adversely affected cigarette industry. The losses which the decline in consumer demand initially entails will cause a decline in the demand for resources in that industry. Workers and other resources released from the contracting cigarette industry can now find employment in the expanding bike industry. Furthermore, the increased demand for resources in the bike industry will mean higher resource prices in that industry than those being paid in the cigarette industry, where declines in resource demand have lowered resource prices. The resulting differential in resource prices will provide the incentive for resource owners to further their self-interests by reallocating their resources from the cigarette to the bike industry. And this, of course, is the precise shift needed to permit the bike industry to expand and the cigarette industry to contract.

The ability of the market system to communicate changes in such basic data as consumer tastes and to elicit appropriate responses from both businesses and resource suppliers is called the **directing** or **guiding function of prices.** By affecting product prices and profits, changes in consumer tastes direct the expansion of some industries and the contraction of others. These adjustments carry through to the resource market as expanding industries demand more resources and contracting industries demand fewer. The resulting changes in resource prices guide resources from the contracting to the expanding industries. In the absence of a market system, some administrative agency, presumably a governmental planning board, would have to undertake the task of directing business institutions and resources into specific lines of production.

Analysis similar to that just outlined would indicate that the market system would adjust appropriately to similar fundamental changes—for example, to changes in technology and changes in the relative supplies of various resources.

Important postscript: Our discussion of how the market system guides resources from less important to more important uses explains why most economists are opposed to long-term legal freezes of product and resource prices. Although freezing prices is a tempting means of controlling inflation which government has tried occasionally in our economy, such freezes undermine the guiding function of prices and interfere with the realization of allocative efficiency through time (Chapter 19).

Initiating progress Adjusting to given changes is one thing; initiating changes, particularly desirable changes, is something else again. Is the competitive market system congenial to technological improvements and capital accumulation, the interrelated changes which lead to greater productivity and a higher level or material well-being for society? This is not an easy question to answer. We state our reply at this point without stopping for qualifications and modifications (see Chapter 28).

TECHNOLOGICAL ADVANCE The competitive market system would seem to contain the incentive for technological advance. The introduction of cost-cutting techniques provides the innovating firm with a temporary advantage over its rivals. Lower production costs mean economic profits for the pioneering firm. By passing a part of its cost reduction on to the consumer through a lower product price, the innovating firm can achieve a sizable increase in sales and lucrative economic profits at the expense of rival firms. Furthermore, the competitive market system would seem to provide an environment conducive to the rapid diffusion of a technological advance. Rivals *must* follow the lead of the most progressive firm or suffer the immediate penalty of losses and the eventual pain of bankruptcy.

We should note that the lower product price which the technological advance permits will cause the innovating industry to expand. This expansion may be the result of existing firms' expanding their rates of output or of new firms entering the industry under the lure of the economic profits initially created by the technological advance. This expansion, that is, the diversion of resources from less progressive to more progressive industries, is as it should be. Sustained efficiency in the use of scarce resources demands that resources be continually reallocated from industries whose productive techniques are relatively less efficient to those whose techniques are relatively more efficient.

CAPITAL ACCUMULATION But technological advance typically entails the use of increased amounts of capital goods. Can the market system provide the capital goods upon which technological advance relies? More specifically, can the entrepreneur as an innovator command through the market system the resources necessary to produce the machinery and equipment upon which technological advance depends?

Obviously, the entrepreneur can. If society registers dollar votes for capital goods, the product market and the resource market will adjust to these votes by producing capital goods. In other words, the market system acknowledges dollar voting for both consumer and capital goods. But who, specifically, will register votes for capital goods? First, the entrepreneur as a receiver of profit income can be expected to apportion a part of that income to the accumulation of capital goods. By so doing, an even greater profit income can be achieved in the future if the innovation proves successful. Furthermore, by paying a rate of interest, entrepreneurs can borrow portions of the incomes of households and use these borrowed funds in casting dollar votes for the production of more capital goods.

COMPETITION AND CONTROL: THE "INVISIBLE HAND"

Though the market system is the organizing mechanism of pure capitalism, it is essential to recognize the role of competition as the mechanism of control in such an economy. The market mechanism of supply and demand communicates the wants of consumers (society) to businesses and through businesses to resource suppliers. It is competition, however, which forces businesses and resource suppliers to make appropriate responses. To illustrate: We have seen that an increase in consumer demand for some product will raise that good's price above the wage, rent, interest, and normal profit costs of production. The resulting economic profits in effect are a signal to producers that society wants more of the product. It is competition—in particular, the ability of new firms to enter the industry—that simultaneously brings an expansion of output and a lowering of price back to a level just consistent with production costs. However, if the industry was not competitive, but was dominated by, say, one huge firm (a monopolist) which was able to prohibit the entry of potential competitors, that firm could continue to enjoy economic profits by preventing the expansion of the industry.

But competition does more than guarantee responses appropriate to the wishes of society. It is competition which forces firms to adopt the most efficient productive techniques. In a competitive market, the failure of some firms to use the least costly production technique means their eventual elimination by other competing firms which do employ the most efficient methods of production. Finally, we have seen that competition provides an environment conducive to technological advance.

A very remarkable aspect of the operation and the adjustments of a competitive market system is that a curious and important identity is involved—the identity of private and social interests. That is, firms and resource suppliers, seeking to further their own self-interest and operating within the framework of a highly competitive market system, will simultaneously, as though guided by an **"invisible hand,"**[2] promote the public or social interest. For example, we have seen that given a competitive environment, business firms use the least costly combination of resources in producing a given output because it is in their private self-interest to do so. To act otherwise would be to forgo profits or even to risk bankruptcy over a period of time. But, at the same time, it is clearly also in the social interest to use scarce resources in the least costly, that is, most efficient, manner. Not to do so would be to produce a given output at a greater cost or sacrifice of alternative goods than is really necessary. Furthermore, in our earlier more-bikes–fewer-cigarettes illustration, it is self-interest,

awakened and guided by the competitive market system, which induces the very responses appropriate to the assumed change in society's wants. Businesses seeking to make higher profits and to avoid losses, on the one hand, and resource suppliers pursuing greater monetary rewards, on the other, negotiate the very changes in the allocation of resources and therefore the composition of output which society now demands. The force of competition, in other words, controls or guides the self-interest motive in such a way that it automatically, and quite unintentionally, furthers the best interests of society. The "invisible hand" concept tells us that when firms maximize their profits, society's national output is also maximized.

An evaluation of the market system

Is the market system the best means of responding to the Fundamental Questions? This is a complex question; any complete answer necessarily leaps the boundary of facts and enters the realm of values. This means there is no scientific answer to the query. The very fact that there exist many competing ways of allocating scarce resources—that is, many different kinds of economic systems (Table 2-3)—is ample evidence of disagreement as to the effectiveness of the market system.

THE CASE FOR THE MARKET SYSTEM

The virtues of the market system are implicit in our discussion of its operation. Two merit emphasis.

Allocative efficiency The basic economic argument for the market system is that it promotes an efficient allocation of resources. The competitive market system, it is argued, guides resources into the production of those goods and services most wanted by society. It forces the use of the most efficient techniques in organizing resources for production, and it is conducive to the development and adoption of new and more efficient production techniques. In short, proponents of the market system argue that the "invisible hand" will in effect harness self-interest so as to provide society with

---

[2] Adam Smith, *The Wealth of Nations* (New York: Modern Library, Inc., originally published in 1776), p. 423.

the greatest output of wanted goods from its avail-able resources. This, then, suggests the maximum economic efficiency. It is this presumption of allo-cative efficiency which makes most economists hes-itant to advocate governmental interference with, or regulation of, free markets unless the reasons for such interference are clear and compelling.

Freedom The major noneconomic argument for the market system is its great emphasis upon per-sonal freedom. One of the fundamental problems of social organization is how to coordinate the eco-nomic activities of large numbers of individuals and businesses. We recall from Chapter 2 that there are basically two ways of providing this coor-dination: one is central direction and the use of co-ercion; the other is voluntary cooperation through the market system. Only the market system can coordinate economic activity without coercion. The market system permits—indeed, it thrives upon—freedom of enterprise and choice. Entrepre-neurs and workers are not herded from industry to industry by government directives to meet the pro-duction targets established by some omnipotent governmental agency. On the contrary, they are free to further their own self-interests, subject, of course, to the rewards and penalties imposed by the market system itself.

So long as effective freedom of exchange is main-tained, the central feature of the market organization of economic activity is that it prevents one person from interfering with another in respect of most of his activities. The consumer is protected from coercion by the seller because of the presence of other sellers with whom he can deal. The seller is protected from coer-cion by the consumer because of other consumers to whom he can sell. The employee is protected from coercion by the employer because of other employers for whom he can work, and so on. And the market does this impersonally and without centralized authority.[3]

To summarize: The competitive market system is allegedly conducive to both allocative efficiency and freedom.

[3] Milton Friedman, *Capitalism and Freedom* (Chicago: The University of Chicago Press, 1962), pp. 14–15.

THE CASE AGAINST THE MARKET SYSTEM

The case against the market system is somewhat more complex. Critics of the market economy base their position on the following points.

Demise of competition Critics argue the capitalistic ideology is permissive of, and even conducive to, the demise of its main controlling mechanism—competition. The alleged weakening of competition as a control mechanism comes from two basic sources.

1 Though desirable from the social point of view, competition is most irksome to the individual pro-ducer subject to its rigors. It is allegedly inherent in the free, individualistic environment of the capital-istic system that profit-seeking entrepreneurs will attempt to break free of the restraining force of competition in trying to better their position. Com-bination, conspiracy, and cut throat competition are all means to the end of reducing competition and escaping its regulatory powers. As Adam Smith put the matter more than two centuries ago: "People of the same trade seldom meet together but the conversation ends in a conspiracy against the public, or in some diversion to raise prices."

2 Some economists believe that the very technolog-ical advance which the market system fosters has contributed to the decline of competition. Modern technology typically requires *(a)* the use of very large quantities of real capital; *(b)* large markets; *(c)* a complex, centralized, and closely integrated management; and *(d)* large and reliable sources of raw materials. Such an operation implies the need for producers who are large-scale not only in the absolute sense but also in relation to the size of the market. In other words, the achievement of maxi-mum productive efficiency through the employ-ment of the best available technology often requires the existence of a small number of relatively large firms rather than a large number of relatively small ones.

To the degree that competition declines, the market system will be weakened as a mechanism for efficiently allocating resources. Producers and resource suppliers will be less subject to the will of consumers; the sovereignty of producers and re-source suppliers will then challenge and weaken the sovereignty of consumers. The "invisible hand'' identity of private and social interests will begin to lose its grip. Furthermore, the protection from coercion which the market system provides is predicated upon the widespread dispersion of economic power. The concentration of economic power which accompanies the decline of competition permits the possessors of that power to engage in coercive acts.

Wasteful and inefficient production   Critics also challenge the assertion that the market system provides the goods most wanted by society. We have just encountered one facet of the critics' position: To the extent that a weakening of competition lessens consumer sovereignty, the market system becomes less proficient in allocating resources in precise accord with the wishes of consumers. But there are other reasons for questioning its efficiency.

UNEQUAL INCOME DISTRIBUTION   Critical socialists, among others, contend that the market system allows the more efficient, or more cunning, entrepreneurs to accumulate vast amounts of property resources, the accumulation process being extended through time by the right to bequeath. This, in addition to differences in the amount and quality of human resources supplied by various households, causes a highly unequal distribution of money incomes in a market economy. The result is that families differ greatly in their ability to express their wants in the market. The wealthy have many more dollar votes than the poor. Hence, it is concluded that the market system allocates resources to the production of frivolous luxury goods for the rich at the expense of the output of necessities for the poor. A country that

   . . . spends money on champagne before it has provided milk for its babies is a badly managed, silly, vain, stupid, ignorant nation. . . . The only way in which such a nation can make itself wealthy and prosperous is by good housekeeping: that is by providing for its wants in order of their importance, and allowing no money to be wasted on whims and luxuries until the necessities have been thoroughly served.[4]

---

[4] George Bernard Shaw, *The Intelligent Woman's Guide to Socialism and Capitalism* (New York: Brentano's, Inc., 1928), pp. 50–55. Used by permission of the Public Trustee and the Society of Authors.

The point is that the claim of ''efficiency'' in the allocation of resources has a hollow ring if the distribution of income and therefore of output does not meet some reasonable standards of fairness or equity. We shall pursue the debate over income inequality in Chapter 37.

MARKET FAILURE: EXTERNALITIES   Critics cite two important cases of **market failure.** First, the market system may fail to register all the benefits and costs associated with the production and consumption of certain goods and services. That is, some benefits and costs are external to the market in that they accrue to parties other than the immediate buyer and seller. Such benefits and costs are called *spillover* or *external* benefits and costs. For example, consumer demand as registered in the market embodies only the satisfactions which accrue to individual consumers who purchase goods and services; it does not reflect the fact that the purchase of such services as vaccinations and education yields widespread benefits or satisfactions to the community (society) as a whole. Similarly, the supply decisions of producers are based upon the costs which the market obligates them to bear and do not reflect external costs, that is, costs borne by society at large such as various forms of environmental pollution. The point is this: Where demand and supply do *not* accurately reflect all the benefits and all the costs of production, that is, where external benefits and costs exist, the market system cannot be expected to bring about an allocation of resources which best satisfies the wants of society.

MARKET FAILURE: PUBLIC GOODS   The second case of market failure arises because the market system tabulates only individual wants. There are many wants involving goods and services which cannot be financed by individuals through the market. For example, such goods and services as highways, flood-control programs, and national defense cannot be purchased in desired amounts by households on an individual basis. These public goods can only be produced and consumed economically on a collective basis. The market system, it is argued, is incapable of registering such social, or collective, wants. Both the externalities and public goods cases of market failure will be pursued in Chapter 6.

INSTABILITY   Finally, many economists feel that the market system is an imperfect mechanism for achieving full employment and price level stability. The problems of unemployment and inflation will be analyzed in detail in Part 2.

Which of these two positions—one for, and the other against, the market system—is correct? To a degree both are. The several criticisms of the market economy are reasonably accurate and certainly too serious to ignore. On the other hand, we cannot judge an issue by the number of arguments pro and con. The basic economic argument for the market system—that it tends to provide an efficient allocation of resources—is not easily undermined. In practice, the market system is—or at least can be—reasonably efficient.

RELEVANCE, REALISM, AND THE MARKET SYSTEM

Does the market system of the American economy function in the same fashion as the market system discussed in this chapter? In principle, yes; in detail, no. Our discussion of the market system provides us with a working model—a rough approximation—of the actual market system of our economy. Our analysis presents a much simplified, yet useful, picture of the real thing. The competitive market system also gives us a norm, or standard, against which the real-world economy can be compared. Specifically, there are two basic differences between the market system as pictured in this chapter and the actual market system of our economy.

Fewness and entry barriers   In many product and resource markets, competition takes place among a few large firms rather than among the many small ones presupposed in the pure form of the market system. Similarly, large labor unions dominate some labor markets. Entry into several highly profitable industries is made difficult by patents, limited access to key resources, cost advantages of large size, entry-deterring pricing strategies, and other barriers. Competition thus is not as vigorous in practice in many industries as our discussion of the market system assumed. This means that the decisions of businesses and resource suppliers are less than perfectly synchronized with those of con-

LAST WORD

Ticket scalping: sin and theology

While commonly condemned, ticket scalping entails a voluntary market transaction which is of benefit to both buyer and seller.

It is sometimes difficult to keep straight the distinction between sin and sanctity in the realm of the market.

"Scalping" is usually defined as the exchange of a good—typically tickets to sports events—at any price greater than that the original seller listed. There are definitional variations: New York prohibits any resale of tickets for more than 25 percent above their face value. Twenty-five percent sin is reputable; 26 percent sin is damnable. Oh, morality *is* a subtle thing.

But if scalping is a sin, just what is the nature of the inherent evil? The pejorative term suggests the extortion of wealth, with the extortioner's gain being the victim's loss. In actuality, there is no redistributional compulsion—no coerced shift of wealth—when tickets are bought, even when the price exceeds the face value.

Ticket scalping is voluntary exchange in which both exchangers gain. The buyer obtains a ticket

sumers, and that changes in the production goals of society are less precisely communicated throughout the economy. Some firms and unions which dominate their respective markets have the power to resist the dictates of consumer sovereignty and,

worth more to him than the money paid; the seller obtains money he values more than the ticket sold. Indeed, if both did not benefit, the exchange would not take place. The reason why voluntary exchange occurs is because goods are not initially owned by those who most value them. Ticket scalping—like all uncoerced trade—is a way of shifting assets to those who value them most.

Scalpers are middlemen who bid tickets away from those who value them less in order to sell them to people who value them more. The middleman is productive: he creates wealth by facilitating desired redistribution of tickets. The scalper's motive is personal gain, but that can be obtained only by sharing the mutual gains of exchange which arise from moving tickets to uses most valued. Scalping enables community preferences to be satisfied more efficiently.

[We are told] that scalping is "deleterious, not only to the event and the promoter, but to the people involved in it." This is fascinating doctrine. If the promoter is injured, it is because he initially underpriced his tickets, not because the tickets are later resold. If the people involved are hurt, it is because they are mysteriously made worse off by making themselves better off. And if the event suffers, it is because it is a bad thing to have an audience composed of those who most want to be there.

Source: William R. Allen, *Midnight Economist: Broadcast Essays IV* (Los Angeles: International Institute for Economic Research, 1982), pp. 36–37, abridged. Reprinted by permission.

as a matter of fact, frequently will find it personally advantageous to do so. Having said this, however, we should note that competition has a way of working its will over long periods of time. For example, foreign producers have found lucrative opportuni-

ties in several product markets such as steel and autos which were dominated by a handful of American producers only a decade or two ago. But the point remains: The actual U.S. economy differs in many respects from the idealized one which we have been discussing.

Government Another major difference between our model market system and the market system of the American economy lies in the economic role of government in the latter. In contrast with the passive, limited government envisioned in the ideology of pure capitalism, the public sector is an active and integral component of our economy. In particular, the economy of the United States has taken note of the important elements of truth in the criticisms of the market system. Through government, society has taken steps designed to correct these shortcomings. Therefore, government pursues policies intended not only to preserve and bolster competition, but also to adjust certain inequities fostered by the market system, to encourage appropriate resource reallocations when external benefits and costs are significant, to meet collective wants, and to help maintain full employment. It is with these and related economic functions of government that the ensuing chapter is concerned.

Is our analysis of the market system realistic? Does it provide a workable description of the market system of American capitalism? One scholar has responded to these questions as follows:

For all the new quality of twentieth-century industrial society, the great principles of self-interest and competition, however watered down or hedged about, still provide basic rules of behavior which no economic organization can afford to disregard entirely . . . the laws of the market can be discerned . . . if we look beneath the surface.[5]

CHAPTER SUMMARY

1 Every economy is confronted with Five Fundamental Questions: **a** At what level should available resources be employed? **b** What goods and services are to be pro-

[5] Robert L. Heilbroner, *The Worldly Philosophers,* 3d ed. (New York: Simon & Schuster, Inc., 1967), pp. 53–54.

duced? **c** How is that output to be produced? **d** To whom should the output be distributed? **e** Can the system adapt to changes in consumer tastes, resource supplies, and technology?

2 In a market economy, the interacting decisions of competing buyers and sellers will determine a system of product and resource prices at any given point in time.

3 Those products whose production and sale yield total revenue sufficient to cover all costs, including a normal profit, will be produced. Those whose production will not yield a normal profit will not be produced.

4 Economic profits designate an industry as prosperous and signal its expansion. Losses mean an industry is unprosperous and result in a contraction of that industry. Industrial expansion and contraction are self-limiting processes. As expansion increases market supply relative to market demand, the price of a product falls to the point where all economic profits disappear. As contraction decreases market supply relative to market demand, the resulting increase in product price eliminates losses and makes the industry normally profitable once again.

5 Consumer sovereignty dominates a competitive market economy. The penalty of losses and the lure of profits force both businesses and resource suppliers to channel their efforts in accordance with the wants of consumers.

6 Competition forces firms to use the least costly, and therefore the most economically efficient, productive techniques.

7 The market system plays a dual role in distributing total output among individual households. The prices commanded by the quantities and types of resources supplied by each household will determine the number of dollar claims against the economy's output which each household receives. Given consumer tastes, product prices are of fundamental importance in determining consumer expenditure patterns. Within the limits of each household's money income, consumer preferences and the relative prices of products determine the distribution of total output.

8 The competitive market system can communicate changes in consumer tastes to resource suppliers and entrepreneurs, thereby prompting appropriate adjustments in the allocation of the economy's resources. The competitive market system also provides an environment conducive to technological advance and capital accumulation.

9 Competition, the primary mechanism of control in the market economy, will foster an identity of private and social interests; as though directed by an "invisible hand," competition harnesses the self-interest motives of businesses and resource suppliers so as to simultaneously further the social interest in using scarce resources efficiently.

10 The basic economic virtue of the market system is its continuing emphasis upon efficiency. It produces what consumers want through the use of the most efficient techniques. Operation and adjustments of the market system are automatic in the sense that they are the result of individual, decentralized decisions, not the centralized decisions of government.

11 Criticisms of the market system are several: **a** The controlling mechanism, competition, tends to weaken over time; **b** inherent income inequalities, inability to register collective wants, and the presence of external benefits and costs prevent the market system from producing that collection of goods most wanted by society; **c** the competitive market system does not guarantee full employment or price level stability.

12 The market system of American capitalism differs from the competitive market system in that the former is characterized by **a** fewness of competitors and barriers to entry in certain markets, and **b** government intervention in the economy to correct the major defects of the market system. Yet, the competitive market system does provide a working model whereby we can understand the market system of the United States economy.

TERMS AND CONCEPTS

Five Fundamental Questions

economic costs

normal versus economic profits

expanding industry versus declining industry

dollar votes

consumer sovereignty

derived demand

directing (guiding) function of prices

"invisible hand"

market failure

QUESTIONS AND STUDY SUGGESTIONS

1 Describe in detail how the market system answers the Fundamental Questions. Why must economic choices be made? Explain: "The capitalistic system is a profit and loss economy."

2 Evaluate and explain the following statements:

a "The most important feature of capitalism is the absence of a central economic plan."

b "Competition is the indispensable disciplinarian of the market economy."

c "Production methods which are inferior in the engineering sense may be the most efficient methods in the economic sense."

3 Explain fully the meaning and implications of the following quotation.

The beautiful consequence of the market is that it is its own guardian. If output prices or certain kinds of remuneration stray away from their socially ordained levels, forces are set into motion to bring them back to the fold. It is a curious paradox which thus ensues: the market, which is the acme of individual economic freedom, is the strictest taskmaster of all. One may appeal the ruling of a planning board or win the dispensation of a minister; but there is no appeal, no dispensation, from the anonymous pressures of the market mechanism. Economic freedom is thus more illusory than at first appears. One can do as one pleases in the market. But if one pleases to do what the market disapproves, the price of individual freedom is economic ruination.[6]

4 Assume that a business firm finds that its profits will be at maximum when it produces $40 worth of product A. Suppose also that each of the three techniques shown in the following table will produce the desired output.

Resource	Price per unit of resource	Technique No. 1	Technique No. 2	Technique No. 3
Labor	$3	5	2	3
Land	4	2	4	2
Capital	2	2	4	5
Entrepreneurial ability	2	4	2	4

[6] Ibid., p. 42.

a Given the resource prices shown, which technique will the firm choose? Why? Will production entail profits or losses? Will the industry expand or contract? When is a new equilibrium output achieved?

b Assume now that a new technique, technique No. 4, is developed. It entails the use of 2 units of labor, 2 of land, 6 of capital, and 3 of entrepreneurial ability. Given the resource prices in the table, will the firm adopt the new technique? Explain your answer.

c Suppose now that an increase in labor supply causes the price of labor to fall to $1.50 per unit, all other resource prices being unchanged. Which technique will the producer now choose? Explain.

d "The market system causes the economy to conserve most in the use of those resources which are particularly scarce in supply. Resources which are scarcest relative to the demand for them have the highest prices. As a result, producers use these resources as sparingly as is possible." Evaluate this statement. Does your answer to question 4c bear out this contention? Explain.

5 Foreigners frequently point out that, comparatively speaking, Americans are very wasteful of food and material goods and very conscious, and overly economical, in their use of time. Can you provide an explanation for this observation?

6 What are the major criticisms of the market system? Carefully evaluate these criticisms. Analyze in detail: "No allocation of resources can be termed 'efficient' unless we define the 'optimal' distribution of income."

CHAPTER 6

The economic functions of government

Now we begin the move from our abstract working model of pure capitalism to a discussion of American capitalism. In so doing we inject a significant dose of reality into our analysis.

All real-life economies are "mixed"; government and the market system share the function of answering the Five Fundamental Questions. Yet, the various economies of the world differ drastically in the particular blend of government direction and market direction which they embody (see Table 2-3). The economy of the Soviet Union leans heavily toward a centrally planned economy. Our economy, on the other hand, is predominantly a market economy. At the same time, the economic functions of government—Federal, state, and local—are of very considerable significance.

It is not an easy matter to quantify the economic role of government. A rough indicator of the relative importance of the market and government is the fact that currently about four-fifths of the total output of our economy is provided by the market system, the remaining one-fifth being produced under the sponsorship of government. But in addition to sponsoring production, government is also involved in a variety of social insurance and welfare programs designed to redistribute income within the private sector of the economy. Data indicate that taxes and total government disbursements—for the purchase of goods and services *and* for welfare activities—are approximately one-third of the national output. Finally, a variety of difficult-to-quantify regulatory programs designed to protect the environment, improve worker health and safety, protect consumers from unsafe products, provide equal access to employment opportunities, and control the pricing behavior of certain industries impose government into virtually every aspect of economic activity. Government's economic role is clearly large and pervasive. Instead of Chapter 3's pure capitalism, our economy can be better described as mixed capitalism. The operation of the private sector through the market system (Chapters 4 and 5) is modified in a variety of significant ways by the public sector.

Economic functions of government

The economic functions of government are many, and they are varied. In fact, the economic role of government is so broad in scope that it is virtually impossible to establish an all-inclusive list of its economic functions. We shall employ the following breakdown of government's economic activities as a pattern for our discussion, recognizing that some overlapping is unavoidable.

First, some of the economic functions of government are designed to strengthen and facilitate the operation of the market system. The two major activities of government in this area are:
1 Providing the legal foundation and a social environment conducive to the effective operation of the market system.
2 Maintaining competition.

Through a second group of functions, government supplements and modifies the operation of the market system. There are three major functions of government here. They involve:
3 Redistributing income and wealth.

4 Adjusting the allocation of resources so as to alter the composition of the national output.
5 Stabilizing the economy, that is, controlling unemployment and inflation caused by business fluctuations, and promoting economic growth.

While this fivefold breakdown of government's functions is a useful way of analyzing its economic role, we shall find that most government activities and policies have *some* impact in all these areas. For example, a program to redistribute income to the poor affects the allocation of resources to the extent that the poor buy somewhat different goods and services from those that wealthier members of society buy. A decline in, say, government military spending for the purpose of lessening inflationary pressures also tends to reallocate resources from public to private uses.

Let us briefly consider the first two functions of government and then analyze the redistributive, allocative, and stabilization roles of government in more detail.

Legal and social framework

Government assumes the task of providing the legal framework and certain basic services prerequisite to the effective operation of a market economy. The necessary legal framework involves such things as providing for the legal status of business enterprises, defining the rights of private ownership, and providing for the enforcement of contracts. Government also establishes legal "rules of the game" to govern the relationships of businesses, resource suppliers, and consumers with one another. Through legislation, government is enabled to referee economic relationships, detect foul play, and exercise authority in imposing appropriate penalties. The basic services provided by government include the use of police powers to maintain internal order, provision of a system of standards for measuring the weight and quality of products, and establishment of a monetary system to facilitate the exchange of goods and services.

The Pure Food and Drug Act of 1906 and its various amendments provide an excellent example of how government has strengthened the operation of the market system. This act sets rules of conduct to govern producers in their relationships with consumers. It prohibits the sale of adulterated and misbranded foods and drugs, requires the net weights and ingredients of products to be specified on their containers, establishes quality standards which must be stated on the labels of canned foods, and prohibits deceptive claims on patent-medicine labels. All these measures are designed to prevent fraudulent activities on the part of producers and, simultaneously, to increase the public's confidence in the integrity of the market system. Similar legislation pertains to labor-management relations and the relations of business firms to one another.

The presumption is that resource allocation will be improved upon by this type of government activity. Supplying a medium of exchange, ensuring the quality of products, defining ownership rights, and enforcing contracts tend to increase the volume of exchange. This widens markets and permits greater specialization in the use of both property and human resources. Such specialization, we saw in Chapter 3, means a more efficient allocation of resources. However, some argue that government has overregulated the interactions of businesses, consumers, and workers, thereby stifling economic incentives and impairing productive efficiency.

Maintaining competition

Competition is the basic regulatory mechanism in a capitalistic economy. It is the force which subjects producers and resource suppliers to the dictates of buyer or consumer sovereignty. With competition, it is the supply and demand decisions of *many* sellers and buyers which determine market prices. This means that individual producers and resource suppliers can only adjust to the wishes of buyers as tabulated and communicated by the market system. Profits and survival await the competitive producers who obey the market system; losses and eventual bankruptcy are the lot of those who deviate from it. With competition, buyers are the boss, the market is their agent, and businesses are their servant.

The growth of monopoly drastically alters this situation. What is **monopoly?** *Broadly defined, it is the situation wherein the number of sellers becomes small enough for each seller to influence total supply* *and therefore the price of the commodity being sold.* What is its significance? Simply this: When monopoly supplants competition, sellers can influence, or "rig," the market in terms of their own self-interests and to the detriment of society as a whole. Through their ability to influence total supply, monopolists can artificially restrict the output of products and thereby enjoy higher prices and, very frequently, persistent economic profits. These above-competitive prices and profits are in direct conflict with the interests of consumers. Monopolists are not regulated by the will of society as are competitive sellers. Producer sovereignty supplants consumer sovereignty to the degree that monopoly supplants competition. The result is that resources are allocated in terms of the profit-seeking interests of monopolistic sellers rather than in terms of the wants of society as a whole. In short, monopoly tends to cause a misallocation of economic resources.

In the United States the government has attempted to control monopoly primarily in two ways. First, in the case of "natural monopolies"—that is, in industries wherein technological and economic realities rule out the possibility of competitive markets—the government has created public commissions to regulate prices and service standards. Transportation, communications, and electric and other utilities are illustrations of industries which are regulated in varying degrees. At local levels of government, public ownership of electric and water utilities is quite common. But, second, in the vast majority of markets, efficient production can be attained with a high degree of competition. The Federal government has therefore enacted a series of antimonopoly or antitrust laws, beginning with the Sherman Act of 1890, for the purpose of maintaining and strengthening competition as an effective regulator of business behavior. The regulatory commissions and antitrust laws will be examined critically in Chapter 34.

Even if the legal foundation of capitalistic institutions is assured and competition is maintained, there will still be a need for certain additional economic functions on the part of government. *The market economy at its best has certain biases and shortcomings which compel government to supplement and modify its operation.*

Redistribution of income

The market system is an impersonal mechanism, and the distribution of income to which it gives rise may entail more inequality than society desires. The market system yields very large incomes to those whose labor, by virtue of inherent ability and acquired education and skills, commands high wages. Similarly, those who possess—by virtue of hard work or easy inheritance—valuable capital and land receive large property incomes. But others in our society have less ability and have received modest amounts of education and training. And these same people typically have accumulated or inherited no property resources. Hence, their incomes are very low. Furthermore, many of the aged, the physically and mentally handicapped, and husbandless women with dependent children earn only very small incomes or, like the unemployed, no incomes at all through the market system. In short, the market system entails considerable inequality in the distribution of money income and therefore in the distribution of total output among individual households. Although progress has been made, poverty amidst overall plenty in our economy persists as a major economic and political issue.

Government has assumed the responsibility for ameliorating income inequality in our society. This responsibility is reflected in a variety of policies and programs. First, *transfer payments* provide relief to the destitute, aid to the dependent and handicapped, and unemployment compensation to the unemployed. Similarly, our social security and Medicare programs provide financial support for the retired and aged sick. All these programs transfer income from government to households which would otherwise have little or none. Second, government also alters the distribution of income by *market intervention,* that is, by modifying the prices established by market forces. Price supports for farmers and minimum-wage legislation are illustrations of government price fixing designed to raise the incomes of specific groups. Finally, the personal income tax has been used historically to take a larger proportion of the incomes of the rich than of the poor and therefore have a kind of Robin Hood effect upon income distribution. However, recent revisions of the personal income tax have significantly reduced its redistributive impact. Indeed, the tax system as a whole is estimated to have a very modest impact upon income distribution.

Reallocation of resources

Economists are cognizant of two major cases of *market failure,* that is, situations in which the competitive market system would either (1) produce the "wrong" amounts of certain goods and services, or (2) fail to allocate any resources whatsoever to the production of certain goods and services whose output is economically justified. The first case involves "spillovers" or "externalities" and the second "public" or "social" goods.

SPILLOVERS OR EXTERNALITIES

We found in Chapter 5 that one of the virtues of a competitive market system is that it would result in an efficient allocation of resources. That is, the "right" or optimal amount of resources would be allocated to each of the various goods and services produced. Hence, the equilibrium output in a competitive market is also identified as the optimal output.

But the conclusion that competitive markets automatically bring about allocative efficiency rests upon the hidden assumption that *all* the benefits and costs associated with the production and consumption of each product are fully reflected in the market demand and supply curves respectively. Stated differently, it is assumed that there are no *spillovers* or *externalities* associated with the production or consumption of any good or service. A *spillover*[1] occurs when some of the benefits or costs associated with the production or consumption of a good "spill over" onto third parties, that is, to parties other than the immediate buyer or seller. Spillovers are also termed *externalities* because they are

benefits and costs accruing to some individual or group external to the market transaction.

Spillover costs When the production or consumption of a commodity inflicts costs upon some third party without compensation, there exists a **spillover cost.** The most obvious examples of spillover costs involve environmental pollution. When a chemical manufacturer or meat-packing plant dumps its wastes into a lake or river, swimmers, fishermen, and boaters—not to mention communities which seek a usable water supply—suffer spillover costs. When a petroleum refinery pollutes the air with smoke or a paint factory creates distressing odors, the community bears spillover costs for which it is not compensated.

How do spillover or external costs affect the allocation of resources? Figure 6-1a tells the story. When spillover costs occur—when producers shift some of their costs onto the community—their production costs are lower than would otherwise be the case. In other words, the supply curve does not include or "capture" all the costs which can be legitimately associated with the production of the good. Hence, the producer's supply curve, S, understates the total costs of production and therefore lies to the right of the supply curve which would include all costs, S_t. By polluting, that is, by creating spillover costs, the firm enjoys lower production costs and the supply curve S. The result, as shown in Figure 6-1a, is that the equilibrium output Q_e is larger than the optimal output Q_o. Stated differently, resources are *overallocated* to the production of this commodity.

Correcting for spillover costs What actions might government take to correct the overallocation of resources associated with spillover costs? More pointedly, how might government "internalize" the external costs? Two basic types of corrective action are common: legislative action and specific taxes.

I LEGISLATION Looking at our examples of air and water pollution, we find that the most direct action is simply to pass *legislation* which prohibits or limits pollution. Such legislation forces potential polluters to bear the costs of more properly disposing of industrial wastes; for example, firms must buy

---

[1] Spillovers may go by other names—for example, external economies and diseconomies, neighborhood effects, and social benefits and costs.

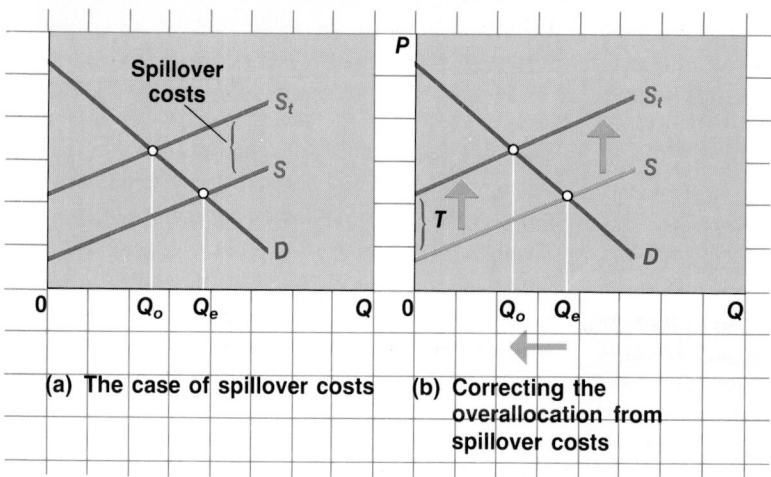

FIGURE 6-1

Spillover costs and the overallocation of resources

With spillover costs in (a) we find that the lower costs borne by businesses, as reflected in *S*, fail to reflect all costs, as embodied in *S$_t$*. Consequently, the equilibrium output *Q$_e$* is greater than the efficient or optimal output *Q$_o$*. This overallocation of resources can be corrected by legislation or, as shown in (b), by imposing a specific tax, *T*, which raises the firm's costs and shifts its supply curve from *S* to *S$_t$*.

and install smoke-abatement equipment or facilities to purify water which has been contaminated by manufacturing processes. Such action forces potential offenders, under the threat of legal action, to bear *all* the costs associated with their production. In short, legislation can shift the supply curve *S* toward *S$_t$* in Figure 6-1b, tending to bring the equilibrium and optimal outputs into equality.

2 SPECIFIC TAXES   A second and less direct action is based upon the fact that taxes are a cost and therefore a determinant of a firm's supply curve (Chapter 4). Government might levy a *specific tax* which equals or approximates the spillover costs per unit of output. Through this tax, government attempts to shove back onto the offending firm those external or spillover costs which private industry would otherwise avoid. Specifically, a specifix tax equal to *T* per unit in Figure 6-1b will increase the firm's costs, shifting the supply curve from *S* to *S$_t$*. The result is that the equilibrium output *Q$_e$* will decline so that it corresponds with the optimal output *Q$_o$* and the overallocation of resources will be eliminated.

Spillover benefits   But spillovers may also take the form of benefits. The production or consumption of

certain goods and services may confer spillover or external benefits on third parties or the community at large for which payment or compensation is not required. For example, chest x-rays and polio immunization shots result in direct benefits to the immediate consumer. But an early diagnosis of tuberculosis and the prevention of a contagious disease yield widespread and substantial spillover benefits to the entire community. Education is another standard example of **spillover benefits.** Education entails benefits to individual consumers: "More educated" people generally achieve higher incomes than do "less educated" people. But education also confers sizable benefits upon society; for example, the economy as a whole benefits from a more versatile and more productive labor force, on the one hand, and smaller outlays in the areas of crime prevention, law enforcement, and welfare programs, on the other. Significant, too, is the fact that political participation correlates positively with the level of education; for example, the percentage of persons who vote increases with educational attainment.

Figure 6-2a shows the impact of spillover benefits upon resource allocation. The existence of spillover benefits simply means that the market demand curve, which reflects only private benefits, understates total benefits. The market demand curve fails to capture all the benefits associated with the provision and consumption of goods and services which entail spillover benefits. Thus D in Figure 6-2a indicates the benefits which private individuals derive from education; D_t is drawn to include these private benefits *plus* the additional spillover benefits accruing to society at large. Thus, while market demand D and supply S_t would yield an equilibrium output of Q_e, this output would be less than the optimal output Q_o. The market system would not produce enough education; resources would be **underallocated** to education.

Correcting for spillover benefits How might the underallocation of resources associated with the presence of spillover benefits be corrected?

I INCREASE DEMAND One approach is to increase demand by providing consumers with purchasing power which can be used *only* to obtain the particular good or service with which spillover benefits are associated. Example: Our food stamp program is designed to improve the diets of low-income families. The food stamps which government provides

to such families can be spent only on food. Stores accepting food stamps are reimbursed with money by the government. A part of the rationale for this program is that improved nutrition will help disadvantaged children perform better in school and disadvantaged adults to be better employees. In brief, the program is designed to help disadvantaged people become productive participants in the economy, an outcome which entails benefits to society as a whole. In terms of Figure 6-2b the program increases the demand for food from from D to D_t, thereby alleviating or eliminating the underallocation of resources.

2 INCREASE SUPPLY An alternative approach works through the supply side of the market. Instead of subsidizing consumers of a particular good, government may find it more convenient and administratively simpler to subsidize producers. A *subsidy* is simply a specific tax in reverse; taxes impose an extra cost on producers, whereas subsidies reduce their costs. In Figure 6-2c we note that a subsidy of U per unit to producers will reduce costs and shift the supply curve downward from S_t to S_t'. As a result, output will increase from Q_e to the optimal

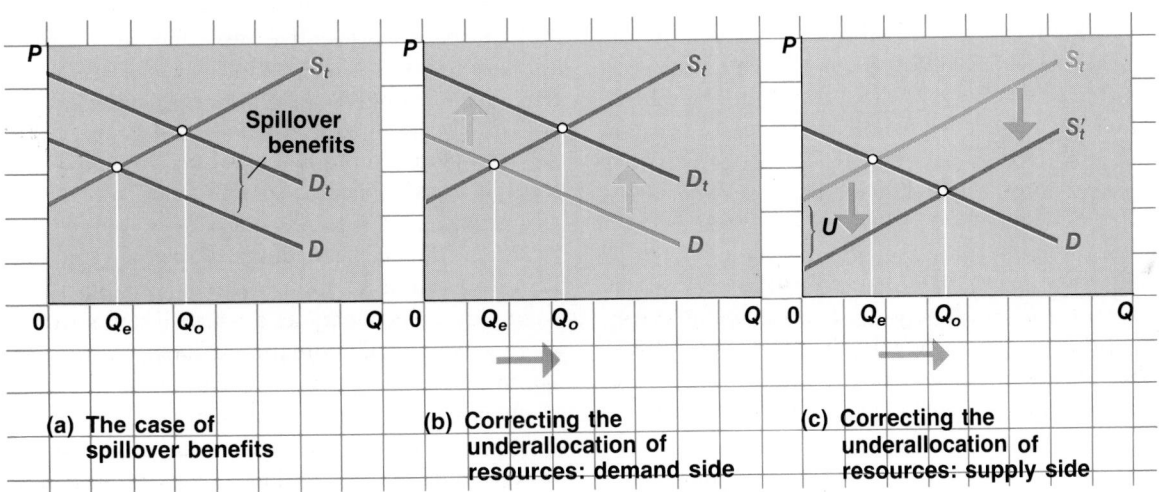

FIGURE 6-2

Spillover benefits and the underallocation of resources

Spillover benefits in (a) cause society's total benefits from a product, as shown by D_t, to be understated by the market demand curve, D. As a result, the equilibrium output Q_e is less than the optimal output Q_o. This can be corrected by a subsidy to consumers, as shown in (b), which increases market demand from D to D_t. Alternatively, the underallocation can be eliminated by providing producers with a subsidy of U, which increases their supply curve from S_t to S_t'.

level Q_o. Hence, the underallocation of resources will be corrected. Public subsidization of higher education, mass immunization programs, and public hospitals and health clinics are cases in point.

3 GOVERNMENT PROVISION   A third policy option arises if spillover benefits are extremely large: Government may simply choose to finance or, in the extreme, to own and operate such industries. This option leads us into a discussion of public goods and services.

PUBLIC GOODS AND SERVICES

Consider the characteristics of *private goods* which are produced through the market system. These goods are *divisible* in that they come in units small enough to be afforded by individual buyers. Furthermore, private goods are subject to the **exclusion principle** in that those who are willing and able to pay the equilibrium price get the product, but those who are unable or unwilling to pay are excluded from the benefits provided by that product.

There are certain kinds of goods and services—called **public** or **social goods**—which would not be produced at all by the market system because their characteristics are essentially opposite those of private goods. Public goods are *indivisible,* involving such large units that they cannot be sold to individual buyers. More importantly, the exclusion principle does *not* apply; that is, there is no effective way of excluding individuals from the benefits of public goods once those goods come into existence. Obtaining the benefits of private goods is predicated upon *purchase;* the benefits from public goods accrue to society from the *production* of such goods.

Illustrations   The classic public goods example is a lighthouse on a treacherous coast or harbor. The construction of a lighthouse might be economically justified in that benefits (fewer shipwrecks) exceed production costs. But the benefit accruing to each individual user would not justify the purchase of such a large and indivisible product. In any event, once in operation, its warning light is a guide to *all* ships. There is no practical way to exclude certain ships from its benefits. Therefore, why should any

ship owner voluntarily pay for the benefits received from the light? The light is there for all to see, and a ship captain cannot be excluded from seeing it if the ship owner chooses not to pay. Economists call this the **free-rider problem;** *people can receive benefits from a good without contributing to its costs.* Given the inapplicability of the exclusion principle, there is no economic incentive for private enterprises to supply lighthouses. If the services of the lighthouse cannot be priced and sold, it will clearly be unprofitable for private firms to devote resources to lighthouses. In short, here is a service which yields substantial benefits but for which the market would allocate no resources. National defense, flood-control, public health, and insect-abatement programs are other public goods. Hence, if society is to enjoy such goods and services, they must be provided by the public sector and financed by compulsory charges in the form of taxes.

Large spillover benefits   While the inapplicability of the exclusion principle rather sharply sets off public from private goods, a variety of other goods and services are provided by government even though the exclusion principle *could* be applied. In particular, such goods and services as education, streets and highways, police and fire protection, libraries and museums, preventive medicine, and sewage disposal could be subject to the exclusion principle, that is, they could be priced and provided by private producers through the market system. But, as noted earlier, these are all services which entail substantial spillover benefits and therefore would be underproduced by the market system. Therefore, government undertakes or sponsors their provision to avoid the underallocation of resources which would otherwise occur. Such goods and services are sometimes called *quasi-public goods.* One can understand the long-standing controversies surrounding the status of medical care and housing. Are these private goods to be provided through the market system, or are they quasi-public goods to be provided by government?

ALLOCATING RESOURCES TO PUBLIC GOODS

Given that the price system would fail to allocate resources for public goods and would underallocate resources for quasi-public goods, what is the mechanism by which such goods get produced?

Public goods are purchased through the government on the basis of group, or collective, choices, in contrast to private goods, which are purchased from private enterprises on the basis of individual choices. More specifically, the types and quantities of the various public goods produced are determined in a democracy by political means, that is, by voting. The quantities of the various public goods consumed are a matter of public policy.[2] These group decisions, made in the political arena, supplement the choices of households and businesses in answering the Five Fundamental Questions.

Assuming these group decisions have been rendered, precisely how are resources reallocated from the production of private goods to the production of public goods? In a full-employment economy, government is faced with the task of freeing resources from private employment to make them available for the production of public goods. The apparent means of releasing resources from private uses is to reduce private demand for them. This is accomplished by levying taxes on businesses and households, thereby diverting some of their incomes—some of their potential purchasing power—out of the income-expenditure streams. With lower incomes, businesses and households will be forced to curtail their investment and consumption spending. *In short, taxes diminish private demand for goods and services, and this decrease in turn prompts a drop in the private demand for resources.* By diverting purchasing power from private spenders to government, taxes free resources from private uses. *Government expenditure of the tax proceeds can then reabsorb these resources in the provision of public goods and services.* For example, corporation and personal income taxes release resources from the

production of investment goods—drill presses, boxcars, warehouses—and consumer goods—food, clothing, and television sets. Government expenditures can reabsorb these resources in the production of guided missiles, military aircraft, and new schools and highways. Government purposely reallocates resources to bring about significant changes in the composition of the economy's total output.

Stabilization

Historically, the most recent and in some ways the most important function of government is that of stabilizing the economy—assisting the private economy to achieve both the full employment of resources and a stable price level. At this point we pause only to outline and assert (rather than fully explain) the stabilization function of government.

The key point is that the level of output depends directly upon total or aggregate expenditures. A high level of total spending means it will be profitable for the various industries to produce large outputs, and this condition, in turn, will necessitate that both property and human resources be employed at high levels. Many economists feel that there are no mechanisms in the capitalistic system to ensure that aggregate spending will be at that particular level which will provide for full employment. There are two unhappy possibilities that might arise:

Unemployment The level of total spending in the private sector may be too low for full employment. The government's obligation is to augment private spending so that total spending—private *and* public—will be sufficient to generate full employment. How can government do this? One answer[3] is by using the same techniques—government spending and taxes—as it uses to reallocate resources to the production of public goods. Specifically, government should increase its own spending on public goods and services on the one hand, and

___

[2] There are differences between *dollar voting*, which dictates output in the private sector of the economy, and *political voting*, which determines output in the public sector. The rich person has many more votes to cast in the private sector than does the poor person. In the public sector, each—at least in theory—has an equal say. Furthermore, the children who cast their votes for bubble gum and comic books in the private sector are banned by virtue of their age from the registering of social choices.

[3] We will find in later chapters that government has means other than its expenditure-tax policies to help achieve economic stability.

reduce taxes in order to stimulate private spending on the other.

2 Inflation   The second possibility is that the economy may attempt to spend in excess of its productive capacity. If aggregate spending exceeds the full-employment output, the excess spending will have the effect of pulling up the price level. Excessive aggregate spending is inflationary. Government's obligation here is to eliminate the excess spending. It can do this primarily by cutting its own expenditures and by raising taxes so as to curtail private spending.

Caution: The real world, unfortunately, is more complex than our discussion implies. Hence, the lamentable situation of simultaneous unemployment and inflation which plagued the 1970s and early 1980s is not susceptible to such simple and self-evident remedies.

The circular flow revisited

In a mixed economy, government is thoroughly integrated into the real and monetary flows which comprise the economy. It is informative to reexamine the redistributional, allocative, and stabilization functions of government in terms of Chapter 3's circular flow model. In Figure 6-3 flows (1) through (4) merely restate Figure 3-2. Flows (1) and (2) show business expenditures for the resources provided by households. Recall that these expenditures are costs to businesses, but represent wage, rent, interest, and profit income to households. Flows (3) and (4) portray households making consumer expenditures for the goods and services produced by businesses.

Now carefully consider the numerous modifications which stem from the addition of government. Flows (5) through (8) tell us that government makes purchases in both product and resource markets. Specifically, flows (5) and (6) represent government purchasing such things as paper clips, computers, and military hardware from private businesses. Flows (7) and (8) reflect government purchases of resources. The Federal government employs and pays salaries to members of Congress, the armed forces, Justice Department lawyers, var-

ious bureaucrats, and so on. State and local governments hire teachers, bus drivers, police, and firefighters. The Federal government might lease or purchase land to expand a military base; a city may buy land to build a new elementary school.

Government then provides public goods and services to both households and businesses as shown by flows (9) and (10). The financing of public goods and services requires tax payments by businesses and households as reflected in flows (11) and (12). We have labeled these flows as *net* taxes to acknowledge that they also include "taxes in reverse" in the form of transfer payments to households and subsidies to businesses. Thus, flow (11) entails not merely corporate income, sales, and excise taxes flowing from businesses to government, but also various subsidies to farmers, shipbuilders, and some airlines.[4] Similarly, government also collects taxes (personal income taxes, payroll taxes) directly from households and makes available transfer payments (for example, welfare payments and social security benefits) as shown by flow (12).

Our expanded circular flow model allows us to more clearly grasp how government can alter the distribution of income, reallocate resources, and change the level of economic activity. The structure of taxes and transfer payments can have a significant impact upon the distribution of income. To illustrate, in flow (12) a tax structure which draws tax revenues primarily from well-to-do households combined with a system of transfer payments to low-income households will result in greater equality in the distribution of income. Flows (6) and (8) imply an allocation of resources which differs from that of a purely private economy. Government buys goods and labor services which differ from those purchased by households. Finally, all governmental flows suggest means by which government might attempt to stabilize the economy. For example, if the economy was experiencing unemployment, an increase in government spending with taxes and transfers held constant would increase aggregate spending, output, and employment. Similarly, given the level of government expendi-

---

[4] Most business subsidies are "concealed" in the form of low-interest loans, loan guarantees, tax concessions, or the public provision of facilities at prices less than costs.

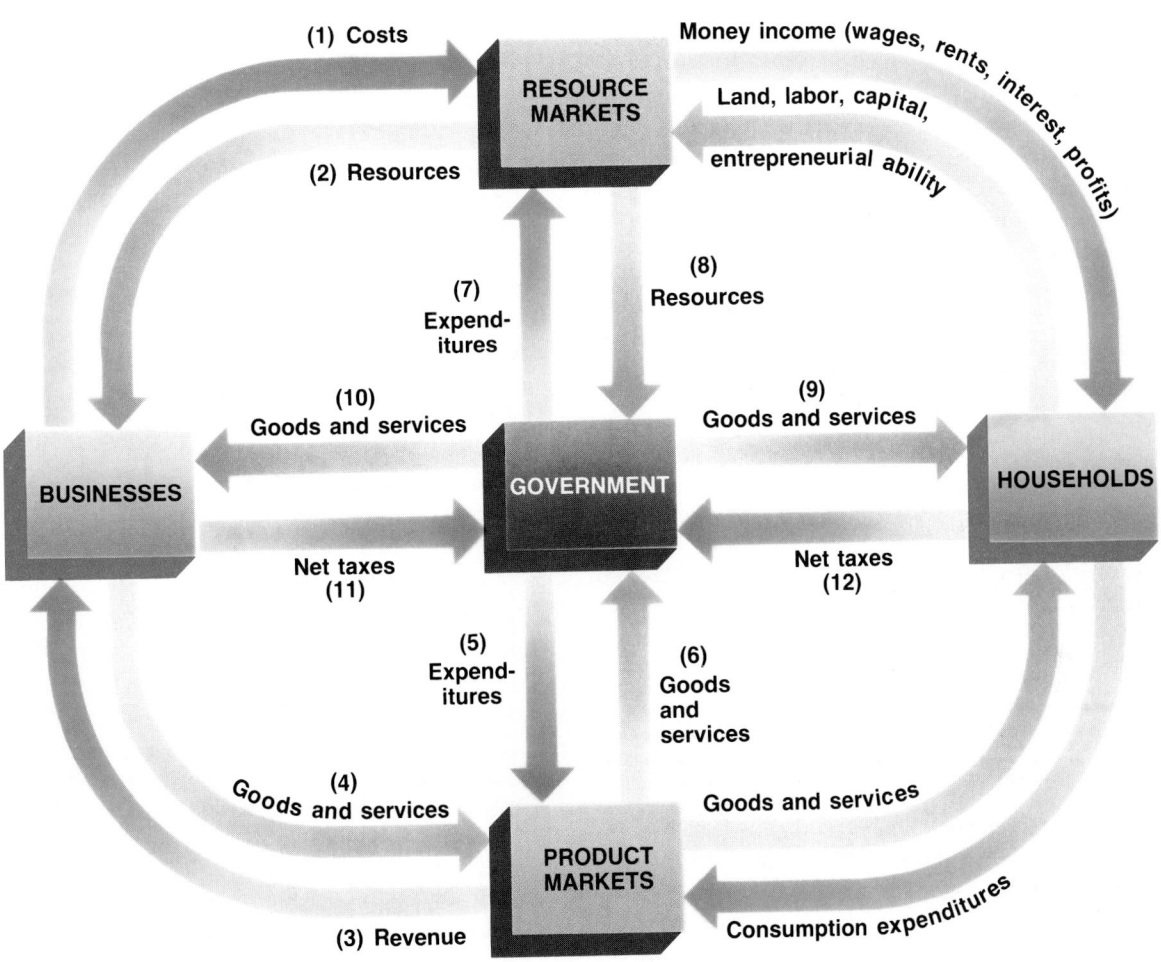

FIGURE 6-3

The circular flow and the public sector

Government expenditures, taxes, and transfer payments affect the distribution of income, the allocation of resources, and the level of economic activity.

tures, a decline in taxes or an increase in transfer payments would increase spendable incomes and boost private spending. Conversely, confronted with inflation the opposite government policies would be in order: reduced government spending, increased taxes,[5] and reduced transfers.

[5] We will find later that the role of taxes in restraining inflation is ambiguous. By reducing spendable incomes, higher taxes are anti-inflationary. But taxes may also add to production costs, thereby increasing the price level.

CHAPTER SUMMARY

1 The American economy can be described as mixed capitalism. It is primarily a market economy, yet government influences the operation of the market system in a variety of ways.

2 One basic function of government is to provide a legal and social framework conducive to the effective functioning of markets.

3 Government also has a responsibility to maintain a reasonable degree of market competition.

4 Government alters the distribution of income by direct market intervention and through the tax-transfer payments system.

5 Spillovers or externalities cause the equilibrium output of certain goods to vary from the optimal output. Spillover costs result in an overallocation of resources which can be corrected by legislation or specific taxes. Spillover benefits are accompanied by an underallocation of resources which can be corrected by subsidies to either consumers or producers.

6 Public goods are typically indivisible and entail benefits from which nonpaying consumers cannot be excluded.

7 The manipulation of taxes and its expenditures is one basic means by which government can help to eliminate unemployment and inflation.

8 The circular flow model is a useful means for envisioning how government performs its redistributional, allocative, and stabilizing functions.

TERMS AND CONCEPTS

mixed capitalism	exclusion principle
monopoly	public or social goods
spillover costs and spillover benefits	free-rider problem

QUESTIONS AND STUDY SUGGESTIONS

1 Carefully evaluate this statement: "The public, as a general rule . . . gets less production in return for a dollar spent by government than from a dollar spent by private enterprise."[6]

2 Why is the American economy called "mixed capitalism"? Enumerate and briefly discuss the main economic functions of government.

3 Explain why, in the absence of spillovers, equilibrium and optimal outputs are identical in competitive markets. What divergences arise between equilibrium and optimal output when **a** spillover costs and **b** spillover benefits are present? How might government correct for these discrepancies? "The presence of spillover costs suggests an underallocation of resources to that product and

[6] National Association of Manufacturers, *The American Individual Enterprise System* (New York: McGraw-Hill Book Company, 1946), p. 952.

LAST WORD

Government and the economy: two views

Martin Feldstein, noted conservative economist, traces our economy's deteriorating performance to an expanded public sector. In contrast Lane Kirkland, President of the AFL–CIO, offers personal reflections on the positive contributions of government.

Anti-government view: . . . the expanded role of government is a major reason, perhaps the major reason, for the deterioration of our economic performance. The government's mismanagement of monetary and fiscal policy has contributed to the instability of aggregate output and to the rapid rise in inflation. Government regulations are a principal cause of lower productivity growth and of the decline in research and development. The growth of government income-transfer programs has exacerbated the instability of family life and perhaps the decline in the birthrate. The low rate of saving and the slow growth of the capital stock reflect tax rules, macroeconomic policies, and the growth of social insurance programs.

the need for governmental subsidies." Do you agree? Explain how zoning and seat belt laws might be used to deal with a problem of spillover costs.

4 What are the basic characteristics of public goods? Explain the significance of the exclusion principle. By what means does government provide public goods?

5 Use your understanding of the characteristics of private and public goods to determine whether the following should be produced through the market system or provided by government: **a** bread; **b** street lighting; **c** bridges; **d** parks; **e** swimming pools; **f** medical care;

. . . the adverse consequences of government policies have been largely the unintended and unexpected by-products of well-meaning policies that were adopted without looking beyond their immediate purpose or understanding the magnitudes of their adverse long-run consequences. Expansionary monetary and fiscal policies were adopted throughout the past fifteen years in the hope of lowering the unemployment rate but without anticipating the higher inflation rate that would eventually follow. High tax rates on investment income were enacted and the social security retirement benefits were increased without considering the subsequent impact on investment and saving. Regulations were imposed to protect health and safety without evaluating the reduction in productivity that would result or the effect of an uncertain regulatory future on long-term research and development activities.

Pro-government view: I grew up in the South in a semirural area and I am not really receptive to the proposition that government is some sort of burden that is on your back. When I grew up, I remember, there were dirt roads one foot outside of the city limits, there was a paved main street in town and that was it. There were outdoor privies everywhere. You went to the well for your water one-half mile outside of town. You had kerosene lamps. If you had a farm, there was a gully on it about 80 feet wide and 50 feet deep and every time it rained it got about two feet wider and two feet deeper, and the land was being washed away. The Social Security system was the county poor farm. And all this existed and it was real and visible.

It was not private enterprise that stopped all those things. It was private enterprise that *did* all those things.

The kerosene was replaced by electricity from the Rural Electrification Administration. The roads were paved by a highway program. The gullies were cured and the land regained by the Soil Conservation Service. The poorhouse was wiped out by Social Security. And the basic ingredient of a big new industry in that part of the world was created by the Civilian Conservation Corps. Practically every pine tree that you see in that state was planted by the CCC. And now that is what the pulp and paper industry lives on. They are thriving on a product which is there because of having government on their backs.

So I think it is crazy to stop basic public investment. It does not make sense to abolish or curtail REA, curtail the highway programs, tinker with Social Security and undermine those public investment programs because they have a price. They also have a tremendous value in terms of a better, stronger economy and in terms of human welfare, human dignity, and human freedom.

Sources: Martin Feldstein (ed.), *The American Economy in Transition* (Chicago: The University of Chicago Press, 1980), pp. 2–4, © 1980 by The University of Chicago; Michael L. Wachter and Susan M. Wachter (eds.), *Toward a New U.S. Industrial Policy?* (Philadelphia: University of Pennsylvania Press, 1981), pp. 36–37.

g mail delivery; *h* housing; *i* air traffic control; *j* libraries.

6 Explain how government might manipulate its expenditures and tax revenues to reduce *a* unemployment and *b* the rate of inflation.

7 "Most governmental actions have simultaneous impacts upon the distribution of income, the allocation of resources, and the levels of unemployment and prices." Use the circular flow model to confirm this assertion for each of the following: *a* the construction of a new high school in Blackhawk County; *b* a 2 percent reduction in the corporate income tax; *c* an expansion of preschool programs for disadvantaged children; *d* a $50 billion increase in spending for the Star Wars defense system; *e* the levying of a tax on air polluters; and *f* an increase in the minimum wage from $3.35 to $4.65.

8 Draw a production possibilities curve with public goods on the vertical axis and private goods on the horizontal axis. Assuming the economy is initially operating on the curve, indicate the means by which the production of public goods might be increased. How might the output of public goods be increased if the economy is initially functioning at a point inside of the curve?

CHAPTER 7

The facts of American capitalism: the private sectors

Chapters 7 and 8 are designed to put meat on our bare-bones model of mixed capitalism. We have discussed the major aggregates of mixed capitalism—business, households, and government—on a very general and somewhat abstract basis. Similarly, a number of references have been made to the economic interrelationships between our economy and the rest of the world. We must now add color to our crude sketch by painting in the factual characteristics of these transactors as they function in our American brand of mixed capitalism. In short, we must breathe reality into our abstract model by adding "the facts" of American economic life. The present chapter contributes factual information pertinent to the *private sectors,* that is, households, businesses, and the international sector. The following chapter does the same for the governmental, or *public, sector.*

Households as income receivers

The household sector of American capitalism is currently composed of some 65 million households. These households play a dual role: They are the ultimate suppliers of all economic resources and simultaneously the major spending group in the economy. Hence, we shall consider households first as income receivers and second as spenders.

There are two related approaches to studying the facts of income distribution.

1 The **functional distribution** of income is concerned with the manner in which society's money income is divided among wages, rents, interest, and profits. Here total income is distributed according to the function performed by the income receiver. Wages are paid to labor, rents and interest compensate property resources, and profits flow to the owners of corporations and unincorporated businesses.

2 The **personal distribution** of income has to do with the way in which the total money income of society is apportioned among individual households. A basic understanding of both the functional and the personal distribution of income is essential to an appreciation of the role of households in American capitalism.

THE FUNCTIONAL DISTRIBUTION OF INCOME

The functional distribution of the nation's total earned income for 1988 is shown in Table 7-1. Clearly the largest source of income for households is the wages and salaries paid to workers by the businesses and governmental units hiring them. In our capitalist system the bulk of total income goes to labor and not to "capital." Proprietors' income—that is, the incomes of doctors, lawyers, small business owners, farmers, and other unincorporated

TABLE 7-1 **The sources of income, 1988**

	Billions of dollars	Percent of total
Wages and salaries	$2905	73
Proprietors' income	325	8
Corporate profits	324	8
Interest	392	10
Rents	19	1
Total earnings	$3964	100

Source: *Survey of Current Business:* January 1989. Details may not add to totals because of rounding.

enterprises—is in fact a combination of wage, profit, rent, and interest incomes. The other three sources of earnings are virtually self-defining. Some households own corporate stock and receive dividend income on their holdings. Many households also own bonds and savings accounts which yield interest income. Rental income results from households providing the buildings, land, and other natural resources to businesses.

Later in Chapter 31 we will consider how functional shares have changed historically.

PERSONAL DISTRIBUTION OF INCOME

Figure 7-1 gives us an overall impression of how total income is distributed among households. Here we divide families into five numerically equal groups or *quintiles* and show the percentage of total income received by each group. We observe that in 1987 the poorest 20 percent of all families received less than 5 percent of total personal income in contrast to the 20 percent they would have received if income were equally distributed. In comparison the richest 20 percent of all families received about 44 percent of personal income. Thus the richest fifth of the population received over nine times as much income as the poorest fifth. Given these data, most economists agree that there is considerable inequality in the distribution of income. The question of how the personal distribution is determined

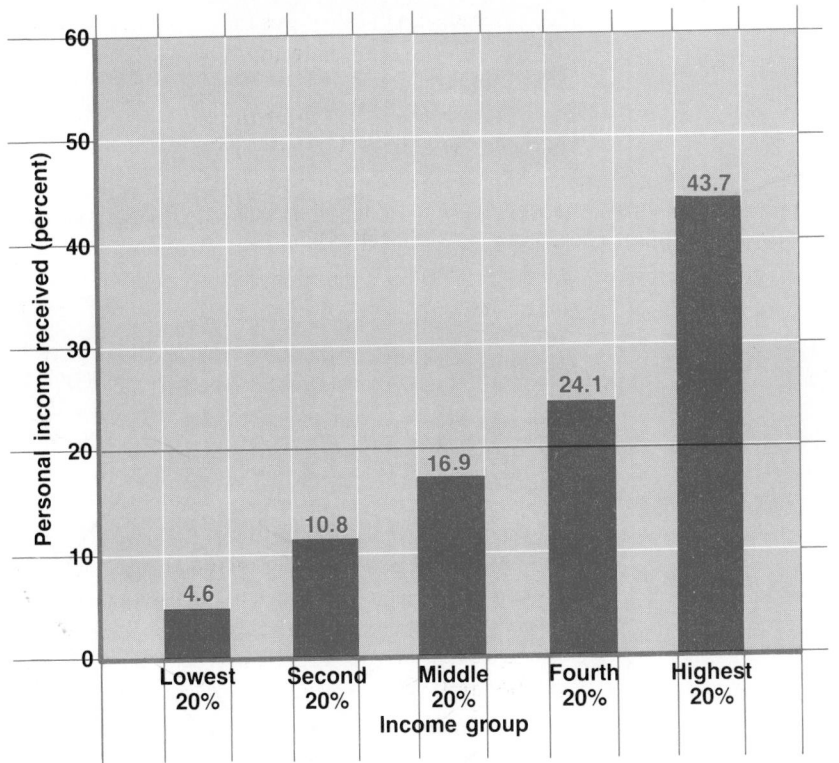

FIGURE 7-1

The distribution of income among families, 1987

Personal income is quite unequally distributed in the United States. An equal distribution would mean that all vertical bars would be equal to the horizontal line drawn at 20 percent; each 20 percent of the families would get 20 percent of total personal income. In fact, the richest fifth of the families gets over nine times as much income as does the poorest fifth.

and the related issue of whether the indicated degree of income inequality is equitable or fair are deferred to later chapters.

Households as spenders

How do households dispose of the income which they earn? In general terms, the answer is simple: A part flows to government in the form of personal taxes, and the remainder is divided between personal consumption expenditures and personal saving. Specifically, the way in which households disposed of their total personal income in 1988 is shown in Table 7-2.[1]

PERSONAL TAXES

Personal taxes, of which the Federal personal income tax is the major component, have risen sharply in both absolute and relative terms since World War II. In 1941, households paid $3.3 billion, or about 3 percent of their $95.3 billion total income, in personal taxes, as compared to $590 billion, or about 15 percent of that year's $3963 billion total income in 1988.

PERSONAL SAVING

Economists define saving as "that part of after-tax income which is *not* consumed"; hence, households have just two choices with their incomes after taxes—to consume or to save.

Let us first consider the saving component of after-tax income. Saving is defined as that portion of current (this year's) income which is not paid out in taxes or in the purchase of consumer goods, but rather, flows into bank accounts, insurance policies, bonds and stocks, and other financial assets.

[1] The income concepts used in Tables 7-1 and 7-2 are different, accounting for the slight quantitative discrepancy between "total income" in the two tables. The distinctions between the various income measures will be explored in Chapter 9.

TABLE 7-2 **The disposition of income, 1988**

	Billions of dollars	Percent of total
Personal taxes	$ 590	15
Personal consumption expenditures	3226	82
Personal savings	147	4
Total income	$3963	100

Source: *Survey of Current Business,* January 1989. Details may not add to totals because of rounding.

Why do households want to save? After all, it is ultimately goods and services which satisfy consumer wants, not the pieces of paper which we call checkbooks, savings account books, certificates of deposit, and bonds. The reasons for saving are many and diverse, but they center around *security* and *speculation.* Households save to provide a nest egg for unforeseen contingencies—sickness, accident, unemployment—for retirement from the work force, to finance the education of children, or simply for the overall financial security of one's family. On the other hand, saving might well occur for speculation. One might channel a part of one's income to the purchase of securities, speculating as to increases in their monetary value.

The desire or willingness to save, however, is not enough. This willingness must be accompanied by the *ability* to save. And, as we shall discover later (Table 12-1), the ability to save depends basically upon the size of one's income. If income is very low, households may *dissave;* that is, they may consume in excess of their after-tax incomes. They manage to do this by borrowing and by digging into savings which they may have accumulated in years when their incomes were higher. However, both saving and consumption vary directly with income; as households get more income, they divide it between saving and consumption. In fact, the top 10 percent of the income receivers account for most of the personal saving in our society.[2]

[2] We will find later that most of the saving in our economy is done by corporations rather than households.

PERSONAL CONSUMPTION EXPENDITURES

Table 7-2 clearly suggests that the bulk of total income flows from income receivers back into the business sector of the economy as personal consumption expenditures.

Since the size and composition of the economy's total output depend to a very considerable extent upon the size and composition of the flow of consumer spending, it is imperative that we examine how households divide their expenditures among the various goods and services competing for their dollars. Consumer expenditures may be classified in several ways. For example, they may be divided into services and products; and products in turn may be subdivided on the basis of their durability. Thus the U.S. Department of Commerce classifies consumer spending as (1) expenditures on durables, (2) expenditures on nondurables, and (3) expenditures on services. If a product generally has an expected life of one year or more, it is called a **durable good;** if its life is less than one year, it is labeled **nondurable.** Automobiles, video recorders, washing machines, personal computers, and most furniture are good examples of consumer durables. Most food and clothing items are representative of nondurables. **Services,** of course, refer to the services which lawyers, barbers, doctors, and others provide to consumers. Note in Table 7-3 that *ours is a service-oriented economy in that slightly over one-half of consumer outlays are for services.*

This threefold breakdown, detailed in Table 7-3, is of considerable importance because it implies that many consumer outlays are discretionary or postponable. During prosperity, durable, or "hard," goods are typically traded in or scrapped before they become utterly useless. This is ordinarily the case with automobiles and most major household appliances. But if a recession materializes, consumers tend to forgo expenditures on durables, having little choice but to put up with an old model car and outdated household appliances. The desire to conserve dollars for the nondurable necessities of food and clothing may cause a radical shrinkage of expenditures on durables. Much the same is true of many services. True, one cannot postpone an operation for acute appendicitis. But education, dental work, and a wide variety of less pressing services can be deferred or, if necessary,

forgone entirely. In brief, the durable goods and services segments of personal consumption expenditures are subject to considerably more variation over a period of time than are expenditures on nondurables.

The business population

Businesses constitute the second major aggregate of the private sector. To avoid any possible confusion, we preface our discussion of the business population with some comments concerning termi-

TABLE 7-3 The composition of personal consumption expenditures, 1988*

Types of consumption	Amount (billions of dollars)	Percent of total
Durable goods	$ 450	14
Motor vehicles and parts	$208	6
Furniture and household equipment	159	5
All others	83	3
Nondurable goods	1047	32
Food	552	17
Clothing and shoes	186	6
Gasoline and oil	79	2
Fuel oil and coal	17	1
All others	213	7
Services	1729	54
Housing	501	16
Household operations	197	6
Medical care	404	13
Transportation	117	4
Personal services, recreation, and others	510	16
Personal consumption expenditures	$3226	100

* Excludes interest paid to businesses.
Sources: *Survey of Current Business,* January 1989. Details may not add to totals because of rounding.

nology. In particular, one must distinguish among a plant, a firm, and an industry.

1 A **plant** is a physical establishment in the form of a factory, farm, mine, retail or wholesale store, or warehouse which performs one or more specific functions in the fabrication and distribution of goods and services.

2 A business **firm,** on the other hand, is the business organization which owns and operates these plants. Although most firms operate only one plant, many firms own and operate a number of plants. Multiplant firms may be "horizontal," "vertical," or "conglomerate" combinations. For example, without exception all the large steel firms of our economy—USX Corporation (United States Steel), Bethlehem Steel, Republic Steel, and the others—are **vertical combinations** of plants; that is, each company owns plants at various stages of the production process. Each steelmaker owns ore and coal mines, limestone quarries, coke ovens, blast furnaces, rolling mills, forge shops, foundries, and, in some cases, fabricating shops. The large chain stores in the retail field—for example, A&P, Kroger, Safeway, J.C. Penney—are **horizontal combinations** in that each plant is at the same stage of production. Other firms are **conglomerates;** they comprise plants which operate across many different markets and industries. For example, International Telephone and Telegraph, apart from operations implied by its name, is involved through affiliated plants on a large-scale basis in such diverse fields as hotels, baking products, educational materials, and insurance (Chapter 34).

3 An **industry** is a group of firms producing the same, or at least similar, products. Though an apparently uncomplicated concept, industries are usually difficult to identify in practice. For example, how are we to identify the automobile industry? The simplest answer is, "All firms producing automobiles." But automobiles are heterogeneous products. While Cadillacs and Buicks are similar products, and Buicks and Fords are similar, and Fords and Chevettes are similar, it is clear that Chevettes and Cadillacs are very dissimilar. At least most buyers think so. And what about trucks? Certainly, small pickup trucks are similar in some respects to station wagons. Is it better to speak of the "motor vehicle industry" rather than of the "automobile industry"? This matter of delineating an industry becomes all the more complex when it is recognized that most enterprises are multiprod-

uct firms. American automobile manufacturers are also responsible for such diverse products as diesel locomotives, buses, refrigerators, guided missiles, and air conditioners. We pose these questions, not with a view to resolving them, but merely to note that industry classifications are rarely clear-cut and always somewhat arbitrary.

Legal forms of business enterprises

The business population is extremely diverse, ranging from giant corporations like General Motors with 1987 sales of $102 billion and 813,000 employees to neighborhood specialty shops and "mom and pop" groceries with one or two employees and sales of only $100 or $150 per day. This diversity makes it desirable to classify business firms by some criterion such as legal structure, industry or product, or size. Table 7-4 shows how the business population is distributed among the three major legal forms: (1) the sole proprietorship, (2) the partnership, and (3) the corporation. Let us define and outline the advantages and disadvantages of each.

SOLE PROPRIETORSHIP

A **sole proprietorship** is literally an individual in business for himself or herself. The proprietor owns or obtains the materials and capital equipment used in the operation of the business and personally supervises its operation.

Advantages   This extremely simple type of business organization has certain distinct advantages:
1 A sole proprietorship is very easy to organize—there is virtually no legal red tape or expense.
2 The proprietor is his or her own boss and has very substantial freedom of action. Since the proprietor's profit income depends upon the enterprise's success, there is a strong and immediate incentive to manage the affairs of the business efficiently.

Disadvantages   But the disadvantages of this form of business organization are great:

TABLE 7-4 **The business population by form of legal organization**

Form	Number of firms	Percent of total
Sole proprietorships*	12,820,000	73
Partnerships	1,644,000	9
Corporations	3,171,000	18
Total	17,635,000	100

*Includes farmers and professional people in business for themselves.

Source: *Statistical Abstract of the United States.* Data are for 1984.

1 With rare exceptions, the financial resources of a sole proprietorship are insufficient to permit the firm to grow into a large-scale enterprise. Specifically, finances are usually limited to what the proprietor has in his or her bank account and to what he or she is able to borrow. Since the mortality rate is relatively great for proprietorships, commercial banks are not overly eager to extend much credit to them.
2 Being in complete control of an enterprise forces the proprietor to carry out all basic management functions. A proprietor must make all basic decisions concerning, for example, buying, selling, and the acquisition and maintenance of personnel, not to mention the technical aspects which might be involved in producing, advertising, and distributing the product. In short, the potential benefits of specialization in business management are usually inaccessible to the typical small-scale proprietorship.
3 Most important of all, the proprietor is subject to *unlimited liability*. This means that individuals in business for themselves risk not only the assets of the firm but also their personal assets. Should the assets of an unsuccessful proprietorship be insufficient to satisfy the claims of creditors, those creditors can file claims against the proprietor's personal property.

PARTNERSHIP

The **partnership** form of business organization is more or less a natural outgrowth of the sole propri-

etorship. As a matter of fact, partnerships were developed in an attempt to overcome some of the major shortcomings of proprietorships. A partnership is almost self-defining. It is a form of business organization wherein two or more individuals agree to own and operate a business. Usually they pool their financial resources and their business acumen. Similarly, they share the risks and the profits or losses which may accrue to them. There are innumerable variations. In some cases, all partners are active in the functioning of the enterprise; in others, one or more partners may be "silent"— that is, they contribute their finances but do not actively participate in the management of the firm.

Advantages   What are the advantages of a partnership arrangement?
1 Like the sole proprietorship, it is easy to organize. Although a written agreement is almost invariably involved, legal red tape is not great.
2 Greater specialization in management is made possible because there are more participants.
3 Again, because there are several participants, the odds are that the financial resources of a partnership will be less limited than those of a sole proprietorship. Partners can pool their money capital and are usually somewhat better risks in the eyes of bankers.

Disadvantages   The partnership often does less to overcome the shortcomings of the proprietorship than first appears and, indeed, raises some new potential problems which the sole proprietorship does not entail.
1 Whenever there are several people participating in management, this division of authority can lead to inconsistent, divided policies or to inaction when action is required. Worse yet, partners may flatly disagree on basic policy. For all these reasons, management in a partnership may be unwieldy and cumbersome.
2 The finances of partnerships are still limited, although generally superior to those of a sole proprietorship. The financial resources of three or four partners may be such as to restrict severely the potential growth of a successful enterprise.
3 The continuity of a partnership is very precarious. The withdrawal or death of a partner generally entails the dissolution and complete reorganization of the firm, potentially disrupting its operations.

4 Finally, unlimited liability plagues a partnership, just as it does a proprietorship. In fact, each partner is liable for all business debts incurred, not only as a result of each partner's own management decisions, but also as a consequence of the actions of any other partner. A wealthy partner risks money on the prudence of less affluent partners.

CORPORATION

Corporations are legal entities, distinct and separate from the individuals who own them. As such, these governmentally designated "legal persons" can acquire resources, own assets, produce and sell products, incur debts, extend credit, sue and be sued, and carry on all those functions which any other type of enterprise performs.

Advantages   The advantages of the corporate form of business enterprise have catapulted this type of firm into a dominant position in modern American capitalism. Although corporations are relatively small in numbers (Table 7-4), they are frequently large in size and scale of operations. Although only 18 percent of all businesses are corporations, they account for roughly nine-tenths of all business sales.

1 The corporation is by far the most effective form of business organization for raising money capital. As this chapter's Last Word reveals, the corporation features unique methods of finance—the selling of stocks and bonds—which allow the firm to tap the savings of untold thousands of households. Through the securities market, corporations can pool the financial resources of extremely large numbers of people. Financing by the sale of securities also has decided advantages from the viewpoint of the purchasers of these securities. First, households can now participate in enterprise and share the expected monetary reward therefrom without having to assume an active part in management. And, in addition, an individual can spread any risks by buying the securities of a variety of corporations. Finally, it is usually easy for the holder of corporate securities to dispose of these holdings. Organized stock exchanges facilitate the transfer of securities among buyers and sellers. Needless to say, this increases the willingness of savers to buy corporate securities. Furthermore, corporations ordinarily have easier access to bank credit than do other types of business organizations. This is the case not only because corporations are better risks but also because they are more likely to provide banks with profitable accounts.

2 Corporations have the distinct advantage of **limited liability.** The owners (stockholders) of a corporation risk *only* what they paid for the stock purchased. Their personal assets are not at stake if the corporation founders on the rocks of bankruptcy. Creditors can sue the corporation as a legal person, but not the owners of the corporation as individuals. Limited liability clearly eases the corporation's task in acquiring money capital.

3 Because of their advantage in attracting money capital, successful corporations find it easier to expand the size and scope of their operations and to realize associated advantages. In particular, corporations may be able to take advantage of mass-production technologies. Similarly, size permits greater specialization in the use of human resources. While the manager of a sole proprietorship may be forced to share her time between production, accounting, and marketing functions, a larger corporation can hire specialized personnel in each of these areas and achieve greater efficiency.

4 As a legal entity, the corporation has a life independent of its owners and, for that matter, of its individual officers. Proprietorships are subject to sudden and unpredictable demise, but, legally at least, corporations are immortal. The transfer of corporate ownership through the sale of stock will not disrupt the continuity of the corporation. In short, corporations have a certain permanence, lacking in other forms of business organization, which is conducive to long-range planning and growth.

Disadvantages   The corporation's advantages are of tremendous significance and typically override any accompanying disadvantages. Yet the following drawbacks of the corporate form of organization merit mentioning:

1 There are some red tape and legal expense in obtaining a corporate charter.

2 From the social point of view, it must be noted that the corporate form of enterprise lends itself to certain abuses. Because the corporation is a legal entity, unscrupulous business owners sometimes can avoid personal responsibility for questionable business activities by adopting the corporate form of enterprise. And, despite legislation to the contrary, the corporate form of organization has been a cornerstone for the issue and sale of worthless securities. Note, however, that these are potential abuses of the corporate form, not inherent defects.

3 A further possible disadvantage of corporations has to do with the taxation of corporate income. Briefly, there is a problem of **double taxation;** that part of corporate income which is paid out as dividends to stockholders is taxed twice—once as a part of corporate profits and again as a part of the stockholders' personal incomes.

4 In the sole proprietorship and partnership forms, those who own the real and financial assets of the firm also directly manage or control those assets.[3] Most observers agree that this is as it should be. But, in larger corporations where the ownership of common stock is widely diffused over tens or hundreds of thousands of stockholders, a fundamental cleavage between ownership and control will arise. The roots of this cleavage lie in the lethargy of the typical stockholder. Most stockholders simply do not exercise their voting rights, or, if they do, merely sign these rights over by proxy to the corporation's present officers. And why not? Average stockholders know little or nothing about the efficiency with which "their" corporation is being managed. Because the typical stockholder may own only 1000 of 15,000,000 shares of common stock outstanding, one vote "really doesn't make a bit of difference"! Not voting, or the automatic signing over of one's proxy to current corporate officials, has the effect of making those officials self-perpetuating.

The **separation of ownership and control** is of no fundamental consequence so long as the actions of the control (management) group and the wishes of the ownership (stockholder) group are in accord. The catch lies in the fact that the interests of the two groups are not always identical. For example, management, seeking the power and prestige which accompany control over a *large* enterprise, may favor unprofitable expansion of the firm's operations. Or a conflict of interest can easily develop with respect to current dividend policies. What portion of corporate earnings after taxes should be paid out as dividends, and what amount

should be retained by the firm as undistributed profits? More obviously, corporation officials may vote themselves large salaries, pensions, bonuses, and so forth, out of corporate earnings which might otherwise be used for increased dividend payments. In short, the separation of ownership and control raises important and intriguing questions about the distribution of power and authority, the accountability of corporate managers, and the possibility of intramural conflicts between managers and shareholders.

INCORPORATE OR NOT?

What determines whether or not a firm incorporates? As our discussion of the corporate form implies, the need for money capital is a critical determinant. The money capital required to establish and operate a barbershop, a shoe-shine stand, or a small gift shop is modest, making incorporation unnecessary. In contrast, modern technology and a much larger dollar volume of business makes incorporation imperative in many lines of production. For example, in most branches of manufacturing—automobiles, steel, fabricated metal products, electrical equipment, household appliances, and so forth—very substantial money requirements for investment in fixed assets and for working capital are involved. Given these circumstances, there is no choice but to incorporate. To exist is to incorporate.

Industrial distribution and bigness

What do the 17.6 million firms which compose the business sector of our economy produce? Table 7-5 measures in several different ways the significance of the various industry classifications. Column 2 indicates the numerical and percentage distribution of the business population among the various industries. Column 3 shows in both absolute and relative terms the portion of the national income originating in the various industries. Column 4 indicates the absolute and relative amounts of employment provided by each industry. Several points in Table 7-5 are noteworthy:

---

[3] The silent-partner arrangement is the exception.

TABLE 7-5 **Industry classes: number of firms, national output originating, and employment provided***

(1) Industry	(2) Number of private businesses		(3) Contribution to national output		(4) Workers employed	
	Thousands	Percent	Billions	Percent	Thousands	Percent
Agriculture, forestry, and fisheries	2,328	13	$ 95	2	3,208	3
Mining	251	1	85	2	721	1
Construction	1,758	10	219	5	4,998	5
Manufacturing	622	4	854	19	19,065	18
Wholesale and retail trade	3,463	20	740	16	24,381	23
Finance, insurance, and real estate	2,272	13	775	17	6,549	6
Transportation, communications, and public utilities	721	4	408	9	5,385	5
Services	6,220	35	794	17	24,196	23
Government			535	12	17,015	16
Rest of world	____	____	30	1		
Total	17,635	100	$4527	100	105,518	100

* Column 2 is for 1984; 3 for 1987; and 4 for 1987.

Source: *Statistical Abstract of the United States, 1988,* p. 496, and *Survey of Current Business.*
Details may not add to totals because of rounding.

1 A large number of firms is engaged in agriculture, but agriculture is relatively insignificant as a provider of incomes and jobs. This implies that agriculture is comprised of a large number of small, competitive producers (Chapter 35).

2 The wholesale and retail industries and the service industries (hotels, motels, personal services, and so forth) are heavily populated with firms and are simultaneously very important sources of employment and incomes in the economy.

3 Table 7-5 reminds us that not all the economy's income and employment originate in private domestic enterprises. Government and foreign enterprises account for about 13 percent of the economy's national income and employ about 16 percent of the labor force.

4 The relatively small number of firms in manufacturing account for almost one-fifth of national income and total employment. These figures correctly suggest that our economy is highly industrialized, characterized by gigantic business corporations in its manufacturing industries. This point merits brief elaboration.

To what degree does big business prevail in our economy? Casual evidence suggests that many of our major industries are dominated by corporate giants which enjoy assets and annual sales revenues calculated in billions of dollars, employ hundreds of thousands of workers, have a hundred thousand or more stockholders, and earn annual profits after taxes running into hundreds of millions of dollars. We have already cited the vital statistics of General Motors, America's largest corporation, for 1987: sales, about $102 **billion;** assets, about $87 **billion;** employees, about 813,000. Remarkably, there are only 22 or 24 nations in the world with annual national outputs in excess of GM's annual sales!

At an aggregate level, *Fortune* magazine's annual listing of data on the nation's largest firms makes clear the dominant role of huge corporations in our economy. Consider, for example, 800 of the largest firms in the American economy.[4] Although these 800 firms comprise only one-hundredth of 1 percent of the nation's business population, they have total assets equal to about one-half the nation's total wealth! In addition, these 800 corporate giants employ approximately one-fourth of the entire labor force.[5]

In 1987 some 187 industrial corporations enjoyed annual sales of over $4 billion; 370 industrial firms realized sales in excess of $2 billion. More generally, the fact that corporations, constituting only 18 percent of the business population, produce about nine-tenths of total business output hints at the dominant role of large corporations in our economy.

But the influential position of giant corporations varies significantly from industry to industry. Big business dominates manufacturing and is pronounced in the transportation, communications, power utilities, and banking and financial industries. At the other extreme are some 2 million farmers whose total sales in 1987 were less than the economy's two largest industrial corporations! In between are a wide variety of retail and service industries wherein relatively small firms are characteristic. More specifically, a look ahead at Table 27-1 reveals a list of industries wherein economic concentration is quite modest. Table 28-1, on the other hand, indicates a number of very basic manufacturing industries wherein economic power is highly concentrated. Despite great diversity by industry, it is reasonably accurate to say that large corporations dominate the American business landscape and grounds exist for labeling the United States a "big business" economy.

[4] The total is comprised of the 500 largest industrial (manufacturing) firms plus the largest 50 firms from each of the following six categories: banking, finance, insurance, retailing, transportation, and public utilities.

[5] Data from Wallace C. Peterson, *Our Overloaded Economy* (Armonk, New York: M. E. Sharpe, Inc., 1982), p. 104.

The international sector

Our economy is deeply enmeshed in a complex web of economic relationships with the rest of the world. Evidence of the growing importance of international trade and finance is all around us. You may be wearing a T-shirt made in Thailand and a wristwatch from Japan; your stereo or television may be from Korea; your bicycle may have been manufactured in England or West Germany. Newspapers feature stories about our seemingly chronic trade deficits, the changing international value of the dollar, trade negotiations with Japan, and the indebtedness of the less developed countries to American banks. It is clear that the "rest of the world" sector has manifold effects upon our domestic economy.

Our immediate goals are modest. We seek some factual understanding of the quantitative importance of the international sector *and* we want to gain some appreciation as to how international trade and finance affects the American economy.

VOLUME, PATTERN, AND LINKAGES

The volume of United States merchandise trade with the rest of the world has increased both absolutely and relatively. In 1960, for example, American merchandise exports and imports were each in the $25 to $30 billion range and constituted about 5 percent of our national output. By 1988 these figures had grown to $315 to $440 billion and 11 to 13 percent of national output.

Table 7-6 helps us identify our major trading partners. Perhaps the most apparent generalization is that most of our trade is with other industrially advanced nations. It is interesting to note that Canada, not Japan, is our major trade partner.

Less obvious is the fact that Table 7-6 implies a complex set of financial linkages which exist between nations. You will note in Table 7-6 that the United States incurred a $125 billion *trade deficit* in 1988; that is, we imported $125 billion more merchandise than we exported in that year. Indeed, we have had large trade deficits for the last 12 years. How are such deficits financed? How does a nation—or an individual—obtain more goods

TABLE 7-6 **U.S. merchandise exports and imports by area, 1988**

Exports to	Value (in billions) of dollars)	Percentage of total	Imports from	Value (in billions) of dollars)	Percentage of total
Industrial countries	$204	65	Industrial countries	$278	63
Canada	72	23	Canada	84	19
Japan	37	12	Japan	87	20
Western Europe	86	27	Western Europe	101	23
Australia, New Zealand, and South Africa	9	3	Australia, New Zealand, and South Africa	6	1
Developing countries	108	34	Developing countries	161	37
OPEC	14	4	OPEC	23	5
Other	95	30	Other	138	31
Eastern Europe	4	1	Eastern Europe	2	1
Total	$316	100	Total	$441	100

Source: *Economic Report of the President, 1989.*

Note: Data are preliminary and are on an international transactions basis and exclude military shipments. Data will not add to totals because of rounding.

from others than is provided to them? The answer is by borrowing from them or by giving up ownership of some of your assets or wealth. And this is precisely what has been happening to the United States. We have been financing our trade deficits by borrowing from (selling securities to) other nations. The United States is now the world's largest debtor nation. Similarly, it is no surprise that nations with which we have very large trade deficits such as Japan (Table 7-6) are acquiring assets in America. Examples: the Japanese now own large amounts of real estate in Hawaii; Japan's Sony recently acquired America's CBS Records.

ECONOMIC IMPLICATIONS

The impacts of global trade and finance upon the United States economy are numerous and important. Let us cite several, some of which are familiar to us.

1 Specialization and living standards It was emphasized in Chapter 3 that individuals and regions within a given nation specialize because productive efficiency is thereby enhanced and living standards increased. Our earlier illustration indicated that Nebraska grows wheat to which its resources are suited and similarly Florida grows oranges. By trading a portion of their outputs, people in both states can enjoy larger aggregate amounts of wheat and oranges than otherwise. The same reasoning applies across international boundaries. International specialization allows each nation to concentrate its resources upon those goods which it can produce most efficiently and to obtain through trade with other nations those products it cannot produce efficiently. Such international specialization contributes to a higher "world income" than would otherwise be the case.

2 Competition A large and growing volume of trade usually means more competition. To illustrate: Not too many years ago our domestic auto-mobile industry was dominated by three large domestic producers. Imported autos were an odd-ity which accounted for only a miniscule portion of the market. But now about one-quarter of all autos sold in the United States are imports. General Motors, Ford, and Chrysler now face a much more competitive environment as they struggle for mar-ket shares with Nissan, Honda, Toyota, Hyundai, Volkswagen, Mercedes, and so on.

Is greater competition a good thing? Although domestic auto producers may not be enamored of it, it is good for consumers. Foreign competition provides consumers with a greater variety of goods and it forces domestic producers to be more effi-cient than otherwise. Recalling Chapter 5's "invisi-ble hand" concept, it is competition which causes an industry's private interest in maximizing profits to coincide with society's interest in using scarce resources efficiently.

3 Finance and banking Dramatic improvements in communications have globalized financial markets and banking industries. Developments in the New York Stock Exchange affect stock markets in Lon-don and Tokyo and vice versa. We have already noted that the United States has become the world's largest debtor nation as a result of large and persistent trade deficits. Furthermore, major American banks have made billions of dollars worth of loans to the less developed nations; poten-tial default on these loans is a threat to individual American banks and a source of apprehension for our entire banking system.

4 Instability and policy Two related points are rele-vant with respect to macroeconomic instability and policy. First, a nation engaged in world trade faces potential sources of instability which would not af-fect a nation "closed" to the world economy. Sec-ond, these new sources of instability complicate domestic stabilization policy and *may* make it less effective. For example, recessions and inflations can be highly contagious among nations. Suppose the nations of western Europe were to incur a rather severe recession. As their incomes declined, they would curtail purchases of American goods. As a result, inventories of unsold American goods would rise and American firms would respond by reducing their production and employment. In short, recession in Europe might contribute to a recession in the United States. Another example: Recall from Chapter 4 that changes in exchange rates can affect a nation's exports and imports and therefore domestic output. For example, if the dol-lar were to *appreciate* vis-a-vis other currencies— that is, if it now took fewer dollars to buy units of foreign monies—domestic output and employment would tend to be depressed. Why? Because if for-eign currencies become relatively cheaper to Amer-icans so do all foreign goods and Americans will respond by shifting their expenditures from domes-tic to foreign goods. In both of these instances pol-icy makers would have to take these developments into account in formulating and applying domestic stabilization policies.

CHAPTER SUMMARY

1 The functional distribution of income shows how society's total income is divided among wages, rents, in-terest, and profits; the personal distribution of income shows how total income is divided among individual households.

2 Households divide their total incomes among personal taxes, saving, and consumer goods. Consumer expendi-tures on durables and some services are discretionary and therefore postponable.

3 Sole proprietorships, partnerships, and corporations are the major legal forms which business enterprises may assume. Though proprietorships dominate numerically, the bulk of total output is produced by corporations. Corporations have grown to their position of dominance in the business sector primarily because they are *a* char-acterized by limited liability, and *b* in a superior posi-tion to acquire money capital for expansion.

4 Manufacturing accounts for a larger percentage of national income in our economy than does any other in-dustrial classification. The wholesale, retail, and service industries are also major sources of income and employ-ment.

5 Ours is a "big business" economy in the sense that many industries are dominated by a small number of large corporations.

6 United States world trade has grown both absolutely and as a proportion of national output. The other indus-trially advanced nations are our major trading partners.

7 International trade yields significant economic bene-fits in the form of *a* the more efficient use of world resources, and *b* enhanced competition. A potential disadvantage is that a nation's international economic interrelationships may entail new sources of macroeconomic instability which complicate policy making.

TERMS AND CONCEPTS

functional and personal distribution of income

durable and nondurable goods

services

plant

firm

horizontal and vertical combinations

conglomerates

industry

sole proprietorship

partnership

corporation

limited liability

double taxation

separation of ownership and control

QUESTIONS AND STUDY SUGGESTIONS

1 Distinguish between functional and personal distributions of income. What effects do you think a change in the personal distribution of income from that shown in Figure 7-1 to one of complete equality would have upon the composition of output and the allocation of resources?

2 Why is the demand for consumer durable goods less stable than that for nondurables?

3 Distinguish clearly between a plant, a firm, and an industry. Why is an "industry" often difficult to define in practice?

4 What are the major legal forms of business organization? Briefly state the advantages and disadvantages of each. How do you account for the dominant role of corporations in our economy? Explain and evaluate the separation of ownership and control which characterizes the corporate form of business enterprise.

5 What are the major industries in American capitalism in terms of *a* the number of firms in operation, and *b* the amount of income and employment provided?

6 Explain and evaluate the following statements:
   a "It is the consumer, and the consumer alone, who casts the vote that determines how big any company should be."
   b "The very nature of modern industrial society requires labor, government, and businesses to be 'big' and their bigness renders impossible the functioning of

LAST WORD

The financing of corporate activity

One of the main advantages of corporations is their ability to finance their operations through the sale of stocks and bonds. It is informative to examine the nature of corporate finance in more detail.

Generally speaking, corporations finance their activities in three different ways. First, a very large portion of a corporation's activity is financed internally out of undistributed corporate profits. Second, like individuals or unincorporated businesses, corporations may borrow from financial institutions. For example, a small corporation which wants to build a new plant or warehouse may obtain the funds from a commercial bank, a savings and loan institution, or an insurance company. Also, unique to corporations, common stocks and bonds can be issued.

A common stock is an ownership share. The purchaser of a stock certificate has the right to vote in the selection of corporate officers and to share in any declared dividends. If you own 1000 of the 100,000 shares issued by Specific Motors, Inc. (hereafter SM), then you own 1 percent of the

the older, small-scale, simpler, and more flexible capitalist system."
   c "The legal form which an enterprise assumes is dictated primarily by the financial requirements of its particular line of production."
   d "If we want capitalism, we must also accept inequality of income distribution."

7 What is the quantitative importance of world trade to

company, are entitled to 1 percent of any dividends declared by the board of directors, and control 1 percent of the votes in the annual election of corporate officials. In contrast, a bond is not an ownership share. A bond purchaser is simply lending money to a corporation. A bond is merely an IOU, in acknowledgment of a loan, whereby the corporation promises to pay the holder a fixed amount at some specified future date and other fixed amounts (interest payments) every year up to the bond's maturity date. For example, one might purchase a ten-year SM bond with a face value of $1000 with a 10 percent stated rate of interest. This means that in exchange for your $1000 SM guarantees you a $100 interest payment for each of the next ten years and then to repay your $1000 principal at the end of that period.

There are clearly important differences between stocks and bonds. First, as noted, the bondholder is not an owner of the company, but is merely a lender. Second, bonds are considered to be less risky than stocks for two reasons. On the one hand, bondholders have a "legally prior claim" upon a corporation's earnings. That is, dividends cannot be paid to stockholders until all interest payments due to bondholders have been paid. On the other hand, holders of SM stock do not know how much their dividends will be or how much they might obtain for their stock if they decide to sell. If Specific Motors falls upon hard times, stockholders may receive no dividends at all and the value of their stock may plummet. Provided the corporation does not go bankrupt, the holder of an SM bond is guaranteed a $100 interest payment each year and the return of his or her $1000 at the end of ten years.

But this is not to imply that the purchase of corporate bonds is riskless. The market value of your SM bond may vary over time in accordance with the financial health of the corporation. If SM encounters economic misfortunes which raise questions about its financial integrity, the market value of your bond may fall. Should you sell the bond prior to maturity you may receive only $600 or $700 for it (rather than $1000) and thereby incur a capital loss. Furthermore, changes in interest rates affect the market prices of bonds. Specifically, increases in interest rates cause bond prices to fall and vice versa. Assume you purchase a $1000 ten-year SM bond this year (1990) when the going interest rate is 10 percent. This obviously means that your bond provides a $100 fixed interest payment each year. But now suppose that by next year the interest rate has jumped to 15 percent and SM must now guarantee a $150 fixed annual payment on its new 1991 $1000 ten-year bonds. Clearly, no sensible person will pay you $1000 for your bond which pays only $100 of interest income per year when new bonds can be purchased for $1000 which pay the holder $150 per year. Hence, if you sell your 1990 bond before maturity, you will suffer a capital loss. Bondholders face another element of risk due to inflation. If substantial inflation occurs over the ten-year period you hold a SM bond, the $100 principal repaid to you at the end of that period will represent substantially less purchasing power than the $1000 you loaned to SM ten years earlier. You will have lent "dear" dollars, but will be repaid in "cheap" dollars.

---

the United States? Explain: "Nations engage in international trade because it allows them to realize the benefits of specialization."

8 How have persistent United States trade deficits been financed? "Trade deficits mean we get more merchandise from the rest of the world than we provide in return. Therefore, trade deficits are economically desirable." Do you agree?

9 Suppose excessive aggregate expenditures in the United States are causing inflation. Explain the effect of *a* appreciation, and *b* depreciation of the dollar upon domestic inflation. How might governmental expenditures and tax policies dealing with inflation (Chapter 6) be altered by each of these changes in the international value of the dollar?

CHAPTER 8

The facts of American capitalism: the public sector

The basic goal of this chapter is to get acquainted with some factual aspects of the public sector. Specifically, what kinds of taxes are used by Federal, state, and local governments? For what purposes and programs are their tax revenues disbursed? Persistent controversy surrounding the scope of government's economic role makes it particularly important that the facts of government be clearly understood and placed in proper perspective.

Two points must be made at the outset:

First, it is with the public sector's role as a receiver and disposer of "income" that this chapter is concerned. While it is through taxation and expenditures that government's impact upon the economy is most directly felt, there are many other ways in which government affects economic life (Chapter 6). For example, government's regulatory activities have increased very significantly in the past two decades (Chapter 34). These activities entail many important implications for output, employment, productivity, the price level, and resource allocation which go far beyond those measured by the tax collections and expenditures involved in the financing of regulatory agencies. In short, a mere examination of public spending and tax revenues does not yield a complete understanding of the economic significance of the public sector.

Second, there is a fundamental difference between the transactions of the private and public sectors of the economy: The former are *voluntary,* and the latter *compulsory.* The receipts and expenditures of households and businesses are the result of voluntary decisions by those two aggregates in buying and selling goods and resources. Government tax revenues are the result of compulsory levies: Households and businesses have no choice but to pay taxes. To a lesser degree, this compulsion appears on the expenditure side of government's transactions. While no one is compelled to use governmentally provided highways, libraries, or health clinics, all physically and mentally capable children who are within stated age brackets must consume public education or its equivalent.

Growth of government

A general impression of the size and growth of government's role in the economy can be achieved by examining government purchases of goods and services and government transfer payments.

GOVERNMENT PURCHASES

Figure 8-1 compares **government purchases** of goods and services with the national output, that is, with the total amount of goods and services produced in the economy for the 1929–1988 period. Total government purchases rose significantly relative to national output over the 1929–1940 period, but then skyrocketed during World War II. However, since the early 1950s government spending for goods and services has hovered around 20 percent of the national output. Of course, the national output has expanded dramatically over the 1929–1985 period so that the *absolute* volume of government spending has increased greatly. Government expenditures on goods and services totaled $964 billion in 1988 as compared to only $9 billion in 1929!

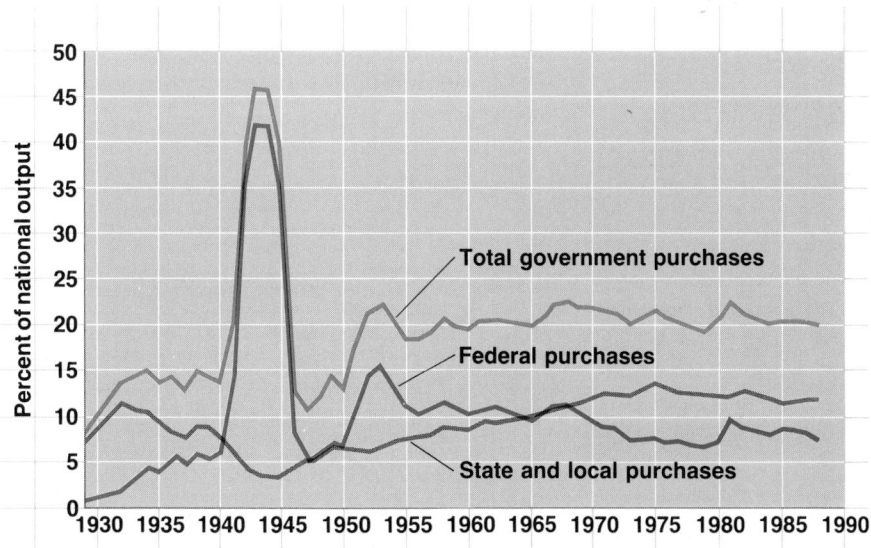

FIGURE 8-1

Government purchases of goods and services as a percent of national output, 1929–1988

Government purchases rose relative to national output over the 1929–1940 period, only to increase dramatically during World War II. Since the early 1950s total government purchases of goods and services have been approximately 20 percent of the national output.

TRANSFER PAYMENTS

Figure 8-1 understates the importance of government because a second type of government outlay—namely, **transfer payments**—is excluded. In addition to purchasing goods and services—armaments, highways, post office buildings, and the services of judges, firefighters, and teachers—government makes disbursements which merely transfer tax revenues from taxpayers in general to specific segments of the populace in the form of social security benefits, unemployment compensation, welfare payments, veterans' benefits, and so forth. Transfer payments have grown rapidly in the past two decades. Transfers rose from $3.7 billion or 4 percent of the national output in 1929 to $586 billion or 12 percent of the national output in 1988. The net result is that tax revenues required to finance both government purchases *and* transfers are equal to approximately one-third of the national output.[1] In 1988 an average tax bill of about $3000 was imposed upon every man, woman, and child in the United States. Or, from a slightly different vantage point, in 1988 the average taxpayer spent about 2 hours and 45 minutes of each 8-hour workday to pay taxes! It should be noted, however, that the size of the public sector is small in the

United States as compared to other industrialized countries. Taxes in Sweden, Norway, France, Great Britain, and West Germany are 51, 46, 45, 39, and 37 percent of national output respectively, as compared to about 30 percent in the United States.

PURCHASES VERSUS TRANSFERS

The distinction between government *purchases* and *transfers* which was made a moment ago deserves elaboration. Government purchases are often called *exhaustive* in that they directly absorb or employ resources, and the resulting production contributes to the national output. Transfer payments, on the other hand, are *nonexhaustive* because, as such, they do not directly absorb resources or account for production.

It is important to note that government purchases and transfers have significantly different impacts upon the allocation of resources. Through government spending on goods, society tends to reallocate resources from private to public goods consumption. Through transfers, government changes the composition of the output of private goods. If government taxes amount to $10, we can expect purchases of private goods and services to decline by roughly that amount. In purchasing public goods and services with this $10 worth of tax

[1] We defer consideration of financing government outlays through deficits until Chapters 14 and 20.

revenue, individuals or groups within the economy, working through government, are in effect negotiating a substitution of public for private goods. Transfer payments are different: Instead of increasing public goods at the expense of private goods, transfers merely tend to "rearrange" private consumption. Though $10 in tax revenues will reduce the private goods consumption of taxpayers by about that amount, households to whom this $10 is transferred can be expected to increase their expenditures on private goods by about $10. But, in all probability, the recipients will purchase somewhat different goods from those bought by the taxpayers. Hence, transfers alter the composition of private goods production.

This distinction between government purchases and transfer payments is relevant for our discussion of the growth of government. One can argue that transfer payments involve a lesser degree of government intervention in the economy than do government purchases.

SOME CAUSES

Recall from Chapter 6 that the desire of the citizenry to correct or alleviate the instability, inefficiency, and inequities which the market system may foster provides a basic rationale for the public sector. Consider a short list of some specific factors which account for the historical growth and present size of government spending and taxes.

1 War and defense   Hot and cold wars have tended to sustain Federal expenditures at high levels for the past four decades. War, national defense, and military-space research are among the major causes of the growth of government spending and taxation which has occurred since 1940. In 1988, expenditures for national defense were on the order of $298 billion.

2 Population growth   There are over twice as many Americans today as there were a scant sixty years ago. This obviously means there are more people for whom public goods and services must be provided. Stated differently, even with a constant level of government spending per person, total government spending would have increased dramatically in recent decades.

3 Urbanization and the demand for public goods   Not only has the size of our population been an important factor underlying the growth of government, but so has the geographic location of the population. In particular, the increasing urbanization of our economy has necessitated massive expenditures on streets, public transportation facilities, police and fire protection, sewers, and so forth. Furthermore, the public has demanded more and better public goods and services to "match" the rising standard of living provided by the private sector of the economy. We want bigger and better highways to accommodate more and better automobiles. We seek more and better educational facilities to upgrade the labor force for the more demanding jobs of private industry.

4 Environmental quality   Population growth and urbanization have contributed to serious and well-publicized problems of environmental quality. In particular, society has become highly aware that the production and consumption of vast quantities of goods can give rise to serious external or spillover costs in the form of air, water, and land pollution. Government has inherited a central role in coping with these environmental problems.

5 Egalitarianism   Since the mid-1960s there has occurred a sharp expansion of programs designed to alleviate poverty and reduce income inequality. Social security, unemployment compensation, welfare, Medicare, food stamps, and public housing are examples. These programs accounted for about 3 percent of national output twenty years ago. Notwithstanding efforts by the Reagan administration to curtail the growth of such programs, they now require approximately 12 percent of national output.

Federal finance

Let us now disaggregate the public sector into Federal, state, and local units of government in order to compare the character of their expenditures and taxes. Table 8-1 tells the story for the Federal government.

FEDERAL EXPENDITURES

Although Table 8-1 reveals a wide variety of Federal expenditures, three important areas of spending stand out: (1) income security, (2) national defense, and (3) interest on the public debt. The *income security* category reflects the myriad of previously mentioned income-maintenance programs which assist the aged, the disabled, the unemployed, the handicapped, the medically indigent, families with no breadwinner, and so forth. *National defense* constitutes over one-fourth of the Federal budget and underscores the high cost of military preparedness. *Interest on the public debt* has grown dramatically in recent years because the public debt itself has grown and interest rates have simultaneously risen. The remaining categories of expenditures listed in Table 8-1 are largely self-explanatory.

FEDERAL RECEIPTS

The receipts side of Table 8-1 makes it clear that the personal income tax, payroll taxes, and the corporate income tax are the basic revenue getters, accounting for 46, 35, and 10 cents of each dollar collected.

Personal income tax   The **personal income tax** is the kingpin of our national tax system and therefore merits rather detailed comment. The present structure of the personal income tax reflects major changes in the income tax code embodied in the **Tax Reform Act (TRA)** of 1986. TRA greatly reduced the number of tax brackets and lowered tax rates, on the one hand, but simultaneously broadened the tax base (the amount of taxable income), on the other.

CHARACTERISTICS   Let us briefly examine the latter change first. The personal income tax is levied upon *taxable income,* that is, on the incomes of households and unincorporated businesses after certain exemptions and deductions have been taken into account. Thus, under TRA an unmarried individual is allowed a $3000 standard deduction and a married couple is allowed $5000. Each individual in a household is also allowed a personal exemption of $2000. For example, a married couple with two dependents would be permitted an $8000 personal exemption. State and local income and property taxes (but not sales taxes), charitable contributions, and home mortgage interest payments are the other major deductibles in determining taxable income.

TRA broadened the tax base (increased taxable

TABLE 8-1 **The federal budget, 1987**

Tax receipts	Billions of dollars	Percent of total	Expenditures	Billions of dollars	Percent of total
Personal income tax	$393	46	Income security	$ 406	40
Payroll taxes	303	35	National defense.	282	28
Corporate income taxes . . .	84	10	Interest on public debt	139	14
Excise taxes.	32	4	Education, training, and health. . . .	70	7
Customs duties	15	2	Agriculture, natural resources, and environment.	41	4
Estate and gift taxes	7	1	Commerce, housing, and transportation	31	3
All other	20	2	All other (net)	35	4
Total receipts	$854	100	Total expenditures	$1004	100

Source: *Economic Report of the President.* Because of rounding, figures may not add up to totals.

TABLE 8-2 **Federal personal income tax rates, 1989***

(1) Total taxable income	(2) Marginal tax rate (4) ÷ (3)	(3) Change in income Δ (1)	(4) Change in taxes Δ (5)	(5) Total tax	(6) Average tax rate (5) ÷ (1)
$ 0	0%	—	—	—	—
29,750	15	$29,750	$ 4,462.50	$ 4,462.50	15%
71,900	28	42,150	11,802.00	16,264.50	22.6
149,250	33	77,350	25,525.50	41,790.00	28
Over 149,250	28	—	—	—	—

*Data are for a married couple filing a joint return.

income) by eliminating or limiting a number of deductions and tax loopholes which existed in the pre-1986 tax code. In particular, most contributions to individual retirement accounts (IRAs) are no longer deductible nor are losses on a variety of "tax shelters." More importantly, prior to 1986 capital gains—which arise when either securities or property are sold at a higher price than one paid for them—were taxed at preferential rates. Under TRA they are taxed as ordinary income.

What about tax rates? TRA substituted two tax rates—15 and 28 percent—for the fourteen pre-TRA rates which ranged from 11 to 50 percent. Columns 1 and 2 of Table 8-2 portray the mechanics of the income tax for a married couple filing a joint return. We observe that the 15 percent rate applies to all taxable income up to $29,750, at which point any *additional* income up to $71,900 is taxable at the 28 percent rate. TRA is complicated, however, by the inclusion of a "hidden" 33 percent tax bracket. For our married couple filing jointly, a 5 percent surcharge is levied on all taxable income between $71,900 and $149,250. That is, the 5 percent surcharge imposes a tax rate of 33 percent (=28 + 5 percent) on the additional $77,350 of taxable income which falls between $71,900 and $149,250. As shown in Table 8-2, TRA specifies that any taxable income which the couple realizes above $149,250 is *not* subject to the 5 percent surcharge so that the 28 percent rate applies once again.[2]

MARGINAL AND AVERAGE TAX RATES   To understand the personal income tax more fully we must grasp the distinction between marginal and average tax rates. The tax rates shown in column 2 of Table 8-2 are marginal tax rates. A **marginal tax rate** is the tax paid on additional or incremental income. By definition, it is the *increase* in taxes paid (column 4) divided by the *increase* in income (column 3). Thus, if our couple's taxable income were to increase from $0 to $29,750 the increase in taxes paid would be $4,462.50 (= .15 × $29,750) as shown in column 4. If the couple's taxable income were to rise by an additional $42,150 (column 3)—that is, from $29,750 to $71,900—a higher marginal tax rate of 28 percent would apply so that an additional tax of $11,802 (= .28 × $42,150) would have to be paid (column 4). A still further increase in taxable income of $77,350 (column 3)—which would increase our couple's total income from $71,900 to $149,250—would be taxed at 33 percent. Specifically, the tax on this additional income would be $25,525.50 (= .33 × $77,350) as shown in column 4.

The marginal tax rates of column 2 tend to

[2] For more on the Tax Reform Act of 1986, see the symposium presented in *The Journal of Economic Perspectives,* Summer 1987. The papers by Joseph A. Pechman and Richard A. Musgrave are especially recommended. See also *Economic Report of the President, 1987,* pp. 79–96.

overstate the personal income tax bite because the rising rates apply only to the income falling within each successive tax bracket. To get a better picture of the tax burden one must consider average tax rates. The **average tax rate** is the total tax paid divided by total taxable income. We note in column 6 of Table 8-2 that for the $0 to $29,750 tax bracket the average tax rate is $4,462.50 (column 4) divided by $29,750 (column 1) or 15 percent, the same as the marginal tax rate. But the couple earning $71,900 does *not* pay 28 percent of its income as taxes as the marginal tax rate would suggest. Rather, its average tax rate is only about 22.6 percent (= $16,264.50 ÷ $71,900). The reason, of course, is that the first $29,750 of income is taxed at 15 percent and only the next $42,150 is subject to the 28 percent rate. Similarly, the average tax rate of a couple earning $149,250 is 28 percent ($41,790 ÷ $149,250) not the 33 percent indicated by the marginal tax rate. What we observe here is that rising marginal tax rates pull up the average tax rate.[3]

By definition, a tax whose average tax rate rises as income increases is called a *progressive tax.* Such a tax claims both a larger absolute amount and a larger proportion of income as income rises. Thus we can say that our current personal income tax is mildly progressive.[4]

LOOPHOLES AND EVASION   Although TRA was successful in closing or limiting many of the loopholes in the personal income tax, several provisions remain which make the tax even less progressive than Table 8-2 indicates. The fact that interest on home mortgages and property taxes remain de-

ductible is of disproportionate benefit to high-income groups. Furthermore, interest on the bonds of state and local governments is exempt from the Federal income tax. Many high-income people can reduce their income tax liabilities very substantially by availing themselves of this loophole. For example, high-income people can reduce the tax rate on their interest income from 33 to zero percent by switching from savings deposits or corporate bonds to tax-exempt state and local bonds.

In addition to legally *avoiding* taxes through the use of loopholes, there is also the unsavory problem of illegal tax *evasion.* Involved here is the concealing of "underground economy" income from such pursuits as selling illegal drugs, prostitution, gambling, and so on. But also involved is the failure of individuals to report interest and dividend income; small-business owners and doctors, among others, who conceal cash payments; waiters and waitresses who conceal or underreport tips; and so forth. The Internal Revenue Service has estimated that tax evasion may reduce personal income tax revenues by as much as 20 percent. It is hoped that the lower marginal tax rates embodied in TRA will reduce incentives to evade taxes.

INDEXATION   A final notable feature of the personal income tax is that it is "indexed" to the rate of inflation to prevent rising prices from pushing taxpayers into higher tax brackets. Thus, as inflation occurs, not only will the size of the standard deduction and the personal exemption be adjusted for the inflation rate, but so will tax brackets. In the face of, say, 10 percent inflation, each of the tax brackets shown in Table 8-2 will be moved up by 10 percent so that families and individuals will not have to pay higher marginal and average tax rates just because the price level has risen.

Payroll taxes   Social security contributions, or **payroll taxes,** are the premiums paid on the compulsory insurance plans, for example, old age insurance and Medicare, provided for by existing social security legislation. These taxes are paid by both employers and employees. Improvements in, and extensions of, our social security programs, plus growth of the labor force, have resulted in very significant increases in payroll taxes in recent years. In 1989 employees and employers each pay a tax of

---

[3]The arithmetic is the same as what you may have encountered in school. You must get a score on an additional or "marginal" examination which is higher than your existing average grade in order to pull your average up!

[4] Note that the marginal tax rate on income above $149,250 falls back to 28 percent which means that the maximum average tax rate will also be 28 percent. You should confirm that a couple earning $250,000 will pay a total tax of $70,000 which is 28 percent of their income. Questions 7 and 8 at the end of this chapter may be helpful in solidifying your understanding of marginal and average tax rates.

7.51 percent on the first $48,000 of an employee's annual earnings.

Corporate income tax TRA entailed changes in the **corporate income tax** similar to those embodied in the personal income tax. The corporate income tax base was broadened while the tax rate was reduced. More specifically, TRA increased corporate tax liabilities by approximately 20 percent by eliminating or tightening a variety of tax loopholes, by reducing the amount of depreciation charges corporations can deduct in calculating taxable income, and by eliminating a special tax credit for new investment. At the same time the general corporate tax rate was cut from 46 to its present 34 percent.

Recall from Chapter 7 that the corporate income tax entails a problem of **double taxation.** That part of corporate income which is paid out as dividends is taxed twice. It is first taxed under the corporate income tax as described in the last paragraph and it is taxed again as personal income to stockholders.

Excise taxes Commodity or consumption taxes may take the form of **sales taxes** or **excise taxes.** The difference between the two is basically one of coverage. Sales taxes fall on a wide range of products, whereas excises are taxes on a small, select list of commodities. As Table 8-1 indicates, the Federal government collects excise taxes imposed upon such commodities as alcoholic beverages, tobacco, and gasoline. However, it does *not* levy a general sales tax; sales taxes are the bread and butter of most state governments.

State and local finance

While the Federal government finances itself largely through personal and corporate income taxation and payroll taxes, state and local governments rely heavily upon sales and **property taxes,** respectively. And although there is considerable overlapping in the types of expenditures made by the three levels of government, income security and national defense account for the majority of Federal expenditures, whereas education leads at both state and local levels.

STATE EXPENDITURES AND RECEIPTS

Note in Table 8-3 that the basic sources of tax revenue at the state level are sales and excise taxes, which account for about 49 percent of all state tax revenues. State personal income taxes, which entail much more modest rates than those employed by the Federal government, are the second most important source of revenue. Taxes on corporate income, property, inheritances, and a variety of licenses and permits constitute the remainder of state tax revenue. On the expenditure side of the picture, the major outlays of state governments are for (1) education, (2) public welfare, (3) health and hospitals, and (4) highway maintenance and construction.

It is important to note that the budget statement shown in Table 8-3 contains aggregated data and therefore tells us little about the finances of individual states. States vary tremendously in the types of taxes employed. Thus although personal income taxes are a major source of revenue for all state governments combined, four states do not use the personal income tax. Furthermore, great variations in the size of tax receipts and disbursements exist among the states.

LOCAL EXPENDITURES AND RECEIPTS

The receipts and expenditures shown in Table 8-4 are for all units of local government, including counties, municipalities, townships, and school districts. One major source of revenue and a single basic use of revenue stand out: The bulk of the revenue received by local government comes from property taxation; most local revenue is spent for education. Other, less important sources of funds and types of disbursements are self-explanatory.

The gaping deficit shown in Table 8-4 is largely removed when nontax sources of income are taken into account: In 1987 the tax revenues of local governments were supplemented by some $156 billion in intergovernmental grants from Federal and state governments. Furthermore, local governments received an additional $59 billion as proprietary income, that is, as revenue from government-owned hospitals and utilities. Finally, lotteries—the subject of this chapter's Last Word—have been a

TABLE 8-3 **Consolidated budget of all state governments, 1987**

Tax receipts	Billions of dollars	Percent of total	Expenditures	Billions of dollars	Percent of total
Sales, excise, and gross receipts taxes	$120	49	Education	$ 62	24
Personal income taxes	76	31	Public welfare	61	23
Corporate income taxes	21	8	Health and hospitals	32	12
Property taxes	5	2	Highways	31	12
Death and gift taxes	3	1	Public safety	19	7
Licenses, permits, and others	22	9	All others	58	22
Total receipts	$247	100	Total expenditures	$263	100

Source: Bureau of the Census, *State Government Finances in 1987.* Because of rounding, figures may not add up to totals.

growing source of nontax revenue for over half of the states.

FISCAL FEDERALISM

Historically, the tax collections of both state and local governments have fallen substantially short of their expenditures. These revenue shortfalls at the state and local levels are largely filled by Federal transfers or grants. It is not uncommon for 15 to 20 percent of all revenue received by state and local governments to come from the Federal government. In fact, in addition to Federal grants to state and local governments, the states also make grants to local governmental units. This system of intergovernmental transfers is called **fiscal federalism.** Concern over large and persistent Federal budget deficits has precipitated declines in Federal grants in recent years, causing state and local governments to increase tax rates, impose new taxes, and restrain expenditures.

TABLE 8-4 **Consolidated budget of all local governments, 1987**

Tax receipts	Billions of dollars	Percent of total	Expenditures	Billions of dollars	Percent of total
Property taxes	$117	74	Education	$168	43
Sales and excises	18	11	Welfare health and hospitals	49	12
Personal and corporate income taxes	10	6	Environment and housing	43	11
Licenses, permits, and others	13	8	Public safety	39	10
			Transportation	27	7
			All others	65	17
Total receipts	$158	100	Total expenditures	$391	100

Source: Bureau of the Census, *Government Finances in 1986–1987.* Because of rounding, figures may not add up to totals.

Apportioning the tax burden

The very nature of public goods and services (see Chapter 6) makes it exceedingly difficult to measure precisely the manner in which their benefits are apportioned among individuals and institutions in the economy. It is virtually impossible to determine accurately the amount by which John Doe benefits from military installations, a network of highways, a public school system, the national weather bureau, and local police and fire protection.

The situation is a bit different on the taxation side of the picture. Statistical studies reveal with somewhat greater clarity the manner in which the overall tax burden is apportioned. Needless to say, this is a question which affects each of us in a vital way. Although the average citizen is concerned with the overall level of taxes, chances are he or she is even more interested in exactly how the tax burden is allocated among individual taxpayers.

BENEFITS RECEIVED VERSUS ABILITY TO PAY

There are two basic philosophies on how the economy's tax burden should be apportioned.

Benefits-received principle The **benefits-received principle** of taxation asserts that households and businesses should purchase the goods and services of government in basically the same manner in which other commodities are bought. It is reasoned that those who benefit most from government-supplied goods or services should pay the taxes necessary for their financing. A few public goods are financed essentially on the basis of the benefits principle. For example, gasoline taxes are typically earmarked for the financing of highway construction and repairs. Those who benefit from good roads pay the cost of those roads. Difficulties immediately arise, however, when an accurate and widespread application of the benefits principle is considered:

1 How does one go about determining the benefits which individual households and businesses receive from national defense, education, and police and fire protection? Recall (Chapter 6) that public goods entail widespread spillover benefits and that the exclusion principle is inapplicable. Even in the seemingly tangible case of highway finance we find it difficult to measure benefits. Individual car owners benefit in different degrees from the existence of good roads. And those who do not own cars also benefit. Businesses would certainly benefit greatly from any widening of their markets which good roads will encourage.

2 Government efforts to redistribute income would be self-defeating if financed on the basis of the benefits principle. It would be absurd and self-defeating to ask poor families to pay the taxes needed to finance their welfare payments! It would be equally ridiculous to think of taxing only unemployed workers to finance the unemployment compensation payments which they receive.

Ability-to-pay principle The **ability-to-pay principle** of taxation stands in sharp contrast to the benefits principle. Ability-to-pay taxation rests on the idea that the tax burden should be geared directly to one's income and wealth. As the ability-to-pay principle has come to be applied in the United States, it contends that individuals and businesses with larger incomes should pay more taxes—both absolutely and relatively—than those with more modest incomes.

What is the rationale of ability-to-pay taxation? Proponents argue that each additional dollar of income received by a household will yield smaller and smaller increments of satisfaction. It is held that, because consumers act rationally, the first dollars of income received in any period of time will be spent upon basic high-urgency goods; that is, upon those goods which yield the greatest benefit or satisfaction. Successive dollars of income will go for less urgently needed goods and finally for trivial goods and services. This means that a dollar taken through taxes from a poor person who has few dollars constitutes a greater sacrifice than does a dollar taken by taxes from the rich person who has many dollars. Hence, in order to balance the sacrifices which taxes impose on income receivers, it is contended that taxes should be apportioned according to the amount of income one receives.

This is appealing, but problems of application exist here, too. In particular, although we might agree that the household earning $50,000 per year has a greater ability to pay taxes than the household receiving a paltry $10,000, exactly *how much more* ability to pay does the first family have as compared with the second? Should the rich person simply pay the *same percentage* of his or her larger income—and hence a larger absolute amount—as taxes? Or should the rich man or woman be made to pay a *larger fraction* of this income as taxes? The problem is that there is no scientific way of measuring one's ability to pay taxes. Thus, in practice, the answer hinges upon guesswork, the tax views of the political party in power, expediency, and the urgency with which government needs revenue. As we shall discover in a few moments, the tax structure of our economy is more in tune with the ability-to-pay principle than with the benefits-received principle.

PROGRESSIVE, PROPORTIONAL, AND REGRESSIVE TAXES

Any discussion of the ability-to-pay and the benefits-received principles of taxation leads ultimately to the question of tax rates and the manner in which tax rates change as one's income increases.

Definitions Taxes are usually seen as being progressive, proportional, or regressive. These designations focus upon the relationship between tax rates and *income* for the simple reason that all taxes—regardless of whether they are levied upon income or upon a product or building or parcel of land—are ultimately paid out of someone's income.

1 A tax is **progressive** if its average rate *increases* as income increases. Such a tax claims not only a larger absolute amount, but also a larger fraction or percentage of income as income increases.

2 A **regressive** tax is one whose average rate *declines* as income increases. Such a tax takes a smaller and smaller proportion of income as income increases. A regressive tax may or may not take a larger absolute amount of income as income expands.

3 A tax is **proportional** when its average rate *remains the same*, regardless of the size of income.

Let us illustrate in terms of the personal income tax. Suppose the tax rates are such that a household pays 10 percent of its income in taxes, regardless of the size of its income. This would clearly be a proportional income tax. Now suppose the rate structure is such that the household with an annual taxable income of less than $1000 pays 5 percent in income taxes, the household realizing an income of

$1000 to $2000 pays 10 percent, $2000 to $3000 pays 15 percent, and so forth. This, as we have already explained, would obviously be a *progressive* income tax. The final case is where the rates decline as taxable income rises: You pay 15 percent if you earn less than $1000; 10 percent if you earn $1000 to $2000; 5 percent if you earn $2000 to $3000; and so forth. This is a *regressive* income tax. In general, progressive taxes are those which bear down most heavily on the rich; regressive taxes are those which hit the poor hardest.

Applications What can we say about the progressivity, proportionality, or regressivity of the major kinds of taxes used in the United States?

1 We have already noted that the Federal *personal income tax* is mildly progressive with marginal tax rates ranging from 15 to 33 percent. Recall that the deductibility of interest on home mortgages and property taxes, along with the exemption of interest income from state and local bonds, erodes the progressivity of the tax.

2 At first glance a *general sales tax* with, say, a 3 percent rate would seem to be proportional. But in fact it is regressive with respect to income. The reason for its regressivity is that a larger portion of a poor person's income is exposed to the tax than is the case with a rich person; the latter avoids the tax on the part of income which is saved, whereas the former is unable to save. Example: "Poor" Smith has an income of $15,000 and spends it all. "Rich" Jones has an income of $30,000 but spends only $20,000 of it. Assuming a 3 percent sales tax applies to the expenditures of each individual, we find Smith will pay $450 (3 percent of $15,000) in sales taxes, and Jones will pay $600 (3 percent of $20,000). Note that whereas *all* of Smith's $15,000 income is subject to the sales tax, only two-thirds of Jones' $30,000 income is taxed. Thus, while Smith pays $450, or 3 percent, of a $15,000 income as sales taxes, Jones pays $600, or just 2 percent, of a $30,000 income. Hence, we conclude that the general sales tax is regressive.

3 The Federal *corporate income tax* is essentially a flat-rate proportional tax with a 34 percent tax rate. But this assumes that corporation owners (shareholders) bear the tax. Some tax experts argue that at least a part of the tax is passed through to consumers in the form of higher product prices. To the extent that this occurs, the tax tends to be regressive like a sales tax.

4 *Payroll taxes* are regressive because they apply to only a fixed absolute amount of one's income. For example, in 1989, payroll tax rates were 7.51 percent, but this figure applies only to the first $48,000 of one's wage income. Thus a person earning exactly $48,000 would pay $3604.80, or 7.51 percent of his or her wage income, while someone with twice that income, or $96,000, would also pay $3604.80—only 3.755 percent of his or her wage income. Note, too, that this regressivity is enhanced because the payroll tax excludes nonwage income. If our individual with the $96,000 wage income also received $48,000 in nonwage (dividend, interest, rent) income, then the payroll tax would amount to only 2.50 percent (= $3604.80 ÷ $144,000) of the total income.

5 Most, but not all, economists feel that *property taxes* on buildings are regressive for essentially the same reasons as are sales taxes. First, property owners add the tax to the rents which tenants are charged. Second, property taxes, as a percentage of income, are higher for poor families than for rich families because the poor must spend a larger proportion of their incomes for housing.[5] The alleged regressivity of the property tax may be reinforced by the fact that property-tax rates are not likely to be uniform as between various political subdivisions. For example, if property values decline in, say, a decaying central-city area, property-tax rates must be increased in the city to bring in a given amount of revenue. But in a wealthy suburb, where the market value of housing is rising, a given amount of tax revenue can be maintained with lower property-tax rates.

SHIFTING AND INCIDENCE OF TAXES

Taxes do not always stick where the government levies them. Some taxes can be shifted among various parties in the economy. It is therefore neces-

sary to locate as best we can the final resting place or **incidence** of the major types of taxes.

Personal income tax   The incidence of the personal income tax generally falls on the individual upon whom the tax is levied; little chance exists for shifting. But there might be exceptions to this. Individuals and groups who can effectively control the price of their labor services may be able to shift a part of the tax. For example, doctors, dentists, lawyers, and other professional people who can readily increase their fees may do so because of the tax. Unions might regard personal incomes taxes as part of the cost of living and, as a result, bargain for higher wages. If they are successful, they may shift a portion of the tax from workers to employers who, by then increasing prices, shift the wage increase to the public. Generally, however, most experts conclude that the individual upon whom the tax is initially levied bears the burden of the personal income tax. The same ordinarily holds true of payroll and inheritance taxes.

Corporate income tax   We have already suggested that the incidence of the corporate income tax is much less certain. The traditional view has it that a firm which is currently charging the profit-maximizing price and producing the profit-maximizing output will have no reason to change price or output when a corporate income tax is imposed. That price and output combination which yields the greatest profit before the tax will still be the most profitable after government takes a fixed percentage of the firm's profits in the form of income taxes. According to this view, the company's stockholders (owners) must bear the incidence of the tax in the form of lower dividends or a smaller amount of retained earnings. On the other hand, some economists argue that the corporate income tax is shifted in part to consumers through higher prices and to resource suppliers through lower prices. In modern industry, where a small number of firms may control a market, producers may not be in the profit-maximizing position initially. The reason? By fully exploiting their market position currently, monopolistic firms might elicit adverse public opinion and governmental censure. Hence, they may await such events as increases in tax rates or wage increases by unions to provide an "excuse" or rationale for price increases with less fear of public criti-

---

[5] Controversy arises in part because empirical research, which compares the value of housing to lifetime (rather than a single year's) income, suggests that this ratio is approximately the same for all income groups. Students interested in this controversy should consult Henry J. Aaron, *Who Pays the Property Tax? A New View* (Washington: Brookings Institution, 1975).

TABLE 8-5 **The probable incidence of taxes**

Type of tax	Probable incidence
Personal income tax	The household or individual upon which it is levied.
Corporate income tax	Disagreement. Some economists feel the firm on which it is levied bears the incidence; others conclude the tax is shifted, wholly or in part, to consumers.
Sales and excise taxes	With exceptions, consumers who buy the taxed products.
Property taxes	Owners in the case of land and owner-occupied residences; tenants in the case of rented property; consumers in the case of business property.

cism. When this actually occurs, a portion of the corporate income tax may be shifted to consumers through higher prices.

Both positions are plausible. Indeed, the incidence of the corporate income tax may well be shared by stockholders and the firm's customers and resource suppliers.

Sales and excise taxes   Sales and excise taxes are the "hidden taxes" of our economy. They are hidden because such taxes are typically shifted by sellers to consumers through higher product prices. There may be some difference in the shiftability of sales taxes and excises, however. Because a sales tax covers a much wider range of products than an excise, there is little chance for consumers to resist the price boosts which sales taxes entail by reallocating their expenditures to untaxed, lower-priced products.

Excises, however, fall on a relatively short, select list of goods. Therefore, the possibility of consumers turning to substitute goods and services is greater. For example, an excise tax on theater tickets which does not apply to other types of entertainment might be difficult to pass on to consumers via price increases. Why? Because price boosts might result in considerable substituting of alternative types of entertainment by consumers. The higher price will cause such a marked decline in sales that a seller will be better off to bear all, or a large portion of, the excise rather than the sharp decline in sales. With many excises, however, modest price increases have little or no effect on sales. Excises on gasoline, cigarettes, and alcoholic bev-

erages are cases in point. Here there are few good substitute products to which consumers can turn as prices rise. For these commodities, the seller is in a better position to shift the tax.

In general, it is safe to say that the bulk of a sales or excise tax will generally be shifted to the consumer through higher product prices.[6]

Property taxes   Many property taxes are borne by the property owner for the simple reason that there is no other party to whom they can be shifted. This is typically true in the case of taxes on land, personal property, and owner-occupied residences. For example, even when land is sold, the property tax is not likely to be shifted. The buyer will tend to discount the value of the land to allow for the future taxes which must be paid on it, and this expected taxation will be reflected in the price a buyer is willing to offer for the land.

Taxes on rented and business property are a different story. Taxes on rented property can be, and usually are, shifted wholly or in part from the owner to the tenant by the simple process of boosting the rent. Business property taxes are treated as a business cost and therefore are taken into account in establishing product price; thus such taxes are ordinarily shifted to the firm's customers.

Table 8-5 summarizes this discussion of the shifting and incidence of taxes.

[6] Later (Chapter 33) we will employ supply and demand analysis as a basis for more sophisticated generalizations as to the shifting and incidence of sales taxes.

THE AMERICAN TAX STRUCTURE

Is the overall tax structure—Federal, state, and local taxes combined—progressive, proportional, or regressive? This is a difficult question to answer because estimates of the distribution of the total tax burden are quite sensitive to assumptions made regarding tax incidence. To what extent are the various taxes shifted and who bears the ultimate burden? For example, we have already cited the disagreement among the experts as to the incidence of the corporate income tax.

An important pre-TRA study for 1985 by Joseph Pechman[7] suggested that the overall tax structure was only mildly progressive. For example, the poorest tenth of all income receivers paid about 17 percent of their income in taxes, while the richest tenth paid slightly in excess of 26 percent. The progressivity of the personal income and corporate income taxes is largely offset by the regressivity of payroll, sales, and excise taxes. This means that the tax system has only a modest effect upon the distribution of income. More recently, the Congressional Budget Office[8] has examined the impact of recent tax legislation—the Tax Reform Act of 1986 in particular—upon the distribution of *Federal* taxes. In comparing the pre-TRA distribution for 1977 with the post-TRA estimates for 1988, it was found that recent tax changes have made the Federal tax system *less* progressive. For example, between 1977 and 1988 the tax burden of the poorest tenth of the population increased from 8.3 to 9.7 percent of their incomes. Conversely, the tax burden of the richest tenth fell from 29.5 to 26.6 percent over the same period. The burdens for all other income receivers were changed only very slightly. The diminished progressivity of the personal income tax and, more importantly, the increasing importance of the regressive payroll tax go far to explain this decline in progressivity. Were the largely regressive tax structures of state and local governments combined with this Federal data the overall tax structure would probably be close to proportional.

[7] Joseph A. Pechman, *Who Paid the Taxes, 1966–1985?* (Washington: The Brookings Institution, 1985).

[8] Congressional Budget Office, *The Changing Distribution of Federal Taxes: 1975–1990* (Washington: 1987).

It is significant to note that, while our tax system does *not* substantially alter the distribution of income, our system of transfer payments has a pronounced effect in reducing income inequality. For example, transfers almost quadrupled the incomes of the poorest fifth of the income receivers. The redistributional effects of transfers will be examined in more detail in Chapter 37.

Tax issues

While the Tax Reform Act of 1986 embodied perhaps the most sweeping changes in the Federal tax code in the past half-century, there is still considerable pressure for further changes in our tax system. These pressures reflect two quite different objectives.

TAXES AND REINDUSTRIALIZATION

Some observers recommend that the entire tax system be recast or restructured so as to encourage the "reindustrialization" of the American economy. The argument essentially is that in the past decade or so the productivity of American workers has stagnated relative to workers in Japan, West Germany, and a number of other industrialized nations. A major consequence is that a number of our basic industries—for example, automobiles, steel, and electronics—have fallen prey to foreign competition. In aggregative terms the United States has been incurring massive balance of international trade deficits or, simply stated, our imports have greatly exceeded our exports.

Some economists contend that we must "reindustrialize" our economy by making massive new investments in machinery and equipment to offset our relative economic decline. Retooled with large amounts of modern machinery and equipment, the productivity of American workers will once again increase. But you will recall from Chapter 2's production possibilities curve that with reasonably full employment, more investment implies offsetting cuts in consumption. Some feel that a major structural overhaul of our present tax system can bring about the required increases in investment and reductions in consumption.[9]

One proposal is that the corporate income tax should be lowered or eliminated. This would greatly enhance the expected profitability of investment and stimulate spending on new plants and equipment. But if the economy is at or close to full employment, how can the required resources be released from the production of consumer goods? A widely discussed means for achieving this is to levy a **value-added tax (VAT)** on consumer goods. VAT is much like a retail sales tax, except that the tax applies only to the difference between the value of a firm's sales and the value of its purchases from other firms.[10] In essence, VAT would amount to a national sales tax on consumer goods. A number of European countries—for example, Great Britain and Sweden—currently use VAT as a major source of revenue. For present purposes the point to note is that VAT penalizes consumption. One can avoid paying VAT by saving rather than consuming. And we know that saving (refraining from consumption) will release resources from consumer goods production and thereby make them available for investment goods production. In short, elimination of the corporate income tax and the installation of VAT will allegedly alter the composition of our national output away from consumption and toward investment with the result that our productivity growth and "competitive edge" will be restored.

CUTTING THE BUDGET DEFICIT

Others feel that higher tax rates or entirely new taxes are required to contain large and persistent Federal budget deficits. As we will discover in Chapter 15, in recent years large Federal deficits have caused the public debt to rise sharply. Because many Federal expenditure programs are regarded to be "politically untouchable," any resolution of the deficit problem will undoubtedly entail tax increases. One option is to introduce VAT.

[9] You might want to reread Chapter 2's section, "A Growing Economy," at this point.

[10] A more detailed look at the concept of value added is found in Chapter 9.

Another is to increase the progressivity of the personal income tax. In particular, some economists feel the anomaly of marginal tax rates rising from 15 to 33 percent and then falling back to 28 percent (column 2 of Table 8-2) cries out for adjustment. The existing structure invites the extension of the 33 percent rate or the imposition of a still higher marginal tax rate on income above $149,250.

CHAPTER SUMMARY

1 Although the absolute level of total government purchases of goods and services has increased greatly, such purchases have been about 20 percent of the national output in the entire post-World War II period.

2 Transfer payments entail the transfer of tax revenues from taxpayers in general to specific segments of the population, for example, those who are retired, unemployed, or indigent. Government purchases and transfers combined amount to about one-third of the national output.

3 Wars and national defense, population growth, urbanization, environmental problems, and egalitarianism have been among the more important causes underlying the historical growth of the public sector.

4 The main categories of Federal spending are for income security, national defense, and interest on the public debt; revenues come primarily from the personal income, payroll, and corporate income taxes.

5 The primary sources of revenue for the states are sales and excise taxes; education, welfare, health and hospitals, and highways are the major state expenditures.

6 At the local level, most revenue comes from the property tax, and education is the most important expenditure.

7 Under our system of fiscal federalism, state and local tax revenues are supplemented by sizable revenue grants from the Federal government.

8 The ability-to-pay principle of taxation is more evident in the American tax structure than is the benefits-received philosophy.

9 The Federal personal income tax is progressive. The corporate income tax is probably progressive. General sales, excise, payroll, and property taxes tend to be regressive.

10 Sales and excise taxes are likely to be shifted; personal income taxes are not. There is disagreement as to whether corporate income taxes are shifted. The incidence of property taxes depends primarily upon whether the property is owner- or tenant-occupied.

11 The pre-TRA tax structure was only mildly progressive. Because recent tax changes have made the Federal tax structure less progressive, the total tax structure is now virtually proportional for most income classes.

12 Current tax issues include *a* restructuring the tax system to promote "reindustrialization," and *b* increasing tax rates or imposing new taxes to reduce large Federal budget deficits.

TERMS AND CONCEPTS

government purchases	**property tax**
transfer payments	**fiscal federalism**
personal income tax	**benefits-received**
Tax Reform Act (TRA) of 1986	**principle**
	ability-to-pay principle
marginal and average tax rates	**progressive tax**
payroll tax	**regressive tax**
corporate income tax	**proportional tax**
double taxation	**tax shifting**
sales and excise taxes	**tax incidence**
	value-added tax (VAT)

QUESTIONS AND STUDY SUGGESTIONS

1 Describe and account for the historical growth of the public sector of the economy. Why might it be significant to distinguish between "transfer payments" and "government purchases of goods and services" in evaluating the impact of the growth of government expenditures?

2 What is the most important source of revenue and the major type of expenditure at the Federal level? At the state level? At the local level?

3 Briefly describe the mechanics of the Federal personal income tax. In what basic ways did the Tax Reform Act of 1986 change the personal income tax? What major tax "loopholes" remain? What is "indexation"?

4 What is "fiscal federalism"? Why does it exist?

5 Distinguish clearly between the benefits-received and the ability-to-pay principles of taxation. Which philoso-

LAST WORD

Lotteries: facts and controversies

State lotteries, which began in 1964, are a potentially important source of public revenue. What are the characteristics of lotteries? And what are the arguments for and against this means of enhancing state revenues?

In 1987 some 28 states and the District of Columbia had lotteries which sold over $12 billion worth of tickets. The average lottery returns about 50 percent of its gross revenues to ticket purchasers as prizes and 40 percent goes to the state treasury. The remaining 10 percent is for designing and promoting the lottery and for commissions to retail outlets which sell tickets. Although states sponsoring lotteries currently obtain only 1 to 2 percent of their total revenues in this way, per capita sales of lottery tickets increased by 14 percent per year over the 1975–1985 period.

Lotteries have been quite controversial. Critics make the following arguments. First, the 40 percent of gross revenues from lotteries which goes to the state governments is in effect a 40 percent tax on ticket purchasers. This tax is higher than the taxes on cigarettes and liquor. Furthermore, research indicates that the "lottery tax" is highly regressive in that there is little relationship between ticket purchases and household incomes. The 5 percent of the adults who patronize lotteries most heavily account for about one-half of total ticket sales; on average these heavy bettors spend about $1200 per year on tickets. Second, critics argue that it is ethically wrong for the state to sponsor gambling. Gambling is generally regarded as immoral and, in other forms, is illegal in most states. It is also held that lotteries may whet the appetite for gambling and generate compulsive gamblers who will impoverish themselves and their families to the end that they become wards of the state.

But there are counterarguments. It is contended, in the first place, that lottery revenue should not be regarded as a tax. Tax collections are compulsory and involve coercion; the purchase of a lottery ticket is voluntary and entails free consumer choice. A second and related argument is that within wide limits it is not appropriate to make moral judgments about how people should spend their incomes. Individuals achieve the maximum satisfaction from their incomes by spending without interference. If some people derive satisfaction from participating in lotteries, they should be free to do so. Finally, lotteries are competitive with illegal gambling and thereby may be socially beneficial in curtailing the power of organized crime.

Two observations seem quite certain at the moment. One is that total lottery revenue will continue to increase. Why? Because more and more states are establishing lotteries and people seem to enjoy gambling, particularly when they feel their losses are being used for "good causes." The other point is that this source of revenue will remain controversial.

Source: Based upon C. T. Clotfelter and P. J. Cook, "Implicit Taxation in Lottery Finance," National Bureau of Economic Research Working Paper No. 2246, May 1987.

phy is more evident in our present tax structure? Justify your answer. To which principle of taxation do you subscribe? Why?

6 Precisely what is meant by a progressive tax? A regressive tax? A proportional tax? Comment upon the progressivity or regressivity of each of the following taxes, indicating in each case your assumption concerning tax incidence:

   a The Federal personal income tax
   b A 3 percent state general sales tax
   c A Federal excise tax on automobile tires
   d A municipal property tax on real estate
   e The Federal corporate income tax

7 Assume that the structure of a personal income tax is such that you would pay a tax of $2000 if your taxable income was $16,000 and a tax of $3000 if your taxable income was $20,000. What is the average tax rate at the $16,000 and $20,000 levels of taxable income? What marginal tax rate applies to taxable income which falls between $16,000 and $20,000? Is this tax progressive, proportional, or regressive? Explain.

8 Calculate the average and marginal tax rates for the following table and indicate whether the tax is progressive, proportional, or regressive. What generalization can you offer concerning the relationship between marginal and average tax rates?

Income	Tax	Average tax rate	Marginal tax rate
$ 0	$ 0	_____	_____
100	10	_____	_____
200	30	_____	_____
300	60	_____	_____
400	100	_____	_____
500	150	_____	

9 Comment on the overall progressivity or regressivity of the United States tax system.

10 Suppose you are convinced that the long-run viability of the United States as a world industrial power necessitates that investment be increased and consumption reduced as proportions of the national output. What specific changes in the tax structure would you recommend to achieve this alteration of output?

11 Design what you consider to be an ideal tax system to raise revenue equal to, say, 20 percent of the national output.

National Income, Employment, and Fiscal Policy

CHAPTER 9

Measuring national output, national income, and the price level

In Part I of this book, we stated that the U.S. economy has not consistently provided for the full employment of available resources. It was also noted in Part I that the levels of employment, production, and prices depend upon the size of certain flows of expenditures and income. Now, in Part 2, we deal at length with how to identify and measure the levels of national output, income, and employment. Part 2 also discusses in detail specific public policies designed to manage, if need be, the price level and the amounts of employment, production, and income in the economy. Specifically, in this chapter we are interested in learning how government statisticians and accountants measure and record the levels of national output, national income, and prices for the entire United States during a particular period. In Chapter 10 we examine the fluctuations which have characterized our economy, emphasizing the effects of unemployment and inflation. Then in Chapters II, 12, and 13, we explain those factors which determine the levels of employment, production, and prices. Chapter 14 explores how fiscal policy—intentional changes of government expenditures and tax collections—might be used to help stabilize output, employment, and the price level.

Our main objectives in the present chapter are as follows. First, we want to explain briefly why it is important to be able to measure the performance of the economy. Second, the key measure of national output—gross national product or GNP—is defined and we show that GNP can be measured either from the vantage point of expenditures on output or by the income generated from the production of that output. Third, several other important measures of national output and income are derived from GNP and their meanings explained. Our fourth goal is to explain how the overall level of prices—the price level—is measured. Fifth, we demonstrate how GNP can be adjusted for changes in the price level—that is, for inflation or deflation—so that changes in the physical amount of the nation's production are more accurately reflected. Finally, we will briefly survey some of the limitations of our measures of national output and income.

The importance of macroeconomic measurement

The present task is that of defining and understanding a group of so-called social or national income accounting concepts which have been designed to measure the overall production performance of the economy. Why do we bother with such a project? Because social accounting does for the economy as a whole what private accounting does for the individual business enterprise or, for that matter, for the household. The business executive is vitally interested in knowing how well his or her firm is doing, but the answer is not always immediately discernible.

Measurement of the firm's flows of income and expenditures is needed to assess the firm's operations for the current year. With this information available, the executive can gauge the economic health of the firm. If things are going well, the accounting data can be used to explain this success. It may be that costs are down or sales and product prices are up, resulting in large profits. If things are going badly, accounting measures can be employed to discover immediate causes. And by examining the accounts over a period of time, the executive can detect growth or decline of profits for the firm and indications of the immediate causes. All this information is valuable in helping the executive make intelligent business decisions.

A system of **national income accounting** does much the same thing for the economy as a whole: It allows us to keep a finger on the economic pulse of the nation. The various measures which make up our social accounting system permit us to measure the level of production in the economy at some point in time and explain the immediate causes of that level of performance. Further, by comparing the national income accounts over a period of time, we can plot the long-run course which the economy has been following; the growth or stagnation of the economy will show up in the national income accounts. Finally, the information supplied by the national income accounts provides a basis for the formulation and application of public policies designed to improve the performance of the economy; without the national income accounts, economic policy would be based upon guesswork. In short, national income accounting allows us to keep tabs on the economic health of society and to formulate intelligently policies which will improve that health.

Gross national product

There are many conceivable measures of the economic well-being of society. It is generally agreed, however, that the best available indicator of an economy's health is its annual total output of goods and services or, as it is sometimes called, the economy's aggregate output. The basic social accounting measure of the total output of goods and services is called the **gross national product** or, simply, **GNP.** It is defined as *the total market value of all final goods and services produced in the economy in one year*. We shall see that all goods *produced* in a particular year may not be *sold;* some may be added to inventories. Any increase in inventories must therefore be included in determining GNP, since GNP measures all current produc-

tion regardless of whether or not it is sold. As you may suspect, our definition of GNP is very explicit and merits considerable comment.

A MONETARY MEASURE

Note, first, that GNP measures the market value of annual output. GNP is a monetary measure. Indeed, it must be if we are to compare the heterogeneous collections of goods and services produced in different years and get a meaningful idea of their relative worth. Put simply, if the economy produces three oranges and two apples in year 1 and two oranges and three apples in year 2, in which year is output greater? There is no answer to this question until price tags are attached to the various products as indicators of society's evaluation of their relative worth. The problem is resolved in Table 9-1, where it is assumed that the money price of the oranges is 20 cents and the price of apples is 30 cents. It can be concluded that year 2's output is greater than that of year 1. Why? Because society values year 2's output more highly; society is willing to pay more for the collection of goods produced in year 2 than of goods produced in year 1.

AVOIDING DOUBLE COUNTING

To measure total output accurately, all goods and services produced in any given year must be counted once, but not more than once. Most products go through a series of production stages before reaching a market. As a result, parts or components of most products are bought and sold many times. Hence, to avoid counting several times the parts of products that are sold and resold, GNP includes only the market value of final goods and ignores transactions involving intermediate goods.

By **final goods** we mean goods and services which are being purchased for final use and not for resale or further processing or manufacturing. Transactions involving **intermediate goods,** on the other hand, refer to purchases of goods and services for further processing and manufacturing or for resale. The sale of final goods is *included* and the sale of intermediate goods is *excluded* from GNP. Why? Because the value of final goods already includes all the intermediate transactions

TABLE 9-1 **Comparing heterogeneous outputs by using money prices** *(hypothetical data)*

Year	Annual outputs	Market value
1	3 oranges and 2 apples	3 at 20 cents + 2 at 30 cents = $1.20
2	2 oranges and 3 apples	2 at 20 cents + 3 at 30 cents = $1.30

involved in their production. To count intermediate transactions separately would involve **double counting** and an exaggerated estimate of GNP.

An example will clarify this point. Suppose there are five stages of production in getting a wool suit manufactured and into the hands of a consumer who, of course, is the ultimate or final user. As Table 9-2 indicates, firm A, a sheep ranch, provides $60 worth of wool to firm B, a wool processor. Firm A pays out the $60 it receives in wages, rents, interest, and profits. Firm B processes the wool and sells it to firm C, a suit manufacturer, for $100. What does firm B do with this $100? As noted, $60 goes to firm A, and the remaining $40 is used by B to pay wages, rents, interest, and profits for the resources needed in processing the wool. And so it goes. The manufacturer sells the suit to firm D, a clothing wholesaler, who in turn sells it to firm E, a retailer, and then, at last, it is bought for $250 by a

consumer, the final user of the product. At each stage, the difference between what a firm has paid for the product and what it receives for its sale is paid out as wages, rent, interest, and profits for the resources used by that firm in helping to produce and distribute the suit.

The basic question is this: How much should we include in GNP in accounting for the production of this suit? The answer: Just $250, the value of the final product. Why? Because this figure includes all the intermediate transactions leading up to the product's final sale. It would be a gross exaggeration to sum all the intermediate sales figures and the final sales value of the product in column 2 and add the entire amount, $710, to GNP. This would be a serious case of double counting, that is, counting the final product *and* the sale and resale of its various parts in the multistage productive process. The production and sale of the suit has

TABLE 9-2 **Value added in a five-stage production process** *(hypothetical data)*

(1) Stage of production	(2) Sales value of materials or product	(3) Value added
	0	
Firm A, sheep ranch	$ 60	$60(= $ 60 − $ 0)
Firm B, wool processor	100	40(= 100 − 60)
Firm C, suit manufacturer	125	25(= 125 − 100)
Firm D, clothing wholesaler	175	50(= 175 − 125)
Firm E, retail clothier	250	75(= 250 − 175)
Total sales values	$710	
Value added (total income)		$250

generated $250, not $710, worth of output and income.

To avoid double counting, national income accountants are careful to calculate only the *value added* by each firm. **Value added** is the market value of a firm's output *less* the value of the inputs which it has purchased from others. Thus, for example, we note in column 3 of Table 9-2 that the value added of firm B is $40, the difference between the $100 value of its output minus the $60 it paid for the inputs provided by firm A. By adding together the values added by the five firms in Table 9-2 the total value of the suit can be accurately determined. Similarly, by calculating and summing the values added by all firms in the economy, national income accountants can determine the GNP, that is, the market value of total output.

GNP EXCLUDES NONPRODUCTION TRANSACTIONS

GNP attempts to measure the annual production of the economy. In so doing, the many nonproduction transactions which occur each year must be carefully excluded. *Nonproduction transactions* are of two major types: (1) purely financial transactions, and (2) secondhand sales.

Financial transactions   Purely financial transactions in turn are of three general types: public transfer payments, private transfer payments, and the buying and selling of securities.

1 We have already mentioned *public transfer payments* (Chapter 8). These are the social security payments, welfare payments, and veterans' payments which government makes to particular households. The basic characteristic of public transfer payments is that recipients make no contribution to *current* production in return for them. Thus, to include them in GNP would be to overstate this year's production.

2 *Private transfer payments*—for example, a university student's monthly subsidy from home or an occasional gift from a wealthy relative—do not entail production but simply the transfer of funds from one private individual to another.

3 *Security transactions,* that is, the buying and selling of stocks and bonds, are also excluded from GNP. Stock market transactions involve merely the swapping of paper assets. As such, these transactions do not directly involve current production. It should be noted, however, that by getting money from the hands of savers into the hands of spenders, some of these security transactions may indirectly give rise to spending which does account for output.

Secondhand sales   The reason for excluding secondhand sales from GNP is fairly obvious: Such sales either reflect no *current* production, or they involve double counting. For example, suppose you sell your 1982 Ford to a friend. This transaction would be excluded in determining GNP because no current production is involved. The inclusion of the sales of goods produced some years ago in this year's GNP would be an exaggeration of this year's output. Similarly, if you purchased a brand new Ford and resold it a week later to your neighbor, we should still want to exclude the resale transaction from the current GNP. Why? Because when you originally bought the new car, its value was included in GNP. To include its resale value would be to count it twice.

TWO SIDES TO GNP: SPENDING AND INCOME

Given a general understanding of the meaning of GNP, we now raise this question: How can the market value of total output—or for that matter, any single unit of output—be measured? Returning to Table 9-2's example, how can we measure, for example, the market value of a suit?

In two ways: First, we can just look at how much a consumer, as the final user, spends in obtaining it. Second, we can add up all the wage, rental, interest, and profit incomes created in its production. This second approach is simply the value-added technique we discussed in Table 9-2. The final-product and value-added approaches are, indeed, two ways of looking at the same thing. *What is spent on a product is received as income by those who contributed to its production.* Indeed, Chapter 3's circular flow model is based upon this notion. If $250 is spent on the suit, that is necessarily the total amount of income derived from its production. You can verify this by noting the incomes generated by firms A, B, C, D, and E in Table 9-2 are $60, $40, $25, $50, and $75 respectively and total to $250. This equality of the expenditure for a product and the income derived from its production is guaranteed, because profit income serves as a balancing item. Profit—or loss—is the income which remains after wage, rent, and interest incomes have been paid by the producer. If the wage, rent, and interest incomes which the firm must pay in getting the suit produced are less than the $250 expenditure for the suit, the difference will be the firm's profits.[1] Conversely, if wage, rent, and interest incomes exceed $250, profits will be negative, that is, losses will be realized, to balance the expenditure on the product and the income derived from its production.

The same line of reasoning is also valid for the output of the economy as a whole. There are two different ways of looking at GNP: One is to look at GNP as the sum of all the expenditures involved in taking that total output off the market. This is called the *output,* or **expenditures, approach.** The other is to look at it in terms of the income derived or created from the production of the GNP. This is called the *earnings,* or *allocations,* or **income, approach** to the determination of GNP. A closer analysis of these two approaches will reveal that they amount to this: *GNP can be determined either by adding up all that is spent to buy this year's total output or by summing up all the incomes derived from the production of this year's output.* Putting this

in the form of a simple equation, we can say that

The amount spent to purchase this year's total output = the money income derived from the production of this year's output

As a matter of fact, this is more than an equation: It is an identity. Buying—that is, spending money—and selling—that is, receiving money income—are actually two aspects of the same transaction. *What is spent on a product is income to those who have contributed their human and property resources in getting that product produced and to market.*

For the economy as a whole, we can expand the above identity to read as in Table 9-3. This summary statement simply tells us that all final goods produced in the American economy are purchased either by the three domestic sectors—households, government, and businesses—or by foreign consumers. It also shows us that, aside from a couple of nonincome allocations, which we discuss later, the total receipts which businesses acquire from the sale of total output are allocated among the various resource suppliers as wage, rent, interest, and profit income. Using this summary as a point of reference, let us next point out in some detail the meaning and significance of the various types of expenditures and the incomes derived from these expenditures.

TABLE 9-3 **The output and income approaches to GNP**

Output, or expenditures, approach		Income, or allocations, approach
Consumption expenditures by households plus Investment expenditures by businesses plus Government purchases of goods and services plus Expenditures by foreigners	= GNP =	Nonincome charges or allocations plus Wages plus Rents plus Interest plus Profits

[1] The term "profits" is used here in the accounting sense so as to include both normal profits and economic profits as defined in Chapter 5.

The expenditures approach to GNP

To determine GNP through the expenditures approach, we must add up all types of spending on finished or final goods and services. But our national income accountants have somewhat more sophisticated terms for the different types of spending than the ones we have employed in Table 9-3. We must therefore familiarize ourselves with these terms and their meanings.

PERSONAL CONSUMPTION EXPENDITURES (C)

What we have called "consumption expenditures by households" is **personal consumption expenditures** to the national income accountants. It entails expenditures by households on *durable consumer goods* (automobiles, refrigerators, video recorders, and so forth), *nondurable consumer goods* (bread, milk, beer, cigarettes, shirts, toothpaste), and *consumer expenditures for services* (of lawyers, doctors, mechanics, barbers). We shall use the letter C to designate the total of these expenditures.

GROSS PRIVATE DOMESTIC INVESTMENT (I_g)

This seemingly complicated term refers to all investment spending by American business firms. What is included as investment spending? Basically three things: (1) all final purchases of machinery, equipment, and tools by business enterprises; (2) all construction; and (3) changes in inventories. This obviously entails more than we have ascribed to the term "investment" thus far. Hence, we must explain why each of these three items is included under the general heading of gross private domestic investment.

The reason for including the first group of items is apparent. This is simply a restatement of our original definition of investment spending as the purchase of tools, machinery, and equipment. The second item—all construction—merits some explanation. It is clear that the building of a new factory, warehouse, or grain elevator is a form of investment. But why include residential construction as investment rather than consumption? The reason is this: Apartment buildings are clearly investment goods because, like factories and grain elevators, they are income-earning assets. Other residential units which are rented are for the same reason investment goods. Furthermore, owner-occupied houses are classified as investment goods because they could be rented out to yield a money income return, even though the owner does not choose to do so. For these reasons all residential construction is considered as investment. Finally, why are changes in inventories counted as investment? Because an increase in inventories is, in effect, "unconsumed output," and that precisely is what investment is!

Inventory changes as investment   Remembering that GNP is designed to measure total current output, we must certainly make an effort to include in GNP any products which are produced *but not sold* this year. In short, if GNP is to be an accurate measure of total production, it must include the market value of any additions to inventories which accrue during the year. Were we to exclude an increase in inventories, GNP would understate the current year's total production. If businesses have more goods on their shelves and in their warehouses at the end of the year than they had at the start, the economy has produced more than it has consumed during this particular year. This increase in inventories must be added to GNP as a measure of *current* production.

What about a decline in inventories? This must be subtracted in figuring GNP, because in such a situation the economy sells a total output which exceeds current production, the difference being reflected in an inventory reduction. Some of the GNP taken off the market this year reflects not current production but, rather, a drawing down of inventories which were on hand at the beginning of this year. And the inventories on hand at the start of any year's production represent the production of previous years. Consequently, a decline in inventories in any given year means that the economy has purchased more than it has produced during the year; that is, society has consumed all of this year's output plus some of the inventories inherited from previous years' production. Remembering that GNP is a measure of the *current* year's output, we must omit any consumption of past production, that is, any drawing down of inventories, in determining GNP.[2]

Noninvestment transactions We have discussed what investment is; it is equally important to emphasize what investment is not. Specifically, investment does *not* refer to the transfer of paper assets or secondhand tangible assets. The buying of stocks and bonds is excluded from the economist's definition of investment, because such purchases merely transfer the ownership of existing assets. The same holds true of the resale of existing assets. Investment is the construction or manufacture of *new* capital assets. The creation of these earning assets gives rise to jobs and income, not the exchange of claims to existing capital goods.

Gross versus net investment We have broadened our concepts of investment and investment goods to include purchases of machinery and equipment, all construction, and changes in inventories. Now let us focus our attention on the three modifiers, "gross," "private," and "domestic," which national income accountants use in describing investment. The second and third terms tell us, respectively, that we are talking about spending by private business enterprises as opposed to governmental (public) agencies and that the firms doing the investing are American—as opposed to foreign—firms.

The term "gross," however, cannot be disposed of so easily. **Gross private domestic investment** includes the production of *all* investment goods—those which are to replace the machinery, equipment, and buildings used up in the current year's production *plus* any net additions to the economy's stock of capital. In short, gross investment includes both replacement and added investment. On the other hand, we reserve the term **net private domestic investment** to refer only to the added in-

[2] Both *planned* and *unplanned* changes in inventories are included as a part of investment. In the former instance firms may intentionally increase their inventories because aggregate sales are growing. In the latter case an unexpected drop in sales may cause firms to have more unsold goods (larger inventories) than they intended.

vestment which has occurred in the current year. A simple example will make the distinction clear. In 1988 our economy produced about $765 billion worth of capital goods. However, in the process of producing the GNP in 1988, the economy used up some $505 billion worth of machinery and equipment. As a result, our economy added $260 (or $765 minus $505) billion to its stock of capital in 1988. Gross investment was $765 billion in 1988, but net investment was only $260 billion. The difference between the two is the value of the capital used up or depreciated in the production of 1988's GNP.

Net investment and economic growth The relationship between gross investment and *depreciation*—the amount of the nation's capital worn out or used up in a particular year—provides a good indicator of whether our economy is expanding, static, or declining. Figure 9-1 illustrates each of these three cases.

1 EXPANDING ECONOMY When gross investment exceeds depreciation, as in Figure 9-1a, the economy is expanding in the sense that its productive capacity—as measured by its stock of capital goods—is growing. More simply, net investment is a positive figure in an expanding economy. For example, as noted above, in 1988 gross investment was $765 billion, and $505 billion worth of capital goods was consumed in producing that year's GNP. This meant that our economy ended 1988 with $260 billion more capital goods than it had on hand at the start of the year. More bluntly stated, we made a $260 billion addition to our "national factory" in 1988. Increasing the supply of capital goods, you will recall, is a basic means of expanding the productive capacity of the economy.

2 STATIC ECONOMY A stationary or static economy reflects the situation in which gross investment and depreciation are equal. This means the economy is standing pat; it is producing just enough capital to replace what is consumed in producing the year's output—no more and no less. This happened in 1942 during World War II. Private investment was purposely restricted by governmental action to free resources to produce war goods. Hence, in 1942

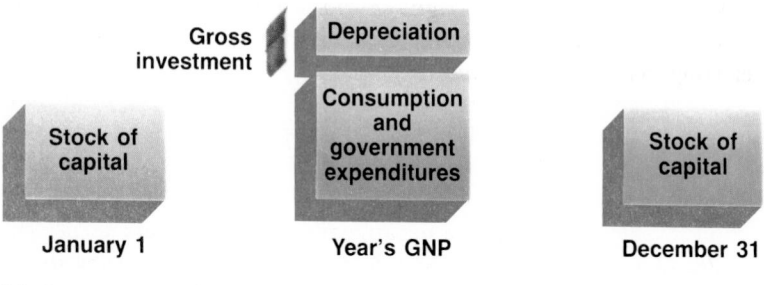

(a) An expanding economy

FIGURE 9-1

Expanding, static and declining economies

In an expanding economy (a), gross investment exceeds depreciation, which means that the economy is making a net addition to its stock of capital facilities. In a static economy (b), gross investment precisely replaces the capital facilities depreciated in producing the year's output, leaving the stock of capital goods unchanged. In a declining economy (c), gross investment is insufficient to replace the capital goods depreciated by the year's production. As a result, the economy's stock of capital declines.

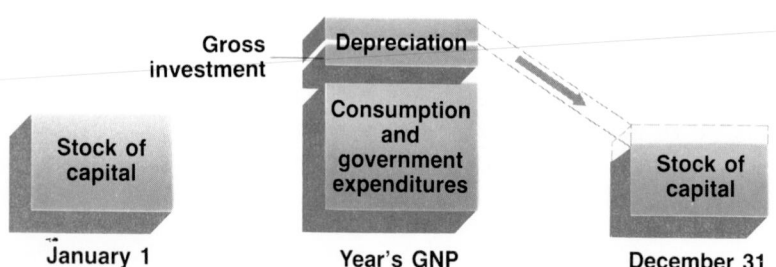

(b) A static economy

(c) A declining economy

gross private investment and depreciation (replacement investment) were approximately equal at $10 billion. This meant that at the end of 1942 our stock of capital was about the same as at the start of that year. In other words, *net* investment was about zero. Our economy was a stationary one in the sense that its productive facilities failed to expand. Figure 9-1b represents the case of a static economy.

3 DECLINING ECONOMY   The unhappy case of a declining economy arises whenever gross investment is less than depreciation, that is, when the economy uses up more capital in a year than it manages to produce. Under such circumstances net investment will be a negative figure—the economy will be *disinvesting*. Depressions foster such circumstances. During bad times, when production and employment are at a low ebb, the nation has a greater

productive capacity than it is currently utilizing. Hence, there is little or no incentive to replace depreciated capital equipment, much less add to the existing stock. Depreciation is likely to exceed gross investment, with the result that the nation's stock of capital is less at the end of the year than it was at the start. This was the case during the heart of the Great Depression. In 1933, for example, gross investment was only $1.6 billion, while the capital consumed during that year was $7.6 billion. Net disinvestment was therefore $6 billion. That is, net investment was a minus $6 billion, indicating that the size of our "national factory" shrunk during that year. Figure 9-1c illustrates the case of a disinvesting, or declining, economy.

We shall use the symbol I to refer to domestic investment spending and attach the subscript g when referring to gross and n when referring to net investment.

GOVERNMENT PURCHASES OF GOODS AND SERVICES (G)

This classification of expenditures *includes* all governmental spending, Federal, state, and local, on the finished products of businesses and all direct purchases of resources—labor, in particular—by government. However, it *excludes* all government transfer payments, because such outlays, as previously noted, do not reflect any current production but merely transfer governmental receipts to certain specific households. The letter G will be used to indicate **government purchases of goods and services.**

NET EXPORTS (X_n)

How do American international trade transactions enter into national income accounting? We can best explain it in this way: First, remember that we are trying to add up all spending in American markets which accounts for or induces the production of goods and services in the American economy. A bit of reflection will lead you to the conclusion that spending by foreigners on American goods will account for American output just as will spending by Americans. Hence, we want to add in what foreigners spend on American goods and services—that

is, we want to add in the value of American exports—in determining GNP by the expenditures approach. On the other hand, we must recognize that a portion of consumption, investment, and government purchases is for goods which have been imported, that is, produced abroad, and therefore does *not* reflect production activity in the United States. The value of imports is subtracted to avoid an overstatement of total production in the United States.

Rather than treat these two items—American exports and imports—separately, our national income accountants merely take the difference between the two. Thus, net exports of goods and services or, more simply, **net exports,** *is the amount by which foreign spending on American goods and services exceeds American spending on foreign goods and services.* For example, if foreigners buy $45 billion worth of American exports and Americans buy $35 billion worth of foreign imports in a given year, net exports would be *plus* $10 billion. It must be emphasized that our definition of net exports might result in a negative figure. If foreigners spend $30 billion on American exports and Americans spend $40 billion on foreign imports, our "excess" of foreign spending over American spending is *minus* $10 billion. Note in Table 9-4 that in 1988 Americans in fact spent $93 billion more on foreign goods and services than foreigners spent on American goods and services, a matter which shall receive our attention in later chapters.

The letter X_n will be used to designate net exports.

$C + I_g + G + X_n =$ GNP

The four categories of expenditures that we have discussed—personal consumption expenditures (C), government expenditures on goods and services (G), gross private domestic investment (I_g), and net exports (X_n)—are comprehensive. They include all possible types of spending. Added together, they measure the market value of the year's output or, in other words, the GNP. That is,

$C + I_g + G + X_n =$ GNP

For 1988 (Table 9-4):

$3226 + $765 + $964 - $93 = $4862

TABLE 9-4 **The income statement for the economy, 1988** *(in billions of dollars)*

Receipts: expenditures approach		Allocations: income approach	
Personal consumption expenditures (C)	$3226	Capital consumption allowance	$505
Gross private domestic investment (I_g)	765	Indirect business taxes	393
Government purchases of goods and services (G)	964	Compensation of employees	2905
Net exports (X_n)	−93	Rents	20
		Interest	392
		Proprietors' income	325
		Corporate income taxes	145
		Dividends	98
		Undistributed corporate profits	79
Gross national product	$4862	Gross national product...............	$4862

Source: U.S. Department of Commerce data. Because of rounding, details may not add up to totals.

The income approach to GNP[3]

How was this $4862 billion of expenditure allocated or distributed as income? It would be most convenient if we could simply say that the total expenditures upon the economy's annual output flow to households as wage, rent, interest, and profit incomes. However, the picture is complicated somewhat by two *nonincome charges* against the value of total output, that is, against GNP. These are (1) a capital consumption allowance, and (2) indirect business taxes.

DEPRECIATION: CAPITAL CONSUMPTION ALLOWANCE

The useful life of most capital equipment extends far beyond the year of purchase. Actual expenditures for capital goods and their productive life are not synchronized in the same accounting period. Hence, to avoid gross understatement of profit and therefore of total income in the year of purchase

---

[3] Some instructors may choose to omit this section because the expenditures approach is more relevant for the analysis of Chapters 11–14.

and overstatement of profit and of total income in succeeding years, individual businesses estimate the useful life of their capital goods and allocate the total cost of such goods more or less evenly over the life of the machinery. The annual charge which estimates the amount of capital equipment used up in each year's production is called "depreciation." Depreciation is essentially a bookkeeping entry designed to provide a more accurate statement of profit income and hence total income provided by a firm in each year.

If profits and total income for the economy as a whole are to be stated accurately, a gigantic depreciation charge must be made against the total receipts of the business sector. This depreciation charge is called a **capital consumption allowance.** Why? Because that is exactly what it is—an allowance for capital goods which have been "consumed" in the process of producing this year's GNP. It is this huge depreciation charge which constitutes the previously noted difference between gross and net investment (I_g and I_n). For present purposes, the significance of this charge is that a part of the business sector's receipts is *not* available for income payments to resource suppliers. Part of the receipts—that is, part of the value of production—is a cost of production which reduces business profits. But, unlike other costs of production, depreciation does not add to anyone's income. In real terms, that is, in terms of physical goods and services, the capital consumption allowance tells us in effect that a portion of this year's GNP must be set aside to replace the machinery and equipment used up in accomplishing its production. In other words, all of GNP cannot be consumed as income by society without impairing the economy's stock of production facilities.

INDIRECT BUSINESS TAXES

The second complicating nonincome charge arises because government levies certain taxes, called **indirect business taxes,** which business firms treat as costs of production and therefore add to the prices of the products they sell. Such taxes include general sales taxes, excises, business property taxes, license fees, and custom duties. We can think of it in this way: A firm produces a product designed to sell at, say, $1. As we have seen, the production of this item creates an equal amount of wages, rental, interest, and profit income. But now government imposes a 3 percent sales tax on all products sold at retail. The retailer merely adds this 3 percent to the price of the product, raising its price from $1 to $1.03 and thereby shifting the burden of the sales tax to consumers.[4]

Obviously, this 3 percent of total receipts which reflects the tax must be paid out to government before the remaining $1 can be paid to households as wage, rent, interest, and profit incomes. Furthermore, this flow of indirect business taxes to government is not earned income, because government contributes nothing directly to the production of the good in return for these sales tax receipts. As a matter of fact, in the case of sales and excise taxes the finished product is being handed to the consumer at the time the tax is levied. In short, we must be careful to exclude indirect business taxes when figuring the total income earned in each year by the factors of production. Part of the value of the annual output reflects the indirect business taxes which are passed along to consumers as

higher product prices. This part of the value of the nation's output is *not* available as either wages, rents, interest, or profits.

Capital consumption allowances and indirect business taxes account for the nonincome allocations listed in Table 9-3. As just noted, what remains are wages, rents, interest, and profits. But, for a variety of reasons, national income statisticians need a more sophisticated breakdown of wages and profits than we have employed thus far in this discussion.

COMPENSATION OF EMPLOYEES

This largest income category comprises primarily the wages and salaries which are paid by businesses and government to suppliers of labor. It also includes an array of wage and salary supplements, in particular payments by employers into social insurance and into a variety of private pension, health, and welfare funds for workers. These wage and salary supplements are a part of the employer's cost of obtaining labor and therefore are treated as a component of the firm's total wage payments.

RENTS

Rents are almost self-explanatory. They consist of income payments received by households which supply property resources.

INTEREST

Interest refers to money income payments which flow from private businesses to the suppliers of money capital. For reasons to be noted later, interest payments made by government are excluded from interest income.

PROPRIETORS' INCOME

What we have loosely termed "profits" is also broken into two basic accounts by national income accountants: One part is called *proprietors' income*

---

[4] In Chapter 33 we shall use supply and demand analysis to find that the shifting of a sales tax is not quite this simple.

or income of unincorporated businesses, and the other, *corporate profits*. Proprietors' income is largely self-defining. It refers to the net income of sole proprietorships, partnerships, and cooperatives. On the other hand, corporate profits cannot be dismissed so easily, because corporate earnings may be distributed in several ways.

CORPORATE PROFITS

Generally speaking, three things can be done with corporate profits: First, a part will be claimed by, and therefore flow to, government as *corporate income taxes*. Second, a part of the remaining corporate profits will be paid out to stockholders as *dividends*. Such payments flow to households, which, of course, are the ultimate owners of all corporations. Third, what remains of corporate profits after both corporate income taxes and dividends have been paid is called *undistributed corporate profits*. These retained corporate earnings, along with capital consumption allowances, are invested currently or in the future in new plants and equipment, thereby increasing the real assets of the investing businesses.

Table 9-4 summarizes our detailed discussions of both the expenditure and income approaches to GNP. The reader will recognize that this is merely a gigantic income statement for the economy as a whole. The left-hand side tells us what the economy produced in 1988 and the total receipts derived from that production. The right-hand side indicates how the income derived from the production of 1988's GNP was allocated. One can determine GNP either by adding up the four types of expenditures on final goods and services or by adding up the nine categories of income and nonincome charges which stem from that output's production. Because output and income are two sides of the same coin, the two sums will necessarily match.

Other social accounts

Our discussion has centered upon GNP as a measure of the economy's annual output. However, there are certain related social accounting concepts of equal importance which can be derived from GNP. To round out our understanding of social accounting, it is imperative that we trace through the process of deriving these related concepts. This procedure will also enhance our understanding of how the expenditure and income approaches to GNP dovetail one another. Our plan of attack will be to start with GNP and make a series of adjustments—subtractions and additions—necessary to the derivation of the related social accounts. The first two of these adjustments we have already mentioned.

NET NATIONAL PRODUCT (NNP)

GNP as a measure of total output has an important defect: It tends to give us a somewhat exaggerated picture of this year's production. Why? *Because it fails to make allowance for that part of this year's output which is necessary to replace the capital goods used up in the year's production.*

Example: Using hypothetical figures, suppose that on January 1, 1990, the economy had $100 billion worth of capital goods on hand. Assume also that during 1990, $40 billion worth of this equipment and machinery is used up in producing a GNP of $800 billion. Thus, on December 31, 1990, the stock of capital goods on hand stands at only $60 billion.

Is it fair to say that the GNP figure of $800 billion measures what this year's production adds to society's well-being? No it is not. It would be much more accurate to subtract from the year's GNP the $40 billion worth of capital goods which must be used to replace the machinery and equipment consumed in producing that GNP. This leaves a *net* output figure of $800 minus $40, or $760 billion.

In short, a figure for *net* output is a better measure of the production available for consumption and additions to the capital stock than is *gross* output. In our system of social accounting, we derive a figure for **net national product** (NNP) by subtracting the capital consumption allowance, which measures replacement investment or the value of the capital used up in a year's production, from GNP. Hence, in 1988:

	Billions
Gross national product	$4862
Capital consumption allowance	−505
Net national product	$4357

NNP, then, is GNP adjusted for depreciation charges. It measures the total annual output which the entire economy—households, businesses, governments, and foreigners—might consume without impairing our capacity to produce in ensuing years.

It is a simple matter, by the way, to adjust Table 9-4 from GNP to NNP. On the income side, we just strike out capital consumption allowance. The other eight allocations should add up to a NNP of $4357 billion. On the expenditure side, one must change *gross* private domestic investment to *net* private domestic investment by subtracting replacement investment as measured by the capital consumption allowance from the former figure. In 1988, a gross investment figure of $765 billion less a depreciation charge of $505 billion results in a net private domestic investment figure of $260 billion and therefore a NNP of $4357 billion.

NATIONAL INCOME (NI)

In analyzing certain problems, we are vitally interested in how much income is *earned* by resource suppliers for their contributions of land, labor, capital, and entrepreneurial ability which go into the year's net production or, alternatively stated, how much it costs society in terms of economic resources to produce this net output. The only component of NNP which does not reflect the current production contributions of economic resources is indirect business taxes. It will be recalled that government contributes nothing directly to production in return for the indirect business tax revenues which it receives; government is *not* considered to be an economic resource. Hence, to get a measure of total wage, rent, interest, and profit incomes

earned from the production of the year's output, we must subtract indirect business taxes from NNP. The resulting figure is called the **national income.** From the viewpoint of resource suppliers, it measures the incomes they have earned for their current contributions to production. From the viewpoint of businesses, national income measures factor or resource costs; national income reflects the market costs of the economic resources which have gone into the creation of this year's output. In 1988:

	Billions
Net national product	$4357
Indirect business taxes	−393
National income	$3964

A glance at Table 9-4 shows that national income can also be obtained through the income approach by simply adding up all the allocations with the exception of capital consumption allowances and indirect business taxes. The seven allocations of GNP which remain after the two nonincome charges have been subtracted constitute the national income.

PERSONAL INCOME (PI)

Personal income (income *received*) and national income (income earned) are likely to differ for the reason that some income which is earned—social security contributions (payroll taxes), corporate income taxes, and undistributed corporate profits—is not actually received by households. Conversely, some income which is received—transfer payments—is not currently earned. Transfer payments, you may recall, are made up of such items as (1) old age and survivors' insurance payments and unemployment compensation, both of which stem from our social security program; (2) welfare payments; (3) a variety of veterans' payments, for example, educational allowances and disability payments; (4) payments out of private pension and welfare programs; and (5) interest payments paid by government and by consumers.[5]

In moving from national income as a measure of income earned to personal income as an indicator of income actually received, we must subtract from national income those three types of income which are earned but not received and add in income received but not currently earned. This is done as follows:

	Billions
National income (income earned)	$3964
Social security contributions	−445
Corporate income taxes	−145
Undistributed corporate profits	−79
Transfer payments	+768
Personal income (income received)	$4063

DISPOSABLE INCOME (DI)

Disposable income is simply personal income less personal taxes. *Personal taxes* are comprised of personal income taxes, personal property taxes, and inheritance taxes, the first of the three being by far the most important. This adjustment is as follows:

	Billions
Personal income (income received before personal taxes)	$4063
Personal taxes	−590
Disposable income (income received after personal taxes)	$3473

[5] Why treat interest payments on government bonds as income *not* currently earned, particularly when interest on the bonds of private firms is included in national income as earned income? The rationale underlying the exclusion is this: Much of the debt has been incurred in connection with (1) war and defense and (2) recessions. Unlike public deficits to finance airports or highways,

Disposable income is the amount of income which households have to dispose of as they see fit. Basically, the choices are two. Remembering that economists conveniently define saving as "not spending," or better, "that part of disposable income which is not spent on consumer goods," it follows that households divide their disposable income between consumption and saving.

RELATIONSHIPS BETWEEN MAJOR SOCIAL ACCOUNTS

We have derived four new social accounting concepts from GNP: (1) net national product (NNP), the market value of the annual output net of capital consumption allowances; (2) national income (NI), income *earned* by the factors of production for their current contributions to production, or the resource costs entailed in getting the year's total output produced; (3) personal income (PI), income *received* by households before personal taxes; and (4) disposable income (DI), income received by households less personal taxes. The relationships between these four concepts are summarized in Table 9-5.

THE CIRCULAR FLOW REVISITED

Figure 9-2 is a synthesis of the expenditures and income approaches to GNP. As a more realistic and more complex expression of the circular flow model of the economy (discussed in Chapters 3 and 6), this figure merits careful study by the reader. Starting at the GNP rectangle in the upper left-hand corner, the expenditures side of GNP is shown by the light blue arrows. Immediately to the right of the GNP rectangle are the nine allocations of GNP and then the various additions and subtractions which are needed in the derivation of NNP, NI, and PI. All allocations or income flows

deficits stemming from the military and recessions yield no production assets (services) to the economy. Hence, interest paid on such debt does *not* reflect the generation of any current output or income. Similar reasoning underlies the inclusion of interest payments by consumers as a part of transfer payments.

TABLE 9-5 **The relationships between GNP, NNP, NI, PI, and DI in 1988**

	Billions
Gross national product (GNP)	$4862
Capital consumption allowance	−505
Net national product (NNP)	$4357
Indirect business taxes	−393
National income (NI)	$3964
Social security contributions	−445
Corporate income taxes	−145
Undistributed corporate profits	−79
Transfer payments	+768
Personal income (PI)	$4063
Personal taxes	−590
Disposable income (DI)	$3473

are depicted by mauve arrows. Note the flow of personal taxes out of PI and the division of DI between consumption and personal saving in the household sector. In the government sector the flows of revenue in the form of four basic types of taxes are denoted on the right; on the left, government disbursements take the form of purchases of goods and services and transfers. The position of the business sector is such as to emphasize, on the left, investment expenditures and, on the right, the three major sources of funds for business investment. Finally, observe the role of the rest of the world in the flow diagram. Spending by people abroad on our exports adds to our GNP, but a portion of our consumption, government, and investment expenditures buy imported products rather than domestically produced goods. The flow emanating from "Rest of the World" correctly indicates that we handle this complication by calculating *net* exports (exports minus imports). Recall that this may be a positive or a negative amount.

The major virtue of Figure 9-2 is that it simultaneously portrays the expenditure and income aspects of GNP, fitting the two approaches to one another. This figure correctly indicates that these flows of expenditure and income are part of a continuous, repetitive process. Cause and effect are

intermingled: Expenditures give rise to income, and out of this income arise expenditures, which again flow to resource owners as income, and so forth.

A final point: The table inside the covers of this book contains an historical summary of the national income accounts since 1929. These data, along with the related statistics which are included, are valuable in providing an empirical underpinning for ensuing discussions of the cyclical ups and downs of the American economy.

Measuring the price level

Thus far our discussion has focused chiefly upon national output and income. Now it is time to consider how the price level is measured.

Measurement of the price level is significant for two reasons. First, it is meaningful for us to know how much the price level has changed, if at all, from one period to another. That is, we need to be aware of whether and to what extent inflation (a rising price level) or deflation (a falling price level) has occurred. Second, because GNP is the market value, or total money value, of all final goods and services produced in a year, money values are used as the common measure when summing a heterogeneous output into a meaningful total. The value of different years' output (GNPs) can be meaningfully compared only if the value of the money itself does not change.

The price level is stated as an index number. A **price index** measures the combined price of a particular collection of goods and services, called a "market basket," in a *given* period relative to the combined price of an identical or similar group of goods and services in a *reference* period. This point of reference, or benchmark, is called the "base year." More formally,

$$\text{Price index in a given year} = \frac{\text{price of market basket in a given year}}{\text{price of the same market basket in the base year}} \times 100$$

By convention, the price ratio between the given year and the base year is multiplied by 100. For example, a price ratio of 2/1 (= 2) is expressed as

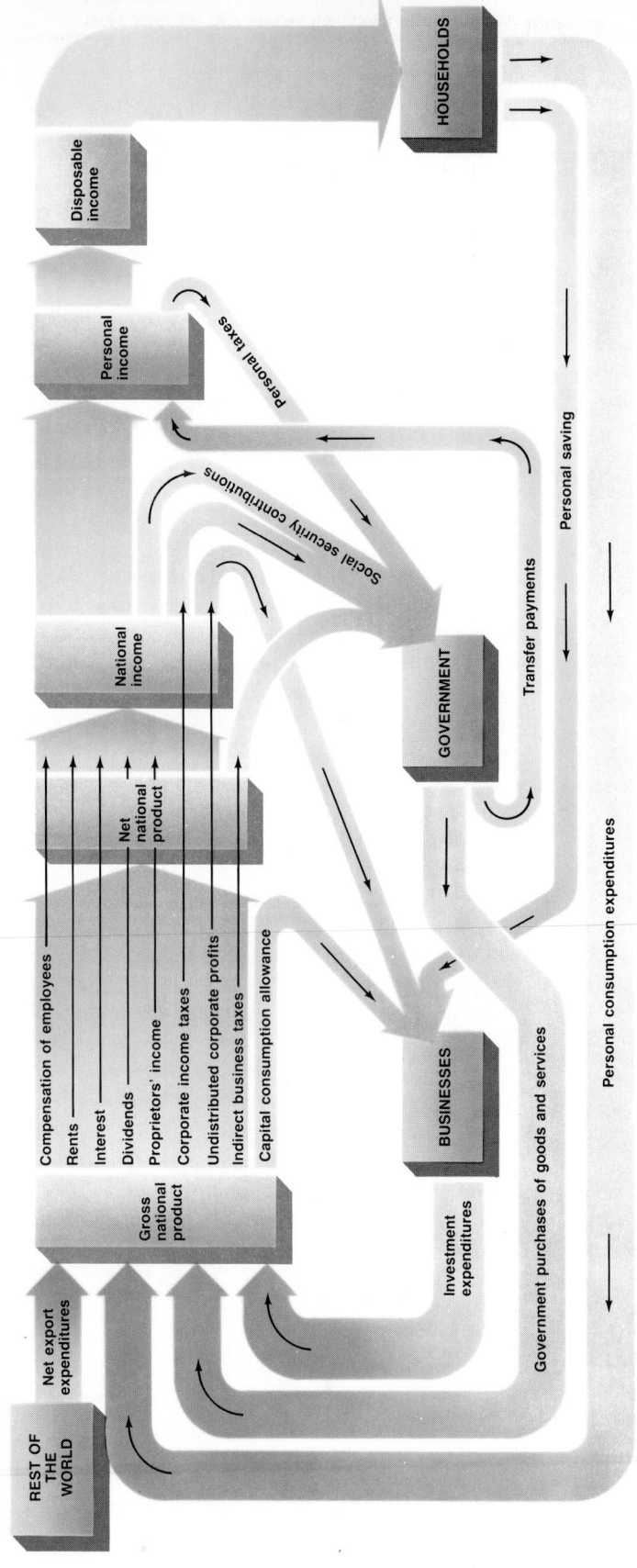

FIGURE 9-2

National output and the flows of expenditure and income

This figure is an elaborate circular flow diagram which fits the expenditures and allocations sides of GNP to one another. The income or allocations flows are shown in mauve; the expenditure flows, in blue. The reader should trace through the income and expenditures flows, relating them to the five basic national income accounting measures.

an index number of 200. Similarly, a price ratio of, say 1/3 (= .33), is expressed as 33.

The Federal government computes indexes of the prices of several different collections or market baskets of goods and services. The best known of these indexes is the consumer price index (CPI), which measures the prices of a fixed market basket of some 300 consumer goods and services purchased by a "typical" urban consumer. The CPI is considered in some detail in this chapter's Last Word. The GNP price index or the **GNP deflator,** however, is more useful than the CPI for measuring the overall price level. The GNP index is broader than the CPI in that the GNP index includes not only the prices of consumer goods and services, but also the prices of investment goods, goods and services purchased by government, and goods and services which enter into world trade. For this reason, the GNP deflator is the price index associated with adjusting money or nominal GNP for price changes. **Nominal GNP** is output valued in terms of the prices existing at the time the output is produced.[6]

Table 9-6 provides a simple example of how a GNP price index or deflator can be computed in a particular year for a hypothetical economy. Observe from column 1 that in 1990 this economy produces only four goods: pizzas (a consumption good); industrial robots (a capital good); paper clips (a good purchased by government); and computer disks (an export good). Suppose that in 1990 the outputs of the four goods are 2, 1, 1, and 1 units, respectively, as shown in column 2. Furthermore, assume that the per unit prices of these four products in 1990 are those shown in column 3. The total price (cost) of the 1990 output therefore is $64, an amount found by summing the expenditures on each of the four goods (column 4).

Now, let us arbitrarily select 1982 as our reference or base year so that we might establish a price index for 1990. The 1982 prices of the components of the 1990 output are listed in column 5 of Table 9-6. From columns 5 and 3, we observe that the prices of pizza and paper clips were lower in 1982 than in 1990, the price of robots was higher, and the price of computer disks did not change. Most

TABLE 9-6 **Computing a GNP price index for 1990 (hypothetical data)**

(1) Product	(2) Quantities in market basket in 1990	(3) Prices of 1990 market basket in 1990	(4) Expenditures on 1990 market basket in 1990 (3) × (2)	(5) Prices of 1990 market basket in 1982 (base year)	(6) Expenditures on 1990 market basket in 1982 (5) × (2)
Pizzas	2	$12	$24	$ 5	$10
Robots	1	18	18	20	20
Paper clips	1	8	8	6	6
Computer disks	1	14	14	14	14
Total price (cost)			$64		$50
GNP price index 1990			$128 \left(= \frac{\$64}{\$50} \times 100\right)$		

[6] Other price indexes in addition to the CPI and the GNP deflator are the *producer price index,* which measures the prices of 3200 commodities at the point of their first commercial sale; the *export price index,* which provides a measure of price changes for all products sold by U.S. businesses to foreign buyers; and the *import price index,* which measures price changes of goods purchased from other countries.

importantly, the total price (cost) of the 1990 output—shown at the bottom of column 6—was $50 in 1982 rather than $64 as in 1990. This fact tells us that the 1990 output would have cost $50 if 1982 prices had persisted. To determine the 1990 price index, we divide the 1990 price of the market basket ($64) by the 1982 price of that same collection of goods ($50). The quotient is then multiplied by 100 to express the price index in its conventional form.

$$\frac{\text{GNP}}{\text{price}}_{\text{index}_{1990}} = \frac{\text{price of market basket}_{1990}}{\text{price of 1990 market basket in the base year}_{1982}} \times 100$$

More concretely,

$$\text{GNP price index}_{1990} = \frac{\$64}{\$50} \times 100 = 128$$

We observe that the price index for 1990 is 128. This index value may be thought of as the price level for 1990.

These same steps can be used to calculate the price level for all years in a series of years. For example, the price index in the 1982 base year is found by discovering the price of the particular collection of goods and services produced in 1982 and comparing this price to the price of that same market basket in the base year. However, in this special case, the "given year" and the "reference year" are both the same. That is,

$$\frac{\text{GNP}}{\text{price}}_{\text{index}_{1982}} = \frac{\text{price of market basket}_{1982}}{\text{price of market basket}_{1982}} \times 100$$

The GNP price index for the 1982 base year therefore is 100. In effect, we automatically set the price index at 100 in the base year.

Likewise, if we wanted to know the GNP price index for 1950, we would determine 1950 output and then estimate what that same or a similar collection of goods and services would have cost in the 1982 base year. For example, if prices on the 1950 output had quadrupled between 1950 and 1982, the price ratio of the market basket would be 1/4 (= .25) and the 1950 GNP price index would be 25 (= .25 × 100).

Once a GNP price index has been constructed for each year in a series of years, comparisons of price levels between years is possible. First exam-

ple: If the price indexes for 1990 and 1982 are 128 and 100, respectively, we can calculate that the price level increased by 28 percent [=(128 − 100)/100] between the two years. Second example: If, as suggested by our previous illustration, the price index for 1950 is 25, we can say that the price level rose by 412 percent [(128 − 25)/25] between 1950 and 1990. Third example: If the price index fell from 100 in 1982 to 98 in 1983, we would know that the price level declined by 2 percent [=(98 − 100)/100].

To summarize: The GNP price index compares the price of each year's output to the price of that same output in the base year or reference year. A series of price indexes for various years enables us to compare price levels between years. An increase in the GNP price index from one year to the next constitutes *inflation;* a decrease in the price index comprises *deflation.*

Nominal and real GNP

Inflation or deflation complicates gross national product because GNP is a price-times-quantity figure. The raw data from which the national income accountants estimate GNP are the total sales figures of business firms; however, these figures embody changes in **both** the quantity of output **and** the level of prices. This means that a change in either the quantity of total physical output or the price level will affect the size of GNP. However, it is the quantity of goods produced and distributed to households which affects their standard of living and not the size of the price tags which these goods bear. The hamburger of 1970 which sold for 65 cents yielded the same satisfaction as will an identical hamburger selling for $2.00 in 1990.

The situation facing our social accountants is this: In gathering statistics from the financial reports of businesses and deriving GNP in various years, government accountants come up with nominal GNP figures. They do **not** know directly to what extent changes in price, on the one hand, and changes in quantity of output, on the other, have accounted for the given increases in nominal GNP. For example, they would not know directly if a 4 percent increase in nominal GNP resulted from a 4 percent rise in output and zero inflation, a zero percent change in output and 4 percent inflation, or some other combination of changes in output and the price level, say, a 2 percent increase in output and 2 percent inflation. The problem, then, is one of adjusting a price-times-quantity figure so it will accurately reflect changes in physical output or quantity, not changes in prices.

Fortunately, national income accountants have been able to revolve this difficulty: They *deflate* GNP for rising prices and *inflate* it when prices are falling. These adjustments give us a picture of GNP for various years *as if* prices and the value of the dollar were constant. A GNP figure which reflects current prices, that is, which is *not* adjusted for changes in the price level, is alternatively called *unadjusted, current dollar, money,* or *nominal GNP.* Similarly, GNP figures which are inflated or deflated for price level changes measure *adjusted, constant dollar,* or **real GNP.**

THE ADJUSTMENT PROCESS

The process for adjusting current dollar or nominal GNP for inflation or deflation is straightforward. The GNP deflator for a specific year, remember, tells us the ratio of that year's prices to the prices of the same goods in the base year. The GNP deflator or GNP price index therefore can be used to inflate or deflate nominal GNP figures. The outcome of this adjustment is that GNP for each year gets expressed in real terms; in other words, *as if* base year prices prevailed. *The simplest and most direct method of deflating or inflating a year's nominal GNP is to express that year's index number in decimal form, and divide it into the nominal GNP.* This yields the same result as the more complex procedure of dividing nominal GNP by the corresponding index number and multiplying the quotient by 100. In equation form:

$$\frac{\text{Nominal GNP}}{\text{price index (in hundredths)}} = \text{real GNP}$$

Or, to illustrate in terms of Table 9-6, nominal GNP in 1990 is $64, the price index for that year is 128 (=1.28 in hundredths), and real GNP in 1990, therefore, is:

$$\frac{\$64}{1.28} = \$50$$

In summary, the real GNP figures measure the value of the total output in the various years *as if* the prices of the products had been constant from the reference or base year throughout all the years being considered. Real GNP thus shows the market value of each year's output measured in terms of constant dollars, that is, dollars which have the same value, or purchasing power, as the base year. Real GNP is clearly superior to nominal GNP as an indicator of the economy's production performance.

INFLATING AND DEFLATING

Table 9-7 provides us with a "real-world" illustration of the **inflating** and **deflating** process. Here we are taking actual nominal GNP figures for selected years and adjusting them with an index of the general price level for these years to obtain real GNP. Note that the base year is 1982. Because the long-run trend has been for the price level to rise, the problem is one of increasing, or *inflating,* the pre-1982 figures. This upward revision of nominal GNP acknowledges that prices were lower in years prior to 1982 and, as a result, nominal GNP figures understated the real output of those years. Column 4 indicates what GNP would have been in all these selected years if the 1982 price level had prevailed. However, the rising price level has caused the nominal GNP figures for the post-1982 years to overstate real output; hence, these figures must be reduced, or *deflated,* as in column 4, in order for us to gauge what GNP would have been in 1984, 1986, and so on, if 1982 prices had actually prevailed. In short, while the *nominal* GNP figures reflect both output and price changes, the *real* GNP figures allow us to estimate changes in real output, because the real GNP figures, in effect, hold the price level constant. Example: For 1988 nominal GNP was $4861.8 billion and the price index was 121.7 or 21.7 percent higher than 1982. To compare 1988's GNP with 1982's we express the 1988 index in hundredths (1.217) and divide it into the nominal GNP of $4861.8 as shown in column 4. The resulting real GNP of $3994.9 is directly comparable to the 1982 base year's GNP because both reflect only changes in output and *not* price level changes. The reader should trace through the computations involved in deriving the real GNP figures

TABLE 9-7 **Adjusting GNP for changes in the price level** (*selected years, in billions of dollars*)

(1) Year	(2) Nominal, or unadjusted, GNP	(3) Price level index,* percent (1982 = 100)	(4) Real, or adjusted, GNP, 1982 dollars
1946	$ 212.4	19.4	$1094.8 (= 212.4 ÷ 0.194)
1951	333.4	25.1	_____
1958	456.8	29.7	$1538.0 (= 456.8 ÷ 0.297)
1964	649.8	32.9	_____
1968	892.7	37.7	$2367.9 (= 892.7 ÷ 0.377)
1972	1212.8	46.5	$2608.1 (= 1212.8 ÷ 0.465)
1974	1472.8	54.0	_____
1980	2732.0	85.7	$3187.8 (= 2732.0 ÷ 0.857)
1982	3166.0	100.0	$3166.0 (= 3166.0 ÷ 1.000)
1984	3772.2	107.7	_____
1986	4240.3	113.9	$3722.8 (= 4240.3 ÷ 1.139)
1988	4861.8	121.7	$3994.9 (= 4861.8 ÷ 1.217)

*U.S. Department of Commerce implicit price deflators.

Source: U.S. Department of Commerce data.

given in Table 9-7 and also determine real GNP for years 1951, 1964, 1974, and 1984, for which the figures have been purposely omitted.[7]

[7] Technical footnote: While this discussion of Table 9-7 provides an intuitive understanding of the process of inflating or deflating GNP with appropriate index numbers, a thorough grasp of the rationale for dividing nominal GNP by an appropriate index to get real GNP calls for further comment. Suppose we want to adjust nominal GNP for 1990 to real GNP (in 1982 prices) so we can determine the growth of real GNP between 1982 and 1990. We know, first, that nominal GNP for 1990 (GNP_{1990}) is equal to the physical output in 1990 (Q_{1990}) times the prices (P_{1990}) at which the output sold. That is,

$$GNP_{1990} = Q_{1990} \cdot P_{1990}$$

We also know from the text's discussion of index numbers that the price index for 1990, using 1982 as the base year, equals the ratio of prices in 1990 to prices in 1982. Thus

$$1990 \text{ price index} = P_{1990}/P_{1982}$$

The text also directs us to divide nominal GNP for 1990

by this 1990 price index to get real GNP for 1990, that is, 1990's output measured at 1982 prices:

$$\frac{GNP_{1990}}{P_{1990}/P_{1982}} = \frac{Q_{1990} \cdot P_{1990}}{P_{1990}/P_{1982}}$$

Inverting and multiplying by the fraction or ratio which represents the 1990 index, we get

$$\frac{GNP_{1990}}{P_{1990}/P_{1982}} = (Q_{1990} \cdot P_{1990}) \cdot \frac{P_{1982}}{P_{1990}}$$

The P_{1990} expressions cancel, leaving

$$\frac{GNP_{1990}}{P_{1990}/P_{1982}} = Q_{1990} \cdot P_{1982}$$

That is to say, by dividing the 1990 nominal GNP (GNP_{1990}) by the 1990 price index (P_{1990}/P_{1982}) we derive real GNP for 1990 or, more specifically, the 1990 output (Q_{1990}) measured in terms of 1982 prices (P_{1982}).

GNP and social welfare

GNP is a reasonably accurate and extremely useful measure of national economic performance. It is not, and was never intended to be, an index of social welfare. GNP is merely a measure of the annual volume of market-oriented activity. And, while GNP may yield a workable impression of material well-being, it is a far cry from being a precise indicator of social welfare:

. . . any number of things could make the Nation better off without raising its real GNP as measured today: we might start the list with peace, equality of opportunity, the elimination of injustice and violence, greater brotherhood among Americans of different racial and ethnic backgrounds, better understanding between parents and children and between husbands and wives, and we could go on endlessly.[8]

There is, nevertheless, a widely held assumption that there should be a strong positive correlation between real GNP and social welfare, that is, greater production should move society toward "the good life." Hence, it is important to understand some of the shortcomings of GNP—some reasons why GNP might understate or overstate real output and why more output will not necessarily make society better off.

NONMARKET TRANSACTIONS

There are certain production transactions which do not appear in the market. Hence, GNP as a measure of the market value of output fails to include these production transactions. Standard examples include the production services of a homemaker, the efforts of the carpenter who repairs his or her own home, or the work of the erudite professor who writes a scholarly but nonremunerative article. Such transactions are *not* reflected in the profit and loss statements of business firms and therefore escape the national income accountants,

[8] Arthur M. Okun, "Social Welfare Has No Price Tag," *The Economic Accounts of the United States: Retrospect and Prospect* (U.S. Department of Commerce, July 1971), p. 129.

causing GNP to be understated. However, some quantitatively large nonmarket transactions, such as that portion of farmers' output which farmers consume themselves, are estimated by national income accountants.

LEISURE

Over a long period of years, leisure has increased very significantly. The workweek declined from about 53 hours at the turn of the century to approximately 40 hours by the end of World War II. Since then the work-week has declined more slowly and is currently about 35 hours. In addition, the expanded availability of paid vacations, holidays, and leave time has reduced the work year. This increased leisure has clearly had a very positive effect upon our well-being. Hence, our system of social accounting understates our well-being by not directly taking cognizance of this. Nor do the accounts reflect the satisfaction—the "psychic income"—which one might derive from one's work.

IMPROVED PRODUCT QUALITY

GNP is a quantitative rather than a qualitative measure. It does not accurately reflect improvements in the quality of products. This is a shortcoming: Quality improvement clearly affects economic well-being every bit as much as does the quantity of goods. To the extent that product quality has improved over time, GNP understates improvement in our material well-being.

THE COMPOSITION AND DISTRIBUTION OF OUTPUT

Changes in the composition and the allocation of total output among specific households may influence economic welfare. GNP, however, reflects only the size of output and does not tell us anything about whether this collection of goods is "right" for society. A switchblade knife and a Beethoven compact disc, both selling for $14.95, are weighted equally in the GNP. And, although the point is a matter for vigorous debate, some economists feel that a more equal distribution of total output would increase national economic well-being. *If these economists are correct, a future trend toward a more nearly equal distribution of GNP would enhance the economic welfare of society. A less nearly equal future distribution would have the reverse effect.* In short, GNP measures the size of the total output but does not reflect changes in the composition and distribution of output which might also affect the economic well-being of society.

PER CAPITA OUTPUT

For many purposes the most meaningful measure of economic well-being is per capita output. Because GNP measures the size of total output, it may conceal or misrepresent changes in the standard of living of individual households in the economy. For example, GNP may rise significantly, but if population is also growing rapidly, the per capita standard of living may be relatively constant or may even be declining.

This is the plight of many of the less developed countries. Consider India. Its national output grew at about 4.3 percent per year over the 1965–1986 period. But annual population growth exceeded 2 percent, resulting in a meager annual increase in per capita output of only 1.8 percent.

GNP AND THE ENVIRONMENT

There are undesirable and much publicized "gross national by-products" which accompany the production and growth of the GNP. These take the form of dirty air and water, automobile junkyards, congestion, noise, and various other forms of environmental pollution. It is quite clear that the costs of pollution affect our economic well-being adversely. These spillover costs associated with the production of the GNP are not now deducted from total output and, hence, GNP overstates our national economic welfare. Ironically, as GNP increases, so does pollution and the extent of this overstatement. As put by one economist, "The ultimate physical product of economic life is garbage."[9] A rising GNP means more garbage—more environmental pollution. In fact, under existing accounting procedures, when a manufacturer pollutes a river and government spends to clean it up, the cleanup expense is added to the GNP while the pollution is not subtracted!

THE UNDERGROUND ECONOMY

Economists agree that there exists a relatively large and perhaps expanding underground or subterranean sector in our economy. Some participants in this sector are engaged in illegal activities such as gambling, loan-sharking, prostitution, and the narcotics trade. These may well be "growth industries." For obvious reasons, persons receiving income from such illegal businesses choose to conceal their incomes. Most of the participants in the underground economy are in legal activities, but do not fully report their incomes to the Internal Revenue Service (IRS). A waiter or waitress may underreport tips from customers. A businessperson may record only a portion of sales receipts for the tax collector. A worker who wants to retain unemployment compensation or welfare benefits may obtain an "off the books" or "cash only" job so there is no record of his or her work activities. To the extent that inflation and high tax burdens squeeze real disposable incomes, the incentive to receive income in forms (for example, cash and barter) which cannot be readily discovered by the IRS is strengthened. Although there is no consensus as to the size of the underground economy, most estimates suggest that it constitutes as much as 5 to 15 percent of the recorded GNP. In 1988, that meant that the official GNP was understated by between $243 and $729 billion. If this additional income had been taxed at, say, a 20 percent average tax rate, the Federal budget deficit for 1988 would have declined from $142 billion to between a $93 billion deficit and a $3 billion surplus.

Additionally, there is some evidence to suggest that the underground economy has been growing relative to the legal economy. If so, then national income accounts will increasingly understate our economy's performance and growth through time.

[9] See the delightful and perceptive essay "Fun and Games with the Gross National Product" by Kenneth E. Boulding, in Harold W. Helfrich, Jr. (ed.), *The Environmental Crisis* (New Haven: Yale University Press, 1970), p. 162.

Finally, to the extent that a proportion of the population is involved in illegal activities or in legal activities wherein income is concealed, our official unemployment statistics will be overstated. And this may pose a problem for policy makers. If the existence of the underground economy distorts such basic economic indicators as GNP and the unemployment rate, policies based upon these indicators may be inappropriate and harmful. Thus an understated GNP and an overstated unemployment rate might prompt policy makers to stimulate the economy. But, as we shall find in Chapter 14, the stimulus may cause unwanted inflation rather than increases in real output and employment.[10]

CHAPTER SUMMARY

1 Gross national product (GNP), a basic measure of society's economic performance, is the market value of all final goods and services produced in a year. Intermediate goods, nonproduction transactions, and secondhand sales are purposely excluded in calculating GNP.

2 GNP may be calculated by summing total expenditures on all final output or by summing the income derived from the production of that output.

3 By the expenditures approach GNP is determined by adding consumer purchases of goods and services, gross investment spending by businesses, government purchases of goods and services, and net exports; GNP = $C + I_g + G + X_n$.

4 Gross investment can be divided into **a** replacement investment (required to maintain the nation's stock of capital at its existing level), and **b** net investment (the net increase in the stock of capital). Positive net investment is associated with a growing economy; negative net investment with a declining economy.

5 By the income or allocations approach GNP is calculated as the sum of compensation to employees, rents, interest, proprietors' income, corporate income taxes, dividends, undistributed corporate profits, and the two nonincome charges (capital consumption allowance and indirect business taxes).

6 Other important national income accounting measures are derived from the GNP. Net national product

(NNP) is GNP less the capital consumption allowance. National income (NI) is total income earned by resource suppliers; it is found by subtracting indirect business taxes from NNP. Personal income (PI) is the total income paid to households prior to any allowance for personal taxes. Disposable income (DI) is personal income after personal taxes have been paid. DI measures the amount of income households have available to consume or save.

7 Price indexes are computed by comparing the price of a specific collection or "market basket" of output in a given period to the price (cost) of the same market basket in a base period and multiplying the outcome (quotient) by 100. The GNP deflator is the price index used to adjust nominal GNP to account for inflation or deflation and thereby to obtain real GNP.

8 Nominal (current dollar) GNP measures each year's output valued in terms of the prices prevailing in that year. Real (constant dollar) GNP measures each year's output in terms of the prices which prevailed in a selected base year. Because it is adjusted for price level changes, real GNP measures the level of production activity.

9 The various national income accounting measures exclude nonmarket and illegal transactions, changes in leisure and product quality, the composition and distribution of output, and the environmental effects of production. Nevertheless, these measures are reasonably accurate and very useful indicators of the nation's economic performance.

TERMS AND CONCEPTS

national income accounting

gross national product (GNP)

final and intermediate goods

double counting

value added

expenditures and income approaches

personal consumption expenditures

gross and net private domestic investment

government purchases of goods and services

net exports

capital consumption allowance

indirect business taxes

net national product

national income

personal income

disposable income

price index

GNP deflator

nominal GNP

real GNP

inflating and deflating

[10] The interested student should consult Joel F. Houston, "The Underground Economy: A Troubling Issue for Policymakers," *Business Review* (Federal Reserve Bank of Philadelphia), September–October 1987, pp. 3–12.

QUESTIONS AND STUDY SUGGESTIONS

1 "National income statistics are a powerful tool of economic understanding and analysis." Explain this statement. "An economy's output is its income." Do you agree?

2 Why do national income accountants include only final goods in measuring total output? How do GNP and NNP differ?

3 What is the difference between gross private domestic investment and net private domestic investment? If you were to determine net national product through the expenditures approach, which of these two measures of investment spending would be appropriate? Explain.

4 Why are changes in inventories included as a part of investment spending? Suppose inventories declined by $1 billion during 1990. How would this affect the size of gross private domestic investment and gross national product in 1990? Explain.

5 The following is a list of national income figures for a given year. All figures are in billions. The ensuing questions will ask you to determine the major national income measures by both the expenditure and income methods. The answers derived by each approach should be the same.

Personal consumption expenditures	$245
Transfer payments	12
Rents	14
Capital consumption allowance (depreciation)	27
Social security contributions	20
Interest	13
Proprietors' income	31
Net exports	3
Dividends	16
Compensation of employees	221
Indirect business taxes	18
Undistributed corporate profits	21
Personal taxes	26
Corporate income taxes	19
Corporate profits	56
Government purchases of goods and services	72
Net private domestic investment	33
Personal saving	16

LAST WORD

The consumer price index

The consumer price index is the most widely reported measure of inflation; therefore, it is important to have some knowledge of its characteristics and limitations.

The consumer price index (CPI) attempts to measure changes in the prices of a market basket of some 300 goods and services purchased by urban consumers. The composition of this market basket was determined on the basis of a survey of the spending patterns of urban consumers over the 1982–1984 period. The index is a "fixed-weight" index in that the composition of the market basket is the same in each year as in the base period (1982–1984).

The "fixed-weight" approach used to construct the CPI differs from the technique used to construct the GNP deflator discussed in this chapter. We previously indicated that the GNP deflator is found by establishing the market basket on the basis of the composition of output in *each* particular year and then determining what the price of that same composition of goods would have been in the base year (Table 9-6). Hence, the composition of the market basket used to construct the GNP index changes from year to year. But in the case of the CPI, the composition of the market basket is fixed in the base period and is assumed not to change from one period to another. The

a Using the above data, determine GNP and NNP by both the expenditure and income methods.

b Now determine NI (1) by making the required subtractions from GNP, and (2) by adding up the types of

reason for this assumption is that the purpose of the CPI is to measure changes in the costliness of a constant standard of living. There are two well-known problems associated with the CPI which lead critics to conclude that this price index overstates increases in the cost of living.

First, consumers in fact do change their spending patterns—the composition of the market basket changes—particularly in response to changes in relative prices. If the price of beef rises, consumers will substitute away from beef and buy fish, veal, or mutton instead. This means that over time consumers are in fact buying a market basket which contains relatively more of the relatively low-priced and relatively less of the relatively high-priced goods and services. The fixed-weight CPI assumes these substitutions have not occurred and it therefore overstates the actual cost of living.

Second, the CPI does not take qualitative improvements into account. To the extent that goods and services have improved since 1982–1984, their prices should be higher. Thus we ought to pay more for medical care today than in the early 1980s because it is generally of higher quality. The same can be said for computers, automobile tires, stereos, and a myriad of other items. The CPI, however, assumes all of the increase in the money or nominal value of the market basket is due solely to inflation rather than quality improvements. Again, the CPI tends to overstate the rate of inflation.

In general, economists feel that the CPI overstates the rate of inflation and perhaps by a significant margin. So what? The major consequence is that this overstatement may contribute to ongoing inflation because the incomes of large numbers of people are tied directly or indirectly to changes in the CPI. For example, some 38 million social security recipients have their monthly check tied or "indexed" to the CPI. And an estimated 4 or 5 million workers have cost-of-living adjustments (COLAs) in their collective bargaining agreements. When prices rise, their money wages automatically increase to further fuel inflation. Furthermore, the wage expectations and demands of virtually all workers—union or nonunion, blue- or white-collar—are linked to the cost of living as measured by the CPI. Thus the CPI is not merely a vehicle for measuring the problem of inflation; it may be part of the problem!

Another consequence of an overstated CPI stems from the "indexing" of personal income tax brackets. This indexing—or adjusting tax brackets upward to account for the rate of inflation—was begun in 1985 to resolve an inequity in the personal income tax. Specifically, the intent of indexing is to prevent inflation from pushing households into higher tax brackets even though their real incomes have not increased. For example, a 10 percent increase in your *nominal* income might put you in a higher marginal tax bracket and increase the proportion of your income paid in taxes (Table 8-2). But if product prices are also rising by 10 percent, your *real* or inflation-adjusted income has remained constant. The result would be an unintended redistribution of real income from taxpayers to the Federal government. The purpose of indexing tax brackets was simply to prevent this redistribution. However, to the extent that the CPI *overstates* inflation, indexing will tend to reduce government's tax share. The Federal government will be deprived of substantial amounts of tax revenue and real income will tend to be redistributed from government to taxpayers.

income which comprise NI.
c Make those adjustments of NI required in deriving PI.
d Make the required adjustments from PI (as determined in 5c) to obtain DI.

6 Use the concepts of gross and net investment to distinguish between an expanding, a static, and a declining economy. "In 1933 net private domestic investment was minus $6 billion. This means in that particular year the economy produced no capital goods at all." Do you agree? Explain: "Though net investment can be positive, negative, or zero, it is quite impossible for gross investment to be zero."

7 Define net exports. Explain how the United States' exports and imports each affect domestic production. Suppose foreigners spend $7 billion on American exports in a given year and Americans spend $5 billion on imports from abroad in the same year. What is the amount of America's net exports? Explain how net exports might be a negative amount.

8 Given the following national income accounting data, compute **a** GNP, **b** NNP, and **c** NI. All figures are in billions.

Compensation of employees	$194.2
U.S. exports of goods and services	13.4
Capital consumption allowance	11.8
Government purchases of goods and services	59.4
Indirect business taxes	12.2
Net private domestic investment	52.1
Transfer payments.................................	13.9
U.S. imports of goods and services	16.5
Personal taxes....................................	40.5
Personal consumption expenditures	219.1

9 Why do national income accountants compare the market value of the total outputs in various years rather than actual physical volumes of production? Explain. What problem is posed by any comparison over time of the market values of various total outputs? How is this problem resolved?

10 Suppose that in 1974 the total output of a hypothetical economy consisted of three goods—X, Y, and Z— produced in the following quantities: X = 4, Y = 1, Z = 3. Also suppose that in 1974 the prices of X, Y, and Z were as follows: X = $3, Y = $12, and Z = $5. Finally, assume that in 1982 the prices of these goods were X = $5, Y = $10, and Z = $10. Determine the GNP price index for 1974, using 1982 as the base year. By what percent did the price level rise between 1974 and 1982?

11 The following table shows nominal GNP and an appropriate price index for a group of selected years. Compute real GNP. Indicate in each calculation whether you are inflating or deflating the nominal GNP data.

Year	Nominal GNP, billions	Price level index, percent (1982 = 100)	Real GNP, billions
1947	$ 235.2	22.1	$_____
1956	428.2	28.1	$_____
1967	816.4	35.9	$_____
1973	1359.3	49.5	$_____
1978	2249.7	72.2	$_____
1983	3405.7	103.9	$_____

12 Which of the following are actually included in deriving this year's GNP? Explain your answer in each case.
  a Interest on an AT&T bond
  b Social security payments received by a retired factory worker
  c The services of a painter in painting the family home
  d The income of a dentist
  e The money received by Smith when he sells a 1983 Chevrolet to Jones
  f The monthly allowance which a college student receives from home
  g Rent received on a two-bedroom apartment
  h The money received by Mac when he resells this year's model Plymouth to Ed
  i Interest received on government bonds
  j A 2-hour decline in the length of the workweek
  k The purchase of an AT&T bond
  l A $2 billion increase in business inventories
  m The purchase of 100 shares of GM common stock
  n The purchase of an insurance policy
  o Wages paid to a domestic servant
  p The market value of a homemaker's services
  q The purchase of a Renaissance painting by a public art museum

13 What would be the most likely effect on real GNP of each of the following: **a** a law mandating an increase in the workweek from 40 hours to 50 hours for every able-bodied adult; **b** the legalization of all of the activities presently undertaken in the underground economy; and **c** a $1 million increase in the production of burglar alarms offset by a $1 million decline in the provision of prenatal health care services? Would society's well-being in each of these situations change in the same direction as the change in real GNP? Explain.

CHAPTER 10

Macroeconomic instability: unemployment and inflation

In an ideal economy, real GNP would expand over time at a brisk, steady pace. Additionally, the price level, as measured by the GNP deflator or the consumer price index, would remain constant or only slowly rise. The result would be neither significant unemployment nor inflation. But experience dramatizes that full employment and a stable price level cannot be taken for granted. Hence, in this and the next several chapters we explore the problem of achieving the goals of full employment and price level stability.

This chapter proceeds as follows: First, we establish an overview of the business cycle—the periodic fluctuations in output, employment, and price levels which characterize our economy. Second, we look in more detail at unemployment: What are the various types of unemployment? How is unemployment measured? Why is unemployment an economic problem? Third, our attention turns to inflation—a serious problem which plagued us throughout the 1970s and into the early 1980s. What are inflation's causes? And consequences?

Overview of the business cycle

Our society seeks economic growth *and* full employment *and* price level stability along with other less quantifiable goals (Chapter 1). The broad spectrum of American economic history reflects remarkable economic growth. Technological progress, rapid increases in productive capacity, and a standard of living which is among the highest in the world are strategic facets of the dynamic character in our economy.

THE HISTORICAL RECORD

But our long-run economic growth has not been steady. Rather, it has been interrupted by periods of economic instability as Figure 10-1 reveals. Periods of rapid economic expansion have sometimes been marred by inflation, that is, increases in the price level. At other times, expansion has given way to recession and depression, that is, low levels of employment and output. Indeed, on a few occasions—most notably in the 1970s and early 1980s—we have had the unhappy experience of a rising price level and abnormally high unemployment simultaneously. In short, the long-term trend of economic growth has been interrupted and complicated by both unemployment and inflation.

PHASES OF THE CYCLE

Generally speaking, the term **business cycle** refers to the recurrent ups and downs in the level of economic activity which extend over a period of several years. Individual business cycles vary substantially in duration and intensity. Yet all embody common phases which are variously labeled by different economists. Figure 10-2 shows us an idealized business cycle. We begin with a cyclical *peak*

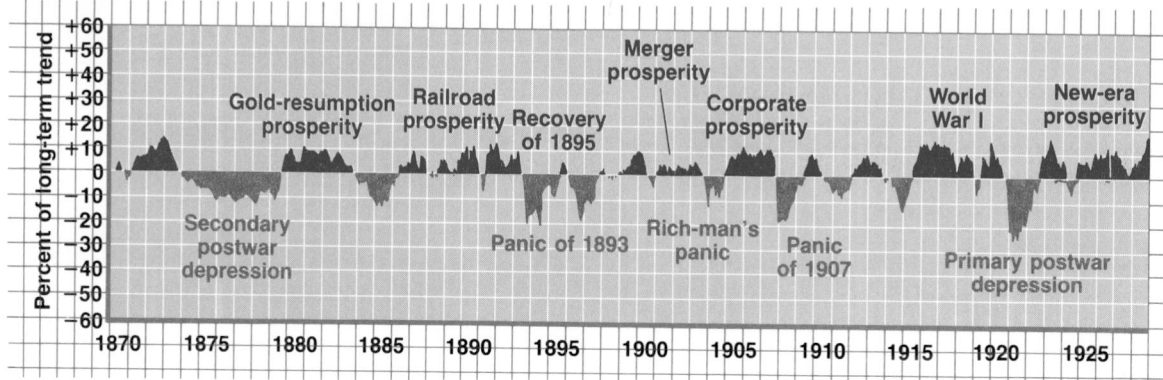

FIGURE 10-1

American business-cycle experience

As indicated by this chart which shows deviations from the long-run trend line of economic activity, the American economy has encountered periods of prosperity and depression. (AmeriTrust Company, Cleveland)

where the economy is at full employment and the national output is also at, or very close to, capacity. The price level is likely to be rising during this cyclical phase, and for reasons we will explore in later chapters, the expansion of business activity is short-circuited. In the ensuing *recession* output and

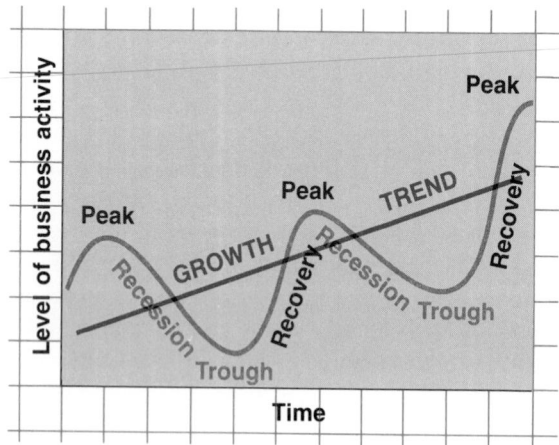

FIGURE 10-2

The business cycle

Economists distinguish between four phases of the business cycle and recognize that the duration and strength of each phase is highly variable. A recession, for example, need not always entail serious and prolonged unemployment. Nor need a cyclical peak always entail full employment.

employment both decline, but prices in our economy tend to be relatively inflexible in a downward direction. The price level is likely to fall only if the recession is severe and prolonged—that is, if a "depression" occurs. In this regard, an old one-liner is that "A recession is when a neighbor loses his job; a depression is when *you* lose *your* job!" The *trough* of the recession or depression is where output and employment "bottom out" at their lowest levels. Finally, in the *recovery* phase the economy's levels of output and employment expand toward full employment. As recovery intensifies, the price level may begin to rise prior to the realization of full employment and capacity production.

Despite common phases, specific business cycles vary greatly in duration and intensity. Indeed, some economists prefer to talk of business *fluctuations,* rather than *cycles,* because cycles imply regularity while fluctuations do not. The Great Depression of the 1930s seriously undermined the level of business activity for an entire decade. By comparison, the business declines of 1924 and 1927 were minor in both intensity and duration, as most of our post-World War II recessions also have been.

CAUSATION: A FIRST GLANCE

Historically, economists have suggested a variety of theories to explain fluctuations in business activ-

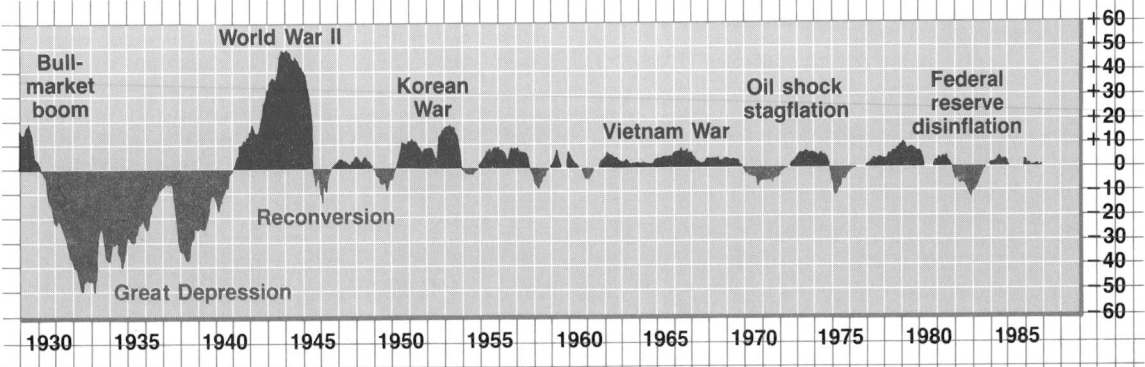

ity. Some theories center upon innovation, contending that major innovations such as the railroad, the automobile, or synthetic fibers have a great impact upon investment and consumption spending and therefore upon output, employment, and the price level. But these major innovations occur irregularly and thus contribute to the variability of economic activity. Other economists have explained the business cycle in terms of political and random events, as is suggested by some of the labeling in Figure 10-1. Wars, for example, can be economically very disruptive. A virtually insatiable demand for war goods during hostilities can generate a period of overfull employment and sharp inflation, frequently followed by an economic slump when peace returns and military spending plummets. Still other economists view the cycle as a purely monetary phenomenon. When government creates too much money, an inflationary boom is generated; a relative paucity of money will precipitate a declining output and unemployment.

Despite this diversity of opinion, most economists believe that the immediate determinant of the levels of national output and employment is the level of total or aggregate expenditures. In an economy that is largely market-directed, businesses produce goods and services only if they can be sold profitably. Crudely stated, if total spending is low, many businesses will not find it profitable to produce a large volume of goods and services. Hence, output, employment, and the level of incomes will all be low. A higher level of total spending will mean that more production will be profitable; thus, output, employment, and incomes will all be

higher also. Once the economy reaches full employment, real output becomes fixed and added spending will simply pull up the price level. Later in this chapter we will find that the relationship between aggregate spending and the price level is more complex and that, in fact, inflation may arise from causes other than a change in total spending.

NONCYCLICAL FLUCTUATIONS

It must *not* be concluded that all changes in business activity are due to the business cycle. On the one hand, there are **seasonal variations** in business activity. For example, the pre-Christmas and pre-Easter buying rushes cause considerable fluctuations each year in the tempo of business activity, particularly in the retail industry. Agriculture, the automobile industry, construction—all are subject to some degree of seasonality.

Business activity is also subject to a **secular trend.** The secular trend of an economy is its expansion or contraction over a long period of years, for example, 25, 50, or 100 years. We simply note at this juncture that the long-run secular trend for American capitalism has been one of rather remarkable expansion (Chapter 21). For present purposes, the importance of this long-run expansion is that the business cycle involves fluctuations in business activity around a long-run growth trend. Note that in Figure 10-1 cyclical fluctuations are measured as deviations from the secular growth trend and that the idealized cycle of Figure 10-2 is drawn against a trend of growth.

CYCLICAL IMPACT: DURABLES AND NONDURABLES

The business cycle is pervasive; it is felt in virtually every nook and cranny of the economy. The interrelatedness of the elements of the economy allows few, if any, to escape the cold hand of depression or the fever of inflation. Yet we must keep in mind that various individuals and various segments of the economy are affected in different ways and in different degrees by the business cycle.

Insofar as production and employment are concerned, those industries producing capital goods and consumer durables are typically hit hardest by recession. The construction industry is particularly vulnerable. Output and employment in nondurable consumer goods industries are usually less sensitive to the cycle. Industries and workers producing housing and commercial buildings, heavy capital goods, farm implements, automobiles, refrigerators, gas ranges, and similar products bear the brunt of bad times. Conversely, these "hard goods" industries seem to be stimulated most by expansion. Two facts go far to explain the vulnerability of these industries to the cycle.

1 Postponability Within limits, the purchase of hard goods is postponable. As the economy slips into bad times, producers frequently forestall the acquisition of more modern production facilities and the construction of new plants. The business outlook simply does not warrant increases in the stock of capital goods. In all probability the firm's present capital facilities and buildings will still be usable and in excess supply. In good times, capital goods are usually replaced before they are completely depreciated. When recession strikes, however, business firms will patch up their outmoded equipment and make it do. As a result, investment in capital goods will decline sharply. Chances are that some firms, having excess plant capacity, will not even bother to replace all the capital which they are currently consuming. Net investment for them may be a negative figure.

Much the same holds true for consumer durables. When recession rolls around and the family budget must be trimmed, it is likely that plans for the purchases of durables such as major appliances and automobiles will first feel the ax. People decide to make repairs to their old appliances and cars rather than buy new models. Food and clothing—consumer nondurables—are a different story. A family must eat and must clothe itself. These purchases are much less postponable. True, to some extent the quantity and most certainly the quality of these purchases will decline. But not so much as is the case with durables.

2 Monopoly power Most industries producing capital goods and consumer durables are industries of high concentration, wherein a relatively small number of large firms dominate the market. As a result, these firms have sufficient monopoly power to temporarily resist lowering prices by restricting output in the face of a declining demand. Consequently, the impact of a fall in demand centers primarily upon production and employment. The reverse holds true in nondurable, or soft, goods industries, which are for the most part quite highly competitive and characterized by low concentration. Price declines cannot be resisted in such industries, and the impact of a declining demand falls to a greater extent on prices than upon the levels of production. Figure 10-3 graphically displays this point. It shows the percentage declines in price and quantity which occurred in ten selected industries as the economy fell from peak prosperity in 1929 to the depth of depression in 1933. Speaking very generally, high-concentration industries make up the top half of the table and low-concentration industries the bottom half. Note the drastic production declines and relatively modest price declines of the high-concentration industries on the one hand, and the large price declines and relatively small output declines which took place in the low-concentration industries on the other.

Armed with this thumbnail sketch of the business cycle, let us now examine unemployment and inflation in more detail.

Unemployment

"Full employment" is an elusive concept to define. A person might initially interpret it to mean that everyone who is in the labor market—100 percent of the labor force—is employed. But such is not the

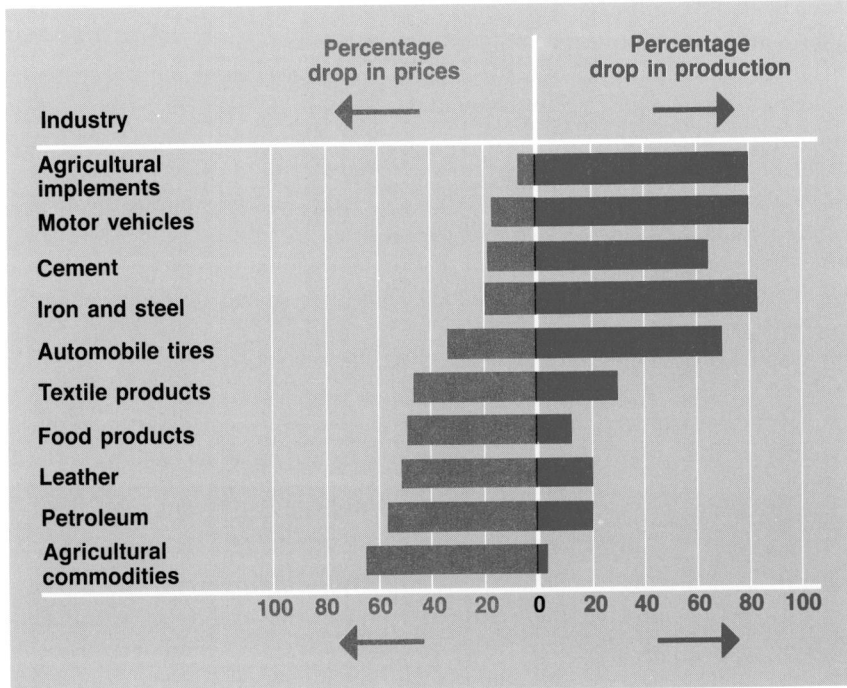

FIGURE 10-3

Relative price and production declines in ten industries, 1929–1933

The high-concentration industries shown in the top half were characterized by relatively small price declines and large declines in output during the early years of the Great Depression. In the low-concentration industries of the bottom half, price declines were relatively large, and production fell by relatively small amounts. [Gardiner C. Means, *Industrial Prices and Their Relative Flexibility* (Washington, 1953), p. 8.]

case. Some unemployment is regarded as normal or warranted.

TYPES OF UNEMPLOYMENT

Let us approach the task of defining full employment by distinguishing among several different types of unemployment.

Frictional unemployment Given freedom to choose occupations and jobs, at any point in time some workers will be "between jobs." Some workers will be in the process of voluntarily switching jobs. Others will have been fired and are seeking reemployment. Still others will be temporarily laid off from their jobs because of seasonality (for example, bad weather in the construction industry) or model changeovers (as in the automobile industry). And there will be some workers, particularly young people, searching for their first jobs. As these people find jobs or are called back from temporary layoffs, other job seekers and temporarily laid-off workers will replace them in the "unemployment pool." Therefore, even though the specific individuals

who are unemployed for these reasons change from month to month, this type of unemployment persists.

Economists use the term **frictional unemployment**—which consists of *search unemployment* and *wait unemployment*—for the group of workers who are either searching for jobs or waiting to take jobs in the near future. The adjective "frictional" correctly implies that the labor market does not operate perfectly and instantaneously—that is, without friction—in matching workers and jobs.

Frictional unemployment is regarded as inevitable and, at least in part, desirable. Why desirable? Because many workers who are voluntarily "between jobs" are moving from low-paying, low-productivity jobs to higher-paying, higher-productivity positions. This means more income for the workers and a better allocation of labor resources—and therefore a larger real output—for the economy as a whole.

Structural unemployment Frictional unemployment shades into a second category, called **structural unemployment.** In this regard, economists use the term "structural" in the sense of "compositional." Important changes occur over time in the "structure" of consumer demand and in technology, which in turn alter the "structure" of the total demand for labor. Because of such changes, some particular skills will be in less demand or may even become obsolete. The demand for other skills will be expanding, including new skills which previously did not exist. Unemployment results because the composition of the labor force does not respond quickly or completely to the new structure of job opportunities. As a result, some workers find that they have no readily marketable talents; their skills and experience have been rendered obsolete and unwanted by changes in technology and consumer demand. Similarly, the geographic distribution of jobs is constantly changing. Witness the migration of industry and employment opportunities from the Snow Belt to the Sun Belt over the past decade.

Examples: (1) Years ago, highly skilled glass-blowers were thrown out of work by the invention of bottle-making machines. (2) More recently, unskilled and inadequately educated blacks have been dislodged from agriculture in the south as a result of the mechanization of agriculture. Many of these workers have migrated to the northern cities and have suffered prolonged unemployment because of insufficient skills. (3) An American shoe worker, unemployed because of import competition, cannot become, say, a computer programmer without considerable retraining and perhaps also geographic relocation. (4) Finally, many oil-field workers in the "oil-patch" states of the United States found themselves structurally unemployed when the world price of oil declined dramatically in the 1980s. At the lower price of oil, less drilling and other oil-related activity took place and consequently widespread layoffs resulted.

The distinction between frictional and structural unemployment is hazy. The difference essentially is that frictionally unemployed workers have salable skills, whereas structurally unemployed workers are not readily reemployable without retraining, additional education, and possibly geographic relocation. Frictional unemployment tends to be more of a short-term character, while structural unemployment is more long-term and therefore regarded as more serious.

Cyclical unemployment By **cyclical unemployment** we mean unemployment caused by the reces-sion phase of the business cycle, that is, by a deficiency of aggregate or total spending. As the overall demand for goods and services decreases, employment falls, and unemployment rises. For this reason, cyclical unemployment is sometimes referred to as *deficient-demand unemployment.* During the recession year 1982, for example, the unemployment rate rose to 9.7 percent. Cyclical unemployment at the depth of the Great Depression in 1933 reached about 25 percent of the labor force.

DEFINING "FULL EMPLOYMENT"

Full employment does *not* mean zero unemployment. Economists regard frictional and structural unemployment as essentially unavoidable; hence, "full employment" is defined as something less than employment of 100 percent of the labor force. Specifically, the **full-employment unemployment rate** is equal to the total of frictional and structural unemployment. Stated differently, the full-employment unemployment rate is achieved when cyclical unemployment is zero. The full-employment rate of unemployment is alternatively referred to as the **natural rate of unemployment.** The real level of national output which is associated with the natural rate of unemployment is called the economy's **potential output.** That is, the economy's potential output is the real output forthcoming when the economy is "fully employed."

From a slightly different vantage point the full or natural rate of unemployment results when labor markets are in balance in the sense that the number of job seekers equals the number of job vacancies. The natural rate of unemployment is some positive amount because it takes time for frictionally unemployed job seekers to find appropriate job openings. And, with regard to the structurally unemployed, it also takes time to achieve the skills and geographic relocation needed for reemployment. If the number of job seekers exceeds the available vacancies, labor markets are not in balance; there is a deficiency of aggregate demand and cyclical unemployment is present. On the other hand, if aggregate demand is excessive there will be a "shortage" of labor in the sense that the number of job vacancies will exceed the number of workers seeking employment. In this situation the actual rate of unemployment is below the natural rate.

This situation of unusually "tight" labor markets is associated with inflation.

The concept of the natural rate of unemployment merits elaboration in two respects.

First, the term does *not* mean that the economy will always operate at the natural rate and thereby realize its potential output. We have already suggested in our brief discussion of the business cycle that the economy frequently operates at an unemployment rate in excess of the natural rate. On the other hand, the economy may on rare occasions achieve an unemployment rate lower than the natural rate. For example, during World War II, when the natural rate was on the order of 3 or 4 percent, the pressure of wartime production resulted in an almost unlimited demand for labor. Overtime work was common as was "moonlighting" (holding more than one job). Furthermore, the government froze some people working in "essential" industries in their jobs, reducing frictional unemployment. The actual rate of unemployment was below 2 percent in the entire 1943–1945 period and actually dropped to 1.2 percent in 1944. The economy was producing beyond its potential output, but incurred considerable inflationary pressure in the process.

The second point is that the natural rate of unemployment itself is *not* an immutable constant, but rather is subject to revision because of the shifting demographics of the labor force or institutional changes (changes in society's laws and customs). For example, in the 1960s it was commonly held that this unavoidable minimum of frictional and structural unemployment was about 4 percent of the labor force. In other words, full employment was said to exist when 96 percent of the labor force was employed. But today, economists generally agree that the natural rate of unemployment is on the order of 5 to 6 percent.

Why is the natural rate of unemployment higher today than in the 1960s? First, the demographic makeup of the labor force has changed. In particular, women and young workers—who traditionally have quite high unemployment rates—have become relatively more important in the labor force. Second, institutional changes have occurred. For example, our unemployment compensation program has been expanded both in terms of numbers of workers covered and size of benefits. This is important because, by cushioning the economic impact of unemployment, unemployment compensation permits unemployed workers to engage in a more leisurely job search, thereby increasing frictional unemployment and the overall unemployment rate.

MEASURING UNEMPLOYMENT

The controversy over the full employment rate of unemployment is complicated by problems encountered in the actual measurement of the rate of unemployment. Table 10-1 is a helpful starting point. The total population is divided into three broad groups. One group is comprised of those under 16 years of age and people who are institutionalized, for example, in mental hospitals or correctional institutions. This first group encompasses people who are not considered to be potential members of the labor force. A second group, labeled "not in labor force," are adults who are potential workers, but for some reason—they are homemakers, in school, or retired—are not employed and are not seeking work. The remaining group is the **labor force,** which constituted about 49 percent of the total population in 1988. The labor force is essentially all people who are able and willing to work. Both those who are employed and those who are unemployed but actively seeking work are counted as being in the labor force. The *unemployment rate* is the percentage of the labor force which is unemployed:

$$\frac{\text{Unemployment}}{\text{rate}} = \frac{\text{unemployment}}{\text{labor force}} \times 100$$

In 1988 the unemployment rate was

$$5.5\% = \frac{6{,}701{,}000}{121{,}669{,}000} \times 100$$

TABLE 10-1 **The labor force, employment, and unemployment, 1988 (in thousands)**

Total population	246,113
Less: Under 16 and institutionalized	−61,500
Not in labor force	−62,944
Equals: Labor force	121,669
Employed	114,968
Unemployed	6,701

Unemployment rates for selected years between 1929 and 1988 are provided on the inside covers of this book.

The Bureau of Labor Statistics (BLS) attempts to determine who is employed and who is not by conducting a nationwide random survey of some 60,000 households each month. A series of questions is asked regarding what members of the household are working, unemployed and looking for work, not looking for work, and so on. Despite the fact that very careful sampling and interview techniques are used, the data collected from this survey have been subjected to a number of criticisms.

1 Part-time employment The official data include all part-time workers as fully employed. In 1988 about 17 million people worked part time because of personal choice. Another 5 million part-time workers either wanted to work full time, but could not find suitable full-time work, or were on short hours because of a temporary slack in consumer demand. These last two groups of workers were, in effect, partially employed and partially unemployed. By counting them as fully employed the official BLS data tend to *understate* the unemployment rate.

2 Discouraged workers One must be actively seeking work in order to be counted as unemployed. Restated, an unemployed individual who is not actively seeking employment is classified as "not in the labor force." The problem is that there is a sizable number of workers who, after unsuccessfully seeking employment for a time, become discouraged and drop out of the labor force. Although the number of **discouraged workers** is larger during recession than during prosperity, an estimated 1 million people fell into this category in 1988. By not counting discouraged workers as unemployed, official data tend to *understate* the unemployment rate.

3 False information Alternatively, the unemployment rate may be *overstated* in that some respondents who are not working may claim they are looking for work, even though that is not the case. Hence, these individuals will be classified as "unemployed," rather than "not in the labor force." The motivation for giving this false information is

that an individual's unemployment compensation or welfare benefits may be contingent upon professed job pursuit. The presence of the underground economy (Chapter 9) may also cause the official unemployment rate to be overstated. An individual fully employed in the South Florida drug traffic or "running numbers" for the Chicago Mafia is likely to identify himself as "unemployed."

The overall point to be made is that, although the unemployment rate is a basic consideration in policy making, it is subject to certain shortcomings. While the unemployment rate is one of the best measures of the economic condition of the nation, it is not an infallible barometer of our economic health.[1]

ECONOMIC COST OF UNEMPLOYMENT

The problems associated with measuring the unemployment rate and defining the full-employment unemployment rate do not disguise an important fact: Above-normal unemployment entails great economic and social costs.

GNP gap and Okun's law The basic economic cost of unemployment is foregone output. *When the economy fails to generate enough jobs for all who are able and willing to work, potential production of goods and services is irretrievably lost.* Stated in terms of Chapter 2's analysis, unemployment keeps society from moving all the way to its production possibilities curve. Economists measure this sacrificed output in terms of the **GNP gap.** This gap is the amount by which the *actual GNP* falls short of *potential GNP.* Potential GNP is determined by assuming that the natural rate of unemployment exists and projecting the economy's "normal" growth rate. Figure 10-4 shows the GNP gap for

[1] To pursue this topic one might consult the Bureau of Labor Statistics, *How the Government Measures Unemployment* (Department of Labor, 1977); Stewart Schwab and John J. Seater, "The Unemployment Rate: Time to Give It a Rest?" *Business Review* (Federal Reserve Bank of Philadelphia), May–June 1977, pp. 11–18; and James J. Hughes and Richard Perlman, *The Economics of Unemployment* (New York: Cambridge University Press, 1984), chap. 1.

recent years and underscores the close correlation between the actual unemployment rate (Figure 10-4b) and the GNP gap (Figure 10-4a). The higher the unemployment rate, the larger the GNP gap.

The late, well-known macroeconomist Arthur Okun quantified the relationship between the unemployment rate and the GNP gap. This relationship, known as **Okun's law,** indicates that *for every*

1 percent that the actual unemployment rate exceeds the natural rate, there is generated a $2\frac{1}{2}$ percent GNP gap. This $1:2\frac{1}{2}$, or $2:5$, unemployment rate–GNP gap link permits one to calculate the absolute loss of output associated with any unemployment rate. For example, in the recession year 1983 the unemployment rate was $9\frac{1}{2}$ percent, or $3\frac{1}{2}$ percent in excess of the then-assumed 6 percent natural rate. Multiplying this $3\frac{1}{2}$ percent by Okun's $2\frac{1}{2}$ figure

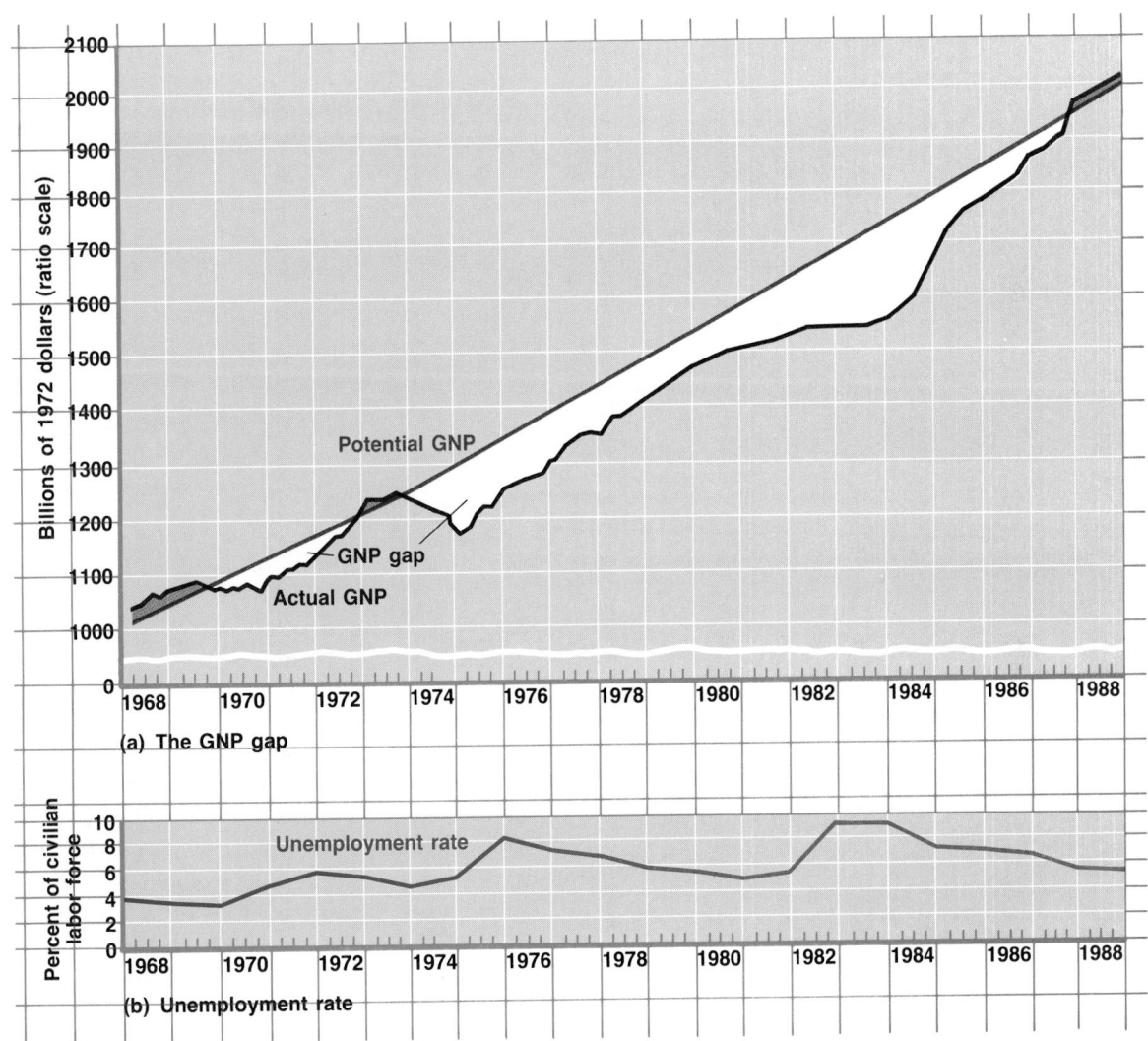

(a) The GNP gap

(b) Unemployment rate

FIGURE 10-4

Potential and actual GNP (a) and the unemployment rate (b)

The difference between potential and actual GNP is the GNP gap. The GNP gap measures the output which the economy sacrifices because it fails to utilize fully its productive potential. Note that a high unemployment rate means a large GNP gap. *(Economic Report of the President and Business Conditions Digest.)*

indicates that the 1983 GNP gap was $8\frac{3}{4}$ percent. Stated differently, 1983's GNP would have been $8\frac{3}{4}$ percent larger than it actually was had the full employment rate of unemployment been realized. Applying this $8\frac{3}{4}$ percent loss to 1983's $3300 billion nominal GNP, we find that the economy sacrificed almost $290 billion ($= \$3300 \times 8\frac{3}{4}$ percent) of output because the natural rate of unemployment was not achieved.

On the other hand, it is important to observe in Figure 10-4 that on occasion the economy's actual output can exceed its potential output. We have already mentioned that this state of affairs existed during World War II when unemployment rates fell below 2 percent. Extra shifts of workers were employed, capital equipment was used beyond its designed capacity, overtime work and moonlighting were common, and so forth. We observe in Figure 10-4 that in the late 1960s the stimulus of the Vietnam war caused actual GNP to exceed potential GNP and again in 1973 an economic boom created a "negative" GNP gap. The potential GNP can occasionally be exceeded, but the excess of actual over potential GNP cannot be sustained indefinitely.

Unequal burdens Aggregate figures conceal the fact that the cost of unemployment is unequally distributed. An increase in the unemployment rate from 6 to, say, 9 or 10 percent would be more tolerable if every worker's hours of work and wage income were reduced proportionally. But in fact this is not the case.

Table 10-2 contrasts unemployment rates for various labor market groups for the recession year 1982 and the full-employment year 1988. Observation of the large variance in the rates of unemployment *within each year* and comparison of the rates *between* the two years yields several generalizations.

First, white-collar workers enjoy lower unemployment rates and are less vulnerable to unemployment during recessions than are blue-collar workers. Reasons for this include the fact that white-collar workers are employed in less cyclically vulnerable industries (services and nondurable goods) or are self-employed. Also, businesses are less inclined to lay off the more-skilled white-collar workers in whom they have made large training investments.

TABLE 10-2 **Unemployment rates by demographic group: recession (1982) and full employment (1988)**

Demographic group	Unemployment rate, 1982 (%)	Unemployment rate, 1988 (%)
Overall	9.7	5.5
Occupation		
Blue-collar	14.2	7.5
White-collar	5.2	3.2
Age		
16–19	23.2	15.3
Black, 16–19	48.0	32.4
White, 16–19	20.4	13.1
Males, 20+	8.8	4.8
Females, 20+	8.3	4.9
Race		
Black	18.9	11.7
White	8.6	4.7
Sex		
Female	9.4	5.6
Male	9.9	5.5
Duration		
15 weeks or more	3.2	1.3

Sources: *Economic Report of the President; Employment and Earnings.*

Second, teenagers incur much higher unemployment rates than do adults. This is so because teenagers have low skill levels, more frequently quit their jobs, are more frequently discharged from jobs, and often have little geographic mobility. Many unemployed teenagers are new labor-market entrants searching for their first job.

Third, the unemployment rate for blacks—both adults and teenagers—has been roughly *twice* that of whites. A number of explanatory factors may be at work here including discrimination in education and in the labor market, the concentration of blacks in the less-skilled (blue-collar) occupations, and the geographic isolation of blacks in central-city areas where the growth of employment opportunities for those first entering the labor market has been minimal.

Fourth, male and female unemployment rates are quite comparable. The lower unemployment rate for women in the 1982 recession year reflects the fact that male workers are dominant in such cyclically vulnerable hard-goods industries as automobiles, steel, and construction.

A final generalization is that the number of persons unemployed for long periods—fifteen weeks or more—as a percentage of the labor force is much less than the unemployment rate. But this figure rises significantly during recessions. The "long-term" unemployed were only 1.3 percent of the labor force in 1988 as compared to the overall 5.5 percent unemployment rate. A very large proportion of unemployment is of relatively short duration. But also observe that the "long-term" unemployed were 3.2 percent of the labor force in the 1982 recession, implying a significant amount of economic hardship.

NONECONOMIC COSTS

Cyclical unemployment is much more than an economic malady; it is a social catastrophe as well. Depression means idleness. And idleness means loss of skills, loss of self-respect, a plummeting of morale, family disintegration, and sociopolitical unrest. Consider the following two commentaries on the Great Depression from Studs Terkel's revealing book *Hard Times*.[2] First, the comments of a young woman who was fortunate enough to attend college:

When I attended Berkeley in 1936, so many of the kids had actually lost their fathers. They had wandered off in disgrace because they couldn't support their families. Other fathers had killed themselves, so the family could have the insurance. Families had totally broken down. Each father took it as his personal failure. These middle-class men apparently had no social sense of what was going on, so they killed themselves.

It was still the Depression. There were kids who didn't have a place to sleep, huddling under bridges on the campus. I had a scholarship, but there were times when I didn't have food. The meals were often three candy bars.

[2] Studs Terkel, *Hard Times* (New York: Avon Books, 1971), pp. 131, 398.

Second, the reminiscences of a craftsman's son:

One of the most common things—and it certainly happened to me—was this feeling of your father's failure. That somehow he hadn't beaten the rap. Sure things were tough, but why should I be the kid who had to put a piece of cardboard into the sole of my shoe to go to school? It was not a thing coupled with resentment against my father. It was simply this feeling of regret, that somehow he hadn't done better, that he hadn't gotten the breaks. Also a feeling of uneasiness about my father's rage against the way things are. . . .

Remember, too, the shock, the confusion, the hurt that many kids felt about their fathers not being able to provide for them. This reflected itself very often in bitter quarrels between father and son. . . .

We had bitter arguments about new ideas. Was Roosevelt right in making relief [welfare payments] available? Was the WPA [a public-works project for the unemployed] a good idea? Did people have the right to occupy their [bankrupt] farms and hold them by force? The old concept that there was something for everybody who worked in America went down the drain with the Great Depression. This created family strains. A lot of parents felt a sense of guilt. . . .

My father led a rough life: he drank. During the Depression, he drank more. There was more conflict in the home. A lot of fathers—mine, among them—had a habit of taking off. They'd go to Chicago to look for work. To Topeka. This left the family at home, waiting and hoping that the old man would find something. And there was always the Saturday night ordeal as to whether or not the old man would get home with his paycheck. Everything was sharpened and hurt more by the Depression.

It is no exaggeration to say that:

A job gives hope for material and social advancement. It is a way of providing one's children a better start in life. It may mean the only honorable way of escape from the poverty of one's parents. It helps to overcome racial and other social barriers. In short . . . a job is the passport to freedom and to a better life. To deprive people of jobs is to read them out of our society.[3]

[3] Henry R. Reuss, *The Critical Decade* (New York: McGraw-Hill Book Company, 1964), p. 133.

History makes it all too clear that severe unemployment is conducive to rapid and sometimes violent social and political change. Witness the movement to the left of American political philosophy during the Depression of the 1930s. The Depression-inspired New Deal was a veritable revolution in American political and economic thinking. Witness also Hitler's ascent to power against a background of unemployment. Furthermore, there can be no question that the heavy concentration of unemployment among blacks and other minorities has been an important cause of the unrest and violence which periodically has plagued cities in America and elsewhere. At a more mundane level, research links increases in suicides, homicides, cardiovascular mortality, and mental illness to high unemployment.[4]

INTERNATIONAL COMPARISONS

Unemployment rates vary greatly among nations of the world over specific periods. The major reason for these differences is that nations have different natural rates of unemployment and also may find themselves in different phases of their business cycles. Column 2 of Table 10-3 lists average unemployment rates approximating U.S. measurement concepts for nine industrialized nations for a recent five-year period. Historically, the United States has had higher unemployment rates than most industrially advanced nations. But this general pattern changed beginning in the mid-1980s. As indicated in column 2, the average annual unemployment rate in the United States over the 1983–1987 period was lower than the unemployment rates of Canada, Australia, France, and the United Kingdom.

Inflation: defined and measured

Now let us turn to inflation as an aspect of macroeconomic instability. The problems posed by infla-

[4] M. Harvey Brenner, "Influence of the Social Environment on Psychopathology: The Historical Perspective," in James E. Barrett et al. (eds.), *Stress and Mental Disorder* (New York: Raven Press, 1979), pp. 8–24.

TABLE 10-3 **Average unemployment and inflation rates for a five-year period in nine countries**

(1) Country	(2) Average annual unemployment rate, 1983–1987 (%)	(3) Average annual inflation rate, 1983–1987 (%)
United States	7.5	3.3
Canada	10.4	4.6
Australia	8.7	7.7
Japan	2.8	1.3
France	10.1	5.7
Germany	7.2	1.6
Italy	6.6	8.9
Sweden	2.8	6.6
United Kingdom	11.3	4.7

Source: Bureau of Labor Statistics, Organization for Economic Cooperation and Development

tion are more subtle than those of unemployment and hence are somewhat more difficult to grasp.

THE MEANING OF INFLATION

What is inflation? *Inflation is a rising general level of prices.* This does not mean, of course, that *all* prices are necessarily rising. Even during periods of rather rapid inflation, some specific prices may be relatively constant and others actually falling. For example, although the United States experienced high rates of inflation in the 1970s and early 1980s, the prices of such products as video recorders, digital watches, and personal computers actually declined. Indeed, as we shall see momentarily, one of the major sore spots of inflation lies in the fact that prices tend to rise very unevenly. Some spring upward; others ascend at a more leisurely pace; others do not rise at all.

MEASURING INFLATION

Inflation is measured by price index numbers such as those introduced in Chapter 9. Recall that a price index measures the general level of prices in reference to a base period.

To illustrate, the consumer price index uses 1982–1984 as the base period in which that period's price level is set equal to 100. In 1988 the price index was at approximately 118. This means that prices were 18 percent higher in 1988 than in 1982–1984 or, more simply put, a given collection of goods which cost $100 in 1982–1984 cost $118 in 1988.

The *rate* of inflation can be calculated for any given year by subtracting last year's (1987) price index from this year's (1988) index, dividing that difference by last year's (1987) index, and multiplying by 100 to express it as a percentage. For example, the consumer price index was 113.6 in 1987 and 118.3 in 1988. Hence, the rate of inflation for 1988 is derived as follows:

$$\text{Rate of inflation} = \frac{118.3 - 113.6}{118.3} \times 100 = 4.1\%$$

The so-called **rule of 70** gives us a different perspective for gaining a quantitative appreciation of inflation. Specifically, the rule allows us to calculate quickly the number of years required for a doubling of the price level. All we need do is divide the number 70 by the annual rate of inflation. That is:

$$\text{Approximate number of years required to double} = \frac{70}{\text{percentage annual rate of increase}}$$

For example, a 3 percent annual rate of inflation will double the price level in about $23(= 70 \div 3)$ years. Inflation of 8 percent per year will double the price level in about $9\ (= 70 \div 8)$ years. Inflation at 12 percent will double the price level in only about 6 years! You should note that the rule of 70 is generally applicable in that it will allow you, for example, to estimate how long it will take for real GNP or your savings account to double.

With this background information in mind, let us next provide an overview of the historical record of inflation in the United States and compare annual inflation rates internationally for a recent period. Then we will survey the causes of inflation and consider its consequences.

THE FACTS OF INFLATION

Figure 10-5 gives us an overview of inflation in the United States since 1920. The figure shows annual increases in the consumer price index, which is constructed using a base period of 1982–1984. That is, the CPI for the 1982–1984 period is arbitrarily set at 100. Although most readers have grown up in an "age of inflation," we observe that our economy has not always been inflation-prone. The price level was remarkably stable in the prosperous 1920s and declined—that is, *deflation* occurred—during the early years of the Great Depression of the 1930s. Prices then rose sharply in the immediate post-World War II period (1945–1948). However, overall price stability characterized the 1951–1965 period wherein the average annual increase in the price level was less than 1½ percent. But the inflation which took hold in the late 1960s and surged ahead in the 1970s introduced Americans to double-digit inflation. In 1979 and 1980 the price level rose at 12 to 13 percent annual rates. By the mid-1980s, however, the annual rate of inflation had diminished to less than 4 percent.

But we must not get the notion that inflation is a distinctly American institution. Virtually all the other industrialized nations—the exceptions being West Germany and Japan—have experienced more rapid rates of inflation in recent years than we have. More concretely, note in column 3 of Table 10-3 that the average annual inflation rates in Italy, Australia, France, Sweden, and the United Kingdom were higher during the 1983–87 period than in the United States. Some nations of the world have had double-digit—or even triple-digit—annual rates of inflation in specific years during the 1980s. Israel's inflation has been so severe that, in one five-year period during the 1980s, the price of a tank of gasoline rose to 30,000 shekels, an amount that would have bought a car five years before. Bolivia's estimated annual inflation rate was about 3400 percent in 1985, which meant that a $20 dinner in 1984 would have cost $680 in 1985. In 1987, Brazil's annual inflation rate was about 400 percent. According to the *Wall Street Journal,* one visitor to Rio's Caesar Park Hotel saw the nightly price of his room double from 1600 cruzados to 3200 cruzados during a three-week stay! The point to be stressed is that, while United

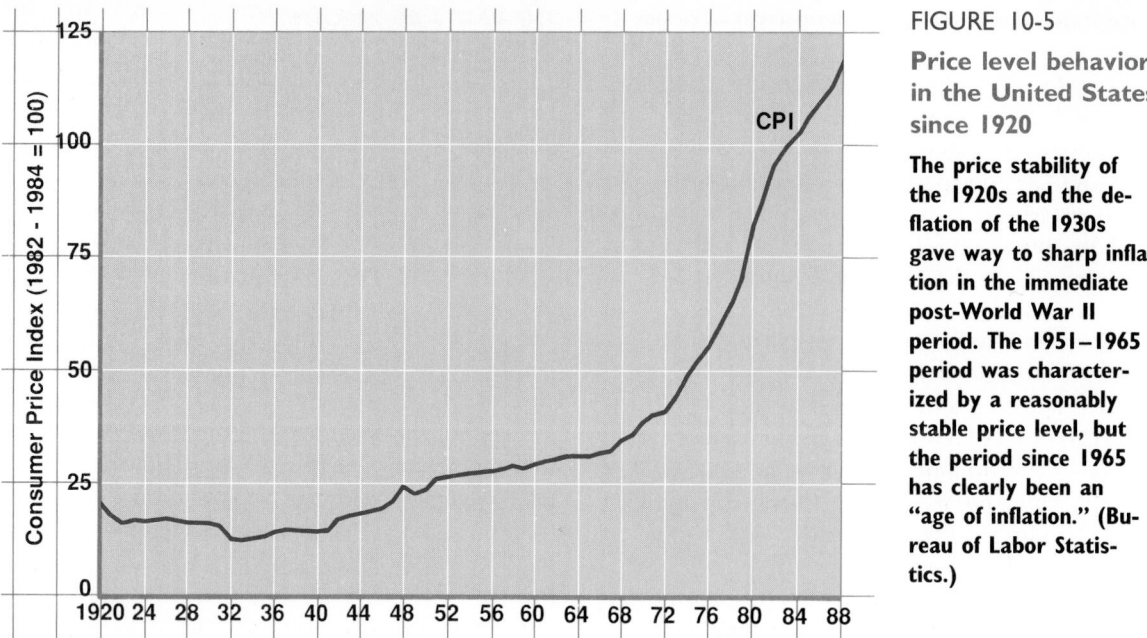

FIGURE 10-5

Price level behavior in the United States since 1920

The price stability of the 1920s and the deflation of the 1930s gave way to sharp inflation in the immediate post-World War II period. The 1951–1965 period was characterized by a reasonably stable price level, but the period since 1965 has clearly been an "age of inflation." (Bureau of Labor Statistics.)

States inflation in the 1970s and early 1980s was both significant and troublesome, it hardly compares with that experienced by many other countries.

CAUSES: THEORIES OF INFLATION

Economists distinguish between two types of inflation.

1 Demand-pull inflation Traditionally, changes in the price level have been attributed to an excess of total demand. The economy may attempt to spend beyond its capacity to produce; it may seek some point beyond its production possibilities curve. The business sector cannot respond to this excess demand by expanding real output because all available resources are already fully employed. Therefore, this excess demand will bid up the prices of the fixed real output, causing **demand-pull inflation.** The essence of demand-pull inflation is often crudely expressed in the phrase "too much money chasing too few goods."

But the relationship between total demand, on the one hand, and output, employment, and the price level, on the other, is more complex than

these terse comments suggest. Figure 10-6 is helpful in unraveling these complications.

In *range 1* total spending—the sum of consumption, investment, government, and net export spending—is so low that the national output is far short of its maximum full-employment level. In other words, a substantial GNP gap exists. Unemployment rates are high and businesses have a great deal of idle productive capacity. Now assume that total demand increases. Real national output will rise and the unemployment rate will fall, but there will be little or no increase in the price level. The reason is that there are large amounts of idle human and property resources which can be put back to work at their *existing* prices. An unemployed worker does not ask for a wage increase during a job interview! In terms of Chapter 4's demand and supply analysis, the usual price-raising effects of the assumed increases in demand do not occur because supply is a horizontal line. The increases in the amount of labor and other resources supplied are possible because idle resources are available and the additional production is profitable. The net result is large output-increasing effects and no price-increasing effects.

As demand continues to rise, the economy enters *range 2* wherein it is approaching full employment and is closer to fully utilizing its available resources. But we note that, before full employment is achieved, the price level may begin to rise. Why so? As production expands, supplies of idle resources do not vanish simultaneously in all sectors and industries of the economy. Bottlenecks begin to develop in some industries even though most have excess production capacity. Some industries are fully utilizing their production capacity before others and cannot respond to further increases in demand for their products by increasing supply. So their prices rise. As labor markets tighten, some types of labor become fully employed and their money wages rise. This increases production costs and prompts businesses to increase their prices. Tight labor markets enhance the bargaining power of unions and increase their ability to obtain sizable wage increases. Businesses are less likely to resist union wage demands because they do not want to be faced with a strike at a time when the economy is becoming increasingly prosperous. Furthermore, with total spending rising, higher costs can be quite easily passed along to consumers through price increases. Finally, as full employment is approached, firms will be forced to employ less efficient (less productive) workers and this contributes to rising costs and prices. The inflation

which occurs in range 2 is sometimes called "premature inflation" because it occurs before the economy reaches full employment.

As total spending increases into *range 3,* full employment will be realized in all sectors of the economy. Industries in the aggregate can no longer respond to increases in demand with increases in output. Real national output is now at a maximum and further increases in demand will merely cause demand-pull inflation. Total demand in excess of society's capacity to produce pulls the price level upward.

Reprise: Chapter 9 drew a distinction between nominal and real GNP that is helpful at this point. So long as the price level is constant (range 1), increases in nominal and real GNP are identical. But with premature inflation (range 2), nominal GNP is rising faster than real GNP, so nominal GNP must be "deflated" to measure changes in physical output. With pure inflation (range 3), nominal GNP is rising—perhaps rapidly—but real GNP is constant.

2 Cost-push or supply-side inflation Inflation may also arise on the supply or cost side of the market. There have been several periods in our recent economic history when the price level has risen despite rather widespread evidence that aggregate demand was not excessive. We have experienced periods wherein output and employment were both *declining* (evidence of a deficiency of total demand), while at the same time the general price level was *increasing.*

The theory of **cost-push inflation** explains rising prices in terms of factors which raise **per unit production cost.** Per unit production cost is the average cost of a particular level of output. This average cost is found by dividing the total cost of the resource inputs by the amount of output produced. That is,

$$\text{Per unit production cost} = \frac{\text{total input cost}}{\text{units of output}}$$

Rising per unit production costs in the economy squeeze profits and reduce the amount of output that firms are willing to supply at the existing price level. As a result, the economywide supply of goods and services declines. This decline in supply in turn drives up the price level. Hence, under this scenario, costs are *pushing* the price level upward,

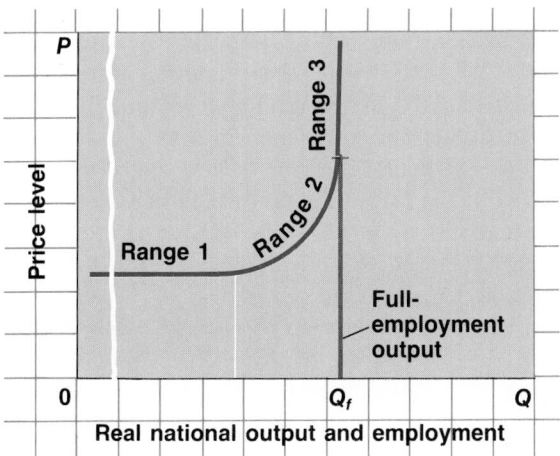

FIGURE 10-6

The price level and the level of employment

As aggregate expenditures increase, the price level generally begins to rise before full employment is reached. At full employment, additional spending tends to be purely inflationary.

rather than demand *pulling* it upward, as in the case of demand-pull inflation.

The two most prominently mentioned sources of cost-push inflation are increases in nominal wages and increases in the prices of nonwage inputs such as raw materials and energy.

Wage-push variant The wage-push variant of cost-push inflation theorizes that, under some circumstances, unions may be a source of inflation. According to this line of reasoning, unions exert some control over nominal wage rates through collective bargaining. Suppose that major unions demand and receive large increases in wages. Moreover, let us assume that these wage gains set the standard for wage increases paid to many nonunion workers. If the economywide wage gains are excessive relative to any offsetting factors such as rises in output per hour, then employers will experience rising per unit production costs. Producers will respond by reducing the amount of goods and services offered for sale. Assuming no change in demand, this decline in supply will result in an increase in the price level. Because the culprit is an excessive increase in nominal wages, this type of inflation is called the *wage-push variant* of cost-push inflation.

Supply-shock variant A second major variant of cost-push inflation, generally labeled *supply shock,* traces rising production costs—and therefore product prices—to abrupt, unanticipated increases in the costs of raw materials or energy inputs. The dramatic run-ups of imported oil prices in 1973–1974 and again in 1979–1980 are good illustrations. As energy prices rose during these periods, the costs of producing and transporting virtually every product in the economy increased. Rapid cost-push inflation ensued.

COMPLEXITIES

The real world happens to be much more complex than our simple distinction between demand-pull and cost-push inflation suggests. In practice it is difficult to distinguish between the two types of inflation. For example, suppose a boost in military spending occurs which increases total spending, causing demand-pull inflation. As the demand-pull stimulus works its way through product and then resource markets, individual firms find their wage costs, material costs, and fuel prices rising. From their perspective they must raise their prices because production costs have risen. Although the inflation in this case is clearly demand-pull, it has the appearance of cost-push to many business firms. It is not easy to label inflation as demand-side or supply-side without knowing the ultimate source—the original cause—of price and wage increases.

Most economists agree that cost-push and demand-pull inflation differ in another important respect. Demand-pull inflation will continue so long as there is excess total spending. On the other hand, cost-push inflation will automatically be self-limiting; that is, it will tend to die out or cure itself. The reason is that reduced supply will cause real national output and employment to fall and these declines serve as constraints upon further cost increases. Stated in different terms, cost-push inflation generates a recession and the recession in turn inhibits additional cost increases. This matter will be addressed in more detail in Chapter 19.

Redistributive effects of inflation

Let us now shift our attention from causes to effects. We first consider how inflation capriciously redistributes income; second, we examine possible effects upon the national output.

As we shall see momentarily, the relationship between the price level and the national output is ambiguous. Historically, real output and the price level have risen and fallen together. In the past two decades or so, however, there have been several occasions in which real output has fallen while prices have continued to rise. We will dodge this issue for a moment by assuming that the real output is constant and at the full-employment level. By holding real output and income constant we can better isolate the effects of inflation upon the distribution of that income. Assuming that the size of the national income pie is fixed, how does inflation affect the size of the slices going to different income receivers?

In answering this question it is critical to understand the difference between money or nominal income and real income.[5] *Money* or **nominal income** consists of the number of dollars one receives as wages, rent, interest, or profits. **Real income** measures the amount of goods and services which one's nominal income can buy. A moment's reflection will make it clear that, if your nominal income increases faster than does the price level, then your real income will rise. Conversely, if the price level increases faster than your nominal income, then your real income will decline. The change in one's real income can be approximated through this simple formula:

Percentage   percentage   percentage
change in = change in − change in
real income   nominal income   price level

Thus, if your nominal income rises by 10 percent in a given year and the price level rises by 5 percent in the same period, your real income will *increase* by about 5 percent. Conversely, a 5 percent increase in nominal income accompanied by 10 percent inflation will *decrease* your real income by approximately 5 percent.[6] The point to remember is that, while inflation reduces the purchasing power of the dollar—that is, it reduces the amount of goods and services a dollar will buy—it does not necessarily follow that a person's real income will fall. The purchasing power of the dollar declines whenever inflation occurs; a decline in your real income or

---

[5] Chapter 9's distinction between nominal and real GNP is pertinent and you may want to refresh yourself on the "inflating" and "deflating" process involved in converting nominal GNP to real GNP (Table 9-7).

[6] A more precise calculation follows Chapter 9's process for changing nominal GNP to real GNP. Hence,

$$\text{Real income} = \frac{\text{nominal income}}{\text{price index (in hundredths)}}$$

Thus, in our first illustration, if nominal income rises by 10 percent from $100 to $110 and the price level (index) increases by 5 percent from 100 to 105, then real income has increased as follows:

$$\frac{\$110}{1.05} = \$104.76$$

The 5 percent increase in real income shown by the simple formula in the text is clearly a good approximation of the 4.76 percent yielded by our more complex formula.

standard of living occurs only when your nominal income fails to keep pace with inflation.

Finally, we must note that the redistributive effects of inflation are quite different, depending upon whether or not it is expected. In the case of **anticipated inflation,** an income receiver *may* be able to take steps to avoid or lessen the adverse effects which inflation would otherwise have upon real income. In the discussion that follows are generalizations which initially assume the presence of **unanticipated inflation.** Then we shall modify our generalizations by taking the anticipation of inflation into account.

FIXED-NOMINAL-INCOME RECEIVERS

Our prior distinction between nominal and real incomes makes it clear that *inflation penalizes people who receive relatively fixed nominal incomes.* Restated, it redistributes income away from fixed income receivers toward others in the economy. The classic case is the elderly couple living on a private pension or annuity which provides a fixed amount of nominal income each month. The pensioner who retired in 1975 on what appeared to be an adequate pension would have found by 1988 that the purchasing power of that pension had been cut by one-half. Similarly, landlords who received rental payments of fixed dollar amounts will be hurt by inflation as they receive dollars of declining value over time. To a lesser extent some white-collar workers, some public sector employees whose income is dictated by fixed pay scales, and families living on fixed levels of welfare and other transfer income will be victims of inflation. Note, however, that the adverse redistributive effect of inflation upon social security recipients has been offset in recent years by substantial increases in the size of benefits. In fact, Congress has *indexed* social security benefits; social security payments are tied to the consumer price index to prevent erosion from inflation.

People living on flexible incomes *may* benefit from inflation. The nominal incomes of such households may spurt ahead of the price level, or cost of living, with the result that their real incomes are enhanced. Workers employed in expanding industries and represented by vigorous unions may keep their nominal wages apace with, or ahead of, the rate of inflation.

On the other hand, some wage earners are hurt by inflation. Those situated in declining industries or without the benefit of strong, aggressive unions may find that the price level skips ahead of their money incomes.

Business executives and other profit receivers **might** benefit from inflation. **If** product prices rise faster than resource prices, business receipts then will grow at a faster rate than will costs. Thus some profit incomes will outdistance the rising tide of inflation.

SAVERS

Inflation also casts its evil eye upon savers. **As prices rise, the real value, or purchasing power, of a nest egg of savings will deteriorate.** Savings accounts, insurance policies, annuities, and other fixed-value paper assets which were once adequate to meet rainy-day contingencies or to provide for a comfortable retirement, decline in real value during inflation. The simplest case is the individual who hoards money as a cash balance. For example, a $1000 cash balance would have lost one-half its real value between 1967 and 1977. Of course, most forms of savings earn interest. But the value of one's savings will still decline if the rate of inflation exceeds the rate of interest. Example: A household may save $1000 in a commercial bank or savings and loan association or buy a $1000 bond at, say, 6 percent interest. But if inflation is 13 percent (as in 1979), the real value or purchasing power of that $1000 will be cut to about $938 at the end of the year. That is, the saver will receive $1060 (equal to $1000 plus $60 of interest), but deflating that $1060 for 13 percent inflation means that the real value of $1060 is only about $938 (equal to $1060 divided by 1.13).

DEBTORS AND CREDITORS

Inflation also redistributes income by altering the relationship between debtors and creditors. Specifically, **unanticipated inflation tends to benefit debtors (borrowers) at the expense of creditors (lenders).** Suppose you borrow $1000 from a bank, which you are to repay in two years. If in that period of time the general level of prices were to double, the $1000 which you repay will have only half the purchasing power of the $1000 originally borrowed. True, if we ignore interest charges, the same number of dollars is repaid as was borrowed. But because of inflation, each of these dollars will now buy only half as much as it did when the loan was negotiated. As prices go up, the value of the dollar comes down. Thus, because of inflation, the borrower is given "dear" dollars but pays back "cheap" dollars. The inflation of the past two decades has been a particular windfall to those who purchased homes in, say, the mid-1960s with fixed-interest-rate mortgages. On the one hand, inflation has greatly reduced the real burden of their mortgage indebtedness. On the other hand, the nominal value of housing has increased more rapidly than the overall price level.

The Federal government, which has amassed a huge $2600 billion of public debt over the decades, has also been a major beneficiary of inflation. Historically, the Federal government has regularly paid off its loans by taking out new ones. Inflation has permitted the Treasury to pay off its loans with dollars which have less purchasing power than the dollars it originally borrowed. Nominal national income and therefore tax collections rise with inflation; the amount of public debt owed does not. This means that inflation reduces the real burden of the public debt to the Federal government. Given the fact that inflation benefits the Federal government in this way, some economists have wondered out loud whether society can really expect government to be particularly zealous in its efforts to halt inflation.

In fact, some nations such as Brazil once used inflation so extensively to reduce the real value of their debts that lenders now force them to borrow money in U.S. dollars or in some other relatively stable currency instead of their own currency. This prevents them from having access to domestic inflation as a means of subtly "defaulting" on their debt. Any inflation which they generate will reduce the value of their own currencies, but not the value of the debt which they must pay back.

ANTICIPATED INFLATION

The redistributive effects of inflation will be less severe or even eliminated if transactors (1) anticipate inflation and (2) have the capacity to adjust their nominal incomes to reflect expected price level changes. For example, the prolonged inflation which began in the late 1960s prompted many unions in the 1970s to insist upon labor contracts which incorporated **cost-of-living adjustment (COLA)** clauses to automatically adjust workers' incomes for inflation. Similarly, the redistribution of income from lender to borrower which we just observed might be altered *if* inflation is anticipated. Suppose that a lender (perhaps a commercial bank or a savings and loan) and a borrower (a household) both agree that 5 percent is a fair rate of interest on a one-year loan, *provided* the price level is stable. But assume inflation has been occurring and both lender and borrower agree it is reasonable to anticipate a 6 percent increase in the price level over the next year. If the bank lends the household $100 at 5 percent, the bank will be paid back $105 at the end of the year. But if 6 percent inflation does occur during the year, the purchasing power of that $105 will have been reduced to about $99. The *lender* will in effect have paid the *borrower* $1 to use the lender's money for a year. The lender can avoid this curious subsidy by simply increasing the interest rate by the amount of the anticipated inflation. Specifically, by charging 11 percent the lender will receive back $111 at the end of the year which, adjusted for the 6 percent inflation, has the real value or purchasing power of about $105. In this instance there is a mutually agreeable transfer of purchasing power from borrower to lender of $5, or 5 percent, for the use of $100 for one year. It is relevant to note that savings and loan institutions have developed variable-interest-rate mortgages to protect themselves from the adverse effects of inflation. Incidentally, these examples imply that, rather than being a cause of inflation, high nominal interest rates may be a consequence of inflation.

Our illustration points out the difference between the real rate of interest, on the one hand, and the money or nominal rate of interest, on the other. The **real interest rate** *is the percentage increase in purchasing power that the lender receives from the borrower.* In our example the real interest rate is 5 percent. The **nominal interest rate** *is the percentage increase in money that the lender receives.* The nominal rate of interest is 11 percent in our example. The difference in these two concepts is that the

real interest rate is adjusted or "deflated" for the rate of inflation while the nominal interest rate is not. Stated differently, the nominal interest rate is the sum of the real interest rate plus the premium paid to offset the expected rate of inflation.

RECAP AND ADDENDA

To summarize: Inflation arbitrarily "taxes" those who receive relatively fixed money incomes and "subsidizes" those who receive flexible money incomes. Unanticipated inflation arbitrarily penalizes savers. Finally, unanticipated inflation benefits debtors at the expense of creditors. It should come as no surprise that the effects of deflation are substantially the reverse. *Assuming no change in total output,* those with fixed money incomes will find their real incomes enhanced. Creditors will benefit at the expense of debtors. And savers will find that the purchasing power of their savings has grown as a result of falling prices.

Two final points must be appended to this discussion. First, the fact that any given family is likely to be an income earner, a holder of financial assets, and an owner of real assets simultaneously is likely to cushion the redistributive impact of inflation. For example, if the family owns fixed-value monetary assets (savings accounts, bonds, and insurance policies), inflation will lessen their real value. But that same inflation is likely to increase the real value of any property assets (a house, land) which the family owns. In short, many families are simultaneously hurt and benefited by inflation. All these effects must be considered before we are able to conclude that the family's net position is better or worse because of inflation.

The second point to be reemphasized is that the redistributive effects of inflation are *arbitrary* in that they occur without regard to society's goals and values. Inflation lacks a social conscience and takes from some and gives to others, whether they be rich, poor, young, old, healthy, or infirm.

Output effects of inflation

We have assumed thus far that the economy's real output is fixed at the full-employment level. As a result, the redistributive effects of inflation and deflation have been in terms of some groups gaining absolutely at the expense of others. *If* the size of the pie is fixed and inflation causes some groups to get larger slices, other groups must necessarily get smaller slices. But, in fact, the level of national output may vary as the price level changes. Stated differently, the size of the pie itself may vary.

There is, frankly, much uncertainty and disagreement as to whether inflation is likely to be accompanied by a rising or a falling real national output. Let us briefly consider three scenarios, the first of which associates inflation with an expanding output and the remaining two with a declining output.

STIMULUS OF DEMAND-PULL INFLATION

Some economists argue that full employment can only be achieved if some modest amount of inflation is tolerated. They base their reasoning on Figure 10-6. We know that the levels of real national output and employment depend upon aggregate spending. If spending is low, the economy will operate in range 1. In this range there is price level stability, but real national output is substantially below its potential and the unemployment rate is high. If aggregate spending now increases to the extent that the economy moves into range 2, we find that society must accept a higher price level—some amount of inflation—to achieve these higher levels of real national output and the accompanying lower unemployment rates. Of course, if further increases in aggregate spending pull the economy into range 3, that spending will be purely inflationary because the full-employment or capacity level of real national output will have been reached.

The critical point for present purposes is that in range 2 there appears to be a tradeoff between output (including employment), on the one hand, and inflation, on the other. Some moderate amount of inflation must be accepted if we are to realize high levels of output and employment. The high levels of spending which give us higher levels of output and low unemployment rates also cause some inflation. Stated differently, an inverse relationship may exist between the inflation rate and the unemployment rate.

This scenario has been criticized in recent years. Some economists feel that any tradeoff between the inflation rate and the unemployment rate is a transitory or short-run phenomenon at best and there is no such tradeoff in the long run. This controversy will be explored in detail in Chapter 19.

COST-PUSH INFLATION AND UNEMPLOYMENT

Let us now detail an equally plausible set of circumstances wherein inflation might cause output and employment to both *decline*. Suppose the level of total spending is initially such that the economy is enjoying full employment *and* price level stability. If cost-push inflation now occurs, the amount of real output which the existing level of total demand will buy will be reduced. That is, a given level of total spending will only be capable of taking a smaller real output off the market when cost-push pressures boost the price level. Hence, real output will fall and unemployment will rise.

Economic events of the 1970s lend support to this scenario. In late 1973 the Organization of Petroleum Exporting Countries (OPEC) became effective and exerted its market power to quadruple the price of oil. The cost-push inflationary effects generated rapid price level increases in the 1973–1975 period. At the same time the unemployment rate rose from slightly less than 5 percent in 1973 to 8.5 percent in 1975. Similar outcomes occurred in 1979–1980 in response to a second OPEC oil price shock.

HYPERINFLATION AND BREAKDOWN

Some economists express anxiety over our first scenario. They are fearful that the mild, "creeping" inflation which might initially accompany economic recovery may snowball into a more severe **hyperinflation.** This term is reserved for extremely rapid inflation whose ultimate impact upon national output and employment tends to be devastating. The contention is that, as prices persist in creeping upward, households and businesses will come to expect them to rise further. So, rather than let their idle savings and current incomes depreciate, people are induced to "spend now" to beat anticipated price rises. Businesses do the same in buying capital goods. Action on the basis of this "inflationary psychosis" intensifies the pressure on prices, and inflation feeds upon itself. Furthermore, as the cost of living rises, labor demands and gets higher nominal wages. Indeed, unions may seek wage increases sufficient not only to cover last year's price level increase but also to compensate for the inflation anticipated during the future life of their new collective bargaining agreement. Prosperity is not a good time for business firms to risk strikes by resisting such demands. Business managers recoup their rising labor costs by boosting the prices they charge consumers. And for good measure, businesses are likely to jack prices up an extra notch or two to be sure that profit receivers keep abreast or ahead of the inflationary parade. As the cost of living moves upward as a result of these price increases, labor once again has an excellent excuse to demand another round of substantial wage increases. But this triggers another round of price increases. The net effect is a cumulative *wage-price inflationary spiral.* Money-wage and price rises feed upon each other, and this helps creeping inflation burst into galloping inflation.

Aside from disruptive redistributive effects, it is alleged that hyperinflation can precipitate economic collapse. Severe inflation encourages a diversion of effort toward speculative, and away from productive, activity. Businesses may find it increasingly profitable to hoard both materials and finished products in anticipation of further price increases. But, by restricting the availability of materials and products relative to the demand for them, such actions will tend to intensify inflationary pressures. Rather than invest in capital equipment, businesses and individual savers may purchase nonproductive wealth—jewels, gold and other precious metals, real estate, and so forth—as hedges against inflation.

In the extreme, as prices shoot up sharply and unevenly, normal economic relationships are disrupted. Business owners do not know what to charge for their products. And consumers do not know what to pay. Resource suppliers will want to be paid with actual output, rather than with rapidly depreciating money. Creditors will avoid debtors to escape the repayment of debts with cheap money. Money becomes virtually worthless and ceases to do its job as a measure of value and medium of exchange. The economy may literally be

thrown into a state of barter. Production and exchange grind toward a halt, and the net result is economic, social, and very possibly political chaos. Hyperinflation has precipitated monetary collapse, depression, and sociopolitical disorder.

Unfortunately, history reveals a number of examples which fit this gloomy scenario. These are typically instances of wartime or war-associated inflation which accelerated into hyperinflation with disastrous results. Consider the effects of World War II upon price levels in Hungary and Japan:

The inflation in Hungary exceeded all known records of the past. In August, 1946, 828 octillion (1 followed by 27 zeros) depreciated pengös equaled the value of 1 prewar pengö. The price of the American dollar reached a value of 3×10^{22} (3 followed by 22 zeros) pengös. Fishermen and farmers in 1947 Japan used scales to weigh currency and change, rather than bothering to count it. Prices rose some 116 times in Japan, 1938 to 1948.[7]

The German inflation of the 1920s was also catastrophic:

The German Weimar Republic is an extreme example of a weak government which survived for some time through inflationary finance. On April 27, 1921, the German government was presented with a staggering bill for reparations payments to the Allies of 132 billion gold marks. This sum was far greater than what the Weimar Republic could reasonably expect to raise in taxes. Faced with huge budget deficits, the Weimar government simply ran the printing press to meet its bills.

During 1922, the German price level went up 5,470 percent. In 1923, the situation worsened; the German price level rose 1,300,000,000,000 times. By October of 1923, the postage on the lightest letter sent from Germany to the United States was 200,000 marks. Butter cost 1.5 million marks per pound, meat 2 million marks, a loaf of bread 200,000 marks, and an egg 60,000 marks. Prices increased so rapidly that waiters changed the prices on the menu several times during the course of a lunch. Sometimes customers had to pay double the price listed on the menu when they ordered.

[7] Theodore Morgan, *Income and Employment,* 2d ed. (Englewood Cliffs, N.J.: Prentice-Hall, Inc., 1952), p. 361.

Photographs of the period show a German housewife starting the fire in her kitchen stove with paper money and children playing with bundles of paper money tied together into building blocks![8]

A closing word of caution is in order. Such dramatic hyperinflations as those just documented are almost invariably the consequence of imprudent expansion of the money supply by government. Given appropriate public policies, there is no reason why mild or creeping inflation need become hyperinflation.

CHAPTER SUMMARY

1 Our economy has been characterized by fluctuations in national output, employment, and the price level. Although characterized by common phases—peak, recession, trough, recovery—business cycles vary greatly in duration and intensity.

2 Although the business cycle has been explained in terms of such ultimate causal factors as innovations, political events, and money creation, it is generally agreed that the level of total spending is the immediate determinant of national output and employment.

3 All sectors of the economy are affected by the business cycle, but in varying ways and degrees. The cycle has greater output and employment ramifications in the capital goods and durable consumer goods industries than it does in nondurable goods industries. Over the cycle, price fluctuations are greater in competitive than in monopolistic industries.

4 Economists distinguish between frictional, structural, and cyclical unemployment. The full-employment or natural rate of unemployment is currently believed to be between 5 and 6 percent. The accurate measurement of unemployment is complicated by the existence of part-time and discouraged workers.

5 The economic cost of unemployment, as measured by the GNP gap, consists of the goods and services which society foregoes when its resources are involuntarily idle. Okun's law suggests that every 1 percent increase in unemployment above the natural rate gives rise to a $2\frac{1}{2}$ percent GNP gap.

[8] Raburn M. Williams, *Inflation! Money, Jobs, and Politicians* (Arlington Heights, Ill.: AHM Publishing Corporation, 1980), p. 2.

LAST WORD

The stock market and macroeconomic instability

How, if at all, do changes in stock prices relate to the macroeconomy?

Stock certificates of hundreds of companies are bought and sold daily in the stock market. Owners of stock shares receive dividends as their portions of the firm's profits. The price of a share of stock for a particular corporation is determined through the interaction of the demand for, and supply of, that stock. Individual stock prices tend to rise and fall in concert with the collective expectations for each firm's future profits. Higher profits normally result in higher dividends to the owners of the stock. And in anticipation of these higher dividends, financial investors are willing to pay a higher price for the stock.

Stock market averages such as the Dow Jones industrial average—the average price of the stocks of a selected list of major United States industrial firms—are closely watched and reported. It is not uncommon for these price averages to change over periods of time, or even to rise or fall sharply during a single day. Many of you will remember "Black Monday," October 19, 1987, when the Dow Jones industrial average experienced a record one-day fall of roughly 20 percent. About $500 billion in stock market wealth evaporated in a single day!

The volatility of the stock market raises an important question: Do changes in stock price averages *cause* macroeconomic instability? There are linkages between the stock market and the economy which might lead us to think the answer to this question is "Yes." Consider a sharp decline in stock prices. Feeling poorer, owners of stock may respond by reducing their spending on goods and services. Because it is less attractive to raise funds by issuing new shares of stock, firms may react by cutting back on their purchases of new capital goods. Research studies find, however, that the consumption and investment impacts of stock price changes are relatively mild. Therefore, although stock price averages do influence total spending, the stock market is *not* a major cause of recession or inflation.

A related question thus emerges: Even though changes in stock prices do not *cause* significant changes in national output and the price level, might not they *predict* such changes? That is, if stock market values are based on expected profits, wouldn't we expect rapid changes in stock price averages to forecast changes in future business conditions? Indeed, stock prices often *do* fall prior to recessions and rise prior to expansions. For this reason stock prices are among a group of eleven variables which constitute an index of leading indicators (Last Word, Chapter 14). This index often provides a useful clue as to the future direction of the economy. But taken alone, stock market prices are not a reliable predictor of changes in national output. Stock prices have fallen rapidly in some instances with no recession following. Black Monday itself did not produce a recession during the following fifteen months. In other instances, recessions have occurred with no prior decline in stock market prices.

In summary, the relationship between stock market prices and the macroeconomy is quite loose. Changes in stock prices are not a major source of macroeconomic instability nor are they totally reliable in forecasting business recessions or expansions.

6 Unemployment rates and inflation rates vary greatly among nations. Unemployment rates differ because nations have different natural rates of unemployment and often are in different phases of their business cycles. Inflation and unemployment rates in the United States have been low over the last few years in comparison to a number of the other industrial nations.

7 Economists discern both demand-pull and cost-push (supply-side) inflation. Two variants of cost-push inflation are wage-push inflation and inflation caused by a supply shock.

8 Unanticipated inflation tends to arbitrarily redistribute income at the expense of fixed-income receivers, creditors, and savers. If inflation is anticipated, individuals and businesses may be able to take steps to lessen or eliminate adverse redistributive effects.

9 The demand-pull theory of inflation suggests that some inflation may be necessary if the economy is to realize high levels of output and employment. However, the cost-push theory of inflation indicates that inflation may be accompanied by declines in real output and employment. Hyperinflation, which is usually associated with injudicious government policy, might undermine the monetary system and precipitate economic collapse.

TERMS AND CONCEPTS

business cycle	**Okun's law**
seasonal variations	**rule of 70**
secular trend	**demand-pull and cost-push inflation**
frictional, structural, and cyclical unemployment	**per unit production cost**
full-employment unemployment rate	**nominal and real income**
natural rate of unemployment	**anticipated versus unanticipated inflation**
potential output	**cost-of-living adjustment (COLA)**
labor force	**nominal and real interest rates**
discouraged workers	**hyperinflation**
GNP gap	

QUESTIONS AND STUDY SUGGESTIONS

1 What are the major phases of the business cycle? How long do business cycles last? How do seasonal variations and secular trends complicate measurement of the business cycle? Why does the business cycle affect output and employment in durable goods industries more severely than industries producing nondurables?

2 Why is it difficult to determine the full-employment unemployment rate? Why is it difficult to distinguish between frictional, structural, and cyclical unemployment? Why is unemployment an economic problem? What are the consequences of the "GNP gap"? What are the noneconomic effects of unemployment? How is the unemployment rate calculated?

3 Given that there exists an unemployment compensation program which provides income for those who are out of work, why worry about unemployment?

4 Use the following data to calculate **a** the size of the labor force and **b** the official unemployment rate. Total population, 500; population under 16 years of age and institutionalized, 120; not in labor force, 150; unemployed, 23; part-time workers looking for full-time jobs, 10.

5 Explain how an *increase* in your nominal income and a *decrease* in your real income might occur simultaneously. Who loses from inflation? From unemployment? If you had to choose between **a** full employment with a 6 percent annual rate of inflation or **b** price stability with an 8 percent unemployment rate, which would you select? Why?

6 If the price index was 110 last year and is 121 this year, what was this year's rate of inflation? What is the "rule of 70"? How long would it take for the price level to double if inflation persisted at **a** 2, **b** 5, and **c** 10 percent per year?

7 Carefully describe the relationship between total spending and the levels of output and employment. Explain the relationship between the price level and increases in total spending as the economy moves from substantial unemployment to moderate unemployment and, finally, to full employment.

8 Explain how a severe "hyperinflation" might lead to a depression.

9 Evaluate as accurately as you can the manner in which each of the following individuals would be affected by unanticipated inflation of 10 percent per year:
   a a pensioned railroad worker
   b a department-store clerk
   c a UAW assembly-line worker
   d a heavily indebted farmer
   e a retired business executive whose current income comes entirely from interest on government bonds
   f the owner of an independent small-town department store

10 A noted television comedian once defined inflation as follows: "Inflation? That means your money today won't buy as much as it would have during the depression when you didn't have any." Is his definition accurate?

11 Assume that in a given year the natural rate of unemployment is 5 percent and the actual rate of unemployment is 9 percent. Use Okun's law to determine the size of the GNP gap in percentage point terms. If the nominal GNP is $500 billion in that year, how much output is being foregone because of unemployment?

CHAPTER 11

Macroeconomic analysis: aggregate demand and aggregate supply

In Chapter 9 we discovered how national output and income are measured. There, we also learned how a price index is constructed and how it is used to compare price levels from one period to the next. In addition, the price index permitted us to convert nominal GNP to real GNP and thus meaningfully to compare GNP in various years. In Chapter 10 we looked at how real GNP, employment, and the price level have fluctuated over time. We also described the economic impacts of changes in real GNP and the price level.

Now, it is time to shift the emphasis from description to analysis by building upon the definitions and facts presented in Chapters 9 and 10. The central purpose of the present chapter is to introduce basic tools which will help us organize our thinking about macroeconomic theories and controversies. To this end we will first discuss the need to look at a market in the aggregate—that is, to combine the myriad of individual markets into a single market. Next, we introduce the concepts of aggregate demand and aggregate supply. The shapes of the aggregate demand and aggregate supply curves will then be explained and the most relevant forces which will cause them to shift will be outlined. We will then consider the notion of the equilibrium levels of prices and real national output. Finally, our focus will turn to the effects of shifts in the aggregate demand and aggregate supply curves on the price level and the size of real national output.

The present chapter provides a skeletal introduction to aggregate demand and supply. The "bare bones" model presented herein will be packed with considerable "sinew and fiber" as

we proceed through Parts 2, 3, and 4. In fact, you may well want to read this chapter again upon completion of Part 4. The reason? While the skeletal framework in this chapter will help you better understand the discussion in the chapters which follow, similarly, the discussion in the ensuing chapters will expand and reinforce your grasp of the basic model presented here.

The need for an aggregate model

In Chapter 4 we examined in some detail the demand and supply curves for single products. There we were interested in discovering how market demand and supply for particular goods establish each product's equilibrium price and quantity. That simple demand and supply model was then used to show how equilibrium prices and quantities change in response to changes in one or more of the determinants of supply and demand.

Single-product demand and supply models such as those found in Chapter 4 are particularly useful for understanding differences in the prices and outputs of various products and services. They help us comprehend why the equilibrium price of a donut is considerably less than the equilibrium price of a diamond, why the price of a barrel of oil is less than the price of a barrel of perfume, and why the annual expenditure on oil is greater than the annual expenditure on diamonds, perfume, and donuts combined. The single-product demand and supply model also helps explain why equilibrium prices and quantities of some individual products change from one period to the next. For example, the model is useful for explaining why the price of medical care has increased relative to other prices over the past two decades, or why the production of personal computers has risen tremendously since their introduction in the late 1970s.

Nevertheless, the single-product demand and supply model leaves several important economic questions unanswered. What causes prices in general to rise or fall? Why does the overall price level remain relatively constant during some periods only to surge upward in others? What determines the sum of all of the equilibrium quantities in specific product markets within a nation—the country's real national output? Why does real national output recede from previous levels in some years while in other periods it grows rapidly?

To answer these questions we need to combine—or aggregate—all the individual markets in the economy into a single overall market. More precisely, we must merge the thousands of individual prices—of pizzas, industrial robots, corn, personal computers, crankshafts, donuts, diamonds, oil, perfume, and so forth—into a single aggregate price or a price level. Similarly, we also must merge the equilibrium quantities of individual products and services into a single entity called real national output. Combining all of the prices of individual products and services into a price level, as well as merging all the equilibrium quantities into real national output, is called **aggregation.** The combined prices (the price level) and the merged equilibrium quantities (real national output) are each referred to as **aggregates.**

The labels on our graph in the simple macroeconomic model therefore become the *price level* (on the vertical axis), not the price of a single product, and *real national output* (on the horizontal axis), not the quantity of a specific product. With these labels in mind, let us gain a preliminary understanding of aggregate demand and aggregate supply.

Aggregate demand

Aggregate demand *is a schedule, graphically represented as a curve, which shows the various amounts of goods and services—the amounts of real national output—which consumers, businesses, and government collectively will desire to purchase at each possible price level.* Other things being equal, the lower the price level, the larger will be the real national output domestic consumers, businesses, government, and foreign buyers will want to purchase. Conversely, the higher the price level, the smaller will be the national output they desire to purchase. Thus, the relationship between the price level and the amount of real national output collectively demanded is inverse or negative.

AGGREGATE DEMAND CURVE

The inverse, or negative, relationship between the price level and national output is apparent in Figure 11-1. Observe that the aggregate demand curve slopes downward and to the right as does the demand curve for an individual product.

Why so? Curiously, the rationale is *not* the same as that which applies to the demand for a single product. That explanation, you may recall, centered upon income and substitution effects. When the price of an individual product falls, the consumer's (constant) money income will enable him or her to purchase more of the product (the

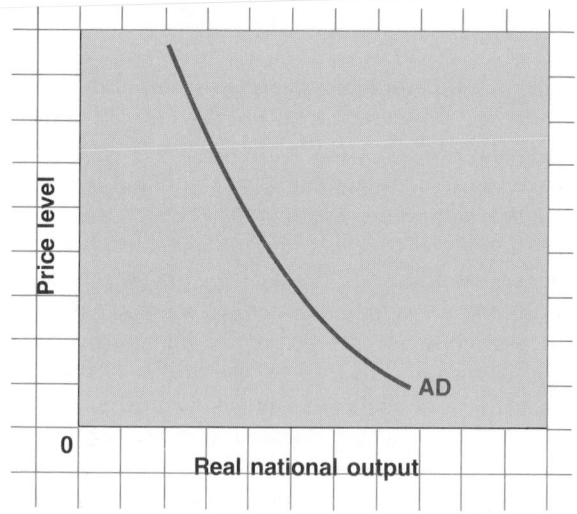

FIGURE 11-1

The aggregate demand curve

The downsloping aggregate demand curve indicates that, the lower the price level, the larger the real national output which will be purchased.

income effect). Furthermore, as price falls, the consumer wants to buy more of the particular product because it becomes relatively less expensive than other goods (the substitution effect).

But these explanations do not work when we are dealing in terms of aggregates. In Figure 11-1 prices in general are falling as we move down the aggregate demand curve so the rationale for the substitution effect (a product becoming cheaper relative to all other products) is not applicable. Similarly, while an individual's demand curve for a specific product assumes the consumer's income to be fixed, the aggregate demand curve implies varying aggregate incomes. Hence, as we move up the aggregate demand curve we move to higher price levels. But recalling our circular flow model, higher prices paid for goods and services will flow to resources suppliers as expanded wage, rent, interest, and profit incomes. As a result, an increase in the price level does *not* necessarily mean a decline in the nominal income of the economy as a whole.

If substitution and income effects do not explain the downsloping aggregate demand curve, what then is the rationale for a downsloping curve? Answer: The rationale for a downsloping aggregate demand curve rests primarily upon three factors: (1) the interest-rate effect; (2) the wealth, or real balances, effect; and (3) the foreign purchases effect.

Interest-rate effect The **interest-rate effect** suggests that the rationale for the downsloping aggregate demand curve lies in the impact of the changing price level upon interest rates and in turn upon consumption and investment spending. More specifically, as the price level rises so will interest rates *and* rising interest rates will in turn cause reductions in certain kinds of consumption and investment spending.

Elaboration: The aggregate demand curve assumes that the supply of money in the economy is fixed. When the price level increases, consumers will need to have more money on hand to make purchases and businesses will similarly require more money to meet their payrolls and purchase other needed inputs. In short, a higher price level will increase the demand for money. Given a fixed supply of money, this increase in demand will drive up the price paid for the use of money. That price, of course, is the interest rate. Higher interest rates

will curtail certain interest-sensitive expenditures by businesses and households. A firm which expects a 10 percent return on a potential capital goods purchase will find that purchase profitable when the interest rate is, say, only 7 percent. But the purchase is unprofitable and therefore will not be made when the interest rate has risen to, say, 12 percent. Similarly, an increase in the interest rate will make some consumers decide *not* to purchase houses or automobiles. To summarize: A higher interest rate curtails certain interest-sensitive business and consumer expenditures.

Conclusion: A higher price level—by increasing the demand for money and the interest rate—causes a reduction in the amount of real output demanded.

Wealth effect A second reason why the aggregate demand curve is downsloping involves the **wealth** or **real balances effect.** The idea here is that at a higher price level the real value or purchasing power of the accumulated financial assets—in particular, assets with fixed money values such as savings accounts or bonds—held by the public will diminish. By eroding the purchasing power of such assets, the public will be poorer in real terms and can therefore be expected to retrench on its spending. A household might feel comfortable in buying a new car or a sailboat if the purchasing power of their financial asset balances is, say, $50,000. But if inflation erodes the purchasing power of these asset balances to, say, $30,000, the family may decide to defer their purchase. Conversely, a decline in the price level will increase the real value or purchasing power of one's wealth and tend to increase spending.

Foreign purchases effect We found in Chapter 9's discussion of national income accounting that imports (American purchases of foreign goods) and exports (foreign purchases of American goods) are important components of total spending. For present purposes the point to be noted is that the volumes of our imports and exports depend upon, among other things, the relative price levels here and abroad. Thus, if the price level rises in the United States relative to foreign countries, American buyers will purchase more imports at the expense of American goods. Similarly, foreigners will also buy fewer American goods, causing American exports to decline. In short, other things being equal, a rise in our domestic price level will increase our imports and reduce our exports, thereby reducing the net exports (exports minus imports) component of aggregate demand in the United States.

Conclusion: The **foreign purchases effect** of a price-level increase results in a decline in the aggregate amount of American goods and services demanded. Conversely, a relative decline in our price level will reduce our imports and increase our exports, thereby increasing the net exports component of American aggregate demand.

NON-PRICE-LEVEL DETERMINANTS OF AGGREGATE DEMAND

We have seen that changes in the price level cause changes in the level of spending by domestic consumers, businesses, government, and foreign buyers in such a way that it is possible to predict changes in the amount of real national output. That is, an increase in the price level, *other things being equal*, will cause a decrease in the quantity of real output demanded. Conversely, a decrease in the price level will increase the amount of real output desired. This relationship is represented graphically as point-to-point movements along a stable aggregate demand curve. However, if one or more of those "other things" change, the entire aggregate demand curve shifts positions. We refer to those "other things" as **non-price-level determinants of aggregate demand.**

To understand what is causing changes in national output, we will need to be able to distinguish between *changes in the quantity of real output demanded* caused by changes in the price level and *changes in aggregate demand* caused by changes in one or more of the non-price-level determinants of aggregate demand. Recall that we drew a similar distinction when discussing single-product demand curves in Chapter 4.

As shown in Figure 11-2, an increase in aggregate demand is depicted by the rightward movement of the curve from AD_1 to AD_2. This shift indicates that, at each price level, the desired amount of real goods and services will be larger than before. Alternatively, a decrease in aggregate demand is shown as the leftward shift of the curve from AD_1

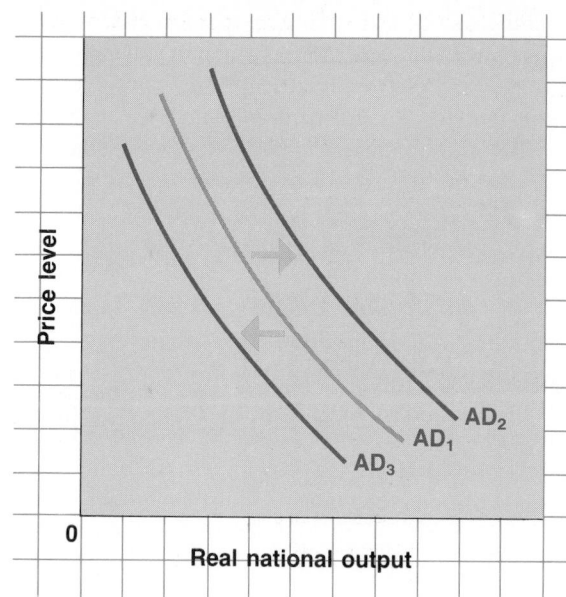

FIGURE 11-2

Changes in aggregate demand

A change in one or more of the non-price-level determinants of aggregate demand listed in Table 11-1 will cause a change in aggregate demand. An increase in aggregate demand is shown as the rightward shift of the AD curve from AD_1 to AD_2; a decrease in aggregate demand, as a leftward shift from AD_1 to AD_3.

to AD_3. This shift tells us that people will now desire to buy less real output at each price level than previously.

To repeat: The changes in aggregate demand shown in the figure take place when changes occur in one or more of the factors previously assumed to be constant. These non-price-level determinants of aggregate demand, or *aggregate demand shifters*, are listed in Table 11-1. Let us examine each element of the table in the order shown.

Consumer spending   Independently of changes in the price level, domestic consumers collectively may decide to alter their purchases of American-produced real output. When this happens the entire aggregate demand curve shifts. It shifts leftward as from AD_1 to AD_3 in Figure 11-2 when consumers decide to buy less output than before at each possible price level. Conversely, the curve moves rightward as from AD_1 to AD_2 when consumers decide to buy more at each possible price level.

TABLE 11-1 **Non-price-level determinants of aggregate demand: factors that shift the aggregate demand curve**

1 Change in consumer spending
  a Consumer wealth
  b Consumer expectations
  c Consumer indebtedness
  d Taxes
2 Change in investment spending
  a Interest rates
  b Profit expectations on investment projects
  c Business taxes
  d Technology
  e Degree of excess capacity
3 Change in government spending
4 Change in net export spending
  a National income abroad
  b Exchange rates

Changes in one or more of several non-price-level factors may change consumer spending and therefore shift the aggregate demand curve. As indicated in Table 11-1, these factors are real consumer wealth, consumer expectations, consumer indebtedness, and taxes.

CONSUMER WEALTH   Consumer wealth consists of all the assets owned by consumers. These holdings include financial assets such as stocks and bonds and physical assets such as houses and land. A sharp decline in the real value of consumer assets tends to cause people to save more (buy fewer products) as a way to restore their wealth. The resulting decline in consumer spending will decrease aggregate demand—that is, shift the aggregate demand curve leftward. Conversely, an increase in the real value of consumer wealth will tend to increase consumption spending at each price level. Hence, the aggregate demand curve will shift rightward. Important point: We are *not* referring in this case to the previously discussed "wealth effect" or "real balance effect." That effect assumes a fixed aggregate demand curve and results from a change in the price level. In contrast, the change in real wealth addressed here is independent of a change in the price level; it is a *non-price-level factor* which shifts the entire aggregate demand curve. An example would be a sharp increase in stock prices

which increases consumer wealth, even though the price level has not changed. Similarly, a sharp decline in the real value of houses and land will reduce consumer wealth, independent of changes in the general price level.

CONSUMER EXPECTATIONS   Changes in expectations about the future can result in changes in consumer spending. For example, when people expect their future real income to rise, they tend to spend more of their current income. Hence, present consumption spending increases (present saving falls), and the aggregate demand curve shifts rightward. Conversely, an expectation that real income will decline in the future tends to reduce present consumption spending and therefore to reduce aggregate demand.

In much the same way, a widely held expectation of surging future inflation is likely to increase aggregate demand today. Why? Because consumers will probably decide to buy products before prices escalate. Conversely, an expectation of lower price levels in the near future is likely to reduce present consumption in that people will postpone some of their present consumption to take advantage of the future lower prices.

CONSUMER INDEBTEDNESS   A high level of consumer indebtedness resulting from past buying sprees financed by installment loans may force consumers to cut present spending as a way to pay off existing consumer debt. The result will be a decline in consumption spending and a leftward shift of the aggregate demand curve. Conversely, when consumers find that their indebtedness is relatively low, their tendency is to increase present consumption spending. This produces an increase in aggregate demand.

TAXES   A reduction in personal income tax rates will increase take-home income and therefore will tend to increase consumer purchases at each possible price level. That is, tax cuts will shift the aggregate demand curve rightward. Tax increases, on the other hand, will reduce consumption spending and shift the aggregate demand curve leftward.

Investment spending Investment spending—the purchase of capital goods—is a second non-price-level determinant of aggregate demand. A decline in the amount of new capital goods desired by businesses at each price level will shift the aggregate demand curve leftward. Conversely, an increase in the desired amount of investment goods will increase aggregate demand. The non-price-level factors which can alter the level of investment spending are listed in Table 11-1. Let us consider each of them.

INTEREST RATES All else being equal, an increase in the interest rate caused by a factor other than a change in the price level will lower investment spending and reduce aggregate demand. We are *not* referring here to the so-called "interest-rate effect." That effect occurs as a result of a change in the price level. Instead, we are referring to a change in the interest rate resulting from, say, a change in the nation's supply of money. An increase in the supply of money tends to reduce the interest rate and thereby increases investment. Conversely, a decrease in the supply of money increases the interest rate and reduces investment.

PROFIT EXPECTATIONS ON INVESTMENT PROJECTS Improved profit expectations on investment projects will increase the demand for capital goods and thereby shift the aggregate demand curve rightward. For example, an anticipated rise in spending by consumers may in turn improve the profit expectations of possible investment projects. Alternatively, if the profit outlook on possible investment projects dims because of an expected decline in consumer spending, investment spending will tend to decline. Consequently, aggregate demand will also decline.

BUSINESS TAXES An increase in business taxes will reduce after-tax profits from corporate investment and therefore will tend to reduce investment spending and aggregate demand. Conversely, tax reductions will increase after-tax profits from corporate investment and can be expected to increase investment spending and push the aggregate demand curve rightward.

TECHNOLOGY New and improved technologies tend to stimulate investment spending and therefore to increase aggregate demand. Example: Recent advances in the high-tech fields of microbiology and electronics have spawned new labs and production facilities to exploit the new technologies.

DEGREE OF EXCESS CAPACITY A rise in excess capacity—unused existing capital—will retard the demand for new capital goods and therefore reduce aggregate demand. Put simply, firms operating factories at well below capacity have little incentive to build new factories. Alternatively, when firms collectively discover that their excess capacity is dwindling, they tend to build new factories and buy more equipment. Hence, investment spending rises and the aggregate demand curve shifts to the right.

Government spending Table 11-1 reminds us that government's desire to buy goods and services is a third non-price-level determinant of aggregate demand. An increase in government purchases of national output at each price level will increase aggregate demand so long as tax collections and interest rates do not change as a result. An example of this type of increase would be a decision by government to expand the U.S. naval fleet. Conversely, a reduction in government spending will reduce aggregate demand. An example would be a cutback in government spending on new highway construction.

Net export spending The final non-price level determinant of aggregate demand is net export spending. When foreign consumers change their purchases of U.S. goods, independent of changes in our price level, the American aggregate demand curve shifts as well. We again specify "independent of changes in our price level" to distinguish clearly from changes in spending associated with the foreign purchases effect. That effect helps explain why a change in the American price level produces a change in real U.S. output. In discussing aggregate demand shifters we are instead addressing changes in net exports caused by factors other than changes in the price level. Increases in net exports (exports minus imports) caused by these other factors push our aggregate demand curve rightward. The logic behind this proposition is as follows. First, a higher level of American exports constitutes an increased *foreign demand* for American goods. Second, a reduction of our imports implies an increased *domestic demand* for American-produced products.

What are the non-price-level factors which alter

net exports? They are primarily national income abroad and exchange rates.

NATIONAL INCOME ABROAD Rising national income in a foreign nation tends to increase the foreign demand for U.S. goods and consequently to increase aggregate demand in America. Why? As income levels rise in a foreign nation, their citizens can afford to buy both more products made at home *and* made in the United States. Hence, our exports rise in step with increases in the levels of national income of our trading partners. Declines in national income abroad have the opposite effect: Our net exports decline, shifting the aggregate demand curve leftward.

EXCHANGE RATES A change in the exchange rate between the dollar and other currencies is a second factor which affects net exports and hence aggregate demand. Suppose that the dollar price of yen rises, which means that the **dollar depreciates** in terms of the yen. Viewed differently, the yen price of dollars falls, meaning that the **yen appreciates.** The upshot of the new relative values of dollars and yen is that consumers in Japan will be able to obtain *more* dollars with any particular number of yen. Similarly, consumers in the United States will be able to obtain *fewer* yen for each dollar. Hence, Japanese consumers will discover that American goods have cheaper price tags in terms of yen. American consumers meanwhile will find that fewer Japanese products can be purchased with a given number of dollars. With respect to our *exports,* for example, a $30 pair of American-made blue jeans now might be bought for, say, 2880 yen as compared to 3600 yen. And in terms of our *imports,* a Japanese watch might now cost $225 rather than, say, $180. Under these circumstances we would expect our exports to rise and imports to fall. This implies an increase in net exports which in turn translates into an increase in U.S. aggregate demand. You are urged to think through the opposite scenario in which the dollar appreciates (yen depreciates).

Recapitulation There are a number of non-price-level determinants (Table 11-1) which influence the amount of real output that domestic consumers, businesses, government, and foreign buyers wish to purchase **at each price level.** Increases in spending brought forth by changes in one or more of the non-price-level determinants of aggregate demand push the aggregate demand curve rightward; conversely, decreases in such spending shift the curve leftward. These shifts in the aggregate demand curve must be distinguished from changes in real national output arising because of changes in the price level. Changes in the price level produce wealth, interest-rate, and foreign purchases effects which explain the downsloping aggregate demand curve. Changes in the non-price-level determinants of aggregate demand cause shifts in the aggregate demand curve itself.

Aggregate supply

Aggregate supply *is a schedule, graphically represented by a curve, indicating the level of real national output which will be available at each possible price level.* Higher price levels create an incentive for enterprises to produce additional output and offer it for sale. Lower price levels cause reductions in output. As a result, the relationship between the price level and the amount of national output businesses offer for sale is direct or positive.

AGGREGATE SUPPLY CURVE

We shall find in our study of macroeconomics that there is great disagreement over the nature and shape of the aggregate supply curve. But for present purposes, it will be useful to think of the aggregate supply curve as comprising three quite distinct segments or ranges. Throughout this discussion we will also assume that the aggregate supply curve itself does not shift when the price level changes. In Chapter 19, this assumption will be relaxed and the discussion of aggregate supply will be extended.

The three segments of the aggregate supply curve are identified as (1) the Keynesian (horizontal), (2) the intermediate (upsloping), and (3) the classical (vertical) range. Let us examine these three ranges and explain the rationale for each. Our task is expedited by the fact that our explanations are essentially those which you are already familiar with from our discussion of Figure 10-6.

We will find that the shape of the aggregate supply curve reflects what happens to per unit production costs as the national output expands or contracts. Recall from the previous chapter that per unit production cost is found by dividing the total cost of the inputs (resources) used by the quantity of output. In other words, the per unit production cost of a particular level of output is the average cost of that output.

Keynesian (horizontal) range In Figure 11-3 we use Q_f to designate the full-employment or potential level of real national output first introduced in Chapter 10. Recall that the natural rate of unemployment occurs at this output level. Observe that the horizontal range of aggregate supply comprises real levels of national output which are substantially less than the full-employment output Q_f. Hence, the horizontal range implies that the economy is in a severe recession or depression and that large amounts of unused machinery and equip-

ment and unemployed workers are therefore available. These idle resources—both human and property—can therefore be put back to work with little or no upward pressure on the price level. As national output expands over this range no shortages or production bottlenecks will be incurred to cause prices to rise. A worker who has been unemployed for two or three months will hardly expect a wage increase when recalled to his or her job. Because producers can acquire labor and other inputs at stable prices, production costs will not rise as output is expanded and hence there is no reason to raise product prices. Conversely, this range also implies that, if real national output is contracting, product and resource prices will be downwardly inflexible. That means real output and employment will fall, but product prices and wages will remain rigid. Indeed, as we will explain in Chapter 12, real output and employment will decline in this range *because* prices and wages are assumed to be inflexible.

This horizontal range has been dubbed the **Keynesian range** after the famous English economist John Maynard Keynes (pronounced "canes") who is the subject of this chapter's Last Word. Keynes—whose theory of employment will be detailed in the next two chapters—examined the functioning of capitalistic economies against the backdrop of the Great Depression of the 1930s when unemployment in the United States was as high as 25 percent. In this lamentable economic condition there was ample room to expand production without fear of higher production costs or higher prices. Conversely, Keynes held that declines in real national output and employment would *not* be cushioned by price and wage reductions.

Classical (vertical) range If we jump to the other extreme, we find that the economy reaches the full or natural rate of unemployment at a real national output of Q_f. The economy is at a point *on* Chapter 2's production possibilities curve and in the short term no further increase in real output is attainable. This means that any further increase in the price level will fail to bring forth additional real output because the economy is already operating at capacity. At full employment individual firms may try to expand production by bidding resources away from other firms. But the resources and addi-

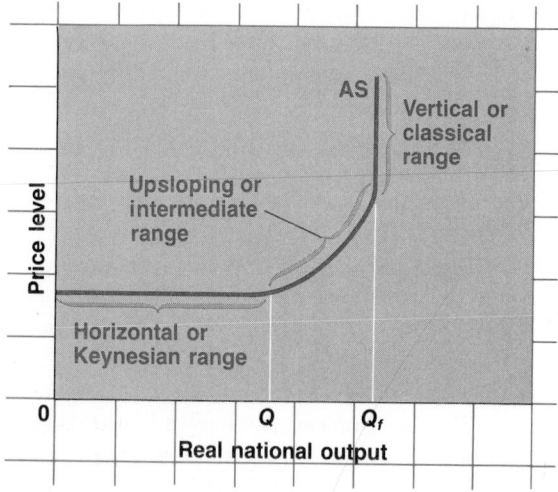

FIGURE 11-3

The aggregate supply curve

The aggregate supply curve shows the level of real national output which will be produced at various price levels. It comprises three ranges: (a) a horizontal or Keynesian range wherein the price level remains constant as national output varies; (b) a vertical or classical range wherein real national output is constant at the full-employment level and the price level can vary; and (c) an intermediate range wherein both real output and the price level are variable.

tional production which one firm gains will be lost by some other firm. Resource prices (costs) and ultimately product prices will rise as a result of this process, but real national output will remain unchanged.

Two diverse points must be made in connection with the vertical range of the aggregate supply curve. First, this range is associated with classical economics—also to be discussed in the next chapter—which concludes there are forces inherent in a market economy which cause full employment to be the norm. Hence, the vertical range is also known as the **classical range** of the aggregate supply curve. The second point is that "full employment" and "full-employment real output" are slippery concepts. This is true not merely because the "full employment or natural unemployment rate" is difficult to quantify (Chapter 10), but also because hours of work and the size of the labor force can sometimes be expanded beyond what is normal. Recall from Figure 10-4 that periodically actual GNP exceeds potential GNP. Thus, in a highly prosperous economy daily working hours and the workweek can be extended. Workers can also engage in "moonlighting," that is, the practice of holding more than one job. Example: During World War II a 10-hour workday and a six-day workweek were not uncommon. Many workers, after completing their normal workday at a regular job, would work a partial or full night shift in a defense plant. Women and young persons, who would not ordinarily have worked, joined the labor force in response to patriotic appeals and high wages. But for our purposes it is acceptable to say there is some specific level of real output which corresponds to full employment.

Intermediate (upsloping) range Finally, in the **intermediate range** between Q and Q_f we observe that an expansion of real output is accompanied by a rising price level. Why? One reason is that the aggregate economy is in fact comprised of innumerable product and resource markets *and* full employment is not reached evenly or simultaneously in the various sectors or industries. Hence, as the economy expands in the QQ_f real output range, the high-tech computer industry, for example, may encounter shortages of skilled workers while the automobile or steel industries are still faced with substantial unemployment. Similarly, in certain

industries raw-material shortages or similar production bottlenecks may begin to appear. Expansion also means that some firms will be forced to use older and less efficient machinery as they approach capacity production. Also, less capable workers may be hired as output expands. For all of these kinds of reasons, per unit production costs rise and firms must receive higher product prices in order for production to be profitable. Hence, in the intermediate range a rising real output is accompanied by a higher price level.

Forewarning: As we have noted, the shape of the aggregate supply curve is a matter of great controversy. We shall find in later chapters that some economists—called *classical* or *new classical economists*—contend the curve is vertical throughout, implying that a change in aggregate demand will be relatively harmless because it only affects the price level while leaving output and employment unchanged. Other economists—known as *Keynesians*—argue that the aggregate supply curve is either horizontal or upsloping and therefore that decreases in aggregate demand have adverse and very costly effects upon output and employment.

NON-PRICE-LEVEL DETERMINANTS OF AGGREGATE SUPPLY

Our discussion of the shape of the aggregate supply curve revealed that real national output increases as the economy moves from left to right through the Keynesian and intermediate ranges of aggregate supply. These changes in output result from *movements along* the aggregate supply curve and need to be distinguished from *shifts* in the aggregate supply curve itself. Said differently, an existing aggregate supply curve identifies the relationship between the price level and real national output, *other things being equal*. But when one or more of these "other things" change, the aggregate supply curve itself shifts. The shift of the curve from AS_1 to AS_2 in Figure 11-4 shows an *increase* in aggregate supply. Over the intermediate and classical range of the aggregate supply curves, this shift is rightward, indicating that businesses collectively will produce more real output at each price level than previously. Over the Keynesian range of the aggregate supply curves, an increase in aggregate

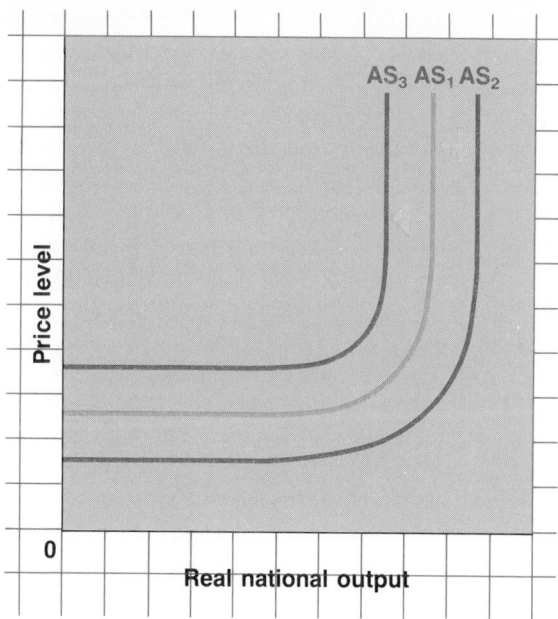

FIGURE 11-4

Changes in aggregate supply

A change in one or more of the non-price-level determinants of aggregate supply listed in Table 11-2 will cause a change in aggregate supply. An increase in aggregate supply is shown as a "rightward" shift of the AS curve from AS_1 to AS_2; a decrease in aggregate supply, as a "leftward" shift from AS_1 to AS_3.

change. We established in earlier chapters that the supply decisions of businesses are made on the basis of production costs and revenues. Businesses are profit seekers and profits arise from the difference between product prices and per unit production costs. Producers respond to higher prices for their products—that is, to higher price levels—by increasing their real output. And, production bottlenecks mean that per unit production costs tend to rise as output expands toward full employment. For this reason the aggregate supply curve slopes upward in its intermediate range.

The present point is that there are factors *other than changes in real national output* which alter per unit production costs. These factors are those listed in Table 11-2. When one or more of them change, per unit production costs change at each price level. That is, the aggregate supply curve shifts positions. Specifically, decreases in per unit production costs of this type shift the aggregate supply curve rightward. Conversely, increases in per unit production costs shift the aggregate supply curve leftward. To repeat: *When per unit production costs change for reasons other than a change in national output, firms collectively alter the amount of national output they produce at each price level.*

We need to establish how changes in the aggregate supply shifters listed in Table 11-2 affect per unit production costs and thereby shift the aggregate supply curve.

supply can best be thought of as a decline in the price level at each level of national output (a downward shift of aggregate supply). For convenience we will refer to an increase in aggregate supply as a "rightward" shift of the curve rather than a "rightward or a downward" shift. Conversely, the shift of the curve from AS_1 to AS_3 will be referred to as a "leftward shift," indicating a *decrease* in aggregate supply. That is, businesses now will produce less real output at each price level than before (or charge higher prices at each level of output).

Table 11-2 summarizes the "other things" which shift the aggregate supply curve when they change. These factors are called **non-price-level determinants of aggregate supply** because they collectively "determine" or establish the location of the aggregate supply curve. The determinants shown in the table have one thing in common: When they change, per unit production costs also

TABLE 11-2 **Non-price-level determinants of aggregate supply: factors that shift the aggregate supply curve**

1 Change in input prices
  a Domestic resource availability
    a_1 land
    a_2 labor
    a_3 capital
    a_4 entrepreneurial ability
  b Prices of imported resources
  c Market power
2 Change in productivity
3 Change in legal-institutional environment
  a Business taxes and subsidies
  b Government regulation

Input prices   Input or resource prices—to be distinguished from the output prices comprising the price level—are an important non-price-level determinant of aggregate supply. All else being equal, higher input prices increase per unit production costs and therefore reduce aggregate supply. Lower input prices produce just the opposite result. Let us examine the following factors which influence input prices: domestic resource availability, the prices of imported resources, and market power.

DOMESTIC RESOURCE AVAILABILITY   We noted in Chapter 2 that a society's production possibilities curve shifts outward when the resources available to it increase. Rightward shifts in the production possibilities curve translate into rightward shifts of our aggregate supply curve. Increases in the supply of domestic resources lower input prices and, as a result, per unit production costs fall. Hence, at any given price level, firms collectively will produce and offer for sale more real national output than before. Conversely, declines in resource supplies tend to increase input prices and to shift the economy's aggregate supply curve to the left.

How might changes in the availability of land, labor, capital, and entrepreneurial resources work to shift the aggregate supply curve? Several examples will help answer this question.

Land   Land resources might become more available, for example, through discoveries of mineral deposits, irrigation of land, or new technical innovations which permit us to transform what were previously "nonresources" into valuable factors of production. An increase in the supply of land resources lowers the price of land inputs and thus lowers per unit production costs. For example, the recent discovery of widely available materials which under low temperatures act as superconductors of electricity is expected eventually to reduce per unit production costs by reducing the loss of electricity during its transmission. The resulting lower price of electricity will increase aggregate supply.

Two examples of reductions in the availability of land resources may also be cited: (1) the widespread depletion of the nation's underground water through irrigation, and (2) the nation's loss of topsoil through intensive farming. Eventually, each of these problems may increase input prices and shift aggregate supply leftward.

Labor   About 75 percent of all business costs are wages or salaries. Hence, all else being equal, changes in wages have a significant impact on per unit production costs and on the location of the aggregate supply curve. An increase in the availability of labor resources reduces the price of labor; a decrease raises labor's price. Examples: The influx of women into the labor force during the past two decades placed a downward pressure on wages and thereby tended to expand American aggregate supply. Emigration of employable workers from abroad also has historically increased the availability of labor in the United States. Conversely, the great loss of life during World War II greatly diminished the postwar availability of labor in the United States, tending to raise per unit production costs. Presently, the AIDS epidemic threatens to reduce the supply of labor and thus diminish the nation's aggregate supply of real output.

Capital   Aggregate supply tends to increase when society adds to its stock of capital. Such an addition would happen, for example, if society decided to save more of its income and to direct the savings toward purchase of capital goods. In much the same way, an improvement in the quality of capital tends to reduce production costs and increase aggregate supply. For example, businesses over the years have replaced equipment of poorer quality with new, superior equipment. Conversely, aggregate supply will decline when the quantity and quality of the nation's stock of capital diminish. Example: In the depths of the Great Depression of the 1930s, our capital stock deteriorated because new purchases of capital were insufficient to offset the normal wearing out and obsolescence of plant and equipment.

Entrepreneurial ability   Finally, note that the amount of entrepreneurial ability available to the economy can change from one period to the next and thereby shift the aggregate supply curve. It is conceivable, for instance, that the recent media focus on individuals who have amassed fortunes through entrepreneurial efforts might increase the number of people who have entrepreneurial aspirations, tending to shift the aggregate supply curve rightward.

PRICES OF IMPORTED RESOURCES   Just as foreign demand for American goods contributes to our aggregate demand, the importation of resources from abroad adds to our aggregate supply. Resources add to our productive capacity whether they be domestic or imported. Imported resources reduce input prices and therefore decrease the per unit cost of producing American real national output. Hence, we may generalize as follows: A decrease in the prices of imported resources expands our aggregate supply; an increase in the prices of these resources reduces our aggregate supply.

Exchange rate fluctuations have been a recent factor which has periodically altered the price of imported resources. To see how this happens, suppose that the dollar price of foreign currency falls—that is, the dollar appreciates—enabling American firms to obtain more foreign currency with each American dollar. This means that American producers face a lower dollar price of imported resources. Under these conditions, we would expect American firms to expand their imports of foreign resources and to realize reductions in per unit production costs at each level of output. And to repeat: Falling per unit production costs of this type shift the American aggregate supply curve to the right.

Conversely, an increase in the dollar price of foreign currency—dollar depreciation—raises the prices of imported resources. As a result, our imports of these resources falls, our per unit production costs jump upward, and our aggregate supply curve moves leftward.

MARKET POWER A change in the degree of market power or monopoly power held by sellers of resources can also affect input prices and aggregate supply. *Market power* is the ability to set a price above that which would occur in a competitive situation. The rise and fall of OPEC's market power during the past two decades provides a good illustration. The tenfold increase in the price of oil that OPEC was able to achieve during the 1970s permeated our economy, drove up per unit production costs, and jolted the American aggregate supply curve leftward. Conversely, a substantial reduction in OPEC's market power during the mid-1980s reduced the cost of manufacturing and transporting products, and as a direct result, increased American aggregate supply.

A change in union market power also can be expected to affect the location of the aggregate supply curve. Some observers believe that unions experienced growing market power in the 1970s, re-

sulting in union wage increases which widened the gap between union and nonunion workers. This higher pay may well have increased per unit production costs and produced leftward shifts of aggregate supply. Alternatively, union market power greatly waned during the 1980s. Consequently, in many industries the price of union labor fell, resulting in lower per unit production costs. The result was an increase in aggregate supply.

Productivity Productivity relates a nation's level of real output to the quantity of input used to produce that output. In other words, **productivity** is a measure of average output, or of real output per unit of input:

$$\text{Productivity} = \frac{\text{real output}}{\text{input}}$$

An increase in productivity means that more real national output can be obtained from the amount of resources—or inputs—currently available.

How does an increase in productivity affect the aggregate supply curve? We first need to discover how a change in productivity alters per unit production costs. Suppose the real national output in a hypothetical economy is 10 units, the input quantity needed to produce that quantity is 5, and the price of each input unit is $2. We would discover that productivity—output per input—is 2 (= 10/5). What would be the per unit cost of output? The answer is found by way of the following formula:

$$\text{Per unit production cost} = \frac{\text{total input cost}}{\text{units of output}}$$

In this case, per unit cost is $1, found by dividing $10 of input cost (= $2 × 5 units of input) by 10 units of output.

Now let us suppose that real national output doubles to 20 units, while the input price and quantity remain constant at $2 and 5 units. That is, suppose productivity rises from 2 (= 10/5) to 4 (= 20/5). Because the total cost of the inputs stays at $10 (= $2 × 5 units of input), the per unit cost of the output falls from $1 to $.50 (= $10 of input cost/20 units of output). Conclusion: *By reducing per unit production costs, an increase in productivity will tend to shift the aggregate supply curve rightward; conversely, a decline in productivity will tend to increase per unit production costs and shift the aggregate supply curve leftward.*

We shall discover in Chapter 21 that productivity growth is a major factor explaining the secular expansion of aggregate supply in the United States and the corresponding growth of real national output. The use of more machinery and equipment per worker, improved production technology, a better-educated and trained labor force, and improved forms of business enterprises have interacted to raise productivity, all else being equal, and increase aggregate supply.

Legal-institutional environment Changes in the legal-institutional setting in which businesses collectively operate may alter per unit costs of output and shift the aggregate supply curve. Two categories of changes of this type are (1) changes in taxes and subsidies, and (2) changes in the extent of regulation.

BUSINESS TAXES AND SUBSIDIES Higher business taxes, such as sales, excise, and social security taxes, can be expected to increase per unit costs and reduce aggregate supply in much the same way that a wage increase does so. Example: An increase in the social security taxes paid by businesses will increase production costs and reduce aggregate supply. Similarly, a business subsidy—a payment or tax break by government to a firm—reduces production costs and increases aggregate supply. Example: During the 1970s, the government subsidized producers of energy from alternative sources such as wind, oil shale, and solar power. The purpose was to reduce production costs and encourage development of energy sources which might substitute for oil and natural gas. To the extent that these subsidies were successful, the aggregate supply curve moved rightward.

GOVERNMENT REGULATION Under most circumstances, it is costly for businesses to comply with government regulations. Hence, regulation increases per unit production costs and shifts the aggregate supply curve leftward. "Supply-side" proponents of deregulation of the economy have argued forcefully that, by increasing efficiency and reducing the paperwork associated with complex regulations, deregulation will reduce per unit costs. In this way, the aggregate supply curve purportedly will shift rightward. Conversely, it is argued

that increases in regulation raise production costs and reduce aggregate supply.

Summary Let us pause to summarize our discussion of aggregate supply. First, the aggregate supply curve comprises three distinct ranges: the Keynesian (horizontal) range, the intermediate (upsloping) range, and the classical (vertical) range. The intermediate range suggests that per unit production costs and therefore the price level rise as output expands toward its potential level. But there are factors other than those associated with rising real output which affect per unit production costs. These other factors are input prices, productivity, and the legal-institutional environment—that is, the non-price-level determinants of aggregate supply listed in Table 11-2. When one or more of these determinants change, the aggregate supply curve shifts positions. A rightward shift of the aggregate supply curve reflects lower per unit production costs and represents an increase in aggregate supply. On the other hand, a leftward shift of the aggregate supply curve implies higher per unit production costs and constitutes a decrease in aggregate supply.

Equilibrium: real output and the price level

We found in Chapter 4 that the intersection of the demand for and supply of a particular product will determine the equilibrium price and output of that good. Similarly, as we see here in Figure 11-5a and b, the intersection of the aggregate demand and aggregate supply curves determines the **equilibrium price level** and **equilibrium real national output**.

First, observe Figure 11-5a where aggregate demand crosses aggregate supply in its intermediate range. We find that the equilibrium price level and level of real national output are P_e and Q_e, respectively. To illustrate why P_e is the equilibrium price and Q_e is the equilibrium level of real national output, let us suppose that the price level were P_1 rather than P_e. We observe from the aggregate supply curve that price level P_1 would entice businesses to produce at most real output level Q_1.

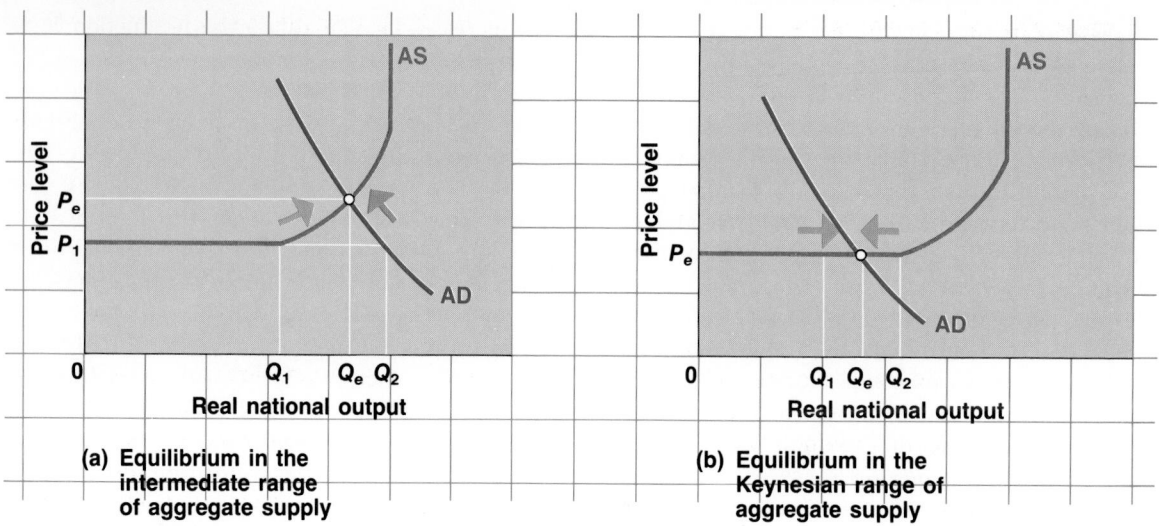

FIGURE 11-5

The equilibrium price level and the equilibrium real national output

The intersection of the aggregate demand and supply curves determines the equilibrium price level and equilibrium real national output. In (a) where aggregate demand intersects aggregate supply in its intermediate range, the price level will change to eliminate underproduction or overproduction of output; in (b) where the aggregate demand curve intersects the aggregate supply curve in its Keynesian range, no change in the price level accompanies the move toward equilibrium real national output.

How much real output would domestic consumers, businesses, government, and foreign buyers wish to purchase at P_1? We see from the aggregate demand curve that the answer is Q_2. The competition among buyers to purchase the available real output of Q_1 will drive up the price level to P_e. As our arrows in Figure 11-5a indicate, the rise in the price level from P_1 to P_e encourages *producers* to increase their real output from Q_1 to Q_e and simultaneously causes *buyers* to scale back their desired level of purchases from Q_2 to Q_e. When equality occurs between the amount of real national output produced and the amount purchased, as it does at P_e, the economy has achieved equilibrium.

In Figure 11-5b we portray aggregate demand intersecting aggregate supply in the Keynesian range where aggregate supply is perfectly horizontal. In this particular case the price level does *not* play a role in bringing about the equilibrium level of real national output. To understand why, first observe that the equilibrium price and real output levels in Figure 11-5b are P_e and Q_e. If the business sector had decided to produce a larger national

output, such as Q_2, it would be unable to dispose of that output. Aggregate demand would be insufficient to take the national output off the market. Faced with unwanted inventories of goods, businesses would reduce their production to the equilibrium level of Q_e—as shown by the leftward pointing arrow—and the market would clear. Conversely, if firms had only produced national output of Q_1, businesses would find that their inventories of goods would quickly diminish because sales of output would exceed production. Businesses would react by increasing production and national output would rise to equilibrium as shown by the rightward pointing arrow.

Changes in equilibrium

The next step in our analysis is to shift the aggregate demand and aggregate supply curves and observe the effects upon real national output (and therefore on employment) and upon the price level.

SHIFTING AGGREGATE DEMAND

Suppose that households and businesses decide to increase their spending. That is, they choose to purchase a larger real output at each possible price level, thereby shifting the aggregate demand curve to the right. Why might they so decide? Our list of non-price-level determinants of aggregate demand (Table 11-1) provides us with several possible reasons. Perhaps consumers become more optimistic in their expectations about future economic conditions. These favorable expectations might stem from new American technological advances which promise to increase the competitiveness of our products in both domestic and world markets and therefore to increase future real income. As a result, consumers now would decide to consume more (save less) of their current incomes. Similarly, firms anticipate that the future business conditions will enhance profits from current investments in new capital. Hence, they increase their investment spending in order to enlarge their productive capacities. As shown in Figure 11-6, the precise effects of an *increase* in aggregate demand

depend upon whether the economy is currently in the Keynesian, intermediate, or classical range of the aggregate supply curve.

In the Keynesian range of Figure 11-6a, where there is a high level of unemployment and much unused production capacity, the effect of an increase in aggregate demand (AD$_1$ to AD$_2$) is to bring about a large increase in real national output (Q_1 to Q_2) and employment with no increase in the price level (P_1). In the classical range of Figure 11-6b, where labor and capital are fully employed, an increase in aggregate demand (AD$_5$ to AD$_6$) would affect the price level only, increasing it from P_5 to P_6. Real national output will remain at the full-employment level Q_f. In the intermediate range of Figure 11-6c an increase in aggregate demand (AD$_3$ to AD$_4$) will raise both real national output (Q_3 to Q_4) *and* the price level (P_3 to P_4). Recalling Chapter 10's discussion of inflation, the price level increases associated with aggregate demand increases in both the classical and intermediate ranges of the aggregate supply curve constitute **demand-pull inflation.** That is, shifts in aggregate demand are pulling up the price level.

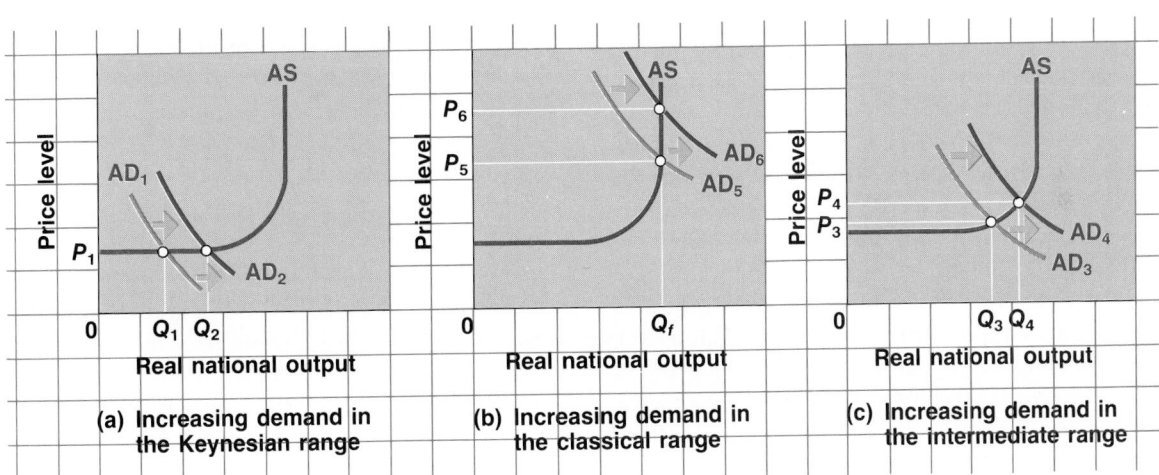

FIGURE 11-6

The effects of increases in aggregate demand

The effects of an increase in aggregate demand depend upon the range of the aggregate supply curve in which it occurs. (a) An increase in aggregate demand in the Keynesian (horizontal) range will increase real national output, but leave the price level unaffected. (b) In the classical (vertical) range an increase in aggregate demand will increase the price level, but real national output cannot increase beyond the full-employment level. (c) An increase in demand in the intermediate range will increase both real national output and the level of prices. The increases in aggregate demand shown in (b) and (c) depict demand-pull inflation.

THE RATCHET EFFECT

What of *decreases* in aggregate demand? Our model predicts that in the Keynesian range real national output will fall and the price level remain unchanged. In the classical range prices fall and real output remains at the full-employment level. In the intermediate range the model suggests that both real national output and the price level will diminish.

But there's an important complicating factor which raises serious doubts about the predicted effects of declines in aggregate demand in the classical and intermediate ranges. The reverse movements of aggregate demand—from AD_6 to AD_5 in Figure 11-6b and from AD_4 to AD_3 in Figure 11-6c—may *not* restore the initial equilibrium positions at least in the short term. The complication is that prices—both of products and resources—tend to be "sticky" or inflexible in a downward direction. What goes up in economics need not come down—at least not down to its original level. Hence, some economists envision a **ratchet effect** (a ratchet is a mechanism which permits one to crank a wheel forward but not backward).

The workings of the ratchet effect are shown in Figure 11-7 where for simplicity's sake we omit the intermediate range of the aggregate supply curve. If aggregate demand increases from AD_1 to AD_2, the economy moves from the P_1Q_1 equilibrium at e_1 in the Keynesian range to the new P_2Q_f equilibrium at e_2 in the classical range. But while prices quite readily move up, they do not easily come down, at least not in the short term. Thus if aggregate demand should reverse itself and decrease from AD_2 to AD_1, the economy will *not* return to the original equilibrium position at e_1. Rather the new, higher price level of P_2 will persist—prices have been ratcheted up from P_1 to P_2—and the decline in aggregate demand will therefore move the economy to equilibrium at e_2'. The price level remains at P_2 and real national output has fallen all the way to Q_2.

Stated differently, the downward inflexibility of prices has ratcheted the Keynesian range of the aggregate supply curve up from the P_1 to the P_2 price level. The original aggregate supply curve was P_1aAS, but downward price inflexibility has ratcheted up the Keynesian range so that the ag-

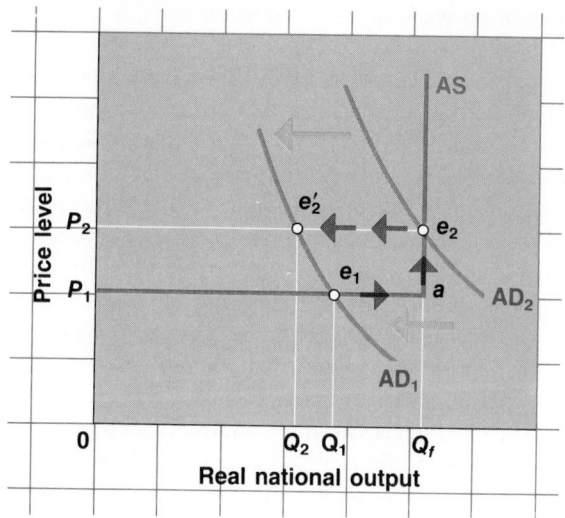

FIGURE 11-7

The ratchet effect

An increase in aggregate demand from AD_1 to AD_2 will move the equilibrium position from e_1 to e_2 with real national output rising from Q_1 to Q_f and the price level from P_1 to P_2. But if prices are inflexible downward, then a decline in aggregate demand from AD_2 to AD_1 will not return the economy to its original equilibrium at e_1. Rather, the new equilibrium will be at e_2' with the price level remaining at P_2 and output falling below the original level to Q_2. The ratchet effect means that the aggregate supply curve has changed from P_1aAS to P_2e_2AS.

gregate supply curve now is P_2e_2AS. Succinctly put, there is an asymmetry in the aggregate supply schedule in that its Keynesian range shifts upward readily and quite rapidly when aggregate demand is expanding, but shifts downward slowly or not at all when aggregate demand declines.

What might cause downward price inflexibility? The answer is complex. In the first place, wages—which typically constitute 75 percent or more of a firm's total costs—tend to be inflexible downward, at least temporarily. Given this inflexibility, it is extremely difficult for firms to reduce their prices and remain profitable. But why are wages inflexible? In the first place, a portion of the labor force works under union contracts wherein wage cuts are prohibited for the duration of the contract. It is not uncommon, incidentally, for collective bargaining agreements in major industries typically to run for three years. Similarly, the wages of nonunion workers are usually adjusted just once a year, rather than quarterly or monthly.

Wage inflexibility is reinforced by the fact that employers may **not** want to reduce wage rates. The reasons are at least twofold. On the one hand, lower wages may well have an adverse impact upon worker morale and hence upon labor productivity (output per worker). While lower wages would tend to lower labor cost per unit of output, lower worker productivity would tend to increase unit labor costs. It is not unreasonable for an employer to fear that the latter might more than counterbalance the former so that a lower wage rate increases, rather than reduces, labor cost per unit of production.

Furthermore, most employers have made an "investment" in the training and experience of their present labor forces. Were they to initiate a wage cut in the face of a decline in aggregate demand, they could expect to lose workers more or less randomly—both some highly trained and some relatively unskilled workers could be expected to quit. To the extent that the highly trained workers find jobs with other firms, the present employer would forgo any chance of getting a return on the investment made in their training. A better option might be to maintain wages and lay off workers on the basis of seniority. Generally, the less senior workers laid off will be the less skilled workers in whom the employer's training investment is least. It is also notable that the minimum wage imposes a legal floor under the wages of the least skilled workers. The important point is that, if production costs are downwardly inflexible, so too will be product prices.

Another part of the explanation of the downward stickiness of prices stems from the fact that in many industries firms have sufficient monopolistic power to resist price cuts for a time when demand declines. A glance back at Figure 10-3 may be helpful. Despite the catastrophic decline in aggregate demand that occurred between 1929 and 1933, firms in the agricultural implements, motor vehicle, cement, iron and steel, and similar industries had a remarkable capacity to resist price cuts, accepting large declines in production and employment as an alternative.

SHIFTING AGGREGATE SUPPLY

Let us examine hypothetical situations as a means of illustrating the effects of a change in aggregate supply upon the equilibrium price level and level of real national output.

First, suppose that foreign suppliers impose dramatic increases in the prices of our imported oil as OPEC did in 1973–1974 and again in 1979–1980. The higher energy prices permeate the world economy and drive up the cost of producing and distributing virtually every domestically produced product and imported resource. Hence, domestic per unit costs of production rise at each output level. The American aggregate supply curve therefore shifts leftward, as shown by the movement from AS_1 to AS_2 in Figure 11-8. Once again recalling Chapter 10's discussion of types of inflation, the price level increase occurring here is clearly **cost-push inflation.**

Note that, given aggregate demand, the effects of a leftward shift in aggregate supply are doubly

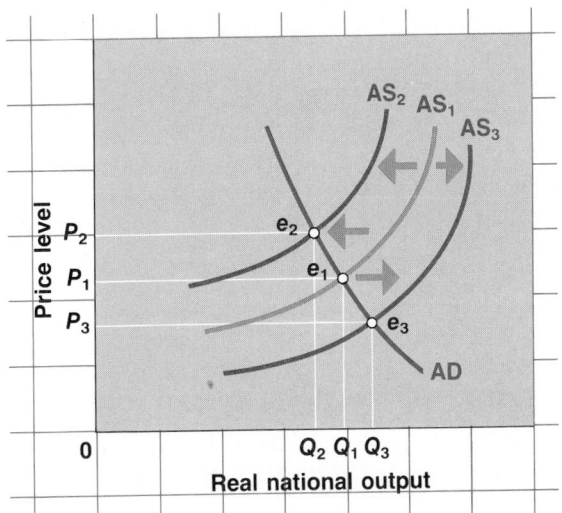

FIGURE 11-8

The effects of changes in aggregate supply

A leftward shift in aggregate supply from AS_1 to AS_2 will cause cost-push inflation in that the price level increases from P_1 to P_2. Real national output will fall from Q_1 to Q_2. A rightward shift of aggregate supply from AS_1 to AS_3 will increase the real national output from Q_1 to Q_3 and tend to reduce the price level from P_1 to P_3.

bad. When aggregate supply shifts from AS_1 to AS_2, real national output will decline from Q_1 to Q_2 *and* the price level will rise from P_1 to P_2. Falling employment and inflation—the combination we label "stagflation"—will occur. We will discuss this problem in detail in Chapter 19.

Alternatively, suppose that one of the factors in Table 11-2 changes such that aggregate supply increases. More specifically, let us suppose the economy experiences a sharp increase in productivity which is not matched by increases in higher paychecks for workers. Or, perhaps a liberalization of our immigration laws increases the supply of labor and pulls wage rates down. Or, finally, maybe lower business tax rates reduce per unit costs (a tax is a cost as viewed by a business), shifting the aggregate supply curve rightward. We see in Figure 11-8 that the shift in the aggregate supply from AS_1 to AS_3 indicates an increase in real output from Q_1 to Q_3 and assuming downward price and wage flexibility, a simultaneous decline in the price level from P_1 to P_3.

Observe that the shift in the aggregate supply curve involves a change in the full-employment level of real national output; in particular, a rightward shift of the curve signifies economic growth and indicates that the economy's potential output has increased. In terms of Chapter 2, the economy's production possibilities curve has moved to the right, which is reflected in the rightward shift of the aggregate supply curve in Figure 11-8.

Unanswered questions: looking ahead

Our elementary aggregate demand and aggregate supply model is a useful framework for developing a more detailed and comprehensive understanding of macroeconomics. Not surprisingly, however, this simple model raises many questions. Are there features of the economy which ensure that the aggregate demand curve always intersects the aggregate supply curve in the classical range; that is, are there automatic mechanisms which ensure full employment of the nation's resources (Chapter 12)? What economic principles underlie the less-

Nation and later the *New Statesman* magazines, and chairman of the National Mutual Life Assurance Society. He also ran an investment company, organized the Camargo Ballet (his wife, Lydia Lopokova, was a renowned star of the Russian imperial Ballet), and built (profitably) the Arts Theatre at Cambridge.*

In addition, Keynes found time to amass a $2 million personal fortune by speculating in stocks, international currencies, and commodities. He was also a leading figure in the "Bloomsbury group," an *avant-garde* group of intellectual luminaries who greatly influenced the artistic and literary standards of England.

Most importantly, Keynes was a prolific scholar. His books encompassed such widely ranging topics as probability theory, monetary economics, and the economic consequences of the World War I peace treaty. His *magnum opus,* however, was the aforementioned *General Theory* which has been described by John Kenneth Galbraith as "a work of profound obscurity, badly written and prematurely published." Yet the *General Theory* convincingly attacked the classical economists' contention that recession would cure itself. Keynes claimed that the capitalistic system contained no automatic mechanism capable of propelling it toward full employment. The economy might languish indefinitely in depression and poverty. Indeed, the massive unemployment of the worldwide depression of the 1930s seemed to provide sufficient empirical evidence that Keynes was right. His basic policy recommendation—a startling one at the time—was for government to increase its spending in order to induce more production and put the unemployed back to work.

* E. Ray Canterbery, *The Making of Economics,* 2d ed. (Belmont, Calif.: Wadsworth Publishing Company, 1980), p. 133.

than-full-employment equilibrium implied by an intersection of aggregate demand and aggregate supply in the Keynesian aggregate supply range (Chapters 12 and 13)? What, if anything, can the government do to keep aggregate demand from periodically declining and producing widespread unemployment (Chapter 14)?

Still other questions include: What role does money and the banking system play in determining the location of the aggregate demand curve and the macroeconomic health of the economy (Chapters 15 through 17)? Have government policies to manage aggregate demand contributed to macroeconomic stability, or, conversely, have they produced the very instability they are designed to counter (Chapter 18)? What set of aggregate demand and supply circumstances explains periods of "stagflation"—simultaneous inflation and recession (Chapter 19)? Where do Federal budget deficits and the national debt fit into this overall framework (Chapter 20)? And, finally, what are the facts and issues of economic growth—rises of real national output and income—and what policies might we enact to generate faster growth (Chapter 21)?

Our answers to these and a host of related questions will form the heart of our ensuing study of macroeconomics.

CHAPTER SUMMARY

1 It is useful for purposes of analysis to consolidate—or aggregate—the outcomes from the enormous number of individual product markets into a composite market in which the key variables are the price level and the level of real national output. This is accomplished through an aggregate demand–aggregate supply model of the economy.

2 The aggregate demand curve shows the level of real national output which the economy will purchase at each possible price level.

3 The rationale for the downsloping aggregate demand curve is based upon the interest-rate effect, the wealth or real balances effect, and the foreign purchases effect. The interest-rate effect indicates that, given the supply of money, a higher price level will increase the demand for money, thereby increasing the interest rate and reducing those consumption and investment purchases which are interest-rate sensitive. The wealth or real balances effect indicates that inflation will reduce the real value or purchasing power of fixed-value financial assets held by households and will thereby cause them to retrench on their consumer spending. The foreign purchases effect suggests that a change in the United States' price level relative to other countries will change the net exports component of American aggregate demand in the opposite direction.

4 The major non-price-level determinants of aggregate demand are spending by domestic consumers, businesses, government, and foreign buyers. Changes in the factors listed in Table 11-1 cause changes in spending by these groups and in turn shift the aggregate demand curve.

5 The aggregate supply curve shows the levels of real national output which will be produced at various possible price levels.

6 The shape of the aggregate supply curve depends upon what happens to per unit production costs—and therefore to the prices which businesses must receive to cover costs and make a profit—as real national output expands. The Keynesian range of the curve is horizontal because, with substantial unemployment, production can be increased without per unit cost or price increases. In the intermediate range, per unit costs increase as production bottlenecks appear and less efficient equipment and workers are employed. Prices must therefore rise as real national output is expanded in this range. The classical range coincides with full employment; real national output is at a maximum and cannot be increased, but the price level will rise in response to an increase in aggregate demand.

7 As indicated in Table 11-2, the major non-price-level determinants of aggregate supply are input prices, productivity, and the legal-institutional environment. All else being equal, a change in one of these factors will change per unit production costs at each level of output and therefore alter the location of the aggregate supply curve.

8 The intersection of the aggregate demand and aggregate supply curves determines the equilibrium price level and real national output.

9 Given aggregate supply, rightward shifts of aggregate demand will *a* increase real national output and employment but not alter the price level in the Keynesian range; *b* increase both real national output and the level of prices in the intermediate range; and *c* increase the price level but not change real national output in the classical range.

10 The ratchet effect is based upon the notion that prices are flexible upward, but relatively inflexible down-

ward. Hence, an increase in aggregate demand will raise the price level, but in the short term prices cannot be expected to fall when demand decreases.

11 The basic aggregate demand and supply model is a springboard for a more detailed and comprehensive study of macroeconomic analysis and issues.

TERMS AND CONCEPTS

aggregation	non-price-level determinants of aggregate supply
aggregates	
aggregate demand	productivity
interest-rate effect	equilibrium price level
wealth or real balances effect	equilibrium real national output
foreign purchases effect	demand-pull inflation
non-price-level determinants of aggregate demand	ratchet effect
aggregate supply	cost-push inflation
Keynesian, classical, and intermediate ranges of the aggregate supply curve	

QUESTIONS AND STUDY SUGGESTIONS

1 Explain in detail why the aggregate demand curve is downsloping. Specify how your explanation differs from the rationale behind the downsloping demand curve for a single product.

2 Explain the shape of the aggregate supply curve, accounting for the differences between the Keynesian, intermediate, and classical ranges of the curve.

3 Suppose that the aggregate demand and supply schedules for a hypothetical economy are as shown on page 199:

   a Use these sets of data to graph the aggregate demand and supply curves. What will be the equilibrium price level and level of real national output in this hypothetical economy? Is the equilibrium level of real national output also the full-employment level of real national output? Explain.

Amount of real national output demanded, billions	Price level (price index)	Amount of real national output supplied, billions
$100	300	$400
200	250	400
300	200	300
400	150	200
400	150	100

b Why will a price level of 150 *not* be an equilibrium price level in this economy? Why *not* 250?

c Suppose that buyers desire to purchase $200 billion of extra real national output at each price level. What factors might cause this change in aggregate demand? What is the new equilibrium price level and level of real national output? Over what range of the aggregate supply curve—Keynesian, intermediate, or classical—has equilibrium changed?

4 Suppose that the hypothetical economy in question 3 had the following relationship between its real national output and the input quantities necessary for producing that level of output:

Input quantity	Real national output
150.0	400
112.5	300
75.0	200

a What is the level of productivity in this economy?
b What is the per unit cost of production if the price of each input is $2?
c Assume that the input price increases from $2 to $3 with no accompanying change in productivity. What is the new per unit cost of production? In what direction would the $1 increase in input price push the aggregate supply curve? What effect would this shift in aggregate supply have upon the price level and the level of real national output?
d Suppose that the increase in input price had *not* occurred but instead that productivity had increased by 100 percent. What would be the new per unit cost of production? What effect would this change in per unit production cost have on the aggregate supply curve? What effect would this shift in aggregate supply have upon the price level and the level of real national output?

5 Will an increase in the American price level relative to price levels in other nations shift our aggregate demand curve? If so, in what direction? Explain. Will a decline in the dollar price of foreign currencies shift the American aggregate supply curve rightward or simply move the economy along an existing aggregate supply curve? Explain.

6 What effects might each of the following have upon aggregate demand or aggregate supply? In each case use a diagram to show the expected effects upon the equilibrium price level and level of real national output. Assume that all other things remain constant.
  a A widespread fear of depression among consumers
  b A large purchase of wheat by the Soviet Union
  c A 5-cent increase in the excise tax on gasoline
  d A reduction in interest rates at each price level
  e A cut in Federal spending for higher education
  f The expectation of a rapid rise in the price level
  g The complete disintegration of OPEC, causing oil prices to fall by one-half
  h A 10 percent reduction in personal income tax rates
  i An increase in labor productivity
  j A 12 percent increase in nominal wages
  k Depreciation in the international value of the dollar
  l A sharp decline in the national incomes of our western European trading partners
  m A decline in the percentage of the American labor force which is unionized

7 What is the relationship between the production possibilities curve discussed in Chapter 2 and the aggregate supply curve discussed in this chapter?

8 Other things being equal, what effect will each of the following have upon the equilibrium price level and level of real national output:
  a An increase in aggregate demand in the classical range of aggregate supply
  b An increase in aggregate supply (assume prices and wages are flexible)
  c An equal increase in both aggregate demand and aggregate supply
  d A reduction in aggregate demand in the Keynesian range of aggregate supply
  e An increase in aggregate demand and a decrease in aggregate supply
  f A decrease in aggregate demand in the intermediate range of aggregate supply (assume prices and wages are inflexible downward)

9 In the accompanying diagram assume that the aggregate demand curve shifts from AD_1 in year 1 to AD_2 in year 2, only to fall back to AD_1 in year 3. Locate the new year 3 equilibrium position on the assumption that prices and wages are **a** completely flexible and **b** completely rigid downward. Which of the two equilibrium positions is more desirable? Which is more realistic? Explain how the price level might be ratcheted upward when aggregate demand increases.

10 "Unemployment can be caused by a leftward shift of aggregate demand or a leftward shift of aggregate supply." Do you agree? Explain.

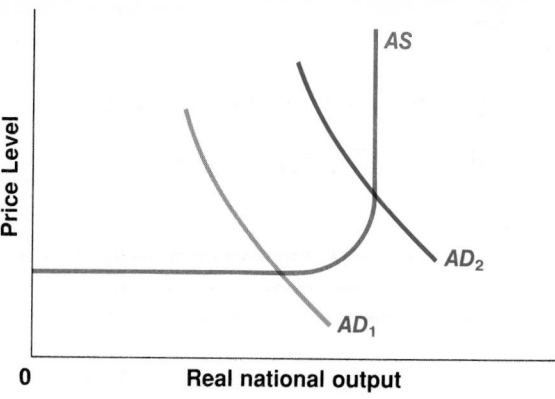

CHAPTER 12

Classical and Keynesian theories of employment

In preceding chapters we began to develop some familiarity with macroeconomic theory and problems through the concepts of aggregate demand and supply. In this and the next chapter we will look at aggregate demand from a different perspective. This new perspective will enable us to answer an important question: Why does aggregate demand—and therefore national output, income, and employment—tend to change by more than an initial change in spending?

Our first goal in this chapter is to contrast the extreme forms of classical and Keynesian employment theories. The comparison we will sketch here is vivid. Classical economics suggests that full employment is the norm of a market economy and that a laissez faire policy is best. Keynesian economics holds that unemployment is characteristic of laissez faire capitalism, and activist government policies are required if we are to avoid the wastes of idle resources. We have seen that the market system can provide for a quite efficient allocation of resources (Chapter 5). The question now is: Can it also achieve and maintain full employment of available resources?

Having contrasted these two widely divergent views, our second objective will be to examine the tools of Keynesian employment theory in greater detail. The Keynesian view has tended to dominate macroeconomics since the Great Depression and, with many modifications and embellishments, provides the core of modern mainstream macroeconomics. In Chapter 13 we use the tools developed in the present chapter to demonstrate how the equilibrium levels of real national output and employment are determined in the Keynesian model. At the end of Chapter 13, we link the Keynesian analysis directly back to the aggregate demand and aggregate supply model introduced in Chapter 11.

Simplifications

Three simplifying assumptions will make it considerably easier to achieve our objectives:

1 Although our analysis eventually will involve an "open economy" in which there are international trade transactions, initially we will assume a "closed economy." That is, our discussion will deal with the domestic economy, deferring the complications arising from exports and imports until midway through Chapter 13.

2 Government will be ignored until Chapter 14, thereby permitting us in Chapters 12 and 13 to determine whether or not laissez faire capitalism is capable of achieving and maintaining full employment.

3 Although saving actually occurs in both the business and household sectors of the economy, we shall for convenience speak as if all saving were personal saving.

Two implications of these assumptions are noteworthy:

First, we found in Chapter 9 that there are four components of aggregate spending: consumption, investment, government purchases, and net exports. Our assumptions 1 and 2 mean that, for the moment, we are concerned only with consumption and investment.

Second, assumptions 2 and 3 permit us to treat net national product (NNP), national income (NI), personal income (PI), and disposable income (DI) as being equal to one another because all the items which in practice distinguish them from one another are due to government (taxes and transfer payments) and business saving (see Table 9-5). This means that if $500 billion worth of goods and services is produced as NNP, we assume that exactly $500 billion worth of DI is received by households to split between consumption and saving.

Now the ground is cleared to rephrase our basic question: Is laissez faire capitalism able to achieve and maintain a sufficiently high level of aggregate demand so as to realize a full-employment national output?

The classical theory of employment

Answers to this question have varied historically. Until the Great Depression of the 1930s, many prominent economists of the nineteenth and early twentieth centuries—now called classical economists[1]—felt that the market system was capable of providing for the full employment of the economy's resources. It was acknowledged that now and then abnormal circumstances would arise in such forms as wars, political upheavals, droughts, speculative crises, gold rushes, and so forth, to push the economy from the path of full employment (see Figure 10-1). But it was contended that when these deviations occurred, automatic adjustments within the market system would soon restore the economy to the full-employment level of output.

We must stress at the outset of our discussion that classical employment theory is not to be regarded simply as an ancient artifact of economic thought. A relatively small number of current economists have reformulated, revitalized, and extended the work of these nineteenth- and twentieth-century economists to generate a "new" classical economics. Indeed, Chapter 18's discussions of monetarism and rational expectations theory explain currently held views of macroeconomics which have strong intellectual roots in classical theory. So too does the distinction between short-run and long-run aggregate supply made in Chapter 19.

The **classical theory of employment** was grounded on two basic notions:

First, it was argued that underspending—that is, a level of spending insufficient to purchase a full-employment output—was most unlikely to occur.

Second, even if a deficiency of total spending were to occur, price-wage (including interest-rate) adjustments would result quite quickly so as to en-

sure that the decline in total spending would *not* entail declines in real output, employment, and real incomes.

SAY'S LAW

Classical theory's denial of the possibility of underspending was based in part upon Say's Law. **Say's Law** is the disarmingly simple notion that the very act of producing goods generates an amount of income exactly equal to the value of the goods produced. That is, the production of any output would automatically provide the income needed to take that output off the market. *Supply creates its own demand.*[2] The essence of Say's Law can be understood most easily in terms of a barter economy. A shoemaker, for example, produces or *supplies* shoes as a means of buying or *demanding* the shirts and stockings produced by other craftsmen. The shoemaker's supply of shoes *is* his demand for other goods. And so it allegedly is for other producers and for the entire economy: Demand must be the same as supply! In fact, the circular flow model of the economy and national income accounting both suggest something of this sort. The income generated from the production of any level of total output would, *when spent,* be just sufficient to provide a matching total demand. Assuming that the composition of output is in accord with consumer preferences, all markets would be cleared of their outputs. It would seem that all that business owners need do to sell a full-employment output is to produce that output; Say's Law guarantees that there will be sufficient consumption spending for its successful disposal.

Saving: a complicating factor   However, there is one obvious omission in this simple application of Say's Law. Although it is an accepted truism that output gives rise to an identical amount of money income (Chapter 9), there is no guarantee that the recipients of this income will spend it all. Some income might be saved (not spent) and therefore not reflected in product demand. Saving would consti-

---

[1] Most notable among this group of classical economists are David Ricardo, John Stuart Mill, F. Y. Edgeworth, Alfred Marshall, and A. C. Pigou.

[2] Attributed to the nineteenth-century French economist J. B. Say.

tute a break, or "leakage," in the income-expenditure flows and therefore would undermine the effective operation of Say's Law. Saving is a withdrawal of funds from the income stream which will cause consumption expenditures to fall short of total output. If households saved some portion of their incomes, supply would not create its own demand. Saving would cause a deficiency of consumption. The consequences? Unsold goods, cutbacks in production, unemployment, and falling incomes.

Saving, investment, and the interest rate But the classical economists argued that saving would not really result in a deficiency of total demand, because each and every dollar saved would be invested by businesses. Investment would allegedly occur to compensate for any deficiency of consumer spending; investment would fill any consumption "gap" caused by saving. Business firms, after all, do not plan to sell their entire output to consumers, but rather to produce a considerable portion of total output in the form of capital goods for sale to one another. Investment spending by businesses is a supplement or an addition to the income-expenditure stream which may fill any consumption gap arising from saving. Thus, if businesses as a group intend to invest as much as households want to save, Say's Law will hold and the levels of national output and employment will remain constant. Whether or not the economy could achieve and sustain a level of spending sufficient to provide a full-employment level of output and income therefore would depend upon whether businesses were willing to invest enough to offset the amount households want to save.

The classical economists argued that capitalism contained a very special market—the *money market*—which would guarantee an equality of saving and investment plans and therefore full employment. That is, the money market—and, more specifically, the *interest rate* (the price paid for the use of money)—would see to it that dollars which leaked from the income-expenditure stream as saving would automatically reappear as dollars spent on investment goods. The rationale underlying the saving and investment equating adjustments of the interest rate was simple and quite plausible. The classical economists contended that, other things being equal, households normally pre-

fer to consume rather than to save. The consumption of goods and services satisfies human wants; idle dollars do not. Hence, it was reasoned that consumers would save only if someone would pay them a rate of interest as a reward for their thriftiness. The greater the interest rate, the more dollars saved; that is, the saving (supply-of-dollars) curve of households would be upsloping, as shown by *S* in Figure 12-1a. And who would be inclined to pay for the use of saving? None other than investors—business owners who seek (demand) money capital to replace and enlarge their plants and their stocks of capital equipment. Because the interest rate is a cost to borrowing businesses, they will be more willing to borrow and invest at low than at high interest rates. This means that the investment (demand-for-dollars) curve of businesses is downsloping, as shown by *I* in Figure 12-1a.

Classical economists concluded that the money market, wherein savers supply dollars and investors demand dollars, would establish an equilibrium price for the use of money—an equilibrium interest rate—at which the quantity of dollars saved (supplied) would equal the number of dollars invested (demanded). In terms of Figure 12-1a, the interest rate would be *r* and the amounts of saving and investment both would be *q*. Saving, said the classicists, does not really constitute a break in the income-expenditure stream or a fatal flaw in Say's Law, because the money market or, more specifically, the interest rate will necessitate that each and every dollar saved will get into the hands of investors and be spent on capital equipment. Therefore, an increase in thriftiness is not a cause for social concern, because this simply shifts the supply-of-saving curve to the right, as from *S* to *S'* in Figure 12-1b. Although saving will momentarily exceed investment and perhaps cause some temporary unemployment, the surplus of saving will drive the interest rate down to a new and lower equilibrium level, *r'*. And this lower interest rate will expand the volume of investment spending until it again equals the amount of saving at *q'*, thereby preserving full employment.

In short, changes in the interest rate would guarantee the operation of Say's Law even in an economy in which substantial saving occurs. As the classical economists saw it, the economy was analogous to a gigantic bathtub in which the volume of water measured the levels of output and employ-

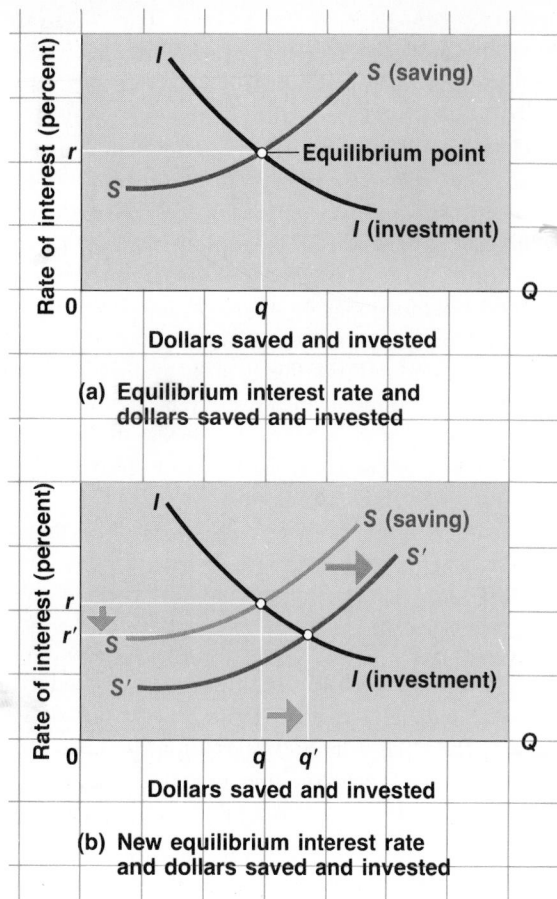

FIGURE 12-1

Classical view of the money market

The classical economists believed that the saving plans of households would be reflected in a supply-of-dollars curve S and the investment plans of businesses in a demand-for-dollars curve I in the money market. In (a) the equilibrium interest rate r, the price paid for the use of money, would equate the amounts households and businesses planned to save and invest, thereby guaranteeing a full-employment level of spending. In (b) an increase in desired saving at each interest rate results in a rightward shift of the supply-of-dollars curve to S'. The equilibrium interest rate therefore falls to r' and the new equilibrium amount of dollars saved and invested increases to q'. At q' the amount of saving and investment is again equal and the full-employment level of spending is again assured.

ment. Any leakage down the drain of saving would be returned to the tub through the spigot of investment. This had to be the case, because the interest rate connected the drainpipe and the spigot!

PRICE-WAGE FLEXIBILITY

The classical economists bolstered their conclusion that full employment is the norm of capitalism with a second basic argument. They argued that the level of output which businesses can sell depends not only upon the level of total spending but also upon the level of product prices. This meant that even if the interest rate should somehow temporarily fail to equate the amounts which households wanted to save with the investment intentions of businesses, any resulting decline in total spending would be offset by proportionate declines in the price level. That is, $40 will buy four shirts at $10, but $20 will buy the same number of shirts provided their price falls to $5. Hence, if households temporarily saved more than businesses were willing to invest, the resulting decline in total spending would not result in a prolonged decline in real output, real income, and the level of employment *if* product prices declined in proportion to the decline in expenditures.

And, according to the classical economists, this is precisely what would happen. Competition among sellers would ensure price flexibility. As declines in product demand became general, competing producers would lower their prices to dispose of accumulating surpluses. In other words, the result of "excess" saving would be to lower prices; and lower prices, by increasing the real value or purchasing power of the dollar, would permit nonsavers to obtain more goods and services with their current money incomes. Saving would therefore lower prices, but not output and employment.

"But," ever-present skeptics have asked, "doesn't this ignore the resource market? Although businesses can sustain their sales in the face of a declining demand by accepting lower product prices, won't they find it unprofitable to do so? As product prices decline, won't resource prices—particularly wage rates—have to decline significantly to permit businesses to produce *profitably* at the now lower prices?" The classical economists replied that wage rates must and would decline. General declines in product demand would be mirrored in declines in the demand for labor and other resources. The immediate result would be a surplus of labor, that is, unemployment, at the wage rate prevailing prior to these declines in the demand for labor. However, though not willing to employ all workers at the original wage rates, producers would find it profitable to employ these workers at lower wage rates. The demand for labor, in other words, is downsloping; those workers unable to locate employment at the old higher wage rates could find jobs at the new lower wage rates.

Would workers be willing to accept lower wage rates? Competition among unemployed workers, according to the classical economists, would force them to do so. In competing for scarce jobs, idle workers would bid down wage rates until these rates (wage costs to employers) were so low that employers would once again find it profitable to hire all available workers. This would happen at the new lower equilibrium wage rate. The classical economists therefore concluded that *involuntary unemployment* was impossible. Anyone who was willing to work at the market-determined wage rate could readily find employment. Competition in the labor market ruled out involuntary idleness.

CLASSICAL THEORY AND LAISSEZ FAIRE

In the classical view these market system adjustments—fluctuations in the interest rate on the one hand, and **price-wage flexibility** on the other—were fully capable of maintaining full employment in a capitalistic economy. Working together, the classical economists felt, the two adjustment mechanisms made full employment a foregone conclusion. The classical economists came to embrace capitalism as a self-regulating economy wherein full employment was regarded as the norm. Capitalism was capable of "running itself." Government assistance in the operation of the economy was deemed unnecessary—nay, harmful. In an economy capable of achieving both full production and full employment, governmental interference could only be a detriment to its efficient operation. The logic of the classical theory led to the conclusion that a laissez faire economic policy was desirable.

Keynesian economics

One embarrassing fact persistently denied the validity of the classical theory of employment—

recurring periods of prolonged unemployment and inflation. While one might explain a minor recession, such as the brief downswings of 1924 and 1927, in terms of wars and similar external considerations, serious and prolonged downswings, such as the Great Depression of the 1930s, were not easily rationalized. There is a remarkable inconsistency between a theory which concludes that unemployment is virtually impossible and the actual occurrence of a ten-year siege of very substantial unemployment. And so various economists came to criticize both the rationale and the underlying assumptions of classical employment theory. They tried to find a better, more realistic explanation of those forces which determine the level of employment.

Finally, in 1936 the renowned English economist John Maynard Keynes, whom you met in Chapter 11's Last Word, came forth with a new explanation of the level of employment in capitalistic economies. In his *General Theory of Employment, Interest, and Money*,[3] Keynes attacked the foundations of classical theory and, in doing so, touched off a major revolution in economic thinking on macroeconomic questions. Although Keynes fathered modern employment theory, many others have since refined and extended his work. In this and the following chapters, we are concerned with Keynesian employment theory, or **Keynesian economics,** as it stands today.

Keynesian employment theory contrasts sharply with the classical position. Its blunt conclusion is that capitalism simply does *not* contain any mechanisms capable of guaranteeing full employment. The economy, it is argued, might come to rest—that is, reach an aggregate output equilibrium—with either considerable unemployment or substantial inflation. Full employment is more of an accident than a norm. Capitalism is *not* a self-regulating system capable of perpetual prosperity; capitalism cannot be depended upon to "run itself." Furthermore, economic fluctuations should not be associated exclusively with external forces such as wars, droughts, and similar abnormalities. Rather, the causes of unemployment and inflation lie to a very considerable degree in the failure of certain fundamental economic decisions—in particular, saving and investment decisions—to be

[3] New York: Harcourt, Brace & World, Inc., 1936.

completely synchronized in a capitalistic system. In addition, product prices and wages tend to be downwardly inflexible; extended and costly periods of recession will prevail before significant declines in prices and wages occur. Internal, in addition to external, forces contribute to economic instability.

Keynesians back these sweeping contentions by rejecting the very mechanisms upon which the classical position is grounded—the interest rate and price-wage adjustments.

THE UNLINKING OF SAVING AND INVESTMENT PLANS

Keynesian theory rejects Say's Law by seriously questioning the ability of the interest rate to match the saving and investment plans of households and businesses. The fact that modern capitalism is amply endowed with an elaborate money market and a wide variety of financial institutions does not diminish this skepticism about the interest rate as a mechanism capable of connecting the saving drain and the investment spigot. Keynesians find untenable the classical contention that business firms would invest more when households increased their rates of saving. After all, does not more saving mean less consumption? Can we really expect business planners to expand their capital facilities as the markets for their products shrink? More generally, the Keynesian view holds that savers and investors are essentially distinct groups that formulate their saving and investment plans for different reasons which, in the case of saving, are largely unrelated to the rate of interest.

1 Savers and investors are different groups Who decides the amounts to be saved and invested in a capitalistic economy? (We continue to ignore government in our discussion.) Business organizations of all kinds and descriptions and, in particular, corporations make the vast majority of investment decisions. And who makes the saving decisions? Here the picture is a bit more cluttered. In a wealthy economy such as that of American capitalism, households save substantial amounts—at least when prosperity prevails. It is true, of course, that business corporations also do a considerable amount of saving in the form of undistributed corporate profits. The important point is that to a signi-

ficant degree, saving decisions and investment decisions are made by different groups of individuals.

2 Savers and investors are differently motivated The nonidentity of savers and investors would not necessarily be fatal to the classical theory if their decisions were motivated and synchronized by some common factor such as the interest rate. But Keynesians contend this is not the case. Saving decisions are motivated by diverse considerations. Some save in order to make large purchases which exceed any single paycheck; households save to make down payments on houses and to buy automobiles or television sets. Some saving is solely for the convenience of having a pool of liquid funds readily available to take advantage of any extraordinarily good buys which one may chance upon. Or saving may occur to provide for the future needs of individuals and their families: Households save to provide for the future retirement of the family breadwinner or to provide a college education for their children. Or saving may be a precautionary, rainy-day measure—a means of protecting oneself against such unpredictable events as prolonged illness and unemployment. Or saving may be merely a deeply ingrained habit that is practiced on an almost automatic basis with no specific purposes in mind. Much saving is highly institutionalized or contractual: for example, payments for life insurance and annuities or participation in a "bond-a-month" program. The basic point is that none of these diverse motives for saving is particularly sensitive to the interest rate. In fact, Keynesians argue that one can readily pose a situation in which, contrary to the classical conception (Figure 12-1), saving is *inversely* related to the interest rate. To illustrate: If a family seeks to provide an annual retirement income of $6000 from saving, it will need to save $100,000 if the interest rate is 6 percent, but only $50,000 if the interest rate is 12 percent!

What, in the Keynesian view, does determine the level of saving? As we shall find momentarily, the primary determinant of both saving and consumption is the level of national income.

Why do businesses purchase capital goods? The motivation for investment spending, as we shall discover in a few pages, is complex. The interest rate—the cost of obtaining money capital with which to invest—*is* a consideration in formulating investment plans. But the interest rate is *not* the only factor. The rate of profit which business firms expect to realize on the investment is also a crucial determinant of the amounts they desire to invest. Furthermore, during a major recession or a depression, profit expectations may be so bleak that the level of investment will be low and possibly declining despite substantial reductions in the interest rate. Interest rate reductions are not likely to stimulate investment spending when it is most sorely needed.

3 Money balances and banks Keynesian employment theory envisions the classical conception of the money market (Figure 12-1) as being oversimplified and therefore incorrect in another sense. Specifically, the classical money market assumes that current saving is the only source of funds for the financing of investment. Keynesian economics holds that there are two other sources of funds which can be made available in the money market: (1) the accumulated money balances held by households, and (2) lending institutions which can add to the money supply.

Keynesian theory stipulates that the public holds money balances not merely to negotiate day-to-day transactions, but also as a form of accumulated wealth not held in savings accounts in banks. Now the important point for present purposes is that, by drawing down or decumulating a portion of these money balances and offering these dollars to investors, a supply of funds in excess of current saving can be made available in the money market. Similarly, as we will find in Chapter 16, when lending institutions make loans, they add to the money supply. Lending by banks and other financial institutions, therefore, is also a means of augmenting current saving as a source of funds for investment. The consequence is that a reduction in the money balances held by households *and* bank lending can give rise to an amount of investment which is in excess of current saving. This implies that Say's Law is invalid and that output, employment, and the price level can fluctuate. More specifically, we shall soon see that an excess of investment over saving results in an increase in total spending which has an expansionary effect on the economy. If the economy is initially in a recession, output and employment will increase; if the economy is already at full employment, the added spending will cause demand-pull inflation.

Conversely, classical theory is incorrect in assuming that all current saving will appear in the money market. If (1) households add some of their current saving to their money balances rather than channel it into the money market, or (2) some current saving is used to retire outstanding bank loans, then the amount of funds made available in the money market will be less than that shown by the classical saving curve in Figure 12-1.[4] This suggests that the amount of current saving will exceed the amount invested. Again, Say's Law does not hold and macroeconomic instability will result. In this case the excess of saving over investment will mean a decline in total demand which is contractionary; output and employment will tend to fall.

---

[4] Technical footnote: It is a relatively simple matter to portray these Keynesian criticisms in terms of the classical conception of the money market. In the first case (Figure a), funds are shifted by households from their accumulated money balances to the money market *and* banks create funds (money) by lending. Adding these amounts horizontally to current saving S, we get the supply-of-funds curve F_1. At the resulting equilibrium interest rate r_1, investment is I_1 and in excess of current saving S_1. In the second case (Figure b), the supply-of-funds curve, F_2, is less than current saving S, because portions of current saving have been added to the money balances of households *and* used to retire bank debt. These portions of current saving have been subtracted horizontally from the S curve to derive the F_2 curve. At the relevant equilibrium interest rate r_2, investment is only I_2 while current saving is greater at S_2. The conclusion is that the money market does *not* ensure the equality of saving and investment; Say's Law is therefore invalid; and the economy is subject to macroeconomic instability.

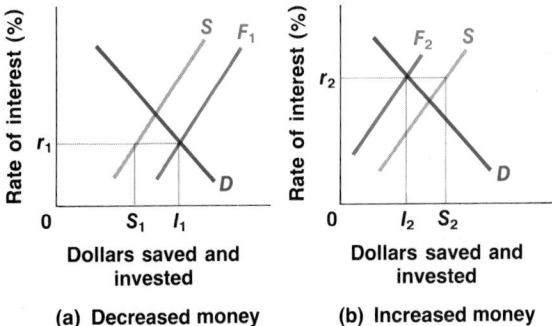

(a) Decreased money balances and bank lending

(b) Increased money balances and bank loan retirement

To summarize: *The Keynesian position is that saving and investment plans can be at odds and thereby can result in fluctuations in total output, total income, employment, and the price level.* It is largely a matter of chance that households and businesses will desire to save and invest identical amounts. Keynesian economists feel they are better plumbers than their classical predecessors by recognizing that the saving drain and the investment spigot are *not* connected.

THE DISCREDITING OF PRICE-WAGE FLEXIBILITY

But what of the second aspect of the classical position—the contention that downward price-wage adjustments will eliminate the unemployment effects of a decline in total spending?

Existence   Keynesians argue that wage-price flexibility simply does not exist to the degree necessary for ensuring the restoration of full employment in the face of a decline in aggregate demand. The market system of capitalism has never been perfectly competitive and now it is riddled by market imperfections and circumscribed by practical and political obstacles which work against downward price-wage flexibility. Recalling Chapter 11's discussion of the ratchet effect, monopolistic producers, dominating many important product markets, have both the ability and the desire to resist falling product prices as demand declines. And in the resource markets, strong labor unions are equally persistent in holding the line against wage cuts. Union collective bargaining agreements shield wages from downward adjustment for the two- or three-year duration of these contracts. In nonunion labor markets it is customary to adjust wages only once a year. Furthermore, employers are often wary of wage cuts, recognizing possible adverse effects upon worker morale and productivity. In short, as a practical matter, downward price-wage flexibility cannot be expected to offset the unemployment effects of a decline in aggregate demand.[5]

Usefulness   Furthermore, even if price-wage declines accompanied a contraction of total spending, it is doubtful that these declines would help reduce

unemployment. The reason? The volume of total money demand cannot remain constant as prices and wages decline. That is, lower prices and wages necessarily mean lower money incomes, and lower money incomes in turn entail further reductions in total spending. The net result is likely to be little or no change in the depressed levels of output and employment.

Keynesians point out that the classicists were tripped up in their reasoning by the fallacy of composition. Because any particular group of workers typically buys only a small amount of what it produces, the product and therefore labor demand curves of a single firm can be regarded as independent of any wage (income) changes accorded its own workers. In other words, it is correct to reason that a decline in its wage rate will move a *single firm* down its stable labor demand curve and result in more workers hired, that is, more employment. But this reasoning, argue Keynesian economists, is not applicable to the economy as a whole, to general wage cuts. Why? Because wages are the major source of income in the economy. Widespread wage declines will therefore result in declines in incomes and also declines in the demand for both products and the labor used in producing them. The result is that employers will hire little or no additional labor after the general wage cuts. What holds true for a single firm—a wage cut for its employees will not adversely affect labor demand—is not true for the economy as a whole—general wage cuts *will* lower money incomes and they will cause the demand for products and labor to decline generally.

Recapitulation: Keynesians argue, in the first place, that prices and wages are in fact not flexible downward and, second, even if they were, that it is highly doubtful that price-wage declines would alleviate widespread unemployment.

---

[5] This is not to say that wages are completely inflexible downward. In the early 1980s large numbers of workers were forced to accept wage freezes, wage cuts, and reduced fringe benefits. Causal factors included (*a*) back-to-back recessions (one of which was so severe as to bring about the highest unemployment rates since the 1930s); (*b*) enhanced foreign competition (for example, the automobile and basic steel industries); and (*c*) industry deregulation (the airlines and trucking).

Classics and Keynes: AD-AS restatement

These two views of the macroeconomic world—classical and Keynesian—can be meaningfully restated and compared in their crude or extreme forms in terms of Chapter 11's aggregate demand and aggregate supply curves.

CLASSICAL VIEW

The classical economists argued that the aggregate supply curve is vertical and therefore exclusively determines the level of real national output. On the other hand, the downsloping aggregate demand curve tends to be stable and solely establishes the price level. These two generalizations merit careful elaboration.

1 Vertical aggregate supply curve The classical position envisions the aggregate supply curve as a vertical line as shown in Figure 12-2a. It is for this reason that we referred to the vertical portion of our aggregate supply curve in Chapter 11 as the "classical range." The vertical aggregate supply curve, remember, is located where the natural or full-employment rate of unemployment is being realized. According to the classical economists, the economy will operate at its full-employment level of output, Q_f, for the reasons previously discussed: Say's Law, flexible interest rates, and responsive prices and wages. It is important to stress that classical economists believe that Q_f does *not* change in response to changes in the price level. Observe, for example, that as the price level falls in Figure 12-2a from P_1 to P_2, real national output remains firmly anchored at Q_f.

But, you might argue, this stability of output seems at odds with Chapter 4's upsloping supply curves for individual products. There we found that lower prices would make production less profitable and cause producers to offer *less* output and presumably employ *fewer* workers. The classical response to your argument is that input costs would fall along with product prices to leave *real* profits unchanged and therefore output unchanged.

Consider a grossly simplified illustration. Sup-

pose we have a one-firm economy in which the firm's owner must receive a *real* profit of $20 in order to be induced to produce the full-employment output of, say, 100 units. Recall from Chapter 10 that what ultimately counts is the *real* reward one receives and not the level of prices. Suppose the owner's only input (aside from personal entrepreneurial talent) is 10 units of labor which are hired at $8 per worker for a total wage cost of $80 ($=10 \times \$8$). Also suppose the 100 units of output sell for $1 per unit so that total revenue is $100 ($=100 \times \$1$). This firm's *money* profit is $20 ($= \$100 - \$80$) and, using the $1 price to designate the base price index of 100 percent, its *real* profit is also $20 ($= \$20 \div 1.00$). Well and good; full employment is achieved. But suppose now that the price level declines by one-half. Would our producer still realize the $20 of real profits needed to induce the production of a 100-unit full-employment output?

The classical answer is Yes. Now that product price is only $.50, total revenue will only be $50 ($= 100 \times \$.50$). But the cost of 10 units of labor will be reduced to $40 ($= 10 \times \$4$) because the wage rate will be halved. Although *nominal* profits fall to $10 ($= \$50 - \$40$), *real* profits remain at $20. In other words, by dividing money profits of $10 by the new price index (expressed as a decimal) we obtain *real* profits of $20 ($= \$10 \div .50$). Generalization: With perfectly flexible wages there would be no change in the real rewards and therefore the production or output behavior of businesses. Under conditions of perfect wage flexibility, a change in the price level will not cause the economy to stray from its full-employment position.

2 Stable aggregate demand The classical economists theorized that money underlies aggregate demand. Specifically, the amount of real national output which can be purchased depends upon (1) the quantity of money which households and businesses possess and (2) the purchasing power or real value of that money as determined by the price level. Recall that the purchasing power of the dollar simply refers to the real quantity of goods and services that a dollar will buy. Thus as we move down the vertical axis of Figure 12-2a the price level is falling. This means that the purchasing power of each dollar increases and therefore the given quantity of money will be capable of pur-

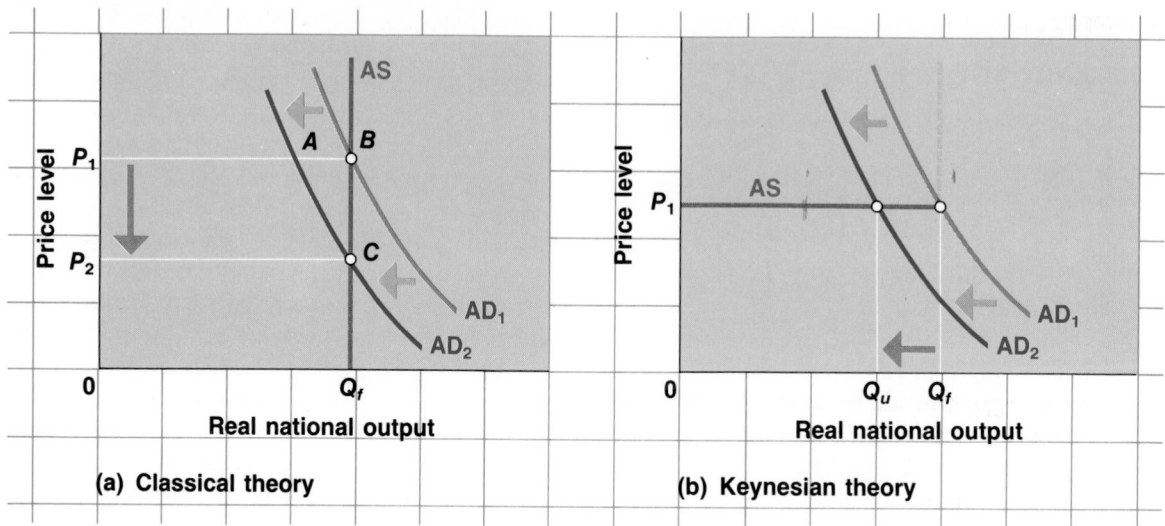

FIGURE 12-2

Classical and Keynesian views of the macroeconomy

According to classical theory (a), aggregate supply will determine the full-employment level of real national output while aggregate demand will establish the price level. Aggregate demand normally is stable, but if it should decline, say, as shown from AD_1 to AD_2, the price level will quickly fall from P_1 to P_2 to eliminate the temporary excess supply of AB and to restore full employment at C. The Keynesian view (b) is that aggregate demand is unstable and that price and wages are downwardly inflexible. An AD_1 to AD_2 decline in aggregate demand has no effect on the price level. Rather, real output falls from Q_f to Q_u and can remain at this equilibrium indefinitely.

chasing a larger quantity of real output. If the price level were to decline by one-half, a given quantity of money would now purchase a real national output which is twice as large. Given a fixed money supply, the price level and real national output are inversely related.

And what of the *location* of the aggregate demand curve? According to the classical economists, aggregate demand will be reasonably stable if the nation's monetary authorities maintain a constant supply of money. Given aggregate supply, increases in the supply of money will shift the aggregate demand curve rightward and spark demand-pull inflation; reductions in the supply of money will shift the curve leftward and trigger deflation. The key to price stability then, according to the classical economists, is to control the nation's money supply so as to prevent unwarranted shifts in aggregate demand. Early classical economists contended that tying the supply of money to the supply of gold would largely ensure that aggregate demand would not expand unduly. We shall find in Chapter 18 that present-day monetarism has its

intellectual roots in classical economics. One reason is that both classical economists and modern monetarists focus upon the money supply as the basic determinant of aggregate demand and the price level.

A final observation: Even if there are declines in the money supply and therefore in aggregate demand, the economy depicted in Figure 12-2a will *not* experience unemployment. Admittedly, the immediate effect of a decline in aggregate demand from AD_1 to AD_2 is an excess supply of output in that the aggregate output of goods and services exceeds aggregate spending by the amount AB. But, given the presumed downward flexibility of product and resource prices, this excess supply will cause product prices to fall along with workers' wages and the prices of other inputs. As a result, the price level will quickly decline from P_1 to P_2 until the amounts of output demanded and supplied are brought once again into equilibrium, this time at C. While the price level has fallen from P_1 to P_2, the level of real national output remains at the full-employment level.

KEYNESIAN VIEW

As noted earlier, the core of the Keynesian theory is that, at least in the short run, product prices and wages are downwardly inflexible, resulting in what is graphically represented as a horizontal aggregate supply curve. Additionally, aggregate demand is subject to periodic changes caused by changes in one or more of the non-price-level determinants of aggregate demand (Table 11-1). Let us explore these two points in terms of Figure 12-2b.

1 Horizontal aggregate supply curve (to full-employment output) The downward inflexibility of prices and wages discussed first in Chapter 11 translates to a horizontal aggregate supply curve as shown in Figure 12-2b. Here, a decline in real national output from, say, Q_f to Q_u will have no impact on the price level. Conversely, an increase in national output from Q_u to Q_f will also leave the price level unchanged. A "Keynesian range" of the aggregate supply curve therefore extends from zero real national output rightward to the full-employment or potential output Q_f. Once full employment is reached, according to the Keynesians, the aggregate supply curve becomes vertical. This view is shown by the vertical red line extending upward from the horizontal aggregate supply curve at Q_f.

2 Unstable aggregate demand Keynesian economists view aggregate demand as being unstable from one period to the next, even if there are no changes in the supply of money. In particular, the investment component of aggregate demand tends to fluctuate, thereby altering the location of the aggregate demand curve. Suppose, for example, that aggregate demand in Figure 12-2b declines from AD_1 to AD_2. Observe that the sole impact of this change in aggregate demand will be upon output and employment in that real national output falls from Q_f to Q_u while the price level remains constant at P_1. Moreover, Keynesians believe that unless there is an fortuitous offsetting increase in aggregate demand, real national output will permanently stay at Q_u, which is below the full-employment level Q_f.

The contrast with the classical view is apparent: *To classical economists,* aggregate demand is stable as long as there were no significant changes in the money supply. Even if aggregate demand did decline, price and wage flexibility would provide an automatic, built-in mechanism which tends to keep the capitalist economy operating at its potential output and natural rate of unemployment. Government macroeconomic policies therefore are unnecessary and counterproductive. *To Keynesians,* volatility of aggregate demand and downward inflexibility of prices mean that unemployment can develop and persist for extended periods in a market economy. Active macroeconomic policies of aggregate demand management by government are essential if the gigantic wastes of recession and depression are to be avoided. For these reasons Keynesians spotlight aggregate demand for special attention. In their simplest models, Keynesians assume that the price level is constant—that is, that the aggregate supply curve is horizontal over the relevant range of analysis as in Figure 12-2b. They also believe that aggregate demand can best be understood in terms of the four components of GNP discussed in Chapter 9: consumption, investment, government purchases, and net exports.

Our task now is to examine these components in some detail, beginning with consumption and investment.

Tools of Keynesian employment theory

According to Keynesian economics, how are the levels of output and employment determined in modern capitalism? The touchstone of any meaningful answer is that *the amount of goods and services produced and therefore the level of employment depend directly upon the level of total or aggregate expenditures.* Subject to the economy's productive potential as determined by the scarce resources available to it, businesses will produce that level of output which they can profitably sell. Both workers and machinery are idled when there are no markets for the goods and services they are capable of producing. Aggregate expenditures and total output and employment vary directly with each other.

Our plan of attack is to analyze the consumption and investment components of aggregate expenditures in the remainder of this chapter. In Chapter 13 we derive the Keynesian private sector model of equilibrium NNP and employment, with net exports included. Chapter 14 adds government expenditures (along with taxes) to the model.

We preface our discussion with two other comments. The first is that unless specified otherwise we assume that the economy is operating within the horizontal Keynesian range of the aggregate supply curve. That is, the economy is presumed to have a substantial amount of excess productive capacity and unemployed labor so that an increase in aggregate demand will increase real output and employment, but *not* the price level. The second point involves terminology. In the Keynesian model we will be developing the notion of *aggregate expenditures* which shows the relationship between real national output and income, on the one hand, and the economy's total spending, on the other. This is in contrast with the macro model we have used thus far wherein *aggregate demand* portrays the relationship between real national output and the price level. In Chapter 13 we shall reconcile Chapter 11's aggregate demand–aggregate supply model and the Keynesian expenditures-output model which we now begin to construct.

Consumption and saving

In terms of absolute size, consumption is the main component of aggregate expenditures (Chapter 9). It is therefore of importance to understand the major determinants of consumption spending. You may also recall that economists define personal saving as "not spending" or "that part of disposable income (DI) which is not consumed"; in other words, disposable income equals consumption plus saving. Hence, in examining the determinants of consumption we are also simultaneously exploring the determinants of saving.

INCOME-CONSUMPTION AND INCOME-SAVING RELATIONSHIPS

There are many considerations which influence the level of consumer spending. But common sense and available statistical data both suggest that the most important determinant of consumer spending is income—in particular, disposable income. And, of course, since saving is that part of disposable in-

come which is not consumed, DI is also the basic determinant of personal saving.

Consider some recent historical data. In Figure 12-3 each dot indicates the consumption–disposable income relationship for each year since 1960 and the blue line is fitted to these points. Note, most obviously, that consumption is directly related to disposable income and, indeed, households clearly spend most of their income. But we can say more. The mauve 45-degree line is added to the diagram as a point of reference. Because this line bisects the 90-degree angle formed by the vertical and horizontal axes of the graph, each point on the 45-degree line must be equidistant from the two axes. We can therefore regard the vertical distance from any point on the horizontal axis to the 45-degree line as either consumption *or* disposable income. If we regard it as disposable income, then the amount (the vertical distance) by which the actual amount consumed in any given year falls short of the 45-degree guideline indicates the amount of saving in any particular year. For example, in 1988 consumption was $3226 billion, and disposable income was $3473; hence, saving in 1988 was $247 billion. That is, disposable income less consumption equals saving. By observing these vertical distances as we move to the right in Figure 12-3, we note that saving also varies directly with the level of disposable income. Not shown in Figure 12-3 is the fact that in years of very low income, for example, some of the worst years of the Great Depression, consumption exceeded disposable income. The dots for these depression years would be located *above* the 45-degree line. Households actually consumed in excess of their current incomes by *dissaving*, that is, by going into debt and liquidating previously accumulated wealth.

To summarize: Figure 12-3 suggests that (1) households consume most of their disposable income and (2) both consumption and saving are directly related to the level of income.

THE CONSUMPTION SCHEDULE

Figure 12-3 embodies historical data; it shows us how much households *actually did consume* (and save) at various levels of DI over a period of years. For analytical purposes we need to show an income-consumption relationship—a consumption schedule—which indicates the various amounts

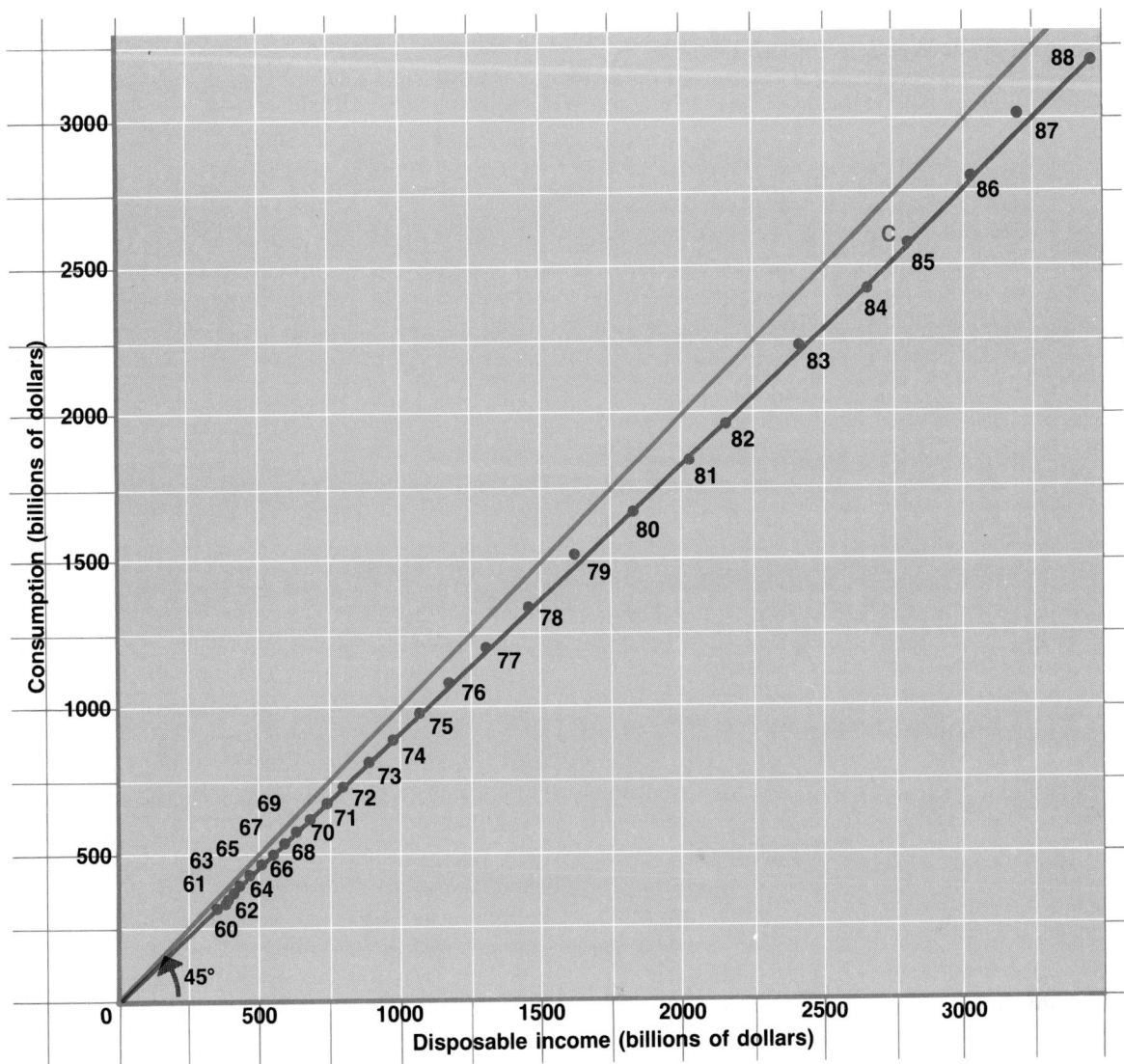

FIGURE 12-3

Consumption and disposable income, 1960–1988

Each dot in this figure shows consumption and disposable income in a given year. The C line generalizes upon the relationship between consumption and disposable income. It indicates a direct relationship and that households consume the bulk of their incomes.

households *plan* to consume at various possible levels of disposable income which might conceivably prevail at some specific *point in time*. A hypothetical **consumption schedule** of the type we require for analysis is shown in columns 1 and 2 of Table 12-1. It is plotted in Figure 12-4a. This consumption schedule reflects the consumption–disposable income relationship suggested by the empirical data of Figure 12-3, and it is consistent with a variety of empirical family budget studies. The rela-

tionship is direct—as common sense certainly would suggest—and, we note that households will spend a *larger proportion* of a small disposable income than of a large disposable income.

THE SAVING SCHEDULE

It is a simple task to derive a **saving schedule.** Because disposable income equals consumption plus saving (DI = $C + S$), we need only subtract

TABLE 12-1 **Keynesian consumption and saving schedules** (*hypothetical data; columns 1 through 3 in billions*)

(1) Level of output and income (NNP = DI)	(2) Consumption, C	(3) Saving, S (1) − (2)	(4) Average propensity to consume (APC) (2)/(1)	(5) Average propensity to save (APS) (3)/(1)	(6) Marginal propensity to consume (MPC) $\Delta(2)/\Delta(1)$*	(7) Marginal propensity to save (MPS) $\Delta(3)/\Delta(1)$*
(1) $370	$375	$−5	1.01	−.01		
					.75	.25
(2) 390	390	0	1.00	.00		
					.75	.25
(3) 410	405	5	.99	.01		
					.75	.25
(4) 430	420	10	.98	.02		
					.75	.25
(5) 450	435	15	.97	.03		
					.75	.25
(6) 470	450	20	.96	.04		
					.75	.25
(7) 490	465	25	.95	.05		
					.75	.25
(8) 510	480	30	.94	.06		
					.75	.25
(9) 530	495	35	.93	.07		
					.75	.25
(10) 550	510	40	.93	.07		

* The Greek letter Δ, delta, means "a change in."

consumption (column 2) from disposable income (column 1) to find the amount saved (column 3) at each level of DI. That is, $DI − C = S$. Hence, columns 1 and 3 of Table 12-1 constitute the saving schedule. This schedule is plotted in Figure 12-4b. Note that there is a direct relationship between saving and DI but that saving constitutes a smaller proportion (fraction) of a small DI than it does of a large DI. If households consume a smaller and smaller proportion of DI as DI goes up, they must save a larger and larger proportion.

Remembering that each point on the 45-degree line indicates a point where DI equals consumption, we see that dissaving would occur at the relatively low DI of, say, $370 billion (row 1), where consumption is actually $375 billion. That is, households will consume in excess of their current incomes by drawing down accumulated savings or by borrowing. Graphically, the vertical distance of the consumption schedule *above* the 45-degree line is equal to the vertical distance of the saving schedule *below* the horizontal axis at the $370 billion level of output and income (see Figure 12-4a and b). In this instance, each of these two vertical distances measures the $5 billion of *dissaving* which

occurs at the $370 billion income level. The **break-even income** is at the $390 billion income level (row 2); this is the level at which households consume their entire incomes. Graphically, the consumption schedule cuts the 45-degree line, and the saving schedule cuts the horizontal axis (saving is zero) at the break-even income level. At all higher incomes, households will plan to save a portion of their income. The vertical distance of the consumption schedule *below* the 45-degree line measures this saving, as does the vertical distance of the saving schedule *above* the horizontal axis. For example, at the $410 billion level of income (row 3), both these distances indicate $5 billion worth of saving (see Figure 12-4a and b).

AVERAGE AND MARGINAL PROPENSITIES

Columns 4 to 7 of Table 12-1 point up additional characteristics of the consumption and saving schedules.

APC and APS That fraction, or percentage, of any given total income which is consumed is called the **average propensity to consume** (APC), and that

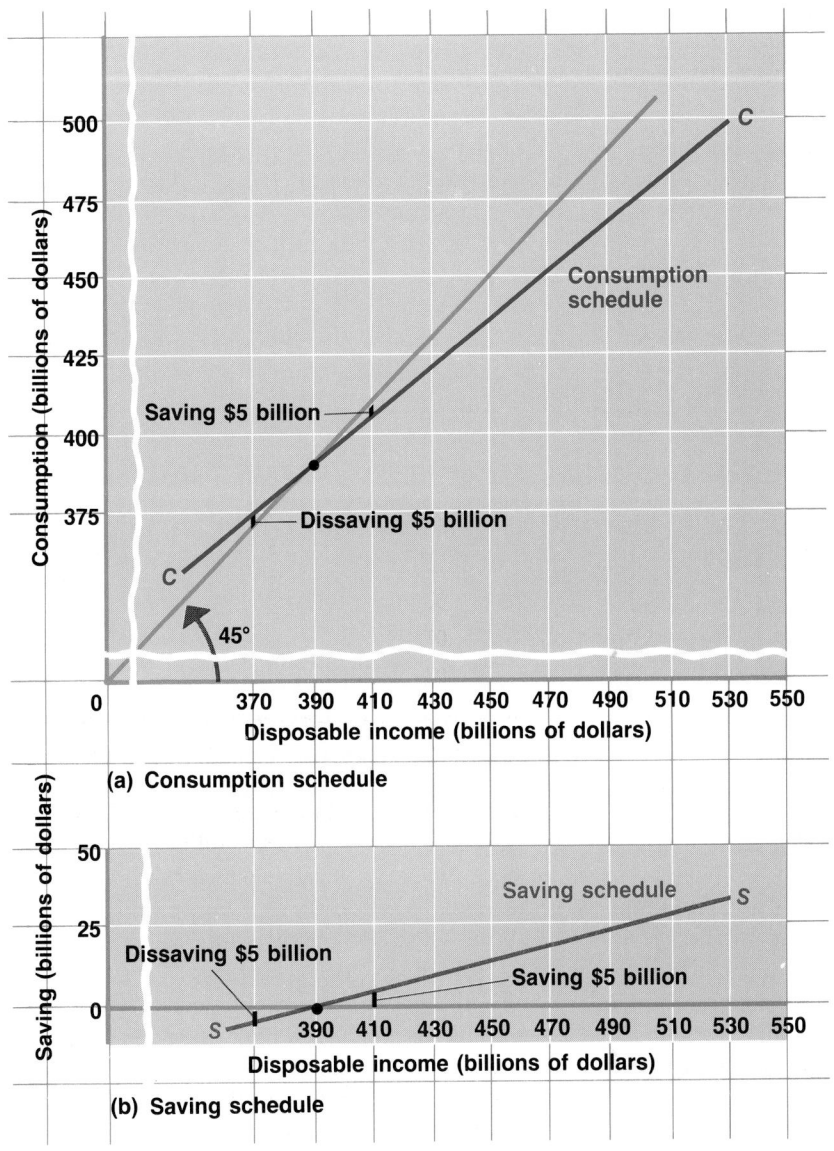

FIGURE 12-4

Consumption (a) and saving (b) schedules

The two parts of this figure show the in-come-consumption and income-saving relation-ships graphically. Each point on the 45-degree line in (a) indicates a point where DI equals consumption. Therefore, because saving equals DI minus consumption, the saving schedule in (b) is found by sub-tracting the consump-tion schedule vertically from the 45-degree guideline. Consumers "break even," that is, consumption equals DI (and saving therefore equals zero) at $390 billion for these hypo-thetical data.

fraction of any total income which is saved is called the **average propensity to save** (APS). That is,

$$APC = \frac{consumption}{income}$$

and

$$APS = \frac{saving}{income}$$

For example, at the $470 billion level of income (row 6) in Table 12-1, the APC is $\frac{450}{470} = \frac{45}{47}$, or about

96 percent, while the APS is obviously $\frac{20}{470} = \frac{2}{47}$, or about 4 percent. By calculating the APC and APS at each of the ten levels of DI shown in Table 12-1, we find that the APC falls and the APS rises as DI increases. This quantifies a point made a moment ago: The fraction of total DI which is consumed declines as DI rises, a movement that makes it nec-essary for the fraction of DI which is saved to rise as DI rises. Indeed, because disposable income is either consumed or saved, the sum of the fraction of any level of DI which is consumed plus the fraction which is saved (not consumed) must exhaust that

level of income. In short, APC + APS = 1. Columns 4 and 5 of Table 12-1 illustrate this point.

MPC and MPS   The fact that households consume a certain portion of some given total income—for example, $\frac{45}{47}$ of a $470 billion disposable income—does not guarantee that they will consume the same proportion of any *change* in income which they might receive. The proportion, or fraction, of any change in income which is consumed is called the **marginal propensity to consume** (MPC), marginal meaning "extra" or "a change in." Or, alternatively stated, the MPC is the ratio of a *change* in consumption to the *change* in income which brought the consumption change about:

$$MPC = \frac{\text{change in consumption}}{\text{change in income}}$$

Similarly, the fraction of any change in income which is saved is called the **marginal propensity to save** (MPS). That is, MPS is the ratio of a *change* in saving to the *change* in income which brought it about:

$$MPS = \frac{\text{change in saving}}{\text{change in income}}$$

Thus, if disposable income is currently $470 billion (row 6) and household incomes rise by $20 billion to $490 billion (row 7), we find that they will consume $\frac{15}{20}$, or $\frac{3}{4}$, and save $\frac{5}{20}$, or $\frac{1}{4}$, of that increase in income (see columns 6 and 7 of Table 12-1). In other words, the MPC is $\frac{3}{4}$, or .75, and the MPS is $\frac{1}{4}$, or .25. *The sum of the MPC and the MPS for any given change in disposable income must always be 1.* That is, consuming and saving out of extra income is an either-or proposition; that fraction of any change in income which is not consumed is, by definition, saved. Therefore the fraction consumed (MPC) plus the fraction saved (MPS) must exhaust the whole increase in income:

MPC + MPS = 1

In our example .75 plus .25 equals 1.

In mathematical terms the MPC is the numerical value of the slope of the consumption schedule or line and the MPS is the numerical value of the slope of the saving schedule or line. As indicated in the appendix to Chapter 1, the slope of any "curve" can be measured by the ratio of the vertical change to the horizontal change involved in moving from one point to another on that line. Thus, in terms of Table 12-1 and Figure 12-4a we see that consumption changes by $15 billion (vertical change) for each $20 billion change in disposable income (horizontal change); that is, the slope of the consumption line is .75 (=$15/$20)—the value of the MPC. We also observe from Table 12-1 and Figure 12-4b that saving changes by $5 billion (vertical change) for every $20 billion change in disposable income (horizontal change). The slope of the saving line therefore is .25 (=$5/$20), which is the value of the MPS.

Economists are not in complete agreement as to the exact behavior of the MPC and MPS as income increases. For many years it was assumed that the MPC declined and the MPS increased as income increased. That is, it was felt that a smaller and smaller fraction of increases in income would be consumed and a larger and larger fraction of these increases would be saved. Many economists now feel that the MPC and MPS for the economy as a whole are relatively constant. Statistical data such as those of Figure 12-3 are consistent with this position. We will assume the MPC and MPS to be constant, not only because of this statistical evidence, but also because a constant MPC and MPS will simplify our analysis considerably.

NONINCOME DETERMINANTS OF CONSUMPTION AND SAVING

The level of disposable income is the basic determinant of the amounts households will consume and save, just as price is the basic determinant of the quantity demanded of a single product. You will recall that changes in determinants other than price, such as consumer tastes, incomes, and so forth (Chapter 4), will cause the demand curve for a given product to shift location. Similarly, there are certain determinants other than income which might cause households to consume more or less at each possible level of DI and thereby change the locations of the consumption and saving schedules. These factors are already familiar to us because we mentioned them in a slightly different context in our earlier discussion of aggregate demand (Chapter 11). There we were focusing upon the downward slope of the aggregate demand curve and upon the factors which shift that curve. Here our interest is how these factors alter the consumption–disposable income and saving–disposable income relationships.

1 Wealth Generally speaking, the greater the amount of wealth households have accumulated, the larger will be the amount of consumption and the smaller the amount of saving out of any level of current income. By *wealth* we mean both real assets (a house, automobiles, television sets, and other durables) and financial assets (cash, savings accounts, stocks, bonds, insurance policies, pensions) which households own. Households save—refrain from consumption—in order to accumulate wealth. Other things being the same, the more wealth households have accumulated, the weaker the incentive to save in order to accumulate additional wealth. Stated differently, an increase in wealth shifts the saving schedule downward and the consumption schedule upward.

Example: The dramatic stock market crash of 1929 had the effect of significantly decreasing the financial wealth of many families almost overnight and was undoubtedly a factor in explaining the low levels of consumption in the depressed 1930s. For the most part, however, the amount of wealth held by households only changes modestly from year to year and therefore does not typically account for large shifts in the consumption and saving schedules.

2 Price level An increase in the price level tends to shift the consumption schedule downward, while a decrease in the price level tends to shift the consumption schedule upward. This generalization is closely related to our discussion of wealth as a determinant of consumption because changes in the price level change the *real value* or *purchasing power* of certain types of wealth. Specifically, the real value of financial assets whose values are fixed in money terms will vary inversely with changes in the price level. This, of course, is the *wealth* or *real balances effect* which you encountered in Chapter 11. Example: Suppose you own a $10,000 government bond. If the price level increases by, say, 10 percent, the real value of your $10,000 financial asset will decrease by approximately 10 percent. Because your real financial *wealth* has been reduced, you will be less inclined to consume out of

current *income.* Conversely, a decrease in the price level will increase your real financial wealth and induce you to consume a larger proportion of your current income.

A notable implication of this discussion is that, whenever we draw (locate) a particular consumption or saving schedule as in Figure 12-4, we are implicitly assuming a constant price level. This means that the horizontal axis of that figure measures *real* disposable income, as opposed to nominal or money, disposable income.[6]

3 Expectations Household expectations concerning future prices, money incomes, and the availability of goods may have a significant impact upon current spending and saving. Expectations of rising prices and product shortages tend to trigger more spending and less saving currently, that is, to shift the consumption schedule upward and the saving schedule downward. Why? Because it is natural for consumers to seek to avoid paying higher prices or having to "do without." Expected inflation and expected shortages induce people to "buy now" to escape higher future prices and bare shelves. The expectation of rising money incomes in the future also tends to make consumers more footloose in their current spending. Conversely, expected price declines, anticipations of shrinking incomes, and the feeling that goods will be abundantly available may induce consumers to retrench on their consumption and build up their savings.

4 Consumer indebtedness The level of consumer debt can also be expected to affect the willingness of households to consume and save out of current income. If households are in debt to the degree that, say, 20 or 25 percent of their current incomes are committed to installment payments on previous purchases, consumers may well be obliged to retrench on current consumption in order to reduce their indebtedness. Conversely, if consumer indebtedness is relatively low, households may consume at an unusually high rate by increasing this indebtedness.

---

[6] In Chapter 13 we will reconcile the constant price level Keynesian analysis with the variable price level embodied in Chapter 11's aggregate demand–aggregate supply model.

5 Taxation   In Chapter 14, where consumption will be plotted against before-tax income, we will find that changes in taxes will shift the consumption and saving schedules. Specifically, we will discover that taxes are paid partly at the expense of consumption *and* partly at the expense of saving. Therefore, an *increase* in taxes will shift *both* the consumption and saving schedules *downward*. Conversely, a tax reduction will be partly consumed and partly saved by households. Thus a tax *decrease* will shift *both* the consumption and saving schedules *upward*.

SHIFTS AND STABILITY

Three final and related points are relevant to our discussion of the consumption and saving schedules.

I Terminology   The movement from one point to another on a given stable consumption schedule (for example, *A* to *B* on C_0 in Figure 12-5a is called a *change in the amount consumed*. The sole cause of this change is a change in the level of disposable income. On the other hand, a *change in the consumption schedule* refers to an upward or downward shift of the entire schedule—for example, a shift from C_0 to C_1 or to C_2 in Figure 12-5a. A relocation of the consumption schedule is obviously caused by changes in any one or more of the nonincome determinants just discussed. A similar distinction in terminology applies to the saving schedule in Figure 12-5b.

2 Schedule shifts   A related point is that, insofar as the first four nonincome determinants of consumption are concerned, the consumption and saving schedules will necessarily shift in opposite directions. If households decide to consume *more* at each possible level of disposable income, this means that they want to save *less,* and vice versa. Graphically, if the consumption schedule shifts upward from C_0 to C_1 in Figure 12-5, the saving schedule will shift downward from S_0 to S_1. Similarly, a downshift in the consumption schedule from C_0 to C_2 means an upshift in the saving schedule from S_0 to S_2. As noted a moment ago, the exception to this involves the fifth nonincome determinant—taxation. We shall discover in Chapter 14

that households will consume less *and* save less in order to pay higher taxes. Hence, a tax increase will lower *both* consumption and saving schedules, whereas a tax cut will shift *both* schedules upward.

3 Stability   Economists of all persuasions are in general agreement that, aside from deliberate gov-

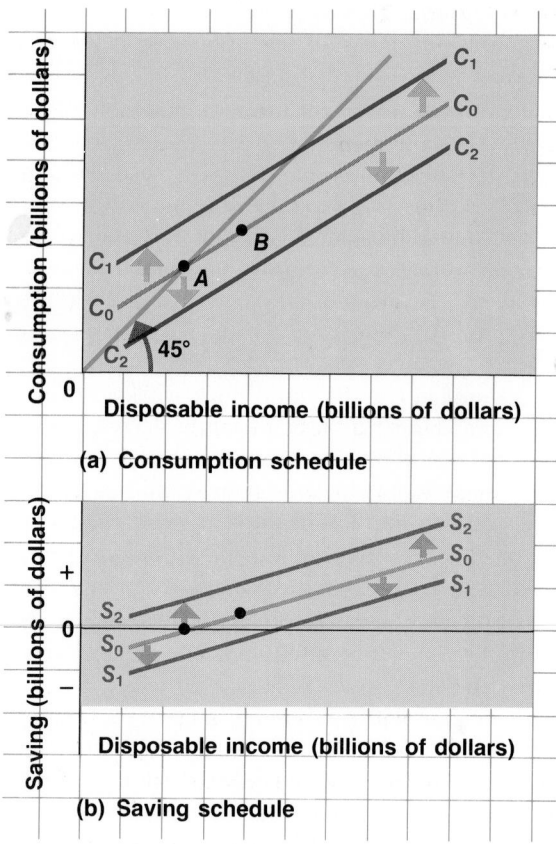

FIGURE 12-5

Shifts in the consumption (a) and saving (b) schedules

A change in any one or more of the nonincome determinants will cause the consumption and saving schedules to shift. If households consume more at each level of DI, they are necessarily saving less. Graphically this means that an upshift in the consumption schedule (C_0 to C_1) entails a downshift in the saving schedule (S_0 to S_1). Conversely, if households consume less at each level of DI, they are saving more. A downshift in the consumption schedule (C_0 to C_2) is reflected in an upshift of the saving schedule (S_0 to S_2).

ernmental actions designed to shift them, the consumption and saving schedules are quite stable. This may be because consumption-saving decisions are strongly influenced by habit or because the nonincome determinants are diverse and changes in them frequently work in opposite directions and therefore tend to be self-canceling.

Investment

Let us now turn to investment, the second component of private spending. Recall that investment refers to expenditures on new plants, capital equipment, machinery, and so forth. What determines the level of net investment spending? There are two basic determinants: (1) the expected rate of net profits which businesses hope to realize from investment spending, and (2) the rate of interest.

EXPECTED RATE OF NET PROFIT

Investment spending is guided by the profit motive; the business sector buys capital goods only when it expects such purchases to be profitable. Consider a simplified example. Suppose the owner of a small cabinetmaking shop is considering investing in a new sanding machine which costs $1000 and has a useful life of only one year. The new machine will presumably increase the firm's output and sales revenue. Specifically, let us suppose that the *net* expected revenue (that is, net of such operating costs as power, lumber, labor, certain taxes, and so forth) from the machine is $1100. In other words, after operating costs have been accounted for, the remaining expected net revenue is sufficient to cover the $1000 cost of the machine and leave a return of $100. Comparing this $100 return or profit with the $1000 cost of the machine, we find that the expected *rate* of net profit on the machine is 10 percent (= $100/$1000).

THE REAL INTEREST RATE

But there is one important cost associated with investing which our example has ignored. And that, of course, is the interest rate—the financial cost the firm must pay to borrow the *money* capital required for the purchase of the *real* capital (the sanding machine).[7] Our generalization is this: If the expected rate of net profits (10 percent) exceeds the interest rate (say, 7 percent), it will be profitable to invest. But if the interest rate (say, 12 percent) exceeds the expected rate of net profits (10 percent), it will be unprofitable to invest.

It should be emphasized that it is the *real* rate of interest, rather than the nominal rate, which is crucial in making investment decisions. Recall from Chapter 10 that the nominal interest rate is expressed in terms of dollars of current value, while the real interest rate is stated in terms of dollars of constant or inflation-adjusted value. In other words, the real interest rate is the nominal rate less the rate of inflation. In our sanding machine illustration we implicitly assumed a constant price level so that all our data, including the interest rate, were in real terms.

But what if inflation is occurring? Suppose a $1000 investment is estimated to yield a real (inflation-adjusted) expected rate of net profits of 10 percent and the nominal interest rate is, say, 15 percent. At first glance one would say the investment is unprofitable and should not be made. But assume now that there is an ongoing inflation of 10 percent per year. This means that the investor will be paying back dollars with approximately 10 percent less in purchasing power. While the nominal interest rate is 15 percent, the real rate is only 5 percent (= 15 percent − 10 percent). Comparing this 5 percent real interest rate with the 10 percent expected real rate of net profits, we find that the investment *is* profitable and should be undertaken.

INVESTMENT-DEMAND CURVE

We must now move from micro to macro, that is, from a single firm's investment decision to an understanding of the total demand for investment

---

[7] The role of the interest rate as a cost in investing in real capital is valid even if the firm does not borrow but, rather, finances the investment internally out of funds saved from past profits. By using this money to invest in the sander, the firm incurs an opportunity cost (Chapter 2) in the sense that it forgoes the interest income which it could have realized by lending the funds to someone else.

goods by the entire business sector. Assume every firm in the economy has estimated the expected rate of net profits from all relevant investment projects and these data have been collected. These estimates can now be *cumulated*—that is, successively summed—by asking: How many dollars' worth of investment projects entail an expected rate of net profit of, say, 16 percent or more? Of 14 percent or more? Of 12 percent or more? And so on.

Suppose we find that there are no prospective investments which will yield an expected net profit of 16 percent or more. But there are $5 billion of investment opportunities with an expected rate of net profits between 14 and 16 percent; an *additional* $5 billion yielding between 12 and 14 percent; still an *additional* $5 billion yielding between 10 and 12 percent; and an *additional* $5 billion in each successive 2 percent range of yield down to and including the 0 to 2 percent range. By *cumulating* these figures we obtain the data of Table 12-2, which are shown graphically by the **investment-demand curve** in Figure 12-6. Note in Table 12-2 that the figure opposite 12 percent, for example, tells us there are $10 billion worth of investment opportunities which will yield an expected net profit of 12 percent *or more;* the $10 billion, in other words, includes the $5 billion of investment which will yield an expected return of 14 percent or more *plus* the $5 billion which is expected to yield between 12 and 14 percent.

TABLE 12-2 **Profit expectations and investment** *(hypothetical data)*

Expected rate of net profit (in percent)	Amount of investment (billions of dollars per year)
16%	$ 0
14	5
12	10
10	15
8	20
6	25
4	30
2	35
0	40

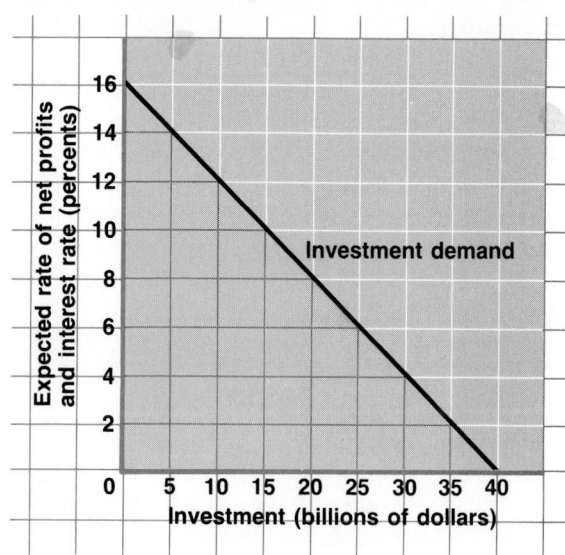

FIGURE 12-6

The investment-demand curve

The investment-demand curve for the economy is derived by arraying all relevant investment projects in descending order of their expected rate of net profitability and applying the rule that investment should be undertaken up to the point at which the interest rate is equal to the expected rate of net profits. The investment-demand curve is downsloping, reflecting an inverse relationship between the interest rate (the financial price of investing) and the aggregate quantity of capital goods demanded.

Given this cumulated information on expected net profit rates of all possible investment projects, we again introduce the real interest rate or financial cost of investing. We know from our sanding machine example that an investment project will be undertaken provided its expected net profit rate exceeds the real interest rate. Let us apply this reasoning to Figure 12-6. If we assume that rate of interest is 12 percent, we find that $10 billion of investment spending will be profitable, that is, $10 billion worth of investment projects entail an expected net profit rate of 12 percent or more. Stated differently, at a financial "price" of 12 percent, $10 billion worth of investment goods will be demanded. Similarly, if the interest rate were lower at, say, 10 percent, then an additional $5 billion of investment projects would become profitable and the total amount of investment goods demanded would be $15 billion (= $10 + $5). At an interest rate of 8 percent, a further $5 billion of investment would become profitable and the total demand for investment goods would be $20 billion. At 6 percent, investment would be $25 billion. And so forth. *By applying the rule that all investment projects should be undertaken up to the point at which the expected rate of net profit equals the interest rate, we discover that the curve of Figure 12-6 is the investment-demand curve.* That is, various possible financial prices of investing (various real interest rates) are shown on the vertical axis and the corresponding quantities of investment goods demanded are revealed on the horizontal axis. By definition, any line or curve embodying such data is the investment-demand curve. Consistent with our product and resource demand curves of Chapter 4, observe the *inverse* relationship between the interest rate (price) and the amount of spending on investment goods (quantity demanded).

This conception of the investment decision allows us to anticipate an important aspect of macroeconomic policy. We shall find in our discussion of monetary policy in Chapter 17 that by changing the supply of money, government can alter the interest rate. This is done primarily to change the level of investment spending. Think of it in this way: At any point in time, business firms in the aggregate have a wide variety of investment projects under consideration. If interest rates are high, only those projects with the highest expected rate of net profit will be undertaken. Hence, the level of investment will be small. As the interest rate is lowered, projects whose expected rate of net profit is less will also become commercially feasible and the level of investment will rise.

A final point: Assuming a fixed supply of money, a change in the price level will influence the amount of investment through the *interest-rate effect* described in Chapter 11. A rise in the price level will increase the amount of money that consumers and businesses desire to have available for purchasing the higher-priced output. That is, if prices rise by, say, 10 percent, then people will want to have 10 percent more money in their billfolds and checking accounts. With a fixed supply of money, this increase in the demand for money balances elevates the price of money—the interest rate—which, in turn, reduces investment. Likewise, lower price levels reduce the demand for money balances, decrease the interest rate, and bolster investment.

SHIFTS IN INVESTMENT DEMAND

In discussing the consumption schedule, we noted that, although disposable income is the key determinant of the amount consumed, there are other factors which affect consumption. These "nonincome determinants," you will recall, cause shifts in the consumption schedule. So it also is with the investment-demand schedule. Given the expected rates of net profit of various possible investments, Figure 12-6 portrays the interest rate as the main determinant of investment. But other factors or variables determine the location of the investment-demand curve. Let us briefly consider several of the more important "noninterest determinants" of investment demand, noting how changes in these determinants might shift the investment-demand curve. We observe at the outset that any factor which increases the expected net profitability of investment will shift the investment-demand curve to the right. Conversely, anything which decreases the expected net profitability of investment will shift the investment-demand curve to the left.

1 Acquisition, maintenance, and operating costs As our sanding machine example revealed, the initial costs of capital goods, along with the estimated costs of operating and maintaining those goods, are clearly important considerations in gauging the expected rate of net profitability of any particular investment. To the extent that these costs rise, the expected rate of *net* profit from prospective investment projects will fall, shifting the investment-demand curve to the left. Conversely, if these costs decline, expected net profit rates will rise, shifting the investment-demand curve to the right. Note that the wage policies of unions may affect the investment-demand curve because wage rates are a major operating cost for most firms.

2 Business taxes Business owners look to expected profits *after taxes* in making their investment decisions. Hence, an increase in business taxes will lower profitability and tend to shift the investment-demand curve to the left; a tax reduction will tend to shift it to the right.

3 Technological change Technological progress—the development of new products, improvements in existing products, the creation of new machinery and new production processes—is a basic stimulus to investment. The development of a more efficient machine, for example, will lower production costs or improve product quality, thereby increasing the expected rate of net profit from investing in the machine. Profitable new products—such as mountain bikes, personal computers, legal drugs, and so on—induce a flurry of investment as firms tool up for expanded production. In short, a rapid rate of technological progress shifts the investment-demand curve to the right, and vice versa.

4 The stock of capital goods on hand   Just as the stock of consumer goods on hand affects household consumption-saving decisions, so the stock of capital goods on hand influences the expected profit rate from additional investment in a given industry. To the extent that a given industry is well stocked with productive facilities and inventories of finished goods, investment will be retarded in that industry. The reason is obvious: Such an industry will be amply equipped to fulfill present and future market demand at prices which yield mediocre profits. If an industry has enough, or even excessive, productive capacity, the expected rate of profit from further investment in the industry will be low, and therefore little or no investment will occur. Excess productive capacity tends to shift the investment-demand curve to the left; a relative scarcity of capital goods shifts it to the right.

5 Expectations   We noted earlier that business investment is based upon *expected* profits. Capital goods are durable—they may have a life expectancy of ten or twenty years—and thus the profitability of any capital investment will depend upon business planners' expectations of the *future* sales and *future* profitability of the product which the capital helps produce. Business expectations may be based upon elaborate forecasts of future business conditions which incorporate a number of "business indicators." Nevertheless, such elusive and difficult-to-predict factors as changes in the domestic political climate, the thrust of foreign affairs, population growth, stock market conditions, and so on, must be taken into account on a subjective or intuitive basis. For present purposes we note that, if business executives are optimistic about future business conditions, the investment-demand curve will shift to the right; a pessimistic outlook will shift it to the left.

INVESTMENT AND INCOME

In order to add the investment decisions of businesses to the consumption plans of households (Chapter 13), we need to express investment plans in terms of the level of disposable income (DI), or NNP. That is, we want to construct an **investment schedule** showing the amounts which business firms as a group plan or intend to invest at each of the various possible levels of income or output. Such a schedule will mirror the investment plans or intentions of business owners and managers in the same way the consumption and saving schedules reflect the consumption and saving plans of households.

We shall assume in our analysis that business investment is geared to long-term profit expectations as influenced by such considerations as technological progress, population growth, and so forth, and therefore is *autonomous* or independent of the level of current disposable income or national output. More specifically, let us suppose that the investment-demand curve is as shown in Figure 12-6 *and* that the current rate of interest is 8 percent. This means that the business sector will find it profitable to spend $20 billion on investment goods. In Table 12-3, columns 1 and 2, we are assuming that this level of investment will be forthcoming at every level of income. The I_n line in Figure 12-7 shows this graphically.

This assumed independence of investment and income is admittedly a simplification. A higher level of business activity may *induce* additional spending on capital facilities, as suggested by columns 1 and 3 of Table 12-3 and I'_n in Figure 12-7. There are at least two reasons why investment might vary directly with income. First, investment is related to profits; much investment is financed internally out of business profits. Therefore, it is very plausible to suggest that as disposable income and NNP rise, so will business profits and therefore the level of investment. Second, at low levels of income and output, the business sector will tend to have unutilized, or excess, productive capacity; that is, many industries will have idle machinery and equipment and therefore little incentive to pur-

TABLE 12-3 **The investment schedule** *(hypothetical data; in billions)*

(1) Level of output and income	(2) Investment, I_n	(3) Investment, I_n'
$370	$20	$10
390	20	12
410	20	14
430	20	16
450	20	18
470	20	20
490	20	22
510	20	24
530	20	26
550	20	28

chase additional capital goods. But, as the level of income rises, this excess capacity disappears and firms are inclined to add to their stock of capital goods. Our simplification, however, is not too severely at odds with reality and will greatly facilitate later analysis.

INSTABILITY OF INVESTMENT

In contrast to the consumption schedule, the investment schedule is unstable. Proportionately, investment is the most volatile component of total spending. Figure 12-8 is informative in that it shows the volatility of investment and also makes clear that this variability is substantially greater than that of GNP. These data also suggest that our simplified treatment of investment as being independent of national output (Figure 12-7) is not especially unrealistic; investment spending does not closely follow GNP.

Some of the more important factors which explain the variability of investment are as follows:

1 Durability Because of their durability, capital goods have a rather indefinite useful life. Within limits, purchases of capital goods are discretionary and therefore postponable. Older equipment or buildings can be scrapped and entirely replaced, on the one hand, or patched up and used for a few more years, on the other. Optimism about the future may prompt business planners to replace their older facilities, that is, to modernize their plants, and this will call for a high level of investment. A slightly less optimistic view, however, may lead to very small amounts of investment as older facilities are repaired and kept in use.

2 Irregularity of innovation We have noted that technological progress is a major determinant of investment. New products and new processes provide a major stimulus to investment. However, history suggests that major innovations—railroads, electricity, automobiles, computers, and so forth—occur quite irregularly, and when they do occur,

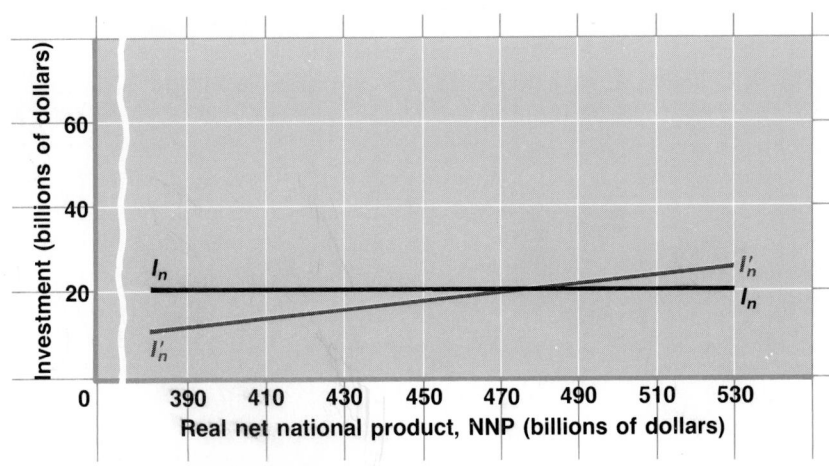

FIGURE 12-7

The investment schedule: two possibilities

Our discussion will be facilitated by employing the investment schedule I_n, which assumes that the investment plans of businesses are independent of the current level of income. Actually, the investment schedule may be slightly upsloping, as suggested by I_n'.

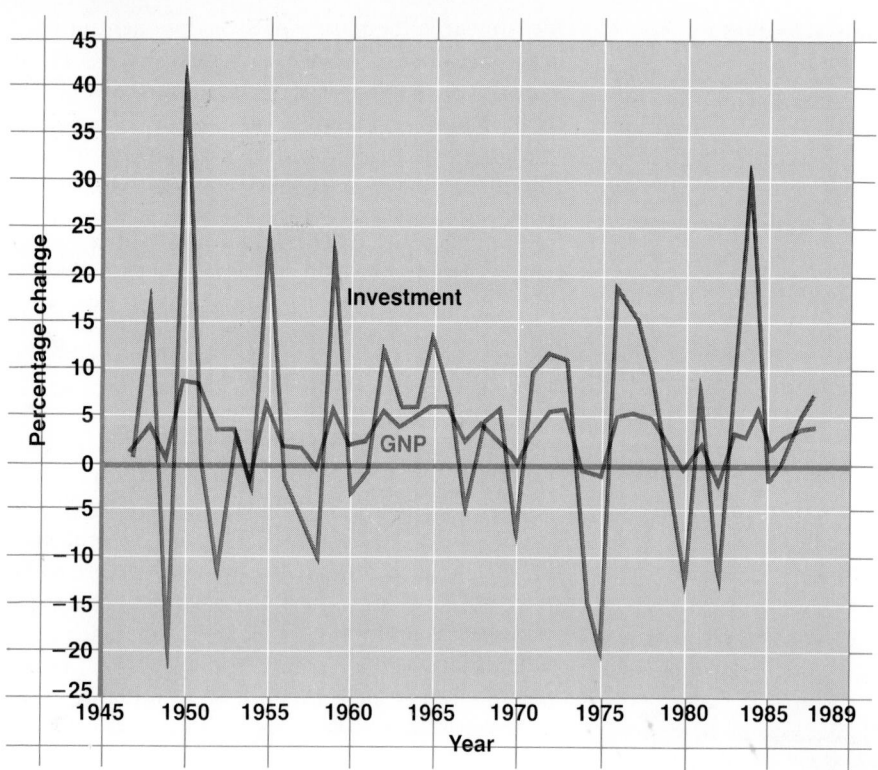

FIGURE 12-8

The volatility of investment

Investment spending is highly volatile. In comparing changes in real investment and real GNP, we observe that the annual percentage changes in investment are greater than the percentage changes in GNP.

these innovations induce a vast upsurge or "wave" of investment spending which in time recedes. A classic illustration: The widespread acceptance of the automobile in the 1920s not only brought about substantial increases in investment in the automobile industry itself, but also induced tremendous amounts of investment in such related industries as steel, petroleum, glass, and rubber, not to mention public investment in streets and highways. But when investment in these related industries was ultimately "completed"—that is, when they had created capital facilities sufficient to meet the needs of the automobile industry—total investment leveled off.

3 Variability of profits We know that business owners and managers invest only when they feel it will be profitable to do so and that, to a significant degree, the expectation of future profitability is influenced by the size of current profits. Current profits, however, are themselves highly variable (line 12 of the table on the inside covers provides information on undistributed corporate profits). Thus, the vari-

ability of profits contributes to the volatile nature of the incentive to invest. Furthermore, the instability of profits may also cause investment fluctuations, because profits are a major source of funds for business investment. American businesses tend to prefer this internal source of financing to increases in external debt or stock issue. In short, expanding profits give business planners both greater incentives and greater means to invest; declining profits have the reverse effects. The fact that actual profits are variable adds to the instability of investment.

4 Variability of expectations We have already discussed how the durability of capital equipment results in the making of investment decisions upon the basis of *expected* net profit. Now, while there is a tendency for business firms to project current business conditions into the future, it is equally true that expectations are sometimes subject to radical revision when some event or combination of events suggests a significant change in future business conditions. What kinds of events make business confidence so capricious? Changes in the domestic political climate, cold-war or energy developments, changes in population growth and therefore in anticipated market demand, court decisions in key labor or antitrust cases, legislative actions, strikes, changes in governmental economic policies, and a host of similar considerations may give rise to substantial shifts in business optimism or pessimism.

The stock market merits specific comment in this regard. Business planners frequently look to the stock market as an index or barometer of the overall confidence of society in future business conditions; a rising "bull" market signifies public confidence in the business future, whereas a falling "bear" market implies a lack of confidence. The stock market, however, is a highly speculative market, and initially modest changes in stock prices can be seriously intensified by participants who jump on the bandwagon by buying when prices begin to rise and by selling when stock prices start to fall. Furthermore, by affecting the amount of proceeds gained through offerings of new stock, upsurges and slumps in stock values also affect the level of investment—that is the amount of capital goods purchased.

For these and similar reasons, it is quite correct to associate most fluctuations in output and employment with changes in investment. In terms of Figure 12-7, we can think of this volatility as being reflected in frequent and substantial upward and downward shifts in the investment schedule.

CHAPTER SUMMARY

1 Classical employment theory envisioned laissez faire capitalism as being capable of providing virtually continuous full employment. This analysis was based on Say's Law and the assumption of price-wage flexibility.

2 The classical economists argued that because supply creates its own demand, general overproduction was improbable. This conclusion was held to be valid even when saving occurred, because the money market, or more specifically, the interest rate, would automatically synchronize the saving plans of households and the investment plans of businesses.

3 Classical employment theory also held that even if temporary declines in total spending were to occur, these declines would be compensated for by downward price-wage adjustments in such a way that real output, employment, and real income would not decline.

4 Keynesian employment theory rejects the notion that the interest rate would equate saving and investment by pointing out that savers and investors are substantially different groups who make their saving and investment decisions for different reasons—reasons which, for savers, are largely unrelated to the interest rate. Furthermore, because of changes in **a** the public's holdings of money balances, and **b** loans made by banks and other financial institutions, the supply of funds may exceed or fall short of current saving to the end that saving and investment will not be equal.

5 Keynesian economists discredit price-wage flexibility on both practical and theoretical grounds. They argue that **a** union and business monopolies, minimum-wage legislation, and a host of related factors have virtually eliminated the possibility of substantial price-wage reductions, and **b** price-wage cuts will lower total income and therefore the demand for labor.

6 The classical and Keynesian views can be illustrated through the aggregate demand and supply model. Classical economists envision **a** a vertical aggregate supply curve which establishes the level of output, and **b** a stable aggregate demand curve which establishes the price level; Keynesians see **a** a horizontal aggregate supply curve at less-than-full-employment levels of output, and **b** an inherently unstable aggregate demand curve.

7 The basic tools of Keynesian employment theory are the consumption, saving, and investment schedules, which show the various amounts that households intend to consume and save and that businesses plan to invest at the various possible income-output levels, given a particular price level.

8 The locations of the consumption and saving schedules are determined by such factors as **a** the amount of wealth owned by households; **b** the price level; **c** expectations of future income, future prices, and product availability; **d** the relative size of consumer indebtedness; and **e** taxation. The consumption and saving schedules are relatively stable.

9 The **average** propensities to consume and save show the proportion or fraction of any level of **total** income that is consumed and saved. The **marginal** propensities to consume and save show the proportion or fraction of any **change** in total income that is consumed or saved.

10 The immediate determinants of investment are **a** the expected rate of net profit and **b** the real rate of interest. The economy's investment-demand curve can be determined by cumulating investment projects and arraying them in descending order according to their expected net profitability and applying the rule that investment will be profitable up to the point at which the real interest rate equals the expected rate of net profit. The investment-demand curve reveals an inverse relationship between the interest rate and the level of aggregate investment.

11 Shifts in the investment-demand curve can occur as the result of changes in **a** the acquisition, maintenance, and operating costs of capital goods; **b** business taxes; **c** technology; **d** the stocks of capital goods on hand; and **e** expectations.

12 We make the simplifying assumption that the level of investment determined by the current interest rate and the investment-demand curve does not vary with the level of aggregate income.

13 The durability of capital goods, the irregular occurrence of major innovations, profit volatility, and the variability of expectations all contribute to the instability of investment spending.

TERMS AND CONCEPTS

classical theory of employment	**average propensities to consume and save**
Say's Law	**marginal propensities to consume and save**
price-wage flexibility	
Keynesian economics	**investment-demand curve**
consumption and saving schedules	**investment schedule**
break-even income	

QUESTIONS AND STUDY SUGGESTIONS

1 Explain the classical economists' conclusion that Say's Law would prevail even in an economy where substantial saving occurred. What arguments have Keynesian economists used in attacking the classical view that Say's Law would result in sustained full employment?

2 "Unemployment can be avoided so long as businesses are willing to accept lower product prices, and workers to accept lower wage rates." Critically evaluate.

LAST WORD

The share economy: making wages flexible

Can greater downward wage flexibility be achieved in order to soften the impact of a decline in aggregate demand upon employment? MIT's Martin Weitzman has offered a proposal to achieve this goal.*

Our comparisons of the classical and the Keynesian conceptions of the macroeconomy clearly suggest that if wages are stable employment will tend to be unstable and vice versa. Most modern economists recognize that long-term union contracts, among other considerations, make wages downwardly inflexible at least in the short run. Hence, the declines in labor demand which accompany recession have their primary effect upon employment. Professor Weitzman's proposal seeks to increase the downward flexibility of wage rates so that the functioning of labor markets corresponds more closely with the classical model and thereby results in greater employment stability.

In essence Weitzman's proposal is that some portion of wages should be tied directly to the firm's profitability; some part of worker compensation should be in the form of profit sharing. For example, instead of paying workers a guaranteed wage rate of $10 per hour, Weitzman suggests that workers be guaranteed $5 per hour (the base wage) and additional compensation equal to some predetermined percentage of the firm's profits (the share wage). Total compensation (base wage + share wage) may exceed or fall short of $10 per hour, depending upon the firm's economic fortunes.

How would employment be affected by such a

plan? Assume initially that workers are receiving $10 per hour—$5 in the form of a guaranteed wage and another $5 as profit-sharing compensation. Now suppose a recession occurs and the employer's sales and profits both decline. As a result, the $5 of profit-sharing income will fall and might decline to zero so that actual wages paid by the firm fall from $10 to $5. Given the new depressed demand for labor, the firm would clearly choose to hire more workers under Weitzman's proposal where wages have now fallen to, $5, than if they were fixed at $10. Aside from reducing cyclical unemployment, Weitzman claims that his wage proposal will create an incentive for employers to hire larger labor forces than otherwise. Under a conventional wage plan a worker would only be employed by a firm if he or she produced output worth more than the $10 guaranteed wage. Under the profit-sharing plan, it would be profitable to hire additional workers so long as they generated additional output worth more than $5 to the firm.

There are a number of criticisms of the profit-sharing wage plan. For example, it has been argued that the plan might jeopardize the historical wage gains of labor and result in "coolie wages." A further criticism is that with lower guaranteed wages employers will be inclined to adopt production techniques which involve the use of relatively more labor and relatively less capital. Because the amount of capital equipment per worker is critical to labor productivity and economic growth, the long-run expansion of real GNP might be impaired. At a more pragmatic level there is the fundamental question as to whether workers will accept the prospect of more jobs and greater employment stability in exchange for a reduced wage guarantee. It should be noted, however, that during the 1980s a growing number of union and nonunion labor contracts *have* contained profit-sharing arrangements. Hence, although a full-blown share economy seems improbable, profit-sharing appears to be an idea which is spreading.

* Martin L. Weitzman, *The Share Economy* (Cambridge, Mass.: Harvard University Press, 1984).

3 Use the aggregate demand–aggregate supply model to compare classical and Keynesian interpretations of *a* the aggregate supply curve, and *b* the aggregate demand curve. Which model do you think is more realistic?

4 Precisely how are the APC and the MPC different? Why must the sum of the MPC and the MPS equal 1? What are the basic determinants of the consumption and saving schedules? Of your own level of consumption?

5 Explain precisely what relationships are shown by *a* the consumption schedule, *b* the saving schedule, *c* the investment-demand curve, and *d* the investment schedule.

6 Explain how each of the following will affect the consumption and saving schedules or the investment schedule:

a A decline in the amount of government bonds which consumers are holding

b The threat of limited, nonnuclear war, leading the public to expect future shortages of consumer durables

c A decline in the real interest rate

d A sharp decline in stock prices

e An increase in the rate of population growth

f The development of a cheaper method of manufacturing pig iron from ore

g The announcement that the social security program is to be restricted in size of benefits

h The expectation that mild inflation will persist in the next decade

i An 8 percent reduction in the price level

7 Explain why an upshift in the consumption schedule typically involves an equal downshift in the saving schedule. What is the exception?

8 Complete the accompanying table that appears at the top of page 228.

a Show the consumption and saving schedules graphically.

b Locate the break-even level of income. How is it possible for households to dissave at very low income levels?

c If the proportion of total income which is consumed decreases and the proportion which is saved increases as income rises, explain both verbally and graphically how the MPC and MPS can be constant at various levels of income.

Level of output and income (NNP = DI)	Consumption	Saving	APC	APS	MPC	MPS
$240	$_____	$−4	_____	_____		
260	_____	0	_____	_____	_____	_____
280	_____	4	_____	_____	_____	_____
300	_____	8	_____	_____	_____	_____
320	_____	12	_____	_____	_____	_____
340	_____	16	_____	_____	_____	_____
360	_____	20	_____	_____	_____	_____
380	_____	24	_____	_____	_____	_____
400	_____	28	_____	_____	_____	_____

9 What are the basic determinants of investment? Explain the relationship between the real interest rate and the level of investment. Why is the investment schedule less stable than the consumption and saving schedules?

10 Assume there are no investment projects in the economy which yield an expected rate of net profit of 25 percent or more. But suppose there are $10 billion of investment projects yielding expected net profit of between 20 and 25 percent; another $10 billion yielding between 15 and 20 percent; another $10 billion between 10 and 15 percent; and so forth. Cumulate these data and present them graphically, putting the expected rate of net profit on the vertical axis and the amount of investment on the horizontal axis. What will be the equilibrium level of aggregate investment if the real interest rate is *a* 15 percent, *b* 10 percent, and *c* 5 percent? Explain why this curve is the investment-demand curve.

11 Linear equations (see appendix to Chapter 1) for the consumption and saving schedules take the general form $C = a + bY$ and $S = -a + (1 - b)Y$, where C, S, and Y are consumption, saving, and national income, respectively. The constant *a* represents the vertical intercept, and *b* is the slope of the consumption schedule.

    a Use the following data to substitute specific numerical values into the consumption and saving equations.

National income (Y)	Consumption (C)
$ 0	$ 80
100	140
200	200
300	260
400	320

    b What is the economic meaning of *b*? Of $(1 - b)$?
    c Suppose the amount of saving which occurs at each level of national income falls by $20, but that the values for *b* and $(1 - b)$ remain unchanged. Restate the saving and consumption equations for the new numerical values and cite a factor which might have caused the change.

12 Suppose that the linear equation for consumption in a hypothetical economy is $C = 40 + .8Y$. Also suppose that income (Y) is $400. Determine *a* the marginal propensity to consume, *b* the marginal propensity to save, *c* the level of consumption, *d* the average propensity to consume, *e* the level of saving, and *f* the average propensity to save.

CHAPTER 13

Equilibrium national output in the Keynesian model

In this chapter we will first use the Keynesian consumption, saving, and investment schedules developed in Chapter 12 to explain the equilibrium levels of output, income, and employment. Next, we will analyze *changes* in the equilibrium levels of output, income, and employment brought about by changes in investment spending. Then, the foreign sector is brought into the model to show how exports and imports affect the equilibrium levels of output, income, and employment. Until government is added to our discussion later in Chapter 14, we will retain the simplifying assumptions of no government and no business saving. Recall that these assumptions permit us to equate NNP and DI. In addition, unless explicitly indicated to the contrary, we will assume that the price level is constant. In other words, the economy is presumed to be functioning within the Keynesian (horizontal) range of the aggregate supply curve. Hence, our analysis will be in terms of *real* national output as opposed to *nominal* national output.

The final section reconciles our newly developed aggregate expenditures model with Chapter 11's aggregate demand and supply model.

Precautionary note: In this and the next chapter we deal with a *model* of the economy which is designed to convey an understanding of the basic determinants of the levels of output and employment. The specific numbers employed are only illustrative; they are not intended to measure the real world.

Expenditures-output approach

In pursuing the important task of determining and explaining the equilibrium level of output, two closely interrelated approaches—the **aggregate expenditures–national output** (or $C + I_n = $ NNP) **approach** and the **leakages-injections** (or, in the initial discussion of this chapter, the $S = I_n$) **approach**—will be employed. Let us first discuss the aggregate expenditures–national output approach (or "expenditures-output approach" for brevity), using both simple arithmetic data and graphic analysis.

TABULAR ANALYSIS

Table 13-1 merely brings together the income-consumption and income-saving data of Table 12-1 and the simplified income-investment data of columns 1 and 2 in Table 12-3.

National output Column 2 of Table 13-1 is the total or national output schedule for the economy. It indicates the various possible levels of total output—that is, the various possible real NNPs—which the business sector of the economy might produce. *Producers are willing to offer each of these ten levels of output in the expectation that they will receive an identical amount of receipts of income from its sale.* That is, the business sector will produce $370 billion worth of output, thereby incurring $370 billion worth of costs (wages, rents, interest, and profit), only if businesses expect that this output can be sold for $370 billion worth of receipts. Some $390 billion worth of output will be offered if businesses feel this output can be sold for $390 billion. And so it is for all the other possible levels of output.

Aggregate expenditures The total, or aggregate, expenditures schedule is shown in column 6 of

TABLE 13-1 Determination of the equilibrium levels of employment, output, and income: the closed private sector (hypothetical data)

(1) Possible levels of employment, millions	(2) Real national output (and income) (NNP = DI),* billions	(3) Consumption, C, billions	(4) Saving, S, billions	(5) Investment, I_n, billions	(6) Aggregate expenditures $(C + I_n)$, billions	(7) Unintended investment (+) or disinvestment (−) in inventories	(8) Tendency of employment, output, and incomes
(1) 40	$370	$375	$−5	$20	$395	$−25	Increase
(2) 45	390	390	0	20	410	−20	Increase
(3) 50	410	405	5	20	425	−15	Increase
(4) 55	430	420	10	20	440	−10	Increase
(5) 60	450	435	15	20	455	−5	Increase
(6) 65	470	450	20	20	470	0	Equilibrium
(7) 70	490	465	25	20	485	+5	Decrease
(8) 75	510	480	30	20	500	+10	Decrease
(9) 80	530	495	35	20	515	+15	Decrease
(10) 85	550	510	40	20	530	+20	Decrease

*If government is ignored and it is assumed that all saving occurs in the household sector of the economy, NNP as a measure of national output is equal to NI, PI, and DI. This means that households receive a DI equal to the value of total output.

Table 13-1. It shows the total amount which will be spent at each possible output-income level. In dealing with the closed private sector of the economy, the aggregate expenditures schedule shows the amount of consumption and planned net investment spending $(C + I_n)$ which will be forthcoming at each output-income level. We use net rather than gross investment because we are employing NNP rather than GNP as a measure of total output. Recall that NNP is GNP minus capital consumption allowances (depreciation). Also, it is worth emphasizing that we are concerned here with *planned* or intended investment as shown in column 5 of Table 13-1. Our analysis will reveal later that imbalances in aggregate expenditures and real national output will result in unplanned or unintended investment in the form of inventory changes (column 7).

Equilibrium NNP Now the question is this: Of the ten possible levels of NNP indicated in Table 13-1, which will be the equilibrium level? That is, which

level of total output will the economy be capable of sustaining? The answer is: *The equilibrium level of output is that output whose production will create total spending just sufficient to purchase that output.* In other words, the equilibrium level of NNP is where the total quantity of goods produced (NNP) is precisely equal to the total quantity of goods purchased $(C + I_n)$. Examination of the national output schedule of column 2 and the aggregate expenditures schedule of column 6 indicates that this equality exists only at the $470 billion level of NNP (row 6). This is the only level of output at which the economy is willing to spend precisely the amount necessary to take that output off the market. Here the annual rates of production and spending are in balance. There is no overproduction, which results in a piling up of unsold goods and therefore cutbacks in the rate of production, nor is there an excess of total spending, which draws down inventories and prompts increases in the rate of production. In short, there is no reason for businesses to vary from this rate of production; $470 billion is therefore the **equilibrium NNP.**

Disequilibrium To enhance our understanding of the meaning of the equilibrium level of NNP, let us examine other possible levels of NNP to see why they cannot be sustained. For example, at the $410 billion level of NNP (row 3), businesses would find that if they produced this output, the income created by this production would give rise to $405 billion in consumer spending. Supplemented by $20 billion of planned investment, the total expenditures $(C + I_n)$ would be $425 billion, as shown in column 6. The economy provides an annual rate of spending more than sufficient to purchase the current $410 billion rate of production. Because businesses are producing at a lower rate than buyers are taking goods off the shelves, an unintended decline in business inventories of $15 billion would occur (column 7) if this situation were sustained. But businesses will adjust to this imbalance between aggregate expenditures and national output by stepping up production. And a higher rate of output will mean more jobs and a higher level of total income. In short, if aggregate expenditures exceed the national output, the latter will be pulled upward. By making the same comparisons of NNP (column 2) and $C + I_n$ (column 6) at all other levels of NNP below the $470 billion equilibrium level, it will be found that the economy wants to spend in excess of the level at which businesses are willing to produce. The excess of total spending at all these levels of NNP will drive NNP upward to the $470 billion level.

The reverse holds true at all levels of NNP above the $470 billion equilibrium level. That is, businesses will find that the production of these total outputs fails to generate the levels of spending needed to take them off the market. Being unable to recover the costs involved in producing these outputs, businesses will cut back on their production. To illustrate: At the $510 billion level of output (row 8), business managers will be disappointed to find that there is insufficient spending to permit the sale of that output. Of the $510 billion worth of income which this output creates, $480 billion is received back by businesses as consumption spending. Though supplemented by $20 billion worth of planned investment spending, total expenditures ($500 billion) fall $10 billion short of the $510 billion quantity produced. If this imbalance persisted, $10 billion of inventories would pile up (column 7). But businesses will react to this un-

intended accumulation of unsold goods by cutting back on the rate of production. This decline in NNP will mean fewer jobs and a decline in total income. The reader should verify that deficiencies of total spending exist at all other levels of NNP in excess of the $470 billion level.

The equilibrium level of NNP exists where the total output, measured by NNP, and aggregate expenditures, $C + I_n$, are equal. Any excess of total spending over total output will drive the latter upward. Any deficiency of total spending will pull NNP downward.

GRAPHIC ANALYSIS

The same analysis can be readily envisioned through a simple graph. In Figure 13-1 the **45-degree line** (which was used in Chapter 12 to delineate graphically how disposable income is divided between consumption and saving) now takes on increased significance. Recall that the special property of the 45-degree line is that at any point on the line, the value of what is being measured on the horizontal axis (in this case NNP) is equal to the value of what is being measured on the vertical axis (here it is aggregate expenditures or $C + I_n$). Having discovered in our tabular analysis that the equilibrium level of national output is determined where $C + I_n$ equals NNP, we can say that the 45-degree line in Figure 13-1 is simply a graphical statement of this equilibrium condition.

Next, we must add the aggregate expenditures schedule to Figure 13-1. To do this we graph the consumption schedule of Figure 12-4a and add to it *vertically* the constant $20 billion amount from Figure 12-7, which, we assume, businesses plan to invest at each possible level of NNP. More directly, we can plot the $C + I_n$ data of column 6 in Table 13-1. Observe that the aggregate expenditures line shows total spending rising with national output and income, but that expenditures do not rise as much as income. This is so because the marginal propensity to consume is fractional. Stated differently, a part of any increase in national output and income will be saved. For our data aggregate expenditures increase by $15 billion for every $20 billion increase in national output and income because $5 billion of each $20 billion income increment is saved.

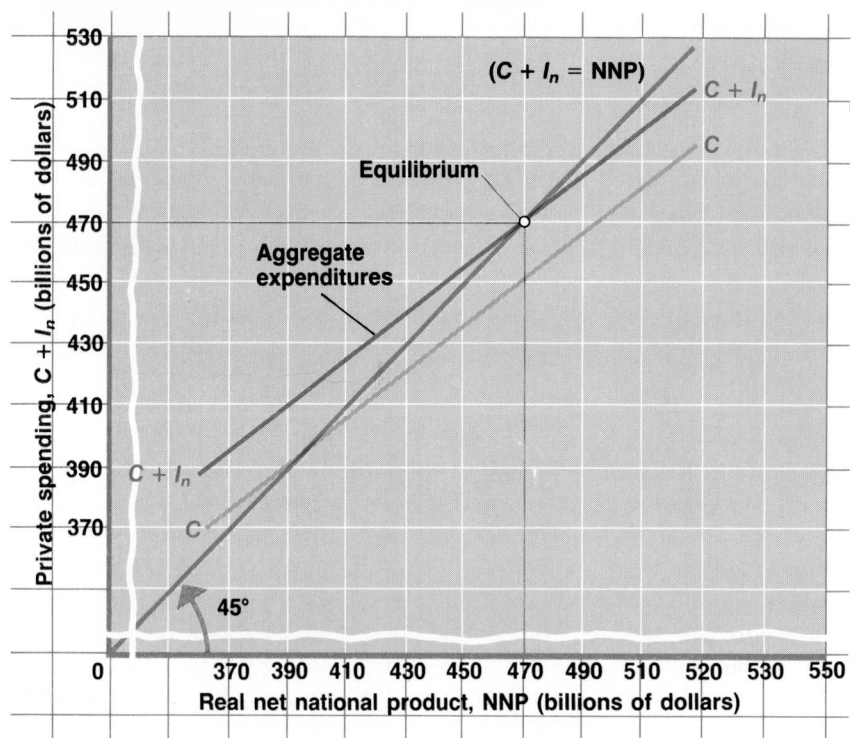

FIGURE 13-1

The aggregate expenditures–national output approach to the equilibrium NNP

The aggregate expenditures schedule, $C + I_n$, is determined by adding a fixed amount of investment to the upsloping consumption schedule. The equilibrium level of NNP is determined where the aggregate expenditures schedule intersects the 45-degree line, in this case at $470 billion.

The question: What is the equilibrium level of NNP? The answer: *Equilibrium is at that NNP which corresponds to the intersection of the aggregate expenditures schedule and the 45-degree line.* Given the nature of the 45-degree line, this intersection locates the only point at which aggregate expenditures (on the vertical axis) are equal to NNP (on the horizontal axis) and this equality *is* the equilibrium condition. Because our aggregate expenditures schedule is based upon the data of Table 13-1, we once again find the equilibrium output to be at the $470 billion level.

It is evident from Figure 13-1 that no levels of NNP above the equilibrium level are sustainable, because $C + I_n$ falls short of NNP; graphically, the aggregate expenditures schedule lies *below* the 45-degree line. For example, at the $510 billion NNP level, $C + I_n$ is only $500 billion. Inventories of unsold goods rise to undesired levels. This unhappy state of affairs will prompt businesses to readjust their production sights downward in the direction of the $470 billion output level.

Conversely, at all possible levels of NNP less than the $470 billion level, the economy desires to spend in excess of what businesses are producing. $C + I_n$ exceeds the value of the corresponding output. Graphically, the aggregate expenditures schedule lies *above* the 45-degree line. At the $410 billion NNP, for example, $C + I_n$ totals $425 billion. Inventories decline as the rate of spending exceeds the rate of production, prompting businesses to raise their production sights in the direction of the $470 billion NNP. Unless there is some change in the consumption-saving plans of households or the investment plans of businesses, the $470 billion level of NNP will be sustained indefinitely.

Leakages-injections approach

The expenditures-output approach to the determination of NNP has the advantage of spotlighting total spending as the immediate determinant of the levels of output, employment, and income. Though the leakages-injections approach is less direct, it does have the advantage of giving emphasis to the reason $C + I_n$ and NNP are unequal at all levels of output except the equilibrium level.

The essence of the leakages-injections approach is this: Under our simplifying assumptions we know that the production of any level of national output will generate an identical amount of disposable income. But we also know a part of that income may be saved—that is, *not* consumed—by households. Saving therefore represents a *leakage*, withdrawal, or diversion of potential spending from the income-expenditures stream. The consequence of saving is that consumption falls short of total output or NNP; hence, by itself consumption is insufficient to take the national output off the market, and this fact would seem to set the stage for a decline in total output. However, the business sector does not intend to sell its entire output to consumers; some of the national output will take the form of capital or investment goods which will be sold within the business sector. Investment can therefore be thought of as an *injection* of spending into the income-expenditures stream which supplements consumption; stated differently, investment is a potential offset to, or replacement for, the leakage of saving.

If the leakage of saving exceeds the injection of investment, then $C + I_n$ will fall short of NNP and this level of NNP will be too high to be sustainable. In other words, any NNP where saving exceeds investment will be an above-equilibrium NNP. Conversely, if the injection of investment exceeds the leakage of saving, then $C + I_n$ will be greater than NNP and NNP will be driven upward. To repeat: Any NNP where investment exceeds saving will be a below-equilibrium NNP. Only where $S = I_n$—where the leakage of saving is exactly offset by the injection of investment—will aggregate expenditures equal the national output. And we know that this equality defines the equilibrium NNP.

It is important to keep in mind that in the closed private economy assumed here, there are only one leakage (saving) and one injection (investment) to worry about. In general terms, a *leakage* is any use of income other than its expenditure on domestically produced output. Hence, in the more realistic models which follow (the section on inter-

national trade in this chapter and Chapter 14), we shall find that the additional leakages of imports and taxes will have to be incorporated into our analysis. Similarly, an *injection* is any supplement to consumer spending on domestic production. So, again, in later models we must add injections of exports and government purchases to our discussion. But for the present, in putting the leakages-injections approach to work, we need only compare the single leakage of saving with the sole injection of investment to assess the impact upon NNP.

TABULAR ANALYSIS

The saving schedule (columns 2 and 4) and the investment schedule (columns 2 and 5) of Table 13-1 are pertinent. Our $C + I_n = $ NNP approach has just led us to conclude that all levels of NNP that are less than $470 billion are unstable because the corresponding $C + I_n$ exceeds these NNPs, driving NNP upward. A comparison of the amounts households and businesses want to save and invest at each of the below-equilibrium NNP levels explains the excesses of total spending. In particular, at each of these relatively low NNP levels, businesses plan to invest more than households want to save. For example, at the $410 billion level of NNP (row 3), households will save only $5 billion, thereby spending $405 of their $410 billion incomes. Supplemented by $20 billion of business investment, aggregate expenditures $(C + I_n)$ are $425 billion. Aggregate expenditures exceed NNP by $15 billion (= $425 − $410) *because* the amount businesses plan to invest at this level of NNP exceeds the amounts households save by $15 billion. It is the fact that a very small leakage of saving at this relatively low income level will be more than compensated for by the relatively large injection of investment spending which causes $C + I_n$ to exceed NNP and induce NNP upward.

Similarly, all levels of NNP above the $470 billion level are also unstable, because here NNP exceeds $C + I_n$. The reason for this insufficiency of aggregate expenditures lies in the fact that at all NNP levels above $470 billion, households will want to save in excess of the amount businesses plan to invest. That is, the saving leakage is not replaced or compensated for by the injection of investment. For example, households will choose to save at the high rate of $30 billion at the $510 billion NNP (row 8). Businesses, however, will plan to invest only $20 billion at this NNP. This $10 billion excess of saving over planned investment will cause total spending to fall $10 billion short of the value of total output. And this deficiency will cause NNP to decline.

Again we verify that the equilibrium NNP is at the $470 billion level. It is only at this point that the saving desires of households and the investment plans of businesses are equal. And only when businesses and households attempt to invest and save at equal rates—where the leakages and injections are equal—will $C + I_n$ = NNP. Only here will the annual rates of production and spending be in balance; only here will unplanned changes in inventories be absent. One can think of it in this way: If saving were zero, consumer spending would always be sufficient to clear the market of any given NNP; that is, consumption would equal NNP. But saving can and does occur, causing consumption to fall short of NNP. Hence, only when businesses are willing to invest at the same rate at which households save will the amount by which consumption falls short of NNP be precisely compensated for.

GRAPHIC ANALYSIS

The leakages-injections approach to determining the equilibrium NNP can be readily demonstrated graphically. In Figure 13-2 we have merely combined the saving schedule of Figure 12-4b and the simplified investment schedule of Figure 12-7. The numerical data for these schedules are repeated in columns 2, 4, and 5 of Table 13-1. It is evident that the equilibrium level of NNP is at $470 billion, where the saving and investment schedules intersect. Only here do businesses and households invest and save at the same rates; therefore, only here will NNP and $C + I_n$ be equal. At all higher levels of NNP, households will save at a rate higher than businesses plan to invest. The fact that the saving leakage exceeds the investment injection causes $C + I_n$ to fall short of NNP, driving NNP downward. At the $510 billion NNP, for example, saving of $30 billion will exceed investment of $20 billion by $10 billion, with the result that $C + I_n$ is $500 billion—$10 billion short of NNP. At all levels of NNP below the $470 billion equilibrium level, businesses will plan to invest at a rate in excess of the amount households save. Here the injection of investment exceeds the leakage of saving so that

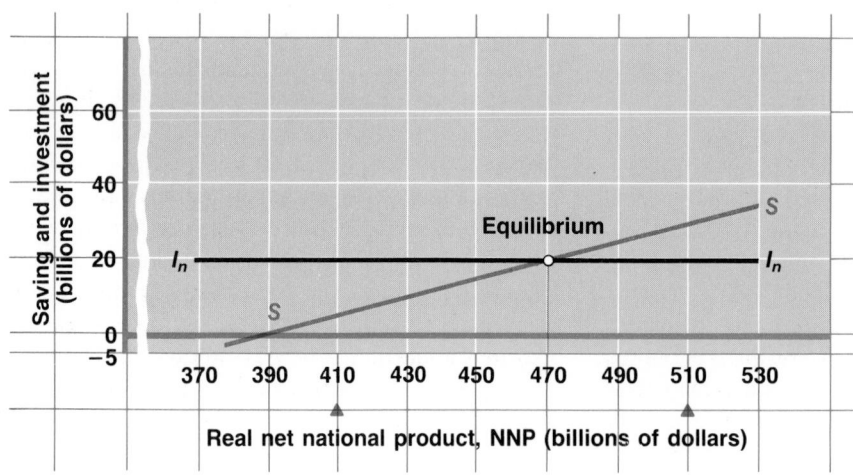

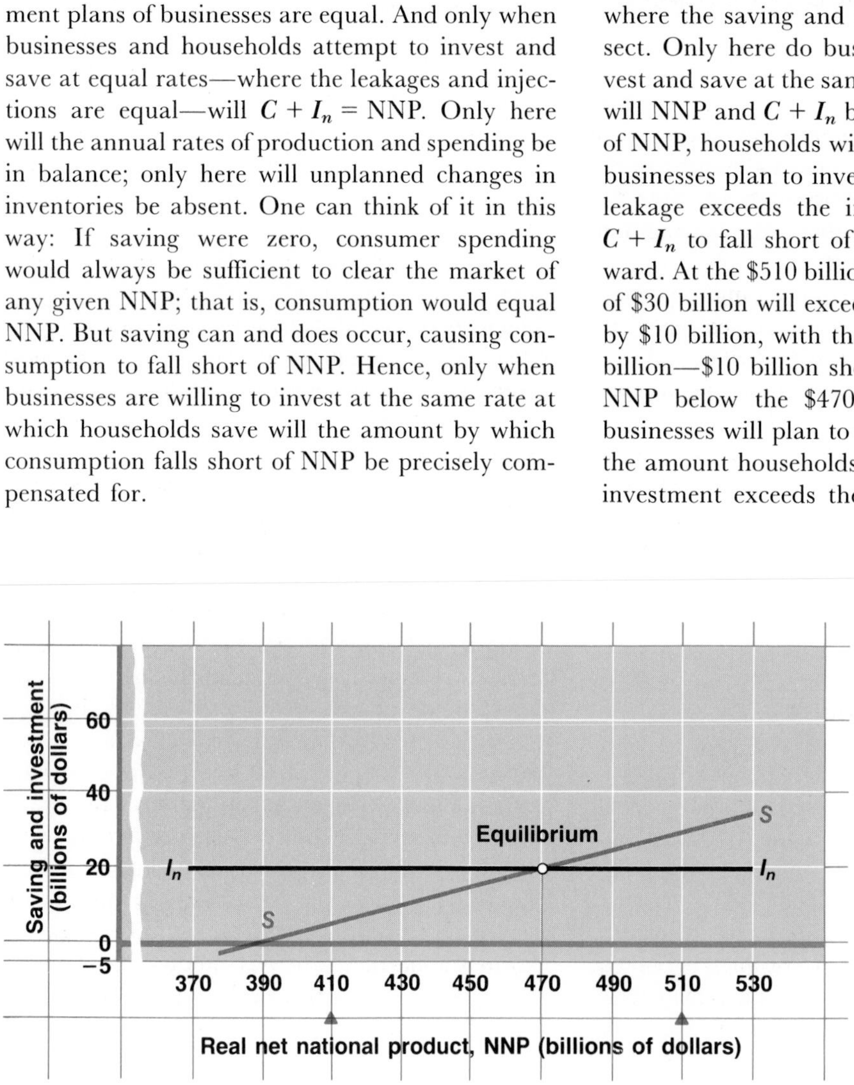

FIGURE 13-2

The leakages-injections approach to the equilibrium NNP

A second approach is to view the equilibrium NNP as determined by the intersection of the saving (S) and the planned investment (I_n) schedules. Only at the point of equilibrium will households plan to save the amount businesses want to invest. It is the consistency of these plans which causes NNP and $C + I_n$ to be equal.

$C + I_n$ exceeds NNP, driving the latter upward. To illustrate: At the $410 billion level of NNP the $5 billion leakage of saving is more than compensated for by the $20 billion that businesses plan to invest. The result is that $C + I_n$ exceeds NNP by $15 billion, inducing businesses to produce a larger NNP.

Planned versus actual investment

We have emphasized that because savers and investors are essentially different groups and are differently motivated, discrepancies in saving and investment can occur and these differences bring about changes in the equilibrium NNP. Now we must recognize that, in another sense, saving and investment must always be equal to one another! This apparent contradiction concerning the equality of saving and investment is resolved when we distinguish between **planned investment** and saving (which need not be equal) and **actual investment** and saving (which by definition must be equal). The catch essentially is that *actual investment consists of both planned and unplanned investment (unplanned changes in inventory investment), and unplanned investment functions as a balancing item which always equates the actual amounts saved and invested in any period of time.*

DISEQUILIBRIUM AND INVENTORIES

Consider, for example, the $490 billion above-equilibrium NNP (row 7 of Table 13-1). What would happen if businesses produced this output, thinking they could sell it? At this level, households save $25 billion of their $490 billion DI, so consumption is only $465 billion. *Planned* investment (column 5) is $20 billion; that is, businesses plan or desire to buy $20 billion worth of capital goods. This means aggregate expenditures $(C + I_n)$ are $485 billion, and sales therefore fall short of production by $5 billion. This extra $5 billion of goods is simply retained by businesses as an *unintended* or *unplanned* increase in inventories (column 7). It is unintended because it results from the failure of total spending to take total output off the market. Remembering that, by definition, changes in in-

ventories are a part of investment, we note the **actual** investment of $25 billion ($20 planned *plus* $5 unintended or unplanned) equals saving of $25 billion, even though saving exceeds *planned* investment by $5 billion. Businesses, not being anxious to accumulate unwanted inventories at this annual rate, will react by cutting back on production.

Now look at the below-equilibrium $450 billion output (row 5 of Table 13-1). Because households save only $15 billion of their $450 billion DI, consumption is $435 billion. Planned investment by businesses is $20 billion, so aggregate expenditures are $455 billion. That is, sales exceed production by $5 billion. How can this be? The answer is that an unplanned decline in business inventories has occurred. More specifically, businesses have unintentionally *dis*invested $5 billion in inventories (column 7). Note once again that *actual* investment is $15 billion ($20 planned *minus* $5 unintended or unplanned) and equal to saving of $15 billion, even though *planned* investment exceeds saving by $5 billion. This unplanned decline in investment in inventories due to the excess of sales over production will induce businesses to increase the NNP by expanding production.

To summarize: At all *above-equilibrium* levels of NNP (where saving exceeds planned investment), actual investment and saving are equal because of unintended increases in inventories which, by definition, are included as a part of actual investment. Graphically (Figure 13-2), the unintended inventory increase is measured by the vertical distance by which the saving schedule lies above the (planned) investment schedule. At all *below-equilibrium* levels of NNP (where planned investment exceeds saving), actual investment will be equal to saving because of unintended decreases in inventories which must be subtracted from planned investment to determine actual investment. These unintended inventory declines are shown graphically as the vertical distance by which the (planned) investment schedule lies above the saving schedule.

ACHIEVING EQUILIBRIUM

These distinctions are important because they correctly suggest that *it is the equality of planned investment and saving which determines the equilib-*

rium level of NNP. We can think of the process by which equilibrium is achieved as follows:

1 A difference between saving and planned investment causes a difference between the production and spending plans of the economy as a whole.

2 This difference between aggregate production and spending plans results in unintended investment or disinvestment in inventories.

3 As long as unintended investment in inventories persists, businesses will revise their production plans downward and thereby reduce the NNP. Conversely, as long as unintended disinvestment in inventories exists, firms will revise their production plans upward and increase the NNP. Both types of movements in NNP are toward equilibrium in that they tend to bring about the equality of planned investment and saving.

4 Only where planned investment and saving are equal will the level of NNP be stable or in equilibrium; that is, only where planned investment equals saving will there be no unintended investment or disinvestment in inventories to drive the NNP downward or upward. Note in column 7 of Table 13-1 that only at the $470 billion equilibrium NNP is there no unintended investment or disinvestment in inventories.

Changes in equilibrium NNP and the multiplier

Thus far, we have been concerned with explaining the equilibrium levels of total output and income. But we saw in Chapter 10 that actually the NNP of American capitalism is seldom stable; rather, it is characterized by long-run growth and punctuated by cyclical fluctuations. Let us turn to the questions of *why* and *how* the equilibrium level of real NNP fluctuates.

The equilibrium level of NNP will change in response to changes in the investment schedule or the saving-consumption schedules. Because investment spending generally is less stable than the consumption-saving schedules, we shall assume that changes in the investment schedule occur. The impact of changes in investment can be readily

envisioned through Figure 13-3a and b. Suppose the expected rate of net profit on investment rises (shifting the investment-demand curve of Figure 12-6 to the right) *or* the interest rate falls (moving down the stable curve). As a result, investment spending increases by, say, $5 billion. This is indicated in Figure 13-3a by an upward shift in the aggregate expenditures schedule from $(C + I_n)_0$ to $(C + I_n)_1$, and in Figure 13-3b by an upward shift in the investment schedule from I_{n0} to I_{n1}. In each of these portrayals the consequence is a rise in the equilibrium NNP from $470 to $490 billion.

Conversely, if the expected rate of net profit from investment decreases *or* the interest rate rises, a decline in investment spending of, say, $5 billion will occur. This is shown by the downward shift of the investment schedule from I_{n0} to I_{n2} in Figure 13-3b and the aggregate expenditures schedule from $(C + I_n)_0$ to $(C + I_n)_2$ in Figure 13-3a. In each case, these shifts cause the equilibrium NNP to fall from the original $470 billion level to $450 billion. The reader should verify these conclusions in terms of Table 13-1 by substituting $25 billion and then $15 billion for the $20 billion planned investment figure in column 5 of the table.

Incidentally—and at the risk of getting ahead of ourselves—the indicated $5 billion changes in investment may be the direct result of economic policy. Looking back at Table 12-2, we find that the initial $20 billion level of investment is associated with an 8 percent interest rate. *If* the economy is in a recession, the monetary authorities may purposely negotiate a reduction in the interest rate to 6 percent (by increasing the money supply), causing a $5 billion increase in investment and thereby in aggregate expenditures to stimulate the economy. Conversely, *if,* with the initial $20 billion of investment, the economy faces a demand-pull inflation problem, the monetary authorities may increase the interest rate to 10 percent (by reducing the money supply), thereby reducing investment and aggregate expenditures to constrain the inflation. Monetary policy—changing the money supply for the purpose of altering interest rates and aggregate expenditures—is the subject of Chapter 17.

When changes in the consumption-saving schedules occur, they will have similar effects. If households want to consume more (save less) at each

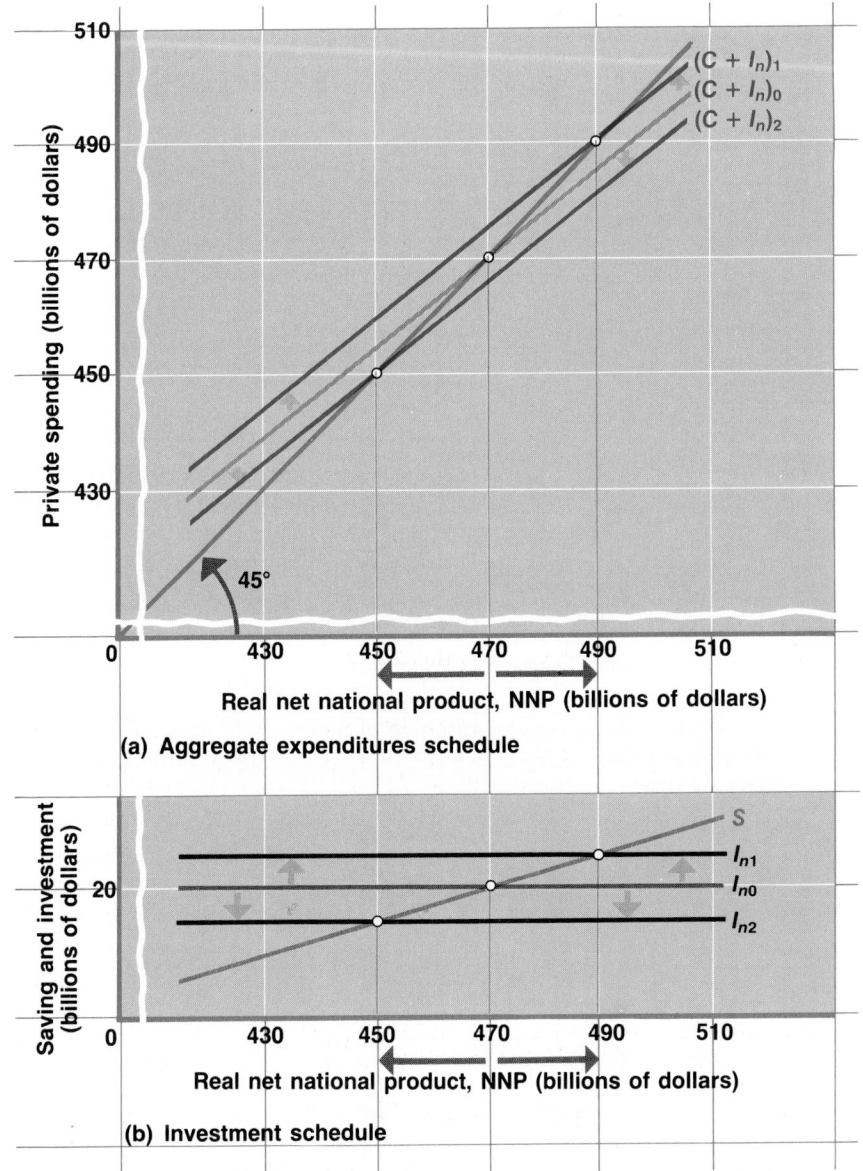

FIGURE 13-3

Changes in the equilibrium NNP caused by shifts in (a) the aggregate expenditures schedule and (b) the investment schedule

An upshift in the aggregate expenditures schedule from, say, $(C + I_n)_0$ to $(C + I_n)_1$ will increase the equilibrium NNP. Conversely, a downshift in the aggregate expenditures schedule from, say, $(C + I_n)_0$ to $(C + I_n)_2$ will lower the equilibrium NNP. In the saving-investment figure an upshift in the investment schedule (I_{n0} to I_{n1}) will raise, and a downshift (I_{n0} to I_{n2}) will lower, the equilibrium NNP.

level of NNP, the aggregate expenditures schedule will shift upward and the saving schedule downward in Figure 13-3a and b, respectively. In either portrayal these shifts will mean an increase in the equilibrium NNP. If households want to consume less (save more) at each possible NNP, the resulting drop in the consumption schedule and the increase in the saving schedule will in turn reduce the equilibrium NNP.

THE MULTIPLIER EFFECT

You have undoubtedly detected a curious feature of these examples: A $5 billion change in investment spending has given rise to a $20 billion change in the output-income level. This surprising result is called the **multiplier effect** or, more simply, the *multiplier*. Specifically, the multiplier is the ratio of a change in equilibrium NNP to the initial change in (investment) spending which caused that change in real NNP. That is:

$$\text{Multiplier} = \frac{\text{change in real NNP}}{\text{initial change in spending}}$$

In this case the multiplier is 4 (change of NNP of 20/change in investment of 5). Or, by rearranging our equation, we can say that:

$$\text{Change in NNP} = \text{multiplier} \times \frac{\text{initial change in spending}}{}$$

Three points about the multiplier must be made at the outset.

1 The "initial change in spending" is usually associated with investment spending for the simple reason that investment seems to be the most volatile component of aggregate expenditures (Figure 12-8). But it is to be emphasized that changes in consumption, government purchases, or exports also will be subject to the multiplier effect.

2 The "initial change in spending" refers to an upshift or downshift in the aggregate expenditures schedule due to an upshift or downshift in one of its components. In Figure 13-3b we find that real NNP has increased by $20 billion because the investment schedule has shifted upward by $5 billion from I_{n0} to I_{n1}. Similarly, an upshift or downshift in the consumption schedule due to a change in one of the nonincome determinants of consumption—wealth, the price level, expectations, consumer in-

debtedness, and so forth—can trigger a multiple change in real NNP.

3 Implicit in our second point is the fact that the multiplier is a two-edged sword that works in both directions. That is, a small increase in spending can give rise to a multiple increase in NNP, or a small decrease in spending can be magnified into a much larger decrease in NNP by the multiplier. Note carefully the effects of the shift in $(C + I_n)_0$ to $(C + I_n)_1$ or to $(C + I_n)_2$ and I_{n0} to I_{n1} or to I_{n2} in Figure 13-3a and b.

Rationale The multiplier is based upon two facts. On the one hand, the economy is characterized by repetitive, continuous flows of expenditures and income wherein the dollars spent by Smith are received as income by Jones. On the other hand, any change in income will cause both consumption and saving to vary in the same direction as, and by a fraction of, the change in income. It follows from these two facts that an initial change in the rate of spending will cause a spending chain reaction which, although of diminishing importance at each successive step, will cumulate to a multiple change in NNP.

The rationale underlying the multiplier effect is illustrated numerically in Table 13-2 for a $5 billion increase in investment spending. Graphically, this is the upshift of the investment schedule from $20 to $25 billion shown in Figure 13-3b. We con-

TABLE 13-2 **The multiplier: a tabular illustration** *(hypothetical data; in billions)*

	(1) Change in income	(2) Change in consumption (MPC = $\frac{3}{4}$)	(3) Change in saving (MPS = $\frac{1}{4}$)
Assumed increase in investment	$ 5.00	$ 3.75	$1.25
Second round	3.75	2.81	0.94
Third round	2.81	2.11	0.70
Fourth round	2.11	1.58	0.53
Fifth round	1.58	1.19	0.39
All other rounds	4.75	3.56	1.19
Totals	$20.00	$15.00	$5.00

tinue to assume that the MPC is three-fourths; the MPS is therefore one-fourth. Also assume that the economy is initially in equilibrium at $470 billion.

The initial increase in investment generates an equal amount of wage, rent, interest, and profit income for the simple reason that spending and receiving income are two sides of the same transaction. How much consumption will be induced by this $5 billion increase in the incomes of households? We find the answer by applying the marginal propensity to consume of three-fourths to this change in income. Thus, the $5 billion income increase causes consumption to rise by $3.75 (= $\frac{3}{4}$ of $5) billion and saving by $1.25 (= $\frac{1}{4}$ of $5) billion. The $3.75 billion which is spent is received by other households as income. They in turn consume three-fourths of this $3.75 billion or $2.81 billion, and save one-fourth, or $0.94 billion. The $2.81 billion which is consumed flows to still other households as income. Though the spending and respending effects of the initial increase in investment diminish with each successive round of spending, the cumulative increase in the output-income level will be $20 billion if the process is carried through to the last dollar. The assumed $5 billion increase in investment will therefore increase the equilibrium NNP by $20 billion, from $470 to $490 billion. Hence, the multiplier is 4 (= $20 billion ÷ $5 billion).

It is no coincidence that the multiplier effect ends at the point where exactly enough saving has been generated to offset the initial $5 billion increase in investment spending. It is only then that the disequilibrium created by the investment increase will be corrected. In this case, NNP and total incomes must rise by $20 billion to create $5 billion in additional saving to match the $5 billion increase in investment spending. Income must increase by 4 times the initial excess of investment over saving, because households save one-fourth of any increase in their incomes (that is, the MPS is one-fourth). As noted, in this example the multiplier—the number of times the ultimate increase in income exceeds the initial increase in investment spending—is 4.

The multiplier and the marginal propensities You may have sensed from Table 13-2 that a relationship of some sort must exist between the MPS and

the size of the multiplier. There is such a relationship: The fraction of an increase in income which is saved—that is, the MPS—determines the cumulative respending effects of any initial change in I_n, G, X_n or C, and therefore the multiplier. More specifically, *the size of the MPS and the size of the multiplier are inversely related.* The smaller the fraction of any change in income which is saved, the greater the respending at each round and, therefore, the greater the multiplier. If the MPS is one-fourth, as in our example, the multiplier is 4. If the MPS were one-third, the multiplier would be 3. If the MPS were one-fifth, the multiplier would be 5. Look again at Table 13-1 and Figure 13-3b. Initially the economy is in equilibrium at the $470 billion level of NNP. Now businesses increase investment by $5 billion so that planned investment of $25 billion exceeds saving of $20 billion at the $470 billion level. This means $470 billion is no longer the equilibrium NNP. The question is: By how much must net national product or income rise to restore equilibrium? The answer is: By enough to generate $5 billion of additional saving to offset the $5 billion increase in investment. Because households save $1 out of every $4 of additional income they receive (MPS = $\frac{1}{4}$), NNP must rise by $20 billion—4 times the assumed increase in investment—to create the $5 billion of extra saving necessary to restore equilibrium. Hence, a multiplier of 4. If the MPS were one-third, NNP would only have to rise by $15 billion (3 times the increase in investment) to generate $5 billion of additional saving and restore equilibrium, and the multiplier therefore would be 3. But if the MPS were one-fifth, NNP would have to rise by $25 billion in order for an extra $5 billion of saving to be forthcoming and equilibrium to be restored, yielding a multiplier of 5.

We can summarize these and all other possibilities by merely saying that *the multiplier is equal to the reciprocal of the MPS.* The reciprocal of any number is the quotient you obtain by dividing 1 by that number. In short, we can say:

$$\text{The multiplier} = \frac{1}{\text{MPS}}$$

This formula provides us with a shorthand method of determining the multiplier. All we need to know is the MPS to calculate the size of the multiplier quickly. Recall, too, from Chapter 12 that since

MPC + MPS = 1, it follows that MPS = 1 − MPC. Therefore, we can also write our multiplier formula as[1]

$$\text{The multiplier} = \frac{1}{1 - \text{MPC}}$$

While we have developed our two multiplier formulas intuitively, the underlying arithmetic is easily understood.[2]

[1] Furthermore, recall that the MPS measures the slope of the saving schedule. In terms of the leakages-injections $(S = I_n)$ approach, this means that if the MPS is relatively large (say, one-half) and the slope of the saving schedule is therefore relatively steep (one-half), any given upward shift in investment spending will be subject to a relatively small multiplier. For example, a $5 billion increase in investment will entail a new point of intersection of the S and I_n schedules only $10 billion to the right of the original equilibrium NNP. The multiplier is only 2. But if the MPS is relatively small (say, one-sixth), the slope of the saving schedule will be relatively gentle. Therefore, a $5 billion upward shift in the investment schedule will provide a new intersection point some $30 billion to the right of the original equilibrium NNP. The multiplier is 6 in this case. The reader should verify these two examples by drawing appropriate saving and investment diagrams.

[2] The algebra underlying the multiplier is that of an "infinite geometric progression" or, simply stated, an infinite series of numbers, each of which is a fixed *fraction* of the previous number. If we designate the fixed fraction as b, the geometric progression is:

$$k = 1 + b + b^2 + b^3 + \cdots + b^n \tag{1}$$

where k is the sum of the progression.

This equation can be readily manipulated to prove that $k = \dfrac{1}{1 - b}$. Multiplying both sides of equation (1) by b we get:

$$bk = b + b^2 + b^3 + b^4 + \cdots + b^{n+1} \tag{2}$$

Now by subtracting equation (2) from equation (1) we find that all the terms on the right side of equation (1) drop out except the first (the "1") *and* that only the last term on the right side of equation (2) remains. Thus we have:

$$k - bk = 1 - b^{n+1}$$

Factor k on the left side:

$$k(1 - b) = 1 - b^{n+1}$$

Significance of the multiplier The significance of the multiplier is this: A relatively small change in the investment plans of businesses or the consumption-saving plans of households can trigger a much larger change in the equilibrium level of NNP. The multiplier magnifies the fluctuations in business activity initiated by changes in spending.

Note that the larger the MPC (the smaller the MPS), the greater will be the multiplier. For example, if the MPC is $\frac{3}{4}$ and the multiplier is therefore 4, a $10 billion decline in planned investment will reduce the equilibrium NNP by $40 billion. But if the MPC is only $\frac{2}{3}$ and the multiplier is thereby 3, the same $10 billion drop in investment will cause the equilibrium NNP to fall by only $30 billion. This makes sense intuitively: A large MPC means the chain of induced consumption shown in column 2 of Table 13-2 dampens down slowly and thereby cumulates to a large change in income. Conversely, a small MPC (a large MPS) causes induced consumption to decline quickly so the cumulative change in income is small.

Incidentally, we will find, in discussing the so-called built-in stabilizers in Chapter 14, that one of the major goals of public policy is to structure a system of taxes and transfer payments which will reduce the MPC and diminish the size of the multiplier, thereby lessening the destabilizing effect of a given change in investment, consumption, government expenditures, or exports.

Generalizing the multiplier The multiplier concept as presented here is sometimes called the *simple multiplier* for the obvious reason that it is based

Now divide by $(1 - b)$:

$$k = \frac{1 - b^{n+1}}{(1 - b)}$$

Since b is a fraction and n is very large, the value of b^{n+1} approaches zero and can be dropped, resulting in:

$$k = \frac{1}{1 - b}$$

In terms of economic content, k indicates the size of the multiplier and b is the MPC. The reader should experiment with equation (1), using MPCs of, say, .5, .6, and .8, to show that a $1 increase in spending will generate $2, $2.50, and $5 of income, respectively.

upon a very simple model of the economy. In terms of the $\dfrac{1}{\text{MPS}}$ formulation, the simple multiplier reflects only the leakage of saving. But, as noted earlier, in the real world successive rounds of income and spending can also be dampened down by other leakages in the form of imports and taxes. That is, in addition to the leakage into saving, some portion of income at each round would be siphoned off as additional taxes, and another part would be used to purchase additional goods from abroad. The result of these additional leakages is that the $\dfrac{1}{\text{MPS}}$ statement of the multiplier can be generalized by changing the denominator to read "fraction of the change in income which is not spent on domestic output" or "fraction of the change in income which leaks, or is diverted, from the income-expenditure stream." The more realistic multiplier which results when all these leakages—saving, taxes, and imports—are taken into account is called the *complex multiplier*. The Council of Economic Advisers, which advises the President on economic matters, has estimated the complex multiplier for the United States to be about 2.

PARADOX OF THRIFT

A curious irony—dubbed the **paradox of thrift**—is suggested by the leakages-injections approach to NNP determination and by our analysis of the multiplier. The paradox is that if society attempts to save more, it may end up actually saving the same amount, or even less. Figure 13-4 is relevant. Sup-

pose I_n and S_1 are the current investment and saving schedules which determine a $470 billion equilibrium NNP. Now assume that households, perhaps anticipating a recession, attempt to save, say, $5 billion more at each income level in order to provide a nest egg against the expected bad times. This attempt to save more is reflected in an upward shift of the saving schedule from S_1 to S_2. But this very upshift creates an excess of saving over planned investment at the current $470 billion equilibrium output. And we know that the multiplier effect will cause this small increase in saving (decline in consumption) to be reflected in a much larger—$20 billion ($5 × 4) in this case—*decline* in equilibrium NNP.

There is a paradox here in several different senses.

1 Note that at the new $450 billion equilibrium NNP, households are saving the same amount they did at the original $470 billion NNP. Society's attempt to save more has been frustrated by the multiple decline in the equilibrium NNP which that attempt itself caused.

2 This analysis suggests that thrift, which has always been held in high esteem in our economy, can be a social vice. From the individual point of view, a penny saved may be a penny earned. But from the social point of view, a penny saved is a penny not spent and therefore causes a decline in someone's income. The act of thrift may be virtuous from the individual's viewpoint but disastrous from the social standpoint because of its potential undesirable effects upon total output and employment.

3 It is ironic, if not paradoxical, that households

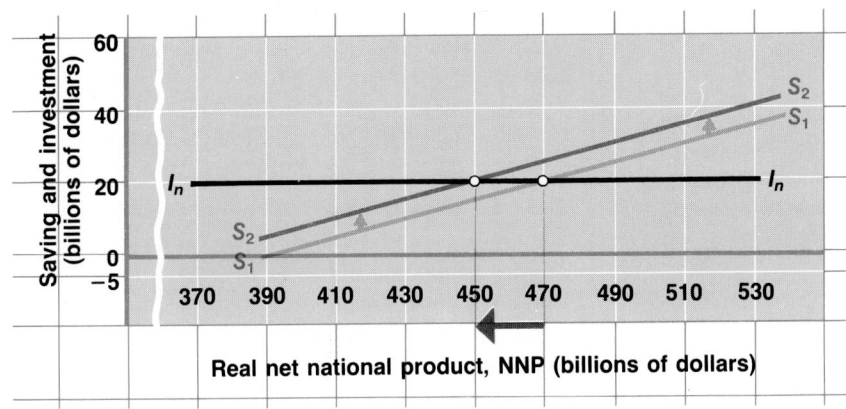

FIGURE 13-4

The paradox of thrift

Unless offset by an upshift in the planned investment schedule, any attempt by households to save more (S_1 to S_2) will be frustrated by a multiple decline in the equilibrium NNP.

may be most strongly induced to save more (consume less) at the very time when increased saving is most inappropriate and economically undesirable, that is, when the economy seems to be backsliding into a recession. An individual fearing the loss of his or her job will hardly be inclined to go on a spending spree. In our scenario more saving has made an anticipated recession a reality.[3]

But the paradox of thrift and its implication that saving is socially undesirable must be altered in two very important respects. First, let us assume that the economy is initially experiencing rather pronounced demand-pull inflation. That is, the economy is operating, not in the horizontal Keynesian range, but in the vertical classical range of the aggregate supply curve. Here the economy is producing at full employment and an excess of aggregate demand is pulling up the price level. If households were to save more (consume less) in this situation, aggregate demand would shift left-

ward and the rate of inflation would be reduced. Look back at Figure 11-6b once again. Assume that the aggregate demand curve is initially at AD_6 with the price level at P_6. An increase in saving will reduce aggregate demand to, say, AD_5 and the price level would tend to decline toward P_5. In this case more saving is socially desirable because it tends to restrain inflation.

The second point is closely related. Recall from our discussion of Figure 2-4 that, other things being equal, an economy which saves *and invests* a larger proportion of its national output will achieve a higher rate of economic growth. A higher rate of saving frees resources from consumption uses so that they *may* be allocated to the production of more investment goods. This additional machinery and equipment enhances the nation's future productive capacity. Thus, if we make the classical assumption that the money market effectively links saving and investment decisions (recall Figure 12-1), then the upshift in the saving schedule from S_1 to S_2 in Figure 13-4 would be matched by an equal upshift in the investment schedule so that the equilibrium level of NNP would remain at $470 billion. In this case real output and employment would be unchanged but the composition of output would be comprised of more investment goods and fewer consumer goods. The result would be a more rapid rate of future economic growth. If rapid growth is a desired social goal, additional saving in this scenario would clearly be virtuous when matched by an equal increase in investment.

Equilibrium versus full-employment NNP

We now turn from the task of explaining to that of evaluating the equilibrium NNP.

Too much emphasis cannot be placed upon the fact that the $470 billion equilibrium NNP embodied in our analysis (Table 13-1 and Figures 13-1 and 13-2) may or may not entail full employment. Remember: The basic theme of Keynesian economics in its extreme form is that capitalism contains no mechanisms capable of automatically creating that particular level of aggregate expenditures which will induce businesses to produce a full-employment noninflationary level of output.

[3] If an upsloping investment schedule (Table 12-3 and Figure 12-7) is substituted for the simplified investment schedule we have employed, the attempt of households to save more will not merely be frustrated but will actually cause a decline in the amount saved. Additionally, a positively sloped investment schedule will increase the size of the multiplier and in effect make it a "supermultiplier." The intrigued reader who wishes to pursue these points should (1) substitute the investment schedule of columns 1 and 3 in Table 12-3 in column 5 of Table 13-1; (2) assume a $5 billion increase in saving; (3) compute (estimate) the new equilibrium point at which planned investment equals saving; (4) compare the original and the new amounts saved; and (5) calculate the size of the multiplier. Note that the size of the multiplier is larger because, for each successive round of income, there will occur not only additional consumption as in our simple multiplier, but also additional investment. Not only does the multiplier process involve a marginal propensity to consume (MPC) of .75, but also a marginal propensity to invest (MPI) of .10, the latter defined as the ratio of a change in investment relative to the change in NNP which induced or resulted in that change in investment. Hence, we must add the MPI to the denominator of our $\dfrac{1}{1 - \text{MPC}}$ formulation of the simple multiplier, making it $\dfrac{1}{1 - (\text{MPC} + \text{MPI})}$. In this case the "supermultiplier" equals $\dfrac{1}{1 - (.75 + .10)} = \dfrac{1}{.15} = 6.67$.

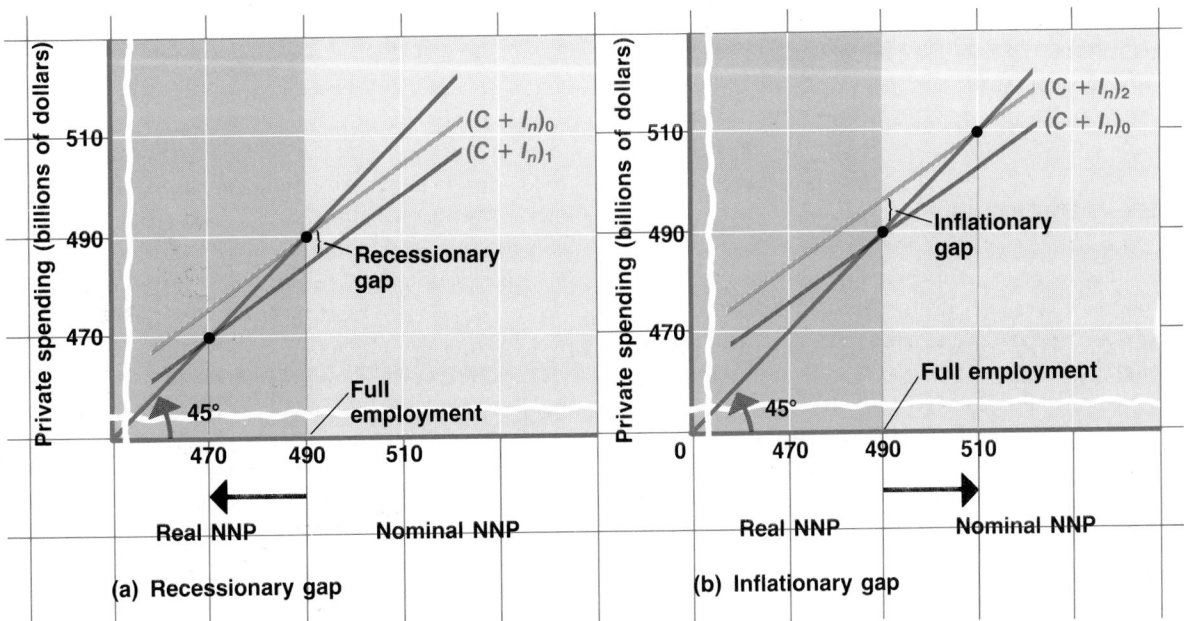

FIGURE 13-5

Recessionary and inflationary gaps

The equilibrium and full-employment NNPs may not coincide. A recessionary gap, shown in (a), is the amount by which aggregate expenditures fall short of the noninflationary full-employment NNP. It will cause a multiple decline in real NNP. The inflationary gap in (b) is the amount by which aggregate expenditures exceed the non-inflationary full-employment level of NNP. This gap will tend to cause a multiple increase in nominal NNP.

The aggregate expenditures schedule might well lie above or below that which would intersect the 45-degree line at the full-employment noninflationary level of output. Indeed, we have assumed thus far that production occurs in the less-than-full-employment Keynesian range of the aggregate supply curve.

RECESSIONARY GAP

Assume in Figure 13-5a that the full-employment noninflationary level of national output is $490 billion. Suppose, too, that the aggregate expenditures schedule is at $(C + I_n)_1$, which, incidentally, happens to be the aggregate expenditures schedule developed and employed in this chapter. This schedule intersects the 45-degree line to the left of the full-employment output, causing the economy's aggregate production to fall $20 billion short of its capacity production. In terms of Table 13-1, the economy is failing to employ 5 million of its 70 mil-

lion available workers and, as a result, is sacrificing $20 billion worth of output.

The amount by which aggregate expenditures fall short of the full-employment level of NNP is called the **recessionary gap** simply because this deficiency of spending has a contractionary or depressing impact upon the economy. In this case, note in Table 13-1 that, assuming the full-employment NNP to be $490 billion, the corresponding level of total expenditures is only $485 billion. Hence, the recessionary gap is $5 billion. In other words, the recessionary gap is the amount by which the aggregate expenditures schedule would have to shift upward in order to realize the full-employment noninflationary NNP. Graphically, the recessionary gap is the *vertical* distance by which the aggregate expenditures schedule $(C + I_n)_1$ falls short of the full-employment point on the 45-degree line. Because the relevant multiplier is 4, we observe that there is a $20 billion differential (equal to the recessionary gap of $5 billion *times* the multiplier of 4) between the equilibrium NNP and the full-employment NNP. This $20 billion gap is the GNP gap (here an NNP gap) which we encountered in Figure 10-4.

INFLATIONARY GAP

If aggregate expenditures happen to be at $(C + I_n)_2$ in Figure 13-5b, a demand-pull inflationary gap will exist. Specifically, the amount by which aggregate spending exceeds the full-employment level of NNP is called an **inflationary gap.** In this case, a $5 billion inflationary gap is assumed to exist, as shown by the *vertical* distance between $(C + I_n)_2$ and the full-employment point on the 45-degree line. That is, the inflationary gap is the amount by which the aggregate expenditures schedule would have to shift downward to realize the full-employment noninflationary NNP.

The effect of this inflationary gap—this excess demand—will be to pull up the prices of the economy's fixed physical volume of production. Businesses as a whole cannot respond to the $5 billion in excess demand by expanding their real outputs, so *demand-pull inflation* will occur.

SIMPLIFICATIONS, COMPLICATIONS, AND POLICY

The astute reader may have sensed that our definitions of the recessionary and inflationary gaps rely upon a simplification, namely, that a full-employment noninflationary level of NNP is attainable. Our earlier discussion of the aggregate supply curve (Figure 11-3) suggests this is not likely to be the case. The intermediate range of the curve precludes the realization of the full-employment noninflationary output. To permit uncluttered definitions of the recessionary and inflationary gaps we have presumed an aggregate supply curve which eliminates the intermediate range and includes only the Keynesian and classical ranges (such as P_1aAS in Figure 11-7).

It is also important to recognize that our Keynesian aggregate expenditures treatment of the inflationary gap poses some complications. Specifically, Figure 13-5b implies that our $5 billion inflationary gap, subject to a multiplier of 4, will simply

cause *money* or *nominal* NNP to rise by $20 billion (to $510 billion) while *real* NNP remains unchanged at $490 billion. To portray this outcome in Figure 13-5b we must modify our horizontal axis so that it measures *real* NNP up to the $490 billion full-employment output and *nominal* NNP for all higher levels of NNP. In other words, the left area designates real changes in NNP and the right area entails nominal changes in NNP.[4]

International trade and equilibrium output

Thus far our aggregate expenditures model has ignored international trade by assuming a closed economy. Let us now relax this assumption, acknowledging the existence of exports and imports and the fact that **net exports** (exports minus imports) may be either positive or negative in a particular period. A glance at line 4 on the inside covers of this book will quickly reveal that net exports in some years have been positive (exports > imports) and in other years negative (imports > exports). Observe that net exports in 1980 were a *positive* $32 billion, for example, while by 1988 they had fallen to a *negative* $93 billion.

How do net exports—that is, exports and imports—relate to aggregate expenditures?

NET EXPORTS AND AGGREGATE EXPENDITURES

First, consider exports. Recall from Chapters 9 and 11 that—like consumption, investment, and government purchases—exports (X) give rise to domestic production, income, and employment. Even though the goods and services produced in re-

---

[4] Our discussion ignores another complication: Full employment (or capacity production) itself is something of an elastic concept because a given number of workers can increase their hours of work just by working overtime, or, as a matter of fact, persons who are not ordinarily in the labor force may be induced to offer their services when job opportunities are abundant. The general validity of our analysis is not impaired by ignoring this refinement.

sponse to such spending are sent abroad, foreign spending on American goods increases production and creates jobs and incomes in the United States. Exports must therefore be added as a new component of aggregate expenditures. Conversely, when an economy is open to international trade, we must acknowledge that a portion of its consumption and investment spending will be for imports (M), that is, for goods and services which were produced abroad rather than in the United States. Hence, in order not to overstate the value of domestic production, we must in effect reduce the sum of consumption and investment expenditures for the portions which were expended on imported goods. Thus, in measuring aggregate expenditures for domestic goods and services, it is necessary to make a subtraction for expenditures on imports. In short, for a private nontrading or closed economy, aggregate expenditures are $C + I_n$. But for a trading or open economy, aggregate spending is $C + I_n + (X - M)$. Or, recalling that net exports (X_n) equals ($X - M$), we can say that aggregate expenditures for a private, open economy are $C + I_n + X_n$.

THE NET EXPORT SCHEDULE

Table 13-3 indicates two distinct potential net export schedules for the hypothetical economy characterized by the data presented earlier in Table 13-1. Similar to consumption and investment schedules, a net export schedule indicates the amount of a particular expenditure—in this case net exports—which will occur at each level of NNP. The net export schedule X_{n1} (columns 1 and 2) tells us that exports exceed imports by $5 billion at each level of NNP. Perhaps exports are $15 billion, for example, while imports are $10 billion. The schedule X_{n2} (columns 1 and 3) reveals that imports are $5 billion higher than exports. That is, perhaps imports are $15 billion while exports are $10 billion. To simplify our discussion we are assuming in both cases that net exports are autonomous or independent of NNP.[5]

The two net export schedules from Table 13-3 are plotted in Figure 13-6b. Schedule X_{n1} indicates that a *positive* $5 billion of net exports are associated with each level of NNP. Conversely, observe that X_{n2} is below the horizontal axis and shows that net exports are a *negative* $5 billion.

TABLE 13-3 **Two net export schedules** *(hypothetical data; in billions)*

(1) Level of NNP	(2) Net exports X_{n1}	(3) Net exports X_{n2}
$370	$+5	$-5
390	+5	-5
410	+5	-5
430	+5	-5
450	+5	-5
470	+5	-5
490	+5	-5
510	+5	-5
530	+5	-5
550	+5	-5

NET EXPORTS AND EQUILIBRIUM NNP

Let us now turn our attention to Figure 13-6a. The aggregate expenditures schedule labeled $C + I_n$ is identical to the one found in Table 13-1 and Figure 13-1; that is, $C + I_n$ reflects the combined consumption and net investment expenditures which will occur at each level of NNP. The equilibrium level of NNP will be $470 billion when there is no foreign sector. Recall that this equilibrium level of output is determined at the intersection of the $C + I_n$ schedule and the 45-degree reference line; only there will aggregate expenditures equal NNP.

But we have stressed that in the real world net exports can be either positive or negative. Hence, exports and imports need not be neutral in their

---

[5] Although our *exports* depend upon *foreign* incomes and are thus independent of domestic NNP, it is recognized that our *imports* do vary directly with our own *domestic* national income. That is, just as our domestic consumption varies directly with our domestic NNP, so do our purchases of foreign goods. As our domestic NNP rises, American households buy not only more Pontiacs and more Pepsi but also more Porsches and more Perrier. However, we will ignore the resulting complications of the positive relationship between imports and domestic NNP in the interest of simplicity.

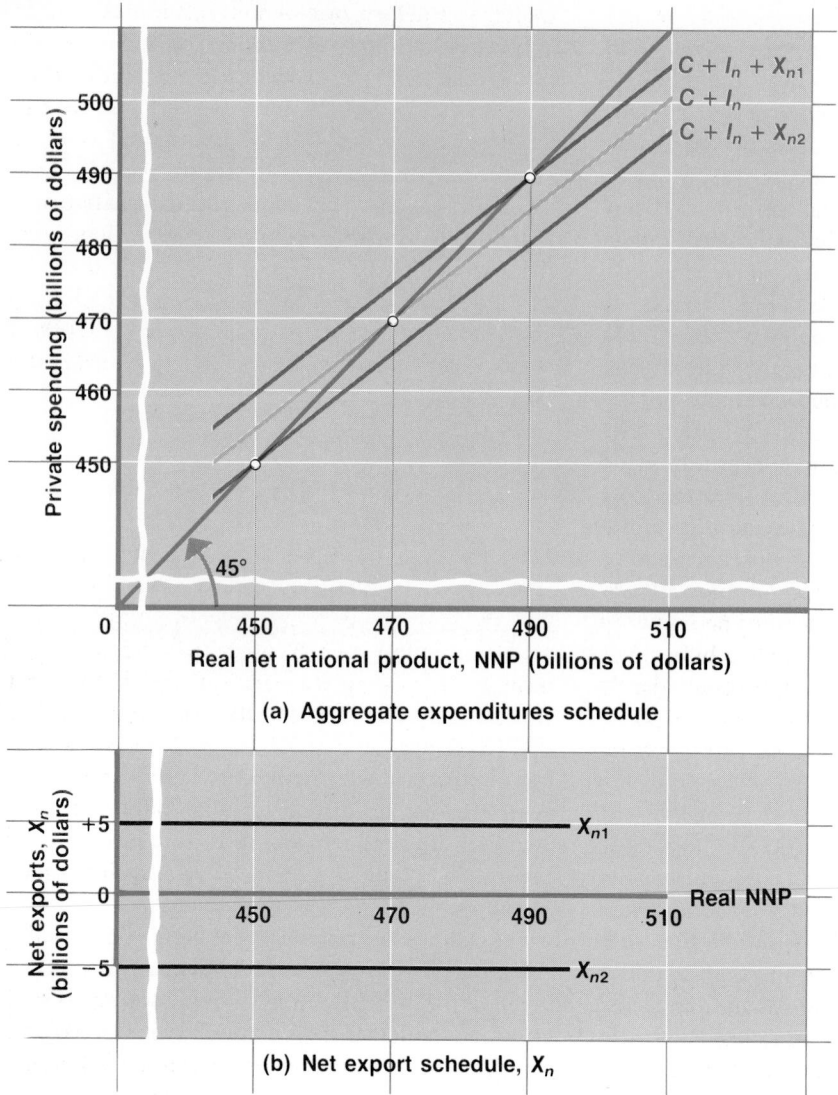

FIGURE 13-6

Net exports and the equilibrium NNP

Positive net exports such as shown by the net export schedule X_{n1} in (b) elevate the aggregate expenditures schedule in (a) from the closed-economy level of $C + I_n$ to the open-economy level of $C + I_n + X_{n1}$. Negative net exports such as depicted by the net export schedule X_{n2} in (b) lower the aggregate expenditures schedule in (a) from the closed-economy level of $C + I_n$ to the open-economy level of $C + I_n + X_{n2}$.

effect upon the equilibrium level of NNP. How will each of the net export schedules presented in Figure 13-6b affect equilibrium NNP?

Positive net exports Let us first suppose that the net export schedule for our hypothetical economy is X_{n1}. The $5 billion of additional net export expenditures by foreigners are accounted for by adding $5 billion to the $C + I_n$ schedule in Figure 13-6a. Restated, aggregate expenditures at each level of NNP are in reality $5 billion higher than indicated by the $C + I_n$ schedule alone. The aggregate expenditures schedule for the open economy

thus becomes $C + I_n + X_{n1}$. Observe that the presence of international trade has increased equilibrium NNP from $470 billion in the simplified closed economy to $490 billion in the more realistic open economy. The reader should verify that the new equilibrium NNP is $490 billion by adding $5 billion to each level of aggregate expenditures in Table 13-1 and then determining where $C + I_n + X_n$ equals NNP.

Generalization: *Positive net exports increase aggregate expenditures beyond what they would be in a closed economy and thus have an expansionary effect on domestic NNP.* In this case, the addition of net exports of $5 billion has increased NNP by $20 billion, implying a multiplier of 4.

Negative net exports A rather natural extension of our line of reasoning enables us to determine the impact of negative net exports upon equilibrium NNP. If net exports are X_{n2} as shown in Figure 13-6b, rather than X_{n1}, $5 billion of net export spending by foreigners must be subtracted from the aggregate expenditure schedule $C + I_n$ in order to establish aggregate expenditures for the open economy. Why is this the case? The $5 billion of negative net exports indicates that our hypothetical economy is importing $5 billion more of goods than it is selling abroad. The aggregate expenditures schedule shown as $C + I_n$ in Figure 13-6a therefore has overstated the expenditures on *domestic* output at each level of NNP. We must in effect reduce the sum of consumption and investment expenditures by the $5 billion net amount expended on imported goods. For example, if imports are $15 billion and exports are $10 billion, we must subtract the $5 billion of *net* imports (= −$5 billion of net exports) from the combined domestic consumption and investment expenditures.

After we subtract $5 billion from the $C + I_n$ schedule in Figure 13-6a, the relevant aggregate expenditures schedule becomes $C + I_n + X_{n2}$ and equilibrium NNP falls from $470 to $450. Again, a change in net exports of $5 billion has resulted in a fourfold change in NNP, telling us that the multiplier is 4. Confirmation of the new equilibrium NNP can be obtained by subtracting $5 billion from aggregate expenditures at each level of NNP in Table 13-1 and ascertaining the new equilibrium NNP.

A corollary to our first generalization emerges: *Negative net exports reduce aggregate expenditures relative to what they would be in the closed economy and hence have a contractionary effect on domestic NNP.* Imports add to the stock of goods available in the economy, but they diminish domestic NNP by reducing expenditures on domestically produced products.

Our generalizations concerning positive and negative net exports and equilibrium NNP allow us to conclude that a decline in net exports—that is, a decrease in exports or an increase in imports—decreases aggregate expenditures and has a contractionary effect on domestic NNP. Conversely, an increase in net exports—the result of either an increase in exports or a decrease in imports—increases aggregate expenditures and has an expansionary effect on domestic NNP. These changes may be in terms of real NNP, nominal NNP, or some combination of the two depending upon where the economy initially is located relative to its potential output. For example, if the full employment level of NNP in Figure 13-6a is $470, then a rise of net exports from zero to $5 billion will create an inflationary gap of $5 billion, *not* a real NNP increase of $20 billion as implied in our earlier discussion.

INTERNATIONAL ECONOMIC LINKAGES

Our analysis of net exports and domestic NNP permits us to demonstrate how circumstances or policies abroad can affect our domestic NNP.

First example: A rising level of national income among our trading partners will enable us to sell more of our goods abroad, thus raising our net exports and increasing our domestic NNP. We should be interested in the prosperity of our trading partners because their good fortune enables them to buy more imports. These purchases stimulate our exports and thereby transfer some of their prosperity to us.

Second example: Suppose that our trading partners impose high tariffs on American goods to reduce their imports and stimulate production in their economies. But their imports are our exports. Thus, when they restrict their imports to stimulate *their* economies, they are reducing our exports and depressing *our* economy. We are likely to retaliate by increasing trade barriers imposed on their products. If so, their exports will decline and therefore their net exports may be unchanged or even fall. In the Great Depression of the 1930s various nations, including the United States, imposed trade barriers in the hope of reducing domestic unemployment. But rounds of retaliation simply throttled world trade and made the world depression worse.

A final example: A depreciation of the dollar relative to other currencies (Chapters 4 and 11) will mean that people abroad will be able to obtain more dollars per unit of their currencies. The price of American goods in terms of these currencies will therefore fall, which will stimulate purchases of our exports. Conversely, American consumers will find they need more dollars to buy foreign goods and consequently will reduce their spending on imports. The resulting higher American exports and lower imports will increase our net exports and expand our NNP. Whether the depreciation of the dollar raises real NNP or produces inflation depends crucially upon the initial location of the economy relative to its full-employment level of output. If the economy initially is operating below its productive capacity, the depreciation of the dollar and the resulting rise in net exports will increase real NNP. Alternatively, if the economy initially is fully employed, the depreciation of the dollar and higher level of net exports will cause domestic inflation. Finally, we remind you that this last example has been cast in terms of a depreciation of the dollar. It will be a worthwhile exercise for you to think through the impact that an *appreciation* of the dollar will have on net exports and equilibrium NNP.

Reconciling two macro models

We have one final challenge before us and it is a reasonably formidable one. The goal is to reconcile the Keynesian model of this chapter which shows the relationship between *aggregate expenditures* and real NNP and which assumes a constant price level with Chapter 11's model which portrays the relationship between real NNP and the *price level*. The Keynesian model, developed during the massive unemployment of the 1930s, assumes that an increase in aggregate expenditures will bring about an increase in national output at the existing or "going" price level. In contrast the aggregate demand–aggregate supply model indicates that the price level will rise as aggregate demand increases in the intermediate and classical ranges of the aggregate supply curve. To repeat: The Keynesian expenditures-output analysis is a *constant* price level model; the aggregate demand–aggregate supply analysis is a *variable* price level model.

DERIVING THE AD CURVE

By using concepts and ideas we are already familiar with we can forge an important link between

our two models by showing how shifts in the aggregate expenditures schedule caused by price level changes permit us to trace out or locate a given downsloping aggregate demand curve.

In the first place, we know from Chapter 12 that there is an inverse relationship between the location of the consumption schedule and the price level. More precisely, an increase in the price level causes the consumption schedule—and therefore the aggregate expenditures schedule—to shift downward and vice versa. A primary reason for this is the *real balances* or *wealth effect* introduced in Chapter 11. An increase in the price level reduces the real value or purchasing power of people's wealth. To restore the value of their wealth, people must save more and therefore consume less. At the higher price level the consumption schedule and therefore the aggregate expenditures schedule will shift downward and real NNP will fall. Conversely, a decline in the price level increases the real value of people's wealth. When individuals are wealthier they are more inclined to consume and less inclined to save out of current real income. At the lower price level the consumption and aggregate expenditures curves shift upward and real NNP rises.

Second, we also know from Chapter 12 that there is an inverse relationship between the location of the investment schedule (Table 12-3 and Figure 12-7) and the price level. An increase in the price level, all else being equal, will increase the interest rate, which in turn will shift the investment and aggregate expenditures schedules downward. This so-called *interest-rate effect,* remember, works as follows: More money will be needed for purchases at the higher price level and, given a fixed supply of money, the increase in money demand will boost the interest rate and reduce investment expenditures. Conversely, a decline in the price level will reduce the demand for money, lower the interest rate, and elevate the investment and aggregate expenditures schedules. Lower price levels in effect will be associated with greater aggregate expenditures and higher equilibrium levels of real NNP.

Finally, we should note that there is an inverse relationship between the price level and the net export schedule. An increase in the price level will move the net export schedule downward and thus reduce aggregate expenditures and equilibrium NNP. Other things being equal, higher prices for

American goods will reduce U.S. export sales abroad and will increase our imports of relatively cheaper foreign products. American net exports, aggregate expenditures on American goods, and American NNP will all fall due to this *foreign purchases effect.* A lower American price level, on the other hand, will produce the opposite effects.

The aggregate demand curve of the variable price-level model, by definition, merely relates the various possible price levels to the corresponding equilibrium NNPs. Consider Figure 13-7. Note, to begin with, that we can "stack" our Keynesian model of Figure 13-7a and the aggregate demand–aggregate supply model of Figure 13-7b vertically because real national output is being measured on the horizontal axis of both models. Now we can

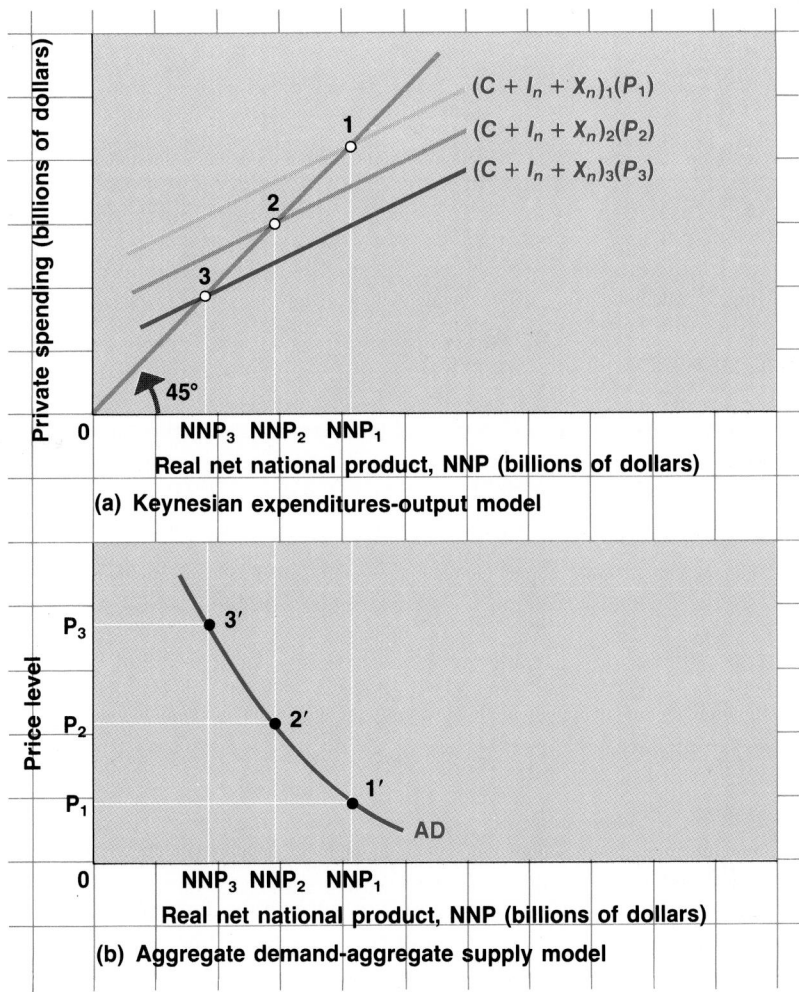

FIGURE 13-7

Deriving the aggregate demand curve from the expenditures-output model

Through the wealth, interest-rate, and foreign purchases effects, the consumption, investment, and net exports schedules and therefore the aggregate expenditures schedule will rise when the price level declines and fall when the price level increases. If the aggregate expenditure schedule is at $(C + I_n + X_n)_2$ when the price level is P_2, we can combine that price level and the equilibrium output, NNP_2, to determine one point ($2'$) on the aggregate demand curve. A lower price level such as P_1 shifts aggregate expenditures to $(C + I_n + X_n)_1$, providing us with point $1'$ on the aggregate demand curve. Similarly, a higher price level at P_3 shifts aggregate expenditures down to $(C + I_n + X_n)_3$ so P_3 and NNP_3 yield another point on the aggregate demand curve at $3'$.

start in the top diagram with the aggregate expenditures schedule $(C + I_n + X_n)_2$. The price level relevant to this aggregate expenditures schedule is P_2 as shown in parentheses to remind us of that fact. From this information we can plot the equilibrium real national output, NNP_2, and the corresponding price level of P_2. This gives us one point—namely $2'$—on Figure 13-7b's aggregate demand curve.

We can now go through the same procedure but assume that the price level is lower at P_1. We know that, other things being equal, a lower price level will: (1) increase the value of wealth, boosting consumption expenditures; (2) reduce the interest rate, promoting investment expenditures; and (3) reduce imports and increase exports, increasing net export expenditures. Consequently, the aggregate expenditures schedule will rise from $(C + I_n + X_n)_2$ to, say, $(C + I_n + X_n)_1$, giving us equilibrium at NNP_1. In Figure 13-7b we locate this new price level–real national output combination, P_1 and NNP_1, at point $1'$.

Similarly, let us now suppose the price level increases from the original P_2 level to P_3. The real value of wealth falls, the interest rate rises, exports fall, and imports rise. Consequently, the consumption, investment, and net export schedules fall, shifting the aggregate expenditures schedule downward from $(C + I_n + X_n)_2$ to $(C + I_n + X_n)_3$ where real output is NNP_3. This permits us to locate a third point on Figure 13-7b's aggregate demand curve, namely point $3'$ where the price level is P_3 and real output is NNP_3.

To summarize: A decrease in the price level shifts the aggregate expenditures schedule upward and thereby increases real NNP. An increase in the price level shifts the aggregate expenditures schedule downward, reducing real NNP. The resulting price level–real NNP combinations yield various points such as $1'$, $2'$, and $3'$, which locate a given downsloping aggregate demand curve.

SHIFTING THE AD CURVE

We know from Chapter 12 that the price level (and its impact upon the real value of wealth, the interest rate, and net exports) is only one of many factors which might shift the aggregate expenditures schedule. For example, the consumption component of aggregate expenditures might be affected by expectations, consumer debt, or tax changes. And the investment component might be altered by changes in profit expectations, technological change, business taxes, and so forth.

Likewise, the net export component of aggregate expenditures might be influenced by changes in exchange rates, tariff policies, and changes in levels of NNP and income in foreign nations. What happens if we *hold the price level constant* and consider shifts in aggregate expenditures caused by these non-price-level determinants of consumption, investment, and net exports? The answer is that the entire aggregate demand curve will shift rightward or leftward. You are reminded that these non-price-level aggregate demand shifters were discussed in Chapter 11 and summarized in Table 11-1.

Consider Figure 13-8. We begin with the aggregate expenditures schedule at $(C + I_n + X_n)_1$ in the top diagram, yielding a real national output of NNP_1. Assume now that more optimistic business expectations cause investment to increase so that the aggregate expenditures schedule rises from $(C + I_n + X_n)_1$ to $(C + I_n + X_n)_2$. (The parenthetical P_1's remind us that in this case the price level is assumed to be constant.) The result, we know, will be a multiplied increase in real NNP from NNP_1 to NNP_2. In the bottom diagram's model this is reflected in an increase in aggregate demand from AD_1 to AD_2 which shows the same multiplied increase in real NNP from NNP_1 to NNP_2. Notice that this change in real NNP is associated with the constant price level P_1 because we are in the horizontal Keynesian range of the aggregate supply curve.

MULTIPLIER WITH PRICE LEVEL CHANGES

Our discussion thus far implies that our two macro models are quite compatible. The aggregate demand curve can be derived from the Keynesian model (Figure 13-7) and the multiplied effect of an initial change in some component of aggregate spending can be envisioned in both models (Figure 13-8). The two models part company, however, when changes in aggregate expenditures and aggregate demand cause price level changes.

Observe Figure 13-9 which merely restates and extends Figure 13-8b. We see that the previously discussed shift in aggregate demand from AD_1 to

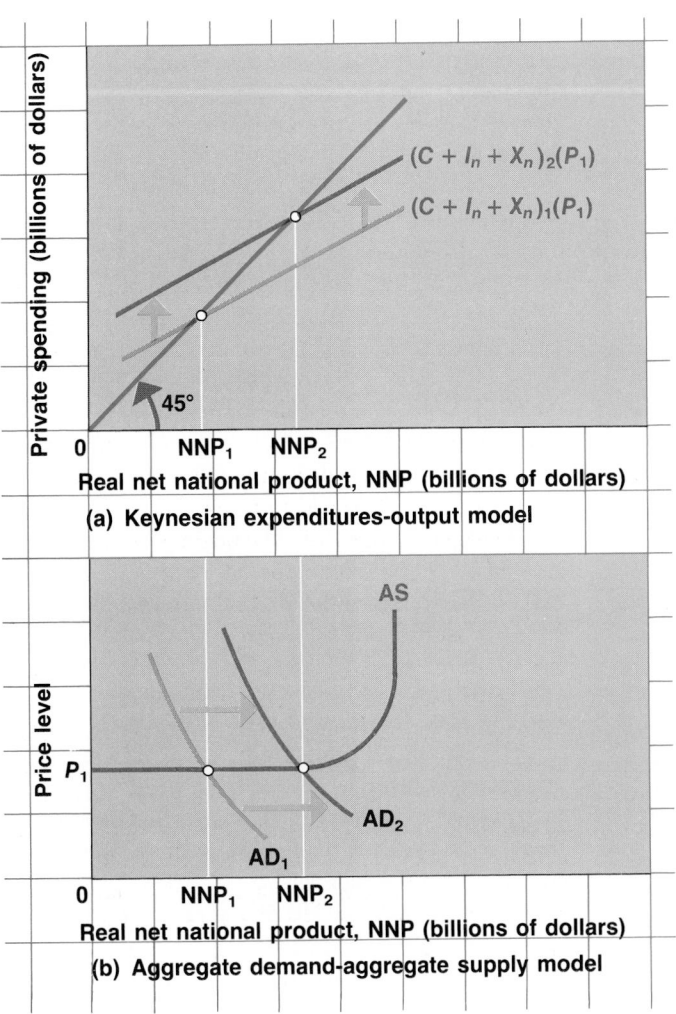

FIGURE 13-8

Shifts in the aggregate expenditures schedule and in the aggregate demand curve

In (a) we assume that some determinant of consumption, invest-ment, or net exports other than the price level shifts the aggre-gate expenditures schedule from $(C + I_n + X_n)_1$ to $(C + I_n + X_n)_2$, thereby increasing real national output from NNP_1 to NNP_2. In (b) we find that the aggregate demand counterpart of this is a rightward shift of the aggregate de-mand curve from AD_1 to AD_2 which is just suf-ficient to show the same increase in real output as in the ex-penditures-output model. We previously summarized the "aggre-gate demand shifters" in Table 11-1.

Figure (a) labels: Private spending (billions of dollars); $(C + I_n + X_n)_2(P_1)$; $(C + I_n + X_n)_1(P_1)$; 45°; NNP_1 NNP_2; Real net national product, NNP (billions of dollars); (a) Keynesian expenditures-output model

Figure (b) labels: Price level; AS; P_1; AD_2; AD_1; NNP_1 NNP_2; Real net national product, NNP (billions of dollars); (b) Aggregate demand-aggregate supply model

AD_2 occurs in the horizontal Keynesian range of aggregate supply. In other words, the economy is assumed to be in a recession with ample excess pro-ductive capacity and a high unemployment rate. Therefore, businesses are willing to produce more output *at existing prices*. Any change in aggregate demand over this range is translated fully into a change in real NNP and employment while the price level remains constant. Stated differently, in the Keynesian range of aggregate supply a "full-strength" multiplier is at work.

We now stress that, if the economy is in the intermediate or classical range of the aggregate supply curve, a part or all of any initial increase in aggregate demand will be dissipated in inflation and therefore *not* reflected in increased real output

and employment. In Figure 13-9 the shift of aggre-gate demand from AD_2 to AD_3 is of the same mag-nitude as the AD_1 to AD_2 shift, but look what hap-pens. Because we are now in the intermediate range of the aggregate supply curve, a portion of the increase in aggregate demand is dissipated in inflation as the price level rises from P_1 to P_2. Thus real NNP rises to only NNP′. If the aggregate sup-ply curve was horizontal, the AD_2 to AD_3 shift would have increased real national output to NNP_3. But inflation has weakened the multiplier so that the actual increase is to NNP′ which is only about half as much.

Our conclusions are twofold. First, *for any given initial increase in aggregate demand, the re-sulting increase in real NNP will be smaller the*

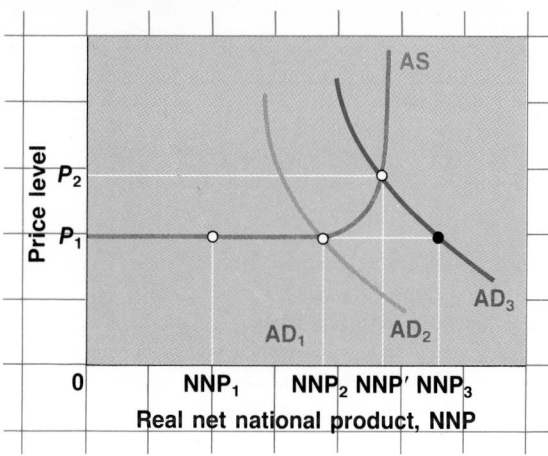

FIGURE 13-9

Inflation and the multiplier

The aggregate demand–aggregate supply model allows us to envision how inflation reduces the size of the multiplier. For the AD_1 to AD_2 increase in aggregate demand the price level is constant and the multiplier is at full strength. Although the increase in aggregate demand from AD_2 to AD_3 is of equal magnitude, it is partly dissipated in inflation (P_1 to P_2) and real output therefore only increases from NNP_2 to NNP'.

larger the increase in the price level. Price level increases weaken the multiplier. You should sketch an increase in demand equal to the AD_2 to AD_3 shift in the vertical classical range to confirm that this increase in spending would be entirely dissipated in inflation. There would be no multiplier because real NNP would be unchanged. Our second and more general conclusion is that *the aggregate expenditures–output model is not sufficient in explaining situations where changes in aggregate expenditures (and hence in aggregate demand) cause the price level to change.*

LOOKING AHEAD

What's next? In Chapter 14 we will embellish our Keynesian expenditures-output and aggregate demand and supply models by moving from a private sector economy to a mixed economy in which government expenditures and taxes are considered. Our main mission will be to explain how government might alter its expenditures and tax collections to alleviate either unemployment or inflation.

LAST WORD

Squaring the economic circle

Humorist Art Buchwald examines the functioning of the multiplier.

WASHINGTON—The recession hit so fast that nobody knows exactly how it happened. One day we were the land of milk and honey and the next day we were the land of sour cream and food stamps.

This is one explanation.

Hofberger, the Chevy salesman in Tomcat, Va., a suburb of Washington, called up Littleton, of Littleton Menswear & Haberdashery, and said, "Good news, the new Novas have just come in and I've put one aside for you and your wife."

Littleton said, "I can't, Hofberger. My wife and I are getting a divorce."

"I'm sorry," Littleton said, "but I can't afford a new car this year. After I settle with my wife, I'll be lucky to buy a bicycle."

Hofberger hung up. His phone rang a few minutes later.

"This is Bedcheck the painter," the voice on the other end said. "When do you want us to start painting your house?"

"I changed my mind," said Hofberger. "I'm not going to paint the house."

"But I ordered the paint," Bedcheck said. "Why did you change your mind?"

"Because Littleton is getting a divorce and he can't afford a new car."

That evening when Bedcheck came home his wife said, "The new color television set arrived from Gladstone's TV Shop."

"Take it back," Bedcheck told his wife.

"Why?" she demanded.

"Because Hofberger isn't going to have his house

painted now that the Littletons are getting a divorce."

The next day Mrs. Bedcheck dragged the TV set in its carton back to Gladstone. "We don't want it."

Gladstone's face dropped. He immediately called his travel agent, Sandstorm. "You know that trip you had scheduled for me to the Virgin Islands?"

"Right, the tickets are all written up."

"Cancel it. I can't go. Bedcheck just sent back the color TV set because Hofberger didn't sell a car to Littleton because they're going to get a divorce and she wants all his money."

Sandstorm tore up the airline tickets and went over to see his banker, Gripsholm. "I can't pay back the loan this month because Gladstone isn't going to the Virgin Islands."

Gripsholm was furious. When Rudemaker came in to borrow money for a new kitchen he needed for his restaurant, Gripsholm turned him down cold. "How can I loan you money when Sandstorm hasn't repaid the money he borrowed?"

Rudemaker called up the contractor, Eagleton, and said he couldn't put in a new kitchen. Eagleton laid off eight men.

Meanwhile, General Motors announced it was giving a rebate on its new models. Hofberger called up Littleton immediately. "Good news," he said, "even if you are getting a divorce, you can afford a new car."

"I'm not getting a divorce," Littleton said. "it was all a misunderstanding and we've made up."

"That's great," Hofberger said. "Now you can buy the Nova."

"No way," said Littleton. "My business has been so lousy I don't know why I keep the doors open."

"I didn't realize that," Hofberger said.

"Do you realize I haven't seen Bedcheck, Gladstone, Sandstorm, Gripsholm, Rudemaker or Eagleton for more than a month? How can I stay in business if they don't patronize my store?"

Source: Art Buchwald, "Squaring the Economic Circle," *Cleveland Plain Dealer,* February 22, 1975. Reprinted by permission.

CHAPTER SUMMARY

1 For a closed no-government economy the equilibrium level of NNP is that at which the aggregate expenditures and national output are equal or, graphically, where the $C + I_n$ line intersects the 45-degree line. At any NNP greater than the equilibrium NNP, national output will exceed aggregate spending, resulting in unintended investment in inventories, depressed profits, and eventual declines in output, employment, and income. At any below-equilibrium NNP, the aggregate expenditures will exceed the national output, thereby resulting in unintended disinvestment in inventories, substantial profits, and eventual increases in NNP.

2 A complementary leakages-injections approach determines the equilibrium NNP at the point where the amount households save and the amount businesses plan to invest are equal. This is at the point where the saving and the planned investment schedules intersect. Any excess of saving over planned investment will cause a shortage of total spending, forcing NNP to fall. Any excess of planned investment over saving will cause an excess of total spending, inducing NNP to rise. These changes in NNP will in both cases correct the indicated discrepancies in saving and planned investment.

3 Shifts in the saving-consumption schedules or in the investment schedule will cause the equilibrium output-income level to change by several times the amount of the initial change in spending. This phenomenon, which accompanies both increases and decreases in spending, is called the multiplier effect. The simple multiplier is equal to the reciprocal of the marginal propensity to save.

4 The paradox of thrift is the notion that the attempt of society to save more, as reflected in an upshift of the saving schedule, may be frustrated by the multiple decline in the equilibrium NNP which will ensue. If demand-pull inflation exists, however, more saving will simply tend to reduce the price level. Furthermore, if the additional saving is invested, the equilibrium NNP will be unchanged and the economy will realize a more rapid rate of growth.

5 The equilibrium level of NNP and the full-employment noninflationary NNP need not coincide. The amount by which aggregate expenditures fall short of the full-employment NNP is called the recessionary gap; this gap prompts a multiple decline in real NNP. The amount by which aggregate expenditures exceed the full-employment NNP is the inflationary gap; it causes demand-pull inflation.

6 Positive net exports increase aggregate expenditures and thus increase domestic NNP; negative net exports decrease aggregate expenditures and therefore reduce domestic NNP. Increases in exports or decreases in imports have an expansionary effect on NNP while decreases in exports or increases in imports have a contractionary effect on NNP.

7 The downsloping aggregate demand curve can be derived from the expenditures-output model by varying the price level and determining how the consequent changes in aggregate expenditures alter the equilibrium level of real national output. Shifts in the aggregate demand curve are associated with shifts in the aggregate expenditures curve caused by non-price-level factors that alter consumption, investment, or net export spending.

8 Assuming a constant price level, the aggregate demand–aggregate supply model would show the same multiplied change in real NNP as portrayed in the expenditures-output model.

9 In the intermediate and classical ranges of the aggregate supply curve the aggregate demand–aggregate supply model tells us that the multiplier will be weakened because a portion of any increase in aggregate demand will be dissipated in inflation.

TERMS AND CONCEPTS

aggregate expenditures–national output approach

leakages-injections approach

equilibrium NNP

45-degree line

planned and actual investment

multiplier effect

paradox of thrift

recessionary and inflationary gaps

net exports

QUESTIONS AND STUDY SUGGESTIONS

1 Explain graphically the determination of the equilibrium NNP by **a** the aggregate expenditures–national output approach and **b** the leakages-injections approach for the private sector of a closed economy. Why must these two approaches always yield the same equilibrium NNP? Explain why the intersection of the aggregate expenditures schedule and the 45-degree line determines the equilibrium NNP.

2 Assuming the level of investment is $16 billion and independent of the level of total output, complete the following table and determine the equilibrium level of output and income which the private sector of this closed economy would provide.

Possible levels of employment, millions	Real national output (NNP = DI), billions	Consumption, billions	Saving, billions
40	$240	$244	$_____
45	260	260	_____
50	280	276	_____
55	300	292	_____
60	320	308	_____
65	340	324	_____
70	360	340	_____
75	380	356	_____
80	400	372	_____

a If this economy has a labor force of 70 million, will there exist an inflationary or a recessionary gap? Explain the consequences of this gap.

b Will an inflationary or a recessionary gap exist if the available labor force is only 55 million? Trace the consequences.

c What are the sizes of the MPC and the MPS?

d Use the multiplier concept to explain the increase in the equilibrium NNP which will occur as the result of an increase in planned investment spending from $16 to $20 billion.

3 Using the consumption and saving data given in question 2 and assuming the level of investment is $16 billion, what are the levels of saving and planned investment at the $380 billion level of national output? What are the levels of saving and actual investment? What are saving and planned investment at the $300 billion level of national output? What are the levels of saving and actual investment? Use the concept of unintended investment to explain adjustments toward equilibrium from both the $380 and $300 billion levels of national output.

4 *Advanced analysis:* Based on the consumption and saving data given in question 2 for a closed economy, what will the equilibrium level of income be if planned investment is $2 billion at the $240 billion level of NNP and increases by $2 billion for every $20 billion increase in NNP? Assuming that businesses want to invest $4 billion more at each level of NNP, what will be the new equilibrium NNP? What is the size of the "supermultiplier" (see footnote 3)? Explain why it is larger than the multiplier derived in question 2.

5 "Planned investment is equal to saving at all levels of NNP; actual investment equals saving only at the equilibrium NNP." Do you agree? Explain. Critically evaluate: "The fact that households may save more than businesses want to invest is of no consequence, because events will in time force households and businesses to save and invest at the same rates."

6 What effect will each of the changes designated in question 6 at the end of Chapter 12 have upon the equilibrium level of NNP? Explain your answers.

7 What is the simple multiplier effect? What relationship does the MPC bear to the size of the multiplier? The MPS? What will the multiplier be when the MPS is 0, 0.4, 0.6, and 1? When the MPC is 1, $\frac{8}{9}$, $\frac{2}{3}$, $\frac{1}{2}$, and 0? How much of a change in NNP will result if businesses increase their level of investment by $8 billion and the MPC in the economy is $\frac{4}{5}$? If the MPC is $\frac{2}{3}$? Explain the difference between the simple and the complex multiplier.

8 Explain the paradox of thrift. What is its significance? "One's view of the social desirability of saving depends upon whether one assumes a Keynesian or classical view of the macroeconomy." Do you agree?

9 The data in columns 1 and 2 of the table below are for a closed economy.

a Use columns 1 and 2 to determine the equilibrium NNP for the closed economy.

b Now open this economy for international trade by including the export and import figures of columns 3 and 4. Calculate net exports and determine the equilibrium NNP for the open economy. Explain why equilibrium NNP differs from the closed economy.

c Given the original $20 billion level of exports, what would be the equilibrium NNP if imports were $10 billion larger at each level of NNP? Or $10 billion smaller at each level of NNP? What generalization concerning the level of imports and the equilibrium NNP is illustrated by these examples?

d What is the size of the multiplier in these examples?

10 Using appropriate diagrams, reconcile the Keynesian aggregate expenditures model and the aggregate demand–aggregate supply model. Explain the following two statements:

a "The Keynesian model is an unemployment model; the aggregate demand–aggregate supply model is an inflation model."

b "The Keynesian model can explain demand-pull inflation, but the aggregate demand–aggregate supply model is needed to explain cost-push inflation."

11 Explain how an upsloping aggregate supply curve might weaken the multiplier effect.

12 *Advanced analysis*: Assume the consumption schedule for the economy is such that $C = 50 + 0.8Y$. Assume further that investment and net exports are autonomous (indicated by I_{n0} and X_{n0}); that is, planned investment and net exports are independent of the level of income and in the amount $I_n = I_{n0} = 30$ and $X_n = X_{n0} = 10$. Recall also that in equilibrium the amount of national output produced (Y) is equal to the aggregate expenditures ($C + I_n + X_n$), or $Y = C + I_n + X_n$.

a Calculate the equilibrium level of income for this economy. Check your work by putting the consumption, investment, and net export schedules in tabular form and determining the equilibrium income.

b What will happen to equilibrium Y if $I_n = I_{n0} = 10$? What does this tell you about the size of the multiplier?

13 *Advanced analysis:* If $I_n = I_{n0} = 50$, $X_n = X_{n0} = 0$, and $C = 30 + 0.5Y$, what is the equilibrium level of income? If $I_n = 10 + 0.1Y$, $X_n = X_{n0} = 0$, and $C = 50 + 0.6Y$, what is the equilibrium level of income? What is the multiplier for this economy?

(1) Real national output (NNP = DI), billions	(2) Aggregate expenditures, closed economy, billions	(3) Exports, billions	(4) Imports, billions	(5) Net exports, billions	(6) Aggregate expenditures, open economy, billions
$200	$240	$20	$30	$_____	$_____
250	280	20	30	_____	_____
300	320	20	30	_____	_____
350	360	20	30	_____	_____
400	400	20	30	_____	_____
450	440	20	30	_____	_____
500	480	20	30	_____	_____
550	520	20	30	_____	_____

Fiscal policy

Chapter 14's basic goal is to add the public sector to the analysis of the equilibrium NNP developed in the two preceding chapters. It is crucial to recall at the outset that the consumption, investment, and import-export decisions of households and businesses are based upon private self-interest and that the sum of these decisions may result in either recession or inflation. In contrast, government is an instrument of society as a whole; hence, within limits government's decisions with respect to spending and taxing can be altered to influence the equilibrium NNP in terms of the general welfare. In particular, we saw in Chapter 6 that a fundamental function of the public sector is to stabilize the economy. This stabilization is achieved in part through *fiscal policy,* that is, through the manipulation of the public budget—government spending and tax collections—for the expressed purpose of increasing output and employment or reducing the rate of inflation. Indeed, one of the basic notions of Keynesian economics is that government has an obligation to behave in this way.

More specific goals of this chapter are to:

1 Analyze the impact of government purchases and taxes upon the equilibrium NNP.

2 Explain how some degree of economic stability is built into our tax system.

3 Survey some shortcomings and problems in the application of fiscal policy.

Legislative mandates

The notion that governmental fiscal actions can exert an important stabilizing influence upon the economy began to gain widespread acceptance during the Depression crisis of the 1930s. Keynesian employment theory played a major role in emphasizing the importance of remedial fiscal measures.

1 Employment Act of 1946 In 1946, when the end of World War II recreated the specter of unemployment, the Federal government formalized in law its area of responsibility in promoting economic stability. The **Employment Act of 1946** proclaims:

The Congress hereby declares that it is the continuing policy and responsibility of the Federal Government to use all practicable means consistent with its needs and obligations and other essential considerations of national policy, with assistance and cooperation of industry, agriculture, labor and State and local governments, to coordinate and utilize all its plans, functions, and resources for the purpose of creating and maintaining, in a manner calculated to foster and promote free competitive enterprise and the general welfare, conditions under which there will be afforded useful employment opportunities, including self-employment, for those able, willing, and seeking to work and to promote maximum employment, production, and purchasing power.

The Employment Act of 1946 is a landmark in American socioeconomic legislation in that it commits the Federal government to take positive action through monetary and fiscal policy to maintain economic stability.

2 CEA and JEC Responsibility for fulfilling the purposes of the act rests with the executive branch; the President must submit an annual Economic Report which describes the current state of the economy and makes appropriate policy recommendations. The act also established a **Council of Economic Advisers** (CEA) to assist and advise the President on economic matters, and a *Joint Economic Committee* (JEC) of the Congress, which has investigated a wide range of economic problems of national interest. In its advisory capacity as "the President's intelligence arm in the eternal war against the business cycle," the CEA and its staff gather and analyze relevant economic data and use them to make forecasts; to formulate programs and policies designed to fulfill the goals of the Employment Act; and to "educate" the President, the Congress, and the general public on problems and policies relevant to the nation's economic health.[1]

3 Humphrey-Hawkins Act of 1978 The *Full Employment and Balanced Growth Act of 1978,* popularly known as the **Humphrey-Hawkins Act,** reaffirms and extends the stabilization goals of the Federal government. The act requires the government to establish five-year goals for the economy and to formulate a program or plan to achieve these goals. Furthermore, the legislation attempted to make more concrete the rather vaguely stated goals of 1946's Employment Act. The specified goals were ambitious and unrealistic. The act sought a 4 percent rate of unemployment and a reduction in the rate of inflation to zero. Other priorities include improving the United States' position in international markets, encouraging the growth of private investment, and reducing the size of the public sector.[2]

[1] Walter W. Heller's *New Dimensions of Political Economy* (New York: W. W. Norton & Company, Inc., 1967) provides an incisive explanation of the functions of CEA and an intriguing account of the Council's operation under Dr. Heller's chairmanship during the 1961–1964 period. Arthur M. Okun's *The Political Economy of Prosperity* (New York: W. W. Norton & Company, Inc., 1970) is also highly recommended. Herbert Stein's *Presidential Economics: The Making of Economic Policy from Roosevelt to Reagan and Beyond* (New York: Simon and Schuster, 1984) is a perceptive history of governmental economic policy.

[2] See the *Economic Report of the President, 1979,* pp. 106–134.

Discretionary fiscal policy

Let us first focus attention upon discretionary fiscal policy. **Discretionary fiscal policy** is the deliberate manipulation of taxes and government spending by the Congress for the purpose of altering real national output and employment, controlling inflation, and stimulating economic growth.

SIMPLIFYING ASSUMPTIONS

To keep a potentially complex discussion as clear as possible, these simplifying assumptions are invoked.

1 We continue to employ in our analysis the simplified investment and net export schedules, wherein the levels of investment and net exports are independent of the level of NNP. Furthermore, we will suppose initially that net exports are zero.
2 We shall assume that the initial impact of government purchases is such that they neither depress nor stimulate private spending. That is, government purchases will not cause any upward or downward shifts in the consumption and investment schedules.
3 It will be presumed that the government's net tax revenues[3] are derived entirely from personal taxes. The significance of this is that, although DI will fall short of PI by the amount of government's tax revenues, NNP, NI, and PI will remain equal.
4 We assume initially that a fixed amount of taxes is collected regardless of the level of NNP.
5 We will suppose initially that the price level is constant. This means changes in aggregate expenditures or aggregate demand will have their full effect upon real output and employment rather than being dissipated wholly or in part by a changing price level. Stated differently, the economy is presumed to be functioning within the horizontal Keynesian range of the aggregate supply curve.
6 Finally, let us assume that the impact of fiscal policy is confined to the demand side of the macroeconomy; there are presumably no intended or unintended effects upon aggregate supply.

[3] By net taxes we mean total tax revenues less "negative taxes" in the form of transfer payments.

These assumptions will permit us to achieve a simple and uncluttered grasp of how changes in government spending and taxes influence the economy. Most of these assumptions will be dropped as we examine the complications and shortcomings that fiscal policy often encounters in the real world.

In our discussion of the private sector of the economy, we implicitly assumed that government purchases of goods and services (G) and tax revenues (T) were both zero. Now let us suppose that G and T each increase from zero to, say, $20 billion, and note the individual impact of each and then the combined impact of the two. As before, we pursue our analysis both tabularly and graphically.

GOVERNMENT PURCHASES AND EQUILIBRIUM NNP

Suppose that government decides to purchase $20 billion worth of goods and services regardless of what the level of NNP might be. Table 14-1 shows the impact upon the equilibrium NNP in terms of simple arithmetic data. Columns 1 through 4 are carried over from Table 13-1 for the private closed economy, wherein, you might recall, the equilibrium NNP was $470 billion. The only new wrinkles

are the additions of net exports (exports minus imports) in column 5 and government purchases in column 6. By adding government purchases to private spending ($C + I_n + X_n$), we get a new higher level of aggregate expenditures as shown in column 7. Comparing columns 1 and 7, we find that aggregate expenditures and the national output are equal at a higher level of NNP; specifically, equilibrium NNP has increased from $470 (row 6) to $550 billion (row 10). *Increases in public spending, like increases in private spending, will boost the aggregate expenditures schedule in relation to the 45-degree line and result in a higher equilibrium NNP.* Note, too, that government spending is subject to the multiplier. A $20 billion increase in government purchases has increased equilibrium NNP by $80 billion (= $550 billion minus $470 billion). That is, the multiplier in this example is 4.

It is important to stress that this $20 billion increase in government spending is *not* financed by increased tax revenues. We shall find momentarily that increased taxes reduce the equilibrium NNP. Stated differently, government spending must entail budget deficits to have the expansionary impact just described. Indeed, Keynes's basic policy recommendation was deficit spending by government to overcome recession or depression.

TABLE 14-1 **The impact of government purchases on equilibrium NNP** *(hypothetical data)*

(1) Real national output and income (NNP = DI), billions	(2) Consumption, C, billions	(3) Saving, S, billions	(4) Investment, I_n, billions	(5) Net exports, X_n, billions		(6) Government purchases, G, billions	(7) Aggregate expenditures $(C + I_n + X_n + G)$ billions, or $(2) + (4) + (5) + (6)$
				Exports, X	Imports, M		
(1) $370	$375	$−5	$20	$10	$10	$20	$415
(2) 390	390	0	20	10	10	20	430
(3) 410	405	5	20	10	10	20	445
(4) 430	420	10	20	10	10	20	460
(5) 450	435	15	20	10	10	20	475
(6) 470	450	20	20	10	10	20	490
(7) 490	465	25	20	10	10	20	505
(8) 510	480	30	20	10	10	20	520
(9) 530	495	35	20	10	10	20	535
(10) 550	510	40	20	10	10	20	550

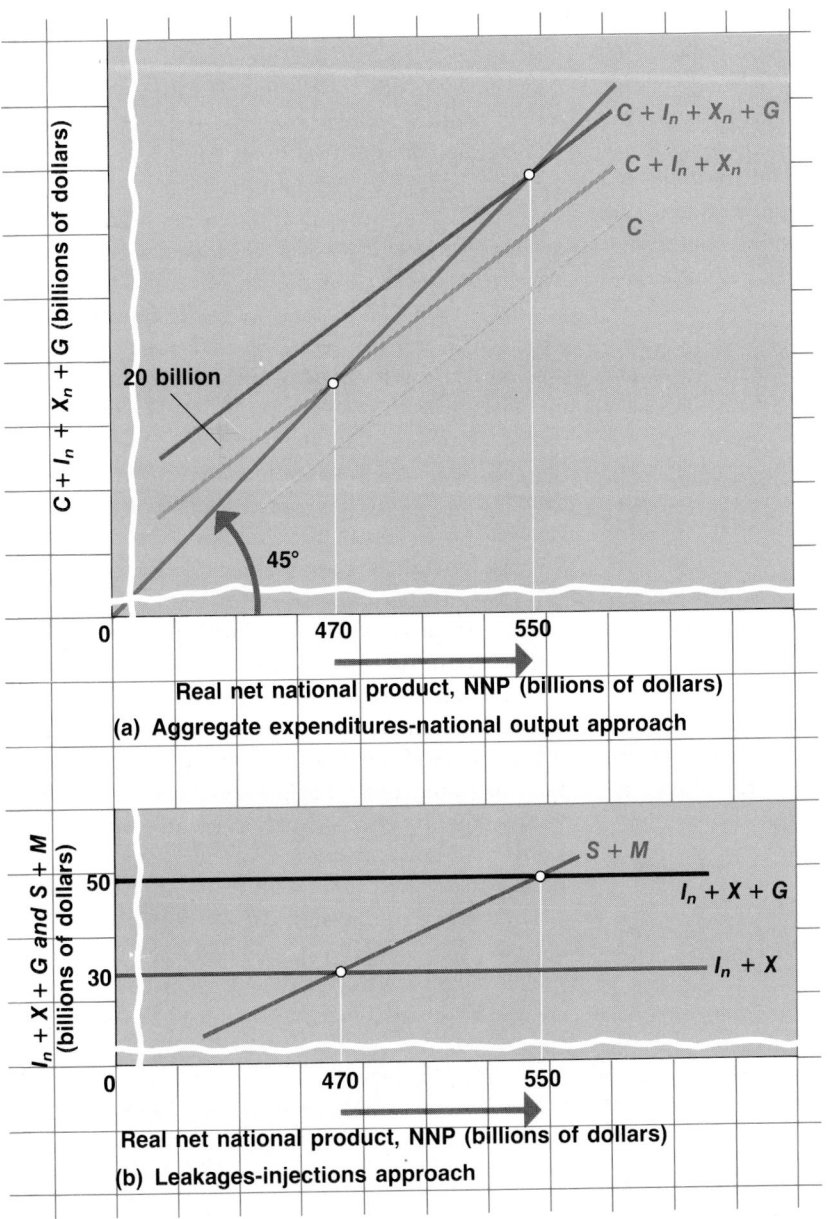

FIGURE 14-1

Government spending and the equilibrium NNP

(a) *The aggregate expenditures–national output approach.* The addition of government expenditures *G* to our analysis raises the aggregate expenditures $(C + I_n + X_n + G)$ schedule and increases the equilibrium level of NNP as would an increase in C, I_n, or X_n. Note that changes in government spending are subject to the multiplier effect.

(b) *Leakages-injections approach.* In terms of the leakages-injections approach, government spending supplements private investment and net export spending $(I_n + X_n + G)$, increasing the equilibrium NNP.

In terms of the leakages-injections approach, government purchases—like investment and exports—are an injection of spending. Leakages of savings and imports cause consumption of domestic output to fall short of domestic disposable income, causing a potential spending gap. This gap may be filled by injections of investment, exports, and government purchases. Observe in Table 14-1 that the $550 billion equilibrium level of NNP (row

10) occurs where $S + M = I_n + X + G$. That is, when taxes are assumed to be zero, $40 + 10 = 20 + 10 + 20$.

Figure 14-1 shows graphically the impact of government purchases. In Figure 14-1a we simply add government purchases, G, vertically to the level of private spending, $C + I_n + X_n$. As a result, the aggregate expenditures schedule (private plus public) has been increased to $C + I_n + X_n + G$, resulting in the indicated $80 billion increase in equilibrium NNP. Figure 14-1b shows the same change in the equilibrium NNP in terms of the leakages-injections approach. Like investment and exports, government spending is an offset to the leakage of saving and imports. Hence, with G added to our discussion, the equilibrium level of NNP is now determined at the point where the amount households save and import is offset exactly by the amount which businesses plan to invest and export *plus* the amount government desires to spend on goods and services. That is, assuming there are no taxes, the equilibrium NNP is determined by the intersection of the $S + M$ schedule and the $I_n + X + G$ schedule. Note that either approach indicates the same new equilibrium NNP.

What of the effect of a *decline* in government spending? Obviously, a decline in G will cause the aggregate expenditures schedule to fall in Figure 14-1a and the $I_n + X + G$ schedule to fall in Figure 14-1b. In either case the result is a multiple *decline* in the equilibrium NNP. You should verify that, if government spending were to decline from $20 to $10 billion, the equilibrium NNP would fall by $40 billion, that is, from $550 to $510 billion, implying a multiplier of 4.

TAXATION AND EQUILIBRIUM NNP

But government also collects tax revenues. How do tax collections affect the equilibrium level of NNP? To answer this question in the simplest way, we will assume that government imposes a **lump-sum tax** which, by definition, is *a tax of a constant amount or, more precisely, a tax which entails the same amount of tax revenue at each level of NNP*. In this instance, let us suppose the lump-sum tax is $20 billion so that government obtains $20 billion of tax revenue at each and every level of NNP.[4] What is the impact of government's increasing tax collections from zero to $20 billion at each level of NNP?

---

[4] This is clearly a regressive tax system because the average tax rate, T/NNP, falls as NNP rises. Most industrially advanced economies have proportional or progressive tax systems. The important modifications to which these latter two systems give rise will be noted shortly.

Table 14-2 is relevant. Taxes are inserted as column 2 and we note in column 3 that disposable (after-tax) income is less than NNP by the amount of the taxes. DI has been reduced by $20 billion— the amount of the taxes—at each level of NNP. And, because DI is made up of consumer spending and saving, we can expect a decline in DI to lower both consumption and saving. But by how much will each decline? The MPC and the MPS hold the answer: The MPC tells us what fraction of a decline in DI will come at the expense of consumption, and the MPS indicates what fraction of a drop in DI will come at the expense of saving. Observing that the MPC equals three-fourths ($= 15/20$) and the MPS equals one-fourth ($= 5/20$), we can conclude that if government collects $20 billion in taxes at each possible level of NNP, the amount of consumption forthcoming at each level of NNP will drop by $15 billion (three-fourths of $20 billion), and the amount of saving at each level of NNP will fall by $5 billion (one-fourth of $20 billion). Observe in columns 4 and 5 of Table 14-2 that the amounts of consumption and saving *at each level of NNP* are $15 and $5 billion smaller, respectively, than in Table 14-1. Thus, for example, before the imposition of taxes, where NNP equaled DI, consumption was $420 billion and saving $10 billion at the $430 billion level of NNP (row 4 of Table 14-1). After taxes are imposed, DI is $410 billion, $20 billion short of the $430 billion NNP, with the result that consumption is only $405 billion and saving is $5 billion (row 4 of Table 14-2).

To summarize: *Taxes cause DI to fall short of NNP by the amount of the taxes. This decline in DI in turn causes both consumption and saving to be less at each level of NNP. The sizes of the declines in C and S are determined by the MPC and the MPS.* Specifically, multiply the tax increase ($20 billion) by the MPC ($\frac{3}{4}$) to determine the decrease in consumption ($15 billion). Similarly, multiply the tax increase ($20 billion) by the MPS ($\frac{1}{4}$) to determine the decrease in saving ($5 billion).

What is the effect upon equilibrium NNP? We calculate aggregate expenditures once again as shown in column 9 of Table 14-2. Note that aggregate spending is $15 billion less at each level of national output than it was in Table 14-1. The reason, of course, is that after-tax consumption, designated by C_a, is $15 billion less at each level of NNP. Comparing national output and aggregate expend-

TABLE 14-2 **Determination of the equilibrium levels of employment, output, and income: private and public sectors (hypothetical data)**

(1) Real national output and income (NNP = NI = PI), billions	(2) Taxes, T, billions	(3) Disposable income, DI, billions, or (1) − (2)	(4) Consumption, C_a, billions	(5) Saving, S_a, billions, or (3) − (4)	(6) Investment, I_n, billions	(7) Net exports, X_n, billions		(8) Government expenditures, G, billions	(9) Aggregate expenditures $(C_a + I_n + X_n + G)$, billions, or (4) + (6) + (7) + (8)
						Exports, X	Imports, M		
(1) $370	$20	$350	$360	$−10	$20	$10	$10	$20	$400
(2) 390	20	370	375	−5	20	10	10	20	415
(3) 410	20	390	390	0	20	10	10	20	430
(4) 430	20	410	405	5	20	10	10	20	445
(5) 450	20	430	420	10	20	10	10	20	460
(6) 470	20	450	435	15	20	10	10	20	475
(7) 490	20	470	450	20	20	10	10	20	490
(8) 510	20	490	465	25	20	10	10	20	505
(9) 530	20	510	480	30	20	10	10	20	520
(10) 550	20	530	495	35	20	10	10	20	535

itures in columns 1 and 9, it is apparent that the aggregate amounts produced and purchased are equal only at the $490 billion NNP (row 7). Observe that the imposition of a $20 billion lump-sum tax has caused equilibrium NNP to fall by $60 billion from $550 billion (row 10 in Table 14-1) to $490 billion (row 7 in Table 14-2).

Our alternative leakages-injections approach confirms this result. Taxes, like saving and imports, are a leakage from the domestic income-expenditures stream. Saving, importing, and paying taxes are all uses of income which do not involve domestic consumption. Consumption will now fall short of national output—thereby creating a potential spending gap—in the amount of after-tax saving and imports *plus* taxes. This gap may be filled by planned investment, exports, and government purchases. Hence, our new equilibrium condition for the leakages-injections approach is: After-tax saving, S_a, plus imports plus taxes equals planned investment plus exports plus government purchases. Symbolically, $S_a + M + T = I_n + X + G$. You should verify in Table 14-2 that this equality of leakages and injections is fulfilled *only* at the $490 billion NNP (row 7).

The impact of the $20 billion increase in taxes is shown graphically in Figure 14-2a and b. In Figure 14-2a the $20 billion *increase* in taxes shows up as a $15 (*not* $20) billion *decline* in the aggregate

expenditures $(C_a + I_n + X_n + G)$ schedule. Under our simplifying assumption that all taxes are personal income taxes, this decline in aggregate expenditures is solely the result of a decline in the consumption component of the aggregate expenditures schedule. The equilibrium NNP shifts from $550 billion to a $490 billion level as a result of this tax-caused drop in consumption.

To generalize: *Increases in taxes will lower the aggregate expenditures schedule relative to the 45-degree line and cause the equilibrium NNP to fall.*

Consider now the leakages-injections approach: The analysis here is slightly more complex because the imposition of $20 billion in taxes has a twofold effect in Figure 14-2b. First, the taxes reduce DI by $20 billion and, with the MPS at one-fourth, cause saving to fall by $5 billion at each level of NNP. In Figure 14-2b this is shown as a shift from $S + M$ (saving before taxes plus imports) to $S_a + M$ (saving after taxes plus imports). Second, the $20 billion in taxes as such appears as a $20 billion additional leakage at each NNP level which must be added to $S_a + M$ (not $S + M$), giving us $S_a + M + T$. Equilibrium now exists at the $490 billion NNP, where the total amount which households save plus imports plus the amount of taxes government intends to collect are equal to the total amount businesses plan to invest plus exports plus the amount of government purchases. The equilibrium condi-

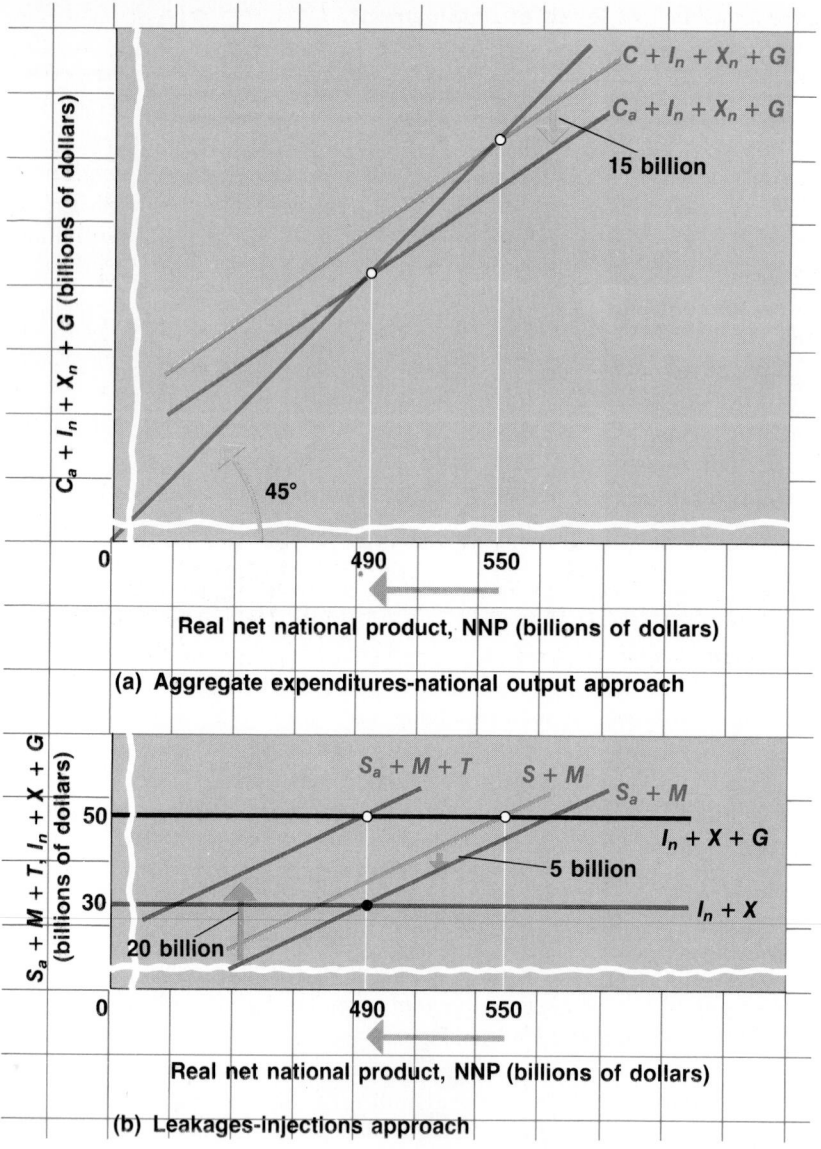

FIGURE 14-2

Taxes and the equilibrium NNP

(a) *The aggregate expenditures–national output approach.* **If the MPC is three-fourths, the imposition of $20 billion of taxes will lower the consumption schedule by $15 billion and thereby cause a decline in the equilibrium NNP. (b)** *The leakages-injections approach.* **Here taxes have a twofold effect. First, with an MPS of one-fourth, the imposition of taxes of $20 billion will reduce disposable income by $20 billion and saving by $5 billion at each level of NNP. This is shown by the shift from S (saving before taxes) + M to S_a (saving after taxes) + M. Second, the $20 billion of taxes constitutes an additional $20 billion leakage at each NNP level, giving us S_a + M + T. By adding government, the equilibrium condition changes from $S + M = I_n + X$ to $S_a + M + T = I_n + X + G$.**

tion for the leakages-injections approach now is $S_a + M + T = I_n + X + G$. Graphically, it is the intersection of the $S_a + M + T$ and the $I_n + X + G$ schedules which determines the equilibrium NNP.

A *decrease* in existing taxes will cause the aggregate expenditures schedule to rise as a result of an upward shift in the consumption schedule in Figure 14-2a. In terms of Figure 14-2b a tax cut will cause a decline in the $S_a + M + T$ schedule. The result in either case is a multiple *increase* in the equilibrium NNP. You should employ both the

expenditures-output and the leakages-injections approaches to confirm that a tax reduction of $10 billion (from the present $20 to $10 billion) will increase the equilibrium NNP from $490 to $520 billion.

BALANCED-BUDGET MULTIPLIER

Note an important and curious thing about our tabular and graphic illustrations. *Equal increases in government spending and taxation increase the equilibrium NNP. That is, if G and T are each increased by a particular amount, the equilibrium level of national output will rise by that same amount.* In our example the $20 billion increases in *G* and *T* cause the equilibrium NNP to increase by $20 billion, from $470 to $490 billion. The rationale for this so-called **balanced-budget multiplier** is revealed in our example. A change in government spending has a more powerful effect upon aggregate expenditures than does a tax change of the same size. Government spending has a *direct* and unadulterated impact upon aggregate expenditures. Government spending is a component of aggregate expenditures and, when government purchases increase by $20 billion as in our example, the aggregate expenditures schedule shifts upward by the entire $20 billion. But a change in taxes affects aggregate expenditures *indirectly* by changing disposable income and thereby changing consumption. Specifically, our lump-sum tax in-

crease shifts the aggregate expenditures schedule downward only by the amount of the tax *times* the MPC. That is, a $20 billion tax increase shifts the aggregate expenditures schedule downward by $15 billion (= $20 billion × ¾). The overall result is a *net* upward shift of the aggregate expenditures schedule of $5 billion which, subject to a multiplier of 4, boosts NNP by $20 billion. This $20 billion increase in NNP is equal to the size of the initial increase in government expenditures and taxes. *That is, the balanced budget multiplier is 1.*

The fact that the balanced budget multiplier is 1 is demonstrated in Figure 14-3. Given the MPC of three-fourths, the tax increase of $20 billion reduces disposable income by $20 billion and decreases consumption expenditures by $15 billion. The $15 billion decline in consumption expenditures in turn *reduces* NNP by $60 billion (= $15 billion × the multiplier of 4). However, observe in Figure 14-3 that the increase in government expenditures of $20 billion *boosts* NNP by $80 billion

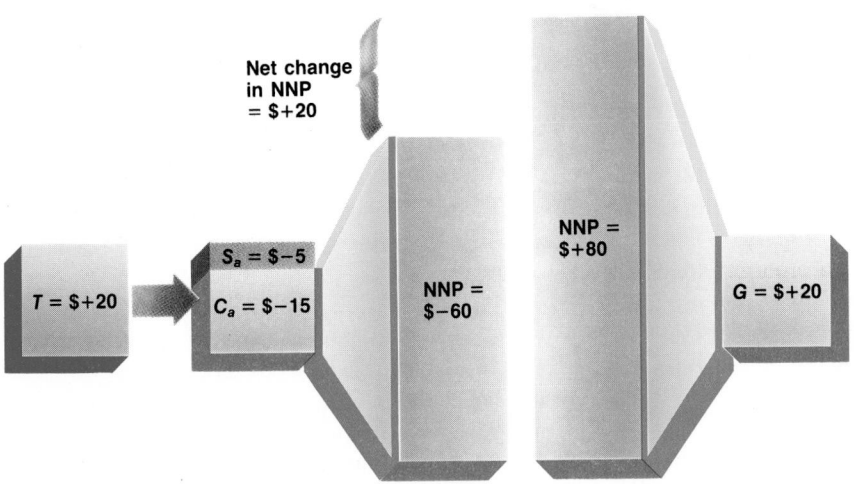

FIGURE 14-3

The balanced-budget multiplier

The balanced budget multiplier is 1. An equal increase in taxes and government expenditures will increase NNP by an amount equal to the increase in the amount of government expenditures and taxes. Given an MPC of three-fourths, a tax increase of $20 billion will reduce disposable income by $20 billion and lower consumption expenditures by $15 billion. Because the multiplier is 4, NNP will therefore decline by $60 billion. The $20 billion increase in government expenditures, however, will produce a more than offsetting increase in NNP of $80 billion. Hence, the net increase in NNP will be $20 billion, which equals the amount of the increase in government expenditures and taxes.

(= $20 billion × the multiplier of 4). Hence, the equal increases of taxes and government expenditures of $20 billion yield a *net* increase of NNP of $20 billion (= $80 billion − $60 billion). *Equal increases in G and T expand NNP by an amount equal to the increase in G and T*. The reader should experiment to verify that the balanced-budget multiplier is valid regardless of the sizes of the marginal propensities to consume and save.

FISCAL POLICY OVER THE CYCLE

Our discussion clearly suggests how fiscal policy might be used to help stabilize the economy. The fundamental purpose of fiscal policy is to eliminate unemployment or inflation. When recession exists, an **expansionary fiscal policy** is in order. This entails (1) increased government spending, *or* (2) lower taxes, *or* (3) a combination of the two. In other words, if the budget is balanced at the outset, fiscal policy should move in the direction of a government budget *deficit* during a recession or depression.

Conversely, when demand-pull inflation stalks the land, a restrictive or **contractionary fiscal policy** is appropriate. A contractionary policy is composed of (1) decreased government spending, *or* (2) higher taxes, *or* (3) a combination of these two policies. Fiscal policy should move toward a *surplus* in the government's budget when the economy is faced with the problem of controlling inflation.[5]

Keep in mind, however, that not only does the difference between government spending and taxes (the size of a deficit or surplus) affect the NNP, but so does the absolute size of the budget. In our balanced-budget multiplier illustration, increases in G

and T of $20 billion increased NNP by $20 billion. If G and T had both increased by only $10 billion, equilibrium NNP would only have risen by $10 billion.

FINANCING DEFICITS AND DISPOSING OF SURPLUSES

Given the size of a deficit, its expansionary effect upon the economy will depend upon the method by which it is financed. Similarly, given the size of a surplus, its deflationary impact will depend upon its disposition.

Borrowing versus new money There are two different ways by which the Federal government can finance a deficit: by borrowing from (selling interest-bearing bonds to) the public, or by issuing new money to its creditors.[6] The impact upon aggregate expenditures will be somewhat different in each case.

1 BORROWING If the government goes into the money market and borrows, it will be competing with private business borrowers for funds. This added demand for funds will drive the equilibrium interest rate upward. We know from Chapter 12 that investment spending is inversely related to the interest rate. Hence, government borrowing will tend to increase the interest rate and thereby "crowd out" some private investment spending and interest-sensitive consumer spending.

2 MONEY CREATION If deficit spending is financed by issuing new money, the crowding-out of private expenditures can be avoided. Federal spending can increase without any adverse effect upon investment or consumption. Thus, we reach the conclu-

[5] Qualification: In our numerical and graphical illustrations we have seen that equal increases in G and T entail a balanced-budget multiplier which is expansionary. Because a change in government spending has a more powerful effect on aggregate expenditures than does an equal change in taxes, an increased budget which results in a relatively small surplus might be slightly expansionary. Hence, if a contractionary fiscal policy is desired, the required surplus must be large enough to offset the balanced-budget multiplier.

[6] This statement implies that government merely prints up new dollar bills to finance its expenditures. We will find in Chapter 17 that the Treasury accomplishes the same result more subtly by borrowing (obtaining loans) from central (Federal Reserve) banks. The Treasury draws checks against these loans to finance its expenditures and, when the recipients deposit these checks in their own accounts at commercial banks, the supply of demand-deposit or checking account money is increased.

sion that *the creation of new money is a more expansionary way of financing deficit spending than is borrowing*.

Debt retirement versus an idle surplus Demand-pull inflation calls for fiscal action by government which will result in a budget surplus. However, the anti-inflationary effect of this surplus depends upon what government does with it.

I DEBT REDUCTION Since the Federal government has an outstanding debt of some $2.6 trillion, it is logical that government should use a surplus to retire outstanding debt. The anti-inflationary impact of a surplus, however, may be reduced somewhat by paying off debt. In retiring debt held by the general public, the government transfers its surplus tax revenues back into the money market, causing the interest rate to fall and thereby stimulating investment and consumption.

2 IMPOUNDING On the other hand, government can realize a greater anti-inflationary impact from its budgetary surplus by simply impounding the surplus funds, that is, by allowing them to stand idle. An impounded surplus means that the government is extracting and withholding purchasing power from the income-expenditure stream. If surplus tax revenues are not reinjected into the economy, there is no possibility of some portion of the surplus being spent. That is, there is no chance that the funds will create inflationary pressure to offset the deflationary impact of the surplus itself. We conclude that *the impounding of a budgetary surplus is more contractionary than the use of the surplus to retire public debt.*

POLICY OPTIONS: *G* OR *T*?

Is it preferable to use government spending or taxes in eliminating recessionary and inflationary gaps? The answer depends to a considerable extent upon one's view as to whether the public sector is too large or too small. Hence, those "liberal" economists, who think that the public sector needs to be enlarged to meet various failures of the market system (Chapter 6), can recommend that aggregate expenditures should be expanded during recessions by increasing government purchases *and* that ag-

gregate expenditures should be constrained during inflationary periods by increasing taxes. Conversely, "conservative" economists, who contend that the public sector is overly large and inefficient, can advocate that aggregate expenditures be increased during recessions by cutting taxes *and* that aggregate expenditures be reduced during inflation by cutting government spending. It is significant that an active fiscal policy designed to stabilize the economy can be associated with either an expanding or a contracting public sector.

Nondiscretionary fiscal policy: built-in stabilizers

To some degree appropriate changes in the relative levels of government expenditures and taxes occur automatically. This so-called automatic or *built-in stability* is not embodied in our discussion of discretionary fiscal policy because we assumed a simple lump-sum tax whereby the same amount of tax revenue was collected at each level of NNP. Built-in stability arises because in reality our net tax system (net taxes equal taxes minus transfers and subsidies) is such that *net tax revenues[7] vary directly with NNP*. Virtually all taxes will yield more tax revenue as NNP rises. In particular, personal income taxes have progressive rates and result in more than proportionate increases in tax collections as NNP expands. Furthermore, as NNP increases and more goods and services are purchased, revenues from corporate income taxes and sales and excise taxes will increase. And, similarly, payroll tax payments increase as economic expansion creates more jobs. Conversely, when NNP declines, tax receipts from all these sources will decline. Transfer payments (or "negative taxes") behave in precisely the opposite way. Unemployment compensation payments, welfare payments, and subsidies to farmers all *decrease* during economic expansion and *increase* during a contraction.

---

[7] From now on, we shall use the term "taxes" in referring to net taxes.

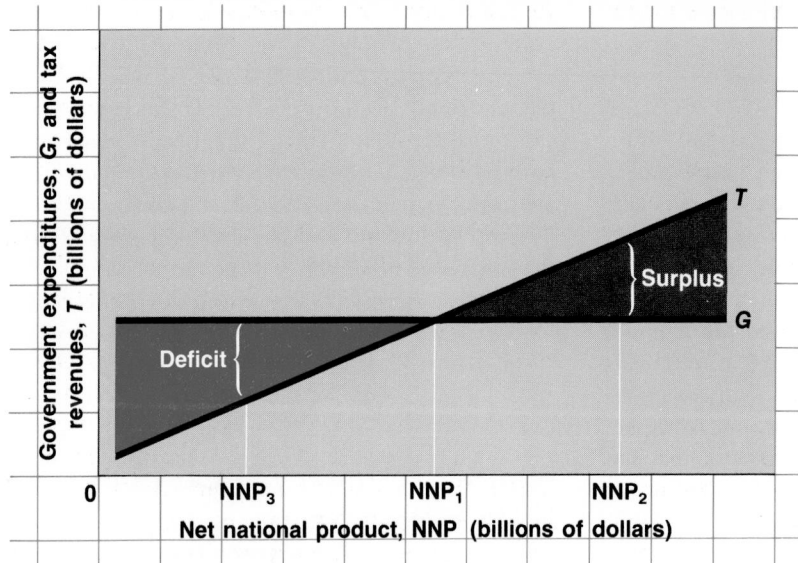

FIGURE 14-4

Built-in stability

If tax revenues vary directly with NNP, then the deficits which will tend to occur automatically during recession will help alleviate that recession. Conversely, the surpluses which tend to occur automatically during expansion will assist in offsetting possible inflation.

AUTOMATIC OR BUILT-IN STABILIZERS

Figure 14-4 is helpful in understanding how the tax system gives rise to built-in stability. Government expenditures G are given and assumed to be independent of the level of NNP; expenditures are decided upon at some fixed level by the Congress. But Congress does *not* determine the *level* of tax revenues; rather, it establishes tax *rates*. Tax revenues then vary directly with the level of NNP which the economy actually realizes. The direct relationship between tax revenues and NNP is shown in the upsloping T line.

The economic importance of this direct relationship between tax receipts and NNP comes into focus when we remember two things. First, taxes are a leakage or withdrawal of potential purchasing power from the economy. Second, it is desirable from the standpoint of stability to increase leakages or withdrawals of purchasing power when the economy is moving toward inflation and to diminish these withdrawals when the economy is tending to slump. In other words, the kind of tax system portrayed in Figure 14-4 builds some stability into the economy by automatically bringing about changes in tax revenues and therefore in the public budget which tend to counter both inflation and unemployment. Generally speaking, a **built-in stabilizer** *is anything which tends to increase the gov-*

ernment's deficit (or reduce its surplus) during a recession and to increase its surplus (or reduce its deficit) during inflation without requiring explicit action by policy makers. And, as Figure 14-4 clearly reveals, this is precisely what our tax system tends to do. As NNP rises during prosperity, tax revenues *automatically* increase and, because they are a leakage, restrain the economic expansion. Stated differently, as the economy moves toward a higher NNP, tax revenues automatically rise and tend to move the budget from a deficit to a surplus. Conversely, as NNP falls during recession, tax revenues *automatically* decline and this reduction in leakages cushions the economic contraction. That is, with a falling NNP, tax receipts decline and tend to move the public budget from a surplus to a deficit. In terms of Figure 14-4, the low level of income NNP_3 will automatically give rise to an expansionary budget deficit; the high and perhaps inflationary income level NNP_2 will automatically generate a contractionary budget surplus.

It is clear from Figure 14-4 that the size of the automatic budget deficits or surpluses and therefore built-in stability depends upon the responsiveness of changes in taxes to changes in NNP. If tax revenues change sharply as NNP changes, the slope of line T in the figure will be steep and the vertical distances between T and G—the deficits or surpluses—will be large. Alternatively, if tax revenues change very little when NNP changes, the slope will be gentle and built-in stability will be low. Changes in public policies or laws which alter the progressivity of the net tax system (taxes minus transfers and subsidies) therefore affect the degree of built-in stability. The Federal government's "indexing" of the personal income tax and lowering of marginal tax rates in the 1980s flattened the slope of T in Figure 14-4. Prior to the 1980s inflation would push taxpayers into higher marginal tax brackets and thus increase government's tax revenues. Now income tax brackets are "indexed," or widened, to adjust for inflation. Also, the Tax Reform Act of 1986 sharply cut marginal rates and consolidated them into fewer brackets. Hence, changes in NNP do not produce as large automatic changes in tax revenue as previously and the economy's degree of built-in stability is less than it once was.

There is no question that the built-in stability provided by our tax system has reduced the severity of business fluctuations. However, the built-in stabilizers are *not* capable of correcting an undesirable change in the equilibrium NNP. All that the stabilizers do is reduce the magnitude or severity of economic fluctuations. Hence, Keynesian economists contend that discretionary fiscal action—that is, changes in tax rates, tax structure, and expenditures—by Congress is required to correct an inflation or a recession of any appreciable magnitude. It is estimated that in the United States the built-in stabilizers are currently strong enough to reduce fluctuations in national income by roughly one-third.

FULL-EMPLOYMENT BUDGET

Built-in stability—the fact that tax revenues vary directly with NNP—makes it hazardous to use the **actual budget** surplus or deficit in any given year as an index of the government's fiscal stance. To illustrate: Suppose the economy is at full employment at NNP_1 in Figure 14-4 and, as we note, the budget is in balance. Now, assume that, during the year, C_a or I_n or X_n declines, causing a recession at NNP_3. The government, let us assume, takes no discretionary fiscal action; therefore, the G and T lines remain in the positions shown in the diagram.

As the economy moves to NNP_3, tax revenues fall and, with government expenditures unaltered, a deficit occurs. But this **cyclical deficit** is clearly *not* the result of positive countercyclical fiscal actions by the government; rather it is the by-product of fiscal inaction as the economy slides into a recession.

The basic point is that we cannot say anything very meaningful about the government's fiscal posture—whether Congress was appropriately manipulating taxes and expenditures—by looking at the historical record of budgetary deficits or surpluses. The actual budget surplus or deficit reflects not only possible discretionary decisions about spending and taxes (as shown in the locations of the G and T lines in Figure 14-4), but also the level of equilibrium NNP (where the economy is operating on the horizontal axis of Figure 14-4). Hence, given that tax revenues vary with NNP, the fundamental problem of comparing deficits or surpluses in year 1 and year 2 is that the level of NNP may be vastly different in each of the two years.

Economists have resolved this problem through the notion of a full-employment budget. Simply stated, the **full-employment budget** *indicates what the Federal budgetary surplus or deficit would be if the economy were to operate at full employment throughout the year*. Figure 14-5 compares the full-employment budget and the actual budget over approximately three decades. Two features stand out.

First, although the actual budget has been in deficit in most years, the full-employment budget is more likely to be in surplus, or at least, closer to balance. Consider 1961 and 1962, years of above-normal unemployment and sluggish economic growth. A look at the actual budget deficits in these years implies that government was appropriately engaged in an expansionary fiscal policy. But the full-employment budget data tell us that this was *not* the case. The full-employment budget data indicate that, *if* the economy had been at full employment, there would have been a budgetary surplus. Our fiscal policy in 1961 and 1962 was in fact contractionary, and this was partially responsible for the less-than-full-employment levels of NNP, the consequent poor tax harvests, and the deficits which occurred in the actual budgets for 1961 and 1962.

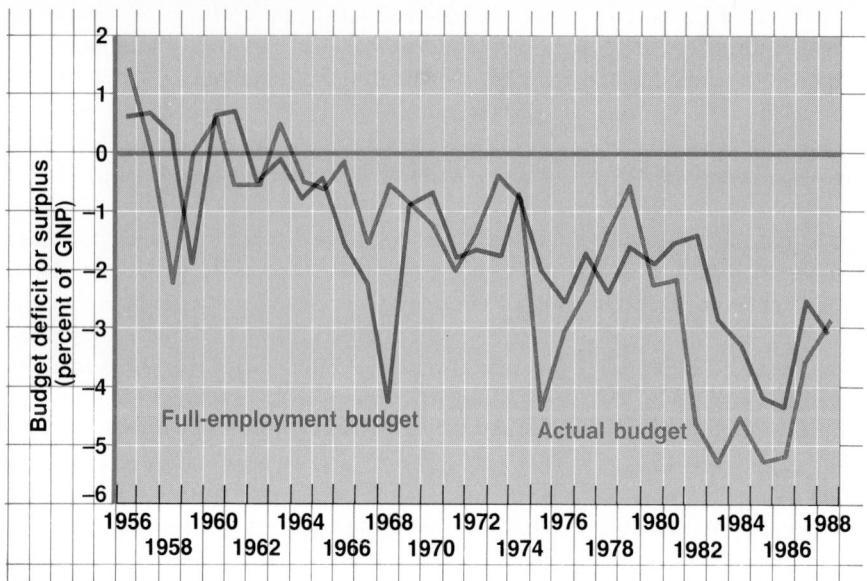

FIGURE 14-5

The full-employment budget and the actual budget

The full-employment budget surplus or deficit is a better indicator of the government's fiscal posture than is the actual surplus or deficit. The actual budget has been in deficit with much greater frequency than the full-employment budget because NNP has been at less than full employment. In the last several years the full-employment budget has been in substantial deficit.

Second, observe the sizable actual *and* full-employment deficits in the latter part of the period. Specifically, note 1987, a year when the economy neared its full-employment or potential output. A major portion of the actual deficit in 1987 resulted from government spending and tax decisions, rather than from the automatic deficiencies in tax revenues brought forth by a below-full-employment NNP. This **structural deficit**—as distinct from a cyclical deficit—meant that tax revenues would have been less than government expenditures even if the economy had achieved its full-employment output. The full-employment budget in 1987 was therefore in substantial deficit, implying an expansionary fiscal policy. We might logically wonder why this combination of near-full-employment and an expansionary fiscal policy did not touch off demand-pull inflation. One important reason was that net exports $(X - M)$ were highly negative in 1987. By reducing aggregate expenditures on domestic NNP, the negative net exports partially canceled the expansionary effects of the sizable deficit in the full-employment budget.

Problems, criticisms, and complications

Unfortunately, there is a great deal of difference between fiscal policy on paper and fiscal policy in practice. It is therefore imperative that we examine some specific problems which may be encountered in enacting and applying appropriate fiscal policy.

PROBLEMS OF TIMING

Several problems of timing may arise in connection with fiscal policy.

1 Recognition lag The recognition lag refers to the time which elapses between the beginning of a recession or inflation and the certain awareness that it is actually happening. It is extremely difficult to predict accurately the future course of economic activity. Although forecasting tools such as the index of leading indicators (see this chapter's Last

Word) provide clues as to the direction of the economy, the economy may be four or six months into a recession or inflation before that fact shows up in relevant statistics and is acknowledged.

2 Administrative lag The wheels of democratic government are often slow in turning. There will typically be a significant lag between the time that the need for fiscal action is recognized and the time that action is actually taken. The $11 billion tax cut which became law in February of 1964 was first proposed to President Kennedy by the Council of Economic Advisers in 1961, and in turn proposed by him in late 1962. The 1968 surcharge on personal and corporate incomes was enacted approximately a year after it was requested by President Johnson. Indeed, Congress has on occasion consumed so much time in adjusting fiscal policy that the economic situation has taken a turnabout in the interim, thereby rendering the policy action completely inappropriate.

3 Operational lag There will also be a lag between the time that fiscal action is taken by Congress and the time that action has an impact upon output, employment, or the price level. Although changes in tax rates can be put into effect quickly, government spending on public works—the construction of dams, interstate highways, and so forth—entails long planning periods and even longer periods of construction. Such spending is of questionable usefulness in offsetting short—for example, six- or eighteen-month—periods of recession. Because of these kinds of problems, discretionary fiscal policy has come to rely increasingly upon tax changes.

POLITICAL PROBLEMS

Fiscal policy is created in the political arena and this greatly complicates its use in stabilizing the economy.

I Other goals Recall that economic stability is *not* the sole objective of government spending and taxing policies. Government is also concerned with the provision of public goods and services and the redistribution of income (Chapter 6). Classic example: During World War II government spending for military goods rose dramatically, causing strong

and persistent inflationary pressures in the early 1940s. The defeat of Nazi Germany and Japan was simply a higher priority goal than achieving price level stability.

Also note that the fiscal policies of state and local governments are frequently procyclical. Thus, like households and private businesses, state and local governments tend to increase expenditures during prosperity and to cut them during recession. During the Great Depression of the 1930s, most of the increase in Federal spending was offset by decreases in state and local spending.

2 Expansionary bias? Rhetoric to the contrary, deficits tend to be politically attractive and surpluses politically painful. That is, there may well be a political bias in favor of deficits; in other words, fiscal policy may embody an expansionary-inflationary bias. Why so? Tax reductions tend to be politically popular. And so are increases in government spending, provided that the given politician's constituents share liberally in the benefits. But higher taxes upset voters and reducing government expenditures can be politically precarious. For example, it might well be political suicide for a farm-state senator to vote for tax increases and against agricultural subsidies. Figure 14-5 is informative. In the 1965–1967 period we find the full-employment budget shifting significantly toward deficits or, in other words, to an expansionary posture. Yet in each of those three years the unemployment rate was below 4 percent and the price level was rising. The proper fiscal stance should have been one of restraint, not stimulus.

3 A political business cycle? Some economists stress that the overriding goal of politicians is not necessarily to act in the interests of the national economy, but rather to get reelected. A few economists have recently put forth the notion of a **political business cycle.** That is, they have argued that politicians might manipulate fiscal policy to maximize voter support, even though their fiscal decisions tend to *destabilize* the economy. According to this view, fiscal policy, as we have described it, may be corrupted for political purposes and thereby be a cause of economic fluctuations.

The suggested scenario goes something like this. The populace, it is assumed, takes economic conditions into account in voting. Incumbents are penalized at the polls if economic conditions are depressed; they are rewarded if the economy is prosperous. Hence, as an election approaches, the incumbent administration (aided by an election-minded Congress) will invoke tax cuts and increases in government spending. Not only will these actions be popular per se, but the resulting stimulus to the economy will push all the critical economic indicators in proper directions. Output and real incomes will rise; unemployment will fall; and the price level will be relatively stable. As a result, incumbents will enjoy a very cordial economic environment in which to stand for reelection.

But after the election, continued expansion of the economy is reflected increasingly in a rising price level and less in growing real incomes. Growing public concern over inflation will prompt politicians to invoke a contractionary fiscal policy. Crudely put, a "made-in-Washington" recession will be engineered by trimming government spending and increasing taxes in order to restrain inflation. Won't this recession hurt incumbents? Not really, because the next election is still two or three years away and the critical consideration for most voters is the performance of the economy in the year or so prior to the election. Indeed, the recession provides a new starting point from which fiscal policy can again be used to generate another expansion in time for the next election campaign!

This possible perversion of fiscal policy is both highly disturbing and inherently difficult to document. Although empirical evidence is mixed and inconclusive, there is some evidence in support of this political theory of the business cycle.

CROWDING-OUT EFFECT

Let us now shift our attention from practical problems in the application of fiscal policy to a basic criticism of fiscal policy itself. The essence of the **crowding-out effect** is that an expansionary (deficit) fiscal policy will tend to increase the interest rate and reduce investment spending, thereby weakening or canceling the stimulus of the fiscal policy. In more detail the scenario is as follows. Assume the economy is in a recession and government invokes discretionary fiscal policy in the form

of an increase in government spending. Government now goes into the money market to finance the deficit. The resulting increase in the demand for money raises the interest rate, that is, the price paid for borrowing money. Because investment spending varies inversely with the interest rate (review Figure 12-6), some investment will be choked off or crowded out.[8] In terms of Figure 14-1 an increase (upshift) in the government component of aggregate expenditures may cause a decrease (downshift) in the private investment component. If investment were to fall by the same amount as the increase in government spending, then fiscal policy would be completely ineffective.

While few would question the logic involved, there is much disagreement as to the size of the crowding-out effect. For example, some economists argue that there will be little crowding-out when there is considerable unemployment. The rationale for this contention is that, given a recession, the stimulus provided by an increase in government spending can be expected to improve business profit expectations which are an important determinant of the location of the investment-demand curve (Figure 12-6). If the investment-demand curve does shift rightward, then investment spending need not fall—it may even increase—even though interest rates are higher.

Another relevant consideration concerns monetary policy, which we discuss in detail in later chapters. The monetary authorities may increase the supply of money by just enough to offset the deficit-caused increase in the demand for money. In this case the equilibrium interest rate would not change and the crowding-out effect would be zero. In the 1980s the monetary authorities restrained the growth of the money supply and, consequently, the crowding-out effects of the large deficits of the 1980s may have been quite large. In comparison, in the 1960s the monetary authorities were strongly disposed to stabilize interest rates. Hence, they would tend to increase the money supply in response to higher interest rates occasioned by government borrowing. As a result, crowding-out was probably inconsequential.

---

[8]Some interest-sensitive consumption spending—for example, automobile purchases—may also be crowded out.

AGGREGATE SUPPLY AND INFLATION

Our discussion thus far has been entirely demand-oriented. Let us now consider a supply-side complication. Tersely stated, the point is simply that, given an upsloping aggregate supply curve, some portion of the potential effect of an expansionary fiscal policy upon real output and employment may be dissipated in the form of inflation. The essence of this point was stressed in Figure 13-9 and is not new to us.

GRAPHIC PORTRAYAL: CROWDING-OUT AND INFLATION

It may be helpful at this juncture to portray fiscal policy and its complications in the context of the aggregate demand–aggregate supply model. Let us suppose in Figure 14-6a that there exists a noninflationary full-employment level of NNP which is at $490 billion. Note that our aggregate supply curve eliminates the intermediate range so that up to full employment the price level is perfectly constant, but after full employment is achieved the classical range prevails so that any further increase in aggregate demand would be purely inflationary.

We begin with aggregate demand at AD₁ which gives us an unemployment equilibrium at $470 billion. This, you may recall, was the private sector equilibrium of Table 13-1. Assume now that an expansionary fiscal policy is undertaken which shifts the aggregate demand curve rightward by $20 billion to AD₂ and the economy therefore achieves full employment without inflation at $490 billion. We know from our previous discussion of discretionary fiscal policy in terms of Tables 14-1 and 14-2 and Figure 14-3 that the expansionary effect of the balanced-budget multiplier when G and T are each $20 billion would be sufficient to

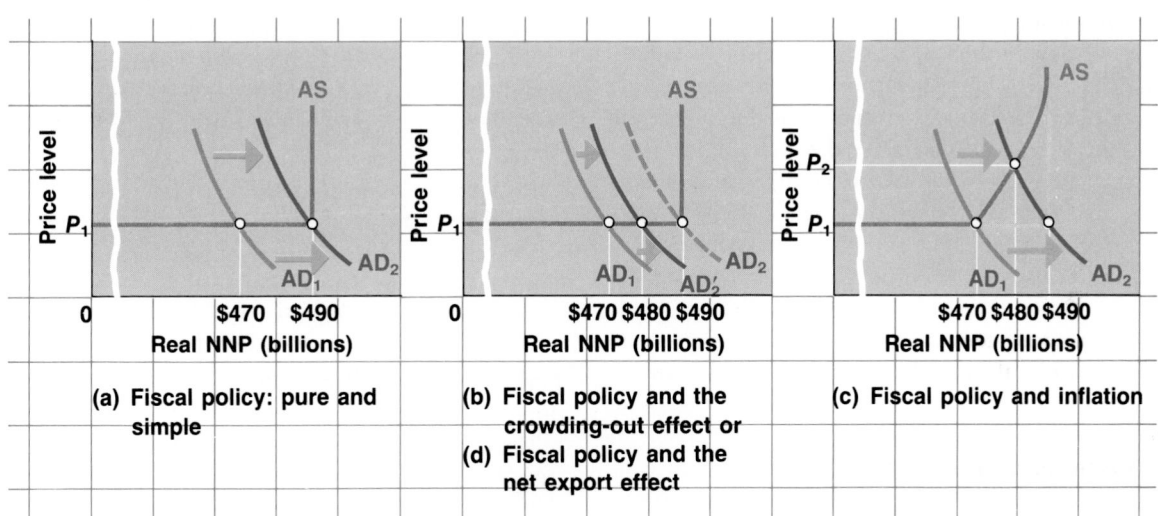

FIGURE 14-6

Fiscal policy: the effects of crowding-out, the net export effect, and inflation

Given a simplified aggregate supply curve, we observe in (a) that fiscal policy is uncomplicated and works at full strength. In (b) it is assumed that some amount of private investment is crowded out by the expansionary fiscal policy so that fiscal policy is weakened. In (c) a more realistic aggregate supply curve reminds us that, when the economy is close to full employment, a part of the impact of an expansionary fiscal policy will be reflected in inflation rather than in increases in real output and employment. Finally, in (d)—which is the same graph as (b)— we assume that fiscal policy increases the interest rate, which attracts foreign financial capital to the United States. The dollar therefore appreciates and our net exports fall, thus weakening the fiscal policy.

achieve this $20 billion increase in equilibrium NNP. You should verify that an increase in G of $5 billion *or* a decrease in T of $6\frac{2}{3}$ billion would bring about the same expansionary effect. In any event, with no offsetting or complicating factors at work this "pure and simple" expansionary fiscal policy moves the economy from recession to full employment.

In Figure 14-6b we muddy the waters by adding the crowding-out effect. While fiscal policy is expansionary and designed to shift aggregate demand from AD_1 to AD_2, some investment may be crowded out so that aggregate demand ends up at AD_2'. Hence, equilibrium NNP increases to only, say, $480 rather than the desired $490 billion. The point is that the crowding-out effect may weaken fiscal policy by some unknown amount.

In Figure 14-6c we switch to a more realistic aggregate supply curve which includes an intermediate range. We ignore the crowding-out effect so that the expansionary fiscal policy is successful in shifting aggregate demand from AD_1 to AD_2. If the aggregate supply curve was shaped as in Figure 14-6a and b, full employment would now be realized at $490 billion and the price level would remain at P_1. But we find that the presence of the upsloping intermediate range on the aggregate supply curve causes a part of the increase in aggregate demand to be dissipated in higher prices with the result that the increase in real NNP is diminished. Specifically, the price level rises from P_1 to P_2 and real national output increases to only $480 billion.

In terms of our aggregate expenditures model (Figures 14-1 and 14-2) we are saying that an expansionary fiscal policy may not increase aggregate expenditures by the full amount of the increase in government expenditures (or the increase in consumption associated with the reduction of a lump-sum tax). If the price level rises—as it does when the aggregate supply curve is upsloping—the increase in government expenditures will be partially offset by declines in consumption, investment, and net exports expenditures. These declines result respectively from the wealth, interest-rate, and foreign purchases effects created by the higher domestic price level. That is, the aggregate demand curve in Figure 14-6c shifts from AD_1 to AD_2, but we move upward along AD_2 to the new equilibrium

price level and level of real national output because of the upsloping aggregate supply curve. Demand-side fiscal policy does not escape the realities imposed by the aggregate supply curve.

FISCAL POLICY IN THE OPEN ECONOMY

Our discussion thus far has been confined to the complications of fiscal policy associated with the closed economy. Additional complications arise when we allow for the fact that our economy is a component of the broader world economy.

Shocks originating from abroad We know from previous discussion that events and policies abroad that affect our net exports have an impact on our economy. Stated in the terms of the present context, we are susceptible to unforeseen international *aggregate demand shocks* which can alter our NNP and render our fiscal actions inappropriate. Example: Suppose we are experiencing a recession and have changed government expenditures and taxes to levels sufficient to bolster aggregate demand and NNP without igniting inflation (as from AD_1 to AD_2 in Figure 14-6a). Now suppose that the economies of our major trading partners unexpectedly and abruptly begin to expand rapidly. Greater employment and rising incomes in those nations translate into more purchases of American goods. Our net exports rise, aggregate demand increases too rapidly, and we experience demand-pull inflation. Had we known in advance that our net exports would rise significantly, we would have enacted a less expansionary fiscal policy. The point is that our growing participation in the world economy brings with it the *complications* of mutual interdependency as well as the *gains* from specialization and trade.

Net export effect An effect which we shall dub the **net export effect** works through international trade to reduce the effectiveness of fiscal policy. We concluded in our discussion of the crowding-out effect that an expansionary fiscal policy might boost interest rates, thus reducing *investment* and thereby weakening fiscal policy. Now we need to ascertain what effect such an increase in the interest rate might have on our *net exports*. Let us suppose that we invoke an expansionary fiscal policy

TABLE 14-3 **Fiscal policy and the net export effect**

(1) **Expansionary fiscal policy**	(2) **Contractionary fiscal policy**
Problem: Recession, slow growth ↓	Problem: Inflation ↓
Expansionary fiscal policy ↓	Contractionary fiscal policy ↓
Higher domestic interest rate ↓	Lower domestic interest rate ↓
Increased foreign demand for dollars ↓	Decreased foreign demand for dollars ↓
Dollar appreciates ↓	Dollar depreciates ↓
Net exports decline (aggregate demand decreases, partially offsetting the expansionary fiscal policy)	Net exports increase (aggregate demand increases, partially offsetting the contractionary fiscal policy)

which brings with it a higher interest rate. The higher interest rate will attract financial capital from abroad where interest rates presumably are unchanged. But foreign financial investors must acquire U.S. dollars before buying the desired American securities. We know that an increase in the demand for a commodity—in this case dollars—will raise its price. So the price of dollars will rise in terms of foreign currencies; or said differently, the dollar will appreciate. What will be the impact of this dollar appreciation on our net exports? Because more units of foreign currencies are needed to buy our goods, foreigners will see our exports as being more expensive; hence, our exports will decline. Conversely, Americans, who can now exchange their dollars for more units of foreign currencies, will buy more imports. The necessary consequence of this complex scenario is that net export expenditures in the United States will diminish and our expansionary fiscal policy will be partially negated.

A return visit to our aggregate demand and supply analysis in Figure 14-6b, now labeled d, will help clarify this point. An expansionary fiscal policy designed to increase aggregate demand from AD_1 to AD_2 may hike the domestic interest rate and ultimately reduce our net exports through the process just described. The decline in the net export component of aggregate demand will partially offset the expansionary fiscal policy. The aggregate demand curve will shift rightward from AD_1 to AD_2', *not* to AD_2, and equilibrium NNP will increase from $470 to $480, *not* to $490. Hence, the net export effect of fiscal policy joins the aforementioned factors of timing, political problems, crowding out, and inflation in complicating the "management" of aggregate demand.

Table 14-3 summarizes the net export effect resulting from fiscal policy. Specifically, column 1 reviews the analysis which we have just discussed (Figure 14-6d). But keep in mind that the net export effect works in both directions. By reducing the domestic interest rate, a *contractionary* fiscal policy tends to *increase* net exports. In this regard, you are urged to follow through the analysis in column 2 of Table 14-3 and relate it to the aggregate demand–aggregate supply model.

SUPPLY-SIDE FISCAL POLICY

Our analysis thus far suggests that the sole impact of fiscal policy is upon the demand side, that is, upon aggregate expenditures and aggregate demand. Economists have come to recognize that fiscal policy—especially tax changes—*may* alter aggregate supply and thereby affect the price level–real output outcomes of a change in fiscal policy.

Suppose in Figure 14-7 that aggregate demand and aggregate supply are presently at AD_1 and AS_1 so that the equilibrium level of real NNP is Q_1 and the price level is P_1. Assume further that it is felt that the level of unemployment associated with Q_1 is too high and that an expansionary fiscal policy is therefore invoked in the form of a tax cut. We know that the demand-side effect is to increase aggregate demand from AD_1 to, say, AD_2. This shift increases real NNP to Q_2, but also boosts the price level to P_2.

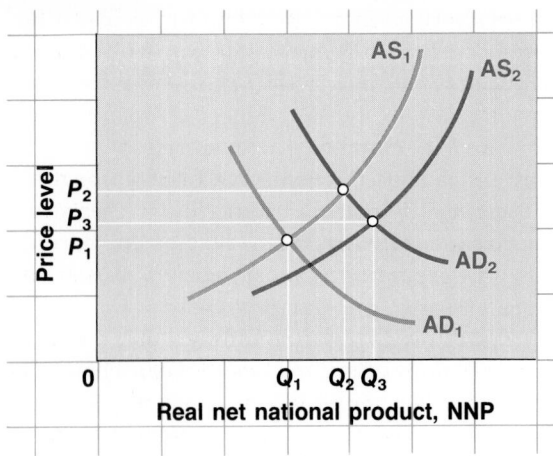

FIGURE 14-7

Supply-side effects of fiscal policy

The traditional view is that tax cuts will increase aggregate demand as from AD_1 to AD_2, thereby increasing both real national output (Q_1 to Q_2) and the price level (P_1 to P_2). If the tax reductions induce favorable supply-side effects, aggregate supply will shift rightward as from AS_1 to AS_2. This allows the economy to realize an even larger output (Q_3 as compared to Q_2) and a lower price level (P_3 as compared to P_2).

Question: How might tax cuts affect aggregate supply? Some economists—appropriately labeled supply-side economists—feel strongly that tax reductions will shift the aggregate supply curve significantly to the right. By what means? Lower taxes will increase disposable incomes and thus increase household saving. Similarly, tax reductions on businesses will increase the profitability of investment. In brief, lower taxes will increase the volumes of both saving and investment, thereby increasing the rate of capital accumulation. Stated differently, the size of our "national factory"—our productive capacity—will grow more rapidly than otherwise. Furthermore, lower personal income tax rates also increase after-tax wages—that is, the price paid for work—and thereby stimulate work incentives. Many of those not already in the labor force will offer their services now that after-tax wages are higher. Those already in the labor force will want to work longer hours and take fewer vacations. Lower tax rates are also a prod to risk takers. Individuals and businesses will be more willing

LAST WORD

The leading indicators

One tool policy makers use to forecast the future direction of real GNP is a monthly index of a group of variables which in the past has provided advance notice of changes in GNP.

"Index of Leading Indicators Falls for Third Month—Recession Feared"; "Index of Leading Indicators Surges Again"; "Decline in Stock Market Drags Down Index of Leading Indicators." Headlines such as these appear regularly in the business sections of our major newspapers. The focus of the articles are the Commerce Department's weighted average—or composite index—of eleven economic variables which has historically reached its peak or trough in advance of the corresponding turns in the business cycle. Hence, changes in the index of leading indicators provide a clue to the future direction of the economy and thus may shorten the length of the "recognition lag" associated with the implementation of macroeconomic policy.

Let us examine the eleven components of the index of leading indicators in terms of a predicted *decline* in GNP, keeping in mind that the opposite changes forecast a *rise* in GNP.

1 Average work week Decreases in the length of the average work week of production workers in manufacturing foretell declines in future manufacturing output and GNP.

to risk their energies and financial capital on new production methods and new products when lower tax rates promise them a larger potential after-tax reward. In short, through all these avenues, lower taxes will shift aggregate supply to the right as from AS_1 to AS_2 in Figure 14-7, thereby reducing inflation and further increasing real NNP. This supply-side rationale for increasing aggregate sup-

2 Initial claims for unemployment insurance Higher first-time claims for unemployment insurance are associated with falling employment and subsequently sagging production.

3 New orders for consumer goods A slump in the number of orders received by manufacturers for consumer goods portends reduced future production—that is, a decline in GNP.

4 Stock market prices Declines in stock prices often are reflections of expected declines in corporate sales and profits. Furthermore, lower stock prices diminish consumer wealth, leading consumers to cut back on their spending. Lower stock market values also make it less attractive for firms to issue new shares of stock as a way to raise funds for investment. Hence, declines in stock prices can bring forth declines in aggregate demand and GNP.

5 Contracts and orders for new plant and equipment A drop in orders for capital equipment and other investment goods implies reduced future aggregate demand and national output.

6 Building permits for houses Decreases in the number of building permits taken out for new homes augur future declines in investment and therefore the distinct possibility that GNP will fall.

7 Vendor performance Somewhat ironically, better performance by sellers of inputs in supplying buyers in a timely fashion indicates slackening business demand and potentially falling GNP.

8 Change in unfilled orders of durable goods Decreases in the dollar amounts of unfilled orders of durable manufactured goods imply falling aggregate demand and therefore ensuing declines in GNP.

9 Change in sensitive raw material prices Declines in certain sensitive raw material prices often precede declines in national output.

10 The money supply Decreases in the money supply are associated with falling GNP. The components of the money supply and its role in the macro economy are the subjects of Chapters 15 through 18.

11 Index of consumer expectations Declines in consumer confidence indicated by this index compiled by the University of Michigan's Survey Research Center foreshadow curtailed consumption expenditures and eventual declines in national output.

It should be emphasized that none of these factors *alone* consistently predicts the future course of the economy. It is not unusual in any month, for example, for one or two of the indicators to be decreasing while the other indicators are increasing. Rather, changes in the *weighted average*—or composite index—of the eleven components are what in the past have provided advance notice of a change in the direction of GNP. The rule of thumb is that three successive monthly declines or increases in the index indicate the economy will soon turn in that same direction.

Although the composite index has correctly signaled business fluctuations on numerous occasions, it has not been an infallible sentinel. At times the index has provided false warnings of recessions which have never happened. In other instances, recessions have so closely followed the downturn in the index that policy makers have not had sufficient time to make use of the "early" warning. Moreover, changing structural features of the economy upon occasion have rendered the existing index obsolete and have necessitated its revision.

Given these caveats, the index of leading indicators can best be thought of as a useful but not totally reliable signaling device which authorities must employ with considerable caution in formulating macroeconomic policy.

---

ply was the basis for the Reagan administration tax cuts in the early 1980s.

Supply-siders also contend that lower tax *rates* need not result in lower tax *revenues*. In fact, lower tax rates that cause a substantial expansion of national output and income can be expected to generate increases in tax revenues. This enlarged tax base will enhance total tax revenues even though tax rates are lower. Thus, while the Keynesian view is that a reduction in tax rates will reduce tax revenues and increase budget deficits, the supply-side view is that tax rate reductions can be structured so that they increase tax revenues and reduce deficits.

Most economists are cautious concerning the supply-side effects of tax cuts. First, they feel that the hoped-for positive effects of a tax reduction upon incentives to work, save and invest, and bear risks are not nearly as strong as supply-siders believe. Second, any rightward shifts of the aggregate supply curve are likely to be realized over an extended period of time, while the demand-side impact will be more immediate. The controversies surrounding supply-side economics will resurface in Chapter 19.

CHAPTER SUMMARY

1 Government responsibility for achieving and maintaining full employment is set forth in the Employment Act of 1946. The Council of Economic Advisers (CEA) was established to advise the President on policies appropriate to fulfilling the goals of the act. The Humphrey-Hawkins Act of 1978 contains specific inflation and unemployment rate objectives.

2 Increases in government spending expand, and decreases contract, the equilibrium NNP. Conversely, increases in taxes reduce, and decreases expand, the equilibrium NNP. Appropriate fiscal policy therefore calls for increases in government spending and decreases in taxes—that is, for a budget deficit—to correct for unemployment. Decreases in government spending and increases in taxes—that is, a budget surplus—are appropriate fiscal policy for correcting demand-pull inflation.

3 The balanced-budget multiplier indicates that equal increases in government spending and taxation will increase the equilibrium NNP by the amount of the increase in government expenditures and taxes.

4 Built-in stability refers to the fact that net tax revenues vary directly with the level of NNP. Therefore, during a recession, the public budget automatically tends toward a stabilizing deficit; conversely, during expansion, the budget automatically tends toward an anti-inflationary surplus. Built-in stability ameliorates, but does not correct, undesired changes in the NNP.

5 The full-employment budget indicates what the Federal budgetary surplus or deficit would be *if* the economy operated at full employment throughout the year. The full-employment budget is a more meaningful indicator of the government's fiscal posture than is its actual budgetary surplus or deficit.

6 The enactment and application of appropriate fiscal policy are subject to certain problems and questions. Some of the most important are these: **a** Can the enactment and application of fiscal policy be better timed so as to maximize its effectiveness in heading off economic fluctuations? **b** Can the economy rely upon Congress to enact appropriate fiscal policy? **c** An expansionary fiscal policy may be weakened if it crowds out some private investment spending. **d** Some of the effect of an expansionary fiscal policy may be dissipated in inflation. **e** Fiscal policy may be rendered ineffective or inappropriate by unforeseen events occurring within the world economy. Also, fiscal policy may precipitate changes in exchange rates which weaken its effects. **f** Supply-side economists contend that Keynesian fiscal policy fails to consider the effects of tax changes upon aggregate supply.

TERMS AND CONCEPTS

Employment Act of 1946	**built-in stabilizers**
Council of Economic Advisers	**actual and full-employment budgets**
Humphrey-Hawkins Act of 1978	**cyclical and structural deficits**
discretionary fiscal policy	**political business cycle**
lump-sum tax	**crowding-out effect**
balanced-budget multiplier	**net export effect**
expansionary and contractionary fiscal policy	

QUESTION AND STUDY SUGGESTIONS

1 Explain graphically the determination of equilibrium NNP through both the aggregate expenditures–national output approach and the leakages-injections approach for the private sector. Now add government spending and taxation, showing the impact of each upon the equilibrium NNP. Explain how discretionary fiscal policy can be used to alleviate inflation and offset a recession.

2 Refer to the tabular data for question 2 at the end of Chapter 13. Now, assuming investment is $16 billion, incorporate government into the table by assuming that it plans to tax and spend $20 billion at each possible level of NNP. Assume net exports are zero, all taxes are personal taxes, and that government spending does not entail shifts in the consumption and investment schedules. Explain the changes in the equilibrium NNP which the addition of government entails.

3 What is the balanced-budget multiplier? Demonstrate the balanced-budget multiplier in terms of your answer to question 2. Explain: "Equal increases in government spending and tax revenues of n dollars will increase the equilibrium NNP by n dollars." Does this hold true regardless of the size of the MPS?

4 Explain how both "conservative" and "liberal" economists might support an activist fiscal policy.

5 Explain the functioning of the built-in stabilizers. Can you suggest ways to strengthen built-in stability?

6 Define the "full-employment budget" and explain its significance. How does it differ from the "actual budget"? What is the difference between a cyclical deficit and a structural deficit?

7 Briefly state and evaluate the major problems encountered in enacting and applying fiscal policy. Explain the notion of a political business cycle. What is the crowding-out effect and why is it relevant to fiscal policy? In what respect is the net export effect similar to the crowding-out effect?

8 Comment upon the following statements:
  a "When faced with inflation, Keynesians recommend higher taxes to restrain demand, while supply-side economists recommend lower taxes to increase aggregate supply."
  b "Keynesians assume demand creates its own supply; supply-siders argue that supply creates its own demand."

9 Demonstrate graphically the potential effects of a tax *increase* upon aggregate demand and aggregate supply.

10 Using Figure 14-4 as a basis for your response, explain the stabilizing or destabilizing effects of fiscal policy if a constitutional amendment requiring an annually balanced budget were passed.

11 Use Figure 14-4 to explain why a deficit increase which causes the economy to expand might be partly self-liquidating. In requesting a tax cut in the early 1960s President Kennedy said, "It is a paradoxical truth that tax rates are too high today and tax revenues are too low and the soundest way to raise tax revenues in the long run is to cut tax rates now." Was his rationale correct?

12 *Advanced analysis:* Assume that, in the absence of any taxes, the consumption schedule for an economy is as shown at the top of the next column:
  a Graph this consumption schedule and note the size of the MPC.
  b Assume now a lump-sum (regressive) tax system is imposed in such a way that the government collects

NNP, billions	Consumption, billions
$100	$120
200	200
300	280
400	360
500	440
600	520
700	600

$10 billion in taxes at all levels of NNP. Calculate the tax rate at each level of NNP. Graph the resulting consumption schedule and compare the MPC and the multiplier with that of the pretax consumption schedule.
  c Now suppose a proportional tax system with a 10 percent tax rate is imposed instead of the regressive system. Calculate the new consumption schedule, graph it, and note the MPC and the multiplier.
  d Finally, impose a progressive tax system such that the tax rate is zero percent when NNP is $100, 5 percent at $200, 10 percent at $300, 15 percent at $400, and so forth. Determine and graph the new consumption schedule, noting the effect of this tax system on the MPC and the multiplier.
  e Explain why the proportional and progressive tax systems contribute to greater economic stability, while the regressive system does not. Demonstrate graphically.

13 *Advanced analysis:* We can add the public sector to the private economy model of question 12 at the end of Chapter 13 as follows. Assume $G = G_0 = 28$ and $T = T_0 = 30$. Because of the presence of taxes, the consumption schedule, $C = 50 + 0.8Y$, must be modified to read $C_a = 50 + 0.8(Y - T)$, where the term $(Y - T)$ is disposable (after-tax) income. Assuming all taxes are on personal income, investment remains $I_n = I_{n0} = 30$. Net exports are again independent of the level of income, that is, $X_n = X_{n0} = 10$. Using the equilibrium condition $Y = C_a + I_n + X_n + G$, determine the equilibrium level of income. Explain why the addition of the public budget with a slight surplus *increases* the equilibrium income. Now substitute $T = 0.2Y$ for $T = T_0 = 30$, and solve again for the level of income.

PART 3

FEDERAL RESERVE BANKS

NEAR-MONIES

MONEY MARKET

DEMAND DEPOSIT

Money, Banking, and Monetary Policy

DISCOUNT RATE

MORAL SUASION

RESERVE RATIO

MONETARY POLICY

EXCESS RESERVES

OPEN-MARKET OPERATIONS

LEAKAGES

VAULT CASH

CHAPTER 15

Money and banking

Money—one of our truly great inventions—constitutes a most fascinating aspect of economic science.

"Money bewitches people. They fret for it, and they sweat for it. They devise most ingenious ways to get it, and most ingenuous ways to get rid of it. Money is the only commodity that is good for nothing but to be gotten rid of. It will not feed you, clothe you, shelter you, or amuse you unless you spend it or invest it. It imparts value only in parting. People will do almost anything for money, and money will do almost anything for people. Money is a captivating, circulating, masquerading puzzle."[1]

Money is also one of the most crucial elements of economic science. It is much more than a passive component of the economic system—a mere tool for facilitating the economy's operation. When operating properly, the monetary system is the lifeblood of the circular flows of income and expenditure which typify all economies. A well-behaved money system is conducive to both full production and full employment. Conversely, a malfunctioning monetary system can make major contributions to severe fluctuations in the economy's levels of output, employment, and prices, *and* can distort the allocation of resources.

In this chapter we are concerned with the nature and functions of money and the basic institutions of the American banking system. Chapter 16 looks into the methods by which individual commercial banks and the banking system as a whole can vary the money supply. In Chapter 17 we discuss how the central banks of the economy attempt to regulate the supply of money so as to promote full employment and price level stability. Finally, Chapter 18 focuses upon *monetarism*—an alternative to the Keynesian macroeconomics of Chapters 12 through 14. Monetarism contends that the money supply is *the* key determinant of output, employment, and the price level.

The structure of the present chapter is as follows. We begin with a review of the functions of money. Next, attention shifts to the supply of money as we pose the rather complicated question: What constitutes money in our economy? Third, we consider what "backs" the supply of money in the United States. Fourth, the demand for money is explained. Fifth, we combine the supply of money and the demand for money to portray and explain the market for money. Finally, the institutional structure of the American financial system will be considered.

The functions of money

What is money? Money is what money does. Anything that performs the functions of money is money. There are three functions of money:

1 Medium of exchange First and foremost, money is a **medium of exchange;** money is usable in buying and selling goods and services. A worker in a bagel bakery does not want to be paid, say, 200 bagels per week. Nor does the bagel bakery wish to receive, say, fresh fish for its bagels. On the other hand, money is readily acceptable as a means of payment. It is a convenient social invention which allows resource suppliers and producers to be paid with a "good" (money) which can be used to buy any one of the full range of goods and services

---

[1] Federal Reserve Bank of Philadelphia, "Creeping Inflation," *Business Review,* August 1957, p. 3.

available in the marketplace. As a medium of exchange, money allows society to escape the complications of barter. And by providing a convenient way of exchanging goods, money allows society to gain the advantages of geographic and human specialization (see Chapter 3, particularly Figure 3-1).

2 Measure of value Money is also a **measure of value.** Society finds it convenient to use the monetary unit as a yardstick for measuring the relative worth of heterogeneous goods and resources. Just as we measure distance in miles or kilometers, we gauge the value of goods and services in terms of dollars. This has distinct advantages. With a money system, we need not state the price of each product in terms of all other products for which it might possibly be exchanged; we need not state the price of cows in terms of corn, crayons, cigars, Chevrolets, croissants, or some other product. This use of money as a common denominator means that the price of each product need be stated *only* in terms of the monetary unit. This use of money permits transactors to readily compare the relative worth of various commodities and resources. Such comparisons facilitate rational decision making. Recall from Chapter 9 the necessity of using money as a measure of value in calculating the size of the GNP. Money is also used as a measure of value for transactions involving future payments. Debt obligations of all kinds are measured in terms of money.

3 Store of value Finally, money serves as a **store of value.** Because money is the most liquid—that is, the most spendable—of all assets, it is a very convenient form in which to store wealth. Most methods of holding money do not yield monetary returns such as one gets by storing wealth in the form of real assets (property) or paper assets (stocks, bonds, and so forth). However, money does have the advantage of being immediately usable by a firm or a household in meeting any and all financial obligations.

The supply of money

Let us now consider the supply of money. Basically, anything which is generally acceptable as a

medium of exchange *is* money. Historically, such diverse items as whales' teeth, elephant tail bristles, circular stones, nails, slaves (yes, human beings), cattle, beer, cigarettes, and pieces of metal have functioned as media of exchange. As we shall see, in our economy the debts of governments and of commercial banks and other financial institutions are currently employed as money.

DEFINING MONEY: *M1*

Neither economists nor public officials are in agreement as to what specific items constitute the economy's money supply. Narrowly defined—and designated as *M1*—the money supply is composed of two items:

1 Currency, that is, coins and paper money in circulation
2 All checkable deposits, that is, deposits in commercial banks and various "thrift" or savings institutions upon which checks can be drawn.[2]

Coins and paper money are debts of government and governmental agencies. Checking accounts represent debts of the commercial bank or savings institution. Let us comment briefly on the components of the *M1* money supply (Table 15-1).

Currency: coins + paper money Ranging from copper pennies to silver dollars, coins constitute the "small change" of our money supply. Coins are a very small portion of our total money supply. Currently, coins constitute only 2 or 3 percent of the total $784 billion *M1* money supply. Coins are essentially "convenience money" in that they permit us to make all kinds of very small purchases.

It is notable that all coins in circulation in the United States are **token money.** This simply means that the **intrinsic value**—that is, the value of the bullion (metal) contained in the coin itself—is less than the face value of the coin. This is purposely the case so as to avoid the melting down of token money for profitable sales as bullion. If our

[2] In the ensuing discussion of the definitions of money several of the quantitatively less significant components are not explicitly discussed in order to sidestep a maze of details. Reference to the statistical appendix of any recent *Federal Reserve Bulletin* will provide the reader with more comprehensive definitions.

TABLE 15-1 **Alternative money definitions for the United States:
M1, M2, and M3**

Money definition or concept	Absolute amount (in billions)	Percentage of concept		
		M1	M2	M3
Currency (coins and paper money)	$ 210	27%	7%	5%
plus Checkable deposits	574	73	19	15
equals M1	$ 784	100%		
plus Noncheckable savings deposits	434		14	11
plus Small time deposits	1836*		60	47
equals M2	$3054		100%	
plus Large time deposits	835*			22
equals M3	$3889			100%

* These figures include other quantitatively smaller components.

Source: *Federal Reserve Bulletin,* February 1989, p. A13. Data are for November 1988.

50-cent pieces each contained, say, 75 cents' worth of silver bullion, it would be highly profitable to melt these coins for sale as bullion. Despite the illegality of such a procedure, 50-cent pieces would tend to disappear from circulation. This is one of the potential defects of commodity money: Its worth as a commodity may come to exceed its worth as money, causing it to cease functioning as a medium of exchange.

Much more quantitatively significant than coins, paper money constitutes about 25 percent of the economy's *M*1 money supply. All of this $200 or so billion of paper currency is in the form of **Federal Reserve Notes,** that is, notes which have been issued by the Federal Reserve Banks with the authorization of Congress. A quick glance at any currency in your wallet will reveal the words "Federal Reserve Note" at the top of the face of the bill and the Reserve Bank of issue in the circle to the left.

Checkable deposits The safety and convenience of using checks have made checking accounts the most important type of money in the United States. After all, you would not think of stuffing, say, $4896.47 in bills and coins in an envelope and dropping it in a mailbox to pay a debt; but to write

and mail a check for a large sum is commonplace. A check must be endorsed (signed on the reverse side) by the person cashing it; the drawer of the check subsequently receives the canceled check as an endorsed receipt attesting to the fulfillment of the obligation. Similarly, because the writing of a check requires endorsement by the drawer, the theft or loss of your bankbook is not nearly so calamitous as if you lost an identical amount of currency. It is, furthermore, more convenient to write a check in many cases than it is to transport and count out a large sum of currency. For all these reasons, *checkbook money* has come to be the dominant form of money in our economy. In terms of dollar volume, about 90 percent of all transactions are carried out by the use of checks.

It might seem strange that checking accounts are a part of the money supply. But the reason for their inclusion is clear: Checks, which are nothing more than a means for transferring the ownership of deposits in banks and other financial institutions, are generally acceptable as a medium of exchange.[3] Furthermore, such deposits can be imme-

---

[3] As a stop at most gas stations will verify, checks are somewhat less generally acceptable as a medium of exchange than is currency!

diately converted into paper money and coins on demand; checks drawn upon these deposits are for all practical purposes the equivalent of currency.

To summarize:

Money, $M1$ = currency + checkable deposits

Evolution of checkable deposits   Table 15-1 shows that **checkable deposits** are clearly the most important component of the $M1$ money supply. It is therefore of some importance to recognize that there exists a spectrum of checkable deposits and to understand how this variety evolved.

By glancing ahead at Figure 15-4 we find that there are many financial institutions which offer checkable deposits in the United States. Commercial banks are perhaps the mainstays of the system. Commercial banks accept the deposits of households and businesses and in turn use these financial resources to extend a wide variety of loans. Commercial bank loans provide short-term working capital to businesses and farmers, finance consumer purchases of automobiles and other durable goods, and so on. The commercial banks are supplemented by a variety of more specialized financial institutions—savings and loan associations (S&Ls), mutual savings banks, and credit unions—which are collectively designated as **thrift** or **savings institutions** or, more simply, "thrifts." **Savings and loan associations** and **mutual savings banks** marshall the savings of households and businesses which are then used, among other things, to finance housing mortgages. **Credit unions** accept the deposits of "members"—usually a group of individuals who work for the same company—and lend these funds to finance installment purchases.

The point to be made is that some twenty years ago only commercial banks provided checkable deposits. Then in the 1970s the various thrift institutions developed new kinds of checkable deposits. For example, the S&Ls created what are called **NOW (negotiable order of withdrawal) accounts.** These accounts are in essence checking accounts based upon savings deposits in the S&Ls. Similarly, credit unions developed **share draft accounts** which are checkable accounts based upon deposits in the credit union. The NOW and share draft accounts were innovative means by which the S&Ls and credit unions could compete for the checking account business of the commercial banks. In fact, the NOW and share draft accounts were highly attractive to depositors because it was permissable to pay interest on such accounts, while commercial banks were prohibited by law from paying interest on their checking (demand deposit) accounts. Not to be outdone, the commercial banks retaliated by developing **ATS (automatic transfer service accounts).** Under this arrangement a bank would automatically transfer funds from your interest-bearing savings account to your checking or demand deposit account as required to replenish the latter account. Thus ATS permitted banks to "get around" the legal prohibition on paying interest on checking accounts. In 1980, the **Depository Institutions Deregulation and Monetary Control Act** authorized all depository institutions to provide checkable deposits and permitted commercial banks to pay interest on the checking accounts of individuals. In 1986, all interest rate ceilings and minimum balance requirements on these accounts were eliminated. The result of all this is that the earlier distinction between commercial bank checking accounts (demand deposits) and the savings deposits of thrift institutions has been virtually erased. While a decade and a half ago it was appropriate to define money as "currency plus the demand deposits of commercial banks," that definition must now read "currency plus all checkable deposits." Checkable deposits include not only the demand deposits (checking accounts) of commercial banks, but also NOW and ATS accounts and share drafts.

Qualification   A technical qualification of our definition of money must be added: Currency and checkable deposits owned by government (the Treasury) and by the Federal Reserve Banks, commercial banks, or other financial institutions are excluded. This exclusion is partly to avoid overstating the money supply and partly because money in the possession of households and businesses—that is, "in circulation"—is more relevant to the level of spending in the economy.[4]

NEAR-MONIES: *M2* AND *M3*

Near-monies are certain highly liquid financial assets such as noncheckable savings accounts, time deposits, and short-term government securities which, although they do not directly function as a medium of exchange, can be readily and without risk of financial loss converted into currency or checkable deposits. Thus, upon demand you may withdraw currency from a **noncheckable savings account** at a commercial bank or thrift institution. Or, alternatively, you may request that funds be transferred from a noncheckable savings account to a checkable account. As the term implies, **time deposits** only become available to a depositor at maturity. For example, a 90-day or 6-month time deposit is only available without penalty when the designated period expires. Although time deposits are somewhat less liquid than noncheckable savings accounts, they can be taken as currency or shifted into checkable accounts when they mature. Thus our monetary authorities offer a second and broader definition of money:

$$\text{Money, } M2 = \begin{array}{l} M1 + \text{noncheckable savings} \\ \text{deposits} + \text{small (less than} \\ \$100,000) \text{ time deposits} \end{array}$$

In other words, **M2** is comprised of the medium of exchange items (currency and checkable deposits) which comprise $M1$ plus other items such as noncheckable savings deposits and small time deposits which can be quite quickly and without loss converted into currency and checkable deposits. Table 15-1 shows that the addition of noncheckable savings deposits and small time deposits yields an $M2$ money supply of $3054 billion as compared to an $M1$ figure of $784 billion.

[4] A paper dollar in the hands of John Doe obviously constitutes just $1 of the money supply. But, if we were to count dollars held by banks as a part of the money supply, the same $1 would count for $2 when deposited in a bank. It would count for a $1 demand deposit owned by Doe and also for $1 worth of currency resting in the bank's vault. This problem of double counting can be avoided by excluding currency resting in banks (and currency redeposited in the Federal Reserve Banks or other commercial banks) in determining the total money supply. The exclusion of currency held by, and demand deposits owned by, government is somewhat more arbitrary. The major reason for this exclusion is that it permits us better to gauge the money supply and rate of spending which occur in the private sector of the economy apart from spending initiated by government policy.

A third "official" definition, **M3,** recognizes that large ($100,000 or more) time deposits—which are usually owned by businesses in the form of certificates of deposit—are also easily convertible into checkable deposits. In fact, there is a going market for these certificates and they can therefore be sold (liquidated) at any time, although perhaps at the risk of a loss. The addition of these large time deposits to $M2$ yields a still broader definition of money:

$$\text{Money, } M3 = \begin{array}{l} M2 + \text{large (}\$100,000 \text{ or} \\ \text{more) time deposits} \end{array}$$

Consulting Table 15-1 again, we find that the $M3$ money supply rises to $3889 billion.

Finally, there are still other slightly less liquid assets such as certain government securities (for example, Treasury bills and U.S. savings bonds) which can be easily converted into $M1$ money. The point to be stressed is that there exists a whole spectrum of assets which vary slightly from one another in terms of their liquidity or "moneyness."

Which definition shall we adopt? While each has its adherents, most economists prefer the simple $M1$ definition. The reason? It includes everything that is *directly* and *immediately* usable as a medium of exchange. If we expand the definition of money beyond currency and checkable deposits, there is simply no logical place to stop because all the additional items in $M2$, $M3$, and beyond are liquid in varying degrees. *We will adopt the narrow $M1$ definition of money in our ensuing discussion and analysis because its components are immediately spendable.* You should be aware, however, that the matter of defining money is controversial and unsettled.

NEAR-MONIES: IMPLICATIONS

Aside from inhibiting a tidy definition of money, the existence of near-monies is important for several related reasons.

I The fact that people have such highly liquid assets available affects their consuming-saving habits. Generally speaking, the greater the amount of financial wealth people have in the form of near-monies, the greater is their willingness to spend out of their money incomes.

2 The conversion of near-monies into money or vice versa can affect the stability of the economy. For example, during the prosperity-inflationary phase of the business cycle, a significant conversion of noncheckable deposits into checkable deposits or currency adds to the money supply and, if not off-set, could enhance inflationary pressures. Needless to say, such conversions can complicate the task of the monetary authorities in controlling the money supply and the level of economic activity.

3 The specific definition of money adopted is important for purposes of monetary policy. For example, the money supply as measured by $M1$ might be constant, while money defined as $M2$ might be increasing. Now, if the monetary authorities feel it is appropriate to have an expanding supply of money, acceptance of our narrow $M1$ definition would call for specific actions to increase currency and checkable deposits. But acceptance of the broader $M2$ definition would suggest that the desired expansion of the money supply is already taking place and that no specific policy action is required.

CREDIT CARDS

You may be curious as to why credit cards—Visa, MasterCard, American Express, and so forth—have been ignored in our discussion of how money is defined. After all, credit cards are a convenient means of making purchases. The answer is that credit cards are *not* really money, but rather a means of obtaining a short-term loan from the commercial bank or other financial institution which has issued the card. When you purchase, say, a box of cassettes with a credit card, the issuing bank will reimburse the store. Then later you reimburse the bank. You will pay an annual fee for the services provided and, if you choose to repay the bank in installments, you will pay a sizable interest charge. Credit cards, in short, are a means of deferring or postponing payment for a short period of time. Your purchase of cassettes is not actually complete until you have paid your credit-card bill. It is worth noting, however, that credit cards—and, indeed, all other forms of credit—allow individuals and businesses to "economize" in the use of money. Credit cards permit you to have less currency and checkable deposits on hand to negotiate

transactions. Stated differently, credit cards facilitate the synchronization of your expenditures and your receipt of income, thereby reducing the cash and checkable deposits you must hold.

What "backs" the money supply?

This is a slippery question; any reasonable complete answer is likely to be at odds with the preconceptions many of us hold with respect to money.

MONEY AS DEBT

The first point to recognize is that the major components of the money supply—paper money and checkable deposits—are debts, or promises to pay. *Paper money is the circulating debt of the Federal Reserve Banks. Checkable deposits are the debts of commercial banks and thrift institutions.*

Furthermore, paper currency and checkable deposits have no intrinsic value. A $5 bill is just a piece of paper, and a checkable deposit is merely a bookkeeping entry. And coins, we already know, have an intrinsic value less than their face value. Nor will government redeem the paper money you hold for anything tangible, such as gold. In effect, we have chosen to "manage" our money supply in seeking to provide the amount of money needed for that particular volume of business activity which one hopes will foster full employment, price level stability, and a healthy rate of economic growth. Most economists feel that such management of the money supply is more sensible than linking the money supply to gold or any other commodity whose supply might arbitrarily and capriciously change (see Chapter 17's Last Word). After all, a substantial increase in the nation's gold stock as the result of new gold discovery or a breakthrough in the extraction of gold from ore might increase the money supply far beyond that amount needed to transact a full-employment level of business activity and therefore cause inflation. Conversely, the historical decline in domestic gold production could reduce the domestic money supply to the point where economic activity was choked off and unemployment and a retarded growth rate resulted. The important point is that paper money cannot be converted into a fixed amount of gold or some other precious metal but is exchangeable only for other pieces of paper money. The government will swap one paper $5 bill for another bearing a different serial number. That is all you can get should you ask the government to redeem some of the paper money you hold. Similarly, check money cannot be exchanged for gold but only for paper money, which, as we have just seen, will not be redeemed by the government for anything tangible.

VALUE OF MONEY

If currency and checkable deposits have no intrinsic characteristics which give them value *and* if they are not backed by gold or other precious metals, then why are they money? What gives a $20 bill or a $100 checking account entry its value? A reasonably complete answer to these questions involves three points.

1 Acceptability Currency and checkable deposits are money for the simple reason they are accepted as money. By virtue of long-standing business practice, currency and checkable deposits perform the basic function of money; they are acceptable as a medium of exchange. Suppose you swap a $20 bill for a shirt or blouse at a clothing store. Why does the merchant accept this piece of paper in exchange for that product? The answer is curious: The merchant accepts paper money because he or she is confident that others will also be willing to accept it in exchange for goods and services. The merchant knows that the paper money can purchase the services of clerks, acquire products from wholesalers, pay the rent on the store, and so forth. Each of us accepts paper money in exchange because we have confidence that it will be exchangeable for real goods and services when we choose to spend it.

2 Legal tender Our confidence in the acceptability of paper money is partly a matter of law; currency has been designated as **legal tender** by government. This means that paper currency must be accepted in the payment of a debt or the creditor forfeits both the privilege of charging interest and the right to sue the debtor for nonpayment. Put more bluntly, the acceptability of paper dollars is bolstered by the fact that government says these dollars are money. The paper money in our economy is basically **fiat money;** it is money because the government says it is, not because of redeemability in terms of some precious metal. The general acceptability of currency is also bolstered by the willingness of government to accept it in the payment of taxes and other obligations due the government.

Lest we be overimpressed by the power of government, it should be noted that the fact that paper currency is generally accepted in exchange is decidedly more important than government's legal tender decree in making these pieces of paper function as money. Indeed, the government has *not* decreed checks (which are also fiat money) to be legal tender, but they nevertheless successfully perform the vast bulk of the economy's exchanges of goods, services, and resources. The fact that governmental agencies—the Federal Deposit Insurance Corporation (FDIC) and the Federal Savings and Loan Association Insurance Corporation (FSLIC)—insure the deposits of commercial banks and S&Ls respectively undoubtedly contributes to the willingness of individuals and businesses to use checkable deposits as a medium of exchange.

3 Relative scarcity At a more fundamental level, the value of money, like the economic value of anything else, is essentially a supply and demand phenomenon. That is, money derives its value from its scarcity relative to its usefulness. The usefulness of money, of course, lies in its unique capacity to be exchanged for goods and services, either now or in the future. The economy's demand for money thus depends upon its total dollar volume of transactions in any given time period plus the amount of money individuals and businesses want to hold for possible future transactions. Given a reasonably constant demand for money, the value or "purchasing power" of the monetary unit will be determined by the supply of money. Let us see why this is so.

MONEY AND PRICES

The real value or purchasing power of money is the amount of goods and services a unit of money will buy. It is apparent, furthermore, that the amount a

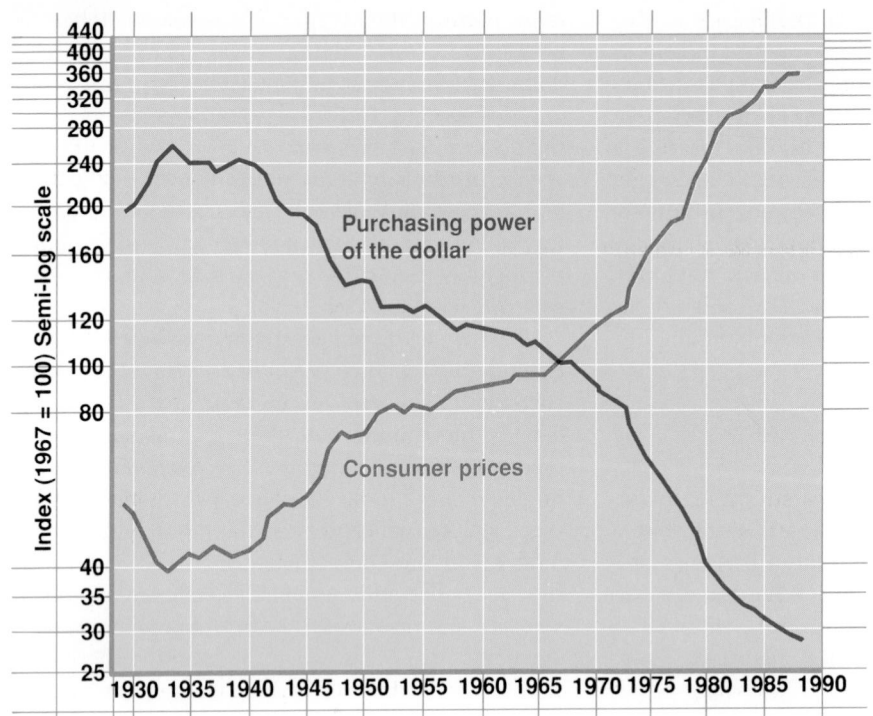

FIGURE 15-1

The price level and the value of money

A reciprocal or inverse relationship exists between the general price level and the purchasing power of the dollar. (This figure is called a "ratio" or "semilog chart" because equal vertical distances measure equal percentage changes rather than equal absolute changes.)

dollar will buy varies inversely with the price level; stated differently, a reciprocal relationship exists between the general price level and the value of the dollar. Figure 15-1 allows us to visualize this inverse relationship. When the consumer price index or "cost-of-living" index goes up, the purchasing power of the dollar necessarily goes down, and vice versa. Higher prices lower the value of the dollar because more dollars will be needed to command a given amount of goods and services. Conversely, lower prices increase the purchasing power of the dollar because you will need fewer dollars to obtain a given quantity of goods and services. If the price level doubles, the value of the dollar will decline by one-half, or 50 percent. If the price level falls by one-half, or 50 percent, the purchasing power of the dollar will double.[5] We noted in Chapter 10 several situations in which a nation's currency became worthless and unacceptable in exchange. With few exceptions these were circumstances where government issued so many pieces of paper currency that the value of each of these units of money was almost totally undermined. The infa-

mous post-World War I inflation in Germany is a notable example. In December of 1919 there were about 50 billion marks in circulation. Exactly four years later this figure had expanded to 496,585,345,900 billion marks! The result? The German mark in 1923 was worth an infinitesimal fraction of its 1919 value.[6] Inflation, you will recall, is frequently the consequence of society's spending

[5] The arithmetic of this relationship is slightly more complex than these examples suggest. If we let P equal the price level expressed as an index number and D equal the value of the dollar, then our reciprocal relationship is

$$D = \frac{1}{P}$$

If P equals 1.00, then D obviously is 1.00. But if the price level rises to 1.20, then D will be .83⅓. Hence, a 20 percent *increase* in the price level will cause a 16⅔ percent *decline* in the value of the dollar.

[6] Frank G. Graham, *Exchange, Prices and Production in Hyperinflation Germany, 1920–1923* (Princeton, N.J.: Princeton University Press, 1930), p. 13.

beyond its capacity to produce. Other things being equal, increases in the money supply tend to increase aggregate demand. Once full employment is reached and total output becomes virtually fixed, this added aggregate demand can only serve to make prices shoot upward. The shirt which sold for $20 in our earlier illustration may, after severe inflation, cost $200. This means that the dollar, which was formerly worth one-twentieth of a shirt, is now worth just one two-hundredths of a shirt. The dollar's value, or purchasing power, has been reduced to 10 percent of its former value by inflation.

How might inflation and the accompanying decreases in the value of the dollar affect the acceptability of paper dollars as money? Households and businesses are willing to accept paper currency as a medium of exchange so long as they know it can in turn be spent by them without any noticeable loss in its purchasing power. But, with spiraling inflation, this is not the case. Runaway inflation, such as Germany faced in the early 1920s, may significantly depreciate the value of money between the time of its receipt and its expenditure. Money will be "hot" money. It is as if the government were constantly taxing away the purchasing power of dollars. Rapid depreciation of the value of the dollar may cause it to cease functioning as a medium of exchange. Businesses and households may refuse to accept paper money in exchange because they do not want to bear the loss in its value which will occur while it is in their possession. (All this despite the fact that government says the paper currency is legal tender!) Without an acceptable medium of exchange, the economy will revert to inefficient barter.

Similarly, people are willing to use money as a store of value so long as there is no unreasonable deterioration in the value of those stored dollars because of inflation. And the economy can effectively employ the monetary unit as a measure of value only when its purchasing power is relatively stable. A yardstick of value which is subject to drastic shrinkage no longer permits buyers and sellers to establish clearly the terms of trade. When the value of the dollar is declining rapidly, sellers will not know what to charge and buyers will not know what to pay for the various goods and services.

MANAGING MONEY

The overriding implication of this discussion of the value of money is this: The major "backing" of paper money is the government's ability to keep the value of money reasonably stable. This entails (1) appropriate fiscal policy, as explained in Chapter 14 and (2) intelligent management or regulation of the money supply, as noted above. Businesses and households accept paper money in exchange for goods and services so long as it will command a roughly equivalent amount of goods and services when they in turn spend it. In our economy a blending of legislation, government policy, and social practice serves as a bulwark against any imprudent expansion of the money supply which might seriously jeopardize money's value in exchange.

What we have said with respect to paper currency also applies to checking account money. In this case money is the debt of the commercial banks and thrift institutions. If you have a checking account worth $200, this merely means that your bank or "thrift" is indebted to you for that number of dollars. You can collect this debt in one of two ways. You can go to the bank or thrift and demand paper currency for your checkable deposit; this simply amounts to changing the debts you hold from the debts of a bank or thrift to government-issued debts. Or, and this is more likely, you can "collect" the debt which the bank or savings institution owes you by transferring this claim by check to someone else. For example, if you buy a $200 coat from a store, you can pay for it by writing a check, which transfers your bank's indebtedness from you to the store. Your bank now owes the store the $200 which it previously owed to you. Why does the store accept this transfer of indebtedness (the check) as a medium of exchange? Because the store can convert it into currency on demand or can in turn transfer the debt to others in making purchases of its choice. Thus, checks, as means of transferring the debts of banks and thrifts, are acceptable as money because of the ability of banks and thrifts to honor these claims.

In turn, the ability of banks and thrifts to honor claims against them depends upon their not creating too many of these claims. We shall find in a moment that a decentralized system of private, profit-seeking banks does not contain sufficient safeguards against the creation of too much check money. Hence, the American banking and financial system has a substantial amount of centralization and governmental control to guard against the imprudent creation of checkable deposits.

Caution: These comments are not to be interpreted to mean that in practice the supplies of currency and checkable-deposit money have been judiciously controlled so as to achieve a high degree of economic stability. Indeed, many economists allege that most of the inflationary woes we have encountered historically are largely the consequence of imprudent increases in the money supply.

RECAP

Let us summarize the major points that have been discussed in this section:

1 In the United States and other advanced economies, all money is essentially the debts of government, commercial banks, and thrift institutions.
2 These debts efficiently perform the functions of money so long as their value, or purchasing power, is relatively stable.
3 The value of money is not rooted in carefully defined quantities of precious metals (as it formerly has been), but rather, in the amount of goods and services money will purchase in the marketplace.
4 Government's responsibility in stabilizing the value of the monetary unit involves (1) the application of appropriate fiscal policies, and (2) effective control over the supply of money.

The demand for money

Our emphasis thus far has been upon what constitutes the supply of money and how the money supply is "backed." We now turn to the demand for money. Our earlier discussion of the functions of money suggests two basic reasons why there is a demand for money, that is, why the public wants to hold money.

TRANSACTIONS DEMAND, D_t

The first reason, of course, is that people want money as a medium of exchange—as a means of conveniently negotiating the purchase of goods and services. Households must have enough money on hand to buy groceries and to pay mortgage and utility bills until the next paycheck is received. Similarly, businesses need money to pay for labor, materials, power, and so on. Money demanded for all such purposes is simply called the **transactions demand** for money. Not surprisingly, the basic determinant of the amount of money demanded for transaction purposes is the level of nominal GNP. The larger the total money value of all goods and services exchanged in the economy, the larger will be the amount of money needed to negotiate these transactions. *The transactions demand for money varies directly with nominal GNP.* Note that we specify *nominal* GNP. Households and firms will want more money for transactions purposes if *either* prices rise *or* real output increases. In both instances there will be a larger dollar volume of transactions to negotiate.

In Figure 15-2a we have graphed the relationship between the transactions demand for money, D_t, and the interest rate. Because the transactions demand for money depends upon the level of nominal GNP and is independent of the interest rate, we show the transactions demand as a vertical line. For simplicity we assume that the amount of money demanded for transactions is unrelated to changes in the rate of interest. That is, higher interest rates will not reduce the amount of money demanded for transactions.[7] Why have we located the transactions demand at $100 billion? While the specific choice of that amount is arbitrary, a rationale can be easily provided. For example, if each dollar held for transactions purposes is spent on the average three times per year *and* nominal GNP is

---

[7] This is a simplification. We would also expect the amount of money held by businesses and households to negotiate transactions to vary inversely with the interest rate. When interest rates are high, consumers and businesses will make an effort to reduce the amount of money held for transactions purposes in order to have more funds to put into interest-earning assets.

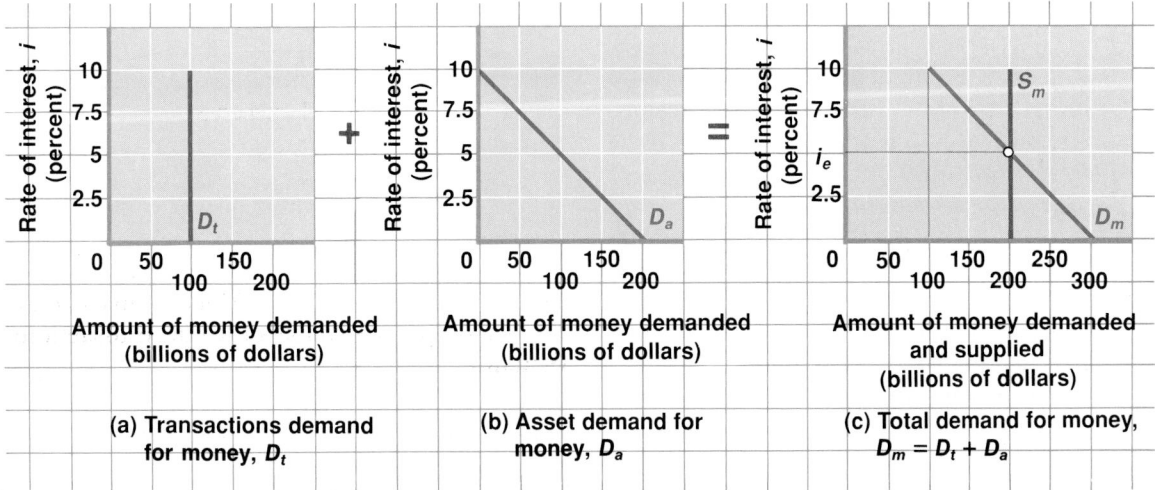

FIGURE 15-2

The demand for money and the money market

The total demand for money, D_m, is determined by horizontally adding the asset demand for money, D_a, to the transactions demand, D_t. The transactions demand is vertical because it is assumed to depend upon nominal GNP rather than the interest rate. The asset demand varies inversely with the interest rate because of the opportunity cost involved in holding currency and checkable deposits which do not pay interest. Combining the money supply (stock), S_m, with total money demand, D_m, portrays the money market and determines the equilibrium interest rate, i_e.

assumed to be $300 billion, then the public would need $100 billion of money to purchase that GNP.

ASSET DEMAND, D_a

The second reason for holding money is rooted in the fact that money functions as a store of value. People may hold their financial assets in a variety of forms—for example, as corporate stocks, private or government bonds, or as $M1$ money. Hence, there is an **asset demand** for money.

What determines the asset demand for money? To get at an answer we must first recognize that each of the various forms in which our financial assets may be held has advantages and disadvantages. To simplify, let us compare holding bonds with holding money as an asset. The advantages of holding money are its liquidity and lack of risk. Money is the most liquid of all assets in that it is immediately usable in the making of purchases. Money is an especially attractive asset to be holding when the prices of goods, services, and other

financial assets are expected to decline. When the price of a bond falls, the bondholder will suffer a loss if the bond must be sold before maturity. There is no such risk with holding money.

The disadvantage of holding money as an asset is that, in comparison with holding bonds, one does *not* earn interest income or, in the case of an interest-bearing checking account, earn as much interest income as on bonds or noncheckable deposits. And idle currency earns no interest at all. Some banks and thrifts require minimum-sized checkable deposits in order for the depositor to be paid interest; hence, many depositors do not achieve these minimum deposit balances and therefore earn no interest. The interest paid upon checkable deposits which exceed the required minimums is less than that paid on bonds and the various noncheckable deposits.

Faced with this information, the problem is to decide how much of your financial assets to hold as, say, bonds and how much as money. The solution depends primarily upon the rate of interest. Think of it this way: By holding money a household or business incurs an opportunity cost (Chapter 2). That is, by holding money interest income is forgone or sacrificed. If a bond pays 10 percent interest, then it costs $10 per year of forgone income to hold $100 as cash or in a noninterest checkable account. It is no surprise that *the asset demand for money varies inversely with the rate of interest.* When the interest rate or opportunity cost of holding money as an asset is low, the public will choose to hold a large amount of money as assets. Conversely, when the interest rate is high, it is costly to "be liquid" and the amount of assets held in the form of money will be small. Stated differently, when it is expensive to hold money as an asset, people will hold less of it; when money can be held cheaply, people will hold more of it. This inverse relationship between the interest rate and the amount of money people will want to hold as an asset is shown by D_a in Figure 15-2b.

TOTAL MONEY DEMAND D_m

As shown in Figure 15-2c, the **total demand** for money, D_m, can be found by adding the asset demand horizontally to the transactions demand. (The vertical blue line in Figure 15-2c represents the transactions demand to which Figure 15-2b's asset demand has been added.) The resulting downsloping line represents the total amount of money the public will want to hold for transactions and as an asset at each possible interest rate. Further note that a change in the nominal GNP—working through the transactions demand for money—will cause the total money demand curve to shift. Specifically, an increase in nominal GNP will mean that the public will want to hold a larger amount of money for transactions purposes and this will shift the total money demand curve to the right. For example, if the nominal GNP increases from $300 to $450 billion and we continue to suppose that the average dollar held for transactions is spent three times per year, then the transactions demand line will shift from $100 to $150 billion. As a result, the total money demand curve will lie $50 billion further to the right at each possible interest rate than was formerly the case. Conversely, a decline in nominal GNP will shift the total money demand curve to the left.

The money market

At the risk of getting ahead of ourselves, we can combine the demand for money with the supply of money to portray the **money market** and determine the equilibrium rate of interest. Hence, in Figure 15-2c we have drawn a vertical line, S_m, to represent the money supply. The money supply is shown as a vertical line on the simplifying assumption that our monetary authorities and financial institutions have provided the economy with some particular *stock* of money, such as the $M1$ total shown in Table 15-1. Just as in a product or resource market (Chapter 4), the intersection of money demand and money supply determines equilibrium price. The "price" in this case is the equilibrium interest rate, that is, the price paid for the use of money.

What if disequilibrium existed in the money market? How would the money market achieve equilibrium? Consider Figure 15-3, which replicates Figure 15-2c and adds two alternative supply-of-money curves.

First, suppose that the supply of money is reduced from $200 billion, shown as S_m, to $150 billion, designated as S_{m1}. Note that the quantity of money demanded exceeds the quantity supplied by $50 billion at the previous equilibrium interest rate of 5 percent. How will the money market adjust? In this case, people will attempt to make up for the shortage of money by selling some of the financial assets they own (we assume for simplicity that these assets are bonds). But one person's receipt of money through the sale of a bond is another person's loss of money through the purchase of that bond. Overall, there is only $150 billion of money available. The collective attempt to get more money by selling bonds will increase the supply of bonds relative to demand in the bond market and drive down bond prices.

Generalization: *Lower bond prices increase interest rates* (Last Word, Chapter 7). For example, a bond selling for its face value of $1,000 and offering a fixed $50 annual interest payment provides a 5 percent interest rate. That is:

$$\frac{\$50}{\$1,000} = 5\%$$

But suppose that the price of this bond drops to $667 because of the increased supply of bonds. The $50 fixed annual interest payment will now yield a $7\frac{1}{2}$ percent interest rate to whomever buys the bond:

$$\frac{\$50}{\$667} = 7\frac{1}{2}\%$$

Because all borrowers must compete by offering to pay lenders interest rates similar to those available on bonds, a higher general interest rate thus emerges. We observe in Figure 15-3 that the interest rate will rise from 5 percent at the money supply of $200 billion to $7\frac{1}{2}$ percent when the money supply is $150 billion. This higher interest rate

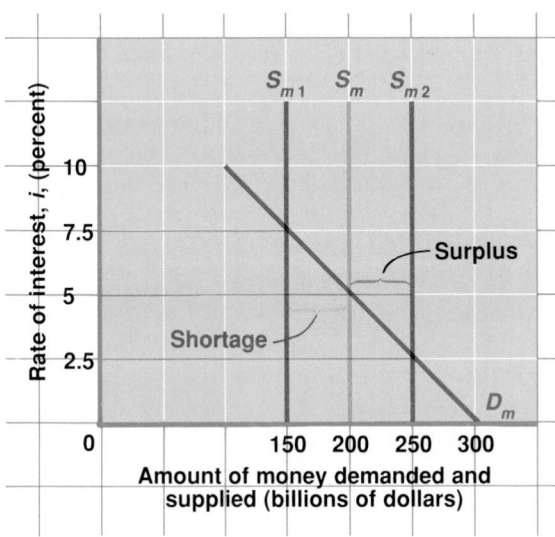

FIGURE 15-3

Restoring equilibrium in the money market

A decrease in the supply of money creates a temporary shortage of money in the money market. People and institutions attempt to gain more money by selling bonds. The supply of bonds therefore increases, which reduces bond prices and raises interest rates. At higher interest rates, people reduce the amount of money they wish to hold. Hence, the amount of money supplied and demanded once again is equal at the higher interest rate. An increase in the supply of money creates a temporary surplus of money, resulting in an increase in the demand for bonds and higher bond prices. Interest rates fall and equilibrium is reestablished in the money market.

raises the opportunity cost of holding money and reduces the amount of money firms and households want to hold. Specifically, the amount of money demanded declines from $200 billion at the 5 percent interest rate to $150 billion at the $7\frac{1}{2}$ percent interest rate. Observe that the money market is back into equilibrium: The quantity of money demanded and supplied are each $150 billion at the $7\frac{1}{2}$ percent interest rate.

Conversely, an increase in the supply of money from $200 billion ($S_m$) to, say, $250 billion ($S_{m2}$) will result in a surplus of money of $50 billion at the initial 5 percent interest rate. People will try to rid themselves of money by purchasing more bonds. But one person's expenditure of money is another person's receipt of money. The collective attempt to buy more bonds therefore will increase the demand for bonds and pull bond prices upward.

Corollary: *Higher bond prices reduce interest rates*. In terms of our example, the $50 interest payment on a bond now priced at, say, $2,000, will yield a bond buyer only a $2\frac{1}{2}$ percent interest rate:

$$\frac{\$50}{\$2,000} = 2\frac{1}{2}\%$$

The point is that interest rates in general will fall as people unsuccessfully attempt to reduce their money holdings below $250 billion by buying bonds. In this case, the interest rate will fall to a new equilibrium at $2\frac{1}{2}$ percent. Because the opportunity cost of holding money now is lower—being liquid is less expensive—consumers and businesses will increase the amount of currency and checkable deposits they are willing to hold from $200 billion to $250 billion. Once again equilibrium in the money market is restored: The quantity of money demanded and supplied are each $250 billion at an interest rate of $2\frac{1}{2}$ percent.

To generalize and recapitulate: (1) Bond prices and interest rates are inversely or negatively related; (2) disequilibriums in the money market cause changes in the price of bonds, and thereby in interest rates; (3) changes in interest rates affect people's willingness to hold money; (4) changes in people's willingness to hold money restore equilibrium in the money market; and (5) the equilibrium interest rate equates the quantities of money supplied and demanded.

In Chapter 17 we will discover how monetary policy attempts to change the money supply so as to alter the equilibrium real interest rate. A higher interest rate will reduce investment and consumption spending, a lower rate will increase investment and consumption spending, and either situation ultimately affects the levels of real output, employment, and prices.

The United States financial system

In the past decade or so the financial sector of our economy has been undergoing sweeping changes and it is fair to say that the financial system is currently in a state of flux. Early regulatory legislation had the effect of rather rigidly defining the mission or the kind of business the various financial institutions were allowed to conduct. For example, commercial banks were to provide checking accounts and make business and consumer loans. The function of the savings and loan associations was to accept savings deposits and provide these savings for mortgage lending. But a combination of competitive pressures, innovation, and deregulation in the recent past has expanded the functions of the various financial institutions and blurred the traditional distinctions between them. We have already noted how the thrift institutions rather ingeniously moved in on the checking account business of the commercial banks, but with the advantage of being able to pay interest to depositors. The commercial banks responded with ATS accounts which allowed them to sidestep the legal prohibition on paying interest on checking accounts. Banks and thrifts have also been encroaching upon the activities of brokerage houses and insurance companies. In turn, nonfinancial firms such as Sears are expanding into banking and finance. Bank holding companies have been created to allow a number of formerly separate banks to be operated as one unit, thus circumventing legal restrictions on branch banking.

The Depository Institutions Deregulation and Monetary Control Act (DIDMCA) of 1980 attempted to cope with these realities by reducing or eliminating many of the historical distinctions between commercial banks and the various thrift institutions. It is fair to say that the DIDMCA is the most fundamental piece of banking legislation passed since the Great Depression of the 1930s. We will identify several of the specific provisions of this legislation shortly when we discuss the various components of the Federal Reserve System. Most important for present purposes, DIDMCA permitted all depository institutions to offer checkable deposits. But in extending the privilege of offering checkable deposits to the thrifts, DIDMCA requires in turn that the thrifts be subject to the same limitations upon the creation of checkable deposits as apply to commercial banks. With these introductory observations in mind, let us examine the overall framework of our financial system.[8]

CENTRALIZATION AND REGULATION

Although the recent trend has been toward the deregulation of the financial system, there remains a considerable amount of centralization and governmental control. This centralization and regulation has historical roots. It became painfully apparent rather early in American history that, like it or not, centralization and public control were prerequisites of an efficient banking system. Congress became increasingly aware of this about the turn of the twentieth century. Decentralized banking fostered the inconvenience and confusion of a heterogeneous currency, monetary mismanagement, and a money supply inappropriate to the needs of the economy. "Too much" money can precipitate dangerous inflationary problems; "too little" money can stunt the economy's growth by hindering the production and exchange of goods and services. The United States and innumerable foreign countries have learned through bitter experience that a decentralized, unregulated banking system is not likely to provide that particular money supply which is most conducive to the welfare of the economy as a whole.

An unusually acute money panic in 1907 was the straw that broke Congress's back. A National Monetary Commission was established to study

[8] For a discussion of various aspects of deregulation of the financial sector, see *Economic Report of the President, 1984,* chap. 5.

the monetary and banking problems of the economy and to outline a course of action for Congress. The end result was the Federal Reserve Act of 1913.

STRUCTURE OF THE FEDERAL RESERVE SYSTEM

The monetary control system which has developed under the frequently amended Federal Reserve Act and DIDMCA is sketched in Figure 15-4. It is important that we understand the nature and functions of the various segments which compose the banking system and the relationships which the parts bear to one another.

Board of Governors   The kingpin of our money and banking system is the **Board of Governors** of the Federal Reserve System ("the Fed"). The seven members of this Board are appointed by the Presi-

dent with the confirmation of the Senate. Terms are long—fourteen years—and staggered so that one member is replaced every two years. The intention is to provide the Board with continuity, experienced membership, and autonomy or independence. The Board is staffed by appointment rather than elections in an attempt to divorce monetary policy from partisan politics.

The Board of Governors has the responsibility of exercising general supervision and control over the operation of the money and banking system of the nation. It is generally agreed that the Board chairman is the most powerful central banker in the world. The Board's actions, which are to be in the public interest and designed to promote the general economic welfare, are made effective through certain control techniques which are designed to alter the money supply. The character and functioning of these control mechanisms will be detailed in Chapter 17.

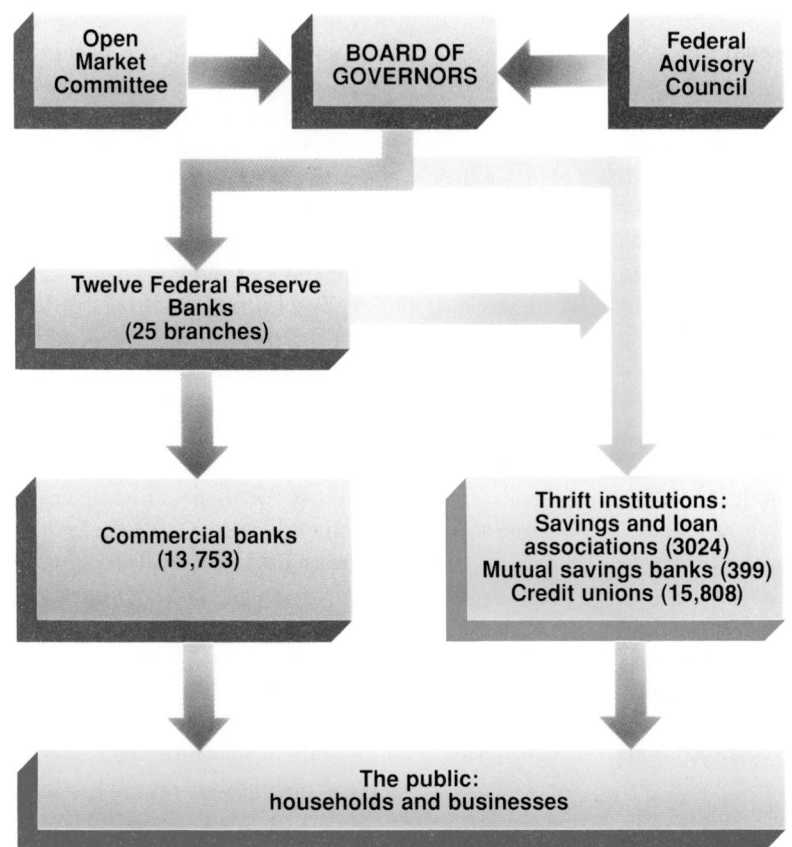

FIGURE 15-4

Framework of the Federal Reserve System and its relationship to the public

With the advice and counsel of the Open Market Committee and the Federal Advisory Council, the Board of Governors makes the basic policy decisions which provide monetary control of our money and banking systems. These decisions are made effective through the twelve Federal Reserve Banks.

Two important bodies assist the Board of Governors in determining basic banking policy. On the one hand, the **Federal Open Market Committee** (FOMC), made up of the seven members of the Board plus five of the presidents of the Federal Reserve Banks, sets the System's policy with respect to the purchase and sale of government bonds in the open market. These open-market operations constitute the most significant technique by which the monetary authorities can affect the money supply (Chapter 17). On the other hand, the **Federal Advisory Council** is composed of twelve prominent commercial bankers, one selected annually by each of the twelve Federal Reserve Banks. The Council meets periodically with the Board of Governors to voice its views on banking policy. However, as its name indicates, the Council is purely advisory; it has no policy-making powers.

It is important to reemphasize that the Fed is essentially an independent institution. It cannot be abolished or rendered ineffective by presidential whim, nor can its role and functions be altered by Congress except by specific legislative action. As noted, the long terms of the Board's members are designed to provide them with security and isolate them from political pressures.

The independence of the Fed has been a matter of ongoing controversy. Proponents of independence contend that the Fed must be protected from political pressures if it is to perform effectively the difficult and highly technical task of managing the money supply. Furthermore, it is argued that it is politically expedient for Congress and the executive branch to invoke expansionary fiscal policies—tax cuts and special-interest spending win votes—and there is thus a need for an independent monetary authority to guard against consequent inflation.

Opponents of an independent Fed argue that it is decidedly undemocratic to have such a powerful agency whose members are not directly subject to the will of the people. A related point is that, because the legislative and executive branches of government bear ultimate responsibility for the economic well-being of the nation, they should have the opportunity to manipulate *all* the policy tools essential to the economy's health. Why should Congress and the administration be responsible for the consequences of policies they do not fully con-

trol? Critics cite instances of the Fed using monetary policy to counter the effects of fiscal policy.

You will be able to clarify your own position on this issue after we have analyzed the functioning of monetary policy in Chapter 17.

The twelve Federal Reserve Banks The twelve **Federal Reserve Banks** have three major characteristics. They are (1) central banks, (2) quasi-public banks, and (3) bankers' banks.

1 CENTRAL BANKS Most nations have one central bank, for example, Britain's Bank of England or West Germany's Bundesbank. The United States has twelve! This partly reflects our geographic size and economic diversity and the fact that we have a large number of commercial banks. It also is the result of a political compromise between proponents of centralization and advocates of decentralization. Figure 15-5 locates the twelve Federal Reserve Banks and indicates the district each serves. It is through these central banks that the basic policy directives of the Board of Governors are made effective. The Federal Reserve Bank of New York City is by far the most important of these central banks. The development of modern communication and transportation facilities has undoubtedly lessened the geographic need for a system of regional banks.

2 QUASI-PUBLIC BANKS The twelve Federal Reserve Banks are quasi-governmental banks. They reflect an interesting blend of private ownership and public control. The Federal Reserve Banks are owned by the member banks in their districts. Upon joining the Federal Reserve System, commercial banks are required to purchase shares of stock in the Federal Reserve Bank in their district. But the basic policies which the Federal Reserve Banks pursue are set by a governmental body—the Board of Governors. The central banks of American capitalism are privately owned but governmentally controlled. And the owners control neither the officials of the central banks nor their policies!

The fact that the Federal Reserve Banks are essentially public institutions is vitally important to an understanding of their operation. In particular, it must be emphasized that the Federal Reserve Banks are ***not*** motivated by profits, as are private

FIGURE 15-5

The twelve Federal Reserve Districts

The Federal Reserve System divides the United States into twelve districts, each of which has one central bank and in some instances one or more branches of the central bank. Hawaii and Alaska are included in the twelfth district. (Federal Reserve Bulletin.)

enterprises. The policies followed by the central banks are those perceived by the Board of Governors to promote the well-being of the economy as a whole. Hence, the activities of the Federal Reserve Banks will frequently be at odds with the profit motive.[9] Also, the Federal Reserve Banks are not in competition with commercial banks. With rare exceptions, the Federal Reserve Banks do not deal with the public, but rather, with the government and the commercial banks.

3 BANKERS' BANKS Finally, the Federal Reserve Banks are frequently called "bankers' banks." This is a shorthand way of saying that the Federal Reserve Banks perform essentially the same functions for depository institutions as depository institutions perform for the public. Just as banks and thrifts accept the deposits of and make loans to the public, so the central banks accept the deposits of and make loans to banks and thrifts. But the Federal Reserve Banks have a third function which banks and thrifts do not perform: the function of issuing currency. Congress has authorized the Federal Reserve Banks to put into circulation Federal Reserve Notes, which constitute the economy's paper money supply.

The commercial banks The workhorses of the American financial system are its 13,753 **commercial banks.** Roughly two-thirds of these are **state banks,** that is, private banks operating under state charters. The remaining one-third received their charters from the Federal government, that is, they are **national banks.** Prior to DIDMCA this distinction was quite important because national banks were required by law to be members of the Federal Reserve System, while state banks had the option of joining or being nonmembers.

In the 1970s the Federal Reserve System experienced a rather sharp decline in its membership. By the close of the 1970s less than 40 percent of all commercial banks belonged to the Fed. The primary reason for this decline was that member commercial banks were required to keep a deposit or "reserve" at the Federal Reserve Banks which does *not* earn interest income. The high interest rates of the 1970s made the opportunity cost (the forgone interest income) of membership very high. The

[9] Though it is not their basic goal, the Federal Reserve Banks have actually operated profitably, largely as the result of Treasury debts held by them. A part of the profits has been used to pay dividends to member banks on their holdings of stock; the bulk of the remaining profits has been turned over to the United States Treasury.

consequence was that many banks withdrew from the Federal Reserve System and therefore the ability of the Fed to control the banking system and the money supply was weakened. DIDMCA responded to this problem by requiring uniform reserves for *all* commercial banks (both state and national banks) and for all other depository institutions, whether or not they are official members of the Federal Reserve System. The act also permits all depository institutions to borrow from the Federal Reserve Banks and to have access to the Fed's check-clearing facilities. As these legislative changes were phased in during the 1980s, the prior distinctions between member commercial banks, nonmember commercial banks, and the various thrift institutions tended to disappear.

The thrift institutions The thrift institutions are regulated by agencies which are separate and apart from the Board of Governors and the Federal Reserve Banks. Thus, for example, the operation of the savings and loan associations is regulated and monitored by the Federal Home Loan Bank. But, as we have just noted, DIDMCA expanded the lending authority of all thrifts, so that S&Ls and mutual saving banks can now make consumer and business loans. DIDMCA also has made the S&Ls and other depository institutions subject to monetary control by the Federal Reserve System. In particular, the thrifts now must meet the same reserve requirements as commercial banks, *and* the thrifts now can borrow from the Fed. We shall find in Chapter 17 that the changing of reserve requirements and the terms under which depository institutions can borrow from the Federal Reserve Banks are two basic means by which the Board of Governors controls the supply of money. Hence, in Figure 15-4 we have noted with mauve arrows that the thrift institutions are partially subject to the control of the Board of Governors and the central banks in that decisions concerning monetary policy will affect the thrifts along with the commercial banks.

Commercial banks and thrift institutions have two basic functions. First, they hold the money deposits of businesses and households. Second, they make loans to the public, and in so doing, increase the economy's supply of money. Detailed analysis of these functions is the main objective of Chapter 16.

LAST WORD

Angola's real currency is beer

Beer is money in the Angolan economy. It serves as a medium of exchange, a measure of value, and a store of value.

Luanda, Angola—Forget about the gold standard and welcome to Angola, where everyone has a little something going on the side and where monetary stability, such as it is, comes packed under pressure in a can—a beer can.

"Beer is the national currency here," said a Portuguese teacher working in Luanda.

As they earnestly seek a more solid footing for the world's wobbly monetary system, economists could perhaps do worse than to take a careful look at the sturdy Angolan model, where the black-market price of a case of 24 cans of imported European beer stands unshaken at 28,000 Angolan kwanzas.

At the official rate of exchange, this works out to $931—equivalent to a monthly salary for a mid-level government official—suggesting that beer is an unaffordable luxury for all but the most affluent Angolans.

In fact, however, almost nobody in Angola could survive by relying exclusively on his or her salary. Besides, the official rate of exchange carries very little weight in Angola. What carries weight is imported beer.

"Everything is more or less related to that," said an Argentine technician employed by the Angolan government. "For the past year, beer has stayed at about the same price."

Imported beer enters the economy by several means. European and U.S. petroleum companies with operations in Angola, for example, all run company stores where their employees can buy imported goods—including beer—for hard currency. And the Angolan government itself runs a huge duty-free retail emporium for diplomats and others with foreign currency.

Known as the Jumbo, the store sprawls near the inland edge of Luanda, filled with imported foods and consumer goods, including 10 brands of Scotch whiskey and seven kinds of imported beer.

It's the beer that catches the eye—the stacked cases of West German, Danish and Belgian ales and lagers seem to stretch forever.

Sold at the official exchange rate, a case of 24 cans of beer here costs 395 kwanzas, or about $13. The lines at the Jumbo's 15 cash registers are dotted with people pushing shopping carts piled high with seven or eight cases.

Outside, the beer is promptly resold on the black market—called the "candongua"—for 28,000 kwanzas a case. It is then broken up and bartered or resold at 1,500 kwanzas a can.

Typically, foreign residents in Luanda pay their household staff in beer. An Angolan family can live, albeit frugally, on two cases a month, bartering or reselling the beer one can at a time.

This eccentric monetary system has developed largely because of the almost complete collapse of Angola's centrally planned official economy.

That collapse is immediately apparent from a visit to almost any state-run store in Luanda—places where ordinary Angolans theoretically buy their monthly rations. The shelves are almost utterly bare—always.

In fact, of 10 basic rationed commodities provided by one such store in central Luanda, only two—beans and sugar—were ever in stock last month.

War and the remarkable inefficiencies of the Angolan productive apparatus are to blame for these shortages. But even when basic goods are produced, they are liable to be purloined and sold on the black market long before they reach the official retailer's shelves.

The reason is simple. Official prices in Angola are tied to the official exchange rate and reflect a wholly artificial world that has not existed in Angola since the early 1970s, when the Portuguese were in power and the official monetary unit was the escudo.

Black market prices, on the other hand are tied to the value of beer, which means they are between 60 and 70 times higher than official prices. They represent the world in which most urban Angolans dwell, or at least those with access to money or beer.

At the Roque Santeró, the largest of Luanda's sprawling, circuslike black markets, they may pay 10,000 kwanzas—or about six cans of beer—for a liter of vegetable oil prominently stamped with the information that it was "furnished by the people of the United States of America," who presumably did not expect it to be sold for profit.

Products shipped as international aid often end up being sold in this manner. In fact, most of the goods for sale at the condonguas probably have been pilfered from somewhere.

Angolans refer to such theft as "fazer desvio"—making detours—and it is the most common means by which people supplement their low official incomes, enabling them to live on the beer economy.

This heady economic activity—quietly tolerated by the government—may explain why the government-run Jumbo is never out of stock.

"They run out of milk," the Argentine technician said. "But beer? They never run out of beer."

Source: Oakland Ross, "Angolan Economy Tied to Beer," *The Globe and Mail, Toronto,* December 12, 1987. Reprinted by permission.

FED FUNCTIONS AND THE MONEY SUPPLY

The Fed performs a wide variety of functions.[10]

First, the Federal Reserve Banks hold deposits, called *reserves,* which are made by banks and thrifts. We will find in Chapter 17 that these deposits are of strategic importance in managing the economy's money supply.

A second important function of the Fed is to provide the mechanism for the collection of checks. If Sarah writes a check on her Salem bank in favor of Sam who deposits it in his San Diego bank, how does the San Diego bank collect the check against the Salem bank? Answer: The Fed handles it in two or three days by adjusting the aforementioned reserves of the two banks. DIDMCA extended this service to all depository institutions; previously, only official members of the Federal Reserve System could avail themselves of this service.

Third, the Federal Reserve Banks act as fiscal agents for the Federal government. The government collects huge sums through taxation, spends equally astronomical amounts, and sells and redeems bonds. The government avails itself of the Fed's facilities in carrying out these activities.

A fourth function is to supervise the operations of member banks. Periodic bank examinations are designed to assess member bank profitability; to ascertain that banks are performing in accordance with the myriad regulations to which they are subject; and to uncover questionable practices or fraud.[11]

Finally—and most important of all—the Federal Reserve System has ultimate responsibility for regulating the supply of money. *The major task of the Federal Reserve authorities is to manage the money supply in accordance with the needs of the economy as a whole.* This task entails making that amount of money available which is consistent with high and rising levels of output and employment and a relatively constant price level. Whereas all the other functions are of a more-or-less routine or service nature, the goal of correctly managing the money supply entails the making of basic and unique policy decisions of a nonroutine character. Chapter 17 discusses Federal Reserve monetary policy and its effectiveness. But before we turn to that subject we must understand how banks create money (Chapter 16).

CHAPTER SUMMARY

1 Anything that functions as *a* a medium of exchange, *b* a measure of value, and *c* a store of value is money.

2 The Federal Reserve System recognizes three "official" definitions of the money supply. $M1$ is comprised of currency and checkable deposits; $M2$ is $M1$ plus noncheckable savings deposits and small (less than $100,000) time deposits; and $M3$ is $M2$ plus large ($100,000 or more) time deposits. In our analysis we concentrate upon $M1$ on the grounds that its components are immediately spendable.

3 Money, which is essentially the debts of government and depository institutions (commercial banks and thrift institutions), has value because of the goods and services which it will command in the market. Maintenance of the purchasing power of money depends to a considerable degree upon the effectiveness with which government manages the money supply.

4 The total demand for money is comprised of the transactions and asset demands for money. The transactions demand varies directly with nominal GNP; the asset demand varies inversely with the interest rate. The money market combines the demand for money with the money supply to determine the equilibrium interest rate.

5 Disequilibriums in the money market are corrected through changes in bond prices. As bond prices change, interest rates move in the opposite direction. At the equilibrium interest rate, bond prices tend to be stable and the amounts of money demanded and supplied are equal.

6 The American banking system is composed of *a* the Board of Governors of the Federal Reserve System, *b* the twelve Federal Reserve Banks, and *c* some 13,753 commercial banks. The Board of Governors is the basic

---

[10] For a detailed look at the service functions of the Federal Reserve Banks, see Board of Governors of the Federal Reserve System, *The Federal Reserve System: Purposes and Functions.* 7th ed. (1984), chaps. 1, 2, 7.

[11] The Federal Reserve is not alone in the task of supervision. The individual states supervise all banks which they charter. The Comptroller of the Currency supervises all national banks. Finally, the Federal Deposit Insurance Corporation has the power to supervise all banks whose deposits it insures. Hence, a member national bank which belongs to the FDIC will be subject to three supervisory agencies—the Federal Reserve, the Comptroller of the Currency, and the FDIC.

policy-making body for the entire banking system. The directives of the Board are made effective through the twelve Federal Reserve Banks, which are simultaneously *a* central banks, *b* quasi-public banks, and *c* bankers' banks. Since the passage of the Depository Institutions Deregulation and Monetary Control Act in 1980, thrift institutions are also subject to those Board of Governor decisions designed to alter the money supply. The banks and thrifts perform the tasks of accepting money deposits and making loans.

7 The major functions of the Federal Reserve System are *a* to hold the deposits or reserves of commercial banks and other depository institutions, *b* to provide facilities for the rapid collection of checks, *c* to act as fiscal agent for the Federal government, *d* to supervise the operations of member banks, and *e* to regulate the supply of money in terms of the best interests of the economy as a whole.

TERMS AND CONCEPTS

medium of exchange

measure of value

store of value

M1, M2, M3

token money

intrinsic value

Federal Reserve Notes

checkable deposits

thrift or savings institutions

savings and loan associations

mutual savings banks

credit unions

NOW (negotiable order of withdrawal) accounts

share draft accounts

ATS (automatic transfer service) account

Depository Institutions Deregulation and Monetary Control Act

near-monies

noncheckable savings accounts

time deposits

legal tender

fiat money

transactions, asset, and total demand for money

money market

Board of Governors

Federal Open Market Committee

Federal Advisory Council

Federal Reserve Banks

commercial banks

state banks

national banks

QUESTIONS AND STUDY SUGGESTIONS

1 Describe how drastic inflation can undermine the ability of money to perform its three basic functions.

2 What are the disadvantages of commodity money? What are the advantages of *a* paper money and *b* check money as compared with commodity money?

3 "Money is only a bit of paper or a bit of metal that gives its owner a lawful claim to so much bread or beer or diamonds or motorcars or what not. We cannot eat money, nor drink money, nor wear money. It is the goods that money can buy that are being divided up when money is divided up."[12] Evaluate and explain.

4 Fully evaluate and explain the following statements:
a "The invention of money is one of the great achievements of the human race, for without it the enrichment that comes from broadening trade would have been impossible."
b "Money is whatever society says it is."
c "When prices of everything are going up, it is not because everything is worth more, but because the dollar is worth less."
d "The difficult questions concerning paper [money] are . . . not about its economy, convenience or ready circulation but about the amount of the paper which can be wisely issued or created, and the possibilities of violent convulsions when it gets beyond bounds."[13]
e "In most modern industrial economies of the world the debts of government and of commercial banks are used as money."

5 What items constitute the *M*1 money supply? What is the most important component of the *M*1 money supply? Why is the face value of a coin greater than its intrinsic value? Distinguish between *M*2 and *M*3. What are near-monies? Of what significance are they? What arguments can you make for including savings deposits in a definition of money?

6 What "backs" the money supply in the United States? What determines the value of money? Who is responsible for maintaining the value of money? Why is it important to be able to alter the money supply? What is meant by *a* "sound money" and *b* "52-cent dollar"?

7 What is the basic determinant of *a* the transactions demand and *b* the asset demand for money? Explain how these two demands might be combined graphically to determine total money demand. How is the equilibrium interest rate determined in the money market? How might *a* the expanded use of credit cards, *b* a shortening

[12] George Bernard Shaw, *The Intelligent Woman's Guide to Socialism and Capitalism* (New York: Brentano's, Inc., 1928), p. 9. Used by permission of the Public Trustee and the Society of Authors.

[13] F. W. Taussig, *Principles of Economics,* 4th ed. (New York: The Macmillan Company, 1946), pp. 247–248.

of worker pay periods, and **c** an increase in nominal GNP affect the transactions demand for money and the equilibrium interest rate?

8 Suppose that a bond has a face value of $10,000 and annually pays a fixed amount of interest of $800. Compute and enter in the space provided either the interest rate which a bond buyer could secure at each of the bond prices listed or the bond price at each of the interest rates shown. State the generalization which can be drawn from the completed table.

Bond price	Interest rate %
$ 8,000	_____
_____	8.9
$10,000	_____
$11,000	_____
_____	6.2

9 Assume the money market is initially in equilibrium and that the money supply is now increased. Explain the adjustments toward a new equilibrium interest rate. Will bond prices be higher or will they be lower at the new equilibrium rate of interest? What effects would you expect this interest-rate change to have upon the levels of output, employment, and prices? Answer the same questions for a decrease in the money supply.

10 What is the major responsibility of the Board of Governors? Discuss the major characteristics of the Federal Reserve Banks. Of what significance is the fact that the Federal Reserve Banks are quasi-public? Do you think the Fed should be an independent institution?

11 What are the two basic functions of commercial banks and thrift institutions? State and briefly discuss the major functions of the Federal Reserve System.

CHAPTER 16

How banks create money

In the last chapter we found that checkable deposits constitute the major proportion of the narrowly defined *M*I money supply. Checkable deposits (the demand deposits of commercial banks plus the NOW accounts and share drafts of the thrift institutions) are used to carry on most of the transactions in our economy. Because the bulk of all checkable deposits are the demand deposits of commercial banks, our discussion in this chapter will focus upon explaining how commercial banks can *create* demand deposit money. More specifically, in this chapter we seek to explain and compare the money-creating abilities of (1) a *single* commercial bank which is part of a multibank system, and (2) the commercial banking *system* as a whole. Throughout the discussion you should keep in mind that thrift institutions also provide checkable deposits and therefore the term "depository institution" is readily substitutable for "commercial bank" in this and the following chapter. Similarly, the term "checkable deposit" can be substituted for "demand deposit."

The balance sheet of a commercial bank

It will be convenient for us to seek our objectives through the commercial bank's balance sheet. An understanding of the basic items which make up a bank's balance sheet, and of the manner in which various transactions change these items, will provide us with a valuable analytical tool for grasping the workings of our monetary and banking systems.

What is a **balance sheet?** It is merely a statement of assets and claims which portrays or summarizes the financial position of a firm—in this case a commercial bank—at some specific point in time. Every balance sheet has one overriding virtue: By definition, it must balance. Why? Because each and every known *asset,* being something of economic value, will be claimed by someone. Can you think of an asset—something of monetary value—which no one claims? A balance sheet balances because the value of assets equals the amount of their owners' claims. The claims shown on a balance sheet are divided into two groups: the claims of the owners of a firm against the firm's assets, called *net worth,* and the claims of nonowners, called *liabilities*. Thus, it can be said that a balance sheet balances because

Assets = liabilities + net worth

A balance-sheet approach to our study of the money-creating ability of commercial banks is invaluable in two specific respects: On the one hand, a bank's balance sheet provides us with a convenient point of reference from which we can introduce new terms and concepts in a more or less orderly manner. On the other hand, the use of balance sheets will allow us to quantify certain strategic concepts and relationships which would defy comprehension if discussed in verbal terms alone.

History as prologue: the goldsmiths

We are about to use balance sheets to explain how a **fractional reserve system of banking** operates. The characteristics and functioning of such a system can be anticipated and more fully understood by pausing to consider a bit of economic history.

When the ancients began to use gold in making transactions, it soon became apparent that it was both unsafe and inconvenient for consumers and merchants to carry gold and to have it weighed and assessed for purity every time a transaction was negotiated. Hence, it became commonplace to deposit one's gold with goldsmiths who possessed vaults or strongrooms which, for a fee, they were willing to make available. Upon receiving a gold deposit, the goldsmith would issue a receipt to the depositor. Soon goods were traded for the goldsmiths' receipts and the receipts became an early form of paper money.

At this point the goldsmiths—now embryonic bankers—utilized a 100 percent reserve system, that is, their circulating paper money receipts were fully backed by gold. But, given the public's acceptance of the goldsmiths' receipts as paper money, the goldsmiths became aware that the gold they stored was rarely redeemed. In fact, the goldsmiths found themselves in charge of "going concerns" wherein the amount of gold deposited in any week or month was likely to exceed the amount withdrawn. Hence, it was only a matter of time until some particularly adroit goldsmith hit upon the idea that paper money could be issued *in excess of* the amount of gold held. The goldsmith would put these additional "receipts" redeemable in gold—paper money—into circulation by making interest-earning loans to merchants, producers, and consumers. Borrowers were willing to accept loans in this form because gold receipts were accepted as a medium of exchange. At this juncture a *fractional reserve system* of banking came into being. If, for example, our ingenious goldsmith made loans equal to the amount of gold stored, then the total value of paper money in circulation would be twice the value of the gold so that reserves would be 50 percent of outstanding paper money.

A system of fractional reserve banking—which is the kind of system we have today—embodies two significant characteristics.

1 Money creation and reserves Banks in such a system can *create money.* When the goldsmith of our illustration made loans by giving borrowers paper money which was not fully backed by gold reserves, money was being created. Obviously, the quantity of such money the goldsmith could create would depend upon the amount of reserves it was deemed prudent to keep on hand. The smaller the amount of reserves deemed necessary, the larger the amount of paper money the goldsmith could create. Although gold is no longer used to "back" our money supply (Chapter 15), bank lending (money creation) today is constrained by the amount of reserves banks feel obligated, or are required, to keep.

2 Bank panics and regulation Banks which operate on the basis of fractional reserves are vulnerable to bank "panics" or "runs." Our goldsmith who has issued paper money equal to twice the value of gold reserves clearly cannot convert all that paper money into gold in the unlikely event that all the holders of that paper money appear simultaneously demanding gold. In fact, there are innumerable instances of European and American banks being ruined by this unfortunate circumstance. On the other hand, a bank panic is highly unlikely *if* the banker's reserve and lending policies are prudent. Indeed, a basic reason why banking systems are highly regulated industries is to prevent bank runs.

A single commercial bank in a banking system

Our goal now is to understand the money-creating potential of a single bank which is part of a multibank banking system. What accounts constitute a commercial bank's balance sheet? How does a single commercial bank create and destroy money? What factors govern the money-creating abilities of such a bank?

FORMATION OF A COMMERCIAL BANK

The answers to these questions demand that we understand the ins and outs of a commercial bank's balance sheet and how certain rather elementary transactions affect that balance sheet. We start with the organization of a local commercial bank.

Transaction 1: the birth of a bank Let us start from scratch. Suppose some farsighted citizens of the metropolis of Wahoo, Nebraska, decide that their town is in need of a new commercial bank to provide all the banking services needed by that growing community. Assuming these enterprising individuals are able to secure a state or national charter for their bank, they then turn to the task of selling, say, $250,000 worth of capital stock (equity shares) to buyers, both in and out of the community. These financing efforts having met with success, the Merchants and Farmers Bank of Wahoo now exists—at least on paper. How does the Wahoo bank's balance statement appear at its birth?

The new owners of the bank have sold $250,000 worth of shares of stock in the bank—some to themselves, some to other people. As a result, the bank now has $250,000 in cash on hand and $250,000 worth of capital stock outstanding. Obviously the cash is an asset to the bank. The cash held by a bank is sometimes dubbed **vault cash** or *till money*. The outstanding shares of stock, however, constitute an equal amount of claims which the owners have against the bank's assets. That is, the shares of stock are the net worth of the bank, though they are assets from the viewpoint of those who possess these shares. The bank's balance sheet would read:

BALANCE SHEET 1: WAHOO BANK

Assets		Liabilities and net worth	
Cash	$250,000	Capital stock	$250,000

Transaction 2: becoming a going concern The newly established board of directors must now get the newborn bank off the drawing board and make it a living reality. The first step will be to acquire prop-

erty and equipment. Suppose the directors, confident of the success of their venture, purchase a building for $220,000 and some $20,000 worth of office equipment. This simple transaction merely changes the composition of the bank's assets. The bank now has $240,000 less in cash and $240,000 worth of new property assets. Using an asterisk (*) to denote those accounts which are affected by each transaction, we find that the bank's balance sheet at the end of transaction 2 appears as follows:

BALANCE SHEET 2: WAHOO BANK

Assets		Liabilities and net worth	
Cash*	$ 10,000	Capital stock	$250,000
Property*	240,000		

Note that the balance sheet still balances, as indeed it must.

Transaction 3: accepting deposits We have already noted that commercial banks have two basic functions: to accept deposits of money and to make loans. Now that our bank is in operation, let us suppose that the citizens and businesses of Wahoo decide to deposit some $100,000 in the Merchants and Farmers Bank. What happens to the bank's balance sheet?

The bank receives cash, which we have already noted is an asset to the bank. Suppose this money is placed in the bank in the form of demand deposits (checking accounts), rather than time deposits or savings accounts. These newly created demand deposits constitute claims which depositors have against the assets of the Wahoo bank. Thus the depositing of money in the bank creates a new liability account—demand deposits. The bank's balance sheet now looks like this:

BALANCE SHEET 3: WAHOO BANK

Assets		Liabilities and net worth	
Cash*	$110,000	Demand deposits*	$100,000
Property	240,000	Capital stock	250,000

You should note that, although there is no direct change in the total supply of money, a change in the composition of the economy's money supply has occurred as a result of transaction 3. Bank money, or demand deposits, have *increased* by $100,000 and currency in circulation has *decreased* by $100,000. Currency held by a bank, you will recall (Chapter 15, footnote 4) is *not* considered to be a part of the economy's money supply.

It is apparent that a withdrawal of cash will reduce the bank's demand-deposit liabilities and its holdings of cash by the amount of the withdrawal. This, too, changes the composition, but not the total supply, of money.

Transaction 4: depositing reserves in a Federal Reserve Bank All commercial banks and thrift institutions which provide checkable deposits must keep a **legal reserve** or, more simply, **reserves.** More precisely, this legal reserve is *an amount of funds equal to a specified percentage of its own deposit liabilities which a member bank must keep on deposit with the Federal Reserve Bank in its district or as vault cash.* We shall simplify our discussion by supposing that our bank keeps its legal reserve *entirely* in the form of deposits in the Federal Reserve Bank of its district. But keep in mind that in reality vault cash is counted as reserves and banks keep a significant portion of their reserves in this form.

The "specified percentage" of its deposit liabilities which the commercial bank must keep as reserves is known as the **reserve ratio.** Why? Because that is exactly what it is—a ratio between the size of the reserves which the commercial bank must keep and the commercial bank's own outstanding deposit liabilities. This ratio is as follows:

$$\frac{\text{Reserve}}{\text{ratio}} = \frac{\text{commercial bank's required reserves}}{\text{commercial bank's demand-deposit liabilities}}$$

Hence, if the reserve ratio were $\frac{1}{10}$, or 10 percent, our bank, having accepted $100,000 in deposits from the public, would be obligated to keep $10,000 as reserves. If the ratio were $\frac{1}{5}$, or 20 percent, $20,000 of reserves would be required. If $\frac{1}{2}$, or 50 percent, $50,000 would be required, and so forth.

Historically, the Board of Governors had the authority to establish and vary the reserve ratio within limits legislated by Congress. The reserve

TABLE 16-1 Reserve requirements of depository institutions

Type of deposit	Current requirement	Statutory limits
Checkable deposits		
$0–41.5 million	3%	3%
Over $41.5 million	12	8–14
Noncheckable nonpersonal savings and time deposits	3	0–9

Source: *Federal Reserve Bulletin.* Data are for January 1989.

ratio limits which now prevail are those legislated in DIDMCA and are shown in Table 16-1. Specifically, a 3 percent reserve is required on the first $41.5 million of demand or other checkable deposits held by an institution. The reserve requirement on an institution's checkable deposits in excess of $41.5 million is currently 12 percent, although the Board of Governors can vary this between 8 and 14 percent. Also, a 3 percent reserve must be kept against noncheckable nonpersonal (business) savings and time deposits. This ratio can be varied between 0 and 9 percent. It is also notable that, after consultation with appropriate congressional committees, the Federal Reserve may impose reserve requirements for 180 days in excess of those specified in Table 16-1.

To make the following discussion relatively simple we shall suppose that the reserve ratio for commercial banks is $\frac{1}{5}$, or 20 percent, and that this requirement applies only to demand deposits. Although on the high side, the 20 percent figure is convenient to use in ensuing computations. And, because we are concerned with checkable (spendable) demand deposits, it is convenient to ignore reserves on noncheckable savings and time deposits in our discussion. The point to be emphasized is that reserve requirements are *fractional,* that is, less than 100 percent. This consideration will be vital in our analysis of the lending ability of the banking system.

The Wahoo bank will just be meeting the required 20 percent ratio between its deposit in the Federal Reserve Bank and its own deposit liabilities by depositing $20,000 in the Federal Reserve

Bank. To distinguish this deposit from the public's deposits in commercial banks, we shall use the term *reserves* in referring to those funds which commercial banks deposit in the Federal Reserve Banks.

But let us suppose that the directors of the Wahoo bank anticipate that their holdings of the public's demand deposits will grow in the future. Hence, instead of sending just the minimum amount, $20,000, they send an extra $90,000, making a total of $110,000. In so doing, the bank will avoid the inconvenience of sending additional reserves to the Federal Reserve Bank each time its own demand-deposit liabilities increase. And we shall see shortly that it is upon the basis of extra reserves that banks can lend and thereby earn interest income.

Actually, of course, the bank would not deposit *all* its cash in the Federal Reserve Bank. However, because (1) banks as a rule hold vault cash only in the amount of $1\frac{1}{2}$ or 2 percent of their total assets, and (2) vault cash can be counted as reserves, we shall find it expedient to assume that all the bank's cash is deposited in the Federal Reserve Bank and therefore constitutes the commercial bank's total reserves. The cumbersome process of adding two assets—"cash" and "deposits in the Federal Reserve Bank"—to determine "reserves" is thereby avoided.

At the completion of this transaction, the balance sheet of the Merchants and Farmers Bank will appear as follows:

BALANCE SHEET 4: WAHOO BANK

Assets		Liabilities and net worth	
Cash*	$ 0	Demand	
Reserves*	110,000	deposits	$100,000
Property	240,000	Capital stock	250,000

There are several points relevant to this transaction which merit comment:

1 EXCESS RESERVES A note on terminology: The amount by which the bank's **actual reserves** exceed its **required reserves** is the bank's **excess reserves.**

That is,

$$\frac{\text{Excess}}{\text{reserves}} = \frac{\text{actual}}{\text{reserves}} - \frac{\text{required}}{\text{reserves}}$$

In this case,

Actual reserves	$110,000
Required reserves	−20,000
Excess reserves	$90,000

The only reliable way of computing excess reserves is to multiply the bank's demand-deposit liabilities by the reserve ratio to obtain required reserves ($100,000 times 20 percent equals $20,000), then to subtract this figure from the actual reserves listed on the asset side of the bank's balance sheet.

To ensure an understanding of this process, the reader should compute excess reserves for the bank's balance sheet as it stands at the end of transaction 4 on the assumption that the reserve ratio is (*a*) 10 percent, (*b*) $33\frac{1}{3}$ percent, and (*c*) 50 percent.

Because the ability of a commercial bank to make loans depends upon the existence of excess reserves, this concept is of vital importance in grasping the money-creating ability of the banking system.

2 CONTROL What is the rationale underlying the requirement that member banks deposit a reserve in the Federal Reserve Bank of their district? One might think that the basic purpose of reserves is to enhance the liquidity of a bank and thereby protect commercial bank depositors from losses; in other words, it would seem that reserves constitute a ready source of funds from which commercial banks can meet large and unexpected withdrawals of cash by depositors. But this reasoning does not hold up under close scrutiny. Although, historically, reserves were looked upon as a source of liquidity and therefore protection for depositors, *legal,* or required, reserves cannot be used for the purpose of meeting unexpected cash withdrawals. If the banker's nightmare should materialize—that is, if everyone having a demand deposit in the bank appeared on the same morning to demand these deposits in cash—the banker could not draw upon required reserves to meet this "bank panic" without violating the legal reserve ratio and thereby incurring the wrath and penalties of the Federal

Reserve authorities. In practice, legal reserves are *not* an available pool of liquid funds upon which commercial banks can rely in times of emergency.[1] As a matter of fact, even if legal reserves were accessible to commercial banks, they would not be sufficient to meet a serious "run" on a bank. Why? Because, as already noted, reserves are *fractional;* that is, demand deposits may be 10 or 20 times as large as a bank's required reserves.

It is not surprising that commercial bank depositors are protected by other means. As noted in Chapter 15, periodic bank examinations are an important device for promoting prudent commercial banking practices. And banking laws restrict banks with respect to the kinds of assets they may acquire; for example, banks are generally prohibited from buying common stocks. Furthermore, the Federal Deposit Insurance Corporation (FDIC) exists to insure the deposit liabilities of commercial banks, while the Federal Savings and Loan Insurance Corporation (FSLIC) similarly protects the depositors of the S&Ls up to $100,000.[2]

If the purpose of reserves is not to provide for commercial bank liquidity, what is their function? *Control* is the basic answer. Legal reserves are a

means by which the Board of Governors can influence the lending ability of commercial banks. The next chapter will explain in detail how the Board of Governors can invoke certain policies which either increase or decrease commercial bank reserves and thereby affect the ability of banks to grant credit. The objective is to prevent banks from *over*extending or *under*extending bank credit. To the degree that these policies are successful in influencing the volume of commercial bank credit, the Board of Governors can help the economy avoid the business fluctuations which give rise to bank runs, bank failures, and collapse of the monetary system. It is in this indirect way—as a means of controlling commercial bank credit and thereby stabilizing the economy—that reserves protect depositors, not as a source of liquidity. As we shall see in a moment, another function of reserves is to facilitate the collection or "clearing" of checks.

3 ASSET AND LIABILITY   Let us pause to note a rather apparent accounting matter which transaction 4 entails. Specifically, *the reserve created in transaction 4 is an asset to the depositing commercial bank but a liability to the Federal Reserve Bank receiving it.* To the Wahoo bank the reserve is an asset. Why? Because it is a claim which this commercial bank has against the assets of another institution—the Federal Reserve Bank. To the Federal Reserve Bank this reserve is a liability, that is, a claim which another institution—the Wahoo bank—has against it. Just as the demand deposit you get by depositing money in a commercial bank is an asset to you and a liability to your commercial bank, so the deposit or reserve which a commercial bank establishes by depositing money in a bankers' bank is an asset to the commercial bank and a liability to the Federal Reserve Bank. An understanding of this relationship is necessary in pursuing transaction 5.

Transaction 5: a check is drawn against the bank   Now let us tackle a very significant and somewhat more complicated transaction. Suppose that Clem Bradshaw, a Wahoo farmer who deposited a substantial portion of the $100,000 in demand deposits which the Wahoo bank received in transaction 3, purchases $50,000 worth of farm machinery from the Ajax Farm Implement Company of Beaver Crossing, Nebraska. Bradshaw very sensibly pays for

---

[1] This amendment must be added: As depositors withdraw cash from a commercial bank, the bank's demand-deposit liabilities will decline. This lowers the absolute amount of required reserves which the bank must keep, thereby freeing some of the bank's actual reserves for use in meeting cash withdrawals by depositors. To illustrate: Suppose a commercial bank has reserves of $20 and demand-deposit liabilities of $100. If the legal reserve ratio is 20 percent, all the bank's reserves are required. Now, if depositors withdraw, say, $50 worth of their deposits as cash, the bank will only need $10 as required reserves to support the remaining $50 of demand-deposit liabilities. Thus $10 of the bank's actual reserves of $20 are no longer required. The bank can draw upon this $10 in helping to meet the cash withdrawals of its depositors. And, of course, if a bank goes out of business, all its reserves will be available to pay depositors and other claimants.

[2] Some observers feel that deposit insurance may have had a perverse effect in that it may have encouraged bankers to make riskier decisions with respect to lending and asset acquisition. One proposed reform is that the size of each bank's insurance premiums should vary directly with the riskiness of its assets, thereby providing a stronger financial incentive to avoid unnecessary risk.

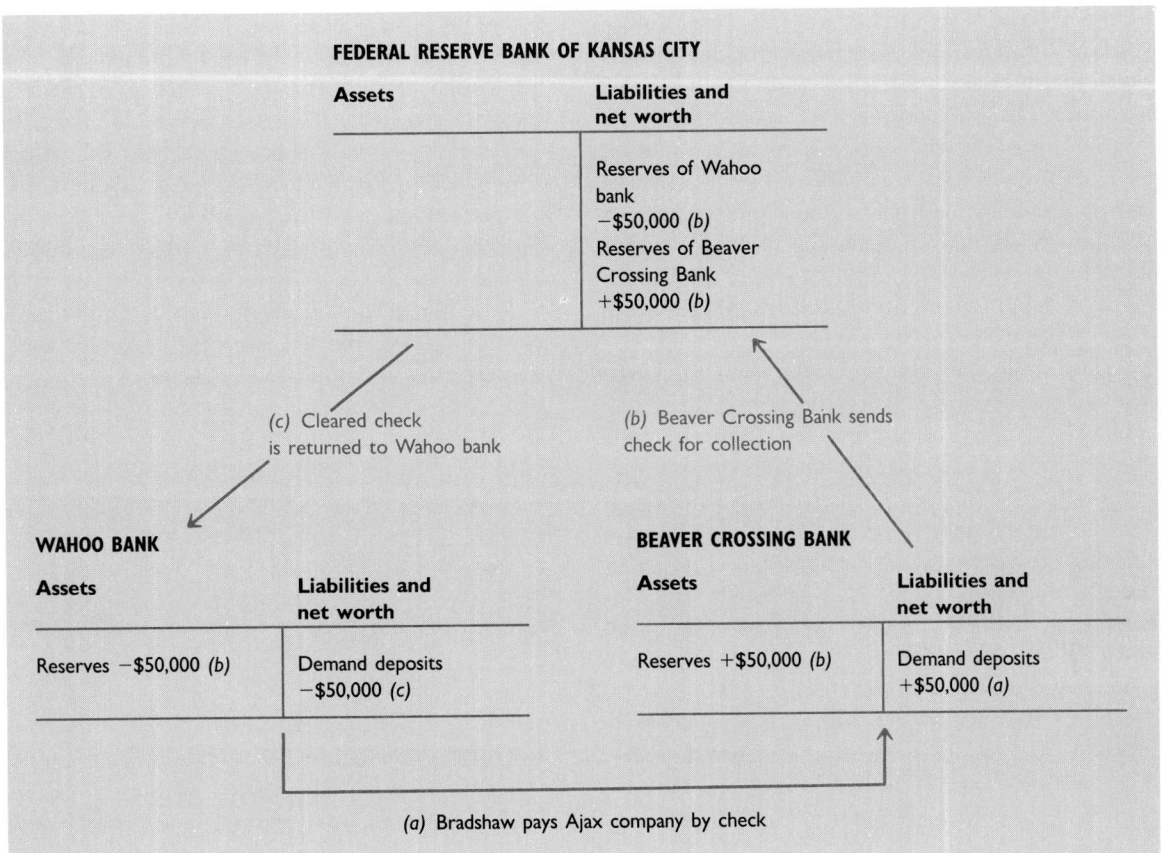

FIGURE 16-1

The collection of a check through a Federal Reserve Bank

The bank against which a check is drawn and cleared loses both reserves and deposits; the bank in which the check is deposited acquires reserves and deposits.

this machinery by writing a $50,000 check, against his deposit in the Wahoo bank, in favor of the Ajax company. We want to determine (1) how this check is collected or cleared, and (2) the effect that the collection of the check has upon the balance sheets of the banks involved in the transaction.

To accomplish this, we must consider the Wahoo bank, the Beaver Crossing bank (the Ajax Company's bank), and the Federal Reserve Bank of Kansas City.[3] To keep our illustration as clear as possible, we shall deal only with the changes which occur in those specific accounts affected by this transaction.

[3] Actually, the Omaha branch of the Federal Reserve Bank of Kansas City would handle the process of collecting this check.

Let us trace this transaction in three related steps, keying the steps by letters to Figure 16-1.

a. Mr. Bradshaw gives his $50,000 check, drawn against the Wahoo bank, to the Ajax company. The Ajax company in turn deposits the check in its account with the Beaver Crossing bank. The Beaver Crossing bank increases the Ajax company's demand deposit by $50,000 when it deposits the check. The Ajax company is now paid off. Bradshaw is pleased over his new machinery, for which he has now paid.

b. Now the Beaver Crossing bank has Bradshaw's check in its possession. This check is simply a claim against the assets of the Wahoo bank. How will the Beaver Crossing bank collect this claim? By sending this check—along with checks drawn on other banks—to the Federal Reserve Bank of Kansas City. Here a clerk will clear, or collect, this check for the Beaver Crossing bank by *increasing* its reserve in the Federal Reserve Bank by $50,000 and by *decreasing* the Wahoo bank's reserve by a like amount. The check is collected merely by making bookkeeping notations to the effect that the Wahoo bank's claim against the Federal Reserve Bank has been reduced by $50,000 and the Beaver Crossing bank's claim increased accordingly. Note these changes on the balance sheets in Figure 16-1.[4]

c. Finally, the cleared check is sent back to the Wahoo bank, and for the first time the Wahoo bank discovers that one of its depositors has drawn a check for $50,000 against his demand deposit. Accordingly, the Wahoo bank reduces Mr. Bradshaw's demand deposit by $50,000 and recognizes that the collection of this check has entailed a $50,000 decline in its reserves at the Federal Reserve Bank. Note that the balance statements of all three banks will still balance. The Wahoo bank will have reduced both its assets and its liabilities by $50,000. The Beaver Crossing bank will have $50,000 more in reserves and in demand deposits. The ownership of reserves at the Federal Reserve Bank will have changed, but total reserves will stay the same.

The point we are making is this: *Whenever a check is drawn against a bank and deposited in another bank, the collection of that check will entail a loss of both reserves and demand (checkable) deposits by the bank upon which the check is drawn.* Con-

versely, if a bank receives a check drawn on another bank, the bank receiving the check will, in the process of collecting it, have its reserves and deposits *increased* by the amount of the check. In our example, the Wahoo bank loses $50,000 in both reserves and deposits to the Beaver Crossing bank. But there is no loss of reserves or deposits for the banking system as a whole. What one bank loses another bank gains.

Bringing all the other assets and liabilities back into the picture, the Wahoo bank's balance sheet looks like this at the end of transaction 5:

BALANCE SHEET 5: WAHOO BANK

Assets		Liabilities and net worth	
Reserves*	$ 60,000	Demand	
Property	240,000	deposits*	$ 50,000
		Capital stock	250,000

The reader should verify that with a 20 percent reserve requirement, the bank's *excess* reserves now stand at $50,000.

Transaction 5 is reversible. If a check drawn against another bank is deposited in the Wahoo bank, the Wahoo bank will receive both reserves and deposits equal to the amount of the check as it is collected.

---

[4] Here is an interesting sidelight: The collection of Bradshaw's check by the Beaver Crossing bank through the Federal Reserve Bank involves the same type of procedure as the collection of a check between two individuals who have deposits in the same commercial bank. Suppose you and I both have checking accounts in the Wahoo bank. I owe you $10 and I pay this debt by check. You deposit the $10 check in the bank. Here a bank clerk collects the check for you by noting a "+$10" in your account and a "−$10" in my account. And that's that. The same thing happens at the Federal Reserve Bank of Kansas City when the Beaver Crossing bank clears a $50,000 check against the Wahoo bank. The banker's bank increases the Beaver Crossing bank's deposit in the Federal Reserve Bank—that is, its reserve—by $50,000 and lowers the Wahoo bank's reserve by the same amount. The check is then cleared.

RECAP

Let us summarize the salient conclusions from the first five transactions we have analyzed:
1 When a bank accepts deposits of cash, the composition of the money supply is changed, but the total supply of money is not directly altered.
2 Commercial banks and other depository institutions are required to keep legal reserve deposits, or simply "reserves," equal to a specified percentage of their own deposit liabilities as cash or on deposit with the Federal Reserve Bank of their district. The reserve ratio indicates the size of this "specified percentage." Reserves are primarily a means by which the monetary authorities can control the lending capabilities of commercial banks.
3 The amount by which a bank's actual reserves

exceed its required reserves is called "excess re-serves."

4 Commercial bank reserves are an asset to the commercial bank but a liability to the Federal Reserve Bank holding them.

5 A bank which has a check drawn and collected against it will lose both reserves and deposits equal to the value of the check to the bank that is receiving the check.

MONEY-CREATING TRANSACTIONS OF A COMMERCIAL BANK

The next three transactions are particularly crucial because they explain (1) how a single commercial bank can literally create money by making loans, (2) how money is destroyed when loans are repaid, and (3) how banks create money by purchasing government bonds from the public.

Transaction 6: granting a loan You will recall that, in addition to accepting deposits, commercial banks have a basic function of granting loans to borrowers. What effect does commercial bank lending have upon the balance sheet of a commercial bank?

Suppose that the Grisley Meat Packing Company of Wahoo decides that the time is ripe to expand its facilities. Suppose, too, that the company needs exactly $50,000—which, by some coincidence, just happens to be equal to the Wahoo bank's excess reserves—to finance this project.

The company approaches the Wahoo bank and requests a loan for this amount. The Wahoo bank is acquainted with the Grisley company's fine reputation and financial soundness and is convinced of its ability to repay the loan. So the loan is granted. The president of the Grisley company hands a promissory note—a high-class IOU—to the Wahoo bank. The Grisley company wants the convenience and safety of paying its obligations by checks. Hence, instead of receiving a bushel basket full of currency from the bank, the Grisley company will get a $50,000 increase in its demand deposit in the Wahoo bank. From the Wahoo bank's standpoint it has acquired an interest-earning asset (the promissory note) and has created demand deposits (a liability) to "pay" for this asset.

In short, the Grisley company has swapped an IOU for the right to draw an additional $50,000

worth of checks against its demand deposit in the Wahoo bank. Both parties are pleased with themselves. The Wahoo bank now possesses a new asset—an interest-bearing promissory note which it files under the general heading of "Loans." The Grisley company, sporting a fattened demand deposit, is now in a position to expand its operations.

At the moment the loan is negotiated, the Wahoo bank's position is shown by balance sheet 6a.

BALANCE SHEET 6a: WAHOO BANK *(when loan is negotiated)*

Assets		Liabilities and net worth	
Reserves	$ 60,000	Demand	
Loans*	50,000	deposits*	$100,000
Property	240,000	Capital stock	250,000

All this looks innocent enough. But a closer examination of the Wahoo bank's balance statement will reveal a startling fact: *When a bank makes loans, it creates money.* The president of the Grisley company went to the bank with something which is *not* money—her IOU—and walked out with something that *is* money—a demand deposit. Contrast this situation with transaction 3 where demand deposits were created, but only by currency going out of circulation. Hence, there was a change in the *composition* of the money supply but no change in the total *supply* of money. When banks lend, they create demand (checkable) deposits which are money. By extending credit the Wahoo bank has "monetized" an IOU. The Grisley company and the Wahoo bank have created and then swapped claims. The claim created by the Grisley company and given to the bank is not money; an individual's IOU is not generally acceptable as a medium of exchange. But the claim created by the bank and given to the Grisley company is money; checks drawn against a demand deposit are acceptable as a medium of exchange. It is through the extension of credit by commercial banks that the bulk of the money used in our economy is created. As we indicated in the previous chapter, this checking account money may be thought of as "debts" of commercial banks and thrift institutions. Checks are bank "debts" in the sense that they are claims which the banks and thrifts promise to pay "upon demand."

But there are important forces which circumscribe the ability of a commercial bank to create demand deposits—that is, "bank money"—by lending. In the present case, the Wahoo bank can expect the newly created demand deposit of $50,000 to be a very active account. The Grisley company would not borrow $50,000 at, say, 9, 12, or 15 percent interest for the sheer joy of knowing the funds were available if needed. Let us assume that the Grisley company awards a $50,000 contract to the Quickbuck Construction Company of Omaha. Quickbuck, true to its name, completes the expansion job and is rewarded with a check for $50,000 drawn by the Grisley company against its demand deposit in the Wahoo bank. The Quickbuck company, having its headquarters in Omaha, does not deposit this check back in the Wahoo bank but instead deposits it in the Fourth National Bank of Omaha. The Fourth National Bank now has a $50,000 claim against the Wahoo bank. This check is collected in the manner described in transaction 5. As a result, the Wahoo bank *loses* both reserves and deposits equal to the amount of the check; the Fourth National Bank *acquires* $50,000 of reserves and deposits. In short, assuming a check is drawn by the borrower for the entire amount of the loan ($50,000) and given to a firm which deposits it in another bank, the Wahoo bank's balance sheet will read as follows *after the check has been cleared against it:*

BALANCE SHEET 6b: WAHOO BANK *(after a check drawn on the loan has been collected)*

Assets		Liabilities and net worth	
Reserves*	$ 10,000	Demand	
Loans	50,000	deposits*	$ 50,000
Property	240,000	Capital stock	250,000

You will note immediately that after the check has been collected, the Wahoo bank is just barely meeting the legal reserve ratio of 20 percent. The bank has *no excess reserves*. This poses an interesting question: Could the Wahoo bank have lent an amount greater than $50,000—an amount greater than its excess reserves—and still have met the 20 percent reserve requirement if a check for the full amount of the loan were cleared against it? The answer is "No." For example, suppose the Wahoo bank had loaned $55,000 to the Grisley company. Collection of the check against the Wahoo bank would have lowered its reserves to $5,000 (= $60,000 − $55,000) and deposits would once again stand at $50,000 (= $105,000 − $55,000). The ratio of actual reserves to deposits would now be $5,000/$50,000, or only 10 percent. The Wahoo bank could thus *not* have lent $55,000.

By experimenting with other figures in excess of $50,000, the reader will find that the maximum amount which the Wahoo bank could lend at the outset of transaction 6 is $50,000. This figure is identical with the amount of excess reserves which the bank had available at the time the loan was negotiated. We conclude that *a single commercial bank in a multibank banking system can lend only an amount equal to its initial preloan excess reserves.* Why? Because when it lends, it faces the likelihood that checks for the entire amount of the loan will be drawn and cleared against the lending bank. A lending bank can anticipate the loss of reserves to other banks equal to the amount it lends.[5]

Transaction 7: repaying a loan If commercial banks create demand deposits—that is, money—when they make loans, it seems logical to inquire whether money is destroyed when the loans are repaid. The answer is "Yes." Using balance sheets 6b and 7, let us see what happens when the Grisley company repays the $50,000 it borrowed.

To simplify, we shall (1) suppose that the loan is repaid not in installments but rather in one lump sum two years after the date of negotiation, and (2) ignore interest charges on the loan. The Grisley company will write a check for $50,000 against its demand deposit, which we assume was $50,000 before the Grisley loan was negotiated. As a result, the Wahoo bank's demand-deposit liabilities decline by $50,000; the Grisley company has given up $50,000 worth of its claim against the bank's assets.

---

[5] Qualification: If some of the checks written on a loan are redeposited back in the lending bank by their recipients, then that bank will be able to lend an amount somewhat greater than its initial excess reserves.

In turn, the bank will surrender the Grisley company's IOU which it has been patiently holding these many months. The bank and the company have reswapped claims. But the claim given up by the Grisley company is money; the claim it is repurchasing—its IOU—is not. The supply of money has therefore been reduced by $50,000; that amount of demand deposits has been destroyed, unaccompanied by an increase in the money supply elsewhere in the economy. The Grisley company's IOU has been "demonetized." This fact is shown in balance sheet 7, where we note that the Wahoo bank's demand deposits and loans both return to zero. You will note that the decline in demand deposits increases the bank's holdings of excess reserves; this provides the basis for new loans to be made.

BALANCE SHEET 7: WAHOO BANK *(after loan has been repaid)*

Assets		Liabilities and net worth	
Reserves	$ 10,000	Demand deposits*	$ 0
Loans*	0		
Property	240,000	Capital stock	250,000

In the highly unlikely event the Grisley company repays the loan with cash, the supply of money will still decline by $50,000. In this case, the Grisley company would repurchase its IOU by handing over $50,000 in cash to the bank. This causes loans to fall on the bank's balance sheet by $50,000 and cash to increase by $50,000. Remember that we specifically excluded currency held by banks from the money supply on the ground that to include such cash would be double counting; it is apparent that this constitutes a $50,000 reduction in the supply of money.

Transaction 8: buying government securities When a commercial bank buys government bonds from the public, the effect is substantially the same as that of lending. New money is created. To illustrate, let us assume that the Wahoo bank's balance sheet initially stands as it did at the end of transaction 5. Now assume that, instead of making a $50,000 loan, the bank buys $50,000 of government securi-

ties from a securities dealer. The bank receives the interest-bearing bonds which appear on its balance statement as the asset "Securities" and gives the dealer an increase in its demand-deposit account. The Wahoo bank's balance sheet would appear as follows:

BALANCE SHEET 8: WAHOO BANK

Assets		Liabilities and net worth	
Reserves	$ 60,000	Demand deposits*	$100,000
Securities*	50,000		
Property	240,000	Capital stock	250,000

The important point is that demand deposits, that is, the supply of money, have been increased by $50,000, as in transaction 6. *Commercial bank bond purchases from the public increase the supply of money in the same way as does lending to the public.* The bank accepts government bonds—which are not money—and gives the securities dealer an increase in its demand deposits—which is money.

Of course, when the securities dealer draws and clears a check for $50,000 against the Wahoo bank, the bank will lose both reserves and deposits in that amount and therefore will just be meeting the legal reserve requirement. Its balance sheet will now read precisely as in 6b except that "Securities" is substituted for "Loans" on the asset side.

Finally, as you undoubtedly suspect, the selling of government bonds to the public by a commercial bank—like the repayment of a loan—will reduce the supply of money. The securities buyer will pay by check and both "Securities" and "Demand deposits" (the latter being money) will decline by the amount of the sale.

PROFITS AND LIQUIDITY

The relative importance of the various asset items on a commercial bank's balance sheet is the result of the banker's pursuit of two conflicting goals. One goal is profits. Commercial banks, like any other business, are seeking profits. This is why the bank wants to make loans and buy securities.

These two items are the major earning assets of commercial banks. On the other hand, a commercial bank must seek safety. For a bank, safety lies in liquidity—specifically such liquid assets as cash and excess reserves. Banks must be on guard for depositors' transforming their demand deposits into cash. Similarly, the possibility exists that more checks will be cleared against a bank than are cleared in its favor, causing a net outflow of reserves. Bankers are thus seeking a proper balance between prudence and profits. The compromise that is achieved determines the relative size of earning assets as opposed to highly liquid assets.

The banking system: multiple-deposit expansion

Thus far we have discovered that a single bank in a banking system can lend dollar for dollar with its excess reserves. Now what of the lending ability of all commercial banks taken as a group? Jumping to our conclusions, we shall find that *the commercial banking system can lend, that is, can create money, by a multiple of its excess reserves. This multiple lending is accomplished despite the fact that each bank in the system can only lend dollar for dollar with its excess reserves.* The immediate task is to uncover how these seemingly paradoxical conclusions come about.

To do this, it is necessary that we keep our analysis as uncluttered as possible. Therefore, we shall rely upon three simplifying assumptions. First, suppose that the reserve ratio for all commercial banks is 20 percent. Second, assume initially that all banks are exactly meeting this 20 percent reserve requirement. No excess reserves exist; all banks are "loaned up." Third, we shall suppose that if any bank becomes able to increase its loans as a result of acquiring excess reserves, an amount equal to these excess reserves will be loaned to one borrower, who will write a check for the entire amount of the loan and give it to someone else, who deposits the check in another bank. This third assumption merely means that we are assuming the worst thing possible that can happen to any lending bank—a check for the entire amount of the loan is drawn and cleared against it and in favor of another bank.

THE BANKING SYSTEM'S LENDING POTENTIAL

To begin, suppose that a junkyard owner finds a $100 bill while dismantling a car which has been on the lot for years. The person deposits the $100 in bank A, which adds the $100 to its reserves. Since we are recording only *changes* in the balance sheets of the various commercial banks, bank A's balance sheet will now appear as shown by the entries designated as *(a₁)*:

BALANCE SHEET: COMMERCIAL BANK A

Assets		Liabilities and net worth	
Reserves	$+100 (a_1) − 80 (a_3)	Demand deposits	$+100 (a_1) + 80 (a_2) − 80 (a_3)
Loans	+ 80 (a_2)		

Recall from transaction 3 that this $100 deposit of currency does *not* alter the money supply; while $100 of demand-deposit money comes into being, an offsetting $100 of currency has gone out of "circulation." What *has* happened is that bank A has acquired *excess reserves* of $80. Of the newly acquired $100 in reserves, 20 percent, or $20, must be earmarked to offset the new $100 deposit and the remaining $80 is excess reserves. Remembering that a single commercial bank, such as bank A, can lend only an amount equal to its excess reserves, we conclude that bank A can lend a maximum of $80. When a loan for this amount is negotiated, bank A's loans will increase by $80, and the borrower will get an $80 demand deposit. Let us add these figures—designated as *(a₂)*—to bank A's balance sheet.

But now we must invoke our third assumption: The borrower draws a check for $80—the entire amount of the loan—and gives it to someone who deposits it in another bank, bank B. As we saw in transaction 6, bank A *loses* both reserves and deposits equal to the amount of the loan *(a₃)*. The net result of all these transactions is that bank A's reserves now stand at $20 (= $100 − $80), loans at $80, and the demand deposits are at $100 (= $100 + $80 − $80). Note that when the dust has settled, bank A is just meeting the 20 percent reserve ratio.

Recalling transaction 5, bank B *acquires* both the reserves and the deposits which bank A has lost. Bank B's balance sheet looks like this (b_1):

BALANCE SHEET: COMMERCIAL BANK B

Assets		Liabilities and net worth	
Reserves	$+80 (b_1) −64 (b_3)	Demand deposits	$+80 (b_1) +64 (b_2) −64 (b_3)
Loans	+64 (b_2)		

When the check is drawn and cleared, bank A *loses* $80 in reserves and deposits and bank B *gains* $80 in reserves and deposits. But 20 percent, or $16, of bank B's newly acquired reserves must be kept as required reserves against the new $80 in demand deposits. This means that bank B has $64 (= $80 − $16) in excess reserves. It can therefore lend $64 (b_2). When the borrower draws a check for the entire amount and deposits it in bank C, the reserves and deposits of bank B both fall by the $64 (b_3). As a result of these transactions, bank B's reserves will now stand at $16 (= $80 − $64), loans at $64, and demand deposits at $80 (= $80 + $64 − $64). Note that after all this has occurred, bank B is just meeting the 20 percent reserve requirement.

We are off and running again. Bank C has acquired the $64 in reserves and deposits lost by bank B. Its balance statement appears as follows (c_1):

BALANCE SHEET: COMMERCIAL BANK C

Assets		Liabilities and net worth	
Reserves	$+64.00 (c_1) −51.20 (c_3)	Demand deposits	$+64.00 (c_1) +51.20 (c_2) −51.20 (c_3)
Loans	+51.20 (c_2)		

Exactly 20 percent, or $12.80, of this new reserve will be required, the remaining $51.20 being excess reserves. Hence, bank C can safely lend a maxi-

mum of $51.20. Suppose it does (c_2). And suppose the borrower draws a check for the entire amount and gives it to someone who deposits it in another bank (c_3).

Bank D—the bank receiving the $51.20 in reserves and deposits—now notes these changes on its balance sheet (d_1):

BALANCE SHEET: COMMERCIAL BANK D

Assets		Liabilities and net worth	
Reserves	$+51.20 (d_1) −40.96 (d_3)	Demand deposits	$+51.20 (d_1) +40.96 (d_2) −40.96 (d_3)
Loans	+40.96 (d_2)		

It can now lend $40.96 (d_2). The borrower draws a check for the full amount and deposits it in another bank (d_3).

Now, if we wanted to be particularly obnoxious, we could go ahead with this procedure by bringing banks E, F, G, H, . . . , N into the picture. We shall merely suggest that you check through computations for banks E, F, and G, to ensure that you have the procedure firmly in mind.

The nucleus of this analysis is summarized in Table 16-2. Data for banks E through N are supplied so you may check your computations. Our conclusion is a rather startling one: On the basis of the $80 in excess reserves (acquired by the banking system when someone deposited $100 of currency in bank A), the *entire commercial banking system* is able to lend $400. Lo and behold, the banking system is able to lend by a multiple of 5 when the reserve ratio is 20 percent! Yet you will note that each single bank in the banking system is lending only an amount equal to its excess reserves. How do we explain these seemingly conflicting conclusions? Why is it that the *banking system* can lend by a multiple of its excess reserves, but *each individual bank* can only lend dollar for dollar with its excess reserves?

The answer lies in the fact that reserves lost by a single bank are not lost to the banking system as a whole. The reserves lost by bank A are acquired by bank B. Those lost by B are gained by C. C loses to D, D to E, E to F, and so forth. Hence, although

TABLE 16-2 **Expansion of the money supply by the commercial banking system**

Bank	(1) Acquired reserves and deposits	(2) Required reserves	(3) Excess reserves, or (1) − (2)	(4) Amount which the bank can lend; new money created = (3)
Bank A	$100.00 (a_1)	$20.00	$80.00	$ 80.00 (a_2)
Bank B	80.00 (a_3, b_1)	16.00	64.00	64.00 (b_2)
Bank C	64.00 (b_3, c_1)	12.80	51.20	51.20 (c_2)
Bank D	51.20 (c_3, d_1)	10.24	40.96	40.96 (d_2)
Bank E	40.96	8.19	32.77	32.77
Bank F	32.77	6.55	26.22	26.22
Bank G	26.22	5.24	20.98	20.98
Bank H	20.98	4.20	16.78	16.78
Bank I	16.78	3.36	13.42	13.42
Bank J	13.42	2.68	10.74	10.74
Bank K	10.74	2.15	8.59	8.59
Bank L	8.59	1.72	6.87	6.87
Bank M	6.87	1.37	5.50	5.50
Bank N	5.50	1.10	4.40	4.40
Other banks	21.97	4.40	17.57	17.57
Total amount of money created				$400.00

reserves can be, and are, lost by *individual* banks in the banking system, there can be no loss of reserves for the banking *system* as a whole.

Hence, we reach the curious conclusion that an individual bank can only safely lend an amount equal to its excess reserves, but the commercial banking system can lend by a multiple of its excess reserves. This contrast, incidentally, is a fine illustration of why it is imperative that we keep the fallacy of composition (Chapter 1) firmly in mind. Commercial banks *as a group* can create money by lending in a manner much different from that of the *individual banks* in that system.

THE MONETARY MULTIPLIER

The rationale involved in this *demand-deposit multiplier,* or **monetary multiplier** is similar to that of the income multiplier discussed in Chapter 13. The income multiplier was based on the fact that the expenditures of one household are received as income by another; the deposit multiplier rests on the fact that the reserves and deposits lost by one bank are received by another bank. And, just as the size of the income multiplier is determined by the reciprocal of the MPS, that is, by the leakage into saving which occurs at each round of spending, so the deposit multiplier m is the reciprocal of the required reserve ratio R, that is, of the leakage into required reserves which occurs at each step in the lending process. In short,

$$\text{Monetary multiplier} = \frac{1}{\text{required reserve ratio}}$$

or, symbolically:

$$m = \frac{1}{R}$$

In this formula, m tells us the maximum amount of

new demand-deposit money which can be created for a *single dollar* of excess reserves, given the value of **R**. To determine the maximum amount of new demand-deposit money, **D**, which can be created by the banking system on the basis of any given amount of excess reserves, **E**, we simply multiply the excess reserves by the monetary multiplier. That is,

$$\begin{array}{c}\text{Maximum} \\ \text{demand-deposit} \\ \text{expansion}\end{array} = \begin{array}{c}\text{excess} \\ \text{reserves}\end{array} \times \begin{array}{c}\text{monetary} \\ \text{multiplier}\end{array}$$

or, more simply,

$$D = E \times m$$

Thus, in our example of Table 16-2:

$$\$400 = \$80 \times 5$$

But keep in mind that, despite the similar rationale underlying the income and deposit multipliers, the former has to do with changes in income and the latter with changes in the supply of money.

Diagrammatic summary   Figure 16-2 summarizes the final outcome from our example of a multiple-deposit expansion of the money supply. We observe that the initial deposit of $100 of currency into the bank (lower box) creates an initial demand deposit of an equal amount (upper left box). Given our assumption of a 20 percent reserve ratio, however, only $20 of currency reserves are needed to "back up" this $100 demand deposit. The excess reserves of $80 permit the creation of $400 of new demand deposits via the making of loans, correctly suggesting a monetary multiplier of 5. The $100 of new reserves thus supports a total supply of money of $500: $100 of initial demand deposit plus $400 of demand deposits created through lending.

Readers might experiment with these two teasers in testing their understanding of multiple credit expansion by the banking system:
1 Rework the analysis in Table 16-2 (at least three or four steps of it) on the assumption that the reserve ratio is 10 percent. What is the maximum amount of money the banking system could create upon acquiring $100 in new reserves and deposits? (No, the answer is not $800!)
2 Explain how a banking system which is "loaned

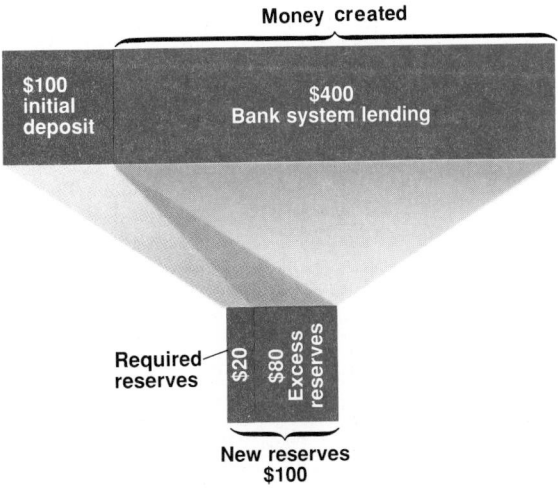

FIGURE 16-2

The outcome of the money expansion process

A deposit of $100 of currency into a checking account creates an initial demand deposit of $100. But if the reserve ratio is 20 percent, only $20 of reserves are legally required to support the $100 demand deposit. The $80 of excess reserves allows the banking system to create $400 of demand deposits through making loans. The $100 of reserves thus supports a total of $500 of money ($100 + $400).

up" and faced with a 20 percent reserve ratio might be forced to *reduce* its outstanding loans by $400 as a result of a $100 cash withdrawal from a demand deposit which forces the bank to draw down its reserves by $100.

SOME MODIFICATIONS

Our discussion of credit expansion has been conducted in a somewhat rarefied atmosphere. There are certain complications which might modify the quantitative preciseness of our analysis.

Other leakages   Aside from the **leakage** of required reserves at each step of the lending process, two other leakages of money from the commercial banks might occur, thereby dampening the money-creating potential of the banking system.

1 CURRENCY DRAINS A borrower may request that a part of his or her loan be paid in cash. Or the recipient of a check drawn by a borrower may present it at the bank to be redeemed partially or wholly in currency rather than added to the borrower's account. Thus, if the person who borrowed the $80 from bank A in our illustration asked for $16 of it in cash and the remaining $64 as a demand deposit, bank B would receive only $64 in new reserves (of which only $51.20 would be excess) rather than $80 (of which $64 was excess). This decline in excess reserves reduces the lending potential of the banking system accordingly. As a matter of fact, if the first borrower had taken the entire $80 in cash and if this currency remained in circulation, the multiple expansion process would have stopped then and there. But the convenience and safety of demand deposits make this unlikely.

2 EXCESS RESERVES Our analysis of the commercial banking system's ability to expand the money supply by lending is based on the supposition that commercial banks are willing to meet precisely the legal reserve requirement. To the extent that bankers hold excess reserves, the overall credit expansion potential of the banking system will be reduced. For example, suppose bank A, upon receiving $100 in new cash, decided to add $25, rather than the legal minimum of $20, to its reserves. Then it would lend only $75, rather than $80, and the money multiplier would be diminished accordingly.[6] In fact, the amount of excess reserves which banks have held in recent years has been very minimal. The explanation is very simple: Excess reserves earn no interest income for a bank; loans and investments do. Hence, our assumption that a bank will lend an amount equal to its excess reserves is reasonable and generally quite accurate.

[6] Specifically, in our $m = \dfrac{1}{R}$ monetary multiplier, we now add to R, the required reserve ratio, the additional excess reserves which bankers choose to keep. For example, if banks want to hold additional excess reserves equal to 5 percent of any newly acquired demand deposits, then the denominator becomes .25 (equal to the .20 reserve ratio plus the .05 addition to excess reserves). The monetary multiplier is reduced from 5 to 1/.25, or 4.

LAST WORD

Bank and thrift failures

The past decade has experienced a rising tide of bank and thrift failures.

Deregulation of the financial industry (Chapter 15) has resulted in increased competition between banks and thrift institutions (savings and loan associations, credit unions, mutual funds, and other financial institutions). Although this increased competition has produced positive overall results, it also has contributed to an unpleasant side-effect: an increasing number of bank and thrift failures (see table).

Two points need to be kept in mind in interpreting this table. On the one hand, these failures constitute only a small percentage of the 14,000 banks and 19,000 thrifts in the United States. On the other hand, for reasons we will soon explore, the number of failures understates the severity of the problem facing some segments of the thrift industry, namely, savings and loan associations (S&Ls).

Earlier in the 1980s, government was forced to bail out two or three major banks experiencing extreme financial difficulties. But *bank* failures in the most recent years have mainly involved small banks operating in agricultural and energy-producing regions. Poor crop prices and declines in energy prices during the 1980s resulted in heavy defaulting on loans, which in turn caused some banks to fail. Nevertheless, banks as a group have remained relatively profitable, and the consensus view is that the banking industry has seen the worst of its troubles. The major remaining problem for large banks is the

Bank and thrift failures, 1980–1988

Year	Banks	Thrifts
1980	10	3
1981	10	11
1982	10	28
1983	42	71
1984	79	27
1985	124	34
1986	145	49
1987	206	48
1988	221	220

Source: Federal Deposit Insurance Corporation and Federal Home Loan Bank Board

possibility that some less developed nations may not be able to pay back their sizeable loans.

The forecast is less optimistic for many *thrifts*. Recent S&L failures have involved some of the largest firms in the industry, and the financial difficulties are more general than for banks. More specifically, nearly 1,000 of the nation's 3,000 S&Ls suffered losses in 1988. Thus, the most recent turmoil in the financial industry is centered upon the S&Ls.

Deregulation of the banking and thrift industry in the early 1980s set the stage for the S&L crisis by leaving the S&Ls without their previously unique role. Prior to the 1980s, banking laws had carved out a near monopoly for the S&Ls on home mortgage loans. When the government lifted interest rate ceilings on deposits in banks and thrifts, competition drove up the interest rates on deposits. But many S&Ls were caught holding fixed-rate, long-term mortgages issued at interest rates far below those needed to keep existing deposits and compete for new deposits. S&Ls responded to the resulting losses by diversifying their loans toward higher-interest commercial loans, consumer loans, loans for office buildings, and the like.

In 1980 government increased deposit insurance from $40,000 per account to $100,000 and some observers believe that this has contributed to the S&L crisis. In an attempt to salvage their enterprises, financially shaky S&Ls offered extraordinarily high interest rates to attract deposits away from competing institutions. Savers, knowing that accounts of $100,000 or less were fully insured by FSLIC, directed funds to these S&Ls. As their interest rates on deposits surged, these S&Ls began to make risky high-interest loans to cover the high costs of their newly acquired funds.

Defaults on many of these risky loans resulted in several large S&L becoming insolvent (having insufficient assets relative to liabilities). Savings and loans in Texas and other "oil patch" states were particularly hard hit. Loan defaults exploded in these areas in response to lower oil prices and accompanying hard times. Many speculative loans on office buildings and other real estate went into default. As indicated in the accompanying table, 220 S&Ls failed in 1988 alone.

The Federal Saving and Loan Insurance Corporation (FSLIC) has covered losses to depositors in failed S&L, but the huge size of the losses has plunged the insurance fund severely into the red. In 1988 the Federal government actively became involved in arranging to sell off or merge insolvent S&Ls. The Federal government has estimated that losses at insolvent thrifts eventually may reach $85 to $105 billion. Some of this amount will be paid for by financially profitable S&Ls through increased premiums to the FSLIC fund. But most of the cost of failed S&Ls will eventually land in the laps of taxpayers. The reason is that Congress has pledged the full credit of the U.S. government to back deposits in insured thrifts. This pledge is designed to assure S&L depositors that their funds are safe, even though the FSLIC itself is "broke." Hence, in 1989, a massive Federal "bailout" of failed S&Ls appeared imminent.

NEED FOR MONETARY CONTROL

Our illustration of the banking system's ability to create money rests upon the assumption that commercial banks are willing to exercise their abilities to create money by lending and that households and businesses are willing to borrow. In reality the willingness of banks to lend on the basis of excess reserves varies cyclically and therein lies the rationale for governmental control of the money supply in order to promote economic stability.

When prosperity reigns banks can be expected to expand credit to the maximum of their ability. Why not? Loans are interest-earning assets and in good times there is little fear of borrowers' defaulting. But, as we shall find in the next two chapters, the money supply has an important effect upon aggregate demand. By lending and thereby creating money to the maximum of their ability during prosperity, commercial banks may contribute to excessive aggregate demand and to the resulting inflation.

Conversely, if depression clouds appear on the economic horizon, bankers may hastily withdraw their invitations to borrow, seeking the safety of liquidity (excess reserves) even if it involves the sacrifice of potential interest income. Bankers may fear the large-scale withdrawal of deposits by a panicky public and simultaneously doubt the ability of borrowers to repay. It is not too surprising that during some years of the Great Depression of the 1930s, banks had considerable excess reserves but lending was at a low ebb. The general point is that during recession banks may decrease the money supply by cutting back on lending. This contraction of the money supply will tend to restrain aggregate demand and to intensify the recession. A rapid shrinkage of the money supply contributed to the Great Depression of the 1930s.

Our overall conclusion is that profit-motivated bankers can be expected to vary the money supply so as to reinforce cyclical fluctuations. It is for this reason that the Federal Reserve System has at its disposal certain policy instruments designed to control the money supply in an anticyclical, rather than procyclical, fashion. It is to an analysis of these policy tools that we now turn.

CHAPTER SUMMARY

1 The operation of a commercial bank can be understood through its balance sheet wherein assets are equal to liabilities plus net worth.

2 Modern banking systems are based upon fractional reserves.

3 Commercial banks are required to keep a legal reserve deposit in a Federal Reserve Bank or as vault cash. This reserve is equal to a specified percentage of the commercial bank's demand-deposit liabilities. Excess reserves are equal to actual reserves minus required reserves.

4 Banks lose both reserves and demand deposits when checks are drawn against them.

5 Commercial banks create money—that is, demand deposits, or bank money—when they make loans. The creation of checkable deposits by bank lending is the most important source of money in our economy. Money is destroyed when loans are repaid.

6 The ability of a single commercial bank to create money by lending depends upon the size of its *excess* reserves. Generally speaking, a commercial bank can lend only an amount equal to the size of its excess reserves. It is thus limited because, in all likelihood, checks drawn by borrowers will be deposited in other banks, causing a loss of reserves and deposits to the lending bank equal to the amount which it has loaned.

7 The commercial banking system as a whole can lend by a multiple of its excess reserves because the banking *system* cannot lose reserves, although individual banks can lose reserves to other banks in the system. The multiple by which the banking system can lend on the basis of each dollar of excess reserves is the reciprocal of the reserve ratio. This multiple credit expansion process is reversible.

8 The fact that profit-seeking banks would tend to alter the money supply in a procyclical fashion underlies the need for the Federal Reserve System to control the money supply.

TERMS AND CONCEPTS

balance sheet

fractional reserve system
of banking

vault cash

legal reserves

reserve ratio

actual, required, and
excess reserves

monetary multiplier

leakages

QUESTIONS AND STUDY SUGGESTIONS

I Why must a balance sheet always balance? What are the major assets and claims on a commercial bank's balance sheet?

2 Why are commercial banks required to have reserves? Explain why reserves are assets to commercial banks but liabilities to the Federal Reserve Banks. What are excess reserves? How do you calculate the amount of excess reserves held by a bank? What is their significance?

3 "Whenever currency is deposited in a commercial bank, cash goes out of circulation and, as a result, the supply of money is reduced." Do you agree? Explain.

4 "When a commercial bank makes loans, it creates money; when loans are repaid, money is destroyed." Explain.

5 Explain why a single commercial bank can safely lend only an amount equal to its excess reserves but the commercial banking system can lend by a multiple of its excess reserves. Why is the multiple by which the banking system can lend equal to the reciprocal of its reserve ratio?

6 Assume that Jones deposits $500 in currency into her demand deposit in the First National Bank. A half-hour later Smith negotiates a loan for $750 at this bank. By how much and in what direction has the money supply changed? Explain.

7 Suppose the National Bank of Commerce has excess reserves of $8,000 and outstanding demand deposits of $150,000. If the reserve ratio is 20 percent, what is the size of the bank's actual reserves?

8 Suppose the Continental Bank has the following simplified balance sheet. The reserve ratio is 20 percent.

c How will the bank's balance sheet appear after checks drawn for the entire amount of the new loans have been cleared against this bank? Show this new balance sheet in column 2.

d Answer questions *a*, *b*, and *c* on the assumption that the reserve ratio is 15 percent.

9 The Third National Bank has reserves of $20,000 and demand deposits of $100,000. The reserve ratio is 20 percent. Households deposit $5,000 in currency into the bank which is added to reserves. How much excess reserves does the bank now have?

10 Suppose again that the Third National Bank has reserves of $20,000 and demand deposits of $100,000. The reserve ratio is 20 percent. The bank now sells $5,000 in securities to the Federal Reserve Bank in its district, receiving a $5,000 increase in reserves in return. How much excess reserves does the bank now have? Why does your answer differ (yes, it does!) from the answer to question 9?

11 What are banking "leakages"? How might they affect the money-creating potential of the banking system? Be specific.

12 Explain why there is a need for the Federal Reserve System to control the money supply.

13 Suppose that Bob withdraws $100 of cash from his checking account at Security Bank and uses it to buy a camera from Joe, who deposits the $100 in his checking account in Serenity Bank. Assuming a reserve ratio of 10 percent and no initial excess reserves, determine the extent to which: **a** Security Bank must reduce its loans and demand deposits because of the cash withdrawal and **b** Serenity Bank can safely increase its loans and demand deposits because of the cash deposit. Have the cash withdrawal and deposit changed the money supply?

Assets			Liabilities and net worth		
	(1)	(2)		(1)	(2)
Reserves	$22,000 _____	_____	Demand deposits	$100,000 _____	_____
Securities	38,000 _____	_____			
Loans	40,000 _____	_____			

a What is the maximum amount of new loans which this bank can make? Show in column 1 how the bank's balance sheet will appear after the bank has loaned this additional amount.

b By how much has the supply of money changed? Explain.

14 Suppose the simplified consolidated balance sheet shown on page 320 is for the commercial banking system. All figures are in billions. The reserve ratio is 25 percent.

a How much excess reserves does the commercial banking system have? What is the maximum amount the banking system might lend? Show in column 1

Assets		Liabilities and net worth	
	(1)		(1)
Reserves	$ 52 _____	Demand deposits	$200 _____
Securities	48 _____		
Loans	100 _____		

how the consolidated balance sheet would look after this amount has been lent.

b Answer question 14a on the assumption that the reserve ratio is 20 percent. Explain the resulting difference in the lending ability of the commercial banking system.

CHAPTER 17

The Federal Reserve Banks and monetary policy

Our attention in Chapter 16 was focused upon the money-creating ability of individual banks and the commercial banking system. Our discussion ended on a disturbing note: Unregulated commercial banking might contribute to cyclical fluctuations in business activity. That is, commercial banks will find it profitable to expand the supply of money during periods of demand-pull inflation and to restrict the money supply in seeking liquidity during depression. It is the purpose of this chapter to see how our monetary authorities attempt to reverse the procyclical tendencies of the commercial banking system through a variety of control techniques. As in Chapter 16 we are here couching our discussion in terms of commercial banks because of their major role in creating demand-deposit money. However, throughout our discussion the term "depository institution" can be substituted for "commercial bank" and "checkable deposits" can be substituted for "demand deposits."

The goals of the present chapter are these: First, the objectives of monetary policy and the roles of participating institutions are briefly discussed. Next, the balance sheet of the Federal Reserve Banks is surveyed, because it is through these central banks that monetary policy is largely implemented. Third, the techniques of monetary control are analyzed in considerable detail. What are the major instruments of monetary control and how do they function? Fourth, the Keynesian perspective of the cause-effect chain through which monetary policy functions is detailed and the effectiveness of monetary policy is evaluated. Finally, a brief, but important, recapitulation of Keynesian employment theory and policy is presented.

Objectives of monetary policy

Before analyzing the techniques through which monetary policy is put into effect, it is essential that we clearly understand the objectives of monetary policy and identify the institutions responsible for the formulation and implementation of that policy.

Certain key points made in Chapter 15 merit reemphasis at the outset of our discussion. The Board of Governors of the Federal Reserve System has the responsibility of supervising and controlling the operation of our monetary and banking systems. It is this Board which formulates the basic policies which the banking system follows. Because it is a public body, the decisions of the Board of Governors are made in what it perceives to be the public interest. The twelve Federal Reserve Banks— the central banks of American capitalism—have the responsibility of implementing the policy decisions of the Board. You will recall that as quasipublic banks, the Federal Reserve Banks are not guided by the profit motive, but rather they pursue those measures which the Board of Governors recommends.

However, to say that the Board follows policies which "promote the public interest" is not enough. We must pinpoint the goal of monetary policy. It will come as no great surprise that *the fundamental objective of* **monetary policy** *is to assist the economy in achieving a full-employment, noninflationary level of total output.* Monetary policy consists of altering the economy's money supply for the purpose of stabilizing aggregate output, employment, and the price level. More specifically, monetary policy entails increasing the money supply during a recession to stimulate spending and, conversely, restricting the money supply during inflation to constrain spending.

The Federal Reserve Board alters the size of the nation's money supply by manipulating the size of excess reserves held by commercial banks. Excess reserves, you will recall, are critical to the money-creating ability of the banking system. The specific techniques by which the Board changes excess reserves in the banking system merit considerable discussion. Once we see how the Federal Reserve controls excess reserves and the money supply, we will turn to an explanation of how changes in the stock of money affect interest rates and aggregate expenditures.

Consolidated balance sheet of the Federal Reserve Banks

Because monetary policy is implemented by the twelve Federal Reserve Banks, it is useful to consider the nature of the balance sheet of these banks. Some of the assets and liabilities found here are considerably different from those found on the balance sheet of a commercial bank. Table 17-1 is a simplified consolidated balance sheet which shows all the pertinent assets and liabilities of the twelve Federal Reserve Banks as of November 30, 1988.

ASSETS

There are two major assets which are important for our ensuing analysis.

Securities The securities shown are government bonds which the Federal Reserve Banks have pur-

chased. These bonds consist largely of debt instruments such as Treasury bills (short-term securities) and Treasury bonds (long-term securities) issued by the Federal government to finance past and present budget deficits. That is, the securities are part of the public or national debt (Chapter 20). Some of these bonds may have been purchased directly from the Treasury, but most are bought in the open market from commercial banks or the public. Although these bonds are an important source of income to the Federal Reserve Banks, they are not bought and sold purposely for income. Rather, as we shall see, they are bought and sold primarily to influence the size of commercial bank reserves and therefore their ability to create money by lending.

Loans to commercial banks For reasons we will discuss soon, commercial banks occasionally borrow from the Federal Reserve Banks. The IOUs which the commercial banks give to these "bankers' banks" in negotiating loans are listed as loans to commercial banks. From the Federal Reserve Banks' point of view, these IOUs are assets, that is, claims against the commercial banks which have borrowed from them. To the commercial banks, these IOUs are liabilities. By borrowing in this way, the commercial banks obtain increases in their reserves in exchange for IOUs.

LIABILITIES

On the liability side we find three major items.

TABLE 17-1 **Twelve Federal Reserve Banks' consolidated balance sheet, November 30, 1988 (in millions)**

Assets		Liabilities and net worth	
Securities	$232,702	Reserves of commercial banks	$ 40,012
Loans to commercial banks	2,328	Treasury deposits	5,198
All other assets	49,390	Federal Reserve Notes (outstanding)	224,535
		All other liabilities and net worth	14,675
Total	$284,420	Total	$284,420

Source: *Federal Reserve Bulletin*, February 1989.

Reserves of commercial banks We are already familiar with this account. It is an asset from the viewpoint of the member banks but a liability to the Federal Reserve Banks.

Treasury deposits Just as businesses and private individuals find it convenient and desirable to pay their obligations by check, so does the United States Treasury. It keeps deposits in the various Federal Reserve Banks and draws checks on them in paying its obligations. To the Treasury such deposits are assets; to the Federal Reserve Banks they are liabilities. The Treasury creates and replenishes these deposits by depositing tax receipts and money borrowed from the public or the banks through the sale of bonds.

Federal Reserve Notes Our paper money supply consists of Federal Reserve Notes which are issued by the Federal Reserve Banks. When in circulation, these pieces of paper money constitute circulating claims against the assets of the Federal Reserve Banks and are therefore treated by them as liabilities. Just as your own IOU is neither an asset nor a liability to you when it is in your own possession, so Federal Reserve Notes resting in the vaults of the various Federal Reserve Banks are neither an asset nor a liability. Only those notes in circulation are liabilities to the bankers' banks. These notes, which come into circulation through commercial banks, are not a part of the money supply until they are in the hands of the public.

The tools of monetary policy

With this cursory understanding of the Federal Reserve Banks' balance sheet, we are now in a position to explore how the Board of Governors of the Federal Reserve System can influence the money-creating abilities of the commercial banking system. What tools or techniques can be employed at the discretion of the Board of Governors to influence commercial bank reserves?

There are three major instruments of monetary control:

1 Open-market operations
2 Changing the reserve ratio
3 Changing the discount rate

OPEN-MARKET OPERATIONS

Open-market operations are the most important means by which the money supply is controlled. The term **open-market operations** refers to the buying and selling of government bonds by the Federal Reserve Banks in the open market—that is, the buying and selling of bonds from or to commercial banks and the general public. How do these purchases and sales of government securities affect the excess reserves of commercial banks?

Buying securities Suppose the Board of Governors orders the Federal Reserve Banks to buy government bonds in the open market. From whom may these securities be purchased? In general, from commercial banks and the public. In either case the overall effect is basically the same—commercial bank reserves are increased.

FROM COMMERCIAL BANKS Let us trace through the process by which the Federal Reserve Banks buy government bonds *from commercial banks*. This transaction is a simple one.

a. The commercial banks give up a part of their holdings of securities to the Federal Reserve Banks.

b. The Federal Reserve Banks pay for these securities by increasing the reserves of the commercial banks by the amount of the purchase.

Just as the commercial bank may pay for a bond bought from a private individual by increasing the seller's demand deposit, so the bankers' bank may pay for bonds bought from commercial banks by increasing the banks' reserves. In short, the consolidated balance sheets of the commercial banks and the Federal Reserve Banks will change as shown on page 324, top left.

The upward arrow shows that securities have moved from the commercial banks to the Federal Reserve Banks. Hence, we have placed a minus sign in front of "Securities" in the asset column of the balance sheet of the commercial banks. For the same reason, we have placed a plus sign in front of "Securities" in the asset column of the balance sheet of the Federal Reserve Banks. The downward arrow indicates that the Federal Reserve Banks have provided reserves to the commercial banks. We therefore have placed a plus sign in front of "Reserves" in the balance sheet for the commercial

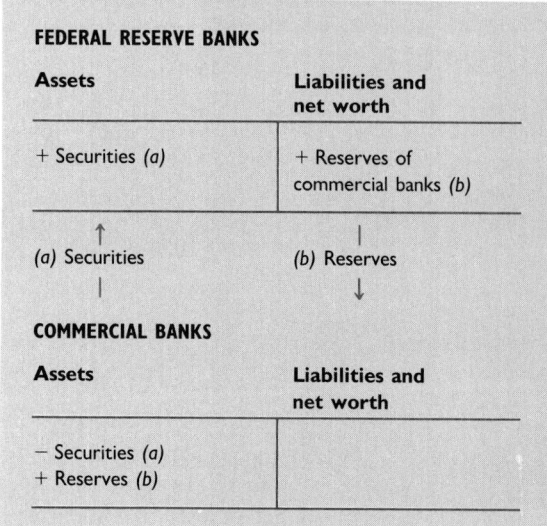

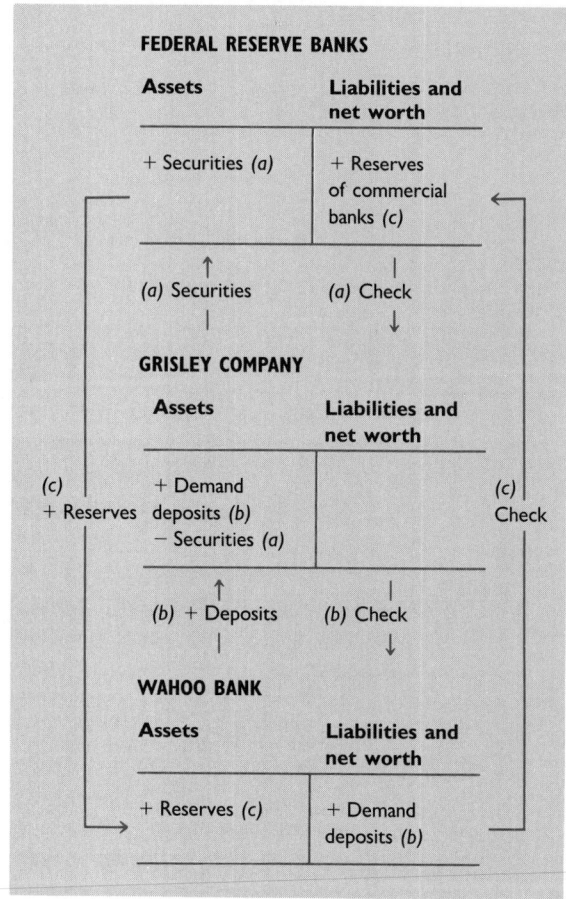

banks. The plus sign in the liability column of the balance sheet of the Federal Reserve Banks indicates that commercial bank reserves have increased; they are a liability to the Federal Reserve Banks.

The most important aspect of this transaction is that, when Federal Reserve Banks purchase securities from commercial banks, the reserves—and therefore the lending ability—of the commercial banks are increased.

FROM THE PUBLIC If the Federal Reserve Banks should purchase securities *from the general public,* the effect on commercial bank reserves would be substantially the same. Suppose that the Grisley Meat Packing Company possesses some negotiable government bonds which it sells in the open market to the Federal Reserve Banks. The transaction goes like this:

a. The Grisley company gives up securities to the Federal Reserve Banks and gets in payment a check drawn by the Federal Reserve Banks on themselves.

b. The Grisley company promptly deposits this check in its account with its Wahoo bank.

c. The Wahoo bank collects this check against the Federal Reserve Banks by sending it to the Federal Reserve Banks for collection. As a result the Wahoo bank receives an increase in its reserves. Balance sheet changes are as follows:

Two aspects of this transaction are noteworthy. First, as with Federal Reserve purchases of securities directly from commercial banks, the reserves and lending ability of the commercial banking system have been increased. This fact is denoted by the plus sign in front of "Reserves," indicating an increase in assets of the Wahoo bank. Second, in this instance the supply of money is directly increased by the central banks' purchase of government bonds, aside from any expansion of the money supply which may occur as the result of the increase in commercial bank reserves. This direct increase in the money supply has taken the form of an increased amount of checking account money in the economy. In this regard, note the plus sign in front of demand deposits in the Wahoo bank. Because these demand deposits are an asset as viewed by the Grisley company, we observe that demand deposits have increased (plus sign) on the Grisley company's balance sheet.

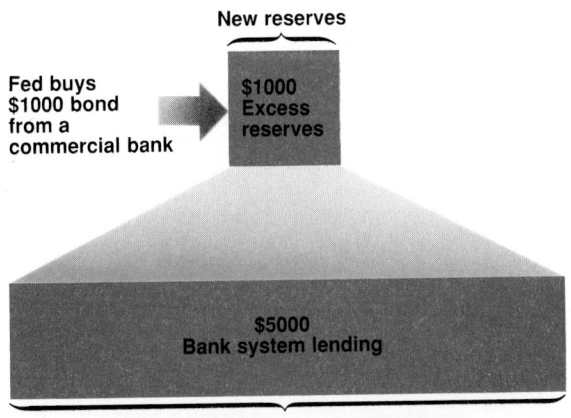

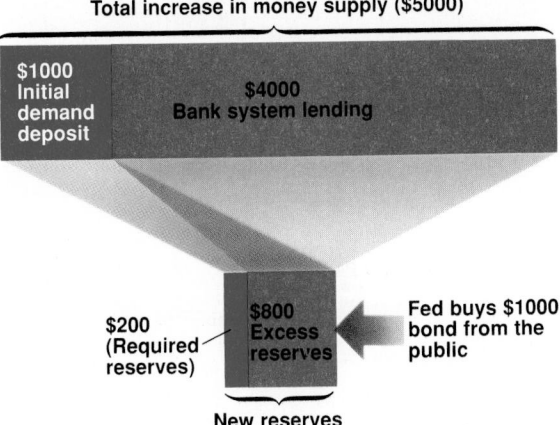

FIGURE 17-1

The Federal Reserve's purchase of bonds and the expansion of the money supply

Assuming that all banks are "loaned up" initially, a Federal Reserve purchase of a $1000 bond from either a commercial bank or the public will increase the money supply by $5000 when the reserve ratio is 20 percent. In the top portion of the diagram, we observe that the purchase of a $1000 bond from a commercial bank creates $1000 of excess reserves which support an expansion of demand deposits of $5000 through making loans. In the lower portion, we note that the purchase of a $1000 bond from the public creates only $800 of excess reserves, because $200 of reserves are required to "back up" the $1000 new demand deposit in the banking system. Hence, the commercial banks can expand the money supply by $4000 by making loans. This $4000 of checking account money *plus* the initial new demand deposit of $1000 together equal $5000 of new money.

You may detect a slight difference between the Federal Reserve Banks' purchases of securities from the commercial banking system and from the public. Assuming all commercial banks are "loaned up" initially, Federal Reserve bond purchases *from commercial banks* will increase the actual reserves and excess reserves of the commercial banks by the entire amount of the bond purchases. Thus, as shown in Figure 17-1, a $1000 bond purchase from a commercial bank would increase both the actual and excess reserves of the commercial bank by $1000. On the other hand, Federal Reserve Bank purchases of bonds *from the public* increase actual reserves but also increase demand deposits. Thus, a $1000 bond purchase from the public would increase actual reserves of the "loaned up" banking system by $1000; but with a 20 percent reserve ratio, the excess reserves of the banking system would only amount to $800. In the case of bond purchases from the public, it is *as if* the commercial banking system had already used one-fifth, or 20 percent, of its newly acquired reserves to support $1000 worth of new demand-deposit money.

However, in each transaction the basic conclusion is the same: *When the Federal Reserve Banks buy securities in the open market, commercial banks' reserves will be increased*. Assuming that the banks lend out their excess reserves, the nation's money supply will rise. Observe in Figure 17-1 that a $1000 purchase of bonds by the Federal Reserve will result in $5000 of additional money, without regard to whether the purchase was made from commercial banks or from the general public.

Selling securities We should now be highly suspicious that Federal Reserve Bank sales of government bonds will reduce commercial bank reserves. Let us confirm these suspicions.

TO COMMERCIAL BANKS Suppose the Federal Reserve Banks sell securities in the open market to *commercial banks:*

a. The Federal Reserve Banks give up securities which the commercial banks acquire.

b. The commercial banks pay for these securities by drawing checks against their deposits—that is, their reserves—in the Federal Reserve Banks. The Federal Reserve Banks collect these checks by reducing the commercial banks' reserves accordingly.

In short, the balance sheet changes appear as follows:

FEDERAL RESERVE BANKS

Assets	Liabilities and net worth
— Securities (a)	— Reserves of commercial banks (b)
↓ (a) Securities	↑ (b) Reserves

COMMERCIAL BANKS

Assets	Liabilities and net worth
— Reserves (b) + Securities (a)	

Note specifically the reduction in commercial bank reserves.

TO THE PUBLIC Should the Federal Reserve Banks sell securities *to the public,* the overall effect would be substantially the same. Let us put the Grisley company on the buying end of government bonds which the Federal Reserve Banks are selling.

a. The Federal Reserve Bank sells government bonds to Grisley, the latter paying with a check drawn on the Wahoo bank.

b. The Federal Reserve Banks clear this check against the Wahoo bank by reducing its reserves.

c. The Wahoo bank returns the Grisley company's check to it, reducing the company's demand deposit accordingly.

The balance sheets change as shown in the next column.

Note that Federal Reserve bond sales of $1000 to the commercial banking system reduce the system's actual and excess reserves by $1000. But a $1000 bond sale to the public reduces excess reserves by $800 because demand-deposit money is also reduced by $1000 by the sale. In the case of bond sales to the public, it is *as if* the commercial banking system had reduced its outstanding de-

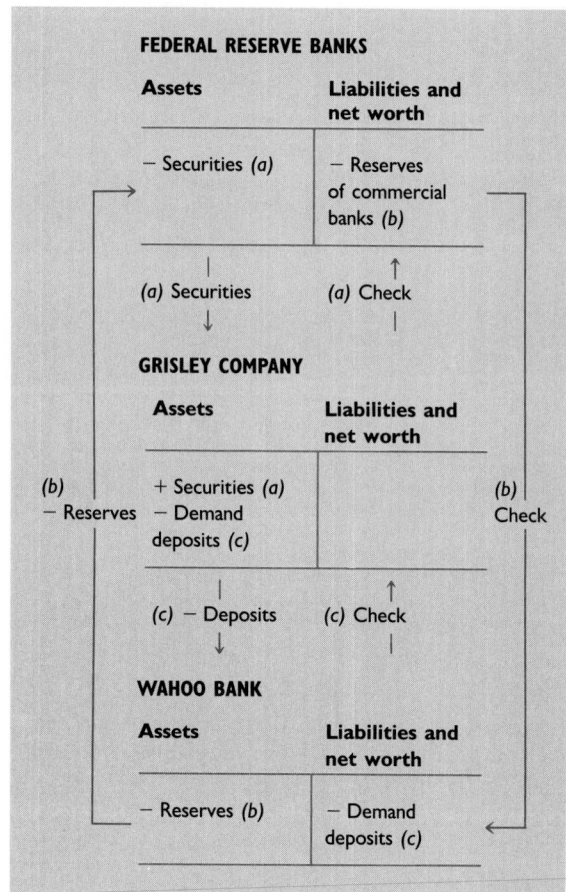

mand deposits by $1000 to cushion the decline in excess reserves to the extent of $200.

In both variations of the Federal Reserve bond sale transaction, however, the basic conclusion is identical: *When the Federal Reserve Banks sell securities in the open market, commercial bank reserves are reduced.* If all excess reserves are presently lent out, this decline in commercial bank reserves will translate into a decline in the nation's money supply. In our example, a $1000 sale of government securities will result in a $5000 decline in the money supply irrespective of whether the sale was made to commercial banks or the general public. You are urged to convince yourself of this fact by reexamining Figure 17-1 and tracing the effects of a *sale* of a $1000 bond by the Federal Reserve Banks either to commercial banks or to the public.

Question: What makes commercial banks and the public willing to sell government securities to, or buy them from, the Federal Reserve Banks? The answer lies in the price of bonds and their interest rates. We know from Chapter 15 that bond prices and interest rates are inversely related. When the Federal Reserve decides to buy government bonds, the demand for them will increase. Hence, government bond prices will rise and their interest rates will decline. The higher bond prices and their lower interest rates will prompt bank and public holders of government bonds to sell them to the Federal Reserve Banks. Conversely, when the Federal Reserve decides to sell government bonds, the additional supply of bonds in the bond market will lower bond prices and raise their interest rates, thereby making government bonds attractive purchases for banks and the public.

THE RESERVE RATIO

How can the Board of Governors influence the ability of commercial banks to lend through manipulation of the legal **reserve ratio?** A simple example will supply a clear answer to this query. Starting with row 2 of Table 17-2, suppose a commercial bank's balance sheet shows that reserves are $5000 and demand deposits $20,000. If the legal reserve ratio stands at 20 percent, the bank's *required* reserves are $4000. Since *actual* reserves are $5000, it is apparent that the *excess* reserves of this bank are $1000. On the basis of this $1000 of excess reserves, we have seen that this single bank

can lend $1000, but the banking system as a whole could create a maximum of $5000 in new checking account money by lending.

Raising the reserve ratio   Now, what if the Board of Governors raised the legal reserve ratio from 20 to 25 percent? (See row 3.) Required reserves would jump from $4000 to $5000, shrinking excess reserves from $1000 to zero. It is apparent that *raising the reserve ratio increases the amount of required reserves banks must keep. Either banks lose excess reserves, diminishing their ability to create money by lending, or else they find their reserves deficient and are forced to contract their checkable deposits and therefore the money supply.* In the case just cited, excess reserves are transformed into required reserves, and the money-creating potential of our *single bank* is reduced from $1000 to zero. The *banking system's* money-creating capacity declines from $5000 to zero.

What if the Board of Governors announced a forthcoming increase in the legal reserve requirement to 30 percent? (See row 4.) The commercial bank would be faced with the prospect of failing to meet this requirement. To protect itself against such an eventuality, the bank would be forced to lower its outstanding demand deposits and at the same time to increase its reserves. To reduce its demand deposits, the bank would be disposed to let outstanding loans mature and to be repaid without extending new credit. To increase reserves, the

TABLE 17-2 **The effects of changes in the reserve ratio upon the lending ability of commercial banks (hypothetical data)**

(1) Legal reserve ratio, percent	(2) Demand deposits	(3) Actual reserves	(4) Required reserves	(5) Excess reserves, or (3) − (4)	(6) Money-creating potential of single bank, = (5)	(7) Money-creating potential of banking system
(1) 10	$20,000	$5000	$2000	$ 3000	$ 3000	$ 30,000
(2) 20	20,000	5000	4000	1000	1000	5,000
(3) 25	20,000	5000	5000	0	0	0
(4) 30	20,000	5000	6000	−1000	−1000	−3,333

bank might sell some of its holdings of securities, adding the proceeds to its reserves. Both courses of action will reduce the supply of money (see Chapter 16, transactions 6 and 8).

Lowering the reserve ratio   What would be the effect if the Board of Governors lowered the reserve ratio from the original 20 to 10 percent? (See row 1.) In this case, required reserves would decline from $4000 to $2000, and as a result, excess reserves would jump from $1000 to $3000. As a result, the single bank's lending or money-creating ability increases from $1000 to $3000 and the banking system's money-creating potential expands from $5000 to $30,000. We can conclude that *lowering the reserve ratio changes required reserves to excess reserves, thereby enhancing the ability of banks to create new money by lending.*

Table 17-2 reveals that a change in the reserve ratio affects the money-creating ability of the *banking system* in two ways.
1 It affects the size of excess reserves.
2 It changes the size of the monetary multiplier.

Thus, for example, in raising the legal reserve ratio from 10 to 20 percent, excess reserves are reduced from $3000 to $1000, on the one hand, and the demand-deposit multiplier is reduced from 10 to 5. Hence, the money-creating potential of the banking system declines from $30,000 (= $3000 × 10) to $5000 (= $1000 × 5).

Although changing the reserve ratio is a potentially powerful technique of monetary control, it is actually used infrequently.

THE DISCOUNT RATE

One of the traditional functions of a central bank is to be a "lender of last resort." That is, central banks will lend to commercial banks which are financially sound, but which have unexpected and immediate needs for additional funds. Thus it is that each Federal Reserve Bank will make short-term loans to commercial banks in its district.

When a commercial bank borrows, it turns over to the Federal Reserve Bank a promissory note or IOU drawn against itself and secured by acceptable collateral—typically United States government securities. Just as commercial banks charge interest on their loans, so do the Federal Reserve Banks

charge interest on the loans they grant to commercial banks. This interest rate is called the **discount rate.**

As a claim against the commercial bank, the borrowing bank's promissory note is an asset to the lending Federal Reserve Bank and appears on its balance sheet as "Loans to commercial banks." To the commercial bank the IOU is a liability, appearing as "Loans from the Federal Reserve Banks" on the commercial bank's balance sheet. In payment of the loan the Federal Reserve Bank will *increase* the reserves of the borrowing commercial bank. Since no required reserves need be kept against loans from the Federal Reserve Banks, *all* new reserves acquired by borrowing from the Federal Reserve Banks would be excess reserves. These changes are reflected in the balance sheets of the commercial banks and the bankers' banks as shown below.

FEDERAL RESERVE BANKS	
Assets	**Liabilities and net worth**
+ Loans to commercial banks	+ Reserves of commercial banks
↑	↓
IOUs	+ Reserves

COMMERCIAL BANKS	
Assets	**Liabilities and net worth**
+ Reserves	+ Loans from the Federal Reserve Banks

It is interesting to note that this transaction is analogous to a private person's borrowing from a commercial bank (see Chapter 16, transaction 6).

The important point, of course, is that *commercial bank borrowing from the Federal Reserve Banks increases the reserves of commercial banks, thereby enhancing their ability to extend credit to the public.*

The Board of Governors of the Federal Reserve System has the power to establish and manipulate the discount rate at which commercial banks can borrow from the Federal Reserve Banks. From the commercial banks' point of view, the discount rate constitutes a cost entailed in acquiring reserves. Hence, when the discount rate is decreased, commercial banks are encouraged to obtain additional reserves by borrowing from the Federal Reserve Banks. Commercial bank lending based upon these new reserves will constitute an increase in the money supply. Conversely, an increase in the discount rate discourages commercial banks from obtaining additional reserves through borrowing from the central banks. An increase in the discount rate therefore is consistent with the monetary authorities' desire to restrict the supply of money.

A PREVIEW: EASY MONEY AND TIGHT MONEY

Suppose the economy is faced with unemployment and deflation. The monetary authorities correctly decide that an increase in the supply of money is needed to stimulate the volume of aggregate expenditures in order to help absorb the idle resources. To induce an increase in the supply of money, the Board of Governors must see to it that the excess reserves of commercial banks are expanded. What specific policies will bring this about?

1 The Board of Governors should order the Federal Reserve Banks to buy securities in the open market. These bond purchases will be paid for by increases in commercial bank reserves.
2 The reserve ratio should be reduced, automatically changing required reserves into excess reserves and increasing the size of the money multiplier.
3 The discount rate should be lowered to induce commercial banks to add to their reserves by borrowing from the Federal Reserve Banks.

For obvious reasons, this set of policy decisions is called an **easy money policy.** Its purpose is to make credit cheaply and easily available, so as to increase the volumes of aggregate expenditures and employment.

Suppose, on the other hand, excessive spending is pushing the economy into an inflationary spiral. The Board of Governors should attempt to reduce total spending by limiting or contracting the supply of money. The key to this goal lies in reducing the reserves of commercial banks. How is this done?

1 The Federal Reserve Banks should sell government bonds in the open market to tear down commercial bank reserves.
2 Increasing the reserve ratio will automatically strip commercial banks of excess reserves and decrease the size of the money multiplier.
3 A boost in the discount rate will discourage commercial banks from building up their reserves by borrowing at the Federal Reserve Banks.

This group of directives is appropriately labeled a **tight money policy.** The objective is to tighten the supply of money in order to reduce spending and control inflationary pressures.

RELATIVE IMPORTANCE

Of the three major monetary controls, open-market operations clearly have evolved as the most important control mechanism. The reasons for this are worth noting.

The discount rate is less important than open-market operations for two interrelated reasons. First, the amount of commercial bank reserves obtained by borrowing from the central banks is typically very small. On the average only 2 or 3 percent of bank reserves are acquired in this way. Indeed, it is often the effectiveness of open-market operations which induces the commercial banks to borrow from the Federal Reserve Banks. That is, to the extent that central bank bond sales make commercial banks temporarily short of reserves, the commercial banks will be prompted to borrow from the Federal Reserve Banks. Hence, rather than being a primary tool of monetary policy, commercial bank borrowing from the Fed occurs largely in response to monetary policy as carried out by open-market operations.

A second consideration is that, while the manipulation of commercial bank reserves through open-market operations and the changing of reserve requirements are accomplished at the initiative of the Federal Reserve System, the discount rate depends upon the initiative of the commercial banks to be effective. For example, if the discount rate is lowered at a time when very few banks are inclined to borrow from the Federal Reserve Banks, the lower rate will have little or no impact upon bank reserves or the money supply.

Nevertheless, some economists point out that a

change in the discount rate may have an important "announcement effect"; that is, a discount rate change may be a very clear and explicit way of communicating to the financial community and the economy as a whole the intended direction of monetary policy. Other economists doubt this, arguing that changes in the discount rate are often "passive" in that the rate is changed to keep it in line with other short-term interest rates, rather than to invoke a policy change.

What about changes in reserve requirements?

Because the impact is so powerful, so blunt, so immediate, and so widespread, the Federal Reserve uses its authority to change reserve requirements only sparingly, particularly during tight money periods when increases in reserve requirements would be appropriate.[1]

The reluctance to increase reserve requirements undoubtedly is related to the fact that reserve balances earn no interest; hence, higher reserve requirements can have substantial adverse effects upon bank profits. In fact, it was the rising opportunity cost associated with high interest rates in the 1970s which caused large numbers of banks to drop their membership in the Federal Reserve System, thereby weakening the potential effectiveness of monetary policy. Recall that the Depository Institutions Deregulation and Monetary Control Act of 1980 responded to this problem by requiring all commercial banks and other depository institutions—whether or not they are members of the Federal Reserve System—to hold reserves in the central banks (Table 16-1). This means that, when used, reserve-requirement changes will be an even more potent technique of monetary policy than in the past.

But there are more positive reasons why open-market operations have evolved as the primary technique of monetary policy. This mechanism of monetary control has the advantage of flexibility—government securities can be purchased or sold in large or small amounts—and the impact upon bank reserves is quite prompt. Yet, compared with reserve-requirement changes, open-market operations work subtly and less directly. Furthermore, quantitatively there is no question about the potential ability of the Federal Reserve Banks to affect commercial bank reserves through bond sales and purchases. A glance at the consolidated balance sheet for the Federal Reserve Banks (Table 17-1) reveals very large holdings of government bonds ($233 billion), the sales of which could theoretically reduce commercial bank reserves from $40 billion to zero.

MINOR SELECTIVE CONTROLS

The three major instruments of monetary policy are supplemented periodically by certain other, less important credit controls in the form of **selective controls** which pertain to the stock market, installment purchases, and moral suasion.

Margin requirement The lesson of the great stock market "crash" of 1929 is that runaway speculation in the stock market can impose serious problems upon the economy.[2] For example, collapsing stock prices may wipe out the wealth of individuals and businesses who hold substantial amounts of stock. This causes them to retrench on their consumption and investment spending and propels the economy into a recession or depression. Similarly, businesses which want to expand will find that depressed stock prices make it difficult to obtain the required funds. To guard against excessive stock market speculation and the possibility of a crash, the Board of Governors of the Federal Reserve System has the authority to specify the **margin requirement**, or minimum percentage down payment which purchasers of stock must make. Thus, the current margin requirement of 50 percent means that only 50 percent of the purchase price of a security may be borrowed, the remaining 50 percent being paid "cash on the barrelhead." This rate can be raised when it is deemed desirable to restrict speculative stock purchases and lowered

---

[1] Lawrence S. Ritter and William L. Silber, *Money,* 5th ed. (New York: Basic Books, Inc., Publishers, 1984), p. 121.

[2] The reader might enjoy Gordon Thomas and Max Morgan-Witts, *The Day the Bubble Burst* (Garden City, N.Y.: Doubleday & Company, Inc., 1979); and John Kenneth Galbraith, *The Great Crash, 1929* (London: Hamish Hamilton, 1955).

to revive a sluggish market. In fact, the 50 percent requirement has applied since 1974.

Consumer credit Congress occasionally has authorized the Board of Governors to invoke specific restraints on consumer credit. Example: Using legislative authority available to him, President Carter ordered the Federal Reserve in the spring of 1980 to impose new restrictions upon consumer borrowing as a part of his anti-inflation program. Specifically, lenders were required to make a "special deposit" in the Federal Reserve Banks equal to 15 percent of any *increase* in the total amount of credit outstanding in the form of credit card purchases or unsecured personal loans. Because these special deposits would earn no interest, they would increase the costs of lenders and discourage further expansions of consumer credit.

Moral suasion The monetary authorities sometimes use the less tangible technique of **moral suasion** or "jawboning" to influence the lending policies of commercial banks. Moral suasion simply means the employment by the monetary authorities of "friendly persuasion"—policy statements, public pronouncements, or outright appeals—warning that excessive expansion or contraction of bank credit might involve serious consequences for the banking system and the economy as a whole. Example: In March of 1980 the Federal Reserve "strongly recommended" that to help fight inflation banks restrict their lending to an annual growth rate of 6 to 9 percent, a figure substantially below the 20 percent growth rate otherwise anticipated.

Monetary policy, equilibrium NNP, and the price level

Although there is universal agreement that the Federal Reserve possesses the tools necessary to change the money supply, there is considerable disagreement as to how changes in the money supply affect the economy. The mainstream—or Keynesian—interpretation of how monetary policy works is the subject of our immediate attention. In Chapter 18 the monetarist perspective of monetary policy is examined in detail.

CAUSE-EFFECT CHAIN: KEYNESIAN VIEW

Precisely how does monetary policy work toward the goal of full employment and price stability? The central factors and relationships are illustrated in Figure 17-2.

Money market The diagram at the left shows the **money market,** wherein the demand for money curve, D_m, and the supply of money curve, S_m, are brought together. Recall from Chapter 15[3] that the total demand for money is comprised of the transactions and the asset demands. The transactions demand is directly related to the level of economic transactions as reflected in the size of the nominal NNP. The asset demand is inversely related to the interest rate. Recall too that the interest rate is the opportunity cost of holding money as an asset; the higher the cost, the smaller the amount of money the public wants to hold. In Figure 17-2a the total demand for money is inversely related to the interest rate. In this presentation an increase in nominal NNP will shift D_m to the right; a decline in nominal NNP will shift D_m to the left.

We complete our portrayal of the money market by adding the money supply, S_m. The money supply is shown as a vertical line on the assumption that it is some fixed amount determined by the Board of Governors' policy independently of the rate of interest. In other words, while monetary policy (the supply of money) helps determine the interest rate, the interest rate does not in turn determine monetary policy. Figure 17-2a tells us that, given the demand for money, if the supply of money is $150 billion, the equilibrium interest rate will be 8 percent. Recall from Chapter 12 that it is the real, not the nominal, rate of interest which is critical for investment decisions. Hence, our discussion here assumes a constant price level and that the 8 percent interest rate portrayed in Figure 17-2a is the real rate of interest.

Investment This 8 percent interest rate is projected off the investment-demand curve of Figure 17-2b. We find that at this 8 percent interest rate it will be profitable for businesses to invest $20 billion. Ob-

[3] You might find it helpful at this point to reread the section entitled "The Demand for Money" in Chapter 15.

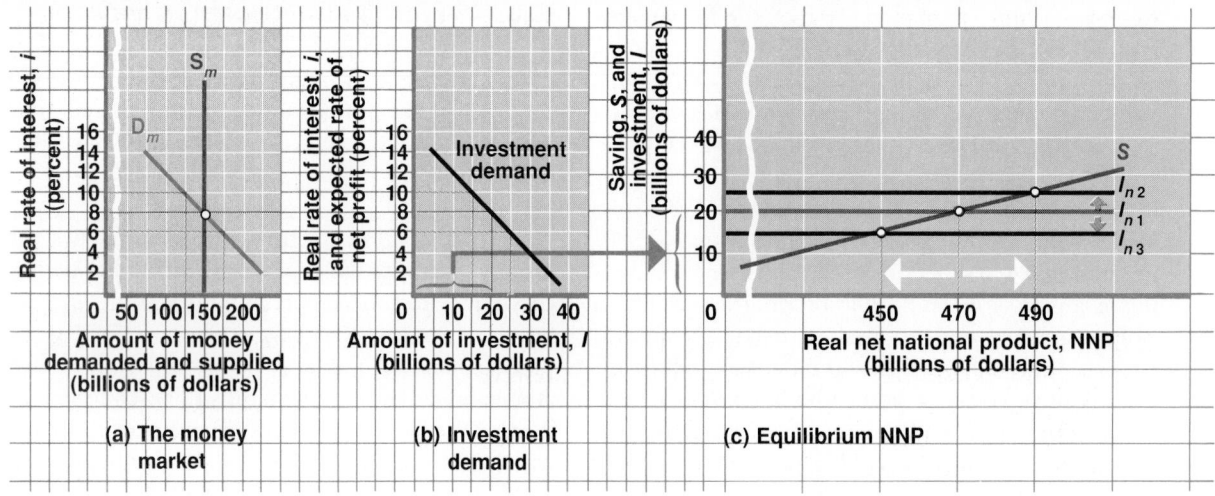

FIGURE 17-2

Monetary policy and the equilibrium NNP: Keynesian view

An easy money policy will lower the interest rate, increase the investment component of aggregate spending, and thereby increase the equilibrium level of NNP. Conversely, a tight money policy will raise the rate of interest, reduce the investment component of aggregate spending, and restrain demand-pull inflation.

serve that more investment will be forthcoming at an interest rate below 8 percent while less investment will occur if the interest rate is above 8 percent. Economists are in general agreement that the investment component of total spending is more likely to be affected by changes in the interest rate than is consumer spending. It is quite true, of course, that consumer purchases of automobiles—which are heavily dependent upon installment credit—are sensitive to interest rates. But overall the interest rate does not seem to be a very crucial factor in determining how households divide their disposable income between consumption and saving.[4]

The impact of changing interest rates upon investment spending is great because of the large size

[4] Indeed, it is not clear whether decreases in the interest rate will tend to increase or decrease the amount of consumption. On the one hand, a lower interest rate may induce some households, particularly those operating small businesses, to save less, because it is now cheap to finance by borrowing. On the other hand, those who save to provide a given retirement income or to accumulate funds for the education of their children find that a lower interest rate will mean that a larger volume of saving will be required to earn the needed income.

and long-term nature of such purchases. Capital equipment, factory buildings, warehouses, and so forth, are tremendously expensive purchases. In absolute terms the interest charges on funds borrowed for these purchases will be considerable. Similarly, the interest cost on a house purchased on a long-term contract will be very large: A one-half percentage point change in the interest rate could easily amount to thousands of dollars on the total cost of a home. It is important to note as well that changes in the interest rate may also affect investment spending by changing the relative attractiveness of capital equipment purchases and bond purchases. If the interest rate rises on bonds, then, given the profit expectations on capital goods purchases, businesses will be more inclined to use business savings to purchase securities than to buy capital equipment. Conversely, given profit expectations on investment spending, a fall in the interest rate makes capital goods purchases more attractive than bond ownership. In short, the impact of changing interest rates will be primarily upon investment spending and, through this channel, upon output, employment, and the level of prices. More specifically, as Figure 17-2b indicates, investment spending varies inversely with the interest rate.

Equilibrium NNP Finally, in Figure 17-2c the $20 billion of investment determined in Figure 17-2b is plugged in the simple leakages-injections model for the private closed economy to determine the equilibrium level of NNP. We observe that I_{n1} equals savings at the NNP level of $470 billion.

EASY MONEY POLICY

If the $470 billion of equilibrium NNP in Figure 17-2c entails widespread unemployment and unused plant capacity, it would be appropriate for the Federal Reserve to institute an *easy money policy*. Recall that an easy money policy is one which makes credit easily and cheaply available. To increase the money supply the Federal Reserve Banks will take some combination of the following actions: (1) buy government securities from banks and the public in the open market, (2) lower the legal reserve ratio, or (3) lower the discount rate. The result will be an increase in excess reserves in the commercial banking system. Because excess reserves are the basis upon which commercial banks can expand the money supply by lending, we can expect the nation's money supply to rise. An increase in the money supply will lower the interest rate, causing investment to increase and equilibrium NNP to expand. The amount by which NNP increases will depend upon the extent of the increase in investment and the size of the economy's income multiplier.

More concretely, if the full-employment NNP is $490 billion, an increase in the money supply from $150 to $175 billion will reduce the interest rate from 8 to 6 percent, as indicated in Figure 17-2a, and increase investment from $20 to $25 billion, as shown in Figure 17-2b. This $5 billion upshift of the investment schedule from I_{n1} to I_{n2} in Figure 17-2c, subject to the relevant income multiplier of 4, will increase equilibrium NNP from $470 billion to the desired $490 billion full-employment level.

TIGHT MONEY POLICY

Conversely, if the original $470 billion NNP generates demand-pull inflation, the Federal Reserve will institute a *tight money policy*. A tight money policy, remember, is one which reduces the avail-

ability of credit and increases its cost. The Federal Reserve Board will order the Federal Reserve Banks to undertake some combination of the following actions: (1) sell government securities to depository institutions and the public in the open market, (2) increase the legal reserve ratio, or (3) increase the discount rate. The outcome will be that banks will discover that their reserves are too low to meet the legal reserve ratio; that is, that their demand deposits are too high relative to their reserves. How can depository institutions meet the reserve ratio when they do not have sufficient reserves? The answer, of course, is that they will need to reduce their demand deposits by refraining from issuing new loans as old loans are paid back. The money supply therefore will shrink, causing the interest rate to rise. The higher interest rate will reduce investment, decreasing aggregate expenditures and restraining demand-pull inflation.

To illustrate: If the full-employment, noninflationary NNP is $450 billion, an inflationary gap of $5 billion will exist. That is, at the $470 billion level of NNP, planned investment exceeds saving—and therefore aggregate expenditures exceed national output—by $5 billion. A decline in the money supply from $150 to $125 billion will increase the interest rate from 8 to 10 percent in Figure 17-2a and reduce investment from $20 to $15 billion in Figure 17-2b. The consequent $5 billion downshift in Figure 17-2c's investment schedule from I_{n1} to I_{n3} will equate planned investment and saving—and therefore aggregate expenditures and national output—at the $450 billion NNP, thereby eliminating the initial $5 billion inflationary gap.

Table 17-3 summarizes the traditional interpretation of how monetary policy works. We recommend that you study this table carefully.

REFINEMENTS AND FEEDBACKS

The components of Figure 17-2 allow us to (1) appreciate some of the factors which determine the effectiveness of monetary policy and (2) note the existence of a "feedback" or "circularity" problem which complicates monetary policy.

Policy effectiveness Figure 17-2 indicates the magnitudes by which an easy or tight money policy will

TABLE 17-3 **Monetary policy: Keynesian interpretation**

(1) Easy money policy	(2) Tight money policy
Problem: unemployment and recession	*Problem:* inflation
Federal Reserve buys bonds, lowers reserve ratio, or lowers the discount rate	Federal Reserve sells bonds, increases reserve ratio, or increases the discount rate
↓	↓
Money supply rises	Money supply falls
↓	↓
Interest rate falls	Interest rate rises
↓	↓
Investment spending increases	Investment spending decreases
↓	↓
Real NNP rises by a multiple of the increase in investment	Inflation declines

change the interest rate, investment, and the equilibrium NNP. These magnitudes are determined by the particular shapes of the demand for money and investment-demand curves. You might pencil in alternative curves to convince yourself that *the steeper the D_m curve, the larger will be the effect of any given change in the money supply upon the equilibrium rate of interest. Furthermore, any given change in the interest rate will have a larger impact upon investment—and hence upon equilibrium NNP—the flatter the investment-demand curve.* In other words, a given change in quantity of money will be most effective when the demand for money curve is relatively steep and the investment-demand curve is relatively flat. Conversely, a given change in the quantity of money will tend to be relatively ineffective when the money-demand curve is flat and the investment-demand curve is steep. As we shall find in Chapter 18, there is considerable controversy as to the precise shapes of these curves and therefore as to the effectiveness of monetary policy.

Feedback effects The alert reader may have sensed in Figure 17-2 a feedback or circularity problem which complicates and influences the effectiveness of monetary policy. Bluntly stated, the nature of the circularity problem is as follows: By reading Figure 17-2 from left to right (as we have) we discover that the interest rate, working through the investment-demand curve, is an important determinant of the equilibrium NNP. Now we must recognize that causation also runs the other way. The level of NNP is a determinant of the equilibrium interest rate. This link comes about because the transactions component of the money-demand curve depends directly upon the level of nominal NNP.

How does this feedback from Figure 17-2c to 17-2a affect monetary policy? It means that the increase in the NNP which an easy money policy brings about will in turn *increase* the demand for money, tending to partially offset or blunt the interest-reducing effect of the easy money policy. Conversely, a tight money policy will tend to reduce the NNP. But this in turn will *decrease* the demand for money and tend to dampen the initial interest-increasing effect of the tight money policy. The feedback also embodies the core of a policy dilemma, as we shall see later.

MONETARY POLICY: AD-AS RESTATEMENT

We can further refine our understanding of monetary policy by reference to our aggregate demand–aggregate supply model. As with fiscal policy (Chapter 14), monetary policy is subject to constraints implicit in the aggregate supply curve. More specifically, the cause-effect chain presented in Figure 17-2 and Table 17-3 indicates that monetary policy primarily affects investment spending and, therefore, real output and the price level. The AD-AS model, and the aggregate supply curve in particular, explains how the change in investment may be divided between changes in real output and changes in the price level.

Consider Figure 17-3. You may recall from Chapter 11 that in locating a given aggregate demand curve we assume that the money supply is fixed. An increase in the money supply shifts the aggregate demand curve rightward. A larger

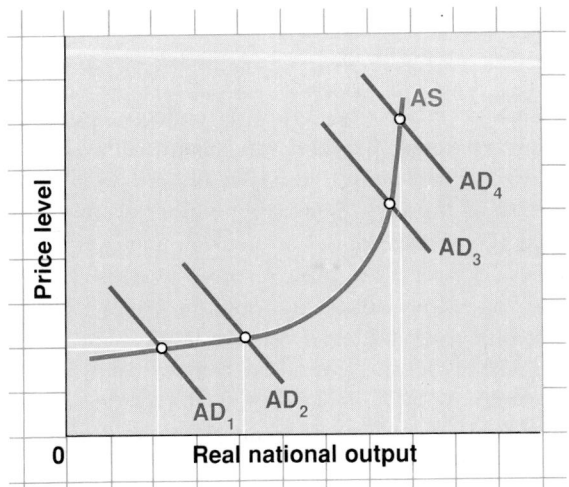

FIGURE 17-3

Monetary policy and the AD-AS model

An easy money policy in the near-horizontal Keynesian range of the aggregate supply curve has its primary effect upon real output and employment rather than the price level. In the near-vertical classical range easy money would be inappropriate because it would cause inflation and bring about little or no increase in real output and employment. The effect of tight money upon the economy is complicated by the downward stickiness of prices and wages.

money supply will permit the economy to purchase a larger real output at any given price level. Conversely, a reduction in the money supply shifts the aggregate demand curve leftward.

We thus note in Figure 17-3 that, if the economy is in the near-horizontal Keynesian or recession range of the aggregate supply curve, an easy money policy will shift the aggregate demand curve rightward as from AD₁ to AD₂ and have a large impact upon real national output and employment and little or no effect upon the price level.

But if the economy was already at or near to full employment, an increase in aggregate demand would have little or no effect upon real output and employment. It would, however, cause a substantial increase in the price level. This is shown in Figure 17-3 by the shift of aggregate demand from AD₃ to AD₄ in the classical or vertical range of the aggregate supply curve. Needless to say, an easy money policy would clearly be inappropriate when the economy was at or near full employment. Fig-

ure 17-3 underscores the reason why: It would be highly inflationary.

It is left to the reader to analyze (1) an easy money policy in the intermediate range and (2) a tight money policy in all three ranges. In analyzing tight money you should distinguish between the case where prices are assumed to be flexible downward and the case where they are inflexible (recall Figure 11-7's ratchet effect). In other words, if prices are sticky in the short run but more flexible over time, then the short-run and long-run effects of a tight money policy may be quite different.

Effectiveness of monetary policy

How well does monetary policy work? Actually, the effectiveness of monetary policy is subject to considerable debate.

STRENGTHS OF MONETARY POLICY

Most economists regard monetary policy as an essential component of our national stabilization policy. Indeed, several specific points can be made on behalf of monetary policy.

1 Speed and flexibility In comparison with fiscal policy, monetary policy can be quickly altered. We have seen (Chapter 14) that the application of appropriate fiscal policy may be seriously delayed by congressional deliberations. In contrast, the Open Market Committee of the Federal Reserve Board can literally buy or sell securities on a daily basis and thereby influence the money supply and interest rates.

2 Isolation from political pressure Recall that the members of the Federal Reserve Board are appointed for 14-year terms. Board members therefore are not subject to intense lobbying and pressure to remain elected. Thus the Board, more easily than Congress, can engage in politically unpopular policies which might be necessary for the long-term health of the economy. Additionally, monetary policy itself is a more subtle and more politically conservative measure than is fiscal policy. Changes in government spending directly affect the allocation of resources and, of course, tax changes can have extensive political ramifications. By contrast, monetary policy works by a more subtle route and therefore seems to be more politically palatable.

3 Monetarism In the next chapter we will examine in some detail the controversy over the relative effectiveness of monetary policy and fiscal policy. Let us merely note here that, although most economists view both fiscal and monetary policies as useful stabilization techniques, there is a group of respected economists—called *monetarists*—who feel that changes in the money supply are the key determinants of the level of economic activity and that fiscal policy is relatively ineffective.

SHORTCOMINGS AND PROBLEMS

It must be recognized, however, that monetary policy entails certain limitations and encounters a number of real-world complications.

1 Cyclical asymmetry If it is pursued vigorously enough, tight money can actually destroy commercial banking reserves to the point where banks are forced to contract the volume of loans. This means a contraction of the money supply. But an easy money policy suffers from a "You can lead a horse to water, but you can't make him drink" problem. An easy money policy can do little more than see to it that commercial banks have the ability—that is, the excess reserves needed—to make loans. It cannot guarantee, however, that the banks' loans will actually be negotiated and the supply of money increased. If the commercial banks, seeking liquidity, are unwilling to lend, the easy money policy efforts of the Board of Governors will be to little avail. Similarly, the public can frustrate the intentions of the Federal Reserve by deciding not to borrow excess reserves. Additionally, the money that the Federal Reserve Banks interject into the system through buying bonds from the public conceivably can be used by the public to pay off existing loans.

Qualification: This cyclical asymmetry has not created a major difficulty for monetary policy except during times of severe depression. During more normal times, higher excess reserves translate into added lending and therefore to an increase in the money supply.

2 Changes in velocity From a monetary point of view (Chapter 18), total expenditures may be regarded as the money supply *multiplied* by the **velocity of money,** that is, the number of times per year the average dollar is spent on goods and services. Hence, if the money supply is $150 billion, total spending will be $600 billion if velocity is 4, but only $450 billion if velocity is 3.

Although the issue is controversial, some Keynesian economists feel that velocity has a habit of changing in the opposite direction from the money supply, thereby tending to offset or frustrate policy-instigated changes in the money supply. In other words, during inflation, when the money supply is restrained by policy, velocity tends to increase. Conversely, when policy measures are taken to increase the money supply during a recession, velocity may very well fall.

Postponing details until Chapter 18, velocity might behave in this manner because of the asset demand for money. We know that an easy money policy, for example, means an increase in the supply of money relative to the demand for it and therefore a reduction in the interest rate (Figure 17-2a). But now that the interest rate—the opportunity cost of holding money as an asset—is lower, the public will hold larger money balances. This means dollars move from hand to hand—from households to businesses and back again—less rapidly. In technical terms, the velocity of money has declined. A reverse sequence of events allegedly causes a tight money policy to induce an increase in velocity.

3 The investment impact Some economists doubt that monetary policy has as much impact upon investment as Figure 17-2 implies. As we have already noted, the combination of a relatively flat money-demand curve and a relatively steep investment-demand curve will mean that a given change in the money supply will not elicit a very large change in investment and, hence, not a large change in the equilibrium NNP (Figure 17-2). Furthermore, the operation of monetary policy as portrayed may be complicated, and at least temporarily offset, by unfavorable changes in the location of the investment-demand curve. For example, a tight money policy designed to drive up interest rates may have little impact on investment spending if the investment demand curve in Figure 17-2b at the same time shifts to the right because of business optimism, technological progress, or expectations of higher future prices of capital. Monetary policy will have to raise interest rates extraordinarily high under these circumstances to be effective in reducing aggregate expenditures. Conversely, a severe recession may undermine business confidence, collapse the investment-demand curve to the left, and thereby tend to frustrate an easy money policy.

THE TARGET DILEMMA

This brings us to one of the most difficult problems of monetary policy. Should the Fed attempt to control the money supply *or* the interest rate? This **target dilemma** arises because the monetary authorities cannot simultaneously stabilize both.

The policy dilemma To understand this dilemma, review the money market diagram of Figure 17-2a. Let us assume that the Fed's policy target is to stabilize the interest rate on the grounds that interest rate fluctuations destabilize investment spending and, working through the income multiplier, destabilize the economy. Now suppose that expansion of the economy increases nominal GNP which in turn increases the transactions demand, and therefore the total demand, for money. As a result, the equilibrium interest rate will rise. In order to stabilize the interest rate—that is, to bring it down to its original level—the Board of Governors will be obligated to increase the supply of money. But this may turn a healthy recovery into an inflationary boom, the very thing that the Federal Reserve System is designed to prevent.

A similar scenario can be applied to recession. As GNP falls, so will money demand and interest rates, provided that the money supply is unchanged. But to prevent interest rates from declining, the Board would have to reduce the money supply. This decline in the supply of money would contribute to a further contraction of aggregate expenditures and intensify the recession.

What if the Fed's policy target is the money supply rather than the interest rate? Then the Fed must tolerate interest rate fluctuations which will contribute to instability in the economy. Simplified explanation: Assume in Figure 17-2a that the Fed achieves its desired money supply target of $150 billion. We know that any expansion of GNP will increase the demand for money and raise the interest rate. This higher interest rate will tend to lower investment spending and choke off an otherwise healthy expansion. The point to be reemphasized is that the monetary authorities cannot simultaneously stabilize both the money supply and the interest rate.

Recent history Because an interest rate target and a money supply target cannot be realized simultaneously, there has occurred an ongoing controversy as to which target is preferable. During most of the post-World War II period the Fed concentrated upon the goal of stabilizing interest rates. But this monetary policy came under considerable criticism in the late 1960s and 1970s because it was felt that it was contributing to the inflation which was gaining momentum during this period. Critics contended that, as inflation-caused increases in nominal GNP increased both money demand and interest rates, the Fed was reacting by increasing the money supply to offset the interest rate rise. But this increase in the money supply was allegedly fueling further increases in the price level, causing the whole process to repeat itself. Monetary policy, in other words, was held to have an inflationary bias.

Against this background a major change in monetary policy occurred in October of 1979. The Board of Governors announced that its policy target would now be to control the money supply and to allow interest rates to fluctuate within much wider limits. This policy prevailed for three years and succeeded in breaking the inflationary feedback process described above. But—as our analysis of Figure 17-2 would lead us to believe—interest rates fluctuated substantially as did real GNP and employment.

In October of 1982 another major policy change was put into effect as the Fed shifted to a more pragmatic, middle-of-the-road position where it will now pay some attention to *both* interest rates and the money supply but will not adhere strictly to either target. This more flexible approach has manifested itself in several ways. For example, following the stock market crash of October 1987, the Fed promptly pumped considerable reserves into the banking system to help meet the immediate needs of the financial community and to stem a possible decline in consumer and business expenditures. This infusion of money occurred even though the economy was nearing full employment.

Additionally, the Federal Reserve has recently shown flexibility in measuring the tightness or easiness of its monetary policy. During the 1980s thrifts and banks developed interest-bearing checkable deposits which are included in $M1$. But transfers of funds from noncheckable deposits—that is, from $M2$ and $M3$—to these interest-bearing accounts caused $M1$ to balloon. Because people were using a portion of this $M1$ more like saving balances than transaction balances, the relationship between changes in $M1$ and changes in nominal NNP severely broke down. Thus, $M1$ became considerably less reliable as a target for monetary policy. In 1988 the Federal Reserve changed its focus from $M1$ to $M2$ and $M3$ (see Chapter 15) in setting its targets for monetary growth.

In short, the Fed's recent policies have had a decidedly "play-it-by-ear" character about them. Whether this type of approach to monetary policy will prove to be more satisfactory than alternative approaches is unclear at this point. Note, finally, that the monetary target dilemma will again surface in Chapter 18.

MONETARY POLICY AND THE INTERNATIONAL ECONOMY

In Chapter 14 we established that linkages among economies of the world complicate domestic fiscal policy. These linkages also relate to monetary policy.

Net export effect   Recall from Chapter 14 that an expansionary fiscal (deficit) policy will increase the demand for money and boost the domestic interest rate. The higher interest rate will increase foreign financial investment in the United States, strengthening the demand for dollars in the foreign exchange market and boosting the international price of the dollar. This currency *appreciation* will pro-

duce lower net exports and hence weaken the stimulus of the fiscal policy (Figure 14-6d).

Will an easy money policy have a similar effect? As outlined in column 1 of Table 17-4, the answer is "No." An easy or expansionary money policy designed to alleviate recession will indeed produce a **net export effect,** but its direction will be exactly opposite to that of an expansionary fiscal policy. An easy money policy will reduce the domestic interest rate rather than increase it. The lower interest rate will discourage the inflow of financial capital to the United States. Hence, the demand for dollars in foreign exchange markets will fall, causing the dollar to *depreciate* in value. Stated simply, it will now take more dollars to buy, say, a yen or a franc. This means that all foreign goods are more expensive to Americans and, conversely, American goods are cheaper to foreigners. Result? Our imports will fall and our exports will rise, or, in short, our net exports will increase. As a result, aggregate expenditures and equilibrium NNP will expand in the United States.

Conclusion: Unlike an expansionary fiscal policy which *reduces* net exports, an easy money policy *increases* net exports. *International flows of financial capital in response to interest rate changes in the United States strengthen domestic monetary policy.* This conclusion holds equally for a tight money

TABLE 17-4 **Monetary policy and the net export effect**

(1) Easy money policy	(2) Tight money policy
Problem: recession, slow growth	Problem: Inflation
Easy money policy (lower interest rate)	Tight money policy (higher interest rate)
↓	↓
Decreased foreign demand for dollars	Increased foreign demand for dollars
↓	↓
Dollar depreciates	Dollar appreciates
↓	↓
Net exports increase (increase in aggregate demand)	Net exports decrease (decrease in aggregate demand)

policy which we know increases the domestic interest rate. In this regard you are urged to follow through the analysis in column 2 of Table 17-4.

Macro stability and the trade balance Now let's go back to Table 17-4 and assume that, in addition to domestic macroeconomic stability, a widely held economic goal is that the United States should achieve an approximate balance in the dollar value of its exports and imports. That is, we should achieve a balance in our international trade. In simple terms, we want to "pay our way" in international trade in that the earnings from our exports are sufficient to finance our imports.

Consider column 1 of Table 17-4 once again, but now suppose that initially the United States has a very large balance of international trade *deficit,* which means our imports substantially exceed our exports so we are *not* paying our own way in world trade. By following through our cause-effect chain in column 1 we find that an easy money policy lowers the international value of the dollar to the end that our exports increase and our imports decline. This increase in net exports tends to correct the assumed initial balance of trade deficit.

Conclusion: *The easy money policy which is appropriate for the alleviation of unemployment and sluggish growth is compatible with the goal of correcting a balance of trade deficit.* Conversely, if initially our exports were greatly in excess of our imports—that is, the United States had a large balance of trade *surplus*—an easy money policy would aggravate the surplus.

Now turn your attention to column 2 of Table 17-4 and assume once again that at the outset the United States has a large balance of trade deficit. In invoking a tight money policy to restrain inflation we would find that net exports would decrease, or, in other words, our exports would fall and imports would rise. This clearly means that the trade deficit would be enlarged.

Conclusion: *A tight money policy invoked to alleviate inflation conflicts with the goal of correcting a balance of trade deficit.* If our initial problem was that of a trade surplus, a tight money policy would tend to resolve that surplus.

Overall we find that an easy money policy alleviates a trade deficit and aggravates a trade surplus. Similarly, a tight money policy alleviates a trade surplus and aggravates a trade deficit. The

point is that certain combinations of circumstances create conflicts or tradeoffs between the use of monetary policy to achieve domestic stability and the realization of balance in the nation's international trade.

Recap: Keynesian employment theory and policy

This is an opportune point at which to recapitulate and synthesize Keynesian employment theory and associated stabilization policies. We want to gain a better understanding of how the many analytical and policy aspects of macroeconomics discussed in this and the eight preceding chapters fit together. Figure 17-4 provides the "big picture" we seek. The overriding virtue of this diagram is that it shows how the many concepts and principles we have discussed relate to one another and how they constitute a coherent theory of what determines the level of resource use in a market economy. Note that those items which constitute, or are strongly influenced by, public policy are shown in red.

Now let us review the substance of Figure 17-4. Reading from left to right, the key point, of course, is that the levels of output, employment, income, and prices are all directly related to the level of aggregate expenditures. The decisions of business firms to produce goods and therefore to employ resources depend upon the total amount of money spent on these goods. To discover what determines the level of aggregate spending, we must examine its four major components.

$$C_a + I_n + X_n + G$$

The absolute level of consumption spending depends upon the position of the consumption schedule and the level of net national product or disposable income. Most economists are convinced that the consumption schedule is quite stable. Therefore, the absolute level of consumption spending usually can be thought of as changing in response to changes in NNP brought about by fluctuations in other components in aggregate expenditures. Furthermore, the slope of the consumption schedule, measured by the MPC (the marginal propensity to consume), is critical in determining the size of the multiplier.

Investment spending is a highly volatile component of aggregate spending and therefore likely to be a cause of fluctuations in the levels of output, employment, and prices. Note that both fiscal policy (taxes in particular) and monetary policy influence investment spending.

We know that net export spending is found by subtracting imports from exports. Both imports and exports are affected by exchange rates, while imports are influenced by the level of domestic NNP and exports by NNP levels in other nations. Exchange rates, in turn, depend upon price levels and interest rates in various nations. By influencing the domestic price level and the interest rate, domestic fiscal and monetary policy thus affect exchange rates.

The government purchases component of aggregate expenditures differs from consumption, investment, and net exports in that it is determined directly by public policy. Consumption, investment, and net export decisions are made in the self-interest of the household and business sectors, respectively. Government spending decisions, on the other hand, are made, at least in part, to fulfill society's interest in high levels of output and employment and a stable price level.

FISCAL AND MONETARY POLICY

Fiscal policy refers, of course, to changes in government spending and tax revenues which are designed to eliminate either an inflationary or a recessionary gap. Figure 17-4 makes the potential stabilizing role of government quite evident; government spending, as one of the four major components of aggregate spending, directly affects output, employment, and the price level. Tax policy, on the other hand, works indirectly through the consumption and investment components of total spending.[5] In particular, reductions in the personal income tax tend to shift the consumption schedule

[5] In our earlier tabular (Table 14-2) and graphic (Figure 14-2) models of the economy, we made the simplifying assumption that all taxes were personal taxes and, therefore, tax changes only affected consumption.

upward; tax increases tend to shift it downward. Cuts in the corporation income tax or other business taxes tend to improve profit expectations, shift the investment-demand curve to the right, and stimulate investment; tax increases weaken profit expectations and reduce the willingness to invest.

Fiscal policy is both *discretionary* and *automatic.* The automatic or built-in stabilizers—the progressiveness of the net tax structure—causes tax collections to vary directly with the level of national income. Discretionary policy consists of the changing of spending levels and the manipulation of tax rates or the tax structure by Congress for the explicit purpose of achieving greater stability in the economy. Keep in mind, however, that government expenditure and taxation policies are used not only to achieve macroeconomic stability, but also to achieve reallocations of resources and to redistribute income. The functioning of monetary policy was just detailed in the discussion of Figure 17-2 and Table 17-3. Finally, we have seen that both fiscal and monetary policy can influence net exports by way of their effects on the domestic interest rate and price level.

Although we have treated fiscal and monetary policy separately, they are in fact interrelated and should be coordinated. This can be illustrated by reference once again to Figure 17-2 and the feedback effects it embodies. The quantitative significance of, say, a given increase in government spending will depend upon whether it is accompanied by an "accommodating" change in the money supply. Suppose it is determined that the actual NNP is $25 billion short of the full-employment level and that the multiplier is 5. Hence, other things being equal, a $5 billion increase in government purchases will move the economy to full employment. But in fact, other things—in particular, the interest rate—cannot be expected to remain unchanged as the economy begins to expand under the impetus of the additional spending (Figure 17-2c). As production and NNP expand, the transactions demand for money will increase and, given the supply of money, interest rates will rise (Figure 17-2a). The higher interest rates will tend to "crowd out" some investment (Figure 17-2b) and thereby partially offset the expansionary impact of the increase in government spending. Unless the money supply is increased to keep the interest rate constant, the income multiplier effect of Chapters

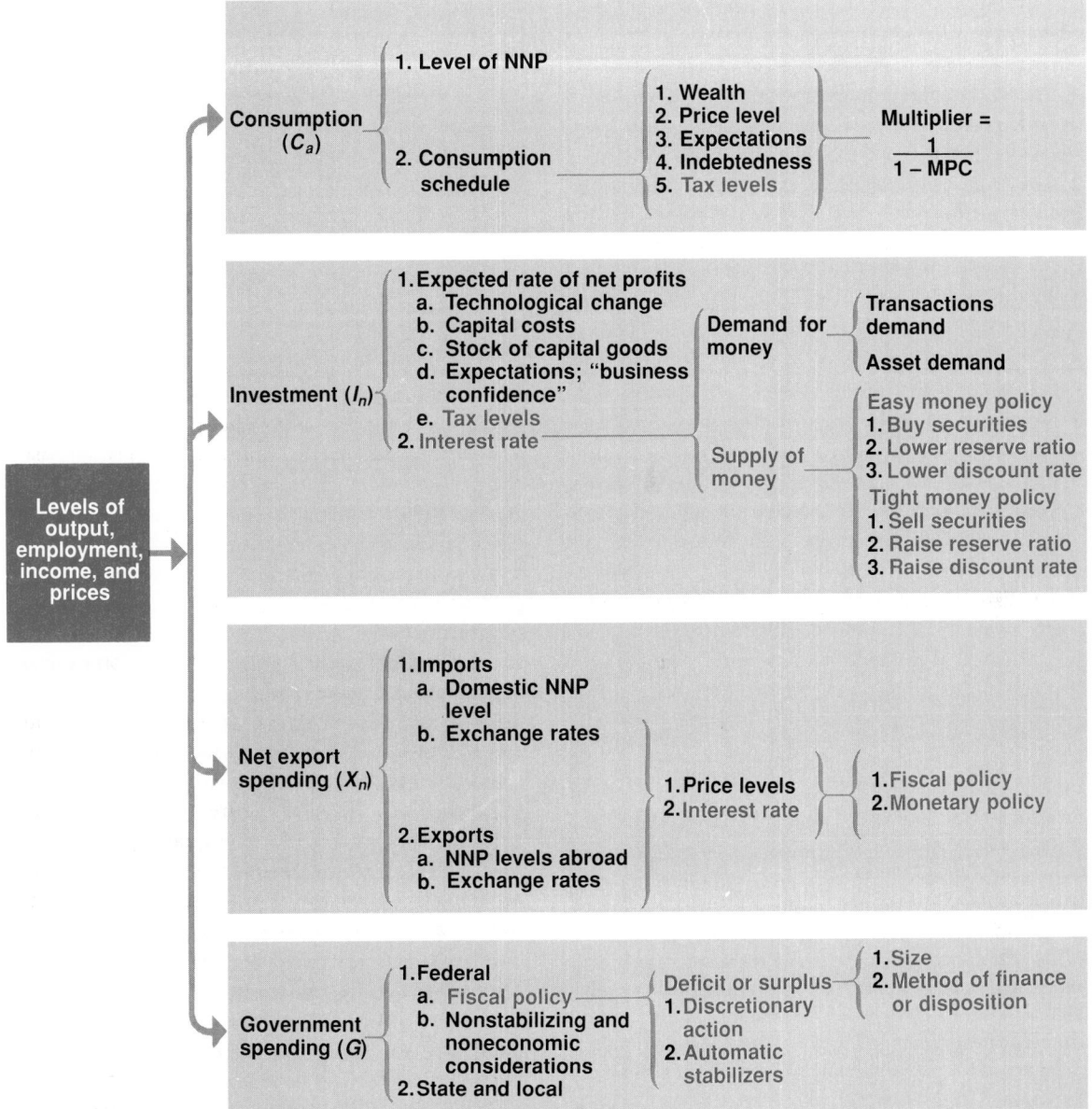

FIGURE 17-4

The Keynesian theory of employment and stabilization policies

This figure integrates the various components of Keynesian employment theory and stabilization policy. Note that determinants which constitute, or are strongly influenced by, public policy are shown in red.

13 and 14 will be diminished because of money market feedbacks which curtail investment and net export spending. The point is that fiscal and monetary policies do not operate in isolation; effective stabilization policy presumes their careful coordination.

CHAPTER SUMMARY

1 Like fiscal policy, the goal of monetary policy is to assist the economy in achieving a full-employment, non-inflationary level of total output.

2 For a consideration of monetary policy, the most important assets of the Federal Reserve Banks are securities and loans to commercial banks. The basic liabilities are the reserves of member banks, Treasury deposits, and Federal Reserve Notes.

3 The three major instruments of monetary policy are *a* open-market operations, *b* changing the reserve ratio, and *c* changing the discount rate.

4 Minor selective controls involve the margin requirement, consumer credit, and moral suasion.

5 Keynesians envision monetary policy as operating through a complex cause-effect chain: *a* Policy decisions affect commercial bank reserves; *b* changes in reserves affect the supply of money; *c* changes in the supply of money alter the interest rate; and *d* changes in the interest rate affect investment, the equilibrium NNP, and the price level. Table 17-3 draws together all the basic notions relevant to the application of easy and tight money policies.

6 The advantages of monetary policy include its flexibility and political acceptability. Further, monetarists feel that the supply of money is the single most important determinant of the level of national output.

7 Monetary policy is subject to a number of limitations and problems. *a* The excess reserves which an easy money policy provides may not be used by banks to expand the supply of money. *b* Policy-instigated changes in the supply of money may be partially offset by changes in the velocity of money. *c* The impact of monetary policy will be lessened if the money-demand curve is flat and the investment-demand curve is steep. The investment-demand curve may also shift so as to negate monetary policy.

8 The monetary authorities face a policy dilemma in that they can stabilize interest rates *or* the money supply, but not both. In the post-World War II period monetary policy has shifted from stabilizing interest rates, to controlling the money supply, and more recently to a more pragmatic position.

9 The impact of an easy money policy upon domestic NNP is strengthened by an accompanying increase in net exports precipitated by a lower domestic interest rate. Likewise, a tight money policy is strengthened by a decline in net exports. In some circumstances, there may be a tradeoff between the use of monetary policy to affect

LAST WORD

Return to a gold standard?

What are the alleged advantages and disadvantages of a monetary system which is tied to gold?

In the past decade or so there has been a modest revival of interest in returning to a gold standard. The Republican Party platform in 1980 hinted at the advantages of returning to the gold standard. And in 1981 President Reagan appointed a Gold Commission to consider the matter.

What is the gold standard? In simple terms a gold standard ties the money supply to gold. The quantity of money is directly linked to the size of the nation's official gold stock and the government is committed to buying and selling gold at a fixed price. If that price is, say, $350 per ounce, then the money supply will increase by $350 whenever government buys an ounce of gold and decrease by $350 whenever it sells an ounce of gold.

Many proponents of the gold standard contend that, if purged of government interference, market economies such as ours are inherently stable; they tend toward a high level of employment and price level stability. It is argued that the economic instability which we have encountered over the years is largely the consequence of misguided and poorly timed attempts by the fiscal and monetary authorities to "manage" the economy. They contend that well-intended changes in the Federal budget and the money supply have intensified, rather than alleviated, cyclical fluctuations.

Proponents hold that the gold standard will function as a disciplining force by limiting the power of government to "manufacture" all the money it might like to spend. More specifically, a pure gold standard would prevent the Treasury from pumping too much money into the economy. If, for example, the supply of money was excessive, the general price level would rise. But under the gold standard the price of gold is fixed, so that gold would now become cheap relative to all other goods and services. The demand for gold would thereby increase and people would buy gold from the Treasury. In making these gold purchases dollars go out of circulation, the supply of money is reduced, and inflation is contained. Under the gold standard the growth of the money supply would be limited to the growth of the gold supply. Because the world's gold supply has been growing rather slowly at about 2 percent per year, it is safe to assume that the United States' money supply would grow slowly. Thus individuals and businesses can make both short- and long-term commitments in dollars, knowing that excessive monetary growth will not cause inflation and alter the value of the dollar. Greater stability in price expectations will in turn help to lower interest rates, stimulate investment, and promote economic growth.

Critics of the gold standard—and there are many—make these points. First, many critics start from the opposite premise of gold standard advocates. They argue that our economy is inherently unstable and that the monetary authorities must have the discretion to increase or decrease the money supply to smooth out fluctuations in real output, the price level, and interest rates. Accepting the gold standard would rule out this stabilizing function. Second, there is no reason to believe that growth in the world's gold stock—and hence in the money supply—will necessarily be slow and stable. For example, a major gold discovery or a technological advance which would permit the economical mining of low-grade ores could trigger a wave of inflation as the United States traded dollars for newly mined gold at a fixed price. Furthermore, if the Soviet Union were to sell gold to buy American grain, required gold purchases under the gold standard would increase the money supply and generate inflation. Do we want to have a monetary system under which our money supply and price levels are determined by the size of Soviet grain harvests? Conversely, some critics have pointed out that a sustained increase in the world's gold stock of 2 percent per year, if realized, would be inadequate to sustain a robust economic expansion in

real GNP of 3 to 5 percent per year.

Finally, and more generally, it is argued that economic *instability* will occur under the gold standard as the fixed price of gold varies over time from the market-determined or equilibrium price. If the supply of and demand for gold tends to establish a market price below the fixed price, gold will be sold to the Treasury, the money supply will increase, and inflation will occur. Conversely, if the market price tends to exceed the fixed price, gold will be purchased from the Treasury, the money supply will decline, and the economy will move toward deflation and recession. It is therefore no surprise, critics argue, that our historical record under the gold standard clearly does not reflect economic stability. Thus in the pre-1913 classical gold standard era:

"The U.S. price level was not stable from year to year, or decade to decade. The price level was approximately the same in 1913 as in 1882, but this gives a misleading suggestion of stability. Prices of goods and services fell 47% in 1882–96, then rose 41% from 1896 to 1913."

"Real economic activity was more variable under the gold standard than in the recent past. Recessions lasted twice as long, on average, from 1879 to 1913 as in 1945–80, and expansions and recoveries were about one-third shorter. Per capita real income, a useful measure of the living standard, rose more slowly. The most reliable statistics suggest that real per capita income rose a bit faster in the disappointing decade of the 1970s than under gold prior to 1913."*

One can expect that the relative merits of the gold standard vis-à-vis a discretionary monetary policy will be debated for some time to come. In Chapter 18 we will find that the debate is complicated by the presence of another option—a proposed "monetary rule" which would obligate the Federal Reserve System to increase the money supply at the same annual rate as the potential growth of our real GNP.

Postscript: The President's Gold Commission did *not* recommend returning to the gold standard.

* Allan H. Meltzer, "An Epistle to the Gold Commissioners," *The Wall Street Journal,* September 17, 1981.

the value of the dollar and thus to correct a trade imbalance and the use of monetary policy to achieve domestic stability.

10 Figure 17-4, which provides a summary statement of Keynesian employment theory and policy, merits careful study by the reader.

TERMS AND CONCEPTS

monetary policy	margin requirement
open-market operations	moral suasion
reserve ratio	money market
discount rate	velocity of money
easy and tight money policies	target dilemma
selective controls	net export effect

QUESTIONS AND STUDY SUGGESTIONS

1 Use commercial bank and Federal Reserve Bank balance sheets in each case to demonstrate the impact of each of the following transactions upon commercial bank reserves:

a The Federal Reserve Banks purchase securities from private businesses and consumers.

b Commercial banks borrow from the Federal Reserve Banks.

c The Board of Governors reduces the reserve ratio.

2 Suppose you are a member of the Board of Governors of the Federal Reserve System. The economy is experiencing a sharp and prolonged inflationary trend. What changes in **a** the reserve ratio, **b** the discount rate, and **c** open-market operations would you recommend? Explain in each case how the change you advocate would affect commercial bank reserves, the money supply, interest rates, and aggregate expenditures.

3 In the table below you will find simplified consolidated balance sheets for the commercial banking system and the twelve Federal Reserve Banks. In columns 1

CONSOLIDATED BALANCE SHEET: ALL COMMERCIAL BANKS

		(1)	(2)	(3)
Assets:				
Reserves	$ 33	____	____	____
Securities	60	____	____	____
Loans	60	____	____	____
Liabilities and net worth:				
Demand deposits	$150	____	____	____
Loans from the Federal Reserve Banks	3	____	____	____

CONSOLIDATED BALANCE SHEET: TWELVE FEDERAL RESERVE BANKS

		(1)	(2)	(3)
Assets:				
Securities	$60	____	____	____
Loans to commercial banks	3	____	____	____
Liabilities and net worth:				
Reserves of commercial banks	$33	____	____	____
Treasury deposits	3	____	____	____
Federal Reserve Notes	27	____	____	____

through 3, indicate how the balance sheets would read after each of the three ensuing transactions is completed. Do not cumulate your answers; that is, analyze each transaction separately, starting in each case from the given figures. All accounts are in billions of dollars.

a Suppose a decline in the discount rate prompts commercial banks to borrow an additional $1 billion from the Federal Reserve Banks. Show the new balance-sheet figures in column 1.

b The Federal Reserve Banks sell $3 billion in securities to the public, who pay for the bonds with checks. Show the new balance-sheet figures in column 2.

c The Federal Reserve Banks buy $2 billion of securities from commercial banks. Show the new balance-sheet figures in column 3.

d Now review each of the above three transactions, asking yourself these three questions: (1) What change, if any, took place in the money supply as a direct and immediate result of each transaction? (2) What increase or decrease in commercial banks' reserves took place in each transaction? (3) Assuming a reserve ratio of 20 percent, what change in the money-creating potential of the commercial banking *system* occurred as a result of each transaction?

4 What is the basic objective of monetary policy? Describe the cause-effect chain through which monetary policy is made effective. Using Figure 17-2 as a point of reference, discuss how **a** the shapes of the demand for money and investment-demand curves and **b** the size of the MPS influence the effectiveness of monetary policy. How do feedback effects influence the effectiveness of monetary policy?

5 The accompanying diagram shows the course of inter-est rates over the 1977–1988 period. Recalling the changes in Fed policy targets which occurred over this period, can you use economic analysis to explain the high degree of interest rate volatility experienced in the late 1979 to mid-1982 period?

6 Evaluate the overall effectiveness of monetary policy. Why have open-market operations evolved as the primary means of controlling commercial bank reserves? Discuss the specific limitations of monetary policy.

7 Explain the observation that the Fed cannot simultaneously stabilize interest rates and the money supply. Explain why the target of stable interest rates might contribute to ongoing inflation.

8 Summarize the theory of employment and show in detail how monetary and fiscal policies might affect the various components of aggregate expenditures.

9 Suppose that the Federal Reserve decides to engage in a tight money policy as a way to reduce demand-pull inflation. Use the aggregate demand–aggregate supply model to show the intent of this policy for a closed economy. Next, introduce the open economy and explain how international flows of financial capital will affect the location of your aggregate demand curve.

10 Design an antirecession stabilization policy, involving both fiscal and monetary policies which is consistent with **a** a relative decline in the public sector, **b** greater income equality, and **c** a high rate of economic growth. Explain: "Truly effective stabilization policy presumes the coordination of fiscal and monetary policy."

11 Explain: "The velocity of money varies directly with the interest rate and inversely with the supply of money."

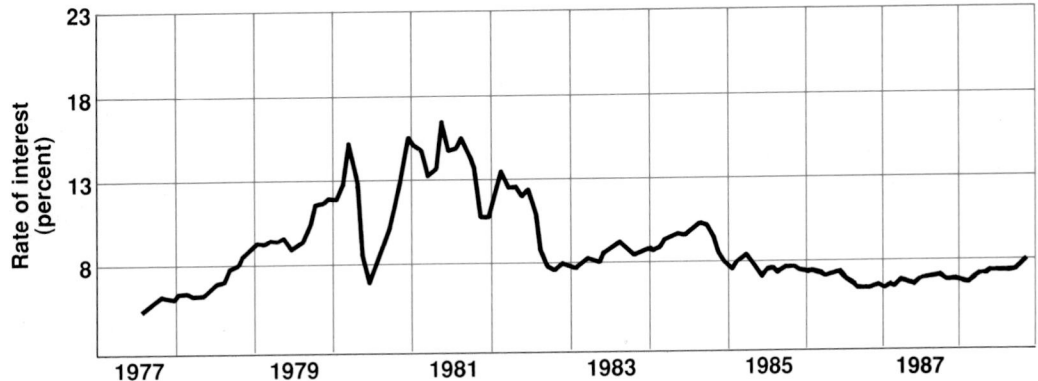

PART 4

WAGE-PRICE CONTROLS

CROWDING-OUT EFFECT

EQUATION OF EXCHANGE

MONETARISM

BUDGET DEFICIT

Problems and Controversies in Macroeconomics

ECONOMIC GROWTH

CAPITAL-OUTPUT RATIO

INDUSTRIAL POLICY

MONETARY RULE

RATIONAL EXPECTATIONS

COST-PUSH INFLATION

PHILLIPS CURVE

VELOCITY

INCOMES POLICIES

CHAPTER 18

Alternative views: monetarism and rational expectations

The Keynesian conception of employment theory and stabilization policy, summarized in the discussion represented by Figure 17-4, is the view of macroeconomics which has dominated the thinking of most economists in all of the market-oriented industrial economies since World War II. In the United States, Democratic and Republican administrations alike have indicated a basic acceptance of the Keynesian precepts, if not the Keynesian label. In the past two decades, however, this theory has been challenged by alternative conceptions of macroeconomics, particularly monetarism and rational expectations theory (RET). Each of these schools of macroeconomic thinking is led by its own set of distinguished scholars. Five Nobel prize winners—Paul Samuelson, Franco Modigliani, and Robert Solow of MIT; James Tobin of Yale; and Lawrence Klein of Pennsylvania—are members of the older generation of Keynesian spokesmen. The University of Chicago's Milton Friedman is the intellectual leader of the *monetarist school.* Winner of the 1976 Nobel Prize in economics, Friedman's pioneering empirical and theoretical research asserts that the role of money in determining the level of economic activity and the price level is much greater than suggested by Keynesian theory. The leading contributors to the *rational expectations theory* (RET)—a facet of the so-called *new classical economics*—are Chicago's Robert Lucas and Minnesota's Thomas Sargent and Neil Wallace.

The primary purpose of this chapter is to present monetarism and RET and compare them with Keynesianism. In Chapter 19, we will continue the discussion of the Keynesian, monetar-ist, and RET perspectives in conjunction with analysis of the problem of simultaneous inflation and unemployment. In Chapter 20, the issues surrounding the troublesome budget deficits and the public debt are explored. Part 4 concludes with an important chapter on the problem of maintaining economic growth.

Basic differences

We begin by contrasting Keynesian economics and monetarism. For purposes of vivid comparison, it will be useful to characterize Keynesianism and monetarism in their polar forms. In reality, the lines between many contemporary Keynesians and monetarists are not so neatly drawn. But at the extreme, Keynesians and monetarists have substantially different views as to the inherent stability of capitalistic economies. They also have important ideological differences, particularly with respect to the role of government. It will be helpful for us to grasp these differences at the outset.

KEYNESIANS: INSTABILITY AND INTERVENTION

Keynesians believe that capitalism and, more particularly, the free-market system suffer from inherent shortcomings. Most important for the present discussion is the Keynesian contention that capitalism contains no mechanism to guarantee macroeconomic stability. Imbalances of planned investment and saving *do* occur and the result is business fluctuations—periodic episodes of inflation or unemployment. In particular, many markets are noncompetitive so that prices and wages tend to be inflexible downward. Hence, fluctuations in aggregate expenditures affect primarily output and employment rather than prices. According to Keynesians, government, therefore, can and should play a positive, activist role in stabilizing the economy; discretionary fiscal and monetary policies are needed to alleviate the severe economic ups and downs which would otherwise characterize capitalism's course.

MONETARISTS: STABILITY AND LAISSEZ FAIRE

The **monetarist** view is that markets are very competitive and that a competitive market system provides the economy with a high degree of macroeconomic stability. Monetarism has its intellectual roots in Chapter 12's classical economics which, you will recall, argues that the price and wage flexibility which competitive markets provide would cause fluctuations in aggregate expenditures to alter product and resource prices rather than output and employment. Thus the market system would provide substantial macroeconomic stability *were it not for governmental interference with the functioning of the economy.* The problem, as the monetarists see it, is that government has fostered and promoted downward wage-price inflexibility through the minimum-wage law, pro-union legislation, farm price supports, pro-business monopoly legislation, and so forth. The free-market system could provide substantial macroeconomic stability, but, despite good intentions, government interference has undermined this capability. Furthermore, as we shall detail momentarily, the monetarists argue that government has contributed to the instability of the system—to the business cycle— through its clumsy and mistaken attempts to achieve greater stability through *discretionary* fiscal and monetary policies.

Given the above comments, it is no surprise that monetarists have a strong *laissez faire* or free-market orientation. Governmental decision making is held to be bureaucratic, inefficient, harmful to individual incentives, and frequently characterized by policy mistakes which destabilize the economy. Furthermore, centralized decision making by government inevitably erodes individual freedoms.[1] The public sector should be kept to the smallest possible size. Keynesians and monetarists therefore are almost diametrically opposed in their conceptions of the private and public sectors. To the Keynesian, the instability of private investment causes the economy to be unstable. Government plays a positive role by applying appropriate stabilization medicine. To the monetarist, government has harmful effects upon the economy. Government creates rigidities which weaken the capacity of the market system to provide substantial stability and it embarks upon monetary and fiscal measures which, although well intentioned, aggravate the very instability they are designed to cure.

The basic equations

Keynesian economics and monetarism each build their analysis upon specific equations.

THE AGGREGATE EXPENDITURES EQUATION

As indicated in previous chapters, Keynesian economics focuses upon aggregate spending and its components. Recall that the basic Keynesian equation is:

$$C_a + I_n + X_n + G = \text{NNP} \tag{1}$$

This theory says in essence that the aggregate amount spent by buyers is equal to the total value of the goods and services sold. In equilibrium, $C_a + I_n + X_n + G$ (aggregate expenditures) is equal to NNP (national output).

EQUATION OF EXCHANGE

Monetarism, as the label suggests, focuses upon money. The fundamental equation of monetarism is the **equation of exchange:**

---

[1] Friedman's philosophy is effectively expounded in two of his books: *Capitalism and Freedom* (Chicago: The University of Chicago Press, 1962), and with Rose Friedman, *Free to Choose* (New York: Harcourt Brace Jovanovich, 1980).

$$MV = PQ \qquad (2)$$

where M is the supply of money; V is the income or circuit **velocity of money,** that is, the number of times per year the average dollar is spent on final goods and services; P is the price level or, more specifically, the average price at which each unit of physical output is sold; and Q is the physical volume of goods and services produced. The label "equation of exchange" is easily understood. The left side, MV, represents the total amount *spent* by purchasers of output, while the right side, PQ, represents the total amount *received* by the sellers of that output.

The difference between the two approaches can be compared with two ways of looking at the flow of water through a sewer pipe—say, at the rate of 6000 gallons per hour. A neo-Keynesian investigator might say that the flow of 6000 gallons an hour consisted of 3000 gallons an hour from a paper mill, 2000 gallons an hour from an auto plant, and 1000 gallons an hour from a shopping center. A monetarist investigator might say that the sewer flow of 6000 gallons an hour consisted of an average of 200 gallons in the sewer at any one time with a complete turnover of the water 30 times every hour.[2]

It should be emphasized at the outset that both the Keynesian and monetarist approaches are useful and insightful to the understanding of macroeconomics. In fact, the Keynesian equation can be quite readily "translated" into monetarist terms. According to the monetarist approach, total spending is simply the supply of money multiplied by its velocity. In short, MV is the monetarist counterpart of $C_a + I_n + X_n + G$. Because MV is the total amount spent on final goods in one year, it is necessarily equal to nominal NNP. Furthermore, we know from Chapter 9 that nominal NNP is the sum of the physical outputs of various goods and services (Q) multiplied by their respective prices (P). That is, NNP $= PQ$. Thus, we can restate the Keynesian $C_a + I_n + X_n + G =$ NNP equation in nominal terms as the monetarist equation of exchange, $MV = PQ$.[3] In a very real sense, the two approaches are two ways of looking at the same thing. But the critical question remains: Which theory is the more accurate portrayal of macroeconomics and therefore the better basis for economic policy?

SPOTLIGHT ON MONEY

The Keynesian equation puts money in a secondary role. Indeed, you will recall (Chapter 17) that the Keynesian conception of monetary policy entails a rather lengthy transmission mechanism. We depict the Keynesian monetary transmission mechanism in Figure 18-1a. Observe that a change in monetary policy alters the nation's supply of money. The change in the money supply in turn affects the interest rate, thereby affecting the level of investment. When the economy initially is operating at less than capacity, changes in investment affect nominal NNP ($= PQ$) by changing real output (Q) through the multiplier effect. Alternatively, when the economy is achieving full employment, changes in investment affect nominal NNP by altering the price level (P).

Keynesians contend there are many loose links in this cause-effect chain with the result that monetary policy is an uncertain and relatively weak stabilization tool when compared with fiscal policy. Remember some of the weaknesses of monetary policy cited in Chapter 17. For example, recall from Figure 17-2 that monetary policy will be relatively ineffective if the demand for money curve is relatively flat and the investment-demand curve is relatively steep. Furthermore, the investment-demand curve may shift adversely so that the impact of a change in the interest rate upon investment spending is muted or offset. Nor will an easy money policy be very effective if banks and other depository institutions are not anxious to lend or the public eager to borrow.

---

[2] Werner Sichel and Peter Eckstein, **Basic Economic Concepts** (Chicago: Rand McNally College Publishing Company, 1974), p. 344.

[3] Technical footnote: It should be noted that there is an important conceptual difference between the Keynesian $C_a + I_n + X_n + G$ and the MV component of the equation of exchange. Specifically, the former indicates planned or *intended* expenditures, while the latter reflects *actual* spending.

(a) Keynesian monetary transmission mechanism

(b) Monetarist monetary transmission mechanism

FIGURE 18-1

Alternative views of the monetary transmission mechanism

Keynesians (a) emphasize the roles of interest rates and investment spending in explaining how changes in the money supply affect nominal NNP. On the other hand, monetarists (b) contend that changes in the money supply cause direct changes in aggregate demand and thereby changes in nominal NNP.

The monetarists believe that money and monetary policy are much more important in determining the level of economic activity than do the Keynesians. In fact, *monetarists hold that changes in the money supply are the single most important factor in determining the levels of output, employment, and prices*. They envision a different cause-effect chain between the supply of money and the level of economic activity than the Keynesian model suggests. Rather than limiting the effect of an increase in money to bond purchases and consequent declines in the interest rate, monetarists theorize that an increase in the money supply drives up the demand for all assets—real or financial—as well as for current output. Hence, under conditions of full employment, the prices of all of these items will rise. Additionally, monetarists contend that the velocity of money is stable—meaning that it does not fluctuate wildly and does not change in response to a change in the money supply itself. Hence, changes in the money supply will have a predictable effect upon the level of nominal NNP $(= PQ)$. More precisely, an increase in M will tend to increase P or Q, or some combination of both P and Q; a decrease in M will tend to produce the opposite effects.

Most monetarists believe that, although a change in M may cause short-run changes in real output and employment as market adjustments occur, the long-run impact of a change in M will be upon the price level. Recall that monetarists believe that the private economy is inherently stable and tends to operate at the full-employment level of output. The exact level of that full-employment output depends upon such "real" factors as the quantity and quality of labor, capital, and land and upon technology (Chapter 21). For present purposes the point to be made is that, if Q is constant at the economy's capacity output, then changes in M will give rise to changes in P.

Monetarism implies a simpler and much more direct transmission mechanism than does the Keynesian model. We summarize the monetarist transmission mechanism in Figure 18-1b. Observe from the diagram that monetarists view changes in the money supply as producing direct changes in aggregate demand which alter nominal NNP. We know from previous discussion that monetarists contend that changes in the money supply affect all components of aggregate demand, not just investment. Furthermore, the changes in aggregate demand allegedly affect nominal NNP in the long run primarily through changes in the price level, not through changes in real output.

Velocity: stable or unstable?

A critical theoretical issue involved in the Keynesian–monetarists debate centers on the question of whether the velocity of money, *V*, is stable. It is important to note that, as used here, the word "stable" is *not* synonymous with the word "constant." Monetarists are well aware that velocity is higher today than it was in 1945. Shorter pay periods, greater use of credit cards, and more rapid means of making payments have increased velocity since 1945. Said differently, these factors have enabled people over the years to reduce their cash and checkbook holdings relative to the size of the nominal NNP.

So what then do monetarists mean when they argue that velocity is stable? According to monetarists, the factors which alter velocity change gradually and predictably. Hence, changes in velocity from one year to the next can be easily anticipated. Moreover, velocity does *not* change in response to changes in the supply of money itself.

If velocity is stable, the equation of exchange tells us that the monetarists are indeed correct in claiming that a direct predictable relationship exists between the money supply and nominal NNP ($= PQ$). Simple example: Suppose that $M = 100$, $V = 1$, and nominal NNP $= 100$. Let us also assume that velocity increases annually at a stable rate of 2 percent. Using the equation of exchange, we therefore can predict that a 5 percent annual growth rate of the money supply will result in about a 7 percent increase in nominal NNP. That is, *M* will increase from 100 to 105, *V* will rise from 1 to 1.02, and nominal NNP will increase from 100 to about 107 ($= 105 \times 1.02$). But if *V* is not stable, the Keynesian contention that money plays only a secondary role in macroeconomics is valid. That is, if *V* is variable and unpredictable from one period to another, the link between *M* and *PQ* will be loose and uncertain. In particular, a steady growth of *M* will not necessarily translate into a steady growth of nominal NNP. (This chapter's Last Word is a minidebate on this very issue.)

MONETARISTS: *V* IS STABLE

What rationale do the monetarists offer for their contention that *V* is stable? Basically, they argue that people have a rather stable desire to hold money relative to holding other financial and real assets and buying current output. The factors which determine the amount of money people and businesses wish to hold at any given time are independent of the supply of money. Most importantly, the amount of money the public will want to hold will depend upon the level of nominal NNP.

Consider a simple example. Suppose that, when the level of nominal NNP is $400 billion, the amount of money which the public wants or *desires* to hold in order to negotiate the purchase of this output is $100 billion. (This implies that *V* is 4.) If we further assume that the *actual* supply of money is $100 billion, we can say that the economy is in equilibrium with respect to money. That is, the *actual* amount of money supplied is equal to the amount the public *desires* to hold.

In the monetarist view an increase in the money supply of, say, $10 billion will upset this equilibrium in that the public will now be holding more money or liquidity than it wants to hold; the actual amount of money being held exceeds the desired amount. What happens? The natural reaction of the public (households and businesses) is to restore its desired balance of money relative to other items such as stocks and bonds, factories and equipment, houses and automobiles, and clothing and toys. The public has more money than it wants; the way to get rid of money is to buy things. But one person's spending of money leaves more cash in someone else's checkable deposit or billfold. That person, too, tries to "spend down" excess cash balances. It is clear that the collective attempt to reduce cash balances will increase aggregate demand, which in turn will boost the nominal NNP. By how much will nominal NNP rise? Because velocity is 4—that is, the typical dollar is spent four times per year—nominal NNP must rise by $40 billion. When nominal NNP reaches $440 billion, the *actual* money supply of $110 billion again will be the amount which the public *desires* to hold, and by definition equilibrium will be reestablished. The basic point is that spending on goods and services will increase until nominal NNP has increased sufficiently to restore the original equilibrium relationship between nominal NNP and the money supply. In fact, the relationship NNP/M defines V. A stable relationship between NNP and M means a stable V.

KEYNESIANS: V IS UNSTABLE

In the Keynesian view the velocity of money is variable and unpredictable. This position can best be understood in reference to the Keynesian conception of the demand for money.[4] The Keynesian view, you will recall, is that money is demanded, not only to use in negotiating transactions, but also to hold as an asset. Money demanded for *transactions* purposes will be "active" money, that is, money which is changing hands and circulating through the income-expenditures stream. In other words, transactions dollars have some positive velocity; for example, the average transactions dollar may be spent, say, six times per year and thereby negotiate $6 worth of transactions. In this case V is 6 for each transactions dollar. But money demanded and held as an *asset* is "idle" money; these dollars do *not* flow through the income-expenditures stream and therefore their velocity is zero. It follows that the overall velocity of the entire money supply will depend upon how it is divided between transactions and asset balances. Obviously, the greater the relative importance of "active" transactions balances, the larger will be V. Conversely, the greater the relative significance of "idle" asset balances, the smaller will be V.

Given this framework, Keynesians discredit the monetarist transmission mechanism—the allegedly dependable relationship between changes in M and changes in NNP—by arguing that a significant portion of any increase in the money supply may go into asset balances, *causing V to fall*. In the very extreme case, assume *all* the increase in the money supply is held by the public as additional asset balances. That is, the public simply hoards the additional money and uses none of it for transactions. The money supply will have increased, but velocity will decline by an offsetting amount so that

[4] It might be a good idea to review Chapter 15's "The Demand for Money" section at this point.

there will be no effect whatsoever upon the size of nominal NNP.

We can consider the Keynesian position at a slightly more sophisticated level by referring back to Figure 15-2. We note that the relative importance of the asset demand for money varies inversely with the rate of interest. Hence, an *increase* in the money supply will *lower* the interest rate. Because it is now less expensive to hold money as an asset, the public will hold larger zero-velocity asset balances. Therefore, the overall velocity of the money supply will fall. Conversely, a *reduction* in the money supply will *raise* the interest rate, making it more costly to hold money as an asset. The resulting decline in asset balances will increase the overall velocity of money. *In the Keynesian view velocity varies (1) directly with the rate of interest and (2) inversely with the supply of money.* If this analysis is correct, the stable relationship between M and nominal NNP embodied in the monetarist's transmission mechanism does *not* exist because V will vary whenever M changes.

Incidentally, at this juncture we can more fully appreciate a point made at the end of Chapter 17 in discussing possible shortcomings of monetary policy. It was indicated that V has the bad habit of changing in the opposite direction than M. Our present discussion reveals the cause-effect chain through which this might occur.

EMPIRICAL EVIDENCE

The stability of V is clearly an empirical question and an appeal to "the facts" would seem sufficient to settle the issue. But, unfortunately, the facts are not easy either to discern or to interpret.

Monetarists think that the weight of empirical evidence clearly supports their position. In Figure 18-2 the money supply and the nominal national output (PQ) are both plotted. Given that $MV = PQ$, the close correlation between M and PQ suggests that V is quite stable. Monetarists reason that the money supply is the critical causal force in determining the nominal NNP; causation runs from M to nominal NNP.

But Keynesians are unimpressed with such data. They offer two arguments by way of rebuttal. First, they point out that by simple manipulation of $MV = PQ$, we find that $V = PQ/M = $ NNP/M.

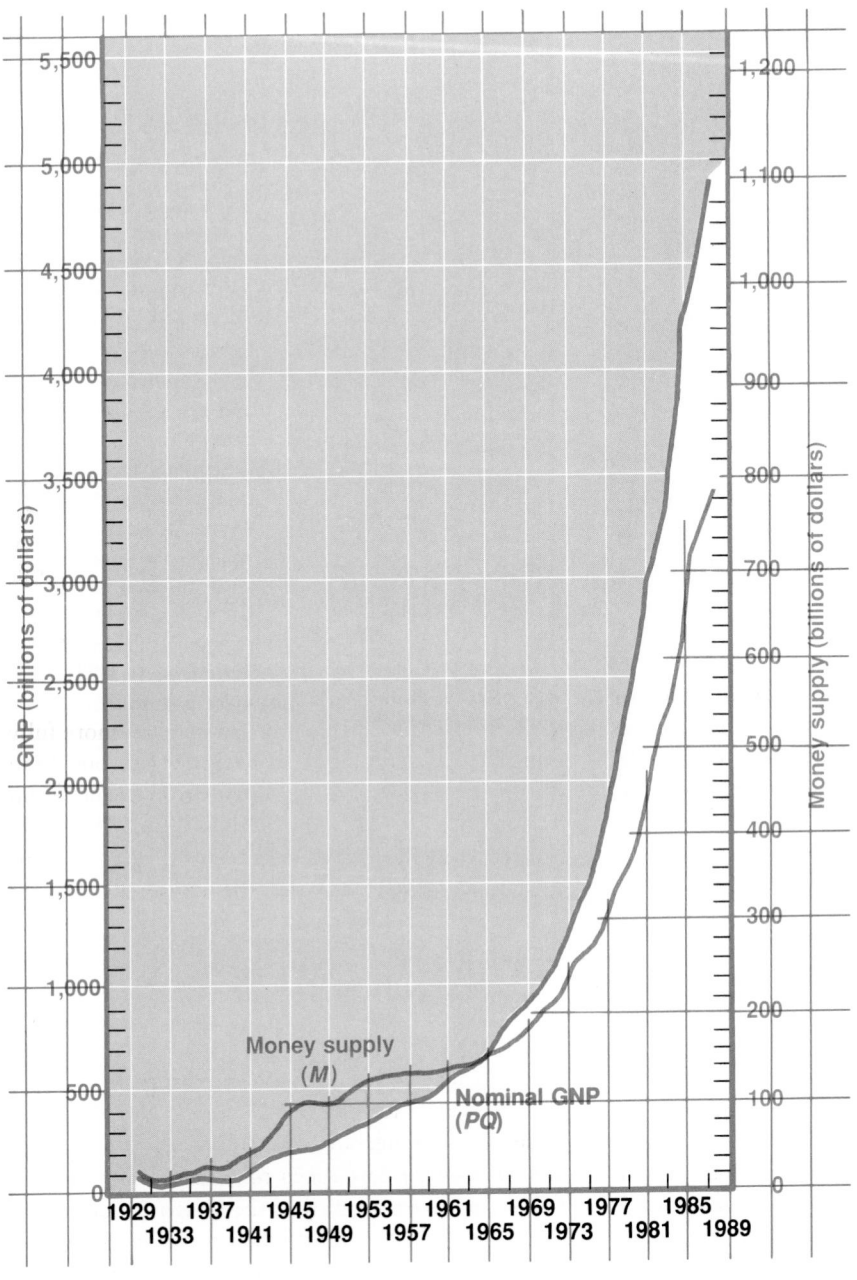

FIGURE 18-2

The money supply
and the GNP,
1929–1988

Monetarists cite the close positive correlation between the money supply and nominal GNP as evidence in support of their position that money is the critical determinant of economic activity and the price level. They assume that the money supply is the "cause" and the GNP is the "effect," an assumption which Keynesians question. Monetarists also feel that the close correlation between *M* and nominal GNP indicates that the velocity of money is stable. *(Economic Report of the President.)*

That is, we can empirically calculate the value of V by dividing each year's nominal output (NNP) by the money supply. Keynesians contend that the resulting data, shown in Figure 18-3, repudiate the monetarist contention that V is stable. For example, observe that there was considerable year-to-year variation in velocity even during the so-called "steady" upward trend of velocity between 1945 and 1982. Also, note the markedly changed behavior of velocity since 1982. Not only did velocity stop growing, in some of these years it actually declined. Keynesians also point out that the close correlation between the velocity of money and the interest rate shown in Figure 18-3 supports their analytical con-

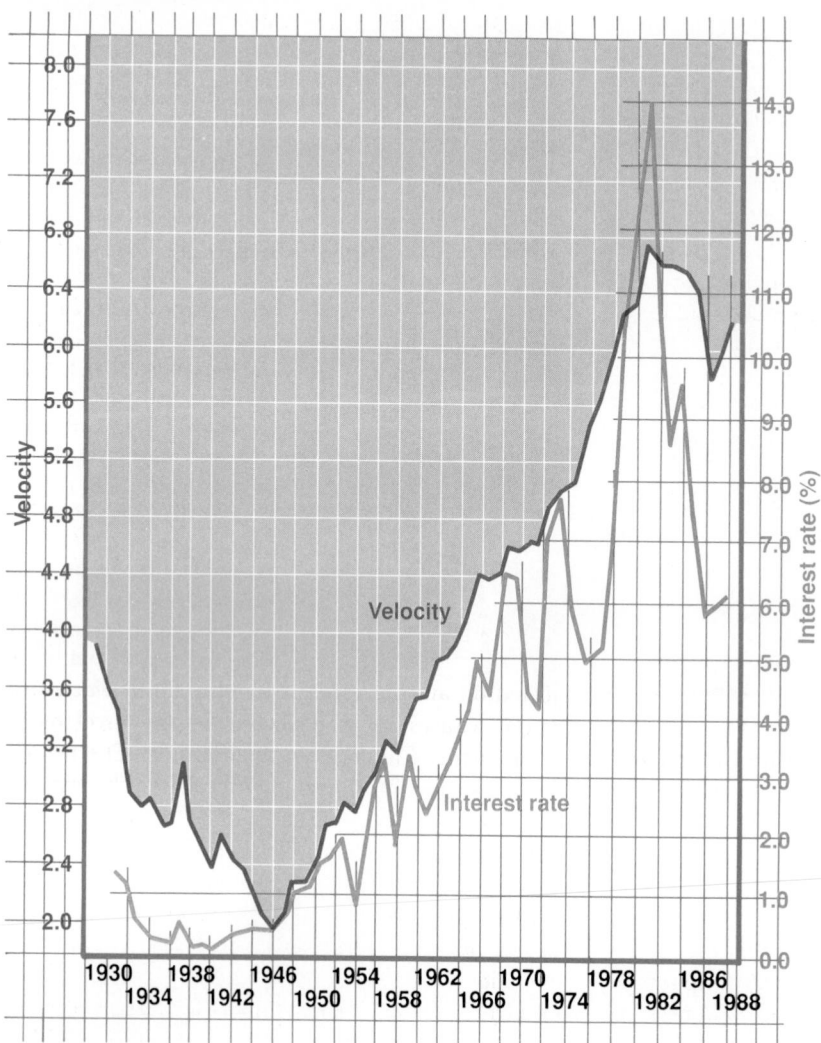

FIGURE 18-3

The velocity of money and the interest rate, 1929–1988

Keynesians argue that the velocity of money varies both cyclically and secularly. Hence, they conclude that any link between a change in the money supply and the subsequent change in nominal NNP is tenuous and uncertain. More specifically, Keynesians contend that velocity varies directly with the rate of interest because a lower interest rate will increase the size of zero-velocity asset balances and therefore lower the overall velocity of money. *(Economic Report of the President.)*

clusion that velocity varies directly with the rate of interest.[5] Velocity, in the Keynesian view, is variable both cyclically and secularly and these variations downgrade the role of money as a determinant of output, employment, and the price level.

Keynesians add this reminder: Given the large size of the money supply, a small variation in velocity can have a very substantial impact on nominal NNP. For example, assume M is $300 billion and V is 5. A modest 10 percent increase in V will cause

a $150 billion increase in nominal NNP. That is, MV—and therefore PQ—are initially $1500 billion (= $300 × 5). Now, if V increases by 10 percent to 5.5, PQ will be $1650 billion (= MV = 300 × 5.5). Stated in terms of the issue at hand, a very small variation in V can offset a large absolute change in M.

Second, Keynesians respond to Figure 18-2 by noting that *correlation* and *causation* are quite different things. Is it not possible that the changes in nominal GNP portrayed in Figure 18-2 were in fact caused by changes in aggregate expenditures, that is, in $C_a + I_n + X_n + G$, as suggested by the Keynesian model? Perhaps a favorable change in

[5] Technical note: The short-term interest rate used here is the rate on three-month Treasury bills.

business expectations increased investment. And is it not also possible that the indicated growth in the nominal national output prompted—indeed, necessitated—that businesses and consumers borrow more money over time from commercial banks in order to finance this rising volume of economic activity? In other words, Keynesians claim that causation may in fact run from aggregate expenditures *to* national output *to* the money supply, rather than from the money supply *to* aggregate demand *to* national output as the monetarists contend. The important point, argue the Keynesians, is that the data of Figure 18-2 are as consistent with the Keynesian view as they are with the monetarist position.

The question of the stability of *V* remains a crucial point of conflict between Keynesians and monetarists.

Policy debates

The differences in the Keynesian and monetarist theories spill over into the area of stabilization policy.

THE FISCAL POLICY DEBATE

Although Keynesians acknowledge the importance of monetary policy, they believe that fiscal policy is a much more powerful and reliable stabilization device. This is implied by the basic equation of Keynesianism. Government spending, after all, is a direct component of aggregate expenditures. And taxes are only one short step removed in that tax changes allegedly affect consumption and investment in dependable and predictable ways.

Monetarists seriously downgrade or, in the extreme, reject fiscal policy as both a reallocative and a stabilization device. They believe that fiscal policy is quite weak and ineffectual because of the **crowding-out effect** (Chapter 14). Monetarists' reasoning goes like this: Suppose government runs a budgetary deficit by selling bonds, that is, by borrowing from the public. By borrowing, they argue, government is competing with private businesses for funds. Thus, government borrowing will increase the demand for money, raise the interest

rate, and thereby crowd out a substantial amount of private investment which otherwise would have been profitable. Hence, the net effect of a budget deficit upon aggregate expenditures is unpredictable and, at best, modest.

Alternatively, the workings of the crowding-out effect can be seen from a more analytical perspective by referring back to Figure 17-2. The financing of the government's deficit will increase the demand for money, shifting the D_m curve of Figure 17-2a to the right. Given the money supply, S_m, the equilibrium interest rate will rise. This increase in the interest rate will be relatively large, according to the monetarists, because the D_m curve is relatively steep.

Furthermore, monetarists believe that the investment-demand curve of Figure 17-2b is relatively flat; that is, investment spending is very sensitive to changes in the interest rate. In short, the initial increase in the demand for money causes a relatively large rise in the interest rate which, projected off an interest-sensitive investment-demand curve, causes a large decline in the investment component of aggregate expenditures. The resulting large contractionary effect offsets the expansionary impact of the fiscal deficit and, on balance, the equilibrium NNP is unaffected. So sayeth Friedman: ". . . in my opinion, the state of the budget by itself has no significant effect on the course of nominal [money] income, on inflation, on deflation, or on cyclical fluctuations."[6] Admittedly, if a deficit was financed by the issuing of new money,[7] the crowding-out effect could be avoided and the deficit would be followed by economic expansion. *But,* the monetarists point out, the expansion would be due, *not* to the fiscal deficit per se, but rather, to the creation of additional money.

Keynesians, for the most part, do not deny that some investment may be crowded out. But they perceive the amount as being small and, hence, they conclude that the net impact of an expansionary fiscal policy upon equilibrium NNP will be substantial. In terms of Figure 17-2, the Keynesian view is that the demand for money curve is rela-

[6] Statement by Friedman in Milton Friedman and Walter Heller, *Monetary vs. Fiscal Policy* (New York: W. W. Norton & Company, Inc., 1969), p. 51.

[7] See Chapter 14, footnote 6.

tively flat and the investment-demand curve is steep. (You may recall that this combination tends to make monetary policy relatively weak and ineffective.) Hence, the increase in D_m will cause a very modest increase in the interest rate which, when projected off a steep investment-demand curve, will result in a very small decrease in the investment component of aggregate expenditures. In other words, little investment will be crowded out. It *is* acknowledged by Keynesians that a deficit financed by creating new money will have a greater stimulus than one financed by borrowing. In terms of Figure 17-2a, for any given increase in D_m there is some increase in S_m which will leave the interest rate, and therefore the volume of investment, unchanged.

MONETARY POLICY: DISCRETION OR RULES?

The Keynesian conception of monetary policy is, of course, that portrayed in Figure 17-2. As just noted, Keynesians believe that the demand for money curve is relatively flat and the investment-demand curve relatively steep, causing monetary policy to be a comparatively weak stabilization tool. We have also seen that, in contrast, monetarists contend that the money demand curve is very steep and the investment-demand curve quite flat, a combination which means that a change in the money supply has a powerful effect upon the equilibrium level of nominal NNP. This is clearly in keeping with monetarism's fundamental contention that the money supply is the critical determinant of the level of economic activity and the price level.

However, most monetarists do *not* advise the use of easy and tight money policies to modify the "downs" and "ups" of the business cycle. Professor Friedman contends that, historically, the *discretionary* changes in the money supply made by the monetary authorities have in fact been a *destabilizing* influence in the economy. Examining the monetary history of the United States from the Civil War up to the establishment of the Federal Reserve System in 1913 and comparing this with the post-1913 record, Friedman concludes that, even if the economically disruptive World War II period is ignored, the latter (post-1913) period was clearly more unstable. Much of this decline in economic

stability after the Federal Reserve System became effective is attributed to faulty decisions on the part of the monetary authorities. *In the monetarist view economic instability is more a product of monetary mismanagement than it is of any inherent destabilizers in the economy.* According to the monetarists, there are two important sources of monetary mismanagement.

Irregular time lags First, there is the matter of *time lags*. Although the monetary transmission mechanism is direct, changes in the money supply have their impact upon nominal NNP only after a rather long and variable time period. Friedman's empirical work suggests that a change in the money supply may significantly change NNP in as short a period as six to eight months or in as long a period as two years. Because it is virtually impossible to predict the time lag involved in a given policy action, there is little chance of determining accurately when specific policies should be invoked or, in fact, which policy measure—easy or tight money—is appropriate. Indeed, given the uncertain duration of this time lag, the use of discretionary monetary policy to "fine-tune" the economy for cyclical "ups" and "downs" may backfire and intensify these cyclical changes. For example, suppose an easy money policy is invoked because the various economic indicators suggest a mild recession. But assume now that within the ensuing six months the economy, for reasons quite unrelated to public policy actions, reverses itself and moves into the prosperity-inflationary phase of the cycle. At this point the easy money policy becomes effective and reinforces the inflation.

Interest rate: wrong target Second, monetarists argue that the monetary authorities have typically attempted to control interest rates for the purpose of stabilizing investment and therefore the economy. Recalling Chapter 17's discussion of the targeting dilemma, the problem with this is that the Board of Governors cannot simultaneously stabilize both the money supply and interest rates. Therefore, in trying to stabilize interest rates, the Fed might *destabilize* the economy.

Consider an example. Suppose the economy is coming out of a recession and is currently approaching full employment, with aggregate expenditures, output, employment, and the price level all increasing. This expanding volume of economic activity will cause the demand for money to increase and therefore cause the interest rate to rise. Now, if the monetary authorities reason that their task is to stabilize interest rates, they will embark upon an easy money policy. But this expansionary monetary policy will add to aggregate expenditures at a time when the economy is already on the verge of an inflationary boom. That is, the attempt to stabilize interest rates will fan existing inflationary fires and tend to make the economy less stable. A similar scenario is applicable to an economy moving into a recession.

The monetary rule Monetarist moral: The monetary authorities should stabilize, not the interest rate, but the rate of growth of the money supply. Specifically, Friedman advocates legislating the **monetary rule** that the money supply be expanded each year at the same annual rate as the potential growth of our real GNP; that is, the supply of money should be increased steadily at 3 to 5 percent per year.

Such a rule . . . would eliminate . . . the major cause of instability in the economy—the capricious and unpredictable impact of countercyclical monetary policy. As long as the money supply grows at a constant rate each year, be it 3, 4, or 5 percent, any decline into recession will be temporary. The liquidity provided by a constantly growing money supply will cause aggregate demand to expand. Similarly, if the supply of money does not rise at a more than average rate, any inflationary increase in spending will burn itself out for lack of fuel.[8]

Keynesian response: Despite a somewhat spotty record, it would be foolish to replace discretionary monetary policy with a monetary rule. Arguing that V is variable both cyclically and secularly, Keynesians contend that a constant annual rate of increase in the money supply could contribute to substantial fluctuations in aggregate expenditures and promote economic instability. Indeed, did we not conclude in Chapter 17 that wide fluctuations in interest rates and investment spending

would accompany any shift from the interest rate target? As one Keynesian has quipped, the trouble with the monetary rule is that it tells the policy maker: "Don't do something, just stand there."[9]

AD-AS RESTATEMENT

It is a helpful exercise at this point to contrast monetarist and Keynesian views in terms of our earlier aggregate demand–aggregate supply model. By bringing aggregate supply into the picture we can see more clearly the implications of each model for real output and the price level. And we can also further our understanding of policy differences. Figure 18-4 shows us the monetarist portrayal on the left and the Keynesian conception on the right.

We begin on the demand side. The key difference here, as we already know, concerns the kinds of factors which will cause a shift in aggregate demand. To the monetarists aggregate demand will shift rightward or leftward primarily as the result of an increase or decrease, respectively, in the money supply. Keynesians are more general, recognizing that in addition to changes in private spending both fiscal and monetary policy can shift the aggregate demand curve.

On the supply side we find that the monetarists view the aggregate supply curve as being very steep or, in the extreme, vertical, while Keynesians conceive of it as being quite flat, or in the extreme case, horizontal. This is nothing new to us as a glance back at Figure 11-3 will confirm. The aggregate supply curve presented there has a horizontal or near-horizontal "Keynesian" range and a vertical or near-vertical "classical" range. The flat Keynesian range reflects the belief that the economy often operates short of the full-employment or capacity level, while a near-vertical range mirrors the classical heritage of monetarism and the belief that flexi-

---

[8] Lawrence S. Ritter and William L Silber, *Money,* 5th ed. (New York: Basic Books, Inc., Publishers, 1984), pp. 141–142.

[9] While a considerable number of economists are sympathetic to the establishment of a monetary rule, virtually all central banks around the world engage in discretionary policy. The interested reader should consult Donald J. Mullineaux, "Monetary Rules and Contracts: Why Theory Loses to Practice," *Business Review* (Federal Reserve Bank of Philadelphia), March–April 1985, pp. 13–19.

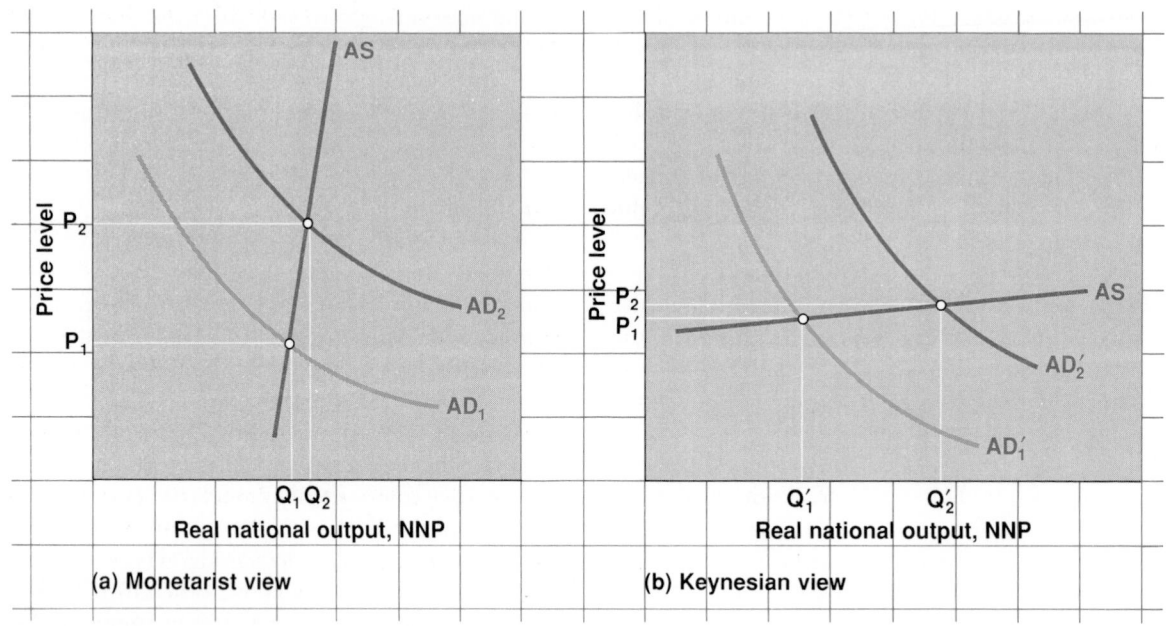

FIGURE 18-4

Monetarism, Keynesianism, and the aggregate demand–aggregate supply model

The monetarist view (a) is that the aggregate supply curve is relatively steep, which means that a change in aggregate demand will have a large effect on the price level but only cause a small change in real output and employment. The Keynesian conception (b) envisions a relatively flat aggregate supply curve which implies that a change in aggregate demand will cause large changes in real output and employment and small changes in the price level.

ble prices and wages continuously move the economy toward full employment.[10]

These different conceptions of the aggregate supply curve are extremely important with respect to stabilization policy. First, in the monetarist view a change in aggregate demand affects primarily the price level and has little impact upon real GNP. This conclusion derives from the assumption that, if the Federal Reserve adheres to a monetary rule, the economy will be operating near or at its full-employment output at all times. If policy makers attempt to use stabilization policy to increase real output and employment, their efforts will be largely in vain. As aggregate demand shifts from AD_1 to AD_2 in Figure 18-4a, we get a very modest increase in real output (Q_1 to Q_2) but a large increase in the price level (P_1 to P_2). The economy will pay a high "price" in terms of inflation to realize very modest increases in output and employment. In comparison, the Keynesian conception indicates that an expansionary policy will have large effects on production and employment and little impact on the price level. This conclusion derives from the assumption that, because of its inherent instability, the private economy may be operating far below its productive potential. Thus in Figure 18-4b we find that the AD_1' to AD_2' increase in aggregate demand will entail a large increase in real output (Q_1' to Q_2') while eliciting only a small price level increase (P_1' to P_2'). To Keynesians, when the economy is operating at less than its capacity, large gains in real output and employment can be obtained at only a small inflationary cost.

Once the economy has reached its full-employ-

[10] Chapter 12's comparison of classical and Keynesian economics and, in particular, the discussion surrounding Figure 12-2, might be fruitfully reread at this point.

ment level of output, of course, the debate between Keynesians and monetarists largely ends. Both would agree that expansionary stabilization policies will produce demand-pull inflation in the classical range of aggregate supply.

The aggregate demand–aggregate supply model also can help clarify the debate over the monetarist's call for a monetary rule. In Figure 18-5 we suppose that the economy is initially operating at the Q_1 full-employment level of NNP. Observe that the aggregate supply curve shifts rightward from AS to AS', depicting a typical or average annual increase in potential real output. Increases in aggregate supply such as this result

from real factors such as added resources and improved technology. The monetarists argue that a monetary rule tying increases in the money supply to the typical rightward shift of the aggregate supply curve will ensure that the aggregate demand curve shifts rightward from AD to AD'. The result? Real NNP will rise from Q_1 to Q_2 and the price level will remain constant at P_1. Hence, say the monetarists, a monetary rule will promote price stability.

Keynesians, we have seen, dispute the close predictable link between changes in the money supply and changes in aggregate demand. They envision the possibility of two quite different scenarios.

Scenario one: During the period in question, the investment demand curve (Figure 17-2b) may shift rapidly to the right because of optimistic business expectations. As a result, the aggregate demand curve in Figure 18-5 will move to some point rightward of AD' and demand-pull inflation will occur. In this case, the monetary rule fails to accomplish its goal of maintaining price stability. According to Keynesians, a contractionary fiscal policy accompanied by a tight money policy can hold the rightward shift of aggregate demand to AD', thereby avoiding the inflation.

Scenario two: Suppose that, during the period in question, the investment demand curve collapses inward because of pessimistic business expectations. Thus there will *not* be the increase from AD to AD' in Figure 18-5. Again the monetary rule flunks the price stability test: The price level falls from P_1 to P_2. By increasing aggregate demand to AD', argue the Keynesians, an expansionary fiscal policy accompanied by an easy money policy can avoid the deflation. Or, if the price level is inflexible downward at P_1, expansionary stabilization policies can avoid the loss of potential output which otherwise would occur (Q_1Q_2).

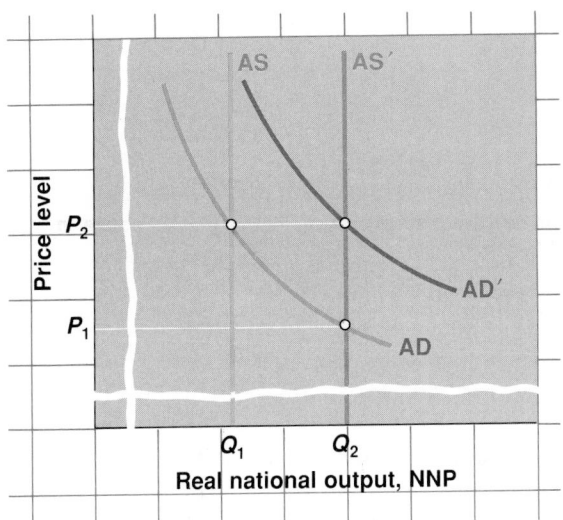

FIGURE 18-5

The monetary rule and the aggregate demand–aggregate supply model

Monetarists favor a monetary rule which would fix the increase in the money supply over time to the average increase in real output. An increase in aggregate demand (AD to AD') thus would match an increase in aggregate supply (AS to AS') and the price level would remain constant. Keynesians counter that the monetary rule will not guarantee that aggregate demand will shift from AD to AD'. Because of instability within the private economy, aggregate demand may either shift to the right of AD', creating demand-pull inflation, or fail to shift all the way to AD', resulting in deflation. Hence, Keynesians argue that the discretionary use of stabilization policies is more likely to maintain price stability than is a monetary rule.

Rational expectations theory

Keynesian economics and monetarism do not stand alone in the battle for the minds of economists, policy makers, and students. Developed largely since the mid-1970s, **rational expectations theory** (RET) has taken shape. Although several variants of RET have emerged, we will confine our discussion to the version which has come to be associated with the *new classical economics*.[11] Other aspects of the new classical economics will be discussed in Chapter 19. Our ultimate goal is to relate RET to the debate over whether stabilization policy should be discretionary, as Keynesians argue, or based on rules, as the monetarists contend. But let us first present some relevant background on RET.

Rational expectations theory follows the general thrust of economic theory in suggesting that people behave rationally. Market participants gather information and process it intelligently to form expectations about things in which they have a monetary stake. If financial investors, for instance, expect stock market prices to fall, they tend to sell the shares they own in anticipation of that decline. The increased availability of stock in the market results in an immediate drop in prices offered per share. When consumers learn that a drought is expected to boost food prices, they have a tendency to purchase storable food products in advance of the price hike. These expectations thus cause an increase in market demand which in turn produces an increase in food prices before the food crop is even harvested.

But rational expectations macroeconomists go beyond these microeconomic examples to argue that businesses, consumers, and workers understand the workings of the economy and are able to use available information to make decisions which best further their own self-interests. People do not merely project past developments into the future; they also assess the anticipated effects of current economic policies upon the future of the economy. In short, "rational" people will use all the relevant information available, including information about how the economy functions and how the government conducts economic policy. This will allow them to forecast the consequences of economic changes—be they policy generated or otherwise—and accordingly make decisions which will maximize their own well-being. This is the essence of rational expectations.

[11] When your children take principles of economics, there will undoubtedly be a *neo* new classical economics (as yet unborn) for them to master!

But RET contains a second basic element which gives it its "new classical" flavor. And that is, like the classical economics of Chapter 12, rational expectations theory assumes that all markets—both product and resource—are highly competitive. Therefore, wages and prices are flexible both upward and downward. Indeed, RET goes further by assuming that new information is quickly (in some cases instantaneously) taken into account in the demand and supply curves of such markets so that equilibrium prices and quantities quickly adjust to new events (technological change), market shocks (a drought or collapse of the OPEC oil cartel), or changes in public policies (an unexpected shift from tight to easy money). Both product and resource prices are highly flexible and change quickly as consumers, businesses, and resource suppliers change their economic behavior in response to new information.

Policy frustration

Let us examine the RET contention that *the aggregated responses of the public to its expectations will tend to render anticipated discretionary stabilization policies ineffective.* Consider monetary policy. Suppose the monetary authorities make pronouncements to the effect that an easy money policy is in the offing. Purpose: To increase real output and employment. But based upon past experience, the public anticipates that this expansionary policy will be accompanied by inflation. As a result, the public will take self-protective actions. Workers will press for higher money wages. Businesses will increase the prices of their products. Lenders will raise their interest rates. All these responses are designed to prevent inflation from having anticipated adverse effects upon the *real* incomes of workers, businesses, and lenders. But collectively this behavior raises wage and price levels. Hence, the increase in aggregate expenditures brought about by the easy money policy is completely dissipated in higher prices and wages; therefore, real output and employment do *not* expand. In Keynesian terms, the increase in real investment spending which the easy money policy was designed to generate (Figure 17-2) never materializes. The expected rate of net profit remains unchanged in that the price of capital rises in lockstep with the prices of the extra production which the capital allows. Also, the nominal interest rate rises proportionately to the price level, thus leaving the real interest rate unchanged. The necessary outcome is that no increase in real investment spending is forthcoming and no expansion of real NNP occurs.

In terms of the monetarists' equation of exchange, the easy money policy increases M and therefore increases aggregate expenditures, MV. But the public's expectation of inflation elicits an increase in P by a percentage amount equal to the increase in MV. Despite the increased MV, real output, Q, and employment are therefore unchanged.

Note carefully what has occurred here. The decision to increase M was made for the purpose of increasing output and employment. But the public, acting upon the expected effects of easy money, has taken actions which have frustrated or nullified the policy's goal. Easy money has been translated into inflation, rather than into desired increases in real output and employment. One can plausibly argue that the economy would have been better off if it had followed a steady money growth policy as suggested by the monetary rule. It was, after all, the government's discretionary easy money policy which prompted unions, businesses, and lenders to raise wages, prices, and interest rates. Why blame these groups for inflation, when the blame should be placed upon government?

AD-AS INTERPRETATION

We can better understand the RET contention of policy ineffectiveness by examining Figure 18-6. This diagram merely restates the classical model from Figure 12-2a. Here we go beyond the steep aggregate supply curve of the monetarists (Figure 18-4a) and portray the curve as being *vertical*. Now, once again, assume an expansionary monetary or fiscal policy shifts the aggregate demand curve rightward from AD_1 to AD_2. Why doesn't this increase in aggregate demand increase real output significantly (as in the Keynesian model of Figure 18-4b) or at least slightly (as in the monetarist model of Figure 18-4a)? According to RET, the answer is that consumers, businesses, and workers will anticipate that an expansionary policy

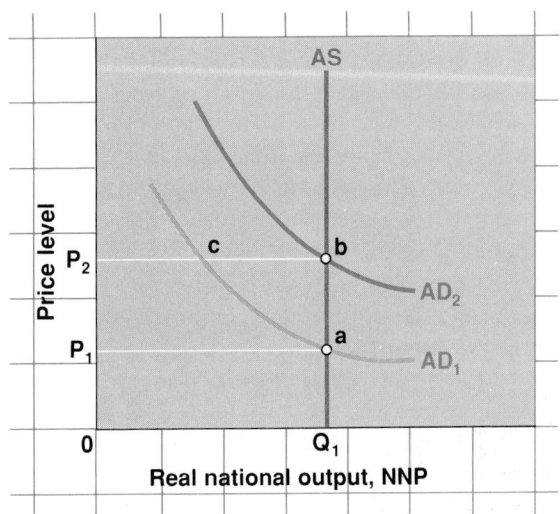

FIGURE 18-6

Rational expectations and the aggregate demand–aggregate supply model

Rational expectations theory implies that the aggregate supply curve is vertical. Strictly interpreted, the theory suggests that an increase in aggregate demand from, say, AD_1 to AD_2 will immediately result in an offsetting increase in the price level (P_1 to P_2) so that real national output will remain unchanged at Q_1. Conversely, a decline in aggregate demand from AD_2 to AD_1 will instantaneously reduce the price level from P_2 to P_1, leaving real national output and employment unchanged.

means rising prices and will have built the expected effects into their market decisions concerning product prices, nominal-wage rates, nominal interest rates, and so forth. Markets will instantaneously adjust, thereby bringing the price level upward from P_1 to P_2. In effect, the economy does not move beyond output Q_1 because the price level rises by precisely the amount required to cancel any impact the expansionary policy might have had upon real output and employment. It is the *combination* of rational expectations and instantaneous market adjustments—in this case upward wage, price, and interest rate flexibility—which dooms the policy change to ineffectiveness. As aggregate demand expands from AD_1 to AD_2, the economy moves upward along the vertical aggregate supply curve directly from point *a* to point *b*. The only result is a higher price level; the *real* incomes of workers, businesses, lenders, and others are all unchanged because they have rationally anticipated the effects of public policy and have incorporated their expectations into market decisions to cause the resulting upshift of nominal wages, nominal profits, and nominal interest rates. Presumably a decline in aggregate demand from AD_2 to AD_1 would have precisely the opposite effects. Instead of causing unemployment, the economy would move directly along the aggregate supply curve from *b* to *a*.

In the "old" classical theory there would be a period of time wherein a decline in aggregate demand would cause a temporary "lapse" from full employment until market adjustments were completed. That is, the economy would first move from *b* to *c* in Figure 18-6, but then in time falling prices and wages would move the economy down AD_1 to full employment at point *a*. But in the RET version of the "new" classical economics, prices would adjust instantaneously so that real output and employment would not deviate from Q_1. In other words, in the "old" classical economics changes in aggregate demand could cause short-run changes in output and employment. But the decision-making process and instantaneous market adjustments of the strict RET form of "new" classical economics preclude this.

PROCYCLICAL POLICY?

Rational expectations theorists claim that discretionary policy may reinforce economic instability. Consider the following scenario. Suppose once again that the economy is sliding into a recession. Government's policy response is to cut taxes by enacting, say, an investment tax credit which allows businesses to subtract 10 percent of their investment expenditures from their taxable incomes. This unexpected windfall will boost anticipated profits on investment projects and thereby stimulate investment spending and aggregate demand. In short, fiscal policy works effectively in the fashion described in Chapter 14. But if this scenario occurs on several occasions, businesses will come to expect that, whenever the economy falls into a recession, policy makers will respond with an investment tax credit or some other form of tax relief. Hence, when recession occurs, businesses will post-

pone investment in anticipation of a forthcoming tax cut which will increase the profitability of that investment. But the decision to defer investment intensifies the downswing. When the tax cut is actually put into effect, there will occur an unusually large spurt of investment. Government tax policy has exaggerated the variability of investment and has intensified both the recession and recovery phases of the cycle. Conclusion: Discretionary policy tends to be procyclical rather that countercyclical. A much better alternative, according to the rational expectations theorists, would be to abandon discretionary policy in favor of rules.

Postscript: While RET supports monetarism in arguing for policy rules, it should be stressed that the rationales are quite different. According to the rational expectations theory, policy is ineffective, not because of policy errors or the inability to time decisions properly, but because of the reaction of the public to the expected effects of these policies. The monetarists are saying, in effect, that discretionary policy doesn't work because the monetary authorities do not have enough information about time lags and such. RET supporters claim that discretionary policy is ineffective because the public has considerable knowledge concerning policy decisions and their impacts. The monetarists base their argument on "ignorance"; RET bases its conclusion on "knowledge."

EVALUATION

There is no question but that RET has caused a substantial stir in economics over the past decade or so. Anyone exposed to RET thinking tends to look at the macroeconomy from a somewhat different perspective. The appeal of RET stems from at least two considerations. First, as is the case with monetarism, RET is an option which might fill the void left by Keynesian economics' alleged inability to explain and to correct by policy the simultaneous inflation and unemployment of the 1970s and early 1980s. Second, RET is strongly rooted in the theory of markets or, in other words, in microeconomics (defined in Chapter 1). Hence, RET purports to provide linkages between macro- and microeconomics which economists have long sought.

But the criticisms of RET are manifold and significantly persuasive so that it is fair to say that at this point the vast majority of economists do *not* subscribe to RET. Let us briefly mention three basic criticisms.

1 Behavior Many economists question that people by and large are, or can be, as well-informed as RET assumes. Can we really expect households, businesses, and workers to understand how the economy works and what the impact will be of, say, the Fed's announced decision to increase its $M1$ money target growth rate from $3\frac{1}{2}$ to 5 percent per year? After all, economists who specialize in forecasting frequently mispredict the *direction* of changes in output, employment, and prices, much less correctly indicate the *amounts* by which such variables will change. RET proponents counter that they are not suggesting that people always make *perfect* forecasts, but rather that they do not make consistent forecasting errors which can be exploited by policy makers. Furthermore, the RET theorists point out that key decision-making institutions—large corporations, major financial institutions, and labor organizations—employ full-time economists to help anticipate impacts of newly implemented public policies. Hence, it is allegedly impossible to fool the important decision-making institutions in the economy on a consistent basis. But the issue of whether people and institutions behave as RET suggests is highly controversial.

2 Sticky prices A second main criticism leveled at RET is that in reality markets—at least many markets—are *not* purely competitive and therefore do not adjust instantaneously (or even rapidly) to changing market conditions. While the stock market and certain commodity markets experience day-to-day or minute-to-minute price changes, many sellers can control within limits the prices they charge. When demand falls, for example, these sellers resist price cuts so that the impact is upon output and employment (see Figure 11-7). This is particularly true of labor markets (Chapter 12) where union and individual contracts keep wages unresponsive to changing market conditions for extended periods of time. Critics ask: If markets adjust quickly and completely as RET suggests, how does one explain the decade of severe unemployment of the 1930s or the high $7\frac{1}{2}$ to $9\frac{1}{2}$ percent unemployment rates which persisted over the 1981–1984 period?

3 Policy and stability A final criticism is that there is substantial evidence to indicate that, contrary to RET predictions, economic policy does affect real GNP and employment. Thus, in the post-World War II period, wherein government has more actively invoked stabilization policies, fluctuations in real output have been less than in earlier periods. Mainstream economists point to studies which indicate that monetary and fiscal policies *do* alter the levels of production and employment and are not merely dissipated in price level changes as RET suggests.

A CONTINUING DEBATE

Our discussion of the theoretical and policy issues raised by monetarism and the new classical economics only skims the surface. In Chapter 19 we will look at these issues from a slightly different slant. There we will have an opportunity, for example, to examine the alternative perspectives on the alleged tradeoff between inflation and unemployment. Additionally, we will develop the important new classical distinction between short-run and long-run aggregate supply. For now, let us simply offer several concluding comments to put the current macroeconomic debate into perspective.

First, from an historical perspective Keynesian economics came to the fore in the late 1930s and dominated macroeconomic theory and policy through the 1950s and into the 1960s. It was then seriously challenged by monetarism in the 1960s and with greater vigor in the 1970s. The 1970s also gave birth to RET and its pointed critique of macro policy.

A second point is that most economists would agree that both Keynesianism and monetarism are inherently plausible. Both theories provide useful frameworks within which the macroeconomy can be analyzed and understood. Economists are in less agreement as to the plausibility and relevance of RET. However, we must be aware that new ideas which seem unrealistic and revolutionary at the outset have a habit of becoming plausible and orthodox in time.

Finally, and perhaps most importantly, the controversy has been healthy in the sense that it has forced economists of all persuasions to rethink some of the very fundamental aspects of macroeconomics. And, as is true of most debates, considerable compromise and revision of positions has occurred. There are very few economists today who would embrace the extreme Keynesian view that "money doesn't matter" or the opposite monetarist extreme that "only money matters." Stated differently, despite important differences between Keynesianism and monetarism, we must not lose sight of the fundamental fact that in both models money affects NNP in the same direction. In both theories an increase in the money supply will increase nominal NNP and vice versa. The debate centers upon the quantitative significance of these changes. Furthermore, thanks to the monetarists' emphasis upon the crowding-out effect, economists and policy makers have become more fully aware of the need to coordinate fiscal and monetary policies. If fiscal policy generates a crowding-out effect of some magnitude which diminishes the effectiveness of fiscal policy, then it is obviously imperative that an appropriate monetary policy be applied simultaneously to negate any potential crowding out of private investment. In addition, economists of all persuasions now stress both aggregate demand and aggregate supply in their analyses. And a legacy of RET is that economists and policy makers are much more sensitive as to how expectations might affect the outcome of a policy change. RET has also been helpful in stressing the links between microeconomics and macroeconomics. We are increasingly aware that what happens to the aggregate levels of output, employment, and prices depends upon how individual product and resource markets function. Thus monetarism and RET have both had a great impact upon macro theory and policy, although the mainstream view continues to be of Keynesian lineage.

CHAPTER SUMMARY

The following statements contrast the Keynesian and monetarist positions on a number of critical points.

1 *Basic differences.* The *Keynesian* view is that the market system is largely noncompetitive and is therefore permissive of macroeconomic instability. An activist stabilization policy, centered upon fiscal policy, is required to remedy this shortcoming. The *monetarist* view is that markets are highly competitive and conducive to macro-

LAST WORD

"*P*-star": a new tool for monetary policy?

The Federal Reserve has recently devised an "experimental indicator" of future inflation based upon the monetarist's equation of exchange. Will this indicator prove to be a useful tool for setting monetary policy?

One of the Federal Reserve's most important tasks when setting monetary policy is to predict the future rate of inflation. For example, suppose that the rate of inflation today is an unacceptably high 8 percent. Should the Fed reduce the growth of the money supply to try to reduce inflation? At first thought the answer may seem to be "Yes." But if the present course of monetary policy is already such that the rate of inflation a year from now will be considerably lower, then a shift to a tight money policy may cause a recession. Alternatively, suppose that today's inflation is a mild 2%, strongly suggesting that the present course of monetary policy is appropriate. But perhaps the existing course of monetary policy will accelerate inflation in a year or two. If so, the Fed may want to tighten its monetary policy today.

economic stability. Monetarists favor a more *laissez faire* policy.

2 *Analytical framework.* To *Keynesians* the basic determinant of real output, employment, and the price level is the level of aggregate expenditures. Hence, their basic equation is $C_a + I_n + X_n + G = $ NNP. The components of aggregate expenditures are determined by a wide variety of factors which, for the most part, are unrelated to

An accurate indicator of future inflation has in the past eluded economists and thus made it difficult to formulate monetary policy. Now, however, a group of Federal Reserve economists believe they have found a reliable predictor of long-run inflation.* These economists refer to their gauge of future inflation as "P-star," for the P^* term in the following equation:

$$P^* = \frac{M2 \times V^*}{Q^*}$$

The P^* in the equation is the predicted future price level. Recall from Chapter 15 that M2 is comprised of M1 *plus* noncheckable savings deposits *plus* small (less than $100,000) time deposits. The V^* term measures the actual annual velocity of M2 over the past 33 years and Q^* is an estimate of the real potential GNP in the future, assuming the economy grows at a maximum noninflationary rate of 2.5 percent annually.

Note that this formula is merely a variation of the equation of exchange ($MV = PQ$). If we multiply each side of the P-star equation by Q^* and reverse sides of the equation, we get: $M2 \times V^* = P^* \times Q^*$. Thus, the only new items here are the M2 term and the asterisks (stars). Proponents of the P-star theory use M2 rather than $M(= M1)$ in the equation because their research shows that, although M2 velocity varies monthly and yearly, it has been constant at 1.65 over longer periods. This means that $1 dollar of M2 will change hands an average of 1.65 times per year over several years.

If, as the Federal Reserve research suggests, the velocity of M2 is indeed *constant* over long periods, then the P-star equation can be useful for shaping monetary policy. If the predicted general level of future prices P^* exceeds the current price level P, then the Fed can expect inflation to rise. Thought of differently, future M2 growth will be too large in relationship to potential GNP, causing inflation to increase. To counter this rising inflation the Fed should reduce the growth of M2 to boost interest rates and slow spending in the economy. Conversely, if P^* is less than P, the future rate of inflation will be less than the present rate. Depending upon the present rate of inflation, an easy money policy might well be in order.

The Federal Reserve cautions that its P-star indicator is experimental and that it will need to test the theory for several years to determine its usefulness as a guide for long-term monetary policy. The Fed also points out, however, that the theory would have accurately predicted coming inflation during the past few decades. At a minimum, the new P-star suggests that the Federal Reserve will continue to pay close attention to M2 along with M1 in conducting its monetary policy.

*Jeffrey J. Hallman, Richard D. Porter, and David H. Small, "M2 Per Unit of Potential GNP as an Anchor for the Price Level," *Federal Reserve Board Staff Study no. 157,* April 1989. For a nontechnical discussion of P-Star see Peter T. Kilborn, "Federal Reserve Sees a Way To Gauge Long-Run Inflation," *The New York Times,* p. A1, June 13, 1989.

the supply of money. *Monetarism* focuses upon the equation of exchange: $MV = PQ$. Because velocity V is basically stable, the critical determinant of real output and employment (Q) and the price level (P) is the supply of money M.

3 *Fiscal policy.* The *Keynesian* position is that because *a* government spending is a component of aggregate expenditures and *b* tax changes have direct and dependable effects upon consumption and investment, fiscal policy is a powerful stabilization tool. *Monetarists* argue that fiscal policy is weak and uncertain in its effects. In particular, unless financed by an increase in the money supply, deficit spending will raise the interest rate and thereby crowd out private investment spending.

4 *Monetary policy.* *Keynesians* argue that monetary policy entails a lengthy transmission mechanism, involving monetary policy decisions, bank reserves, the interest rate, investment, and finally the nominal NNP. Uncertainties at each step in the mechanism limit the effectiveness and dependability of monetary policy. Money matters, but its manipulation through monetary policy is not as powerful a stabilization device as is fiscal policy. More specifically, the combination of a relatively flat demand for money curve and a relatively steep investment-demand curve makes monetary policy relatively ineffective. *Monetarists* believe that the relative stability of *V* indicates a rather dependable link between the money supply and the nominal NNP. However, monetarists think that because of *a* variable time lags in becoming effective and *b* the incorrect use of the interest rate as a guide to policy, the application of discretionary monetary policy to "fine-tune" the economy is likely to fail. In practice, monetary policy has tended to destabilize the economy. Monetarists therefore recommend a monetary rule whereby the money supply is increased in accordance with the long-term growth of real NNP.

The following statements contain the essence of rational expectations theory (RET).

5 RET is based upon two basic assumptions: *a* consumers, businesses, and workers understand how the economy works; are able to assess the future effects of policy and other changes; and adjust their decisions to further their own self-interests; *b* markets are highly competitive and prices and wages adjust quickly to changes in demand and supply.

6 RET holds that, when the public reacts to the expected effects of stabilization policy, the effectiveness of such policy will be negated. This theory therefore supports policy rules as opposed to discretionary policy.

TERMS AND CONCEPTS

Keynesians	crowding-out effect
monetarists	monetary rule
equation of exchange	rational expectations theory
velocity of money	

QUESTIONS AND STUDY SUGGESTIONS

1 Explain: "The debate between Keynesians and monetarists is an important facet of the larger controversy over the role of government in our lives."

2 State and explain the basic equations of Keynesianism and monetarism. Can you "translate" the Keynesian equation into the monetarist equation?

3 In 1988 the money supply (*M*1) was approximately $788 billion and the nominal GNP was about $4862 billion. What was the velocity of money in 1988? Figure 18-3 indicates that velocity increased steadily between the mid-1940s and 1982 and then leveled off or declined. Can you think of reasons to explain these trends?

4 What is the transmission mechanism for monetary policy according to *a* Keynesians and *b* monetarists? What significance do the two schools of thought apply to money and monetary policy as a determinant of economic activity? According to monetarism, what happens when the actual supply of money exceeds the amount of money which the public wants to hold?

5 Why do monetarists recommend that a "monetary rule" be substituted for discretionary monetary policy? Explain: "One cannot assess what monetary policy is doing by just looking at interest rates." Indicate how an attempt to stabilize interest rates can be destabilizing to the economy.

6 Answer the ensuing questions on the basis of the following information for a hypothetical economy in year 1: money supply = $400 billion; long-term annual growth of real NNP = 3 percent; velocity = 4. Assume that the banking system initially has no excess reserves and that the reserve requirement is 10 percent. Also, suppose that velocity is constant and that the economy initially is operating at its full employment level of output.

    a What is the level of nominal NNP in year 1 in this economy?

    b Suppose that the Federal Reserve adheres to the monetarist's rule through open-market operations. What amount of bonds will it have to sell to, or buy from, commercial depository institutions or the public between years 1 and 2 in order to meet its monetary rule?

7 Explain why monetarists assert fiscal policy is weak and ineffective. What specific assumptions do *a* monetarists and *b* Keynesians make with respect to the shapes of the demand for money and investment-demand curves? Why are the differences significant?

8 Indicate the precise relationship between the demand for money and the velocity of money. Discuss in detail: "The crucial issue separating Keynesians from monetarists is whether or not the demand for money is sensitive to changes in the rate of interest." Explain the Keynesian contention that a change in *M* is likely to be accompanied by a change in *V* in the opposite direction.

9 Explain and evaluate these statements in terms of the Keynesian–monetarist controversy:

a "If the national goal is to raise income, it can be achieved only by raising the money supply."

b "The size of a Federal budget deficit is not important. What is important is how the deficit is financed."

c "There is no reason in the world why, in an equation like $MV = PQ$, the V should be thought to be independent of the rate of interest. There is every plausible reason for the velocity of circulation to be a systematic and increasing function of the rate of interest."

d "Monetarists assume that the PQ side of the equation of exchange is 'passive'; Keynesians assume it is 'active.'"

e "If expectations are rational, then monetary policy cannot be used to stabilize production and employment. It only determines the price level."

10 Explain how rational expectations might be an impediment to discretionary stabilization policies. Do you favor discretionary policies or rules? Justify your position.

11 Use the aggregate demand–aggregate supply model to sketch graphically the **a** monetarist, **b** Keynesian, and **c** rational expectations theories of the macroeconomy. Carefully compare the implications of each for public policy. In what respect, if any, does your RET portrayal differ from the "old" classical model of Figure 12-2a?

CHAPTER 19

The inflation–unemployment relationship: Keynesian, new classical, and supply-side views

In Chapter 18, the basic ideas of monetarism and the rational expectations theory (RET) were presented and contrasted with the mainstream Keynesian perspective. We observed that there are differing views on such matters as the degree to which the private economy is inherently unstable, the route through which monetary policy affects the economy, and the effectiveness of monetary and fiscal policy. This chapter takes the discussion of alternative macroeconomic theories further by examining various explanations of the simultaneous occurrence of inflation and unemployment. Additionally, our discussion of alternative views now becomes more inclusive; in particular, we examine supply-side economics.

This chapter's specific goals are as follows. First, we derive and examine the so-called *Phillips Curve*, which has been used by Keynesian economists to explain the apparent tradeoff between unemployment and inflation. Next, an alternative theory—dubbed the *natural rate hypothesis*—is explored to explain the economy's encounters with stagflation. This theory is associated with the *new classical economics*. Then, we explore the new classical distinction between short-run and long-run aggregate supply. This distinction will permit us to expand our earlier analysis of demand-pull and cost-push inflation. Finally, policy proposals designed to deal with stagflation are discussed.

The Phillips Curve

Let us first discuss some important matters which will help you follow our description and analysis of the Phillips Curve.

ANALYTICAL AND HISTORICAL BACKGROUND

Our Keynesian analysis of Chapters 12 through 14 focused upon aggregate expenditures as the fundamental determinant of real national output and employment. The simplest Keynesian model implies that the economy may realize *either* unemployment (a recessionary gap) *or* inflation (an inflationary gap), but *not both* unemployment and inflation *simultaneously*. In terms of the aggregate demand and supply model, the simple Keynesian analysis assumes a "reverse L"-shaped aggregate supply curve (Figure 12-2b). Over the horizontal (Keynesian) range of the aggregate supply curve, increases in aggregate demand will expand real output and employment at a constant price level until full employment is achieved. Further increases in aggregate demand will place the economy in the vertical (classical) range of aggregate supply, over which real output will remain constant, but inflation will occur. Presumably some "right" level of aggregate demand which intersects the aggregate supply curve precisely at the full-employment level of output would give us the best of all possible macroeconomic worlds: full employment *and* a stable price level (Q_f in Figure 12-2b).

In the view of most economists, this simple Keynesian model did in fact provide a generally satisfactory explanation of the economy's macro behavior over the four decades prior to the 1970s.

That is, the Great Depression, the World War II inflationary boom, and most of our macroeconomic ups and downs in the 1950s and 1960s could be interpreted and understood reasonably well within the context of Keynesian analysis. But this situation changed in the 1970s. The coexistence of inflation and unemployment—indeed, the simultaneous occurrence of *increasing* unemployment and a *rising* price level—became common and the central macroeconomic problem of the 1970s and early 1980s. Specifically, there were two serious stagflationary episodes—1973–1975 and 1978–1980—which were not readily explainable in terms of the simple Keynesian expenditures model. These unusual periods can be better understood, however, by (1) explicitly taking into account the more realistic *upsloping,* or intermediate range, of aggregate supply; and (2) allowing for leftward shifts of the aggregate supply curve.

THE PHILLIPS CURVE: CONCEPT AND DATA

The more realistic aggregate supply and demand model is shown in Figure 19-1. Recall that the aggregate demand curve slopes downward as a result of the wealth, interest rate, and foreign purchases effects. With respect to aggregate supply, recall that the three ranges of the curve—the horizontal Keynesian range, the upsloping intermediate range, and the vertical classical range—depend upon what happens to production costs as real national output expands. It is the intersection of aggregate demand and aggregate supply which determines real national output (and employment), on the one hand, and the price level, on the other.

In Figure 19-1 we perform a simple mental experiment. Suppose that in some given period aggregate demand expands from AD_0 to AD_2. This shift might result from a change in any one of the non-price-level determinants of aggregate demand discussed in Chapter 11. For example, businesses may decide to buy more investment goods or government may decide to increase its expenditures in order to provide more public goods. Whatever the cause of the aggregate demand increase, we observe that the price level rises from P_0 to P_2, while real output expands from Q_0 to Q_2.

Now let's compare what would have happened if the increase in aggregate demand had been

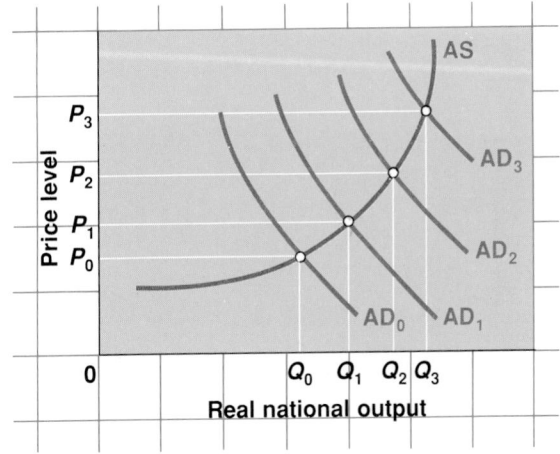

FIGURE 19-1

The effect of changes in aggregate demand upon real national output and the price level

Comparing the effects of various possible increases in aggregate demand yields the conclusion that the larger the increase in aggregate demand, the greater will be the resulting inflation and the greater the increase in real national output. Because real national output and the unemployment rate are inversely related, we can generalize that, given aggregate supply, high rates of inflation should be accompanied by low rates of unemployment.

larger, say, from AD_0 to AD_3. The new equilibrium tells us that both the amount of inflation and the growth of real output would have been greater (and the unemployment rate thereby smaller). Similarly, suppose aggregate demand in our given year had only increased modestly from AD_0 to AD_1. We find that, as compared with our original AD_0 to AD_2 shift, the amount of inflation and the growth of real output would have been smaller (and the unemployment rate therefore larger). The generalization embodied in this mental experiment is that *the greater the rate of growth of aggregate demand, the greater will be the resulting inflation and the greater the growth of real national output (and the lower the unemployment rate).* Conversely, if aggregate demand grows more slowly, the smaller will be the resulting inflation and the slower the growth of real output (and the higher the unemployment rate). More simply stated, our generalization is that *high rates of inflation should be accompanied by low rates of unemployment and*

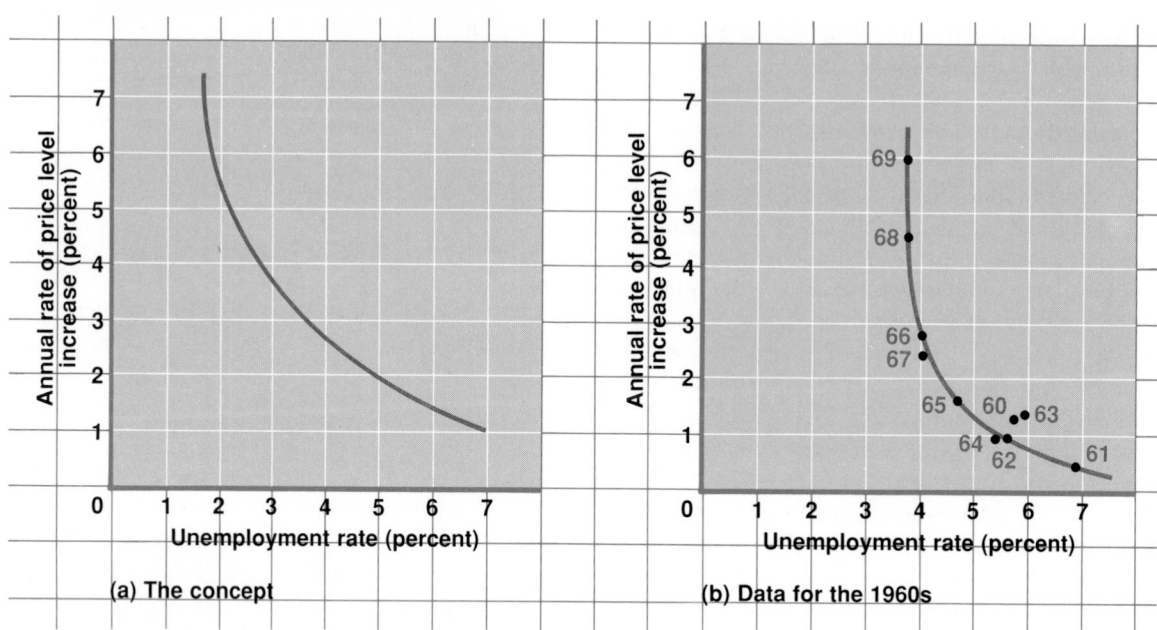

FIGURE 19-2

The Phillips Curve: concept and empirical data

The Phillips Curve purported to show a stable relationship between the unemployment rate and the rate of inflation. Because this relationship is inverse, there would presumably be a tradeoff between unemployment and inflation. Data points for the 1960s seemed to confirm the Phillips Curve concept.

vice versa. Figure 19-2a generalizes what the expected relationship should look like.

Do the facts fit the theory? Pioneering empirical work by economists in the late 1950s and 1960s seemed to verify the existence of this inverse relationship which came to be known as the **Phillips Curve.**[1] Thus, for example, Figure 19-2b shows the relationship between the unemployment rate and the rate of inflation for the 1961–1969 period. The red line generalizing upon the data portrays the expected inverse relationship. On the basis of this kind of empirical evidence economists believed that a stable, predictable tradeoff existed between unemployment and inflation. Furthermore, national economic policy was predicated upon the existence

[1] Named after A. W. Phillips, who developed this concept in Great Britain. See his "The Relationship between Unemployment and the Rate of Change in Money Wage Rates in the United Kingdom, 1862–1957," *Economica,* November 1958, pp. 283–299.

of this tradeoff. Let us consider the logic underlying the Phillips Curve and then discuss why the indicated relationship seemed to break down in the 1970s and early 1980s.

LOGIC OF THE PHILLIPS CURVE

How can the Phillips Curve be explained? What causes the apparent tradeoff between full employment and price level stability? Basically, there are two sets of complementary considerations which explain why inflation might occur before full employment is realized. Given our derivation of the Phillips Curve concept, it is no surprise that the factors underlying the Phillips Curve are those which Keynesians use to explain the intermediate range of the aggregate supply curve.

1 Labor market imbalances A partial explanation lies in certain imbalances—"bottlenecks" and structural problems—which arise in labor markets as the economy expands toward full employment. The basic point here is that "the" labor market in the United States in fact comprises an extremely large number of individual labor markets which are stratified and distinct both occupationally and geographically. This labor market diversity suggests the possibility that, as the economy expands, full employment will *not* be realized simultaneously in each individual labor market. While full employment and labor shortages may exist for some occupations and some areas, unemployment will persist for other occupations and regions. This disparity means that in an expanding economy, even though the overall unemployment rate may be, say, $6\frac{1}{2}$ or 7 percent, scarcities will develop for specific kinds of labor and for labor in certain geographic areas, and the wage rates of such workers will rise. Rising wage rates mean higher costs and necessitate higher prices. The net result is rising prices even though the economy as a whole is still operating short of full employment.

It is fair to ask why labor market adjustments do not eliminate these bottleneck problems. Why, for example, do not unemployed laborers become craftworkers? The answer, of course, is that such shifts cannot be made with sufficient speed to eliminate labor market bottlenecks. The training for a new occupation is costly in terms of both time and money. Furthermore, even if an unemployed laborer has the ability, time, and money to acquire new skills and to relocate, an unemployed laborer in Kalamazoo may just not be aware of the shortage of skilled craftworkers in Kenosha. Then, too, artificial restrictions upon the shiftability of workers sustain structural imbalances. For example, discrimination on the basis of race, ethnic background, or sex can keep qualified workers from acquiring available positions. Similarly, licensing requirements and union restrictions upon the number of available apprenticeships inhibit the leveling out of imbalances between specific labor markets. In brief, labor market adjustments are neither sufficiently rapid nor complete enough to prevent production costs and product prices from rising *before* overall full employment is achieved.

2 Market power A complementary, but more controversial, explanation of the Phillips Curve is based upon the assumption that labor unions and big businesses both possess significant amounts of monopoly or market power with which to raise wages and prices and that this power becomes easier to exert as the economy approaches full employment. Hence, the "wage-push" inflationary scenario goes something like this: As the economy moves toward full employment, employers have more difficulty finding qualified new workers, and unions become more aggressive in their wage demands. Furthermore, increasing prosperity will tend to enhance the willingness of businesses to grant these demands. On the one hand, firms will hesitate to resist union demands and risk a costly strike at the very time when business activity is becoming increasingly profitable. On the other hand, economic expansion provides a favorable environment in which monopoly power can be used to pass wage increases on to consumers in the form of higher product prices. The result is a rising price level in the absence of excess aggregate demand.

STABILIZATION POLICY DILEMMA

If the Phillips Curve remains fixed as in Figure 19-2, policy makers are faced with a dilemma. Traditional fiscal and monetary policies merely alter aggregate demand. They do nothing to correct the labor market imbalances and the market power which bring forth inflation before full employment is attained. More specifically, the manipulation of aggregate demand through fiscal and monetary measures simply has the effect of moving the economy *along* the given Phillips Curve. Hence, the expansionary fiscal policy and the easy money policy which combine to boost aggregate demand and achieve a lower rate of unemployment will simultaneously generate a higher rate of inflation. Conversely, a restrictive fiscal policy and a tight money policy can be used to reduce the rate of inflation, but only at the cost of a higher unemployment rate and more forgone production. *Policies to manage aggregate demand can be used to choose a point on the Phillips Curve, but such policies do not improve upon the "unemployment rate–inflation rate" trade-off embodied in the Phillips Curve.* Given the presence of the Phillips Curve, it is impossible to achieve "full employment without inflation."

Stagflation: a shifting curve?

How well did the concept of a stable Phillips Curve hold up during the 1970s and 1980s? The answer is "Not very well!" In fact, events of the 1970s and early 1980s were clearly at odds with the inflation rate—unemployment rate tradeoff embodied in the Phillips Curve. Figure 19-3 enlarges upon Figure 19-2b by adding data for the 1970–1988 period. The relatively clear-cut inverse relationship of the 1961–1969 period now becomes obscure and highly questionable. Note in Figure 19-3 that in many years of the 1970s the economy experienced *more* inflation and *more* unemployment or, in a

word, **stagflation.** Trace, for example, the data points for the 1972–1974 period. At best, these more recent data suggest that the Phillips Curve has been shifting to the right, that is, to a less desirable position where any given level of unemployment is accompanied by more inflation or, alternatively stated, each level of inflation is accompanied by more unemployment. The gray and black downsloping lines suggest such rightward shifts. At worst, the data suggest that there is no dependable tradeoff between unemployment and inflation.

SUPPLY SHOCKS

What happened to cause bouts of stagflation in the 1970s and early 1980s? The answer supplied by Keynesian economists is that a series of cost- or **supply shocks** occurred. And the fact that these disturbances arose on the cost or supply side makes a difference. Remember that the inverse relationship between the rate of inflation and the unemployment rate shown in Figure 19-2a was derived by changing the level of *aggregate demand* in the intermediate range of the aggregate supply curve in Figure 19-1. Now look at our cost-push inflation model which we have graphed as Figure 19-4. Here we find that a decrease (leftward shift) of *aggregate supply* causes the unemployment rate and the price level to vary *directly*. That is, both increase to give us stagflation. This, say the Keynesians, is essentially what happened during the period 1973–1975 and again in 1978–1980.

Let us consider the series of more-or-less random shocks which raised unit production costs and shifted the aggregate supply curve leftward, as from AS_1 to AS_2 in Figure 19-4, to generate the Great Stagflation of 1973–1975. More technically, let us consider how changes in several of the non-price-level determinants of aggregate supply (Chapter 11) contributed to stagflation.

I OPEC and energy prices First and foremost, the effective formation of the Organization of Petroleum Exporting Countries (OPEC) oil cartel resulted in a dramatic quadrupling of oil prices. This meant that the cost of producing and distributing virtually every good and service rose sharply.

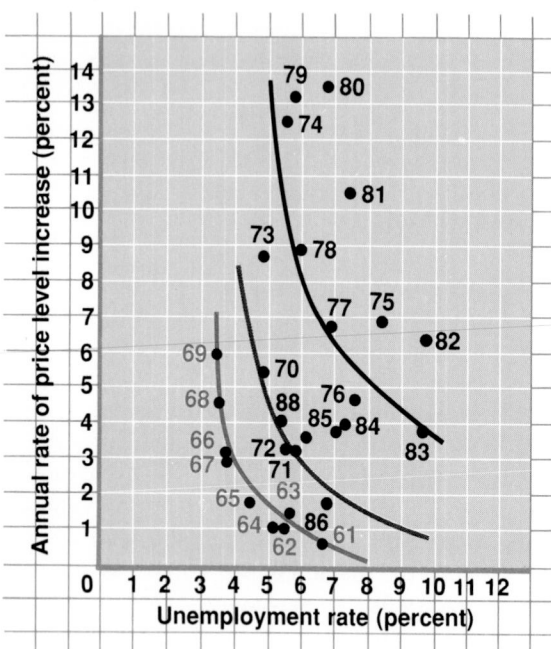

FIGURE 19-3

Inflation rates and unemployment rates, 1961–1988

Data points for the 1961–1988 period suggest no clear relationship between unemployment rates and rates of inflation. This raises questions as to the stability or existence of the Phillips Curve. Some economists feel the curve shifted to the right in the 1970s and early 1980s as suggested by the gray and black curves.

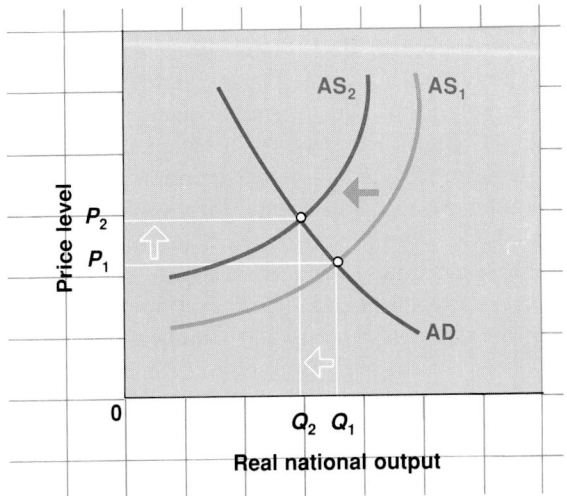

FIGURE 19-4

Aggregate supply and stagflation

According to the mainstream interpretation, in 1973–1975 a series of supply shocks, including sharply increased energy costs, higher agricultural commodity prices, higher import prices, diminishing productivity growth, and inflationary expectations, shifted the aggregate supply curve leftward. The result was stagflation—a higher price level accompanied by a decline in real national output. A similar scenario occurred in 1978–1980.

2 Agricultural shortfalls Severe worldwide agricultural shortfalls occurred in 1972 and 1973, particularly in Asia and the Soviet Union. In response, American agricultural exports expanded sharply, thereby reducing domestic supplies of agricultural commodities. The resulting higher prices for raw agricultural products in the United States meant higher costs to the industrial sectors producing food and fiber products. These higher costs were passed on to consumers as higher prices.

3 Depreciated dollar In the 1971–1973 period, the dollar was reduced in value to achieve greater balance in international trade and finance. Depreciation of the dollar means that it now takes more dollars to buy a unit of foreign money; this in turn causes the prices of all American imports to rise. In brief, a depreciated dollar sharply boosts American import prices. To the extent that American imports

are production inputs, unit production costs increase and the aggregate supply curve will shift leftward.

4 Demise of wage-price controls In the 1971–1974 period the Nixon administration had imposed wage and price controls which had the effect of suppressing inflationary pressures in the economy. When abandoned in 1974, both businesses and input suppliers pushed up their prices rapidly to recoup the price increases they had been forced to forgo during the control period. This upsurge increased unit costs and product prices.

5 Productivity decline The stagflation episodes of the 1970s and early 1980s were not due solely to the four rather dramatic supply shocks just discussed. More subtle considerations involving productivity and expectations were also at work. As we will discover in Chapter 21, the rate of growth of labor productivity—that is, the efficiency of labor—began to decline in the mid-1960s and continued to fall more-or-less persistently throughout the 1970s. This decline in the growth rate of labor productivity—in output per worker-hour—also tended to increase unit production costs.

Why so? The answer is that an increase in unit labor costs (that is, labor cost per unit of output) approximates the difference between the increase in nominal-wage rates and the increase in labor productivity. More precisely:

$$
\begin{array}{ccc}
\text{Percentage} & \text{percentage} & \text{percentage} \\
\text{change in} & \text{change in} & \text{change in} \\
\text{unit labor} & \approx \text{nominal-wage} & - \text{labor} \quad (1) \\
\text{costs} & \text{rates} & \text{productivity}
\end{array}
$$

For example, if hourly nominal wages are currently $5.00 and a worker produces 10 units per hour, then unit labor costs will be $.50. Now, if nominal wages increase by 10 percent to $5.50 per hour and productivity also increases by 10 percent to 11 units per hour, then unit labor costs will be unchanged. That is, $5.00/10 = $5.50/11 = $.50. In terms of our equation 10 percent (change in nominal wages) *minus* 10 percent (change in productivity) *equals* no increase in unit labor costs. Similarly, if nominal wages were to rise by 10 percent and labor productivity does not rise at all, unit labor costs would rise by 10 percent. That is, if the wage rate was $5.00 initially and output per hour was 10 units, labor costs would be $.50. But with wages now $5.50 and output still at 10 units per hour, unit labor costs would now be $.55, which is a 10 percent increase. In our equation 10 percent *minus* zero percent *equals* a 10 percent increase in unit labor costs. Since labor costs are 70 to 80 percent of total production costs, it is no surprise that product prices rise roughly in accord with increases in unit labor costs.

What we should consider from our simple equation when we think about stagflation is that, given the size of nominal-wage increases, a decline in the rate of growth of labor productivity will boost unit production costs and contribute to a leftward shift in the aggregate supply curve.

6 Inflationary expectations and wages The inflation of the 1970s had its genesis in the inflation of the late 1960s which in turn was caused by expanded military spending on the Vietnam war. Hence, by the early 1970s workers had been exposed to a period of accelerating inflation. As a result, the nominal-wage demands of labor began to embody the expectation of an increasing rate of inflation. Most employers, expecting to be able to pass on higher wage costs in this context of mounting inflation, did not resist labor's demands for larger and larger increases in nominal wages. In fact, many workers had cost-of-living adjustments (COLAs) in their collective bargaining contracts, so their nominal-wage rates automatically rose with the price level. In any event, demands for larger and larger nominal-wage increases would increase unit production costs and tend to shift aggregate supply from AS₁ to AS₂ in Figure 19-4.

Note that equation (1) relating unit labor costs to wages and productivity is an appropriate vehicle in which to incorporate both **inflationary expectations** *and* declining labor productivity as causes of stagflation. If nominal wages are being pushed up at an accelerating rate by organized labor and the growth rate of labor productivity is simultaneously falling, there will be a double impetus for unit labor costs—and ultimately product prices—to rise.

Synopsis All of these factors combined in the 1970s to adversely shift the aggregate supply curve to yield the worst possible macroeconomic world—

falling output and rising unemployment combined with a rising price level (Figure 19-4). The numerical dimensions of the 1973–1975 stagflation were quite remarkable. The unemployment rate shot up from 4.9 percent in 1973 to 8.5 percent in 1975, contributing to a $49 billion *decline* in real GNP. In the same period the price level increased by 21 percent. Like a bad dream the 1973–1975 stagflation scenario essentially recurred in 1978–1980. In this instance an enormous $21 per barrel increase in oil prices was imposed by OPEC. Coupled with rising prices of agricultural commodities, the price level rose by 26 percent over the 1978–1980 period, while unemployment jumped from 6.1 to 7.6 percent. Real GNP grew by a very modest 2 percent annual rate over the three-year period.

Regardless of the causes of stagflation, it was quite clear to most economists in the 1970s that the Phillips Curve did not represent a stable relationship. There was evidence that adverse (leftward) shifts in aggregate supply were at work, which seemed to explain those unhappy occasions when the inflation rate and the unemployment rate increased simultaneously. To many economists the experience during the 1970s and the early 1980s suggested that the Phillips Curve was shifting to the right and confronting the economy with higher rates of inflation and unemployment than had previously been the case.

STAGFLATION'S DEMISE: 1982–1988

A return look at Figure 19-3 reveals a rather dramatic inward collapse of the inflation-unemployment points between 1982 and 1988. By 1988 the stagflation of the 1970s and early 1980s had nearly subsided. One important precursor to this favorable trend was the deep recession of 1981–1982, largely caused by an extremely tight money policy. The recession propelled the unemployment rate to 9.7 percent in 1982. Under conditions of extreme labor market slack, workers accepted smaller increases in their nominal wages—or in some cases wage reductions—to help preserve their jobs. Firms, in turn, were forced to restrain price hikes to maintain their relative shares of a greatly diminished market.

Other significant factors were also at work. Intensive foreign competition throughout the 1982–

1988 period suppressed wage and price hikes in several basic industries such as automobiles and steel. Deregulation of the airline and trucking industries also resulted in wage reductions or so-called "wage-givebacks." A decline in OPEC's monopoly power produced a stunning fall in the price of oil and its derivative products. All of these factors combined to reduce unit production costs and hence tended to shift the aggregate supply curve rightward (as from AS_2 to AS_1 in Figure 19-4). Meanwhile, a record-long peacetime economic expansion created 15 million new jobs between 1982 and 1988. The previously high unemployment rate therefore fell dramatically. More specifically, the unemployment rate fell from 9.6 percent in 1983 to 6.2 percent in 1987 and to 5.4 percent by the end of 1988. As an inspection of Figure 19-3 reveals, the inflation-unemployment points represented for 1987 and 1988 therefore are located in fairly close proximity to the points associated with the Phillips Curve for the 1960s.

Important point: Like the situations in 1973–1974 and 1979–1980, unemployment and inflation moved in the *same* direction during several years within the 1983–1988 period. That is, unemployment and inflation did *not* move in opposite directions as implied by the Phillips Curve for the 1960s. During the Great Stagflation of the mid-1970s, inflation and unemployment simultaneously *increased;* during several of the years of the economic expansion of 1983–1988, inflation and unemployment simultaneously *declined.*

The natural rate hypothesis

We have seen that the standard Keynesian explanation for the scattering of inflation rate-unemployment points to the right of the 1960s Phillips Curve is that a series of supply shocks occurred which shifted the aggregate supply curve *leftward* and thus moved the Phillips Curve rightward and upward as suggested in Figure 19-3. In turn, the inward collapse of inflation rate-unemployment points in the 1980s came about because of *rightward* shifts of the aggregate supply curve. This Keynesian view holds that a tradeoff between the inflation rate and the unemployment rate still exists, but that changes in aggregate supply may

change the menu of inflation and unemployment choices—that is, may shift the Phillips Curve itself—during some abnormal periods.

A second explanation of simultaneously higher rates of unemployment and inflation is associated with new classical thinking and is called the **natural rate hypothesis.** It questions the very existence of the concept of a downsloping Phillips Curve as portrayed in Figure 19-3. This view concludes that the economy is stable in the long run at the natural rate of unemployment. We know from Chapter 10 that the natural rate of unemployment is the rate achieved when the labor market experiences neither a shortage nor a surplus of workers. Alternatively stated, it is the rate of unemployment which exists when cyclical unemployment is zero.

According to the natural rate hypothesis, misguided Keynesian full-employment policies, based on the incorrect assumption that a stable Phillips Curve *does* exist, will result in an increasing rate of inflation. The natural rate hypothesis has its empirical roots in Figure 19-3, where one can argue that a vertical line located at a presumed 6 percent natural rate of unemployment summarizes the inflation-unemployment "relationship" better than the traditional downsloping Phillips Curve. According to the natural rate hypothesis, any particular rate of inflation is compatible with the economy's natural rate of unemployment.

There are two variants of the natural rate interpretation of the inflation-unemployment data points shown in Figure 19-3: the adaptive expectations and rational expectations theories.

ADAPTIVE EXPECTATIONS THEORY

One variant of the natural rate hypothesis is the **theory of adaptive expectations.** This theory is so named because it assumes that people form their expectations of future inflation on the basis of previous and present rates of inflation and only gradually change their expectations as experience unfolds. The adaptive expectations theory was advanced and popularized by Milton Friedman and is consistent with both the traditional monetarist and emerging new classical perspectives.

The adaptive expectations theory holds that there may be a short-run tradeoff between inflation and unemployment, but in the long run no such tradeoff exists. Any attempt to reduce the unemployment rate below the natural rate sets in motion forces which destabilize the Phillips Curve and shift it rightward. Hence, as we shall discover momentarily, the adaptive expectations view distinguishes between a "short-run" and "long-run" Phillips Curve.

Short-run Phillips Curve   Consider Phillips Curve PC_1 in Figure 19-5. Suppose that the economy initially is experiencing a mild 3 percent rate of infla-

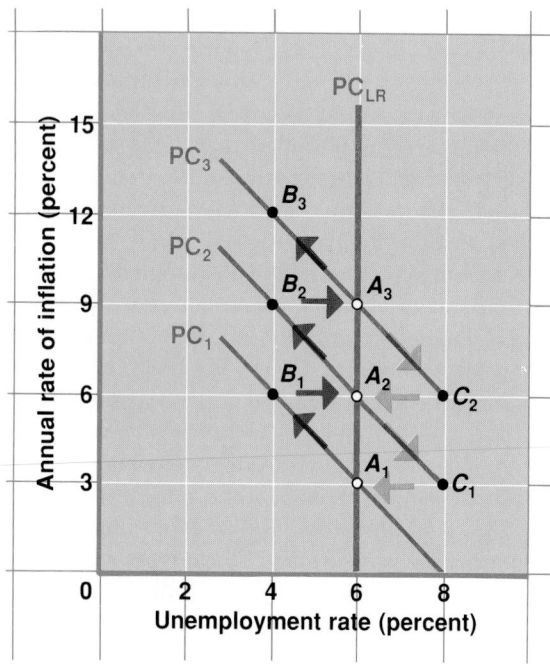

FIGURE 19-5

The adaptive expectations theory

The expansion of aggregate demand may temporarily increase profits and therefore output and employment (A_1 to B_1). But nominal wages will soon rise, reducing profits and thereby negating the short-run stimulus to production and employment (B_1 to A_2). Consequently, in the long run there is no tradeoff between the rates of inflation and unemployment; the long-run Phillips Curve is vertical. This suggests that Keynesian expansionary policies will generate increasing inflation rather than a lower rate of unemployment. On a more positive note, it also suggests that restrictive Keynesian stabilization policies can reduce inflation without creating permanent increases in unemployment.

tion and a natural rate of unemployment, which, for purposes of illustration, is assumed to be 6 percent. According to the adaptive expectations theory, such short-run curves as PC_1 exist because the actual rate of inflation is not always the same as the expected rate. Establishing an additional point on Phillips Curve PC_1 will help clarify this notion. We begin at point A_1, where the assumption is that nominal wages are set on the expectation that the 3 percent rate of inflation will continue. But now suppose that government mistakenly judges the full-employment unemployment rate to be 4 percent instead of 6 percent. This misjudgment might come about because the economy temporarily achieved a 4 percent rate of unemployment in an earlier period. To achieve the targeted 4 percent rate of unemployment, let us suppose that government invokes expansionary fiscal and monetary policy.

The resulting increase in aggregate demand boosts the rate of inflation to 6 percent. Given the level of money or nominal wages, *which were set on the expectation that the rate of inflation would continue to be 3 percent,* the higher product prices raise business profits. Firms respond to expanded profits by increasing output and therefore hiring additional workers. In the short run, the economy moves to point B_1, which, in contrast with A_1, entails a lower rate of unemployment (4 percent) and a higher rate of inflation (6 percent). This movement from A_1 to B_1, you will note, is generally consistent with our earlier interpretation of the Phillips Curve. Presumably, the economy has accepted some inflation as the "cost" of achieving a reduced level of unemployment. But the natural rate theorists interpret the movement from A_1 to B_1 quite differently. They see it as only a temporary manifestation of the following principle: *When the actual rate of inflation is higher than expected, the unemployment rate will fall.*

Long-run vertical Phillips Curve   Point B_1 is *not* a stable equilibrium position, according to the adaptive expectations theory. The reason is that workers will recognize that their real wages and incomes have fallen; that is, their nominal wages have not been rising as fast as inflation. Workers will therefore demand and receive nominal wage increases to restore the purchasing power they have lost. But, as nominal wages rise to restore the previous level of real wages which existed at A_1, business profits will fall to their earlier level. This profit reduction means that the original motivation of businesses to increase output and employ more workers will disappear. Consequence? Unemployment returns to its natural level at point A_2. Note, however, that the economy is now faced with a higher actual *and* expected rate of inflation—6 percent rather than 3 percent. That is, the higher level of aggregate demand which originally moved the economy from A_1 to B_1 still exists. Therefore, the inflation it engendered still persists.

In view of the now-higher 6 percent expected rate of inflation, the short-run Phillips Curve shifts upward from PC_1 to PC_2. In brief, an "along-the-Phillips Curve" kind of movement from A_1 to B_1 on PC_1 is merely a short-run or transient phenomenon. In the long run—after nominal wages catch up with price level increases—unemployment will return to the natural rate at A_2 and a new short-run Phillips curve PC_2 will exist at the higher expected rate of inflation.

The process may now be repeated. Government may reason that certain extraneous, chance events have frustrated its expansionist policies. Hence, government tries again. Policy measures are used to increase aggregate demand and the scenario repeats itself. Prices rise momentarily ahead of nominal wages, profits expand, and output and employment increase (A_2 to B_2). But, in time, workers now press for, and are granted, higher nominal wages to restore their level of real wages. Profits, therefore, fall to their original level, causing employment to gravitate back to the normal rate at A_3. Government's "reward" for trying to force the actual rate of unemployment below the natural rate is the perverse one of a still higher (9 percent) rate of inflation.

If we conceive of A_1B_1, A_2B_2, A_3B_3, and so forth, as indicating a series of short-run Phillips Curves, the adaptive expectations theory can be interpreted as saying that, ironically, governmental attempts through policy to move along the short-run Phillips Curve (A_1 to B_1 on PC_1) *cause* the curve to shift to a *less* favorable position (PC_2, then PC_3, and so on). In other words, a stable Phillips Curve with the dependable series of unemployment rate–inflation rate tradeoffs which it implies simply does not exist. There is, in fact, no *stable* rate of inflation (such as 6 percent at B_1) which can be

accepted as the "cost" of reduced unemployment in the *long run*. To keep unemployment at the desired 4 percent level, government must *continuously* expand the level of aggregate demand. The "cost" of a 4 percent unemployment rate is *not* a constant 6 percent annual rate of inflation at B_1, but rather an increasing rate of inflation, that is, an annual rate of inflation that increases from 6 percent (B_1) to 9 percent (B_2) to 12 percent (B_3), and so forth. Stated differently, the *long-run relationship* between unemployment and inflation is shown by the vertical line through A_1, A_2, and A_3. The Phillips Curve tradeoff portrayed earlier in Figure 19-2 does not exist.

Disinflation Can this adaptive expectations scenario be employed to explain **disinflation**—reductions in the rate of inflation—as well as inflation itself? Advocates of this hypothesis answer in the affirmative. Suppose in Figure 19-5 that the economy is at point A_3 where the inflation rate is 9 percent and the unemployment rate is 6 percent. A significant decline in aggregate demand such as that associated with the 1981–1982 recession can be expected to reduce inflation below the 9 percent expected rate, say, to 6 percent. Business profits will fall because product prices are rising less rapidly than wages. The nominal wage increases, remember, were set on the assumption that the 9 percent rate of inflation would continue. In response to the profit decline, firms will reduce their employment and consequently the unemployment rate will rise. The economy will temporarily slide downward from point A_3 to C_2 along short-run Phillips Curve PC_3. According to the natural rate theorists, *when the actual rate of inflation is lower than the expected rate, the unemployment rate will rise.*

Firms and workers will eventually adjust their expectations to the new 6 percent rate of inflation and thus newly negotiated wage increases will decline. Hence, profits will be restored, employment will rise, and the unemployment rate will return to its natural rate of 6 percent at point A_2. Because the expected rate of inflation is now 6 percent, the short-run Phillips Curve PC_3 will shift leftward to PC_2. If aggregate demand falls further, the scenario will continue. Inflation will decline from 6 percent to, say, 3 percent, moving the economy from A_2 to C_1 along PC_2. The reason once again is that the lower-than-expected rate of inflation (lower prices) has squeezed profits and reduced employment. But, in the long run, firms can be expected to respond to the lower profits by reducing their nominal wage increases. Profits will therefore be restored and unemployment will return to its natural rate at A_1 as the short-run Phillips Curve moves from PC_2 to PC_1. Once again it is evident that the long-run Phillips Curve is vertical at the natural rate of unemployment.

To repeat: According to the adaptive expectations theory, any particular rate of inflation is compatible in the long run with the natural rate of unemployment.

RATIONAL EXPECTATIONS THEORY

The adaptive expectations theory assumes that changes in nominal wages lag behind changes in the price level. It is this lag which gives rise to *temporary* increases in profits which in turn *temporarily* stimulate employment.

The **rational expectations theory**—introduced in Chapter 18—is the second variant of the natural rate hypothesis. This theory, recall, contends that businesses, consumers, and workers generally understand how the economy functions and effectively use available information to protect or further their own self-interests. In particular, people understand how government policies will affect the economy and anticipate these impacts in their own decision making. In the present context let us suppose that, when government invokes expansionary policies, workers anticipate inflation and a subsequent decline in real wages. Therefore, workers incorporate this expected inflation into their nominal wage demands. If we make the assumption that workers correctly and fully anticipate the amount of price inflation and adjust their current nominal wage demands accordingly so as to maintain their real wages, then even the temporary increases in profits, output, and employment will *not* occur. In this case, instead of the temporary increase in employment shown by the movement from A_1 to B_1 in Figure 19-5, the movement will be directly from A_1 to A_2. Fully anticipated inflation by labor means there will be no short-run decline in unemployment. Price inflation, fully anticipated in the nominal-wage demands of workers, will generate a vertical line through A_1, A_2 and A_3 in Figure 19-5.

Policy implication: Keynesian measures to achieve a misspecified full-employment rate of unemployment will generate an increasing rate of inflation, not a lower rate of unemployment. Note, incidentally, that the adaptive and rational expectations theories are consistent with the conservative philosophy that government's attempts to do good deeds typically fail and at considerable cost to society. In this instance the "cost" is in the form of accelerating inflation. Indeed, an activist fiscal policy will be ineffective in achieving its goals.

Recap: Interpretations of the Phillips Curve have changed dramatically over the past three decades. The original idea of a stable tradeoff between unemployment and inflation gave way to the adaptive expectations view that, while a short-run tradeoff existed, no such tradeoff was available in the long run. The more recent rational expectations theory stresses that macroeconomic policy is ineffective because it is anticipated by workers. Hence, the conclusion is that there does not even exist a short-run tradeoff between unemployment and inflation. Taken together, the natural rate hypotheses (adaptive and rational expectations theories) conclude that demand-management policies cannot influence real output and employment in the long run, but only the price level. This conclusion is clearly contrary to the predictions of the original Phillips Curve (Figure 19-2b).

Which view is correct? Does an inverse relationship exist between the unemployment rate and the inflation rate as the original Phillips Curve suggested? Or is there no long-run tradeoff as the natural rate theory contends? Perhaps the safest statement that can be made is that most economists accept the notion of a short-run tradeoff while recognizing that in the long run such a tradeoff is much less likely.

Aggregate supply revisited

The distinction made between short-run Phillips Curves and the long-run vertical Phillips Curve has stimulated important new thinking about aggregate supply.

Recall from Figures 19-1 and 19-2a that the

Phillips Curve was derived by shifting aggregate demand rightward along a supposedly *stable* aggregate supply curve. Firms responded to the increasing price level by producing more and increasing their employment. Thus, the unemployment rate fell as the price level increased.

The natural rate theory correctly suggests, however, that the aggregate supply curve in Figure 19-1 is stable only so long as nominal or money wages do not increase in response to the rise in the price level. Once workers fully recognize that the rise in the price level has occurred, they will demand and receive higher money wages so as to restore their real wages. An increase in nominal wages, other things being equal, will cause a leftward shift of the aggregate supply curve. That is, a change in nominal wages is one of the non-price-level determinants of aggregate supply (Table 11-2).

Implication: The simplified aggregate supply curve—with its Keynesian, intermediate, and classical ranges—needs to be refined to take into consideration changes in nominal wages that are induced by changes in the price level. Stated differently, new classical economists point out that a critical distinction must be made between short-run and long-run aggregate supply.

DEFINITIONS

As used in this particular context, *the short run is a period in which input prices—particularly nominal wages—remain fixed in the presence of a change in the price level*. There are two basic reasons why input prices may remain constant for a time even though the price level has changed. First, it is plausible that workers may not immediately be aware of the existence of a higher or a lower price level. If this is true, they will have no knowledge their real wages have changed and hence will not adjust their wage demands accordingly. Second, many employees are hired under conditions of fixed-wage contracts. Unionized employees, for example, receive nominal wages based on the terms of their collective bargaining agreements. Additionally, most managers and many professionals receive set salaries established in annual contracts.

The upshot of these two factors—lack of information about the price level and the existence of

labor contracts—is that changes in the price level normally do not immediately result in change in nominal wages.

On the other hand, the *long run is a period in which input prices (wages) are fully responsive to changes in the price level*. Given sufficient time, workers are able to gain full information about price level changes and consequently can ascertain the effects upon their real wage. Specifically, workers will be aware that a price level increase has reduced their real wage; likewise, they will know that a price level decline has increased their real wage. Additionally, and more importantly, workers and employers in the long run are freed from their existing labor contracts and can negotiate changes in nominal wages and salaries.

Keeping these definitions in mind, let us further embellish Chapter 11's discussion of aggregate supply.

SHORT-RUN AGGREGATE SUPPLY

Consider the **short-run aggregate supply curve** shown as $AS(P_1)$ in Figure 19-6a. This curve is constructed on the basis of two assumptions: (1) that the initial price level is P_1, and (2) that nominal wages have been established on the expectation that the price level P_1 will persist. To remind us of these two assumptions, we have appended the parentheses (P_1) to the label placed on the aggregate supply curve AS. Observe from point A_1 and the vertical white line intersecting it that the economy is operating at its potential level of real output Q_p at price level P_1. This potential real output is the real production forthcoming when the economy is operating at its natural rate of unemployment.

Now let us determine the consequence of *unexpected* changes in the price level by initially examining an *increase* in the price level from P_1 to P_2. Recalling that nominal wages are fixed in the short run, it is apparent that the higher product prices associated with P_2 will enhance profits. In response to the higher profits, producers will increase their output from Q_p to Q_2 as indicated by the move from A_1 to A_2 on $AS(P_1)$. Observe that at Q_2 the economy is operating beyond its potential output. How is that possible? Answer: It is made possible by extending work-hours of part-time and full-time

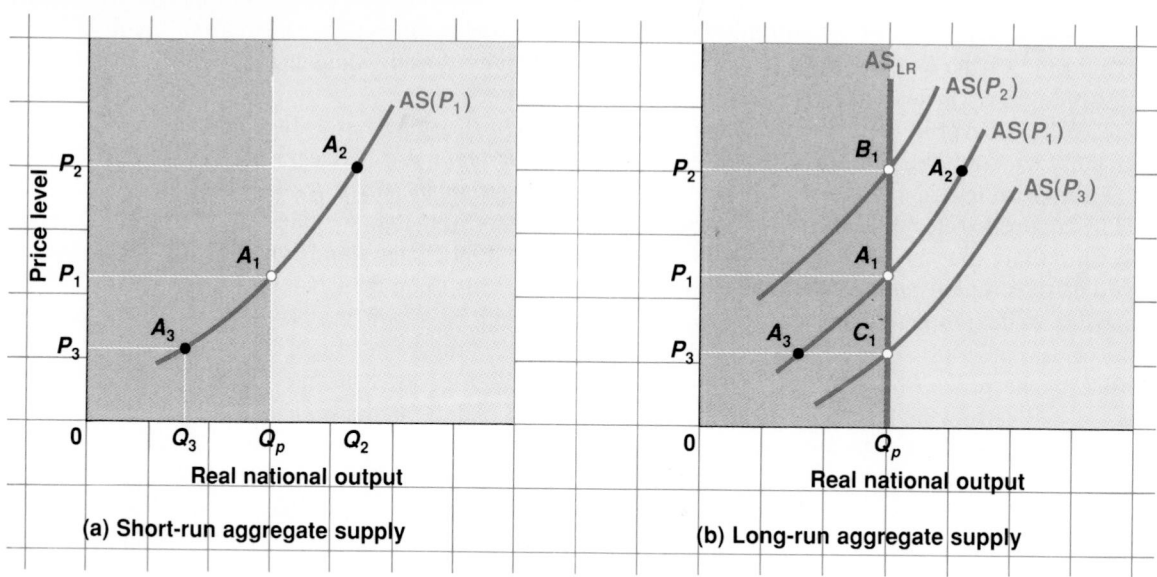

FIGURE 19-6

Short-run and long-run aggregate supply

In the short run (a), input prices such as nominal wages are assumed to be fixed based upon price level P_1. Hence, an increase in the price level will bolster profits and entice firms to expand real output. Alternatively, a decrease in the price level will reduce profits and real output. The short-run AS curve therefore slopes upward. In the long run (b), a price level rise will result in an increase in nominal wages and thus a leftward shift of the short-run AS curve. Conversely, a decrease in the price level will produce a decline in nominal wages and a rightward shift of the short-run AS curve. The long-run AS curve therefore may be thought of as being vertical.

workers, enticing new workers such as homemakers and retirees into the labor force, and hiring and training the structurally unemployed. Hence, the nation's unemployment rate will decline below its natural rate.

And how will producers respond when there is a *decrease* in the price level from P_1 to P_3? In this case firms will discover that their profits have diminished or disappeared. After all, product prices have dropped while nominal wages have not. Producers therefore will reduce employment and production and, as revealed by point A_3, real output will fall to Q_3. This decline in real output will be accompanied by an unemployment rate which is greater than the natural rate.

LONG-RUN AGGREGATE SUPPLY

By definition, nominal wages are assumed to be fully responsive in the long run to changes in the price level. What are the implications of this assumption for aggregate supply?

In Figure 19-6b we again assume that the economy initially is at point A_1 (P_1 and Q_p). Our previous discussion indicated that an *increase* in the price level from P_1 to P_2 will move the economy from point A_1 to A_2 along the short-run aggregate supply curve AS(P_1). In the long run, workers will discover that their real wages have fallen as a result of this increase in the price level. They will therefore presumably demand and receive higher nominal wages to restore their previous level of real wages. Result? The short-run aggregate supply curve will shift leftward from AS(P_1) to AS(P_2). This short-run AS curve will now reflect the *higher* price level P_2 and the expectation that P_2 will continue. Figure 19-6b shows that the leftward shift in the short-run aggregate supply to curve AS(P_2) will move the economy from A_2 to B_1. Real output will fall to its potential level and the unemployment rate will return to its natural rate.

Conversely, a *decrease* in the price level from P_1 to P_3 will produce an opposite scenario. As previously noted, the economy will initially move from point A_1 to point A_3, at which profits will be squeezed or eliminated because prices have fallen and nominal wages have not. But this is simply the short-run response. Given enough time, the lower price level P_3, which has increased the real wage, together with the higher unemployment associated with the reduction in real output, will diminish nominal wages. We know that sufficiently lower nominal wages will shift the short-run aggregate supply curve rightward from $AS(P_1)$ to $AS(P_3)$ and real output will return to Q_p at point C_1. By tracing a line between the long-run equilibrium points B_1, A_1, and C_1, a **long-run aggregate supply curve** appears. Observe that it is vertical at the potential level of output, Q_p.

KEYNESIAN VERSUS NEW CLASSICAL POLICY IMPLICATIONS

The conception of aggregate supply presented in Figure 19-6 implies that wage and price flexibility will drive the economy toward full employment. For this reason this model is closely identified with **new classical economics.**

According to new classical thinking, fully *anticipated* price level changes do *not* change the level of real output because nominal wages immediately change in the same direction and by the same percentage as the price level. Hence, only the long-run aggregate supply curve is relevant when price level changes are anticipated in advance. For this reason, government stabilization policies allegedly fail to affect real output. This is simply the rational expectations view.

To be sure, *unanticipated* changes in the price level—so-called **price level surprises**—*do* produce short-term fluctuations in real output. These temporary changes in real output, say the new classical economists, result from unanticipated changes in aggregate demand and supply. In other words, temporary changes in real output arise from aggregate demand or supply shocks. Example: Suppose that an unanticipated increase in the foreign demand for American goods increases our price level. As a consequence, the economy will move along its short-run aggregate supply curve to

a higher level of real output. But in the long run, nominal wages and other input prices will increase in response to the higher price level and the economy will return to its potential real output.

New classical generalization: *Although price level surprises may create short-run macroeconomic instability, the economy is stable in the long run at the full-employment level of output.*

Modern Keynesians dismiss the assumptions of accurate information and forward-looking behavior which underlie the RET aspect of new classical economics. But modern Keynesians do not quarrel with the distinction between short- and long-run aggregate supply. Instead, today's Keynesians contend that experience has shown that the adjustment of nominal wages critical to the vertical long-run aggregate supply curve is painfully slow. More precisely, because nominal wages tend to be inflexible downward, years may go by before the economy moves from a point such as A_3 to C_1 in Figure 19-6b. Keynesians therefore call for active use of stabilization policies to reduce the high costs associated with severe unemployment or inflation. New classical economists, on the other hand, view the long run as either instantaneous or relatively short; hence, they advocate a hands-off policy by government to permit the economy to adjust *itself* to the full-employment level of real output.

Demand-pull and cost-push inflation

Let us now apply the distinction between short-run and long-run aggregate supply to demand-pull and cost-push inflation.

DEMAND-PULL INFLATION

Demand-pull inflation occurs when an increase in aggregate demand pulls up the price level. We earlier depicted this type of inflation by shifting an aggregate demand curve rightward along a stable aggregate supply curve (Figure 11-6b and 11-6c). In our more sophisticated version of aggregate supply, however, an increase in the price level will eventually result in an increase in nominal wages and thus a leftward shift of the short-run aggregate supply curve itself. This circumstance is shown in Figure 19-7a. Initially suppose that the price level is P_1, determined at the intersection of aggregate demand curve AD_1 and aggregate supply curve $AS(P_1)$. The aggregate supply curve $AS(P_1)$ is a short-run curve based upon the nominal wages associated with the price level P_1. These nominal wages were set on the expectation that P_1 would persist. Observe that the economy is achieving its potential real output Q_p.

Now consider the effects of an increase in aggregate demand such as shown by the rightward shift from AD_1 to AD_2. This shift in aggregate demand can result from any one of a number of factors, including an increase in the money supply, an increase in investment spending, and so forth (Table 11-1). Whatever its cause, the increase in aggregate demand increases the price level from P_1 to P_2 and expands output to Q_2. To this point, nothing new has been said. But now we must ask what will happen to the short-run aggregate supply

curve once workers realize their real wages have fallen and once their existing contracts have expired? Our answer is that nominal wages will rise, and as they do, the short-run aggregate supply curve will shift leftward, as from $AS(P_1)$ to $AS(P_2)$. Consequently, the price level will further increase to P_3 and the equilibrium level of output will return to its potential level Q_p.

Generalization: *In the short run, demand-pull inflation will drive up the price level and increase real output; in the long run, only the price level will rise.* In the long run, the increase in aggregate demand has only moved the economy along its vertical aggregate supply curve AS_{LR}.

COST-PUSH INFLATION

Cost-push inflation arises from factors which increase the cost of production at each price level—that is, shift the aggregate supply curve leftward—

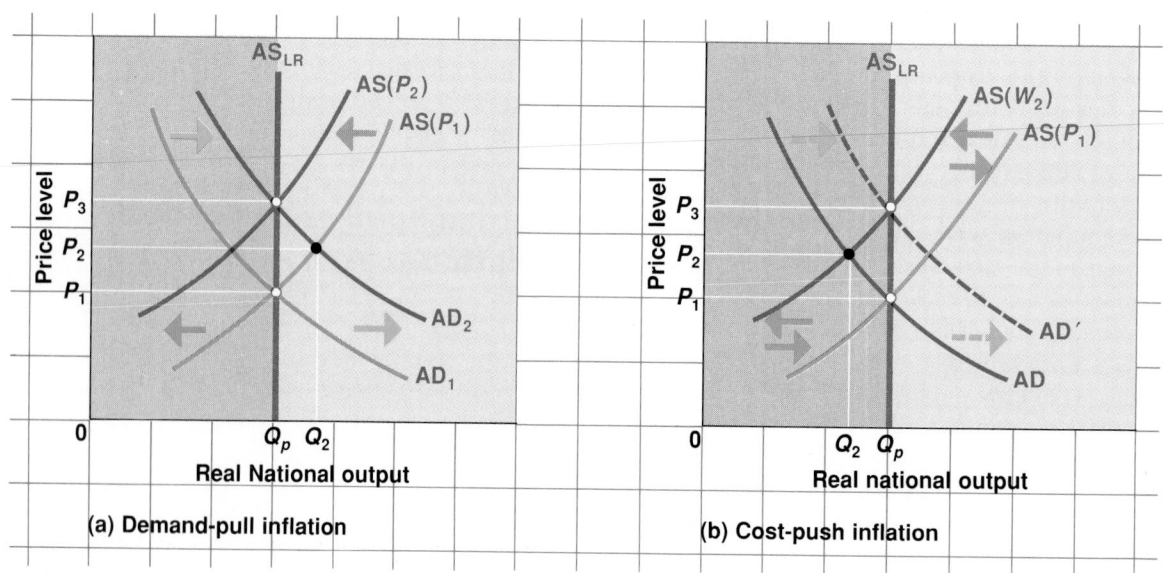

FIGURE 19-7

Demand-pull and cost-push inflation revisited

In (a) an increase in AD will drive up the price level and increase real output in the short run. But, in the long run, nominal wages will rise and AS will shift leftward. Hence, real output will return to its previous level and the price level will rise still further. In (b) cost-push inflation occurs when AS shifts leftward. If government counters the decline in real output by increasing AD to the broken line, the price level will rise even further. On the other hand, if government allows a recession to occur, nominal wages eventually will fall and the AS curve will shift back rightward to its original location. Observe that the long-run AS curves are vertical in both (a) and (b).

and therefore cause the price level to rise (Figure 11-8). But our previous analysis has, in effect, considered only short-run aggregate supply. We must now examine the cost-push theory in its long-run context.

Consider Figure 19-7b in which the economy is initially assumed to be operating at the P_1 and Q_p levels of price and output. Now let us suppose that, by exerting monopoly power, labor unions are able to secure nominal wage gains in excess of advances in labor productivity. Moreover, suppose that many nonunion employers, wishing to deter unionism in their own enterprises, respond by increasing the nominal wages they pay to keep them proportionate to union wage scales. As wages rise, the short-run aggregate supply curve shifts leftward, as depicted by the move from AS(P_1) to AS(W_2). Consequently, the price level rises from P_1 to P_2. Note that the new aggregate supply curve is labeled AS(W_2) rather than AS(P_2). Curve AS(W_2) has resulted from a wage rate hike and therefore is the *cause* of the price level rise from P_1 to P_2. The shift of the aggregate supply curve from AS(P_1) to AS(W_2) is not a *response* to a price level increase as was the case in our previous discussions of short- versus long-run aggregate supply.

Cost-push inflation creates a major dilemma for policy makers. If aggregate demand in Figure 19-7b remains at AD, it is clear that real output will decline from Q_p to Q_2. Government can counter this recession and its attendant unemployment by using stabilization policies to increase aggregate demand to AD'. But there is a potential policy trap ready to snare its victim. An increase in aggregate demand to AD' will further aggravate inflation by increasing the price level from P_2 to P_3. And the P_2 to P_3 increase in the price level is not likely to be a one-time boost. Why? The reason is that we can expect that wage earners will respond to their decline in real wages by seeking and receiving increases in nominal wages. If successful, the higher nominal wages will cause a further increase in production costs. This will shift the short-run aggregate supply curve to a position to the left of AS(W_2). In this case, the leftward shift of the short-run aggregate supply curve is in *response* to the higher price level P_3 which was caused by the rightward shift of aggregate demand to AD'. You may wish to draw in this leftward shift of AS to convince yourself that a leftward shift of aggregate supply will regenerate the stagflation problem. In short, government will have to increase aggregate demand once again to restore the Q_p level of output. But if government does so, the scenario may simply repeat itself.

The point to note is that shifts in the short-run aggregate supply curve may occur when government applies expansionary demand management policy to alleviate output reductions resulting from cost-push inflation. These shifts in short-run aggregate supply frustrate the attainment of full employment.

Alternatively, suppose that government recognizes the aforementioned policy trap and decides *not* to increase aggregate demand from AD to AD'. That is, suppose government instead implicitly decides to allow a cost-push induced recession to run its course. Widespread layoffs, plant shutdowns, and business failures eventually will occur. Hence, there will be sufficient slack in labor markets to reduce nominal wages and thereby undo the initial leftward shift of short-run aggregate supply. Restated, a severe recession will in time shift the short-run aggregate supply from AS(W_2) back to AS(P_1). The price level will therefore return to P_1 and the potential level of output will be restored along long-run aggregate supply AS$_{LR}$.

Two generalizations emerge from our analysis:
1 *If government attempts to maintain full employment under conditions of cost-push inflation, an inflationary spiral is likely to occur.*
2 *If government takes a hands-off approach to cost-push inflation, a recession will probably occur.* Although the recession can be expected eventually to undo the initial rise in production costs, the economy in the meanwhile will experience high unemployment and a loss of real output.

Policy options

Given (1) our experiences with stagflation over the past two decades or so and (2) the difficulties in using demand-management policies to deal with stagflation (Figure 19-7b), it is no surprise that the United States and other mixed economies have sought out additional policy options. In terms of Figure 19-7b these policies were designed to prevent the aggregate supply curve from shifting leftward as from AS(P_1) to AS(W_2). Or, alternatively, if the economy already found itself with stagflation at the intersection of AD and AS(W_2), the goal would be to shift the aggregate supply curve rightward toward AS(P_1). Similarly, in terms of the Phillips Curve (whether conceived of as a down-sloping curve or a vertical line) the policy goal is to shift the curve leftward to provide a better inflation rate–unemployment rate tradeoff for society. In particular, economists who interpreted the data points for the 1970s and 1980s in Figure 19-3 as reflecting rightward shifts of the Phillips Curve sought means of shifting the curve back to the more desirable position which seemed relevant for the 1960s.

Generally speaking, three categories of policies have been proposed: (1) market policies; (2) wage-price, or incomes, policies; and (3) the set of policies prescriptions which have come to be identified as "supply-side economics." Let us treat these proposals in the order stated.

MARKET POLICIES

Two kinds of **market policies** can be distinguished. *Employment and training policy* is intended to reduce or eliminate imbalances and bottlenecks in labor markets. A *procompetition policy* attempts to reduce the market power of unions and large corporations. Recall that labor market imbalances and market power constitute the traditional logic underlying the Phillips Curve.

Employment and training policy   The goal of employment and training policy is to improve the efficiency of labor markets so that any given level of aggregate demand will be associated with a lower level of unemployment. In other words, the purpose of employment and training policy is to achieve a better matching of workers to jobs, thereby reducing labor market imbalances or bottlenecks. Several different kinds of programs will provide a better matching of workers to jobs. Three of these are vocational training, job information, and antidiscrimination programs.

I VOCATIONAL TRAINING   Programs of vocationally oriented education and training will permit marginal and displaced workers to be more quickly re-

employed. Various government programs provide for both institutional and on-the-job training for the unemployed, for disadvantaged youth, and for older workers whose skills are meager or obsolete.

2 JOB INFORMATION   A second type of employment and training policy is concerned with improving the flow of job information between unemployed workers and potential employers and with enhancing the geographic mobility of workers. For example, a number of attempts have been made in recent years to modernize the United States Employment Service in order to increase its effectiveness in bringing job seekers and employers together.

3 NONDISCRIMINATION   Another facet of employment and training policy is concerned with the reduction or elimination of artificial obstacles to employment. Prejudice and discrimination have been an important roadblock in the matching of workers and jobs; discrimination is a basic factor in explaining why unemployment rates for blacks are roughly twice as high as for whites. The Civil Rights Act of 1964 attempts to improve the use of labor resource by removing discrimination because of race, religion, sex, or ethnic background as an obstacle to employment or union membership.

Procompetition policy   A second avenue for improving the tradeoff between the unemployment rate and rate of inflation is to reduce the monopoly or market power of unions and businesses. The contention of this policy is that the monopoly power of unions must be reduced so that they will be less able to push up wage rates ahead of average productivity increases. Similarly, more competition in the product market will reduce the power of large corporations to raise prices.

How can the economy be made more competitive? A basic recommendation is to apply our existing antitrust (antimonopoly) laws much more vigorously to big businesses and to remove remaining legal restrictions upon entry to certain regulated industries such as communications, transportation, and power generation and distribution. Similarly, the elimination of tariffs and other restrictions upon foreign imports will tend to increase the competitiveness of American markets. On the labor front, it is periodically argued that the antimonopoly laws should be applied to unions or that collective bargaining should be less centralized. Also recall that Chapter 12's Last Word outlined a proposal to link a portion of wages to profits in order to make wages more flexible downward. The purpose is to shift the burden of a decline in demand from unemployment to wages.

WAGE-PRICE (INCOMES) POLICIES

A second general approach accepts the existence of monopoly power and labor market imbalances as more-or-less inevitable facts of economic life, and seeks to alter the behavior of labor and product-market monopolists so as to make their wage and price decisions more compatible with the twin goals of full employment and price level stability. Although they differ primarily in degree, it is meaningful to distinguish between **wage-price guideposts** and **wage-price controls.** In essence, guideposts and controls differ in that guideposts rely upon the voluntary cooperation of labor and business, whereas controls have the force of law.

Wage-price guideposts and wage-price controls are sometimes called **incomes policies.** The reason for this label is that a person's real income—the amount of goods and services one can obtain with one's nominal income—depends upon the size of that nominal income and the prices of the goods and services he or she buys. Guideposts and controls are designed to constrain both nominal incomes and prices paid, thereby affecting real incomes.

There have been five periods in our recent history when incomes policies have been applied:
1 Comprehensive controls during World War II
2 Selective controls during the Korean war in the early 1950s
3 Guideposts during the early 1960s under the Kennedy–Johnson administrations
4 The Nixon administration's wage-price controls of 1971–1974
5 The Carter administration's guideposts of 1978
Our discussion will center upon the guideposts of the early 1960s and the 1971–1974 controls.

Kennedy–Johnson guideposts In the period from 1962 to 1966, the Kennedy and Johnson administrations set forth "guideposts for noninflationary

wage and price behavior."[2] The guideposts were essentially a set of wage and price rules which, if followed by labor and management, would provide some assurance that the government's plan to stimulate the economy would be translated into increases in real national output and employment, rather than dissipated in price increases.

I WAGE GUIDEPOST *The basic wage guidepost was that nominal wage rates in all industries should rise in accordance with the rate of increase in labor productivity for the nation as a whole.* Referring back to equation (1) in our earlier discussion of the productivity decline, we know that nominal wage rate increases which are equal to the rate of productivity growth will be noninflationary. That is, unit labor costs will be unchanged and there will be no reason for producers to raise their prices.

Of course, the productivity increases of some industries will exceed, while those of others will fall short of, the overall or average increase in national productivity. Hence, for an industry whose productivity rises by less than national productivity, unit labor costs will rise. For example, if national productivity rose by 3 percent while productivity rose by only 1 percent in industry X, then, with nominal wage rates increasing by 3 percent, that industry would experience approximately a 2 percent *increase* in its unit labor costs. Conversely, if productivity rose by 5 percent in industry Y, then the 3 percent increase in nominal wages would *decrease* its unit labor costs by about 2 percent.

2 PRICE GUIDEPOST *The basic price guidepost was that prices should change to compensate for changes in unit labor costs.* This meant that in industries whose rate of productivity was equal to the national average, prices would be constant because unit labor costs would be unchanged. For industries where productivity rose by less than the national average, prices could be increased by enough to cover the resulting increase in unit labor costs. Industry X, cited earlier, could increase its prices by 2 percent. For industries where productivity increases exceeded the national average, prices would be expected to fall in accordance with the resulting decline in unit labor costs. Industry Y

[2] *Economic Report of the President, 1962,* pp. 185–190.

should lower its prices by 2 percent. These price increases and decreases would cancel out and leave the overall price level unchanged.

Nixon wage-price controls In 1971 controls were put into effect by President Nixon. Faced with stagflation, taxes were cut by some $7 to $8 billion to stimulate aggregate demand and, it was hoped, boost output and employment. The problem, however, was to prevent this expansionary fiscal policy from being translated into additional inflation rather than into increases in employment and real output. The Nixon response was to order a freeze on wages, prices, and rents. More precisely, the President's executive order made it illegal to (1) increase wages or salaries, (2) charge more for a product than the highest price charged in the 30-day period prior to the freeze, and (3) raise the rents landlords charged tenants. The Nixon freeze was followed by formal wage and price controls which set maximum legal limits on wage and price hikes. These controls were phased out in 1974, which, you will recall, was in time to reinforce the stagflation already being generated by OPEC, agricultural shortfalls, and the depreciation of the dollar.

The wage-price policy debate There has been heated and prolonged debate in the United States as to the desirability and efficacy of incomes policies. The debate centers on two points.

I WORKABILITY AND COMPLIANCE Critics argue that the voluntary *guideposts* approach is doomed to failure because it asks business and labor leaders to abandon their primary functions and to forgo the goals of maximum profits and higher wages. A union leader will not gain favor with the rank and file by reducing wage demands; nor does a corporate official become endeared to stockholders by bypassing potentially profitable price increases. For these reasons little voluntary cooperation can be expected from labor and management.

Wage and price *controls* have the force of law and, therefore, labor and management can be forced to obey. Nevertheless, problems of enforcement and compliance can be severe, particularly if wage and price controls are quite comprehensive and if they are maintained for an extended time. The basic problem is that, over time, strong eco-

nomic incentives develop to evade controls. For example, it can be highly profitable to violate controls upon products and resources which are particularly scarce. The reason is that to be effective, the maximum legal price will be less than the free-market price; therefore, it will be profitable to violate the controls. Hence, it is not surprising that, despite strong patriotic motivation for compliance and the sizable enforcement bureaucracy which accompanied the World War II controls, illegal *black markets*—where prices were above legal limits—flourished for many products. Furthermore, firms can effectively circumvent price controls by lowering the quality or size of their product. If the price of a candy bar is frozen at 40 cents, its price can be effectively doubled by reducing its size by one-half!

Proponents of incomes policies point out that inflation is frequently fueled by *inflationary expectations*. Workers demand unusually large nominal wage increases because they expect future inflation to diminish their real incomes. Employers acquiesce in these demands because they, too, anticipate an inflationary environment in which higher costs can be easily passed along to consumers. It is argued that a strong wage-price control program can quell inflationary expectations by convincing labor and management that the government does not intend to allow inflation to continue. Therefore, workers do not need anticipatory wage increases. And firms are put on notice that they may not be able to shift higher costs to consumers via price increases. Expectations of inflation can generate inflation; wage-price controls can undermine those expectations.

2 ALLOCATIVE EFFICIENCY AND RATIONING Opponents of incomes policies argue that effective guideposts or controls interfere with the allocative function of the price system. They believe that product and resource prices must be allowed to fluctuate freely and fully in response to changing market conditions—that is, to changes in demand, changes in resource supplies, and changes in technology—in order for allocative efficiency to be sustained through time (Chapter 5). Effective price controls would prohibit the market system from making these adjustments. For example, if an increase in the demand for some product should occur, its price could *not* rise to signal society's wish for more

output and therefore more resources in this area of production.

A related point is that controls strip the market mechanism of its rationing function, that is, of its ability to equate quantity demanded and quantity supplied, and product shortages will result. Question: Which buyers are to obtain the product and which are to do without? One possibility is that the product can be rationed on a first-come-first-served basis or by favoritism. But this is likely to be highly arbitrary and inequitable; those who are first in line or those able to cultivate a friendship with the seller get as much of the product as they want while others get none at all. In the interest of equity, government may have to undertake the task of impartially rationing the product to all consumers. This was done for a wide variety of products during World War II by issuing ration coupons to buyers on an equitable basis. Note, however, that governmental rationing contributes to the problems of compliance and bureaucracy that were noted earlier.

Defenders of incomes policies respond as follows: If effective guideposts or controls are imposed upon a competitive economy, then in time the resulting rigidities will undoubtedly impair allocative efficiency. But is it correct to assume that resource allocation will be efficient in the absence of a wage-price policy? After all, cost-push inflation allegedly arises *because* big labor and big businesses possess monopoly power and consequently have the capacity to distort the allocation of resources. In short, it is not at all clear that a wage-price policy would further distort resource allocation in an economy already characterized by monopoly and allocative inefficiency.

Effectiveness How effective have incomes policies been? The evidence, in a word, is "mixed." Most economists would agree that the use of direct wage-price controls during World War II did contain—or at least defer—the serious inflation which would otherwise have occurred. On the other hand, the 1962 wage and price guideposts did little to arrest the growing demand-pull inflation of the mid-1960s. Additionally, empirical evidence suggests the wage and price controls of 1971–1974 not only failed to achieve their purposes, but may have worsened stagflation by causing inefficiencies in the allocation of resources.[3]

SUPPLY-SIDE ECONOMICS

In the past decade or so, some economists—many of them with conservative leanings and with intellectual roots in classical economics—have stressed the low growth of productivity and real output as basic causes of stagflation and the overall poor performance of our economy in the 1970s. These **supply-side economists** assert that Keynesian economics does not come to grips with stagflation because its focal point is aggregate demand. Writing in the 1930s against the background of the Great Depression, Keynes focused upon the problems of unemployment and excess productive capacity. As you are well aware, his basic conclusion was that depressions are the result of a deficiency of aggregate expenditures and, therefore, the expansion of demand through appropriate fiscal policy would restore full employment. Production costs and aggregate supply play a passive role in the simple Keynesian model. Given the availability of idle resources, the aggregate amount of output supplied would respond to an increase in aggregate expenditures. Supply-side economists contend that changes in aggregate supply—shifts in the long-run aggregate supply curve—must be recognized as an "active" force in determining both the levels of inflation *and* unemployment. Economic disturbances can be generated on the supply side, as well as on the demand side. Most importantly for present purposes, by emphasizing the demand side, Keynesians have neglected certain supply-side policies which might alleviate stagflation.

The tax "wedge" Supply-side economists note that the historical growth of the public sector has increased the nation's tax bill both absolutely and as a percentage of the national income. In the Keynesian view, higher taxes represent a withdrawal of purchasing power from the economy and therefore have a contractionary or anti-inflationary effect (Chapter 14). Supply-siders argue to the contrary: They contend that sooner or later most taxes are incorporated into business costs and shifted forward to consumers in the form of higher prices.

[3] The interested reader can find a review of the studies of the effects of the 1971–1974 wage and price controls in Alan Blinder, *Economic Policy and the Great Stagflation* (New York: Academic Press, 1979), chapter 6.

Taxes, in short, entail a cost-push effect. Supply-side economists point out that in the 1970s and early 1980s state and local governments negotiated substantial increases in sales and excise taxes and that the Federal government has boosted dramatically payroll (social security) taxes. These are precisely the kinds of taxes which are incorporated in business costs and reflected in higher prices. The point is that many taxes constitute a "wedge" between the costs of resources and the price of a product. As government has grown, this **tax wedge** has increased, tending to shift the aggregate supply curve leftward.

Tax-transfer disincentives But supply-side economists contend that taxes have even more important adverse effects. The spectacular growth of our tax-transfer system in the 1960s and 1970s allegedly has had negative effects upon incentives to work, invest, innovate, and assume entrepreneurial risks. In short, the tax-transfer system has eroded the productivity of our economy and the decline in efficiency has meant higher production costs and stagflation. The argument essentially is that higher taxes will reduce the after-tax rewards of workers and producers, thereby making work, innovations, investing, and risk bearing less financially attractive. Supply-side economists stress the importance of *marginal tax rates* because these rates are most relevant to the decisions to undertake *additional* work and *additional* saving and investing.

INCENTIVES TO WORK Supply-siders argue that how long and how hard individuals work depends upon how much additional *after-tax* earnings will be derived from this extra work. In order to induce more work—to increase aggregate inputs of labor—marginal tax rates on earned incomes should be reduced. Stated differently, lower marginal tax rates increase the attractiveness of work and simultaneously increase the opportunity cost of leisure. Hence, individuals will choose to substitute work for leisure. This increase in productive effort can occur in many ways: by increasing the number of hours worked per day or per week; by encouraging workers to postpone retirement; by inducing more people to enter the labor force; by making people willing to work harder; by discouraging long periods of unemployment; and so forth.

TRANSFER DISINCENTIVES Supply-side economists also contend that the existence of a wide variety of public transfer programs has eroded incentives to work. For example, the existence of unemployment compensation and welfare programs has made the loss of one's job less of an economic crisis than formerly. The fear of being unemployed and therefore the need to be a disciplined, productive worker is simply less acute than previously. Indeed, most transfer programs are structured to discourage work. For example, our social security and aid to families with dependent children programs are such that transfers are reduced sharply if recipients earn income. These programs simply encourage recipients *not* to be productive. Why? Because they impose a "tax" in the form of a loss of transfer benefits on those who work.

INCENTIVES TO SAVE AND INVEST The rewards to saving and investing have also been reduced by high marginal tax rates. Assume you save $1000 at 10 percent, so that you earn $100 interest per year. If your marginal tax rate is, say, 40 percent, your after-tax interest earnings will fall to $60 and the after-tax interest rate you receive is only 6 percent. While you might be willing to save (forgo current consumption) for a 10 percent return on your saving, you might prefer to consume when the return is only 6 percent. Saving, remember, is the prerequisite of investment. Thus supply-side economists recommend lower marginal tax rates on saving. They also call for lower taxes on investment income to ensure there are ready investment outlets for the economy's enhanced pool of saving. Recall from Chapter 12 that one of the determinants of investment spending is the *after-tax* net profitability of that spending. In short, lower marginal tax rates encourage saving and investing to the end that workers will find themselves equipped with more and technologically superior machinery and equipment. Therefore, labor productivity will rise, and as equation (1) in this chapter reminds us, this will hold down increases in unit labor costs and the price level.

Overregulation Supply-siders also claim that government involvement in the economy in the form of regulation has also had adverse effects upon productivity and costs. Two points should be noted in this regard. First, it is held that "industrial" regulation—government regulation of specific industries such as transportation or communications—frequently has the effect of providing firms in the regulated industry with a kind of legal monopoly or cartel. That is, governmental regulation in effect protects such firms from the rigors of competition with the result that these firms tend to be less efficient and incur higher costs of production than they would otherwise. Second, there has occurred a substantial increase in the "social" regulation of industry in the past decade or so. A new array of government regulations has been imposed upon industry in response to the problems of pollution, product safety, worker health and safety, and equal access to job opportunities. Supply-side economists point out that social regulation has increased significantly the costs of doing business. The overall impact of both varieties of regulation is that costs and prices are higher and there is a tendency toward stagflation.

REAGANOMICS: THE PROGRAM

The elements of supply-side economics which we have just outlined provided the intellectual underpinnings for the economic policies of the Reagan administration (1981–1988). More specifically, **Reaganomics** consisted of the following four policies:

1 The growth of the Federal government was restrained by freezes and cuts in spending on social and welfare programs. Defense spending, however, was increased significantly.
2 Substantial reductions in government regulation of private businesses occurred.
3 The administration encouraged the Federal Reserve System to hold the growth rate of the money supply to a rate considered to be noninflationary, yet sufficiently expansive to allow for economic growth.
4 Personal and corporate income tax rates were reduced sharply beginning in 1981. The tax system was reformed in 1986 such that the marginal tax rate on income of wealthy taxpayers fell from 50 percent to 28 percent.

It is generally agreed that the basic component of supply-side economics and Reaganomics is the use of tax cuts as an antistagflation measure. It is this consideration which we now examine.

ERTA, TRA, and the Laffer Curve The tax cuts of the Reagan administration took two forms: the **Economic Recovery Tax Act of 1981** (ERTA) and the **Tax Reform Act of 1986** (TRA). The major provisions of ERTA were (1) a 25 percent cut in personal income taxes over a three-year period; (2) a reduction in capital gains tax rates; and (3) the more rapid write-off against taxes of business expenditures on new plant and equipment. The purpose was to reduce the tax wedge and, more importantly, stimulate incentives to work and to save and invest. Although TRA was designed to be "revenue-neutral"—that is, to maintain the existing level of tax revenues—it lowered marginal income tax rates. To offset these lower rates, TRA simultaneously broadened the tax base (the amount of taxable income). ERTA and TRA were to be the primary means of shifting Figure 19-4's aggregate supply curve from AS_2 toward AS_1, thereby alleviating inflation, increasing real output, and reducing the unemployment rate.

The notion of tax cuts—especially a mammoth cut such as that embodied in ERTA—in a time of inflation generated considerable controversy. Keynesian and other economists flatly objected. The demand-side orientation of Keynesians led them to contend that the ERTA tax cuts would generate very large budget deficits which would tend to accelerate the rate of inflation.

But Arthur Laffer, a prominent supply-side economist, argued that lower tax *rates* are quite compatible with constant or even enlarged tax *revenues*. A tax cut need not result in inflationary deficits. His position is based on what has come to be known as the **Laffer Curve,** which, as shown in Figure 19-8, depicts the relationship between tax rates and tax revenues. The basic notion is that, as tax rates increase from zero to 100 percent, tax revenue will increase from zero to some maximum level (at M) and then decline to zero. Tax revenues decline beyond some point because higher tax rates presumably discourage economic activity and therefore the tax base (national output and income) diminishes. This is easiest to envision at the extreme where tax rates are 100 percent. Tax revenues here are reduced to zero because the 100 per-

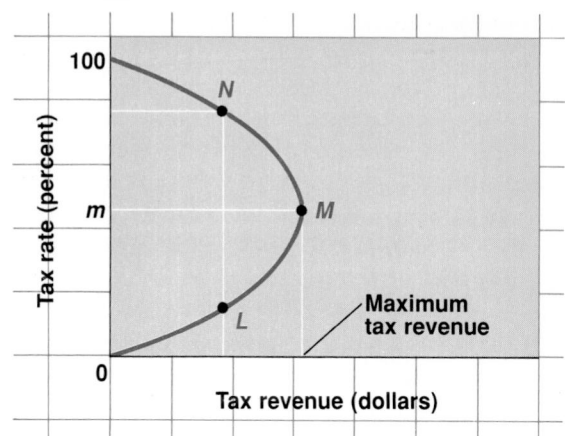

FIGURE 19-8

The Laffer Curve

The Laffer Curve suggests that up to point *M* higher tax rates will result in larger tax revenues. But still higher rates will have adverse effects upon incentives to produce, reducing the size of the national income tax base to the extent that tax revenues decline. It follows that, if tax rates are above *Om*, tax reductions will result in increases in tax revenues. The controversial empirical question is to determine at what actual tax rates will tax revenues begin to fall.

cent confiscatory tax rate has brought production to a halt. A 100 percent tax rate applied to a tax base of zero yields no revenue. Professor Laffer's contention was that we were at some point such as *N* where tax rates were so high that production had been discouraged to the extent that tax revenues were below the maximum at *M*. If the economy is at *N*, then lower tax *rates* are quite compatible with constant tax *revenues*. In Figure 19-8 we simply lower tax rates, moving from point *N* to point *L*, and government will collect an unaltered amount of tax revenue. Laffer's reasoning is that lower tax rates will stimulate incentives to work, save and invest, innovate, and accept business risks, thereby triggering a substantial expansion of national output and income. This enlarged tax base will sustain tax revenues even though tax rates are lower.

According to supply-side economists, the avoidance of a deficit will be abetted in two additional ways. First, tax avoidance and evasion will decline. High marginal tax rates prompt taxpayers to avoid taxes through the use of various tax shel-

ters (for example, buying municipal bonds on which the interest is tax free) or to conceal income from the Internal Revenue Service. Lower tax rates will reduce the inclination to engage in such activities. Second, the stimulus to production and employment which a tax cut provides will reduce government transfer payments. For example, more job opportunities will reduce unemployment compensation payments and thereby tend to reduce a budget deficit.

Criticisms As they relate to the Laffer Curve, the ERTA tax cuts and the TRA reductions in marginal tax rates have been subject to considerable criticism.

I TAXES: INCENTIVES AND TIME A fundamental criticism has to do with the question of the sensitivity of economic incentives to changes in tax rates. Skeptics point out that there is ample empirical evidence to suggest that the impact of a tax reduction upon incentives will be small, of uncertain direction, and relatively slow to emerge. For example, with respect to incentives to work:

. . . the major empirical studies of the impact of income taxation on the supply of labor have found quite mixed results: some individuals work harder if the tax burden is eased and others work less because their after-tax income goals are achieved with less effort.[4]

Furthermore, any positive effects which tax cuts may have upon real output may be slow to appear:

In the long run, most tax changes that increase total capital formation and thereby raise the rate of economic growth will eventually raise (tax) revenues. However, the long run is likely to be very long indeed since a major proportionate increase in savings and investment will cause only a tiny proportionate increase in the capital stock every year, and it is the latter which is important to economic growth. Consequently, the long run must be measured in terms of decades rather than years.[5]

[4] Testimony of Otto Eckstein in Senate Budget Committee, *Leading Economists' Views of Kemp–Roth* (Washington, 1978), p. 53.

[5] Testimony of R. G. Penner, ibid., p. 139.

2 REINFORCING INFLATION Most economists take the position that the demand-side effects of a tax cut exceed the supply-side effects. Hence, they predicted the ERTA tax cuts would generate large increases in aggregate demand which would overwhelm any increase in aggregate supply, resulting initially in large budget deficits and eventually in soaring inflation.

3 POSITION ON CURVE Skeptics note that the Laffer Curve is merely a logical proposition which asserts that there must be some level of tax rates between zero and 100 percent at which tax revenues will be maximized. Economists of all persuasions can agree with this statement. But the issue at hand is an empirical question: Where is our economy located on that curve? If it is *assumed*—as Laffer did—that we were at *N* in Figure 19-8, then the ERTA tax cuts were on a sound footing. But critics contend that where the United States was located on the curve in 1981 was undocumented and unknown. If the economy was actually at any point southwest of *M*, then lower tax rates would greatly *reduce* tax revenues and create budget deficits which would intensify inflation once the economy reached full employment.

REAGANOMICS: DID IT WORK?

The real world is admittedly a very imperfect laboratory in which to judge the success of a vast socioeconomic experiment such as Reaganomics. It is also recognized that Congress did not accept all the expenditure reductions which the Reagan administration requested in its program. Finally, we must acknowledge that the Reagan years witnessed significant declines in inflation and interest rates, a record-long peacetime economic expansion, and the attainment of full employment. Having acknowledged these points, it is nevertheless fair to say that, *as such,* supply-side economics largely failed to accomplish its goals.

The facts are that any immediate expansionary effects of the ERTA tax cuts were apparently overwhelmed by the tight money (high interest rate) policy which was part of the Reagan program. Hence, the economy fell into a severe recession in 1980–1982. It is quite true that the inflation rate fell sharply from annual rates of 13.5 to 10.4 percent in 1980 and 1981 to 3.2 percent by 1983. Since 1983 the inflation rate has remained relatively low. But most economists feel that the decline in inflation was due to the severe restraint the Federal Reserve's tight money policy imposed upon aggregate demand rather than the rightward shift of aggregate supply predicted by supply-side economists. It is also notable that fortuitous reductions in oil prices have been important in slowing the rate of inflation. We also know that the ERTA tax cuts have been a primary cause of the burgeoning budget deficits which the Federal government has incurred since 1982. The prediction of the Laffer Curve that lower taxes would yield increased tax revenues simply did not bear fruit. We will see in Chapter 20 that these large deficits may have crowded out some unknown amount of private investment and tended to depress both export-dependent and import-competing industries. A record-high U.S. balance of trade deficit has resulted. Furthermore, there is little or no evidence to suggest that Reaganomics has had any significant positive impacts upon saving and investment rates or incentives to work. In fact, the savings rate trended downward during the 1980s. There was a resurgence of labor productivity in 1983 and 1984, but this is normal during an economic recovery. Productivity growth since 1984 has not been impressive.

Is the post-1982 economic recovery evidence that Reaganomics has taken hold? While it is difficult to say with certainty, a quite convincing case can be made that the recovery is largely attributable to the expansionary effects of the large recent Federal deficits to which ERTA gave rise and not to improved saving and investment rates or enhanced incentives. The recovery, in other words, is essentially a "Keynesian" demand-side phenomenon and not readily attributable to supply-side considerations.

Longer-run effects of Reaganomics are unclear at this point. Will anticipated changes in work incentives, risk taking, and saving and investment rates yet emerge? Will labor productivity increase? Will inflation reassert itself now that the economy is nearing full employment and large budget deficits still exist? These are debatable questions. But the evidence to date casts considerable doubt upon the central supply-side proposition that tax cuts can significantly shift the nation's aggregate supply curve rightward more rapidly than its historical pace.

Recap: alternative macroeconomic perspectives

Macroeconomics is currently in a state of flux. We have seen here and in Chapter 18 that a number of competing theories exist which attempt to explain how the national economy operates. In particular, the central ideas and policy implications of Keynesianism, monetarism, rational expectations theory, and supply-side economics have been presented.

Table 19-1 summarizes major aspects of these contending theories and policy perspectives and is worthy of your careful study. In reviewing the table, you will note that no direct reference is made

TABLE 19-1 **Alternative macroeconomic theories and policies**

| | | Natural rate hypothesis | | |
Issue	Keynesianism	Monetarism	Rational expectations	Supply-side economics
View of the private economy	Inherently unstable	Stable in long run at natural rate of unemployment	Stable in long run at natural rate of unemployment	May stagnate in absence of proper work, saving, and investment incentives
Cause of the observed instability of the private economy	Investment plans unequal to saving plans (changes in AD); AS shocks	Inappropriate monetary policy	Unanticipated AD and AS shocks in the short run	Changes in AS
Appropriate macro policies	Active fiscal and monetary policy; occasional use of income policies	Monetary rule	Monetary rule	Policies to increase AS
How changes in the money supply affect the economy	By changing the interest rate, which changes investments, and real NNP	By directly changing AD which changes NNP.	No effect because outcomes are anticipated	By influencing investment and thus AS
View of the velocity of money	Unstable	Stable	No consensus	No consensus
How fiscal policy affects the economy	Changes AD and NNP via the multiplier process	No effect unless money supply changes	No effect because outcomes are anticipated	Affects NNP and price level via changes in AS
View of cost-push inflation	Possible (wage-push, AS shock)	Impossible in the long run in the absence of excessive money supply growth	Impossible in the long run in the absence of excessive money supply growth	Possible (productivity decline, higher costs due to regulation, etc.)

to the terminology "new classical economics." Keep in mind that this viewpoint is simply that associated in a general way with the natural rate hypothesis which asserts that the economy tends automatically to achieve equilibrium at its full potential level of output—that is, at its natural rate of unemployment. The natural rate hypothesis is supported by economists of the monetarist and rational expectations persuasions.

CHAPTER SUMMARY

1 Using the aggregate demand–aggregate supply model to compare the impacts of small and large increases in aggregate demand upon the price level and real national output yields the generalization that high rates of inflation should be associated with low rates of unemployment and vice versa. This relationship is known as the Phillips Curve and empirical data prior to the 1970s were generally consistent with this inverse relationship. Labor market imbalances and monopoly power are used to explain the Phillips Curve tradeoff.

2 In the 1970s the Phillips Curve seems to have shifted rightward, a shift which is consistent with stagflation. A series of supply shocks in the form of higher energy and food prices, a depreciated dollar, and the demise of the Nixon wage-price freeze were involved in the 1973–1975 stagflation. More subtle factors such as inflationary expectations and a decline in the rate of productivity growth also contributed to stagflationary tendencies. Following the recession of 1981–1982, the Phillips Curve shifted inward toward its original position. By 1988 stagflation had largely subsided.

3 The adaptive expectations variant of the natural rate hypothesis argues that in the long run the traditional Phillips Curve tradeoff does not exist. Expansionary demand-management policies will shift the short-run Phillips Curve upward, resulting in increasing inflation with no permanent decline in unemployment.

4 The rational expectations variant of the natural rate hypothesis contends that the inflationary effects of expansionary policies will be anticipated and reflected in nominal wage demands. As a result, there will be no short-run increase in employment and thus no short-run Phillips Curve.

5 In the short run—where nominal wages are fixed—an increase in the price level will bolster profits and result in greater real output. Conversely, a decrease in the price level will reduce profits and real output. Hence, the short-run aggregate supply curve is upward-sloping. In the long run—where nominal wages are variable—price level increases will cause increases in nominal wages and thus leftward shifts of the short-run aggregate supply curve. Conversely, price level declines will shift the short-run aggregate supply curve rightward. The long-run aggregate supply curve therefore tends to be vertical at the potential level of output.

6 In the short run demand-pull inflation will tend to increase the price level *and* real output. Once nominal wages have increased, however, the temporary increase in real output will dissipate.

7 In the short run cost-push inflation will increase the price level and reduce real output. Unless government expands aggregate demand, nominal wages eventually will decline under conditions of recession and the short-run aggregate supply curve will shift back to its initial location. Hence, prices and real output will return to their original levels.

8 Market policies, wage-price (incomes) policies, and supply-side policies have been proposed as means of preventing or alleviating stagflation.

9 Market policies consist of employment and training programs designed to reduce labor market imbalances and procompetition policies which reduce the market power of unions and corporations.

10 Incomes policies take the form of wage-price guideposts or controls. Economists have debated the desirability of such policies in terms of their workability and their impact upon resource allocation.

11 Supply-side economists trace stagflation to the growth of the public sector and, more specifically, to the growing tax "wedge" between production costs and product prices, the adverse effects of the tax-transfer system upon incentives, and government overregulation of businesses. Based upon the Laffer Curve, supply-side adherents advocated sizable tax cuts such as the Economic Recovery Tax Act of 1981 as a remedy for stagflation. Evidence has cast considerable doubt on the validity of the supply-side view.

TERMS AND CONCEPTS

Phillips Curve

stagflation

supply shocks

inflationary expectations

natural rate hypothesis

theory of adaptive expectations

disinflation

rational expectations theory

short-run aggregate supply curve

long-run aggregate supply curve

new classical economics

price-level surprises

demand-pull inflation

cost-push inflation

market policies

wage-price guideposts

wage-price controls

incomes policies

supply-side economics

tax wedge

Reaganomics

Economic Recovery Tax Act of 1981

Tax Reform Act of 1986

Laffer Curve

QUESTIONS AND STUDY SUGGESTIONS

1 Employ the aggregate demand–aggregate supply model to derive the Phillips Curve. What events occurred in the 1970s to cast doubt upon the stability and existence of the Phillips Curve?

2 Use an appropriate diagram to explain the adaptive expectations rational for concluding that in the long run the Phillips Curve is a vertical line.

3 Explain rational expectations theory and its relevance to analysis of the Phillips Curve.

4 Assume the following information is relevant for an industrially advanced economy in the 1990–1992 period:

LAST WORD

"Real" business cycle theory

A handful of prominent new classical economists stand traditional economic theory on its head by arguing that business cycles are caused by real factors affecting aggregate supply rather than by fluctuations in aggregate demand.

Traditional Keynesians and monetarists hold that business cycles result mainly from changes in aggregate demand. But new classical economists tend to rule out demand changes as causes of permanent changes in real output. They contend that flexible nominal wages and changes in other input prices return real output to its potential level through rapid adjustments in short-run aggregate supply (Figures 19-6b and 19-7a). Yet, historical evidence clearly shows that long-lasting business recessions and booms *do* occur. If changes in aggregate demand are not the reason for these observed fluctuations, what are the reasons?

A small, but influential, group of new classical economists has hypothesized that business cycles are caused by factors which disturb the long-run growth trend of aggregate supply. According to this novel view, recessions begin on the supply side of the economy, not on the demand side as traditionally assumed. In other words, "real" factors—technology, resource availability, and productivity—which affect aggregate supply are the alleged causes

Year	Price level index	Rate of increases in labor productivity	Index of industrial production	Unemployment rate	Average hourly wage rates
1990	167	4 %	212	4.5%	$6.00
1991	174	3	208	5.2	$6.50
1992	181	2.5	205	5.8	$7.10

of business cycles. In contrast, traditional theory envisions "monetary" factors affecting aggregate demand as the usual source of cyclical instability.

An example focusing upon a recession will clarify the new classical thinking. Suppose that productivity—output per worker—declines because an increase in the world price of oil makes it prohibitively expensive to operate certain types of machinery. This decline in productivity implies a reduction in the economy's ability to produce real output and therefore a leftward shift of its long-run (vertical) aggregate supply curve. As national output falls in response to the decline in aggregate supply, less money is needed to exchange the reduced volume of goods and services. That is, the decline in output reduces the demand for money. Moreover, the slowdown in business activity lessens business borrowing from banks, causing a drop in the supply of money. In this scenario, changes in the supply of money respond passively to changes in the demand for money. The decline in the money supply in turn reduces aggregate demand (shifts the AD curve leftward) to the same extent as the initial decline in aggregate supply. The result is that real equilibrium output is lower, while the price level remains unchanged. Like the Keynesian model, then, the real business cycle theory allows for a decline in real output in the presence of a constant price level.*

Another facet of this theory is that the drop in productivity will be accompanied by a decline in the average real wage rate. Firms reduce their hourly pay because less output is being produced in each hour of work. The labor market would clear if people were willing to take jobs at the lower set of real wages. Therefore, although total employment falls, the economy's "true" unemployment rate remains at its natural rate. In effect, at the lower real wage more people are now choosing leisure rather than work. The official unemployment rate tends to rise during recessions only because some job seekers continue to hold out for a return to work at the previous higher real wage. According to the "real" business cycle theorists, these people should be regarded as *voluntarily unemployed*. If they properly were excluded from the official unemployment rolls, the reported rate of unemployment would be the same as the natural rate, the latter remaining unchanged.

The policy implications of the real business cycle theory are as unusual and controversial as the theory itself. First, demand-management policies are inappropriate and doomed to fail. Expansionary stabilization policy in this situation will not increase real output; instead, it will cause inflation. Second, the "voluntary" unemployment which accompanies "real" recessions is not of social concern. Jobs are available for everyone willing to work for reduced real wages. Third, deviations of aggregate supply from its long-term growth trend should not be the source of social concern. According to real business cycle theorists, gains from "real" business booms roughly match the output losses arising from "real" downturns. The *net* long-run costs of business cycles therefore are allegedly very modest. Hence, the emphasis of public policy should be on stimulating long-term economic growth rather than on trying to stabilize the economy.

Conventional economists vigorously reject the real business cycle theory on the grounds that it does not square with the facts of past business cycles. But, at a minimum, the theory makes it evident that conventional macroeconomic theory is not the only analytical game in town.

* You are urged to test your comprehension of the real business cycle theory by using the AD-AS model to diagram it.

Describe in detail the macroeconomic situation faced by this society. Is cost-push inflation in evidence? What policy proposals would you recommend?

5 Evaluate or explain the following statements:
  a "Taken together, the adaptive expectations and rational expectations theories imply that demand-management policies cannot influence the real level of economic activity in the long run."
  b "The essential difference between the adaptive expectations theory and rational expectations theory is that inflation is unanticipated in the former and anticipated in the latter."

6 Use graphical analysis to show (1) demand-pull inflation in the short run and long run, and (2) cost-push inflation in the short run and long run. Assume in the second case that government does *not* increase aggregate demand to offset the real output effect of the cost-push inflation.

7 Suppose that the potential level of real national output (Q) for a hypothetical economy is $250 and that the price level (P) initially is 100. Use the short-run aggregate supply schedules shown below to answer the questions that follow.

AS(P_{100})		AS(P_{125})		AS(P_{75})	
P	Q	P	Q	P	Q
125	280	125	250	125	310
100	250	100	220	100	280
75	220	75	190	75	250

a What will be the level of real national output in the *short run* if the price level unexpectedly rises from 100 to 125 because of an increase in aggregate demand? Falls unexpectedly from 100 to 75 because of a decrease in aggregate demand? Explain each situation.
b What will be the level of real national output in the *long run* when the price level rises from 100 to 125? Falls from 100 to 75? Explain each situation.
c Show the circumstances described in **a** and **b** on graph paper and derive the long-run aggregate supply curve.

8 Explain the Kennedy-Johnson wage-price guideposts, indicating in detail the relationship between nominal wages, productivity, and unit labor costs. What specific problems are associated with the use of wage-price guideposts and controls? Evaluate these problems and note the arguments in favor of guideposts and controls. Would you favor a special tax on firms which grant wage increases in excess of productivity increases?

9 "Controlling prices to halt inflation is like breaking a thermometer to control the heat. In both instances you are treating symptoms rather than causes." Do you agree? Does the correctness of the statement vary when applied to demand-pull and to cost-push inflation? Explain.

10 What reasons do supply-side economists give to explain leftward shifts of the AS curve? Using the Laffer Curve, explain why they recommend tax cuts to remedy stagflation.

11 Review Table 19-1 and explain to your satisfaction each of the elements contained therein. If an item makes little sense to you, search this and previous chapters to find explicit or implicit explanations of the particular point made in the table.

CHAPTER 20

Budget deficits and the public debt

F ederal deficits and our rapidly expanding public debt have received a great amount of publicity in the past few years. Headlines proclaiming "Exploding Federal Debt," "National Debt Threatens You," and "Runaway Deficits Possible" can hardly escape our attention.

In this chapter we will examine with some care the issues of persistent Federal deficits and the mounting public debt to which these deficits have given rise. After presenting relevant definitions, we first gain perspective by comparing several different budget philosophies. Next, we examine the quantitative dimensions of the public debt. How large is the debt? How can it be most meaningfully measured? Our third objective is to consider a number of problems associated with the public debt. We will find that some of these are essentially false or bogus problems, while others are of some substance. Fourth, we want to assess the great upsurge in the size of deficits and in the public debt which have occurred in the past decade. We seek to understand why many economists envision these deficits as having adverse effects upon our domestic investment and upon our international trade. Finally, we briefly examine several proposals designed to reduce or eliminate budget deficits.

Deficits and debt: definitions

At the outset it is important to have clearly in mind what we mean by deficits and the public debt. Recall from Chapter 14 that a **budget deficit** is the amount by which government's expenditures exceed its revenues during a particular year. Thus, for example, during 1988 the Federal government spent $1116 billion and its receipts were only $974 billion, giving rise to a $142 billion deficit. The national or **public debt** is the total accumulation of the Federal government's total deficits and surpluses which have occurred through time. Hence, at the end of 1988 the public debt was about $2600 billion.

Note that the term "public debt" as ordinarily used does *not* include the entire public sector; in particular, state and local finance is omitted. In fact, while the Federal government has been incurring very large deficits, state and local governments in the aggregate have been enjoying quite substantial surpluses. For example, in 1988 all state and local governments combined had a budgetary surplus in excess of $55 billion.

Budget philosophies

Is it desirable to incur deficits and thereby realize a growing public debt? Or should the budget be balanced annually, if necessary by legislation or constitutional amendment? Indeed, we saw in Chapter 14 that the essence of countercyclical fiscal policy is that the Federal budget should move toward a deficit during recession and toward a surplus during inflation. This correctly suggests that the use of an activist fiscal policy is unlikely to result in a balanced budget in any particular year. Is this a matter of concern? Let us approach this question by examining the economic implications of several contrasting budget philosophies.

ANNUALLY BALANCED BUDGET

Until the Great Depression of the 1930s, the **annually balanced budget** was generally accepted without question as a desirable goal of public finance. Upon examination, however, it becomes evident that an annually balanced budget largely rules out government fiscal activity as a countercyclical, stabilizing force. Worse yet, an annually balanced budget actually intensifies the business cycle. To illustrate: Suppose that the economy encounters a siege of unemployment and falling incomes. As Figure 14-4 indicates, in such circumstances tax receipts will automatically decline. In seeking to balance its budget, government must either (1) increase tax rates, (2) reduce government expenditures, or (3) employ a combination of these two. The problem is that all these policies are contractionary; each one further dampens, rather than stimulates, aggregate demand.

Similarly, an annual balanced budget will intensify inflation. Again, Figure 14-4 tells us that, as money incomes rise during the course of inflation, tax collections will automatically increase. To avoid the impending surplus, government must either (1) cut tax rates, (2) increase government expenditures, or (3) adopt a combination of both. It is clear that all three of these policies will add to inflationary pressures.

The basic conclusion is evident: *An annually balanced budget is not economically neutral; the pursuit of such a policy is procyclical, not countercyclical.* Despite this and other problems, there is considerable support for a constitutional amendment requiring an annually balanced budget.

More recently, several prominent conservative economists have advocated an annually balanced budget, not so much because of a fear of deficits and a mounting public debt per se, but rather because they feel an annually balanced budget is essential in constraining an undesirable and uneconomic expansion of the public sector. Budget deficits, they argue, are a manifestation of political irresponsibility. Deficits allow politicians to give the public the benefits of government spending programs while currently avoiding the associated cost of paying higher taxes. In other words, these fiscal conservatives believe government has a tendency to grow larger than it should because there is less popular opposition to this growth when it is financed by deficits rather than taxes. Wasteful governmental expenditures are more likely to creep into the Federal budget when deficit financing is readily available. Conservative economists and politicians want legislation or a constitutional amendment to force a balanced budget in order to slow the growth of government. They view deficits as a symptom of a more fundamental problem—government encroachment upon the vitality of the private sector.[1]

CYCLICALLY BALANCED BUDGET

The notion of a **cyclically balanced budget** envisions government exerting a countercyclical influence and at the same time balancing its budget. In this case, however, the budget would not be balanced annually—after all, there is nothing sacred about twelve months as an accounting period—but rather, over the course of the business cycle.

The rationale of this budget philosophy is simple, plausible, and appealing. To offset recession, government should lower taxes and increase spending, thereby purposely incurring a deficit. During the ensuing inflationary upswing, taxes would be raised and government spending slashed. The resulting surplus could then be used to retire the Federal debt incurred in financing the recession. In this way government fiscal operations would exert a positive countercyclical force, and the government could still balance its budget—not annually, but over a period of years.

The basic problem with this budget philosophy is that the upswings and downswings of the business cycle may not be of equal magnitude and duration (Figure 10-1), and hence the goal of stabilization comes into conflict with balancing the budget over the cycle. For example, a long and severe slump, followed by a modest and short period of prosperity, would mean a large deficit during the

---

[1] See, for example, J. Buchanan and R. Wagner, *Democracy in Deficit: The Political Legacy of Lord Keynes* (New York: Academic Press, 1977).

slump, little or no surplus during prosperity, and therefore a cyclical deficit in the budget.

FUNCTIONAL FINANCE

According to **functional finance,** the question of a balanced budget—either annually or cyclically—is of secondary importance. The primary purpose of Federal finance is to provide for noninflationary full employment, that is, to balance the economy, not the budget. If the attainment of this objective entails either persistent surpluses or a large and growing public debt, so be it. According to this philosophy, the problems involved in government deficits or surpluses are relatively minor compared with the highly undesirable alternatives of prolonged recession or persistent inflation. The Federal budget is first and foremost an instrument for achieving and maintaining macroeconomic stability. Government should not hesitate to incur any deficits and surpluses required in achieving this goal.

In response to those who express concern about the large Federal debt which the pursuit of functional finance might entail, proponents of this budget philosophy offer three arguments. First, our tax system is such that tax revenues automatically increase as the economy expands. Hence, given government expenditures, a deficit which is successful in stimulating equilibrium NNP will be partially self-liquidating (Figure 14-4). Second, given its taxing powers and the ability to create money, the government's capacity to finance deficits is virtually unlimited. Finally, it is contended that the problems of a large Federal debt are substantially less burdensome than most people think. It is to the matter of the public debt that we now turn.

The public debt: facts and figures

Because modern fiscal policy endorses unbalanced budgets for the purpose of stabilizing the economy, its application will quite possibly lead to a growing public debt. Let us now briefly consider the public debt—its causes, its characteristics, its size, and the burdens and benefits associated with it.

Growth of the public debt, as Table 20-1 indicates, has been substantial since 1929. As noted, the public debt is the accumulation of all past deficits, minus surpluses, of the Federal budget.

CAUSES

Why has our public debt increased historically? Or, stated differently, what has caused us to incur large and persistent deficits? From a long-run historical perspective the answer is twofold: wars and recessions. A considerable portion of the public debt has arisen from the deficit financing of wars. For example, the public debt grew more than fivefold during World War II and it also increased substantially during World War I. Why so? Consider the World War II situation and the options it posed. The task was to reallocate a substantial portion of the economy's resources from civilian to war goods production. Accordingly, government expenditures for armaments and military personnel soared. The financing options were threefold: Increase taxes, print the needed money, or practice deficit financing. Government feared that tax financing would entail tax rates so high that they would diminish incentives to work. The national interest required attracting more people into the labor force and encouraging those already participating to work longer hours. Very high tax rates were felt to interfere with these goals. Printing and spending additional money was correctly perceived to be highly inflationary. Hence, much of World War II was financed by selling bonds to the public, thereby draining off spendable income and freeing resources from civilian production so they would be available for defense industries.

A second source of the public debt is recessions and, more specifically, the built-in stability which characterizes our fiscal system. In periods when the national income declines or fails to grow, tax collections automatically decline and tend to cause deficits. Thus the public debt rose during the Great Depression of the 1930s and, more recently, during the recessions of 1974–1975 and 1980–1982.

Aside from these two historical factors, we must append a third consideration which has accounted for much of the large deficits of the early 1980s. The Economic Recovery Tax Act of 1981 provided for substantial cuts in both individual and corpo-

TABLE 20-1 **Quantitative significance of the public debt: the public debt and interest payments in relation to GNP, 1929–1988***

(1) Year	(2) Public debt, billions	(3) Gross national product, billions	(4) Interest payments, billions	(5) Public debt as percentage of GNP, (2) ÷ (3)	(6) Interest payments as percentage of GNP, (4) ÷ (3)	(7) Per capita public debt
1929	$ 16.9	$ 103.9	$ 0.7	16%	0.7%	$ 134
1940	50.7	100.4	1.1	51	1.1	384
1946	271.0	212.4	4.2	128	2.0	1917
1950	256.9	288.3	4.5	89	1.6	1667
1955	274.4	405.9	5.1	68	1.3	1654
1960	290.5	515.3	6.8	56	1.3	1610
1965	322.3	705.1	8.4	46	1.2	1659
1970	380.9	1015.5	14.1	37	1.3	1858
1975	541.4	1598.4	23.0	34	1.4	2507
1980	908.5	2732.0	53.3	33	2.0	3989
1982	1136.8	3166.0	84.6	36	2.7	4889
1984	1564.1	3772.2	115.6	41	3.1	6600
1985	1817.0	4014.9	130.1	45	3.2	7594
1986	2120.1	4240.3	135.4	50	3.2	8775
1987	2345.6	4526.7	143.0	55	3.2	9616
1988	2600.8	4861.8	154.2	53	3.2	10,568

* In current dollars.

Source: *Economic Report of the President, 1989; Economic Indicators,* February, 1989.

rate income taxes. The Reagan administration and Congress did *not* make offsetting reductions in government outlays, thereby building a *structural deficit* into the Federal budget in the sense that the budget would not balance even if the economy were operating at the full-employment level. Unfortunately, the economy was not at full employment during most of the early 1980s. In particular, the 1981 tax cuts combined with the severe 1980–1982 recession to generate rapidly rising annual deficits which were $146 billion in 1982 and accelerated to $206 billion by 1986.

Without being too cynical one might also assert that deficits and a growing public debt are the result of a lack of political will and determination. Remember: Spending tends to gain votes; tax increases precipitate political disfavor. Thus, while opposition to deficits is widely expressed by both politicians and their constituencies, *specific* proposals to raise taxes or cut either domestic or defense programs typically encounter more opposition than support. Hence, college students may favor smaller deficits so long as funds for student loans are not eliminated in the process.

To summarize: Much of the public debt has been caused by wartime finance, recessions, and, more recently, by tax cuts.

QUANTITATIVE ASPECTS

Let us now examine more systematically the size of the public debt. The public debt is estimated to be $2600 billion—that's $2.6 trillion—in 1988. That amount is more than twice what the debt was a mere six years ago! How much is $2.6 trillion? Two trillion 600 million $1 bills placed end-to-end would stretch 240 million miles or, in other words, from the earth to the sun and back—and then some. Or, a stack of $1000 bills 4 inches high would make you a millionaire; it would take a stack 174 miles high to designate our $2.6 trillion public debt.[2]

But we must not fear large or virtually incomprehensible numbers per se. The reason will become clear when we put the size of the public debt into better perspective.

Debt and GNP A bald statement of the absolute size of the debt glosses over the fact that the wealth and productive ability of our economy have also increased tremendously over the years. It is safe to say that a wealthy nation has greater ability to incur and carry a large public debt than does a poor nation. In other words, it is more realistic to measure changes in the public debt *in relation to* changes in the economy's GNP. Column 5 in Table 20-1 presents such data. Note that instead of the fifty-fold increase in the debt between 1940 and 1988 shown in column 2, we find that the relative size of the debt is about the same as in 1940. However, our data also show that the relative size of the debt has increased significantly since the early 1970s. Column 7 indicates that on a per capita basis the debt has increased more or less steadily through time.

Interest charges Many economists feel that the primary burden of the debt is the annual interest charge that accrues as a result of the debt. The absolute size of these interest payments is shown in column 4. We observe that interest payments have increased dramatically beginning in the 1970s. This reflects not only increases in the debt, but, more importantly, periods of very high interest rates. Interest on the debt is now the third largest item of expenditures in the Federal budget (Table 8-1). Interest charges as a percentage of the GNP are shown in column 6. We find that interest payments as a proportion of GNP have increased significantly in recent years. This ratio reflects the level of taxation (the average tax rate) which is re-

quired to service the public debt. In other words, in 1988 government had to collect taxes equal to 3.2 percent of the gross national product simply to pay interest on its debt.

Ownership Approximately one-fourth of the total public debt is held by governmental agencies and our central banks, the remaining three-fourths being held by state and local governments, private individuals, commercial banks, insurance companies, and so on. Only about 13 percent of the total debt is held by foreigners. This latter statistic is significant because, as we shall see shortly, the implications of internally and externally held debt are quite different.

Accounting and inflation While the data presented in Table 20-1 appear to be straightforward and unassailable, this in fact is not the case. Robert Eisner, past President of the American Economic Association, argues that governmental accounting procedures do not reflect the government's actual financial position. He points out that private firms have a separate capital budget because, in contrast to current expenses on labor and raw materials, expenditures for capital equipment represent tangible money-making assets. The Federal government treats expenditures for highways, harbors, and public buildings in the same fashion as it does, for example, welfare payments, while in fact the former outlays are investments in physical assets. According to Eisner, the reported 1988 Federal budget deficit would be nearly halved if the Federal government employed a capital budget which included depreciation costs.

Eisner also reminds us that inflation works to the benefit of debtors. A rising price level reduces the real value or purchasing power of the dollars paid back by borrowers. Taking this "inflationary tax" into account further reduces the size of the deficit. Finally, by adding the amount of state and local budget surpluses to the capital-budget-adjusted and inflation-adjusted Federal budget deficit, Eisner is able to show that a $42 billion government budget *surplus* occurred in 1988! All of this is quite controversial. But the important point is that there are different ways of measuring the public debt and government's overall financial position. Some of these alternative views differ significantly from the basic data presented in Table 20-1.

---

[2] These illustrations are from *U.S. News & World Report*, September 6, 1985, p. 33. Updated. You are invited to verify the implied arithmetic.

Economic implications: false issues

How does the public debt and its growth affect the operation of the economy? Can a mounting public debt bankrupt the nation at some point? Does the debt somehow place an unwarranted economic burden upon our children and grandchildren?

These are essentially false or bogus issues. The debt is not about to bankrupt the government or the nation. Nor, except under certain specific circumstances, does the debt place a burden upon future generations.

GOING BANKRUPT?

Can a large public debt somehow bankrupt the government, making it unable to meet its financial obligations? The basic answer to this question is "No" and the rationale for this response entails the following three points.

1 Refinancing The first point to note is that there is no reason why the public debt need be reduced, much less eliminated. In practice, as portions of the debt fall due each month, government does not typically cut expenditures or raise taxes to provide funds to *retire* the maturing bonds. (We know that with depressed economic conditions, this would be unwise fiscal policy.) Rather, the government simply *refinances* the debt, that is, sells new bonds and uses the proceeds to pay off holders of the maturing bonds.

2 Taxation Government has the constitutional authority to levy and collect taxes. If acceptable to voters, a tax increase is an option which government has for gaining sufficient revenue to pay interest and principal on the public debt. Financially distressed private households and corporations *cannot* raise revenue via taxes; government *can*. Private households and corporations *can* go bankrupt; government *cannot*.

3 Creating money A final, important consideration that makes bankruptcy difficult to imagine is that the Federal government has the power to print money with which to pay both principal and interest on the debt. A government bond simply obligates the government to redeem that bond for some specific amount of money on its maturity date. Government can use the proceeds from the sale of other bonds *or* it can create the needed money to retire the maturing bonds. As we will find later, the creation of new money to pay interest upon or to retire debt *may* be inflationary. But the present point is that it is difficult to conceive of governmental bankruptcy when government has the power to create new money by simply running the printing presses.

SHIFTING BURDENS

Does the public debt impose a burden upon future generations? We noted earlier that per capita debt in 1988 was $10,568. Does this mean that each newborn child in 1988 enters the world with a pat on the backside from an obstetrician and is then in effect handed a $10,568 bill from Uncle Sam? Not really!

We first must ask: To whom do we owe the public debt? The answer is: For the most part, we owe it to ourselves. About 87 percent of our government bonds are held internally, that is, they are owned and held by citizens and institutions—banks, businesses, insurance companies, governmental agencies, and trust funds—within the United States. Thus *the public debt is also a public credit.* While the public debt is a liability to the American people (as taxpayers), most of that same debt is simultaneously an asset to the American people (as bondholders). Retirement of the public debt would therefore call for a gigantic transfer payment whereby American individuals would pay higher taxes and the government in turn would pay out most of those tax revenues to those same taxpaying individuals and institutions in the aggregate in redeeming the bonds which they hold. Although a redistribution of income would result from this gigantic financial transfer, it need not entail any immediate decline in the economy's aggregate wealth or standard of living. The repayment of an internally held public debt entails no leakage of purchasing power from the economy of the country as a whole. The new babies who on the average inherit the $10,568 per person public debt obligation will also be bequeathed that same amount of government bonds.

We noted earlier that the public debt increased sharply during World War II. Was some of the economic burden of World War II, for example, shifted to future generations by the decision to finance military purchases through the sale of government bonds? Again, the answer is "No." Recalling the production possibilities curve, we can see that the economic cost of World War II consisted of the civilian goods which society had to forgo in shifting scarce resources to war goods production. Regardless of whether the financing of this reallocation was achieved through higher taxes or borrowing, the real economic burden of the war would have been essentially the same. In short, the burden of the war was borne almost entirely by the persons who lived during the war; they were the ones who did without a multitude of consumer goods to permit the United States to arm itself and its allies.[3]

Synopsis: Thus far we have said two things about the economic implications of the public debt. First, given that the government (1) need only refinance (not retire) the debt, (2) has the power to tax, and (3) has the power to create money, there is no fear of the government going bankrupt. Second, the debt is not a means of shifting economic burdens from one generation to another.

Economic implications: substantive issues

Having made these happy points, we must be careful not to whitewash the public debt. It does pose some real and potential problems, although economists vary in the importance they attach to these problems.

---

[3] Wartime production may cause a nation's stock of capital to cease to grow or to dwindle as resources are shifted from the production of capital goods and to the production of war goods. As a result, future generations inherit a smaller stock of capital goods than they otherwise would. This occurred in the United States during World War II (see table on inside covers, line 2). But, again, this shifting of costs is independent of how a war is financed.

INCOME DISTRIBUTION

The distribution of government bond ownership is undoubtedly uneven. Some people own more than their $10,568 per capita share; others less; others none at all. Although our knowledge of the ownership of the public debt by income class is very limited, there is a presumption that ownership is concentrated among the wealthier groups in society. Because the tax system is only mildly progressive, the payment of interest on the public debt probably increases income inequality. If greater income equality is one of our social goals, then this redistributive effect is clearly undesirable.

INCENTIVES

Table 20-1 indicates that the present public debt necessitates annual interest payments well in excess of $150 billion. With no increase in the size of the debt, this annual interest charge must be paid out of tax revenues. These added taxes may tend to dampen incentives to bear risk, to innovate, to invest, and to work. In this indirect way, the existence of a large public debt can impair economic growth. As noted earlier, the ratio of interest payments to the GNP indicates the level of taxation needed to pay interest on the debt. Hence, some economists are concerned by the fact that this ratio has increased quite sharply in recent years (column 6 of Table 20-1).

EXTERNAL DEBT

External debt—our U.S. debt held by the citizens and institutions of foreign countries—is a burden. This part of the public debt obviously is not "owed to ourselves," and in real terms the payment of interest and principal requires the transfer of a portion of our real output to other nations. It is worth noting that foreign ownership of the public debt has increased in recent years. In 1960 only about 5 percent of the debt was foreign-owned; currently foreign ownership is about 13 percent. The assertion that "we owe the debt to ourselves" and the implication that the debt should be of little or no concern is somewhat less accurate than it was a scant two or three decades ago.

CROWDING-OUT AND THE STOCK OF CAPITAL

This brings us to a potentially more serious problem. As an exception to our earlier comments, there is one important way by which the public debt can transfer a real economic burden to future generations. And that is by causing future generations to inherit a smaller stock of capital goods—a smaller "national factory," so to speak. This possibility involves Chapter 14's **crowding-out effect** which, you will recall, is the notion that deficit financing will increase interest rates and thereby reduce investment spending. If this should happen, future generations would inherit an economy with a smaller productive capacity and, hence, other things being equal, the standard of living would be lower than otherwise.

How might this come to pass? Let us suppose that the economy is operating at its full-employment or potential level of output and that the Federal budget is initially in balance. Now for some reason government increases its level of spending. We know from our earlier discussion of the economic burden of World War II that the impact of an increase in government spending will fall upon the population living at the time it occurs. Think of Chapter 2's production possibilities curve with "government goods" on one axis and "private goods" on the other. In a full-employment economy an increase in government spending will move the economy *along* the curve in the direction of the government-goods axis which clearly means that fewer private goods will be available.

But the rub is that private goods may be either consumer or investment goods. If the increased government goods are provided at the expense of consumer goods, then the present generation bears the entire burden in the form of a lower current standard of living. The current investment level is not affected and therefore neither is the size of the national factory inherited by future generations. But if the increase in government goods entails a reduction in the production of capital goods, then the present generation's level of consumption (standard of living) will be unimpaired. However, in the future our children and grandchildren will inherit a smaller stock of capital goods and therefore will realize lower income levels than otherwise.

Two scenarios Let us now sketch the two scenarios which tend to give us the two results just described.

First scenario: Suppose the presumed increase in government spending is financed by an increase in taxation, say, personal income taxes. We know that most income is consumed and that, therefore, consumer spending will fall by almost as much as the increase in taxes. In this case the burden of the increase in government spending falls primarily upon today's generation in the form of fewer consumer goods.

Second scenario: Assume that the increase in government spending is financed by increasing the public debt. In this case the government goes into the money market and competes with private borrowers for funds. Given the supply of money, this increase in the demand for money will increase the interest rate which is, of course, the "price" paid for the use of money. In Figure 20-1 the curve I_{d1} merely reproduces the investment-demand curve of Figure 12-6. (Ignore curve I_{d2} for the moment.) The investment-demand curve is downsloping, indicating that investment spending varies inversely with the interest rate. In this instance government deficit financing drives up the interest rate, causing private investment to fall. For example, if government borrowing increases the interest rate from, say, 6 to 10 percent, investment spending would fall from $25 to $15 billion. In other words, $10 billion of private investment would be crowded out. Our conclusion is that the assumed increase in public goods production is much more likely to come at the expense of investment goods when financed by deficits. In comparison with tax financing the future generation inherits a smaller national factory and therefore realizes a lower standard of living with deficit financing.

Two qualifications But there are two important loose ends to our discussion which might mitigate or even eliminate the size of the economic burden shifted to future generations in our second scenario.

I PUBLIC INVESTMENT Our discussion has glossed over the character of the increase in government spending. Just as private goods may involve consumption or investment, so it is with public goods. If the increase in government spending is essen-

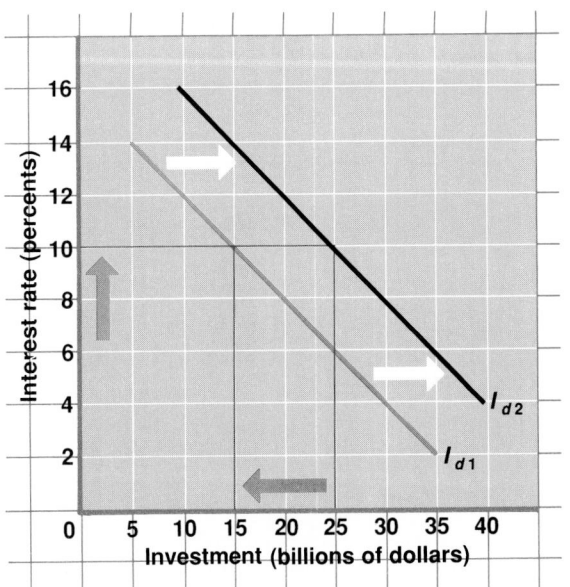

FIGURE 20-1

The investment-demand curve and the crowding-out effect

The crowding-out effect suggests that, given the location of the investment-demand curve (I_{d1}), an increase in the interest rate caused by a government deficit will reduce private investment spending and thereby decrease the size of the "national factory" inherited by future generations. In this case an increase in the interest rate from 6 to 10 percent crowds out $10 billion of private investment. However, if the economy is initially in a recession, the government deficit may improve business profit expectations and shift the investment-demand curve rightward as from I_{d1} to I_{d2}. This shift may offset the crowding-out effect wholly or in part.

tially consumption-type outlays—such as subsidies for school lunches or the provision of limousines for government officials—then our second scenario's conclusion that the debt increase has shifted a burden to future generations is correct. But what if the government spending is primarily investment-type outlays, for example, for the construction of highways, harbors, and flood-control projects? Similarly, what if they are "human capital" investments in education and health?

Like private expenditures on machinery and equipment, **public investments** increase the economy's future productive capacity. Hence, in

this case the capital stock of future generations need not be diminished, but rather its composition is changed so there is more public capital and less private capital.

2 UNEMPLOYMENT The other qualification relates to our assumption that the initial increase in government expenditures occurs when the economy is operating at full employment. Again our production possibilities curve reminds us that, *if* the economy is at less than full employment or, graphically, operating at a point inside the production possibilities frontier, then an increase in government expenditures can move the economy *to* the curve without any sacrifice of either current consumption or capital accumulation. Hence, if unemployment exists initially, deficit spending by government need *not* entail a burden for future generations in the form of a smaller national factory.

Let us look at this from a somewhat more sophisticated perspective. Consider Figure 20-1 once again. We have already explained that, if deficit financing increases the interest rate from 6 to 10 percent, a crowding-out effect of $10 billion will occur. But now we are saying that the increase in government spending will stimulate a recession economy via the multiplier effect, thereby improving business profit expectations and causing a rightward shift of investment demand to I_{d2}. As a result, we note in the case shown that, despite the higher 10 percent interest rate, investment spending remains at $25 billion. Of course, the increase in investment demand might be smaller or larger than that portrayed in Figure 20-1. In the former case the crowding-out effect would not be fully offset; in the latter case it would be more than offset. The basic point is that an increase in investment demand serves as an offset to any crowding-out effect.

Deficits in the 1980s

Federal deficits and the growing public debt have been pushed into the economic spotlight in the 1980s. This is the case in part because of the unusually large size of recent deficits. It also reflects an intertwined group of economic problems which are associated with the deficits.

RECENT CONCERNS

Growing concern over deficits and the public debt spring from several sources.

1 First, there is the matter of size. As Table 20-2 makes clear, the absolute size of annual Federal deficits increased enormously in the 1980s, as did the public debt. The average annual deficit for the decade of the 1970s was approximately $35 billion. In the 1980s annual deficits have averaged five times that amount. As a consequence, the public debt nearly tripled in the 1980–1988 period (Table 20-1). Furthermore, projections by the Congressional Budget Office (CBO) envision continuing annual deficits well into the 1990s.

2 A related point has to do with the burgeoning interest costs associated with the debt. Reference to column 4 of Table 20-1 indicates that interest payments on the public debt have increased more than tenfold since 1970. Interest payments were $154 billion in 1988, an amount greater than the entire deficit in that year! Because interest payments are a part of government expenditures, the debt in a sense feeds upon itself through interest charges. Recognizing that interest payments on the debt are the only component of government spending which cannot be cut by Congress, the spiraling of such payments complicates the problem of controlling government spending and therefore the size of future deficits.

3 A further point of concern is that our current large annual deficits have been occurring in a peacetime economy which is currently operating quite close to full employment. Recall that historically deficits—particularly sizable ones—have been associated with wartime finance and recessions. While the 1980–1982 recession undoubtedly contributed to large deficits, it is clear that our continuing deficits reflect the 1981 tax cuts and the fact that government spending was not reduced by a compensating amount. Glancing back at Figure 14-4, the 1981 tax cuts have shifted the tax line downward so that even at a full-employment level of output (NNP_1 in the diagram) sizable structural deficits can be expected.

TABLE 20-2 **Recent annual Federal deficits**
(selected years, in billions of dollars)

Year	Deficit	Year	Deficit
1970	$12	1983	179
1973	6	1984	173
1977	46	1985	197
1979	16	1986	206
1980	61	1987	158
1981	64	1988	142
1982	146		

Source: *Economic Report of the President, 1989*, p. 401.

Large deficits during times of full employment raise several concerns. First, the greatest potential for significant "crowding out" occurs when the economy is fully employed. Second, the expansionary effect of such deficits may generate demand-pull inflation. Finally, as stated by the Council of Economic Advisors in 1987:

Persistent large Federal deficits throughout an economic expansion could pose a difficult dilemma for macroeconomic policy in the event of a significant economic downturn. In such a downturn, Federal receipts automatically decline and transfer payments expand. Either a sharply contractionary fiscal policy would need to be adopted during a recession to prevent a further increase in the Federal deficit, or the share of the deficit in GNP would have to be allowed to expand to levels not previously experienced in the United States in peacetime.[4]

4 A final point of concern is that large budget deficits make it difficult for the nation to achieve a balance in its international trade. More specifically, as we shall see momentarily, large annual budget deficits tend to promote imports and stifle exports. Furthermore, budget deficits are thought to be a main cause of two related phenomena which have been much in the news: (1) our recently attained status as the "world's leading debtor nation" and

---

[4] *Economic Report of the President, 1987* (Washington, D.C.: 1987), p. 67–68.

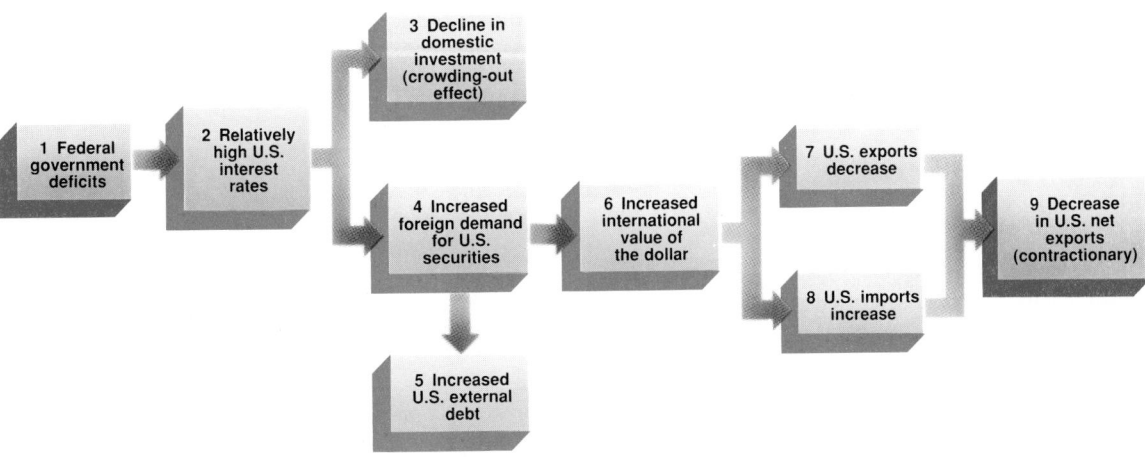

FIGURE 20-2

Possible effects of recent large deficits

Many economists are in general agreement that the large deficits of the 1980s have had the effects shown above. Deficits have increased domestic interest rates, resulting in both the crowding out of private investment and an increase in the demand for American securities. The latter has both increased our externally held debt and increased the demand for dollars. The strong demand for dollars has increased the international value of the dollar, making our exports more expensive to foreigners and imports cheaper to Americans. The consequent decline in our net exports has had a contractionary effect upon our economy.

(2) the so-called "selling off of America" to foreign investors.

DEFICIT-RELATED PROBLEMS

Let us trace out the manifold effects of these large recent deficits as perceived by many economists.[5] The cause-effect chain is quite lengthy, but it yields important insights. Figure 20-2 is a helpful guide for our discussion.

Beginning with boxes 1 and 2, we note once again that in financing its deficits government must go into the money market to compete with the private sector for funds. We know that this drives up interest rates.[6] High interest rates in turn have two important effects. First, as shown in box 3, they discourage private investment spending which, of course, is the crowding-out effect discussed earlier.

Because the economy is reasonably close to full employment, it is felt that the crowding-out effect is likely to be large. Therefore, although they are willing to admit that the short-run impact of deficits is expansionary, a number of economists are expressing concern that the long-run effect will be to retard the economy's growth rate. They envision deficits being used to finance defense spending and consumption-type government goods at the expense of investment in modernized factories and equipment. Deficits, it is contended, are forcing the economy on to a slower long-run growth path.

The second effect, shown by box 4, is that high interest rates on both American government and private securities make financial investment in the

[5] See, for example, Alice M. Rivlin (ed.), *Economic Choices 1984* (Washington: The Brookings Institution, 1984).

[6] During much of the early 1980s our expansionary deficit fiscal policy was accompanied by a tight money policy, that is, a policy which restricted growth of the money supply to combat inflation. This particular policy-mix is especially conducive to high interest rates. Deficit financing increases the demand for money at the time when the monetary authorities are restricting its supply.

United States more attractive for foreigners. While the resulting inflow of foreign funds is helpful in financing both the deficit and private investment, box 5 reminds us that this inflow represents an increase in our external debt. Recall that paying interest upon and retiring debts to foreigners entail a reduction in future national output available to our domestic economy.

Box 6 indicates that in order to purchase high-yielding American securities, foreigners must first buy American dollars with their own currencies. This increases the worldwide demand for dollars and increases the international price or exchange value of the dollar. To illustrate: Suppose that prior to our incurring large deficits the dollar ($) and the French franc (F) exchanged in the market at a rate of $1 = F10. But now the financing of our large deficits increases interest rates in the United States and thereby increases the demand for dollars with which to buy American securities. Suppose this raises the price of the dollar to, say, $1 = F11.

This rise in the international value of the dollar will tend to depress our exports (box 7) and increase our imports (box 8), giving rise to an "unfavorable" balance of trade. Let us see how this comes about. We know that exchange rates link the price levels of the nations of the world. Hence, when the value of the dollar increases—when dollars become more expensive to foreigners—then all American goods become more expensive to foreign buyers. In our example the increase in the value of the dollar from $1 = F10 to $1 = F11 increases the prices of all American goods by 10 percent to the French. The American product that formerly cost 10 francs now costs 11 francs. How will the French react to this? Answer: By buying fewer American goods. In other words, American exports will fall. Conversely, at the higher exchange rate Americans now get 11 rather than 10 francs for a dollar, so French goods are cheaper to Americans. Hence, we buy more French goods; our imports rise. Or, to bring these two developments together, American net exports (exports *minus* imports) fall. Indeed, we found in Chapter 9 that our net exports, or *trade balance*, was a *minus* $93 billion in 1988.

Net exports, you may recall from Chapter 11 and Chapter 13, are a component of aggregate demand. When net exports decline, this has a contractionary effect on the economy as shown in box 9. As our exports fall, unemployment will rise in

American exporting industries such as agriculture and computers. American import-competing industries such as automobiles and basic steel will also be adversely affected. The increase in the value of the dollar makes Japanese and German imports of these products cheaper and the American auto and steel industries find themselves with excess productive capacity and redundant labor. Note that the foregoing comments reiterate our earlier analysis (Chapter 14) that an expansionary fiscal policy may be less stimulating to the economy than the simple Keynesian model suggests. We have found that the expansionary impact of a deficit might be softened by both the *crowding-out effect* (box 3) and the negative *net export effect* (box 9) to which it might give rise.

There are a few further loose ends to this rather complex story.

1 The inflow of foreign funds does augment domestic funds and thereby helps to keep American interest rates lower than would otherwise be the case. Stated differently, the inflow of foreign funds to the United States tends to diminish the size of the crowding-out effect. From the standpoint of the foreign nations transferring their funds to the United States, their domestic investment and long-term economic growth will be smaller than otherwise.

2 Deficit-caused high interest rates in America impose an increased burden on heavily indebted underdeveloped countries such as Mexico and Brazil. Their dollar-denominated debts to American banks and the banks of other industrially advanced nations become more costly to service when American interest rates rise. Similarly, if declining American net exports lead to protectionism, these nations will have more difficulty selling their products in the United States. This means they will have greater difficulty in earning dollars to pay interest and principal on their debts. In short, our large deficits—particularly through the upward pressure they exert on domestic interest rates—pose something of a threat to the international credit system and to American banks.

3 The unfavorable trade imbalance means that we are not exporting enough goods to pay for our imports. The difference has been paid for in two ways. First, we have borrowed heavily from people and institutions in foreign lands. In the late 1980s, the United States became the world's leading debtor nation. Second, considerable amounts of U.S. as-

sets such as factories, shopping centers, and farms have been sold to foreign investors. To pay our debts and repurchase these assets, it will be necessary in the future to export more than we import. In other words, in the future we will be forced to consume and invest less than we produce.

POLICY RESPONSES

Federal deficits have been persistent; only once (1969) in the past twenty-five years has the Federal budget shown a surplus. And, as we have seen, deficits have ballooned in size in the 1980s. Many *Keynesian economists* feel that our recent deficits have had desirable stimulating effects upon the economy. But Keynesians are increasingly concerned that these deficits will eventually produce demand-pull inflation.

Alternatively, *new classical economists* led by Robert Barro of Harvard argue that deficits have little concrete effect on the economy. They believe that people are generally aware that deficits today will necessitate higher future taxes to pay for added interest expense resulting from the deficits. Households therefore allegedly respond to deficits by spending less today—that is, by saving more—in anticipation of having less future after-income available for consumption. Because the increase in private saving perfectly offsets the increase in the government's borrowing, the interest rate does not change. Thus, neither a crowding-out effect nor a trade deficit necessarily emerges.

But the vast majority of economists reject this view, claiming instead that the 1980s provide ample evidence of negative effects of large deficits. In fact, some economists attribute the stock market crash of October 1987 (Last Word, Chapter 10) largely to government failure to come to grips with the large Federal budget deficit.

In any event, concern with large deficits and an expanding public debt has spawned a variety of responses to which we now turn.

Constitutional amendment Perhaps the most extreme proposal to emerge is that a constitutional amendment be passed which mandates that Congress balance the budget each year. This proposed **balanced budget amendment** is based upon the assumption that Congress will continue to act "irresponsibly" because government spending enhances and tax increases diminish a politician's popular support. Political rhetoric notwithstanding, Federal deficits allegedly will continue until a constitutional amendment forces a balanced budget. Critics of this proposal remind us that an annually balanced budget has a procyclical or destabilizing effect upon the economy.

Gramm-Rudman-Hollings Act In December of 1985 Congress passed the **Gramm-Rudman-Hollings Act** which mandated annual reductions in the Federal deficit to ensure that the budget be brought into balance by 1991. The act was revised in 1987 to allow a more gradual reduction in the budget deficits and a balanced budget by 1993. The budget deficit must be reduced to $146 billion in 1989, to $110 billion in 1990, and thereafter trimmed by roughly $35 billion per year until balance is achieved in 1993. It should be noted that these deficits are substantially less than those predicted by the Congressional Budget Office in the absence of Gramm-Rudman-Hollings.

If the President and Congress cannot agree upon sufficient spending cuts or tax hikes to achieve the required deficit targets, a series of automatic spending cuts will be forced upon the administration so the targets are realized. A few programs such as social security and certain basic welfare programs are exempt from the cuts, but most are not. Half of the required cuts would come from national defense and the other half from such domestic programs as education, agricultural subsidies, unemployment benefits, transportation, science and space, and so on.

Tax increases The Gramm-Rudman-Hollings law mandated spending cuts if deficit targets are not otherwise realized. It makes no provision for tax boosts. But many observers feel that the budget cannot be balanced by 1993 on the basis of spending cuts alone. Hence, many proposals for tax increases are being aired. These include a value-added tax which, you may recall from Chapter 8, is akin to a national sales tax. Others suggest a special tax on imported oil which would make the Treasury the beneficiary of reduced oil prices rather than consumers. Still others say that the 1981 cuts in personal income taxes which contributed to current deficits must be reversed wholly or in part. However, this chapter's Last Word presents the controversial view that tax increases simply induce more government spending and are therefore unlikely to be helpful in deficit reduction.

Other proposals Concern with balancing the budget has prompted a variety of other deficit-reduction proposals. Two proposals of significance are the call for greater "privatization" of the economy and for reform which would enable the President to veto spending measures on a line-item basis.

PRIVATIZATION **Privatization** is a rather awkward term which refers to government divesting itself of certain assets and programs through their sale to private firms. This is in keeping with the conservative belief that most economic activities can be performed more efficiently in the private sector than in the public sector. More important for present purposes, the sale of government programs and assets would provide revenue to help reach Gramm-Rudman-Hollings deficit targets. Hence, it has been proposed that the Navy's petroleum reserves in California and Wyoming, Amtrak, Washington's Dulles and International Airports, the Federal Housing Administration, and the Bonneville Power Administration, among other entities, be sold to private firms. While privatization is very controversial, there are precedents. Margaret Thatcher's conservative government in Great Britain has sold off over $25 billion worth of state-owned enterprises in the past decade.

2 LINE-ITEM VETO The **line-item veto** would permit the President to veto individual spending items in appropriation bills. A typical appropriations bill merges hundreds of programs and projects into a single piece of legislation. Governors of forty-three states currently possess line-item veto authority for their state budgets, but the President does not have that kind of veto power for the Federal budget. Proponents of this reform argue that it would allow the President to cull from appropriation bills projects for which local or regional benefits are less than the costs to the nation's taxpayers. Hence, the line-item veto would tend to reduce government spending and help the Federal government balance its budget. Opponents argue that the line-item veto would give far too much power to the President—power, they say, which might easily be abused for political purposes.

LAST WORD

Will higher taxes increase the deficit?

Two Ohio University economists have recently argued that higher taxes will not significantly alter the size of Federal budget deficits and, in fact, are likely to *increase* them.

An evident means of reducing or eliminating Federal deficits is to increase taxes. But there is some evidence to suggest that higher taxes may result in even larger deficits. The reasoning underlying this curious conclusion is quite straightforward. Elected officials, it is argued, are primarily interested in being reelected and, to that end, are under great pressure to increase the funding of programs held in high esteem by their particular constituents. Thus, politicians may justify a tax increase for a popular purpose such as deficit reduction only to divert the additional revenue to spending programs favored by special interest groups whose political support is sought.

Examining data for the 1966–1986 period, these researchers conclude that the average Federal tax rate (measured as a percentage of personal income) and the Federal deficit (measured as a percentage

POSITIVE ROLE OF DEBT

Having completed this survey of imagined and real problems associated with deficits and the public debt, let us conclude our discussion on a more positive note. We must not forget that debt—both pubof GNP) are in fact positively related. In other words, higher tax rates *are* associated with larger, not smaller, deficits. Using more sophisticated analysis, the authors hold constant nontax factors such as the unemployment rate, unanticipated inflation, and wars, which also have a great influence on the size of Federal deficits. This analysis suggests that a $1.00 increase in taxes will lead to a $1.58 increase in government spending or, in other words, a $.58 *increase* in the deficit. If the Federal government obtains more financial resources, legislators will spend not only all of the incremental tax revenues but also "a little bit more." The authors argue that their findings "raise serious doubts as to whether tax increases will be effective in reducing the deficit." Indeed, they suggest that "tax increases may worsen rather than improve the problem." A deficit-reducing strategy based on tax increases may well be counterproductive.

What alternative strategies might work in reducing or eliminating deficits? One is to use "arbitrary restraints" such as a constitutional amendment requiring an annually balanced budget or legislation such as Gramm-Rudman-Hollings. A second proposal is to limit all legislators to one term of, say, six years, to alter the legislator–constituency relationship so that politicians are under much less pressure to spend on behalf of constituent pressure groups.

Based upon Lowell Gallaway and Richard Vedder, "The 'Optimal' Budget Deficit: A Theoretical and Empirical Analysis," Ohio Economic Studies, mimeographed, no date; and Richard Vedder, Lowell Gallaway, and Christopher Frenze, "Federal Tax Increases and the Budget Deficit, 1947–1986: Some Empirical Evidence," prepared for the Joint Economic Committee, April 29, 1987, mimeographed.

lic and private—plays a positive role in a prosperous and growing economy. We know that as income expands, so does saving. Keynesian employment theory and fiscal policy tell us that if aggregate expenditures are to be sustained at the full-employment level, this expanding volume of saving

or its equivalent must be obtained and spent by consumers, businesses, or government. The process by which saving is transferred to spenders is *debt creation*. Now, in fact, consumers and businesses do borrow and spend a great amount of saving. But if households and businesses are not willing to borrow and thereby to increase private debt sufficiently fast to absorb the growing volume of saving, an increase in public debt must absorb the remainder or the economy will falter from full employment and fail to realize its growth potential.

CHAPTER SUMMARY

1 A budget deficit is the excess of government expenditures over its receipts; the public debt is the total accumulation of its deficits and surpluses over time.

2 Budget philosophies include the annually balanced budget, the cyclically balanced budget, and functional finance. The basic problem with an annually balanced budget is that it is procyclical rather than countercyclical. Similarly, it may be difficult to balance the budget over the course of the business cycle if upswings and downswings are not of roughly comparable magnitude. Functional finance is the view that the primary purpose of Federal finance is to stabilize the economy and the problems associated with consequent deficits or surpluses are of secondary importance.

3 Historically, growth of the public debt has been caused by the deficit financing of wars and by recessions. The large deficits of the 1980s are primarily the result of tax reductions.

4 The public debt was $2.6 trillion in 1988. Since the 1970s the debt and associated interest charges have both been increasing as a percentage of the GNP. The debt has also been rising on a per capita basis.

5 The argument that a large public debt may bankrupt the government is false because **a** the debt need only be refinanced rather than refunded and **b** the Federal government has the power to levy taxes and create money.

6 The crowding-out effect aside, the public debt is not a vehicle for shifting economic burdens to future generations.

7 More substantive problems associated with the public debt include the following: **a** Payment of interest on the debt probably increases income inequality. **b** Interest payments on the debt require higher taxes which may impair incentives. *c* Paying interest or principal upon the portion of the debt held by foreigners entails a transfer of real output abroad. *d* Government borrowing to refinance or pay interest on the debt may increase interest rates and crowd out private investment spending.

8 Federal budget deficits have been much larger in the 1980s than in earlier years. Many economists perceive that these large deficits have increased interest rates in the United States which in turn have *a* crowded out private investment and *b* increased the foreign demand for American securities. The increased demand for American securities has increased the international value of the dollar, causing American exports to fall and American imports to rise. Declining net exports have a contractionary effect upon our domestic economy.

9 Proposed remedies for the large deficits and public debt increases of the 1980s include *a* a proposed constitutional amendment mandating an annually balanced budget; *b* the revised Gramm-Rudman-Hollings Act which requires annual deficit reductions until a balanced budget is achieved in 1993; *c* proposals for new Federal taxes or higher rates for existing taxes; *d* greater privatization of the economy by selling public assets and programs to the private sector; and *e* giving the President line-item veto authority.

TERMS AND CONCEPTS

budget deficit	crowding-out effect
public debt	public investments
annually balanced budget	balanced budget amendment
cyclically balanced budget	Gramm-Rudman-Hollings Act
functional finance	privatization
external debt	line-item veto

QUESTIONS AND STUDY SUGGESTIONS

1 Assess the potential for using fiscal policy as a stabilization device under *a* an annually balanced budget, *b* a cyclically balanced budget, and *c* functional finance.

2 What have been the major sources of the public debt historically? Why were deficits so large in the 1980s?

3 Discuss the various ways of measuring the size of the public debt. How does an internally held public debt differ from an externally held public debt? What would be the effects of retiring an internally held public debt? An externally held public debt? Distinguish between refinancing and retiring the debt.

4 Explain or evaluate each of the following statements:
a "A national debt is like a debt of the left hand to the right hand."
b "The least likely problem arising from a large public debt is that the government will go bankrupt."
c "The basic cause of our growing public debt is a lack of political courage."

5 Is the crowding-out effect likely to be larger during recession or when the economy is near full employment? Can you use the aggregate demand–aggregate supply model to substantiate your answer?

6 Some economists argue that the quantitative importance of the public debt can best be measured by interest payments on the debt as a percentage of the GNP. Can you explain why?

7 Explain the essence of the revised Gramm-Rudman-Hollings Act. Would you favor a constitutional amendment requiring that the Federal budget be balanced annually? Do you favor "privatization," either as a means of reducing budget deficits or as a vehicle for reducing the size of the public sector? Do you favor giving the President the authority to veto line-items of appropriation bills?

8 Is our $2.6 trillion public debt a burden to future generations? If so, in what sense? Why might deficit financing be more likely to reduce the future size of our "national factory" than tax financing of government expenditures?

9 Trace the cause-and-effect chain through which large deficits might affect domestic interest rates, domestic investment, the international value of the dollar, and our international trade. Comment: "There is too little recognition that the deterioration of America's position in world trade is more the result of our own policies than the harm wrought by foreigners."

10 Explain how a significant decline in the nation's budget deficit would be expected to reduce *a* the size of our trade deficit, *b* the total debt Americans owe to foreigners, and *c* foreign purchases of U.S. assets such as factories and farms.

CHAPTER 21

Economic growth

Previous chapters have concentrated upon the causes of short-run fluctuations in employment and price levels and upon policies which might mitigate such instability. Of equal importance is the issue of economic growth to which we now turn.

Although punctuated by periods of cyclical instability, economic growth in the United States has been impressive. For example, during this century real output has increased twelvefold and population has tripled to yield approximately a quadrupling of the goods and services available to the average American.

Our discussion of growth will be organized as follows. First, we want to understand how growth is defined and why it is important. Our second goal is to gain some analytical perspective on economic growth. Our third objective is to present and assess the long-term growth record of the United States. Fourth, we want to understand the quantitative importance of the various factors which contribute to growth. Fifth, we seek to explain the slowdown in the productivity growth of American labor which began in the 1970s. Finally, we will briefly examine the controversy surrounding growth and take a fleeting look at policies to promote growth.

Growth economics

Employment theory and stabilization policy are of a static or short-run character. They assume the economy has fixed amounts of resources or inputs available and therefore is capable of producing some capacity or full-employment level of national output. The central question of employment theory is: What must be done to utilize fully the nation's *existing* productive capacity? In contrast, growth economics is concerned with the question of how to *increase* the economy's productive capacity or full-employment GNP.

TWO DEFINITIONS

Economic growth is defined and measured in two related ways. Specifically, economic growth may be defined (1) as the increase in real GNP or NNP which occurs over a period of time, or (2) as the increase in real GNP or NNP *per capita* which occurs over time. Both definitions are useful. For example, if one is concerned with the question of military potential or political preeminence, the first definition is more relevant. But per capita output is clearly superior for comparisons of living standards among nations or regions. While India's GNP is almost 50 percent larger than Switzerland's, the latter's standard of living is over 60 times as great as India's. Our attention in this chapter is primarily upon the growth of real output and income per capita.

Economic growth by either definition is usually calculated in terms of annual percentage *rates* of growth. For example, if real GNP was $200 billion last year and is $210 billion this year, we can calculate the rate of growth by subtracting last year's real GNP from this year's real GNP and comparing the difference to last year's real GNP. Specifically, the growth rate in this particular case is ($210 − $200)/$200, or 5 percent.

IMPORTANCE OF GROWTH

Why is growth a widely held economic goal? The answer is almost self-evident: The growth of total output relative to population means a higher standard of living. An expanding real output means greater material abundance and implies a more satisfactory answer to the economizing problem. Our question can be answered from a slightly different perspective. *A growing economy is in a superior position to meet new needs and resolve socioeconomic problems both domestically and internationally.* A growing economy, by definition, enjoys an increment in its annual real output which it can use to satisfy existing needs more effectively or to undertake new programs. An expanding real wage or salary income makes new opportunities available to any given family—a trip to Europe, a new stereo, a college education for each child, and so forth—without the sacrifice of other opportunities and enjoyments. Similarly, a growing economy can, for example, undertake new programs to alleviate poverty and clean up the environment *without* impairing existing levels of consumption, investment, and public goods production. *Growth lessens the burden of scarcity.* A growing economy, unlike a static one, can consume more while simultaneously increasing its capacity to produce more in the future. By easing the burden of scarcity—that is, by relaxing society's production constraints—economic growth allows a nation to realize existing economic goals more fully and to undertake new output-absorbing endeavors.

ARITHMETIC OF GROWTH

People sometimes wonder why economists get so excited about seemingly minuscule changes in the rate of growth. Does it really matter very much whether our economy grows at 4 percent or 3 percent? It matters a great deal! For the United States, which has a current real GNP of about $3995 billion, the difference between a 3 and a 4 percent growth rate is about $40 billion worth of output per year. For a very poor country, a .5 percent change in the growth rate may well mean the difference between starvation and mere hunger.

Furthermore, when envisioned over a period of years, an apparently small difference in the rate of growth becomes exceedingly important because of the "miracle" of compound interest. Example: Suppose Alphania and Betania have identical GNPs. But Alphania begins to grow at a 4 percent annual rate, while Betania grows at only 2 percent. Recalling our "rule of 70" of Chapter 10, Alphania would find that its GNP would double in only about eighteen years ($= 70 \div 4$); Betania would take thirty-five years ($= 70 \div 2$) to accomplish the same feat. The importance of the growth rate is undeniable.

One can also reasonably argue that the realization of growth is of greater importance than achieving economic stability. For example, the elimination of a recessionary gap might increase the national income by, say, 6 percent on a one-time basis. But a 3 percent annual growth rate will increase the national income by 6 percent in two years and will continue to provide that 6 percent biannual increment indefinitely.

Causes: ingredients of growth

What are the sources of economic growth? Basically, there are six strategic ingredients in the growth of any economy. Four of these factors relate to the physical ability of an economy to grow. They are (1) the quantity and quality of its natural resources, (2) the quantity and quality of its human resources, (3) the supply or stock of capital goods, and (4) technology. These four items may be termed the **supply factors** in economic growth. These are the physical agents of greater production. It is the availability of more and better resources, including the stock of technological knowledge, which permits an economy to produce a greater real output.

But the ability to grow and the actual realization of growth may be quite different things. Specifically, two additional considerations contribute to growth. First, there is a **demand factor** in growth. In order to realize its growing productive potential, a nation must provide for the full employment of its expanding supplies of resources. This requires a growing level of aggregate demand. Second, there is the **allocative factor** in growth. To achieve its productive potential, a nation must provide not only for the full employment of its resources, but also for full production from them. The ability to expand production is not a sufficient condition for the expansion of total output; the actual employment of expanded resource supplies *and* the allocation of those resources in such a way as to get the maximum amount of useful goods produced are also required.

It is notable that the supply and demand factors in growth are related. For example, unemployment tends to retard the rate of capital accumulation and may slow expenditures for research. And, conversely, a low rate of innovation and investment can be a basic cause of unemployment.

These factors can be placed in proper perspective by recalling Chapter 2's production possibilities curve, reproduced in Figure 21-1. This is a best-performance curve in that it indicates the various *maximum* combinations of products the economy can produce, given the quantity and quality of its natural, human, and capital resources, and its stock of technological knowledge. An improvement in any of the supply factors will push the produc-

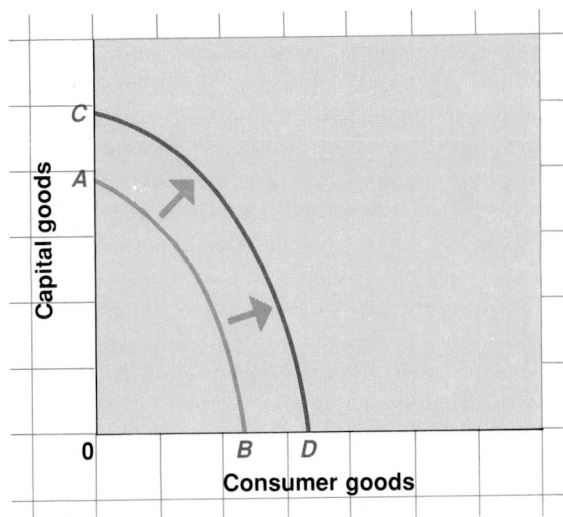

FIGURE 21-1

Economic growth and the production possibilities curve

Economic growth is indicated by an outward shift of the production possibilities curve, as from *AB* to *CD*. Increases in the quantity and quality of resources and technological advance permit this shift; full employment and allocative efficiency are essential to its realization.

tion possibilities curve to the right, as indicated by the shift from *AB* to *CD* in Figure 21-1. Increases in the quantity or quality of resources and technological progress push the curve to the right. But the demand and allocative factors remind us that the economy need not realize its maximum productive potential; the curve may shift to the right and leave the economy behind at some level of operation *inside* the curve. In particular, the economy's enhanced productive *potential* will not be *realized* unless (1) aggregate demand increases sufficiently to sustain full employment, and (2) the additional resources are employed efficiently so they make the maximum possible contribution to the national output.

Example: The net increase in the labor force of the United States is roughly 2 million workers per year. As such, this increment raises the productive capacity, or potential, of the economy. But the realization of the extra output these additional workers are capable of producing presumes they are able to find jobs and that these jobs are in those firms and industries where their talents are fully utilized. Society doesn't want new labor-force entrants to be unemployed; nor does it want pediatricians working as plumbers.

Although demand and allocative considerations are important, discussions of growth focus primarily upon the supply side. Growth is concerned with those factors detailed in Table 11-2 which can shift the aggregate supply curve rightward. Or, in terms of Figure 19-6b, growth is depicted as a rightward shift of the long-run vertical aggregate supply curve. Figure 21-2 provides us with a commonly used framework for discussing the supply factors in growth. It merely indicates that there are two fundamental ways by which any society can increase its real output and income: (1) by increasing its inputs of resources, and (2) by increasing the productivity of those inputs. Let us focus our attention upon inputs of labor. By so doing we can say that *our real GNP in any year depends upon the input of labor (measured in worker-hours) multiplied by* **labor productivity** *(measured as real output per worker per hour)*. That is,

Total output = worker-hours × labor productivity

Hypothetical illustration: Assume an economy with 10 workers, each of whom works 2000 hours

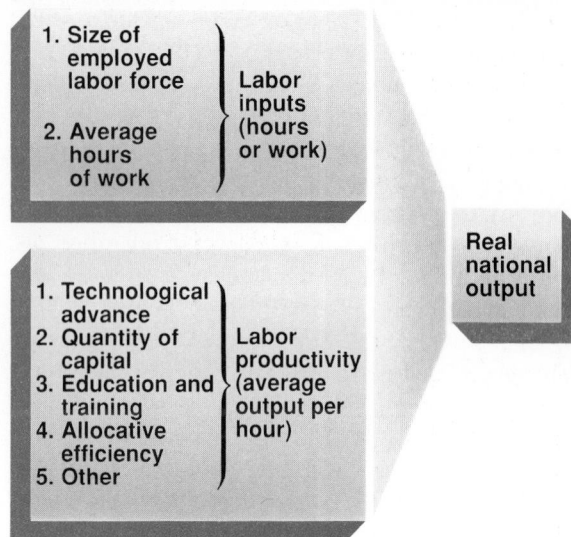

FIGURE 21-2

The determinants of real output

Real GNP can be usefully viewed as the product of the quantity of labor inputs multiplied by labor productivity.

per year (50 weeks at 40 hours per week) so that total input of worker-hours is 20,000 hours. If productivity—average real output per worker-hour—is $5, then total output or real GNP will be $100,000 (= 20,000 × $5).

What determines the number of hours worked each year? And, more importantly, what determines labor productivity? Figure 21-2 provides us with a framework for answering these questions. The hours of labor input depend upon the size of the employed labor force and the length of the average workweek. Labor force size in turn depends upon the size of the working age population and the labor force participation rate, that is, the percentage of the working age population which is actually in the labor force. The average workweek is governed by legal and institutional considerations and by collective bargaining.

Productivity is determined by such factors as technological progress, the quantity of capital goods with which workers are equipped, the quality of labor itself, and the efficiency with which the various inputs are allocated, combined, and managed. Stated differently, productivity increases

when the health, training, education, and motivation of workers are improved; when workers have more and better machinery and natural resources with which to work; when production is better organized and managed; and when labor is reallocated from less efficient industries to more efficient industries.

It is worth noting that Figure 21-2 complements Figure 17-4 on page 341. The latter figure outlines the determinants of the *demand* for national output. Figure 21-2 summarizes those factors which determine a nation's capacity to *supply* or produce aggregate output. By locating Figure 21-2 to the left of Figure 17-4 one obtains a more complete model of the economy which sketches the determinants of both the demand for, and the supply of, national output.

Growth record of the United States

Table 21-1 gives us a rough idea of economic growth in the United States over past decades as viewed through our two definitions of growth. Column 2 summarizes the economy's growth as measured by increases in real GNP. Although not steady, the growth of real GNP has been quite remarkable. *The real GNP has increased almost fivefold since 1940.* But our population has also grown significantly. Hence, using our second definition of growth, we find in column 4 that *real per capita GNP was almost 3 times larger in 1988 than it was in 1940.* Internationally, our economy is in virtual dead heat with Switzerland in providing the world's highest per capita GNP.

What about our *rate* of growth? Data presented in Table 21-2 suggest that the post-World War II growth rate of the United States' real GNP has been more than 3 percent per year, while real GNP per capita has grown at almost 2 percent per year.

These bare numbers must be modified in several respects.

l The figures of Tables 21-1 and 21-2 do *not* fully take into account improvements in product quality, and thereby may understate the growth of eco-

TABLE 21-1 Real GNP and per capita GNP, 1929–1988

(1) Year	(2) GNP, billions of 1982 dollars	(3) Population, millions	(4) Per capita GNP, 1982 dollars (2) ÷ (3)
1929	$ 710	122	$ 5,820
1933	499	126	3,960
1940	773	132	5,553
1945	1355	140	9,679
1950	1204	152	7,921
1955	1495	166	9,006
1960	1665	181	9,199
1965	2088	194	10,763
1970	2416	205	11,785
1975	2695	214	12,593
1980	3187	228	13,978
1985	3618	239	15,138
1988	3995	246	16,240

Source: *Economic Report of the President, 1989.*

nomic well-being. Purely quantitative data do not provide an accurate comparison between an era of iceboxes and one of refrigerators.

2 The increases in real GNP and per capita GNP shown in Table 21-1 were accomplished despite very sizable increases in leisure. The seventy-hour workweek is a thing of the distant past. The standard workweek is now less than forty hours. The result again is an understatement of economic well-being.

3 On the other hand, these measures of growth do *not* take into account adverse effects which growth may have upon the environment and the quality of life itself. To the extent that growth debases the physical environment and creates a stressful work environment our data will overstate the benefits of growth.

4 It is also important to stress that the United States' growth record is less impressive than those of many other industrially advanced nations. For example, the growth record of Japan has averaged more than twice that of the United States over the past four decades and there is genuine concern that Japan will overtake America as the world's leading industrial power.

TABLE 21-2 Growth of real GNP and real GNP per capita in selected countries

	Growth rates of real GNP		Growth rates of real GNP per capita	
	1870–1969	1948–1988	1870–1969	1948–1988
United States	3.7%	3.3%	2.0%	1.9%
Japan	4.2	7.1	—	5.9
Germany	3.0	5.0	1.9	4.2
United Kingdom	1.9	2.6	1.3	2.2
France	2.0	4.1	1.7	3.3
Italy	2.2	4.4	1.5	3.9
Canada	3.6	4.5	1.8	2.7

Source: U.S. Department of Commerce, *Historical Statistics of the United States: Colonial Times to 1970* (Washington, 1975), p. 225; and *Economic Report of the President, 1989,* p. 27.

Accounting for growth

Edward F. Denison of The Brookings Institution has spent most of his professional career attempting to quantify the relative importance of the various factors which contribute to economic growth. His conceptual framework corresponds quite closely to the factors shown in Figure 21-1 and is therefore highly relevant to our discussion. Denison's most recent estimates are shown in Table 21-3. Over the 1929–1982 period Denison calculates that real national income grew by 2.9 percent per year. He then estimates what percentage of this annual growth was accounted for by each of the factors shown in the table. Let us use Denison's Table 21-3 as a focal point for a series of brief comments on the ingredients in American economic growth.

INPUTS VERSUS PRODUCTIVITY

The most evident conclusion one can derive from Denison's data is that *productivity growth has been*

TABLE 21-3 The sources of growth in U.S. real national income, 1929–1982

Sources of growth		Percent of total growth
(1) Increase in quantity of labor		32
(2) Increase in labor productivity		68
(3) Technological advance	28	
(4) Quantity of capital	19	
(5) Education and training	14	
(6) Economies of scale	9	
(7) Improved resource allocation	8	
(8) Legal-human environment and other	−9	
		100

Source: Edward F. Denison, *Trends in American Economic Growth, 1929–1982* (Washington: The Brookings Institution, 1985), p. 30. Details may not add to totals because of rounding.

the most important force underlying the growth of our real national output and income. Note that increases in the quantity of labor (item 1) account for only about one-third of the increase in real national income over this period; the remaining two-thirds is attributable to rising labor productivity (item 2).

QUANTITY OF LABOR

Our population and labor force have both expanded significantly through time. For example, over the 1929–1982 period considered by Denison, our total population grew from 122 to 232 million and the labor force increased from 49 to 110 million workers. Historical reductions in the length of the average workweek have tended to reduce labor inputs, but the workweek has declined very modestly since World War II. Declining birthrates in the past twenty years or so have slowed the rate of population growth. However, largely because of increased participation by women in labor markets, our labor force continues to grow by about 2 million workers per year.

TECHNOLOGICAL ADVANCE

We note in Table 21-3 that technological advance (item 3) is an important engine of growth, accounting for 28 percent of the increase in real national income realized over the 1929–1982 period. Technological advance is broadly defined so as to include, not merely new production techniques, but also new managerial techniques and new forms of business organization. More generally, technological advance involves the discovery of new knowledge which permits the combining of a given amount of resources in new ways so as to result in a larger output.

In practice, technological advance and capital formation (investment) are closely related processes; technological advance often entails investment in new machinery and equipment. The idea that there is a more efficient way to catch a rabbit than running it down led to investment in the bow and arrow. And it is clearly necessary to construct new nuclear power plants in order to apply nuclear power technology. However, modern crop-rotation practices and contour plowing are ideas which contribute greatly to output, although they do not necessarily entail the use of new kinds or increased amounts of capital equipment.

Casual observation suggests that, historically, technological advance has been both rapid and profound. Gas and diesel engines, conveyor belts, and assembly lines come to mind as highly significant developments of the past. More recently, the lamp of technology has freed the automation jinni and with it the potential wonders of the push-button factory. Supersonic jets, the transistor and integrated circuitry, computers, xerography, containerized shipping, and nuclear power—not to mention recent breakthroughs in superconductivity—are technological achievements which were in the realm of fantasy a mere generation ago. Table 21-3 merely confirms the importance of such developments in the economic growth process.

QUANTITY OF CAPITAL

Some 19 percent—almost one-fifth—of the annual growth of real national income over the indicated period was attributable to increases in the quantity of capital (item 4). It is no surprise that a worker will be more productive when equipped with a larger amount of capital goods. And how does a nation acquire more capital? Capital accumulation results from saving and the investment in plant and equipment which these savings make possible.

It must be emphasized that the critical consideration from the standpoint of labor productivity is the amount of capital goods *per worker*. Our aggregate stock of capital might expand during a given time period, but if the labor force increases more rapidly, then labor productivity will fall because *each worker* will be less well equipped. Indeed, we will find later in this chapter that something of this sort happened in the 1970s and contributed to a slowing of productivity growth.

To what extent has real capital per worker increased? One long-run estimate concludes that in the 1889 to 1969 period the stock of capital goods increased sixfold and, over this same period, labor-hours doubled. Hence, the quantity of capital goods per labor-hour was roughly three times as large in 1969 than it was in 1889.[1] While the capital stock is not easy to calculate, data suggest that the amount of capital equipment (machinery and buildings) per worker is currently about $30,000.[2]

Two addenda are in order. First, we shall see shortly that the United States has been investing a smaller percentage of its GNP in recent years than have most other industrially advanced nations. This helps to explain our relatively less impressive growth performance (Table 21-2). The second point is that investment is not only private, but also public. There is concern that our **infrastructure**—our highways and bridges, port facilities, public transit systems, waste water treatment facilities, municipal water systems, airports, and so on—is encountering growing problems of deterioration, technological obsolescence, and insufficient capacity to serve future growth. Indeed, this chapter's Last Word addresses this issue and suggests that a substantial portion of our poor productivity performance over the past decade or two is attributable to insufficient public investment in the infrastructure.

EDUCATION AND TRAINING

Ben Franklin once said that "He that hath a trade hath an estate." This is an archaic way of saying that education and training improve a worker's productivity and result in higher earnings. Like investment in real capital, investment in human capital is an important means of increasing labor productivity. Denison's estimates in Table 21-3 indicate that 14 percent of the growth in our real national income is attributable to such improvements in the quality of labor (item 5).

Perhaps the simplest measure of labor force quality is the level of educational attainment. Figure 21-3 reflects the gains realized in the past three decades. Currently over four-fifths of the labor force has received at least a high school education. Of this group almost 22 percent acquired a college education or more. Only about 6 percent of the civilian labor force has received no more than an elementary school education. It is clear that educa-

[1] Solomon Fabricant, *A Primer on Productivity* (New York: Random House, Inc., 1969), chap. 5.

[2] David Alan Aschauer, "Is the Public Capital Stock Too Low?" *Chicago Fed Letter* (Federal Reserve Bank of Chicago), October 1987, p. 1.

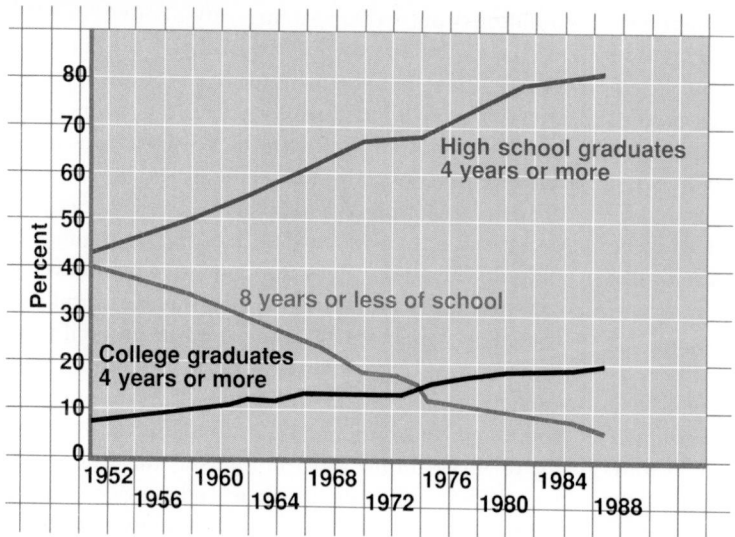

FIGURE 21-3

Recent changes in the educational attainment of the labor force

The percentage of the labor force completing high school and college has been rising steadily in recent years, while the percentage who did not go to high school or complete elementary school has been falling. (Statistical Abstract of the United States.)

tion has become accessible to more and more people.[3]

It must be added that there are persistent concerns about the quality of American education. You may recall that scores on Scholastic Aptitude Tests (SATs) declined in the 1960s and 1970s. Furthermore, the performance of American students in science and mathematics compares unfavorably to students in many other industrialized countries.

SCALE ECONOMIES AND RESOURCE ALLOCATION

Table 21-3 also tells us that labor productivity has increased because of economies of scale (item 6) and improved resource allocation (item 7). Let us consider the latter factor first.

Improved resource allocation simply indicates that over time workers have reallocated themselves

[3] For a fascinating discussion of human resources in the United States, see Victor R. Fuchs, *How We Live* (Cambridge, Mass.: Harvard University Press, 1983).

from relatively low-productivity employments to relatively high-productivity employments. For example, over the 1929–1982 period a great deal of labor has been reallocated from agriculture—where labor productivity is relatively low—to manufacturing—where labor productivity is relatively high. As a result, the average productivity of American workers in the aggregate has increased. Similarly, we know that historically labor market discrimination has denied many women and minorities access to those jobs wherein they would be most productive. The decline of such discrimination over time has increased labor productivity. We will find in Chapter 39 that tariffs, import quotas, and other barriers to international trade are conducive to the allocation of labor to relatively unproductive employments. The long-run movement toward freer international trade has therefore improved the allocation of labor and enhanced productivity.

Economies of scale will be discussed in some detail in Chapter 24. At this point let us assert that there may be production advantages which are derived from market and firm size. For example, a large corporation might be able to select a more efficient production technique from those now available than could a small-scale firm. A large manufacturer of automobiles can use elaborate assembly lines, featuring computerization and robotics, while smaller producers must settle for more primitive technologies. The contribution of economies of scale shown in Table 21-3 means that markets have increased in scope and firms have increased in size so that overall more efficient production methods are being utilized. Accordingly, labor productivity increases.

DETRIMENTS TO GROWTH

Unfortunately, some developments detract from labor productivity and the growth of real national income. The legal and human environment entry in Table 21-3 (item 8) aggregates these detriments to productivity growth. Over the 1929–1982 period considerable changes were made with respect to the regulation of industry, environmental pollution, worker health and safety, and so forth, which have impacted negatively on growth. The expansion of government regulation of business in such areas as pollution control and worker health and safety diverted investment spending away from productivity-increasing capital goods and toward equipment which provides cleaner air and water and greater worker protection from accident and illness. A firm required to spend $1 million on a new scrubber to meet government standards for air pollution does not have that $1 million available to spend on machinery and equipment which would enhance worker productivity. The diversion of resources to deal with dishonesty and crime and the effects of such considerations as work stoppages because of labor disputes and the impact of bad weather on agricultural output are also included in item 8.

This point is worth adding. Worker safety, clean air and water, and the overall "quality of life" may come at the expense of productivity. But the reverse is also true. That is, we cannot assume that productivity advances automatically enhance society's welfare; productivity growth may entail opportunity costs of other things (a clean environment) which we value more highly. Productivity measures output per hour of work, not overall "well-being" per hour of work.

OTHER FACTORS

There are a number of other difficult-to-quantify considerations which play significant roles in determining an economy's growth rate. For example, there is no doubt that the generous and varied supplies of natural resources with which the United States has been blessed have been an important contributor to our economic growth.[4] We enjoy an abundance of fertile soil, quite desirable climatic and weather conditions, ample quantities of most mineral resources, generous sources of power, and so forth. It is generally agreed that, with the possible exception of the Soviet Union, the United States has a larger variety and greater quantity of natural resources than any other nation.

While an abundant natural resource base is often very helpful to the growth process, we must not conclude that a meager resource base dooms a nation to slow growth. Although Japan's natural resources are severely constrained, its post-World War II growth has been remarkable (Table 21-2). On the other hand, some of the very underdeveloped countries of Africa and South America have substantial amounts of natural resources.

There are additional unmeasurable factors which bear upon a nation's growth rate. In particular, the overall social-cultural-political environment of the United States generally has been conducive to economic growth. Several interrelated factors contribute to this favorable environment. First, as opposed to many other nations, there are virtually no social or moral taboos upon production and material progress. Indeed, American social philosophy has embraced the notion that material advance is an attainable and highly desirable economic goal. The inventor, the innovator, and the business executive are generally accorded high degrees of prestige and respect in American society. Second, Americans have traditionally possessed healthy attitudes toward work and risk taking; our society has benefited from a willing labor

---

[4] Denison omits land (natural resources) from Table 21-3 on the grounds (no pun intended) that, unlike inputs of labor and capital, there have been no changes in land inputs to contribute to the growth of real national income. That is, the quantity of land does not change and any qualitative changes are minuscule.

force and an ample supply of entrepreneurs. Third, our market system is replete with personal and corporate incentives which encourage growth; our economy rewards actions which increase output. Finally, our economy has been characterized by a stable political system wherein internal order, the right of property ownership, the legal status of enterprise, and the enforcement of contracts have been fostered. Though not subject to quantification, this bundle of characteristics has undoubtedly provided an excellent foundation for American economic growth.

AGGREGATE DEMAND, INSTABILITY, AND GROWTH

As embodied in Table 21-3, Denison's analysis is designed to explain the growth of *actual*, as opposed to *potential* or full-employment, real national income. The 2.9 percent annual growth rate which the table attempts to explain embodies changes in real national income caused by fluctuations in aggregate demand. Denison recognizes that our growth rate would have been higher—3.2 percent per year—if the economy's potential output had been realized year after year. Deviations from full employment due to a deficiency of aggregate demand cause the actual rate of growth to fall short of the potential rate. A glance back at Figure 10-4 reminds us vividly of the extent to which the actual performance of our economy frequently falls short of its potential output. Looking back into history, we find that the Great Depression of the 1930s was a serious blow to the United States' long-run growth record. Between 1929 and 1933 our real GNP (measured in 1982 prices) actually *declined* from $710 to $499 billion! In 1939 the real GNP was approximately at the same level as in 1929 (see line 17 on table inside front cover). More recently it is estimated that the 1980–1982 recession cost the United States over $600 billion in lost output and income.

But this is only a part of the picture. Cyclical unemployment can have certain harmful "carryover" effects upon the growth rate in subsequent years of full employment through the adverse effects it may have upon other factors in growth. For example, unemployment depresses investment and capital accumulation. Furthermore, the expansion of research budgets may be slowed by recession so that technological progress diminishes; union resistance to technological change may stiffen; and so forth. Though it is difficult to quantify the impact of these considerations upon the growth rate, they undoubtedly can be of considerable importance.

REPRISE

Our discussion of United States' economic growth suggests that increases in labor productivity have been decidedly more important than increases in labor inputs in expanding real GNP. But growth in labor productivity does not just happen. It is brought about by technological progress, by increases in the quantity of real capital per worker, by improvements in the quality of labor, by shifting labor from low-productivity to high-productivity employment, and by a variety of other factors. Nor can productivity growth and the expansion of real output be taken for granted. Many of the so-called less developed countries of the world have put forth substantial efforts to achieve economic growth but have realized little or no success. Similarly, growth rates for the industrially advanced nations are erratic, particularly because of fluctuations in aggregate demand.

The productivity slowdown

In the 1970s—and to a lesser degree in the 1980s—the United States experienced a much-publicized productivity slowdown. Table 21-4 portrays the course of United States labor productivity in the post-World War II period. Observe in column 2 that for about two decades following World War II (1948–1966) labor productivity increased at a vigorous average annual rate of 3.2 percent, only to decline rather precipitously in the 1966–1973 period. This was followed by a dismal productivity performance in the 1973–1981 period, and a modest resurgence of productivity growth in the 1980s. Although labor productivity growth has been slowing worldwide, American productivity growth has been less than that realized by other major industrialized nations. The United States still enjoys the

TABLE 21-4 **Growth of labor productivity and real per capita GNP, 1948–1987**

(1) Period	(2) Productivity growth rate	(3) Real per capita GNP growth rate
1948–1966	3.2%	2.2%
1966–1973	2.0	2.0
1973–1981	0.7	1.1
1981–1987	1.5	1.8

Source: *Economic Report of the President, 1988*, p. 67. End points of calculations are cyclical peaks.

highest absolute level of output per worker, but our productivity advantage is diminishing.

SIGNIFICANCE

The significance of our productivity slowdown is manifold.

1 Standard of living Productivity growth is the basic source of improvements in real wage rates and the standard of living. Real income per worker-hour can only increase at the same rate as real output per worker-hour. More output per hour means more real income to distribute for each hour worked. The simplest case is the classic one of Robinson Crusoe on his deserted island. The number of fish he can catch or coconuts he can pick per hour *is* his real income or wage per hour. We observe in column 3 of Table 21-4 that the broadest measure of living standards—the growth of real per capita GNP—followed the path of labor productivity. Living levels thus measured grew by only 1.1 percent per year during the severe 1973–1981 productivity stagnation as compared to 2.2 percent in the 1948–1966 postwar decades.

2 Inflation We discovered in our discussion of incomes policies in Chapter 19 that productivity increases tend to offset increases in nominal-wage rates and thereby have an ameliorating effect on cost-push inflationary pressures. Other things

being equal, a decline in the rate of productivity growth contributes to rapidly rising unit labor costs and a higher rate of inflation. Many economists believe that productivity stagnation contributed to the unusually high inflation rates of the 1970s.

3 World markets Our slow rate of productivity growth as compared to our major international trading partners tends to increase the relative prices of American goods in world markets. The result is a decline in our competitiveness and a loss of international markets for American producers.

CAUSES OF THE SLOWDOWN

There is no consensus among experts as to why American productivity growth has slowed and fallen behind the rates of Japan and western Europe. Indeed, the fact that so many factors may bear upon a country's productivity performance may preclude a simple explanation of the slowdown. Given this caveat, let us survey some of the possible causes of the slowdown which have been put forward by various analysts.

1 Investment There is a high positive correlation between the percentage of a nation's GNP devoted to investment goods and the productivity increases it achieves. A worker using a bulldozer can move more dirt per hour than can that same worker equipped with an ordinary shovel. As Figure 21-4 indicates, the United States has been investing a smaller proportion of its GNP and realizing a lower rate of productivity growth than other western capitalist countries. Why has investment in recent years been relatively low in the United States?

A number of plausible reasons have been offered. First, the uncertain stagflation environment of the 1970s tended to dampen business incentives to invest. Indeed, the fact that stock prices were depressed while construction costs soared tended to induce firms to expand by buying existing businesses rather than by building *new* plants and equipment. Inflation also tended to squeeze *real* after-tax profits and thereby impinged upon the ability to invest. And the overall sluggishness of the economy in the 1970s undoubtedly acted as a depressant upon investment. Businesses are not anx-

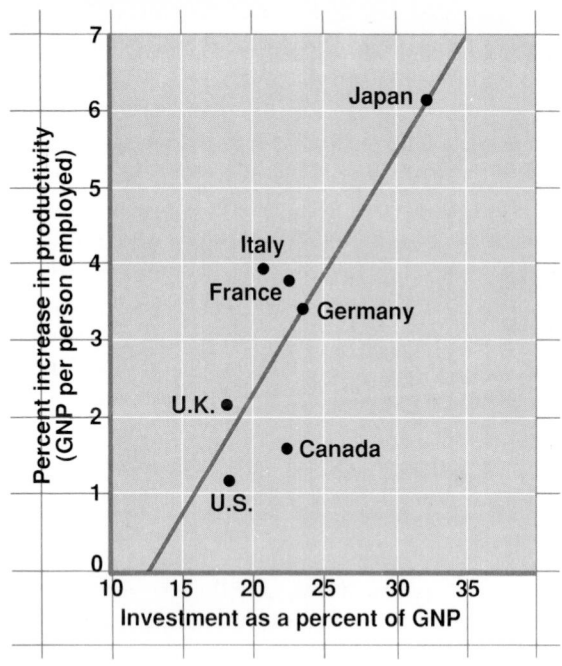

FIGURE 21-4

Investment and the growth of productivity

The larger the proportion of GNP which a nation invests, the greater its rate of productivity growth. [Organization for Economic Co-operation and Development, Historical Statistics 1960–1982 (Paris: OECD, 1984), Tables 1.3, 1.7, 3.7, and 6.8. Data are for 1960–1982.]

ious to add to their capital facilities when existing machinery and equipment are being underutilized.

In addition to the decline in investment spending as a percentage of GNP, the composition of investment spending changed in the late 1960s and 1970s. As noted earlier, the expansion of government regulation of businesses in the areas of pollution control and worker health and safety diverted some investment spending away from output-increasing capital goods and toward capital which may have increased total utility in society, but did not directly increase output itself. In addition, some economists suggest that high marginal tax rates on corporate and personal incomes have reduced after-tax profitability and therefore discouraged the undertaking of new investment projects. Finally, the dramatic increases in the price of energy which occurred in the 1970s may have caused highly productive, capital-intensive techniques to become relatively less attractive. In particular,

high energy prices increased the costs of operating capital equipment. This in effect raised the price of capital relative to the price of labor. Producers were therefore more inclined to use less productive, labor-intensive techniques.

2 Capital per worker   We must also recall that the critical relationship for productivity growth is the amount of capital available per worker-hour. In the late 1960s and in the 1970s the labor force grew unusually fast as post-World War II "baby boom" workers entered the labor force and as women increased their participation rate. Specifically, in the 1948–1966 period the annual increase in worker-hour *input* was 0.4 percent, but between 1966 and 1978 it averaged 1.4 percent. The stock of capital simply did not expand during this period at a sufficient rate to keep the quantity of capital per worker from declining.

3 Labor quality   Aside from its rapid expansion, the average *quality* of the labor force may have diminished in the late 1960s and 1970s. The large number of young baby boom workers who entered the labor force had little experience and training and therefore were less productive. Similarly, the labor force participation of women increased significantly over the 1966–1981 period. Many of these entrants were married women who had little or no prior labor force experience and therefore also had relatively low productivity. Finally, the average level of educational attainment of the labor force has been increasing more slowly in recent years. The median number of years of school completed by the adult population was 12.3 in 1960 and increased to only 12.9 by 1986.

4 Technological progress   Technological advance—usually reflected in improvements in the quality of capital goods and improvements in the efficiency with which inputs are combined—may also have faltered. Technological progress is fueled by expenditures for formal research and development (R & D) programs, and R & D spending in the United States declined as a percentage of GNP between the mid-1960s and the late 1970s. Specifically, R & D outlays rose steadily in the postwar period to a peak of 3 percent of the GNP by the mid-1960s, only to decline to about 1 percent by the late 1970s. This decline was partly the consequence of decreasing Federal support and partly the result of businesses' reaction to the economic instability and uncertainty associated with the 1970s.

5 Industrial relations A very different view of the productivity slowdown stresses that forces of an institutional nature—the way work is organized, the attitudes and behavior of workers and managers, communication between labor and management, and the division of authority among managers and workers—account for much of our poor productivity performance vis-à-vis Japan and western Europe. The argument here is that American industrial relations are characterized by an adversarial relationship between managers and their employees. Feeling alienated from their employers, workers do not participate in the decisions which govern their daily work lives; they do not identify with the objectives of their firms, and they therefore are not motivated to work hard and productively. Managers are judged, rewarded, and motivated by short-term profit performance and thus, it is argued, give little attention to long-term plans and strategies which are critical to the realization of high rates of productivity growth. Japanese industries, by way of contrast, provide lifetime employment security for a sizable portion of their work force, allow for worker participation in decision making, and use bonuses to provide a direct link between the economic success of a firm and worker incomes. Furthermore, the direct interest that workers have in the competitiveness and profitability of their enterprise reduces the need for supervisory personnel. The result of all this is a commonality of interest and cooperation between management and labor, greater flexibility in job assignment, and enhanced willingness of workers to accept technological change. Lifetime employment is also conducive to heavy investment by employers in the training and retraining of their workers. The implication is that an overhaul of our industrial relations system is a key to revitalizing our productivity growth.

A RESURGENCE?

There is some evidence to suggest that the United States may have turned the corner with respect to its productivity slowdown. While Table 21-4's 1.5 percent productivity growth figure for the 1980s is meager in comparison to the immediate postwar decades, it represents a considerable improvement over the 0.7 percent figure of the 1973–1981 era. Although it remains to be seen whether these improved figures reflect only a short-run improvement or a more permanent trend, it is quite evident that many of the factors which depressed productivity growth have dissipated or been reversed. For example, inflation has been brought under control, and therefore its depressing effect upon investment has been reduced. Similarly, business tax rates have been reduced and regulatory controls have been relaxed. Since 1977 research and development spending has been increasing as a percentage of gross national product. In 1987 this figure stood at $3\frac{3}{4}$ percent of GNP. Important innovations involving computerization and robotics may be providing a significant stimulus to productivity. The inexperienced baby boom workers who flooded labor markets in the 1960s and 1970s are now becoming more mature, more productive workers. While American industrial relations remain distinctly different from the cooperative "shared vision" of Japanese managers and workers, the problems imposed by recession and increasing foreign competition are pushing American workers and managers in that direction. "Quality circles" and "employee involvement" plans are increasingly common in American industry. But to repeat: Whether the recent revival of productivity is transitory or permanent is unclear at this point. In any event, the vigorous productivity growth of the postwar period continues to elude us.

Is growth desirable?

So much for the causes of American economic growth and the details of the recent productivity slowdown. We now turn to the task of evaluation. Up to this point we have taken for granted that growth is a desirable state of affairs. In fact, growth is an issue of considerable controversy.

THE CASE AGAINST GROWTH

In recent years serious questions have been raised as to the desirability of continued economic growth for already affluent nations. A number of interrelated arguments comprise this antigrowth sentiment.

1 Pollution Concern with environmental deterioration is an important component of the antigrowth position. The basic point here is that industrialization and growth result in serious problems of pollution, industrial noise and stench, ugly cities, traffic jams, and many other of the disamenities of modern life. These adverse external or spillover costs are held to be the consequence of the hard fact that the production of the GNP changes the form of resources, but does not destroy them. Virtually all inputs in the productive process are eventually returned to the environment in some form of waste. The more rapid our growth and the higher our standard of living, the more waste there is for the environment to absorb—or attempt to absorb. In an already wealthy society, further growth may mean only the satisfaction of increasingly trivial wants at the cost of mounting threats to our ecological system. Antigrowth economists feel that future growth should be purposely constrained.

2 Problem resolution? There is little compelling evidence that economic growth has been a solvent for socioeconomic problems, as its proponents claim. Antigrowth economists assert, for example, that the domestic problem of poverty—income inequality—is essentially a problem of distribution, not production. The requisites for solving the poverty problem are commitment and political courage, not further increases in output. In general, there is no compelling evidence that growth has been, or will be, a palliative for domestic problems.

3 Human obsolescence and insecurity Antigrowth economists contend that rapid growth—and in particular the changing technology which is the core of growth—poses new anxieties and new sources of insecurity for workers. Both high-level and low-level workers face the prospect of having their hard-earned skills and experience rendered obsolete by an onrushing technology.

4 Growth and human values Critics of growth also offer a group of related arguments which say, in effect, that while growth may permit us to "make a living," it does not provide us with "the good life."

We may, in fact, be producing more, but enjoying it less. Must not the loss of aesthetic and instinctual gratification suffered by ordinary working people over two centuries of technological innovation that changed them from artisans and craftsmen into machine-minders and dial-readers be entered on the liability side of the balance sheet of economic growth? More specifically, it is charged that growth means industrialization, uncreative and unsatisfying mass-production jobs, and workers who are alienated in that they have little or no control over the decisions which affect their lives.

IN DEFENSE OF GROWTH

However, many economists defend growth as a high-priority goal, making such arguments as follow.

1 Living standards The primary defense of economic growth is the noted one that it is the basic path to material abundance and rising standards of living (Table 21-1). *Growth makes the unlimited wants—scarce resources dilemma less acute.* More specifically:

In a growing economy public choices are less agonizing and divisive. It is possible to modernize the armed forces; keep the nation's infrastructure in repair; provide for the elderly, the sick, and the needy; improve education and other public services; and still have private incomes that rise after taxes.[5]

2 Growth and the environment Growth proponents feel that the connection between growth, on the one hand, and the environment, on the other, is overdrawn. To a considerable degree these are separable issues. If society should flatly abandon the goal of growth and produce a constant real output every year, it would still have to make choices about the composition of output which would affect the environment and the quality of life. Society would still have to weigh the relative merits of enjoying the natural beauty of a forest or cutting the timber for productive uses. And, if the timber were cut, soci-

---

[5] Alice M. Rivlin (ed.), *Economic Choices of 1984* (Washington: The Brookings Institution, 1984), p. 2.

ety would have to decide whether it would be used for housing or billboards.

Pollution is not so much a by-product of growth as it is a shortcoming of the price system. Specifically, much of the environment—streams, lakes, oceans, and the air—are treated as "common property" and no charge is made for their use. Hence, our environmental resources are overused and debased. Recalling Chapter 6's terminology, environmental pollution is a case of spillover or external costs, and the correction of this problem entails regulatory legislation or the imposition of specific taxes ("effluent charges") to remedy the price system's flaw and eliminate the misuse of the environment. There are, to be sure, serious pollution problems. But limiting growth is the wrong response. "The way to control pollution is to control pollution, not growth."[6]

3 Income inequality Growth is the only practical way of achieving a more equitable distribution of income in our society. "It is inevitably less likely that a middle-class electorate will vote to redistribute part of its own income to the poor than it will be willing to allocate a slightly larger share of a growing total."[7] In fact, the distribution of income in the United States is approximately the same today as it was at the end of World War II (Chapter 37); it follows that the primary means for improving the economic position of the poor is to move the entire distribution of income upward through growth. Similarly, a no-growth policy would virtually eliminate the prospect for the world's poor to improve their economic positions.

4 Nonmaterial considerations Defenders of growth argue that its retardation or cessation will not automatically foster humanistic goals or promote "the good life." Indeed, we should expect the contrary. For example, the ending of growth will not mean the elimination of production-line work; historically, growth has been accompanied by a *decline* in

[6] Marc J. Roberts, "On Reforming Economic Growth," in Mancur Olson and Hans H. Landsberg (eds.), *The No-Growth Society* (New York: W. W. Norton & Company, Inc., 1973), p. 125.

[7] Robert M. Solow, "Is the End of the World at Hand?" *Challenge,* March–April 1973, p. 41.

the fraction of the labor force so employed. Nor has growth uniformly made labor more unpleasant or hazardous. New machinery is usually less taxing and less hazardous than the machinery it replaces. Air-conditioned workplaces are more pleasant than the sweaty factories of old.

Furthermore, why would the retardation or prohibition of growth reduce materialism or alienation? Would we not expect the results to be quite the opposite? The loudest protests against materialism are heard in those nations and from those groups who now enjoy the highest levels of material abundance! More positively, it is the high standards of living which growth provides that make it possible for more people "to take the time for education, reflection, and self-fulfillment."[8]

Growth policies

If one is willing to accept the view that on balance economic growth is a desirable goal, then the question as to what public policies might best stimulate growth naturally arises. In part, we summarize views which were treated in detail in earlier chapters.

1 *Keynesian economists* stress the demand side of growth. They tend to envision slow growth as the consequence of inadequate aggregate demand and the resulting GNP gaps. In particular, they emphasize low interest rates (easy money policy) to stimulate investment spending. If necessary, fiscal policies can be used to constrain government spending and consumption so that a high level of investment will not be inflationary.

2 In contrast, *supply-side economists* emphasize those factors which will increase the potential or capacity output of the economy over time. Their goal is to shift Figure 11-3's aggregate supply curve rightward. In particular, they want to stimulate saving, investment, work effort, and entrepreneurial risk taking, primarily by the use of tax reductions. Thus, for example, by lowering or eliminating the tax on interest *income,* the return on saving will increase and therefore so will the amount of saving. Similarly, by lowering or eliminating the deduction of interest *expenses* on one's personal in-

[8] Roberts, op. cit., p. 133.

come tax, consumption will be discouraged and saving encouraged. Some economists favor the introduction of a national consumption tax as a full or partial replacement for the personal income tax (Chapter 8). The idea is to penalize consumption and thereby encourage saving. On the investment side of the picture, the proposal generally is to reduce or eliminate the corporate income tax or, more specifically, to allow generous tax credits for business investment spending. It is reasonably accurate to say that Keynesians put more emphasis upon the short-run goal of maintaining high levels of real national output by manipulating aggregate expenditures, while supply-siders take a longer-run perspective by stressing those factors which cause the full-employment or capacity output of the economy to increase.

3 There are other potential growth-stimulating policies which economists of various persuasions recommend. For example, some advocate the use of an **industrial policy** whereby government would take a direct, active role in shaping the structure and composition of industry so as to promote growth. Thus government might take steps to hasten the expansion of high-productivity industries and to speed the movement of resources out of low-productivity industries. The details of industrial policy and the controversy surrounding it are discussed in Chapter 34's Last Word. Government might also increase its expenditures on basic research and development to stimulate technological progress. Similarly, increased expenditures on education may help increase the quality and productivity of labor.

While the litany of potential growth-enhancing policies is long and involved, most economists agree that it is no simple matter to increase a nation's growth rate.

CHAPTER SUMMARY

1 Economic growth may be defined either in terms of **a** an expanding real national output (income) or **b** an expanding per capita real output (income). Growth lessens the burden of scarcity and provides increases in the national output which can be used in the resolution of domestic and international socioeconomic problems.

LAST WORD

The infrastructure and productivity

The productivity slowdown of the 1970s and 1980s has never been convincingly explained. David Aschauer, a University of Michigan economist, argues that our productivity slowdown may be attributable largely to inadequate public investment in the economy's infrastructure.

Our national infrastructure refers to the public investments in dams, power installations, highways, harbors, airports, sewers, mass transit systems, and similar facilities, which are conducive to the efficient production and distribution of goods and services. Aschauer calls our attention to several significant relationships between the infrastructure, on the one hand, and private investment and productivity growth, on the other.

First, he suggests that public capital—that is, the infrastructure—and private capital are complementary. In other words, investments in new highways and bridges accelerate the transportation of goods from factories to consumers and modern power plants lower energy costs and therefore the costs of running private manufacturing plants. As evidence

2 The supply factors in economic growth are **a** the quantity and quality of a nation's natural resources, **b** the quantity and quality of its human resources, **c** its stock of capital facilities, and **d** its technology. Two other factors—a sufficient level of aggregate demand and allocative efficiency—are essential if the economy is to realize its growth potential.

of this complementarity, Aschauer shows that high rates of public investment are associated with high rates of private profit. For example, in the 1965–1969 period public investment was 2.3 percent of GNP each year and private profit rates were 13.3 percent. But in 1980–1984 public investment was only 0.4 percent of GNP per year and profit rates were only 7.9 percent.

Second, Aschauer also presents data to show that public investment and productivity growth are closely related. For example, in the 1950–1970 period the public capital stock or infrastructure grew at a 4.1 percent annual rate and productivity growth was 2.0 percent per year. In the 1971–1985 era, however, the yearly increase in the infrastructure fell to only 1.6 percent and the annual productivity increase plummeted to 0.8 percent. Aschauer contends that, of this 1.2 percentage point decline in productivity growth (= 2.0 percent − 0.8 percent) which occurred between these two periods, a full 1 percentage point is explainable by our relative neglect of the infrastructure.

Finally, international comparisons are considered to bolster the argument. The accompanying figure shows the relationship between productivity growth and public investment as a percentage of national output for seven industrially advanced nations. The picture is quite clear: Those nations such as Japan, which devote a large proportion of their GNP to infrastructure investment, enjoy high rates of productivity growth. Those who spend relatively little on their infrastructure, such as the United States, realize low rates of productivity growth.

The policy implications of these arguments are almost self-evident. While others have attributed

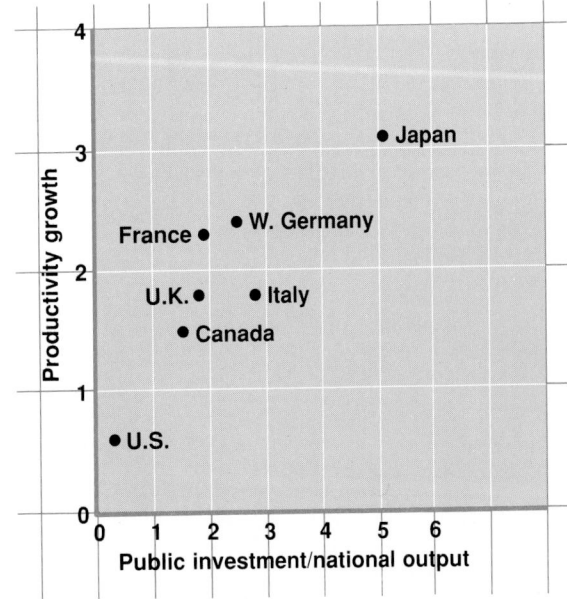

our productivity slowdown to such factors as high energy prices, insufficient research and development spending, and the adverse effects of high marginal tax rates on incentives to work and invest, Aschauer contends that we can stimulate our productivity growth simply by reversing the deterioration of the nation's infrastructure. "By reorienting our public spending to upgrade and expand the public capital stock, we can heighten the productivity of our workforce and improve the competitive position of the United States in the increasingly open international marketplace."

Source: Based on David Alan Aschauer, "Is the Public Capital Stock Too Low?" *Chicago Fed Letter,* October 1987; and "Rx for Productivity: Build Infrastructure," *Chicago Fed Letter,* September 1988.

---

3 The post-World War II growth rate of real GNP for the United States has been over 3 percent; real GNP per capita has grown at about 2 percent.

4 The real GNP of the United States has grown, partly because of increased inputs of labor, and primarily because of increases in the productivity of labor. Technological progress, increases in the quantity of capital per worker, improvements in the quality of labor, economies of scale, and the improved allocation of labor are among the more important factors which increase labor productivity.

5 The rate of productivity growth declined sharply in the 1970s, causing a slowdown in the rise of our living standards and contributing to inflation. Although productivity has risen in the 1980s, it remains substantially below the levels realized in the two decades following World War II.

6 Critics of economic growth *a* cite adverse environmental effects; *b* argue that domestic and international problems are essentially matters of distribution, not production; *c* contend that growth is a major source of human obsolescence and insecurity; and *d* argue that growth is frequently in conflict with certain human values.

7 Proponents of growth stress that *a* growth means a better solution to the wants-means dilemma; *b* environmental problems are only loosely linked to growth; *c* growth is the only feasible means by which greater income equality can be realized; and *d* growth is more consistent with "the good life" than is stagnation.

TERMS AND CONCEPTS

economic growth

supply, demand, and allocative factors in growth

labor productivity

infrastructure

industrial policy

QUESTIONS AND STUDY SUGGESTIONS

1 Why is economic growth important? Explain why the difference between a 2.5 percent and a 3.0 percent annual growth rate might be of great importance.

2 What are the major causes of economic growth? "There are both a demand and a supply side to economic growth." Explain. Illustrate the operation of both sets of factors in terms of the production possibilities curve. Relate Figure 21-4 to the production possibilities curve.

3 Suppose an economy's real GNP is $30,000 in year 1 and $31,200 in year 2. What is the growth rate of its GNP? Assume that population was 100 in year 1 and 102 in year 2. What is the growth rate of GNP per capita? Between 1948 and 1988 the nation's price level has risen by over 400 percent while its real output has increased by almost 250 percent. Use the aggregate demand–aggregate supply model to show these outcomes graphically.

4 Briefly describe the growth record of the United States. Compare the rates of growth in real GNP and real GNP per capita, explaining any differences. To what extent might these figures understate or overstate economic well-being?

5 To what extent have increases in our real GNP been the result of more labor inputs? Of increasing labor productivity? Discuss the factors which contribute to productivity growth in order of their quantitative importance.

6 Using examples, explain how changes in the allocation of labor can affect labor productivity.

7 How do you explain the close correlation which exists between changes in the rate of productivity growth and changes in real wage rates (see Figure 30-1)? Discuss the relationship between productivity growth and inflation.

8 Account for the recent slowdown in the United States' rate of productivity growth. What are the consequences of this slowdown? "Most of the factors which contributed to poor productivity growth in the 1970s are now behind us and are unlikely to recur in the near future." Do you agree?

9 In Chapter 19 we saw that the Reagan administration's economic program involved *a* restraining the growth of government by cutting social and welfare programs; *b* less governmental regulation of business; *c* reductions in corporate and personal income taxes; and *d* a tight money policy to control inflation. Assess the potential impact of each policy upon long-run economic growth.

10 "If we want economic growth in a free society, we may have to accept a measure of instability." Evaluate. The noted philosopher Alfred North Whitehead once remarked that "the art of progress is to preserve order amid change and to preserve change amid order." What did he mean? Is this contention relevant for economic growth? What implications might this have for public policy? Explain.

11 Comment on the following statements:
   a "Technological advance is destined to play a more important role in economic growth in the future than it has in the past."
   b "Income inequality is a matter of redistribution, not of further growth."
   c "The issues of economic growth and environmental pollution are separable and distinct."

12 What specific policies would you recommend to increase the productivity of American workers?

PART 5

The Economics of the Firm and Resource Allocation

CHAPTER 22

Demand, supply, and elasticity

Scarce resources and unlimited wants, you will recall, are the foundation of economic science. The efficient management of scarce resources is a major goal of our economic system. Furthermore, there are two major facets to the problem of achieving efficient resource use. The first, which we have examined in Parts 2, 3, and 4 of this book, centers upon the full employment of available resources. The second aspect of the economizing problem—the one to which we now turn—has to do with allocating employed resources among alternative uses in the most efficient manner. Stated differently, Parts 2, 3, and 4 focused upon the first of the Five Fundamental Questions posed in Chapter 5: "Can the economy achieve the full employment of its available resources?" Part 5 deals with the remaining four questions: "Can the economy produce that output most desired by society?" "Will the production of that output be organized in the most efficient manner?" "Can the economy satisfactorily distribute that output?" "Is the economy capable of maintaining efficiency in the use of its resources in the face of changes in the relative supplies of resources, changes in consumer tastes, and changes in technology?" All four of these questions have an important bearing on the problem of achieving and maintaining an efficient allocation of available resources.

We are well aware that one of the major characteristics of capitalistic economies is their heavy reliance upon the market system as a means for allocating resources (Chapter 5). Our major topics of discussion, then, are individual prices and the market system. Specifically, our basic goal in this and ensuing chapters is to acquire a comprehensive understanding of the operation and relative efficiency of the *market* or *price system* in allocating resources within the framework of American capitalism. As a means to achieving this primary goal, we also seek a thorough analysis of *individual* prices under a variety of contrasting market arrangements.

In Chapter 4 we familiarized ourselves with the rudiments of demand and supply analysis. In the present chapter we seek a more sophisticated understanding of demand and supply. Specifically, the tasks of this chapter are threefold. First, a brief summary of the elements of demand and supply analysis is presented. Second, we shall consider the concept of elasticity as applied to both demand and supply. Third, as an application of supply and demand analysis we will examine the potential effects of legally fixed prices upon individual markets.

Demand, supply, and market price[1]

Demand and supply both refer to schedules. The demand schedule shows the relationship between various possible prices of a product and the quantities which consumers will purchase at each of these prices (Table 22-1, columns 1 and 2). The price–quantity-demand relationship thus portrayed is an inverse or negative one. Consumers typically buy less at a high price than at a low price. This commonsense relationship is called the *law of demand.* Graphically the demand curve is downsloping (*DD* in Figure 22-1).

The supply schedule embodies the relationship

[1] This review is not a substitute for Chapter 4. The student is strongly urged to reread Chapter 4 at this point.

TABLE 22-1 **The demand for, and supply of, corn** *(hypothetical data)*

(1) Total quantity demanded per week	(2) Price per bushel	(3) Total quantity supplied per week	(4) Surplus (+) or shortage (−) (arrow indicates effect on price)
2,000	$5	12,000	+10,000 ↓
4,000	4	10,000	+ 6,000 ↓
7,000	3	7,000	0
11,000	2	4,000	− 7,000 ↑
16,000	1	1,000	−15,000 ↑

between possible product prices and the quantities which producers will supply at each of those prices (Table 22-1, columns 2 and 3). The relationship between price and quantity supplied is a direct or positive one. The *law of supply* states that producers will find it profitable to devote more resources to the production of a good when its price is high than they will when it is low. When graphed, this direct relationship results in an upsloping supply curve (*SS* in Figure 22-1).

The intersection of demand and supply determines the market, or equilibrium, price and quantity. Both Table 22-1 and Figure 22-1 show that the demand and supply data assumed here result in an equilibrium price of $3 and an equilibrium quantity of 7000 units. Competition causes any other price to be unstable. The excess demand or shortages which accompany *below*-equilibrium prices will prompt competing buyers to bid up the price, as consumers want to avoid doing without the product. A rising price will (1) induce firms to allocate more resources to the production of this good, and (2) ration some consumers out of the market. These adjustments are illustrated in Figure 22-1 by the arrows pointing up the supply curve and up the demand curve. The excess supply or surpluses which result at any *above*-equilibrium price will induce competing sellers to cut their prices to work off these excess stocks. The falling price will (1) prompt firms to allocate fewer resources to this line of production, and (2) ration some additional buyers into the market. These adjustments are shown by the arrows pointing down the supply and demand curves in Figure 22-1.

Changes in the determinants of either demand or supply can cause the demand and supply schedules (curves) to shift. Variations in consumer tastes, incomes, the prices of related goods, consumer expectations, and the number of buyers in the market all will account for shifts in demand. Changes in any of those factors which affect production costs—for example, resource prices, technology, or changes in taxes and subsidies—will cause supply to shift.

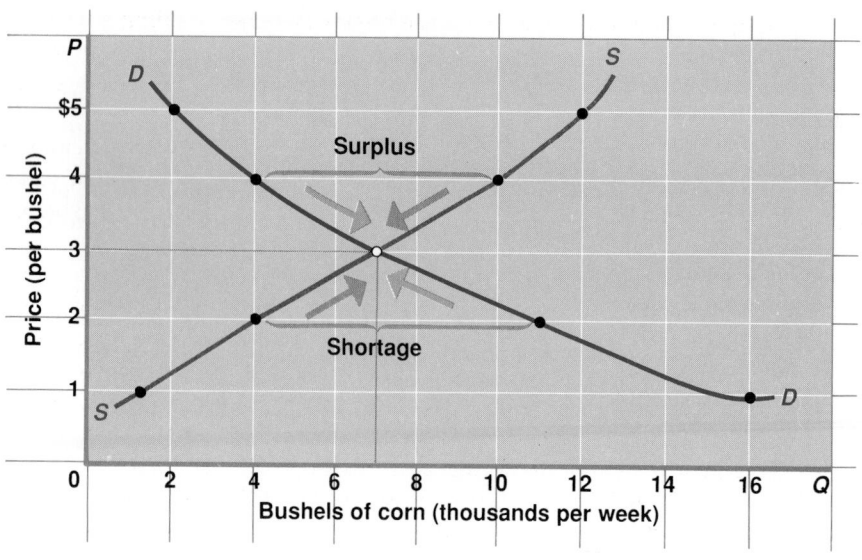

FIGURE 22-1

The equilibrium price for corn as determined by market demand and market supply

Equilibrium price and equilibrium quantity are determined by the intersection of demand *DD* and supply *SS*.

The relationship between a change in demand and the resulting changes in equilibrium price and quantity is a direct one. An inverse relationship exists between a change in supply and the ensuing change in price. However, the relationship between a change in supply and the ensuing change in quantity is direct.

Price elasticity of demand

The law of demand tells us that consumers will respond to a price decline by buying more of a product. But the degree of responsiveness of consumers to a price change may vary considerably from product to product. Furthermore, we will find that consumer responsiveness typically varies substantially between different price ranges for the same product.

Economists measure how responsive, or sensitive, consumers are to a change in the price of a product by the concept of *price elasticity*. The demand for some products is such that consumers are relatively responsive to price changes; modest price changes give rise to very considerable changes in the quantity purchased. The demand for such products is said to be *relatively elastic* or simply *elastic*. For other products, consumers are relatively unresponsive to price changes; that is, substantial price changes result only in modest changes in the amount purchased. In such cases demand is *relatively inelastic* or simply *inelastic*.

THE PRICE ELASTICITY FORMULA

Economists measure the degree of elasticity or inelasticity by the *coefficient E_d* in this **price elasticity formula**:

$$E_d = \frac{\text{percentage change in quantity demanded}}{\text{percentage change in price}}$$

One calculates these *percentage* changes by dividing the change in price by the original price and the consequent change in quantity demanded by the original quantity demanded. Thus, our formula restated:

$$E_d = \frac{\substack{\text{change in quantity} \\ \text{demanded}}}{\substack{\text{original quantity} \\ \text{demanded}}} \div \frac{\text{change in price}}{\text{original price}}$$

Use of percentages But why use percentages rather than absolute amounts in measuring consumer responsiveness? The answer is that if we use absolute changes, our impression of buyer responsiveness will be arbitrarily affected by the choice of units. To illustrate: If the price of product X falls from \$3 to \$2 and consumers, as a result, increase their purchases from 60 to 100 pounds, we get the impression that consumers are quite sensitive to price changes and therefore that demand is elastic. After all, a price change of "one" has caused a change in the amount demanded of "forty." But by changing the monetary unit from dollars to pennies (why not?), we find a price change of "one hundred" causes a quantity change of "forty," giving the impression of inelasticity. The use of percentage changes avoids this problem. The given price decline is 33 percent whether measured in terms of dollars (\$1/\$3) or in terms of pennies (100¢/300¢).

Ignore minus sign We know from the downsloping demand curve that price and quantity demanded are inversely related. This means that the price elasticity coefficient of demand will always yield a *negative* number. For example, if price declines, then quantity demanded will increase. This means that the numerator in our formula will be positive and the denominator negative, yielding a negative coefficient. Conversely, for an increase in price, the numerator will be negative but the denominator positive, again yielding a negative coefficient.

It is conventional for economists to ignore the minus sign and to simply present the *absolute value* of the elasticity coefficient. This is done to avoid an ambiguity which might otherwise arise. It can be confusing to say that an elasticity coefficient of −4 is greater than one of −2; this possible confusion can be avoided if we simply say a coefficient of 4 indicates greater elasticity than one of 2. Hence, in all that follows we ignore the minus sign in the coefficient of price elasticity of demand and merely show the absolute value. Incidentally, the noted ambiguity does not arise with supply because price and quantity are positively related.

Interpretations   Now let us interpret our formula. Demand is **elastic** if a given percentage change in price results in a *larger* percentage change in quantity demanded. Example: If a 2 percent decline in price results in a 4 percent increase in quantity demanded, demand is elastic. In all such cases, where demand is elastic, the elasticity coefficient will obviously be greater than 1; in this case it will be 2. If a given percentage change in price is accompanied by a relatively smaller change in the quantity demanded, demand is **inelastic.** Illustration: If a 3 percent decline in price gives rise to only a 1 percent increase in the amount demanded, demand is inelastic. Specifically, the elasticity coefficient is .33 in this instance. It is apparent that the elasticity coefficient will always be less than 1 when demand is inelastic. The borderline case which separates elastic and inelastic demands occurs where a percentage change in price and the accompanying percentage change in quantity demanded happen to be equal. For example, a 1 percent drop in price causes a 1 percent increase in the amount sold. This special case is termed *unit elasticity,* because the elasticity coefficient is exactly 1, or unity.

It must be emphasized that when economists say demand is "inelastic," they do not mean consumers are completely unresponsive to a price change. The term **perfectly inelastic** demand designates the extreme situation wherein a change in price results in no change whatsoever in the quantity demanded. Approximate examples: an acute diabetic's demand for insulin or an addict's demand for heroin. A demand curve parallel to the vertical axis—such as D_1 in Figure 22-2—shows this situation graphically. Conversely, when economists say demand is "elastic," they do not mean that consumers are completely responsive to a price change. In the extreme situation, wherein there is some small price reduction which would cause buyers to increase their purchases from zero to all they could obtain, we say that demand is **perfectly elastic.** A perfectly elastic demand curve is a line parallel to the horizontal axis; D_2 in Figure 22-2 is illustrative. We shall find later in Chapter 25 that such a demand curve applies to a firm which is selling in a purely competitive market.

REFINEMENT: MIDPOINTS FORMULA

An annoying problem arises in applying the price elasticity formula. To illustrate: In calculating the elasticity coefficient for corn for the $5–$4 price range in Table 22-2, should we use the $5–2000-bushel price–quantity combination or the $4–4000-bushel combination as a point of reference in calculating the percentage changes in price and quantity which the elasticity formula requires? Our choice will influence the outcome. Using the $5–2000-bushel reference point, we find that the percentage decrease in price is 20 percent and the percentage increase in quantity is 100 percent. Substituting in the formula, the elasticity coefficient is 100/20, or 5. But, using the $4–4000-bushel reference point, we find that the percentage increase in price is 25 percent and the percentage decline in quantity is 50 percent. The elasticity coefficient is therefore 50/25, or 2, in this case. Although the formula indicates that demand is elastic in both cases, the two solutions involve a considerable difference in the degree of elasticity. In other instances—experiment, for example, with the $3–$2 price range—the formula may indicate a slightly elastic demand for one price–quantity combination and slight inelasticity of demand for the other.

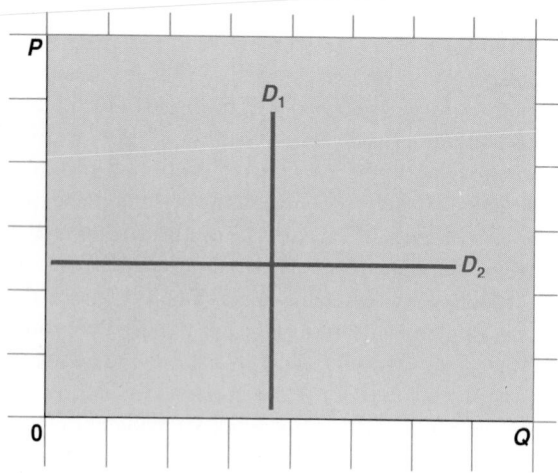

FIGURE 22-2

Perfectly inelastic and elastic demand

A perfectly inelastic demand curve, D_1, graphs as a line parallel to the vertical axis; a perfectly elastic demand curve, D_2, is drawn parallel to the horizontal axis.

TABLE 22-2 **Price elasticity of demand as measured by the total-revenue test and the elasticity coefficient (hypothetical data)**

(1) Total quantity demanded per week	(2) Price per bushel	(3) Total revenue (expenditures)	(4) Total-revenue test	(5) Elasticity coefficient, E_d (approximate)
2,000	$5	$10,000		
			Elastic	$\dfrac{2,000}{6,000/2} \div \dfrac{1}{9/2} = 3.00$
4,000	4	16,000		
			Elastic	$\dfrac{3,000}{11,000/2} \div \dfrac{1}{7/2} = 1.91$
7,000	3	21,000		
			Elastic	$\dfrac{4,000}{18,000/2} \div \dfrac{1}{5/2} = 1.11$
11,000	2	22,000		
			Inelastic	$\dfrac{5,000}{27,000/2} \div \dfrac{1}{3/2} = 0.56$
16,000	1	16,000		

Economists have reached a workable compromise to this problem by using the *averages* of the two prices and the two quantities under consideration for reference points. In the $5–$4 price-range case, the price reference is $4.50 and the quantity reference 3000 bushels. The percentage change in price is now about 22 percent and the percentage change in quantity about 67 percent, giving us an elasticity coefficient of 3. Instead of gauging elasticity at either one of the extremes of this price–quantity range, this solution estimates elasticity at the midpoint of the $5–$4 price range. More positively stated, we can refine our earlier statement of the elasticity formula to read:

$$E_d = \frac{\text{change in quantity}}{\text{sum of quantities}/2} \div \frac{\text{change in price}}{\text{sum of prices}/2}$$

Substituting data for the $5–$4 price range, we get

$$E_d = \frac{2000}{6000/2} \div \frac{1}{9/2} = 3.00$$

In column 5 of Table 22-2 we have calculated the elasticity coefficients for the demand data of Table 22-1, using the midpoints formula. It is a worthwhile exercise to verify each of the calculations in Table 22-2. Furthermore, be certain you are able to interpret the coefficients correctly. For example, the 3.00 coefficient means that a 1 percent change in price will change the quantity demanded by 3 percent.

THE TOTAL-REVENUE TEST

Perhaps the easiest way to gauge whether demand is elastic or inelastic is to note what happens to total revenue or receipts—total expenditures from the buyer's viewpoint—when the price of a product changes.

I Elastic demand If demand is *elastic,* a *decrease* in price will result in an *increase* in total revenue. Why? Because even though a lesser price is being received per unit, enough additional units are now being sold to more than make up for the lower price. This is illustrated in Figure 22-3a for the $5–$4 price range of our demand curve from Table 22-1. (Ignore Figure 22-3b for the moment.) Total revenue, of course, is price times quantity. Hence, the area shown by the rectangle OP_1AQ_1 is total revenue ($10,000) when price is P_1 ($5) and quantity demanded is Q_1 (2000 bushels). Now when price declines to P_2 ($4), causing the quantity demanded to increase to Q_2 (4000 bushels), total revenue changes to OP_2BQ_2 ($16,000), which is obvi-

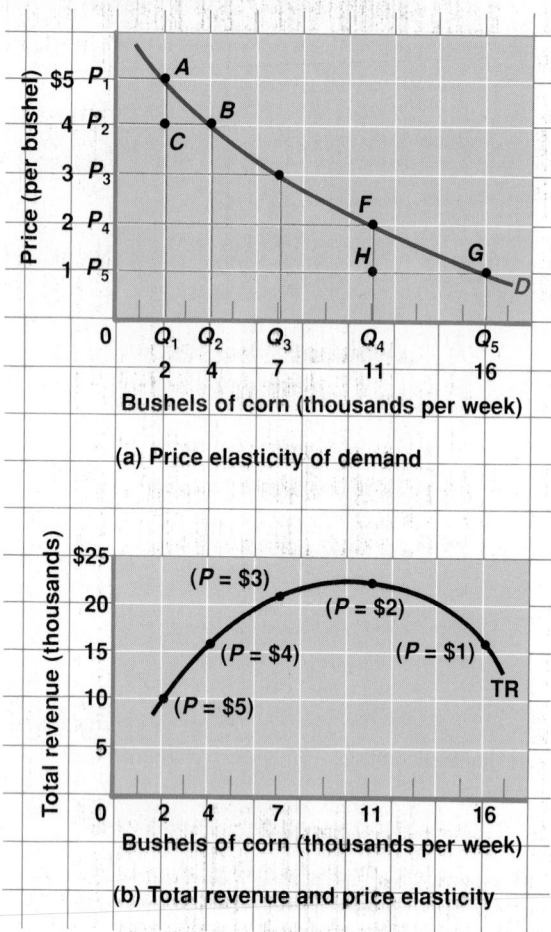

(a) Price elasticity of demand

(b) Total revenue and price elasticity

FIGURE 22-3

Elasticity and total revenue

If demand is elastic, as in the $5–$4 price range of (a), a change in price will cause total revenue to change in the opposite direction. Conversely, if demand is inelastic, as in the $2–$1 price range of (a), price and total revenue will move in the same direction. In (b) a total revenue curve is plotted to confirm that, when prices and total revenue change in opposite directions, demand is elastic. Conversely, when prices and total revenue change in the same direction, demand is inelastic.

ously larger than OP_1AQ_1. It is larger because the *loss* in revenue due to the lower price per unit (area P_2P_1AC) is *less* than the *gain* in revenue due to the larger sales (area Q_1CBQ_2) which accompanies the lower price. Specifically, the $1 price reduction applies to the original 2000 bushels (Q_1) for a loss

of $2000. But the lower price increases sales by 2000 bushels (Q_1 to Q_2) with a resulting gain in revenue of $8000 (= 2000 × $4). Hence, the *net increase* in total revenue is $6000 (= $8000 − $2000). This reasoning is reversible: If demand is elastic, a price *increase* will cause total revenue to *decrease*. Why? Because the *gain* in total revenue caused by the higher unit price (area P_2P_1AC) is *less* than the *loss* in revenue associated with the accompanying fall in sales (Q_1CBQ_2). Generalization: *If demand is elastic, a change in price will cause total revenue to change in the opposite direction.*

2 Inelastic demand   If demand is *inelastic*, a price *decrease* will cause total revenue to *decrease*. The modest increase in sales which occurs will be insufficient to offset the decline in revenue per unit, and the net result is that total revenue declines. This situation exists for the $2–$1 price range of our demand curve, as shown in Figure 22-3a. Initially, total revenue is OP_4FQ_4 ($22,000) when price is P_4 ($2) and quantity demanded is Q_4 (11,000 bushels). If we reduce price to P_5 ($1), quantity demanded will increase to Q_5 (16,000 bushels). Total revenue will change to OP_5GQ_5 ($16,000), which is clearly less than OP_4FQ_4. It is smaller because the loss in revenue due to the lower unit price (area P_5P_4FH) *is larger* than the *gain* in revenue due to the accompanying increase in sales (area Q_4HGQ_5). More specifically, the $1 decline in price applies to 11,000 bushels (Q_4) with a consequent revenue loss of $11,000. The increase in sales which accompanies this lower price is 5000 bushels (Q_4 to Q_5) which results in a revenue gain of $5000 (= 5000 × $1). The overall result is a *net decrease* in total revenue of $6000 (= $5000 − $11,000). Again, our analysis is reversible: If demand is inelastic, a price increase will increase total revenue. Generalization: *If demand is inelastic, a change in price will cause total revenue to change in the same direction.*

3 Unit elasticity   In the special case of *unit elasticity,* an increase or decrease in price will leave total revenue unchanged. The loss in revenue due to a lower unit price will be exactly offset by the gain in revenue brought about by the accompanying increase in sales. Conversely, the gain in revenue due to a higher unit price will be exactly offset by the loss in revenue associated with the accompanying decline in the amount demanded.

Columns 3 and 4 of Table 22-2 apply the **total-revenue test** to the entire demand curve for corn. Figure 22-3b confirms our findings. Here we have graphed the five total revenue–quantity demanded points from columns 1 and 3 of Table 22-2 and drawn a curve to generalize on this relationship. The height of the total revenue curve measures the rectangular area under the demand curve in Figure 22-3a at each price–quantity combination. We observe that in the $5–$4 price range total revenue does indeed increase as price is reduced. Similarly, we find that total revenue also increases for the $4–$3 and the $3–$2 price declines. Note in column 5 of Table 22-2 that our elasticity coefficients indicate demand is in fact elastic for all of these price ranges. For the $2–$1 price range we note in Figure 22-3b that total revenue declines. This indicates an inelastic demand which column 5 of Table 22-2 confirms to be the case. Over the range of price reductions in which total revenue increases, demand is elastic; over the range in which price reductions are associated with a decline in total revenue, demand is inelastic.[2] Question 11 at the end of the chapter is highly recommended at this point.

Reprise Table 22-3 provides a convenient summary of the characteristics of price elasticity of demand and merits careful study.

CHARACTERISTICS

The alert reader may have detected two subtle but notable characteristics of elasticity from our applications of the elasticity formula and the total-revenue test.

Elasticity and price range First, elasticity typically varies over the different price ranges of the same

[2]To keep our discussion relatively uncluttered we have rather severely limited the number of price–quantity demanded combinations in our demand curve. There is some unspecified price–quantity demanded combinations slightly above $2 and slightly less than 11,000 bushels of corn at which a small change in price would leave total revenue unchanged, indicating unit elasticity of demand.

demand schedule or curve. For all straight-line and most other demand curves—including our illustrative demand for corn in Table 22-2—demand tends to be more elastic in the upper left portion than in the lower right portion. This is essentially a consequence of the arithmetic properties of the elasticity measure. Specifically, in the upper left portion the percentage change in quantity tends to be large because the original quantity from which the percentage quantity change is derived is small. Similarly, in this portion the percentage change in price tends to be small because the original price from which the percentage price change is calculated is large. The relatively large percentage change in quantity divided by the relatively small change in price yields an elastic demand. The reverse holds true for the lower right portion of the demand curve. Here the percentage change in quantity tends to be small because the original quantity from which the percentage change is determined is large. Similarly, the percentage change in price tends to be large because the original price from which the relative price change is calculated is small. The small percentage change in quantity divided by the relatively large percentage change in price results in an inelastic demand.

Elasticity versus slope The second characteristic of price elasticity of demand is that the graphic appearance, that is, the slope, of a demand curve is *not* a sound basis upon which to judge its elasticity. For example, in Figure 22-3a we find that because the demand curve has a steeper slope at relatively higher prices and a flatter slope at relatively lower prices, one is tempted to associate an inelastic demand with high prices and an elastic demand with low prices. But this is faulty reasoning. Have we not just discovered that the elasticity formula and the total-revenue test indicate that the reverse is true? The catch lies in the fact that the slope—the flatness or steepness—of a demand curve is based upon *absolute* changes in price and quantity, while elasticity has to do with *relative* or *percentage* changes in price and quantity. The difference between slope and elasticity can also be made quite clear by calculating elasticity for various price–quantity combinations on a straight-line demand curve. You will find that, although the slope is by definition constant throughout, demand is elastic in the high-price range and inelastic in the low-

TABLE 22-3 **Price elasticity of demand: a summary**

Absolute value of elasticity coefficient	Terminology	Description	Impact on total revenue (expenditures) of a price:	
			Increase	Decrease
Greater than 1 $(E_d > 1)$	"Elastic" or "relatively elastic"	Quantity demanded changes by a larger percentage than does price	Total revenue decreases	Total revenue increases
Equal to 1 $(E_d = 1)$	"Unit" or "unitary elastic"	Quantity demanded changes by the same percentage as does price	Total revenue is unchanged	Total revenue is unchanged
Less than 1 $(E_d < 1)$	"Inelastic" or "relatively inelastic"	Quantity demanded changes by a smaller percentage than does price	Total revenue increases	Total revenue decreases

price range. Question 11 at the end of this chapter is again relevant.

DETERMINANTS OF PRICE ELASTICITY OF DEMAND

There are no ironclad, exceptionless generalizations concerning the determinants of the elasticity of demand. The following points, however, are usually accepted as valid and helpful.

1 Substitutability Generally speaking, the larger the number of good substitute products available, the greater the elasticity of demand. We shall find in Chapter 25 that in a purely competitive market, where by definition there is an extremely large number of perfect substitutes for the product of any given seller, the demand curve to that single seller will be perfectly elastic (Figure 25-1). If one competitive seller of wheat or corn raises its price, buyers will turn to the readily available perfect substitutes of its many rivals. At the other extreme, we have already noted that the diabetic's demand for insulin is undoubtedly highly inelastic. It is worth noting that the elasticity of demand for a product depends upon how narrowly the product is defined.

The demand for Texaco motor oil is more elastic than is the overall demand for motor oil. A number of other brands are readily substitutable for Texaco's oil, but there is no good substitute for motor oil per se.

2 Proportion of income Other things being equal, the larger a good bulks in one's budget, the greater will tend to be the elasticity of demand for it. A 10 percent increase in the price of pencils or chewing gum will amount to only a few pennies and elicit little response in terms of amount demanded. A 10 percent increase in the price of automobiles or housing means price increases of, say, $1500 and $15,000 respectively. These latter increases are significant fractions of the annual incomes of many families, and quantities purchased could be expected to diminish significantly.

3 Luxuries versus necessities The demand for "necessities" tends to be inelastic; the demand for "luxuries" tends to be elastic. Bread and electricity are generally regarded as necessities; we "can't get along" without them. A price increase will not reduce significantly the amount of bread consumed or the amounts of lighting and power used in a household. Note the very low price elasticities of these goods in Table 22-4. A more extreme case: One does not decline an operation for acute appendicitis because the physician's fee has just gone up! On the other hand, French cognac and emeralds are luxuries which, by definition, can be forgone without undue inconvenience. If the price of cognac or emeralds rises, one need not purchase and, in so deciding, one will encounter no great hardship. The demand for salt tends to be highly inelastic on several counts. It is a "necessity"; unsalted cooking leaves much to be desired. There are few good substitutes available. Finally, salt is a negligible item in the family budget.

4 Time Generally speaking, the demand for a product tends to be more elastic the longer the time period under consideration. One aspect of this generalization has to do with the fact that many consumers are creatures of habit. When the price of a product rises, it takes time to seek out and experiment with other products to see if they are acceptable to us. Consumers may not immediately reduce their purchases to any significant degree when the price of beef rises by, say, 10 percent. But, given time, they may shift their affections to chicken or fish for which they have now "developed a taste." Another facet of this generalization has to do with product durability. Studies show that the "short-run" demand for gasoline is more inelastic at 0.2 than is the "long-run" demand at 0.7. Why so? Because in the long run, large, gas-guzzling automobiles wear out and, in a context of rising gasoline prices, are replaced by smaller, higher-mileage cars.

A recent empirical study of commuter rail transportation in the Philadelphia area estimates that the "long-run" elasticity of demand is almost three times as great as the "short-run" elasticity. Specifically, short-run commuter responses (defined as those which occur immediately at the time of a fare change) are inelastic at 0.68. In contrast, the long-run response (defined as those which occur over a four-year period) is elastic at 1.84. The greater long-run elasticity is attributable to the fact that over time potential rail commuters are able to make choices concerning automobile purchases and the locations of residences and employment. In any event, these different elasticities led to the prediction that the commuter system, which has about 100,000 riders, could immediately *increase* daily revenues by $8000 by increasing the price of a one-way ticket by $.25 or about 9 percent. Why? Because short-run demand is inelastic. But in the long-run the same 9 percent fare increase is estimated to *reduce* total revenue per day by over $19,000 because demand is elastic. The implication is that a fare increase which is profitable in the short run may lead to financial difficulties in the long run.[3]

Table 22-4 shows estimated price elasticities of demand for a variety of products. It is recommended that you use the elasticity determinants just discussed to explain or rationalize each of these elasticity coefficients.

TABLE 22-4 Selected price elasticities of demand

Product	Price elasticity
Bread	.15
Beef	.64
Lamb and mutton	2.65
Eggs	.32
Restaurant meals	2.27
Electricity (household)	.13
Medical care	.31
Tobacco products	.46
Automobile tires	.86
Newspapers and magazines	.42
Clothing and shoes	.20
Housing	.01
Movies	.87

Sources: H. S. Houthakker and Lester D. Taylor, *Consumer Demand in the United States: Analyses and Projections*, 2d ed. (Cambridge, Mass.: Harvard University Press, 1970); and P. S. George and G. A. King, *Consumer Demand for Food Commodities in the United States with Projections for 1980* (Berkeley: University of California, 1971).

[3] Richard Voith, "Commuter Rail Ridership: The Long and the Short Haul," *Business Review* (Federal Reserve Bank of Philadelphia), November–December 1987, pp. 13–23.

SOME PRACTICAL APPLICATIONS

The concept of price elasticity of demand is a notion of great practical significance, as the following examples will make evident.

1 Wage bargaining The United Automobile Workers once contended that automobile manufacturers should raise wages and simultaneously cut automobile prices. Arguing that the elasticity of demand for automobiles was about 4, the UAW concluded that a price cut would help check inflation, boost the total revenue of manufacturers, and preserve or even increase the profits of producers. A spokesman for the Ford Motor Company, however, claimed that available studies suggest an elasticity of demand for automobiles in the 0.5–1.5 range. He held that price cuts would therefore shrink profits or result in losses for manufacturers. In this case, the elasticity of demand for automobiles was a strategic factor in labor-management relations and wage bargaining.[4]

2 Bumper crops Another example: Studies indicate that the demand for most farm products is highly inelastic, perhaps on the order of 0.20 or 0.25. As a result, increases in the output of farm products due to a good growing season or to productivity increases depress both the prices of farm products and the total revenues (incomes) of farmers. For farmers as a group, the inelastic nature of the demand for their products means that a bumper crop may be undesirable. For policy makers it means that higher total farm income depends upon the restriction of farm output (Chapter 35).

3 Automation The impact of automation, that is, of rapid technological advance, upon the level of employment depends in part upon the elasticity of demand for the product being manufactured. Suppose a firm installs new laborsaving machinery, resulting in the technological unemployment of, say, 500 workers. Suppose too that a part of the cost reduction resulting from this technological advance is passed on to consumers in the form of reduced product prices. Now, the effect of this price reduction upon the firm's sales and therefore the quantity of labor it requires will depend upon the elasticity of product demand. An elastic demand might increase sales to the extent that some of, all, or even more than the 500 displaced workers are reabsorbed by the firm. An inelastic demand will mean that few, if any, of the displaced workers will be reemployed, because the increase in the volume of the firm's sales and output will be small.

4 Airline deregulation The initial effect of deregulating the airlines in the late 1970s was to increase the profits of many carriers. The reason was that deregulation increased competition among the airlines, thereby lowering air fares. Lower fares, coupled with an elastic demand for air travel,[5] increased revenues. Because the additional costs associated with flying full, as opposed to partially empty, aircraft are minimal, revenues increased ahead of costs and profits were enhanced. Unfortunately for the airlines, this profitability was not to last. The reasons were threefold: The competitive scramble for new routes tended to compete profits away; rising fuel prices increased operating costs; and persistent "fare wars" cut into profits.

5 Excise taxes Government pays attention to the elasticity of demand when selecting goods and services upon which to levy excise taxes. Assume a $1 tax is currently levied upon some product and 10,000 units are sold. Tax revenue is $10,000. If the tax is now raised to, say, $1.50, and the consequent higher price causes sales to decline to 5,000 because of an elastic demand, tax revenue will *decline* to $7,500. A higher tax on a product, the demand for which is elastic, will bring in less tax revenue. Hence, it behooves legislatures to seek out products for which demand is inelastic—for example, liquor, gasoline, and cigarettes—when levying excises. A more sophisticated look at the effects of excise taxes will be presented in Chapter 33.

---

[4] See the statement by Theodore Yntema, vice president of finance, Ford Motor Company, before the Subcommittee on Antitrust and Monopoly of the Committee on the Judiciary, United States Senate, Feb. 4–5, 1958.

[5] For a summary of studies on the elasticity of demand for air travel, see George W. Douglas and James C. Miller, III, *Economic Regulation of Domestic Air Transport* (Washington, D.C.: The Brookings Institution, 1974), pp. 34–38.

6 Heroin and street crime The fact that the demand for heroin by addicts is highly inelastic poses some awkward tradeoffs in the area of law enforcement. The approach typically used in attempting to reduce heroin addiction is to restrict supply, that is, to make the drug less readily available by cracking down on its shipment into the United States. But what will happen if this policy is successful? Given the highly inelastic demand, the street price to addicts will rise sharply while the amount purchased will decrease only slightly. From the drug pushers' point of view this means increased revenues and profits. From the addicts' point of view it means greater total expenditures on heroin. Because much of the income which addicts spend on heroin is derived from crime—shoplifting, burglary, prostitution, muggings, and so on—these kinds of crime will increase as addicts increase their total expenditures for heroin. Here, the effort of law-enforcement authorities to control the spread of drug addiction may increase the amount of crime committed by addicts.[6]

7 Minimum wage The Federal minimum wage prohibits employers from paying covered workers less than $3.35 per hour. Critics contend that the imposition of an above-equilibrium minimum wage moves employers back up their downsloping labor demand curves and causes unemployment, particularly among teenage workers. On the other hand, workers who remain employed at the minimum wage will receive higher incomes than otherwise. The amount of income lost by the unemployed and the income gained by those who keep their jobs will clearly depend upon the elasticity of demand for teenage labor. A number of research studies suggest that demand is quite inelastic, possibly as low as 0.15 or 0.25. If these estimates are correct, it means that the income gains associated with the minimum wage exceed the income losses. The case made by critics of the minimum wage would be stronger if the demand for teenage workers was elastic.[7]

These examples could be multiplied, but the main point is clear. Elasticity of demand is vitally important to businesses, farmers, labor, and government policy makers.

ELASTICITY OF SUPPLY

The concept of price elasticity also applies to supply. If producers are responsive to price changes, supply is elastic. If they are relatively insensitive to price changes, supply is inelastic.

The elasticity formula is pertinent in determining the degree of elasticity or inelasticity of supply. The only required alteration is the substitution of "percentage change in quantity *supplied*" for "percentage change in quantity *demanded*."

The main determinant of the **elasticity of supply** is the amount of *time* which a producer has to respond to a given change in product price. Generally speaking, we can expect a greater output response—and therefore greater elasticity of supply—the longer the amount of time a producer has to adjust to a given price change. Why? Because a producer's response to an increase in the price of product X depends upon its ability to shift resources from the production of other products[8] to the production of X. And the shifting of resources takes time: the greater the time, the greater the resource "shiftability." Hence, the greater will be the output response and the elasticity of supply.

In analyzing the impact of time upon the elasticity of supply, economists find it useful to distinguish between the immediate market period, the short run, and the long run.

1 The market period The immediate **market period** is so short a time that producers cannot respond to a change in demand and price. Example: Suppose a small truck farmer brings an entire season's output of tomatoes—one truckload—to market. The supply curve will be perfectly inelastic; the farmer will sell the truckload whether the price is high or low. Why? Because he cannot offer more

---

[6] For an excellent discussion of this point, see Robert Paul Thomas, *Microeconomic Applications: Understanding the American Economy* (Belmont, Calif.: Wadsworth Publishing Company, 1981), chap. 10.

[7] Sar A. Levitan and Richard S. Belous, *More Than Subsistence: Minimum Wages for the Working Poor* (Baltimore: The Johns Hopkins University Press, 1979), p. 16.

[8] The prices of which we assume remain constant.

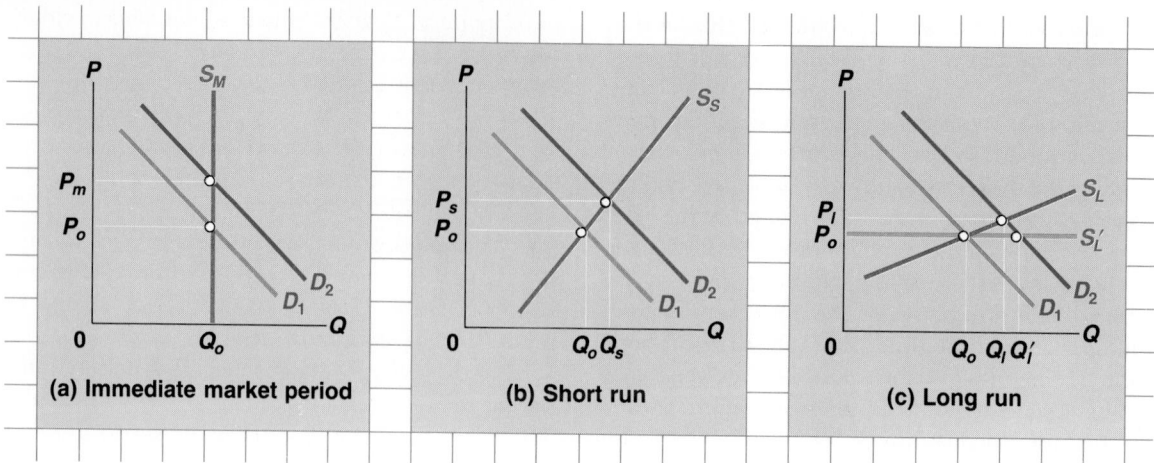

FIGURE 22-4

Time and the elasticity of supply

The greater the amount of time producers have to adjust to a change in demand, the greater will be their output response. In the immediate market period (a) there is insufficient time to change output, and so supply is perfectly inelastic. In the short run (b) plant capacity is fixed, but output can be altered by changing the intensity of its use; supply is therefore more elastic. In the long run (c) all desired adjustments—including changes in plant capacity—can be made, and supply becomes still more elastic.

tomatoes than his one truckload if the price of tomatoes should be higher than he had anticipated. Even though he might like to offer more, tomatoes cannot be produced overnight. It will take another full growing season to respond to a higher-than-expected price by producing more than one truckload. Similarly, because the product is perishable, the farmer cannot withhold it from the market. If the price is lower than he had anticipated, he will still sell the entire truckload. Costs of production, incidentally, will not be important in making this decision. Even though the price of tomatoes may fall far short of production costs, the farmer will nevertheless sell out to avoid a total loss through spoilage. In a very short time, then, our farmer's supply of tomatoes is fixed; only one truckload can be offered no matter how high the price. The perishability of the product forces the farmer to sell all, no matter how low the price.

Figure 22-4a illustrates the truck farmer's perfectly inelastic supply curve in the market period. Note that this and other truck farmers are unable to respond to an assumed increase in demand; they do not have time to increase the amount supplied. The price increase from P_o to P_m simply rations a

fixed supply to buyers, but elicits no increase in output.[9]

2 The short run   In the **short run,** the plant capacity of individual producers and of the industry is presumed to be fixed. But firms do have time to use their plants more or less intensively. Thus, in the short run, our truck farmer's plant, which we shall consider as being comprised of land and farm machinery, is presumed fixed. But he does have time in the short run to cultivate tomatoes more intensively by applying more labor and more fertilizer and pesticides to the crop. The result is a greater output response to the presumed increase in demand; this greater output response is reflected in a more elastic supply of tomatoes, as shown by S_s in Figure 22-4b. Note that the increase in demand is met by a larger quantity adjustment (Q_o to Q_s) and a smaller price adjustment (P_o to P_s) than in the

[9] The supply curve need not be perfectly inelastic (vertical) in the market period. If the product is not perishable, producers may choose, at low current prices, to store some of their product for future sale. This will cause the market supply curve to have some positive slope.

market period; price is therefore lower than in the market period.

3 The long run The **long run** is a time period sufficiently long so that firms can make all desired resource adjustments; individual firms can expand (or contract) their plant capacities, and new firms can enter (or existing firms can leave) the industry. In the "tomato industry" our individual truck farmer is able to acquire additional land and buy more machinery and equipment. Furthermore, more farmers may be attracted to tomato production by the increased demand and higher price. These adjustments mean an even greater supply response, that is, an even more elastic supply curve S_L. The result, shown in Figure 22-4c, is a small price effect (P_o to P_l) and a large output effect (Q_o to Q_l) in response to the assumed increase in demand.

The solid supply curve in Figure 22-4c entails a new long-run equilibrium price P_l which is somewhat higher than the original price, P_o, in Figure 22-4a. Why higher? The presumption is that tomato farming is an **increasing-cost industry,** meaning simply that the industry's expansion causes the prices of relevant resources to rise. The increased demand for fertilizer and farm equipment has pushed their prices up somewhat; the expanded demand for land has increased its market or rental value. In short, it is common and realistic to expect the expansion of an industry to result in "increasing costs." Hence, while P_o was sufficient for profitable production in Figure 22-4a, a higher price, P_l, is required for profitable production in the enlarged industry. If the tomato industry hired very small or negligible portions of relevant resources, then its increased demand for these inputs would leave their prices unchanged. In this **constant-cost industry** case the long-run supply curve would be perfectly elastic, as shown by the dashed curve S_L' in Figure 22-4c. The new price would be equal to the original price, P_o, in Figure 22-4a. We shall discuss these cases more fully in Chapter 25.

You may have noted that no mention has been made of a total-revenue test for elasticity of supply. Indeed, there is none. Supply shows a positive or direct relationship between price and the amount supplied; that is, the supply curve is upsloping. Thus, regardless of the degree of elasticity or ine-

lasticity, price and total receipts will always move together.

One final point: While our discussion has focused upon price elasticity of demand and supply, there are other important elasticity concepts. Cross elasticity of demand (which measures the sensitivity of consumer purchases of one product to a change in the price of some other product) and income elasticity (which gauges the sensitivity of consumer purchases of a product to a change in income) are considered in this chapter's Last Word.

Applications: legal prices

Supply and demand analysis and the elasticity concept will be applied repeatedly in the remainder of this book. Let us strengthen our understanding of these analytical tools and their significance by examining some of the implications of legal prices.

On occasion the general public and government are of the opinion that the forces of supply and demand result in prices that are either unfairly high to buyers or unfairly low to sellers. In such instances government may intervene by legally limiting how high or low the price may go. Let us examine what happens to the functioning of the market when legal price fixing occurs.

PRICE CEILINGS AND SHORTAGES

A **price ceiling** *is the maximum legal price which a seller may charge for a product or service.* The rationale for ceiling prices on specific products is that they purportedly enable consumers to obtain some "essential" good or service which they could not afford at the equilibrium price. Rent controls and usury laws (which specify maximum interest rates which may be charged to borrowers) are examples. On a more general basis ceiling prices or general price controls have been used in attempting to restrain the overall rate of inflation in the economy. Price controls were invoked during World War II and used to a lesser extent during the Korean conflict. Similarly, President Nixon froze prices, wages, and rents in the early 1970s.

World War II price controls   Let us turn back the clock to World War II and analyze the effects of a ceiling price upon, say, butter. The booming wartime prosperity of the early 1940s was shifting the demand for butter to the right so that, as in Figure 22-5, the equilibrium or market price P was, say, $1.20 per pound. On the one hand, the rapidly rising price of butter was contributing to inflation and, on the other, rationing out of the butter market those families whose money incomes were not keeping pace with the soaring cost of living. Hence, to help stop inflation and to keep butter on the tables of the poor, government imposed a ceiling price P_c of, say, $0.90 per pound. Note that to be effective a ceiling price must be **below** the equilibrium price. A ceiling price of, say, $1.50 would have no immediate impact upon the butter market.

What will be the effects of this ceiling price? The rationing ability of the free market will be rendered ineffective. At the ceiling price there will be a persistent shortage of butter. That is, the quantity of butter demanded at P_c is Q_d and the quantity supplied is only Q_s; hence, a persistent excess demand or shortage in the amount Q_sQ_d occurs. The size of this shortage varies directly with the price elasticities of supply and demand. The important

point is that the legal price P_c prevents the usual market adjustment wherein competition among buyers would bid up price, thereby simultaneously inducing more production and rationing some buyers out of the market until the shortage disappears at the equilibrium price and quantity, P and Q.

Now, by preventing this market-clearing adjustment process from occurring, the ceiling price poses problems born of the market disequilibrium. First, how is the available supply Q_s to be apportioned among buyers who want the amount Q_d? Should the supply be distributed on a first-come, first-served basis, that is, to those who are willing and able to stand in line the longest? Or should the grocer distribute butter on the basis of favoritism? The point is that an unregulated shortage is hardly conducive to the equitable distribution of butter. Hence, to avoid catch-as-catch-can distribution, government must establish some formal system of rationing the product to consumers. This was accomplished during World War II by issuing ration coupons to individuals on an equitable basis. An effective rationing system entails the printing of ration coupons equal to Q_s pounds of butter and the equitable distribution of these coupons among consumers so that, for example, the rich family of four and the poor family of four will both get the same number of coupons.

But the use of ration coupons does not prevent a second problem from arising. Specifically, the demand curve in Figure 22-5 tells us there are many buyers who are willing to pay more than the ceiling price. And, of course, it is more profitable for grocers to sell above the ceiling price. Hence, despite the sizable enforcement bureaucracy which accompanied World War II price controls, illegal **black markets**—markets wherein products were bought and sold at prices above the legal limits—flourished for many goods. The counterfeiting of ration coupons was also a problem.

Rent controls   Ceiling prices also entail the larger problem of prohibiting the price movements which are essential to preserve allocative efficiency through time. Example: Rent controls in New York City have contributed to a persistent housing shortage. Although the short-term effect of such controls may be to keep housing within reach of some of the poor, their longer-term impact is to inhibit alleviation of the housing shortage. Given

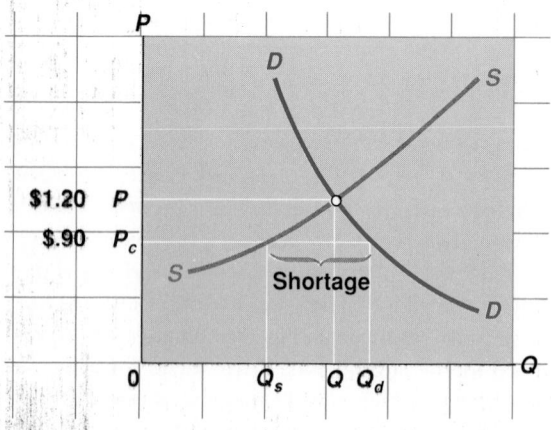

FIGURE 22-5

Price ceilings result in persistent shortages

Because the imposition of a price ceiling such as P_c results in a persistent product shortage, as indicated by the distance Q_sQ_d, government must undertake the job of rationing the product in order to achieve an equitable distribution.

low rents, investors are reluctant to construct new housing and investing in repairs tends to be unprofitable. The point is that rent controls prevent the rent increases needed to signal the profitable allocation of more resources to the construction of new housing and the renovation of old housing in New York City.

Credit card interest ceilings In 1986 several bills were introduced in Congress to impose a nationwide interest rate ceiling on credit card accounts. In fact, several states now have such laws and others have legislation under consideration. The basic rationale for interest rate ceilings is that the banks and retail stores issuing such cards are presumably "gouging" users and, in particular, lower-income users by charging interest rates that average about 18 percent.

What are likely to be the responses to the legal imposition of below-equilibrium interest rates on credit cards? According to a study by the Federal Reserve,[10] profits on bank-issued credit cards have been low, while retail store cards have generally entailed losses for their issuers. Hence, lower interest income associated with a legal interest ceiling would necessitate adjustments by issuers to reduce costs or enhance revenues. What forms might these responses take? First, card issuers might tighten credit standards so as to reduce nonpayment losses and collection costs. In particular, low-income people and young people who have not yet established their creditworthiness would find it more difficult to obtain credit cards. Second, the annual fee charged card holders might be increased as might the fee charged merchants for processing credit card sales. Similarly, card users might be charged a fee for every transaction. Third, card users are now provided with a "grace period" wherein the credit provided is interest-free. It is possible that this period would be shortened or eliminated. Finally, retail stores which issue cards might be expected to increase their merchandise prices to help offset the decline of interest income. This would mean that customers who pay cash would in effect be subsidizing customers who use credit cards. Empirical studies of states which now have ceilings on credit card interest rates have confirmed our first and final predictions.

Rock concerts Below-equilibrium pricing should not be associated solely with government policies. Superstar rock personalities such as Bruce Springsteen or Michael Jackson frequently price their concert tickets below the market-clearing price. Tickets are usually rationed on a first-come, first-served basis and black market "scalping" is commonplace. Why should rock stars want to subsidize their fans—at least those who are fortunate enough to obtain tickets—with below-equilibrium prices? Why not set ticket prices at a higher, market-clearing level and realize more income from a tour? The answer is that the long lines of fans waiting hours or days for the bargain-priced tickets catch the attention of the press, as does an occasional attempt by those who do not get tickets to "crash" a sold-out concert. The millions of dollars worth of free publicity undoubtedly stimulates record sales from which a major portion of any rock group's income is derived. Hence, the "gift" of below-equilibrium ticket prices which a rock star gives to fans is not without associated benefits to the star. The gift also imposes costs upon fans—the opportunity cost of the time spent waiting in line to buy tickets.[11]

PRICE FLOORS AND SURPLUSES

Price floors—*minimum prices fixed by government which are above equilibrium prices*—have generally been invoked when society has felt that the free functioning of the market system has failed to provide a sufficient income for certain groups of resource suppliers or producers. Minimum-wage legislation and the support of agricultural prices are the two most widely discussed examples of government price floors. Let us examine price floors as applied to a specific farm commodity.

Suppose the going market price for corn is $2 per bushel, and as a result of this price, farmers realize extremely low incomes. Government de-

[10] Glenn B. Canner and James T. Fergus, "The Economic Effects of Proposed Ceilings on Credit Card Interest Rates," *Federal Reserve Bulletin,* January 1987, pp. 1–13.

[11] For details, consult Thomas, op. cit., chap. 6.

cides to lend a helping hand by establishing a legal floor price of, say, $3 per bushel.

What will be the effects? At any price above the equilibrium price, quantity supplied will exceed quantity demanded; that is, there will be a persistent excess supply or surplus of the product. Farmers will be willing to produce and offer for sale more than private buyers are willing to purchase at the price floor. The size of this surplus will vary directly with the elasticity of demand and supply. The greater the elasticity of demand and supply, the greater the resulting surplus. As is the case with a ceiling price, the rationing ability of the free market has been disrupted by the imposition of a legal price.

Figure 22-6 provides us with a graphic illustration of the effect of a price floor. Let SS and DD be the supply and demand curves for, say, corn. Equilibrium price and quantity are obviously P and Q, respectively. If government imposes a price floor of P_f, farmers will be willing to produce Q_s, but private buyers will only take Q_d off the market at that price. The surplus entailed is measured by the excess of Q_s over Q_d.

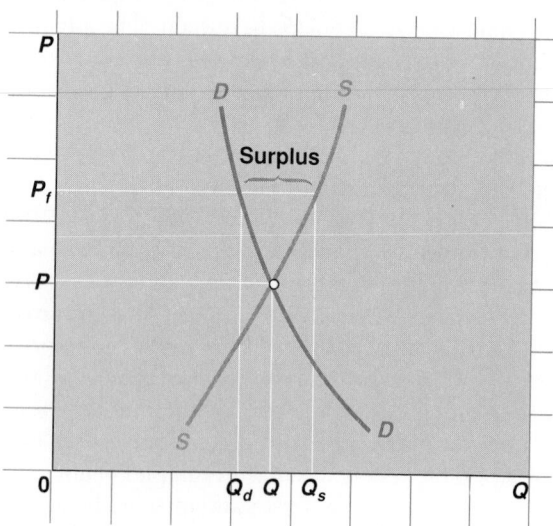

FIGURE 22-6

Price floors result in persistent surpluses

A price floor such as P_f gives rise to a persistent product surplus as indicated by the distance Q_dQ_s. Government must either purchase these surpluses or take measures to eliminate them by restricting product supply or increasing product demand.

LAST WORD

Cross and income elasticity of demand

In addition to price elasticity of demand, two other elasticity concepts are of significance.

We have seen that *price elasticity of demand* measures the effect of a change in a product's price upon the quantity of *that* product demanded. The concept of *cross elasticity of demand* measures how sensitive consumer purchases of *one* product (say X) are to a change in the price of some *other* product (say Y). Our formula for the coefficient of cross elasticity of demand is similar to simple price elasticity except that we are relating the percentage change in the consumption of X to a percentage change in the price of Y:

$$E_{xy} = \frac{\text{percentage change in quantity demanded of X}}{\text{percentage change in price of Y}}$$

The astute reader will observe that this elasticity concept allows us to quantify and more fully understand substitute and complementary goods as introduced in Chapter 4. If cross elasticity of demand is *positive*—that is, the quantity demanded of X varies directly with a change in the price of Y—then X and Y are *substitute goods*. For example, an increase in the price of butter (Y) will cause consumers to buy more margarine (X). The larger the positive coefficient, the greater the substitutability between the two products. When cross elasticity is *negative*, then we know that X and Y "go together" and are *complementary goods*. Thus an increase in the price of cameras will decrease the amount of film purchased. The larger the negative coefficient, the greater the complementarity between the two goods. A zero or near-zero coefficient suggests that the two products are unrelated or *independent goods*. For example, we would not expect a change in the price of butter to have any significant impact upon the purchases of film.

The concept of *income elasticity of demand* measures the percentage change in the quantity of a product demanded which results from some percentage change in consumer incomes:

$$E_i = \frac{\begin{array}{c} \text{percentage change} \\ \text{in quantity demanded} \end{array}}{\text{percentage change in income}}$$

For most goods the income elasticity coefficient will be *positive*. Again recalling Chapter 4, those products of which more is purchased as incomes increase are called *normal* or *superior goods*. But the positive elasticity coefficient varies greatly among products. For example, the income elasticity of demand for automobiles has been estimated to be about +3.00, while for most farm products it is only on the order of +0.20. A *negative* income elasticity coefficient designates an *inferior good*. Margarine, potatoes, cabbage, bus tickets, used clothing, and muscatel wine are likely candidates. Consumers tend to *decrease* their purchases of such products as incomes *increase*.

The practical significance of income elasticity coefficients is that they help us predict which industries are likely to be prosperous, expanding industries and which will probably be unprosperous, declining industries. Specifically, other things being equal, a high positive income elasticity implies that that industry will share more than proportionately in the overall income growth of the economy. A small positive or, worse yet, a negative coefficient implies a declining industry. For example, the indicated high positive income elasticity of demand for automobiles portends long-run prosperity for that industry, while the low income elasticity of demand for most agricultural products suggests chronic problems for that industry.

Government inherits the task of coping with the surplus which a price floor entails. There are two general approaches open to government. First, it might invoke certain programs to restrict supply (for example, acreage allotments by which farmers agree to take a certain amount of land out of production) or to increase demand (for example, research on new uses for agricultural products) in order to reduce the difference between the equilibrium price and the price floor and thereby the size of the resulting surplus. If these efforts are not wholly successful, then, secondly, government must purchase the surplus output (thereby subsidizing farmers) and store or otherwise dispose of it. We shall have more to say about agricultural surpluses in Chapter 35.

RECAPITULATION

Price ceilings and price floors rob the free-market forces of supply and demand of their ability to bring the supply decisions of producers and the demand decisions of buyers into accord with one another. Freely determined prices automatically ration products to buyers; legal prices do not. Therefore, government must accept the administrative problem of rationing which stems from price ceilings and the problem of buying or eliminating surpluses which price floors entail. Legal prices entail controversial tradeoffs. The alleged benefits of price ceilings and floors to consumers and producers respectively must be set against costs associated with consequent shortages and surpluses. Furthermore, our discussions of World War II price controls, rent controls, and interest rate ceilings on credit cards point out that governmental interference with the market can have unintended side effects which are clearly undesirable. Rent controls are likely to discourage housing construction and repair. Instead of protecting low-income families from high interest charges, interest rate ceilings may simply make credit unavailable to them.

CHAPTER SUMMARY

l The present chapter extends the rudiments of demand and supply analysis developed in Chapter 4. The summarizing statements pertinent to that chapter should be reviewed at this point.

2 Price elasticity of demand measures the responsiveness of consumers to price changes. If consumers are relatively sensitive to price changes, demand is elastic. If consumers are relatively unresponsive to price changes, demand is inelastic.

3 The price elasticity formula measures the degree of elasticity or inelasticity of demand. The formula is

$$E_d = \frac{\text{percentage change in quantity demanded}}{\text{percentage change in price}}$$

The averages of the prices and quantities under consideration are used as reference points in determining the percentage changes in price and quantity. If E_d is greater than 1, demand is elastic. If E_d is less than 1, demand is inelastic. Unit elasticity is the special case in which E_d equals 1. A perfectly inelastic demand curve is portrayed by a line parallel to the vertical axis; a perfectly elastic demand curve is shown by a line above and parallel to the horizontal axis.

4 Price elasticity of demand can be determined by observing the effect of a price change upon total revenue from the sale of the product. If price and total revenue move in opposite directions, demand is elastic. If price and total revenue move in the same direction, demand is inelastic. In the case where demand is of unit elasticity, a change in price will leave total revenue unchanged.

5 The number of available substitutes, the size of an item in one's budget, whether the product is a luxury or necessity, and the time period involved are all considerations which influence elasticity of demand.

6 Elasticity varies at different price ranges on a demand curve, tending to be elastic in the northwest segment and inelastic in the southeast segment. It is not correct to judge elasticity by the steepness or flatness of a demand curve on a graph.

7 The elasticity concept is also applicable to supply. Elasticity of supply depends upon the shiftability of resources between alternative employments. This shiftability in turn varies directly with the amount of time producers have to adjust to a given price change.

8 Legally fixed prices upset the rationing function of equilibrium prices. Effective price ceilings result in persistent product shortages and, if an equitable distribution of the product is sought, government will have to ration the product to consumers. Price floors give rise to product surpluses; government must purchase these surplus products *or* eliminate them by imposing restrictions on production or by increasing private demand.

TERMS AND CONCEPTS

price elasticity formula	**elasticity of supply**
elastic versus inelastic demand	**market period**
	short run and long run
perfectly inelastic demand	**increasing- and constant-cost industries**
perfectly elastic demand	**price ceiling**
total-revenue test	**price floor**

QUESTIONS AND STUDY SUGGESTIONS

1 Answer questions 1, 3, and 10 at the end of Chapter 4.

2 In some industries, for example, the petroleum industry, producers justify their reluctance to lower prices by arguing that the demand for their products is inelastic. Explain.

3 How will the following changes in price affect total revenue (expenditures)—that is, will total revenue *increase, decline,* or *remain unchanged?*
   a Price falls and demand is inelastic.
   b Price rises and demand is elastic.
   c Price rises and supply is elastic.
   d Price rises and supply is inelastic.
   e Price rises and demand is inelastic.
   f Price falls and demand is elastic.
   g Price falls and demand is of unit elasticity.

4 What are the major determinants of elasticity of demand? Use these determinants in judging whether the demand for each of the following products is elastic or inelastic: **a** oranges; **b** cigarettes; **c** Winston cigarettes; **d** gasoline; **e** butter; **f** salt; **g** automobiles; **h** football games; **i** diamond bracelets; and **j** this textbook.

5 Why is it difficult to judge elasticity of demand or supply by merely observing the appearance of a demand or supply curve on a graph?

6 Empirical estimates suggest the following demand elasticities: 0.6 for physicians' services; 4.0 for foreign travel; and 1.2 for radio and television receivers. Use the generalizations for the determinants of elasticity developed in this chapter to explain each of these figures.

7 What effect would a rule stating that university students live in university dormitories have upon the elasticity of demand for dormitory space? What impact might this in turn have upon room rates?

E_s	Quantity supplied	Product price	Quantity demanded	Total revenue	E_d
	28,000	$10	10,000	$_____	
_____	22,500	9	13,000	_____	_____
_____	17,000	8	17,000	_____	_____
_____	13,000	7	22,000	_____	_____
_____	11,000	6	25,000	_____	_____

8 Determine the elasticity of demand and supply for the demand and supply schedules above. Use the total-revenue test to check the answers given by the E_d formula.

9 Suppose you are sponsoring an outdoor rock concert. Your major costs—for the band, land rent, and security—are largely independent of attendance. Use the concept of elasticity of demand to explain how you might go about establishing ticket prices in order to maximize profits.

10 What is the elasticity of the supply of Rembrandt paintings? Can you relate your answer to the extremely high prices paid for classical art at auctions?

11 Graph the accompanying demand data and then use either the elasticity coefficient or the total-revenue test to determine price elasticity of demand for each possible price change. What can you conclude about the relationship between the slope of a curve and its elasticity? Explain in a nontechnical way *why* demand tends to be elastic in the northwest segment of the demand curve and inelastic in the southeast segment. Graph the total revenue data below the demand curve (see Figure 22-3) and generalize upon the relationship between price elasticity and total revenue.

Product price	Quantity demanded
$5	1
4	2
3	3
2	4
1	5

12 How would you expect the elasticity of supply of product X to differ in a situation of full employment in industry X, on the one hand, and of considerable unemployment in the industry, on the other? Explain.

13 "If the demand for farm products is highly price inelastic, a bumper crop may reduce farm incomes." Evaluate and illustrate graphically.

14 Suppose you are chairperson of a state tax commission that is responsible for establishing a program to raise new revenue through the use of excise taxes. Would elasticity of demand be important to you in determining those products upon which excises should be levied? Explain.

15 Why is it desirable for ceiling prices to be accompanied by government rationing? And for price floors to be accompanied by surplus-purchasing or output-restricting or demand-increasing programs? Show graphically why price ceilings entail shortages and price floors result in surpluses. What effect, if any, does the elasticity of demand and supply have upon the size of these shortages and surpluses? Explain.

16 New York City has had rent controls since 1941. What effect do you think they have had upon the amount of housing demanded? Upon the construction of new housing? Explain: "Rent controls are a kind of self-fulfilling prophecy. They are designed to cope with housing shortages, but instead create such shortages." Can you predict the economic consequences of usury laws? Show diagrammatically the expected effect of the minimum wage upon the employment of low-wage workers.

17 Explain the error in the following argument: "For the past four years the prices of automobiles have been rising and each year people have purchased more autos. Price and quantity are directly related and the economists' law of demand is incorrect."

18 In the 1950s the local Boy Scout troop in Jackson, Wyoming decided to gather and sell at auction the elk antlers shed by the thousands of elk which winter in the area. The buyers were mainly local artisans who used the antlers to make belt buckles, buttons, and tie clasps. The price per pound was 6¢ and the troop took in $500 annually. In the 1970s a fad developed in Asia which involved grinding antlers into powder and sprinkling it on food to secure purported aphrodisiac benefits. In 1979 the price per pound of elk antlers in the Jackson auction was $6 per pound and the Boy Scouts earned $51,000! Show graphically and explain these dramatic increases in price and total revenue. Assuming no shift in the supply curve of elk antlers, use the midpoints formula to calculate the coefficient for the elasticity of supply.

19 In 1987 the average price of a home rose from $97,000 in April to $106,800 in May. During the same period home sales fell from 724,000 to 616,000 units. If we assume that mortgage interest rates and all other factors affecting home sales are constant, what do these figures suggest about the elasticity of demand for housing?

CHAPTER 23

The theory of consumer behavior[1]

In Chapter 22 we extended our understanding of demand and supply by introducing the concept of price elasticity and by discussing legal price ceilings and floors as applications of demand and supply analysis. The present chapter is devoted to further consideration of the demand side of the market. In Chapter 24 we shall discuss production costs, which, we shall discover, are the major determinant of supply. The goal of Chapters 25 to 28 is to use our understanding of demand and supply in analyzing pricing and output decisions under a variety of specified market structures.

The two main objectives of the present chapter are as follows. First, we seek a more sophisticated explanation of the law of demand. Second, we want to understand how consumers allocate their money incomes among various goods and services. Why does a consumer buy some specific bundle of goods rather than any one of a number of other collections of goods which are available?

[1] Some instructors may choose to omit this chapter. This can be done without impairing the continuity and meaning of ensuing chapters.

Two explanations of the law of demand

The law of demand may be treated as a common-sense notion. A high price usually does discourage consumers from buying; a low price typically does encourage them to buy. Now let us explore two complementary explanations of the downsloping nature of the demand curve which will back up our everyday observations.[2]

INCOME AND SUBSTITUTION EFFECTS

You may recall from Chapter 4 that the law of demand—the downsloping demand curve—can be explained in terms of the income and substitution effects. Whenever the price of a product decreases, two things happen to cause the amount demanded to increase.

Income effect If the price of a product—say, steak—declines, the real income or purchasing power of anyone buying that product will increase. This increase in real income will be reflected in increased purchases of a variety of products, including steak. For example, with a constant money income of, say, $20 per week you can purchase 10 pounds of steak at a price of $2 per pound. But if the price of steak falls to $1 per pound and you buy 10 pounds of steak, $10 per week is freed for buying more of this and other commodities. A decline in the price of steak increases the real income of the

[2] A third explanation, based upon *indifference curves,* is in some respects more precise and more sophisticated than the two we now discuss. An introduction to indifference curve analysis is provided in the appendix to this chapter.

451

consumer, enabling him or her to purchase a larger quantity of steak.[3] This is called the **income effect.**

2 Substitution effect The lower price of a product means that it is now cheaper relative to all other products. And consumers will tend to substitute the cheaper product for other products which are now relatively more expensive. In our example, as the price of steak falls—the prices of other products being unchanged—steak will become more attractive to the buyer. At $1 per pound it is a "better buy" than at $2 per pound. Consequently, the lower price will induce the consumer to substitute steak for some of the now relatively less attractive items in the budget. Steak may well be substituted for pork, chicken, veal, fish, and a variety of other foods. A lower price increases the relative attractiveness of a product and makes the consumer willing to buy more of it. This is known as the **substitution effect.**

The income and substitution effects combine to make a consumer able and willing to buy more of a specific good at a low price than at a high price.

LAW OF DIMINISHING MARGINAL UTILITY

A second explanation centers upon the notion that, although consumer wants in general may be insatiable, wants for specific commodities can be fulfilled. In a given span of time, wherein the tastes of buyers are unchanged, consumers can get as much of specific goods and services as they want. The more of a specific product consumers obtain, the less anxious they are to get more units of the same product. This can be most readily seen for durable goods. A consumer's want for an automobile, when he or she has none, may be very strong; the desire for a second car is much less intense; for a third or fourth, very weak. Even the wealthiest of families rarely have more than a half-dozen cars, despite the fact that their incomes would allow them to purchase and maintain a whole fleet of them.

Economists put forth the idea that specific consumer wants can be fulfilled with succeeding units of a commodity in the **law of diminishing mar-**

ginal utility. Let us dissect this law to see exactly what it means. Recall (Chapter 2) that a product has utility if it has the power to satisfy a want. **Utility** is want-satisfying power. Two characteristics of this concept must be emphasized: First, "utility" and "usefulness" are by no means synonymous. Paintings by Picasso may be useless in the functional sense of the term yet be of tremendous utility to art connoisseurs. Second, and implied in the first point, utility is a subjective notion. The utility of a specific product will vary widely from person to person. A bottle of muscatel wine may yield substantial utility to the Skid Row alcoholic, but zero or negative utility to the local temperance union president. A pair of eyeglasses has great utility to someone who is extremely far- or nearsighted, but no utility to a person having 20-20 vision.

By *marginal* utility we simply mean the extra utility, or satisfaction, which a consumer gets from one additional unit of a specific product. In any relatively short time wherein the consumer's tastes can be assumed not to change, the marginal utility derived from successive units of a given product will decline.[4] Why? Because a consumer will eventually become relatively saturated, or "filled up," with that particular product. The fact that marginal utility will decline as the consumer acquires additional units of a specific product is known as the law of diminishing marginal utility.

We have noted that utility is a subjective concept. As a result, it is not susceptible to precise quantitative measurement. But for purposes of illustration, let us assume that we can measure satisfaction with units we shall call "utils." This mythical unit of satisfaction is merely a convenient pedagogical device which will allow us to quantify our thinking about consumer behavior. Thus, in Table 23-1, we can illustrate the relationship between the quantity obtained of a product—say, fast-food hamburgers—and the accompanying extra utility derived from each successive unit. Here we assume that the law of diminishing marginal utility

---

[3] We assume here that steak is a *normal* or *superior* good.

[4] For a time the marginal utility of successive units of a product may increase. A third can of beer may yield a larger amount of extra satisfaction than the first or second. But beyond some point, we can expect the marginal utility of added units to decline. In the case of beer, this decline may be abrupt.

TABLE 23-1 **The law of diminishing marginal utility as applied to hamburgers (hypothetical data)**

Unit of hamburgers	Marginal utility, utils	Total utility utils
First	10	10
Second	6	16
Third	2	18
Fourth	0	18
Fifth	−5	13

sets in with the first hamburger consumed. Each successive hamburger yields less and less extra utility than the previous one as the consumer's want for hamburgers comes closer and closer to fulfillment. *Total utility* can be found for any number of hamburgers by cumulating the marginal-utility figures as indicated in Table 23-1. The third hamburger has a marginal utility of 2 utils; 3 hamburgers yield a total utility of 18 utils (= 10 + 6 + 2). Notice that marginal utility becomes zero for the fourth hamburger and negative for the fifth.

Now, how does the law of diminishing marginal utility explain why the demand curve for a specific product is downsloping? If successive units of a good yield smaller and smaller amounts of marginal, or extra, utility, then the consumer will buy additional units of a product only if its price falls. The consumer for whom these utility data are relevant may buy, say, 2 hamburgers at a price of $1. But, owing to diminishing marginal utility from additional hamburgers, a consumer will choose *not* to buy more at this price, because giving up money really means giving up other goods, that is, alternative ways of getting utility. Therefore, additional hamburgers are "not worth it" unless the price (sacrifice of other goods) declines. (When marginal utility becomes negative, McDonalds or Burger King would have to pay *you* to consume another hamburger!) From the seller's viewpoint, diminishing marginal utility forces the producer to lower the price in order to induce buyers to take a larger quantity of the product. This rationale supports the notion of a downsloping demand curve.

Theory of consumer behavior

In addition to providing a basis for explaining the law of demand, the idea of diminishing marginal utility also plays a key role in explaining how consumers should allocate their money income among the many goods and services which are available for them to buy.

CONSUMER CHOICE AND BUDGET RESTRAINT

We can picture the situation of the typical consumer being something like this:

1 Rational behavior The average consumer is a fairly rational person, and attempts to dispose of his or her money income in such a way as to derive the greatest amount of satisfaction, or utility, from it. Typical consumers want to get "the most for their money" or, more technically, to maximize total utility.

2 Preferences We may suppose, too, that the average consumer has rather clear-cut preferences for various goods and services available in the market. We assume that buyers have a good idea of how much marginal utility they will get from successive units of the various products which they might choose to purchase.

3 Budget restraint The consumer's money income is limited in amount. Because a consumer supplies limited amounts of human and property resources to businesses, the money income received will be limited. With a few possible exceptions—the Rockefellers, Bob Hope, Michael Jackson, and Saudi Arabia's King Fahd—all consumers are subject to a *budget restraint*.

4 Prices The goods and services available to consumers have price tags on them. Why? Because they are scarce in relation to the demand for them, or, stated differently, their production entails the use of scarce and therefore valuable resources. In the ensuing examples we shall suppose that product prices are not affected by the amounts of specific goods which the individual consumer buys;

pure competition exists on the buying or demand side of the market.

Obviously, if a consumer has a limited number of dollars and the products he or she wants have price tags on them, the consumer will be able to purchase only a limited amount of goods. The consumer cannot buy everything wanted when each purchase exhausts a portion of a limited money income. It is precisely this point which brings the economic fact of scarcity home to the individual consumer.

In making his choices, our typical consumer is in the same position as the Western prospector . . . who is restocking for his next trip into the back country and who is forced by the nature of the terrain to restrict his luggage to whatever he can carry on the back of one burro. If he takes a great deal of one item, say baked beans, he must necessarily take much less of something else, say bacon. His job is to find that collection of products which, in view of the limitations imposed on the total, will best suit his needs and tastes.[5]

The consumer must make compromises; choices must be made among alternative goods to obtain with limited money resources the most satisfying mix of goods and services.

UTILITY-MAXIMIZING RULE

The question then boils down to this: Of all the collections of goods and services which a consumer can obtain within the limit of his or her budget, which specific collection will yield the greatest utility or satisfaction? Bluntly put, the rule to be followed in maximizing satisfactions is that *the consumer's money income should be allocated so that the last dollar spent on each product purchased yields the same amount of extra (marginal) utility*. We shall call this the **utility-maximizing rule.** When the consumer is "balancing his margins" in accordance with this rule, there will be no incentive to alter his or her expenditure pattern. The consumer will be in *equilibrium* and, barring a change in tastes, income, or the prices of the various goods,

[5]E. T. Weiler, *The Economic System* (New York: The Macmillan Company, 1952), p. 89.

he or she will be worse off—total utility will decline—by any alteration in the collection of goods purchased.

A numerical illustration will help explain the validity of the rule. For simplicity's sake we limit our discussion to just two products. Keep in mind that the analysis can readily be extended to any number of goods. Suppose that consumer Brooks is trying to decide which combination of two products—A and B—she should purchase with her limited daily income of $10. Obviously, Brooks's preferences for these two products and their prices will be basic data determining the combination of A and B which will maximize her satisfactions. Table 23-2 summarizes Brooks's preferences for products A and B. Column 2a shows the amount of extra or marginal utility Brooks will derive from each successive unit of A. Column 3a reflects Brooks's preferences for product B. In each case the relationship between the number of units of the product obtained and the corresponding marginal utility re-

TABLE 23-2 The utility-maximizing combination of products A and B obtainable with an income of $10* (hypothetical data)

(1)	(2) Product A: price = $1		(3) Product B: price = $2	
Unit of product	(a) Marginal utility, utils	(b) Marginal utility per dollar (MU/price)	(a) Marginal utility, utils	(b) Marginal utility per dollar (MU/price)
First	10	10	24	12
Second	8	8	20	10
Third	7	7	18	9
Fourth	6	6	16	8
Fifth	5	5	12	6
Sixth	4	4	6	3
Seventh	3	3	4	2

* It is assumed in this table that the amount of marginal utility received from additional units of each of the two products is independent of the quantity of the other product. For example, the marginal utility schedule for product A is independent of the amount of B obtained by the consumer.

flects the law of diminishing marginal utility. Diminishing marginal utility is assumed to occur with the first unit of each product purchased.

But before we can apply the utility-maximizing rule to these data, we must put the marginal-utility information of two columns 2a and 3a on a per-dollar-spent basis. Why? Because a consumer's choices will be influenced not only by the extra utility which successive units of, say, product A will yield, but also by how many dollars (and therefore how many units of alternative good B) she must give up to obtain those added units of A. Example: Suppose you prefer a compact disc whose marginal utility is, say, 36 utils to a movie whose marginal utility is just 24 utils. But if the CD's price is $12 and the movie only $6, the choice would be for the movie rather than the CD! Why? Because the *marginal utility per dollar spent* would be 4 utils for the movie (4 = 24 ÷ $6) as compared to only 3 utils for the CD (3 = 36 ÷ $12). You could buy two movies for $12 and, assuming the marginal utility of the second movie is, say, 16 utils, your total utility would be 40 utils. Forty units of satisfaction from two movies is clearly superior to 36 utils derived from the same $12 expenditure on one CD. The point is this: To make the amounts of extra utility derived from differently priced goods comparable, marginal utility must be put on a per-dollar-spent basis. This is done in columns 2b and 3b. These figures are obtained by dividing the marginal-utility data of columns 2a and 3a by the assumed prices of A and B—$1 and $2, respectively.

Now we have Brooks's preferences—on unit and per dollar bases—and the price tags of A and B before us. Brooks stands patiently with $10 to spend on A and B. In what order should she allocate her dollars on units of A and B to achieve the highest degree of utility within the limits imposed by her money income? And what specific combination of A and B will she have obtained at the time that she exhausts her $10?

Concentrating on columns 2b and 3b of Table 23-2, we find that Brooks should first spend $2 on the first unit of B. Why? Because its marginal utility per dollar of 12 utils is higher than A's. But now Brooks finds herself indifferent about whether she should buy a second unit of B or the first unit of A, because the marginal utility per dollar of both is 10. So she buys both of them. Brooks now has 1 unit of A and 2 of B. Note that with this combina-

tion of goods the last dollar spent on each yields the same amount of extra utility. Does this combination of A and B therefore represent the maximum amount of utility which Brooks can obtain? The answer is "No." This collection of goods only costs $5 [= (1 × $1) + (2 × $2)]; Brooks has $5 of income remaining, which she can spend to achieve a still higher level of total utility.

Examining columns 2b and 3b again, we find that Brooks should spend the next $2 on a third unit of B because the marginal utility per dollar for the third unit of B is 9 as compared to 8 for the second unit of A. But now, with 1 unit of A and 3 of B, we find she is again indifferent to a second unit of A and a fourth unit of B. Let us again assume Brooks purchases one more unit of each. Marginal utility per dollar is now the same at 8 utils for the last dollar spent on each product, *and Brooks's money income of $10 is exhausted* [(2 × $1) + (4 × $2)]. *The utility-maximizing combination of goods attainable by Brooks is 2 units of A and 4 of B.*[6] By summing the marginal utility information of columns 2a and 3a we find that Brooks is realizing 18 (= 10 + 8) utils of satisfaction from the 2 units of A and 78 (= 24 + 20 + 18 + 16) utils of satisfaction from the 4 units of B. Her $10 of income, optimally spent, yields 96 (= 18 + 78) utils of satisfaction. Table 23-3 summarizes this step-by-step process for maximizing consumer utility and merits careful study by the reader.

It is to be emphasized that there are other combinations of A and B which are obtainable with $10. But none of these will yield a level of total utility as high as do 2 units of A and 4 of B. For example, 4 units of A and 3 of B can be obtained for $10. However, this combination violates the utility-maximizing rule; total utility here is only 93 utils, clearly inferior to the 96 utils yielded by 2 of A and 4 of B. Furthermore, there are other combinations of A and B (such as 4 of A and 5 of B *or* 1 of A and 2 of B) wherein the marginal utility of the last dollar spent is the same for both A and B. But all such combinations are either unobtainable with

---

[6] To simplify, we assume in this example that Brooks spends her entire income; she neither borrows nor saves. Saving can be regarded as a utility-yielding commodity and incorporated in our analysis. It is treated thus in question 5 at the end of the chapter.

TABLE 23-3 Sequence of purchases in achieving consumer equilibrium

Potential choice	Marginal utility per dollar	Purchase decision	Income remaining
1 { First unit of A	10	First unit of B for $2	$8 = $10 − $2
{ First unit of B	12		
2 { First unit of A	10	First unit of A for $1	$5 = $8 − $3
{ Second unit of B	10	and second unit of B for $2	
3 { Second unit of A	8	Third unit of B for $2	$3 = $5 − $2
{ Third unit of B	9		
4 { Second unit of A	8	Second unit of A for $1	$0 = $3 − $3
{ Fourth unit of B	8	and fourth unit of B for $2	

Brooks's limited money income (as 4 of A and 5 of B) or fail to exhaust her money income (as 1 of A and 2 of B) and therefore do not yield her the maximum utility attainable.

ALGEBRAIC RESTATEMENT

We are now in a position to restate the utility-maximizing rule in simple algebraic terms. Our rule merely says that a consumer will maximize her satisfaction when she allocates her money income in such a way that the last dollar spent on product A, the last on product B, and so forth, yield equal amounts of additional, or marginal, utility. Now the marginal utility per dollar spent on A is indicated by MU of product A/price of A (column 2b of Table 23-2) and the marginal utility per dollar spent on B by MU of product B/price of B (column 3b of Table 23-2). Our utility-maximizing rule merely requires that these ratios be equal. That is,

$$\frac{\text{MU of product A}}{\text{price of A}} = \frac{\text{MU of product B}}{\text{price of B}}$$

and, of course, the consumer must exhaust her available income. Our tabular illustration has shown us that the combination of 2 units of A and 4 of B fulfills these conditions in that

$$\frac{8}{1} = \frac{16}{2}$$

and the consumer's $10 income is spent.

If the equation is not fulfilled, there will be some reallocation of the consumer's expenditures between A and B, from the low to the high marginal-utility-per-dollar product, which will increase the consumer's total utility. For example, if the consumer were to spend $10 on 4 of A and 3 of B, we would find that

$$\frac{\text{MU of A: 6 utils}}{\text{price of A: \$1}} < \frac{\text{MU of B: 18 utils}}{\text{price of B: \$2}}$$

The last dollar spent on A provides only 6 utils of satisfaction, and the last dollar spent on B provides 9 (= 18 ÷ $2). On a per dollar basis, units of B provide more extra satisfaction than units of A. Hence, the consumer will increase her total satisfaction by purchasing more of B and less of A. As dollars are reallocated from A to B, the marginal utility from additional units of B will decline as the result of moving *down* the diminishing marginal-utility schedule for B, and the marginal utility of A will rise as the consumer moves *up* the diminishing marginal-utility schedule for A. At some new combination of A and B—specifically, 2 of A and 4 of B—the equality of the two ratios and therefore consumer equilibrium will be achieved. As we already know, the net gain in utility is 3 utils (= 96 − 93).

Marginal utility and the demand curve

It is a quite simple step from the utility-maximizing rule to the construction of an individual's downsloping demand curve. Recall from Chapters 4 and 22 that the basic determinants of an individual's demand curve for a specific product are (1) preferences or tastes, (2) money income, and (3) the prices of other goods. The utility data of Table 23-2 reflect our consumer's preferences. Let us continue to suppose that her money income is given at $10. And, concentrating upon the construction of a simple demand curve for product B, let us assume that the price of A—representing "other goods"—is given at $1. We should now be able to derive a simple demand schedule for B by considering alternative prices at which B might be sold and determining the corresponding quantity our consumer will choose to purchase. Of course, we have already determined one such price-quantity combination in explaining the utility-maximizing rule: Given tastes, income, and the prices of other goods, the rational consumer will purchase 4 units of B at a price of $2. Now assume the price of B falls to $1. This means that the marginal-utility-per-dollar data of column 3b will double, because the price of B has been halved; the new data for column 3b are in fact identical to those shown in column 3a. The purchase of 2 units of A and 4 of B is no longer an equilibrium combination. By applying the same reasoning used to develop the utility-maximizing rule, we now find Brooks's utility-maximizing position entails 4 units of A and 6 of B. That is, we can sketch Brooks's demand curve for B as in Table 23-4. This, of course, confirms the downsloping demand curve discussed in earlier chapters.

Recall that at the beginning of this chapter it was indicated that the increased purchases of a good whose price had fallen could be understood in terms of the substitution and income effects. Although our analysis does not permit us to sort out these two effects quantitatively, we can see intuitively how each is involved in the increased purchase of product B.

TABLE 23-4 **The demand schedule for product B**

Price per unit of B	Quantity demanded
$2	4
1	6

The *substitution effect* can be understood by referring back to our utility-maximizing rule. Before the price of B declined, Brooks was in equilibrium in that $MU_A(8)/P_A(\$1) = MU_B(16)/P_B(\$2)$, when purchasing 2 units of A and 4 units of B. But after B's price falls from $2 to $1, $MU_A(8)/P_A(\$1) < MU_B(16)/P_B(\$1)$ or, more simply stated, the last dollar spent on B now yields more utility (16 utils) than does the last dollar spent on A (8 utils). This indicates that a switching of expenditures from A to B is needed to restore equilibrium; that is, a *substitution* of now cheaper B for A will tend to occur in the bundle of goods which Brooks purchases.

What about the *income effect?* The assumed decline in the price of B from $2 to $1 increases Brooks's real income. Before the price decline, Brooks was in equilibrium when buying 2 of A and 4 of B. But at the lower $1 price for B, Brooks would have to spend only $6 rather that $10 on this same combination of goods. She has $4 left over to spend on more of A, more of B, or more of both products. In short, the decline in the price of B has caused Brooks's *real* income to increase so that she can now obtain larger amounts of A and B with the same $10 *money* income. The portion of the 2-unit increase in her purchase of B which is due to this increase in real income is the income effect.

The time dimension

The theory of consumer behavior has been generalized to take the economic value of *time* into account. Both consumption and production activities have a common characteristic—they take time. And time is a valuable economic resource; by working—by using an hour in productive activity—one may earn $6, $10, or $50, depending upon one's education, skills, and so forth. By using that hour for leisure or in consumption activities, one incurs the opportunity cost of forgone income; you sacrifice the $6, $10, or $50 you could have earned by working.

THE VALUE OF TIME

In the marginal-utility theory of consumer behavior economists traditionally have assumed that consumption is an instantaneous act. However, it is logical to argue that the "prices" of consumer goods should include, not merely the market price, but also the value of the time required in the consumption of the good. In other words, the denominators of our earlier marginal-utility/price ratios are incomplete because they do not reflect the "full price"—market price *plus* the value of the consumption time—of the product.

Imagine a consumer who is considering the purchase of a round of golf, on the one hand, and a concert, on the other. The market price of the golf game is $5 and the concert is $8. But the golf game is more time-intensive than the concert. Suppose you will spend four hours on the golf course, but only two hours at the concert. If your time is worth, say, $4 per hour—as evidenced by the $4 wage rate you can obtain by working—then we must recognize that the "full price" of the golf game is $21 (the $5 market price *plus* $16 worth of time). Similarly, the "full price" of the concert is $16 (the $8 market price *plus* $8 worth of time). We find that, contrary to what market prices alone would indicate, the "full price" of the concert is really *less* than the "full price" of the golf game. If we now invoke the simplifying assumption that the marginal utilities derived from successive golf games and concerts are identical, traditional theory would indicate that one should consume more golf games than concerts because the market price of the former is lower ($5) than the latter ($8). But when time is taken into account, the situation is reversed and golf games are more expensive ($21) than are concerts ($16). Hence, it is rational in this case to consume more concerts than golf games!

SOME IMPLICATIONS

By taking time into account, we can explain certain observable phenomena which the traditional theory does not. It may be rational for the unskilled worker or retiree whose time has little or no market value to ride a bus from Peoria to Pittsburgh. But the corporate executive, whose time is very valuable, will find it cheaper to fly, even though bus fare is only a fraction of plane fare. It is sensible for the retiree, living on a modest social security check and having ample time, to spend many hours shopping for bargains. It is equally intelligent for the highly paid physician, working 55 hours per week, to pa-

LAST WORD

The water-diamond paradox

Water is clearly one of the most useful products in the world; our very survival depends upon it. Yet water is very cheap. In contrast, diamonds—which are merely decorative and have little practical value—are very expensive. Why do prices apparently fail to measure the usefulness of goods? Our theory of consumer behavior and the distinction between total and marginal utility help resolve this paradox.

The explanation of the water-diamond paradox lies in two related considerations. First, the supplies of the two products are much different. Water is plentiful and, as a consequence, its price is low and we therefore consume large quantities of it. In doing so we extend our use of water to uses wherein the utility from the last unit of water—water's marginal utility—is very low. For example, we water our lawns, make ice cubes, and wash our

tronize fast-food restaurants and to buy a new television set over the phone. Affluent Americans are observed by foreigners to be "wasteful" of food and other material goods, but "overly economical" in the use of time. Americans who visit less developed countries find that time is used casually or "squandered," while material goods are very highly prized and carefully used. These differences are not a paradox or a case of radically different temperaments. The differences are primarily a quite rational reflection of the fact that the high labor productivity which is characteristic of an advanced society gives

cars. In contrast, diamonds are rare and costly to mine, cut, and polish. Therefore, their supply is restricted and they are available only at a high price. The utility from an extra diamond thus is high—that is, the marginal utility of diamonds is very large.

The second consideration relates back to the utility-maximizing rule which simply states that consumers should purchase any good until the ratio of its marginal utility to price is the same as that for all other goods. Although the *marginal* utility of water may be low because it is plentiful and its price is low, the *total* utility derived from its consumption is exceedingly large because of the great quantity consumed. Conversely, the total utility derived from diamonds is low. Why so? Because the very high price which reflects the scarcity of diamonds causes consumers to purchase relatively few of them. In short, the total utility derived from water is relatively great and the total utility derived from diamonds is relatively small, but it is *marginal* utility which is relevant to the price people are willing to pay for a good. Water yields much more total utility to us than do diamonds, even though the utility of an additional gallon of water is much less than the utility of an additional diamond. Society would gladly give up *all* of the diamonds in the world if that were necessary to obtain *all* of the water in the world. But society would rather have an *additional* diamond than an *additional* gallon of water, given the abundant stock of water available.

time a high market value, whereas precisely the opposite is true in a less developed country.

A final point: As labor productivity has increased historically with the growth of our economy, time has become more valuable in the labor market. Or, stated differently, time used on pure leisure and various consumer activities has become more expensive. As a result, we make a great effort to use nonwork time more "productively." Where possible, we try to increase the pleasure or utility yield per hour by consuming more per unit of time. In some cases this means making consumption more goods-intensive; for example, by buying or renting a motorized golf cart, the time required for a round of golf can be reduced. One watches the news on television because it takes less time than reading the newspaper. In other instances, we consume two or more items simultaneously. After dinner, the consumer "may find himself drinking Brazilian coffee, smoking a Dutch cigar, sipping a French cognac, reading *The New York Times,* listening to a Brandenburg Concerto and entertaining his Swedish wife—all at the same time, with varying degrees of success."[7] But the yield from certain uses of time—pure idleness, cultural pursuits, and the "cultivation of mind and spirit"— cannot be readily increased. Hence, time tends to be shifted from these uses to areas where the yield is greater. This helps explain why, although economic development may bring affluence in the form of goods, it also increases the relative scarcity of time and creates a more hectic life-style. Economic growth, it is argued, cannot produce abundance in all respects; total affluence—an abundance of *both* goods and time—is a logical fallacy. Advanced economies are goods-rich and time-poor, while less developed countries are time-rich and goods-poor!

CHAPTER SUMMARY

1 The law of demand can be explained in terms of the income and substitution effects or the law of diminishing marginal utility.

2 The income effect says that a decline in the price of a product will enable the consumer to buy more of it with a fixed money income. The substitution effect points out that a lower price will make a product relatively more attractive and therefore increase the consumer's willingness to substitute it for other products.

3 The law of diminishing marginal utility states that beyond some point, additional units of a specific com-

[7] Staffan B. Linder, *The Harried Leisure Class* (New York: Columbia University Press, 1970), p. 79. This delightful book is required reading for the person who wants to pursue the many implications of the increasing value of time.

modity will yield ever-declining amounts of extra satisfaction to a consumer. It follows that a lower price will be needed to induce the consumer to increase purchases of such a product.

4 We may assume that the typical consumer is rational and acts on the basis of rather well-defined preferences; consumers act sensibly and know roughly the satisfaction they will derive from successive units of various products available to them. Because income is limited and goods have prices on them, the consumer cannot purchase all the goods and services he or she might like to have. The consumer should therefore select that attainable combination of goods which will maximize his or her utility or satisfaction.

5 The consumer's utility will be maximized when income is allocated so that the last dollar spent on each product purchased yields the same amount of extra satisfaction. Algebraically, the utility-maximizing rule is fulfilled when

$$\frac{\text{MU of product A}}{\text{price of A}} = \frac{\text{MU of product B}}{\text{price of B}}$$

and the consumer's income is spent.

6 The utility-maximizing rule and the demand curve are logically consistent.

7 The theory of consumer choice has been generalized by taking into account the value of the time required in the consumption of various goods and services.

TERMS AND CONCEPTS

income effect	**utility**
substitution effect	**utility-maximizing rule**
law of diminishing marginal utility	

QUESTIONS AND STUDY SUGGESTIONS

1 Explain the law of demand through the income and substitution effects, using a price increase as a point of departure for your discussion. Explain the law of demand in terms of diminishing marginal utility.

2 Mrs. Peterson buys loaves of bread and quarts of milk each week at prices of $1 and 80 cents, respectively. At present she is buying these two products in amounts such that the marginal utilities from the last units purchased of the two products are 80 and 70 utils, respectively. Is she buying the best, that is, the utility-maximizing, combination of bread and milk? If not, how should she reallocate her expenditures between the two goods?

3 Assume you are choosing between two goods, X and Y, and your marginal utility from each is as shown below. If your income is $9 and the prices of X and Y are $2 and $1 respectively, what quantities of each will you purchase in maximizing utility? Specify the amount of total utility you will realize. Assume that, other things remaining unchanged, the price of X falls to $1. What quantities of X and Y will you now purchase? Using the two prices and quantities you have derived for X, graph your demand curve for X.

Units of X	MU$_x$	Units of Y	MU$_y$
1	10	1	8
2	8	2	7
3	6	3	6
4	4	4	5
5	3	5	4
6	2	6	3

4 "Nothing is more useful than water: but it will purchase scarce any thing; scarce any thing can be had in exchange for it. A diamond, on the contrary, has scarce any value in use; but a very great quantity of other goods may frequently be had in exchange for it."[8] Explain.

5 Columns 1 through 4 of the following table show the marginal utility, measured in terms of utils, which Mr. Black would get by purchasing various amounts of products A, B, C, and D. Column 5 shows the marginal utility Black gets from saving. Assume that the prices of A, B, C, and D are $18, $6, $4, and $24, respectively, and that Black has a money income of $106.

 a What quantities of A, B, C, and D will Black purchase in maximizing his satisfactions?
 b How many dollars will Black choose to save?
 c Check your answers by substituting them into the algebraic statement of the utility-maximizing rule.

---

[8] Adam Smith, *The Wealth of Nations* (New York: Modern Library, Inc., originally published in 1776), p. 28.

Column 1		Column 2		Column 3		Column 4		Column 5	
Units of A	MU	Units of B	MU	Units of C	MU	Units of D	MU	No. of $ saved	MU
1	72	1	24	1	15	1	36	1	5
2	54	2	15	2	12	2	30	2	4
3	45	3	12	3	8	3	24	3	3
4	36	4	9	4	7	4	18	4	2
5	27	5	7	5	5	5	13	5	1
6	18	6	5	6	4	6	7	6	$\frac{1}{2}$
7	15	7	2	7	$3\frac{1}{2}$	7	4	7	$\frac{1}{4}$
8	12	8	1	8	3	8	2	8	$\frac{1}{8}$

6 "In the long run it may be irrational to purchase goods on the basis of habit; but in the short run habitual buying may prove to be a very sensible means of allocating income." Do you agree? Explain.

7 How can time be incorporated into the theory of consumer behavior? Foreigners frequently point out that, comparatively speaking, Americans are very wasteful of food and other material goods and very conscious of, and overly economical in, their use of time. Can you provide an explanation for this observation?

8 Explain: **a** "Before economic growth, there were too few goods; after growth, there is too little time." **b** "It is irrational for an individual to take the time to be completely rational in economic decision making."

9 In the last decade or so there has been a dramatic expansion of small retail convenience stores—such as Kwik Shops, 7-Elevens, Gas 'N Shops—despite the fact that their prices are generally much higher than those charged by the large supermarkets. Can you explain their success?

10 *Advanced analysis.* Let $MU_a = z = 10 - x$ and $MU_b = z = 21 - 2y$, where z is marginal utility measured in utils, x is the amount spent on product A, and y is the amount spent on B. Assume the consumer has $10 to spend on A and B; that is, $x + y = 10$. How is this $10 best allocated between A and B? How much utility will the marginal dollar yield?

Indifference curve analysis

A more sophisticated explanation of consumer behavior and consumer equilibrium is based upon (1) budget lines and (2) indifference curves.

THE BUDGET LINE: WHAT IS OBTAINABLE

*A **budget line** simply shows the various combinations of two products which can be purchased with a given money income.* For example, if the price of product A is $1.50 and the price of B is $1.00, then the consumer could purchase all the combinations of A and B shown in Table 1 with $12 of money income. We note that at one extreme the consumer might spend all of his or her income on 8 units of A and have nothing left to spend on B. Or, by giving up 2 units of A and thereby "freeing" $3, the consumer could have 6 units of A and 3 of B. And so on to the other extreme, at which the consumer could buy 12 units of B at $1.00 each, thereby expending his or her entire money income on B and having nothing left to spend on A.

Figure 1 shows the budget line graphically. Note that the slope of the budget line measures the ratio of the price of B to the price of A; more pre-

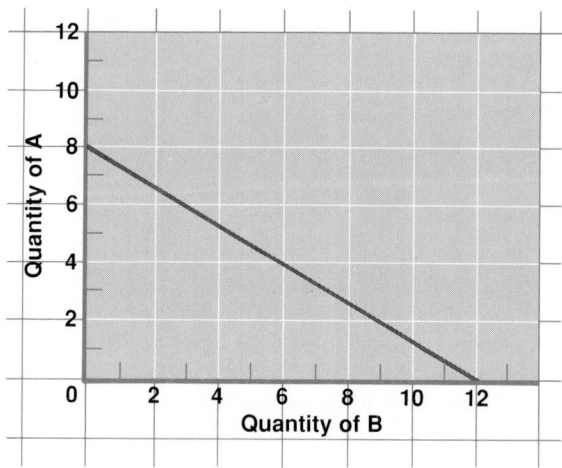

FIGURE 1

A consumer's budget line

The budget line shows all the various combinations of any two products which can be purchased, given the prices of the products and the consumer's money income.

cisely, the absolute value of the slope is $P_B/P_A = \$1.00/\$1.50 = 2/3$. This is merely the mathematical way of saying that the consumer must forgo 2 units of A (measured on the vertical axis) at $1.50 each in order to make available $3 to spend on 3 units of B (measured on the horizontal axis). In other words, in moving down the budget or price line, 2 of A (at $1.50 each) must be given up to obtain 3 of B (at $1.00 each). This yields a slope of $\frac{2}{3}$.

Two other characteristics of the budget line merit comment.

1 Income changes The location of the budget line varies with money income. Specifically, an *increase* in money income will shift the budget line to the *right;* a *decrease* in money income will move it to the *left*. To verify these statements, simply recalculate Table 1 on the assumption that money income is (*a*) $24 and (*b*) $6 and plot the new budget lines in Figure 1.

TABLE 1 **The budget line: combinations of A and B obtainable with an income of $12 (hypothetical data)**

Units of A (price = $1.50)	Units of B (price = $1.00)	Total expenditures
8	0	$12 (= $12 + $0)
6	3	$12 (= $9 + $3)
4	6	$12 (= $6 + $6)
2	9	$12 (= $3 + $9)
0	12	$12 (= $0 + $12)

2 Price changes A change in product prices will also shift the budget line. A decline in the prices of both products—which is the equivalent of a real income increase—will shift the curve to the right. You can verify this assertion by recalculating Table 1 and replotting Figure 1 on the assumption that $P_A = \$.75$ and $P_B = \$.50$. Conversely, an increase in the prices of A and B will shift the curve to the left. Again, assume $P_A = \$3$ and $P_B = \$2$ and rework Table 1 and Figure 1 to substantiate this statement. Note in particular what happens if we change P_B while holding P_A (and money income) constant. The reader should verify that, if we lower P_B from $\$1.00$ to $\$.50$, the budget line will fan outward to the right. Conversely, by increasing P_B from, say, $\$1.00$ to $\$1.50$, the line will fan to the left. In both instances the line remains "anchored" at 8 units on the vertical axis because P_A has not changed.

INDIFFERENCE CURVES: WHAT IS PREFERRED

We know budget lines reflect "objective" market data having to do with income and prices. The budget line reveals the combinations of A and B which are obtainable, given money income and prices. Indifference curves, on the other hand, embody "subjective" information about consumer preferences for A and B. By definition, *an **indifference curve** shows all combinations of products A and B which will yield the same level of satisfaction or utility to the consumer*. Table 2 and Figure 2 present a hypothetical indifference curve involving products A and B. The consumer's subjective preferences are such that he or she will realize the same total utility from each combination of A and B shown in the table or curve; hence, the consumer will be indifferent as to which combination is actually obtained.

It is essential to understand several characteristics of indifference curves.

1 Downsloping Indifference curves are downsloping for the simple reason that both product A and product B yield utility to the consumer. Hence, in moving from combination j to combination k, the consumer is obtaining more of B and thereby increasing his or her total utility; therefore, some of A must be taken away to decrease total utility by a

TABLE 2 **An indifference schedule (hypothetical data)**

Combination	Units of A	Units of B
j	12	2
k	6	4
l	4	6
m	3	8

precisely offsetting amount. In brief, "more of B" necessitates "less of A" so that the quantities of A and B are inversely related. And any curve which reflects inversely related variables is downsloping.

2 Convex to origin But, as viewed from the origin, a downsloping curve can be concave (bowed outward) or convex (bowed inward). A concave curve has an increasing (steeper) slope as one moves down the curve, while a convex curve has a diminishing (flatter) slope as one moves down it. (Recall that the production possibilities curve of Figure 2-1

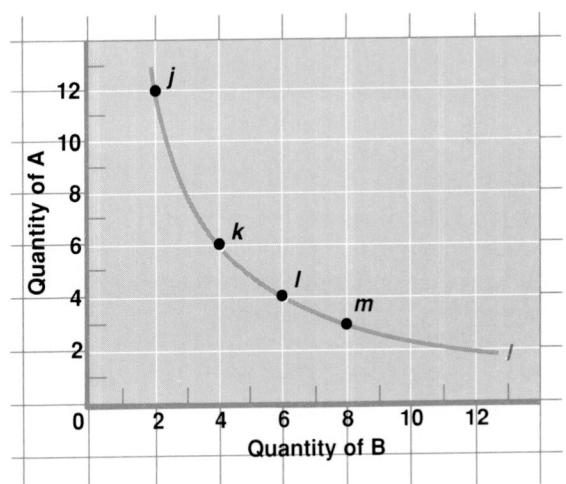

FIGURE 2

A consumer's indifference curve

Every point on an indifference curve represents some combination of products A and B which is equally satisfactory to the consumer; that is, each combination of A and B embodies the same level of total utility.

is concave, reflecting the law of increasing opportunity costs.) We note in Figure 2 that *the indifference curve is convex as viewed from the origin.* That is, the slope diminishes or becomes flatter as we move from *j* to *k*, to *l*, to *m*, and so on down the curve. Technically, the slope of the indifference curve measures the **marginal rate of substitution** (MRS) because it shows the rate, at the margin, at which the consumer is prepared to substitute one good for the other (B for A) so as to remain equally satisfied. The diminishing slope of the indifference curve means the willingness to substitute B for A *diminishes* as one moves down the curve.

What is the rationale for this convexity; that is, for a diminishing MRS? The answer is that a consumer's subjective willingness to substitute B for A (or vice versa) will depend upon the amounts of B and A which he or she has to begin with. Consider Table 2 and Figure 2 once again, beginning at point *j*. Here, in relative terms, the consumer has a substantial amount of A and very little of B. This means that "at the margin" B is very valuable (that is, its marginal utility is high), while A is less valuable at the margin (its marginal utility is low). It follows that the consumer will be willing to give up a substantial amount of A to get, say, 2 more units of B. In this particular case, the consumer is willing to forgo 6 units of A to get 2 more units of B; the MRS is $\frac{6}{2}$, or 3. But at point *k* the consumer now has less A and more B. This means that A will now be somewhat more valuable, and B somewhat less valuable, at the margin. Hence, considering the move from point *k* to point *l*, the consumer is only willing to give up 2 units of A to get 2 more units of B so the MRS is now only $\frac{2}{2}$, or 1. Having still less of A and more of B at point *l*, the consumer is only willing to give up 1 unit of A in return for 2 more of B and, hence, the MRS falls to $\frac{1}{2}$. In general, as the amount of B *increases,* the marginal utility of additional units of B *decreases.* Similarly, as the quantity of A *decreases,* its marginal utility *increases.* This means in Figure 3 that in moving down the curve the consumer will be willing to give up smaller and smaller amounts of A as an offset to acquiring each additional unit of B. The result is a curve with a diminishing slope, that is, one which is convex when viewed from the origin. Alternatively stated, the MRS declines as one moves southeast along the indifference curve.

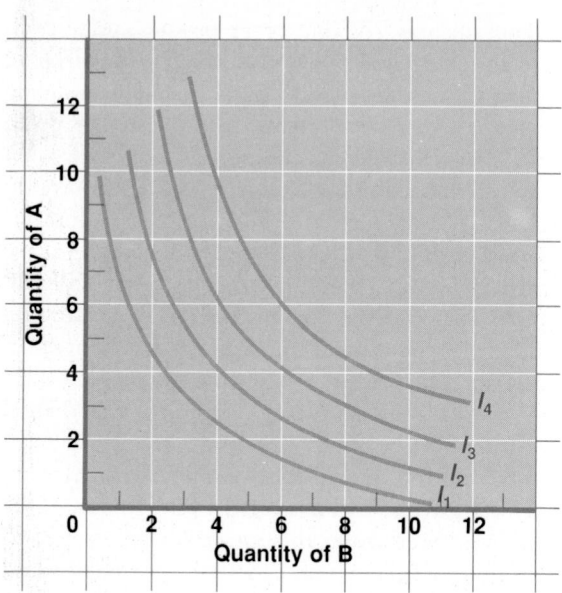

FIGURE 3

An indifference map

An indifference map is comprised of a set of indifference curves. Each successive curve further from the origin indicates a higher level of total utility. That is, any combination of products A and B shown by a point on I_4 is superior to any combination of A and B shown by a point on I_3, I_2, or I_1.

3 Indifference map The single indifference curve of Figure 2 reflects some constant (but unspecified) level of total utility or satisfaction. It is possible—and useful for our analysis—to sketch a whole series of indifference curves or, in other words, an **indifference map** as shown in Figure 3. Each curve reflects a different level of total utility. Specifically, each curve to the *right* of our original curve (labeled I_3 in Figure 3) reflects combinations of A and B which yield *more* utility than I_3. Each curve to the *left* of I_3 reflects *less* total utility than I_3. In other words, *as we move out from the origin each successive indifference curve entails a higher level of utility.* This can be simply demonstrated by drawing a line in a northeasterly direction from the origin and noting that its points of intersection with each successive curve entail larger amounts of *both* A and B and therefore a higher level of total utility.

EQUILIBRIUM AT TANGENCY

Noting that the axes of Figures 1 and 3 are identical, we can now determine the consumer's **equilibrium position** by combining the budget line and the indifference map as shown in Figure 4. Recall that, by definition, the budget line indicates all combinations of A and B which the consumer can attain, given his or her money income and the prices of A and B. The question is: Of these attainable combinations, which will the consumer most prefer? The answer is: That combination which yields the greatest satisfaction or utility. Specifically, *the utility-maximizing combination will be the one lying on the highest attainable indifference curve.* In terms of Figure 4 the consumer's utility-maximizing or equilibrium combination of A and B is at point X where the budget line is *tangent* to I_3. Why not, for example, point Y? Because Y is on a lower indifference curve, I_2. By trading "down" the budget line—by shifting dollars from purchases of A to purchases of B—the consumer can get on an indifference curve further from the origin and thereby increase total utility from the same income. Why not Z? Same reason: Point Z is on a lower indifference curve, I_1. By trading "up" the budget line—by reallocating dollars from B to A—it is possible for the consumer to get on higher indifference curve I_3 and increase total utility. How about point W on indifference curve I_4? While it is true that W entails a higher level of total utility than does X, point W is beyond (outside) the budget line and hence *not* attainable to the consumer. Point X is the best or optimal *attainable* combination of products A and B. At this point we note that, by definition of tangency, the slope of the highest obtainable indifference curve equals the slope of the budget line. Because the slope of the indifference curve reflects the MRS and the slope of the budget line is P_B/P_A, the optimal or equilibrium position is where

$$MRS = P_B/P_A$$

DIGRESSION: THE MEASUREMENT OF UTILITY

The alert reader may have sensed an important difference between the marginal-utility theory and

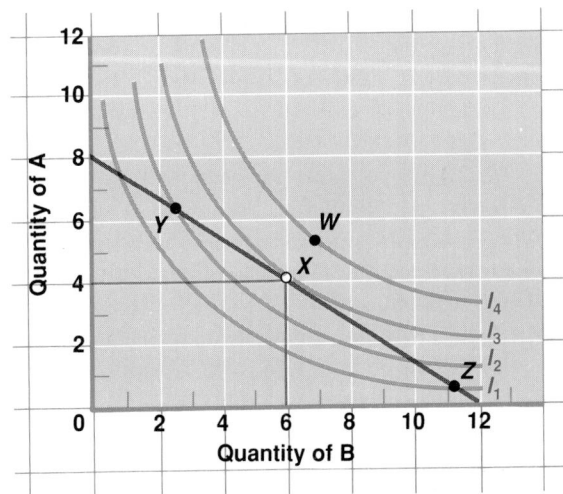

FIGURE 4

The consumer's equilibrium position

The consumer's equilibrium position is at point X, where the budget line is tangent to the highest attainable indifference curve, I_3. In this case the consumer will buy 4 units of A at $1.50 per unit and 6 of B at $1 per unit with a $12 money income. Points Z and Y also represent attainable combinations of A and B, but yield less total utility as is evidenced by the fact they are on lower indifference curves. While W would entail more utility than X, it is outside the budget line and therefore unattainable.

the indifference curve theory of consumer demand. The marginal-utility theory assumes that utility is *numerically* measurable. That is, the consumer is assumed to be able to say *how much* extra utility he or she derives from an extra unit of A or B. Given the prices of A and B, the consumer must be able to measure the marginal utility derived from successive units of A and B in order to realize the utility-maximizing (equilibrium) position as previously indicated by

$$\frac{\text{Marginal utility of A}}{\text{price of A}} = \frac{\text{marginal utility of B}}{\text{price of B}}$$

The indifference curve approach poses a less stringent requirement for the consumer: He or she need only be able to specify whether a given combination of A and B yields more, less, or the same amount of utility than some other combination of A and B. The consumer need only be able to say, for example, that 6 of A and 7 of B yield more (or less) satisfaction than 4 of A and 9 of B; indifference curve analysis does *not* require the consumer to specify *how much* more (or less) satisfaction will be realized.

When the equilibrium situations in the two approaches are compared we find that (1) in the indifference curve analysis the MRS equals P_B/P_A; however, (2) in the marginal-utility approach the ratio of marginal utilities equals P_B/P_A. We therefore deduce that the MRS is equivalent in the marginal-utility approach to the ratio of marginal utilities of the two goods.[9]

DERIVING THE DEMAND CURVE

In our earlier comments on the characteristics of the budget line we noted that, given the price of A, an increase in the price of B will cause the budget line to fan inward to the left. This knowledge can now be used to derive a demand curve for product B. In Figure 5a we have simply reproduced Figure 4 showing our initial consumer equilibrium at point X. The budget line involved in determining this equilibrium position assumes a money income of $12 and that $P_A = \$1.50$ and $P_B = \$1.00$. Let us examine what happens to the equilibrium position if we increase P_B to $1.50, holding money income and the price of A constant.

The result is shown in Figure 5a. The budget line fans to the left, yielding a new equilibrium point of tangency with indifference curve I_2 at point X'. At X' we find the consumer is buying 3 units of B and 5 of A as compared to 4 of A and 6 of B at X. Our interest is in B and we note that we have sufficient information to locate the demand curve for product B. That is, we know that at equilibrium point X the price of B is $1.00 and 6 units are purchased; at equilibrium point X' the price of B is $1.50 and 3 units are purchased. These data are shown graphically as a demand curve for B in

[9] Technical footnote: If we begin with the utility-maximizing rule, $MU_A/P_A = MU_B/P_B$, then multiply through by P_B and divide through by MU_A, we obtain $P_B/P_A = MU_B/MU_A$. In indifference curve analysis we know that the optimal or equilibrium position is where MRS = P_B/P_A. Hence, MRS also equals MU_B/MU_A.

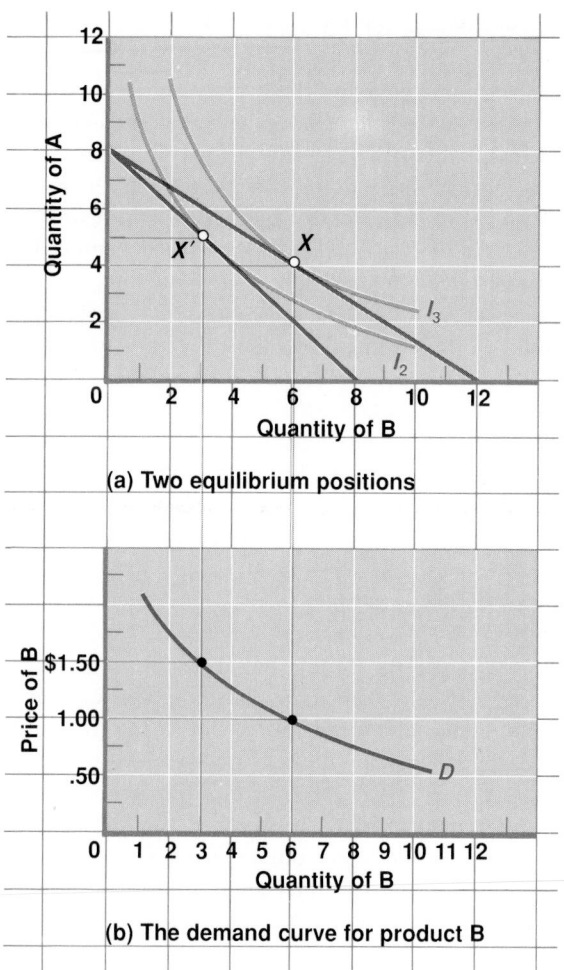

(a) Two equilibrium positions

(b) The demand curve for product B

FIGURE 5

Deriving the demand curve

When the price of B is increased from $1.00 to $1.50 in (a) the equilibrium position moves from X to X', decreasing the quantity demanded from 6 to 3 units. The demand curve for B is determined in (b) by plotting the $1.00–6 units and the $1.50–3 units price-quantity combinations for B.

Figure 5b. Note that the horizontal axes of Figure 5a and b are identical; both measure the quantity demanded of B. Hence, we can simply drop gray perpendiculars from Figure 5a down to the horizontal axis of Figure 5b. On the vertical axis of Figure 5b we merely locate the two chosen prices of B. Connecting these prices with the relevant quantities demanded, we locate two points on the demand curve for B. In drawing the demand curve as shown, we assume that all the "in-between" price-quantity points are similarly derived. The point is that, by simple manipulation of the price of B in an indifference curve–budget line context, a downsloping demand curve for B can be derived. Notice that we have derived the law of demand under the correct assumption of "other things being equal" since *only* the price of B has been changed. The price of A as well as the consumer's income and tastes have remained constant when deriving the consumer's demand curve for product B.

APPENDIX SUMMARY

I The indifference curve approach to consumer behavior is based upon the consumer's budget line and indifference curves.

2 The budget line shows all combinations of two products which the consumer can purchase, given money income and the prices of the products.

3 A change in product prices or money income will shift the budget line.

4 An indifference curve shows all combinations of two products which will yield the same level of total utility to the consumer. Indifference curves are downsloping and convex to the origin.

5 An indifference map consists of a number of indifference curves; the further from the origin, the higher the level of utility associated with each curve.

6 The consumer will select that point on the budget line which puts him or her on the highest attainable indifference curve.

7 Changing the price of one product shifts the budget line and determines a new equilibrium position. A downsloping demand curve can be determined by plotting the price-quantity combinations associated with the old and new equilibrium positions.

APPENDIX TERMS AND CONCEPTS

budget line

indifference curve

marginal rate of substitution

indifference map

equilibrium position

APPENDIX QUESTIONS AND STUDY SUGGESTIONS

I What information is embodied in a budget line? What shifts will occur in the budget line as money income *a* increases and *b* decreases? What shifts will occur in the budget line as the price of the product shown on the horizontal axis *a* increases and *b* decreases?

2 What information is contained in an indifference curve? Why are such curves *a* downsloping and *b* convex to the origin? Why does total utility increase as the consumer moves to indifference curves further from the origin? Why can't indifference curves intersect?

3 Using Figure 4, explain why the point of *tangency* of the budget line with an indifference curve is the consumer's equilibrium position. Explain why any point where the budget line *intersects* an indifference curve will *not* be equilibrium. Explain: "The consumer is in equilibrium where $MRS = P_B/P_A$."

4 Assume that the data in the accompanying table indicate an indifference curve for Mr. Chen. Graph this curve, putting A on the vertical and B on the horizontal axis. Assuming the prices of A and B are \$1.50 and \$1.00, respectively, and that Chen has \$24 to spend, add the resulting budget line to your graph. What combination of A and B will Chen purchase? Does your answer meet the $MRS = P_B/P_A$ rule for equilibrium?

Units of A	Units of B
16	6
12	8
8	12
4	24

5 Explain graphically how indifference analysis can be used to derive a demand curve.

6 *Advanced analysis*: Demonstrate that the equilibrium condition $MRS = P_B/P_A$ is the equivalent of the utility-maximizing rule $MU_A/P_A = MU_B/P_B$.

CHAPTER 24

The costs of production

Product prices are determined by the interaction of the forces of demand and supply. Preceding chapters have focused our attention upon the factors underlying demand. As we observed in Chapter 4, the basic factor underlying the ability and willingness of firms to supply a product in the market is the cost of production. The production of any good requires the use of economic resources which, because of their relative scarcity, bear price tags. The amount of any product which a firm is willing to supply in the market depends upon the prices (costs) and the productivity of the resources essential to its production, on the one hand, and the price which the product will bring in the market, on the other. The present chapter is concerned with the general nature of production costs. Product prices are introduced in the following several chapters, and the supply decisions of producers are then explained.

Economic costs

The economist's notion of costs goes back to the basic fact that resources are scarce and have alternative uses. Thus, to use a bundle of resources in the production of some particular good means that certain alternative production opportunities have been forgone. *Costs in economics have to do with the forgoing of the opportunity to produce alternative goods and services.* More specifically, the **economic,** or **opportunity cost** of any resource in producing some good is its value or worth in its best alternative use. This conception of costs is clearly embodied in the production possibilities curve of Chapter 2. Note, for example, that at point *C* in Table 2-1 the opportunity cost of producing 100,000 *more* pizzas is the 3,000 industrial robots which must be forgone. The steel that is used for armaments is not available for the manufacture of automobiles or apartment buildings. And if an assembly-line worker is capable of producing automobiles or washing machines, then the cost to society in employing this worker in an automobile plant is the contribution the worker would otherwise have made in producing washing machines. The cost to you in reading this chapter is the alternative uses of your time which you must forgo while you do it.

EXPLICIT AND IMPLICIT COSTS

Let us now consider costs from the viewpoint of an individual firm. Given the notion of opportunity costs, we can say that *economic costs are those payments a firm must make, or incomes it must provide, to resource suppliers in order to attract these resources away from alternative lines of production.* These payments or incomes may be either explicit or implicit. The monetary payments—that is, the "out-of-pocket" or cash expenditures which a firm makes to those "outsiders" who supply labor services, materials, fuel, transportation services, power, and so forth—are called **explicit costs.** In other words, explicit costs are payments to non-owners of the firm for the resources which they supply. But, in addition, a firm may use certain resources which the firm itself owns. Our notion of opportunity costs tells us that, regardless of whether a resource is owned or hired by an enterprise, there is a cost involved in using that resource in a specific employment. The costs of such self-owned, self-employed resources are nonexpenditure or **implicit costs.** To the firm, those implicit costs are the money payments which the self-employed resources could have earned in their best alternative employments.

Example: Suppose Brooks operates a corner grocery as a sole proprietor. She owns outright her store building and supplies all her own labor and money capital. Though her enterprise has no explicit rental or wage costs, implicit rents and wages are incurred. By using her own building for a grocery, Brooks sacrifices the $800 monthly rental income which otherwise she could have earned by renting it to someone else. Similarly, by using her money capital and labor in her own enterprise, Brooks sacrifices the interest and wage incomes which she otherwise could have earned by supplying these resources in their best alternative employments. And, finally, by running her own enterprise, Brooks forgoes the earnings she could have realized by supplying her managerial efforts in someone else's firm.

NORMAL PROFITS AS A COST

The minimum payment required to keep Brooks's entrepreneurial talents engaged in this enterprise is called a **normal profit.** As is true of implicit rent or implicit wages, her normal return for the performing of entrepreneurial functions is an implicit cost. If this minimum, or normal, return is not realized, the entrepreneur will withdraw her efforts from this line of production and reallocate them to some more attractive line of production. Or the individual may cease being an entrepreneur in favor of becoming a wage or salary earner.

In short, *the economist includes as costs all payments—explicit and implicit, the latter including a normal profit—required to attract and retain resources in a given line of production.*

ECONOMIC, OR PURE, PROFITS

Our discussion of economic costs correctly suggests that economists and accountants use the term "profits" differently. *Accounting profits are the firm's total revenue less its explicit costs.* But economists define profits differently. **Economic profits** *are total revenue less* all *costs (explicit and implicit, the latter including a normal profit to the entrepreneur).* Therefore, when an economist says that a firm is just covering its costs, it is meant that all explicit and implicit costs are being met and that the entrepreneur is receiving a return just large enough to retain his or her talents in the present line of production. If a firm's total receipts exceed all its economic costs, any residual accrues to the entrepreneur. This residual is called an *economic, or pure, profit.* In short:

$$\begin{matrix} \text{Economic} \\ \text{profits} \end{matrix} = \begin{matrix} \text{total} \\ \text{revenue} \end{matrix} - \begin{matrix} \text{opportunity cost} \\ \text{of all inputs} \end{matrix}$$

An economic profit is *not* a cost, because by definition it is a return in excess of the normal profit required to retain the entrepreneur in this particular line of production. In Chapter 31 we shall find that economic profits are associated with risk bearing and monopoly power.

Figure 24-1 shows the relationships between the various cost and profit concepts and merits

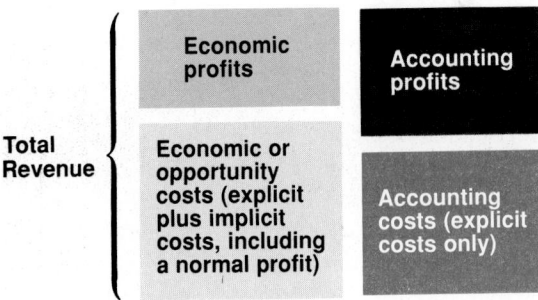

FIGURE 24-1

Economic and accounting profits

Economic profits are equal to total revenue less opportunity costs. Opportunity costs are the sum of explicit and implicit costs and include a normal profit to the entrepreneur. Accounting profits are equal to total revenue less accounting (explicit) costs.

close examination. It is also recommended that at this point you consider question 2 at the end of this chapter.

SHORT RUN AND LONG RUN

The costs which a firm or an industry incurs in producing any given output will depend upon the types of adjustments it is able to make in the amounts of the various resources it employs. The quantities employed of many resources—most labor, raw materials, fuel, power, and so forth—can be varied easily and quickly. Other resources require more time for adjustment. For example, the capacity of a manufacturing plant, that is, the size of the factory building and the amount of machinery and equipment therein, can only be varied over a considerable period of time. In some heavy industries it may take several years to alter plant capacity.

Short run: fixed plant   These differences in the time necessary to vary the quantities of the various resources used in the productive process make it essential to distinguish between the short run and the long run. The **short run** refers to a period of time too brief to permit an enterprise to alter its plant capacity, yet long enough to permit a change in the level at which the fixed plant is utilized. The firm's plant capacity is fixed in the short run, but output can be varied by applying larger or smaller amounts of labor, materials, and other resources to that plant. Existing plant capacity can be used more or less intensively in the short run.

Long run: variable plant   From the viewpoint of existing firms, the **long run** refers to a period of time extensive enough to allow these firms to change the quantities of *all* resources employed, including plant capacity. From the viewpoint of an industry, the long run also encompasses enough time for existing firms to dissolve and leave the industry or for new firms to be created and to enter the industry. *While the short run is a "fixed-plant" time period, the long run is a "variable-plant" time period.*

Illustrations   Some examples will make clear the distinction between the short run and the long run.

If a General Motors plant were to hire an extra 100 workers or to add an entire shift of workers, this would be a short-run adjustment. If the same GM plant were to add a new wing to its building and install more equipment, this would be a long-run adjustment.

It is important to note that the short run and the long run are *conceptual* rather than specific calendar time periods. In light manufacturing industries, changes in plant capacity may be negotiated almost overnight. A small firm making T-shirts can increase its plant capacity in a few days or less by ordering and installing a couple of new cutting tables and several extra sewing machines. But heavy industry is a different story. It may take Exxon several years to construct a new oil refinery.

We now want to analyze production costs in the short-run, or fixed-plant, period. Following this we consider costs in the long-run, or variable-plant, period.

Production costs in the short run

A firm's costs of producing any output will depend not only upon the prices of needed resources, but also upon technology—the quantity of resources it takes to produce that output. It is the latter, technological aspect of costs with which we are concerned for the moment. In the short run a firm can change its output by adding variable resources to a fixed plant. Question: How does output change as more and more variable resources are added to the firm's fixed resources?

LAW OF DIMINISHING RETURNS

The answer is provided in general terms by the **law of diminishing returns,** also called the "law of diminishing marginal product" and the "law of variable proportions." This engineering law states that *as successive units of a variable resource (say, labor) are added to a fixed resource (say, capital or land), beyond some point the extra, or marginal, product attributable to each additional unit of the* *variable resource will decline.* Stated somewhat differently, if additional workers are applied to a given amount of capital equipment, as is the case in the short run, eventually output will rise by smaller and smaller amounts as more workers are employed. Two examples will illustrate this law.

Rationale Suppose a farmer has a fixed amount of land—say, 80 acres—in which corn has been planted. Assuming the farmer does not cultivate the cornfields at all, the yield will be, say, 40 bushels per acre. If the land is cultivated once, output may rise to 50 bushels per acre. A second cultivation may increase output to 57 bushels per acre, a third to 61, and a fourth to, say, 63. Further cultivations will add little or nothing to total output. Successive cultivations add less and less to the land's yield. If this were not the case, the world's needs for corn could be fulfilled by extremely intense cultivation of this single 80-acre plot of land. Indeed, if diminishing returns did not occur, the world could be fed out of a flowerpot.

The law of diminishing returns also holds true in nonagricultural industries. Assume a small planing mill is manufacturing wood furniture frames. The mill has a given amount of equipment in the form of lathes, planers, saws, sanders, and so forth. If this firm hired just one or two workers, total output and productivity (output per worker) would be very low. These workers would have a number of different jobs to perform, and the advantages of specialization would be lost. Time would also be lost in switching from one job operation to another, and the machines would stand idle much of the time. In short, the plant would be understaffed, and production therefore would be inefficient. Production would be inefficient because there is too much capital relative to labor. These difficulties would disappear as more workers were added. Equipment would be more fully utilized, and workers could now specialize on a single job. Time would no longer be lost as the result of job switching. Thus, as more workers are added to the initially understaffed plant, the extra or marginal product of each will tend to rise as a result of more efficient production. But this cannot go on indefinitely. As still more workers are added, problems of overcrowding will arise. Workers must wait in line to use the machinery, so now *workers* are underutil-

ized. Total output increases at a diminishing rate because, given the fixed plant size, each worker will have less capital equipment to work with as more and more labor is hired. The extra, or marginal, product of additional workers declines because the plant is more intensively staffed. There now is more labor in proportion to the fixed amount of capital goods. In the extreme case, the continuous addition of labor to the plant would use up all standing room, and production would be brought to a standstill.

It is to be emphasized that the law of diminishing returns assumes that all units of variable inputs—workers in this case—are of equal quality. That is, each successive worker is presumed to have the same innate ability, motor coordination, education, training, work experience, and so forth. Marginal product ultimately diminishes, not because successive workers are qualitatively inferior, but because more workers are being used relative to the amount of capital goods available.

Numerical example Table 24-1 presents a more explicit numerical illustration of the law of diminishing returns. Column 2 indicates the **total product** which will result from combining each level of labor input in column 1 with an assumedly fixed amount of capital goods. Column 3, **marginal product,** shows us the *change* in total output associated with each additional input of labor. Note that with no labor inputs, total product is zero; an empty plant will yield no output. The first two workers reflect increasing returns, their marginal products being 10 and 15 units of output respectively. But then, beginning with the third worker, marginal product—the increase in total product—diminishes continuously and actually becomes zero with the eighth worker and negative with the ninth. **Average product** or output per worker (also called "labor productivity") is shown in column 4. It is calculated simply by dividing total product (column 2) by the corresponding number of workers (column 1).

Graphic portrayal Figure 24-2a and b shows the law of diminishing returns graphically and is useful in helping to understand more fully the relationships between total, marginal, and average product. Note first that total product goes through three

TABLE 24-1 **The law of diminishing returns** *(hypothetical data)*

(1) Inputs of the variable resource (labor)	(2) Total product	(3) Marginal product $\Delta 2/\Delta 1$		(4) Average product (2)/(1)
0	0			—
		10	Increasing marginal returns	
1	10			10
		15		
2	25			$12\frac{1}{2}$
		12		
3	37			$12\frac{1}{3}$
		10	Diminishing marginal returns	
4	47			$11\frac{3}{4}$
		8		
5	55			11
		5		
6	60			10
		3		
7	63			9
		0	Negative marginal returns	
8	63			$7\frac{7}{8}$
		−1		
9	62			$6\frac{8}{9}$

phases: It rises initially at an increasing rate; then it increases but at a decreasing rate; finally it reaches a maximum and declines. Geometrically, marginal product is the slope of the total product curve. Stated differently, marginal product measures the rate of change in total product associated with each successive worker. Hence, the three phases of total product are also reflected in marginal product. Where total product is increasing at an increasing rate, marginal product is necessarily rising. Here extra workers are adding larger and larger amounts to total product. Similarly, where total product is increasing but at a decreasing rate, marginal product is positive but falling. Each additional worker adds less to total product than did preceding workers. When total product is at a maximum, marginal product is zero. When total product declines, marginal product becomes negative.

Average product also reflects the same general "increasing-maximum-diminishing" relationship between variable inputs of labor and output as does marginal product. But note this technical point concerning the relationship between marginal product and average product: Where marginal product exceeds average product, the latter must rise. And wherever marginal product is less than average product, then average product must be declining. It follows that marginal product intersects average product where the latter is at a maximum. This relationship is a matter of mathematical necessity. When one adds a number to a total which is greater than the current average of that total, the average must rise. And when one adds a number to a total which is less than the current average of that total, the average necessarily falls. You raise your average grade in a course only when your score on an additional (marginal) examination is greater than the average of all your past scores. If your grade on an additional exam is below your current average, your average will be pulled down. In our production example, so long as the amount an additional worker adds to total product exceeds the average product or "productivity" of all workers already employed, average product will rise. Conversely, when an extra worker adds an amount to the total product which is less than the present average product, then that worker will lower average product or "productivity."

The law of diminishing returns is embodied in the shapes of all three curves. But, as our earlier definition of the law of diminishing returns indi-

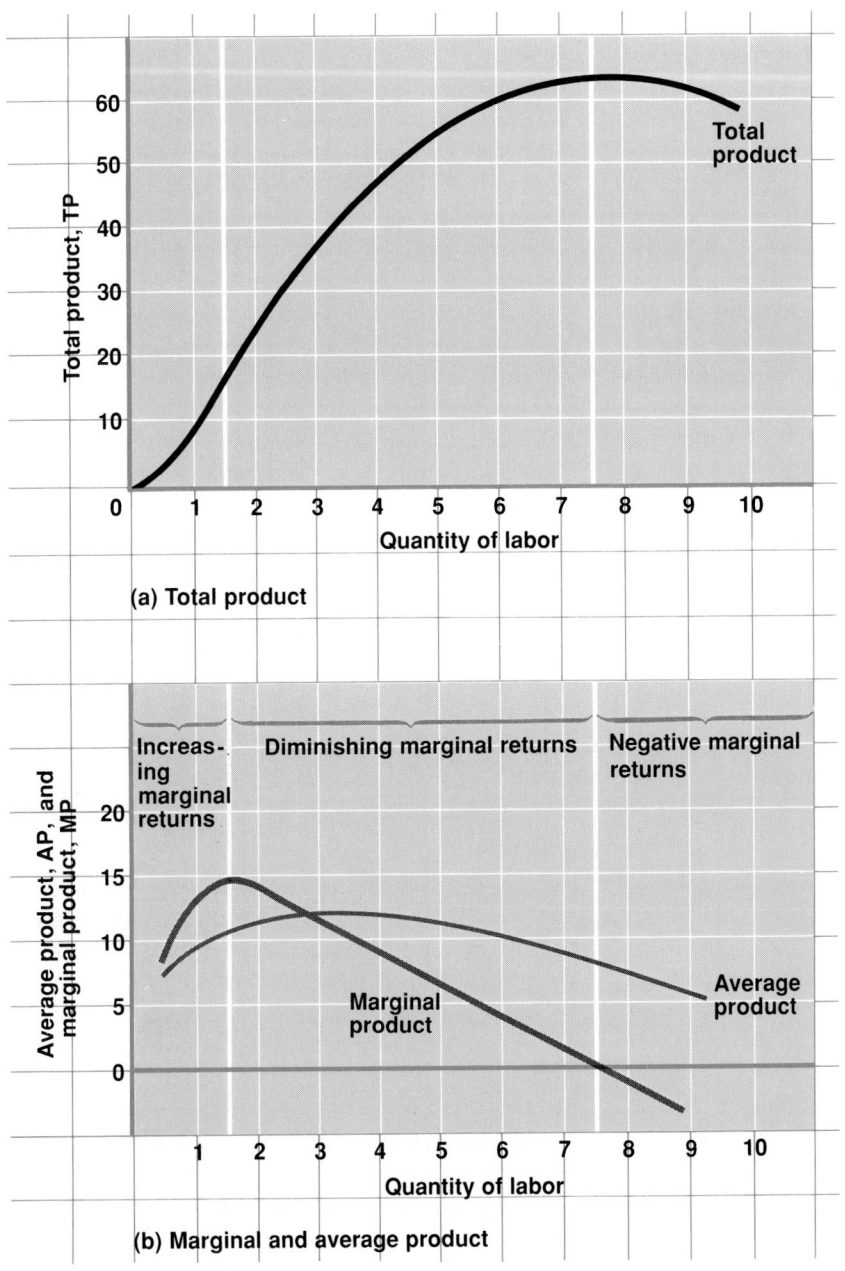

(a) Total product

Increasing marginal returns

Diminishing marginal returns

Negative marginal returns

Marginal product

Average product

(b) Marginal and average product

FIGURE 24-2

The law of diminishing returns

As a variable resource (labor) is added to fixed amounts of other resources (land or capital), the resulting total product will eventually increase by diminishing amounts, reach a maximum, and then decline as in (a). Marginal product in (b) reflects the changes in total product associated with each input of labor. Average product is simply output per worker. Note that marginal product intersects average product at the maximum average product.

cates, economists are most concerned with marginal product. We therefore discern the stages of increasing, diminishing, and negative marginal product (returns) in Figure 24-2. Glancing back at columns 1 and 3 of Table 24-1, we observe increasing returns for the first two workers, decreasing returns for workers 3 through 8, and negative returns for the ninth worker.

FIXED, VARIABLE, AND TOTAL COSTS

The production data described by the law of diminishing returns must be coupled with resource prices to determine the total and per unit costs of producing various outputs. We have emphasized that in the short run some resources—those associated with the firm's plant—are fixed. Others are variable. This correctly suggests that in the short run, costs can be classified as either fixed or variable.

Fixed costs Fixed costs *are those costs which in total do not vary with changes in output.* Fixed costs are associated with the very existence of a firm's plant and therefore must be paid even if the firm's output is zero. Such costs as interest on a firm's bonded indebtedness, rental payments, a portion of depreciation on equipment and buildings, insurance premiums, and the salaries of top management and key personnel are generally fixed costs. In column 2 of Table 24-2 we have assumed that the firm's total fixed costs are $100. Note that, by definition, this fixed-cost figure prevails at all levels of output, including zero.

Variable costs Variable costs *are those costs which change with the level of output.* They include payments for materials, fuel, power, transportation services, most labor, and similar variable resources. In column 3 of Table 24-2 we find that the total of variable costs changes directly with output. But note that *the increases in variable costs associated with each one-unit increase in output are not constant.* As production begins, variable costs will for a time increase by a *decreasing* amount; this is true through the fourth unit of output. Beyond the fourth unit, however, variable costs rise by *increasing* amounts for each successive unit of output. The explanation of this behavior of variable costs lies in the law of diminishing returns. Because of increasing marginal product, smaller and smaller increases in the amounts of variable resources will be needed for a time to get each successive unit of output produced. And, because all units of the variable resources are priced the same, this means that total variable costs will increase by decreasing amounts. But when marginal product begins to decline as diminishing returns are encountered, it will be necessary to use larger and larger additional

TABLE 24-2 **Total- and average-cost schedules for an individual firm in the short run (hypothetical data)**

Total-cost data				Average-cost data			
(1)	(2)	(3)	(4)	(5)	(6)	(7)	(8)
Total product	Total fixed cost	Total variable cost	Total cost	Average fixed cost	Average variable cost	Average total cost	Marginal cost
(Q)	(TFC)	(TVC)	(TC) TC = TFC + TVC	(AFC) $AFC = \dfrac{TFC}{Q}$	(AVC) $AVC = \dfrac{TVC}{Q}$	(ATC) $ATC = \dfrac{TC}{Q}$	(MC) $MC = \dfrac{\text{change in TC}}{\text{change in } Q}$
0	$100	$ 0	$ 100				
1	100	90	190	$100.00	$90.00	$190.00	$ 90
2	100	170	270	50.00	85.00	$135.00	80
3	100	240	340	33.33	80.00	$113.33	70
4	100	300	400	25.00	75.00	$100.00	60
5	100	370	470	20.00	74.00	94.00	70
6	100	450	550	16.67	75.00	91.67	80
7	100	540	640	14.29	77.14	91.43	90
8	100	650	750	12.50	81.25	93.75	110
9	100	780	880	11.11	86.67	97.78	130
10	100	930	1030	10.00	93.00	103.00	150

amounts of variable resources to produce each successive unit of output. Total variable costs will therefore increase by increasing amounts.

Total cost   **Total cost** is self-defining: It is the *sum of fixed and variable costs at each level of output*. It is shown in column 4 of Table 24-2. At zero units of output, total cost is equal to the firm's fixed costs. Then for each unit of production—1 through 10—total cost varies by the same amounts as does variable cost.

Figure 24-3 shows graphically the fixed-, variable-, and total-cost data of Table 24-2. Note that total variable cost is measured vertically from the horizontal axis and total fixed cost is added vertically to total variable cost in locating the total-cost curve.

The distinction between fixed and variable costs is of considerable significance to the business manager. Variable costs are those costs which businesses can control or alter in the short run by changing levels of production. On the other hand,

fixed costs are clearly beyond the business executive's present control; such costs are incurred in the short run and must be paid regardless of output level.

PER UNIT, OR AVERAGE, COSTS

Producers are certainly interested in their total costs, but they are equally concerned with their *per unit*, or *average, costs*. In particular, average-cost data are more usable for making comparisons with product price, which is always stated on a per unit basis. Average fixed cost, average variable cost, and average total cost are shown in columns 5 to 7 of Table 24-2. It is important that we know how these unit-cost figures are derived and how they vary as output changes.

1 AFC   **Average fixed cost** (AFC) is found by dividing total fixed cost (TFC) by the corresponding output (Q). That is

$$AFC = \frac{TFC}{Q}$$

Whereas total fixed costs are, by definition, independent of output, AFC will decline so long as output increases. As output increases, a given total fixed cost of $100 is being spread over a larger and larger output. When output is just 1 unit, total fixed costs and AFC are equal at $100. But at 2 units of output, total fixed costs of $100 become $50 worth of fixed costs per unit; then $33.33, as $100 is spread over 3 units; $25, when spread over 4 units; and so forth. This is what business executives commonly refer to as "spreading the overhead." We find in Figure 24-4 that AFC graphs as a continually declining amount as total output is increased.

2 AVC   **Average variable cost** (AVC) is calculated by dividing total variable cost (TVC) by the corresponding output (Q):

$$AVC = \frac{TVC}{Q}$$

AVC declines initially, reaches a minimum, and then increases again. Graphically, this provides us with a U-shaped or saucer-shaped AVC curve, as is shown in Figure 24-4.

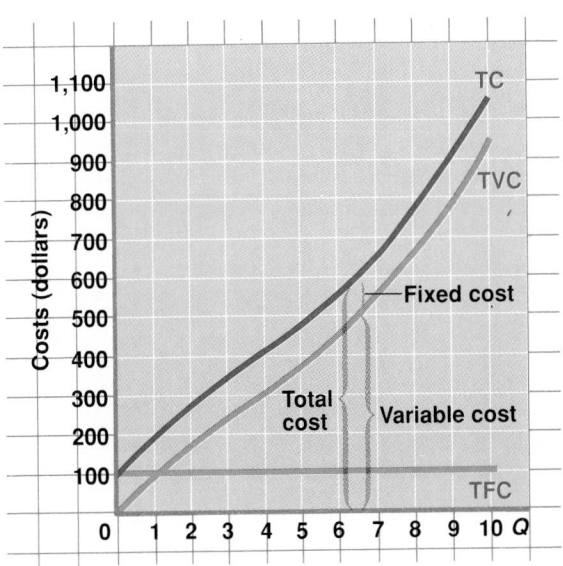

FIGURE 24-3

Total cost is the sum of fixed and variable costs

Total variable costs (TVC) change with output. Fixed costs are independent of the level of output. The total cost (TC) of any output is the vertical sum of the fixed and variable costs of that output.

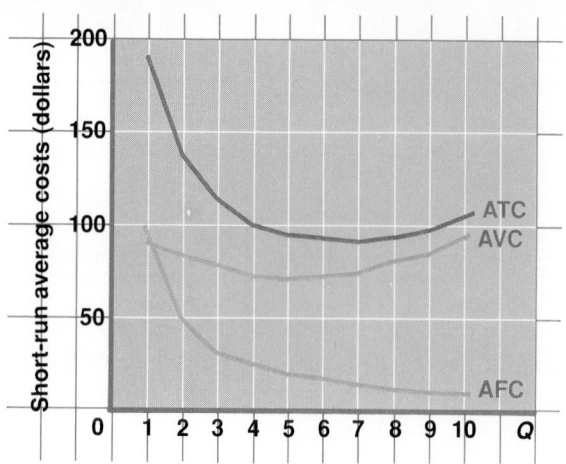

FIGURE 24-4

The average-cost curves

Average total cost (ATC) is the vertical sum of average variable cost (AVC) and average fixed cost (AFC). AFC necessarily falls as a given amount of fixed costs is apportioned over a larger and larger output. AVC initially falls because of increasing marginal returns but then rises because of diminishing marginal returns.

Because total variable cost reflects the law of diminishing returns, so must the AVC figures, which are derived from total variable cost. Because of increasing returns, it takes fewer and fewer additional variable resources to produce each of the first 4 units of output. As a result, variable cost per unit will decline. AVC hits a minimum with the fifth unit of output, and beyond this point AVC rises as diminishing returns necessitate the use of more and more variable resources to produce each additional unit of output. In more direct terms, at low levels of output production will be relatively inefficient and costly, because the firm's fixed plant is understaffed. Not enough variable resources are being combined with the firm's plant; production is inefficient, and per unit variable costs are therefore relatively high. As output expands, however, greater specialization and a more complete utilization of the firm's capital equipment will make for more efficient production. As a result, variable cost per unit of output will decline. As more and more variable resources are added, some point will eventually be reached where diminishing returns are incurred. The firm's capital equipment will now be

staffed more intensively, and therefore each added input will not increase output by as much as preceding inputs. This means that AVC will increase.

You can verify the U or saucer shape of the AVC curve by returning to Table 24-1. Assume the price of labor is, say, $10 per unit. By dividing average product (output per worker) into $10 (price per worker), you will determine labor cost per unit of output. Because we have assumed labor to be the only variable output, labor cost per unit of output *is* variable cost per unit of output or AVC. When average product is initially low, AVC will be high. As workers are added, average product rises and this causes AVC to fall. When average product is at its maximum, AVC will be at its minimum. Then, as still more workers are added and average product declines, AVC will rise. The "hump" of the average-product curve is reflected in the saucer or U shape of the AVC curve. A glance ahead at Figure 24-6 will confirm this line of reasoning graphically.

3 ATC   Average total cost (ATC) can be found by dividing total cost (TC) by total output (Q) or, more simply, by adding AFC and AVC for each of the ten levels of output. That is,

$$\text{ATC} = \frac{\text{TC}}{Q} = \text{AFC} + \text{AVC}$$

These data are shown in column 7 of Table 24-2. ATC is found by adding vertically the AFC and AVC curves, as in Figure 24-4. Thus the vertical distance between the ATC and AVC curves reflects AFC at any level of output.

MARGINAL COST

There remains one final and very crucial cost concept—marginal cost. **Marginal cost** (MC) *is the extra, or additional, cost of producing one more unit of output.* MC can be determined for each additional unit of output simply by noting the *change* in total cost which that unit's production entails.

$$\text{MC} = \frac{\text{change in TC}}{\text{change in } Q}$$

Our data are structured so that the "change in Q"

is always "1," so we have defined MC as the cost of *one* more unit of output.

In Table 24-2 we find that production of the first unit of output increases total cost from $100 to $190. Therefore, the additional, or marginal, cost of that first unit is $90. The marginal cost of the second unit is $80 (= $270 − $190); the MC of the third is $70 (= $340 − $270); and so forth. MC for each of the 10 units of output is shown in column 8 of Table 24-2. MC can also be calculated from the total-variable-cost column. Why? Because the only difference between total cost and total variable cost is the constant amount of fixed costs ($100). Hence, the *change* in total cost and the *change* in total variable cost associated with each additional unit of output are always the same.

Marginal cost is a strategic concept because it designates those costs over which the firm has the most direct control. More specifically, MC indicates those costs which are incurred in the production of the last unit of output and, simultaneously, the cost which can be "saved" by reducing total output by the last unit. Average-cost figures do *not* provide this information. For example, suppose the firm is undecided as to whether it should produce 3 or 4 units of output. At 4 units of output Table 24-2 indicates that ATC is $100. But the firm does not increase its total costs by $100 by producing, nor does it "save" $100 by not producing, the fourth unit. Rather, the change in costs involved here is only $60, as the MC column of Table 24-2 clearly reveals. A firm's decisions as to what output level to produce are typically marginal decisions, that is, decisions to produce a few more or a few less units. Marginal cost reveals the change in costs which one more unit or one less unit of output entails. When coupled with marginal revenue, which we will find in Chapter 25 indicates the change in revenue from one more or one less unit of output, marginal cost allows a firm to determine whether it is profitable to expand or contract its level of production. The analysis in the next four chapters centers upon these marginal calculations.

Marginal cost is shown graphically in Figure 24-5. Note that marginal cost declines sharply, reaches a minimum, and then rises rather sharply. This mirrors the fact that variable cost, and therefore total cost, increases first by decreasing amounts and then by increasing amounts (see Figure 24-3 and columns 3 and 4 of Table 24-2).

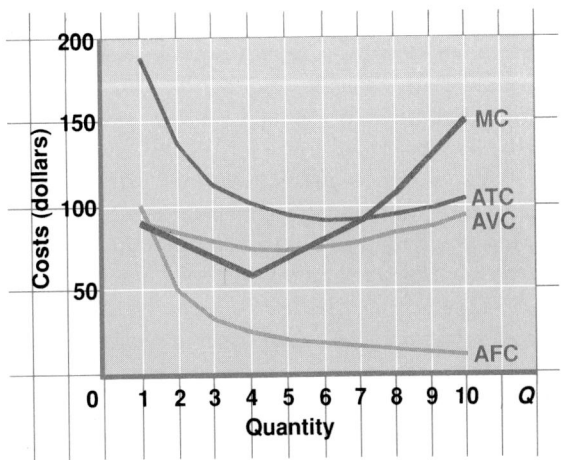

FIGURE 24-5

The relationship of marginal cost to average total cost and average variable cost

Marginal cost (MC) cuts both ATC and AVC at their minimum points. This is so because whenever the extra or marginal amount added to total cost (or variable cost) is less than the average of that cost, the average will necessarily fall. Conversely, whenever the marginal amount added to total (or variable) cost is greater than the average of total (or variable) cost, the average must rise.

MC and marginal product The shape of the marginal-cost curve is a reflection of, and the consequence of, the law of diminishing returns. The relationship between marginal product and marginal cost can be readily grasped by looking back to Table 24-1. If each successive unit of a variable resource (labor) is hired at a constant price, the marginal cost of each extra unit of output will *fall* so long as the marginal product of each additional worker is *rising*. This is so because marginal cost is simply the (constant) price or cost of an extra worker divided by his or her marginal product. Hence, in Table 24-1 suppose each worker can be hired at a cost of $10. Because the first worker's marginal product is 10 and the hiring of this worker increases the firm's costs by $10, the marginal cost of each of these 10 extra units of output will be $1 (= $10 ÷ 10). The second worker also increases costs by $10, but the marginal product is 15, so that the marginal cost of each of these 15 extra units of output is $.67 (= $10 ÷ 15). In general, so long as marginal product is rising, marginal cost will be falling. But as diminishing returns set in—in this case, with the third worker—marginal cost will begin to rise. Thus, for the third worker, marginal cost is $.83 (= $10 ÷ 12); $1.00 for the fourth worker; $1.25 for the fifth; and so on. The relationship between marginal product and marginal cost is evident: *Given the price (cost) of the variable resource, increasing returns (that is, a rising marginal product) will be reflected in a declining marginal cost and diminishing returns (that is, a falling marginal product) in a rising marginal cost.* The MC curve is a mirror reflection of the marginal product curve. Once again, examine Figure 24-6. When marginal product is rising, marginal cost is necessarily falling. When marginal product is at its maximum, marginal cost is at its minimum. And when marginal product is falling, marginal cost is rising.

Relation of MC to AVC and ATC   It is also notable that the marginal cost curve intersects both the AVC and ATC curves at their minimum points. As noted earlier, this marginal-average relationship is a matter of mathematical necessity, which a commonsense illustration can make readily apparent. Suppose a baseball pitcher has allowed his opponents an average of 3 runs per game in the first three games he has pitched. Now, whether his average falls or rises as a result of pitching a fourth (marginal) game will depend upon whether the additional runs he allows in that extra game are fewer or more than his current 3-run average. If he allows fewer than 3 runs—for example, 1—in the fourth game, his total runs will rise from 9 to 10, and his average will fall from 3 to $2\frac{1}{2}$ (= 10 ÷ 4). Conversely, if he allows more than 3 runs—say, 7—in the fourth game, his total will increase from 9 to 16 and his average will rise from 3 to 4 (= 16 ÷ 4).

So it is with costs. When the amount added to total cost (marginal cost) is less than the average of total cost, ATC will fall. Conversely, when marginal cost exceeds ATC, ATC will rise. This means in Figure 24-5 that so long as MC lies below ATC, the latter will fall, and where MC is above ATC, ATC will rise. Therefore, at the point of intersection where MC equals ATC, ATC has just ceased to fall but has not yet begun to rise. This, by definition, is the minimum point on the ATC curve. *The*

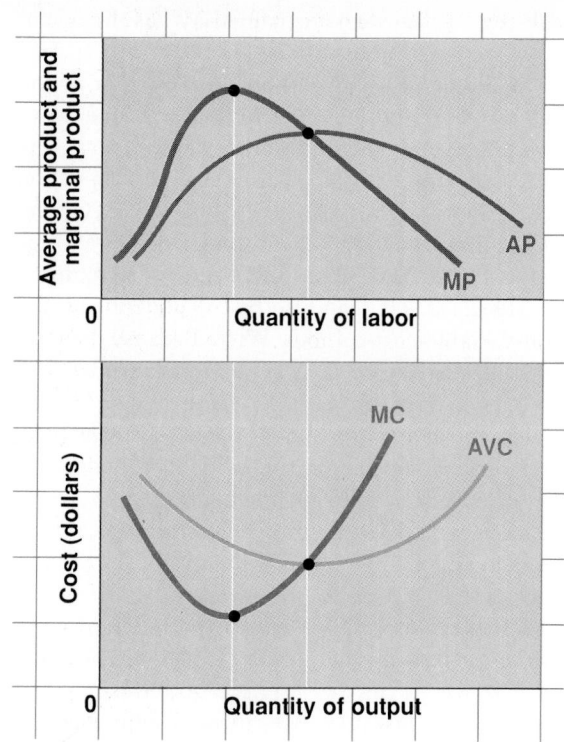

FIGURE 24-6

The relationship between productivity curves and cost curves

The marginal cost (MC) and average-variable-cost (AVC) curves are mirror images of the marginal product (MP) and average-product (AP) curves respectively. Assuming labor is the only variable input and that its price (the wage rate) is constant, MC is found by dividing the wage rate by MP. Hence, when MP is rising, MC is falling; when MP reaches its maximum, MC is at its minimum; and when MP is diminishing, MC is rising. A similar relationship holds between AP and AVC.

marginal-cost curve intersects the average-total-cost curve at the latter's minimum point. Because MC can be defined as the addition either to total cost *or* to total variable cost resulting from one more unit of output, this same rationale explains why the MC curve also crosses the AVC curve at the latter's minimum point. No such relationship exists for the MC curve and the average-fixed-cost curve, because the two are not related; marginal cost embodies only those costs which change with output, and fixed costs by definition are independent of output.

SHIFTING THE COST CURVES

Changes in either resource prices or technology will cause the cost curves to shift. For example, if fixed costs had been higher—say, $200 rather than the $100 we assumed in Table 24-2—then the AFC curve in Figure 24-5 would be shifted upward. The ATC curve would also be located at a higher position because AFC is a component of ATC. Note that the positions of the AVC and MC curves would be unaltered, however, because their locations are based on the prices of variable rather than fixed resources. Thus, if the price (wage) of labor or some other variable input were to rise, the AVC, ATC, and MC curves would all shift upward, but the position of AFC would remain unchanged. Reductions in the prices of fixed or variable resources will entail cost curve shifts exactly opposite to those just described.

If a more efficient technology were discovered, then the productivity of all inputs would increase. As a result, the cost figures in Table 24-1 would all be lower. To illustrate, if labor is the only variable input and wages are $10 per hour and average product is 10 units, then AVC would be $1. But if a technological improvement increases the average product of labor to 20 units, then AVC will decline to $.50. More generally, an upshift in the productivity curves shown in the top portion of Figure 24-6 will mean a downshift in the cost curves portrayed in the bottom portion of that diagram.

Let us now turn to the relationship between output and unit costs when all inputs are variable.

Production costs in the long run

In the long run all desired resource adjustments can be negotiated by an industry and the individual firms which it comprises. The firm can alter its plant capacity; it can build a larger plant or revert to a smaller plant than that assumed in Table 24-2. The industry can also change its plant size; the long run is an amount of time sufficient for new firms to enter or existing firms to leave an industry. The impact of the entry and exodus of firms into and from an industry will be discussed in the next chapter; here we are concerned only with changes in plant capacity made by a single firm. And in considering these adjustments, we couch our analysis in terms of ATC, making no distinction between fixed and variable costs because all resources, and therefore all costs, are variable in the long run.

Suppose a single-plant manufacturing enterprise starts out on a small scale and then, as the result of successful operations, expands to successively larger plant sizes. What will happen to average total costs as this growth occurs? The answer is this: For a time successively larger plants will bring lower average total costs. However, eventually the building of a still larger plant may cause ATC to rise.

Figure 24-7 illustrates this situation for five possible plant sizes. ATC-1 is the average-total-cost curve for the smallest of the five plants, and ATC-5 for the largest. The relationship of the five plant sizes to one another is clearly that stated above. Constructing a larger plant will entail lower minimum per unit costs through plant size 3. But beyond this point a larger plant will mean a higher level of minimum average total costs.

The white lines perpendicular to the output axis are crucial. They indicate those outputs at which the firm should change plant size in order to realize the lowest attainable per unit costs of production. To illustrate in terms of Figure 24-7: For all outputs up to 20 units, the lowest per unit costs are attainable with plant size 1. However, if the firm's volume of sales expands to some level greater than 20 but less than 30 units, it can achieve lower per unit costs by constructing a larger plant—plant size 2. Although *total* cost will be higher at the greater levels of production, the cost *per unit* of output will be less than before. For any output between 30 and 50 units, plant size 3 will yield the lowest per unit costs. For the 50- to 60-unit range of output, plant size 4 must be built to achieve the lowest unit costs. Lowest per unit costs for any output in excess of 60 units demand the construction of the still larger plant of size 5.

Tracing these adjustments, we can conclude that the long-run ATC curve for the enterprise will comprise segments of the short-run ATC curves for the various plant sizes which can be constructed. *The long-run ATC curve shows the least per unit cost at which any output can be produced after the firm*

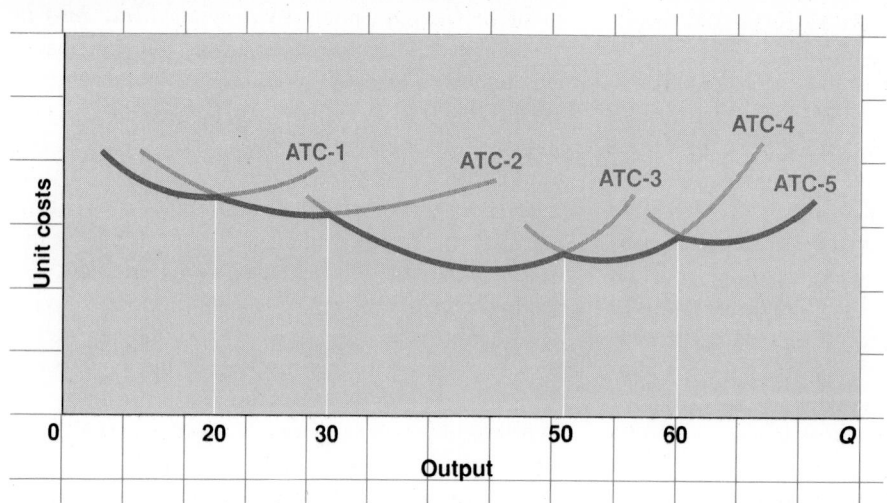

FIGURE 24-7

The long-run average-cost curve: five possible plant sizes

The long-run average-cost curve is made up of segments of the short-run cost curves (ATC-1, ATC-2, etc.) of the various-sized plants from which the firm might choose. Each point on the bumpy planning curve shows the least unit cost attainable for any output when the firm has had time to make all desired changes in its plant size.

has had time to make all appropriate adjustments in its plant size. In Figure 24-7 the heavy, bumpy curve is the firm's long-run ATC curve or, as it is often called, the firm's planning curve.

In most lines of production the choice of plant sizes is much wider than that assumed in our illustration. In fact, in many industries the number of possible plant sizes is virtually unlimited. This means that in time quite small changes in the vol-

ume of output (sales) will prompt appropriate changes in the size of the plant. Graphically, this implies there is an unlimited number of short-run ATC curves, as suggested by Figure 24-8. The minimum ATC of producing each possible level of output is shown by the long-run ATC curve. Rather than being comprised of *segments* of short-run ATC curves as in Figure 24-7, the long-run ATC curve is made up of all the *points of tangency* of the theoreti-

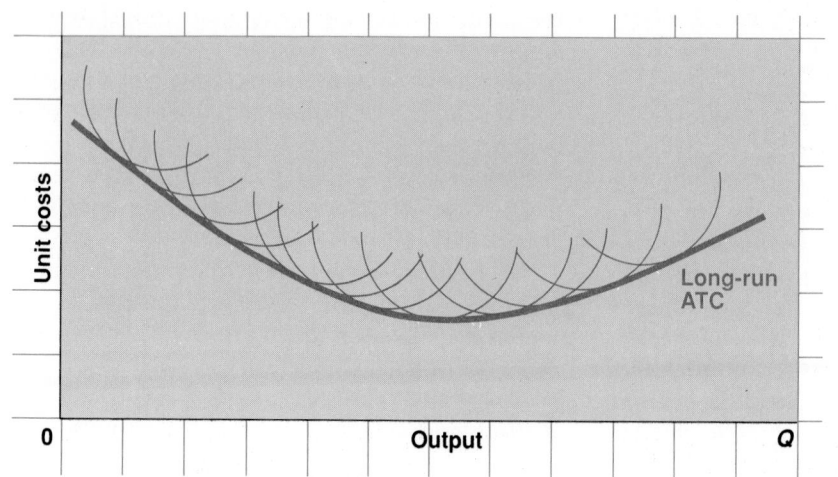

FIGURE 24-8

The long-run average-cost curve: unlimited number of plant sizes

If the number of possible plant sizes is very large, the long-run average-cost curve approximates a smooth curve. Economies of scale, followed by diseconomies of scale, cause the curve to be U-shaped.

cally unlimited number of short-run ATC curves from which the long-run ATC curve is derived. Hence, the planning curve is smooth rather than bumpy. Note that, with the exception of the minimum point on the long-run ATC curve, the long-run ATC curve is *not* tangent to the short-run ATC curves at the minimum points of the latter. Where the long-run ATC curve is diminishing, the points of tangency are to the left of the minimum points on the short-run ATC curves. Conversely, where long-run ATC is rising, the tangency points are to the right of the minimum points on the short-run ATC curves.

ECONOMIES AND DISECONOMIES OF SCALE

We have patiently accepted the contention that for a time a larger and larger plant size will entail lower unit costs but that beyond some point successively larger plants will mean higher average total costs. Now we must explain this point. Exactly why is the long-run ATC curve U-shaped? It must be emphasized, first of all, that the law of diminishing returns is *not* applicable here, because it presumes that one resource is fixed in supply and, as we have seen, the long run assumes that all resources are variable. Also, our discussion assumes that resource prices are constant. What, then, is our explanation? The U-shaped long-run average-cost curve is explainable in terms of what economists call economies and diseconomies of large-scale production.

Economies of scale **Economies of scale** or, more commonly, economies of mass production, explain the downsloping part of the long-run ATC curve, as indicated in Figure 24-9a. As the size of a plant increases, a number of considerations will for a time give rise to lower average costs of production.

I LABOR SPECIALIZATION Increased specialization in the use of labor is feasible as a plant increases in size. The hiring of more workers means that jobs can be divided and subdivided. Instead of performing five or six distinct operations in the productive process, each worker may now have just one task to perform. Workers can be used full time on those particular operations at which they have special skills. In a small plant skilled machinists may

spend half their time performing unskilled tasks. This makes for higher production costs. Further, the dividing of work operations which large scale allows will give workers the opportunity to become very proficient at the specific tasks assigned them. The jack-of-all-trades who is burdened with five or six jobs will not be likely to become very efficient in any of them. When allowed to concentrate on one task, the same worker may become highly efficient. Finally, greater specialization tends to eliminate the loss of time which accompanies the shifting of workers from one job to another.

2 MANAGERIAL SPECIALIZATION Large-scale production also permits better utilization of, and greater specialization in, management. A supervisor capable of handling twenty workers will be underutilized in a small plant hiring only ten people. The production staff can be doubled with no increase in administrative costs. In addition, small firms will not be able to use management specialists to best advantage. In a small plant a sales specialist may be forced to divide his or her time between several executive functions—for example, marketing, personnel, and finance. A larger scale of operations will mean that the marketing expert can devote full time to supervising sales and product distribution while appropriate specialists are added to perform other managerial functions. Greater efficiency and lower unit costs are the net result.

3 EFFICIENT CAPITAL Small firms are often not able to utilize the technologically most efficient productive equipment. In many lines of production the most efficient machinery is available only in very large and extremely expensive units. Furthermore, effective utilization of this equipment demands a high volume of production. This means only large-scale producers are able to afford and operate efficiently the best available equipment.

To illustrate: In the automobile industry the most efficient fabrication method entails the use of robotics and elaborate assembly-line equipment. The efficient use of this equipment demands an annual output of an estimated 200,000 to 400,000 automobiles (Chapter 28). Only very large-scale producers can afford to purchase and use this equipment efficiently. The small-scale producer is between the devil and the deep blue sea. To fabricate automobiles with the use of other equipment is

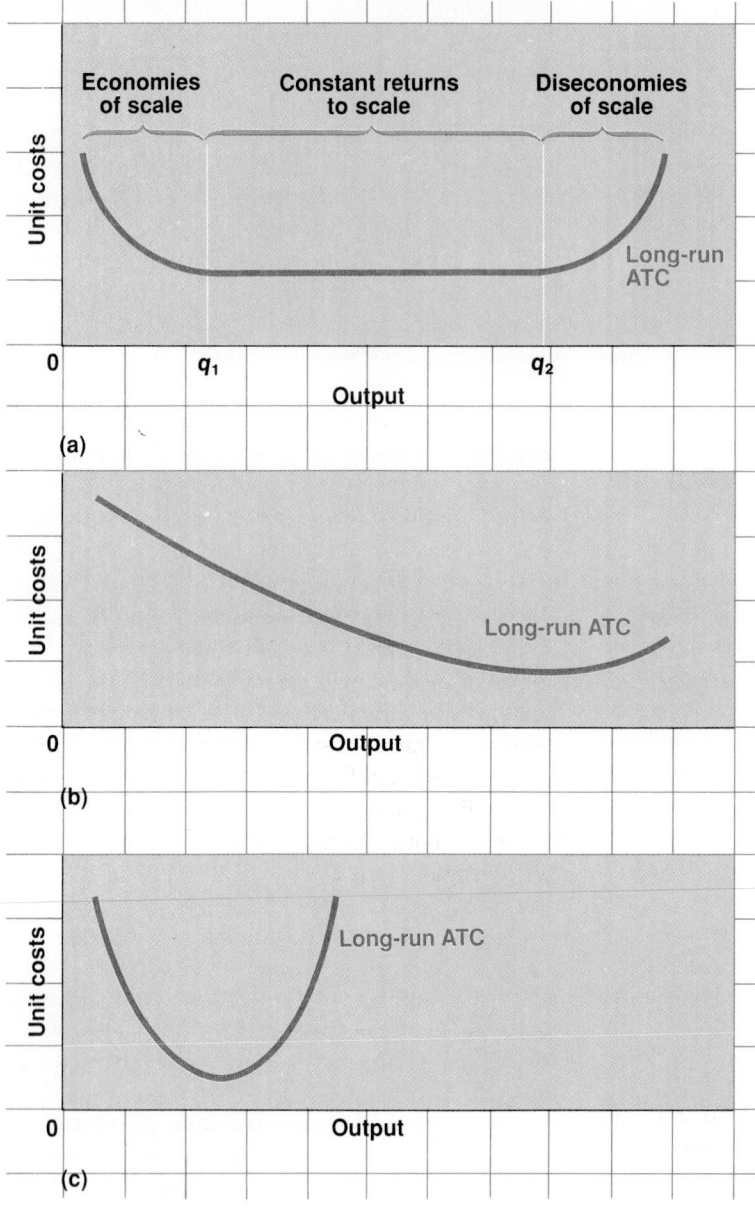

FIGURE 24-9

Various possible long-run average-cost curves

(a) Where economies of scale are rather rapidly exhausted and diseconomies not encountered until a considerably large scale of output has been achieved, long-run average costs will be constant over a wide range of output. (b) When economies of scale are extensive and diseconomies remote, the ATC will fall over a wide range of production. (c) If economies of scale are exhausted quickly, followed immediately by diseconomies, minimum unit costs will be encountered at a relatively low output.

inefficient and therefore more costly per unit. The alternative of purchasing the most efficient equipment and underutilizing it with a small level of output is also inefficient and costly.

4 BY-PRODUCTS The large-scale producer is in a better position to utilize by-products than is a small firm. The large meat-packing plant makes glue, fertilizer, pharmaceuticals, and a host of other products from animal remnants which would be discarded by smaller producers.

All these technological considerations—greater specialization in the use of labor and management and the ability to use the most efficient equipment and the effective utilization of by-products—will contribute to lower unit costs for the producer which is able to expand its scale of operations.

From a slightly different perspective, an increase in *all* resources of, say, 10 percent will cause a more-than-proportionate increase in output of, say, 20 percent. The necessary result will be a decline in ATC.

Diseconomies of scale But in time the expansion of a firm *may* give rise to diseconomies and therefore higher per unit costs.

The main factor causing **diseconomies of scale** has to do with certain managerial problems involved in efficiently controlling and coordinating a firm's operations as it becomes a large-scale producer. In a small plant a single key executive may render all the basic decisions relative to the plant's operation. Because of the firm's smallness, the executive is close to the production line and can, therefore, readily comprehend the various aspects of the firm's operations, easily digest the information gained from subordinates, and render clear and efficient decisions.

This neat picture changes, however, as a firm grows. The management echelons between the executive suite and the assembly line become many; top management is far removed from the actual production operations of the plant. It becomes impossible for one person to assemble, understand, and digest all the information essential to rational decision making in a large-scale enterprise. Authority must be delegated to innumerable vice-presidents, second vice-presidents, and so forth. This expansion in the depth and width of the management hierarchy entails problems of communication, coordination, and bureaucratic red tape and the possibility that the decisions of various subordinates will fail to mesh. The result is impaired efficiency and rising average costs. Again, thought of differently, an increase in *all* resources of, say, 10 percent will cause a less-than-proportionate increase in output of, say, 5 percent. As a consequence, ATC will increase. Diseconomies of scale are illustrated by the rising portion of the long-run cost curve in Figure 24-9a.

Constant returns to scale In some instances there may exist a rather wide range of output between the output level at which economies of scale are exhausted and the point at which diseconomies of scale are encountered. That is, there will exist a range of **constant returns to scale** over which long-run average cost is constant. The $q_1 q_2$ output

range of Figure 24-9a is relevant. Here a given percentage increase in *all* inputs of, say, 10 percent will cause a proportionate 10 percent increase in output. Thus, ATC does not change.

Relevance Economies and diseconomies of scale are something more than a plausible pipe dream of economic theorists. Indeed, in most American manufacturing industries economies of scale have been of great significance. Firms which have been able to expand their scale of operations to realize the economies of mass production have survived and flourished. Those unable to achieve this expansion have found themselves in the unenviable position of being high-cost producers, doomed to a marginal existence or ultimate insolvency.

There is some difference of opinion among economists as to the relevance of diseconomies of scale. On the one hand, some feel that the existence and continued growth of such gigantic corporations as General Motors, AT&T, Exxon, and Prudential Life Insurance seem to cast doubt on the concept. In practice, computerized information and communication systems have often been developed and applied for the purpose of overcoming or forestalling the decision-making problems embodied in the notion of diseconomies of scale. In cases where these efforts are successful, the long-run average-cost curve would fall and then become more or less constant as economies of scale are exhausted. On the other hand, there is case study and anecdotal evidence to suggest that diseconomies of scale are a fact of industrial life and, when encountered, can be significant. Large firms often design their organizational structures in the hope of avoiding diseconomies of scale. For example, among its many subdivisions, General Motors has established five automobile-producing divisions (Chevrolet, Buick, Oldsmobile, Pontiac, and Cadillac), each of which is largely autonomous and competing. A degree of decentralization has been sought which will allow full realization of economies of scale yet help to avoid diseconomies of scale.[1]

Despite such efforts, former executives of large corporations attest to the reality of diseconomies of scale. To illustrate, a former General Motors presi-

[1]See Leonard W. Weiss, *Economics and American Industry* (New York: John Wiley & Sons, Inc., 1961), pp. 347–350.

dent has commented thusly on GM's Chevrolet division:

Chevrolet is such a big monster that you twist its tail and nothing happens at the other end for months and months. It is so gigantic that there isn't any way to really run it. You just sort of try to keep track of it.

Similarly, a former GM vice president provided this insider's view of Chevrolet:

One of the biggest . . . problems was in the manufacturing staff. It was overburdened with layer upon layer of management. . . . A plant manager reported to a city manager who reported to a regional manager who reported to a manager of plants who reported to me, the general manager. Consequently, the manager of the Chevrolet Gear and Axle plant on Detroit's near east side who was only a few miles from my office, was almost light years away in terms of management reporting channels.

More generally, Adams and Brock[2] have recently examined the steel and automobile industries and concluded that the hierarchical, bureaucratic managements which accompany the large size of firms in those industries tend to inhibit efficiency. They also contend that in recent years many large and highly diversified corporations have chosen to divest themselves of various divisions and subsidiaries in the interest of enhancing managerial efficiency.

It is also of interest that the notion of economies of scale has been invoked in debate over the national defense budget. The Air Force warned that the estimated cost of each MX intercontinental missile would rise by approximately 50 percent (from about $79 million to $119 million per missile) in 1985 because Congress decided to reduce the number purchased from 40 to 21 missiles. The higher price allegedly reflects higher unit costs due to the loss of scale economies in production.

MES AND INDUSTRY STRUCTURE

Our comments correctly imply that economies and diseconomies of scale are an important determi-

[2] Walter Adams and James W. Brock, *The Bigness Complex* (New York: Pantheon Books, 1986), chap. 3. The above two quotations are cited in Adams and Brock.

nant of the structure of an industry. To elaborate this point it is helpful to introduce the concept of **minimum efficient scale** (MES) which is simply the smallest level of output at which a firm can minimize long-run average costs. In Figure 24-9a this occurs at Oq_1 units of output. Because of the extended range of constant returns to scale we also observe that firms producing substantially larger outputs could also realize the minimum attainable average costs. Specifically, firms would be equally efficient within the q_1q_2 range. We would therefore not be surprised to find an industry with such cost conditions to be populated by firms of quite different sizes. The meatpacking, furniture, wood products, and small appliance industries provide approximate examples. To repeat: With an extended range of constant returns to scale, relatively large and relatively small firms could coexist in an industry and be equally viable.

Compare this with Figure 24-9b where economies of scale are extensive and diseconomies are remote. Here the long-run average-cost curve will decline over a long range of output. Such is the case in the automobile, aluminum, steel, and a host of other heavy industries. This means that, given consumer demand, efficient production will be achieved only with a small number of industrial giants. Small firms cannot realize the minimum efficient scale and will not be viable. In the extreme, economies of scale might extend beyond the market's size, resulting in what is termed a natural monopoly (Chapter 26). A **natural monopoly,** by definition, is a market situation wherein unit costs are minimized by having a single firm produce the particular good or service.

Where economies of scale are few and diseconomies quickly encountered, minimum efficient size occurs at a small level of output as shown in Figure 24-9c. In such industries a given level of consumer demand will support a large number of relatively small producers. Many of the retail trades and some types of farming fall into this category. So do certain types of light manufacturing, for example, the baking, clothing, and shoe industries. Fairly small firms are as efficient as, or more efficient than, large-scale producers in such industries.

The point to be made is that the shape of the long-run average-cost curve, as determined by economies and diseconomies of scale, can be significant in determining the structure and competitiveness of an industry. Whether an industry is "competitive"—populated by a relatively large number of small firms—or "concentrated"—dominated by a few large producers—is sometimes a reflection of an industry's technology and the resulting shape of its long-run average-cost curve. But we must be cautious in making this statement because industry structure does not depend upon cost conditions alone. Government policies, the geographic size of a market, managerial ability, and a variety of other factors must be considered in explaining the structure of a given industry.[3] Indeed, this chapter's Last Word presents empirical evidence which suggests that many industries are much more concentrated—that is, are less competitive—than can be justified on the basis of economies of scale.

CHAPTER SUMMARY

I Economic costs include all payments which must be received by resource owners in order to ensure the continued supply of these resources in a particular line of production. This definition includes explicit costs, which flow to resource suppliers who are separate from a given enterprise, and also implicit costs, which are the remuneration of self-owned and self-employed resources. One of the implicit cost payments is a normal profit to the entrepreneur for functions performed.

2 In the short run a firm's plant capacity is fixed. The firm can use its plant more or less intensively by adding or subtracting units of variable resources, but the firm does not have sufficient time to alter its plant size.

3 The law of diminishing returns describes what happens to output as a fixed plant is used more intensively. The law states that as successive units of a variable resource such as labor are added to a fixed plant, beyond some point the resulting marginal product associated with each additional worker will decline.

4 Because some resources are variable and others fixed, costs can be classified as variable or fixed in the short run. Fixed costs are those which are independent of the level of output. Variable costs are those which vary with output. The total cost of any output is the sum of fixed and variable costs at that output.

5 Average fixed, average variable, and average total

[3] See, for example, Michael Keeley, "The Economics of Firm Size," *Economic Review* (Federal Reserve Bank of San Francisco), Winter 1984, pp. 5–21.

costs are simply fixed, variable, and total costs per unit of output. Average fixed costs decline continuously as output increases, because a fixed sum is being apportioned over a larger and larger number of units of production. Average variable costs are U-shaped, reflecting the law of diminishing returns. Average total cost is the sum of average fixed and average variable costs; it too is U-shaped.

6 Marginal cost is the extra, or additional, cost of producing one more unit of output. Graphically, the marginal cost curve intersects the ATC and AVC curves at their minimum points.

7 Lower resource prices shift the cost curves downward as does technological progress. Higher input prices shift the cost curves upward.

8 The long run is a period of time sufficiently long for a firm to vary the amounts of all resources used, including plant size. Hence, in the long run all costs are variable. The long-run ATC, or planning, curve is composed of segments of the short-run ATC curves, which represent the various plant sizes a firm is able to construct in the long run.

9 The long-run ATC curve is generally U-shaped. Economies of scale are first encountered as a small firm expands. A number of considerations—particularly greater specialization in the use of labor and management, the ability to use the most efficient equipment, and the more complete utilization of by-products—contribute to these economies of scale. Diseconomies of scale stem from the managerial complexities which accompany large-scale production. The relative importance of economies and diseconomies of scale in an industry is often an important determinant of the structure of that industry.

TERMS AND CONCEPTS

economic (opportunity) cost	variable costs
explicit and implicit costs	total costs
normal and economic profits	average fixed cost
short run and long run	average variable cost
law of diminishing returns	average total cost
total, marginal, and average product	marginal cost
fixed costs	economies and diseconomies of scale
	constant returns to scale
	minimum efficient scale
	natural monopoly

QUESTIONS AND STUDY SUGGESTIONS

1 Distinguish between explicit and implicit costs, giving examples of each. What are the explicit and implicit costs of going to college? Why does the economist classify normal profits as a cost? Are economic profits a cost of production?

2 Gomez runs a small firm which makes pottery. He hires one helper at $12,000 per year, pays annual rent of $5,000 for his shop, and materials cost $20,000 per year. Gomez has $40,000 of his own funds invested in equipment (pottery wheels, kilns, and so forth) which could earn him $4,000 per year if alternatively invested. Gomez has been offered $15,000 per year to work as a potter for a competitor. He estimates his entrepreneurial talents to be worth $3,000 per year. Total annual revenue from pottery sales is $72,000. Calculate accounting profits and economic profits for Gomez's pottery.

3 Which of the following are short-run and which are long-run adjustments? *a* Texaco builds a new oil refinery; *b* Acme Steel Corporation hires 200 more workers; *c* a farmer increases the amount of fertilizer used on his corn crop; and *d* an Alcoa plant adds a third shift of workers.

4 Why can the distinction between fixed and variable costs be made in the short run? Classify the following as fixed or variable costs: advertising expenditures, fuel, interest on company-issued bonds, shipping charges, payments for raw materials, real estate taxes, executive salaries, insurance premiums, wage payments, depreciation and obsolescence charges, sales taxes, and rental payments on leased office machinery. "There are no fixed costs in the long run; all costs are variable." Explain.

5 List the fixed and variable costs associated with owning and operating an automobile. Suppose you are considering whether to drive your car or fly 1000 miles to Fort Lauderdale for spring break. Which costs—fixed, variable, or both—would you take into account in making your decision? Would any implicit costs be relevant? Explain.

6 Use the data at the top of page 488 to calculate marginal product and average product. Plot total, marginal, and average product and explain in detail the relationship between each pair of curves. Explain why marginal product first rises, then declines, and ultimately becomes negative. What bearing does the law of diminishing returns have upon short-run costs? Be specific. "When marginal product is rising, marginal cost is falling. And when marginal product is diminishing, marginal cost is rising." Illustrate and explain graphically and through a numerical example.

LAST WORD

Economies of scale and industrial concentration

Is market concentration explainable in terms of economies of scale?

It is sometimes argued that industrial concentration—the dominance of a market by a small number of firms—is fully justified on the basis of economies of scale. That is, if a firm's long-run average-cost curve declines over an extended range of output, total consumption of the product may only support a few efficient (minimum unit cost) producers (Figure 24-9b).

Research studies suggest that industrial concentration is generally *not* warranted on the basis of economies of scale. The minimum efficient scale (MES)—that is, the smallest plant size at which minimum unit cost would be attained—has been determined for a number of industries, twelve of which are listed in the accompanying table. Column 2 compares the MES output with domestic consumption of each product to determine the percentage of total consumption which a single MES plant could produce. We find, for example, that a cigarette manufacturer of minimum efficient scale could produce about 6.6 percent of the domestic consumption of cigarettes. Furthermore, by dividing the percentage of domestic consumption which an MES plant could produce into 100 percent (total domestic consumption), one can calculate the number of efficient plants which consumption will support. Thus we observe in column 3 that 15 MES plants (= 100 percent ÷ 6.6 percent) are compatible with domestic cigarette consumption.

Minimum efficient plant sizes as a percentage of domestic consumption

(1) Industry	(2) Minimum efficient scale as a percentage of domestic consumption	(3) Number of efficient plants compatible with domestic consumption
Diesel engines (small)	25.5%	4
Turbogenerators	23.0	4
Electric motors	15.0	7
Refrigerators	14.1	7
Cellulosic synthetic fiber	11.1	9
Passenger automobile production	11.0	9
Commercial aircraft	10.0	10
Cigarettes	6.6	15
Printing paper	4.4	23
Beer brewing	3.4	29
Bicycles	2.1	48
Petroleum refining	1.9	53

Source: F. M. Scherer, *Industrial Market Structure and Economic Performance,* 2d ed. (Boston: Houghton Mifflin Company, 1980), pp. 96–97.

We find that in a few industries—small diesel engines, turbogenerators, electric motors, and refrigerators—some level of concentration is required to realize scale economies. But for most of the industries shown, the minimum efficient plant sizes are small in comparison to the domestic market for each product. This in turn suggests that economies of scale do *not* provide a rationale or justification for a high degree of concentration (for example, an oligopoly) in most of the studied industries. The fact that the four largest firms in the beer industry actually provide 77 percent of domestic beer output and the four largest cigarette manufacturers control 90 percent of the domestic cigarette market (Table 28-1) is not explainable solely in terms of economies of scale.

There are some qualifications which must be appended. The data cited in the table refer only to *production* economies. Multiplant firms—and therefore higher levels of industrial concentration than those suggested by column 3 of the table—may be justified on the basis of other nonproduction advantages. For example, a large multiplant firm may be able to economize on management services by drawing upon a common pool of accountants, lawyers, and financial planners to serve all of its plants. Similarly, a multiplant firm may realize economies in advertising, raising money capital, or in product distribution. On the other hand, it is conceivable that diseconomies could be associated with some aspects of multiplant operation. In any event, even when adjustments are made for such factors, the general conclusion remains that economic concentration in many industries cannot be justified on the basis of economies of scale.

Inputs of labor	Total product	Marginal product	Average product
1	15	————	————
2	34	————	————
3	51	————	————
4	65	————	————
5	74	————	————
6	80	————	————
7	83	————	————
8	82	————	————

7 Assume a firm has fixed costs of $60 and variable costs as indicated in the table below. Complete the table. When finished, check your calculations by referring to question 4 at the end of Chapter 25.

   a Graph fixed cost, variable cost, and total cost. Explain how the law of diminishing returns influences the shapes of the variable cost and total-cost curves.
   b Graph AFC, AVC, ATC, and MC. Explain the derivation and shape of each of these four curves and the relationships which they bear to one another. Specifically, explain in nontechnical terms why the MC curve intersects both the AVC and ATC curves at their minimum points.

   c Explain how the locations of each of the four curves graphed in question 7b would be altered if (1) total fixed cost had been $100 rather than $60, and (2) total variable cost had been $10 less at each level of output.

8 Indicate how each of the following would shift the **a** marginal cost curve, **b** average variable cost curve, **c** average fixed cost curve, and **d** average total cost curve of a manufacturing firm. In each case specify the direction of the shift.
   a A reduction in business property taxes
   b An increase in the nominal wages of production workers
   c A decrease in the price of electricity
   d An increase in insurance rates on plant and equipment
   e An increase in transportation costs

9 Use the concepts of economies and diseconomies of scale to explain the shape of a firm's long-run ATC curve. What is the concept of minimum efficient scale? What bearing may the exact shape of the long-run ATC curve have upon the structure of an industry?

Total product	Total fixed cost	Total variable cost	Total cost	Average fixed cost	Average variable cost	Average total cost	Marginal cost
0	$————	$ 0	$————	$————	$————	$————	
1	————	45	————	————	————	————	$————
2	————	85	————	————	————	————	————
3	————	120	————	————	————	————	————
4	————	150	————	————	————	————	————
5	————	185	————	————	————	————	————
6	————	225	————	————	————	————	————
7	————	270	————	————	————	————	————
8	————	325	————	————	————	————	————
9	————	390	————	————	————	————	————
10	————	465	————	————	————	————	————

CHAPTER 25

Price and output determination: pure competition

Chapters 22 to 24 have provided us with the basic tools of analysis necessary to understand how product price and output are determined. But a firm's decisions concerning price and production will vary depending upon the character of the industry in which it is operating. There is no such thing as an "average" or "typical" industry. Detailed examination of the business sector of our economy reveals an almost infinite number of different market situations; no two industries are alike. At one extreme we may find a single producer dominating a market. At the other we discover thousands upon thousands of firms, each of which supplies a minute fraction of market output. Between these extremes lies an almost unlimited variety of market structures.

Prelude: four market models

Any attempt to examine each specific industry would be an endless and impossible task. There are simply too many of them. Hence, we seek a more realistic objective—to define and discuss several basic market structures, or models. In so doing, we shall acquaint ourselves with the *general* way in which price and output are determined in most of the market types which characterize our economy.

Economists envision four relatively distinct market situations—(1) pure competition, (2) pure monopoly, (3) monopolistic competition, and (4) oligopoly. They will be considered in this order here and in the next three chapters. These four market models differ in terms of the number of firms in the industry, whether the product is standardized or differentiated, and how easy or difficult it is for new firms to enter the industry.

Aided by Table 25-1, let us briefly indicate the main characteristics of these four models, acknowledging that more detailed definitions are to follow. In **pure competition** there are a very large number of firms producing a standardized product (for example, wheat or corn). New firms can enter the industry very easily. At the other extreme **pure monopoly** (Chapter 26) refers to a market in which one firm is the sole seller of a product or service (a local electric company). The entry of additional firms is blocked so that the firm *is* the industry. Because there is only one product, there is obviously no product differentiation. **Monopolistic competition** (Chapter 27) is characterized by a relatively large number of sellers who are producing differentiated products (women's clothing, furniture, books). Differentiation is the basis for product promotion and development. Entry to a monopolistically competitive industry is quite easy. Finally, **oligopoly** (Chapter 28) is earmarked by a

TABLE 25-1 **Characteristics of the four basic market models**

Characteristic	Market Model			
	Pure competition	Monopolistic competition	Oligopoly	Pure monopoly
Number of firms	A very large number	Many	Few	One
Type of product	Standardized	Differentiated	Standardized or differentiated	Unique; no close substitutes
Control over price	None	Some, but within rather narrow limits	Circumscribed by mutual interdependence; considerable with collusion	Considerable
Conditions of entry	Very easy, no obstacles	Relatively easy	Significant obstacles present	Blocked
Nonprice competition	None	Considerable emphasis on advertising, brand names, trademarks, etc.	Typically a great deal, particularly with product differentiation	Mostly public relations advertising
Examples	Agriculture	Retail trade, dresses, shoes	Steel, automobiles, farm implements, many household appliances	Local utilities

few sellers and this "fewness" means that pricing and output decisions are interdependent. Each firm is affected by the decisions of rivals and must take these decisions into account in determining its own price-output behavior. Products may be standardized (such as steel or aluminum) or differentiated (automobiles and typewriters). Generally, entry to oligopolistic industries is very difficult. Again, these definitions will be embellished as we examine each model in detail and the characteristics that are outlined in Table 25-1 will come into sharper focus.

We shall find it convenient from time to time to distinguish between the characteristics of a purely competitive market and those of all other basic market arrangements—pure monopoly, monopolistic competition, and oligopoly. To facilitate such comparisons we shall employ **imperfect competition** as a generic term to designate all those market structures which deviate from the purely competitive market model.

Pure competition: concept and occurrence

Let us focus our attention upon pure competition, beginning with an elaboration of our definition.

1 Very large numbers A basic feature of a purely competitive market is the presence of a large number of independently acting sellers, usually offering their products in a highly organized market. Markets for farm commodities, the stock market, and the foreign exchange market are illustrative.

2 Standardized product Competitive firms are producing a standardized or homogeneous product. Given price, the consumer is indifferent as to the seller from which the product is purchased. In a competitive market the products of firms B, C, D, E, and so forth, are looked upon by the buyer as perfect substitutes for that of firm A. Because of product standardization, there is no reason for *nonprice competition,* that is, competition on the basis of differences in product quality, advertising, or sales promotion.

3 "Price taker" In a purely competitive market *individual firms* exert no significant control over product price. This characteristic follows from the preceding two. Under pure competition each firm produces such a small fraction of total output that increasing or decreasing its output will have no perceptible influence upon total supply or, therefore, product price. To illustrate, assume there are 10,000 competing firms, each of which is currently producing 100 units of output. Total supply is therefore 1,000,000. Now suppose one of these 10,000 firms cuts its output to 50 units. Will this affect price? No. And the reason is clear: This restriction of output by a single firm has an almost imperceptible impact on total supply—specifically, the total quantity supplied declines from 1,000,000 to 999,950. This is clearly not enough of a change in total supply to affect product price noticeably. In short, the individual competitive producer is a **price taker;** the competitive firm cannot adjust market price, but can only adjust to it.

Stated differently, the individual competitive producer is at the mercy of the market; product price is a given datum over which the producer exerts no influence. The firm can get the same price per unit for a large output as it can for a small output. To ask a price higher than the going market price would be futile. Consumers will not buy anything from firm A at a price of $2.05 when its 9999 competitors are selling an identical, and therefore a perfect substitute, product at $2 per unit. Conversely, because firm A can sell as much as it chooses at $2 per unit, there is no reason for it to charge some lower price, say, $1.95. Indeed, to do so would shrink its profits.

4 Free entry and exit New firms are free to enter and existing firms are free to leave purely competitive industries. In particular, no significant obstacles—legal, technological, financial, or other—exist to prohibit new firms from coming into being and selling their outputs in competitive markets.

Relevance Pure competition is quite rare in practice. This does not mean, however, that an analysis of how competitive markets work is an irrelevant exercise in logic.

1 In the first place, there are a few industries which more closely approximate the competitive model than they do any other market structure. For example, as we shall discover in Chapter 35, much can be learned about American agriculture by understanding the functioning of competitive markets.

2 Moreover, pure competition provides the simplest context in which to apply the revenue and cost concepts developed in previous chapters. Pure competition is a clear and meaningful starting point for any discussion of price and output determination.

3 Finally, in the concluding section of this chapter we shall discover that the operation of a purely competitive economy provides us with a standard, or norm, against which the efficiency of the real-world economy can be compared and evaluated.

In short, pure competition is a market model of considerable analytical and some practical importance.

Our analysis of pure competition centers upon four major objectives. First, we will examine demand from the competitive seller's viewpoint. Second, we seek an understanding of how a competitive producer adjusts to market price in the short run. Next, the nature of long-run adjustments in a competitive industry is explored. Finally, we want to evaluate the efficiency of competitive industries from the standpoint of society as a whole.

Demand to a competitive seller

Because each competitive firm offers a negligible fraction of total supply, the individual firm cannot perceptibly influence the market price which the forces of total demand and supply have established. The competitive firm does *not* have a price policy, that is, the ability to adjust price. Rather, the firm can merely *adjust to* the market price, which it must regard as a given datum determined by the market. As noted, the competitive seller is said to be a *price taker,* rather than a *price maker.*

PERFECTLY ELASTIC DEMAND

Stated technically, the demand curve facing the individual competitive firm is *perfectly elastic.* Columns 1 and 2 of Table 25-2 show a perfectly elastic demand curve where market price is assumed to be $131. Note that the firm cannot obtain a higher price by restricting output; nor need it lower price in order to increase its volume of sales.

But a word of caution is in order. We are *not* saying that the *market* demand curve is perfectly elastic in a competitive market. Indeed, it is not, but rather, it is typically a downsloping curve as a

TABLE 25-2 **The demand and revenue schedules for an individual purely competitive firm (hypothetical data)**

Firm's demand or average-revenue schedule		Revenue data	
(1) Product price (average revenue)	**(2)** Quantity demanded (sold)	**(3)** Total revenue	**(4)** Marginal revenue
$131	0	$ 0	
131	1	131	$131
131	2	262	131
131	3	393	131
131	4	524	131
131	5	655	131
131	6	786	131
131	7	917	131
131	8	1048	131
131	9	1179	131
131	10	1310	131

glance ahead at Figure 25-7b indicates. As a matter of fact, the total-demand curves for most agricultural products are quite *in*elastic, even though agriculture is the most competitive industry in our economy. We are saying that the demand schedule faced by the *individual firm* in a purely competitive industry is perfectly elastic. The distinction comes about in this way. For the industry—that is, for all firms producing a particular product—a larger volume of sales can be realized only by accepting a lower product price. All firms, acting independently but simultaneously, can and do affect total supply and therefore market price. But not so for the individual firm. If a single producer increases or decreases output, the outputs of all other competing firms being constant, the effect on total supply and market price is negligible. The single firm's demand or sales schedule is therefore perfectly elastic, as shown in Figures 25-1 and 25-7a. This is an instance in which the fallacy of composition is worth remembering. What is true for the group of firms (a downsloping, less than perfectly elastic, demand curve) is *not* true for the individual, purely competitive firm (a perfectly elastic demand curve).

AVERAGE, TOTAL, AND MARGINAL REVENUE

A moment's reflection reveals that the firm's demand schedule is simultaneously a revenue schedule. What appears in column 1 of Table 25-2 as price per unit to the purchaser is revenue per unit, or **average revenue,** to the seller. To say that a buyer must pay a price of $131 per unit is to say that the revenue per unit, or average revenue, received by the seller is $131. Price and average revenue are the same thing looked at from different points of view.

Total revenue for each level of sales can readily be determined by multiplying price by the corresponding quantity which the firm can sell. Multiply column 1 by column 2, and the result is column 3. In this case, total revenue increases by a constant amount, $131, for each additional unit of sales. Each unit sold adds exactly its price to total revenue.

Whenever a firm is pondering a change in its output, it will be concerned with how its revenue will *change* as a result of that shift in output. What will be the additional revenue from selling another

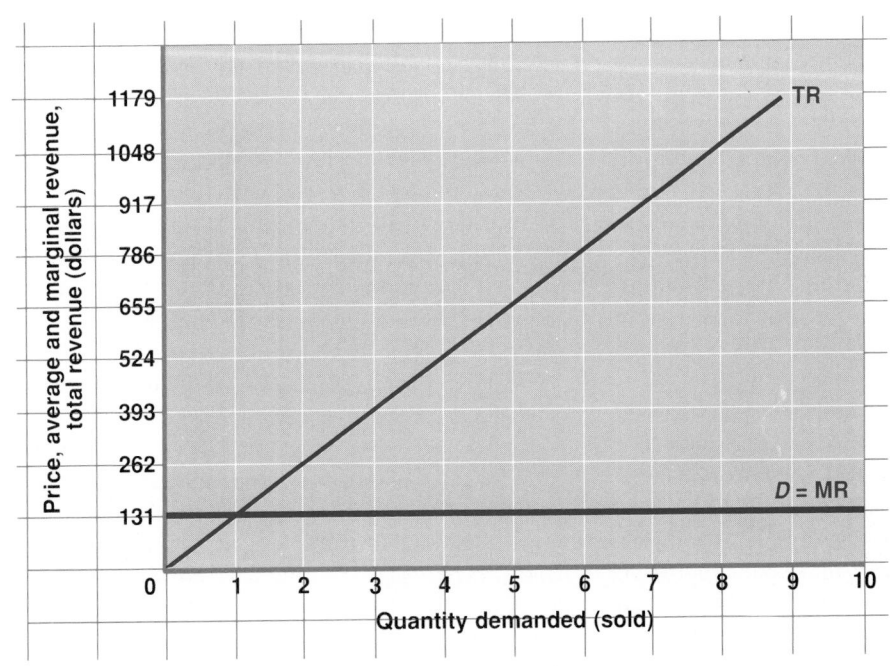

FIGURE 25-1

Demand, marginal revenue, and total revenue of a purely competitive firm

Because it can sell additional units of output at a constant price, the marginal-revenue curve (MR) of a purely competitive firm coincides with its perfectly elastic demand curve (D). The firm's total-revenue curve (TR) is a straight upsloping line.

unit of output? **Marginal revenue** is the addition to total revenue, that is, the extra revenue, which results from the sale of one more unit of output. In other words, in Table 25-2, marginal revenue is simply the change in total revenue associated with the sale of another unit of the product. In column 3 we note that total revenue is obviously zero when zero units are being sold. The first unit of output sold increases total revenue from zero to $131. Marginal revenue—the increase in total revenue resulting from the sale of the first unit of output—is therefore $131. The second unit sold increases total revenue from $131 to $262, so marginal revenue is again $131. Indeed, you will note in column 4 that marginal revenue is a constant figure of $131. Why? Because total revenue increases by a constant amount with every extra unit sold. Under purely competitive conditions, product price is constant to the individual firm; added units therefore can be sold without lowering product price. This means that each additional unit of sales adds exactly its price—$131 in this case—to total revenue. And marginal revenue *is* this increase in total revenue. Marginal revenue is constant under pure competition because additional units can be sold at a constant price.

GRAPHIC PORTRAYAL

The competitive firm's demand curve and total- and marginal-revenue curves are shown graphically in Figure 25-1. The demand or average-revenue curve is perfectly elastic. The marginal-revenue curve coincides with the demand curve because the market is a purely competitive one, and as a result, product price is constant to the single firm. Each extra unit of sales increases total revenue by $131. Total revenue is a straight line up to the right. Its slope is constant—that is, it is a straight line—because marginal revenue is constant.

Profit maximization in the short run: two approaches

In the short run the competitive firm has a fixed plant and is attempting to maximize its profits or, as the case may be, minimize its losses by adjusting its output through changes in the amounts of variable resources (materials, labor, and so forth) it employs. The economic profits it seeks are defined as the difference between total revenue and total costs. Indeed, this points out the direction of our analysis. The revenue data of the previous section and the cost data of Chapter 24 must be brought together in order that the profit-maximizing output for the firm can be determined.

There are two complementary approaches to determining the level of output at which a competitive firm will realize maximum profits or minimum losses. The first involves a comparison of total revenue and total costs; the second, a comparison of marginal revenue and marginal costs. Both approaches are applicable not only to a purely competitive firm but also to firms operating in any of the other three basic market structures. To ensure an understanding of output determination under pure competition, we shall invoke both approaches, emphasizing the marginal approach. Also, hypothetical data in both tabular and graphic form will be employed to bolster our understanding of the two approaches.

TOTAL-REVENUE–TOTAL-COST APPROACH

Given the market price of its product, the competitive producer is faced with three related questions: (1) Should we produce? (2) If so, what amount? (3) What profit (or loss) will be realized?

At first glance, the answer to question 1 seems obvious: "You should produce if it is profitable to do so." But the situation is a bit more complex than this. In the short run a part of the firm's total costs is variable costs, and the remainder is fixed costs. The latter will have to be paid "out of pocket" even when the firm is closed down. In the short run a firm takes a loss equal to its fixed costs when it is producing zero units of output. This means that, although there may be no level of output at which the firm can realize a profit, the firm might still produce, provided that in so doing, it can realize a loss which is less than the fixed-cost loss it will face in closing down. In other words, the correct answer to the "Should we produce?" question is this: *The firm should produce in the short run if it can realize either (1) an economic profit or (2) a loss which is less than its fixed costs.*

Assuming the firm *will* produce, the second question becomes relevant: "How much should be produced?" The answer here is fairly evident: *In*

the short run the firm should produce that output at which it maximizes profits or minimizes losses.

Now let us examine three cases which will demonstrate the validity of these two generalizations and answer our third query by indicating how profits and losses can be readily calculated. In the first case the firm will maximize its profits by producing. In the second case it will minimize its losses by producing. In the third case the firm will minimize its losses by closing down. Our plan of attack is to assume the same short-run cost data for all three cases and to explore the firm's production decisions when faced with three different product prices.

Profit-maximizing case   In all three cases we employ cost data with which we are already familiar. Columns 3 through 5 of Table 25-3 merely repeat the fixed-, variable-, and total-cost data which were developed in Table 24-2. Assuming that market price is $131, we can derive total revenue for each level of output by simply multiplying output times price, as we did in Table 25-2. These data are presented in column 2. Then in column 6 the profit or loss which will be encountered at each output is found by subtracting total cost (column 5) from

TABLE 25-3 **The profit-maximizing output for a purely competitive firm: total-revenue–total-cost approach (price = $131)** *(hypothetical data)*

(1) Total product	(2) Total revenue	(3) Total fixed cost	(4) Total variable cost	(5) Total cost	(6) Total economic profit (+) or loss (−), = (2) − (5)
0	$ 0	$100	$ 0	$ 100	$−100
1	131	100	90	190	− 59
2	262	100	170	270	− 8
3	393	100	240	340	+ 53
4	524	100	300	400	+124
5	655	100	370	470	+185
6	786	100	450	550	+236
7	917	100	540	640	+277
8	1048	100	650	750	+298
9	1179	100	780	880	+299
10	1310	100	930	1030	+280

total revenue (column 2). Now we have all the data needed to answer the three questions.

Should the firm produce? Yes, because it can realize a profit by doing so. How much? Nine units, because column 6 tells us that this is the output at which total economic profits will be at a maximum.

The size of that profit in this **profit-maximizing case**? $299.

Figure 25-2a compares total revenue and total cost graphically. Total revenue is a straight line, because under pure competition each additional unit adds the same amount—its price—to total

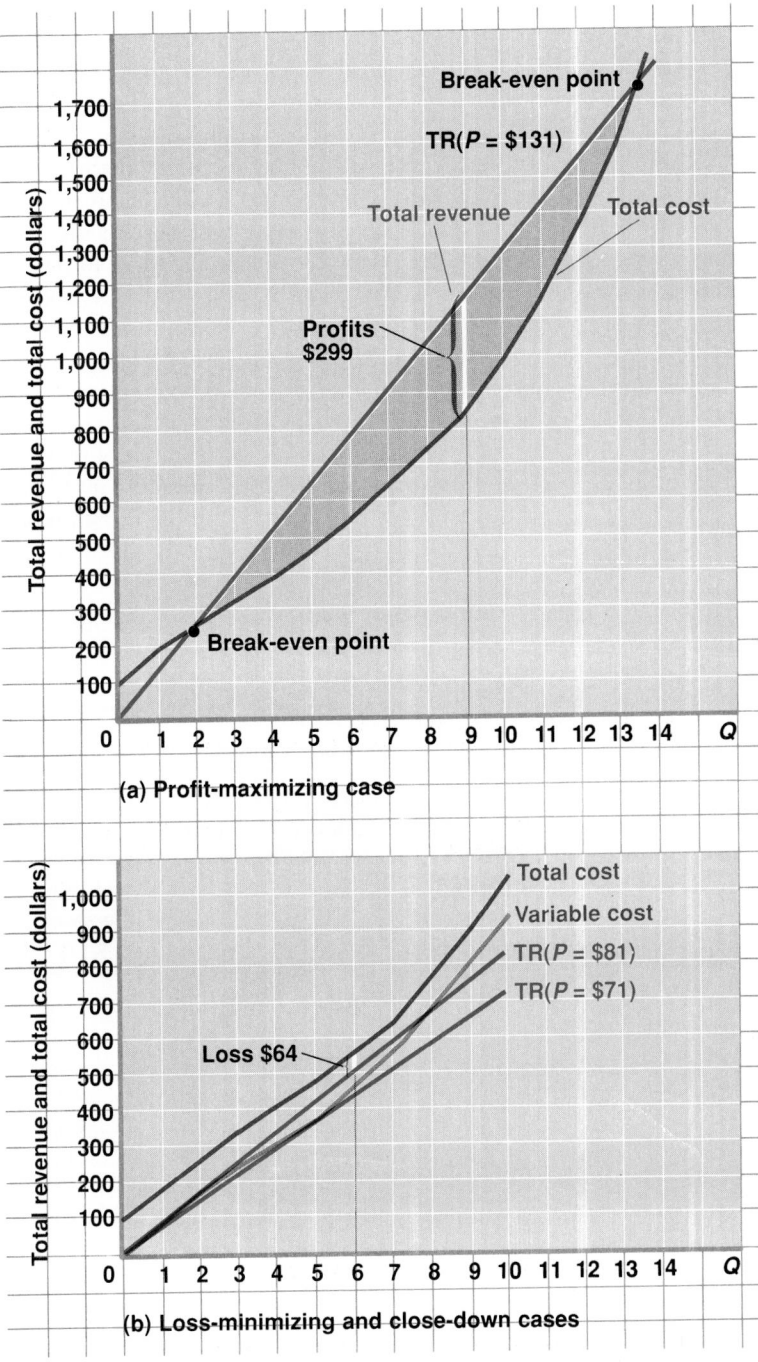

(a) Profit-maximizing case

(b) Loss-minimizing and close-down cases

FIGURE 25-2

The profit-maximizing (a), loss-minimizing, and close-down cases (b), as shown by the total-revenue–total-cost approach

A firm's profits are maximized in (a) at that output at which total revenue exceeds total cost by the maximum amount. A firm will minimize its losses in (b) by producing at that output at which total cost exceeds total revenue by the smallest amount. However, if there is no output at which total revenue exceeds variable costs, the firm will minimize losses in the short run by closing down.

revenue (Table 25-2). Total costs increase with output; more production requires more resources. But the rate of increase in total costs varies with the relative efficiency of the firm. Specifically, the cost data reflect Chapter 24's law of diminishing returns. That is, for a time the rate of increase in total cost is less and less as the firm utilizes its fixed resources more efficiently. Then, after a time, total cost begins to rise by ever-increasing amounts because of the inefficiencies which accompany greater utilization of the firm's plant. Comparing total cost with total revenue in Figure 25-2a, we note that a **break-even point** occurs at about 2 units of output. And if our data were extended beyond 10 units of output, another such point would be incurred where total cost would catch up with total revenue, as is shown in Figure 25-2a. Any output outside these points will entail losses. Any output within these break-even points will entail an economic profit. The maximum profit is achieved where the vertical difference between total revenue and total cost is greatest. For our particular data this is at 9 units of output and the resulting maximum profit is $299.

Loss-minimizing case Assuming no change in costs, the firm may not be able to realize economic profits if the market yields a price considerably below $131. To illustrate: Suppose the market price is $81. As column 6 of Table 25-4 indicates, at this price all levels of output will entail losses. But the firm will *not* close down. Why? Because, by producing, the firm can realize a loss considerably less than the fixed-cost loss it would incur by closing down, that is, producing zero units of output. Specifically, in this **loss-minimizing case,** the firm will minimize its losses by producing 6 units of output. The resulting $64 loss is clearly preferable to the $100 loss which closing down would involve. Stated differently, by producing 6 units the firm earns a total revenue of $486, sufficient to pay all the firm's variable costs ($450) and also a substantial portion—$36 worth—of the firm's $100 of fixed costs. In general terms, whenever total revenue exceeds total *variable* costs, the firm will produce because all variable costs as well as some portion of total fixed costs can be paid out of revenue. If the firm were to close down, all of its total fixed costs would have to be paid out of the entrepre-

TABLE 25-4 **The loss-minimizing outputs for a purely competitive firm: total-revenue–total-cost approach (prices = $81 and $71)** *(hypothetical data)*

Product price = $81						Product price = $71		
(1) Total product	(2) Total revenue	(3) Total fixed cost	(4) Total variable cost	(5) Total cost	(6) Total economic profit (+) or loss (−), = (2) − (5)	(7) Total revenue	(8) Total cost	(9) Total economic profit (+) or loss (−), = (7) − (8)
0	$ 0	$100	$ 0	$ 100	$−100	$ 0	$ 100	$−100
1	81	100	90	190	−109	71	190	−119
2	162	100	170	270	−108	142	270	−128
3	243	100	240	340	− 97	213	340	−127
4	324	100	300	400	− 76	284	400	−116
5	405	100	370	470	− 65	355	470	−115
6	486	100	450	550	− 64	426	550	−124
7	567	100	540	640	− 73	497	640	−143
8	648	100	650	750	−102	568	750	−182
9	729	100	780	880	−151	639	880	−241
10	810	100	930	1030	−220	710	1030	−320

neur's pocket. By producing some output, the firm's loss will be an amount less than its total fixed cost. There are, you will note, several other outputs which entail a loss less than the firm's $100 fixed costs; but at 6 units of output the loss is minimized.

Close-down case Assume finally that the market price is a mere $71. Given short-run costs, column 9 of Table 25-4 clearly indicates that at all levels of output, losses will exceed the $100 fixed-cost loss the firm will incur by closing down. It follows that, in this **close-down case,** the firm will minimize its losses by halting production, that is, by producing zero units of output.

Figure 25-2b demonstrates the loss-minimizing and close-down cases graphically. In the loss-minimizing case, the total revenue line TR ($P = $81) exceeds total variable cost by the maximum amount at 6 units of output. Here total revenue is $486, and the firm recovers all its $450 of variable costs and also $36 worth of its fixed costs. The firm's minimum loss is $64, clearly superior to the $100 fixed-cost loss involved in closing down. In the close-down case, the total-revenue line TR ($P = $71) lies below the total-variable-cost curve at all points; there is no output at which variable costs can be recovered. Therefore, the firm, by producing, would incur losses in excess of its fixed costs. The firm's best choice is to close down and pay its $100 fixed-cost loss out of pocket.

MARGINAL-REVENUE–MARGINAL COST APPROACH

An alternative means for determining the amounts which a competitive firm will be willing to offer in the market at each possible price is for the firm to determine and compare the amounts that each *additional* unit of output will add to total revenue, on the one hand, and to total cost, on the other. That is, the firm should compare the *marginal revenue* (MR) and the *marginal cost* (MC) of each successive unit of output. Any unit of output whose marginal revenue exceeds its marginal cost should be produced. Why? Because on each such unit, the firm is gaining more in revenue from its sale than it adds costs in getting that unit produced. Hence, the unit of output is adding to total profits or, as the case may be, subtracting from losses. Similarly,

if the marginal cost of a unit of output exceeds its marginal revenue, the firm should avoid producing that unit. It will add more to costs than to revenue; such a unit will not "pay its way."

MR = MC rule In the initial stages of production, where output is relatively low, marginal revenue will usually (but not always) exceed marginal cost. It is therefore profitable to produce through this range of output. But at later stages of production, where output is relatively high, rising marginal costs will cause the reverse to be true. Marginal cost will exceed marginal revenue. Production of units of output falling in this range is obviously to be avoided in the interest of maximizing profits. Separating these two production ranges will be a unique point at which marginal revenue equals marginal cost. This point is the key to the output-determining rule: *The firm will maximize profits or minimize losses by producing at that point where marginal revenue equals marginal cost.* For convenience we shall call this profit-maximizing guide the **MR = MC rule.** For most sets of MR and MC data, there will be no nonfractional level of output at which MR and MC are precisely equal. In such instances the firm should produce the last complete unit of output whose MR exceeds its MC.

Three characteristics Three features of this MR = MC rule merit comment.

I First, a qualification: The rule assumes that the firm will choose to produce rather than close down. Shortly, we shall note that marginal revenue must be equal to, or must exceed, average variable cost, or the firm will find it preferable to close down rather than produce the MR = MC output.

2 It is to be emphasized that the MR = MC rule is an accurate guide to profit maximization for all firms, be they purely competitive, monopolistic, monopolistically competitive, or oligopolistic. The rule's application is *not* limited to the special case of pure competition.

3 A third and related point is that the MR = MC rule can be conveniently restated in a slightly different form when being applied to a purely competitive firm. You will recall that product price is determined by the broad market forces of supply and demand, and although the competitive firm can sell as much or as little as it chooses at that price, the firm cannot manipulate the price itself. In tech-

nical terms the demand, or sales, schedule faced by a competitive seller is perfectly elastic at the going market price. The result is that product price and marginal revenue are equal; that is, each extra unit sold adds precisely its price to total revenue as shown in Table 25-2 and Figure 25-1. Thus, under pure competition—and *only* under pure competition—we may substitute price for marginal revenue in the rule, so that it reads as follows: *To maximize profits or minimize losses the competitive firm should produce at that point where price equals marginal cost* ($P = MC$). This **$P = MC$** rule is simply a special case of the MR = MC rule.

Now let us apply the MR = MC or, because we are considering pure competition, the **$P = MC$** rule, using the same three prices employed in our total-revenue–total-cost approach to profit maximization.

Profit-maximizing case   Table 25-5 reproduces the unit- and marginal-cost data derived in Table 24-2. It is, of course, the marginal-cost data of column 5 in Table 25-5 which we wish to compare with price (equal to marginal revenue) for each unit of output. Suppose first that market price, and therefore

marginal revenue, is $131, as shown in column 6. What is the profit-maximizing output? It is readily seen that each and every unit of output up to and including the ninth adds more to total revenue than to total cost. That is, price, or marginal revenue, exceeds marginal cost on all the first 9 units of output. Each of these units therefore adds to the firm's profits and should be produced. The tenth unit, however, will not be produced, because it would add more to costs ($150) than to revenue ($131).

The level of economic profits realized by the firm can be readily calculated from the unit-cost data. Multiplying price ($131) times output (9), we find total revenue to be $1179. Total cost of $880 is found by multiplying average total cost ($97.78) by output (9).[1] The difference of $299 (= $1179 − $880) is economic profits. An alternative means of

[1] In most instances the unit-cost data are rounded figures. Therefore, economic profits calculated from them will typically vary by a few cents from the profits determined in the total-revenue–total-cost approach. We here ignore the few-cents differentials and make our answers consistent with the results of the total-revenue–total-cost approach.

TABLE 25-5 **The profit-maximizing output for a purely competitive firm: marginal-revenue-equals-marginal-cost approach (price = $131)** *(hypothetical data)*

(1) Total product	(2) Average fixed cost	(3) Average variable cost	(4) Average total cost	(5) Marginal cost	(6) Price = marginal revenue	(7) Total economic profit (+) or loss (−)
0						$−100
1	$100.00	$90.00	$190.00	$ 90	$131	− 59
2	50.00	85.00	135.00	80	131	− 8
3	33.33	80.00	113.33	70	131	+ 53
4	25.00	75.00	100.00	60	131	+124
5	20.00	74.00	94.00	70	131	+185
6	16.67	75.00	91.67	80	131	+236
7	14.29	77.14	91.43	90	131	+277
8	12.50	81.25	93.75	110	131	+298
9	11.11	86.67	97.78	130	131	+299
10	10.00	93.00	103.00	150	131	+280

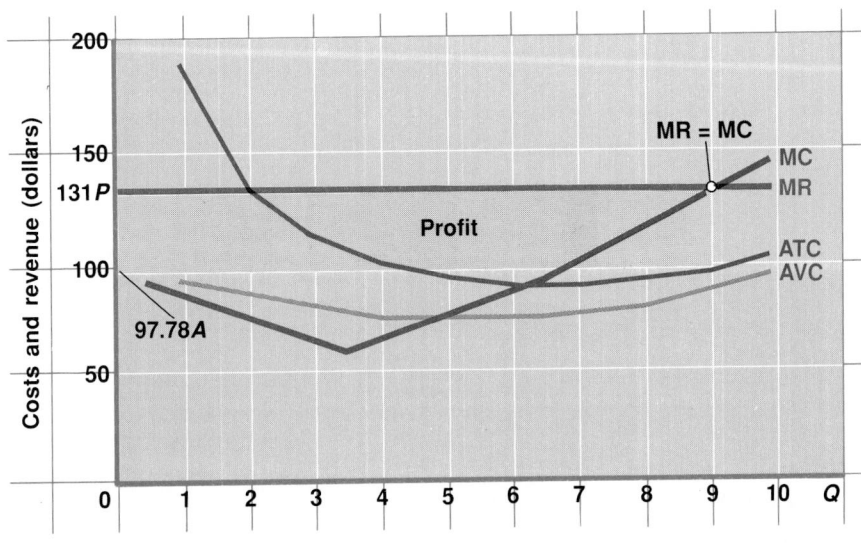

FIGURE 25-3

The short-run profit-maximizing position of a purely competitive firm

The $P = MC$ output allows the competitive producer to maximize profits or minimize losses. In this case price exceeds average total cost at the $P = MC$ output of 9 units. Economic profits per unit of AP are realized; total economic profits are indicated by the gray rectangle.

calculating economic profits is to determine profit *per unit* by subtracting average total cost ($97.78) from product price ($131) and multiplying the difference (per unit profits of $33.22) by the level of output (9). By verifying the figures in column 7 of Table 25-5 the skeptical reader will find that any output other than that indicated to be most profitable by the MR (P) = MC rule will entail either losses or profits less than $299.

Figure 25-3 makes the comparison of price and marginal cost graphically. Here per unit economic profit is indicated by the distance *AP*. When multiplied by the profit-maximizing output, the resulting total economic profit is shown by the gray rectangular area.

It should be noted that the firm is seeking to maximize its *total* profits, not its *per unit* profits. Per unit profits are largest at 7 units of output, where price exceeds average total cost by $39.57 ($131 minus $91.43). But by producing only 7 units, the firm would be forgoing the production of two additional units of output which would clearly contribute to total profits. The firm is happy to accept lower per unit profits if the resulting extra units of sales more than compensate for the lower per unit profits.

Loss-minimizing case Now let us apply the same reasoning on the assumption that market price is $81 rather than $131. Should the firm produce? If so, how much? And what will the resulting profits or losses be? The answers, respectively, are "Yes," "Six units," and "A loss of $64."

Column 6 of Table 25-6 shows the new price (equal to marginal revenue) alongside the same unit- and marginal-cost data presented in Table 25-5. Comparing columns 5 and 6, we find that the first unit of output adds $90 to total cost but only $81 to total revenue. One might be inclined to conclude: "Don't produce—close down!" But this would be hasty. Remember that in the very early stages of production, marginal product is low, making marginal cost unusually high. The price–marginal-cost relationship might improve with increased production. And it does. On the next 5 units—2 through 6—price exceeds marginal cost. Each of these 5 units adds more to revenue than to cost, more than compensating for the "loss" taken on the first unit. Beyond 6 units, however, MC exceeds MR (P). The firm should therefore produce at 6 units. In general, the profit-seeking producer should always compare marginal revenue (or price under pure competition) with the *rising* portion of the marginal-cost schedule or curve.

Will production be profitable? No, it will not. At 6 units of output, average total costs of $91.67 exceed price of $81 by $10.67 per unit. Multiply by the 6 units of output, and we find the firm's total loss is $64. Then why produce? Because this loss is less than the firm's $100 worth of fixed costs—the $100 loss the firm would incur in the short run by closing down. Looked at differently, the firm re-

TABLE 25-6 **The loss-minimizing outputs for a purely competitive firm: marginal-revenue-equals-marginal-cost approach (prices = $81 and $71) (hypothetical data)**

(1) Total product	(2) Average fixed cost	(3) Average variable cost	(4) Average total cost	(5) Marginal cost	(6) $81 price = marginal revenue	(7) Profit (+) or loss (−), $81 price	(8) $71 price = marginal revenue	(9) Profit (+) or loss (−), $71 price
0						$−100		$−100
				$ 90	$81		$71	
1	$100.00	$90.00	$190.00			−109		−119
				80	81		71	
2	50.00	85.00	135.00			−108		−128
				70	81		71	
3	33.33	80.00	113.33			− 97		−127
				60	81		71	
4	25.00	75.00	100.00			− 76		−116
				70	81		71	
5	20.00	74.00	94.00			− 65		−115
				80	81		71	
6	16.67	75.00	91.67			− 64		−124
				90	81		71	
7	14.29	77.14	91.43			− 73		−143
				110	81		71	
8	12.50	81.25	93.75			−102		−182
				130	81		71	
9	11.11	86.67	97.78			−151		−241
				150	81		71	
10	10.00	93.00	103.00			−220		−320

ceives enough revenue per unit ($81) to cover its average variable costs of $75 and also provide $6 per unit, or a total of $36, to apply against the payment of fixed costs. Therefore, the firm's loss is only $64 (= $100 − $36), rather than $100.

This case is shown graphically in Figure 25-4. Whenever price exceeds the minimum average variable cost but falls short of average total cost, the firm can pay a part of, but not all, its fixed costs by producing. In this instance total variable costs are shown by the area *OVGF*. Total revenue, however, is *OPEF*, greater than total variable costs by *VPEG*. This excess of revenue over variable costs can be applied against total fixed costs, represented

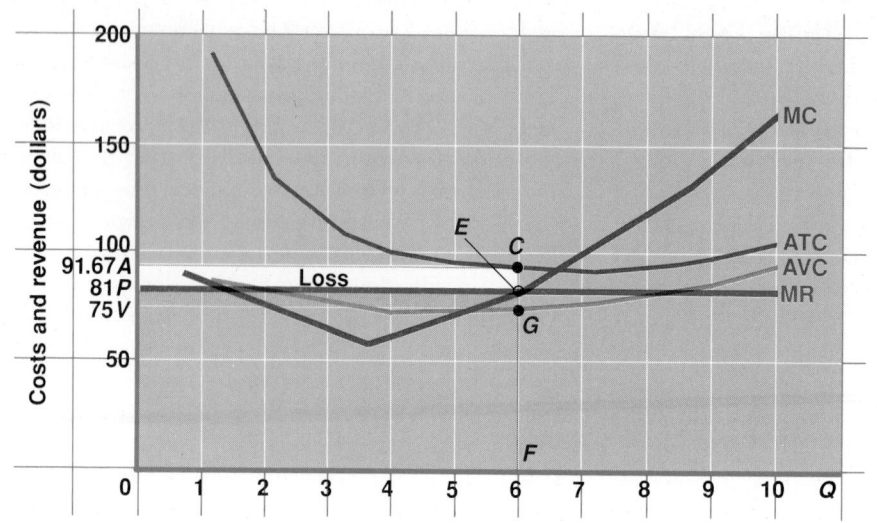

FIGURE 25-4

The short-run loss-minimizing position of a purely competitive firm

If price exceeds the minimum AVC but is less than ATC, the *P* = MC output of 6 units will permit the firm to minimize its losses. In this instance losses are *AP* per unit; total losses are shown by the area *PACE*.

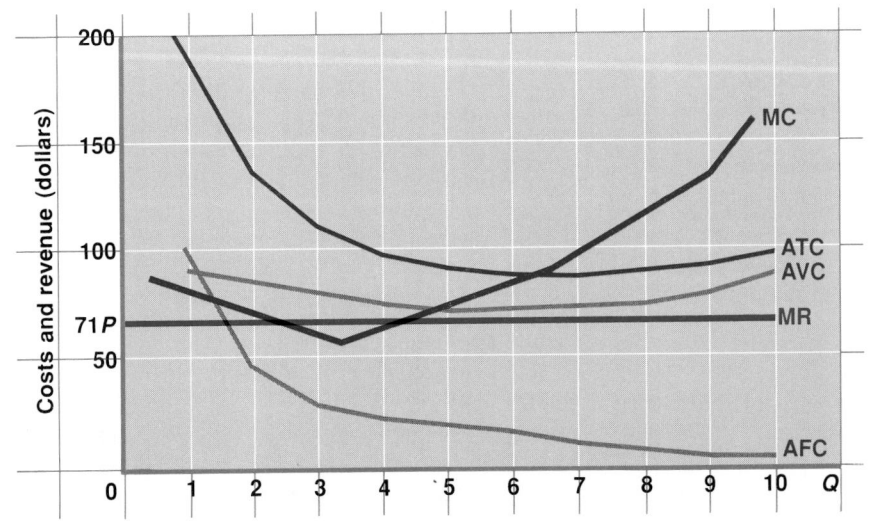

FIGURE 25-5

The short-run close-down position of a purely competitive firm

If price falls short of minimum AVC, the competitive firm will minimize its losses in the short run by closing down. There is no level of output at which the firm can produce and realize a loss smaller than its fixed costs.

by area *VACG*. Stated differently, by producing 6 units the firm's loss is only area *PACE;* by closing down, its loss would be its fixed costs shown by the larger area *VACG*.

Close-down case Suppose now that the market yields a price of only $71. In this case it will pay the firm to close down, to produce nothing. Why? Because there is no output at which the firm can cover its average variable costs, much less its average total cost. In other words, the smallest loss it can realize by producing is greater than the $100 worth of fixed costs it will lose by closing down. The smart thing is to close down. This can be verified by comparing columns 3 and 8 of Table 25-6 and can be readily visualized in Figure 25-5. Price comes closest to covering average variable costs at the MR (*P*) = MC output of 5 units. But even here, price or revenue per unit would fall short of average variable cost by $3 (= $74 − $71). By producing at the MR (*P*) = MC output, the firm would lose its $100 worth of fixed costs *plus* $15 ($3 on each of the 5 units) worth of variable costs, for a total loss of $115. This clearly compares unfavorably with the $100 fixed-cost loss the firm would incur by choosing to close down and thereby produce no output. In short, it will pay the firm to close down rather than operate at a $71 price or, for that matter, at any price less than $74.

The close-down case obligates us to modify our MR (*P*) = MC rule for profit maximization or loss minimization. *A competitive firm will maximize profits or minimize losses in the short run by producing at that output at which* MR (*P*) = MC, *provided that price exceeds the minimum average-variable-cost figure.*

Marginal cost and the short-run supply curve Now the astute reader will recognize that we have simply selected three different prices and asked how much the profit-seeking competitive firm, faced with certain costs, would choose to offer or supply in the market at each of these prices. This information—product price and corresponding quantity supplied—constitutes the supply schedule for the competitive firm. Table 25-7 summarizes the supply schedule data for the three prices we have chosen—$131, $81, and $71. The reader is urged to apply the MR (*P*) = MC rule (as modified by the close-down case) to verify the quantity-supplied data for the $151, $111, $91, and $61 prices and calculate the corresponding profits or losses. We confirm that the supply schedule is upsloping. In this instance, price must be $74 (equal to minimum average variable cost) or greater before any output is supplied. And because the marginal cost of successive units of output is increasing, the firm must get successively higher prices in order for it to be profitable to produce these additional units of output.

Figure 25-6 generalizes upon our application of the MR (*P*) = MC rule. Here we have drawn the appropriate cost curves. Then from the vertical

TABLE 25-7 **The supply schedule of a competitive firm confronted with the cost data of Table 25-5 (hypothetical data)**

Price	Quantity supplied	Maximum profit (+) or minimum loss (−)
$151	10	$_____
131	9	+299
111	8	_____
91	7	_____
81	6	− 64
71	0	−100
61	0	_____

axis we have extended a series of marginal-revenue lines from some of the various possible prices which the market might set for the firm. The crucial

prices are P_2 and P_4. Our close-down case reminds us that at any price *below* P_2—that price which is equal to the minimum average variable cost—the firm should close down and supply nothing. Actually, by producing Q_2 units of output *at* a price of P_2, the firm will just cover its variable costs, and its loss will be equal to its fixed costs. The firm therefore would be indifferent as between closing down *or* producing Q_2 units of output. But at any price *below* P_2, such as P_1, the firm will close down and supply zero units of output.

P_4 is strategic because it is the price at which the firm will just break even by producing Q_4 units of output, as indicated by the MR (P) = MC rule. Here total revenue will just cover total costs (including a normal profit). At P_3 the firm supplies Q_3 units of output and, in so doing, minimizes its losses. At any other price between P_2 and P_4 the firm will minimize its losses by producing to the point where MR (P) = MC. At any price above P_4

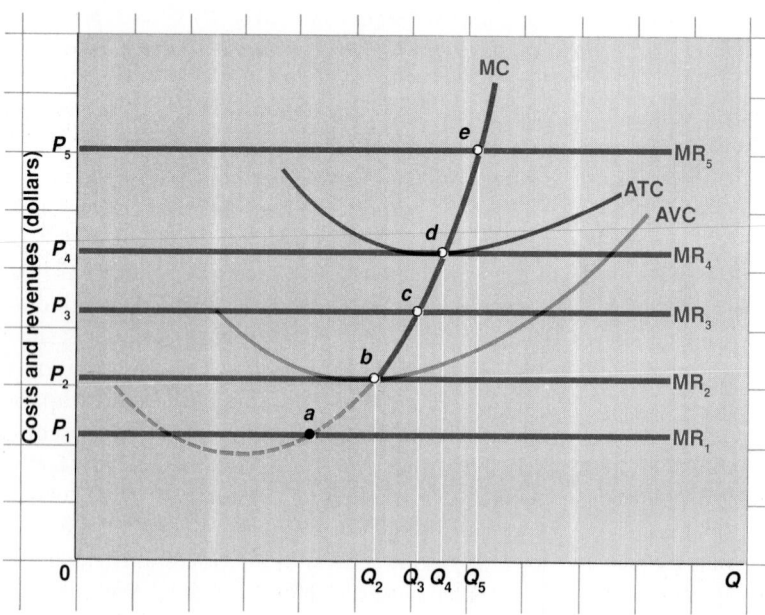

FIGURE 25-6

The P = MC rule and the competitive firm's short-run supply curve

Application of the P = MC rule, as modified by the close-down case, reveals that the (solid) segment of the firm's MC curve which lies above AVC is the firm's short-run supply curve. More specifically, at price P_1, P = MC at point a, but the firm will produce no output because P_1 is less than minimum AVC. At price P_2 the firm is in equilibrium at point b where it produces Q_2 units and incurs a loss equal to its fixed costs. At P_3 equilibrium is at point c where output is Q_3 and losses are less than fixed costs. Equilibrium is at point d if price is P_4; in this case the firm breaks even because at output Q_4 price equals ATC. At price P_5 the firm reaches an equilibrium at point e and maximizes its economic profit by producing Q_5 units.

the firm will maximize its economic profits by producing to the point where MR (P) = MC. Thus at P_5 the firm will realize the greatest profits by supplying Q_5 units of output. The basic point is this: Each of the various MR (P) = MC intersection points shown as *b, c, d,* and *e* in Figure 25-6 indicates a possible product price (on the vertical axis) and the corresponding quantity which the profit-seeking firm would supply at that price (on the horizontal axis). These points, by definition, locate the supply curve of the competitive firm. Because nothing would be produced at any price below the minimum average variable cost, we can conclude that *the portion of the firm's marginal-cost curve which lies above its average-variable-cost curve is its* **short-run supply curve.** The heavy segment of the marginal-cost curve is the short-run supply curve in Figure 25-6. This is the link between production costs and supply in the short run.

It is pertinent to remember from Chapter 24 that changes in such factors as the prices of variable inputs or in technology will shift the marginal cost or short-run supply curve to a new location. For example, an increase in wages would shift the supply curve upward as viewed from the horizontal axis (leftward as viewed from the vertical axis), constituting a decease in supply. Similarly, technological progress which increases the productivity of labor would shift the marginal cost or supply curve downward as viewed from the horizontal axis (rightward as viewed from the vertical axis). This

represents an increase in supply. You should determine how (1) a specific tax on the product and (2) a per unit subsidy on this product would shift the supply curve.

RECAPITULATION

Let us now pause to summarize the main points we have made concerning short-run competitive pricing. Table 25-8 provides a convenient check sheet on the total-revenue–total-cost and MR = MC approaches to determining the competitive firm's profit-maximizing output. This table warrants careful study by the reader. In the MR = MC approach it is noteworthy that in deciding whether or not to produce, it is the comparison of price with minimum average *variable* cost which is all-important. Then, in determining the profit-maximizing or loss-minimizing amount to produce, it is the comparison—or better yet, the equality—of MR (P) and MC which is crucial. Finally, in determining the actual profit or loss associated with the MR (P) = MC output, price and average *total* cost must be contrasted. A final basic conclusion implied in Table 25-8 is that the segment of the short-run marginal-cost curve which lies above the average-variable-cost curve is the competitive firm's short-run supply curve. This conclusion stems from the application of the MR (P) = MC rule and the necessary modification suggested by the close-down case.

TABLE 25-8 **Summary of competitive output determination in the short run**

	Total-revenue–total-cost approach	Marginal-revenue–marginal-cost approach
Should the firm produce?	Yes, if TR exceeds TC or if TC exceeds TR by some amount less than total fixed cost.	Yes, if price is equal to, or greater than, minimum average variable cost.
What quantity should be produced to maximize profits?	Produce where the excess of TR over TC is a maximum or where the excess of TC over TR is a minimum (and less than total fixed costs).	Produce where MR or price equals MC.
Will production result in economic profit?	Yes, if TR exceeds TC. No, if TC exceeds TR.	Yes, if price exceeds average total cost. No, if average total cost exceeds price.

FIRM AND INDUSTRY: EQUILIBRIUM PRICE

Now one final wrap-up step remains. Having developed the competitive firm's short-run supply curve through the application of the MR (P) = MC rule, we must determine which of the various price possibilities will actually be the equilibrium price. Recalling Chapter 4, we know that in a purely competitive market, equilibrium price is determined by *total*, or market, supply and total demand. To derive total supply, we know that the supply schedules or curves of the individual competitive sellers must be summed. Thus in Table 25-9, columns 1 and 3 repeat the individual competitive firm's supply schedule just derived in Table 25-7. Let us now conveniently assume that there are a total of 1000 competitive firms in this industry, each having the same total and unit costs as the single firm we have been discussing. This allows us to calculate the total- or market-supply schedule (columns 2 and 3) by multiplying the quantity-supplied figures of the single firm (column 1) by 1000.

Now, in order to determine equilibrium price and output, this total-supply data must be compared with total-demand data. For purposes of illustration, let us assume total-demand data are as shown in columns 3 and 4 of Table 25-9. Comparing the total quantity supplied and total quantity demanded at the seven possible prices, we readily determine that the equilibrium price is $111 and that equilibrium quantity is 8000 units for the industry and 8 units for each of the 1000 identical firms.

Will these conditions of market supply and demand make this a prosperous or an unprosperous industry? Multiplying product price ($111) by output (8), we find the total revenue of each firm to be $888. Total cost is $750, found by multiplying average total cost of $93.75 by 8, or simply by looking at column 5 of Table 25-3. The $138 difference is the economic profit of each firm. Another way of calculating economic profits is to determine *per unit* profit by subtracting average total cost ($93.75) from product price ($111) and multiplying the difference (per unit profits of $17.25) by the firm's equilibrium level of output (8). For the industry, total economic profit is $138,000. This, then, is a prosperous industry.

Figure 25-7a and b shows this analysis graphically. The individual supply curves of each of the 1000 identical firms—one of which is shown as *ss* in Figure 25-7a—are summed horizontally to get the total-supply curve *SS* of Figure 25-7b. Given total demand *DD*, equilibrium price is found to be $111, and equilibrium quantity for the industry is 8000 units. This equilibrium price is given and unalterable to the individual firm; that is, the typical firm's demand curve is perfectly elastic at the equilibrium price, as indicated by *dd*. Because price is given and constant to the individual firm, the marginal-revenue curve coincides with the demand curve. This $111 price exceeds average total cost at the firm's equilibrium MR (P) = MC output, resulting in a situation of economic profits similar to that already portrayed in Figure 25-3.

Assuming that no changes in cost or market demand occur, these diagrams reveal a genuine *short-run* equilibrium situation. There are no shortages or surpluses in the market to cause price or total quantity to change. Nor can any of the firms making up the industry improve their profits by altering their output. Note, too, that higher unit and marginal costs, on the one hand, or a weaker market demand situation, on the other, could have posed a loss situation similar to Figure 25-4. The student is urged to sketch, in Figure 25-7a and b, how higher costs and a less favorable demand could cause a short-run equilibrium situation entailing losses.

TABLE 25-9 Firm and market supply and market demand *(hypothetical data)*

(1) Quantity supplied, single firm	(2) Total quantity supplied, 1000 firms	(3) Product price	(4) Total quantity demanded
10	10,000	$151	4,000
9	9,000	131	6,000
8	8,000	111	8,000
7	7,000	91	9,000
6	6,000	81	11,000
0	0	71	13,000
0	0	61	16,000

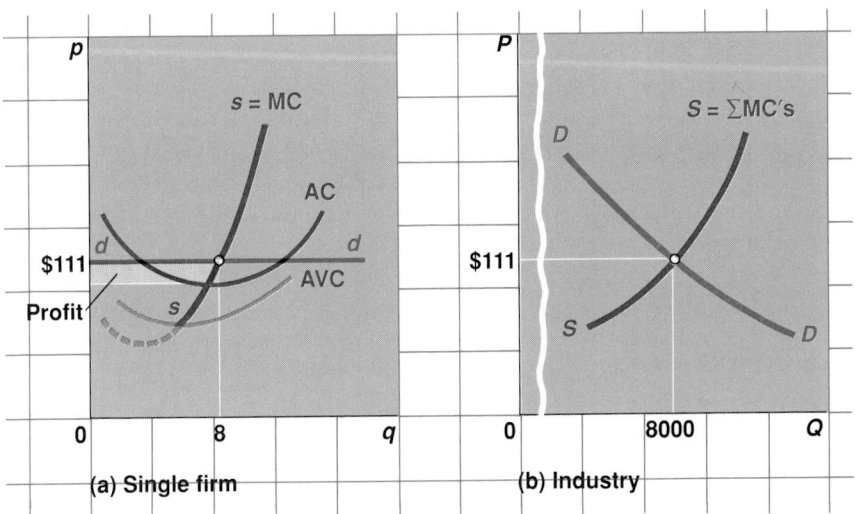

FIGURE 25-7

Short-run competitive equilibrium for a firm (a) and the industry (b)

The horizontal sum of the 1000 firms' supply curves (**ss**) determines the industry supply curve (**SS**). Given industry demand (**DD**), the short-run equilibrium price and output for the industry are $111 and 8000 units. Taking the equilibrium price as given datum, the representative firm establishes its profit-maximizing output at 8 units and, in this case, realizes the economic profit shown by the gray area.

Figure 25-7a and b underscores a point made earlier: Product price is a given datum to the *individual* competitive firm, but at the same time, the supply plans of all competitive producers *as a group* are a basic determinant of product price. If we recall the fallacy of composition, we find there is no inconsistency here. Though each firm, supplying a negligible fraction of total supply, cannot affect price, the sum of the supply curves of all the many firms in the industry constitutes the industry supply curve, and this curve does have an important bearing upon price. In short, under competition, equilibrium price is a given datum to the individual firm and simultaneously is the result of the production (supply) decisions of all firms taken as a group.

Profit maximization in the long run

The long run permits firms to make certain adjustments which time does not allow in the short run. In the short run there are a given number of firms

in an industry, each of which has a fixed, unalterable plant. True, firms may close down in the sense that they produce zero units of output in the short run; but they do not have sufficient time to liquidate their assets and go out of business. By contrast, in the long run firms already in an industry have sufficient time either to expand or to contract their plant capacities, and, more important, the number of firms in the industry may either increase or decrease as new firms enter or existing firms leave. We want to discover how these long-run adjustments modify our conclusions concerning short-run output and price determination.

ASSUMPTIONS AND GOAL

It will facilitate our analysis greatly to make certain simplifying assumptions, none of which will impair the general validity of our conclusions.
1 We shall suppose that the only long-run adjustment is the entry and exodus of firms. Furthermore, for simplicity's sake we shall ignore the short-run adjustments already analyzed, in order to grasp more clearly the nature of long-run competitive adjustments.

2 It will also be assumed that all firms in the industry have identical cost curves. This allows us to talk in terms of an "average," or "representative," firm with the knowledge that all other firms in the industry are similarly affected by any long-run adjustments which occur.

3 We assume for the moment that the industry under discussion is a constant-cost industry. This means simply that the entry and exodus of firms will *not* affect resource prices or, therefore, the locations of the unit-cost schedules of the individual firms.

Our goal is to describe long-run competitive adjustments both verbally and through graphic analysis. It will be well to state in advance the basic conclusion we seek to explain: *After all long-run adjustments are completed, that is, when long-run equilibrium is achieved, product price will be exactly equal to, and production will occur at, each firm's point of minimum average total cost.* This conclusion follows from two basic facts: (1) Firms seek profits and shun losses, and (2) under competition, firms are free to enter and leave industries. If price initially exceeds average total costs, the resulting economic profits will attract new firms to the in-

dustry. But this expansion of the industry will increase product supply until price is brought back down into equality with average total cost. Conversely, if price is initially less than average total cost, the resulting losses will cause firms to leave the industry. As they leave, total product supply will decline, bringing price back up into equality with average total cost.

Our conclusion can best be demonstrated and its significance evaluated by assuming that the average or representative firm in a purely competitive industry is initially in long-run equilibrium. This is shown in Figure 25-8a, where price and minimum average total cost are equal at, say, $50. Economic profits here are zero; hence, the industry is in equilibrium or "at rest," because there is no tendency for firms to enter or leave the industry. As we know, the going market price is determined by total, or industry, demand and supply, as shown by D_1D_1 and S_1S_1 in Figure 25-8b. (The market supply schedule, incidentally, is a *short-run* schedule; the industry's long-run supply schedule will be developed in our discussion.) By examining the quantity axes of the two graphs, we note that if all firms are identical, there must be 1000 firms in the

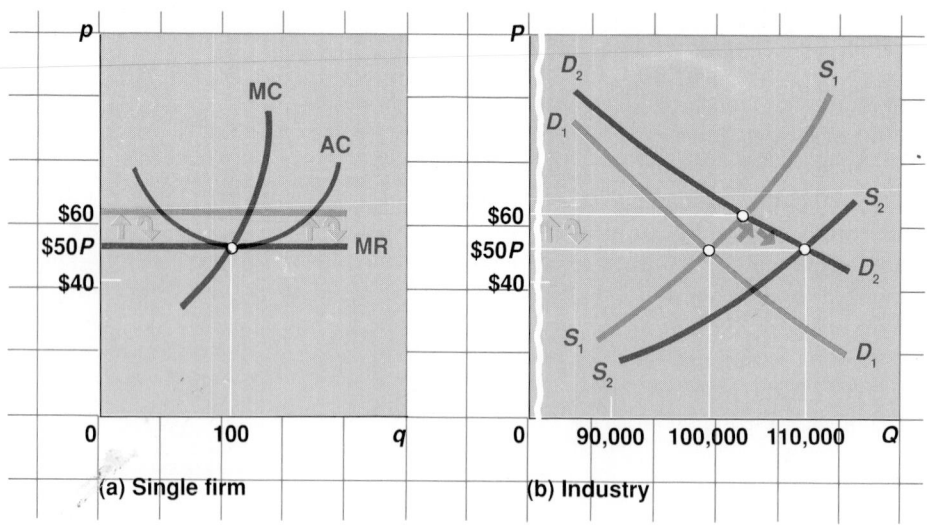

FIGURE 25-8

Temporary profits and the reestablishment of long-run equilibrium in a representative firm (a) and the industry (b)

A favorable shift in demand (D_1D_1 to D_2D_2) will upset the original equilibrium and cause economic profits. But profits will cause new firms to enter the industry, increasing supply (S_1S_1 to S_2S_2) and lowering product price until economic profits are once again zero.

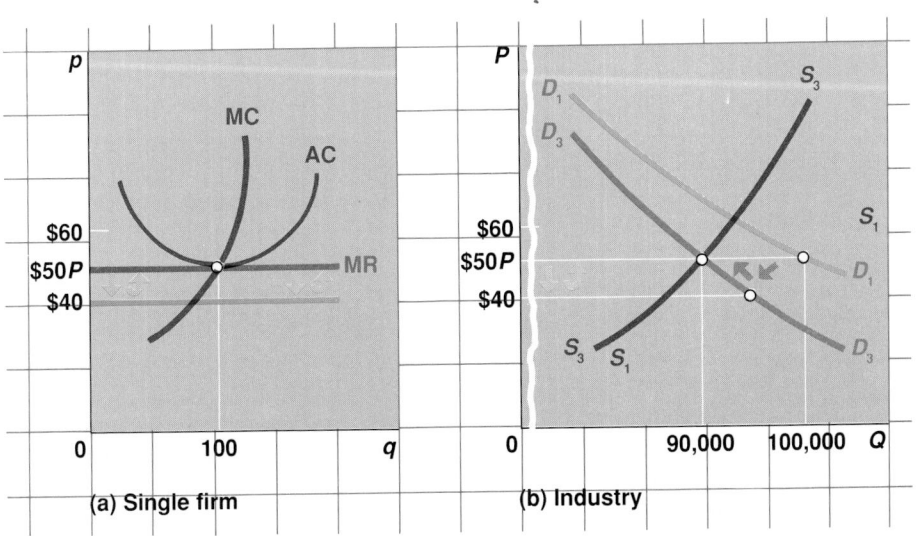

FIGURE 25-9

Temporary losses and the reestablishment of long-run equilibrium in a representative firm (a) and the industry (b)

An unfavorable shift in demand (D_1D_1 to D_3D_3) will upset the original equilibrium and cause losses. But losses will cause firms to leave the industry, decreasing supply (S_1S_1 to S_3S_3) and increasing product price until all losses have disappeared.

industry, each producing 100 units, to achieve the industry's equilibrium output of 100,000 units.

ENTRY OF FIRMS ELIMINATES PROFITS

Now our model is set up. Let us upset the serenity of the long-run equilibrium in Figure 25-8 and trace subsequent adjustments. Suppose that a change in consumer tastes increases product demand from D_1D_1 to D_2D_2. This favorable shift in demand will make production profitable; the new price of $60 exceeds average total cost of $50. *These economic profits will lure new firms into the industry.* Some of the entrants will be newly created firms; others will shift from less prosperous industries. But as the firms enter, the market supply of the product will increase, causing product price to gravitate downward from $60 toward the original $50 level. Assuming, as we are, that the entry of new firms has no effect upon costs, economic profits will persist, and entry will therefore continue until short-run market supply has increased to S_2S_2. At this point, price is again equal to minimum average total cost at $50. The economic profits caused by the boost in demand have been competed away to zero, and as a result, the previous

incentive for more firms to enter the industry has disappeared. Long-run equilibrium has been restored at this point.

Figure 25-8 tells us that upon the reestablishment of long-run equilibrium, industry output is 110,000 units and that each firm in the now expanded industry is producing 100 units. We can therefore conclude that the industry is now composed of 1100 firms; that is, 100 new firms have entered the industry.

EXODUS OF FIRMS ELIMINATES LOSSES

To strengthen our understanding of long-run competitive equilibrium, let us throw our analysis into reverse. In Figure 25-9a and b, the heavy lines show once again the initial long-run equilibrium situation used as a point of departure in our previous analysis of how the entry of firms eliminates economic profits.

Now let us suppose that consumer demand falls from D_1D_1 to D_3D_3. This forces price down to $40, making production unprofitable. *In time the resulting losses will induce firms to leave the industry.* The reason is that the owners can realize a normal profit elsewhere as opposed to the below-normal profit (losses) now confronting them. As capital equipment wears out and contractual obligations expire, some firms will simply toss in the sponge. As this exodus of firms proceeds, however, industry supply will decrease, moving from S_1S_1 toward S_3S_3. And as this occurs, price will begin to rise from $40 back toward $50. Assuming costs are unchanged by the exodus of firms, losses will force firms to leave the industry until supply has declined to S_3S_3, at which point price is again exactly $50, barely consistent with minimum average total cost. The exodus continues until losses are eliminated and long-run equilibrium is again restored.

Observe in Figure 25-9a and b that total quantity supplied is now 90,000 units and each firm is producing 100 units. This means that the industry is now populated by only 900 firms rather than the original 1000. Losses have forced 100 firms out of business. The careful reader may have noted that we have sidestepped the question of which firms will leave the industry when losses occur by assuming all firms have identical cost curves. In the "real world" entrepreneurial talents are likely to differ so that, even if resource prices are the same for all firms, inferior entrepreneurs would incur higher costs and therefore tend to be the first to leave the industry when product demand declined. Similarly, other resources may be heterogeneous and also give rise to cost differences. For example, firms with less productive labor forces will tend to be high-cost producers and likely candidates to quit the industry when product demand decreases.

Our prestated conclusion has now been verified. Competition, as reflected in the entry and exodus of firms, forces price into equality with the minimum long-run average total cost of production, and each firm produces at the point of minimum long-run average total cost. Observe, too, that these expanding- and declining-industry cases comprise an explanation of the functioning of consumer sovereignty, a concept which we encountered in a more elementary form in Chapter 5.

LONG-RUN SUPPLY FOR A CONSTANT-COST INDUSTRY

We now ask: What is the character of the **long-run supply curve** which evolves from this analysis of

the expansion or contraction of a competitive industry? Even though our discussion is concerned with the long run, we have noted that the market supply curves of Figures 25-8b and 25-9b are short-run industry supply curves. However, the analysis itself permits us to sketch the nature of the long-run supply curve for this competitive industry. The crucial factor in determining the shape of the industry's long-run supply curve is the effect, if any, which changes in the number of firms in the industry will have upon the costs of the individual firms in the industry.

In the foregoing analysis of long-run competitive equilibrium we assumed the industry under discussion was a **constant-cost industry.** By definition, this means that the expansion of the industry through the entry of new firms will have no effect upon resource prices or, therefore, upon production costs. Graphically, the entry of new firms does **not** change the position of the long-run average-cost curves of the individual firms in the industry. When will this be the case? For the most part, when the industry's demand for resources is small in relation to the total demand for those resources. And this is most likely to be the situation when the industry is employing unspecialized resources which are being demanded by many other industries. In short, when the particular industry's demand for resources is a negligible component of the total demand, the industry can expand without significantly affecting resource prices and costs.

What will the long-run supply curve for a constant-cost industry look like? The answer is contained in our previous discussion of the long-run adjustments toward equilibrium which profits or losses will initiate. Here we assumed that entrance or departure of firms would not affect costs. The result was that the entry or exodus of firms would alter industry output but always bring product price back to the original $50 level, where it is just consistent with the unchanging minimum average total cost of production. Specifically, we discovered that the industry would supply 90,000, 100,000, or 110,000 units of output, all at a price of $50 per unit. In technical terms, *the long-run supply curve of a constant-cost industry is perfectly elastic.*

This is demonstrated graphically in Figure 25-10, where the illustrative data from Figures 25-8 and 25-9 are retained. Suppose that industry demand is originally D_1D_1, industry output is Q_1

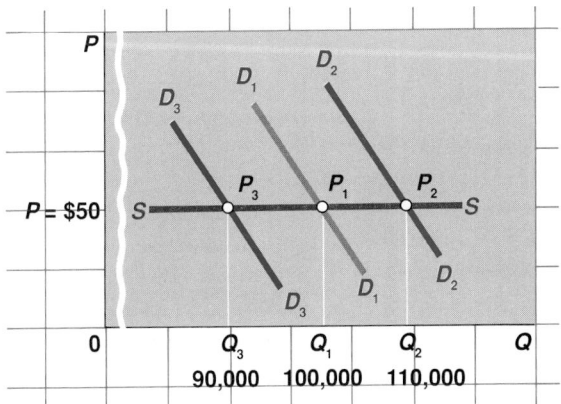

FIGURE 25-10

The long-run supply curve for a constant-cost industry is perfectly elastic

Because the entry or exodus of firms does not affect resource prices or, therefore, unit costs, an increase in demand (D_1D_1 to D_2D_2) will cause an expansion in industry output (Q_1 to Q_2) but no alteration in price ($Q_1P_1 = Q_2P_2$). Similarly, a decrease in demand (D_1D_1 to D_3D_3) will cause a contraction of output (Q_1 to Q_3) but no change in price ($Q_1P_1 = Q_3P_3$). This means that the long-run industry supply curve (SS) will be perfectly elastic.

(100,000), and product price is Q_1P_1 ($50). This situation, referring to Figure 25-8, is one of long-run equilibrium. Now assume that demand increases to D_2D_2, upsetting this equilibrium. The resulting economic profits will attract new firms. Because this is a constant-cost industry, entry will continue and industry output will expand until price is driven back down to the unchanged minimum average-total-cost level. This will be at price Q_2P_2 ($50) and output Q_2 (110,000).

This analysis, now using Figure 25-9 as a reference point, is reversible. A decline in short-run industry demand from D_1D_1 to D_3D_3 will cause an exodus of firms and ultimately a restoration of equilibrium at price Q_3P_3 ($50) and output Q_3 (90,000). A line which connects all points, such as these three, shows the various price–quantity supplied combinations which would be most profitable when it has had enough time to make *all* desired adjustments to assumed changes in industry demand. By definition, this line is the industry's long-run supply curve. In a constant-cost industry this line, SS in Figure 25-10, is perfectly elastic.

LONG-RUN SUPPLY FOR AN INCREASING-COST INDUSTRY

But constant-cost industries are a special case. Most industries are **increasing-cost industries** in that their average cost curves shift upward as the industry expands and downward as the industry contracts. In most instances the entry of new firms will affect resource prices and therefore unit costs for the individual firms in the industry. When an industry is using a significant portion of some resource whose total supply is not readily increased, the entry of new firms will increase resource demand in relation to supply and boost resource prices. This is particularly so in industries which are using highly specialized resources whose initial supply is not readily augmented. The result of higher resource prices will be higher long-run average costs for firms in the industry. The higher costs, it should be noted, take the form of an upward shift in the long-run average-cost curve for the representative firm.

The net result is that when an increase in product demand causes economic profits and attracts new firms to the industry, a two-way squeeze on profits will occur to eliminate those profits. On the one hand, the entry of new firms will increase market supply and lower product price and, on the other, the entire average-total-cost curve of the representative firm will shift upward. This means that the equilibrium price will now be higher than it was originally. The industry will only produce a larger output at a higher price. Why? Because expansion of the industry has increased average total costs, and in the long run product price must cover these costs. A greater output will be forthcoming at a higher price, or, more technically, the industry supply curve for an increasing-cost industry will be upsloping. Instead of getting either 90,000, 100,000, or 110,000 units at the same price of $50, in an increasing-cost industry 90,000 units might be forthcoming at $45; 100,000 at $50; and 110,000 at $55. The higher price is required to induce more production because costs per unit of output increase as the industry expands.

This can be seen graphically in Figure 25-11. Original market demand, industry output, and price are D_1D_1, Q_1 (100,000), and Q_1P_1 ($50) respectively. An increase in demand to D_2D_2 will upset this equilibrium and give rise to economic

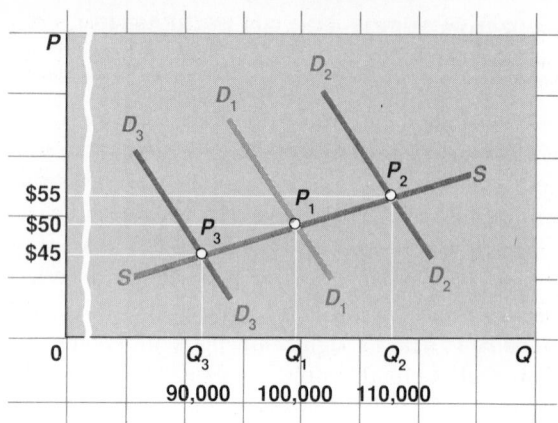

FIGURE 25-11

The long-run supply curve for an increasing-cost industry is upsloping

In an increasing-cost industry the entry of new firms in response to increases in demand (D_3D_3 to D_1D_1 to D_2D_2) will bid up resource prices and thereby increase unit costs. As a result, an increased industry output (Q_3 to Q_1 to Q_2) will be forthcoming only at higher prices ($Q_2P_2 > Q_1P_1 > Q_3P_3$). The long-run industry supply curve (SS) is therefore upsloping.

profits. As new firms enter, (1) industry supply will increase, tending to drive product price down, and (2) resource prices will rise, causing the average total costs of production to rise. Because of these average-total-cost increases, the new long-run equilibrium price will be established at some level *above* the original price, such as Q_2P_2 ($55). Conversely, a decline in demand from D_1D_1 to D_3D_3 will make production unprofitable and cause an exodus of firms from the industry. The resulting decline in the demand for resources relative to their supply will lower resource prices and cause average total costs of production to decline. Hence, the new equilibrium price will be established at some level *below* the original price, such as Q_3P_3 ($45). Connecting these three equilibrium positions, we derive an upsloping long-run supply curve as shown by SS in Figure 25-11.

Which situation—constant- or increasing-cost —is characteristic of American industry? Economists generally agree that increasing-cost industries are most common. Agriculture and extractive industries such as mining and lumbering are increasing-cost industries because each utilizes a

very large portion of some basic resource— farmland, mineral deposits, and timberland. Expansion will significantly affect the demand for these resources and result in higher costs. It is less easy to generalize with respect to manufacturing industries. In their early stages of development, such industries may well be relatively constant-cost industries.[2] But as continued expansion increases the importance of these industries in resource markets, they may in time become increasing-cost industries.

Pure competition and efficiency

Whether a purely competitive industry is one of constant or increasing costs, the final long-run equilibrium position for each firm will have the same basic characteristics. As shown in Figure 25-12, price (and marginal revenue) will settle at the level where they are equal to minimum average cost. However, we discovered in Chapter 24 that the marginal-cost curve intersects, and is therefore equal to, average cost at the point of minimum average cost. In the long-run equilibrium position, "everything is equal." MR (P) = AC = MC. This triple equality is of more than geometric interest. It tells us that, although a competitive firm may realize economic profits or losses in the short run, it will barely break even by producing in accordance with the MR (P) = MC rule in the long run. Furthermore, this triple equality suggests certain conclusions concerning the efficiency of a purely com-

[2] Under certain, very special circumstances, an industry may be for a time a *decreasing-cost industry*. For example, as more mines are established in a given locality, each firm's costs in pumping out water seepage may decline. With more mines pumping, the seepage into each is less, and pumping costs are therefore reduced. Furthermore, with only a few mines in an area, industry output might be so small that only relatively primitive and therefore costly transportation facilities are available. But as the number of firms and industry output expand, a railroad might build a spur into the area and thereby significantly reduce transportation costs. Under such special conditions, a firm's long-run supply curve may shift *downward*. We will have more to say about this kind of cost economy in Chapter 36.

petitive economy which are of great social significance. It is to an evaluation of competitive pricing from society's point of view that we now turn.

Economists agree that, subject to certain limitations and exceptions, a purely competitive economy will lead to the most efficient use of society's scarce resources. That is, *a competitive price economy will tend to allocate the limited amounts of resources available to society in such a way as to maximize the satisfactions of consumers.* Actually, the efficient use of limited resources requires that two conditions—which we shall call allocative efficiency and productive efficiency—be fulfilled. First, to achieve **allocative efficiency** resources must be apportioned among firms and industries so as to obtain the particular mix of products which is most wanted by society (consumers). Allocative efficiency is realized when it is impossible to alter the composition of total output so as to achieve a net gain for society. Second, **productive efficiency** requires that each good embodied in this optimum product mix be produced in the least costly way. To facilitate our discussion of how these

conditions would be achieved under purely competitive conditions, let us examine the second point first.

1 Productive efficiency: *P* = AC We have just noted that, in the long run, competition forces firms to produce at the point of minimum average total cost of production and to charge that price which is just consistent with these costs. This is clearly a most desirable situation from the consumer's point of view. It means that firms must use the best available (least-cost) technology or they will not survive. Stated differently, it means that the minimum amount of resources will be used in the production of any given output. For example, glance back at the final equilibrium position shown in Figure 25-9a. Each firm in the industry is producing 100 units of output by using $5000 (equal to average cost of $50 *times* 100 units) worth of resources. If that same output had been produced at a total cost of, say, $7000, resources would be being used inefficiently. Society would be faced with the net loss of $2000 worth of alternative products. Note, too, that consumers benefit from the lowest product price which is possible under the cost conditions which currently prevail. Finally, the costs involved in each instance are only those costs essential in producing a product. Because products are standardized in competitive industries, there will be no selling or promotional costs which must be added to production costs in determining product price.

2 Allocative efficiency: *P* = MC But the competitive production of *any* collection of goods does not necessarily make for an efficient allocation of resources. Production must not only be technologically efficient, but it must also entail the "right goods," that is, the goods that consumers want the most. The competitive market system will see to it that resources are allocated so as to result in a total output whose composition best fits the preferences of consumers.

Let us see precisely how this comes about. We must first grasp the social meaning of competitive product and resource prices. *The money price of any product—product X—is society's measure, or index, of the relative worth of that product at the margin.* Similarly, recalling the notion of opportunity costs, we see that *the marginal cost of producing X measures the value, or relative worth, of the other goods*

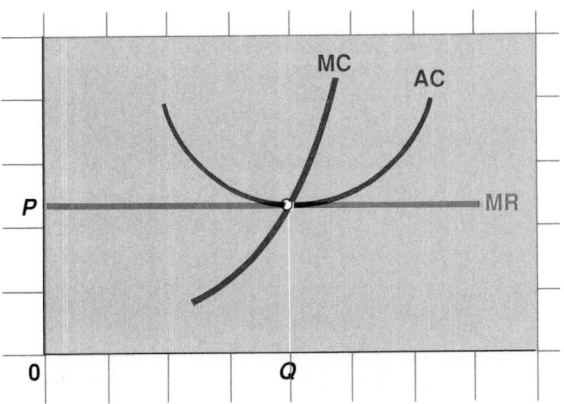

FIGURE 25-12

The long-run equilibrium position of a competitive firm, *P* = AC = MC

The equality of price and minimum average cost indicates that the firm is using the most efficient known technology and is charging the lowest price *P* and producing the greatest output *Q* consistent with its costs. The equality of price and marginal cost indicates that resources are being allocated in accordance with consumer preferences.

that the resources used in the production of an extra unit of X could otherwise have produced. In short, product price measures the benefit, or satisfaction, which society gets from additional units of X, and the marginal cost of an additional unit of X measures the sacrifice, or cost to society, of other goods in using resources to produce more of X. Now, under competition, the production of each product will occur up to that precise point at which price is equal to marginal cost (Figure 25-12). The profit-seeking competitor will realize the maximum possible profit only by equating price and marginal cost. To produce short of the MR (P) = MC point will mean less than maximum profits to the individual firm and an *under*allocation of resources to this product from society's standpoint. The fact that price exceeds marginal cost indicates that society values additional units of X more highly than the alternative products which the appropriate resources could otherwise produce. To illustrate, if the price of a shirt is $10 and its marginal cost is $8, the production of an additional shirt will cause a net increase in total output of $2. Society will gain a shirt valued at $10, while the alternative products sacrificed by allocating more resources to shirts would only be valued at $8. Whenever society can gain something valued at $10 by giving up something valued at $8, the initial allocation of resources must have been inefficient.

For similar reasons, the production of X should not go beyond the output at which price equals marginal cost. To do so would entail less than maximum profits for producers and an *over*allocation of resources to X from the standpoint of society. To produce X at some point at which marginal cost exceeds price means that resources are being used in the production of X at the sacrifice of alternative goods which society values more highly than the added units of X. For example, if the price of a shirt is $10 and its marginal cost is $13, then the production of one less shirt would result in a net increase in society's total output of $3. Society would lose a shirt valued at $10, but the reallocation of the freed resources to their best alternative uses would increase the output of some other good valued at $13. Again, whenever society is able to give up something valued at $10 in return for something valued at $13, the original allocation of resources must have been inefficient.

Our conclusion is that *under pure competition, profit-motivated producers will produce each commodity up to that precise point at which price and marginal cost are equated. This means that resources are efficiently allocated under competition.* Each good is produced to the point at which the value of the last unit is equal to the value of the alternative goods sacrificed by its production. To alter the production of X would necessarily reduce consumer satisfactions. To produce X beyond the P = MC point would result in the sacrifice of alternative goods whose value to society exceeds that of the extra units of X. To produce X short of the P = MC point would involve the sacrifice of units of X which society values more than the alternative goods resources can produce.

A further attribute of purely competitive markets is their ability to restore efficiency in the use of resources when disrupted by dynamic changes in the economy. In a competitive economy, any changes in consumer tastes, resource supplies, or technology will automatically set in motion appropriate realignments of resources. As we have already explained, an increase in consumer demand for product X will increase its price. Disequilibrium will occur in that, at its present output, the price of X will now exceed its marginal cost. This will create economic profits in industry X and stimulate its expansion. Its profitability will permit the industry to bid resources away from now less pressing uses. Expansion in this industry will end only when the price of X is again equal to its marginal cost, that is, when the value of the last unit produced is once again equal to the value of the alternative goods society forgoes in getting that last unit of X produced. Similarly, changes in the supplies of particular resources or in the techniques pertinent to various industries will upset existing price–marginal-cost equalities by either raising or lowering marginal cost. These inequalities will cause business executives, in either pursuing profits or shunning losses, to reallocate resources until price once again equals marginal cost in each line of production. In so doing, they correct any inefficiencies in the allocation of resources which changing economic data may temporarily impose upon the economy.

A final point: The highly efficient allocation of resources which a purely competitive economy fosters comes about because businesses and resource suppliers freely seek to further their own self-interests. That is, the "invisible hand" (Chapter 5) is at work in a competitive market system. In a competitive economy, businesses employ resources until the extra, or marginal, costs of production equal the price of the product. This not only maximizes the profits of the individual producers but simultaneously results in a pattern of resource allocation which maximizes the satisfactions of consumers. The competitive market system organizes the private interests of producers along lines which are fully in accord with the interests of a society as a whole.

QUALIFICATIONS

Our conclusion that a purely competitive market system results in both productive and allocative efficiency must be qualified in several important respects.

The income distribution problem The contention that pure competition will allocate resources efficiently—that is, will produce the collection of goods and services which maximizes the satisfaction of consumer wants—is predicated upon some given distribution of money income. In other words, money income is distributed among households in some specific way, and this distribution results in a certain structure of demand. The competitive market system then brings about an efficient allocation of resources or, stated differently, an output of goods and services whose composition maximizes the fulfillment of these particular consumer demands. But what if the distribution of money income is altered so that the structure of demand changes? Would the competitive market system negotiate a new allocation of resources? The answer, of course, is "Yes"; the market system would reallocate resources and therefore change the composition of output to maximize the fulfillment of this new pattern of consumer wants. The problem, then, is, Which of these two "efficient" allocations of resources is the "most efficient"? Which allocation of resources yields the greatest level of satisfaction to society? There is no *scientific* answer to this question because we do not know how to measure and compare the satisfaction derived by various individuals from goods and services. If all people were precisely alike in their ca-

pacities to obtain satisfaction from income, economists could recommend that income be distributed equally and that the allocation of resources which would be appropriate to *that* distribution would be the "best" or "most efficient" of all. But, in fact, people are different by virtue of their education, experiences, and environment, not to mention their inherited mental and physical characteristics. Such differences can be used to argue for an unequal distribution of income.

The basic point for present purposes is that the distribution of income associated with the workings of a purely competitive market system is quite unequal and therefore may lead to the production of trifles for the rich while denying the basic needs of the poor. Hence, many economists believe that the distribution of income which pure competition provides should be modified by public action. They maintain that allocative efficiency is hardly a virtue if it comes in response to an income distribution which offends prevailing standards of equity. The question of income inequality will be accorded detailed treatment in Chapter 37.

Market failure: spillovers and public goods The purely competitive model implicitly assumes there are no substantial market spillovers. But, in fact, spillover costs or benefits may be significant. Under competition each producer will assume only those costs which it *must* pay. This correctly implies that in some lines of production there are significant costs which producers can and do avoid, usually by polluting the environment. Recall from Chapter 6 that these avoided costs accrue to society and are aptly called *spillover* or *external costs*. On the other hand, the consumption of certain goods and services, such as chest x-rays and polio shots, yields widespread satisfactions, or benefits, to society as a whole. These satisfactions are called *external* or *spillover benefits*.

Now the significance of spillover costs and benefits for present purposes is this: The profit-seeking activities of producers will bring about an allocation of resources which is efficient from society's point of view only if marginal cost embodies *all* the costs which production entails and product price accurately reflects *all* the benefits which society gets from a good's production. Only in this case will competitive production at the MR (P) = MC point balance the *total* sacrifices and satisfactions of society and result in an efficient allocation of resources. To the extent that price and marginal cost are not accurate indexes of sacrifices and satisfactions—in other words, to the extent that spillover costs and benefits exist—production at the MR (P) = MC point will *not* signify an efficient allocation of resources (see Figures 6-1 and 6-2).

Remember, too, the point of the lighthouse example in Chapter 6: The market system does not provide for social or public goods, that is, for goods to which the exclusion principle does **not** apply. Despite its other virtues, the competitive price system ignores an important class of goods and services—national defense, flood-control programs, and so forth—which can and do yield satisfaction to consumers but which cannot be priced and sold through the market system.

Productive techniques Purely competitive markets may not always entail the use of the most efficient productive techniques or the development of improved techniques. There are both a static or "right now" aspect and a dynamic or "over time" aspect of this general criticism.

The static aspect involves the **natural monopoly** problem which was introduced in Chapter 24. In certain lines of production, existing technology may be such that a firm must be a large-scale producer in order to realize the lowest unit costs of production. Given consumer demand, this suggests that a relatively small number of efficient, large-scale producers is needed if production is to be carried on efficiently. In other words, existing mass-production economies might be lost if such an industry were populated by the large number of small-scale producers which pure competition requires.

The dynamic aspect of this criticism concerns the willingness and ability of purely competitive firms to undertake technological advance. The progressiveness of pure competition is debated by economists. For present purposes we merely call attention to the belief of some authorities that a purely competitive economy would **not** foster a very rapid rate of technological progress. They argue, first, that the incentive for technological advance may be weak under pure competition because the profit rewards accruing to an innovating firm as the result of a cost-reducing technological improve-

LAST WORD

The theory of contestable markets

The concept of contestable markets suggests that the market power of imperfectly competitive producers may be severely constrained by potential industry entrants.

As noted in this chapter, the outcomes of purely competitive markets set standards of efficiency by which imperfectly competitive markets are judged. Both allocative and productive efficiency are realized when an industry is purely competitive. It has recently been argued by Princeton's William Baumol that the *potential* entry of firms to industries which are *not* purely competitive may also bring about the efficient results associated with pure competition.

More specifically, Baumol has developed the notion of a *contestable market* which means a market in which firm entry and exit are costless or virtually so. Envision a contestable market which is oligopolistic, that is, comprised of three or four large firms. The contestability of the market means that it is subject to "hit and run" entry by other firms because they can enter and leave virtually without cost. It follows that any economic profits or production inefficiencies on the part of the several firms in the industry will attract new entrants. (Productive inefficiencies imply that profits are being forgone by existing producers and new entrants can realize such profits by producing efficiently.) Hence, in contestable markets the mere

ment will be quickly competed away by rival firms which readily adopt the new technique. Second, the small size of the typical competitive firm and the fact that it tends to "break even" in the long

presence of potential competition will force existing firms to produce efficiently and to charge prices which yield only a normal profit. Stated differently, incumbent firms are forced to behave as would purely competitive firms in order to forestall entry of other firms. We thus realize the socially desirable outcomes of purely competitive markets in contestable markets even though the latter are populated by only a few firms. The important factor which promotes these outcomes is not the number of firms in the industry, but costless entry and exit.

The most cited example of a contestable market is the airline industry. Assume there are just two airlines flying the Omaha–Chicago route. If entry and exit were costly, the market would *not* be contestable and the two incumbent airlines might realize substantial economic profits from their protected market position. But in fact additional airlines can enter and leave this particular segment of the air transportation market with minimal cost. The reason is that the relevant capital equipment—the airplanes themselves—are highly mobile! Hence, if an additional airline were to enter and find the Omaha–Chicago route to be unprofitable, it could simply "pull out" by flying its equipment to some other route. The important point is that the awareness of the possibility of costless entry will compel the two airlines currently flying the Omaha–Chicago route to provide their transportation services efficiently and at prices which yield only a normal profit.

The main policy implication of contestable markets is that the focus of antimonopoly policy should shift from the current structure or competitive conditions within an industry to the conditions of entry. The primary criticism of contestable market theory is that its applicability is extremely limited. Critics contend that there are few, if any, industries—including the aforementioned airline industry—where entry and exit are costless.

run raise serious questions as to whether such producers could finance substantial programs of organized research. We will return to this controversy in Chapter 28.

Range of consumer choice A purely competitive economy might not provide for a sufficient range of consumer choice or for the development of new products. This criticism, like the previous one, has both a static and a dynamic aspect. Pure competition, it is contended, entails product standardization, whereas other market structures—for example, monopolistic competition and, frequently, oligopoly—entail a wide range of types, styles, and quality gradations of any product. This product differentiation widens the consumer's range of free choice and simultaneously allows the buyer's preferences to be more completely fulfilled. Similarly, critics of pure competition point out that, just as pure competition is not likely to be progressive with respect to the development of new productive techniques, neither is this market structure conducive to the improvement of existing products or the creation of completely new ones.

The question of the progressiveness of the various market structures in terms of both productive techniques and product development will be a recurring one in the following three chapters.[3]

CHAPTER SUMMARY

1 American industry is characterized by differing degrees of competition. The market models of *a* pure competition, *b* pure monopoly, *c* monopolistic competition, and *d* oligopoly are classifications into which most industries can be fitted with reasonable accuracy.

2 A purely competitive industry comprises a large number of independent firms producing a standardized product. Pure competition assumes that firms and resources are mobile among different industries. No single firm can influence market price in a competitive industry; the firm's demand curve is perfectly elastic and price therefore equals marginal revenue.

3 Short-run profit maximization by a competitive firm can be analyzed by a comparison of total revenue and total cost or through marginal analysis. A firm will maximize profits by producing that output at which total rev-

[3] Instructors who want to consider agriculture as a case study in pure competition should insert Chapter 35 at this point.

enue exceeds total cost by the greatest amount. Losses will be minimized by producing where the excess of total cost over total revenue is at a minimum and less than total fixed costs.

4 Provided price exceeds minimum average variable cost, a competitive firm will maximize profits or minimize losses in the short run by producing that output at which price or marginal revenue is equal to marginal cost. If price is less than average variable cost, the firm will minimize its losses by closing down. If price is greater than average variable cost but less than average total cost, the firm will minimize its losses by producing the $P = MC$ output. If price exceeds average total cost, the $P = MC$ output will provide maximum economic profits for the firm.

5 Applying the MR $(P) = MC$ rule at various possible market prices leads to the conclusion that the segment of the firm's short-run marginal-cost curve which lies above average variable cost is its short-run supply curve.

6 In the long run, competitive price will tend to equal the minimum average cost of production. This is so because economic profits will cause firms to enter a competitive industry until those profits have been competed away. Conversely, losses will force the exodus of firms from the industry until product price once again barely covers unit costs.

7 The long-run supply curve is perfectly elastic for a constant-cost industry, but is upsloping for an increasing-cost industry.

8 In a purely competitive economy the profit-seeking activities of producers will result in an allocation of resources which maximizes the satisfactions of consumers. The long-run equality of price and minimum average cost indicates that competitive firms will use the most efficient known technology and charge the lowest price consistent with their production costs. The equality of price and marginal cost indicates that resources will be allocated in accordance with consumer tastes. The competitive price system will reallocate resources in response to a change in consumer tastes, technology, or resource supplies so as to maintain allocative efficiency over time.

9 Economists recognize four possible deterrents to allocative efficiency in a competitive economy. **a** There is no reason why the competitive market system will result in an optimal distribution of income. **b** In allocating resources, the competitive model does not allow for spillover costs and benefits or for the production of public goods. **c** A purely competitive industry may preclude the use of the best-known productive techniques and foster a slow rate of technological advance. **d** A competitive system provides neither a wide range of product choice nor an environment conducive to the development of new products.

TERMS AND CONCEPTS

pure competition	loss-minimizing case
pure monopoly	close-down case
monopolistic competition	MR $(P) = MC$ rule
oligopoly	short-run supply curve
imperfect competition	long-run supply curve
price taker	constant-cost industry
average, total, and marginal revenue	increasing-cost industry
	allocative efficiency
profit-maximizing case	productive efficiency
break-even point	

QUESTIONS AND STUDY SUGGESTIONS

1 Briefly indicate the basic characteristics of pure competition, pure monopoly, monopolistic competition, and oligopoly. Under which of these market classifications does each of the following most accurately fit: **a** a supermarket located in your home town; **b** the steel industry; **c** a Kansas wheat farm; **d** the commercial bank in which you or your family has an account; **e** the automobile industry. In each case justify your classification.

2 Strictly speaking, pure competition never has existed and probably never will. Then why study it?

3 Use the following demand schedule to determine total and marginal revenues for each possible level of sales.

Product price	Quantity demanded	Total revenue	Marginal revenue
$2	0	$_____	
2	1	_____	$_____
2	2	_____	_____
2	3	_____	_____
2	4	_____	_____
2	5	_____	_____

a What can you conclude about the structure of the industry in which this firm is operating? Explain.
b Graph the demand, total-revenue, and marginal-revenue curves for this firm.
c Why do the demand and marginal-revenue curves coincide?

d "Marginal revenue is the change in total revenue." Do you agree? Explain verbally and graphically, using the data in the table.

4 Assume the following unit-cost data are for a purely competitive producer:

Total product	Average fixed cost	Average variable cost	Average total cost	Marginal cost
0				
1	$60.00	$45.00	$105.00	$45
2	30.00	42.50	72.50	40
3	20.00	40.00	60.00	35
4	15.00	37.50	52.50	30
5	12.00	37.00	49.00	35
6	10.00	37.50	47.50	40
7	8.57	38.57	47.14	45
8	7.50	40.63	48.13	55
9	6.67	43.33	50.00	65
10	6.00	46.50	52.50	75

a At a product price of $32, will this firm produce in the short run? Why, or why not? If it does produce, what will be the profit-maximizing or loss-minimizing output? Explain. Specify the amount of economic profit or loss per unit of output.

b Answer the questions of 4a on the assumption that product price is $41.

c Answer the questions of 4a on the assumption that product price is $56.

d Complete the short-run supply schedule for the firm, and indicate the profit or loss incurred at each output (columns 1 to 3).

(1) Price	(2) Quantity supplied, single firm	(3) Profit (+) or loss (−)	(4) Quantity supplied, 1500 firms
$26	_____	$_____	_____
32	_____	_____	_____
38	_____	_____	_____
41	_____	_____	_____
46	_____	_____	_____
56	_____	_____	_____
66	_____	_____	_____

e Explain: "That segment of a competitive firm's marginal-cost curve which lies above its average-variable-cost curve constitutes the short-run supply curve for the firm." Illustrate graphically.

f Now assume there are 1500 identical firms in this competitive industry; that is, there are 1500 firms, each of which has the same cost data as shown here. Calculate the industry supply schedule (column 4).

g Suppose the market demand data for the product are as follows:

Price	Total quantity demanded
$26	17,000
32	15,000
38	13,500
41	12,000
46	10,500
56	9,500
66	8,000

What will equilibrium price be? What will equilibrium output be for the industry? For each firm? What will profit or loss be per unit? Per firm? Will this industry expand or contract in the long run?

5 Why is the equality of marginal revenue and marginal cost essential for profit maximization in all market structures? Explain why price can be substituted for marginal revenue in the MR = MC rule when an industry is purely competitive.

6 Explain: "A competitive producer must look to average variable cost in determining whether or not to produce in the short run, to marginal cost in deciding upon the best volume of production, and to average total cost to calculate profits or losses." Why might a firm produce at a loss in the short run rather than close down?

7 Using diagrams for both the industry and a representative firm, illustrate competitive long-run equilibrium. Employing these diagrams, show how *a* an increase, and *b* a decrease, in market demand will upset this long-run equilibrium. Trace graphically and describe verbally the adjustment processes by which long-run equilibrium is restored. Assume the industry is one of constant costs.

8 Distinguish carefully between a constant-cost and an increasing-cost industry. Answer question 7 on the assumption that the industry is one of increasing costs. Compare the long-run supply curves of a constant-cost and an increasing-cost industry.

9 Suppose a decrease in demand occurs in a competitive increasing-cost industry. Contrast the product price and industry output which exist after all long-run adjustments are completed with those which originally prevailed.

10 In long-run equilibrium, $P = AC = MC$. Of what significance for economic efficiency is the equality of P and AC? The equality of P and MC? Distinguish between productive efficiency and allocative efficiency in your answer.

11 Explain why some economists believe that an unequal distribution of income might impair the efficiency with which a competitive market system allocates resources. What other criticisms can be made of a purely competitive economy?

CHAPTER 26

Price and output determination: pure monopoly

L et us now jump to the opposite end of the industry spectrum (Table 25-1) and examine the characteristics, the bases, the price-output behavior, and the social desirability of pure monopoly. How is a pure monopoly defined? What conditions underlie the existence of a pure monopoly? How does a monopolist's price-output behavior compare with that of a purely competitive industry? Stated differently, do monopolists achieve the allocative and productive efficiency associated with pure competition? If not, are there policies by which government can improve the price-output behavior of a pure monopolist?

Pure monopoly: an introduction

Absolute or **pure monopoly** exists when a single firm is the sole producer of a product for which there are no close substitutes. Let us first examine the characteristics of pure monopoly and then provide a few examples.

CHARACTERISTICS

1 **Single seller** A pure, or absolute, monopolist is a one-firm industry. A single firm is the only producer of a given product or the sole supplier of a service; hence, the firm and the industry are synonymous.

2 **No close substitutes** It follows from this first characteristic that the monopolist's product is unique in the sense that there are no good, or close, substitutes. From the buyer's point of view, this means that there are no reasonable alternatives. The buyer must buy the product from the monopolist or do without.

The fact there are no close substitutes for the monopolized product has interesting implications in terms of advertising. Depending upon the type of product or service involved, a monopolist may or may not engage in extensive advertising and sales promotion. For example, a pure monopolist selling a luxury good such as diamonds might advertise heavily in an attempt to increase the demand for the product. Perhaps the result will be that more people will buy diamonds rather than take vacations, for example. Local public utilities, on the other hand, normally see no point in large expenditures for advertising: Local citizens who want water, gas, electric power, and telephone service already know from whom they must buy these necessities.

If pure monopolists of the public utility variety do advertise, such advertising is likely to be of a public relations, or goodwill, character rather than highly competitive, as is the advertising associated with, say, cigarettes, detergents, and beer. Because they have no immediate rivals, monopolists, in trying to induce more people to buy their products, need not invoke the ours-is-better-than-theirs type of advertising which characterizes radio and television. Rather, the monopolist's pitch is likely to be, "We're really nice fellows and certainly wouldn't do anything to exploit other firms, our employees, or, heaven forbid, consumers."

3 "Price maker" We have emphasized that the individual firm operating under pure competition exercises no influence over product price; it is a "price taker." This is so because it contributes only a negligible portion of total supply. In vivid contrast, the pure monopolist is a *price maker;* the firm exercises considerable control over price. And the reason is obvious: It is responsible for, and therefore controls, the total quantity supplied. Given a downsloping demand curve for its product, the monopolist can cause product price to change by manipulating the quantity of the product supplied. If it is advantageous, we can expect this power to be so used.

4 Blocked entry If, by definition, a pure monopolist has no immediate competitors, there must be a reason for this lack of competition. And there is: The existence of monopoly depends upon the existence of barriers to entry. Be they economic, technological, legal, or other, certain obstacles must exist to keep new competitors from coming into the industry if monopoly is to persist. Entry under conditions of pure monopoly is blocked. More on this in a moment.

EXAMPLES

In most cities the governmentally owned or regulated public utilities—the gas and electric companies, the water company, the cable TV company, and the telephone company—are all monopolies or virtually so. There are no close substitutes for the services provided by these public utilities. Of course, there is almost always *some* competition.

Candles or kerosene lights are very imperfect substitutes for electricity; telegrams, letters, and messenger services can be substituted for the telephone. But such substitutes are either costly, inconvenient, or unappealing.

The classic example of a private, unregulated monopoly is the De Beers diamond syndicate which effectively controls 80 to 85 percent of the world's supply of diamonds. Although monopoly in the very strict sense of the term is virtually nonexistent in American industry, there have been and are a number of approximations.

The principal instances of companies that in recent years have maintained positions even approaching monopoly for any significant length of time are Western Electric (with about 85 percent of the domestic telephone equipment market); General Motors (with a diesel locomotive market share averaging 77 percent between 1956 and 1971); IBM (whose general-purpose digital computer systems market share ranged between 72 and 82 percent during the 1960s and early 1970s); Eastman Kodak (with about 90 percent of domestic amateur film production and roughly 65 percent of all film sales . . .); Dow Chemical (with 90 percent of U.S. magnesium production until new entry took place in 1969); Xerox (with 75 to 80 percent of electrostatic copier revenues during the 1960s, declining to 55 percent by 1978 after key patents expired); and Campbell (with approximately 85 percent of canned soup sales, ignoring such substitutes as dehydrated soups and the homemade alternative).[1]

Professional sports leagues also embody monopoly power. The leagues grant member clubs franchises to be the sole suppliers of their services in designated geographic areas. Aside from Chicago, New York, and one or two other extremely large metropolitan areas, the larger cities of the United States are served by a single professional baseball, football, hockey, or basketball team. If you want to see a live major-league professional basketball game in Phoenix or Seattle, you must patronize the Suns and the Sonics respectively.

Monopoly may also have a geographic dimension. A small town may be served by only one airline or railroad. The local bank, movie, or book-

[1] F. M. Scherer, *Industrial Market Structure and Economic Performance,* 2d ed. (Chicago: Rand McNally College Publishing Company, 1980), p. 67.

store may approximate a monopoly in a small and geographically isolated community.

IMPORTANCE

Analysis of pure monopoly is important for at least two reasons. First, a not insignificant amount of economic activity—perhaps 5 or 6 percent of the GNP—is carried out under conditions which approach pure monopoly. Second, a study of pure monopoly provides us with valuable insights concerning the more realistic market structures of monopolistic competition and oligopoly, which will be discussed in Chapters 27 and 28. These two market situations combine in differing degrees the characteristics of pure competition and pure monopoly.

Barriers to entry

The absence of competitors which characterizes pure monopoly is largely explainable in terms of barriers to entry, that is, considerations which prohibit additional firms from entering an industry. These barriers are also pertinent in explaining the existence of oligopoly and monopolistic competition between the market extremes of pure competition and pure monopoly. In the case of pure monopoly, entry barriers are sufficiently great to block completely all potential competition. Somewhat less formidable barriers permit the existence of oligopoly, that is, a market dominated by a few firms. Still weaker barriers result in the fairly large number of firms which characterizes monopolistic competition. The virtual absence of entry barriers helps explain the very large number of competing firms which is the basis of pure competition. The important point is this: Barriers to entry are pertinent not only to the extreme case of pure monopoly but also to the "partial monopolies" which are so characteristic of our economy. What forms do these entry barriers assume?

ECONOMIES OF SCALE: COSTS

Modern technology in some industries is such that efficient, low-cost production can be achieved only if producers are extremely large both absolutely and in relation to the market. Where economies of scale are very significant, a firm's average-cost schedule will decline over a wide range of output (Figure 24-9b). Given market demand, the achieving of low unit costs and therefore low unit prices for consumers depends upon the existence of a small number of firms or, in the extreme case, only one firm. The automobile, aluminum, and basic steel industries are a few of many heavy industries which reflect such conditions. If three firms currently enjoy all available economies of scale and each has roughly one-third of a market, it is easy to see why new competitors may find it extremely difficult to enter this industry. On the one hand, new firms entering the market as small-scale producers will have little or no chance to survive and expand. Why? Because as small-scale entrants they will be unable to realize the cost economies enjoyed by the existing "Big Three" and therefore will be unable to realize the profits necessary for survival and growth. New competitors in the basic steel and automobile industries will not come about as the result of the successful operation and expansion of small "backyard" producers. They simply will not be efficient enough to survive. The other option is to start out big, that is, to enter the industry as a large-scale producer. In practice, this is extremely difficult. It will be very difficult for a new and untried enterprise to secure the money capital needed to obtain capital facilities comparable to those accumulated by any of the Big Three in the automobile industry. The financial obstacles in the way of starting big are so great in many cases as to be prohibitive.

Caution: Recall from Chapter 24's Last Word that in most industries the minimum efficient scale of operation can be realized by a firm producing a very small percentage of domestic consumption. This suggests that a high degree of industrial concentration—pure monopoly or oligopoly—is frequently not justified in terms of economies of scale.

PUBLIC UTILITIES: NATURAL MONOPOLIES

In a few industries, economies of scale are particularly pronounced, *and* at the same time competition is impractical, inconvenient, or simply unworkable. Such industries are called *natural monopolies,* and most of the so-called public utilities—the electric and gas companies, bus firms, cable television, and water and communication facilities—can be so classified. These industries are generally given exclusive franchises by government. But in return for this sole right to supply electricity, water, or bus service in a given geographic area, government reserves the right to regulate the operations of such monopolies to prevent abuses of the monopoly power it has granted.

Let us examine some illustrations. It would be exceedingly wasteful for a community to have a number of firms supplying water or electricity. Technology is such in these industries that heavy fixed costs on generators, pumping and purification equipment, water mains, and transmission lines are required. This problem is aggravated by the fact that capital equipment must be sufficient to meet the peak demands which occur on hot summer days when lawns are being watered and air conditioners operated. These heavy fixed costs mean that unit costs of production decline with the number of cubic feet of water or kilowatt hours of electricity supplied by each firm. The presence of several water and electricity suppliers would divide the total market and reduce the sales of each competitor. Each firm would be pushed back up its declining average-cost curve. Firms would underutilize their fixed plants, with the result that unit cost and therefore electricity and water rates would be unnecessarily high. In addition, competition might prove to be extremely inconvenient. For example, the presence of a half-dozen telephone companies in a municipality could entail the inconvenience of having six telephones and six telephone books—not to mention six telephone bills—to ensure communications with all other residents in the same town.

Natural monopolies have low marginal costs and, following the MR = MC rule, find it advantageous to expand output. As a result, cutthroat price competition tends to break out when a number of firms exist in these public utilities industries. The result may be losses, the bankruptcy of weaker rivals, and the eventual merger of the survivors. The evolving pure monopoly may be anxious to recoup past losses and to profit fully from its new position of market dominance by charging exorbitant prices for its goods or services.

To spare society from such disadvantageous results, government will usually grant an exclusive franchise to a single firm to supply water, natural gas, electricity, telephone service, or bus transportation. In return government reserves the right to designate the monopolist's geographic area of operation, to regulate the quality of its services, and to control the prices which it may charge. The result is a regulated or government-sponsored monopoly—monopoly designed to achieve low unit costs but regulated to guarantee that consumers will benefit from these cost economies. We shall examine some of the problems associated with regulation later in this chapter and in Chapter 34.

LEGAL BARRIERS: PATENTS AND LICENSES

We have already noted that government frequently gives exclusive franchises to natural monopolies. Government also creates legal entry barriers in awarding patents and licenses.

Patents By granting an inventor the exclusive right to control a product for seventeen years, American patent laws are aimed at protecting the inventor from having the product or process usurped by rival enterprises which have not shared in the time, effort, and money outlays which have gone into its development. By the same token, of course, patents may provide the inventor with a monopoly position for the life of the patent. Patent control figured prominently in the growth of many modern-day industrial giants—National Cash Register, General Motors, Xerox, Polaroid, General Electric, du Pont, to name a few. The United Shoe Machinery Company provides a notable example of how patent control can be abused to achieve monopoly power. In this case United Shoe became the exclusive supplier of certain essential shoemaking machines through patent control. It extended its monopoly power to other types of shoemaking machinery by requiring all lessees of its patented machines to sign a "tying agreement" in which shoe manufacturers agreed also to lease all other shoemaking machinery from United Shoe. This allowed United Shoe to monopolize the market until partially effective antitrust action was taken by the government in 1955.

Research, of course, underlies the development of patentable products. Firms which gain a measure of monopoly power by their own research or by purchasing the patents of others are in a strategic position to consolidate and strengthen their market position. The profits provided by one important patent can be used to finance the research required to develop new patentable products. Monopoly power achieved through patents may well be cumulative.

Licenses Entry into an industry or occupation may be limited by government through the issuing of licenses. For example, at the national level the Federal Communications Commission licenses radio and television stations. In many large cities one must obtain a municipal license to drive a taxicab. It is generally acknowledged that the consequent restriction of the supply of cabs creates monopolistic earnings for cab owners and drivers. In a few instances government might license itself to provide some product and thereby create a public monopoly. For example, the sale of liquor in a number of states is exclusively through state-owned retail outlets. Similarly, many states have in effect "licensed" themselves to run lotteries (Chapter 8).

OWNERSHIP OF ESSENTIAL RAW MATERIALS

The institution of private property can be used by a monopoly as a means of achieving an effective obstacle to potential rivals. A firm owning or controlling a raw material which is essential in the production process can prohibit the creation of rival firms. There are several classic examples. The Aluminum Company of America retained its monopoly position in the aluminum industry for many years by virtue of its control of all basic sources of bauxite, the major ore used in aluminum fabrication. At one time the International Nickel Company of Canada (now called Inco) controlled approximately 90 percent of the world's known nickel reserves. As noted earlier, most of the world's known diamond mines are owned or effectively controlled by the De Beers Company of South Africa. Similarly, it is very difficult for new professional sports leagues to evolve when existing leagues have contracts with the best players and leases on the major stadiums and arenas.

UNFAIR COMPETITION

A firm's rivals may be eliminated and the entry of new competitors blocked by aggressive, cutthroat tactics. Familiar techniques entail product disparagement, pressure on resource suppliers and banks to withhold materials and credit, the hiring away of strategic personnel, and aggressive price cutting designed to bankrupt competitors. Though many of these facets of **unfair competition** are now illegal or fringe upon illegality they are of more than historical interest. For example, although Federal legislation prohibits price cutting intended to reduce competition, how is one to distinguish in practice between legitimate price competition based upon cost advantages and price competition designed to bankrupt rivals?

TWO IMPLICATIONS

Our discussion of barriers to entry suggests two noteworthy points.

1 Relatively rare Barriers to entry are rarely complete; indeed, this is merely another way of stating our earlier point that pure monopoly is relatively rare. Although, as we have seen, research and technological advance may strengthen the market position of a firm, technology may also undermine existing monopoly power. Existing patent advantages may be circumvented by the development of new and distinct, yet substitutable, products. New sources of strategic raw materials may be found. It is probably only a modest overstatement to say that monopoly in the sense of a one-firm industry persists over time only with the sanction or aid of government—for example, the postal service's monopoly on the delivery of first-class mail.

2 Desirability? It is implied in our discussion that monopolies may be desirable or undesirable from the standpoint of economic efficiency. The public utilities and economies-of-scale arguments suggest that market demand and technology may be such that efficient low-cost production presupposes the existence of monopoly. On the other hand, our comments upon materials ownership, patents, licensing, and unfair competition as sources of monopoly imply more undesirable connotations of business monopoly.

With these points in mind, let us analyze the price-output behavior of a pure monopolist. Important insights with respect to the social desirability of monopoly will be revealed.

Price and output determination

Let us assume a pure monopolist which, through, say, patent and materials control, is able to block the entry of new firms to the market. Suppose, too, that the monopolist is unhampered by the existence or the prospect of a regulatory commission. In short, we have a monopolist which is ideally situated to exploit the market fully.[2] The pure monopolist will determine its profit-maximizing output on the basis of its cost and demand data.

MONOPOLY DEMAND

The crucial difference between a pure monopolist and a purely competitive seller lies on the demand side of the market. We recall from Chapter 25 that the purely competitive seller faces a perfectly elastic demand schedule at the market price determined by industry supply and demand. The competitive firm is a "price taker" which can sell as much or as little as it wants at the going market price. It follows that each additional unit sold will add a constant amount—its price—to the firm's total revenue. In other words, marginal revenue for the competitive seller is constant and equal to product price. This means that total revenue increases by a constant amount, that is, by the con-

TABLE 26-1 **Revenue and cost data of a pure monopolist (hypothetical data)**

Revenue data				Cost data			
(1) Quantity of output	(2) Price (average revenue)	(3) Total revenue	(4) Marginal revenue	(5) Average total cost	(6) Total cost	(7) Marginal cost	(8) Profit (+) or loss (−)
0	$172	$ 0			$ 100		$−100
1	162	162	$162	$190.00	190	$ 90	− 28
2	152	304	142	135.00	270	80	+ 34
3	142	426	122	113.33	340	70	+ 86
4	132	528	102	100.00	400	60	+128
5	122	610	82	94.00	470	70	+140
6	112	672	62	91.67	550	80	+122
7	102	714	42	91.43	640	90	+ 74
8	92	736	22	93.73	750	110	− 14
9	82	738	2	97.78	880	130	−142
10	72	720	−18	103.00	1030	150	−310

[2] It is assumed for the moment that the monopolist cannot engage in price discrimination, that is, the practice of charging different prices to different buyers.

stant price of each unit sold. A glance back at Table 25-2 and Figure 25-1 will refresh you on the price, marginal-revenue, and total-revenue relationships for the purely competitive firm.

The monopolist's demand curve—indeed, the demand curve of *any* imperfectly competitive seller—is much different. Because the pure monopolist *is* the industry, its demand, or sales, curve is the industry demand curve.[3] And the industry demand curve is not perfectly elastic, but rather is downsloping. This is illustrated by columns 1 and 2 of Table 26-1. There are three implications of a downsloping demand curve which must be understood.

1 Price exceeds marginal revenue In the first place, a downsloping demand curve means that a pure monopoly can increase its sales only by charging a lower unit price for its product. *Furthermore, the fact that the monopolist must lower price to boost sales causes marginal revenue to be less than price (average revenue) for every level of output except the first.* The reason? Price cuts will apply not only to the extra output sold but also to *all* other units of output which otherwise could have been sold at a higher price. Each additional unit sold will add to total revenue its price *less* the sum of the price cuts which must be taken on all prior units of output.

Figure 26-1 is helpful on this point. Here we have extracted two price–quantity combinations—$142-3 and $132-4—from the monopolist's demand curve. By lowering price from $142 to $132, the monopolist can sell one more unit and thus gain as revenue the fourth unit's price of $132. This gain is designated as the gray rectangle in Figure 26-1. But to sell this fourth unit for $132, the monopolist must lower price on the first three units from $142 to $132. This $10 price reduction on 3 units results in a $30 revenue loss as indicated by the light red rectangle in Figure 26-1. The *net* change in total revenue or, in other words, marginal revenue, from selling the fourth unit is $102, the $132 gain minus the $30 loss.

[3] Recall in Chapter 25 that we presented separate diagrams for the purely competitive industry *and* for a single firm in that industry. Because with pure monopoly the firm and the industry are one and the same, we need only a single diagram.

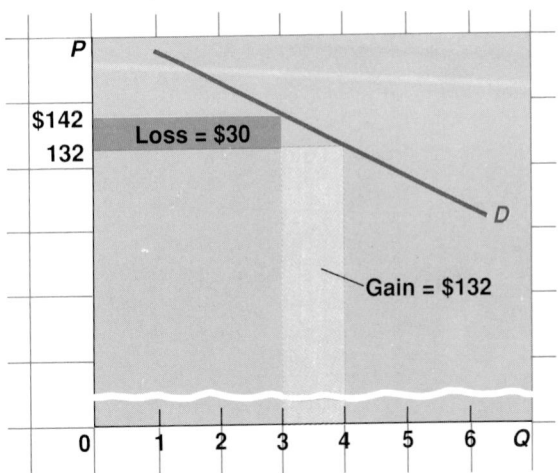

FIGURE 26-1

Price and marginal revenue under pure monopoly

A pure monopolist—or, in fact, any imperfect competitor with a downsloping demand curve—must reduce price to sell more output. As a consequence, marginal revenue will be less than price. In our example, by reducing price from $142 to $132 the monopolist gains $132 from the sale of the fourth unit. But from this gain must be subtracted $30 which reflects the $10 price cut which has been made on each of the first three units. Hence, the fourth unit's marginal revenue is $102 (= $132 − $30), considerably less than its $132 price.

Similarly, looking at Table 26-1 once again, we observe that the marginal revenue of the second unit of output is $142 rather than its $152 price, because a $10 price cut must be taken on the first unit to increase sales from 1 to 2 units. Similarly, to sell 3 units the firm must lower price from $152 to $142. The resulting marginal revenue will be just $122—the $142 addition to total revenue which the third unit of sales provides less $10 price cuts on the first 2 units of output. It is this rationale which explains why the marginal-revenue data of column 4 of Table 26-1 fall short of product price in column 2 for all levels of output except the first. Because marginal revenue is, by definition, the increase in total revenue associated with each additional unit of output, the declining marginal-revenue figures mean that total revenue will increase at

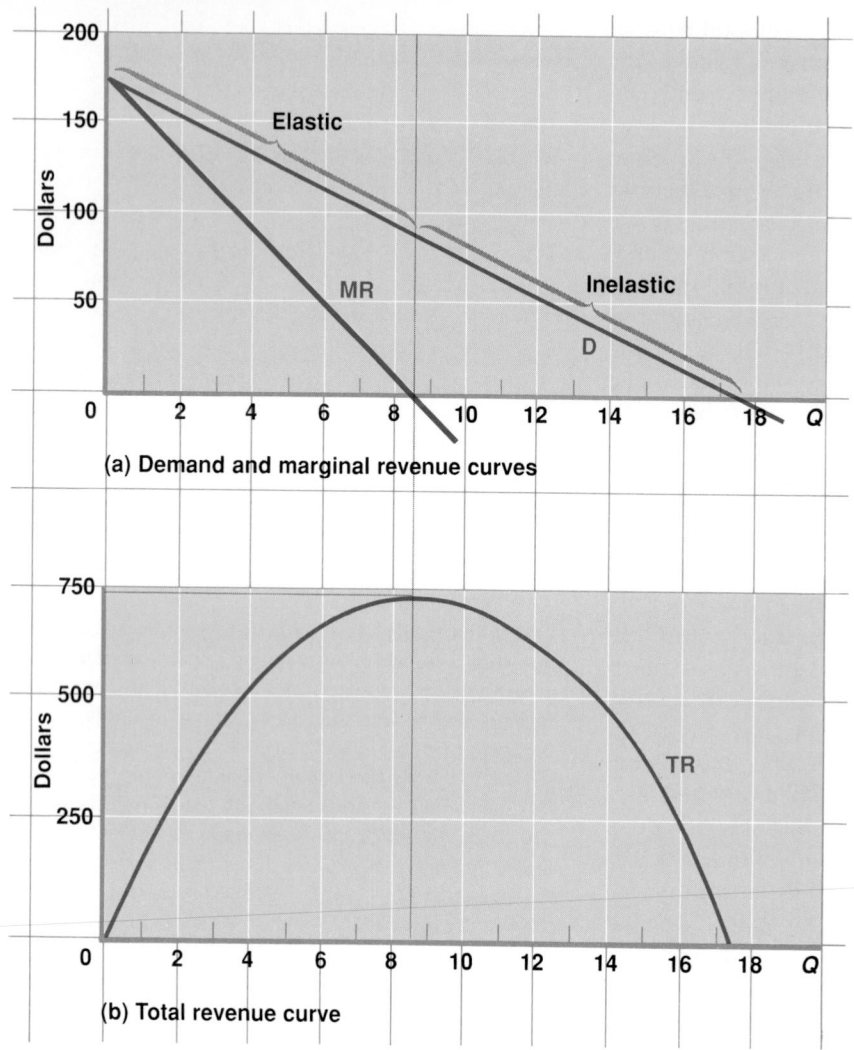

FIGURE 26-2

Demand, marginal revenue, and total revenue of an imperfectly competitive firm

Because it must lower price to increase its sales, an imperfectly competitive firm's marginal-revenue curve (MR) lies below its downsloping demand curve (D). Total revenue (TR) increases at a decreasing rate, reaches a maximum, and then declines. Note that, because MR is the change in TR, a unique relationship exists between MR and TR. In moving down the elastic segment of the demand curve, TR is increasing and, hence, MR is positive. When TR reaches its maximum, MR is zero. And in moving down the inelastic segment of the demand curve, TR is declining, so MR is negative. A monopolist or other imperfectly competitive seller will never choose to lower price into the inelastic segment of its demand curve because by doing so it will simultaneously reduce total revenue and increase production costs, thereby lowering profits.

a diminishing rate as shown in column 3 of Table 26-1.

The relationships between the demand, marginal-revenue, and total-revenue curves are por-

trayed graphically in Figure 26-2a and b. In drawing this diagram we have extended the demand and revenue data of columns 1 through 4 of Table 26-1 by continuing to assume that successive $10 price cuts will each elicit one additional unit of sales. That is, 11 units can be sold at $62, 12 at $52, and so forth. In addition to the fact that the marginal-revenue curve lies *below* the demand curve, note the special relationship between total revenue and marginal revenue. Because marginal revenue is, by definition, the change in total revenue, we observe that so long as total revenue is increasing, marginal revenue is positive. When total revenue reaches its maximum, marginal revenue is zero. And when total revenue is diminishing, marginal revenue is negative.

2 Price maker The second implication of a downsloping demand curve is this: In all imperfectly competitive markets in which such demand curves are relevant—that is, purely monopolistic, oligopolistic, and monopolistically competitive markets—firms have a price policy. By virtue of their ability to influence total supply, the output decisions of such firms necessarily affect product price. This is most evident, of course, in the present case of pure monopoly, where one firm controls total output. Faced with a downsloping demand curve, wherein each output is associated with some unique price, the monopolist unavoidably determines price in deciding what volume of output to produce. The monopolist simultaneously chooses both price and output. In columns 1 and 2 of Table 26-1 we find that the monopolist can sell only an output of 1 unit at a price of $162, only an output of 2 units at a price of $152 per unit, and so forth.[4]

But all this is not to imply that the monopolist is "free" of market forces in establishing price and output or that the consumer is somehow completely at the monopolist's mercy. In particular, the monopolist's downsloping demand curve means that high prices are associated with low volumes of sales and, conversely, low prices with larger outputs. So long as the location of the monopolist's demand curve is fixed, it cannot raise

price without losing sales, or gain sales without charging a lower price.

3 Price elasticity The total-revenue test for price elasticity of demand is the basis for our third conclusion. Recall from Chapter 22 that the total-revenue test tells us that, when demand is elastic, a decline in price will increase total revenue. Similarly, when demand is inelastic, a decline in price will reduce total revenue. Beginning at the top of the demand curve in Figure 26-2, observe that for all price reductions from $172 down to approximately $82, total revenue increases (and marginal revenue therefore is positive). This means that demand is elastic in this price range. Conversely, for price reductions below $82, total revenue decreases (marginal revenue is negative), which indicates that demand is inelastic.

The generalization which emerges from these observations is that a monopolist will never choose a price-quantity combination where total revenue is decreasing (marginal revenue is negative). Stated differently, *the profit-maximizing monopolist will always want to avoid the inelastic segment of its demand curve in favor of some price-quantity combination in the elastic segment.* By lowering price into the inelastic range, total revenue will decline. But the lower price is associated with a larger output and therefore increased total costs. Lower revenue and higher costs mean diminished profits.

The question which now arises is this: What specific price-quantity combination on the elastic segment of the demand curve will the pure monopolist choose? This depends not only upon demand and marginal-revenue data but also upon costs.

COST DATA

On the cost side of the picture we shall assume that, although the firm is a monopolist in the product market, it hires resources competitively and employs the same technology as our competitive firm in the preceding chapter. This permits us to use the cost data developed in Chapter 24 and applied in Chapter 25, thereby facilitating a comparison of the price-output decisions of a pure monopoly with those of a pure competitor. Columns 5 through 7 of Table 26-1 merely restate the pertinent cost concepts of Table 24-2.

---

[4] The notion of a supply curve does not apply in a purely monopolistic (or any other imperfectly competitive) market because of the ability of the seller to control product price. A supply curve shows the amounts producers will offer at various *given* prices which may confront them in the market. But prices are not "given" to the pure monopolist; it does not respond to a fixed price, but rather, sets the price itself.

EQUATING MARGINAL REVENUE AND MARGINAL COST

A profit-seeking monopolist will employ the same rationale as a profit-seeking firm in a competitive industry. It will produce each successive unit of output so long as it adds more to total revenue than it does to total costs. In technical language, the firm will produce up to that output at which marginal revenue equals marginal cost.

A comparison of columns 4 and 7 in Table 26-1 indicates that the profit-maximizing output is 5 units; the fifth unit is the last unit of output whose marginal revenue exceeds its marginal cost. What price will the monopolist charge? The downsloping demand curve of columns 1 and 2 in Table 26-1 indicates that there is only one price at which 5 units can be sold: $122.

This same analysis is presented graphically in Figure 26-3, where the demand, marginal-revenue, average-total-cost, and marginal-cost data of Table 26-1 have been drawn. A comparison of marginal revenue and marginal cost again indicates that the profit-maximizing output is 5 units or, more generally, Q_m. The unique price at which Q_m can be sold is found by extending a perpendicular up from the profit-maximizing point on the output axis and

then at right angles from the point at which it hits the demand curve to the vertical axis. The indicated price is P_m. To charge a price higher than P_m, the monopolist must move up the demand curve, and this means that sales will fall short of the profit-maximizing level Q_m. Specifically, the firm will be failing to produce units of output whose marginal revenue exceeds their marginal cost. If the monopolist charges less than P_m, it would involve a volume of sales in excess of the profit-maximizing output.

Columns 2 and 5 of Table 26-1 indicate that, at 5 units of output, product price of $122 exceeds average total cost of $94. Economic profits are therefore $28 per unit; total economic profits are then $140 (= 5 × $28). In Figure 26-3, per unit profit is indicated by the distance AP_m, and total economic profits—the gray area—are found by multiplying this unit profit by the profit-maximizing output Q_m.

The same profit-maximizing combination of output and price can also be determined by comparing the total revenue and total costs incurred at each possible level of production. The reader should employ columns 3 and 6 of Table 26-1 to verify all the conclusions we have reached through the use of our marginal-revenue–marginal-cost

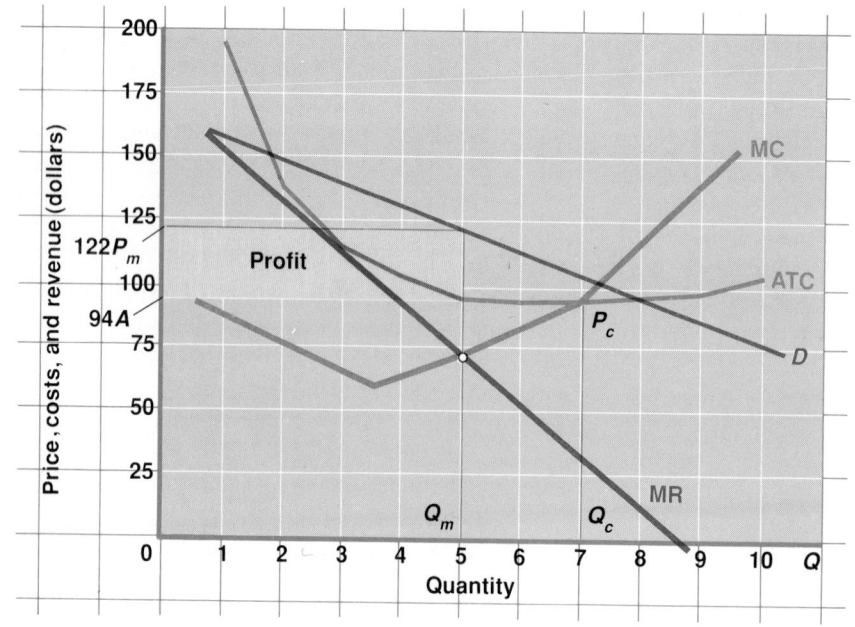

FIGURE 26-3

The profit-maximizing position of a pure monopolist

The pure monopolist maximizes profits by producing the MR = MC output. In this instance profit is AP_m per unit, and total profits are measured by the gray rectangle.

analysis. Similarly, an accurate graphing of total revenue and total cost against output will also show the greatest differential (the maximum profit) at 5 units of output.

MISCONCEPTIONS CONCERNING MONOPOLY PRICING

Our analysis explodes some popular fallacies concerning the behavior of monopolies.

1 Not highest price Because a monopolist can manipulate output and price, it is often alleged that a monopolist "will charge the highest price it can get." This is clearly a misguided assertion. There are many prices above P_m in Figure 26-3, but the monopolist shuns them solely because they entail a smaller-than-maximum profit. *Total* profits are the difference between *total* revenue and *total* costs, and each of these two determinants of profits depends upon the quantity sold as much as upon the price and unit cost.

2 Total, not unit, profits The monopolist seeks maximum *total* profits, not maximum *unit* profits. In Figure 26-3 a careful comparison of the vertical distance between average cost and price at various possible outputs indicates that per unit profits are greater at a point slightly to the left of the profit-maximizing output Q_m. This is more readily seen in Table 26-1, where unit profits are $32 at 4 units of output as compared with $28 at the profit-maximizing output of 5 units. In this instance the monopolist is accepting a lower-than-maximum per unit profit for the simple reason that the additional sales more than compensate for the lower unit profits. A profit-seeking monopolist would rather sell 5 units at a profit of $28 per unit (for a total profit of $140) than 4 units at a profit of $32 per unit (for a total profit of only $128).

3 Losses It must also be emphasized that pure monopoly does not guarantee economic profits. True, the likelihood of economic profits is greater for a pure monopolist than for a purely competitive producer. In the long run the latter is doomed by the free and easy entry of new firms to a normal profit; barriers to entry permit the monopolist to

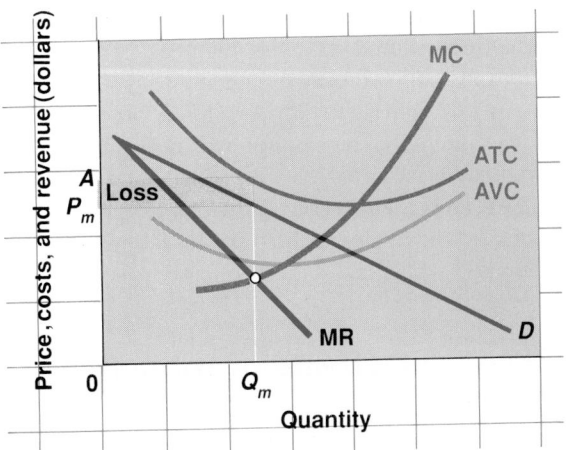

FIGURE 26-4

The loss-minimizing position of a pure monopolist

If demand *D* is weak and costs are high, the pure monopolist may be unable to make a profit. Because P_m exceeds AVC at Q_m, it will minimize losses in the short run by producing at that output where MR = MC. Loss per unit is AP_m, and total losses are indicated by the light red rectangle.

perpetuate economic profits in the long run.[5] Unlike the competitive situation, entry barriers keep out potential entrants who would increase supply, drive price down, and eliminate economic profits. Of course, like the pure competitor, the monopolist will not persistently operate at a loss. Faced with losses, the firm's owners will choose to move their resources to alternative industries which offer higher returns. Thus we can expect the monopolist to realize a normal profit or better in the long run. However, if the demand and cost situation faced by the monopolist is sufficiently less favorable than shown in Figure 26-3, short-run losses will be realized. Despite its dominance in the market, the monopolist shown in Figure 26-4 realizes a loss of

[5] A related point is that the distinction between the short run and the long run is less important under monopoly than it is under pure competition. With pure competition the entry or exit of firms guarantees that economic profits will be zero in the long run. But with pure monopoly barriers to entry prevent the competing away of economic profits by new firms.

an amount shown by the light red area by virtue of weak demand and relatively high costs. Yet it continues to operate for the time being because its total loss is less than its fixed costs. More precisely, observe that at Q_m the monopolist's price P_m exceeds its average variable cost. Perhaps this firm is the sole surviving enterprise producing, say, brass spittoons or slide rules, which are no longer in great demand.

Economic effects of monopoly

Let us now evaluate pure monopoly from the standpoint of society as a whole. Our discussion will encompass (1) price, output, and resource allocation; (2) some difficulties involved in making cost comparisons between competitive and monopolistic firms; (3) technological progress; and (4) the distribution of income.

PRICE, OUTPUT, AND RESOURCE ALLOCATION

In Chapter 25 we concluded that pure competition would result in both "productive efficiency" and "allocative efficiency." Productive efficiency is realized because the free entry and exodus of firms would force firms to operate at the optimal rate of output where unit costs of production would be at a minimum. Product price would be at the lowest level consistent with average total costs. To illustrate: In Figure 26-3 the competitive firm would sell Q_c units of output at a price of $Q_c P_c$. Allocative efficiency is reflected in the fact that production under competition would occur up to that point at which price (the measure of a product's value to society) would equal marginal cost (the measure of the alternative products forgone by society in the production of any given commodity).

Figure 26-3 indicates that, *given the same costs,* a purely monopolistic firm will produce much less desirable results. As we have already discovered, the pure monopolist will maximize profits by producing an output of Q_m and charging a price of P_m. It can be readily seen that *the monopolist will find it profitable to sell a smaller output and to charge a higher price than would a competitive producer.*[6]

[6] In Figure 26-3 the price-quantity comparison of monopoly and pure competition is from the vantage point of the single purely competitive *firm* of Figure 25-7a. An equally illuminating approach is to start with the purely competitive *industry* of Figure 25-7b, which is reproduced below. Recall that the competitive industry's supply curve S is the horizontal sum of the marginal-cost curves of all the firms in the industry. Comparing this with industry demand D, we get the purely competitive price and output of P_c and Q_c. Now suppose that this industry becomes a pure monopoly as a result of a wholesale merger or one firm's somehow buying out all its competitors. Assume, too, that no changes in costs or market demand result from this dramatic change in the industry's structure. What were formerly, say, 100 competing firms are now a pure monopolist consisting of 100 branch plants.

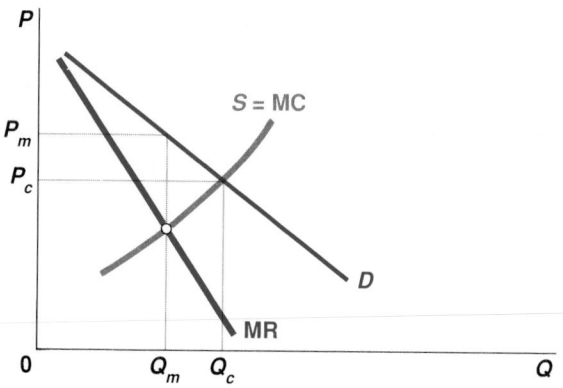

The industry supply curve is now simply the marginal-cost curve of the monopolist, the summation of the MC curves of its many branch plants. The important change, however, is on the market demand side. From the viewpoint of each individual competitive firm, demand was perfectly elastic, and marginal revenue was therefore equal to price. Each firm equated MC to MR (and therefore to P) in maximizing profits (Chapter 25). But industry demand and individual demand are the same to the pure monopolist; the firm *is* the industry, and thus the monopolist correctly envisions a downsloping demand curve D. This means that marginal revenue MR will be less than price; graphically the MR curve lies below the demand curve. In choosing the profit-maximizing MC = MR position, the monopolist selects an output Q_m which is smaller, and a price P_m which is greater, than would be the case if the industry were organized competitively.

Output Q_m is short of the Q_c point where average total costs are minimized (the intersection of MC and ATC). Glancing at column 5 of Table 26-1, we see that ATC at the monopolist's 5 units of output is $94.00 as compared to the $91.43 which would result under pure competition. Furthermore, at Q_m units of output, product price is considerably greater than marginal cost. This means that society values additional units of this monopolized product more highly than it does the alternative products which resources could otherwise produce. In other words, the monopolist's profit-maximizing output results in an underallocation of resources; the monopolist finds it profitable to restrict output and therefore employ fewer resources than are justified from society's standpoint.

COST COMPLICATIONS

To this point our evaluation of pure monopoly has led us to conclude that, *given identical costs,* a purely monopolistic firm will find it profitable to charge a higher price, produce a smaller output, and foster an allocation of economic resources inferior to that of a purely competitive industry. These contrasting results are rooted in the barriers to entry which characterize monopoly.

Now we must muddy the waters by recognizing that costs may *not* be the same for purely competitive and monopolistic producers. Unit costs incurred by a monopolist may be either larger or smaller than those facing a purely competitive firm. Several potentially conflicting considerations are involved: (1) economies of scale, (2) the notion of "X-inefficiency," (3) monopoly-preserving expenditures, and (4) the "very long-run" perspective which allows for technological progress. The first three issues are examined in this section and technological progress is taken up in the ensuing section.

Economies of scale revisited The assumption that the unit costs available to the purely competitive and the purely monopolistic firm are the same may not hold in practice. Given production techniques and therefore production costs, consumer demand may not be sufficient to support a large number of competing firms producing at an output which per-

mits each of them to realize all *existing* economies of scale. In such instances a firm must be large in relation to the market—that is, it must be monopolistic—to produce efficiently (at low unit cost).

This point is shown diagrammatically in Figure 26-5. The argument is that with pure competition or some approximation thereof each firm would have only a small share of the market such as Q_c. This small share forces each firm back up the long-run average-cost curve so that unit costs are high (AC_c). Economies of scale are *not* being realized and average costs are therefore high. But with monopoly (or oligopoly) the single (or each of the few) firm(s) can achieve existing scale economies and lower unit costs. In other words, a monopolist or oligopolist may realize output Q_m with the consequent lower average cost of AC_m. Presumably these lower costs—even after allowing for an economic profit—translate into a lower product price than competitive firms would be able to charge.

How important is this exception? Most economists feel that it applies for the most part only to public utilities and is therefore not significant enough to undermine our general conclusions concerning the restrictive nature of monopoly. Evidence suggests that the large corporations which populate many manufacturing industries now have more monopoly power than can be justified on the grounds that these firms are merely availing themselves of existing economies of scale.[7] Again, Chapter 24's Last Word provides relevant evidence which suggests that most industries could be quite competitive—substantially more competitive than is now the case—without sacrificing economies of scale.

X-inefficiency While economies of scale *might* argue in favor of monopoly in a few cases, the notion of X-inefficiency tends to suggest that monopoly costs might be *higher* than those associated with more competitive industries. What is X-inefficiency? Why might it plague monopolists more than competitors?

All the average-cost curves used in this and other chapters are based upon the assumption that

---

[7] For an excellent summary of research on this issue see Scherer, op. cit., chap. 4.

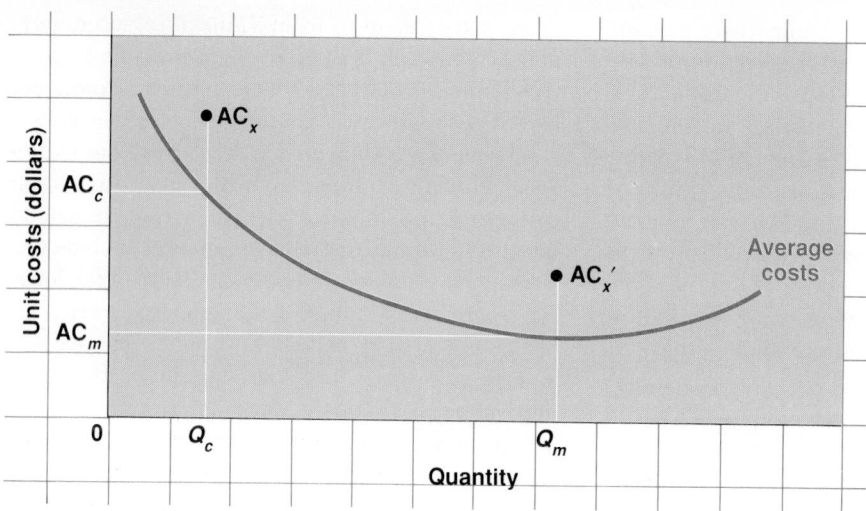

FIGURE 26-5

Economies of scale and X-inefficiency

This diagram serves to demonstrate two unrelated points. First, given the existence of extensive economies of scale, we note that a monopolist can achieve low unit costs of AC_m at Q_m units of output. In contrast, if the market were divided among a number of competing firms so that each produced only Q_c, then scale economies would be unrealized and unit costs of AC_c would be high. The second point is that X-inefficiency—the inefficient internal operation of a firm—results in higher-than-necessary costs. For example, unit costs might be AC_x rather than AC_c for Q_c units of output and AC'_x rather than AC_m for the Q_m level of output.

the firm chooses from *existing* technologies that one which is the most efficient or, in other words, that technology which permits the firm to achieve the minimum average cost for each level of output.[8] **X-inefficiency** is said to occur when a firm's actual costs of producing any output are greater than the minimum possible costs.[9] In Figure 26-5 X-inefficiency is represented by unit costs of AC_x (as opposed to AC_c) for output Q_c and average costs of AC'_x (rather than AC_m) for output Q_m. Any

point above the average-cost curve in Figure 26-5 is attainable but reflects internal inefficiency or "bad management" on the part of the firm.

Why does X-inefficiency occur when it tends to reduce profits? The answer is that managers may often have goals—for example, firm growth, an easier work life, the avoidance of business risk, providing jobs for incompetent friends and relatives—which conflict with cost minimization. Or X-inefficiency may arise because a firm's workers are poorly motivated. Or a firm may simply become lethargic and relatively inert, relying upon rules-of-thumb in decision making as opposed to relevant calculations of costs and revenues.

For present purposes the relevant question is whether monopolistic firms are more susceptible to X-inefficiency than are competitive producers. Presumably this is the case. At the level of theory firms in competitive industries are continuously under pressures from rivals which force them to be internally efficient as a matter of survival. But monopolists and oligopolists are sheltered from competitive forces and such an environment is conducive to

[8] You may recall that Table 5-1 defined the most efficient productive technique in a simplified way. A more sophisticated discussion of how a firm minimizes production costs is presented in the "Optimal Combination of Resources" section of Chapter 29.

[9] This concept is attributed to Harvey Leibenstein, "Allocative Efficiency vs. X-efficiency," *American Economic Review*, June 1966, pp. 392–415. Also see his *Beyond Economic Man* (Cambridge, Mass.: Cambridge University Press, 1976), and "X-Efficiency: From Concept to Theory," *Challenge*, September–October 1979, pp. 13–22.

X-inefficiency. Empirical evidence on X-inefficiency is largely anecdotal and sketchy, but it does suggest that X-inefficiency is greater the smaller the amount of competition. For example, a reasonable estimate is that X-inefficiency may be 5 percent or more of costs for monopolists, but only 3 percent for an "average" oligopolistic industry wherein the four largest firms produce 60 percent of total output.[10] In the words of one authority: "The evidence is fragmentary, but it is persuasive. 'X-inefficiency' exists, and it is more apt to be reduced when competitive pressures are strong than when firms enjoy insulated market positions."[11]

Monopoly-preserving expenditures There is still another reason why monopoly might entail higher costs and a greater efficiency loss than suggested by Figures 26-3 and 26-5. In particular, a firm may go to considerable expense to acquire or maintain monopoly privileges granted by government. To illustrate: A monopolist's barrier to entry may depend upon legislation or an exclusive license provided by government as, for example, in radio and television broadcasting. In an effort to sustain or enhance the consequent economic profits, the monopolist may spend substantial amounts on legal fees, lobbying, and public relations advertising to persuade government to grant or sustain its privileged position. These expenditures add nothing to the firm's output, but clearly increase its costs.

TECHNOLOGICAL PROGRESS: DYNAMIC EFFICIENCY

We have already noted that our condemnation of monopoly must be qualified in those instances where *existing* mass-production economies might be lost if an industry comprises a large number of small, competing firms. Now we must consider the issue of **dynamic efficiency,** which focuses upon the question of whether monopolists are more

[10] William G. Shepherd, *The Economics of Industrial Organization*, 2d ed. (Englewood Cliffs, N.J.: Prentice-Hall, Inc., 1985), p. 134. For a rather extensive review of case study evidence of X-inefficiency, see F. M. Scherer, op. cit., pp. 464–466.

[11] Scherer, op. cit., p. 466.

likely to develop more efficient production techniques over time than are competitive firms. Are monopolists more likely to improve productive technology, thereby lowering (shifting downward) their average-cost curves, than are competitive producers? Although we will concentrate upon changes in productive techniques, the same question applies to product improvement. Do monopolists have greater means and incentives to improve their products and thus enhance consumer satisfaction? This is fertile ground for honest differences of opinion.

The competitive model Competitive firms certainly have the incentive—indeed, a market mandate—to employ the most efficient *known* productive techniques. We have seen that their very survival depends upon being efficient. But at the same time, competition tends to deprive firms of economic profit—an important means and a major incentive to develop *new* improved productive techniques or *new* products. The profits of technological advance may be short-lived to the innovating competitor. An innovating firm in a competitive industry will find that its many rivals will soon duplicate or imitate any technological advance it may achieve; rivals will share the rewards but not the costs of successful technological research.

The monopoly model In contrast, we have seen that—thanks to entry barriers—a monopolist may persistently realize substantial economic profits. Hence, the pure monopolist will have greater financial resources for technological advance than will competitive firms. But what about the monopolist's incentives for technological advance? Here the picture is clouded.

There is one imposing argument which suggests that the monopolist's incentives to develop new techniques or products will be weak: The absence of competitors means that there is no automatic stimulus to technological advance in a monopolized market. Because of its sheltered market position, the pure monopolist can afford to be inefficient and lethargic. The keen rivalry of a competitive market penalizes the inefficient; an inefficient monopolist does not face this penalty simply because it has no rivals. The monopolist has every reason to become satisfied with the status quo, to become complacent. It might well pay the monopolist to withhold or "file" technological improvements in both productive techniques and products in order to exploit existing capital equipment fully. New and improved techniques and products, it is argued, may be suppressed by monopolists to avoid any losses caused by the sudden obsolescence of existing machinery and equipment. And, even when improved techniques are belatedly introduced by monopolists, the accompanying cost reductions will accrue to the monopolist as increases in profits and only partially, if at all, to consumers in the form of lower prices and an increased output. Proponents of this view point out that in a number of industries which approximate monopoly—for example, steel and aluminum—the interest in research has been minimal. Such advances as have been realized have come largely from outside the industry or from the smaller firms which make up the "competitive fringe" of the industry.

Basically, there are at least two counterarguments:

1 Technological advance is a means of lowering unit costs and thereby expanding profits. As our analysis of Figure 26-3 implies, lower costs will give rise to a profit-maximizing position which involves a larger output and a lower price than previously. Any expansion of profits will not be of a transitory nature; barriers to entry protect the monopolist from profit encroachment by rivals. In short, technological progress is profitable to the monopolist and therefore will be undertaken.
2 Research and technological advance may be one of the monopolist's barriers to entry; hence, the monopolist must persist and succeed in the area of technological advance or eventually fall prey to new competitors. Technological progress, it is argued, is essential to the maintenance of monopoly.

A mixed picture Which view is more accurate? Frankly, economists are not sure. Most economists do not envision pure monopoly as a particularly progressive market structure. At the same time, they acknowledge that agriculture, the industry which most nearly fits the competitive model, has only on rare occasions provided itself with innovations in product and method. Government research and the oligopolistic firms which produce farm equipment have provided this competitive industry with most of its improvements in products and techniques. As we shall see in Chapter 28, one can

make a case that oligopolistic industries, wherein firms are large enough to have the ability to finance research and at the same time are compelled to engage in such research because of the presence of a moderate number of rivals, *may* be more conducive to technological advance than any other market structure.

Now what can be offered by way of a summarizing generalization on the economic efficiency of pure monopoly? Simply this: In a static economy, wherein economies of scale are equally accessible to purely competitive and monopolist firms, pure competition will be superior to pure monopoly in that pure competition forces use of the best-known technology and allocates resources in accordance with the wants of society. However, when economies of scale available to the monopolist are not attainable by small competitive producers, or in a dynamic context in which changes in the rate of technological advance must be considered, the inefficiencies of pure monopoly are somewhat less evident.

INCOME DISTRIBUTION

Business monopoly probably contributes to inequality in the distribution of income. By virtue of their market power, monopolists charge a higher price than would a purely competitive firm with the same costs; monopolists are in effect able to levy a "private tax" upon consumers and thereby to realize substantial economic profits. These monopolistic profits, it should be noted, are not widely distributed because corporate stock ownership is largely concentrated in the hands of upper income groups. The owners of monopolistic enterprises tend to be enriched at the expense of the rest of society.

Price discrimination

Let's extend our understanding of monopoly and its consequences by considering (1) price discrimination and (2) government regulation of natural monopolies.

To this juncture we have assumed that the

monopolist charges a uniform price to all buyers. Under certain conditions the monopolist might be able to exploit its market position more fully and thus increase profits by charging different prices to different buyers. In so doing the seller is engaging in price discrimination. **Price discrimination** *takes place when a given product is sold at more than one price and these price differences are not justified by cost differences.*

CONDITIONS

The opportunity to engage in price discrimination is not readily available to all sellers. In general, price discrimination is workable when three conditions are realized.

1 Most obviously, the seller must be a monopolist or, at least, possess some degree of monopoly power, that is, some ability to control output and price.

2 The seller must be able to segregate buyers into separate classes wherein each group has a different willingness or ability to pay for the product. This separation of buyers is usually based upon different elasticities of demand as later illustrations will make clear.

3 The original purchaser cannot resell the product or service. If those who buy in the low-price segment of the market can easily resell in the high-price segment, the resulting decline in supply would increase price in the low-price segment and the increase in supply would lower price in the high-price segment. The price discrimination policy would thereby be undermined. This correctly suggests that service industries—for example, the transportation industry or legal and medical services—are especially susceptible to price discrimination.

ILLUSTRATIONS

Price discrimination is widely practiced in our economy. The sales representative who must communicate important information to corporate headquarters has a highly inelastic demand for long-distance telephone service and pays the high daytime rate. The college student making a periodic "reporting in" call to the folks at home has an elastic demand and defers the call to take advantage of lower evening or weekend rates. Electric utilities frequently segment their markets by end uses, such as lighting and heating. The absence of reasonable substitutes means that the demand for electricity for illumination is inelastic and the price per kilowatt hour for this use is high. But the availability of natural gas and petroleum as alternatives to electrical heating makes the demand for electricity less inelastic for this purpose and the price charged is lower. Similarly, industrial users of electricity are typically charged lower rates than residential users because the former may have the alternative of constructing their own generating equipment while the individual household does not. Movie theaters and golf courses vary their charges on the basis of time (higher rates in the evening and on weekends when demand is strong) and age (ability to pay). Railroads vary the rate charged per ton mile of freight according to the market value of the product being shipped. The shipper of 10 tons of television sets or costume jewelry will be charged more than the shipper of 10 tons of gravel or coal. Physicians and lawyers frequently set their fees for a given service on the basis of ability to pay; a rich person may pay a higher fee for a divorce or an appendectomy than a poor person. A manufacturer sells the same whiskey at a high price under a prestige label, but at a lower price under a different label. An appliance or tire manufacturer sells its product directly to the public at one price and through Sears or Ward's at a lower price. Airlines charge high fares to traveling executives, whose demand for travel tends to be inelastic, and offer a variety of lower fares in the guise of "family rates" and "standby fares" to attract vacationers and others whose demands are more elastic. Hotels and restaurants frequently give discounts to retired people.

CONSEQUENCES

The economic consequences of price discrimination are essentially twofold. First, it is not surprising that a monopolist will be able to increase its profits by practicing price discrimination. Second, other things being equal, a discriminating monopolist will produce a larger output than a nondiscriminating monopolist.

1 More profits The simplest way to understand why price discrimination can yield additional profits is to look again at our monopolist's downsloping demand curve in Figure 26-3. Although the profit-maximizing uniform price is $122, the segment of the demand curve lying above the profit area in Figure 26-3 tells us that there are buyers of the product who would be willing to pay *more than P_m* ($122) rather than forgo the product. If the monopolist can identify and segregate each of these buyers and thereby charge the maximum price each would pay, the sale of any given level of output will be more profitable. In columns 1 and 2 of Table 26-1 we note that the buyers of the first 4 units of output would be willing to pay more than the equilibrium price of $122. If the seller could somehow practice perfect price discrimination by extracting the maximum price each buyer would pay, total revenue would increase from $610 (= $122 × 5) to $710 (= $122 + $132 + $142 + $152 + $162) and profits would thereby increase from $140 (= $610 − $470) to $240 (= $710 − $470).

2 More production But, other things being the same, the discriminating monopolist will in fact choose to produce a larger output than the nondiscriminating monopolist. Recall that when the nondiscriminating monopolist lowers price to sell additional output, the lower price will apply not only to the additional sales but also to *all* prior units of output. As a result, marginal revenue is less than price and, graphically, the marginal-revenue curve lies below the demand curve. The fact that marginal revenue is less than price is a disincentive to increased production. But when a perfectly discriminating monopolist lowers price, the reduced price applies *only* to the additional unit sold and *not* to prior units. Hence, price and marginal revenue are equal for any unit of output. Graphically, the perfectly discriminating monopolist's marginal-revenue curve will coincide with its demand curve and the disincentive to increased production is removed. As indicated in Table 26-1, because marginal revenue now equals price, the monopolist will find that it is profitable to produce 7, rather than 5, units of output. The additional revenue from the sixth and seventh units is $214 (= $112 + $102). Thus total revenue for 7 units is $924 (= $710 + $214). Total costs for 7 units are $640,

so profits are $284. Questions 5 and 6 at the end of this chapter may be helpful in comparing the price and output decisions of a nondiscriminating and a discriminating monopolist.

Regulated monopoly

Most purely monopolistic industries are natural monopolies and therefore subject to social regulation. In particular, the prices or rates which public utilities—railroads, telephone companies, natural gas and electricity suppliers—can charge are determined by a Federal, state, or local regulatory commission or board.

Figure 26-6 shows the demand and cost conditions of a natural monopoly. Because of heavy fixed costs, demand cuts the average-cost curve at a point where average cost is still falling. It would obviously be inefficient to have a number of firms in such an industry because, by dividing the market, each firm would move further to the left on its average-cost curve so that unit costs would be substantially higher. The relationship between market demand and costs is such that the attainment of low unit costs presumes only one producer.

We know by application of the MR = MC rule that P_m and Q_m are the profit-maximizing price and output which the unregulated monopolist would choose. Because price exceeds average total cost, the monopolist enjoys a substantial economic profit which is likely to contribute to income inequality. Furthermore, price exceeds marginal cost, which indicates an underallocation of resources to this product or service. The question is: Can government regulation bring about better results from society's point of view?

SOCIALLY OPTIMAL PRICE: $P =$ MC

If the objective of our regulatory commission is to achieve allocative efficiency, it should attempt to establish a legal (ceiling) price for the monopolist that is equal to *marginal cost*. Remembering that each point on the market demand curve designates a price-quantity combination, and noting that

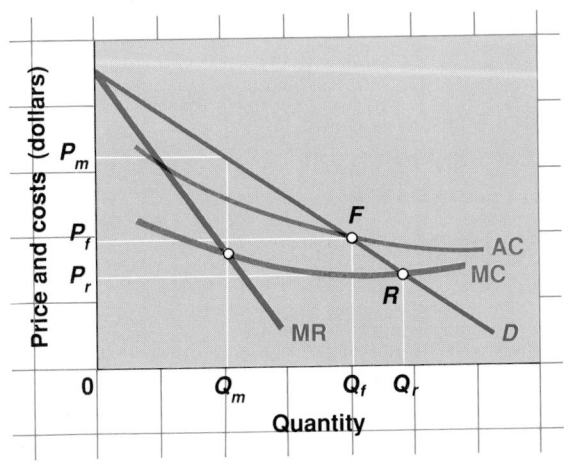

FIGURE 26-6

Regulated monopoly

Price regulation can improve the social consequences of a natural monopoly. The socially optimal price P_r will result in an efficient allocation of resources but is likely to entail losses and therefore call for permanent public subsidies. The "fair-return" price P_f will allow the monopolist to break even, but will not fully correct the underallocation of resources.

marginal cost cuts the demand curve only at point R, it is clear that P_r is the only price which is equal to marginal cost. The imposition of this maximum or ceiling price causes the monopolist's effective demand curve to become $P_r RD$; the demand curve becomes perfectly elastic, and therefore $P_r = $ MR, out to point R, where the regulated price ceases to be effective. The important point is that, given the legal price P_r, the monopolist will maximize profits or minimize losses by producing Q_r units of output, because it is at this output that MR $(P_r) = $ MC. By making it illegal to charge more than P_r per unit, the regulatory agency has eliminated the monopolist's incentive to restrict output in order to benefit from a higher price. In short, by imposing the legal price P_r and letting the monopolist choose its profit-maximizing or loss-minimizing output, the allocative results of pure competition can be simulated. Production takes place where $P_r = $ MC, and this equality indicates an efficient allocation of resources to this product or service.[12] This price which achieves allocative efficiency is called the **socially optimal price.**

"FAIR-RETURN" PRICE: $P = AC$

But the socially optimal price P_r is likely to pose a problem of losses for the regulated firm. The price which equals marginal cost is likely to be so low that average total costs are not covered as is shown in Figure 26-6. The inevitable result is losses. The reason for this lies in the basic character of public utilities. Because they are required to meet "peak" demands (both daily and seasonally) for their product or service, they tend to have substantial excess productive capacity when demand is relatively "normal." This high level of investment in capital facilities means that unit costs of production are likely to decline over a wide range of output. In technical terms, the market demand curve in Figure 26-6 cuts marginal cost at a point to the left of the marginal-cost–average-total-cost intersection, so the socially optimal price is necessarily below AC. Therefore, to enforce a socially optimal price upon the regulated monopolist would mean short-run losses, and in the long run, bankruptcy for the utility.

What to do? One option would be a public subsidy sufficient to cover the loss which marginal-cost pricing would entail. Another possibility is to condone price discrimination in the hope that the additional revenue gained thereby will permit the firm to cover costs. In practice, regulatory commissions have pursued a third option; they have tended to back away somewhat from the objective of allocative efficiency and marginal-cost pricing. Most regulatory agencies in the United States are concerned with establishing a **"fair-return" price.** This is so in no small measure because, as the courts have envisioned it, an unembellished socially optimum price would lead to losses and eventual bankruptcy and thereby deprive the monopoly's owners of their private property without "due process of law." Indeed, the Supreme

---

[12] While "allocative efficiency" is achieved, "productive efficiency" would only be achieved by chance. In Figure 26-6 we note that production takes place at Q_r which is less than the output at which average costs are minimized. Can you redraw Figure 26-6 to show those special conditions whereby both allocative and productive efficiency are realized?

Court has held that the regulatory agencies must permit a "fair return" to owners.

Remembering that total costs include a normal or "fair" profit, we see that the "fair" or "fair-return" price in Figure 26-6 would be P_f, where price equals *average* cost. Because the demand curve cuts average cost only at point F, it is clear that P_f is the only price which permits a fair return. The corresponding output at regulated price P_f will be Q_f.

DILEMMA OF REGULATION

A comparison of the results of the socially optimum price ($P = $ MC) and the fair-return price ($P = $ AC) suggests a policy dilemma, sometimes termed the **dilemma of regulation.** When price is set to achieve the most efficient allocation of resources ($P = $ MC), the regulated utility is likely to suffer losses. Survival of the firm would presumably depend upon permanent public subsidies out of tax revenues. On the other hand, although a fair-return price ($P = $ AC) allows the monopolist to cover costs, it only partially resolves the underallocation of resources which the unregulated monopoly would foster. That is, the fair-return price would only increase output from Q_m to Q_f, whereas the socially optimum output is Q_r. Despite this problem, the basic point is that regulation can improve upon the results of monopoly from the social point of view. Price regulation can simultaneously reduce price, increase output, and reduce the economic profits of monopolies. We will have more to say about the problems of implementing the effective regulation of natural monopolies in Chapter 34.

CHAPTER SUMMARY

1 A pure monopolist is the sole producer of a commodity for which there are no close substitutes.

2 Barriers to entry, in the form of **a** economies of scale, **b** natural monopolies, **c** patent ownership and research, **d** the ownership or control of essential raw materials, and **e** unfair competition help explain the existence of pure monopoly and other imperfectly competitive market structures. Barriers to entry which are very formidable in the short run may prove to be surmountable in the long run.

LAST WORD

Railroad monopoly and Wyoming coal

A study has concluded that the monopoly power of railroads is depressing coal production in Wyoming and costing the state millions of dollars in lost severance taxes.

The market for Wyoming coal has been depressed the past several years. While recession and energy conservation are contributing factors, falling world crude oil prices have been the primary cause. Given the competitive structure of the Wyoming coal industry, one would expect these conditions to reduce the price of coal which in turn would help sustain its competitive position. But in fact, although the prices received by Wyoming mining firms have fallen, steady and dramatic increases in the *delivered* price of Wyoming coal have occurred because of increased rail rates. Average shipping rate increases for the 1980–1983 period have been on the order of 36 percent. The higher delivered prices have caused buyers (largely power producers) to switch to cheaper local coal or alternative fuels.

The study's authors contend that the Burlington Northern and Union Pacific railroads have substantial monopoly power over the Wyoming coal fields they serve. The former is the only coal carrier in the Powder River Basin where most of the state's coal is mined and the Union Pacific is the only shipper in the Hanna Basin of southern Wyoming. The authors employ empirical analysis in attempting to measure the monopoly power of the railroads. More specifically, they calculate the rates of return on the railroads' investments which they find to be above-normal when adjusted for the riskiness of the industry. They also conclude that the railroads are earning an economic profit in shipping Wyoming coal. Furthermore, the transportation of Wyoming coal is found to be subject to economies of scale which is also indicative of the existence of monopoly power. They conclude that "the strong possibility of monopoly power exists for these railroads."

What are the economic implications of the monopoly power of the railroads for Wyoming's economy? The authors estimate that the elimination of this monopoly power would cause rail rates and the delivered price of coal to fall by approximately 8 percent overall. Estimating the price elasticity of demand for Wyoming coal to be 1.85, this price reduction would increase coal sales by about 15 percent. This would entail positive effects upon production and employment both in and beyond the coal industry. The 15 percent increase in sales would also increase the state government's coal severance tax revenue by approximately 15 percent because this tax is levied upon the "mine-mouth" value of coal production (which would not change) rather than the reduced delivered price. The authors observe that the overall effects of the elimination of the railroad monopoly in Wyoming would be "extremely beneficial" for the state.

Source: Extracted from Scott E. Atkinson and Joe Kerkvliet, *Falling World Oil Prices and the Role of Railroads in the Market for Wyoming Coal* (Office of Research and Graduate Studies, University of Wyoming, 1984).

3 The pure monopolist's market situation differs from that of a competitive firm in that the monopolist's demand curve is downsloping, causing the marginal-revenue curve to lie below the demand curve. Like the competitive seller, the pure monopolist will maximize profits by equating marginal revenue and marginal cost. Barriers to entry may permit a monopolist to acquire economic profits even in the long run. It is noteworthy, however, that *a* the monopolist does not charge "the highest price it can get"; *b* the maximum total profit sought by the monopolist rarely coincides with maximum unit profits; *c* high costs and a weak demand may prevent the monopolist from realizing any profit at all; and *d* the monopolist will want to avoid the inelastic range of its demand curve.

4 Given the same costs, the pure monopolist will find it profitable to restrict output and charge a higher price than would a competitive seller. This restriction of output causes resources to be misallocated, as is evidenced by the fact that price exceeds marginal cost in monopolized markets. However, the costs of monopolists and competitive producers may not be the same. On the one hand, economies of scale may make lower unit costs accessible to monopolists but not to competitors. On the other hand, there is evidence that X-inefficiency—the failure to produce with the least-costly combination of inputs—is more common to monopolists than it is to competitive firms and that monopolists may make sizable expenditures to maintain monopoly privileges conferred by government.

5 Economists disagree as to how conducive pure monopoly is to technological advance. Some feel that pure monopoly is more progressive than pure competition because its ability to realize economic profits provides for the financing of technological research. Others, however, argue that the absence of rival firms and the monopolist's desire to exploit fully its existing capital facilities weaken the monopolist's incentive to innovate.

6 Monopoly tends to increase income inequality.

7 A monopolist can increase its profits by practicing price discrimination, provided it can segregate buyers on the basis of different elasticities of demand and the product or service cannot be readily transferred between the segregated markets. Other things being equal, the discriminating monopolist will produce a larger output than will the nondiscriminating monopolist.

8 Price regulation can be invoked to eliminate wholly or partially the tendency of monopolists to underallocate resources and to earn economic profits. The "socially optimum" price is determined where the demand and marginal-cost curves intersect; the "fair-return" price is determined where the demand and average-cost curves intersect.

TERMS AND CONCEPTS

pure monopoly	**socially optimal price**
unfair competition	**fair-return price**
X-inefficiency	**the dilemma of**
dynamic efficiency	**regulation**
price discrimination	

QUESTIONS AND STUDY SUGGESTIONS

1 "No firm is completely sheltered from rivals; all firms compete for the dollars of consumers. Pure monopoly, therefore, does not exist." Do you agree? Explain.

2 Discuss the major barriers to entry. Explain how each barrier can foster monopoly or oligopoly. Which barriers, if any, do you feel give rise to monopoly that is socially justifiable?

3 How does the demand curve faced by a purely monopolistic seller differ from that confronting a purely competitive firm? Why does it differ? Of what significance is the difference? Why is the pure monopolist's demand curve not perfectly inelastic?

4 Use the accompanying demand schedule to calculate total revenue and marginal revenue. Plot the demand, total revenue, and marginal revenue curves and carefully explain the relationships between them. Explain why the marginal revenue of the fourth unit of output is $3.50, even though its price is $5.00. Use Chapter 22's total revenue test for price elasticity to designate the elastic and inelastic segments of your graphed demand curve. What generalization can you make regarding the relationship between marginal revenue and elasticity of demand? Suppose that somehow the marginal cost of successive units of output were zero. What output would the profit-seeking firm produce? Finally, use your analysis to explain why a monopolist would never produce in that range of its demand curve which is inelastic.

Price	Quantity demanded	Price	Quantity demanded
$7.00	0	$4.50	5
6.50	1	4.00	6
6.00	2	3.50	7
5.50	3	3.00	8
5.00	4	2.50	9

5 Suppose a pure monopolist is faced with the demand schedule shown below and the same cost data as the competitive producer discussed in question 4 at the end of Chapter 25. Calculate total and marginal revenue and determine the profit-maximizing price and output for this monopolist. What is the level of profits? Verify your answer graphically and by comparing total revenue and total cost. If this firm could engage in perfect price discrimination, that is, if it could charge each buyer the maximum acceptable price, what would be the level of output? Of profits?

Price	Quantity demanded	Total revenue	Marginal revenue
$115	0	$_____	
100	1	_____	$_____
83	2	_____	_____
71	3	_____	_____
63	4	_____	_____
55	5	_____	_____
48	6	_____	_____
42	7	_____	_____
37	8	_____	_____
33	9	_____	_____
29	10	_____	

6 Draw a diagram showing the relevant demand, marginal-revenue, average-cost, and marginal-cost curves and the equilibrium price and output for a nondiscriminating monopolist. Use the same diagram to show the equilibrium position of a monopolist which is able to practice perfect price discrimination. Compare equilibrium outputs, total revenues, and economic profits in the two cases. Comment upon the economic desirability of price discrimination.

7 Assume a pure monopolist and a purely competitive firm have the same unit costs. Contrast the two with respect to *a* price, *b* output, *c* profits, *d* allocation of resources, and *e* impact upon the distribution of income. Since both monopolists and competitive firms follow the MC = MR rule in maximizing profits, how do you account for the different results? Why might the costs of a purely competitive firm and a monopolist *not* be the same? What are the implications of such cost differences?

8 Carefully evaluate the following widely held viewpoint. Can you offer any arguments to the contrary?

A monopoly is usually not under pressure to *invent* new products or methods. Nor does it have strong incentives to *innovate:* to apply those new inventions in practice and bring new products to the market. *The monopoly may choose to invent and innovate, but it will do so only at its own pace.* No competitor forces its hand. Even if its capital is outdated or its products mediocre, a monopolist may prefer to protect and continue them rather than to replace them with better ones.[13]

9 Critically evaluate and explain:

a "Because they can control product price, monopolists are always assured of profitable production by simply charging the highest price consumers will pay."

b "The pure monopolist seeks that output which will yield the greatest per unit profit."

c "An excess of price over marginal cost is the market's way of signaling the need for more production of a product."

d "The more profitable a firm, the greater its monopoly power."

e "The monopolist has a price policy; the competitive producer does not."

f "With respect to resource allocation, the interests of the seller and of society coincide in a purely competitive market but conflict in a monopolized market."

---

[13] William G. Shepherd, *Public Policies Toward Business,* 7th ed., (Homewood, Ill.: Richard D. Irwin, Inc., 1985), p. 42.

g "In a sense the monopolist makes a profit for not producing; the monopolist produces profits more than it does goods."

10 Assume a monopolistic publisher has agreed to pay an author 15 percent of the total revenue from the sales of a text. Will the author and the publisher want to charge the same price for the text? Explain.

11 Suppose a firm's demand curve lies below its average-total-cost curve at all levels of output. Can you conceive of any circumstance by which production might be profitable?

12 Are colleges and universities engaging in price discrimination when they charge full tuition to some students and provide financial aid to others? What are the advantages and disadvantages of this practice?

13 Explain verbally and graphically how price (rate) regulation may improve the performance of monopolies. In your answer distinguish between **a** socially optimal (marginal-cost) pricing and **b** fair-return (average-cost) pricing. What is the "dilemma of regulation"?

14 It has been proposed that natural monopolists should be allowed to determine their profit-maximizing outputs and prices and then government should tax their profits away and distribute them to consumers in proportion to their purchases from the monopoly. Is this proposal as socially desirable as requiring monopolists to equate price with marginal cost or average cost?

CHAPTER 27

Price and output determination: monopolistic competition

Pure competition and pure monopoly are the exception, not the rule, in American capitalism. Most market structures fall somewhere between these two extremes. In Chapter 28 we shall discuss oligopoly, a market structure which stands close to pure monopoly. In the present chapter we are concerned with monopolistic competition. Monopolistic competition correctly suggests a blending of monopoly and competition; more specifically, monopolistic competition involves a very considerable amount of competition with a small dose of monopoly power intermixed.

Our basic objectives in this chapter are (1) to define and discuss the nature and prevalence of monopolistic competition, (2) to analyze and evaluate the price-output behavior of monopolistically competitive firms, and (3) to explain and assess the role of nonprice competition, that is, competition based upon product quality and advertising, in monopolistically competitive industries.

Monopolistic competition: concept and occurrence

First of all, let us recall, and also expand upon, the definition of monopolistic competition.

RELATIVELY LARGE NUMBERS

Monopolistic competition refers to that market situation in which a relatively large number of small producers are offering similar but not identical products. The contrasts between this and pure competition are important. Monopolistic competition does not require the presence of hundreds or thousands of firms but only a fairly large number— say 25, 35, 60, ot 70.

Several important characteristics of monopolistic competition follow from the presence of relatively large numbers. In the first place, each firm has a comparatively small percentage of the total market, so each has a very limited amount of control over market price. Then too, the presence of a relatively large number of firms also ensures that collusion—concerted action by the firms to restrict output and rig price—is all but impossible. Finally, with numerous firms in the industry, there is no feeling of mutual interdependence among them; each firm determines its policies without considering the possible reactions of rival firms. And this is a very reasonable way to act in a market in which one's rivals are very numerous. After all, the 10 or 15 percent increase in sales which firm X may realize by cutting price will be spread so thinly over its 20, 40, or 60 rivals that, for all practical purposes, the impact upon their sales will be imperceptible. Rivals' reactions can be ignored because the impact of one firm's actions upon each of its many rivals is so small that these rivals will have no reason to react.

PRODUCT DIFFERENTIATION

Also in contrast to pure competition, monopolistic competition has the fundamental feature of **product differentiation.** Purely competitive firms produce a standardized or homogeneous product; monopolistically competitive producers turn out variations of a given product. In fact, product differentiation may take a number of different forms.

1 Product quality Most obviously, product differentiation may take the form of physical or qualitative differences in the products themselves. "Real" differences involving functional features, materials, design, and workmanship are vitally important aspects of product differentiation. Personal computers, for example, may differ in terms of hardware capacity, software, graphics, and the degree to which they are "user-friendly." There are literally scores of competing principles of economics texts which differ in terms of content, organization, presentation and readability, pedagogical aids, graphics and design, and so forth. Any city of reasonable size will have a variety of retail stores selling men's and women's clothing which vary greatly in terms of styling, materials, and quality of workmanship. Similarly, one fast-food hamburger chain may feature sesame seed buns, while a competitor stresses the juiciness of its hamburgers.

2 Services Services and the conditions surrounding the sale of a product are important aspects of product differentiation. One grocery store may stress the helpfulness of its clerks who bag your groceries and carry them to your car. A "warehouse" competitor may leave the bagging and carrying to its customers, but feature lower prices. "One-day" clothes cleaning is frequently preferred to cleaning of roughly equal quality which takes three days. The "snob appeal" of a store, the courteousness and helpfulness of clerks, the firm's reputation for servicing or exchanging its products, and the availability of credit are all service aspects of product differentiation.

3 Location Products may also be differentiated on the basis of location and accessibility. Small minigroceries or convenience stores successfully compete with large supermarkets, even though the former have a much more limited range of products and charge significantly higher prices. They compete on the basis of location—being close to customers and being situated on much-traveled streets—and by staying open 24 hours a day. Similarly, a gas station's close proximity to the interstate highway gives it a locational advantage which allows it to sell gasoline at a higher price than could a gas station in a town 2 or 3 miles from the interstate.

4 Promotion and packaging Product differentiation may also arise from largely imaginary differences created through advertising, packaging, and the use of brand names and trademarks. The association of a celebrity's name with such products as jeans or perfume may enhance those products in the eyes of buyers. Many consumers regard a given toothpaste packaged in a "pump" container to be preferable to the same toothpaste in a conventional tube. While there are a variety of aspirin-type products, product promotion and advertising may convince many consumers that Bayer or Anacin is superior and worth a substantially higher price than a generic substitute.

One important implication of product differentiation is that, despite the presence of a relatively large number of firms, monopolistically competitive producers do have limited amounts of control over the prices of their products. Consumers have preferences for the products of specific sellers and *within limits* will pay a higher price to satisfy those preferences. Sellers and buyers are no longer linked at random, as in a purely competitive market.

NONPRICE COMPETITION

As the above discussion makes clear, under monopolistic competition economic rivalry centers not only on price, but also upon such nonprice factors as product quality, advertising, and conditions associated with the sale of a product. Because products are differentiated, it can be supposed that they can be varied over time and that the differentiating features of each firm's product will be susceptible to advertising and other forms of sales promotion. Great emphasis is placed upon trademarks and brand names as means of convincing consumers that a firm's product is better than rivals' products.

EASY ENTRY

Entry into monopolistically competitive industries tends to be relatively easy. The fact that monopolistically competitive producers are typically small-sized firms, both absolutely and relatively, suggests that economies of scale and capital requirements are few. On the other hand, as compared with pure competition, there may be some added financial barriers posed by the need for deriving a product different from one's rivals and the obligation to advertise that product. Existing firms may hold patents on their products and copyrights on their brand names and trademarks, enhancing the difficulty and cost of successfully imitating them.

In short, monopolistic competition refers to industries that comprise a relatively large number of firms, operating noncollusively, in the production of differentiated products. Nonprice competition accompanies price competition. Ease of entry makes for competition by new firms in the long run.

ILLUSTRATIONS

Table 27-1 lists a group of manufacturing industries which approximate monopolistic competition. In addition, retail stores in metropolitan areas are generally monopolistically competitive; grocery stores, gasoline stations, barber shops, dry cleaners, clothing stores, and so forth, operate under conditions similar to those we have described.

Price and output determination

Let us now analyze the price-output behavior of a monopolistically competitive firm. To facilitate this task we assume initially that the firms in the indus-

TABLE 27-1 Percentage of output* produced by firms in selected low-concentration manufacturing industries

Industry	Four largest firms	Eight largest firms	Twenty largest firms
Men's and boys' suits and coats	25%	37%	57%
Mattresses and bedsprings	23	31	43
Prefab metal buildings	21	31	50
Women's and misses' suits and coats	19	28	40
Book publishing	17	30	56
Upholstered furniture	17	25	39
Wood furniture	16	23	37
Metal house furniture	16	26	44
Paperboard boxes	15	26	43
Bolts, nuts, and rivets	13	23	38
Fur goods	12	19	33
Metal doors	11	17	30
Women's and misses' dresses	6	10	17

* As measured by value of industry shipments. Data are for 1982.

Source: Bureau of the Census, *1982 Census of Manufacturers.*

try are producing *given* products and are engaging in a *given* amount of promotional activity. Later we shall note how product variation and advertising modify our discussion.

THE FIRM'S DEMAND CURVE

Our explanation is couched in terms of Figure 27-1a. The basic feature of this diagram, which sets it off from our analyses of pure competition and pure monopoly, is the elasticity of the firm's individual demand, or sales, curve. *The demand curve faced by a monopolistically competitive seller is highly, but not perfectly, elastic.* It is much more elastic than the demand curve of the pure monopolist, because the

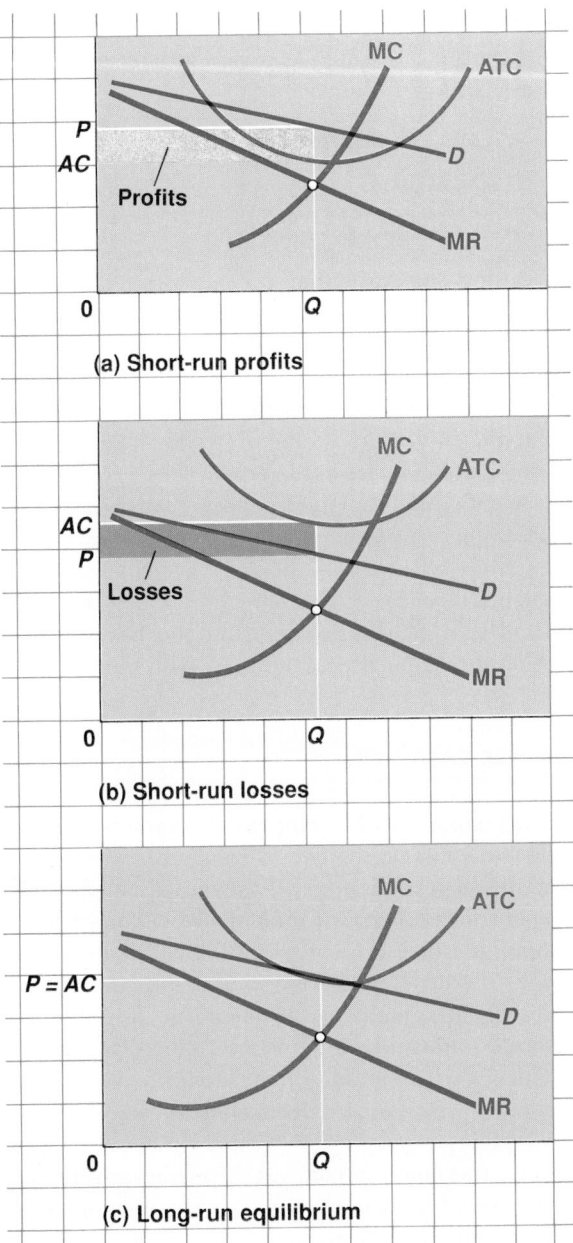

FIGURE 27-1

Monopolistically competitive firms tend to realize a normal profit in the long run

The economic profits shown in (a) will induce new firms to enter, causing the profits to be competed away. The losses indicated in (b) will cause an exodus of firms until normal profits are restored. Thus in (c), where price just covers unit costs at the MR = MC output, the firm's long-run equilibrium position is portrayed.

monopolistically competitive seller is faced with a relatively large number of rivals producing close-substitute goods. The pure monopolist, of course, has no rivals at all. Yet, for two reasons, the monopolistically competitive seller's sales curve is not perfectly elastic as is the purely competitive producer's: First, the monopolistically competitive firm has fewer rivals, and, second, the products of these rivals are close but not perfect substitutes.

Generally speaking, the precise degree of elasticity embodied in the monopolistically competitive firm's demand curve will depend upon the exact number of rivals and the degree of product differentiation. The larger the number of rivals and the weaker the product differentiation, the greater will be the elasticity of each seller's demand curve, that is, the closer the situation will be to pure competition.

THE SHORT RUN: PROFITS OR LOSSES

The firm will maximize its profits or minimize its losses in the short run by producing that output designated by the intersection of marginal cost and marginal revenue, for reasons with which we are now familiar. The representative firm of Figure 27-1a produces an output Q, charges a price P, and is fortunate enough to realize a total profit of the size indicated in gray. But a less favorable cost and demand situation may exist, putting the monopolistically competitive firm in the position of realizing losses in the short run. This is illustrated by the light red area in Figure 27-1b. In the short run the monopolistically competitive firm may either realize an economic profit or be faced with losses.

THE LONG RUN: BREAK EVEN

In the long run, however, the *tendency* is for monopolistically competitive firms to earn a normal profit or, in other words, to break even. In the short-run profits case, Figure 27-1a, we can expect the economic profits to attract new rivals, because entry is relatively easy. As new firms enter, the demand curve faced by the typical firm will fall (shift to the left) and become more elastic. Why? Because each firm has a smaller share of the total demand and now faces a larger number of close-substitute products. This in turn tends to cause the disappearance of economic profits, When the demand curve is tangent to the average-cost curve at the profit-maximizing output, as shown in Figure 27-1c, the firm is just breaking even. Output Q is the equilibrium output for the firm; as Figure 27-1c clearly indicates, any deviation from that output will entail average costs which exceed product price and, therefore, losses for the firm. Furthermore, economic profits have been competed away, and there is no incentive for more firms to enter. In the short-run losses case, Figure 27-1b, we can expect an exodus of firms to occur in the long run. Faced with fewer substitute products and blessed with an expanded share of total demand, surviving firms will find that their losses disappear and gradually give way to approximately normal profits.[1]

Note that we have been very careful to say that the representative firm in a monopolistically competitive market *tends* to break even, that is, earn a normal profit, in the long run. There are certain complicating factors which prevent us from being more dogmatic. First, some firms may achieve a measure of product differentiation which cannot be duplicated by rivals even over a long span of time. A given gasoline station may have the only available location at the busiest intersection in town. Or a firm may hold a patent which gives it a slight and more-or-less permanent advantage over imitators. Such firms may realize a sliver of economic profits even in the long run. Second, remember that entry is not completely unrestricted. Because of product differentiation, there are likely to be greater financial barriers to entry than otherwise would be the case. This again suggests that some economic profits may persist even in the long run. A third consideration may work in the opposite direction, causing losses—below-normal profits—to persist in the long run. The proprietors of a corner delicatessen persistently accept a return less than they could earn elsewhere, because their business is a way of life to them. The suburban barber ekes out a meager existence, because cutting hair is "all he wants to do." With all things considered, however, the

long-run normal profit equilibrium of Figure 27-1c is probably a reasonable portrayal of reality.

Wastes of monopolistic competition

Recalling our evaluation of competitive pricing in Chapter 25, we know that economic efficiency requires the triple equality of price, marginal cost, and average cost. The equality of price and marginal cost is necessary for the realization of **allocative efficiency**, that is, the allocation of the right amount of resources to the product. The equality of price with minimum average total cost suggests the achievement of **productive efficiency** or the use of the most efficient (least-cost) technology; this equality means that consumers will enjoy the largest volume of the product and the lowest price which prevailing cost conditions will allow.

EXCESS CAPACITY

In monopolistically competitive markets neither allocative nor productive efficiency is realized. An examination of Figure 27-1c suggests that the monopolistic element in monopolistic competition causes a modest underallocation of resources to goods produced under this market structure. Price exceeds marginal cost in long-run equilibrium, thereby indicating that society values additional units of this commodity more than the alternative products which the needed resources can otherwise produce.

Furthermore, in contrast to purely competitive firms, we observe in Figure 27-1c that monopolistically competitive firms produce somewhat short of the most efficient (least unit cost) output. Production entails higher unit costs than the minimum attainable. This in turn means a somewhat higher price than would result under competition. Consumers do **not** benefit from the largest output and lowest price which cost conditions permit. Indeed, monopolistically competitive firms must charge a higher than competitive price in the long run in order to achieve a normal profit. Looked at differently, if each firm were able to produce at the most efficient output, a smaller number of firms could

---

[1] For simplicity's sake we assume constant costs; shifts in the cost curves as firms enter or leave would complicate our discussion slightly, but would not alter the conclusions.

produce the same total output, and the product could be sold to consumers at a lower price. Monopolistically competitive industries tend to be overcrowded with firms, each of which is underutilized, that is, operating short of optimal capacity. This is typified by many kinds of retail establishments, for example, the thirty or forty gasoline stations, all operating with excess capacity, that populate a medium-sized city. Underutilized plants and consumers penalized through higher than competitive prices for this underutilization—these are the so-called **wastes of monopolistic competition.**

REDEEMING FEATURES?

But we must not be hypercritical of monopolistic competition. In many monopolistically competitive industries the price and output results are not drastically different from those of pure competition. The highly elastic nature of each firm's demand curve guarantees that the results are nearly competitive. Furthermore, the product differentiation which characterizes monopolistic competition means that buyers can select from a number of variations of the same general product. This is conducive to the better fulfillment of the diverse tastes of consumers. In fact, there is a tradeoff between product differentiation and the production of a given product at the minimum average cost. The stronger the product differentiation (the less elastic the demand curve), the further to the left of the minimum average costs will production take place. But the greater the product differentiation, the more the likelihood that diverse tastes will be fully satisfied. In other words, the greater the excess capacity problem, the wider the range of consumer choice.

Nonprice competition

For reasons cited above, we can conclude that the situation portrayed in Figure 27-1c may not be the most beneficial to society. It can also be surmised that it is not very satisfying to the monopolistically competitive producer which barely captures a normal profit for its efforts. We can therefore expect monopolistically competitive producers to take steps to improve upon the long-run equilibrium position. But how can this be accomplished? The answer lies in product differentiation. Each firm has a product which is currently distinguishable in some more-or-less tangible way from those of its rivals. The product is presumably subject to further variation, that is, to product development. Then, too, the emphasis upon real product differences and the creation of imaginary differences may be achieved through advertising and related sales promotion. In short, the profit-realizing firm of Figure 27-1a is loath to stand by and watch new competitors encroach upon its profits by duplicating or imitating its product, copying its advertising, and matching its services to consumers. Rather, the firm will attempt to sustain these profits and stay ahead of competitors through further product development and by enhancing the quantity and quality of advertising. In this way it might prevent the long-run tendency of Figure 27-1c from becoming a reality. True, product development and advertising will add to the firm's costs. But they can also be expected to increase the demand for its product. If demand increases by more than enough to compensate for development and promotional costs, the firm will have improved its profit position. As Figure 27-1c suggests, the firm may have little or no prospect of increasing profits by price cutting. So why not practice **nonprice competition?**

PRODUCT DIFFERENTIATION AND PRODUCT DEVELOPMENT

The likelihood that easy entry will promote product variety and product improvement is possibly a redeeming feature of monopolistic competition which may offset, wholly or in part, the "wastes" associated with this market structure. There are really two somewhat distinct considerations here: (1) product differentiation at a point in time, and (2) product improvement over a period of time.

┃ Differentiation Product differentiation means that at any point in time the consumer will be offered a wide range of types, styles, brands, and quality gradations of any given product. Compared with the situation under pure competition, this correctly suggests possible advantages to the consumer. The range of choice is widened, and variations and shadings of consumer tastes are more fully met by producers. But skeptics warn that product differentiation is not an unmixed blessing. Product proliferation may reach the point where the consumer becomes confused and rational choice is then rendered time-consuming and difficult. Variety may add spice to the consumer's life, but only up to a point. A woman shopping for lipstick may be bewildered by the vast array of products from which she might choose. Revlon alone offers 157 shades of lipstick, of which 41 are "pink"! Worse yet, some observers fear that the consumer, faced with a myriad of similar products, may rely upon such a dubious expedient as judging product quality by price; that is, the consumer may irrationally assume that price is necessarily an index of product quality.

2 Development Product competition is an important avenue of technological innovation and product betterment over a period of time. Such product development may be cumulative on two different senses. First, a successful product improvement by one firm obligates rivals to imitate or, if they can, improve upon this firm's temporary market advantage or suffer the penalty of losses. Second, profits realized from a successful product improvement can be used to finance further improvements. Again, however, there are notable criticisms of the product development which may occur under monopolistic competition. Critics point out that many product alterations are more apparent than real, consisting of frivolous and superficial changes in the product which do *not* improve its durability, efficiency, or usefulness. A more exotic container, bright packaging, or "shuffling the chrome" is frequently the focal point for product development. It is argued, too, that particularly in the cases of durable and semidurable consumer goods, development may follow a pattern of "planned obsolescence," wherein firms improve their product only by that amount necessary to make the average consumer dissatisfied with last year's model.

Do the advantages of product differentiation, properly discounted, outweigh the "wastes" of monopolistic competition? It is difficult to say, short of examining specific cases; and even then, concrete conclusions are difficult to come by.

ADVERTISING

A monopolistically competitive producer may gain at least a temporary edge on rivals by manipulating the product. The same result may be achieved by manipulating the consumer through advertising and sales promotion. While product differentiation adapts the product to consumer demand, advertising adapts consumer demand to the product.

The purpose of advertising to a monopolistically competitive firm is simple. The firm hopes to increase its share of the market and to increase consumer loyalty to its particular differentiated product. In technical terms, it is hoped that advertising will shift the firm's demand curve rightward and simultaneously reduce its price elasticity.

There is considerable controversy as to the economic and social desirability of advertising. This controversy is not an unimportant one. Advertising and promotional expenditures in the United States were estimated to be almost $110 billion in 1987.[2] This exceeded by a wide margin the amount all state and local governments spent on public welfare. Hence, if advertising is generally wasteful, any potential virtues of monopolistically competitive markets are thereby dimmed, and the need for corrective public policies is indicated.

Let us survey the basic claims for and the charges against advertising. As we proceed through our discussion, bear in mind that advertising is not confined to monopolistic competition. Product differentiation and heavy advertising are also characteristic of many oligopolistic industries (Chapter 28). Hence, our comments are equally germane to these industries.

The case for advertising Some of the arguments in favor of advertising follow:
I Advertising allegedly provides the information which assists consumers in making rational choices. In a dynamic, complex economy there is an acute need for the consumer to be closely acquainted with new firms, new products, and improvements in existing products. Advertising is the medium which disperses such information.

---

[2] However, advertising expenditures have been relatively constant as a percentage of the GNP. For example, advertising outlays were about 2.3 percent of GNP in both 1937 and 1987.

2 Advertising supports national communications. Radio, television, magazines, and newspapers are financed in part through advertising.

3 Advertising is said to be a stimulant to product development. Successful advertising is frequently based upon unique and advantageous features of a firm's product. Hence, a firm is obligated to improve its product to provide "sales points" for competing successfully in the advertising sphere.

4 Through successful advertising a firm can expand its production and thereby realize greater economies of scale. As shown in Figure 27-2, by shifting the firm's demand curve to the right through advertising, production will expand from, say, Q_1 to Q_2. Despite the fact that advertising outlays will shift the firm's average-cost curve upward, unit costs will nevertheless decline from, say, AC_1 to AC_2. Greater productive efficiency resulting from economies of scale more than offsets the increase in unit costs due to advertising. Consumers will therefore get the product at a lower price with advertising than they would in its absence.

5 It is held that advertising is a force which promotes competition. By providing information about a wide variety of substitute products, advertising tends to diminish monopoly power. In fact, intensive advertising is frequently associated with the introduction of new products designed to compete with existing brands. Could the Hyundai and Isuzu automobiles have gained a foothold in the American market without advertising?

6 Advertising allegedly promotes full employment by inducing high levels of consumer spending. This is particularly crucial, it is argued, in a wealthy society such as ours, where much of total production takes the form of luxury or semiluxury goods which fulfill no basic wants. One need not advertise to sell food to a hungry man, but advertising and sales promotion are essential in persuading families that they need a second car, a video recorder, or a home computer. Stability in an opulent society calls for want-creating activities—in particular, advertising—or high levels of production and employment will not be sustainable.

The case against advertising Some of the arguments on the other side of the picture allegedly "debunk" the claims for advertising; others raise new points.

1 Critics of advertising point out that the basic objective of advertising is to persuade, not to inform.

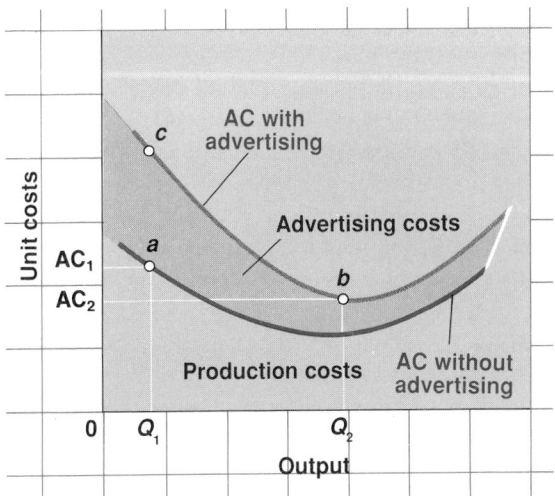

FIGURE 27-2

The possible effects of advertising upon a firm's output and average costs

Proponents of advertising contend that advertising will expand the firm's production from, say, *a* to *b* and lower unit costs as economies of scale are realized. Some critics argue that advertising is more likely to increase costs and leave output largely unchanged, as is suggested by the movement from *a* to *c*.

Few would claim that a television beer commercial which focuses upon the "less filling–tastes great" controversy conveys much useful information to consumers. Competitive advertising is often based upon misleading and extravagant claims which confuse and frequently insult the intelligence of consumers, not enlighten them. Indeed, advertising may well persuade consumers in some cases to pay high prices for much-acclaimed but inferior products, forgoing better but unadvertised products selling at lower prices.

2 Advertising expenditures as such are relatively unproductive; they add little or nothing to the well-being of society. Advertising diverts human and property resources from other more pressing areas. For example, timber, which is sorely needed in the production of housing, is squandered on unsightly billboards and on producing the paper used for the ubiquitous advertising supplements in local newspapers. Advertising allegedly constitutes an inefficient use of scarce resources.

3 Significant external costs come with advertising. Billboards blot out roadside scenery and generally debase the countryside. The consumption of unhealthy products such as tobacco and alcohol rises. Advertising's support of national communications may have unfavorable effects upon the accuracy and quality of those communications. Will a newspaper present an unprejudiced report of the labor dispute in which its major advertiser is involved? Will a television newscast conveniently ignore the fact that antitrust action has been initiated against its sponsor?

4 Much advertising tends to be self-canceling. The million-dollar advertising campaign of one detergent manufacturer is largely offset by equally expensive campaigns waged by its rivals. Little additional detergent is actually used. Each firm has about the same portion of the market as it had originally. And the cost, and therefore the price, of detergent is higher. In Figure 27-2 self-canceling advertising may move the firm from point *a* to point *c*, not from *a* to *b*. This chapter's Last Word concerns the possibility that advertising may be excessive from the viewpoint of individual firms.

5 It is claimed that advertising promotes the growth of monopoly. On the one hand, extensive advertising creates financial barriers to entry and thereby intensifies the market power which firms already possess. This is held to be the case in the tobacco industry, where producers as a group may spend in excess of $600 million per year on advertising and related promotional activities. The three major domestic auto manufacturers—GM, Ford, and Chrysler—currently spend over $2 billion for advertising per year. Furthermore, by creating brand loyalties, consumers become less responsive to price cutting by competitors, thereby enhancing the monopoly power possessed by the firm which is advertising its product.

6 Most economists are reluctant to accept advertising as an important determinant of the levels of output and employment. There has been little evidence of economic stagnation in the post-World War II years that would seem remediable by advertising and promotional outlays. Furthermore, the most volatile aspect of aggregate demand is not so much highly advertised consumer goods as it is little-advertised investment goods. It is also argued that advertising expenditures are procyclical; they fluctuate *with* total spending, intensifying unemployment during bad times and adding to inflationary pressures during prosperous times.

EMPIRICAL EVIDENCE

The main research interest of economists has centered upon the impact of advertising on the degree of competition in various industries. Two quite distinct schools of thought have evolved. The **anticompetitive view** argues that advertising is essentially a form of *persuasion* which enhances product differentiation in the minds of consumers and thereby allows each firm to exercise a greater degree of monopoly or market power at the expense of consumers. Advertising persuades consumers that there are fewer good substitute products available. More technically stated, advertising makes the firm's demand curve less elastic, allowing it to charge higher prices and realize enhanced profits. Advertising reduces active competition among existing firms in the industry and, serving as a barrier to entry, protects established firms from new potential rivals. In contrast, the **procompetitive view** envisions advertising as *information,* that is, as a relatively inexpensive means of increasing the number of substitute products **known** to buyers. Hence, advertising makes the demand curve of any particularly monopolistically competitive or oligopolistic seller more elastic, and both prices and profits tend to be reduced. Greater knowledge of product availability through advertising effectively increases the number of substitutes and makes the industry more competitive.

There are important empirical studies which lend credence to both of these views. For example, Comanor and Wilson have examined the role of advertising in forty-one industries manufacturing consumer goods and reached the general conclusion that advertising is anticompetitive. Specifically, they report that "the heavy volume of advertising expenditures in some industries serves as an important barrier to new competition in the markets served by these industries."[3] The prices of the heavily advertised goods exceed their marginal costs, reflecting a misallocation of resources. Furthermore, for many of the studied industries expenditures for advertising were found to be "excessive" and wasteful of scarce resources.

[3] William S. Comanor and Thomas A. Wilson *Advertising and Market Power* (Cambridge, Mass.: Harvard University Press, 1974), p. 239.

In contrast, Eckard has concluded that advertising is a procompetitive force. He reasons that, if advertising promotes monopoly power, then industries which advertise most heavily should be the ones which increase their prices the most and their outputs the least over time (recall Figure 26-3). Examining price and output changes of some 150 major industries over the 1963–1977 period, Eckard found that generally those industries with higher-than-average levels of advertising had *lower*-than-average rates of price increases and had *higher*-than-average rates of output increase. Conclusion: Rather than contributing to monopoly power, advertising generally enhances competition.[4]

There are also a number of other industry studies which suggest that advertising enhances competition and has economically desirable results. For example, a study of the eyeglasses industry compared prices in states where professional codes of ethics permitted optometrists to advertise with those where codes prohibited or restricted advertising. The conclusion was that prices of eyeglasses were from 25 to 40 percent higher in states where advertising was restricted.[5] A similar study of retail drug prices, comparing states where advertising was permitted with those in which it was not, found that prescription drug prices were about 5 percent lower in states which permitted advertising.[6] Finally, a study of the toy industry yielded the conclusion that television advertising had the effect of bringing about substantial price reductions.

Advertising cuts distribution margins on advertised brands for two reasons: *first,* advertising causes goods to turn over rapidly so they can be sold profitably with smaller markups; and *second,* advertising creates product identity—which, in differentiated products, permits the public to compare prices between stores, thus setting a limit on the retailer's freedom to mark up. Products which are both heavily advertised and are fast sellers will be pulled through the distribution channels with the lowest markups of all.[7]

Evidence on the economic effects of advertising is mixed because studies are usually plagued by data problems and difficulties in determining cause and effect. Suppose it is found that firms which do a great deal of advertising seem to have considerable monopoly power and large profits. Does this mean that advertising creates barriers to entry which in turn generate monopoly power and profits? Or do entry barriers associated with factors quite remote from advertising cause monopoly profits which in turn allow firms to spend lavishly in advertising their products? In any event, at this time there is simply no consensus as to the economic implications of advertising.[8]

MONOPOLISTIC COMPETITION AND ECONOMIC ANALYSIS

Our discussion of nonprice competition correctly implies that the equilibrium situation of a monopolistically competitive firm is actually much more complex than the previous graphic analysis indicates. Figure 27-1a, b, and c *assumes* a given product and a given level of advertising expenditures. But we now know these are not given in practice. The monopolistically competitive firm must actually juggle three variable factors—price, product, and promotion—in seeking maximum profits. What specific variety of product, selling at what price, and supplemented by what level of promotional activity, will result in the greatest level of profits attainable? This complex situation is not

[4] E. Woodrow Eckard, Jr., "Advertising, Concentration, and Consumer Welfare," *Review of Economics and Statistics,* May 1988, pp. 340–343.

[5] Lee and Alexandra Benham, "Regulating the Professions: A Perspective on Information Control," *Journal of Law and Economics,* October 1975, pp. 421–447. Also see John E. Kwoka, Jr., "Advertising and the Price and Quality of Optometric Services," *American Economic Review,* March 1984, pp. 211–216.

[6] John F. Cady, *Restricted Advertising and Competition: The Case of Retail Drugs* (Washington, D.C.: American Enterprise Institute, 1976).

[7] Robert L. Steiner, "Does Advertising Lower Consumer Prices?" *Journal of Marketing,* October 1973, p. 21.

[8] The reader who wishes to pursue this topic should consult Mark S. Albion and Paul W. Farris, *The Advertising Controversy: Evidence on the Economic Effects of Advertising* (Boston, Mass.: Auburn House Publishing Company, 1981).

readily expressed in a simple, meaningful economic model. At best we can note that each possible combination of price, product, and promotion poses a different demand and cost (production plus promotion) situation for the firm, some one of which will allow it maximum profits. In practice, this optimum combination cannot be readily forecast but must be sought by the process of trial and error. And even here, certain limitations may be imposed by the actions of rivals. A firm may not risk the elimination of advertising expenditures for fear its share of the market will decline sharply, to the benefit of its rivals who do advertise. Similarly, patents held by rivals will rule out certain desirable product variations.

CHAPTER SUMMARY

I The distinguishing features of monopolistic competition are: **a** There is a large enough number of firms so that each has little control over price, mutual interdependence is absent, and collusion is virtually impossible; **b** products are characterized by real and imaginary differences and by varying conditions surrounding their sale; **c** economic rivalry entails both price and nonprice competition; and **d** entry to the industry is relatively easy. Many aspects of retailing, and some industries wherein economies of scale are few, approximate monopolistic competition.

2 Monopolistically competitive firms may earn economic profits or incur losses in the short run. The easy entry and exodus of firms give rise to a tendency for them to earn a normal profit in the long run.

3 The long-run equilibrium position of the monopolistically competitive producer is less socially desirable than that of a purely competitive firm. Under monopolistic competition, price exceeds marginal cost, suggesting an underallocation of resources to the product, and price exceeds minimum average total cost, indicating that consumers do not get the product at the lowest price which cost conditions would allow. However, because the firm's demand curve is highly elastic, these "wastes" of monopolistic competition should not be overemphasized.

4 Product differentiation provides a means by which monopolistically competitive firms can offset the long-run tendency for economic profits to approximate zero. Through product development and advertising outlays, a firm may strive to increase the demand for its product more than nonprice competition increases its costs.

LAST WORD

Do firms advertise too much?

It is debatable whether advertising is excessive from the consumer's point of view. But simple analysis suggests that advertising may often be excessive from the vantage point of individual firms.

Imperfectly competitive firms face a dilemma when it comes to advertising and other forms of nonprice competition. Let us consider this dilemma in terms of the Acme and Ajax corporations which are rivals in the manufacture and sale of blue jeans.

The four cells in the accompanying figure show what daily profits would be with either "large" or "small" advertising budgets; specifically, the number above the diagonal indicates Ajax's profits and the number below the diagonal shows Acme's profits. For example, if Acme chooses a large advertising budget and Ajax a small one (cell B), Acme will gain market share at Ajax's expense and, hence, Acme's profits will be $1200 and Ajax's only $600. Cell C portrays the opposite set of circumstances. Because their advertising efforts are about equal in cells A and D, both firms realize one-half of the market and thereby receive equal profits. But profits are greater in cell D because advertising expenditures are smaller than in cell A. That is, the lower expenditures on advertising in cell A more than compensate for any lost revenue which the firms may experience because of reduced sales.

A dilemma arises because the dynamics of the situation leads to an outcome at cell A where advertising expenditures are large. To illustrate, assume both firms initially have small advertising bud-

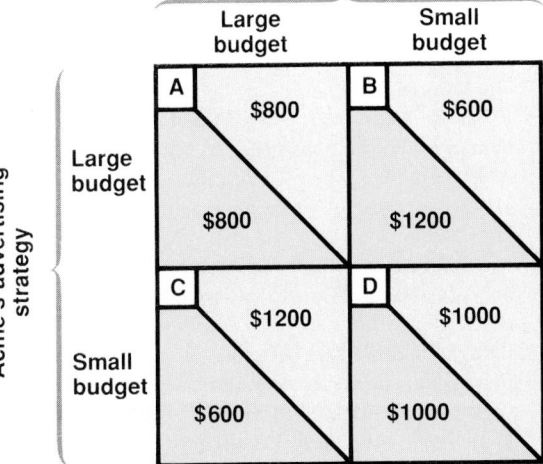

Ajax's advertising strategy

Acme's advertising strategy

	Large budget	Small budget
Large budget	A $800 / $800	B $600 / $1200
Small budget	C $1200 / $600	D $1000 / $1000

gets and are each realizing $1000 profits. But Acme now recognizes that if it increases its advertising expenditures *and Ajax does not,* then Acme's profits will increase to $1200 (cell D to B). However, this move by Acme will cause Ajax's profits to fall to $600. Ajax can increase its profits by also shifting to a large advertising budget (cell B to A). Ajax's profits are now $800, rather than $600. Ajax's large advertising budget strategy has taken some sales from Acme and lowered its profits from $1200 to $800. An identical scenario evolves if we begin again with cell D and assume Ajax (rather than Acme) takes the initiative to increase its advertising budget.

In short, cells B and C are not a stable or equilibrium outcome and, assuming there is no collusion among the two firms, the dynamics of the situation moves the outcome to cell A where advertising budgets are large and profits are less than with smaller advertising budgets (cell D). Because much advertising is done in response to the advertising of one's rivals and is self-cancelling, firms may end up with larger advertising budgets and smaller profits than otherwise attainable. Bluntly put, there is too much advertising from the seller's perspective.

5 Although subject to certain dangers and problems, product differentiation affords the consumer a greater variety of products at any point in time and improved products over time. Whether these features fully compensate for the "wastes" of monopolistic competition is a complex and unresolved question.

6 There is sharp disagreement as to the economic benefits of advertising. Proponents justify advertising on the grounds that it *a* aids consumers in exercising rational choices, *b* supports national communications, *c* speeds product development, *d* permits firms to realize economies of scale, *e* promotes competition, and *f* encourages spending and a high level of employment. Critics assert that advertising *a* confuses rather than informs; *b* misallocates resources away from more urgent employments; *c* involves a variety of external costs; *d* results in higher, not lower, costs and prices; *e* promotes monopoly; and *f* is not a strategic determinant of spending and employment. Empirical evidence reveals no consensus as to whether advertising is an anti- or procompetitive force.

7 In practice the monopolistic competitor seeks that specific combination of price, product, and promotion which will maximize its profits.

TERMS AND CONCEPTS

monopolistic competition

product differentiation

wastes of monopolistic competition

nonprice competition

anti- and procompetitive views of advertising

QUESTIONS AND STUDY SUGGESTIONS

1 How does monopolistic competition differ from pure competition? From pure monopoly? Explain fully what product differentiation entails.

2 Compare the elasticity of the monopolistically competitive producer's demand curve with that of *a* a pure competitor, and *b* a pure monopolist. Assuming identical long-run costs, compare graphically the prices and outputs which would result under pure competition and monopolistic competition. Contrast the two market structures in terms of allocative and productive efficiency. Explain: "Monopolistically competitive industries are characterized by too many firms, each of which produces too little."

3 "Monopolistic competition is monopoly up to the point at which consumers become willing to buy close-substitute products and competitive beyond that point." Explain.

4 "Competition in quality and in service may be quite as effective in giving the buyer more for her money as is price competition." Do you agree? Explain why monopolistically competitive firms frequently prefer nonprice to price competition.

5 Critically evaluate and explain:

a "In monopolistically competitive industries economic profits are competed away in the long run; hence, there is no valid reason to criticize the performance and efficiency of such industries."

b "In the long run monopolistic competition leads to a monopolistic price but not to monopolistic profits."

6 Do you agree or disagree with the following statements? Why?

a "The amount of advertising which a firm does is likely to vary inversely with the real differences in its product."

b "If each firm's advertising expenditures merely tend to cancel the effects of its rivals' advertising, it is clearly irrational for these firms to maintain large advertising budgets."

7 Carefully evaluate the two views expressed in the following statements:

a "It happens every day. Advertising builds mass demand. Production goes up—costs come down. More people can buy—more jobs are created. These are the ingredients of economic growth. Each stimulates the next in a cycle of productivity and plenty which constantly creates a better life for you."

b "Advertising constitutes 'inverted education'—a costly effort to induce people to buy without sufficient thought and deliberation and therefore to buy things they don't need. Furthermore, advertising outlays vary directly with the level of consumer spending." Which view do you feel is the more accurate? Justify your position.

8 Compare the anticompetitive and the procompetitive views of advertising. Which do you feel is more accurate?

CHAPTER 28

Price and output determination: oligopoly

In many of our manufacturing, mining, and wholesaling industries, a few firms are dominant. Such industries are called oligopolies. It is with these industries that the present chapter is concerned. Specifically, we have five objectives. (1) We seek first to define oligopoly, assess its occurrence, and note the reasons for its existence. (2) The major goal is to survey the possible courses of price-output behavior which oligopolistic industries might follow. (3) The role of nonprice competition, that is, competition on the basis of product development and advertising, in oligopolistic industries is discussed. (4) Next, some comments with respect to the economic efficiency and social desirability of oligopoly are offered. (5) Finally, many of the salient points found in the chapter are underscored in a brief case study of the automobile industry.

Oligopoly: concept and occurrence

What are the basic characteristics of oligopoly? How frequently is it encountered in our economy? Why has this industry structure developed?

FEWNESS

The outstanding feature of **oligopoly** is "fewness." When a relatively small number of firms dominate the market for a good or service, the industry is oligopolistic. But what specifically is meant by "a few" firms? This is necessarily vague, because the market model of oligopoly covers a great deal of ground, ranging between pure monopoly, on the one hand, and monopolistic competition, on the other. Thus oligopoly encompasses the aluminum industry, in which three firms tend to dominate an entire national market, and the situation in which, say, ten or fifteen gasoline stations may enjoy roughly equal shares of the petroleum products market in a medium-sized town. Generally, when we hear of the "Big Three," "Big Four" or "Big Six," we can be relatively certain that the indicated industry is oligopolistic.

Homogeneous or differentiated products Oligopolies may be **homogeneous** or **differentiated;** that is, the firms in an oligopolistic industry may produce standardized or differentiated products. Many industrial products—steel, zinc, copper, aluminum, lead, cement, industrial alcohol, and so forth—are virtually standardized products in the physical sense and are produced under oligopolistic conditions. On the other hand, many consumer goods industries—automobiles, tires, detergents, greeting cards, breakfast cereals, cigarettes, and a host of household appliances—are differentiated oligopolies.

Concentration ratios Table 28-1 lists a number of major industries in which "fewness" is present in varying degrees. The data show the four-firm sales **concentration ratio,** which is simply the percentage of total industry sales accounted for by the four largest firms in each industry. Thus we note, for example, that 90 percent of the cigarettes and 79 percent of the household detergents produced in the United States are manufactured by the four largest firms in each industry.

TABLE 28-1 **Percentage of output* produced by firms in selected high-concentration manufacturing industries**

Industry	Percentage of industry output produced by four largest firms
Primary lead	100
Household refrigerators and freezers	94
Motor vehicles	92
Household laundry equipment	91
Electric lamps (bulbs)	91
Cigarettes	90
Small arms ammunition	87
Primary copper	87
Cereal breakfast foods	86
Flat glass	85
Greeting card publishing	84
Turbines and generators	84
Beer and ale	80
Household vacuum cleaners	80
Household detergents	79
Telephones	76
Gypsum products	76
Sewing machines	72
Tires and inner tubes	66
Primary aluminum	64
Aircraft	64

* As measured by value of shipments. Data are for 1982.
Source: Bureau of the Census, *Concentration Ratios in Manufacturing.*

While concentration ratios generally provide useful insights as to the competitiveness or monopolization of various industries, they are subject to several noteworthy shortcomings. First, the concentration ratios pertain to the nation as a whole, while the relevant markets for some products are actually highly localized because of high transportation costs. For example, the concentration ratio for ready-mix concrete is only 6 percent, suggesting a highly competitive industry. But the sheer bulk of this product limits the relevant market to a given town or metropolitan area and in such localized markets we typically find oligopolistic suppliers. We have already suggested that at the local level, some aspects of the retail trade—particularly in small- and medium-sized towns—are characterized by oligopoly. Second, definitions of industries are somewhat arbitrary and it is important to be aware of **interindustry competition,** that is, competition between two products associated with different industries. Hence, Table 28-1's high concentration ratios for the aluminum and copper industries probably understate the degree of competition because aluminum and copper compete in many applications, for example, in the market for electrical transmission lines. Third, the data are for American products and therefore tend to overstate monopoly power because they do not take into account the **import competition** of foreign suppliers. The automobile industry is a highly relevant illustration. While Table 28-1 tells us that four American firms account for 92 percent of the domestic production of motor vehicles, it ignores the fact that about 25 percent of the automobiles purchased in the United States are imports. Finally, concentration ratios tell us nothing about the actual market performance of various industries. Industries X and Y may have identical four-firm concentration ratios of, say, 85 percent. Industry X may be characterized by vigorous price competition and technological progress as evidenced by improved product and production techniques. In contrast, the firms of industry Y may price their products collusively and be technologically stagnant. From society's viewpoint the "competitive" performance of industry X is clearly superior to the "monopolistic" performance of Y, a fact concealed by the identical concentration ratios. Nevertheless, used with caution and tempered with common sense, concentration ratios serve as helpful indicators of the degree of monopoly power embodied in various industries.[1]

UNDERLYING CAUSES

Why are certain industries composed of only a few firms? The answer lies primarily in cost economies, other barriers to entry, and mergers.

Economies of scale   We discovered in Chapter 24 that, where economies of scale are substantial (see Figure 24-9b), reasonably efficient production will be possible only with a small number of producers; in other words, efficiency requires that the productive capacity of each firm be large relative to the total market. Indeed, it is an unstable situation for an industry to have a large number of high-cost firms, each of which is failing to realize existing economies of scale. In Figure 24-7, for example, a firm currently operating with the small and inefficient plant size indicated by ATC-1 will recognize that this short-run position is unsatisfactory; it can realize substantially lower unit costs and a larger profit by expanding its plant to ATC-2. The same can be said for the move to ATC-3. However, given a reasonably stable market demand, all the many firms with small (ATC-1) plant sizes cannot now survive. The profitable expansion to larger plant sizes by some will necessarily come at the expense of rivals. The realization of economies of scale by some firms implies that the number of rival producers is simultaneously being reduced through failure or merger.

Historically, what has happened in many industries is that technological progress has made more and more economies of scale attainable over time. Thus many industries started out with a primitive technology, few economies of scale, and a relatively large number of competitors. But then, as technology improved and economies of scale became increasingly pronounced, the less alert or less aggressive firms fell by the wayside and a few

producers emerged. For example, estimates suggest that over eighty firms populated the automobile industry in its infancy. Over the years, the development of mass-production techniques reduced the field through failure and combination. Now the Big Three—General Motors, Ford, and Chrysler—account for about 90 percent of domestically produced automobile sales.

But why, you may ask, aren't new firms created to enter the automobile industry? The answer, of course, is that to achieve the low unit costs essential to survival, any new entrants must necessarily start out as large producers. This may require several billions of dollars worth of investment in machinery and equipment alone. Economies of scale can be a formidable barrier to entry. They explain not only the evolution of oligopoly in many industries, but also why such industries are not likely to become more competitive. We should temper these comments, however, by recalling from Chapter 24's Last Word that the degree of concentration in many industries is in excess of that warranted by economies of scale.

Other barriers   We must note that the development or persistence of some oligopolies can be traced at least in part to other entry barriers. In the electronics, chemical, and aluminum industries, the ownership of patents and the control of strategic raw materials have been important. And perhaps prodigious advertising outlays may provide an added financial barrier to entry, as some economists argue has been the case in the cigarette industry.

The urge to merge   The final factor in explaining oligopoly or fewness is merger. The motivation for merger has diverse roots. Of immediate relevance is the fact that the combining of two or more formerly competing firms by merger may increase their market share substantially and enable the new and larger production unit to achieve greater economies of scale. Another significant motive underlying the "urge to merge" is the market power which may accompany merger. A firm that is larger both absolutely and relative to the market may have greater ability to control the market for, and the price of, its product than does a smaller more competitive producer. Furthermore, the large size which merger entails may give the firm the advantage of being a "big buyer" and permit it to

[1] See F. M. Scherer, *Industrial Market Structure and Economic Performance*, 2d ed. (Chicago: Rand McNally College Publishing Company, 1980), chap. 3, for a more sophisticated discussion of the problems involved in measuring the degree of monopoly power.

demand and obtain lower prices (costs) from input suppliers than previously.

MUTUAL INTERDEPENDENCE

Regardless of the means by which oligopoly evolves, it is clear that rivalry among a small number of firms, interjects a new and complicating factor into our discussion: **mutual interdependence.** Imagine three firms, A, B, and C, each of which has about one-third of the market for a particular product. If A cuts price, its share of the market will increase. But B and C will be directly, significantly, and adversely affected by A's price cutting. Hence, we can expect some *reaction* on the part of B and C to A's behavior: B and C may match A's price cut or even undercut A, thereby precipitating a price war. This response correctly suggests that no firm in an oligopolistic industry will dare to alter its price policies without attempting to calculate the most likely reactions of its rivals. To be sure, cost and demand data are important to the oligopolist in establishing price, but to these we must add the reaction of rivals—a highly uncertain factor. The situation faced by oligopolistic producers resembles that of participants in games of strategy, such as poker, bridge, or chess. There is no means of knowing beforehand the best way to play your cards in a poker game, because this depends upon the way other participants play theirs. Players must pattern their actions according to the actions and expected reactions of rivals.

It is to be emphasized that the mutual interdependence resulting from fewness, and the consequent need for a firm to weigh the possible reactions of rivals in altering its price policy, are unique features of oligopoly. The large number of rivals, which characterizes pure competition and monopolistic competition, and the absence of rivals, which is the earmark of pure monopoly, rule out mutual interdependence in these market structures. Indeed, a good, workable definition of oligopoly is this: *Oligopoly exists when the number of firms in an industry is so small that each must consider the reactions of rivals in formulating its price policy.*

Recap: Oligopoly exists when a small number of firms dominate the market for a homogeneous or differentiated product. Oligopoly occurs because of economies of scale, other entry barriers such as patents or the ownership of raw materials, and mergers. Fewness results in mutual interdependence with respect to pricing policies.

Price-output behavior

The theories of competitive, monopolistic, and monopolistically competitive markets as presented in prior chapters are quite standard and widely accepted segments of microeconomics. But economic analysis offers no standard portrait of oligopoly. In general, there are two major reasons why it is difficult to use formal economic analysis in explaining the price behavior of oligopolies.

1 The previously noted fact that oligopoly encompasses a diversity of specific market situations works against the development of a single, generalized explanation or model of how an oligopoly determines price and output. Pure competition, monopolistic competition, and pure monopoly all refer to rather clear-cut market arrangements; oligopoly does not. It includes the "tight" oligopoly situation in which two or three firms dominate an entire market as well as the "loose" oligopoly situation in which six or seven firms share, say, 70 or 80 percent of a market while a "competitive fringe" of firms share the remainder. It includes both product differentiation and standardization. It encompasses the cases in which firms are acting in collusion and those in which they are acting independently. It embodies the situations in which barriers to entry are very strong and those in which they are not quite so strong. In short, the many breeds, or strains, of oligopoly preclude the development of any simple market model which provides a general explanation of oligopolistic behavior.

2 The element of mutual interdependence which fewness adds to the analysis is a most significant complication. To be specific, the inability of a firm to predict with certainty the reactions of its rivals makes it virtually impossible to estimate the demand and marginal-revenue data faced by an oligopolist. And without such data, firms cannot determine their profit-maximizing price and output even in theory, as we shall presently make clear.

Despite these analytical difficulties, two interrelated characteristics of oligopolistic pricing stand out. On the one hand, oligopolistic prices tend to be inflexible, or "sticky." Prices change less frequently in oligopoly than they do under pure competition, monopolistic competition, and in some instances, pure monopoly. Figure 10-3 provides some interesting data on this point. On the other hand, when oligopolistic prices do change, firms are likely to change their prices together; oligopolistic price behavior suggests the presence of incentives to act in concert or collusively in setting and changing prices.

Four variants

To gain insight into oligopoly pricing we will examine four rather distinct models: (1) the kinked de-

mand curve, (2) collusive pricing, (3) price leadership, and (4) cost-plus pricing.

KINKED DEMAND: NONCOLLUSIVE OLIGOPOLY

Again imagine an oligopolistic industry comprised of just three firms, A, B, and C, each having about one-third of the total market for a differentiated product. Assume the firms are "independent" in the sense that they do not engage in collusive practices in setting prices. Suppose, too, that the going price for firm A's product is PQ and its current sales are Q, as shown in Figure 28-1a. Now the question is, "What does the firm's demand, or sales, curve look like?" We have just noted that mutual interdependence, and the uncertainty of rivals' reactions which interdependence entails,

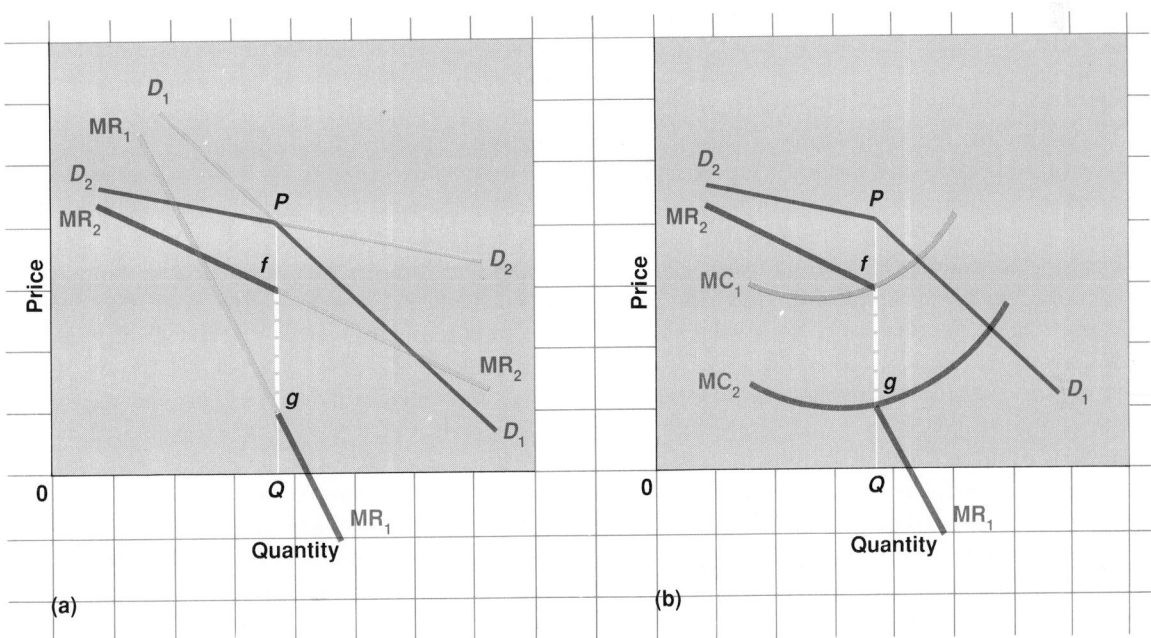

FIGURE 28-1

The kinked demand curve

The nature of a noncollusive oligopolist's demand and marginal-revenue curves as shown in (a) will depend upon whether its rivals will match (D_1D_1 and MR_1MR_1) or ignore (D_2D_2 and MR_2MR_2) any price changes which it may initiate from the current price PQ. In all likelihood an oligopolist's rivals will ignore a price increase but follow a price cut. This causes the oligopolist's demand curve to be kinked (D_2PD_1) and the marginal-revenue curve to have a vertical break, or gap (fg) as shown in (b). Furthermore, because any shift in marginal costs between MC_1 and MC_2 will cut the vertical (dashed) segment of the marginal-revenue curve, no change in either price PQ or output Q will occur.

make this question difficult to answer. The location and shape of an oligopolist's demand curve depend upon how the firm's rivals will react to a price change introduced by A. There are two plausible assumptions about the reactions of A's rivals with which we might experiment.

Match or ignore?   One possibility is that firms B and C will exactly match any price change initiated by A. In this case, A's demand and marginal-revenue curves will look something like D_1D_1 and MR_1MR_1 in Figure 28-1a. If A cuts price, its sales will increase very modestly, because its two rivals will follow suit and thereby prevent A from gaining any price advantage over them. The small increase in sales which A (and its two rivals) will realize is at the expense of other industries; A will gain no sales from B and C. If A raises the going price, its sales will fall only modestly. Why? Because B and C match its price increase, so A does not price itself out of the market. The industry now loses some sales to other industries, but A loses no customers to B and C.

The other obvious possibility is that firms B and C will simply ignore any price change invoked by A. In this case, the demand and marginal-revenue curves faced by A will resemble D_2D_2 and MR_2MR_2 in Figure 28-1a. The demand curve in this case is considerably more elastic than under the assumption that B and C will match A's price changes. The reasons are clear. If A lowers its price and its rivals do not, A will gain sales significantly at the expense of its two rivals because it will be underselling them. Conversely, if A raises its price and its rivals do not, A will be pricing itself out of the market and will lose many customers to B and C, which are now underselling it. Because of product differentiation, however, A's sales do not fall to zero when it raises its price; some of A's customers will pay the higher price because they have strong preferences for A's product.

Now, which is the most logical assumption for A to make as to how its rivals will react to any price change it might initiate? The answer is "some of each"! Common sense and observation of oligopolistic industries suggest that price declines will be matched as a firm's competitors act to prevent the price cutter from taking their customers, but that price increases will be ignored, because rivals of the price-increasing firm stand to gain the business lost

by the price booster. In other words, the dark blue D_2P segment of the "rivals ignore" demand curve seems relevant for price increases, and the dark blue PD_1 segment of the "rivals follow" demand curve is more realistic for price cuts. It is logical, or at least a good guess, that an oligopolist faces a **"kinked" demand curve** on the order of D_2PD_1 as shown in Figure 28-1b. (Ignore the MC_1 and MC_2 curves for the moment.) The curve is highly elastic above the going price, but much less elastic or even inelastic below the current price. Note also that if it is correct to suppose that rivals will follow a price cut but ignore an increase, the marginal-revenue curve of the oligopolist will also have an odd shape. It, too, will be made up of two segments—the dark blue MR_2f part of the marginal-revenue curve appropriate to D_2D_2 and the dark blue gMR_1 chunk of the marginal-revenue curve appropriate to D_1D_1 in Figure 28-1a. Because of the sharp differences in elasticity of demand above and below the going price, there occurs a gap, or what we can treat as a vertical segment, in the marginal-revenue curve. In Figure 28-1b the marginal-revenue curve is shown by the two blue lines connected by the dashed vertical segment, or gap.

Price inflexibility   This analysis is important in that it goes far to explain why price changes may be infrequent in noncollusive oligopolistic industries.
I The kinked-demand schedule gives each oligopolist good reason to believe that any change in price will be for the worse. A substantial number of a firm's customers will desert it if it raises its price. If it lowers its price, its sales at best will increase very modestly. Even if a price cut increases its total revenue somewhat, the oligopolist's costs may well increase by a more-than-offsetting amount. If the dark blue PD_1 segment of its sales schedule is *inelastic* in that E_d is less than 1, the firm's profits will surely fall.[2] A price decrease will lower the firm's total revenue, and the production of a somewhat larger output will increase total costs. Worse yet, a price cut by A may be *more* than met by B and C; A's initial price cut may precipitate a **price war;** so the amount sold by A may actually decline as its

---

[2] Recall from Figure 26-2 that a demand curve is elastic to the left of the point where marginal revenue intersects the horizontal axis and inelastic to the right of that point.

rival firms charge still lower prices. These are all good reasons on the demand side of the picture why noncollusive oligopolies might seek "the quiet life" and follow live-and-let-live, or don't-upset-the-applecart, price policies. More specifically, if the resulting profits are satisfactory to the several firms at the existing price, it may seem prudent to them not to alter that price.

2 The other reason for price inflexibility under noncollusive oligopoly works from the cost side of the picture. The broken marginal-revenue curve which accompanies the kinked demand curve suggests that within limits, substantial cost changes will have no effect upon output and price. To be specific, any shift in marginal cost between MC_1 and MC_2 as shown in Figure 28-1b will result in no change in price or output; MR will continue to equal MC at output Q at which price PQ will be charged.

Shortcomings The kinked-demand analysis has been subjected to two major criticisms. First, the analysis *does not explain how the going price gets to be at PQ (Figure 28-1) in the first place.* Rather, it merely helps to explain why oligopolists may be reluctant to deviate from an existing price which yields them a "satisfactory" or "reasonable" profit. The kinked demand curve explains price inflexibility but not price itself. Second, oligopoly prices are not as rigid—particularly in an upward direction—as the kinked-demand theory implies. During inflationary periods such as the 1970s and the early 1980s, oligopolistic producers raised their prices frequently and substantially. Such price increases might be better explained in terms of collusive oligopoly.

COLLUSIVE OLIGOPOLY

The condition of oligopoly—a small number of mutually interdependent firms—is conducive to collusion. **Collusion** occurs when firms in an industry reach an explicit or tacit (unspoken) agreement to fix prices, divide or share the market, or otherwise restrict competition among themselves. The disadvantages and uncertainties of the noncollusive, kinked-demand model to producers are obvious. There is always the danger of a price war breaking out. In particular, in a general business

recession each firm will find itself with excess capacity and therefore it can reduce per unit costs by increasing its market share. Then, too, the possibility is always present that a new firm may surmount entry barriers and initiate aggressive price cutting to gain a foothold in the market. In addition, the kinked demand curve's tendency toward rigid prices may adversely affect profits if general inflationary pressures increase costs. Stated differently, collusive control over price may permit oligopolists to reduce uncertainty, increase profits, and perhaps even prohibit the entry of new rivals.

Price and output Where will price and output be established under **collusive oligopoly?** To answer this question we must construct a highly simplified situation. Assume once again there are three firms—A, B, and C—producing in this instance homogeneous products. Each firm has identical cost curves. Each firm's demand curve is indeterminate unless we know how its rivals will react to any price change. Therefore, let us suppose each firm assumes that its two rivals will match either a price cut or a price increase. In other words, each firm's demand curve is of the D_1D_1 type in Figure 28-1a. Assume further that the demand curve for each firm is identical. Given identical cost and identical demand and marginal revenue data, we can say that Figure 28-2 represents the position of each of our three oligopolistic firms.

What price and output combination should each firm choose? If firm A were a pure monopolist, the answer would be clear enough: Establish output at Q, where marginal revenue equals marginal cost, charge the corresponding price PQ, and enjoy the maximum profit attainable. However, firm A *does* have two rivals selling identical products, and if A's assumption that its rivals will match its price[3] proves to be incorrect, the consequences could be disastrous for A. Specifically, if B and C actually charge prices below PQ, then firm A's demand curve will shift quite sharply to the left as its potential customers turn to its rivals, which are now selling the same product at a lower price. Of course, A can retaliate by cutting its price too; but this will have the effect of moving all three

---

[3] Recall that this is the assumption upon which A's demand curve in Figure 28-2 is based.

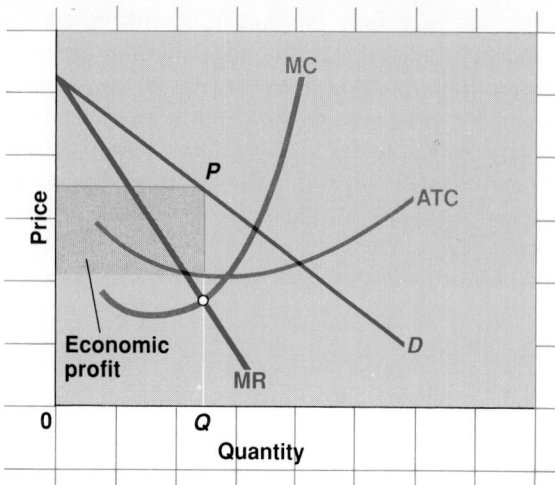

FIGURE 28-2

Collusion and the tendency toward joint-profit maximization

If oligopolistic firms are faced with identical or highly similar demand and cost conditions, they will tend to behave collusively and maximize joint profits. The price and output results are essentially the same as those of pure (unregulated) monopoly; each oligopolist charges price PQ and produces output Q.

firms down their demand curves, lowering their profits, and perhaps even driving them to some point where average cost exceeds price. So the question becomes, "Will B and C want to charge a price below *PQ*?" Under the assumptions we have made, and recognizing that A will have little choice except to match any price they may set below *PQ*, the answer is "No." Faced with the same demand and cost circumstances, B and C will find it in their interest to produce *Q* and charge *PQ*. This is a curious situation; each firm finds it most profitable to charge the same price *PQ*, but only if its rivals will actually do so! How can the three firms realize the *PQ*-price and *Q*-quantity solution in which each is keenly interested? How can this be made a reality so that all three can avoid the less profitable outcomes associated with either higher or lower prices? The answer is evident: The firms will all be motivated to collude—to "get together and talk it over"—and agree to charge the same price *PQ*. In addition to reducing the omnipresent possibility of price warring, each firm will realize the maximum profit. And for society, the result is likely to be

about the same as if the industry were a pure monopoly composed of three identical plants (Chapter 26).

Cartels and such Collusion may assume a variety of forms. The most comprehensive form of collusion is the **cartel** which typically involves a formal written agreement with respect to both price and production. Output must be controlled—that is, the market must be shared—in order to maintain the agreed-upon price.

OPEC The most spectacularly successful international cartel of recent years has been OPEC (the Organization of Petroleum Exporting Countries). Comprised of thirteen nations, OPEC was extremely effective in the 1970s in restricting oil supply and raising prices. The cartel was able to raise world oil prices from $2.50 to $11.00 per barrel within a six-month period in 1973–1974. By early 1980 price hikes had brought the per barrel price into the $32 to $34 range. The result was enormous profits for cartel members, a substantial stimulus to worldwide inflation, and serious international trade deficits for oil importers.

OPEC was highly effective in the 1970s for several reasons. First, OPEC dominated the world market for oil. If a nation imported oil, it was almost obligated to do business with OPEC. Second, the world demand for oil was strong and expanding in the 1970s. Finally, the "short-run" demand for oil was highly inelastic, which meant that a small restriction of output by OPEC would result in a relatively large price increase. Thus, as shown in Figure 28-3, in 1973–1974 and again in 1979–1980 OPEC was able to achieve dramatic increases in oil prices and only incur a very modest decline in sales. Given this inelastic demand, higher prices meant greatly increased total revenues to OPEC members. The accompanying smaller output meant lower total costs. The combination of more total revenue and lower total costs resulted in greatly expanded profits.

Why was the demand for oil inelastic? The answer in part is that few energy substitutes are immediately available. Automobiles run only on gasoline; a home with an oil furnace must be heated with fuel oil; and so on. Furthermore, during the earlier years of cheap energy, American consumers and producers acquired large stocks of energy-

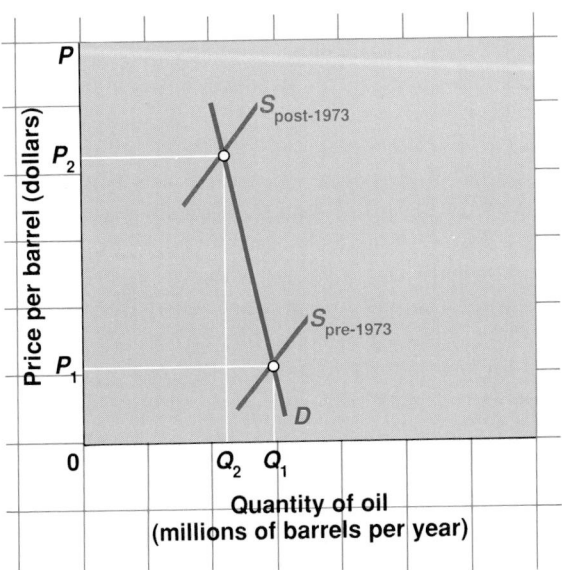

FIGURE 28-3

The OPEC cartel and the world oil market

Because of the inelasticity of the demand for oil, in 1973–1974 and again in 1979–1980 the OPEC cartel was able to obtain a dramatic increase in the price of oil (P_1 to P_2) accompanied by only a very modest decline in production and sales (Q_1 to Q_2).

intensive durable and investment goods. That is, with gas selling at about 32 cents per gallon in the 1970–1972 period, it was not unreasonable to buy a large gas-guzzling automobile. It would not be economically rational to sell that relatively new automobile in 1973 or 1974 in the face of a substantial increase in gas prices. Hence, it is not surprising that the "short-run" elasticity of demand for gasoline is estimated to be in the .20 to .40 range. That is, a 10 percent increase in the price of gasoline will only result in a 2 to 4 percent decrease in consumption. Similarly, most of our stock of residential and commercial buildings in the 1970s was constructed during the cheap energy period; hence, they were built with a rather cavalier attitude concerning the use of insulation, weatherstripping, thermopane windows, and so forth. And pre-1973 low energy prices made it rational for producers to equip their workers with large amounts of energy-intensive machinery and equipment. In brief, in the "short run" our economy is locked in to stocks of durable and investment goods which we continue to use at about the same intensity, regardless

of the price of oil. Hence, the demand for oil is inelastic. The important point is that the inelastic demand was highly advantageous to the OPEC cartel, allowing it to translate relatively small production cutbacks into very large increases in prices, revenues, and profits. We shall discuss momentarily the serious weakening of the OPEC cartel in the 1980s.

ELECTRICAL EQUIPMENT CONSPIRACY Cartels are illegal in the United States and hence collusion has been less formal. For example, in 1960 an extensive price-fixing and market-sharing scheme involving heavy electrical equipment such as transformers, turbines, circuit breakers, and switchgear was uncovered. Elaborate sub rosa schemes were developed by such participants as General Electric, Westinghouse, and Allis-Chalmers to rig prices and divide the market.

The manner in which prices were fixed, bids controlled, and markets allocated may be illustrated by *power switch gear assemblies* . . . five companies and twelve individuals were involved. It was charged that at least twenty-five meetings were held between the middle of November 1958 and October 1959 in various parts of the country. . . .

At these periodic meetings, a scheme or formula for quoting nearly identical prices to electric utility companies, private industrial corporations and contractors was used by defendant corporations, designated by their representatives as a "phase of the moon" or "light of the moon" formula. Through cyclic rotating positioning inherent in the formula one defendant corporation would quote the low price, others would quote intermediate prices and another would quote the high price; these positions would be periodically rotated among the defendant corporations. This formula was so calculated that in submitting prices to these customers, the price spread between defendant corporations' quotations would be sufficiently narrow so as to eliminate actual price competition among them, but sufficiently wide so as to give an appearance of competition. This formula was designed to permit each defendant corporation to know the exact price it and every other defendant corporation would quote on each prospective sale.

At these periodic meetings, a cumulative list of sealed bid business secured by all of the defendant corporations was also circulated and the representatives present would compare the relative standing of each corporation according to its agreed upon percentage of the total sales pursuant to sealed bids. The representatives present would then discuss particular future bid invitations and designate which defendant corporation should submit the lowest bid therefor, the amount of such bid, and the amount of the bid to be submitted by others.[4]

Some twenty-nine manufacturers and forty-six company officials were indicted in this "great electrical conspiracy" which violated our antitrust laws. Substantial fines, jail penalties, and lawsuits by victimized buyers were the final outcome.

In innumerable other instances collusion is still less formal. **Gentlemen's agreements** frequently are struck at cocktail parties, on the golf course, or at trade association meetings where competing firms reach a verbal agreement on product price, leaving market shares to the ingenuity of each seller as reflected in nonprice competition. Although they too collide with the antitrust laws, the elusive character of gentlemen's agreements makes them more difficult to detect and prosecute successfully.

Obstacles to collusion In practice cartels and similar collusive arrangements are difficult to establish and maintain. Let us briefly consider several important barriers to collusion.

1 DEMAND AND COST DIFFERENCES When oligopolists' costs and product demands differ, it is more difficult to reach an agreement on price. Where products are differentiated and changing frequently over time, we would expect this to be the case. Indeed, even with highly standardized products, we would expect that firms might have somewhat different market shares and would operate with differing degrees of productive efficiency. Thus it is likely that even homogeneous oligopolists would have somewhat different demand and cost curves. In either event, differences in costs and demand will mean that the profit-maximizing price for each firm will differ; there will be no single price which is readily acceptable to all. Price collusion

[4] Jules Backman, *The Economics of the Electrical Machinery Industry* (New York: New York University Press, 1962), pp. 135–138, abridged. Reprinted by permission.

therefore depends upon the ability to achieve compromises and concessions—to arrive at a degree of "understanding" which in practice is often difficult to attain. For example, the MR = MC positions of firms A, B, and C may call for them to charge $12, $11, and $10 respectively, but this price cluster or range may be unsatisfactory to one or more of the firms. Firm A may feel that differences in product quality justify only a $1.50, rather than a $2, price differential between its product and that of firm C. In short, cost and demand differences make it difficult for oligopolists to agree on a single price or a "proper" cluster of prices; these differentials are therefore an obstacle to collusion.

2 NUMBER OF FIRMS Other things being equal, the larger the number of firms, the more difficult it is to achieve a cartel or some other form of price collusion. Agreement on price by three or four producers that control an entire market is much more readily accomplished than it is in the situation where ten firms each have roughly 10 percent of the market, or where the Big Three have, say, 70 percent of the market, while a "competitive fringe" of eight or ten smaller firms does battle for the remainder.

3 CHEATING There is also a more-or-less persistent temptation for collusive oligopolists to engage in clandestine price cutting, that is, to make secret price concessions in order to get additional business. The technical aspects of cheating can be grasped by looking back at Figure 28-2 where the oligopolist in selling Q units at price PQ. At first glance it would seem that additional sales would violate the MR = MC rule and therefore *reduce* profits. But this is an instance of price discrimination where, through secrecy, the buyers of Q units and the buyers of additional units are separated into two markets. This separation through secrecy means that the sales of units beyond Q add their full price to marginal revenue; that is, additional sales through secret price concessions do *not* require a price cut on all prior units sold. Marginal revenue is equal to price for these additional units so that the sale of this extra output via cheating will be profitable out to the point at which *price* equals marginal cost.

The difficulty with cheating is that buyers who are paying PQ may get wind of the lower-priced sales and demand similar treatment. Or buyers receiving price concessions from one oligopolist may use this concession as a wedge to get even larger price concessions from the firm's rivals. The attempt of buyers to play sellers against one another may precipitate price warring among the firms. In short, although it is potentially profitable, the use of secret price concessions is a threat to the maintenance of collusive oligopoly over time. Collusion is more likely to persist when cheating is deterred because it is easy to detect.

4 RECESSION Recession is usually an enemy of collusion because slumping markets cause average costs to rise. In technical terms, as the oligopolists' demand and marginal-revenue curves shift to the left (Figure 28-2), each firm moves back to a higher point on its average-cost curve. The firms find they have substantial excess productive capacity, sales are down, unit costs are up, and profits are being squeezed. Under such conditions, businesses may feel they are in a better position to avoid serious profit reductions by price cutting in the hope of gaining sales at the expense of rivals.

5 POTENTIAL ENTRY The enhanced prices and profits which result from collusion will tend to attract new entrants. Such entry would increase market supply and thereby reduce prices and profits. Therefore, successful collusion requires that the colluding oligopolists are able to block the entry of new producers.

6 LEGAL OBSTACLES: ANTITRUST Our antitrust laws (Chapter 34) prohibit cartels and the kind of price-fixing collusion we have been discussing. It is for these reasons that less obvious means of price rigging—such as price leadership—have evolved in the United States.

OPEC IN DISARRAY The highly successful OPEC oil cartel of the 1970s fell into disarray in the 1980s, and the reasons for OPEC's decline relate closely to the obstacles to collusion we have just enumerated. First, the dramatic runup of oil prices in the 1970s stimulated the search for new oil reserves, and soon non-OPEC nations, which OPEC could not block from entering world markets, became a part of the world oil industry. Great Britain, Norway, Mexico, and the Soviet Union have all become major world oil suppliers. As a result, OPEC's share of world oil production fell from about 50 percent during 1973–1979 to only 30 percent in 1985. Second, on the demand side, oil conservation, worldwide recession in the early 1980s, and the expanded use of alternative energy sources (such as coal and solar and nuclear power) all reduced the demand for oil. The amount of oil demanded in the industrialized countries was about 20 percent less in 1985 than in 1979. The combination of greater production by non-OPEC nations and a decline in world demand generated an "oil glut" and seriously impaired OPEC's ability to control world oil prices. Third, OPEC has had a serious cheating problem stemming from the relatively large number of members (thirteen) and the diversity of their economic circumstances. Saudi Arabia is the dominant cartel member; it has the largest oil reserves and is probably the lowest-cost producer. Saudi Arabia has favored a "moderate" pricing policy because it has feared that very high oil prices would hasten the development of alternative energy sources (for example, solar power and synthetic fuels) and increase the attractiveness of existing substitutes such as coal and wood. Such developments would greatly reduce the value of its vast oil reserves. Saudi Arabia also has a small population and a very high per capita GNP. But other members—for example, Nigeria and Venezuela—are very poor, have large populations, and are burdened with large external debts. These members have immediate needs for cash. Hence, there has been substantial cheating whereby some members have exceeded assigned production quotas and have sold oil at prices below those agreed upon by the cartel. Iran, in need of additional oil revenues to finance its costly and prolonged war with Iraq, sought to increase its production quotas at Saudi Arabia's expense. Furthermore, when increasing world supply and declining demand have made it necessary for OPEC to cut production in order to maintain prices, there has been a great deal of disagreement as to how the needed cuts should be allocated among members.

In 1985 and 1986 it was generally agreed that the OPEC cartel was unraveling. OPEC's official price of $34 a barrel in 1979 had fallen to $28 by the summer of 1985. Then in early 1986 oil prices dropped dramatically to about $10 per barrel. By 1988 the price had recovered to at about $14 per barrel. Does this mean OPEC is a matter of history? Not necessarily. A recent report of the U.S. Geological Survey argues to the contrary. While the world has plenty of oil for the next six or seven decades, it is a fact that about one-half of the world's proven reserves are in the Middle East. This suggests that sometime in the future the Middle East may again be able to exert monopolistic control over world oil supplies.

PRICE LEADERSHIP: TACIT COLLUSION

Price leadership is still a less formal means by which oligopolists can coordinate their price behavior without engaging in outright collusion. Formal agreements and clandestine meetings are not involved.[5] Rather, a practice evolves whereby the "dominant" firm—usually the largest or the most efficient in the industry—initiates price changes, and all other firms more-or-less automatically follow that price change. The importance of price leadership is evidenced in the fact that such industries as farm machinery, anthracite coal, cement, copper, gasoline, newsprint, tin cans, lead, sulfur, rayon, fertilizer, glass containers, steel, automobiles, and nonferrous metals are practicing, or have in the recent past practiced, price leadership.

Consider the case of the cigarette industry, which provides a classic example of tight price leadership. In this instance the Big Three, producing from 68 to 90 percent of total output, evolved a highly profitable practice of price leadership which resulted in virtually identical prices over the entire 1923 to 1941 period.

In 1918 American Tobacco tried to lead a price rise, but Reynolds (the largest seller) refused to follow. In 1921, American cut its price and Reynolds retaliated with a further cut, which American and the other sellers were forced to match. This experience apparently had a profound educational impact on American and the other major brand sellers, none of whom challenged Reynolds' leadership again for a decade. Between 1923 and 1941, virtual price identity prevailed continuously among the "standard" brands. During

this period there were eight list price changes. Reynolds led six of them, five upward and one downward, and was followed each time, in most cases within 24 hours of its announcement. The other two changes were downward revisions during 1933 led by American and followed promptly by the other standard brand vendors. American also attempted to lead a price increase in 1941, but Reynolds again refused to follow and the change was rescinded. Throughout this period, the return on invested capital realized by Reynolds, American, and Liggett & Myers averaged 18 percent after taxes—roughly double the rate earned by American manufacturing industry as a whole.[6]

Since 1946 cigarette pricing has been somewhat less rigid, reflecting both successful antitrust action and the development of increasingly heterogeneous product lines.

The examination of price leadership in a variety of industries suggests that the price leader is likely to observe the following tactics. First, because price changes always entail some risk that rivals will not follow, price adjustments will be made infrequently. The price leader will *not* respond pricewise to minuscule day-to-day changes in cost and demand conditions. Price will be changed only when cost and demand conditions have been altered significantly and on an industrywide basis. That is, the price leader will typically revise price upward in response to industrywide wage increases, an increase in taxes, or an increase in the price of some basic input such as energy. In the automobile industry price adjustments are usually made on the occasion of the introduction of new models each fall. Second, impending price adjustments are often communicated by the price leader to the industry through speeches by major executives, trade publication interviews, and so forth. By publicizing "the need to raise prices" the price leader can elicit a consensus among its competitors for the actual increase. Finally, the price leader does not necessarily choose the price which maximizes short-run profits for the industry. The reason for this is that the industry may want to discourage new firms from entering. If barriers to entry are based upon cost advantages (economies

---

[5] A word of caution: Upon (legal) investigation what initially appears to be price leadership occasionally turns out to be a more formal conspiracy.

[6] F. M. Scherer, *Industrial Pricing: Theory and Evidence* (Chicago: Rand McNally & Company, 1970), p. 38.

of scale) of existing firms, these cost barriers may be surmounted by new entrants *if* product price is set high enough. Stated differently, new firms which are relatively inefficient because of their small size may survive and grow if the industry's price is very high. To discourage new competitors and thereby maintain the current oligopolistic structure of the industry, price may be established below the short-run profit-maximizing level.

COST-PLUS PRICING

A final model of oligopolistic price behavior centers upon what is variously known as *markup, rule-of-thumb,* or **cost-plus pricing.** In this case the oligopolist uses a formula or procedure to estimate cost per unit of output and a markup is applied to cost in order to determine price. Unit costs, however, vary with output and therefore the firm must assume some typical or target level of output. For example, the firm's average-cost figure may be that which is realized when the firm is operating at, say, 75 or 80 percent of capacity. A markup, usually in the form of a percentage, is applied to average cost in determining price. For example, an appliance manufacturer may estimate unit costs of dishwashers to be $250, to which a 50 percent markup is applied. This yields a $375 price to retailers.

But why is the markup 50 percent, rather than 25 or 100 percent? The answer is that the firm is seeking some target profit or rate of return on its investment. To illustrate, General Motors has been using cost-plus pricing for over forty years:

GM begins its pricing analysis with an objective of earning, on the average over the years, a return of approximately 15 per cent after taxes on total invested capital. Since it does not know how many autos will be sold in a forthcoming year, and hence what the average cost per unit (including prorated overhead) will be, it calculates costs on the assumption of *standard volume*—that is, operation at 80 per cent of conservatively rated capacity. A *standard price* is next calculated by adding to average cost per unit at standard volume a sufficient profit margin to yield the desired 15 per cent after-tax return on capital. A top level price policy committee then uses the standard price as the initial basis of its price decision, making (typically small) adjustments upward or downward to take into account actual and potential competition,

business conditions, long-run strategic goals, and other factors.[7]

Two final points. First, cost-plus pricing has special advantages for multiproduct firms which would otherwise be faced with the difficult and costly process of estimating demand and cost conditions for perhaps hundreds of different products. In practice, it is virtually impossible to allocate correctly certain common overhead costs such as power, lighting, insurance, and taxes to specific products. Second, this method of pricing is *not* inconsistent with outright collusion or price leadership. If the several producers in an industry have roughly similar costs, adherence to a common pricing formula will result in highly similar prices and price changes. As we shall find in the case study which concludes this chapter, General Motors uses cost-plus pricing *and* is the price leader in the automobile industry.

Role of nonprice competition

We have noted that, for several reasons, oligopolists have an aversion to price competition. This aversion may lead to some more-or-less informal type of collusion on price. In the United States, however, price collusion is usually accompanied by nonprice competition. It is typically through nonprice competition that each firm's share of the total market is determined. This emphasis upon nonprice competition has its roots in two basic facts.

I Price cuts can be quickly and easily met by a firm's rivals. Because of this the possibility of significantly increasing one's share of the market through price competition is small; rivals will promptly cancel any potential gain in sales by matching price cuts. And, of course, the risk is always present that price competition will precipitate disastrous price warring. Nonprice competition is less likely to get out of hand. More positively stated, oligopolists seem to feel that more permanent advantages can be gained over rivals through nonprice competition because product variations, improvements in productive techniques, and successful advertising gimmicks cannot be duplicated

[7] Ibid., p. 46.

so quickly and so completely as can price reductions.

2 There is a more evident reason for the tremendous emphasis which oligopolists put upon nonprice competition: Manufacturing oligopolists are typically blessed with substantial financial resources with which to support advertising and product development. Hence, although nonprice competition is a basic characteristic of both monopolistically competitive and oligopolistic industries, the latter are typically in a financial position to indulge in nonprice competition more fully.

Oligopoly and economic efficiency

Is oligopoly an "efficient" market structure from society's standpoint? More specifically, how does the price–output behavior of the oligopolist compare with that of a purely competitive firm? Given that there exists a variety of oligopoly models—kinked demand, collusion, price leadership, and cost-plus pricing—it is difficult to make such a comparison.

TWO VIEWS

Two distinct views have evolved regarding the economic consequences of oligopoly. They focus upon the issue of dynamic efficiency which was brought up in Chapter 26. The **traditional view** holds that, because oligopoly is close to monopoly in structure, we should expect it to operate in a roughly similar way. Being characterized by barriers to entry, oligopoly can be expected, according to this view, to result in a restriction of output short of the point of lowest unit costs and a corresponding market price which yields substantial, if not maximum, economic profits. Indeed, one may even argue that oligopoly is actually less desirable than pure monopoly for the simple reason that pure monopoly in the United States is frequently subject to government regulation to mitigate abuses of such market power. Informal collusion among oligopolists may yield price and output results similar to pure monopoly, yet at the same time maintain the outward appearance of several independent and "competing" firms.

The traditional view is challenged by the **Schumpeter–Galbraith view,** which holds that large oligopolistic firms with market power are requisite to a rapid rate of technological progress. It is argued, first, that modern research to develop new products and new productive techniques is incredibly expensive. Therefore, only large oligopolistic firms are able to finance extensive research and development (R & D) activities. Second, the existence of barriers to entry gives the oligopolist some assurance that it will realize any profit rewards to which successful R & D endeavors may give rise. In Galbraith's words:

The modern industry of a few large firms [is] an excellent instrument for inducing technical change. It is admirably equipped for financing technical development. Its organization provides strong incentives for undertaking development and for putting it into use. . . . In the modern industry shared by a few large firms, size and the rewards accruing to market power combine to insure that resources for research and technical development will be available. The power that enables the firm to have some influence on prices insures that the resulting gains will not be passed on to the public by imitators (who have stood none of the costs of development) before the outlay for development can be recouped. In this way market power protects the incentive to technical development.[8]

Bluntly put, small competitive firms have neither the *means* nor the *incentives* to be technologically progressive; large oligopolists do.

If the Schumpeter–Galbraith view is correct, it suggests that over time oligopolistic industries will foster rapid product improvement, lower unit production costs, lower prices, and perhaps a greater output and more employment than would the same industry organized competitively. And there is anecdotal and case-study evidence which suggests that many oligopolistic manufacturing industries—for example, television and other electronics prod-

---

[8] John Kenneth Galbraith, *American Capitalism,* rev. ed. (Boston: Houghton Mifflin Company, 1956), pp. 86–88. Also see Joseph Schumpeter, *Capitalism, Socialism, and Democracy* (New York: Harper & Row Publishers, Inc., 1942).

ucts, home appliances, automobile tires—have been characterized by substantial improvements in product quality, falling relative prices, and expanding levels of output and employment.

Those who embrace the traditional view are not without counterarguments. They contend that oligopolists have a strong incentive to impede innovation and restrain technological progress. The larger corporation wants to maximize profits by exploiting fully all its capital assets. Why rush to develop and introduce a new product (for example, fluorescent lights) when that product's success will render obsolete all equipment designed to produce an existing product (incandescent bulbs)?[9] Furthermore, it is not difficult to cite oligopolistic industries wherein it is generally agreed that interest in research and development has been modest at best: The steel, cigarette, and aluminum industries are cases in point.

TECHNOLOGICAL PROGRESS: THE EVIDENCE

Which view is more nearly correct? Empirical studies have yielded ambiguous results. The consensus, however, seems to be that giant oligopolies are probably *not* the fountainhead of technological progress. For example, a study[10] of sixty-one important inventions made during the 1880 to 1965 period indicates that over half were the work of independent inventors, quite disassociated from the industrial research laboratories of corporate enterprise. Such substantial advances as air conditioning, power steering, the ballpoint pen, cellophane, the jet engine, insulin, xerography, the helicopter, and the catalytic cracking of petroleum have this individualistic heritage. Other equally important advances have been provided by small- and medium-sized firms. According to this study, about two-thirds—forty out of sixty-one—of the basic inventions of this century have been fathered by independent inventors or the research activities

of relatively small firms. This is not to deny that in a number of oligopolistic industries—for example, the aircraft, chemical, petroleum, and electronics industries—research activity has been pursued vigorously and fruitfully. But even here the picture is clouded by the fact that a very substantial portion of the research carried on in the aircraft-missile, electronics, and communications industries is heavily subsidized with public funds.

It is of interest that some leading researchers in this field have tentatively concluded that technological progress in an industry may be determined more by the industry's scientific character and "technological opportunities" than by its market structure. There may simply be more ways to progress in the electronics and computer industries than in the brickmaking and cigarette industries, regardless of whether they are organized competitively or oligopolistically.

Automobiles: a case study[11]

The automobile industry provides an informative case study of oligopoly, illustrating many of the points made in this chapter. It also indicates that market structure is not permanent and, in particular, that foreign competition can upset the oligopolists' "quiet life."

Market structure Although there were over eighty auto manufacturers in the early 1920s, a number of mergers (most notably the combining of Chevrolet, Pontiac, Oldsmobile, Buick, and Cadillac into General Motors), many failures during the Great Depression of the 1930s, and the increasing importance of entry barriers—all tended to reduce numbers in the industry. Currently, three large firms dominate the market for domestically produced automobiles. General Motors (GM) is preeminent with about 55 percent of the market; Ford has 22 to 24 percent; and Chrysler, having bought out Amer-

[9] See Daniel Hamberg, "Invention in the Industrial Research Laboratory," *Journal of Political Economy*, April 1963, pp. 95–115.

[10] John Jewkes, David Sawers, and Richard Stillerman, *The Sources of Invention*, rev. ed. (New York: St. Martin's Press, Inc., 1968).

[11] This section draws heavily upon Walter Adams and James W. Brock, "The Automobile Industry," in Walter Adams (ed.), *The Structure of American Industry*, 7th ed. (New York: The Macmillan Company, 1986), pp. 126–171.

ican Motors in 1987, has about 18 to 20 percent. These firms are gigantic: According to *Forbes* magazine, GM, Ford, and Chrysler were the first, third, and twelfth largest manufacturing companies in United States in 1987 as measured by sales. And all three are leading truck manufacturers, produce a variety of household appliances, are involved in defense contracting, and have extensive overseas interests. GM has a virtual monopoly in producing buses and diesel locomotives in the United States.

Entry barriers Entry barriers are substantial as is evidenced by the fact that it has been about six decades since an American firm successfully entered the automobile industry. The primary barrier is economies of scale. It is estimated that the minimum efficient scale for a producer is about 300,000 units of output per year. However, given the uncertainties of consumer tastes, experts feel that a truly viable firm must produce at least two different models. Hence, to have a reasonable prospect of success a new firm would have to produce about 600,000 autos per year. The estimated cost of an integrated plant (involving the production of engines, transmissions, other components, and product assembly) might be as much as $3 billion. Other entry barriers include extensive advertising and the existence of far-flung dealer networks (GM has over 10,000 dealers and Ford has 5,500) which provide spare parts and repair service. A newcomer would face the expensive task of overcoming existing brand loyalties. Given that the domestic automobile industry spent $2.32 billion on advertising in 1987, this is no small matter.

Price leadership and profits The indicated industry structure—a few firms with high entry barriers—has been fertile ground for collusive or coordinated pricing. In practice, price leadership has characterized the industry for the past fifty years. GM has traditionally been the price leader. Each fall, when the new models are introduced, GM establishes prices for its basic models and Ford and Chrysler set the prices of their comparable models accordingly. (The details of how GM establishes its prices were outlined in the earlier section on cost-plus pricing.)

In the past several decades automobile prices have moved up steadily and at a rate significantly in excess of the overall rate of inflation. And despite large periodic declines in demand and sales, automobile prices have displayed considerable downward rigidity. (Rebates and financing subsidies during periods of slack demand are the exception to this rule.) Furthermore, price behavior has frequently been perverse in the sense that prices have been *increased* in the face of *declining* sales.

Over the years price leadership has proved to be very profitable. For example, over the 1947–1977 period the Big Three earned an average profit rate significantly greater than that of all United States manufacturing corporations taken as a whole. However, the fortunes of the Big Three have fluctuated dramatically since the late 1970s, with Chrysler being saved from bankruptcy in 1979 by a government bailout.

Styling and technology In addition to advertising, nonprice competition has centered upon styling and technological advance. In practice the former has been stressed over the latter. As early as the 1920s GM recognized that the replacement market was becoming increasingly important as compared to the market for first-time purchasers. Therefore, its strategy—later adopted by the other manufacturers—became one of annual styling changes accompanied by model proliferation. The purpose is to achieve higher sales and profits by encouraging consumers to replace their autos with greater frequency.

Technological progress in the industry presents a mixed picture. With respect to manufacturing processes, the industry has not altered its basic production techniques since Ford's introduction of the moving assembly line some seventy years ago. However, the industry has done a good job of adapting and improving upon new production technologies which others have pioneered.

Performance with respect to automotive technology offers a different picture. Since the 1920s, the industry's main attention has been on styling, not on engineering innovation. Progress has occurred. . . . But progress has been slow, the sources of innovations have frequently been supplier firms or foreign automobile manufacturers, and American manufacturers have often been slow to adopt improvements. The major changes have been in power brakes and steering, automatic transmission, and air conditioning, and even in these areas the pioneering work was frequently done elsewhere. Until the 1970s, there had been no fundamental changes in the basic engine, carburation, ignition, and suspension systems. Some manufacturers abroad have been more innovative in this area, offering diesel engines, Wankel engines, stratified charge engines, fuel injection, and pneumatic suspension systems. Other entrepreneurs have proposed fundamental alternatives to the internal combustion engine, such as steam and electric vehicles. Turbines frequently appeared to be a potential alternative. Yet, until pollution control requirements tightened in the 1970s, the auto companies showed at most only sporadic interest in fundamental changes and alternatives.

If the large size and tight concentration of the automobile companies had any special value for technological progress, it should have been in these risky areas of fundamental change. Yet, the record of the industry, particularly in the post-war period, is woefully lacking.[12]

Foreign competition In recent years the automobile market in the United States has become more competitive than the tight oligopolistic structure of the domestic industry would suggest. GM, Ford, and Chrysler have been challenged in the past two decades by foreign (particularly Japanese) producers. While the Big Three account for 96 percent of domestic *production,* they only account for about 75 percent of domestic *sales.*

The reasons for the growth of foreign competition are manifold. The OPEC-inspired increases in gasoline prices in the 1970s prompted a shift in consumer demand toward smaller, fuel-efficient imports from Japan and Germany. Many analysts contend that domestic producers seriously misjudged the scope and apparent permanence of this shift. In addition, many consumers perceive that imports have quality advantages. Indeed, the aforementioned emphasis of domestic producers upon styling rather than fundamental qualitative changes may have returned to plague them in the 1980s. Finally, lower overseas wages and higher labor productivity have given the Japanese and Koreans a substantial cost advantage on compact cars. It must be appended that import competition is centered upon the small-car segment of the market; foreign producers have negligible shares of the intermediate and large-car segments. Additionally, the relatively rapid decline in the international value of the dollar which began in early 1985 has greatly reduced the cost disadvantage facing American firms.

The response of the domestic automobile industry to enhanced foreign competition has been essentially twofold. In the first place, the industry—with the support of organized labor—successfully lobbied government for protection. The result, beginning in 1981, was "voluntary" import quotas on Japanese cars which effectively restrained competition. The reduced foreign competition allowed domestic manufacturers to boost their prices to consumers. For example, one authoritative estimate suggests that the import quotas strengthened the domestic oligopoly to the extent that on the average domestic producers earned an additional $400 in profits on each car sold in 1983. Given that the output of domestic producers was 7 million cars in 1983, the aggregate increase in profits of domestic manufacturers was $2.8 billion.[13] These estimates clearly indicate that American consumers have a great stake in free international trade and the competition it generates (Chapter 39).

An interesting and adverse side effect is that, although the import quotas officially expired in early 1985, the Japanese government has replaced them with its own quota system. The reason is that the restricted supply of Japanese automobiles in the American market permitted Japanese manufacturers to increase their prices and profits. Thus, the original import quotas have created what is in effect a Japanese export cartel.

The second response of domestic producers has been to co-opt and mitigate foreign competition by initiating an elaborate network of joint ownership arrangements and joint ventures with foreign producers. For example, Chrysler owns about one-fourth of Mitsubishi and imports both compact cars and parts from the latter. Mitsubishi in turn is a part owner of Korea's Hyundai Motor Company. General Motors has a joint production arrange-

[12] Lawrence J. White, "The Automobile Industry," in Walter Adams (ed.), *The Structure of American Industry,* 5th ed. (New York: The Macmillan Company, 1977), p. 205.

[13] Carving Up the Car Buyer," *Newsweek,* March 5, 1984, pp. 72–73. The estimates are those of Robert Crandall of The Brookings Institution. The import quotas further hurt American consumers by restricting the supply and increasing the prices of Japanese cars.

ment with Toyota in California and has significant ownership shares in other lesser-known Japanese auto manufacturers. Ford owns about one-fourth of Mazda. These arrangements cast a cloud of doubt over the contention that foreign competition has had an important "disciplining" effect upon American auto manufacturers. One can certainly contend that these joint-ownership and joint-production arrangements have the effects of enhancing concentration in the worldwide automobile industry and reducing independent decision making.

We have now finished our analysis of the four basic product market models—pure competition, pure monopoly, monopolistic competition, and oligopoly. The reader is advised to reexamine Table 25-1 to ensure that the main characteristics of each of these models are clearly understood.

CHAPTER SUMMARY

Oligopolistic industries are characterized by the presence of a few firms, each of which has a significant fraction of the market. Firms thus situated are mutually interdependent; the behavior of any one firm directly affects, and is affected by, the actions of rivals. Products may be virtually uniform or significantly differentiated. Underlying reasons for the evolution of oligopoly are economies of scale, other entry barriers, and the advantages of merger.

2 There are four major variants of oligopoly: **a** the kinked-demand model, **b** collusive oligopoly, **c** price leadership, and **d** cost-plus pricing.

3 Noncollusive oligopolists in effect face a kinked demand curve. This curve and the accompanying marginal-revenue curve help explain the price rigidity which characterizes such markets; they do not, however, explain the level of price.

4 The uncertainties inherent in noncollusive pricing are conducive to collusion. There is a tendency for collusive oligopolists to maximize joint profits—that is, to behave somewhat like pure monopolists. Demand and cost differences, the presence of a "large" number of firms, "cheating" through secret price concessions, recessions, and the antitrust laws are all obstacles to collusive oligopoly.

LAST WORD

The beer industry: oligopoly brewing?

As any beer can collector knows, the beer industry was once populated by hundreds of firms and an even larger number of brands. But this industry has increasingly become concentrated and is now an oligopoly.

The brewing industry has undergone profound changes since World War II which have tended to increase the degree of concentration in the industry. In 1947 slightly over 400 independent brewing companies existed in the United States. By 1967 the number had declined to 125 and by 1980 only 41 survived. While the five largest brewers sold only 19 percent of the nation's beer in 1947, the Big Five (Anheuser-Busch, Miller, Stroh, Heileman, and Coors) sold about 88 percent in 1987. Anheuser-Busch and Miller are dominant with 40 and 21 percent of the market respectively. Why the change?

Changes on the demand side of the market have contributed to the "shake-out" of small brewers from the industry. First, there is evidence that in the 1970s consumer tastes shifted from the stronger-flavored beers of the small brewers to the light, dry products of the larger brewers. Second, there has been a relative shift from the consump-

5 Price leadership is a less formal means of collusion whereby the largest or most efficient firm in the industry initiates price changes and the other firms follow.

6 With cost-plus or markup pricing, oligopolists esti-

tion of beer in taverns to consumption in the home. The significance of this change lies in the fact that taverns were usually supplied with kegs from local brewers to avoid the relatively high cost of shipping kegs. But the acceptance of metal containers for home consumption made it possible for large, somewhat distant brewers to compete with the local brewers because the former could now ship their products by truck or rail without breakage.

Developments on the supply side of the market have been even more profound. In particular, technological advances have speeded up the bottling or closing lines so that, for example, the number of cans of beer which could be filled and closed per minute increased from 900 to 1500 between 1965 and the late 1970s. Currently the most modern canning lines can close 2000 cans per minute. Large plants are also able to reduce labor costs through the automating of brewing and warehousing. Furthermore, plant construction costs per barrel are about one-third less for a 4.5-million-barrel plant than for a 1.5-million-barrel plant. As a consequence of these and other economies, it is estimated that unit production costs decline sharply up to the point at which a plant produces 1.25 million barrels per year. Average costs continue to decline, but less significantly, up to the 4.5-million-barrel capacity at which all scale economies seem to be exhausted. Evidence of the importance of scale economies is reflected in statistics which show that over time there has been a steady decline in breweries producing less than 1 million barrels per year. Given that the construction of a modern 4-million-barrel capacity brewery is about $250 million, economies of scale may now constitute a significant barrier to entry.

Although mergers have occurred, they have not been a fundamental cause of increased concentration in the brewing industry. Rather, mergers have been largely the result of failing small breweries selling out.

On the other hand, the ascendancy of the Miller Brewing Company from the seventh to the second largest producer in the 1970s was due in large measure to advertising and product differentiation. When Miller was acquired by the Phillip Morris Company in 1970, the new management made two salient changes. First, Miller High Life beer was "repositioned" into that segment of the market where potential sales were the greatest. Sold previously as the "champagne of beers," High Life had appealed heavily to upper-income consumers and women who only drank beer occasionally. Miller's new television ads featured young blue-collar workers who were inclined to be greater beer consumers. Second, Miller then developed its low-calorie Lite beer which was extensively promoted with the infusion of Phillip Morris advertising dollars. Lite proved to be the most popular new product in the history of the beer industry and contributed significantly to Miller's ascendancy in the industry.

But Anheuser-Busch has successfully fought off Miller's attempt to become the number one firm in the industry. Indeed, Miller's market share of 21 percent in 1984 was approximately the same as it was in 1979, while Anheuser-Busch's share increased from 27 to 34 percent over the same period. Undoubtedly, a lavish advertising budget has helped Anheuser-Busch to retain and enhance its dominant position. In 1987 it spent over $304 million on advertising as compared to Miller's $171 million.

Source: This synopsis is based upon Kenneth G. Elzinga, "The Beer Industry," in Walter Adams (ed.), *The Structure of American Industry*, 7th ed. (New York: Macmillan Publishing Co., Inc., 1986), pp. 203–238. Updated.

mate their unit costs at some target level of output and add a percentage "markup" to determine price.

7 Market shares in oligopolistic industries are usually determined on the basis of nonprice competition. Oligopolists emphasize nonprice competition because *a* advertising and product variations are less easy for rivals to match, and *b* oligopolists frequently have ample resources to finance nonprice competition.

8 The traditional view holds that the price–output results of oligopoly are similar to those of pure monopoly. The Schumpeter–Galbraith view is that oligopoly is conducive to technological progress and therefore results in better products, lower prices, and larger levels of output and employment than if the industry were organized more competitively.

TERMS AND CONCEPTS

oligopoly	price war
homogeneous and differentiated oligopoly	collusion
	cartel
concentration ratio	gentlemen's agreement
interindustry competition	price leadership
	cost-plus pricing
import competition	traditional and Schumpeter–Galbraith views
mutual interdependence	
kinked demand curve	

QUESTIONS AND STUDY SUGGESTIONS

1 Why do oligopolies exist? List five or six oligopolists whose products you own or regularly purchase. What distinguishes oligopoly from monopolistic competition?

2 "Fewness of rivals means mutual interdependence, and mutual interdependence means uncertainty as to how those few rivals will react to a price change by any one firm." Explain. Of what significance is this for determining demand and marginal revenue? Other things being equal, would you expect mutual interdependence to vary directly or inversely with the degree of product differentiation? With the number of firms? Explain.

3 What assumptions concerning a rival's responses to price changes underlie the kinked demand curve? Why is there a gap in the marginal-revenue curve? How does the kinked demand curve help explain oligopolistic price rigidity? What are the shortcomings of the kinked-demand model?

4 Why might price collusion occur in oligopolistic industries? Assess the economic desirability of collusive pricing. Explain: "If each firm knows that the price of each of its few rivals depends on its own price, how can the prices be determined?" What are the main obstacles to collusion? Apply these obstacles to the weakening of OPEC in the 1980s.

5 Assume the demand curve shown in question 4 in Chapter 26 applies to a pure monopolist which has a constant marginal cost of $4. What price and output will be most profitable for the monopolist? Now assume the demand curve applies to a two-firm industry (a "duopoly") and that each firm has a constant marginal cost of $4. If the firms collude, what price and quantity will maximize their joint profits? Demonstrate why it might be profitable for one of the firms to cheat. If the other firm becomes aware of this cheating, what will happen?

6 Explain how price leadership might evolve and function in an oligopolistic industry. Is cost-plus pricing compatible with collusion?

7 "Oligopolistic industries have both the means and the inclination for technological progress." Do you agree? Explain.

8 "If oligopolists really want to compete, they should do so by cutting their prices rather than by squandering millions of dollars on advertising and other forms of sales promotion." Do you agree? Why don't oligopolists usually compete by cutting prices?

9 Under what circumstances might the price–output results of pure monopoly be superior from society's viewpoint to those of oligopoly?

10 Using Figure 28-2, explain how a collusive oligopolist might increase its profits by offering secret price concessions to buyers. On the diagram, indicate the amount of additional profits which the firm may realize. What are the risks involved in such a policy?

11 Review the case study of the automobile industry and identify aspects of industry structure and behavior which are oligopolistic. What responses have domestic producers made to increasing foreign competition?

12 Assume that the diagram in Chapter 27's Last Word (page 553) pertains to pricing strategies rather than advertising strategies. In particular, substitute "low price" for "large budget" and "high price" for "small budget" in the diagram and again assume that the figures in each cell show profit payoffs to the two oligopolists. Use the diagram to explain (1) the mutual interdependence which characterizes oligopolistic industries and (2) why the two firms might find collusive pricing to be mutually advantageous. If the firms reach a collusive agreement to charge high prices, explain why each would have an incentive to cheat.

CHAPTER 29

Production and the demand for economic resources

The preceding four chapters have been concerned with the pricing and output of goods and services under a variety of product market structures. In producing any commodity, a firm must hire productive resources which, directly or indirectly, are owned and supplied by households. It is appropriate that we now turn from the pricing and production of goods to the pricing and employment of resources needed in accomplishing production. In terms of our circular flow diagram of the economy (Chapter 3), we now shift our attention from the bottom loop of the diagram, where firms supply and households demand products, to the top loop, where households supply and businesses demand resources. It is in part this reversal of roles which makes necessary a separate discussion of resource pricing.

Significance of resource pricing

There are a number of intertwined reasons for studying resource pricing.

1 Money incomes The most basic fact about resource prices is that they constitute a major determinant of money incomes. The expenditures which businesses make in acquiring economic resources flow as wage, rent, interest, and profit incomes to those households which in turn supply the human and property resources at their disposal.

2 Resource allocation Another important aspect of resource pricing is that, just as product prices ration finished goods and services to consumers, so resource prices allocate scarce resources among various industries and firms. An understanding of the manner in which resource prices negotiate the allocation of resources is particularly significant in view of the fact that, in a dynamic economy, the efficient allocation of resources over time calls for continuing shifts in resources among alternative uses.

3 Cost minimization To the firm, resource prices are costs, and to realize maximum profits a firm must produce the profit-maximizing output with the most efficient (least costly) combination of resources. Given technology, it is resource prices which play the major role in determining the quantities of land, labor, capital, and entrepreneurial ability that are to be combined in the productive process (Table 5-1).

4 Policy issues Finally, aside from these objective facets of resource pricing, there are a myriad of ethical questions and public policy issues surrounding the resource market. In particular, the amoral nature of resource prices results in considerable inequality in the personal distribution of income. Too, the age-old question of the sizes of the income shares going to specific groups is still very much alive. What is the proper distribution of the national income between "capitalist income" (profits, interest, and rents) and "labor income" (wages)? Should a special tax be levied on "excess" profits? Is it desirable for government to establish a wage floor in the form of a legal minimum wage? What about legal ceilings on interest rates? Are current government subsidies to the incomes of farmers justifiable? Chapter 37 is concerned with the facts and ethics of income distribution.

Complexities of resource pricing

Economists are in substantial agreement as to the basic principles of resource pricing. Yet there exists considerable disagreement and sometimes an element of confusion as to the variations in these general principles which must be made as they are applied to specific resources and particular markets. While economists are in general agreement that the pricing and employment of economic resources, or factors of production, are a supply and demand phenomenon, they also recognize that in particular markets, resource supply and demand may assume strange and often complex dimensions. This is further complicated by the fact that the operation of supply and demand forces may be muted or even largely supplanted by the policies and practices of government, business firms, or labor unions, not to mention a host of other institutional considerations.

Our major objective in this chapter is a limited one: to explain the basic factors which underlie the demand for economic resources. We shall couch our discussion in terms of labor, recognizing that the principles we outline are also generally applicable to land, capital, and entrepreneurial ability. In Chapter 30 we shall combine our understanding of resource demand with a discussion of labor supply in analyzing wage rates. Then in Chapter 31 we shall incorporate the supply side of the markets for property resources in analyzing the prices of, and returns to, land, capital, and entrepreneurial talent.

Marginal productivity theory of resource demand

The least complicated approach to resource demand is that which assumes a firm is hiring some specific resource in a competitive market and in turn is selling its product in a competitive market. The simplicity of this situation lies in the fact that under competition the firm can dispose of as little or as much output as it chooses at the going market price. The firm is selling such a negligible fraction of total output that it exerts no influence whatever on product price. Similarly, in the resource market, competition means that the firm is hiring such a small fraction of the total supply of the resource that its price is unaffected by the quantity the firm purchases.

RESOURCE DEMAND AS A DERIVED DEMAND

Having specified these simplified conditions, we can note the most crucial point: The demand for resources is a **derived demand**, that is, derived from the finished goods and services which resources help produce. Resources do not directly satisfy consumer wants, but do so indirectly by producing goods and services. No one wants to consume an acre of land, a John Deere tractor, or the labor services of a farmer, but households do want to consume the various food and fiber products which these resources help produce.

MARGINAL REVENUE PRODUCT (MRP)

The derived nature of resource demand correctly implies that the strength of the demand for any resource will depend upon (1) the productivity of the resource in helping to create a good, and (2) the market value or price of the good it is producing. In other words, a resource which is highly productive in turning out a commodity highly valued by society will be in great demand. On the other hand, demand will be very weak for a relatively unproductive resource which is only capable of producing some good not in great demand by households. There will be no demand for a resource which is phenomenally efficient in the production of something which no one will want to purchase!

The roles of productivity and product price in determining resource demand can be brought into sharper focus through Table 29-1. Here it is assumed that a firm is adding one variable resource—labor—to its fixed plant. Columns 1 through 3 remind us that the law of diminishing returns will be applicable in this situation, causing the **marginal product** (MP) of labor to fall beyond some point.[1] For simplicity's sake, it is here assumed that diminishing marginal product sets in with the first worker hired.

But we have already emphasized that the derived demand for a resource depends not only upon the productivity of that resource but also upon the price of the commodity it produces. Column 4 adds this price information. Note that product price is constant, in this case at $2, because we are supposing a competitive product market. Multiplying column 2 by column 4, we get the total-revenue data of column 5. From these total-revenue data we can readily compute **marginal revenue product** (MRP)—*the increase in total revenue resulting from*

[1] It might be helpful to review the subsection entitled "Law of Diminishing Returns" in Chapter 24 at this point.

the use of each additional variable input (labor, in this case). This is indicated in column 6.

RULE FOR EMPLOYING RESOURCES: MRP = MRC

The MRP schedule—columns 1 and 6—constitutes the firm's demand schedule for labor. To explain why this is so, we must first discuss the rule which guides a profit-seeking firm in hiring any resource. *To maximize profits, a firm should hire additional units of any given resource so long as each successive unit adds more to the firm's total revenue than it does to its total costs.* Economists have special terms which designate what each additional unit of labor or other variable resource adds to total cost and what it adds to total revenue. We have just noted that, by definition, MRP measures how much each successive worker adds to total revenue. The amount which each additional unit of a resource adds to the firm's total (resource) cost is called **marginal resource cost** (MRC). Thus we can restate our rule for hiring resources as follows: *It will be profitable for a firm to hire additional units of a*

TABLE 29-1 **The demand for a resource: pure competition in the sale of the product (hypothetical data)**

(1) Units of resource	(2) Total product	(3) Marginal product (MP), or Δ(2)	(4) Product price	(5) Total revenue, or (2) × (4)	(6) Marginal revenue product (MRP) or Δ(5)
0	0		$2	$ 0	
		7			$14
1	7		2	14	
		6			12
2	13		2	26	
		5			10
3	18		2	36	
		4			8
4	22		2	44	
		3			6
5	25		2	50	
		2			4
6	27		2	54	
		1			2
7	28		2	56	

resource up to the point at which that resource's MRP is equal to its MRC. If the number of workers a firm is currently hiring is such that the MRP of the last worker exceeds his or her MRC, the firm can clearly profit by hiring more workers. But if the number being hired is such that the MRC of the last worker exceeds the MRP, the firm is hiring workers who are not "paying their way," and it can thereby increase its profits by laying off some workers. The reader will recognize that this **MRP = MRC rule** is very similar to the MR = MC profit-maximizing rule employed throughout our discussion of price and output determination. The rationale of the two rules is the same, but the point of reference is now *inputs* of resources, rather than *outputs* of product.

MRP IS A DEMAND SCHEDULE

Just as product price and marginal revenue are equal in a purely competitive product market, so *resource price and marginal resource cost are equal when a firm is hiring a resource competitively.* In a purely competitive labor market the wage rate is set by the total, or market, supply of, and the market demand for, labor. Because it hires such a small fraction of the total supply of labor, a single firm cannot influence this wage rate. This means that total resource cost increases by exactly the amount of the going wage rate for each additional worker hired; the wage rate and MRC are equal. It follows that so long as it is hiring labor competitively, *the firm will hire workers to the point at which their wage rate (or MRC) is equal to their MRP.*[2]

Accordingly, employing the data in column 6 of Table 29-1, we find that if the wage rate is $13.95, the firm will hire only one worker. This is so because the first worker adds $14 to total revenue and slightly less—$13.95—to total costs. For each successive worker, however, we find that MRC exceeds MRP, indicating that it will not be profitable to hire any of those workers. If the wage rate is

[2] The logic here is the same as that which allowed us to change the MR = MC profit-maximization rule to *P* = MC for the purely competitive seller of Chapter 25.

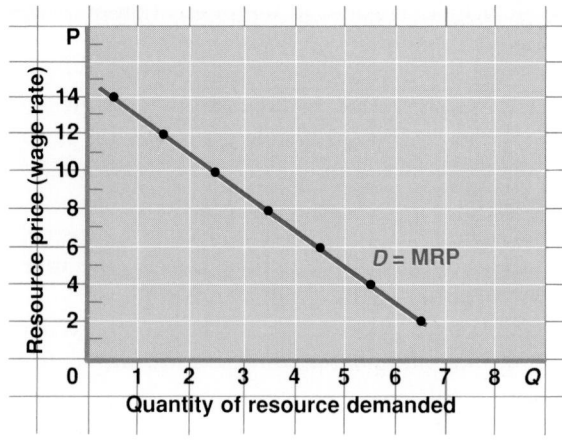

FIGURE 29-1

The purely competitive seller's demand for a resource

The MRP curve is the resource demand curve. The location of the curve depends upon the marginal productivity of the resource and the price of the product. Under pure competition product price is constant; therefore, diminishing marginal productivity is the sole reason why the resource demand curve is down-sloping.

$11.95, we apply the same reasoning and discover that it will pay the firm to hire both the first and second workers. Similarly, if the wage rate is $9.95, three will be hired. If $7.95, four. If $5.95, then five. And so forth. It is evident that *the MRP schedule constitutes the firm's demand for labor, because each point on this schedule (curve) indicates the number of workers which the firm would hire at each possible wage rate which might exist.* This is shown graphically in Figure 29-1.[3]

[3] The rationale employed here is familiar to us. Recall in Chapter 25 that we applied the price-equals-marginal-cost or *P* = MC rule for the profit-maximizing *output* to discover that the portion of the competitive firm's short-run marginal-cost curve lying above average variable cost is the short-run *product* supply curve (Figure 25-6). Presently we are applying the MRP = MRC rule for the profit-maximizing *input* to the firm's MRP curve and determining that this curve is the input or *resource* demand curve.

RESOURCE DEMAND UNDER IMPERFECT COMPETITION

Our analysis of labor demand becomes slightly more complex when we assume that the firm is selling its product in an imperfectly competitive market. Pure monopoly, oligopoly, and monopolistic competition in the product market all mean that the firm's product demand curve is downsloping; that is, the firm must accept a lower price in order to increase its sales. Table 29-2 takes this into account. The productivity data of Table 29-1 are retained in columns 1–3, but it is now assumed in column 4 that product price must be lowered in order to sell the marginal product of each successive worker. The MRP of the purely competitive seller falls for one reason: Marginal product diminishes. But the MRP of the imperfectly competitive seller falls for two reasons: Marginal product diminishes, **and** product price falls as output increases.

It must be emphasized that the lower price which accompanies every increase in output applies in each case not only to the marginal product of each successive worker but also to all prior units which otherwise could have been sold at a higher price. To illustrate: The second worker's marginal product is 6 units. These 6 units can be sold for $2.40 each or, as a group, for $14.40. But this is *not* the MRP of the second worker. Why? Because in order to sell these 6 units, the firm must take a 20-cent price cut on the 7 units produced by the first worker—units which could have been sold for $2.60 each. Thus, the MRP of the second worker is only $13.00 [= $14.40 − (7 × 20 cents)]. Similarly, the third worker's MRP is $8.40. Although the 5 units this worker produces are worth $2.20 each in the market, the third worker does not add $11.00 to the firm's total revenue when account is taken of the 20-cent price cut which must be taken on the 13 units produced by the first two workers. In this case the third worker's MRP is only $8.40 [= $11.00 − (13 × 20 cents)]. And so it is for the other figures in column 6.

The net result is that the MRP curve—the resource demand curve—of the imperfectly competitive producer tends to be less elastic than that of a purely competitive producer. At a wage rate or MRC of $11.95, both the purely competitive and the imperfectly competitive seller will hire two workers. But at $9.95, the competitive firm will hire three and the imperfectly competitive firm only two. And at $7.95, the purely competitive firm will take on four employees and the imperfect com-

TABLE 29-2 **The demand for a resource: imperfect competition in the sale of the product (hypothetical data)**

(1) Units of resource	(2) Total product	(3) Marginal product (MP), or Δ(2)	(4) Product price	(5) Total revenue, or (2) × (4)	(6) Marginal revenue product (MRP), or Δ(5)
0	0		$2.80	$ 0	
1	7	7	2.60	18.20	$18.20
2	13	6	2.40	31.20	13.00
3	18	5	2.20	39.60	8.40
4	22	4	2.00	44.00	4.40
5	25	3	1.85	46.25	2.25
6	27	2	1.75	47.25	1.00
7	28	1	1.65	46.20	−1.05

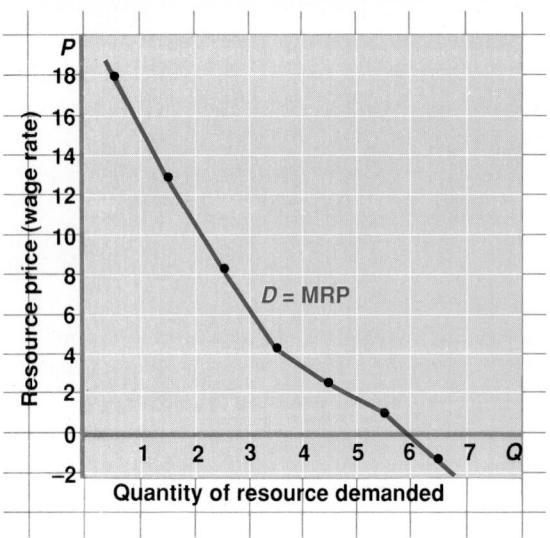

FIGURE 29-2

The imperfectly competitive seller's demand for a resource

An imperfectly competitive seller's resource demand curve slopes downward because marginal product diminishes and product price falls as output increases.

output in the product market. Other things being equal, the imperfectly competitive seller will produce less of a product than would a purely competitive seller. In producing this smaller output, it will demand fewer resources.

But one important qualification is pertinent. We noted in Chapters 26 and 28 that the market structures of pure monopoly and oligopoly *might* be conducive to technological progress and to a higher level of production, more employment, and lower prices in the long run than would a purely competitive market. The resource demand curve in these cases would not be restricted.

MARKET DEMAND FOR A RESOURCE

Can we now derive the market demand curve for a resource? Yes, we can. You will recall that the total, or market, demand curve for a product is developed by summing horizontally the demand curves of all individual buyers in the market. Similarly, the market demand curve for a particular resource can be derived in essentially the same fashion, that is, by summing the individual demand or MRP curves for all firms hiring that resource.[5]

petitor only three. This difference in elasticity can be readily visualized by graphing the MRP data of Table 29-2 as in Figure 29-2 and comparing them with Figure 29-1.[4]

It is not surprising that the imperfectly competitive producer is less responsive to wage cuts in terms of workers employed than is the purely competitive producer. The relative reluctance of the imperfect competitor to employ more resources and thereby produce more output when resource prices fall is merely the resource market reflection of the imperfect competitor's tendency to restrict

[4] Note that the points in Figures 29-1 and 29-2 are plotted one-half way between each number of workers because MRP is associated with the *addition* of one more worker. Thus, in Figure 29-2, for example, the MRP of the second worker ($13.00) is plotted not at 1 or 2, but rather at $1\frac{1}{2}$. This "smoothing" technique also allows us to present a continuously downsloping curve rather than one which moves downward in discrete steps as each worker is hired.

[5] The matter is actually not quite this simple. The resource demand, or MRP, curve *for each firm* is drawn on the assumption that product price is constant. However, if a lowering of resource price causes *all firms* in this industry to hire more of the resource and thereby expand total output, we can expect product price to decline. The result is that the resource market demand curve will not be quite identical with the sum of the individual firms' demand curves for that resource. Recall that the resource demand curve of Figure 29-2 is steeper or less elastic than the curve of Figure 29-1 *because* the latter is based on a constant product price and the former upon the assumption that product price falls as output or product supply increases. So it is for the case at hand. A simple horizontal summing of the resource demand curves of the individual firms is unrealistically based upon an unchanging product price. The true market demand curve takes cognizance of the fact that product price will fall as *industry* output expands, and, hence, this curve will be steeper or less elastic than that based upon a constant product price. For details, consult Campbell R. McConnell and Stanley L. Brue, *Contemporary Labor Economics,* 2d ed. (New York: McGraw-Hill Book Company, 1989), pp. 125–127.

Changes in resource demand

What will alter the demand for a resource, that is, shift the demand curve? The very derivation of resource demand immediately suggests two related factors—the resource's productivity and the market price of the product it is producing. And our previous analysis of changes in product demand (Chapter 4) suggests another factor—changes in the prices of other resources.

CHANGES IN PRODUCT DEMAND

Because resource demand is a derived demand, it is not surprising that any change in the demand for the product will affect product price and therefore the MRP of the resource. The relevant generalization is that, other things being equal, *a change in the demand for the product that a particular type of labor is producing will shift labor demand in the same direction.* Thus, in Table 29-1, assume an increase in product demand which boosts product price from $2 to $3. If you calculate the new labor demand curve and plot it in Figure 29-1, you will find that it lies to the right of the old curve. Similarly, a drop in product demand and price will shift the labor demand curve to the left. Real-world examples: The 1987 stock market crash resulted in a decline in the volume of stocks traded daily and a consequent decline in the demand for stockbrokers, causing widespread layoffs on Wall Street. Similarly, the dramatic increases in the prices of oil, natural gas, and electricity which have occurred since the mid-1970s led to a rebirth of the demand for woodburning stoves. An interesting labor market impact was an increase in the demand for chimney sweeps. Finally, in late 1987 McDonald's used television commercials aimed at attracting housewives and retirees to work in its 1600 company-owned restaurants. Why did this recruitment campaign begin in 1987 rather than a decade or two earlier? A major reason was that more and more women were devoting their time to labor market work and thus had less time for meal preparation. The result was an increase in the demand for restaurant meals and an increase in the demand for fast-food workers which could not be entirely filled by teenagers, the traditional source of labor for fast-food restaurants.

PRODUCTIVITY CHANGES

Other things being unchanged, *a change in the productivity of labor will shift the labor demand curve in the same direction.* For example, if we were to double the MP data of column 3 in Table 29-1 we would find that the MRP data would also double, indicating an increase in labor demand.

Recall (Chapter 21) that the productivity of any resource can be altered in several ways. (1) The marginal productivity data for, say, labor will depend upon the quantities of other resources with which it is combined. The greater the amount of capital and land resources with which labor is combined, the greater will be the marginal productivity and the demand for labor. (2) Technological improvements will have the same effect. The better the quality of the capital, the greater the productivity of labor. Steelworkers employed with a given amount of real capital in the form of modern oxygen furnaces are more productive than when employed with the same amount of real capital embodied in the old open-hearth furnaces. (3) Improvements in the quality of the variable resource itself—labor—will increase the marginal productivity and therefore the demand for labor. In effect, we have a new demand curve for a different, more skilled, kind of labor.

All these considerations, incidentally, are important in explaining why the average level of (real) wages is higher in the United States than in most foreign nations. American workers are generally healthier and better trained than those of foreign nations, and in most industries they work with a larger and more efficient stock of capital goods and more abundant natural resources than do the workers of most other countries. This spells a strong demand for labor. On the supply side of the market, labor is *relatively* scarce as compared with most foreign nations. A strong demand and a relatively scarce supply result in high wage rates. This will be discussed further in Chapter 30.

PRICES OF OTHER RESOURCES

Just as changes in the prices of other products will change the demand for a specific commodity, so changes in the prices of other resources can be expected to alter the demand for a particular resource. And just as the effect of a change in the price of product X upon the demand for product Y depends upon whether X and Y are substitute or complementary goods (Chapter 4), so the effect of a change in the price of resource A upon the demand for resource B will depend upon their substitutability or their degree of complementarity.

Substitute resources Suppose in a certain production process that technology is such that labor and capital are substitutable for one another. In other words, a firm can produce some given output with a relatively small amount of labor and a relatively large amount of capital or vice versa. Now assume a decline in the price of machinery occurs. The resulting impact upon the demand for labor will be the net result of two opposed effects: the substitution effect and the output effect. First, the decline in the price of machinery will prompt the firm to substitute machinery for labor. This is the obvious adjustment to make if the firm seeks to produce any given output in the least costly fashion. At given wage rates, smaller quantities of labor will now be employed. In short, this **substitution effect** will decrease the demand for labor. Second, because the price of machinery has fallen, the costs of producing various outputs will also have declined. With lower costs, the firm will find it profitable to produce and sell a larger output. This greater output will increase the demand for all resources, including labor. For a reduction in the price of machinery, this **output effect** will increase the demand for labor.

The substitution and output effects are clearly working in opposite directions. For a decline in the price of machinery, the substitution effect decreases and the output effect increases the demand for labor. The net impact upon labor demand will depend upon the relative sizes of the two opposed effects. If the substitution effect outweighs the output effect, the reduction in the price of capital will cause the demand for labor to decline. If the reverse holds true, the demand for labor will increase. To generalize: *If the substitution effect outweighs the output effect, a change in the price of a substitute resource will cause the demand for labor to change in the same direction. If the output effect exceeds the substitution effect, a change in the price of a*

substitute resource will cause the demand for labor to change in the opposite direction.

Complementary resources Recall from Chapter 4 that certain products, such as cameras and film or computers and software, are called complementary goods in that they "go together" and are jointly demanded. Resources may also be complementary in that an increase in the quantity of one of them employed in the production process will require an increase in the amount used of the other as well, and vice versa. Suppose that a small manufacturer of metal products uses punch presses as its basic piece of capital equipment. Each press is designed to be operated by one worker; the machine is not automated—it won't run itself—and a second worker would be wholly redundant.

Assume that a significant technological advance in the production of these presses substantially reduces their costs. Now there can be no negative substitution effect because labor and capital must be used in fixed proportions, one person for one machine. Capital cannot be substituted for labor. But there is a positive output effect for labor. Other things being equal, the reduction in the price of capital goods means lower production costs. It will therefore be profitable to produce a larger output. In doing so the firm will use both more capital and more labor. When labor and capital are complementary, a decline in the price of machinery will increase the demand for labor through the output effect. Conversely, in the case of an *increase* in the price of capital, the output effect will reduce the demand for labor. Our generalization is that *a change in the price of a complementary resource will cause the demand for labor to change in the opposite direction.*

Recapitulation: The demand curve for labor will *increase* (shift rightward) when:
1 The demand for (and therefore the price of) the product produced by that labor increases
2 The productivity (MP) of labor increases
3 The price of a substitute input decreases, provided the output effect is greater than the substitution effect
4 The price of a substitute input increases, provided the substitution effect exceeds the output effect
5 The price of a complementary input decreases

Elasticity of resource demand

The considerations just discussed are responsible for shifts in the location of resource demand curves. Such changes in demand are to be carefully distinguished from a change in the quantity of a resource demanded. The latter, you will recall, does not entail a shift in the resource demand curve but rather a movement from one point to another on a stable resource demand curve, because of a change in the price of the specific resource under consideration. To illustrate: In Table 29-1 and Figure 29-1 we note that an increase in the wage rate from $5.95 to $7.95 will reduce the quantity of labor demanded from five to four workers.

This raises a question: What determines the sensitivity of producers to changes in resource prices? Or, more technically, what determines the elasticity of resource demand? Several long-standing generalizations provide some important insights in answering this question.

1 Rate of MP decline A purely technical consideration—the rate at which the marginal product of the variable resource declines—is important. *If the marginal product of labor declines slowly as it is added to a fixed amount of capital, the MRP, or demand curve for labor, will decline slowly and tend to be highly elastic.* A small decline in the price of such a resource will give rise to a relatively large increase in the amount demanded. Conversely, if the marginal productivity of labor declines sharply, the MRP, or labor demand curve, will decline rapidly. This means that a relatively large decline in the wage rate will be accompanied by a very modest increase in the amount of labor hired; resource demand will be inelastic.

2 Ease of resource substitutability The degree to which resources are substitutable for one another is a highly important determinant of elasticity. *The larger the number of good substitute resources available, the greater will be the elasticity of demand for a particular resource.* If a furniture manufacturer finds that some five or six different types of wood are equally satisfactory in making coffee tables, a rise in the price of any one type of wood may cause a very sharp drop in the amount demanded as the producer readily substitutes other woods. At the other extreme, it may be impossible to substitute; bauxite is absolutely essential in the production of aluminum ingots. This means that the demand for it by aluminum producers tends to be inelastic.

It is significant to note that *time* can play an important role in the input substitution process. For example, a firm's truck drivers may obtain a substantial wage increase with little or no immediate decline in employment. But over time, as the firm's trucks wear out and are replaced, the company may purchase larger trucks and thereby be able to deliver the same total output with fewer drivers. Alternatively, as the firm's trucks depreciate, it might turn to entirely different means of transportation. As a second example, it is notable that the Boeing 737-300 airplane was specifically designed to require only two pilots rather than the customary three.

3 Elasticity of product demand The elasticity of demand for any resource will depend upon the elasticity of demand for the product which it helps produce. *The greater the elasticity of product demand, the greater the elasticity of resource demand.* The derived nature of resource demand would lead us to expect this relationship. A small rise in the price of a product with great elasticity of demand will give rise to a sharp drop in output and therefore a relatively large decline in the amounts of the various resources demanded. This correctly implies that the demand for the resource is elastic. Indeed, our comparisons of resource demand when output is being sold competitively (Table 29-1 and Figure 29-1) on the one hand, and under imperfectly competitive conditions (Table 29-2 and Figure 29-2) on the other, have already suggested that, other things being the same, the greater the elasticity of product demand, the greater the elasticity of resource demand.

4 Labor cost–total cost ratio *Finally, the larger the proportion of total production costs accounted for by a resource, the greater will be the elasticity of demand for that resource.* The rationale here is rather evident. In the extreme, if labor costs were the only production cost, then a 20 percent increase in wage rates would shift the firm's cost curves upward by 20 percent. Given the elasticity of product demand, this substantial increase in costs would cause a relatively large decline in sales and a sharp decline in the amount of labor demanded. Labor demand would tend to be elastic. But if labor costs were only 50 percent of production costs, then a 20 percent increase in wage rates would only increase costs by 10 percent. Given the same elasticity of product demand, a relatively small decline in sales and therefore in the amount of labor would result. The demand for labor would tend to be inelastic.

Optimal combination of resources

Up to this point we have centered our discussion upon one variable input, namely, labor. But we know that in the long run firms are able to vary the amounts of *all* the resources which they use. It is therefore important to consider what combination of resources a firm will choose when all are variable. While our analysis will proceed on the basis of two resources, it can readily be extended to any number one chooses to consider.

Our discussion focuses upon two interrelated questions:

1 What is the least-cost combination of resources to use in producing *any* given level of output?
2 What combination of resources will maximize a firm's profits?

THE LEAST-COST RULE

When is a firm producing *any* given output with the **least-cost combination of resources?** The answer is: When the last dollar spent on each resource entails the same marginal product. That is, *the cost of any output is minimized when the marginal product per dollar's worth of each resource used is the same.* If we are thinking in terms of just two resources, labor and capital, the cost-minimizing position occurs where

$$\frac{\text{MP of labor}}{\text{price of labor}} = \frac{\text{MP of capital}}{\text{price of capital}} \qquad (1)$$

It is not difficult to see why the fulfillment of this condition means least-cost production. Suppose, for example, that the prices of capital and labor are both $1 per unit, but that capital and labor are currently being employed in such

amounts that the marginal product of labor is 9 and the marginal product of capital is 5. Our equation immediately tells us that this is clearly *not* the least costly combination of resources: MP_L/P_L is 9/1 and MP_C/P_C is 5/1. If the firm spends a dollar less on capital and shifts that dollar to labor, it will lose the 5 units of output produced by the marginal dollar's worth of capital, but will gain the 9 units of output from the employment of an extra dollar's worth of labor. *Net* output will increase by 4 $(= 9 - 5)$ units for the same total cost. Note that this shifting of dollars from capital to labor will push the firm down its MP curve for labor and back up its MP curve for capital, moving the firm toward a position of equilibrium where equation (1) is fulfilled. At that point the MP of both labor and capital might be, for example, 7.

Whenever the same total cost results in a greater total output, it means that the cost per unit—and therefore the total cost of any given level of output—is being reduced. Stated somewhat differently, to be able to produce a *larger* output with a *given* total-cost outlay is the same thing as being able to produce a *given* output with a *smaller* total-cost outlay. And as we have seen, the cost of producing any given output can be reduced so long as $MP_L/P_L \neq MP_C/P_C$. But when dollars have been shifted among capital and labor to the point at which equation (1) holds, then there are no further changes in the amounts of capital and labor employed which will further reduce costs. The least-cost combination of capital and labor is being realized for that output.

All the long run[6] cost curves developed in Chapter 24 and applied in the ensuing product market chapters implicitly assume that each possible level of output is being produced with the least costly combination of inputs. If this were not the case, then presumably there would exist lower attainable positions for the cost curves, and consequently there would be some other (larger) output and lower price at equilibrium. In terms of Chapter 26 a firm which combines resources in violation of the least-cost rule would incur X-inefficiency.

Note that the producer's least-cost rule is analogous to the consumer's utility-maximizing rule of

---

[6] We specify long run because the application of the least-cost rule assumes that the quantities of both labor and capital are variable.

Chapter 23. In achieving the utility-maximizing collection of goods, the consumer considers both his or her preferences as reflected in diminishing marginal-utility data *and* the prices of the various products. Similarly, a producer wants to minimize costs, just as the consumer seeks to maximize utility. In pursuing this combination of resources, the producer must consider both the productivity of the resource as reflected in diminishing marginal productivity data *and* the prices (costs) of the various resources. A firm may well find it profitable to employ very small amounts of an extremely productive resource if its price is particularly high. Conversely, it may be sensible to hire large amounts of a relatively unproductive resource if its price should turn out to be sufficiently low.

THE PROFIT-MAXIMIZING RULE

In order to maximize profits it is not sufficient to simply minimize costs. There are many different levels of output which a firm can produce in the least costly way. But there is only one unique output which will maximize profits. Recalling our earlier analysis of product markets, this profit-maximizing *output* is where marginal revenue equals marginal cost (MR = MC). Let us now derive a comparable rule from the standpoint of resource *inputs*.

The derivation of such a rule is quite simple. In deriving the demand schedule for labor early in this chapter we determined that the profit-maximizing quantity of labor to employ is that quantity at which the wage rate, or price of labor (P_L), equals the marginal *revenue* product of labor (MRP_L) or, more simply, $P_L = MRP_L$.

The same rationale applies to any other resource—for example, capital. Capital will also be employed in the profit-maximizing amount when its price equals its marginal revenue product, or $P_C = MRP_C$. Thus, in general, we can say that when hiring resources *in competitive markets,* a firm will realize the **profit-maximizing combination of resources** when each input is employed up to the point at which its price equals its marginal revenue product:

$$P_L = MRP_L$$
$$P_C = MRP_C$$

This rule is alternatively expressed as

$$\frac{MRP_L}{P_L} = \frac{MRP_C}{P_C} = 1 \qquad (2)$$

Note in equation (2) that it is not sufficient that the MRPs of the two resources be **proportionate to** their prices; the MRPs must be **equal to** their prices and the ratios therefore equal to 1. For example, if $MRP_L = \$15$, $P_L = \$5$, $MRP_C = \$9$, and $P_C = \$3$, the firm would be underemploying both capital and labor even though the ratios of MRP to resource price were identical for both resources. That is, the firm could expand its profits by hiring additional amounts of both capital and labor until it had moved down their downsloping MRP curves to the points at which MRP_L was equal to \$5 and MRP_C was \$3. The ratios would now be 5/5 and 3/3 and obviously equal to 1.[7]

---

[7] It is not a difficult matter to demonstrate that equation (2) is consistent with (indeed, the equivalent of) the $P = MC$ rule for determining the profit-maximizing output which we encountered in Chapter 25. We begin by taking the reciprocal of equation (2):

$$\frac{P_L}{MRP_L} = \frac{P_C}{MRP_C} = 1$$

We recall that, assuming pure competition in the product market, marginal revenue product, MRP, is found by multiplying marginal product, MP, by product price, P_x. Thus we can write:

$$\frac{P_L}{MP_L \cdot P_x} = \frac{P_C}{MP_C \cdot P_x} = 1$$

Multiplying through by product price, P_x, we get:

$$\frac{P_L}{MP_L} = \frac{P_C}{MP_C} = P_x$$

The two ratios measure marginal cost. That is, if we divide the cost of an additional input of labor or capital by the associated marginal product we have the addition to total cost, that is, the *marginal cost,* of each additional unit of output. For example, if the price of an extra worker (P_L) is \$10 and that worker's marginal product (MP_L) is, say, 5 units, then the marginal cost of each of those 5 units is \$2. The same reasoning applies to capital. We thus obtain:

$$MC_x = P_x$$

Our conclusion is that equation (2) in the text, showing the profit-maximizing combination of *inputs,* is the equivalent of our earlier $P = MC$ rule which identified the profit-maximizing *output*.

A subtle, but significant, point must be added: Although we have separated the two for discussion purposes, the profit-maximizing position of equation (2) subsumes the least-cost position of equation (1).[8] That is, a firm which is maximizing its profits *must* be producing the profit-maximizing output with the least costly combination of resources. If it is *not* using the least costly combination of labor and capital, then it could produce the same output at a smaller total cost and realize a larger profit. Thus, a necessary condition for profit maximization is the fulfillment of equation (1). But equation (1) is not a sufficient condition for profit maximization. It is quite possible for a firm to produce the "wrong" output, that is, an output which does not maximize profits, but to produce that output with the least costly combination of resources.

NUMERICAL ILLUSTRATION

A numerical illustration may be helpful in grasping the least-cost and profit-maximizing rules. In col-

[8] Note that if we divide the MRP numerators in equation (2) by product price we obtain equation (1).

umns 2, 3, 2', and 3' of Table 29-3 we show the total products and marginal products for various amounts of labor and capital which are assumed to be the only inputs needed in the production of product X. Both inputs are subject to the law of diminishing returns. We also assume that labor and capital are supplied in competitive resource markets at $8 and $12 respectively and that product X is sold competitively at $2 per unit. For both labor and capital we can determine the total revenue associated with each input level by multiplying total product by the $2 product price. These data are shown in columns 4 and 4'. This allows us to calculate the marginal revenue product of each successive input of labor and capital as shown in columns 5 and 5'.

Consider the following question: What is the least-cost combination of labor and capital to use in producing, say, 50 units of output? Answer: 3 units of labor and 2 units of capital. Note from columns 3 and 3' that in hiring 3 units of labor $MP_L/P_L = 6/8 = 3/4$ and for 2 units of capital

TABLE 29-3 **The least-cost and profit-maximizing combination of labor and capital (hypothetical data)***

Labor (price = $8)					Capital (price = $12)				
(1) Quantity	(2) Total product	(3) Marginal product	(4) Total revenue	(5) Marginal revenue product	(1') Quantity	(2') Total product	(3') Marginal product	(4') Total revenue	(5') Marginal revenue product
0	0	0	$ 0	$ 0	0	0	0	$ 0	$ 0
1	12	12	24	24	1	13	13	26	26
2	22	10	44	20	2	22	9	44	18
3	28	6	56	12	3	28	6	56	12
4	33	5	66	10	4	32	4	64	8
5	37	4	74	8	5	35	3	70	6
6	40	3	80	6	6	37	2	74	4
7	42	2	84	4	7	38	1	76	2

* To simplify, it is assumed in this table that the productivity of each resource is independent of the quantity of the other. For example, the total and marginal product of labor is assumed not to vary with the quantity of capital employed.

$MP_C/P_C = 9/12 = 3/4$, so equation (1) is fulfilled. And columns 2 and 2' indicate that this combination of labor and capital does, indeed, result in the specified 50 (= 28 + 22) units of output. How can we verify that costs are actually minimized? First, note that the total cost of employing 3 units of labor and 2 of capital is $48 [= (3 × $8) + (2 × $12)] or, alternatively stated, cost per unit of output is $.96 (= $48/50). Observe that there are other combinations of labor and capital which will yield 50 units of output. For example, 5 units of labor and 1 unit of capital will produce 50 (= 37 + 13) units, but we find that total cost is now higher at $52 [= (5 × $8) + (1 × $12)] which means that average unit cost has risen to $1.04 (= $52/50). Note that by employing 5 units of labor and 1 of capital the least-cost rule would be violated in that $MP_L/P_L = 4/8$ is less than $MP_C/P_C = 13/12$, indicating that more capital and less labor should be employed to produce this output. Similarly, 50 units of output also could be produced with 2 units of labor and 3 of capital. The total cost of the 50 units of output would again be $52 [= (2 × $8) + (3 × $12)], or $1.04 per unit. Here equation (1) is not fulfilled in that $MP_L/P_L = 10/8$ which exceeds $MP_C/P_C = 6/12$. This inequality suggests that the firm should use more labor and less capital. To recapitulate: While there may be several combinations of labor and capital capable of producing any given output—in this case 50 units—only that combination which fulfills equation (1) will minimize costs.

Second question: Will 50 units of output maximize the firm's profits? Answer: No, because the profit-maximizing rule stated in equation (2) is **not** fulfilled when employing 3 units of labor and 2 of capital. We know that in order to maximize profits any given input should be employed until its price equals its marginal revenue product ($P_L = MRP_L$ and $P_C = MRP_C$). But for 3 units of labor we find in column 5 that labor's MRP is $12 while its price is only $8. This means it is profitable to hire more labor. Similarly, for 2 units of capital we observe in column 5' that MRP is $18 and capital's price is only $12, indicating that more capital should be employed. Stated differently, when hiring 3 units of labor and 2 of capital to produce 50 units of output, the firm is underemploying both inputs. Labor and capital are both being used in less than profit-maximizing amounts. We find that the marginal

revenue products of labor and capital are equal to their prices and equation (2) is fulfilled when the firm is employing 5 units of labor and 3 units of capital. This is therefore the profit-maximizing combination of outputs.[9] The firm's total cost will be $76, which is made up of $40 (= 5 × $8) worth of labor and $36 (= 3 × $12) worth of capital. Total revenue of $130 is determined by multiplying total output of 65 (= 37 + 28) by the $2 product price or, alternatively, by simply summing the total revenue attributable to labor ($74) and to capital ($56). The difference between total revenue and total cost is, of course, the firm's economic profit which in this instance is $54 (= $130 − $76). Note that equation (2) is fulfilled when 5 units of labor and 3 of capital are employed: $MRP_L/P_L = 8/8 = MRP_C/P_C = 12/12 = 1$. The reader is urged to experiment with other combinations of labor and capital to demonstrate that they will yield an economic profit less than $54.

Our example also verifies our earlier assertion that a firm which is using the profit-maximizing combination of inputs is also necessarily producing the resulting output with the least cost. That is, in fulfilling equation (2) the firm is automatically fulfilling equation (1). In this case for 5 units of labor and 3 of capital we observe that $MP_L/P_L = 4/8 = MP_C/P_C = 6/12$. Questions 5 and 7 at the end of this chapter are also recommended to further your understanding of the least-cost and profit-maximizing combination of inputs.[10]

---

[9] Given that we are dealing with discrete (nonfractional) increases in the two outputs, you should also be aware that in fact the employment of 4 units of labor and 2 of capital is equally profitable. Stated differently, the fifth unit of labor's MRP and its price are equal (at $8), so that the fifth unit neither adds to, nor subtracts from, the firm's profits. The same reasoning applies to the third unit of capital.

[10] Footnote 5 in Chapter 30 modifies our least-cost and profit-maximizing rules for the situation in which a firm is hiring resources under imperfectly competitive conditions. Where there is imperfect competition in the resource market, the marginal resource cost (MRC)—the cost of an extra input—exceeds the resource price (P). Hence, we must substitute MRC for P in the denominators of equations (1) and (2).

Marginal productivity theory of income distribution

Our discussion of resource pricing provides us with the cornerstone of the view that economic justice is one of the outcomes of a competitive capitalist economy. Recall that Table 29-1 tells us, in effect, that labor receives an income payment equal to the marginal contribution which it makes to the firm's revenue. Bluntly stated, labor is paid what it is worth. Therefore, if one is willing to accept the ethical proposition "To each according to what one creates," the marginal productivity theory seems to provide a fair and equitable distribution of income. Because the marginal productivity theory is equally applicable to capital and land, the distribution of all incomes can be held as equitable.

At first glance an income distribution whereby workers and owners of property resources are paid in accordance with their contribution to output sounds eminently fair. But there are serious criticisms of the **marginal productivity theory of income distribution.**

1 Inequality   Critics argue that the distribution of income resulting from the marginal productivity theory is likely to be highly unequal because productive resources are very unequally distributed in the first place. Aside from differences in genetic endowments, individuals encounter substantially different opportunities to enhance their productivity through education and training. Some members of society may not be able to participate in production at all because of mental or physical handicaps and would obtain no income under a system of distribution based solely upon marginal productivity. The ownership of property resources is also highly unequal. Many landlords and capitalists obtain their property by inheritance rather than through their own productive effort. Hence, income from inherited property resources is at odds with the "To each according to what one creates" proposition. This line of reasoning can lead one to advocate government policies to modify the income distribution resulting from payments made strictly according to marginal productivity.

LAST WORD

Input substitution: the case of cabooses

Substituting among inputs—particularly when jobs are at stake—can be quite controversial.

We have found that a firm will achieve the least-cost combination of inputs when the last dollar spent on each makes the same contribution to total output. This rule also implies that a firm is unimpeded in changing its input mix in response to technological changes or changes in input prices. Unfortunately, in the real world the substitution of new capital for old capital and the substitution of capital for labor may be controversial and difficult to achieve.

Consider the case of railroad cabooses. The railroads claim that technological advance has made the caboose obsolete. In particular, railroads want to substitute a "trainlink" which can be attached to the coupler of the last car of a train. This small black box contains a revolving strobe light and instruments which monitor train speed, airbrake pressure, and other relevant data which it transmits to the locomotive engineer. The trainlink costs only

2 Monopsony and monopoly   The marginal productivity theory rests upon the assumption of competitive markets. We will find in Chapter 30 that labor markets, for example, are riddled with imperfections. Some employers exert monopsony power in hiring workers. And some workers, through labor unions and professional associations, brandish monopoly power in selling their services. Indeed,

$4000 in comparison to $80,000 for a new caboose. And, of course, the trainlink replaces one member of the train crew.

The railroads cite substantial cost economies—perhaps as much as $400 million per year—from this rearrangement of capital and labor inputs. But the United Transportation Union (UTU) which represents railroad conductors and brakemen fears that the recent trend toward the demise of the caboose portends a decline in the demand for its members. The union therefore has made a concerted, but largely unsuccessful, effort to halt the elimination of cabooses on trains. The UTU argues that the elimination of cabooses will reduce railroad safety.

The union contends that, unlike humans, trainlink cannot detect broken wheels or axles nor overheated bearings. From the vantage point of the railroads this looks like featherbedding, that is, the protection of unnecessary jobs. The railroads contend that available data show no safety differences between trains using and those not using cabooses. Indeed, safety may be enhanced without cabooses because many injuries are incurred by crew who are riding in cabooses.

While cabooses are virtually extinct in Europe, they are the rule in Canada. In the United States the railway unions have lobbied successfully for legislation in four states which makes cabooses mandatory. In all other states the use of cabooses remains a matter of collective bargaining negotiations. In any event, the case of cabooses indicates clearly that input substitution is not as simple as economic analysis would suggest.

the process of collective bargaining over wages suggests a power struggle over the division of income. In this struggle market forces—and income shares based upon marginal productivity—are pushed into the background. In short, we will find that, because of real-world market imperfections, wage rates and other resource prices frequently do *not* measure contributions to national output.

CHAPTER SUMMARY

1 Resource prices are a major determinant of money incomes, and simultaneously perform the function of rationing resources to various industries and firms.

2 The fact that the demand for any resource is derived from the product it helps produce correctly suggests that the demand for a resource will depend upon its productivity and the market value (price) of the good it is producing.

3 The marginal revenue product schedule of any resource is the demand schedule for that resource. This follows from an application of the rule that a firm hiring under competitive conditions will find it most profitable to hire a resource up to the point at which the price of the resource equals its marginal revenue product.

4 The demand curve for a resource is downsloping, because the marginal product of additional inputs of any resource declines in accordance with the law of diminishing returns. When a firm is selling in an imperfectly competitive market, the resource demand curve will fall for a second reason: Product price must be reduced in order to permit the firm to sell a larger output. The market demand for a resource can be derived by summing horizontally the demand curves of all firms hiring that resource.

5 The demand for a resource will change, that is, a resource demand curve will shift, as the result of *a* a change in the demand for, and therefore the price of, the product the resource is producing; *b* changes in the productivity of the resource due either to increases in the quantity or improvements in the quality of the resources with which a given resource is being combined, or improvements in the quality of the given resource itself; and *c* changes in the prices of other resources.

6 A decline in the price of resource A will typically result in a reduction in the demand for resource B (the substitution effect). But this reduction may be offset by the fact that the decline in the price of A will lower production costs, increasing the equilibrium output and therefore the demand for resource B (the output effect). There is no substitution effect, only an output effect, for resources which are complementary or jointly demanded.

7 The elasticity of resource demand will be greater *a* the slower the rate at which the marginal product of the resource declines, *b* the larger the number of good substitute resources available, *c* the greater the elasticity of demand for the product, and *d* the larger the proportion of total production costs attributable to the resource.

8 Any level of output will be produced with the least costly combination of resources when the marginal product per dollar's worth of each input is the same, that is, when

$$\frac{\text{MP of labor}}{\text{price of labor}} = \frac{\text{MP of capital}}{\text{price of capital}}$$

9 A firm will employ the profit-maximizing combination of resources when the price of each resource is equal to its marginal *revenue* product or, algebraically, when

$$\frac{\text{MRP of labor}}{\text{price of labor}} = \frac{\text{MRP of capital}}{\text{price of capital}} = 1$$

TERMS AND CONCEPTS

derived demand

marginal product

marginal revenue product

marginal resource cost

MRP = MRC rule

substitution and output effects

least-cost combination of resources

profit-maximizing combination of resources

marginal productivity theory of income distribution

QUESTIONS AND STUDY SUGGESTIONS

I What is the significance of resource pricing? Explain in detail how the factors determining resource demand differ from those underlying product demand. Explain the meaning and significance of the notion that the demand for a resource is a *derived* demand. Why do resource demand curves slope downward?

2 Complete the following labor demand table for a firm which is hiring labor competitively and selling its product in a competitive market.

a How many workers will the firm hire if the going wage rate is $27.95? $19.95? Explain why the firm will not hire a larger or smaller number of workers at each of these wage rates.

b Show in schedule form and graphically the labor demand curve of this firm.

c Now redetermine the firm's demand curve for labor on the assumption that it is selling in an imperfectly competitive market and that, although it can sell 17 units at $2.20 per unit, it must lower product price by 5 cents in order to sell the marginal product of each successive worker. Compare this demand curve with that derived in question 2b. Explain any differences.

3 Distinguish between a change in resource demand and a change in the quantity of a resource demanded. What specific factors might give rise to a change in resource demand? A change in the quantity of a resource demanded?

4 What factors determine the elasticity of resource demand? What effect will each of the following have upon the elasticity *or* the location of the demand for resource C, which is being used in the production of commodity X? Where there is any uncertainty as to the outcome, specify the causes of that uncertainty.
  a An increase in the demand for product X.
  b An increase in the price of substitute resource D.
  c An increase in the number of resources which are substitutable for C in producing X.
  d A technological improvement in the capital equipment with which resource C is combined.
  e A decline in the price of complementary resource E.
  f A decline in the elasticity of demand for product X due to a decline in the competitiveness of the product market.

5 Suppose the productivity of labor and capital are as shown on the next page. The output of these resources sells in a purely competitive market for $1 per unit. Both

Units of labor	Total product	Marginal product	Product price	Total revenue	Marginal revenue product
I	17		$2	$_____	
2	31	_____	2	_____	$_____
3	43	_____	2	_____	_____
4	53	_____	2	_____	_____
5	60	_____	2	_____	_____
6	65	_____	2	_____	_____

labor and capital are hired under purely competitive conditions at $1 and $3 respectively.

Units of capital	MP of capital	Units of labor	MP of labor
1	24	1	11
2	21	2	9
3	18	3	8
4	15	4	7
5	9	5	6
6	6	6	4
7	3	7	1
8	1	8	$\frac{1}{2}$

a What is the least-cost combination of labor and capital to employ in producing 80 units of output? Explain.

b What is the profit-maximizing combination of labor and capital for the firm to employ? Explain. What is the resulting level of output? What is the economic profit?

c When the firm is employing the profit-maximizing combination of labor and capital as determined in 5b, is this combination also the least costly way of producing the profit-maximizing output? Explain.

6 Using the substitution and output effects, explain how a decline in the price of resource A *might* cause an increase in the demand for substitute resource B. If resources C and D are complementary and used in fixed proportions, what will be the impact of an increase in the price of C upon the demand for D?

7 In each of the following four cases MRP_L and MRP_C refer to the marginal revenue products of labor and capital, respectively, and P_L and P_C refer to their prices. Indicate in each case whether the conditions are consistent with maximum profits for the firm. If not, state which resource(s) should be used in larger amounts and which resource(s) should be used in smaller amounts.

    a $MRP_L = \$8$; $P_L = \$4$; $MRP_C = \$8$; $P_C = \$4$.
    b $MRP_L = \$10$; $P_L = \$12$; $MRP_C = \$14$; $P_C = \$9$.
    c $MRP_L = \$6$; $P_L = \$6$; $MRP_C = \$12$; $P_C = \$12$.
    d $MRP_L = \$22$; $P_L = \$26$; $MRP_C = \$16$; $P_C = \$19$.

8 *Advanced analysis:* Demonstrate algebraically that the condition for the profit-maximizing level of output is the equivalent of the condition for the profit-maximizing combination of inputs.

9 If each input is paid in accordance with its marginal revenue product, will the resulting distribution of income be ethically just?

CHAPTER 30

The pricing and employment of resources: wage determination

Armed with some understanding of the strategic factors underlying resource demand, we must now introduce supply as it characterizes the markets for labor, land, capital, and entrepreneurial ability to see how wages, rents, interest, and profits are determined.

We discuss wages prior to other resource prices because to the vast majority of households the wage rate is the most important price in the economy; it is the sole or basic source of income. Indeed, about three-fourths of the national income is in the form of wages and salaries.

Our basic objectives in discussing wage determination are to (1) understand the forces underlying the general level of wage rates in the United States; (2) see how wage rates are determined in particular labor markets by presenting several representative labor market models; (3) analyze the impact of unions upon the structure and level of wages; (4) discuss the economic effects of the minimum wage; (5) explain wage differentials; and (6) introduce and briefly discuss the concept of investment in human capital.

Throughout this chapter we shall rely upon the marginal productivity theory of Chapter 29 as an explanation of labor demand.

Meaning of wages

Wages, or wage rates, are the price paid for the use of labor. Economists often employ the term "labor" broadly to apply to the payments received by (1) workers in the popular sense of the term, that is, blue- and white-collar workers of almost infinite variety; (2) professional people—lawyers, physicians, dentists, teachers, and so forth; and (3) owners of small businesses—barbers, plumbers, television repairers, and a host of retailers—for the labor services they provide in operating their own businesses.[1]

Though in practice wages may take the form of bonuses, royalties, commissions, and monthly salaries, we shall use the term "wages" to mean wage rates per unit of time—per hour, per day, and so forth. This designation has the advantage of reminding us that the wage rate is a price paid for the use of units of labor service. It also permits us to distinguish clearly between "wages" and "earnings," the latter depending upon wage rates *and* the number of hours or weeks of labor service supplied in the market.

It is important, too, to make a distinction between money or nominal wages and real wages. **Nominal wages** are the amount of money received per hour, per day, per week, and so on. **Real wages,** on the other hand, are the quantity of goods and services which one can obtain with one's nominal wages; real wages are the "purchasing power" of nominal wages. One's real wages de-

[1] This broad definition of labor, incidentally, encompasses individuals who would be considered as profit receivers in national income accounting. Hence, under this definition, wages would clearly amount to more than three-fourths of the national income.

pend upon one's nominal wages and the prices of the goods and services purchased. You may recall from Chapter 11 that the percentage change in real wages can be determined by subtracting the percentage change in the price level from the percentage change in nominal wages. Thus an 8 percent increase in nominal wages during a year when the price level increases by 5 percent yields a 3 percent increase in real wages. Note that nominal wages and real wages need not move together. For example, nominal wages may rise and real wages simultaneously decline *if* product prices rise more rapidly than do nominal wages. Unless otherwise indicated, our discussion will be couched in terms of real wage rates by assuming that the level of product prices is constant.

General level of wages

Wages tend to differ among nations, among regions, among various occupations, and among individuals. Wage rates are vastly higher in the United States than in China or India; they are generally higher in the north and east of the United States than in the south; plumbers are paid more than cotton pickers; physician Abrams may earn twice as much as physician Bennett for the same number of hours of work. Wage rates also differ by sex and race.

Our approach will involve moving from the general to the specific. In this section we are concerned with explaining why the general level of wages is higher in the United States than in most foreign nations. This explanation will be largely applicable to regional wage differences within nations. In the following section we shall seek to explain wages in terms of markets for specific types of labor. In both of these discussions a supply and demand approach will offer the most fruitful results.

The general or average level of wages, like the general level of prices, is a composite concept encompassing a wide range of different specific wage rates. This admittedly vague concept is a useful point of departure in making and explaining international and interregional wage comparisons. Statistical data indicate that the general level of real wages in the United States is among the highest in the world. The simplest explanation of this fact is that in the United States the demand for labor has been great in relation to the supply.

ROLE OF PRODUCTIVITY

Let us look behind these forces of demand and supply. We know that the demand for labor—or any other resource—depends upon its productivity. In general, the greater the productivity of labor, the greater the demand for it. And, given the total supply of labor, the stronger the demand, the greater the average level of real wages. The demand for American labor has been strong because it is highly productive. But why the high productivity? The reasons are several:

1 Capital American workers are used in conjunction with large amounts of capital equipment. For example, a recent estimate indicates that total physical capital (machinery and buildings) per worker is approximately $30,000.[2]

2 Natural resources Natural resources are very abundant in relation to the size of the labor force. The United States is richly endowed with arable land, basic mineral resources, and ample sources of industrial power. The fact that American workers have large amounts of high-quality natural resources to work with is perhaps most evident in agriculture where, historically, the growth of physical productivity has been dramatic (Chapter 35).

3 Technology The level of technological advance is generally higher in the United States than in most foreign nations. American workers in many industries use not only more capital equipment but better (technologically superior) equipment than do the vast majority of foreign workers. Similarly, work methods are steadily being improved through detailed scientific study and research.

4 Labor quality The health, vigor, education and training, and work attitudes of American workers

---

[2] David Alan Aschauer, "Is the Public Capital Stock Too Low?" *Chicago Fed Letter* (Federal Reserve Bank of Chicago), October 1987, p. 1.

have been generally superior to those of the labor of most other nations. This means that, even with the same quantity and quality of natural and capital resources, American workers would be more efficient than many of their foreign counterparts.

5 Other factors Less tangible, yet important, items underlying the high productivity of American labor are *(a)* the efficiency and flexibility of American management; *(b)* a business, social, and political environment which puts great emphasis upon production and productivity; and *(c)* the vast size of the domestic market, which provides the opportunity for firms to realize mass-production economies.

The reader will recognize that the aforementioned factors are merely a restatement of the cornerstones of economic growth (Chapter 21). It is also notable that the productivity of labor depends to a very great degree upon considerations other than the quality of labor itself, that is, upon the quantity and quality of the property resources at the worker's disposal.

REAL WAGES AND PRODUCTIVITY

The dependence of real hourly wages upon the level of productivity is indicated in Figure 30-1. Note the relatively close relationship in the long run between real hourly wages and output per

labor-hour. When one recalls that real income and real output are two ways of viewing the same thing, it is no surprise that *real income (earnings) per worker can increase only at about the same rate as output per worker.* More real output per hour means more real income to distribute for each hour worked. The simplest case is the classic one of Robinson Crusoe on the deserted island. The number of coconuts he can pick or fish he can catch per hour *is* his real wage per hour.

SECULAR GROWTH

But simple supply and demand analysis suggests that, even if the demand for labor is strong in the United States, increases in the supply of labor will cause the general level of wages to decline over time. It is certainly true that the American population and the labor force have grown significantly over the decades. However, these increases in the supply of labor have been more than offset by increases in the demand for labor stemming from the productivity-increasing factors discussed above. The result has been a long-run, or secular, increase in wage rates, as suggested by Figure 30-2. One authoritative study indicates that, for the 1889–1969 period, labor productivity, as measured by output per labor-hour, grew at an annual rate of 2.4 percent. This rate of growth translates into a doubling of real output and real wage rates in

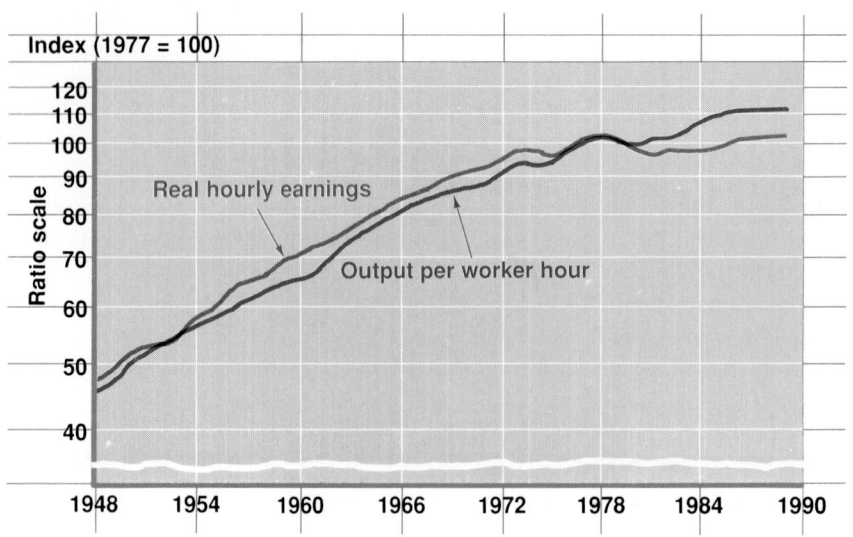

FIGURE 30-1

Output per hour and real average hourly earnings

Over a long period of years there has been a close relationship between real hourly earnings and output per worker-hour. *(Department of Labor, Monthly Labor Review.)*

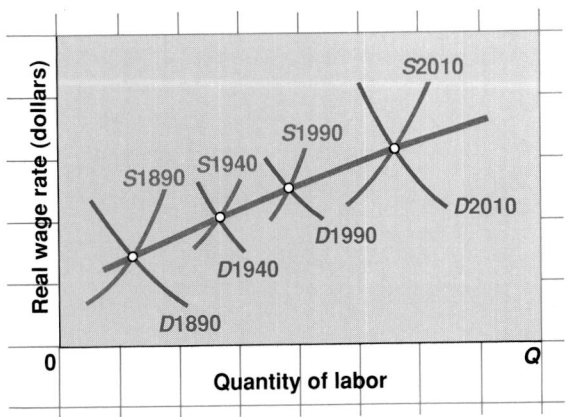

FIGURE 30-2

The secular trend of real wages in the United States

The productivity of American labor has increased substantially in the long run, causing the demand for labor to increase in relation to the supply. The result has been increases in real wages.

about thirty years (recall the "rule of 70"), and for the entire eighty-year period under consideration, something in excess of a sixfold increase in real wages per labor-hour.[3] Recall from Chapter 21 that the rate of productivity growth diminished significantly in the 1970s and early 1980s. Specifically, the annual rate of productivity growth was only 0.7 percent over the 1973–1981 period. In the 1980s, however, there has been a modest resurgence of productivity.

Wages in particular labor markets

We now turn from the general level of wages to specific wage rates. The question now is this: What determines the wage rate received by some specific type of worker? Demand and supply analysis again provides a revealing approach. Our analysis covers some half-dozen basic market models.

[3] Solomon Fabricant, *A Primer on Productivity* (New York: Random House, Inc., 1969), p. 14.

COMPETITIVE MODEL

A purely **competitive labor market** has the following characteristics: (1) a large number of firms are competing with one another in hiring a specific type of labor, (2) numerous qualified workers who have identical skills are independently supplying this type of labor service, and (3) "wage taker" behavior pertains to both firms and workers in that neither can exert control over the market wage rate.

Market demand Let us suppose that there are many—say, 200—firms demanding a particular type of semiskilled or skilled labor.[4] The total, or market, demand for this labor can be determined by summing horizontally the labor demand curves (the MRP curves) of the individual firms, as suggested in Figure 30-3a and b.

Market supply On the supply side of the picture, we assume there is no union; workers compete freely for available jobs. The supply curve for a particular type of labor will be upsloping, reflecting the fact that, in the absence of unemployment, hiring firms as a group will be forced to pay higher wage rates to obtain more workers. Why? Because the firms must bid these workers away from other industries, occupations, and localities. Within limits, workers have alternative job opportunities; that is, they may work in other industries in the same locality, or they may work in their present occupations in different cities or states. In a full-employment economy the group of firms in this particular labor market must pay higher and higher wage rates to attract this type of labor away from these alternative job opportunities. Similarly, higher wages are necessary to induce individuals not currently in the labor force to seek employment.

Stated more technically, the market supply curve rises because it is an *opportunity cost* curve. In order to attract workers to this particular employment the wage rate paid must cover the oppor-

[4] These firms need not be in the same industry; industries are defined in terms of the products they produce and not of the resources they employ. Thus, firms producing wood-frame furniture, window and door frames, and cabinets will all demand carpenters.

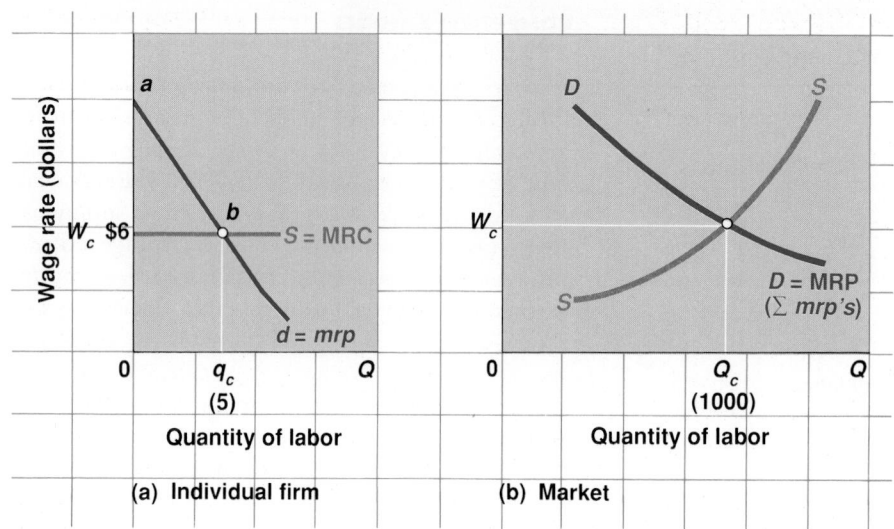

FIGURE 30-3

The supply of, and the demand for, labor in a single competitive firm (a) and in a competitive market (b)

In a competitive labor market the equilibrium wage rate W_c and number of workers employed Q_c are determined by supply SS and demand DD, as shown in (b). Because this wage rate is given to the individual firm hiring in the market, its labor supply curve, $S = MRC$, is perfectly elastic, as in (a). The firm finds it most profitable to hire workers up to the MRP = MRC point. The area $Oabq_c$ represents the firm's total revenue of which OW_cbq_c is its total wage cost; the remaining area W_cab is available for paying nonlabor resources.

tunity costs of alternative uses of time spent, either in other labor markets, in household activities, or in leisure. Higher wages attract more people to this employment—people who were not attracted by lower wages because their opportunity costs were too high.

Market equilibrium The equilibrium wage rate and the equilibrium level of employment for this type of labor are determined by the intersection of the labor demand and labor supply curves. In Figure 30-3b the equilibrium wage rate is W_c ($6), and the number of workers hired is Q_c (1000). To the individual firm the wage rate W_c is given. Each of the many hiring firms employs such a small fraction of the total available supply of this type of labor that none can influence the wage rate. Technically, the supply of labor is perfectly elastic to the individual firm, as shown by S in Figure 30-3a. Each individual firm will find it profitable to hire workers up to the point at which the going wage rate is equal to labor's MRP. This is merely an

application of the MRP = MRC rule developed in Chapter 29. (Indeed, the demand curve in Figure 30-3a is based upon Table 29-1.) As Table 30-1 indicates, *because resource price is given to the individual competitive firm, the marginal cost of that resource* (MRC) *will be constant and equal to resource price (the wage rate).* In this case the wage rate and hence the marginal cost of labor are constant to the individual firm. Each additional worker hired adds precisely his or her wage rate ($6 in this case) to the firm's total resource cost. The firm then will maximize its profits by hiring workers to the point at which their wage rate, and therefore marginal resource cost, equals their marginal revenue product. In Figure 30-3a the "typical" firm will hire q_c (five) workers.

It is significant to note that the firm's total revenue from the hiring of q_c workers can be found by summing their MRPs. In this case the total revenue from the five workers is indicated by the area $Oabq_c$ in Figure 30-3a. Of this total revenue, the area OW_cbq_c is the firm's total wage cost and the

TABLE 30-1 **The supply of labor: pure competition in the hire of labor (hypothetical data)**

(1) Units of labor	(2) Wage rate	(3) Total labor cost (wage bill)	(4) Marginal resource (labor) cost
0	$6	$ 0	
1	6	6	$6
2	6	12	6
3	6	18	6
4	6	24	6
5	6	30	6
6	6	36	6

triangular area $W_c ab$ represents additional revenue available to reward other inputs such as capital, land, and entrepreneurship.

MONOPSONY MODEL

We have just seen that in a purely competitive labor market each employer hires too small an amount of labor to influence the wage rate. Each firm is a "wage taker" in that it can hire as little or as much labor as it needs at the market wage, as reflected in its perfectly elastic labor supply curve.

Let us now consider the case of **monopsony,** which describes an employer which has monopolistic buying (hiring) power. Monopsony entails the following characteristics:
1 The given firm's employment is a large portion of the total employment of a particular kind of labor.
2 This type of labor is relatively immobile, either geographically or in the sense that, if workers sought alternative employment, they would have to acquire new skills.
3 The firm is a "wage maker" in that the wage rate it must pay varies directly with the number of workers it chooses to employ.

In some instances the monopsonistic power of employers is virtually complete in the sense that there is only one major employer in a labor market. For example, the economies of some towns and cities depend almost entirely upon one major firm. A silver-mining concern may be the basic source of employment in a remote Colorado town. A New England textile mill, a Wisconsin paper mill, or a farm-belt food processor may provide a large proportion of the employment in its locality. Anaconda Mining is the dominant employer in Butte, Montana. In other cases *oligopsony* may prevail; three or four firms may each hire a large portion of the supply of labor in a particular market. Our study of oligopoly correctly suggests that there is a strong tendency for oligopsonists to act in concert— much like a monopsonist—in hiring labor.

The important point is this: When a firm hires a considerable portion of the total available supply of a particular type of labor, its decision to employ more or fewer workers will affect the wage rate paid to that labor. Specifically, *if a firm is large in relation to the labor market, it will have to pay a higher wage rate in order to obtain more labor.* For simplicity's sake let us suppose there is only one employer of a particular type of labor in a specified geographic area. In this extreme case, the labor supply curve to that firm and the total supply curve for the labor market are identical. This supply curve, for reasons already made clear, is upsloping, indicating that the firm must pay a higher wage rate to attract more workers. This is shown by *SS* in Figure 30-4. The supply curve is in effect the average-cost-of-labor curve from the firm's perspective; each point on it indicates the wage rate (cost) per worker which must be paid to attract the corresponding number of workers.

But the higher wages involved in attracting *additional* workers will also have to be paid to *all* workers currently employed at lower wage rates. If not, labor morale will surely deteriorate, and the employer will be plagued with serious problems of labor unrest because of the wage-rate differentials existing for the same job. As for cost, the payment of a uniform wage to all workers will mean that the cost of an extra worker—the marginal resource (labor) cost (MRC)—will exceed the wage rate by the amount necessary to bring the wage rate of all workers currently employed up to the new wage level. Table 30-2 illustrates this point. One worker can be hired at a wage rate of $6. But the hire of a second worker forces the firm to pay a higher wage

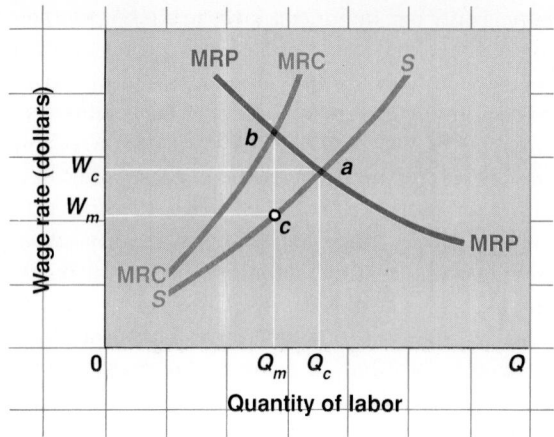

FIGURE 30-4

The wage rate and level of employment in a monopsonistic labor market

In a monopsonistic labor market the employer's marginal resource (labor) cost curve (MRC) lies above the labor supply curve (S). Equating MRC with labor demand MRP at point b, the monopsonist will hire Q_m workers (as compared with Q_c under competition) and pay the wage rate W_m (as compared with the competitive wage W_c).

of $7. Marginal resource (labor) cost is $8—the $7 paid the second worker plus a $1 raise for the first worker. Stated differently, total labor cost is $14 (= 2 × $7) rather than $13, which would be the case if the first worker was paid $6 and the second

TABLE 30-2 **The supply of labor: monopsony in the hire of labor (hypothetical data)**

(1) Units of labor	(2) Wage rate	(3) Total labor cost (wage bill)	(4) Marginal resource (labor) cost
0	$ 5	$ 0	
1	6	6	$ 6
2	7	14	8
3	8	24	10
4	9	36	12
5	10	50	14
6	11	66	16

paid $7. Hence, the MRC of the second worker is $8 (= $14 − $6), not the $7 wage rate paid the second worker. Similarly, the marginal labor cost of the third worker is $10—the $8 which must be paid to attract this worker from alternative employments plus $1 raises for the first two workers. The important point is that *to the monopsonist, marginal resource (labor) cost will exceed the wage rate.* Graphically, the MRC curve (columns 1 and 4 in Table 30-2) will lie above the average-cost, or supply, curve of labor (columns 1 and 2 in Table 30-2). This is shown graphically in Figure 30-4.

How much labor will the firm hire, and what wage rate will it pay? To maximize profits the firm will equate marginal resource (labor) cost with the MRP.[5] The number of workers hired by the monopsonist is indicated by Q_m, and the wage rate paid, W_m, is indicated by the corresponding point on the resource supply, or average-cost-of-labor, curve. It is particularly important to contrast these results with those which a competitive labor market would have yielded. With competition in the hire of labor, the level of employment would have been greater (Q_c), and the wage rate would have been higher (W_c). It simply does not pay the monopsonist to hire workers up to the point at which the wage rate and labor's MRP are equal. *Other things being equal, the monopsonist maximizes its*

---

[5] The fact that MRC exceeds resource price when resources are hired or purchased under imperfectly competitive (monopsonistic) conditions calls for appropriate adjustments in Chapter 29's least-cost and profit-maximizing rules for hiring resources. [See equations (1) and (2) in the "Optimal Combination of Resources" section of Chapter 29.] Specifically, we must substitute MRC for resource price in the denominators of our two equations. That is, with imperfect competition in the hiring of both labor and capital, equation (1) becomes

$$\frac{MP_L}{MRC_L} = \frac{MP_C}{MRC_C} \tag{1'}$$

and equation (2) is restated as

$$\frac{MRP_L}{MRC_L} = \frac{MRP_C}{MRC_C} = 1 \tag{2'}$$

As a matter of fact, equations (1) and (2) can be regarded as special cases of (1') and (2') in which firms happen to be hiring under purely competitive conditions and resource price is therefore equal to, and can be substituted for, marginal resource cost.

profits by hiring a smaller number of workers and thereby paying a less-than-competitive wage rate. In the process, society gets a smaller output,[6] and workers get a wage rate less by *bc* than their marginal revenue product. Just as a monopolistic seller finds it profitable to restrict product output to realize an above-competitive price for its goods, so the monopsonistic employer of resources finds it profitable to restrict employment in order to depress wage rates and therefore costs, that is, to realize below-competitive wage rates.[7]

In fact, monopsonistic labor markets are not common in our economy. There are typically a large number of potential employers for most workers, particularly when these workers are occupationally and geographically mobile. Also, as we shall see momentarily, unions often counteract monopsony power in labor markets. Nevertheless, economists have found evidence of monopsony in such diverse labor markets as those for nurses, professional athletes, public school teachers, newspaper employees, and some building trades workers.

In the case of nurses the major employers in most localities are a relatively small number of hospitals. Furthermore, the highly specialized skills of nurses are not readily transferable to other occupations. It has been found in accordance with the monopsony model that, other things being equal, the smaller the number of hospitals in a town or city (that is, the greater the degree of monopsony), the lower the beginning salaries of nurses.[8]

The market for professional athletes is also of interest. Although *potential* employers are quite numerous, the market is characterized by ingenious collusive devices by which employers have attempted with considerable success to limit competition in the hire of labor. The National Football League, the National Basketball Association, and the American and National Baseball Leagues have established systems of rules which tend to tie a player to one team and prevent him from selling his talents to the highest bidder on the open (competitive) market. In particular, through the new player draft, the team which selects or "drafts" a player has the exclusive right to bargain a contract with that player. Furthermore, the so-called reserve clause in each player's contract gives his team the exclusive right to purchase his services for the next season. Though recent court cases and collective bargaining agreements which stipulate "free agency" for experienced players have tended to make the labor markets for professional athletes somewhat more competitive, collusive monopsony persists.

As detailed in this chapter's Last Word, empirical studies have shown that prior to 1976 baseball players (despite very high salaries) were paid substantially less than their estimated MRPs, which is, of course, consistent with Figure 30-4. However, beginning in 1976 players were allowed to become "free agents"—in other words, they became free to sell their services to any interested team—after their sixth season of play. A comparison of the salaries of the first group of free agents with their estimated MRPs indicates that the competitive bidding of teams for free agents brought their salaries and MRPs into close accord as our competitive model suggests.

SOME UNION MODELS

Thus far, we have been content to assume that workers are actively competing in the sale of their labor services. In a good many markets, workers "sell" their labor services collectively through unions. To envision the economic impact of unions in the simplest context, let us suppose a union is formed in an otherwise competitive labor market. That is, a union is now bargaining with a relatively large number of employers. Later we shall consider the case where the union faces a large single employer, that is, a monopsonist.

---

[6] This is analogous to the monopolist's restricting output as it sets product price and output on the basis of marginal revenue, not product demand. In this instance, resource price is set on the basis of marginal labor (resource) cost, not resource supply.

[7] Will a monopsonistic employer also be a monopolistic seller in the product market? Not necessarily. The New England textile mill may be a monopsonistic employer, yet face severe domestic and foreign competition in selling its product. In other cases—for example, the automobile and steel industries—firms have both monopsonistic and monopolistic (oligopolistic) power.

[8] C. R. Link and J. H. Landon, "Monopsony and Union Power in the Market for Nurses," *Southern Economic Journal,* April 1975, pp. 649–659.

Unions seek many goals. The basic economic objective, however, is to raise wage rates. The union can pursue this objective in several different ways.

Increasing the demand for labor   From the union's point of view, the most desirable technique for raising wage rates is to increase the demand for labor. As shown in Figure 30-5, an increase in the demand for labor will result in *both* higher wage rates and more jobs. The relative sizes of these increases will depend upon the elasticity of labor supply.

But how might a union increase labor demand? The answer is by altering one or more of the determinants of labor demand (Chapter 29). Specifically, a union can attempt to (1) increase the demand for the product or service it is producing, (2) enhance labor productivity, or (3) alter the prices of other inputs. Let us briefly explore these techniques in the order stated.

I INCREASE PRODUCT DEMAND   Unions may attempt to increase the demand for the products they help produce—and hence increase the derived demand for their own labor services—by advertising, political lobbying, or "featherbedding."

Union television ads urging consumers to "buy the union label" are relevant. More specifically,

the International Ladies Garment Workers Union (ILGWU) has joined with its employers to finance advertising campaigns to bolster the demand for their products. And in 1984 the Communications Workers of America (CWA) helped finance a $2 million "Call or Buy Union" campaign to convince telephone users to choose the long-distance services and equipment of AT&T and Western Union Corporation, which together provided almost 100,000 CWA jobs.

On the political front it is not surprising to find construction unions lobbying for new highway or urban renewal projects. Similarly, teachers' unions and associations push for increased public spending on education. Unions connected with the aerospace industry might lobby to increase military spending. And it is no accident that some unions have vigorously supported their employers in seeking protective tariffs or import quotas designed to exclude competing foreign products. In the 1980s the steelworkers and the automobile workers both sought such forms of protection. Thus, a decline in the supply of imported cars through tariffs or negotiated agreements between nations, will increase their prices, thereby increasing the demand for highly substitutable American-made autos and boosting the derived demand for American auto workers.

Some unions have sought to expand the demand for labor by forcing make-work, or "featherbedding," rules upon employers. Prior to fairly recent court rulings, the Railway Brotherhoods forced railroads to hire train crews of a certain minimum size; diesel engines had to have a fireman even though there was no fire.

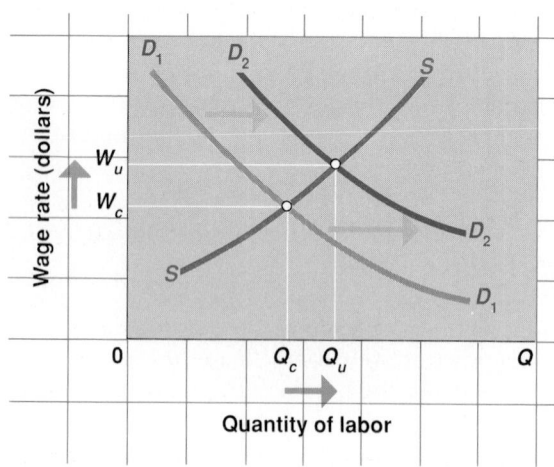

FIGURE 30-5

Unions and the demand for labor

When unions can increase the demand for labor (D_1D_1 to D_2D_2), higher wage rates (W_c to W_u) and a larger number of jobs (Q_c to Q_u) can be realized.

2 INCREASE PRODUCTIVITY   While many of the decisions which affect labor productivity—for example, decisions concerning the quantity and quality of real capital—are made unilaterally by management, it is significant to note that there is a growing interest in establishing joint labor-management committees designed to increase labor productivity.

3 INCREASE PRICES OF SUBSTITUTES   Unions might enhance the demand for their own labor by effecting an increase in the prices of substitute resources. A good example is that unions—whose workers are generally paid significantly more than the mini-

mum wage—strongly support increases in the minimum wage. An alleged reason for this position is that unions want to increase the price of potentially substitutable low-wage, nonunion labor. A higher minimum wage for nonunion workers will deter employers from substituting them for union workers, thereby bolstering the demand for union workers. Similarly, unions can also increase the demand for their labor by supporting public actions which *reduce* the price of a complementary resource. For example, unions in industries which use large amounts of energy might actively oppose rate increases proposed by electric or natural gas utilities. Where labor and energy are complementary, energy price increase might reduce the demand for labor through Chapter 29's output effect.

Unions recognize that their capacity to influence the demand for labor is tenuous and uncertain. As many of our illustrations imply, unions are frequently trying to forestall *declines* in labor demand rather than actually increasing it. In view of these considerations, it is not surprising that union efforts to increase wage rates have concentrated upon the supply side of the market.

Exclusive or craft unionism Unions may boost wage rates by reducing the supply of labor. Historically, the labor movement has favored policies designed to restrict the supply of labor to the economy as a whole in order to bolster the general level of wages. Labor unions have supported legislation which has (1) restricted immigration, (2) reduced child labor, (3) encouraged compulsory retirement, and (4) enforced a shorter workweek.

More relevant for present purposes is the fact that specific types of workers have adopted through unions a host of techniques designed to restrict their numbers. This has been especially true of *craft unions*—unions which comprise workers of a given skill, such as carpenters, bricklayers, and plumbers. These unions have in many instances forced employers to agree to hire only union workers, thereby giving the union virtually complete control of the supply of labor. Then, by following restrictive membership policies—long apprenticeships, exorbitant initiation fees, the limitation or flat prohibition of new members—the union causes an artificial restriction of the labor supply. As indicated in Figure 30-6, this results in higher wage rates. For obvious reasons, this approach to achiev-

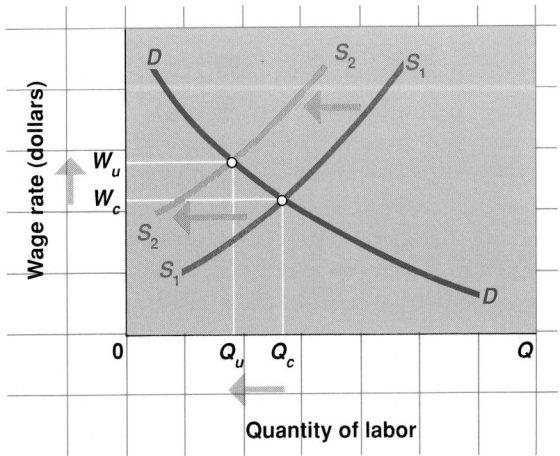

FIGURE 30-6

Exclusive or craft unionism

By reducing the supply of labor (S_1S_1 to S_2S_2) through the use of restrictive membership policies, exclusive unions achieve higher wage rates (W_c to W_u). However, the restriction of labor supply also reduces the number of workers employed (Q_c to Q_u).

ing wage increases is called **exclusive unionism.** Higher wages are the result of excluding workers from the union and therefore from the supply of labor.

Occupational licensing is another widely used means of restricting the supplies of specific kinds of labor. Here a group of workers in an occupation will pressure state or municipal governments to pass a law which provides that, say, barbers (physicians, plumbers, beauticians, egg graders, pest controllers) can practice their trade only if they meet certain specified requirements. These requirements might specify the level of educational attainment, amount of work experience, the passing of an examination, and personal characteristics ("the practitioner must be of good moral character"). The licensing board which administers the law is typically dominated by members of the licensed occupation. The result is self-regulation which is conducive to policies that reflect self-interest. In short, the imposition of arbitrary and irrelevant entrance requirements or the construction of an unnecessarily stringent examination can restrict the number of entrants to the occupation. Ostensibly, the purpose of licensing is to protect consumers from incompetent practitioners. But in fact licensing laws are frequently abused in that the number of qualified workers is artificially restricted, resulting in above-competitive wages and earnings for those in the occupation as suggested by Figure 30-6. Furthermore, licensing requirements often specify a residency requirement which tends to inhibit the interstate movement of qualified workers. It is estimated that some 600 occupations are now licensed in the United States.

Many economists feel that the very high earnings of physicians have been attributable in part to the ability of the American Medical Association (AMA) to control the licensing of doctors. Practicing physicians must be licensed and licenses are awarded only to graduates of medical schools approved by the AMA. By restricting the number of approved schools and by indirectly influencing the number of medical school acceptances, the AMA has allegedly restricted the supply of physicians relative to demand and thereby increased the incomes of licensed doctors.[9]

Inclusive or industrial unionism Most unions, however, do not attempt to limit their membership. On the contrary, they seek to organize all available or potential workers. This is characteristic of the so-called *industrial unions*—unions, such as the automobile workers and steelworkers, which seek all unskilled, semiskilled, and skilled workers in a given industry as members. A union can afford to be exclusive when its members are skilled craftsmen for whom substitute workers are not readily available in quantity. But a union that comprises largely unskilled and semiskilled workers will undermine its own existence by limiting its membership and thereby causing numerous highly substitutable nonunion workers to be readily available for employment.

If an industrial union is successful in including virtually all workers in its membership, firms will be under great pressure to come to terms at the wage rate demanded by the union. Why? Because by going on strike the union can deprive the firm of its entire labor supply.

[9] See, for example, Richard B. Freeman, *The Over-Educated American* (New York: Academic Press, 1976), pp. 118–120.

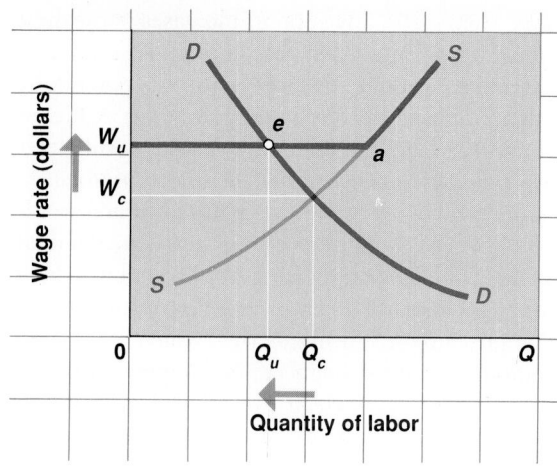

FIGURE 30-7

Inclusive or industrial unionism

By organizing virtually all available workers and thereby controlling the supply of labor, inclusive industrial unions may impose a wage rate, such as W_u, which is above the competitive wage rate W_c. The effect is to change the labor supply curve from SS to W_uaS. At the W_u wage rate, employers will cut employment from Q_c to Q_u.

Inclusive unionism is illustrated in Figure 30-7. Initially, the competitive equilibrium wage rate is W_c, and the level of employment is Q_c. Now suppose an industrial union is formed, and it imposes a higher, above-equilibrium wage rate of, say, W_u. The imposition of this wage rate changes the supply curve of labor to the firm from the preunion SS curve to the postunion W_uaS curve shown by the dark orange line.[10] No workers will be forthcoming at a wage rate less than that demanded by the union. If the employers decide it is better to pay this higher wage rate than to suffer a

[10] Technically, the imposition of the wage rate W_u makes the labor supply curve perfectly elastic over the W_ua range in Figure 30-7. If employers hire any number of workers within this range, the union-imposed wage rate is effective and must be paid, or the union will supply no labor at all—the employers will be faced with a strike. If the employers want a number of workers in excess of W_ua, they will have to bid up wages above the union's minimum. This situation will only occur if the market demand curve for labor shifts rightward so that it intersects the aS range of the labor supply curve.

strike, they will cut back on employment from Q_c to Q_u.

In slightly more technical terms, by agreeing to the union's W_u wage demand, individual employers become "wage takers" at this wage and therefore face a perfectly elastic labor supply curve over the $W_u a$ range. Because labor supply is perfectly elastic, MRC is equal to the W_u wage over this range. The Q_u level of employment results from employers equating MRC $(= W_u)$ with MRP as embodied in the labor demand curve.

Note that at W_u there is an excess supply or surplus of labor in the amount ea. In the absence of the union—that is, in a purely competitive labor market—we might expect these unemployed workers to accept lower wages and the wage rate would thereby fall to the W_c competitive equilibrium level. But this doesn't happen because workers are acting collectively through their union. Workers cannot individually offer to work for less than W_u; nor can employers contractually pay less.

WAGE INCREASES AND UNEMPLOYMENT

Have unions in fact been successful in raising the wages of their members? Although we defer a detailed treatment of this question until Chapter 38, the best evidence suggests that union members on the average achieve a 10 to 15 percent wage advantage over nonunion workers.

As Figures 30-6 and 30-7 suggest, the wage-raising actions of both exclusive and inclusive unionism cause employment to decline. A union's success in achieving above-equilibrium wage rates is tempered by the consequent decline in the number of workers employed. This unemployment effect can act as a restraining influence upon union wage demands. A union cannot expect to maintain solidarity within its ranks if it seeks a wage rate so high that joblessness will result for, say, 20 or 30 percent of its members.

The unemployment impact of wage increases might be mitigated from the union's standpoint in two ways. First, the normal growth of the economy increases the demand for most kinds of labor through time. Thus a rightward shift of the labor demand curves in Figures 30-6 and 30-7 could offset, or more than offset, any unemployment effects which would otherwise be associated with the indi-

cated wage increases. There would still be an employment restricting aspect to the union wage increases but it would take the form, not of an absolute decline in the number of jobs, but rather of a decline in the rate of growth of job opportunities.

Second, the size of the unemployment effect will depend upon the elasticity of demand for labor. The more inelastic the demand, the smaller will be the amount of unemployment which accompanies a given wage-rate increase. If they have sufficient bargaining strength, unions *may* obtain provisions in their collective bargaining agreements which reduce the substitutability of other inputs for labor and thereby reduce the elasticity of demand for union labor. For example, a union may be able to force employer acceptance of rules which forestall the introduction of new machinery and equipment. Or the union may bargain successfully for severance or layoff pay which increases the cost to the firm of substituting capital for labor when wage rates are increased. Similarly, the union might be able to gain a contract provision which prohibits the firm from subcontracting production to nonunion (lower-wage) firms, thus effectively restricting the substitution of cheaper labor for union workers. For these and other reasons the unemployment restraint upon union wage demands may be less pressing than our exclusive and inclusive union models suggest.

BILATERAL MONOPOLY MODEL

Now let us suppose that a strong industrial union is formed in a labor market which is monopsonistic rather than competitive. In other words, let us combine the monopsony model with the inclusive unionism model. The result is a case of **bilateral monopoly.** The union is a monopolistic "seller" of labor in that it controls the labor supply and can exert an influence over wage rates; it faces a monopsonistic employer (or combination of oligopsonistic employers) of labor who can also affect wages by altering its employment. Is this an extreme or special case? Not at all. In such important industries as steel, automobiles, meatpacking, and farm machinery, "big labor"—one huge industrial union—bargains with "big business"—a few huge industrial giants.

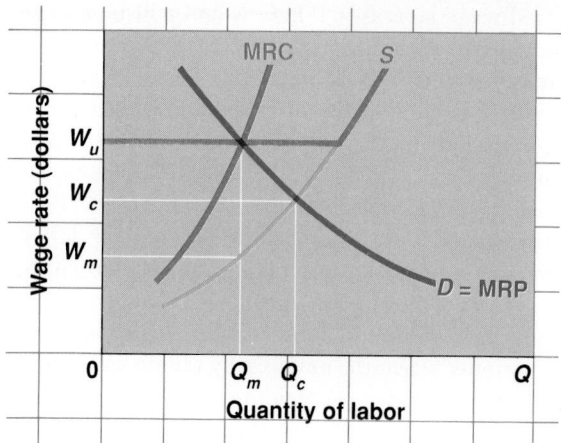

FIGURE 30-8

Bilateral monopoly in the labor market

When a monopsonistic employer seeks the wage rate W_m and the inclusive union it faces seeks an above-equilibrium wage rate such as W_u, the actual outcome is logically indeterminate.

This situation is shown in Figure 30-8, which merely superimposes Figure 30-7 upon 30-4. The monopsonistic employer will seek the below-competitive-equilibrium wage rate W_m and the union presumably will press for some above-competitive-equilibrium wage rate such as W_u. Which of these two possibilities will result? We cannot say with any certainty. The outcome is logically indeterminate in the sense that economic theory does not explain what the resulting wage rate will be. We should expect the resulting wage to lie somewhere between W_m and W_u. Beyond that, about all we can say is that the party with the most bargaining power and the most effective bargaining strategy will be able to get its opponent to agree to a wage close to the one it seeks.[11]

These comments suggest another important feature of the bilateral monopoly model. It is possible that the wage and employment outcomes might

[11] Economists have developed a number of bargaining theories. The ambitious reader should consult Bevars D. Mabry, *Economics of Manpower and the Labor Market* (New York: Intext Educational Publishers, 1973), chap. 13; and Campbell R. McConnell and Stanley L. Brue, *Contemporary Labor Economics*, 2d ed. (New York: McGraw-Hill Book Company, 1989), chap. 7.

be more socially desirable than the term bilateral monopoly would imply. Monopoly on one side of the market *might* in effect cancel out the monopoly on the other side of the market, yielding competitive or near-competitive results. If either the union or management prevailed in this market—that is, if the actual wage rate were determined at either W_u or W_m—employment would be restricted to Q_m (where MRP = MRC), which is below the competitive level. But now let us suppose the monopoly power of the union roughly offsets the monopsony power of management and a bargained wage rate of about W_c, which is the competitive wage, is agreed upon. Once management agrees to this wage rate, its incentive to restrict employment disappears; no longer can the employer depress wage rates by restricting employment. Thus management equates the bargained wage rate W_c (= MRC) with MRP and finds it most profitable to hire Q_c workers. In short, with monopoly on both sides of the labor market, it may be possible that the resulting wage rate and level of employment will be closer to competitive levels than if monopoly existed on only one side of the market.

THE MINIMUM-WAGE CONTROVERSY

Since the passage of the Fair Labor Standards Act in 1938, the United States has had a Federal **minimum wage.** The minimum wage has ranged from about 40 to 50 percent of the average wage paid to manufacturing workers and is currently $3.35 per hour. Roughly 90 percent of all nonsupervisory workers are covered. Proposals now in Congress call for a $4.55 minimum wage by 1992. Our analysis of the effects of union wage-fixing raises the much-debated question of the efficacy of this minimum-wage legislation as an antipoverty device.

Case against the minimum wage Critics, reasoning in terms of Figure 30-7, contend that the imposition of effective (above-equilibrium) minimum wages will simply push employers back up their MRP or labor demand curves because it is now profitable to hire fewer workers. The higher wage costs may even force some firms out of business. The result is that some of the poor, low-wage workers whom the minimum wage was designed to help will now find themselves out of work. Is it not obvious, critics query, that a worker who is unemployed at a minimum wage of $3.35 per hour is clearly worse off than if he or she were employed at the market wage rate of, say, $2.50 per hour?

A second major criticism is that the minimum wage is poorly targeted as an antipoverty device. The minimum wage is designed to provide a "living wage" which will allow less-skilled workers to earn enough so that they and their families can escape poverty. However, critics argue that the primary impact of the minimum wage is upon teenage workers, many of whom belong to relatively affluent families.

Case for the minimum wage Advocates allege that critics have analyzed the impact of the minimum wage in an unrealistic context. Figure 30-7, advocates claim, assumes a competitive and static market. The imposition of a minimum wage in a monopsonistic labor market (Figure 30-8) suggests that the minimum wage can increase wage rates without causing unemployment; indeed, higher minimum wages may even result in more jobs by eliminating the monopsonistic employer's motive to restrict employment. Furthermore, the imposition of an effective minimum wage may increase labor productivity, shifting the labor demand curve to the right and offsetting any unemployment effects which the minimum wage might otherwise induce. But how might a minimum wage increase productivity? First, a minimum wage may have a *shock effect* upon employers. That is, firms using low-wage workers may tend to be inefficient in the use of labor; the higher wage rates imposed by the minimum wage will presumably shock these firms into using labor more efficiently, and so the productivity of labor rises. Second, it is argued that higher wages will tend to increase the real incomes and therefore the health, vigor, and motivation of workers, making them more productive.

Evidence Which view is correct? The consensus from the large number of research studies of the minimum wage is that it does cause some unemployment, particularly among teenage (16 to 19 years) workers. Specifically, it is estimated that a 10 percent increase in the minimum wage will reduce teenage employment by 1 to 3 percent. Young adults (age 20 to 24) are also adversely af-

fected; a 10 percent increase in the minimum wage would reduce employment for this group by 1 percent or less. Blacks and women, who are disproportionately represented in low-wage occupations, tend to suffer larger declines in employment than do white males. The other side of the coin, of course, is that those who remain employed receive higher incomes and tend to escape poverty. The overall antipoverty effect of the minimum wage may thus be a mixed, ambivalent one. Those who lose their jobs are plunged deeper into poverty; those who remain employed tend to escape poverty.[12]

Wage differentials

We have discussed the general level of wages and the role of supply and demand in a series of specific labor market situations. We now consider the wage differences which persist between different occupations and different individuals in the same occupations. Why does a corporate executive or professional athlete receive $300,000, $500,000, or even $1,000,000 or more per year while laundry workers and retail clerks get a paltry $10,000 or $11,000 per year? Why is the average annual salary $485,000 for major-league baseball players as compared to $27,000 for acute-care nurses and $26,000 for schoolteachers? What rationale lies behind Chrysler Corporation paying its chairman, Lee Iacocca, total compensation of over $23 million in 1987? Table 30-3 indicates the substantial **wage differentials** which exist among certain common occupational groups. Our objective is to explain these kinds of differences.

Once again the forces of supply and demand provide a general answer. If the supply of a particular type of labor is very great in relation to the demand for it, the resulting wage rate will be low. But if demand is great and the supply relatively

---

[12] See Sar A. Levitan and Richard S. Belous, *More Than Subsistence: Minimum Wages for the Working Poor* (Baltimore: The Johns Hopkins University Press, 1979); empirical data are from Charles Brown, Curtis Gilroy, and Andrew Kohen, "The Effect of the Minimum Wage on Employment and Unemployment," *Journal of Economic Literature*, June 1982, pp. 487–528.

TABLE 30-3 **Average hourly and weekly earnings in selected industries, September 1988**

Industry	Average hourly gross earnings	Average weekly gross earnings
Motor vehicles	$16.12	$725
Bituminous coal	16.11	694
Construction	13.12	504
Chemicals	12.75	541
Printing and publishing	10.70	412
Fabricated metals	10.30	433
Food products	9.12	372
Hotels and motels	6.44	202
Retail trade	6.39	185
Laundries and dry cleaning	6.35	216
Apparel and finished textiles	6.19	230

Source: U.S. Department of Labor, *Employment and Earnings,* November 1988.

small, wages will be very high. Though it is a good starting point, this supply and demand explanation is not particularly revealing. We want to know *why* supply and demand conditions differ in various labor markets. To do this we must probe those factors which lie behind the supply and demand of particular types of labor.

If (1) all workers were homogeneous, (2) all jobs were equally attractive to workers, and (3) labor markets were perfectly competitive, all workers would receive precisely the same wage rate. As such, this is not a particularly startling statement. It merely suggests that in an economy having one type of labor and in effect one type of job, competition would result in a single wage rate for all workers. The statement is important in that it suggests the reasons why wage rates do differ in practice. (1) Workers are not homogeneous. They differ in capacities and in training and, as a result, fall into noncompeting occupational groups. (2) Jobs vary in attractiveness; the nonmonetary aspects of various jobs are not the same. (3) Labor markets are typically characterized by imperfections.

NONCOMPETING GROUPS

Workers are not homogeneous; they differ significantly in their mental and physical capacities *and* in their education and training. Hence, at any point in time the labor force can be thought of as falling into a number of **noncompeting groups,** each of which may be composed of one or several occupations for which the members of this group qualify. For example, a relatively small number of workers have the inherent abilities to be brain surgeons, concert violinists, and research chemists, and even fewer have the financial means of acquiring the necessary training. The result is that the supplies of these particular types of labor are very small in relation to the demand for them and that the consequent wages and salaries are high. These and similar groups do not compete with one another nor with other skilled or semiskilled workers. The violinist does not compete with the surgeon, nor does the garbage collector or retail clerk compete with either the violinist or the surgeon.

This is not to say that each of the thousands of specific occupations in the United States constitutes a noncompeting group of workers or that workers fall into isolated occupational compartments. A number of unskilled or semiskilled occupations may well belong to one noncompeting group. For example, gasoline station attendants, farmhands, and unskilled construction workers may all be classified in the same group, because each is capable of doing the others' jobs. Yet none of the workers in this group currently offers effective competition for computer programmers or electricians, who find themselves in other, more exclusive groups.

Over time, of course, workers may move from one noncompeting group to another as they are able to develop their native capacities through education and training. The assembly-line worker who has an IQ of 130 may become an accountant or a lawyer by going to night school. But here another obstacle arises: Higher education is a costly business. Our ambitious but low-income laborer does not have the same opportunity of entering the higher-paid occupational groups as do the off-spring of the lawyers and accountants who are already in those groups. And, needless to say, differences in inherent capacities provide an even more permanent obstacle to occupational mobility. Both native capacity and the opportunity to train oneself are unequally distributed, causing the wage differentials of noncompeting groups to persist.

The concept of noncompeting groups is a flexible one; it can be applied to various subgroups and even to specific individuals in a given group. Some especially skilled surgeons are able to command fees considerably in excess of their run-of-the-mill colleagues who perform the same operations. Michael Jordan, Larry Bird, Earvin "Magic" Johnson, Patrick Ewing, and a few others demand and get salaries many times that of the average professional basketball player. Why? Because in each instance their less-talented colleagues are only imperfect substitutes.

EQUALIZING DIFFERENCES

If a group of workers in a particular noncompeting group is equally capable of performing several different jobs, one might expect that the wage rate would be identical for each of these jobs. But this is not the case. A group of high school graduates may be equally capable of becoming bank clerks or unskilled construction workers. But these jobs pay different wages. In virtually all localities, construction laborers receive higher wages than do bank clerks.

These differences can be explained on the basis of the *nonmonetary aspects* of the two jobs. The construction job involves dirty hands, a sore back, the hazard of accidents, and irregular employment, both seasonally and cyclically. The banking job entails a white shirt, pleasant air-conditioned surroundings, and little fear of injury or layoff. Other things being equal, it is easy to see why workers will prefer picking up a deposit slip rather than a shovel. The result is that contractors must pay higher wages than banks pay to compensate for the unattractive nonmonetary aspects of construction jobs. These wage differentials are called **equalizing differences** because they must be paid to compensate for the nonmonetary differences in various jobs.

MARKET IMPERFECTIONS

The notion of noncompeting groups helps explain wage differentials between various jobs for which limited numbers of workers are qualified. Equalizing differences aid in understanding wage differentials on certain jobs for which workers in the same noncompeting group are equally qualified. Market imperfections in the form of various immobilities help explain wage differences paid on identical jobs.

1 Geographic immobilities Workers take root geographically. They are reluctant to leave friends, relatives, and associates, to force their children to change schools, to sell their houses, and to incur the costs and inconveniences of adjusting to a new job and a new community. Geographic mobility is likely to be particularly low for older workers who have seniority rights and substantial claims to pension payments upon retirement. Similarly, an optometrist or dental hygienist who is qualified to practice in one state may not meet the licensing requirements of other states, and therefore his or her ability to move geographically is impeded. Then, too, workers who may be willing to move may simply be ignorant of job opportunities and wage rates in other geographic areas. As Adam Smith noted over two centuries ago, "A man is of all sorts of luggage the most difficult to be transported." The reluctance or inability of workers to move causes geographic wage differentials for the same occupation to persist.

2 Institutional immobilities Geographic immobilities may be reinforced by artificial restrictions on mobility which are imposed by institutions. In particular, we have already noted that craft unions find it to their advantage to restrict their membership. After all, if carpenters and bricklayers become plentiful, the wages they can command will decline. Thus the low-paid nonunion carpenter of Brush, Colorado, may be willing to move to Chicago in the pursuit of higher wages. But his chances of successfully doing so are slim. He may be unable to get a union card; and no card, no job. The professions impose similar artificial restraints. For example, at most universities individuals lacking advanced degrees are automatically not considered for employment as teachers. Quite apart from one's competence as a teacher and one's command of the subject matter, a "union card"—an M.A. or preferably a Ph.D.—is the first requisite for employment.

3 Sociological immobilities Finally, we must acknowledge sociological immobilities. Despite legislation to the contrary, women workers frequently receive less pay than men working at the same job. The consequence of racial and ethnic discrimination is that blacks, Hispanics, and other minority groups are often forced to accept lower wages on given jobs than fellow workers receive. We shall have more to say on the matter of discrimination in Chapter 38.

A final point: It is typical that all three of these considerations—noncompeting groups, equalizing differences, and market imperfections—will play a role in the explanation of actual wage differentials. For example, the differential between the wages of a physician and a construction worker is largely explainable on the basis of noncompeting groups. Physicians fall into a noncompeting group where, because of mental and financial requisites to entry, the supply of labor is small in relation to demand, and wages are therefore high. In construction work, where mental and financial prerequisites are much less significant, the supply of labor is great in relation to demand and wages are low when compared with those of physicians. However, were it not for the unpleasantness of the construction worker's job and the fact that his craft union pursues restrictive membership policies, the differential would probably be even greater than it is.

Investment in human capital

We have just seen that the concept of noncompeting groups is a very important part of the explanation of wage differentials. Let us probe more carefully the question of why these noncompeting groups exist.

THE CONCEPT

According to *human capital theory,* noncompeting groups—and therefore wage differentials—exist to a large extent because of differing amounts of investment in human capital. A **human capital investment** is any action which improves the skills and abilities or, in other words, the productivity, of workers. Like business purchases of machinery and equipment, expenditures which increase one's productivity can be regarded as investments because *current* expenditures or costs are incurred with the intention that these costs will be more than compensated for by an enhanced *future* flow of earnings. Generally speaking, investments in human capital are of three kinds. Each of them is for the purpose of enhancing the productivity of workers and thereby increasing their wages and incomes.

First, expenditures on *education*—including general and specific education, formal and informal education, on-the-job training, and so forth—are the most obvious and perhaps most important kind of investment in human capital. Education contributes to a labor force which is more skilled and more productive. Second, expenditures on *health* are also significant. Better health—the consequence of expenditures on preventive medicine and medical care, improved diet, and better housing—gives rise to greater vigor, longevity, and higher productivity among workers. Finally, expenditures on *mobility* which shifts workers from relatively low to relatively high productivity uses are a less obvious form of investment in human capital. Like education, the geographic movement of workers involves incurring present costs to realize a future gain in the form of a higher market value of their labor services. In short, employable persons have embodied within themselves a future flow of labor services. According to human capital theory, the productivity and therefore the market value of labor services (one's wages) are determined to a great degree by the amount which the individual, his or her family, and employers have chosen to invest in education and training, health, and location.

THE INVESTMENT DECISION

It may seem odd or even repugnant to analyze investment in workers in the same way one would explore the decision to buy a machine. But, in fact, the two decisions are very similar. The current purchase of a machine (real capital) will give rise to a

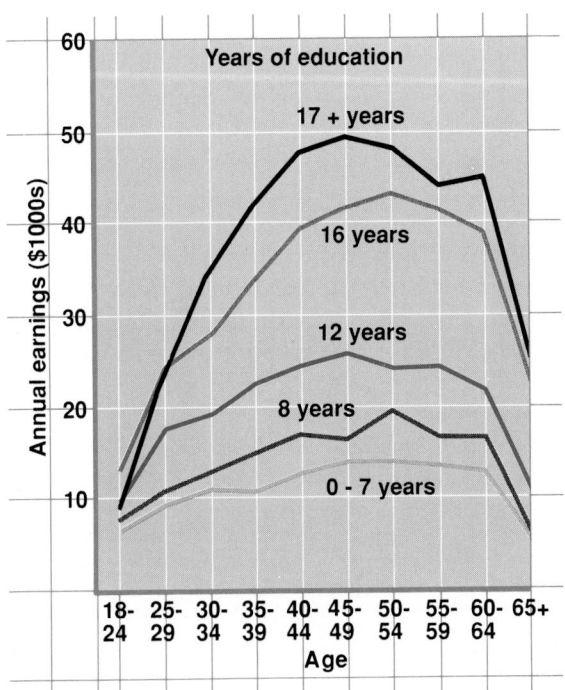

FIGURE 30-9

Education levels and individual income

Investment in education yields a return in the form of an income differential enjoyed throughout one's work-life. (*U.S. Bureau of the Census.* Data are for males in 1985.)

future flow of additional net revenues over the estimated years of life of the machine. Potential investors can discount this lifetime flow of earnings, compare their present value with the cost of the machine, and determine a rate of return on the investment. By comparing this rate of return with the interest rate (that is, the financial cost of investing), a firm can rationally decide whether the purchase of this machine is profitable.[13] Similarly, one might subject the decision to invest in, say, a four-year college education to the same analysis. Figure 30-9 indicates that individuals with larger investments in education achieve higher incomes during their work careers than do those who have made

smaller education investments. The economic return from investment in a college education can therefore be regarded as the *additional* lifetime earnings which the college graduate will earn as compared with the earnings of a high school graduate. The present value of this difference in lifetime earnings can be determined and compared with the cost of the education, and the rate of return on the investment in the college education can be calculated. This rate will be useful to the individual in determining whether investment in additional education is economically justifiable. It will also be helpful to society in determining the proper balance between investment in people and investment in machinery.

EXPLANATORY VALUE

Proponents contend that, in addition to accounting for a portion of wage differentials, the theory of human capital explains a number of phenomena which would otherwise be minor mysteries. Why do we educate younger, rather than older, people? Why are younger people more mobile than older people? Answer to both questions: Younger people have a longer expected working life over which to realize returns on their investments in education or mobility and this makes the rate of return higher. The concept of human capital is also a part of the explanation of the rising level of real wages which the United States has enjoyed historically (Figure 30-2). If our economy had the same natural resources and real capital we now possess, but a completely uneducated and untrained labor force or even a labor force with the educational and skill levels of, say, 1929, our GNP and real wage levels would obviously be much lower than they now are. Recall (see Table 21-3) that improved education and training are of considerable importance in explaining the economic growth which our economy has enjoyed.

CRITICISM

Human capital theory is not without its detractors. In particular, human capital theory assumes the existence of a direct and significant relationship between investment in human capital and produc-

---

[13] The reader may find it helpful to review the derivation of the investment-demand curve in Chapter 12.

Pay and performance in professional baseball

Professional baseball has provided an interesting "laboratory" in which the predictions of wage theory have been empirically tested.

Until 1976 professional baseball players were bound to a single team through the so-called "reserve clause" which prevented players from selling their talents on the open (competitive) market. Stated differently, the reserve clause conferred monopsony power upon the team which originally drafted a player. As we have seen in the present chapter, labor market theory would lead us to predict that this monopsony power would permit teams to pay wages less than a player's marginal revenue product (MRP). However, since 1976 major league players have been able to become "free agents" at the end of their sixth season of play and at that time can sell their services to any team. Orthodox theory suggests that free agents should be able to increase their salaries and bring them more closely into accord with their MRPs. Research tends to confirm both of the indicated predictions.

Scully* found that before baseball players could

* Gerald W. Scully, "Pay and Performance in Major League Baseball," *American Economic Review*, December 1974, pp. 915–930.

become free agents their salaries were substantially below their MRPs. Scully estimated a player's MRP as follows. First, he determined the relationship between a team's winning percentage and its revenue. Then he estimated the relationship between various possible measures of player productivity and a team's winning percentage. He found the ratio of strikeouts to walks for pitchers and the slugging averages for hitters (all nonpitchers) to be the best indicators of a player's contribution to the winning percentage. These two estimates were combined to calculate the contribution of a player to a team's total revenue.

As noted, Scully calculated that prior to free agency the estimated MRPs of both pitchers and

TABLE I **Marginal revenue products and salaries of professional baseball pitchers, 1968–1969**

(1) Performance	(2) Marginal revenue product	(3) Salary
1.60	$ 57,600	$31,100
1.80	80,900	34,200
2.00	104,100	37,200
2.20	127,400	40,200
2.40	150,600	43,100
2.60	173,900	46,000
2.80	197,100	48,800
3.00	220,300	51,600
3.20	243,600	54,400
3.40	266,800	57,100
3.60	290,100	59,800

* Strikeout-to-walk ratio.

Source: Scully, op. cit., p. 923.

tivity. Specifically, the hypothesized cause-effect chain is:

Investment in human capital
(expenditures on education)
causes
Increases in worker productivity
which cause
Higher wage rates and higher earnings

But some authorities feel that the cause-effect relationship may be much more complex and less clear. For example, if we find that the average person who invests in a college education earns, say, $3500 more per year than the average high school graduate, can we be certain that the additional earnings are *solely* the result of investing in college? Critics of human capital theory say "No." They argue that "other things are *not* equal" in that stu-

hitters were substantially greater than player salaries. Table 1 shows the relevant data for pitchers. Column 1 indicates pitcher performance as measured by lifetime strikeout-to-walk ratio. A higher ratio indicates a better pitcher. Column 2 indicates MRP after player training costs are taken into account and column 3 shows actual average salary for pitchers in each quality class. As expected, salaries were far less than MRPs. Even the lowest quality pitchers (those with a 1.60 strikeout-to-walk ratio) received on the average salaries amounting to only about 54 percent of their MRPs. Observe, too, that the gap between MRP and average salary widens as player quality improves. "Star" players were exploited more than other players. The best pitchers received salaries which were only about 21 percent of their MRPs, according to Scully. The same general results apply to hitters. For example, the least productive hitters on the average received a salary equal to about 37 percent of their MRPs.

Sommers and Quinton† have assessed the economic fortunes of fourteen players who constituted the "first family" of free agents. In accordance with the predictions of labor market theory, their research indicates that the competitive bidding of free agency has brought the salaries of free agents more closely into accord with their estimated MRPs. The data for the five free-agent pitchers are shown in Table 2 where we find a surprisingly close correspondence between estimated MRPs and salaries. Although MRP and salary differences are larger for hitters, Sommers and Quinton conclude that the overturn of the monopsonistic reserve clause "has forced owners into a situation where there is a

† Paul M. Sommers and Noel Quinton, "Pay and Performance in Major League Baseball: The Case of the First Family of Free Agents," *Journal of Human Resources*, Summer 1982, pp. 426–435.

TABLE 2 Estimated marginal revenue products and player costs, 1977

(1) Pitcher	(2) Marginal revenue product	(3) Annual contract cost*
Garland	$282,091	$230,000
Gullett	340,846	349,333
Fingers	303,511	332,000
Campbell	205,639	210,000
Alexander	166,203	166,667

* Includes annual salary, bonuses, the value of insurance policies and deferred payments, etc.

Source: Sommers and Quinton, op. cit., p. 432.

greater tendency to pay players in relation to their contribution to team revenues."

How have baseball team owners reacted to the escalating salaries under free agency? In early 1986 the players' union filed a grievance charging that the twenty-six professional baseball clubs had acted in concert against signing any of the players who became free agents in 1985. In fact, of the sixty-two players who became free agents in 1985, only two had signed contracts with a different team before the season began. In effect, the players charged that owners had attempted to restore some of the monopsony power which they previously had possessed. Such collusive action is illegal because it violates the basic collective bargaining agreement which exists between players and owners. In the fall of 1987 an arbitrator ruled that baseball owners had conspired to "destroy" the free-agent market and affected players may be awarded financial damages.

---

dents who go to college have greater innate ability and are more highly motivated than those who do not attend college.

. . . the only reason that education is correlated with income is that the combination of ability, motivation, and personal habits that it takes to succeed in education happen to be the same combination that it takes to be a productive worker.[14]

According to this view, the people with 16 years of education in Figure 30-9 would have received higher incomes than those with 12 years of education even if they had chosen not to invest in a col-

[14] Alice M. Rivlin, "Income Distribution—Can Economists Help?" *American Economic Review*, May 1975, p. 10.

lege education. The reason? They possess the ability and the motivation—not to mention family connections—to succeed in the labor market; the fact that they attended college is quite incidental to this success. Does education increase one's labor market productivity? Or do those who acquire more education earn more largely because they are inherently more able and more highly motivated? The issue raised here is very important for public policy. For example, if human capital theory is correct, then additional expenditures on education and job training for low-income workers should be an effective means of reducing poverty and lessening income inequality. But if the critics of human capital theory are correct, such a policy will be ineffective and wasteful.[15,16]

CHAPTER SUMMARY

1 Wages are the price paid per unit of time for the services of labor.

2 The general level of wages in the United States is higher than in most foreign nations because the demand for labor is great in relation to the supply. The strong demand for American labor is based upon its high productivity, which in turn depends upon the quantity and quality of the capital equipment and natural resources used by labor, the quality of the labor force itself, the efficiency of management, a favorable sociopolitical environment, and the vast size of the domestic market. Over time these factors have caused the demand for labor to increase in relation to the supply, accounting for the long-run rise of real wages in the United States.

3 The determination of specific wage rates depends upon the structure of the particular labor market. In a competitive market the equilibrium wage rate and level of employment will be determined by the intersection of labor supply and demand.

4 Under monopsony, however, the marginal resource cost curve will lie above the resource supply curve, because the monopsonist must bid up wage rates in hiring extra workers and pay that higher wage to *all* workers. The monopsonist will hire fewer workers than under competitive conditions in order to achieve less-than-competitive wage rates (costs) and thereby greater profits.

5 A union may raise competitive wage rates by *a* increasing the derived demand for labor, *b* restricting the supply of labor through exclusive unionism, and *c* directly enforcing an above-equilibrium wage rate through inclusive unionism.

6 In many important industries, the labor market takes the form of bilateral monopoly, in which a strong union "sells" labor to a monopsonistic employer. The outcome of this labor market model is logically indeterminate.

7 Economists disagree about the desirability of the minimum wage as an antipoverty mechanism. While it causes unemployment for some low-income workers, it raises the incomes of others who retain their jobs.

8 On the average, unionized workers realize wage rates which are 10 to 15 percent higher than comparable nonunion workers.

9 Wage differentials are largely explainable in terms of *a* noncompeting groups, that is, differences in the capacities and training of different groups of workers; *b* equalizing differences, that is, wage differences which must be paid to offset nonmonetary differences in jobs; and *c* market imperfections in the form of geographic, artificial, and sociological immobilities.

10 Investment in human capital takes the form of expenditures on education and training, health, and location and is generally regarded as an important concept in explaining wage differentials.

[15] For more on human capital theory, see Ronald G. Ehrenberg and Robert S. Smith, *Modern Labor Economics: Theory and Public Policy,* 3d ed. (Glenview, Ill.: Scott, Foresman and Company, 1988), chap. 9; and Campbell R. McConnell and Stanley L. Brue, *Contemporary Labor Economics,* 2d ed. (New York: McGraw-Hill Book Company, 1989), chap. 4.

[16] Some instructors may choose to assign Chapter 38 at this point.

TERMS AND CONCEPTS

nominal and real wages	**bilateral monopoly**
competitive labor market	**the minimum wage**
monopsony	**wage differentials**
exclusive and inclusive unionism	**noncompeting groups**
	equalizing differences
occupational licensing	**human capital investment**

QUESTIONS AND STUDY SUGGESTIONS

1 Explain why the general level of wages is higher in the United States than in most foreign nations. What is the most important single factor underlying the long-run increase in average real wage rates in the United States?

2 Describe wage determination in a labor market in which workers are unorganized and many firms are actively competing for the services of labor. Show this situation graphically, using W_1 to indicate the equilibrium wage rate and Q_1 to show the number of workers hired by the firms as a group. Compare the labor supply curve of the individual firm with that of the total market and explain any differences. In the firm's diagram identify total revenue, total wage cost, and revenue available for the payment of nonlabor resources.

a Suppose now that the formerly competing firms form an employers' association which hires labor as a monopsonist would. Describe verbally the impact upon wage rates and employment. Adjust the market graph you have just drawn, showing the monopsonistic wage rate and employment level as W_2 and Q_2, respectively.

b Using the monopsony model, explain why hospital administrators frequently complain about a "shortage" of nurses. Do you have suggestions for correcting this shortage?

3 Describe the techniques which unions might employ to raise wages. Evaluate the desirability of each from the viewpoint of **a** the union, and **b** society as a whole. Explain: "Craft unionism directly restricts the supply of labor; industrial unionism relies upon the market to restrict the number of jobs."

4 Assume a monopsonistic employer is paying a wage rate of W_m and hiring Q_m workers, as is indicated in Figure 30-8. Now suppose that an industrial union is formed and that it forces the employer to accept a wage rate of W_c. Explain verbally and graphically why in this instance the higher wage rate will be accompanied by an *increase* in the number of workers hired.

5 Complete the labor supply table in the next column for a firm hiring labor competitively.

a Show graphically the labor supply and marginal resource (labor) cost curves for this firm. Explain the relationships of these curves to one another.

b Compare these data with the labor demand data of question 2 in Chapter 29. What will the equilibrium wage rate and level of employment be? Explain.

c Now redetermine this firm's supply schedule for labor on the assumption that it is a monopsonist and

Units of labor	Wage rate	Total labor cost (wage bill)	Marginal resource (labor) cost
0	$14	$_____	$_____
1	14	_____	_____
2	14	_____	_____
3	14	_____	_____
4	14	_____	_____
5	14	_____	_____
6	14	_____	

that, although it can hire the first worker for $6, it must increase the wage rate by $3 to attract each successive worker. Show the new labor supply and marginal labor cost curves graphically and explain their relationships to one another. Compare these new data with those of question 2 for Chapter 29. What will be the equilibrium wage rate and the level of employment? Why do these differ from your answer to question 5b?

6 A critic of the minimum wage has contended, "The effects of minimum wage legislation are precisely the opposite of those predicted by those who support them. Government can legislate a minimum wage, but cannot force employers to hire unprofitable workers. In fact, minimum wages cause unemployment among low-wage workers who can least afford to give up their small incomes." Do you agree? What bearing does the elasticity of labor demand have upon this assessment? What factors might possibly offset the potential unemployment effects of a minimum wage?

7 On the average do union workers receive higher wages than comparable nonunion workers?

8 What are the basic considerations which help explain wage differentials? What long-run effect would a substantial increase in safety for underground coal miners have upon their wage rates in comparison to other workers?

9 "Many of the lowest-paid people in society—for example, short-order cooks—also have relatively poor working conditions. Hence, the notion of equalizing wage differentials is disproved." Do you agree? Explain.

10 What is meant by investment in human capital? Use this concept to explain **a** wage differentials, and **b** the long-run rise in real wage rates in the United States. What basic criticism is made of human capital theory?

CHAPTER 31

The pricing and employment of resources: rent, interest, and profits

Wages were accorded a rather lengthy discussion in Chapter 30. In contrast, the discussions of the income shares—rent, interest, and profits—found in the present chapter are relatively brief. There are two reasons for this difference in emphasis. (1) Wage incomes are clearly the major component of the national income. As we will find in the concluding section of this chapter, 70 to 80 percent of the national income is in the form of wage and salary incomes, the remainder accruing as rent, interest, and profit incomes. (2) The economic theories of rent, interest, and profits are quite unsettled; there are honest differences among authorities as to definitions, explanations, and implications where nonwage incomes are concerned. For these two reasons we shall concentrate upon the basic features of rent, interest, and profit determination and forgo the many controversial points and the sometimes ambiguous details which are encountered in more advanced discussions of these income shares.

Economic rent

To most people the term "rent" means the seemingly exorbitant sum one must pay for a two-bedroom apartment or a dormitory room. To the business executive, "rent" is a payment made for the use of a factory building, machinery, or warehouse facilities. Closer examination finds these commonsense definitions of rent to be confusing and ambiguous. Dormitory room rent, for example, includes interest on the money capital the university has borrowed in financing the dormitory's construction, wages for custodial and maid service, utility payments, and so forth. Economists therefore use the term "rent" in a narrower but less ambiguous sense: **Economic rent** *is the price paid for the use of land and other natural resources which are completely fixed in total supply*. It is the unique supply conditions of land and other natural resources—their fixed supply—which make rental payments distinguishable from wage, interest, and profit payments.

Let us examine this feature and some of its implications through simple supply and demand analysis. To avoid complications, assume, first, that all land is of the same grade or quality—in other words, that each available acre of land is equally productive. Suppose, too, that all land has just one use, being capable of producing just one product—say, corn. And assume that land is being rented in a competitive market—that many corn farmers are demanding and many landowners offering land in the market.

In Figure 31-1, *SS* indicates the supply of arable farmland available in the economy as a whole and D_2 the demand of farmers for the use of that land. As with all economic resources, demand is a derived demand. It is downsloping because of the

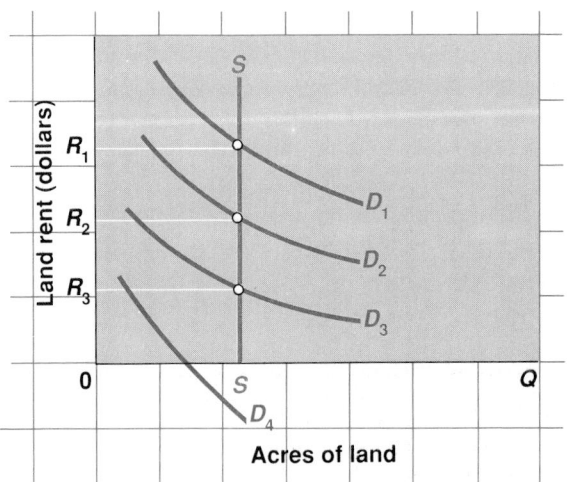

FIGURE 31-1

The determination of land rent

Because the supply of land and other natural resources is perfectly inelastic (SS), demand is the sole active determinant of land rent. An increase (D_2 to D_1) or decrease (D_2 to D_3) in demand will cause considerable changes in rent (R_2 to R_1 and R_2 to R_3). If demand is very small (D_4) relative to supply, land will be a "free good."

law of diminishing returns and the fact that, for farmers as a group, product price must be diminished to sell additional units of output.

The unique feature of our analysis is on the supply side: For all practical purposes the supply of land is perfectly inelastic, as reflected in SS. Land has no production cost; it is a "free and nonreproducible gift of nature." The economy has so much land, and that's that. It is true, of course, that within limits existing land can be made more usable by clearing, drainage, and irrigation. But these programs constitute capital improvements and not changes in the amount of land as such. Furthermore, such variations in the usability of land are a very small fraction of the total amount of land in existence and therefore do not undermine the basic argument that land and other natural resources are in virtually fixed supply.

The fixed nature of the supply of land means that demand is the only active determinant of land rent; supply is passive. And what determines the demand for land? Those factors discussed in Chap-

ter 29—the price of the product grown on the land, the productivity of land (which depends in part upon the quantity and quality of the resources with which land is combined), and the prices of those other resources which are combined with land. If, in Figure 31-1, the demand for land should increase from D_2 to D_1 or decline from D_2 to D_3, land rent would change from R_2 to R_1 or R_3, but the amount of land supplied would remain unchanged at $0S$. Changes in economic rent will have no impact upon the amount of land available; the supply of land is simply not augmentable. In technical terms, there is a large price effect and no quantity effect when the demand for land changes. If demand for land is only D_4, land rent will be zero; land will be a "free good" because it is not scarce enough in relation to demand for it to command a price. This situation was approximated in the freeland era of American history.

LAND RENT IS A SURPLUS

The perfect inelasticity of the supply of land must be contrasted with the relative elasticity of such property resources as apartment buildings, machinery, and warehouses. These resources are *not* fixed in total supply. A higher price will give entrepreneurs the incentive to construct and offer larger quantities of these property resources. Conversely, a decline in their prices will induce suppliers to allow existing facilities to depreciate and not be replaced. The same general reasoning applies to the total supply of labor. Within limits, a higher average level of wages will induce more workers to enter the labor force, and lower wages will cause them to drop out of the labor force. In other words, the supplies of nonland resources are upsloping or, stated differently, the prices paid to such resources perform an **incentive function.** A high price provides an incentive to offer more; a low price, to offer less.

Not so with land. Rent serves no incentive function, because the total supply of land is fixed. If rent is $10,000, $500, $1, or $0 per acre, the same amount of land will be available to society to make a contribution to production. Rent, in other words, could be eliminated without affecting the productive potential of the economy. For this reason economists consider rent to be a *surplus,* that is, a payment which is not necessary to ensure that land will be available to the economy as a whole.[1]

A SINGLE TAX ON LAND?

If land is a free gift of nature, costs nothing to produce, and would be available even in the absence of rental payments, why should rent be paid to those who by historical accident or inheritance happen to be landowners? Socialists have long argued that all land rents are unearned incomes. Therefore, they argue, land should be nationalized—owned by the state—so that any payments for its use can be utilized by the state in furthering the well-being of the entire population rather than by a landowning minority.

In the United States, criticism of rental payments has taken the form of a **single-tax movement** which gained considerable support in the late nineteenth century. Spearheaded by Henry George's provocative book *Progress and Poverty* (1879), this reform movement centered upon the notion that economic rent might be taxed away completely without impairing the available supply of land or, therefore, the productive potential of the economy as a whole.

George observed that as population grew and the geographic frontier closed, landowners came to enjoy larger and larger rents from their landholdings. These increments in rent were simply the result of a growing demand for a resource whose supply was perfectly inelastic; some landlords were receiving fabulously high incomes, not through rendering any productive effort, but solely as the

result of holding advantageously located land. Henry George took the position that these increases in land rent belonged to the economy as a whole; he held that land rents should be taxed away and spent for public uses.

As George saw it, the fact that the tax burden was imposed on the landowner was perfectly justifiable; land rent, after all, was unearned income. Population growth and the closing of the geographic frontier were conferring windfall rental income upon landowners, and government was fully justified in taxing away such rental income. Indeed, George held that there was no reason to tax away only 50 percent of the landowner's unearned rental income. Why not take 70 or 90 or 99 percent? In seeking popular support for his ideas on land taxation, Henry George proposed that taxes on rental income be the *only* tax levied by government.

George's case for taxing land was based not only on equity or fairness, but also on efficiency grounds. In particular, unlike virtually every other tax, a tax on land does *not* alter or distort the allocation of resources. For example, a tax on wages will reduce after-tax wages and might weaken incentives to work. An individual who decides to participate in the labor force at a $6 before-tax wage rate may decide to drop from the labor force and go on welfare when an income tax reduces the after-tax wage rate to, say, $4.50. Similarly, a property tax on buildings lowers the returns to those who invest in such property, causing them in time to reallocate their money capital toward other investment opportunities. But no such reallocations of resources occur when land is taxed.[2] The most profitable use for land before it is taxed remains the most profitable use after the tax is imposed. Of course, a landlord could withdraw land from production when a tax is imposed, but this would mean no rental income at all.

Criticisms Critics of the single tax on land make these points: First, current levels of government spending are such that a land tax alone would clearly not bring in enough revenue; it cannot be considered realistically as a *single* tax. Second, as noted earlier, in practice most income payments

---

[1] The alert reader will have observed that a portion—in some instances a major portion—of wage and salary incomes may be a surplus in that these incomes exceed the minimum amount necessary to keep an individual in his or her current line of work. For example, in 1988 the *average* salary paid to major league baseball players was about $485,000 per year. In the next best occupational option as, say, a college coach, a player might earn only $40,000 or $50,000 per year. Most of his current income is therefore a surplus. Observe that in the twilight of their careers, professional athletes sometimes accept sizable salary reductions rather than seek employment in alternative occupations.

[2] For a more formal analysis of this point, look ahead to Figure 33-6 and the accompanying discussion.

combine elements of interest, rent, wages, and profits. Land is typically improved in some manner by productive effort, and economic rent cannot be readily disentangled from payments for capital improvements. As a practical matter, it would be very difficult to determine how much of any given income payment is actually rent. Third, the question of unearned income goes beyond land and land ownership. One can readily argue that many individuals and groups other than landowners benefit from the receipt of "unearned" income associated with the overall advance of the economy. For example, consider the capital gains income received by an individual who, some twenty or twenty-five years ago, chanced to purchase (or inherit) stock in a firm which has experienced rapid growth (say, IBM or Xerox). How is this income different from the rental income of the landowner? Finally, historically a piece of land is likely to have changed ownership many times. Hence, *former* owners may have been the beneficiaries of past increases in land rent. It is hardly fair to tax *current* owners who paid the competitive market price for land.

PRODUCTIVITY DIFFERENCES

Our analysis thus far has proceeded upon the assumption that all units of land are of the same grade. In practice, this is plainly not so. Different acres vary greatly in productivity. These productivity differences stem primarily from differences in soil fertility and such climatic factors as rainfall and temperature. It is these factors which explain why Iowa soil is excellently suited to corn production, the plains of eastern Colorado are much less so, and desert wasteland of New Mexico is incapable of corn production. These differences in productivity will be reflected in resource demand. Competitive bidding by farmers will establish a high rent for the very productive Iowa land. The less productive Colorado land will command a much lower rent, and the New Mexico land no rent at all. Location may be equally important in explaining differences in land rent. Other things being equal, renters will pay more for a unit of land which is strategically located with respect to materials, labor, and customers than for a unit of land whose location is remote from these markets. Witness the extremely high land rents in large metropolitan areas.

The rent differentials to which quality differences in land would give rise can be easily seen by looking at Figure 31-1 from a slightly different point of view. Suppose, as before, that only one agricultural product, say corn, can be produced on four grades of land, *each* of which is available in the fixed amount $0S$. When combined with identical amounts of capital, labor, and other cooperating resources, the productivity—or, more specifically, the marginal revenue productivity—of each grade of land is reflected in demand curves D_1, D_2, D_3, and D_4. Grade 1 land is the most productive, as reflected in D_1, whereas grade 4 is the least productive, as is shown by D_4. The resulting economic rents for grades 1, 2, and 3 land will be R_1, R_2, and R_3 respectively, the rent differentials mirroring the differences in the productivity of the three grades of land. Grade 4 land is so poor in quality that it would not pay farmers to bring it fully into production; it would be a "free" and only partially used resource.

ALTERNATIVE USES AND COSTS

We have also supposed, thus far, that land has only one use. Actually, we know that land usually has a number of alternative uses. An acre of Iowa farmland may be useful in raising not only corn, but also wheat, oats, milo, and cattle, or it may be useful as a site for a house or factory. What is the importance of this obvious point? It indicates that, although land is a free gift of nature and has no production cost from the viewpoint of society as a whole, the rental payments of individual producers are *costs*. The total supply of land will be available to society even if no rent at all is paid for its use, but, from the standpoint of individual firms and industries, land has alternative uses, and therefore payments must be made by specific firms and industries to attract that land from those other uses. Such payments by definition are costs. Once again the fallacy of composition (Chapter 1) has entered our discussion. From the standpoint of society, there is no alternative but for land to be used by society. Therefore to society, rents are a surplus, not a cost. But because land has alternative uses, the rental payments of corn farmers or any other individual user are a cost; such payments are required to attract land from alternative uses.

Interest

The interest rate is the price paid for the use of money. More precisely, the interest rate is the amount of money one is required to pay for the use of one dollar for a year. Two aspects of this income payment are notable.

1 Because it is paid in kind, interest is typically stated as a percentage of the amount of money being borrowed rather than as an absolute amount. It is less clumsy to say that one is paying 12 percent interest than to proclaim that interest is "$120 per year per $1000." Furthermore, stating interest as a percentage facilitates the comparison of interest paid on loans of much different absolute amounts. By expressing interest as a percentage, we can immediately compare an interest payment of, say, $432 per year per $2880 and one of $1800 per year per $12,000. In this case both interest payments are 15 percent—a fact not at all obvious from the absolute figures.

It is worth noting that a **Truth in Lending Act** was passed in 1968 which requires lenders to state in concise and uniform language the costs and terms of consumer credit. In particular, the act requires that interest must be stated as an annual rate. Nevertheless, as this chapter's Last Word explains, it is not always a simple matter to determine how much interest one is being charged.

2 Money is *not* an economic resource. As such, money is not productive; it is incapable of producing goods and services. However, businesses "buy" the use of money, because money can be used to acquire capital goods—factory buildings, machinery, warehouses, and so forth. And these facilities clearly do make a contribution to production. Thus, in hiring the use of money capital, business executives are ultimately buying the use of real capital goods.

DETERMINING THE INTEREST RATE

The theory of interest rate determination and its relationship to aggregate investment have been

presented in Part 3 and need only be summarized at this point.[3] Glancing back at Figure 17-2, we recall in Figure 17-2a that the total demand for money is comprised of the **transactions** and **asset demands.** The former is directly related to the level of nominal GNP, while the latter is inversely related to the interest rate. Graphed against the interest rate, the total demand for money curve is downsloping. The money supply is a vertical line on the assumption that the monetary authorities determine some stock of money (money supply) independent of the rate of interest. The intersection of the demand for money curve and the money supply curve determines the equilibrium rate of interest.

The investment decision   Now consider Figure 17-2b which shows how the interest rate relates to the purchase of real capital. You may remember that the investment-demand curve is constructed by aggregating all possible investment projects and ranking them from highest to lowest in terms of their expected rates of net profits. By projecting the equilibrium interest rate of Figure 17-2a off the investment-demand curve of Figure 17-2b, we determine the amount of investment which the business sector will find profitable to undertake. All investment projects whose expected rate of net profits exceeds the equilibrium interest rate will be undertaken.

Nominal and real interest rates   The above discussion of the role of the interest rate in the investment decision embodies the hidden assumption that there is no inflation. If inflation occurs, we must distinguish between money or nominal interest rates and real interest rates. The **nominal interest rate** is the rate of interest expressed in terms of dollars of current value. The **real interest rate** is the rate of interest expressed in terms of dollars of constant or inflation-adjusted value. The real interest rate is the nominal rate less the rate of inflation.

An example is helpful in elucidating this distinction. Suppose that the nominal interest rate

---

[3] It is recommended that the reader review the following sections: "The Demand for Money" in Chapter 15; "Monetary Policy, Equilibrium NNP, and the Price Level," in Chapter 17; and "Investment" in Chapter 12.

and the rate of inflation are both 10 percent. If you borrow $100, you must pay back $110 a year from now. However, because of 10 percent inflation each of these 110 dollars will be worth 10 percent less. Hence, the real value or purchasing power of your $110 repayment at the end of the year is only $100. In terms of inflation-adjusted dollars you are borrowing $100 and at year's end paying back $100. While the nominal interest rate is 10 percent, the real interest rate is zero. In other words, by subtracting the 10 percent inflation rate from the 10 percent nominal interest rate we determine that the real interest rate is zero.

This distinction is relevant to the present discussion because it is the real interest rate, not the nominal rate, which is important in making investment decisions. Thus in the late 1970s and early 1980s nominal interest rates were unusually high; 12, 15, and 18 percent rates were not uncommon. At first glance one would think that these high nominal rates would choke off investment; after all, there are relatively few investment opportunities which promise an expected rate of return in excess of 15 or 18 percent. But this didn't occur; investment spending was quite strong during this period. The reason was that, given the anticipation of continuing inflation, prospective investors planned to repay their borrowings in dollars of depreciated real value. In other words, while nominal interest rates were very high, inflation made real interest rates much lower and investment continued unabated. To repeat: It is the real interest rate, not the nominal rate, which is critical to the investment decision.

RANGE OF RATES

Although economists often find it convenient to think in terms of a single interest rate, in fact there exists a whole cluster or range of interest rates. Table 31-1 lists most of the interest rates which are frequently referred to in the media. Note that these rates range from 7 to 18 percent. Why the differences?

1 Risk The varying degrees of risk on loans are important. The greater the chance the borrower will not repay the loan, the more interest the lender will charge to compensate for this risk.

TABLE 31-1 **Selected interest rates, November 1988**

Type of interest rate	Annual percentage
30-year Treasury bond rate (Federal government security used to finance the public debt)	9.13%
90-day Treasury bill rate (Federal government security used to finance the public debt)	8.01
Prime interest rate (Interest rate charged by banks to their best corporate customers)	10.05
30-year mortgage rate (Fixed-interest rate on loans for houses)	9.05
4-year automobile loan rate (Bank interest rate on loans for new automobiles)	10.93
Tax-exempt municipal bond rate (Interest-rate paid on a low-risk bond issued by a state or local government)	7.41
Consumer credit card rate (Interest rate charged for credit card purchases)	17.78

2 Maturity The length or maturity of a loan also affects the interest rate. Other things being equal, long-term loans usually command higher rates of interest than do short-term loans, because the long-term lender suffers the inconvenience and possible financial sacrifice of forgoing alternative uses for his or her money for a greater period of time.

3 Loan size Given two loans of equal length and risk, the interest rate usually will be somewhat higher on the smaller of the two loans. This is so because the administrative costs of a large and a small loan are about the same absolutely.

4 Taxability We noted in Chapter 8 that the interest on certain state and municipal bonds is exempt from Federal income taxation. Because lenders are interested in their after-tax rate of interest, states and local governments can attract lenders even though they pay lower interest rates. Thus, a high-income lender may prefer a 7 percent interest rate on a tax-exempt municipal bond as compared to a 9 percent taxable interest rate on a corporate bond.

5 Market imperfections Market imperfections are also important in explaining some interest rate differentials. The small-town bank which monopolizes the local money market may charge high interest rates on loans to consumers because households find it inconvenient to "shop around" at banks in somewhat distant cities. The large corporation, on the other hand, is able to survey a number of rival investment houses in floating a new bond issue and thereby can secure the lowest obtainable rate.

To circumvent the difficulties involved in discussing the whole structure of interest rates, economists talk of "the" interest rate or the **pure rate of interest.** This pure rate is best approximated by the interest paid on long-term, virtually riskless bonds such as the long-term bonds of the United States government (30-year Treasury bonds). This interest payment can be thought of as being made solely for the use of money over an extended time period, because the risk factor and administrative costs are negligible and the interest on such securities is not distorted by market imperfections. Thus, at the end of 1988 the pure interest rate was about 9 percent.

ROLE OF THE INTEREST RATE

The interest rate is an extremely important price in that it simultaneously affects both the *level* and *composition* of investment goods production.

Interest and national output Our discussion of Figure 12-6 reminds us that, other things being equal, a change in the equilibrium rate of interest will move businesses along the aggregate investment-demand curve, thereby changing the level of investment and the equilibrium level of NNP. Indeed, the big message of Chapter 17 was that the interest rate is an "administered price." This means, of course, that the monetary authorities purposely manipulate the supply of money in order to influence the interest rate and thereby the levels

of output, employment, and prices. Recall that an easy (low interest rate) monetary policy increases investment and expands the economy; a tight (high interest rate) monetary policy chokes off investment and constrains the economy.

Interest and the allocation of capital Prices, you will recall, are rationing devices. The interest rate is no exception; it performs the function of allocating money capital and therefore physical capital to various firms and investment projects. It rations the available supply of money or liquidity to those investment projects whose rate of return or expected profitability is sufficiently high to warrant payment of the going interest rate. If the expected rate of net profits of additional physical capital in, say, the computer industry is 14 percent and the required funds can be secured at an interest rate of 10 percent, the computer industry will be in a position, in terms of profit, to borrow and expand its capital facilities. If the expected rate of net profits of additional capital in, say, the steel industry is expected to be only 8 percent, it will be unprofitable for this industry to accumulate more capital goods. In short, the interest rate allocates money, and ultimately physical capital, to those industries in which it will be most productive and therefore most profitable. Such an allocation of capital goods is obviously in the interest of society as a whole.

But the interest rate does not perform perfectly the task of rationing capital to its most productive uses. Large oligopolistic borrowers are in a better position than competitive borrowers to pass interest costs on to consumers by virtue of their ability to control supply and thereby manipulate their prices. And, too, the sheer size and prestige of large industrial concerns might allow them to obtain money capital on favorable terms, whereas the market for money capital screens out less-well-known firms whose profit expectations might actually be superior.

Business profits
and economic profits

As is the case with rent, economists find it advantageous to define profits more narrowly than do accountants. To accountants, "profit" is what remains of a firm's total revenue after it has paid individuals and other firms for materials, capital, and labor supplied to the firm. To the economist, this conception is too broad and therefore ambiguous. The difficulty, as the economist sees it, is that this view of profits takes into account only **explicit costs,** that is, payments made by the firm to outsiders. It therefore ignores **implicit costs,** that is, payments to similar resources which are owned and self-employed by a firm. In other words, this concept of profits fails to allow for implicit wage, rent, and interest costs. **Economic,** or **pure, profits** are what remain after *all* opportunity costs—both explicit and implicit wage, rent, and interest costs and a normal profit—have been subtracted from a firm's total revenue (Chapter 24). Economic profits may be either positive or negative (losses).

An example may sharpen these comments. As the economist sees it, farmers who own their land and equipment and provide all their own labor are grossly overstating their economic profits if they merely subtract their payments to outsiders for seed, insecticides, fertilizer, gasoline, and so forth, from their total revenues. Actually, much or possibly all of what remain are the implicit rent, interest, and wage costs which the farmers forgo in deciding to self-employ the resources they own rather than make them available in alternative employments. Interest on the capital or wages for the labor contributed by farmers are no more profits than are the payments which would be made if outsiders had supplied these resources. In short, the accountant's definition and the economist's definition of profits are compatible only if the accountant includes both explicit and implicit costs in determining total costs. Economic profits are a residual—the total revenue remaining after *all* costs are taken into account.

ECONOMIC PROFITS AND THE ENTREPRENEUR

Speaking very generally, the economist views profits as the return to a very special type of human resource—entrepreneurial ability. The functions of the entrepreneur were summarized in Chapter 2. They entail (1) taking the initiative to combine other resources in the production of some good or service; (2) making the basic, nonroutine policy

decisions for the firm; (3) introducing innovations in the form of new products or production processes; and (4) bearing the economic risks associated with all these functions.

A part of the entrepreneur's return, you will recall, is called a **normal profit.** This is the minimum return or payment necessary to retain the entrepreneur in some specific line of production. By definition, this normal profit payment is a cost (Chapter 24). However, we know that a firm's total revenue may exceed its total costs (explicit, implicit, the latter inclusive of a normal profit). This extra or excess revenue above all costs is an economy, or pure, profit. This residual—which is *not* a cost because it is in excess of the normal profit required to retain the entrepreneur in the industry—accrues to the entrepreneur. The entrepreneur, in other words, is the residual claimant.

Economists offer several theories to explain why this residual of economic profit might occur. As we will see in a moment, these explanations relate to:

1 The risks which the entrepreneur necessarily bears by functioning in a dynamic and therefore uncertain environment or by undertaking innovational activity.

2 The possibility of attaining monopoly power.

SOURCES OF ECONOMIC PROFIT

Our understanding of economic profits and the entrepreneur's functions can be both deepened and widened by describing an artificial economic environment within which pure profits would be zero. Then, by noting real-world deviations from this environment, we can lay bare the sources of economic profit.

In a purely competitive *static economy,* pure profits would be zero. By a **static economy** we mean one in which all the basic data—resource supplies, technological knowledge, and consumer tastes—are constant and unchanging. A static economy is a changeless one in which all the determinants of cost and supply data, on the one hand, and demand and revenue data, on the other, are constant. Given the static nature of these data, the economic future is perfectly foreseeable; economic uncertainty is nonexistent. The outcome of price and production policies is accurately predictable.

Furthermore, the static nature of such a society precludes any type of innovational change. Under pure competition any pure profits (positive or negative) which might have existed initially in various industries will disappear with the entry or exodus of firms in the long run. All costs—both explicit and implicit—will therefore be precisely covered in the long run, leaving no residual in the form of pure profits (Figure 25-12).

The notion of zero economic profits in a static, competitive economy enhances our understanding of profits by suggesting that the presence of profits is linked to the dynamic nature of real-world capitalism and the accompanying uncertainty. Furthermore, it indicates that economic profits may arise from a source apart from the directing, innovating, risk-bearing functions of the entrepreneur. And that source is the presence of some degree of monopoly power.

Uncertainty, risk, and profits In a dynamic economy the future is always uncertain. This means that the entrepreneur necessarily assumes risks. Profits can be thought of in part as a reward for assuming these risks.

In linking pure profits with uncertainty and risk bearing, it is important to distinguish between risks which are insurable and those which are not. Some types of risks—for example, fires, floods, theft, and accidents to employees—are measurable in the sense that actuaries can estimate their average occurrence with considerable accuracy. As a result, these risks are typically insurable. Firms can avoid, or at least provide for, them by incurring a known cost in the form of an insurance premium. It is the bearing of **uninsurable risks,** then, which is a potential source of economic profits.

What are such uninsurable risks? Basically, they are uncontrollable and unpredictable changes in demand (revenue) and supply (cost) conditions facing the firm. Some of these uninsurable risks stem from unpredictable changes in the general economic environment or, more specifically, from the business cycle. Prosperity brings substantial windfall profits to most firms, whereas depression means widespread losses. In addition, changes are constantly taking place in the structure of the economy. Even in a full-employment, noninflationary economy, changes are always occurring in consumer tastes, resource supplies, and so forth. These changes continually alter the revenue and cost data faced by individual firms and industries, leading to changes in the structure of the business population as favorably affected industries expand and adversely affected industries contract. Changes in government policies are pertinent at both levels. Appropriate fiscal and monetary policies of government may reverse a recession, whereas a tariff may alter significantly the demand and revenue data of the protected industry.

The point is this: Profits and losses can be associated with the bearing of uninsurable risks stemming from both cyclical and structural changes in the economy.

Uncertainty, innovations, and profits The uncertainties just discussed are external to the firm; they are beyond the control of the individual firm or industry. One other extremely important dynamic feature of capitalism—innovation—occurs at the initiative of the entrepreneur. Business firms deliberately introduce new methods of production and distribution to affect their costs favorably and new products to influence their revenue favorably. The entrepreneur purposely undertakes to upset existing cost and revenue data in a way which hopefully will be profitable.

But once again, uncertainty enters the picture. Despite exhaustive market surveys by well-established firms, new products or modifications of existing products may prove to be economic failures. Three-dimensional movies, not to mention Edsel and Corvair automobiles, come readily to mind as product failures. Similarly, of the many new novels, textbooks, records, and tapes which appear every year, only a handful garner large profits. Nor is it known with certainty whether a new machine will actually provide the cost economies predicted for it while it is still in the blueprint stage. Innovations purposely undertaken by entrepreneurs entail uncertainty, just as do those changes in the economic environment over which an individual enterprise has no control. In a sense, then, innovation as a source of profits is merely a special case of risk bearing.

Under competition and in the absence of patent laws, innovational profits will be temporary. Rival firms will imitate successful (profitable) innovations, thereby competing away all economic profits. Nevertheless, innovational profits may always exist in a progressive economy as new, successful innovations replace those older innovations whose associated profits have been eroded or competed away.

Monopoly profits Thus far, we have emphasized that profits are related to the uncertainties and uninsurable risks surrounding dynamic events which enterprises are exposed to or initiate themselves. The existence of monopoly in some form or another is a final source of economic profits. As explained previously, because of its ability to restrict output and deter entry, a monopolist may persistently enjoy economic profits, provided demand is strong relative to cost (Figure 26-3). This profit stems from the monopolist's ability to restrict output and influence product price to its own advantage.

There are both a causal relationship and a notable distinction between uncertainty, on the one hand, and monopoly, on the other, as sources of profits. The causal relationship involves the fact that an entrepreneur can reduce uncertainty, or at least manipulate its effects, by achieving monopoly power.[4] The competitive firm is unalterably exposed to the vagaries of the market; the monopolist, however, can control the market to a degree and thereby offset or minimize potentially adverse effects of uncertainty. Furthermore, innovation is an important source of monopoly power; the short-run uncertainty associated with the introduction of

new techniques or new products may be borne for the purpose of achieving a measure of monopoly power

The notable distinction between profits stemming from uncertainty and from monopoly has to do with the social desirability of the two sources of profits. Bearing the risks inherent in a dynamic and uncertain economic environment and the undertaking of innovations are socially desirable functions. The social desirability of monopoly profits, on the other hand, is very doubtful. Monopoly profits typically are founded upon output restriction, above-competitive prices, and a contrived misallocation of resources.

FUNCTIONS OF PROFITS

Profit is the prime mover, or energizer, of the capitalistic economy. As such, profits influence both the level of resource utilization and the allocation of resources among alternative uses. It is profits—or better, the *expectation* of profits—which induce firms to innovate. And innovation stimulates investment, total output, and employment. Innovation is a fundamental aspect of the process of economic growth, and it is the pursuit of profit which underlies most innovation. However, profit expectations are highly volatile, with the result that investment, employment, and the rate of growth have been unstable. Profits have functioned imperfectly as a spur to innovation and investment.

Perhaps profits perform more effectively the task of allocating resources among alternative lines of production. Recall the message of Chapters 5 and 25: Entrepreneurs seek profits and shun losses. The occurrence of economic profits is a signal that society wants that particular industry to expand. Indeed, profit rewards are more than an inducement for an industry to expand; they also are the financial means by which firms in such industries can add to their productive capacities. Losses, on the other hand, signal society's desire for the afflicted industries to contract; losses penalize businesses which fail to adjust their productive efforts to those goods and services most preferred by consumers. This is not to say that profits and losses result in an allocation of resources which is now and forever attuned to consumer preferences. In particular, the presence of monopoly in both prod-

---

[4] The extensive efforts of large corporations to avoid risk and uncertainty constitute a major theme running through John Kenneth Galbraith's writings. He argues as follows: In resource markets, corporations vertically integrate their structure so as to guarantee themselves reliable sources of materials. Similarly, they finance their capital investment internally to insulate themselves from the vagaries of capital markets. The modern corporation reduces product market uncertainty by supplanting consumer sovereignty with "producer sovereignty," using advertising and other sales techniques to "manage" consumers so they will buy those goods corporations want to sell at the prices they want to charge. Finally, uncertainties of a larger sort—economic fluctuations—are mitigated indirectly by inducing government to undertake appropriate countercyclical policies. Galbraith's *Economics and the Public Purpose* (Boston: Houghton Mifflin Company, 1973) and *The New Industrial State* (Boston: Houghton Mifflin Company, 1967) are relevant.

uct and resource markets impedes the shiftability of firms and resources, as also do the various geographic, artificial, and sociological immobilities discussed in Chapter 30.

Income shares

The discussions of Chapters 30 and 31 would be incomplete without a brief empirical summary as to the importance of wages, rent, interest, and profits as proportions or relative shares of the national income. Table 31-2 provides an historical look at income shares in terms of the income categories used in our national income accounts. Unfortunately, these accounting conceptions of income do not neatly fit the economist's definitions of wages, rent, interest, and profits. In particular, the national income-accounting conceptions are often mixtures of these four types of income. Notable example: Much of "proprietors' income" is wages and salaries, but most unincorporated businesses provide their own capital and entrepreneurial talent and, in the case of farming, they provide their own land. Hence, a portion of proprietors' income is interest, profits, and rent. Recognizing this kind of limitation, what do our national income data tell us about the relative size and trends of income shares?

CURRENT SHARES

Looking at the most recent 1982–1988 figures in the table, we note immediately the dominant role of labor income. Defining labor income narrowly as "wages and salaries," labor currently receives almost 75 percent of the national income. But some economists argue that since proprietors' income is largely comprised of wages and salaries, it should be added to the official "wages and salaries" category to determine labor income. When we use this broad definition, labor's share rises to about 80 percent of national income. Interestingly, although we label our system a "capitalist economy," the capitalist share of national income—which we will define as the sum of "corporate profits," "interest," and "rent"—is only about 20 percent of the national income.

TABLE 31-2 **Relative shares of national income, 1900–1988 (decade or period averages of shares for individual years)**

(1) Decade	(2) Wages and salaries	(3) Pro- prietors' income	(4) Cor- porate profits	(5) Interest	(6) Rent	(7) Total
1900–1909	55.0%	23.7%	6.8%	5.5%	9.0%	100%
1910–1919	53.6	23.8	9.1	5.4	8.1	100
1920–1929	60.0	17.5	7.8	6.2	7.7	100
1930–1939	67.5	14.8	4.0	8.7	5.0	100
1939–1948	64.6	17.2	11.9	3.1	3.3	100
1949–1958	67.3	13.9	12.5	2.9	3.4	100
1954–1963	69.9	11.9	11.2	4.0	3.0	100
1963–1970	71.7	9.6	12.1	3.5	3.2	100
1971–1981	75.9	7.1	8.4	6.4	2.2	100
1982–1988	73.8	6.8	8.6	9.8	1.1	100

Source: Irving Kravis, "Income Distribution: Functional Share," *International Encyclopedia of Social Sciences,* vol. 7 (New York: The Macmillan Company and Free Press, 1968), p. 134, updated.

HISTORICAL TRENDS

What can be deduced from Table 31-2 with respect to historical trends? Let us concentrate on the dominant wage share. Using the narrow definition of labor's share as simply "wages and salaries," we note an increase from about 55 to almost 75 percent in this century.

Structural changes Although there are several tentative explanations of these data, one prominent theory stresses the structural changes which have occurred in our economy. Two specific points are made. First, noting the relative constancy of the capitalist share (the sum of columns 4, 5, and 6)—which was roughly 20 percent in both the 1900–1909 and the 1982–1988 periods—we find that the expansion of labor's share has come primarily at the expense of the share going to proprietors. This suggests that the evolution of the corporation as the dominant form of business enterprise (Chapter 7) is an important explanatory factor. Put bluntly, individuals who would have operated their own corner groceries in the 1920s are the hired managers of corporate supermarkets in the 1980s or 1990s. Second, the changing output-mix and therefore the industry-mix which have occurred historically have tended to increase labor's share. Overall, there has been a long-term change in the composition of output and industry which has been away from land- and capital-intensive production and toward labor-intensive production. Again, crudely stated, there has been an historical reallocation of labor from agriculture (where labor's share is quite low) to manufacturing (where labor's share is rather high) and, finally, to private and public services (where labor's share is very high). These shifts account for much of the growth of labor's share reflected in column 2 of Table 31-2.

Unions? One is tempted to explain an expanding wage share in terms of the growth of labor unions. But there are difficulties with this approach. First, the growth of the labor movement in the United States does not fit very well chronologically with the growth of labor's share of the national income. Much of the growth of "wages and salaries" occurred between 1900 and 1939; much of the growth in the labor movement came in the last few years of the 1930s and the war years of the early 1940s. Sec-

ond, recall from Chapter 30 the possibility that wage increases for union members may come at the expense of the wages of unorganized workers. That is, in obtaining higher wages, unions restrict employment opportunities (Figures 30-6 and 30-7) in organized industries. Unemployed workers and new labor-force entrants therefore seek jobs in the nonunion sectors. The resulting increases in labor supply tend to depress wage rates in nonunion jobs. If this scenario is correct, then higher wages for union workers may be achieved, not at the expense of the capitalist share, but rather at the expense of the nonunion wage share. Overall, the total labor share—union plus nonunion—could well be unaffected by unions. Finally, if the national income is disaggregated into industry sectors (as in Table 7-5) and the historical trend of the wage share in each sector is examined, we reach a curious conclusion. Generally speaking, labor's share has grown more rapidly in those sectors where unions are weak than in sectors which are highly unionized.

Pursuit and escape Other economists perceive substantial stability in the shares of national income that go to labor and capital. That is, if we recognize that most of "proprietors' income" is wages and therefore define labor's share broadly as the sum of "wages and salaries" and "proprietors' income," we note a fairly high degree of stability in labor's share historically. Labor's share, defined as the sum of columns 2 and 3, and the capitalist share, composed of columns 4, 5, and 6, have divided the national income roughly on an 80–20 percent basis throughout the entire period. Economists who have treated the statistics in this way have attempted to explain the stability of labor's share. The **pursuit and escape theory,** for example, is an intriguing explanation with considerable intuitive appeal. Labor and business are envisioned in effect as being engaged in a contest of pursuit and escape. Labor attempts to encroach upon the capitalist share—profits, in particular—by increasing money or nominal wages. But businesses can escape this encroachment in either of two ways: (1) through increasing productivity, which has the effect of absorbing increases in nominal wages and preserving profits; and (2) by increasing product prices as a means of passing increases in wage costs on to consumers. According to the theory, it has been the effective use of these two escape techniques which explains the perceived historical stability of labor's share.[5]

CHAPTER SUMMARY

1 Economic rent is the price paid for the use of land and other natural resources whose total supplies are fixed.

2 Rent is a surplus in the sense that land would be available to the economy as a whole even in the absence of all rental payments. The notion of land rent as a surplus gave rise to the single-tax movement of the late 1800s.

3 Differences in land rent are explainable in terms of differences in productivity due to the fertility and climatic features of land and in its location.

4 Land rent is a surplus rather than a cost to the economy as a whole; however, because land has alternative uses from the standpoint of individual firms and industries, rental payments of firms and industries are correctly regarded as costs.

5 Interest is the price paid for the use of money. The theory of interest envisions a total demand for money comprised of transactions and asset demands. The supply of money is primarily the consequence of monetary policy.

6 The equilibrium interest rate influences the level of investment and helps ration financial and physical capital to specific firms and industries. The real interest rate, not the nominal rate, is critical to the investment decision.

7 Economic, or pure, profits are the difference between a firm's total revenue and its total costs, the latter defined to include implicit costs, which include a normal profit. Profits accrue to entrepreneurs for assuming the uninsurable risks associated with the organizing and directing of economic resources and innovating. Profits also result from monopoly power.

8 Profit expectations influence innovating and investment activities and therefore the level of employment. The basic function of profits and losses, however, is to induce that allocation of resources which is in general accord with the tastes of consumers.

[5] See Clark Kerr, "Labor's Income Share and the Labor Movement," in George W. Taylor and Frank C. Pierson (eds.), *New Concepts in Wage Determination* (New York: McGraw-Hill Book Company, 1957), pp. 260–298. For a more detailed analysis of income shares, see Campbell R. McConnell and Stanley L. Brue, *Contemporary Labor Economics*, 2d ed. (New York: McGraw-Hill Book Company, 1989), chap. 17.

LAST WORD

Determining the price of credit

There are a variety of lending practices which can cause the effective interest rate to be quite different than what it appears to be.

Borrowing and lending—receiving and granting credit—are a way of life. Individuals receive credit when they negotiate a mortgage loan and when they use their credit cards. Conversely, individuals make loans when they open a savings account in a commercial bank or thrift institution or buy a government bond.

Despite the passage of the Truth in Lending Act of 1968, it remains difficult to determine exactly how much interest one pays and receives in borrowing and lending. A few illustrations will be helpful. Let us suppose that you borrow $10,000 which you agree to repay plus $1,000 of interest at the end of the year. In this instance the interest rate is 10 percent. To determine the interest rate (r) one merely compares interest paid with the amount borrowed:

$$r = \frac{\$1,000}{\$10,000} = 10\%$$

But in some cases a lender, say, a bank, will *discount* the interest payment at the time the loan is made. Thus, instead of giving the borrower $10,000, the bank discounts the $1,000 interest payment in advance, giving the borrower only $9,000. This increases the interest rate:

$$r = \frac{\$1,000}{\$9,000} = 11\%$$

While the absolute amount of interest paid is the same, in this second case the borrower has only $9,000 available for the year.

An even more subtle point is that, in order to simplify their calculations, many financial institutions assume a 360-day year (twelve 30-day months). This means the borrower has the use of the lender's funds for five days less than the normal year. This use of a "short year" also increases the interest rate paid by the borrower.

The interest rate paid can change dramatically if a loan is repaid in installments. Suppose a bank lends you $10,000 and charges interest in the amount of $1,000 to be paid at the end of the year. But the loan contract requires you to repay the $10,000 loan in 12 equal monthly installments. The effect of this is that the *average* amount of the loan outstanding during the year is only $5,000. Hence:

$$r = \frac{\$1,000}{\$5,000} = 20\%$$

Here interest is paid on the total amount of the loan ($10,000) rather than the outstanding balance (which averages $5,000 for the year), making for a much higher interest rate.

Another fact which influences the effective interest rate is whether or not interest is *compounded*. Suppose you deposit $10,000 in a savings account which pays a 10 percent interest rate compounded semiannually. In other words, interest is paid on your "loan" to the bank twice a year. At the end of the first six months, $500 of interest (10% of $10,000 for one-half a year) is added to your account. At the end of the year, interest is calculated on $10,500 so that the second interest payment is $525 (10% of $10,500 for one-half a year). Hence:

$$r = \frac{\$1,025}{\$10,000} = 10.25\%$$

This means that a bank advertising a 10 percent interest rate compounded semiannually is actually paying more interest to its customers than a competitor paying a simple (noncompounded) interest rate of 10.20 percent.

"Let the buyer beware" is a fitting motto in the world of credit.

9 The largest share of the national income goes to labor. Narrowly defined as "wages and salaries," labor's relative share has increased through time. When more broadly defined to include "proprietors' income," labor's share has been about 80 percent and the capitalist share about 20 percent of national income since 1900.

TERMS AND CONCEPTS

economic rent	pure rate of interest
incentive function	explicit and implicit costs
single-tax movement	
Truth in Lending Act	economic or pure profit
transactions and asset demands for money	normal profit
	static economy
nominal versus real interest rate	uninsurable risks
	pursuit and escape theory

QUESTIONS AND STUDY SUGGESTIONS

1 How does the economist's usage of the term "rent" differ from everyday usage? "Though rent need not be paid by society to make land available, rental payments are very useful in guiding land into the most productive uses." Explain.

2 Explain why economic rent is a surplus to the economy as a whole but a cost of production from the standpoint of individual firms and industries. Explain: "Rent performs no 'incentive function' in the economy." What arguments can be made for and against a heavy tax on land?

3 If money capital, as such, is not an economic resource, why is interest paid and received for its use? What considerations account for the fact that interest rates differ greatly on various types of loans? Use these considerations to explain the relative size of the interest rates charged on the following: *a* a ten-year $1000 government bond; *b* a $20 pawnshop loan; *c* an FHA thirty-year mortgage loan on a $97,000 house; *d* a 24-month $12,000 commercial bank loan to finance the purchase of an automobile; and *e* a 60-day $100 loan from a personal finance company.

4 What is the basic determinant of the transactions demand for money? The asset demand for money? Combine these graphically with the supply of money to determine the equilibrium interest rate. Comment: "The interest rate is an administered price."

5 What are the major economic functions of the interest rate? Of economic profits? How might the fact that more and more businesses are financing their investment activities internally affect the efficiency with which the interest rate performs its functions?

6 Distinguish between nominal and real interest rates. Which is more relevant in making investment decisions? If the nominal interest rate is 12 percent and the inflation rate is 8 percent, what is the real rate of interest? At various times during the 1970s savers earned nominal rates of interest on their savings accounts which were less than the rate of inflation so that their savings earned negative real interest. Why, then, did they save?

7 Historically, usury laws which put below-equilibrium ceilings on interest rates have been used by some states on the grounds that such laws will make credit available to poor people who could not otherwise afford to borrow. Critics of such laws contend that it is poor people who are most likely to be hurt by such laws. Which view is correct?

8 How do the concepts of business profits and economic profits differ? Why are economic profits smaller than business profits? What are the three basic sources of economic profits? Classify each of the following in accordance with these sources: **a** the profits acquired by a firm from developing and patenting a ball-point pen containing a permanent ink cartridge; **b** the profit of a restaurant which results from construction of a new highway past its door; **c** the profit received by a firm benefiting from an unanticipated change in consumer tastes.

9 Why is the distinction between insurable and uninsurable risks significant for the theory of profits? Carefully evaluate: "All economic profits can be traced to either uncertainty or the desire to avoid it."

10 Explain the absence of economic profit in a purely competitive, static economy. Realizing that the major function of profits is to allocate resources in accordance with consumer preferences, evaluate the allocation of resources in such an economy.

11 What has happened to the wage, profit, interest, and rent shares of national income over time? Explain the alleged growth of labor's share in terms of structural changes in the economy. Explain the alleged stability of labor's share in terms of the "pursuit and escape" theory.

CHAPTER 32

General equilibrium: the market system and its operation

Drawing together the discussion of product and resource markets—the dominant theme of Part 5—is the basic purpose of this chapter.[1] We have analyzed the various categories of individual product and resource markets in some detail. Our present goal is to reemphasize that the many diverse markets of our economy are interwoven into a highly complex *market system*. This market system is responsible for the production of about four-fifths or more of our national product and therefore for the allocation of a comparable proportion of available resources. It is imperative that we grasp how this market system works.

[1] As a prologue to the present chapter, it might be helpful for the reader to scan Chapter 5 and the concluding section of Chapter 25, which summarizes the efficiency aspects of competitive pricing.

Partial and general equilibrium

Our discussion of prices has been compartmentalized; we have examined representative product and resource prices at one time, in isolation, and apart from any detailed interrelationships each may bear to the other. In the jargon of the economist, we have been concerned with **partial equilibrium analysis**—a study of equilibrium prices and outputs in the many specific markets which are the component *parts* of the market system.

But the economy is not merely a myriad of isolated and unrelated markets. On the contrary, it is an interlocking network of prices wherein changes in one market are likely to elicit numerous and significant changes in other markets. Hence, our vantage point now shifts from individual markets and prices in isolation to an analysis of the market system as a whole. In technical language, our discussion now shifts to **general equilibrium analysis**—an overall, big-picture view of the interrelationships among all the various markets and prices (parts) which make up the market *system*.

We shall attempt to grasp the interrelatedness of various industries and markets through a series of three general equilibrium illustrations. We begin with an examination of the multitudinous effects of oil price increases in the 1970s. Next we turn to a hypothetical model of two industries which makes explicit use of the formal analytical tools of microeconomics. A third and final model views the interdependence of the various sectors of the economy through what is called input-output analysis. The chapter closes with a discussion of the relevance of general equilibrium analysis for economic understanding.

Market interrelationships: OPEC and oil prices

Just as a rock dropped into a pond causes widening circles of ripples, any change in the economy precipitates further changes which radiate outward with gradually diminishing force. And just as these ripples sometimes reach shore and rebound eventually to affect the initial point of impact, so too are there feedback effects of initial changes occurring in single markets in the economy. This process of reverberation continues throughout the domestic economy—indeed, throughout the world economy—as a new equilibrium is approached in all markets.

To gain insight as to the interrelatedness of markets, let us consider one of the most dramatic series of price changes of recent history—the dramatic run-up of oil prices in the 1970s. More specifically, in 1973–1974 the OPEC (Organization of Petroleum Exporting Countries) oil cartel—which then accounted for 90 percent of world oil exports—was able to restrict production and increase oil prices by about $8 per barrel. In relative terms the price of a barrel of oil quadrupled within a few months. Then in 1979–1980 OPEC succeeded in imposing a much larger price increase of about $21 per barrel. Thus the barrel of oil which sold for $2.50 in 1972 was priced at $34 in 1980.

According to partial equilibrium analysis, the restriction of output by OPEC would simply reduce the supply of oil, increase its equilibrium price, and reduce its equilibrium output. And that would be the end of the matter. But this narrow perspective would conceal most of the important ramifications of the price increase. What were some of the more salient implications of these oil price increases? Although the two are not neatly separable, let us first consider impacts upon the domestic economy and then turn to international effects.

THE UNITED STATES ECONOMY

One of the initial effects of much higher oil prices was for users to conserve in the use of oil and derivative products and to seek substitute products. For example, many power producers converted their plants from oil to natural gas or coal. Wood-burning stoves and furnaces became popular in homes once again. High oil prices affected locational decisions as many firms moved from the Snow Belt to the Sun Belt.

The prices of products derived from oil—for example, plastics and commercial fertilizer—rose sharply, causing higher costs and a variety of adjustments for manufacturers and farmers who used these products as inputs. The rise in gasoline prices from about $.30 per gallon in the pre-OPEC era to $.65 per gallon in 1974 had far-reaching effects on both automobile users and producers. The immediate effect of the sharply higher gasoline prices was to cause drivers to curtail the use of their cars. Thus, carpools suddenly became popular. Resort owners were adversely affected as many drivers canceled or cut short their vacation plans. The demands for goods and services complementary to automobiles—car washes, motor oil, tires, and auto repairs—tended to decline. The demand for substitutes—for example, public transportation—tended to increase. Over time, automobile purchasers redirected their expenditures from large gas-guzzling American-made cars to compact fuel-efficient imports from Japan and West Germany. The OPEC-inspired upsurge in oil and gasoline prices was an important contributor to the growing share of imports in the United States automobile market in the 1970s and early 1980s.

Households which used oil for heating also took steps to conserve. This was reflected in increased demands for insulation, weatherstripping, thermopane windows, storm doors, and so forth. Impacts upon resource markets were predictable and, in some cases, quite profound. Less labor was needed in the production of domestic automobiles and more was needed in the production and installation of insulation. Less capital was used to build gas stations and more was employed in oil-drilling rigs and offshore platforms. More generally, high energy prices rendered obsolete the plants and equipment of some industries. In some cases this was the direct result of higher operating costs. Capital goods which were economic and usable when oil was $2 per barrel became uneconomic when oil was priced at $10, $15, or $25 per barrel. In other instances the obsolescence reflected the impact of higher oil prices upon the structure of product demand. The plants of American auto producers were heavily committed to the production of large fuel-inefficient cars, the demand for which lagged as consumers shifted to more fuel-efficient imports.

Many more subtle ripples emanating from higher oil and gas prices stemmed from the fact that the demands for oil and gas are inelastic. For example, the elasticity of demand for gasoline is estimated to be in the .20 to .40 range, which means that a 10 percent increase in its price will only result in a 2 to 4 percent decrease in consumption. Recalling our total revenue (expenditures) test for elasticity (Chapter 22), this means that after a price increase consumers will spend a larger portion of their income on oil and gasoline and therefore will have less to spend upon a whole host of other goods and services which are unrelated to oil and gasoline as either substitutes or complements. From a slightly different perspective, the OPEC oil price increases were the equivalent of a gigantic tax levied upon imported oil. American consumers and manufacturers were forced to pay this tax and the OPEC nations served as tax collectors. This "OPEC tax"—which totaled as much as $40 to $50 billion per year—had significant contractionary effects. In technical terms, the net exports (exports minus imports) component of aggregate demand declined, tending to shift the curve to the left. More simply stated, after paying the OPEC tax, American consumers and businesses found themselves with less to spend on domestic consumption and investment goods.

The impacts of higher oil prices were so pervasive as to be an important factor in the stagflation of the 1970s. As noted, higher energy prices confronted American producers with higher per unit production costs. Indeed, it is difficult to think of any industry whose production and transportation costs were not increased by OPEC's price boosts. In terms of the cost-push inflation model, these cost increases shifted the aggregate supply curve leftward and brought about both a higher price level and reductions in real output and employment.

It must be emphasized that not all American industries were affected negatively by OPEC's oil price increases. American oil-producing companies in particular benefited greatly and enjoyed soaring profits. The economies of oil-producing states such as Texas and Louisiana boomed in the 1970s. And we have already suggested that industries producing substitutes for oil prospered. Thus the American coal industry experienced a revitalization in the 1970s.

THE WORLD ECONOMY

The economic impacts of the increase in OPEC oil prices transcended national boundaries. We have noted that the price boosts gave rise to gigantic transfers of real income from oil-importing nations such as the United States to OPEC and other oil-exporting countries. In real terms these transfers reflected the fact that higher oil prices shifted the "terms of trade" against the oil-importing nations and in favor of oil-exporting nations. The United States and other oil importers were forced to exchange larger amounts of their real output to obtain a barrel of imported oil than was previously the case, tending to lower our domestic standard of living.

But the financial aspects of these transfers also posed problems. In particular, the United States for many years has had international trade deficits; that is, the value of our merchandise exports has been less than that of our merchandise imports. Or, simply put, the United States has not been "paying its way" in international trade. The large boosts in the price of imported oil greatly intensified this problem.

Higher oil prices also had dramatic effects upon foreign exchange markets. The international value of the dollar—that is, the price of the dollar in terms of other currencies—is largely determined by the forces of supply and demand. Therefore, when OPEC raised oil prices, the resulting increase in the United States' expenditures for its oil imports increased the supply of dollars in foreign exchange markets. This increase in the supply of dollars relative to demand tended to reduce the international value of the dollar. Using Chapter 4's terminology, the dollar depreciated. This depreciation had important consequences. Most importantly, it reinforced the cost-push inflation which was occurring. When the dollar's value declines, the effect is to increase the price of *all* goods which Americans import. When the dollar depreciates, it takes more dollars to buy a given amount of a foreign currency and, therefore, more dollars to buy a foreign product. A British woolen suit, selling for

£50 in Britain, will cost an American buyer only $100 when the dollar is worth half a pound. That same suit will cost an American $200 if the dollar depreciates to one-fourth of a pound. In short, the decline in the international value of the dollar boosted the prices of all imports and reinforced our domestic inflation.

The impact of the oil price increases was particularly devastating for the many non-oil-producing, less developed countries (LDCs) of Africa, Asia, and Latin America. They were dependent upon petroleum as an energy source in developing their economies. But by having to pay much higher prices for oil, they were forced to sacrifice not only sorely needed consumer goods, but also the capital goods essential for long-term economic growth. Furthermore, stagflation in the industrially advanced nations curtailed demand for LDC exports. Hence, most of the LDCs were forced to borrow. Indeed, LDC debts to the wealthier nations increased almost sevenfold between 1973 and 1982. As we shall see in Chapter 41, that huge debt constitutes something of a threat to the banking systems of the industrially advanced nations.

General equilibrium: a two-industry model

Let us now consider a hypothetical illustration which explicitly embodies the formal tools of economic analysis. In Figure 32-1, which is merely a somewhat sophisticated version of Figure 3-2, the discussion focuses upon two product markets, X and Y. And although each industry would actually employ a number of different inputs, it will facilitate our analysis to concentrate only upon the labor market relevant to each industry. It is assumed that industry X uses type A labor and Y uses type B labor. We also assume that both product markets and resource (labor) markets are purely competitive.

BEHIND THE CURVES

A word or two is in order to remind us of the concepts which underlie the demand and supply curves of both product and resource markets. The

product demand curves are downsloping because of *diminishing marginal utility* (Chapter 23). Successive units of a given product yield less and less additional satisfaction or utility to buyers, so that consumers will purchase more of that product only if its price falls. The upsloping product supply curves are based upon the concept of *increasing marginal costs* (Chapter 24). Because extra units of output are more costly, firms must receive a higher price before it will be profitable for them to produce this extra output. The downsloping labor demand curves are based upon the law of diminishing returns or *diminishing marginal productivity* (Chapter 29). Beyond some point, the addition of labor or any other variable resource to fixed resources will result in smaller and smaller increases in total output. And as we recall these concepts from earlier chapters, do not overlook the obvious link between the upsloping product supply curve and the downsloping resource demand curve. It is the diminishing marginal productivity of the resource which *causes* marginal costs to increase as output is increased. If each successive unit of labor (hired at a constant wage cost) adds less and less to output, then the cost of *each* successive unit of output must be more and more. Finally, the upsloping labor supply curves reflect the *rising opportunity costs* involved in attracting additional workers (Chapter 30). A firm or an industry must pay higher and higher wage rates to obtain larger amounts of labor service.

INITIAL CONDITIONS

We assume long-run equilibrium initially, so that P_{x1} and w_{a1} are the equilibrium product price and wage rate for industry X, and P_{y1} and w_{b1} represent the equilibrium price and wage for industry Y. Firms are making normal profits, and there is therefore no reason for either industry to expand or contract. The two labor markets are similarly "at rest"; there is therefore no incentive for workers to move out of or into either market.

Suppose now that something happens to upset this equilibrium. What will be the character of the resulting adjustments? Specifically, let us say that a change occurs in consumer preferences or tastes so that consumer demand for X increases and consumer demand for Y simultaneously decreases.

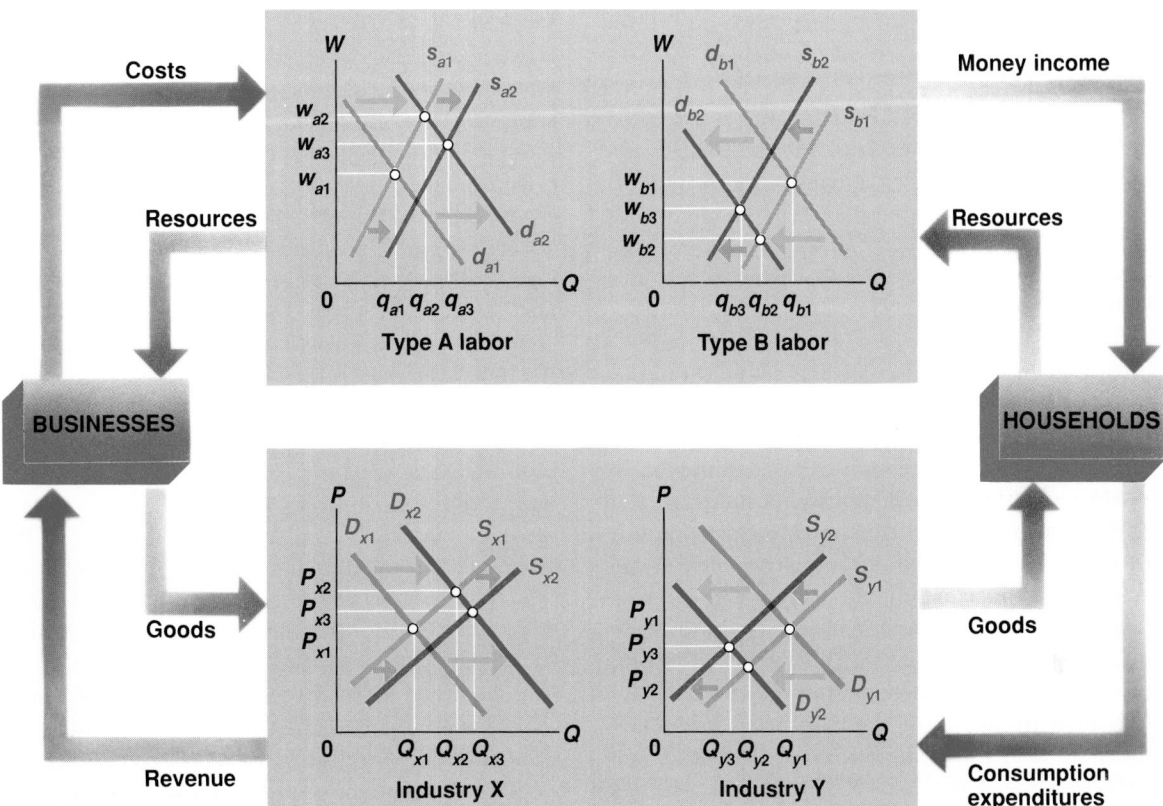

FIGURE 32-1

General equilibrium and the interaction of product and resource markets

These diagrams show the short-run and long-run adjustments resulting from an assumed increase in the demand for product X and assumed decline in the demand for product Y. Emphasis here is upon product and resource market interactions, and the diagrams therefore conceal many of the less obvious repercussions. For example, the given changes in demand for X and Y will affect the demands for substitute and complementary goods and alter the distribution of income.

SHORT-RUN ADJUSTMENTS

What short-run adjustments will occur in response to these changes in consumer demand? First of all, production, which was normally profitable in industry X before demand rose from D_{x1} to D_{x2}, now results in economic profits. Firms in industry X, faced with the new higher price of P_{x2}, find it profitable to move to some point further up and to the right on their marginal-cost curves (Figure 25-6). Collectively, these marginal-cost curves are the supply curve S_{x1} for the industry. Thus, in Figure 32-1 existing firms find it profitable to expand output as a group from Q_{x1} to Q_{x2}.

But to expand output, the firms in industry X must acquire more resources, such as type A labor. Remembering that the demand for resources is a *derived demand*, it is no surprise that the expansion of output by firms in X will increase the demand for labor from d_{a1} to, say, d_{a2}. Workers in this labor market are willing to offer more of their services, perhaps by working longer hours or more days per week, moving up s_{a1} in response to the higher wage rate w_{a2}.

An opposite set of short-run adjustments will be experienced in industry Y. Product demand falls to, say, D_{y2}, causing price to fall from P_{y1} to P_{y2}. At this lower price, individual firms incur losses.

These firms will react by moving down and to the left on their marginal-cost curves as they seek their loss-minimizing positions. The decline in demand for product Y is reflected back in the resource market. In particular, the demand for type B labor falls from d_{b1} to d_{b2}, causing the equilibrium wage rate to decline to w_{b2} and employment to fall to q_{b2}.

LONG-RUN ADJUSTMENTS

But we have only traced the first round of market adjustments. At the conclusion of these short-run adjustments, the production of X still yields an economic profit, while losses persist in industry Y. The presumed changes in consumer demand have made X a prosperous, expanding industry and Y an unprosperous, declining industry. This means that, given sufficient time, new firms will enter industry X, while firms will tend to leave industry Y.

As new firms enter X, the industry supply curve will shift to the right from S_{x1} to, say, S_{x2}. This increase in supply tends to bring price back down to, say, P_{x3}. Equilibrium output of X has further increased to Q_{x3}. If P_{x3} and Q_{x3} represent a new long-run equilibrium, as we assume is the case, we can note in passing that industry X must be an increasing-cost industry. Why? Because the new long-run equilibrium entails a higher price than the initial equilibrium price P_{x1} (Figure 25-11). If this were a constant-cost industry, the new price would be the same as the original price. It is to be emphasized that, in the new equilibrium position, consumers are getting a larger output of X—which is, of course, precisely what they wanted. In other words, these adjustments are a manifestation of *consumer sovereignty*.

Losses in industry Y induce firms to leave the industry. As they do, industry supply will decline from S_{y1} to, say, S_{y2}. This raises price somewhat from P_{y2} to P_{y3}. If we assume industry Y is also an increasing-cost industry, contraction of the industry will lower unit costs. Thus, in the new long-run equilibrium position at P_{y3}, price will be lower than originally, production will be normally profitable once again, and industry size will be stabilized.

These long-run adjustments have counterparts in the resource markets. The supply curve for type B labor, s_{b1}, is drawn on the assumption that other wage rates—for example, the wage rate received by type A labor—are given. The same holds true for the type A labor supply curve, s_{a1}. But our short-run changes in the demand for labor have increased the wage rate for type A labor and reduced the wage rate for type B labor. The stage is set for some of type B labor to shift from industry Y, where job opportunities and wage rates have been declining, to industry X, where employment has been expanding and wage rates have been increasing. Thus we would expect the supply of type A labor to increase from s_{a1} to, say, s_{a2} and the supply of type B labor to fall from s_{b1} to, say, s_{b2}. As a result, wage rates for type A labor fall somewhat from w_{a2} to w_{a3}. And for type B labor, wage rates tend to go back up from w_{b2} to, say, w_{b3}.

But note several related points about these labor market adjustments. First, we are assuming that type B labor can become qualified as type A labor without too much difficulty and retraining. In practice, occupational shifts may actually be complicated and costly to achieve. A second and closely related point is that supply shifts might take a substantial period of time. As suggested, type B workers may in fact require additional education, job retraining, and geographical relocation before becoming type A workers. Finally, because of various immobilities (Chapter 30), we would not expect the supply curve shifts to be sufficiently great to restore the wage rates of the original equilibrium. The new equilibrium wage rate will be w_{a3} (higher than w_{a1}) for type A labor and w_{b3} (lower than w_{b1}) for type B labor. Indeed, these long-run wage adjustments are consistent with and a factor in, the assumed increasing-cost character of industries X and Y.

FURTHER ADJUSTMENTS

But this is only the beginning of the repercussions which stem from our original change in the structure of consumer demand. There are innumerable more subtle adjustments which we might take into account.

Other industries Consider now a third industry—call it industry Z. Will the initial increase in the price of X have any impact upon industry Z? It might! Recall that one of the determinants of the demand for Z is the prices of related goods, and X just might be "related" to Z. But any shift in the demand for Z which stems from the increase in the price of X depends on precisely how products X and Z are related. Recall (Chapter 4) that any two products might be *substitutes* (butter and margarine), *complements* (gasoline and oil), or *independent goods* (raisins and wristwatches). If X and Z are independent goods, then a rise in the price of X will have no significant effect on the demand for Z. But if X and Z are substitutes, the rise in the price of X will increase the demand for Z. Therefore, a series of adjustments will be precipitated in the product and resource markets for Z similar to those just sketched for X. And if X and Z are complements, the higher price for X will lower the demand for Z. This would precipitate adjustments in Z like those already traced for industry Y.

Other resources The initial changes in the demands for type A and type B labor may have an impact upon other resource markets. Suppose that technology in industry X is such that labor and capital must be used in virtually fixed proportions, for example, one machine is needed for every two workers. This means that the expansion in the employment of type A labor will stimulate the demand for relevant kinds of capital goods.

Income distribution It is also quite evident that our short-run and long-run adjustments will alter the distribution of income. Workers and entrepreneurs associated with industry X will receive higher incomes; those in industry Y, lower incomes. It is realistic to assume some differences in tastes which will be transformed into further changes in the structure of consumer demand. These new changes in demand will trigger new rounds of short-run and long-run adjustments.

We could go on, but the basic point is clear. The adjustments stemming from our initial changes in demand are much more complex and go far beyond the simple supply and demand shifts portrayed in Figure 32-1. *Any initial disturbance such as a change in demand, a change in technology, or a change in resource supply will set off a highly complex economic chain reaction.* This chapter's Last Word is a fascinating case study of the seem-ingly endless chain of economic repercussions triggered by the virtual suspension of American cotton exports to England during the Civil War.

EFFICIENCY IMPLICATIONS

The competitive market system is conducive to the efficient use of resources. We found in Chapter 25 that under pure competition both "allocative efficiency" and "productive efficiency" are realized. In nontechnical terms, the "right" amount of each good will be produced and per unit production costs for each good will be minimized. Furthermore, given the distribution of income, free choice by consumers enable them to spend their incomes so as to maximize their satisfaction or utility (Chapter 23).

But we must also recall a number of real-world complications. In particular, the competitive market system would not allocate resources to the production of public goods. Nor would it take into account spillover benefits and costs (Chapters 6 and 33). Stated differently, government would have to employ its taxation and expenditure powers to provide the economy with public goods. It would also need to use legislation or specific taxes and subsidies to correct the misallocations of resources caused by spillover costs and benefits. Furthermore, the personal distribution of income which the competitive market system would yield might not be regarded by society as equitable or just, again implying the need for governmental intervention. Finally, we are aware that in the real world our market system is imperfectly competitive (Chapters 26 through 28) with the result that resources are utilized less efficiently and resource reallocations are more sluggish and less complete than our discussion of Figure 32-1 implies.

General equilibrium: input-output analysis

The relatively simple general equilibrium model just explored serves the major purpose of emphasizing the interrelatedness of the many decision

TABLE 32-1 **A simplified input-output table** *(hypothetical data)*

	Consuming or using sectors					
Producing sectors	(1) Metal	(2) Machinery	(3) Fuel	(4) Agriculture	(5) Households (labor)	(6) Total output
(1) Metal	10	65	10	5	10	100
(2) Machinery	40	25	35	75	25	200
(3) Fuel	15	5	5	5	20	50
(4) Agriculture	15	10	50	50	525	650
(5) Labor (households)	100	200	100	550	50	1000

makers who comprise the economy. Further appreciation of the intricate interrelationships between the various sectors or industries of the economy can be gained through **input-output analysis.**

INPUT-OUTPUT TABLE

Table 32-1 is a very much simplified hypothetical input-output table for an economy.[2] Listed down the left side of the table are the five producing sectors (industries) of the economy. Column 6 shows the total output associated with each of the five sectors; the metal sector produces 100 units, the machine sector 200 units, and so on. These same five sectors are also the consuming sectors of the economy and are shown in this capacity across the top of the table. Looking across each of the horizontal rows of figures, we can see how the total output of each sector is disposed of, or consumed, among the five sectors. For example, of the 200

[2] Wassily W. Leontieff is largely responsible for input-output analysis. See his simplified discussion of "Input-Output Economics," *Scientific American,* October 1951, pp. 15–21. Table 32-1 and portions of the accompanying discussion are from Francis M. Boddy, "Soviet Economic Growth," in Robert T. Holt and John E. Turner (eds.), *Soviet Union: Paradox and Change* (New York: Holt, Rinehart and Winston, Inc., 1962), pp. 77–79, with permission of the publisher. Currently national input-output tables divide the economy into over 400 industries, producing an input-output matrix which has over 400 rows and columns.

units of output of the machinery sector, 40 units go to the metal sector, 25 to the machinery sector itself (because it takes machines to produce machines), and 35, 75, and 25 units go to the fuel, agriculture, and household sectors, respectively, thereby exhausting the units produced.

Following through on this disposition-of-output procedure for all five sectors, we find that each vertical column must and does show the units of output of each producing sector which are consumed as inputs by the five sectors. For example, we find in column 2 that to produce 200 units of machinery, inputs of 65 units of metal, 25 of machinery, 5 of fuel, 10 of agricultural products, and 200 of labor are required. In this way, the table vividly reveals the highly interdependent character of the various sectors or industries. Any given industry or sector employs the outputs of other sectors—and indeed, some of its own output—as its inputs. And the outputs of that given sector are similarly the inputs of the other sectors. To cite a real-world example: While outputs of steel are inputs in the production of railroad cars, these railroad cars are, in turn, used to transport both finished steel and the various inputs—coke, pig iron, and so forth—which are necessary to the production of steel.

INTERDEPENDENCE

The interdependence of the economy's sectors or industries can be further demonstrated by tracing the repercussions of an assumed change in the output of some commodity.

Consider, for example, the repercussions of a 20-unit (10 percent) increase in machinery production. This means that a 10 percent increase in the production of all the outputs which are used as inputs in the production of machinery is required.[3] These inputs, as we know, are listed in column 2 of the table. Applying the 10 percent figure, we find that 6.5 additional units (outputs) of metal, 2.5 units of machinery, 0.5 unit of fuel, 1 unit of agricultural products, and 20 units of labor will be needed to produce another 20 units of machinery.

But this is just the beginning: Many further adjustments are also required. Because each sector which supplies inputs to the machinery sector must expand *its* output, these supplying sectors in turn will require more inputs from other sectors. Example: The additional 6.5 units of metal needed as inputs to produce the extra 20 units of machinery will in turn call for an appropriate—6.5 percent, in this case—increase in the production of all the inputs shown in column 1 to be needed in producing metal. The same reasoning, of course, is applicable to the fuel, agriculture, and labor sectors. That is, the 0.5-unit increase in fuel production required in producing the extra 20 units of machinery will call for an appropriate (1 percent) increase in the production of all the inputs listed in column 3, and similarly for the agricultural and labor sectors. Note that the production of 20 more units of machinery output requires as inputs the production of 2.5 units of machinery. This 2.5-unit increase will require "second-round" increases (of 1.25 percent here) in the inputs of all the resources shown in column 2 in the same general fashion as did the initial 20-unit increase in machinery output.

The reader will clearly recognize that the chain reaction is by no means at an end. All the repercussions cited in these examples call for still further adjustments similar to those already described. The crucial point, of course, is that, because of the high degree of interrelatedness among the sectors of the economy, a change in the figure in any one "cell" or "box" of the input-output table will precipitate an almost endless series of adjustments in

other figures. In our illustration, the expansion of production in one sector has nearly innumerable repercussions which reach into virtually every nook and cranny of the economy. This is why economists sometimes remark, not entirely facetiously, that "in economics everything depends upon everything else."

General equilibrium and economic understanding

General equilibrium analysis can be very useful in evaluating the overall operation of the economy, in understanding specific economic problems, and in formulating policies. A failure to recognize price and sector interrelationships is an important source of misunderstanding and faulty reasoning about major economic problems. Furthermore, input-output analysis lends itself to an abundance of practical applications.

AN ILLUSTRATION

Let us consider an example which reinforces the assertation that it may be essential to go beyond partial equilibrium analysis to understand certain economic issues. Many people favor protective tariffs levied on, say, Japanese or German autos, because the immediate effect will be to increase the price of foreign autos and therefore increase the demand for American-made autos. The result is that output and employment rise in the American auto industry. But this ignores the fact that incomes in Japan and Germany will decline as a result of their inability to sell autos in the United States. And with smaller incomes they will be less able to buy from American industries exporting machine tools, computers, grains, aircraft, and so forth. The increase in employment in the protected industry may well be offset, wholly or in part, by the indirect, subtle declines in employment in American export industries. As a matter of fact, apart from any decline in domestic employment stemming from tariff-induced declines in exports, general equilibrium analysis reminds us that the extra resources which are shifted into the expand-

---

[3] We invoke here one of the simplifying assumptions underlying the input-output table, namely, that production occurs under conditions of constant returns to scale (see Chapter 24).

ing auto industry must come from other industries. In other words, in a full-employment economy the tariff-inspired expansion of the auto industry will entail a contraction in the production of other goods.

FORECASTING AND PLANNING

Input-output analysis has resulted in empirical measurement of the various interactions between sectors of the economy, and these measurements have proved of considerable value as an instrument of economic forecasting and planning. Assume for the moment a much more detailed input-output table containing 50 or even 500 individual sectors with each box filled with accurate empirical data. Now, for example, if the government should decide to undertake the production of fifty new supersonic bombers, the impact of this decision upon affected sectors could be quite accurately predicted; we can forecast quantitatively "what it will take" in terms of the outputs of all the many affected industries to fulfill this goal. Input-output analysis also has considerable relevance for the less developed nations, many of which seek growth through some form of planning (Chapter 41) and for more advanced centrally planned systems, such as the Soviet Union (Chapter 42). By revealing the quantitative interrelationships among various sectors of the economy, input-output analysis allows the planners to determine how realistic—how feasible—planned production targets actually are. By tracing the repercussions of, say, a planned increase in steel production of 10 percent, the Central Planning Board of the U.S.S.R. can estimate what outputs of coal, iron ore, transportation, labor, relevant capital equipment, and all other inputs used in the production of steel will be needed to fulfill this target. In this way, potential bottlenecks to the realization of this goal (or others) may be uncovered; for example, transportation problems may be revealed, or it may be found that the additional plant capacity required conflicts severely with the planned production of housing or the planned expansion of the chemicals industry. Appropriate adjustments may therefore be made in the production targets for steel or other products to make the plan more realistic and more consistent with the constraints imposed by technology and overall scarcities of

LAST WORD

The English cotton famine

The relevance of general equilibrium analysis is illustrated by the myriad effects of the marked decline of American cotton exports to England during the Civil War.

The Civil War led to a near suspension of English imports of American cotton, which in 1860 had accounted for about four-fifths of the English supply. The price of cotton at Liverpool rose from 8 pence per pound in June of 1860 to a peak of $31\frac{1}{2}$ pence in July of 1864. The effects of this cotton famine provide some notion of the interrelationships of prices: the famine was severe (imports of cotton fell by three-fifths from 1861 to 1862) and the cotton industry was very large (employing about 500,000 people in a total labor force of 9 million), so wide effects are noticeable.

The famine led to a great decrease in the demand for cotton fabrication, and hence in the demand for the services of cotton mills and their laborers. The margin between the prices of raw cotton and cloth (taking 39-inch shirtings as an example) declined from 7 pence a pound in 1860, almost equal to the cost of the raw cotton, to 1 or 2 pence in 1862 and 1863. Wage (piece) rates fell an unknown amount, and workers' earnings fell much more when they were forced to work with the inferior Surat cotton.

Of course a large expansion took place in rival fabrics. The production of flax quadrupled between 1861 and 1864 in Ireland, and yarn imports rose greatly; even so, prices of linen goods rose about 60 per cent between 1862 and 1864. Similarly, the wool industry experienced a great boom: imports of wool rose by a third during the period, and raw wool prices rose more than 40 per cent, but the

Yorkshire industry was overtaxed and processing margins increased by half. Some migration of cotton workers and entrepreneurs to Yorkshire, and of weavers of woolens to Lancashire, helped the latter area.

The unemployment in Lancashire caused great distress. The big decrease in consumer expenditures in the area hit shopkeepers hard, and landlords even harder: families doubled up, marriages fell by more than a third, and poor rates increased. By 1863 about one-fourth of the families requiring public assistance were not directly connected with the textile industry.

Of course the effects reached to industries for which cotton textiles was an important customer. The textile machinery industry had a bad slump until 1864, and the warehouses of the region suffered also. The Lancashire and Yorkshire Railway, unlike other English roads, had a decline in both freight and passenger traffic in 1862 and 1863.

We could cast our net farther to uncover more relationships of substitution and complementarity and buyer and seller, and subject only to the limitations of imagination and energy, we shall continue to find them. In Birmingham, to give only one example, the button and needle industries had to discharge many workers, but the edged-tool industry expanded greatly to provide tools for new cotton plantings in India and Egypt.

Perhaps this brief and highly incomplete sketch is sufficient to illustrate the basis for the economist's faith, for such it is, in the general interdependence of economic phenomena. It does not seem bold to conjecture that everyone in England was somehow affected by the cotton famine: as a consumer, in the price of clothing; as a laborer, in the altered directions of consumer spending; in the effects on transport, banking, and commerce; as a capitalist, in the return on investments in textiles and other industries.

Source: George J. Stigler, *The Theory of Price*, rev. ed. (New York: The Macmillan Company, 1952), pp. 288–289. Copyright © 1952 by the Macmillan Company. Reprinted by permission.

economic resources. This is not to say that input-output analysis guarantees that planned production targets will necessarily be met or that it is a panacea for the less developed countries. But properly conceived input-output analysis does provide a useful planning tool.

General equilibrium analysis provides a much broader perspective for analyzing the effects of given economic disturbances or policies than does partial equilibrium analysis. Partial equilibrium analysis shows merely "the big splash" of an initial disturbance; general equilibrium analysis traces the waves and ripples emanating from the big splash. In some instances the waves and ripples are relatively unimportant; in others they may prove to be a tidal wave which completely changes conclusions one would draw from the big splash viewed in isolation. As we noted in Chapter 1, a basic task of the economist is that of ascertaining which waves and ripples are important to the analysis of a given question and which can be safely ignored. In any event, a grasp of the general equilibrium point of view is essential in understanding and evaluating our economy.

CHAPTER SUMMARY

1 General equilibrium analysis is concerned with the operation of the entire market system and the interrelationships among different markets and prices. These interrelationships are important in that they might modify or negate the immediate affects of economic disturbances or policies which partial equilibrium analysis reveals.

2 The dramatic increases in oil prices which occurred in 1973–1974 and in 1979–1980 provide an interesting case study of the multitude of market responses which came into play both domestically and internationally.

3 Demand and supply analysis for both product and resource markets can be used to analyze the many market adjustments triggered by an initial change in market demand or supply.

4 The input-output table provides a kind of general equilibrium analysis which reveals the overall fabric of the economy by focusing upon the interdependencies that exist among the various sectors or industries which it comprises. Input-output analysis has practical applications to economic forecasting and planning.

TERMS AND CONCEPTS

partial equilibrium analysis

input-output analysis

general equilibrium analysis

QUESTIONS AND STUDY SUGGESTIONS

1 Compare partial and general equilibrium analysis. In what respect is each useful?

2 Trace through the market system the economic effects of: **a** the development of a synthetic fiber which never wears out, fades, or stains; **b** a permanent increase in the demand for leather; **c** a sharp decline in the size of the labor force; **d** the development of a new production technique which cuts the cost of home computers by 50 percent; **e** the imposition of a 20 percent excise tax on shoes; **f** the discovery of an effective vaccine for the common cold.

3 Use your understanding of general equilibrium analysis to trace through the market repercussions of the following developments:

a For health reasons there has been a shift of consumer demand from red meat to seafood.

b Because of the greater use of preventive measures, such as fluoridated water and regular dental care, the demand for dental services has declined.

4 Assume a drought in the Great Plains reduces the supply of wheat. Given that wheat is a basic ingredient in the production of bread and that potatoes are a consumer substitute for bread, use supply and demand diagrams to explain the effects of the drought upon **a** the price of wheat, **b** the supply and price of bread, and **c** the demand for and price of potatoes. Sketch the nature of the relevant resource market adjustments.

5 Explain the following statements:

a "Allocative efficiency does not mean distributive justice."

b "There is an 'efficient' or 'optimum' allocation of resources for every conceivable distribution of money income."

6 What is an input-output table? Using Table 32-1, trace some of the repercussions of a 5-unit (10 percent) increase in fuel production. What insights might input-output analysis provide as to the operation of a capitalistic system? How might input-output analysis be used as a "mechanism of coordination" in a centrally planned system?

7 In early 1986 the OPEC oil cartel fell into severe disarray and per barrel oil prices fell from $28 to about $10. List some of the economic repercussions of a substantial reduction in the price of oil for the United States. In particular, trace the expected effects upon our automobile, coal, steel, airline, and oil-exploration industries. What impact might a price cut have upon the locational decisions of firms within the United States? What implications will the price cut have upon American banks which have made large loans to less developed oil producing countries such as Mexico? What might the effects be upon the world distribution of real income? Upon exchange rates?

8 "Economic growth is more important than achieving allocative efficiency through a competitive market system. The reason is that the realization of allocative efficiency involves a one-shot increase in real national output, while economic growth entails continuous increases in the national output over time." Do you agree? Explain. What relationship, if any, do you envision between allocative efficiency and economic growth?

PART 6

NEGATIVE INCOME TAX
NEGATIVE INCOME TAX
NEGATIVE INCOME TAX
NEGATIVE INCOME TAX
NEGATIVE INCOME TAX
NEGATIVE INCOME TAX
NEGATIVE INCOME TAX
NEGATIVE INCOME TAX
NEGATIVE INCOME TAX
NEGATIVE INCOME TAX
NEGATIVE INCOME TAX

WAGNER ACT
WAGNER ACT
WAGNER ACT
WAGNER ACT
WAGNER ACT
WAGNER ACT
WAGNER ACT
WAGNER ACT
WAGNER ACT
WAGNER ACT
WAGNER ACT
WAGNER ACT
WAGNER ACT

AGGLOMERATION
AGGLOMERATION
AGGLOMERATION
AGGLOMERATION
AGGLOMERATION
AGGLOMERATION
AGGLOMERATION
AGGLOMERATION
AGGLOMERATION
AGGLOMERATION
AGGLOMERATION

LORENZ CURVE
LORENZ CURVE
LORENZ CURVE
LORENZ CURVE
LORENZ CURVE
LORENZ CURVE
LORENZ CURVE
LORENZ CURVE
LORENZ CURVE
LORENZ CURVE
LORENZ CURVE
LORENZ CURVE
LORENZ CURVE
LORENZ CURVE

PRICE SUPPORTS
PRICE SUPPORTS
PRICE SUPPORTS
PRICE SUPPORTS
PRICE SUPPORTS
PRICE SUPPORTS
PRICE SUPPORTS
PRICE SUPPORTS
PRICE SUPPORTS
PRICE SUPPORTS
PRICE SUPPORTS
PRICE SUPPORTS
PRICE SUPPORTS

Current Economic
Problems

INTERINDUSTRY COMPETITION
INTERINDUSTRY COMPETITION
INTERINDUSTRY COMPETITION
INTERINDUSTRY COMPETITION
INTERINDUSTRY COMPETITION
INTERINDUSTRY COMPETITION
INTERINDUSTRY COMPETITION
INTERINDUSTRY COMPETITION
INTERINDUSTRY COMPETITION
INTERINDUSTRY COMPETITION
INTERINDUSTRY COMPETITION
INTERINDUSTRY COMPETITION
INTERINDUSTRY COMPETITION

NATURAL MONOPOLY
NATURAL MONOPOLY
NATURAL MONOPOLY
NATURAL MONOPOLY
NATURAL MONOPOLY
NATURAL MONOPOLY
NATURAL MONOPOLY
NATURAL MONOPOLY
NATURAL MONOPOLY
NATURAL MONOPOLY
NATURAL MONOPOLY
NATURAL MONOPOLY
NATURAL MONOPOLY

RIGHT-TO-WORK LAWS
RIGHT-TO-WORK LAWS
RIGHT-TO-WORK LAWS
RIGHT-TO-WORK LAWS
RIGHT-TO-WORK LAWS
RIGHT-TO-WORK LAWS
RIGHT-TO-WORK LAWS
RIGHT-TO-WORK LAWS
RIGHT-TO-WORK LAWS
RIGHT-TO-WORK LAWS
RIGHT-TO-WORK LAWS
RIGHT-TO-WORK LAWS
RIGHT-TO-WORK LAWS

PEAK PRICING
PEAK PRICING
PEAK PRICING
PEAK PRICING
PEAK PRICING
PEAK PRICING
PEAK PRICING
PEAK PRICING
PEAK PRICING
PEAK PRICING
PEAK PRICING
PEAK PRICING
PEAK PRICING
PEAK PRICING

INFRASTRUCTURE
INFRASTRUCTURE
INFRASTRUCTURE
INFRASTRUCTURE
INFRASTRUCTURE
INFRASTRUCTURE
INFRASTRUCTURE
INFRASTRUCTURE
INFRASTRUCTURE
INFRASTRUCTURE
INFRASTRUCTURE
INFRASTRUCTURE
INFRASTRUCTURE

SHERMAN ACT
SHERMAN ACT
SHERMAN ACT
SHERMAN ACT
SHERMAN ACT
SHERMAN ACT
SHERMAN ACT
SHERMAN ACT
SHERMAN ACT
SHERMAN ACT
SHERMAN ACT
SHERMAN ACT
SHERMAN ACT
SHERMAN ACT

OASDHI
OASDHI
OASDHI
OASDHI
OASDHI
OASDHI
OASDHI
OASDHI
OASDHI

INCOME INEQUALITY
INCOME INEQUALITY
INCOME INEQUALITY
INCOME INEQUALITY
INCOME INEQUALITY
INCOME INEQUALITY
INCOME INEQUALITY
INCOME INEQUALITY
INCOME INEQUALITY
INCOME INEQUALITY
INCOME INEQUALITY
INCOME INEQUALITY
INCOME INEQUALITY

DISCRIMINATION
DISCRIMINATION
DISCRIMINATION
DISCRIMINATION
DISCRIMINATION
DISCRIMINATION
DISCRIMINATION
DISCRIMINATION
DISCRIMINATION
DISCRIMINATION
DISCRIMINATION
DISCRIMINATION
DISCRIMINATION
DISCRIMINATION

CHAPTER 33

Government and economic policy

By this point you should have a pretty good idea about government's role in the economy. In particular, you should be aware of the five economic functions of government: (1) providing the legal foundation and social environment conducive to the effective operation of the market system, (2) maintaining competition, (3) redistributing income and wealth, (4) adjusting the allocation of resources to provide public goods and correct for externalities, and (5) stabilizing the economy. We discussed these functions in Chapter 6. In Chapter 8 we examined the growth of the public sector and presented the facts of government expenditures and taxes. Our intent in this chapter is to extend and deepen our understanding of government and in the process identify some of the problems which it faces in carrying out its economic functions.

First, we return to the topic of market failure introduced in Chapter 6, providing here a fuller discussion of public goods and externalities by using some of our recently acquired tools of marginal analysis. Our attention then turns to an analytical examination of taxes. We learned in Chapter 8 how taxes are apportioned in the United States and who bears the burdens of the various taxes. Now we want to use our microeconomic tools to study the basic principles of tax incidence and tax burden. Next, the difficulties society has in revealing its true preferences through majority voting are scrutinized. This is followed by a closely related discussion of *government failure:* the contention that certain characteristics of the public sector hinder government's ability to assist the market system in achieving an efficient allocation of resources. The chapter ends with a brief discussion of the conservative and liberal stances on economic free-

dom. It will become apparent that this is a chapter on selected topics and problems of **public finance**—*the study of public expenditures and revenues*—and **public choice theory**—*the economic analysis of government decision making.*

We shall find that each of the chapters in Part 6 involve economic problems which government has attempted to resolve—with varying degrees of success. Chapter 34 examines the problem of monopoly and anticompetitive business practices, Chapter 35 probes the farm problem, and Chapter 36 analyzes the economic difficulties of urban America. In Chapter 37 we look at the problems of poverty and income inequality, and in Chapter 38 we investigate such labor market issues as unionism, discrimination, and migration. Our present analysis will enhance our understanding of the possibilities and pitfalls associated with government involvement in each of these areas.

Public goods: extending the analysis

Recall that a *private* good is divisible—it comes in small enough units to be afforded by individual buyers. It is also subject to the exclusion principle—those who are unable or unwilling to pay are excluded from the benefits provided by the product. The upshot is that we can conceive of a market demand curve for a private good as the horizontal summation of the demand curves representing each of the individual buyers (review Table 4-2 and Figure 4-2). For example, if Adams wants to buy 3 hot dogs at $1 each; Benson, 1 hot dog; and Conrad, 2 hot dogs; the market demand will reflect that 6 hot dogs (= 3 + 1 + 2) are demanded at a $1 price. The market demand resulting from the sum of the desires of each of the potential individual buyers creates a possibility for the sellers to gain revenue and thereby garner a profit, that is, obtain total revenue in excess of the costs of production. The equilibrium amount of a private good produced and purchased is dictated by product price, which we know is jointly determined by market demand and supply. This equilibrium output is optimal in that it maximizes the combined well-being of the buyers and sellers who are the only people directly affected by the transactions.

A serious snag develops, however, if we attempt to apply this same line of thinking to a public good. A *public good,* remember, is one which is indivisible and for which the exclusion principle does not apply. Once the good is provided, the producer has no way of excluding nonpayers from receiving its indivisible benefits. Because they will obtain the benefit from a public good whether or not they pay for it, potential buyers will *not* reveal their true preferences for it. In other words, they will *not* make voluntary payments for the public good in the marketplace. Hence, *the market demand curve for a public good will be either nonexistent or significantly understated.* The demand for the product expressed in the marketplace therefore will *not* generate sufficient revenue to cover the costs of production, even though the collective benefits of the good may match or exceed the relevant economic costs.

DEMAND FOR PUBLIC GOODS

How might society's optimal (allocatively efficient) amount of a public good be determined—at least in theory—in view of this problem? To maintain simplicity, let us suppose that Adams and Benson are the only people in the economy and that their true demand schedules for a particular public good, say, national defense, are those shown as columns 1 and 2 and columns 1 and 3 of Table 33-1. These demand schedules are "phantom" demand curves in that the two people will not actually reveal them in the marketplace.

TABLE 33-1 **Demand for a public good, two individuals (*hypothetical data*)**

(1) Price	(2) Quantity demanded, Adams	(3) Quantity demanded, Benson
$5	0	1
4	1	2
3	2	3
2	3	4
1	4	5

Suppose that government decides to produce 1 unit of this public good. Because the exclusion principle does not apply, neither Adams nor Benson will voluntarily offer to pay for the single unit because each can consume it without paying. Recall that Adams' consumption of the good does not preclude Benson from also consuming it. But the combined amount of money our two citizens are willing to pay, rather than each not having this one unit of the good, can be determined through the information in Table 33-1. In columns 1 and 2 we see that Adams would be willing to pay $4 for the first unit of the public good; in columns 1 and 3 we observe that Benson would be willing to pay $5 for the first unit. The $9 price that these two individuals are jointly willing to pay is the sum of the amounts each is willing to pay. Similarly, the collective price they are willing to pay for the second unit of the public good is $7 (= $3 by Adams plus $4 by Benson). We could then employ this same procedure for the third unit, and so on. Looking at the collective price they are willing to pay for each additional unit, we construct a collective demand schedule for a public good. Rather than adding the *quantities demanded* at each price as when determining the market demand for a private good, we are adding the *prices* people collectively are willing to pay for the last unit of the public good at each quantity demanded.

In Figure 33-1 we show the same summing procedure graphically, employing the data from Table 33-1 to illustrate the adding-up process. Observe

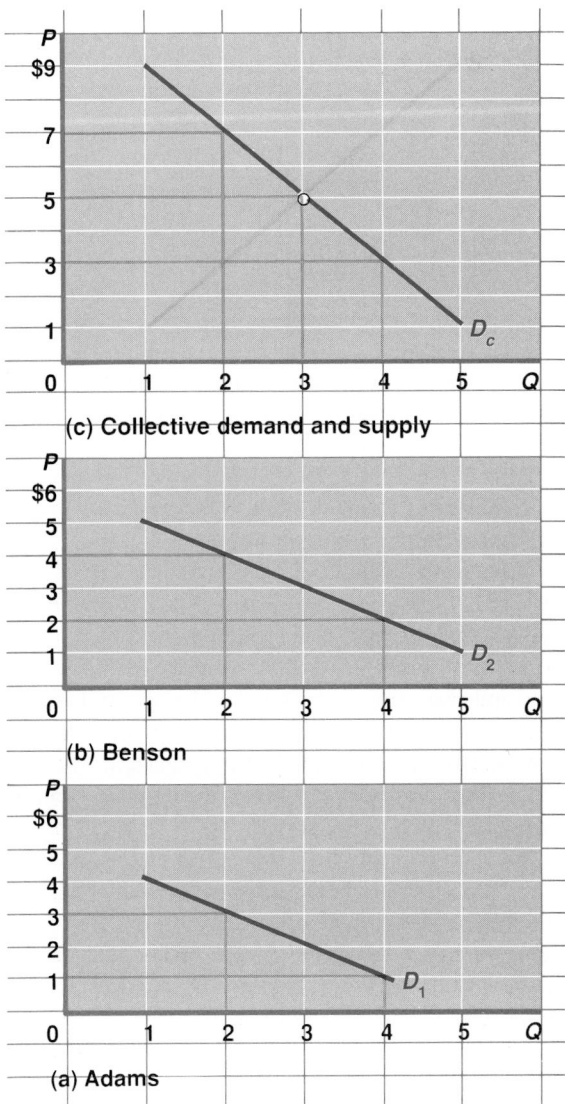

FIGURE 33-1

Graphically the collective demand curve D_c for the public good shown in (c) is found by summing vertically the individual demand curves D_1 and D_2 exhibited in (a) and (b). Government should provide 3 units of the public good, because at that quantity the combined marginal benefit, as measured by citizens' willingness to pay for the last unit (shown by D_c), equals the good's marginal cost (shown by S).

that we are summing Adams' and Benson's demand curves for the public good *vertically* to derive the collective demand curve. The height of the collective demand curve D_c at 2 units of output, for example, is $7—the sum of the amount that Adams and Benson together are willing to pay for the second unit (= $3 + $4). Likewise, the height of the collective demand curve at 4 units of the public good is $3 (= $1 + $2).

You will note that our collective demand curve D_c is based upon the monetary value of the perceived benefits of the various extra units that are equally available to both persons for simultaneous consumption. The curve predictably slopes downward because of the law of diminishing marginal utility: Successive units of the public good will yield less added satisfaction than the previous units.

THE OPTIMAL QUANTITY OF A PUBLIC GOOD

The optimal quantity of the public good alluded to in Figure 33-1 can now be determined. Observe in Figure 33-1c that the supply curve for the public good is upsloping in the usual sense. The short-run law of diminishing returns, which gives rise to the upsloping supply curve, is applicable whether one is making missiles (public goods) or mufflers (private goods). In this case, the optimal quantity of the public good will be 3 units, shown by the intersection of the collective demand and supply curves. Recalling that a supply curve reflects marginal costs, we note that if, say, 2 units are produced, the collective willingness to pay for that second unit (= $7) will exceed the good's marginal cost of production (= $3). This situation implies an underproduction of the good and therefore an *underallocation* of resources to this use. On the other hand, the sum of the amount our two people are willing to pay for the fourth unit (= $3) of the public good is less than that unit's marginal cost (= $7); hence, the fourth unit would entail an overproduction of the good and an *overallocation* of resources to this use. The optimum quantity of the public good is 3 units, where the combined willingness to pay for the extra unit—the combined marginal benefit to the two consumers—just matches the marginal cost of that unit ($5 = $5). Hence, the "marginal benefit equals marginal cost" principle used to determine the optimal amount of a public good is analogous to the MR = MC output rule and the MRP = MRC input rule for maximizing profit.

BENEFIT-COST ANALYSIS

We have demonstrated that economic theory provides some guidance to efficient decision making in the public sector. This guidance can be helpful in understanding **benefit-cost analysis.**

Suppose government is contemplating some specific project, for example, a flood-control project. The basic nature of the economizing problem (Chapter 2) tells us that any decision to use more resources in the public sector will involve both a benefit and a cost. The benefit is the extra satisfaction resulting from the output of more public goods; the cost is the loss of satisfaction associated with the accompanying decline in the production of private goods. Should the resources under consideration be shifted from the private to the public sector? The answer is "Yes" *if* the benefits from the extra public goods exceed the cost resulting from having fewer private goods. The answer is "No" *if* the value or cost of the forgone private goods is greater than the benefits associated with the extra public goods.

But benefit-cost analysis can do more than merely indicate whether a public program is worth undertaking. It can also provide guidance concerning the extent to which a given project should be pursued. Economic questions, after all, are not simply questions to be answered by "Yes" or "No," but rather, matters of "how much" or "how little." In the case of flood control we note first that

a flood-control project is a public good in that the exclusion principle is not readily applicable. Now, should government undertake a flood-control project in a given river valley? And, if so, what is the proper size or scope for the project?

Table 33-2 provides us with some answers. Here we list a series of increasingly ambitious and increasingly costly flood-control plans. To what extent, if at all, should government undertake flood control? The answers depend upon costs and benefits. Costs in this case are largely the capital costs of constructing and maintaining levees and reservoirs; benefits take the form of reduced flood damage.

In the first place, a quick glance at all the plans indicates that for each plan total benefits (column 4) exceed total costs (column 2), indicating that a flood-control project on this river is economically justifiable. This can be seen directly in column 6 where total annual costs (column 2) are subtracted from total annual benefits (column 4). But a second question remains: What is the optimal size or scope for this project? The answer is determined by comparing the additional, or *marginal,* costs and the additional, or *marginal,* benefits associated with each plan. The guideline is the one we established when discussing the optimal amount of a public good: Pursue an activity or project as long as the marginal benefits (column 5) exceed the marginal costs (column 3). Stop the activity or project at, or as close as possible to, that point at

TABLE 33-2 **Benefit-cost analysis for a flood-control project**

(1) Plan	(2) Total annual cost of project	(3) Marginal cost	(4) Total annual benefit (reduction in damage)	(5) Marginal benefit	(6) Net benefit, or (4) − (2)
Without protection	$ 0		$ 0		$ 0
A: Levees	3,000	$ 3,000	6,000	$ 6,000	3,000
B: Small reservoir	10,000	7,000	16,000	10,000	6,000
C: Medium reservoir	18,000	8,000	25,000	9,000	7,000
D: Large reservoir	30,000	12,000	32,000	7,000	2,000

Source: Adapted from Otto Eckstein, *Public Finance,* 3d ed. (Englewood Cliffs, N.J.: Prentice-Hall, Inc., 1973), p. 23. Used with permission.

which marginal benefits equal marginal costs. In this case Plan C—the medium-sized reservoir—is the best plan. Plans A and B are too modest; in both cases marginal benefits exceed marginal costs. Plan D entails marginal costs ($12,000) in excess of marginal benefits ($7000) and therefore cannot be justified. Plan D isn't economically justifiable; it involves an overallocation of resources to this flood-control project. Plan C is closest to the optimum; it expands flood control so long as marginal benefits exceed marginal costs.

Regarded from a slightly different vantage point, the **marginal benefit = marginal cost rule** will determine which plan entails the maximum excess of total benefits (column 4) over total costs (column 2) or, in other words, the plan which yields the maximum *net* gain or benefit to society. We confirm directly in column 6 that the maximum net benefit (of $7000) is associated with Plan C.

It is worth noting that benefit-cost analysis shatters the myth that "economy in government" and "reduced government spending" are synonymous. "Economy" is concerned with efficiency in resource use. If a government program yields marginal benefits which are less than the marginal benefits attainable from alternative private uses—that is, if costs exceed benefits—then the proposed public program should *not* be undertaken. But if the reverse is true—if benefits exceed costs—then it would be uneconomical or "wasteful" *not* to spend on that governmental program. Economy in government does *not* mean the minimization of public spending; rather, it means allocating resources between the private and public sectors until no net benefits can be realized from further reallocations.

MEASUREMENT PROBLEMS

Benefit-cost analysis is extremely helpful in promoting clear thinking about the public sector and is in fact very useful in actual studies involving projects such as flood control, pollution cleanup, and highway construction. But we must acknowledge that the benefits and costs associated with public goods are partially spillovers or externalities which are difficult to measure. For example, consider the possible benefits and costs associated with the construction of a new freeway in a major metropolitan area. In addition to estimating the obvious

costs—land purchase and costs of construction—the responsible agency must also estimate the spillover cost of additional air pollution which results from an enlarged flow of traffic. Furthermore, more traffic may call for increased expenditures for traffic police. What about benefits? Improved transportation means a widening of markets, more competition, and a greater opportunity for the community to specialize and improve economic efficiency. But what is the monetary value of this benefit? And the freeway may help make more jobs accessible to the central-city poor. Again, what is the dollar value of these benefits? The point is that the full costs and benefits associated with government programs are not easily calculated, and benefit-cost analysis is frequently difficult to apply.

Externalities revisited

Our next goal is to extend our earlier analysis of government policies to correct the market failure we call *externalities* or *spillovers*. Recall that a spillover is a cost or benefit accruing to some individual or group—some third party—which is external to the market transaction. An example of a spillover cost is pollution; an example of a spillover benefit is an immunization shot. A review of Figure 6-1 will remind us that the overallocation of resources to the production of a particular good which results when spillover costs are present might be remedied either by passing legislation which limits the activity or by imposing an excise tax on the output. Conversely, another look at Figure 6-2 should reveal that the underallocation of resources associated with spillover benefits can be remedied by granting a subsidy to either the producer or consumer of the good.

During the past several decades economists have explored other approaches to solving the externality problem. Let us examine two of these now.

INDIVIDUAL BARGAINING

According to the **Coase theorem,** named after its originator Ronald Coase, negative or positive spillovers do *not* require government intervention in situations where (1) the ownership of property is clearly defined, (2) the number of people involved is small, and (3) the costs of bargaining are negligible. Government should confine its role under these circumstances to encouraging bargaining between the affected individuals or groups. Because the economic self-interests of the parties are at stake, bargaining will enable them to find an acceptable solution to the externality through discussion with one another. Property rights place a price tag on an externality, creating an opportunity cost for both parties. Hence, a compelling incentive emerges for the parties to find ways to solve the externality problem.

Extended example: Suppose that an owner of a large parcel of forest land is considering contracting with a logging company to clear-cut (totally cut) thousands of acres of old-growth fir trees. The complication is that the forest surrounds a lake which has a nationally known resort located on its shore. The resort is located on land owned by the resort owner. The unspoiled beauty of the general area attracts vacationers from all over the nation to the resort. Should state or local government intervene in some way?

According to the Coase theorem, the forest owner and the resort owner can resolve this type of situation without government intervention. How? As long as *one* of the parties to the dispute has property rights to what is at issue, an incentive will exist for *both* parties to negotiate a solution acceptable to each. In our example, the owner of the timberlands holds the property rights to the land which is to be logged. The owner of the resort therefore has an incentive to negotiate with the forest owner to reduce the logging impact. Clearly, excessive logging of the forest surrounding the resort will reduce tourism and therefore revenues to the resort owner.

Less obvious, but equally strong, is the economic incentive of the forest owner to explore the possibility of an agreement with the resort owner. Why? The answer draws directly upon the idea of opportunity cost. One important cost incurred by the owner in logging the forest is the forgone payment which the forest owner could be expected to obtain from the resort owner for agreeing *not* to clear-cut the fir trees. The resort owner undoubtedly will be willing to make a lump-sum or annual payment to the owner of the forest to avoid or minimize the spillover cost. Or, perhaps the owner of the resort will be willing to buy the forested land at a relatively high price to prevent the logging. As viewed by the forest owner, a payment to preclude logging or a purchase price above the value of the land as a tree farm are *costs* of logging the land.

We would predict a negotiated agreement which both parties in this situation would regard as being better than clear-cutting the firs. According to the Coase theorem, government would not need to intervene to correct for this potential externality.

Moreover, a surprising facet of this idea is that an efficient outcome is independent of which of the two parties is assigned the property rights. As an admittedly extreme example, suppose that government had in advance assigned to the resort owner a "property" right consisting of a legal prohibition of tree cutting within several miles of the resort without permission of the resort owner. Now, we would expect to see the owner of the forest land seeking out the resort owner to discuss the situation. And the resort owner would discover a new opportunity cost. Under the new arrangement of property rights, the resort owner will be able to secure a payment from the owner of the timberland in exchange for allowing, say, selective cutting of some of the older trees on an annual basis. This potential payment is an opportunity cost of *not* allowing tree cutting, as viewed by the resort owner. Once again the two parties would have an economic incentive to negotiate a mutually acceptable agreement. In so doing they would eliminate or lessen the externality.

Unfortunately, many negative externalities involve large numbers of affected parties and high bargaining costs. Therefore, private bargaining may not remedy such negative externalities. The acid-rain problem in the United States and Canada, as just one example, affects many millions of people spread out over two nations. We cannot expect the vast number of affected parts to somehow independently negotiate an agreement which reduces the externality. Furthermore, there will be a public good problem in getting people voluntarily to pay their share of a payment which would be sufficient to get those causing the problem to change their technology or levels of output. The reason is that all of the affected parties will share in any benefit from a negotiated reduction of acid rain, whether they pay to reduce the problem or not. In circumstances such as these, we must rely mainly upon government or governments to find a solution to the externality. Nevertheless, the Coase theorem reminds us that clearly defined property rights can be a factor in reducing or eliminating some externalities.

CREATING A MARKET FOR EXTERNALITY RIGHTS

One of the more novel policy approaches suggested to remedy negative externalities relates to our discussion of the Coase theorem. The idea is to create a **market for externality rights.**[1] Let us confine our discussion to pollution, although other externalities might also lend themselves to this approach. The rationale for creating a market for pollution rights is that the air, rivers, lakes, oceans, and public lands, such as parks and streets, are all primary objects for pollution because the *rights* to use these resources are either held "in common" by society or are unspecified by law. As a result, no specific private individual or institution has any incentive to restrict the use or maintain the purity or quality of these resources because no one has the right to realize a monetary return from doing so. We maintain the property we own—we paint and repair our homes periodically—in part because we will capture the value of these improvements at the time of resale. But, as long as the "rights" to air, water, and certain land resources are commonly held and these resources made freely available, there will be no incentive to maintain them or restrict their use. Hence, these natural resources are "overconsumed" and thereby polluted.

The proposal is therefore made that an appropriate pollution-control agency should determine the amount of pollutants which can be discharged into the water or air of a given region each year and still maintain the quality of the water or air at some acceptable standard. For example, the agency may determine that 500 tons of pollutants may be discharged into Metropolitan Lake and be "recycled" by Nature. Hence, 500 pollution rights, each enti-

[1] J. H. Dales, *Pollution, Property and Prices* (Toronto: University of Toronto Press, 1968).

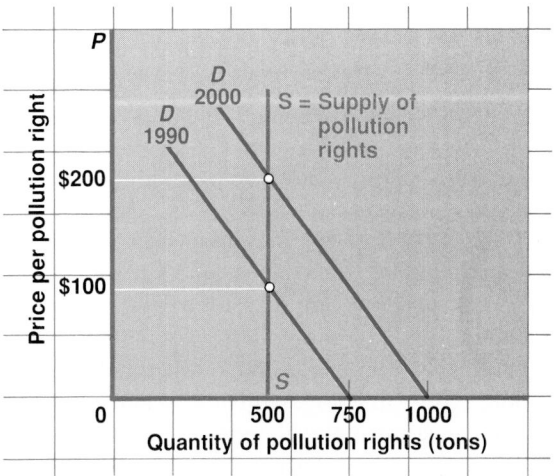

FIGURE 33-2

The market for pollution rights

Pollution can be controlled by having a public body determine the amount of pollution which the atmosphere or a body of water can safely recycle and sell these limited rights to polluters. The effect is to make the environment a scarce resource with a positive price. Economic and population growth will increase the demand for pollution rights over time, but the consequence will be an increase in the price of pollution rights rather than more pollution.

tling the owner to dump 1 ton of pollutants into the lake in the given year, are made available for sale each year. The resulting supply of pollution rights is fixed and therefore perfectly inelastic, as shown in Figure 33-2. The demand for pollution rights will take the same downsloping form as will the demand for any other input. At high prices, polluters either will stop polluting or will pollute less by acquiring pollution-abatement equipment. Thus, an equilibrium market price for pollution rights—in this case $100—will be determined at which an environment-preserving quantity of pollution rights will be rationed to polluters. Note that without this market—that is, if the use of the lake as a dump site for pollutants were free—750 tons of pollutants would be discharged into the lake and it would be "overconsumed," or polluted, in the amount of 250 tons.

And over time, as human and business populations expand, demand will increase, as from D_{1990}

to D_{2000}. *Without* a market for pollution rights, pollution would occur in 2000 in the amount of 500 tons beyond that which can be assimilated by Nature. *With* the market for pollution rights, price will rise from $100 to $200 and the amount of pollutants will remain at 500 tons—the amount which the lake can recycle.

This proposal has a number of advantages. Potential polluters are confronted with an explicit monetary incentive not to pollute: They must buy pollution rights to do so. Conservation groups can fight pollution by buying up and withholding pollution rights, thereby reducing actual pollution below governmentally determined standards. As the demand for pollution rights increases over time, the growing revenue from the sale of the given quantity of pollution rights could be devoted to environment improvement. Similarly, with time the rising price of pollution rights should stimulate the search for improved techniques to control pollution.

Although administrative and political problems have dissuaded government from creating a full-scale market for pollution rights, in fact a market for air pollution rights has emerged. Under terms of the Clean Air Act, the Environmental Protection Agency (EPA) has set air pollution standards for the various regions of the country. In regions where the minimum standards are not being met, new pollution sources are not allowed to enter unless existing sources are reduced or eliminated. Additionally, each existing firm in these regions is forced to reduce air pollution to meet standards that have been set for it by the EPA. In 1977 the EPA began allowing firms which reduce their pollution below the standards set for them to sell pollution rights to new or existing firms. For example, a new firm desiring to locate in the area might be able to buy the right to emit, say, 20 tons of nitrous oxide annually from an existing firm which has reduced its emissions below its allowable limit for that pollutant. The price for the right to emit these 20 tons of nitrous oxide will depend upon the supply of, and demand for, the pollution right. A growing market for such rights has recently emerged.[2]

---

[2] This market is discussed in Timothy Tregarthen, "Selling the Right to Pollute: Pioneer in the Market for Particulates," *The Margin,* April 1988, pp. 8–9.

Tax incidence and burden

Our attention now turns from public goods and externalities to the tax side of public finance theory. We have already discussed taxation in considerable detail in Chapter 8 and we will now present an extension to that material. Specifically, we will expand Chapter 8's discussion of tax incidence, demonstrating the importance of elasticity of supply and demand in determining who bears the burden of an excise tax or sales tax. This analysis will then provide a logical bridge to a discussion of other aspects of the total burden of a tax.

ELASTICITY AND TAX INCIDENCE

The concepts of supply and demand *and* the notion of elasticity are useful in determining who pays a sales or excise tax. Suppose that Figure 33-3 shows the market for a certain domestic wine and that the no-tax equilibrium price and quantity are $4 per bottle and 15 million bottles. Now assume that government levies a specific sales or excise tax of $1 per bottle on this wine. Who actually pays this tax—producers or consumers? In technical terms (Chapter 8), what is the incidence of this tax?

Division of burden Assuming that government imposes the tax upon sellers (suppliers), it can be viewed as an addition to the supply price of the product. Therefore, the tax has the effect of shifting the supply curve upward by the amount of the tax. Thus, while sellers were willing to offer, for example, 5 million bottles of untaxed wine at $2 per bottle, they must now receive $3 per bottle—$2 plus the $1 tax—to offer the same 5 million bottles. Sellers must now get $1 more for each quantity supplied in order to receive the same per unit price as they were getting before the tax. The tax causes an upward shift in the supply curve as shown in Figure 33-3, where S is the "no-tax" supply curve and S_t is the "after-tax" supply curve.

Careful comparison of after-tax supply and demand with the pretax equilibrium reveals that the new equilibrium price is $4.50 per bottle, compared with the before-tax price of $4.00. In this particular case, one-half of the tax is paid by consumers in the form of a higher price and the other

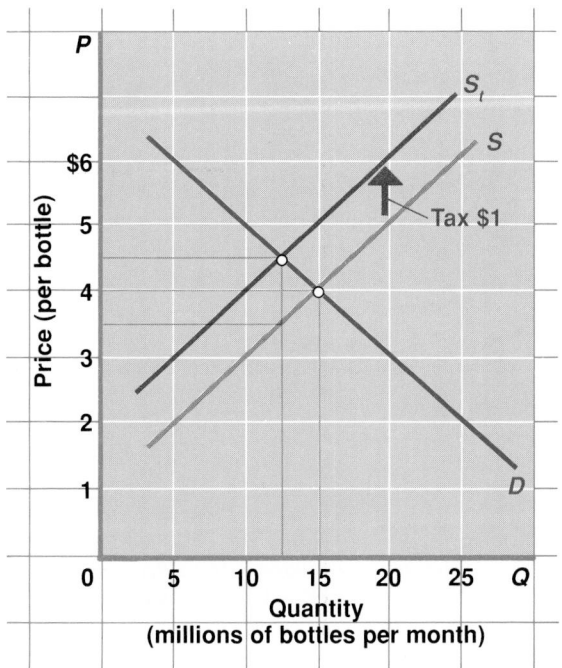

FIGURE 33-3

The incidence of a sales tax

The imposition of a sales tax of a specified amount, say, $1 per unit, shifts the supply curve upward by the amount of the tax. This results in a higher price ($4.50) to the consumer and a lower after-tax price ($3.50) to the producer. In this particular case the burden of the tax is shared equally by consumers and producers.

half by producers in the form of a lower after-tax price. Consumers pay 50 cents more per bottle and, after remitting the $1 tax per unit to government, producers receive $3.50, or 50 cents less than the $4.00 before-tax price. In this instance, consumers and producers share the burden of the tax equally; producers shift half the tax forward to consumers in the form of a higher price and bear the other half themselves.

Elasticities If the elasticities of demand and supply were different from those shown in Figure 33-3, the incidence of the tax would also be different. Two generalizations are relevant.

1 *Given supply, the more inelastic the demand for the product, the larger the portion of the tax shifted for-*

ward to consumers. The easiest way to verify this is to sketch graphically the extreme cases where demand is perfectly elastic and perfectly inelastic. In the first case the incidence of the tax is entirely upon sellers; in the second instance the tax is shifted entirely to consumers. Figure 33-4 contrasts the more likely cases where demand might be relatively elastic (D_e) or relatively inelastic (D_i) in the relevant price range. In the elastic demand case of Figure 33-4a, a small portion of the tax (PP_e) is shifted forward to consumers and most of the tax (PP_a) is borne by producers. In the inelastic demand case of Figure 33-4b, most of the tax (PP_i) is shifted to consumers and only a small amount (PP_b) is paid by producers.

Note, too, that the decline in equilibrium quantity is smaller, the more inelastic the demand. This recalls an earlier application of the elasticity concept: Revenue-seeking legislatures tend to put heavy excise taxes upon liquor, cigarettes, automobile tires, and other products whose demand tends to be inelastic.

2 *Given demand, the more inelastic the supply, the larger the portion of the tax borne by producers.* While the demand curves are identical, the supply curve is elastic in Figure 33-5a and inelastic in Figure 33-5b. For the elastic supply curve we find that most of the tax (PP_e) is shifted forward to consumers and only a small portion (PP_a) is borne by producers or sellers. But where supply is inelastic, the reverse is true. The major portion of the tax (PP_b) falls upon sellers and a relatively small amount (PP_i) is shifted to buyers. Quantity also declines less with an inelastic supply than it does with an elastic supply.

Gold is an example of a product for which supply is inelastic and therefore for which the burden of an excise tax would fall mainly upon producers. On the other hand, the supply of baseballs is elastic. Hence, much of an excise tax on baseballs would most probably get passed forward to consumers.

EXCESS BURDEN OF A TAX

We have just observed that an excise tax on producers in a market characterized by typical supply and demand curves is borne partly by producers and partly by consumers. Additional attention to

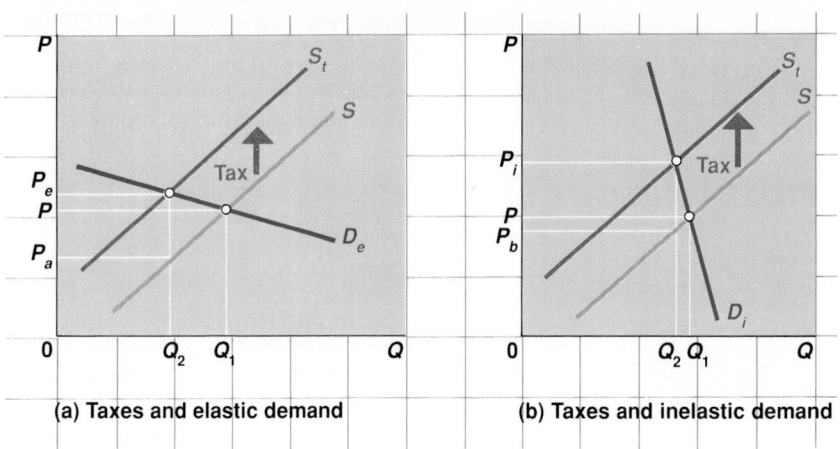

FIGURE 33-4

Demand elasticity and the incidence of a sales tax

In (a) we find that, if demand is elastic in the relevant price range, price will rise modestly (P to P_e) when a sales tax is levied. Hence, the producer bears most of the tax burden. But if demand is inelastic as in (b), the price to the buyer will increase substantially (P to P_i) and most of the tax is shifted to consumers.

the burden of an excise tax is now warranted. Figure 33-6 is identical to Figure 33-3 but contains additional detail important to our discussion.

The $1 excise tax on wine increases the market price from $4 to $4.50 per bottle and reduces the

equilibrium quantity from 15 to 12.5 million bottles. Government's tax revenue is $12.5 million (= $1 × 12.5 million bottles), an amount shown as the rectangle labeled *efac* in Figure 33-6. In this case, the elasticities of supply and demand are such

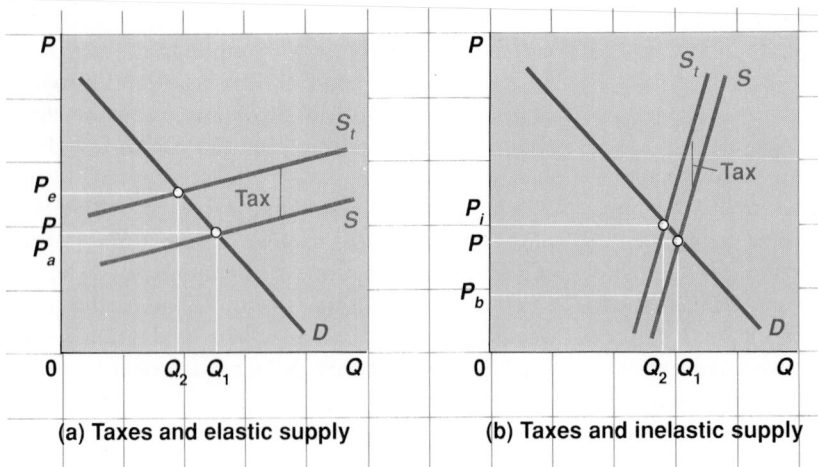

FIGURE 33-5

Supply elasticity and the incidence of a sales tax

Part (a) indicates that with an elastic supply a sales tax results in a large price increase (P to P_e) and the tax is therefore paid largely by consumers. But if supply is inelastic as in (b), the price rise will be small (P to P_i) and sellers will have to bear most of the tax.

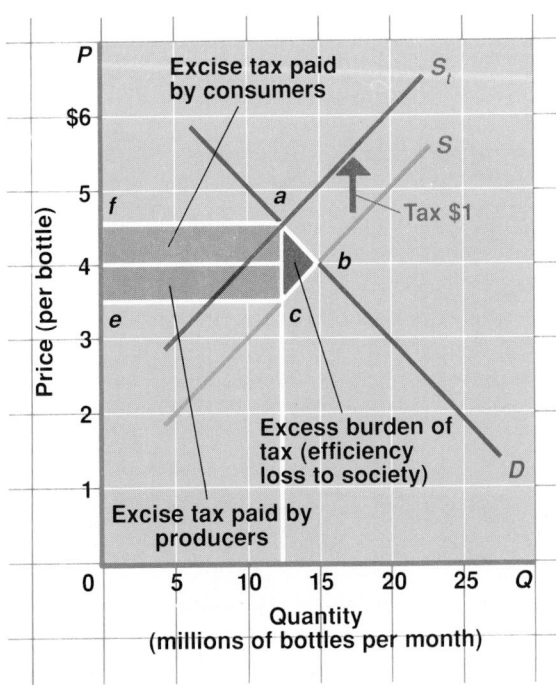

FIGURE 33-6

Excess burden of a tax

The levy of a $1 excise tax per bottle of wine increases the price per bottle to $4.50 and reduces the equilibrium quantity by 2.5 million bottles. Government's tax revenue is $12.5 million (area *efac*). The excess burden or the efficiency loss of the tax is the amount shown as triangle *abc*. The total burden of the tax is the tax revenue plus the excess burden.

that consumers and producers each pay one-half of this total amount, or $6.25 million apiece (=$.50 × 12.5 million bottles). Government, of course, uses this $12.5 million of tax revenue to provide public goods and services of value. Thus there is no loss of well-being to society as a whole from this transfer from consumers and producers to government.

The $1 tax on wine required that consumers and producers collectively pay $12.5 million of tax, but also *has reduced the equilibrium amount of wine produced and consumed by 2.5 million bottles.* The fact that 2.5 million more bottles of wine were demanded and supplied prior to the imposition of the tax correctly implies they provided benefits in *excess* of their costs of production. We can see this from the following simple analysis. The *ab* segment

of demand curve *D* in Figure 33-6 indicates the willingness to pay—the marginal benefit—associated with each of these 2.5 million bottles consumed prior to the tax. The *cb* segment of supply curve *S*, on the other hand, reflects the marginal cost of each of the bottles of wine. For all but the very last one of these 2.5 million bottles, we observe that the marginal benefit (shown by *ab*) exceeds the marginal cost (shown by *cb*). The reduction of well-being associated with the fact that these 2.5 million bottles are not produced is indicated by the triangle *abc*. This triangle shows the **excess burden of the tax,** or the *efficiency loss* to society resulting from the tax. To repeat: *The excess burden of an excise tax is the loss of net benefit accruing to society because consumption and production of the taxed product are reduced below their optimal levels.*

The point we wish to make here is that society's total tax burden exceeds the $12.5 million of tax revenue actually collected by government. The total tax burden consists of the tax revenue *efac* plus the triangle *abc* in the diagram. Area *efac* represents a transfer of income from taxpayers to government; area *abc*, on the other hand, represents a net loss to society. The excess burden of a tax is the extent to which a tax imposes a total burden beyond the amount of the tax collected. That is:

Excess burden = total burden − tax revenue

Most taxes create total tax burdens in excess of the revenue they generate, *but the amount of excess burden depends crucially upon supply and demand elasticities.* Glancing back to Figure 33-4, we observe that the triangle indicating the amount of the excess burden is substantially greater in Figure 33-4a, where demand is relatively elastic, than in Figure 33-4b, where demand is relatively inelastic. Similarly, the excess burden of the tax is shown to be greater in Figure 33-5a than in Figure 33-5b, indicating a larger excess burden where supply is more elastic.

The major principle which emerges from our analysis is that the degree of excess burden (total burden minus tax revenue) of an excise or sales tax varies from market to market depending upon the elasticities of supply and demand. Other things being equal, the greater the elasticity of supply and demand, the greater the excess burden of a particular tax. Two taxes which yield equal revenues do not necessarily entail equal total tax burdens. This fact complicates government's job of determining the best way to collect its needed tax revenues. Government must consider the excess burdens of taxes in designing an optimal tax system.

Qualification: Other tax goals in many instances may be more important than the goal of minimizing excess burdens. As one example, the government may wish to impose taxes which are progressive as a way to redistribute income (Chapter 8). As a second example, the $1 tax on wine in Figure 33-4 may have been intended to reduce consumption of wine from 15 to 12.5 million bottles. Government may have reasoned that certain negative externalities result from the consumption of alcoholic beverages and therefore imposed an excise tax to adjust the market supply curve for these costs and reduce the amount of resources allocated to wine (Figure 6-1b).

Revealing preferences through majority voting

Which public goods should be produced and in what amounts? In what circumstances and through what methods should government intervene to correct for externalities? How should the tax burden of financing government be apportioned? These and many other decisions concerning government are made collectively in the United States through a democratic process which relies heavily upon majority voting. Candidates for office in effect offer voters alternative policy packages and we elect people who we think will make the best decisions on our collective behalf. Voters "retire" officials who do not adequately represent their collective wishes and elect persons who convince them they will better reflect the collective wants of the electorate. Additionally, citizens periodically have opportunities at the state and local level to vote directly on ballot issues which involve public expenditures or new legislation. Although this democratic process generally works well at revealing society's true preferences, it is not without its shortcomings. Just as the market fails in some cases to allocate resources efficiently, our system of voting in some instances produces inefficiencies

and inconsistencies. We will now explore some of these potential voting difficulties.

INEFFICIENT VOTING OUTCOMES

We know that providing a public good having a total benefit greater than its total cost will add to society's well-being. Unfortunately, majority voting raises the possibility of voting outcomes which are economically inefficient. Voters may defeat a proposal to provide a public good even though it may yield total benefits that exceed its total cost. Conversely, majority voting raises the possibility that voters may adopt a proposal to provide a public good costing more than the benefits it could yield.

Illustration Suppose that a public good, say, national defense, can be provided at a total expense of $900. Also, suppose that there are only three individuals—Adams, Benson, and Conrad—in the society and they will share the $900 tax expense equally. That is, Adams, Benson, and Conrad will each pay $300 of tax if the good is provided. Suppose Adams is willing to pay $700 to have this good; Benson, $250; and Conrad, $200. What might be the result if a majority vote is determined on whether or not this good will be provided? Although people do not always vote strictly on the basis of their own economic interest, it is entirely likely that Benson and Conrad will vote "No" because they will incur tax expenses of $300 each while gaining benefits of only $250 and $200, respectively. The majority vote in this case will defeat the proposal even though the total benefit of $1150 (= $700 for Adams + $250 for Benson + $200 for Conrad) exceeds the total cost of $900.

We could easily construct an example illustrating the converse, in which the majority might favor the provision of a public good even though its total cost exceeds its total benefit. (In fact, you will be asked to do just that in end-of-chapter question 9). The point is that an inefficiency may take the form of either an overproduction or underproduction of a specific public good, and therefore an overallocation or underallocation of resources for that particular use. In Chapter 6 we saw that government might improve allocative efficiency (resources channeled to their highest valued use) by providing public goods which the market system would not make available. Now we have extended that analysis to reveal that government might fail to provide some public goods whose production is economically justifiable while providing other goods whose creation is not economically warranted.

The basic tenet our example illustrates is that people have only a single vote no matter how much they might gain from a public good. If buying votes were legal, Adams would be willing to purchase a vote from either Benson or Conrad, paying for it with some of the prospective personal gain. In the marketplace specific goods are normally available to people who have strong preferences for them even though a majority of consumers conclude that the product prices exceed the marginal utilities of the goods. A consumer can buy such products as beef tongues and fresh squid in some supermarkets, but it is doubtful these products would be available under a system which used majority voting to stock the shelves. On the other hand, one cannot easily "buy" national defense once the majority has decided it is not worth buying. To repeat: *Because it fails to incorporate the strength of the preferences of the individual voter, majority voting may produce economically inefficient outcomes.*

Interest groups and logrolling We should note that ways do exist through which inefficiencies associated with majority voting *may* get resolved. Two examples: First, those who have strong preference for a public good may band together into an interest group and use advertisements, mailings, and the like to try to convince others of the merits of a public good. In terms of our example, Adams might make a major effort to convince Benson and Conrad that it is actually in their interest to vote for national defense; that is, that national defense is actually worth more than the $250 and $200 values they now place upon it. Such appeals are commonplace in contemporary American politics.

Second, **logrolling**—*the trading of votes to secure favorable outcomes on decisions which otherwise would be adverse*—can turn an inefficient outcome into an efficient one. Perhaps Benson has a strong preference for a different public good, say, a new road, which Adams and Conrad do not think is worth the tax expense. Now, an opportunity has developed for Adams and Benson to agree to trade votes to ensure the provision of *both* national de-

fense and the new road. The majority vote (Adams and Benson) in our three-person society will result in a positive vote for both national defense and the road. Without the logrolling, each would have been rejected. This logrolling will add to society's well-being if, as was true for national defense, the road creates a positive overall net benefit.

A word of caution: Logrolling need not always increase economic efficiency. It would be easy to construct a scenario in which both national defense and the road individually cost more than the total benefits they each provide, and yet both would be provided because of vote trading. All that is necessary for the road and national defense to be provided is that Adams and Benson each secure net gains from their favored public good. In other words, the tax cost imposed upon Conrad by the expenditures for national defense and the road could exceed Conrad's benefits by such a large amount that it swamped the combined net benefit received by Adams and Benson from the public goods. Under conditions of majority voting and logrolling, government will provide each of the public goods and shift a large net burden to Conrad. This scenario is familiar to political scientists who call this practice "pork-barrel politics" (getting public goods for constituents from the public barrel).

Our conclusion is that logrolling can either increase or diminish economic efficiency depending upon the circumstances.

THE PARADOX OF VOTING

Another difficulty with majority voting is called the **paradox of voting**—a situation where society may not be able to rank its preferences consistently through majority voting.

Consider Table 33-3 where we again suppose there is a community consisting of just three voters: Adams, Benson, and Conrad. Suppose the community has three alternative public goods from which to choose: national defense, a road, and a weather warning system. We would expect each member of the community to arrange the order of the three alternatives according to her or his preferences and then select the most preferred option. This implies that each voter will state that they prefer national defense to a road, and a road to a weather warning system, or whatever. We can then attempt to deter-

TABLE 33-3 **Paradox of voting**

Public good	Preferences		
	Adams	Benson	Conrad
National defense	1st choice	3d choice	2d choice
Road	2d choice	1st choice	3d choice
Weather warning system	3d choice	2d choice	1st choice

Voting outcomes	
Election	**Winner**
(1) National defense vs. road	National defense (preferred by Adams and Conrad)
(2) Road vs. weather warning system	Road (preferred by Adams and Benson)
(3) National defense vs. weather warning system	Weather warning system (preferred by Benson and Conrad)

mine the collective preference scale of the community using a majority voting procedure. More specifically, a vote can be held between any two of the public goods and the winner of the contest matched against the third public good.

We list the three goods and the assumed individual preferences of the three voters in the top portion of Table 33-3. In the lower part of the table, the outcomes of various elections are listed. The upper portion of the table indicates that Adams prefers national defense to the road and the road to the weather warning system. This also implies that Adams prefers national defense to the weather warning system. We see that Benson values the road more than the weather warning system and the warning system more than national defense. Benson therefore prefers the road to national defense. Finally, Conrad's first choice is the weather warning system, second choice is national defense, and third choice is the road.

Consider the outcomes of three hypothetical elections decided through majority vote. First, let us match national defense against the road in an election. We observe in Table 33-3 that national defense will win this contest because a majority of

voters, Adams and Conrad, prefer national defense to a road. This outcome is reported in row (1) of the lower portion of the table, where the election outcomes are summarized. Next we hold an election to see whether this community wants a road or a weather warning system and note that a majority of voters, Adams and Benson, prefer the road to the weather warning system, as shown in row (2).

We have determined that the majority in this community prefer national defense to a road *and* prefer a road to a weather warning system. It therefore might seem logical to conclude that the community prefers national defense to a weather warning system. But it does not!

To demonstrate this point consider a direct election between national defense and the weather warning system. We discover in row (3) that a majority of voters, Benson and Conrad, prefer the weather warning system to national defense. As indicated in Table 33-3, majority voting falsely implies that this community is irrational: it seems to prefer national defense to a road *and* a road to a weather warning system, but would rather have a weather warning system than national defense. The problem is not one of irrational preferences, but rather one of a flawed procedure for determining those preferences. We see that majority voting can yield opposing outcomes depending upon how the vote on public expenditures or other public issues is ordered. Majority voting thus fails under some circumstances to make *consistent* choices that reflect the community's underlying preferences. As a consequence, government might find it difficult to provide the "correct" public goods by acting in accordance with majority voting.

MEDIAN-VOTER MODEL

One final aspect of majority voting deserves comment because of the insights into real-world phenomena that it reveals. The **median-voter model** suggests that *under majority rule the median voter will in a sense determine the outcomes of elections.* The median voter is the person holding the middle position on an issue: One-half of the other voters have stronger preferences for an expenditure on a public good, amount of taxation, the degree of government regulation, or whatever, and the remaining one-half have weaker—or negative—preferences.

To illustrate this principle let us again suppose a society composed of Adams, Benson, and Conrad. This time let us assume that agreement has been reached between the three that as a society they need a weather warning system. Each individual independently is to submit a total dollar amount which he or she thinks should be spent on the warning system, given the fact that each will be taxed one-third of that amount. An election then will be held to determine the actual size of the system. Because each person can be expected to vote for his or her own proposal, no majority will occur if all the proposals are placed on the ballot at the same time. Thus, the group decides that they will first vote between two of the proposals and then match the winner of that vote against the remaining proposal.

The three proposals are as follows: Adams desires a $400 system; Benson wants an $800 system; Conrad opts for a $300 system. Which proposal will win? The median-voter model suggests it will be the $400 proposal submitted by the median voter, who is Adams. One-half of the other voters favors a more costly system; one-half favors a less costly system. To understand why the $400 system will be the outcome we need to conduct two elections.

First, suppose that the $400 proposal is matched against the $800 proposal. Adams naturally will vote for her own $400 proposal, but how will Benson and Conrad vote? Conrad—who proposed a $300 expenditure for the warning system—will vote for the $400 proposal rather than the one for $800. Adams's $400 proposal is selected by a 2-to-1 majority vote. Next, we match the $400 proposal against the $300 proposal. Again the $400 proposal is victorious, because it gets a vote from Adams and one from Benson, who proposed the $800 expenditure and for that reason clearly prefers a $400 expenditure to a $300 one. Adams—the median voter in this case—in a sense is the person who has decided the proper level of expenditure on a weather warning system for this society.

Although we purposely contrived a simple illustration, the idea behind it has the power to explain much. We *do* note a tendency for public choices to match up closely with the median view. In fact, we often observe political candidates taking one set of positions to win the nomination of their political parties; that is, they appeal to the median voter *within the party* to get the nomination. They then tend to shift their views more closely to the political center when they square off against their opponent from the opposite political party. In effect, they redirect their appeal toward the median voter *within the total population.*

Two interesting implications of the median voter model merit comment. First, there will be many people dissatisfied by the extent of government involvement in the economy. The size of government will to a large extent be determined by the median preference, leaving many people desiring a much larger, or a much smaller, public sector. In the marketplace you can buy no zucchinis, 2 zucchinis, or 200 zucchinis, depending on how much you enjoy zucchinis. In the public sector we get the number of Stealth bombers and interstate highways that the median voter prefers.

A second and related point is that some people may choose to "vote with their feet" by moving into political jurisdictions in which the median voter's preferences are closer to their own. For example, someone may move from the city to a suburb where the level of government services and therefore taxes are lower. Or they may move into an area that is known for its excellent, but expensive, school system. Demographic changes within political jurisdictions also occur which change the median preference.

For these reasons, and because our personal preferences for government activity are not static, the median preference within political jurisdictions can and does shift over time. Additionally, information about people's preference is imperfect, leaving much room for politicians to mistake the true median position.

Public sector failure[3]

Our discussion of the problem of achieving the optimal output of public goods and the problems in voting for that output makes it clear that the eco-

[3] This section is based upon the excellent discussion of public sector failure found in James D. Gwartney and Richard Stroup, *Economics: Private and Public Choice,* 3d ed. (New York: Academic Press, 1983), chap. 30. The interested reader should also consult Richard B. McKenzie and Gordon Tullock, *Modern Political Economy* (New York: McGraw-Hill Book Company, 1978).

nomic functions of government are not always performed effectively and efficiently. Indeed, just because the economic results of the market are not entirely satisfactory, it does not necessarily follow that the political process will yield superior results. It is fair to say that there is considerable public disenchantment with, and distrust of, government. This antigovernment sentiment has diverse roots, but it stems in part from the apparent failure of costly government programs to resolve socioeconomic ills. For example, it is argued that foreign aid programs have contributed little or nothing to the economic growth of the less developed nations. We hear reports that well-financed state and Federal school enrichment programs have had no perceptible impact upon the educational attainment of students. Some programs have allegedly fostered the very problems they were designed to solve: Our farm programs were originally designed to save the family farm, but in fact have heavily subsidized large corporate farms which in turn have driven family farms out of business. Public housing programs have destroyed more living units than they have constructed. There are also charges that government agencies have become mired in a blizzard of paperwork. The popular press tells us that social workers in New York City spend 70 to 80 percent of their time doing paperwork, leaving only 20 to 30 percent of their time to work with the people they are supposed to be helping. It is alleged that the public bureaucracy embodies great duplication of effort; that obsolete programs persist; that various agencies work at cross purpose; and so on. The apparent inability of government to control inflation and simultaneously achieve a high level of employment is also an important factor in the public's skepticism toward government.

Coincident with this popular disenchantment, there has evolved a body of literature which alleges that, just as certain limitations or failures are embodied in the private sector's market system, so there are also more-or-less inherent deficiencies in the political processes and bureaucratic agencies which comprise the public sector. Some aspects of this *public choice theory* were dealt with in our discussion of voting problems. We might agree that government has a legitimate role to play in dealing with instances of market failure; that is, government should make adjustments for spillover costs and benefits, provide public goods and services,

temper income inequality, and so forth. We might also accept benefit-cost analysis as an important guide to economically efficient decision making in the public sector. But a more fundamental question remains: Are there inherent problems or shortcomings within the public sector which constrain governmental decision making as a mechanism for promoting economic efficiency? In fact, casual reflection suggests that there may be significant divergence between "sound economics" and "good politics." We know that the former calls for the public sector to pursue various programs so long as marginal benefits exceed marginal costs. Good politics, however, suggests that politicians should support those programs and policies which will maximize their chances of getting elected and retained in office.

Let us now briefly consider some reasons given by public choice theorists for **public sector failure,** that is, some reasons why the public sector may function inefficiently in an economic sense.

SPECIAL INTERESTS AND "RENT SEEKING"

Ideally, public decisions promote the general welfare or, at least, the interests of the vast majority of the citizenry. But it is contended that, in fact, government often promotes the goals of small special-interest groups to the detriment of the public at large. Stated differently, efficient public decision making is often impaired by a **special-interest effect.**

How can this happen? In part the answer is inherent in the definition of a special-interest issue: This is an issue, program, or policy from which a small number of people individually will receive *large* gains at the expense of a vastly larger number of persons who individually suffer *small* losses. The small group of potential beneficiaries will be well informed and highly vocal on this issue, pressing politicians for approval. The large numbers who face very small losses will generally be uninformed and indifferent on this issue; after all, they have little at stake. Crudely put, politicians feel they will clearly lose the support of the small special-interest group which supports the program if they vote against it. But the politicians will *not* lose the support of the large group of uninformed voters who will evaluate them on other issues in which these voters have a stronger interest. Furthermore, the politicians' inclination to support special-interest legislation is enhanced by the fact that such groups are often more than willing to help finance the campaigns of "right-minded" politicians. The result is that the politician will support the special-interest program, even though it may *not* be economically desirable from a social point of view.

This pursuit through government of a transfer of wealth at someone else's or society's expense is called **rent-seeking behavior.** As used here the term "rent" means any payment to a resource supplier, business, or other organization above that which would accrue under competitive market conditions. Corporations, trade associations, labor unions, professional organizations, and the like employ a vast amount of resources in their attempt to secure "rent" directly or indirectly dispensed by government. Government provides this "rent" through legislation and policies which increase payments to some groups, leaving other people or society at large less well off.

Examples of special-interest or rent-seeking groups realizing legislation and policies which are unjustified on the basis of efficiency or equity are manifold: tariffs on foreign products which limit competition and raise prices to consumers (Chapter 39); tax loopholes which benefit only the wealthy (Chapter 8); public work projects which cost more than the benefits they yield; occupational licensing which goes beyond that needed to protect customers (Chapter 30); large subsidies to farmers by taxpayers (Chapter 35); and so forth. You will discover that this chapter's Last Word is also highly relevant as an example of a successful special-interest or rent-seeking activity.

CLEAR BENEFITS, HIDDEN COSTS

It is also contended that the vote-seeking politician will not *objectively* weigh all the costs and benefits of various programs, as economic rationality demands, in deciding which to support and which to reject. Given that political officeholders must seek voter support every few years, politicians will tend to favor programs which entail immediate and clear-cut benefits, on the one hand, and vague, difficult-to-identify, or deferred, costs, on the other.

Conversely, politicians will look askance at programs which embody immediate and easily identifiable costs along with future benefits which are diffuse and vague. The point here is that such biases in the area of public choice can lead politicians to reject economically justifiable programs and to accept programs which are economically irrational. Example: A proposal to construct and expand mass-transit systems in large metropolitan areas may be economically rational on the basis of objective benefit-cost analysis of the sort illustrated in Table 33-2. But if (1) the program is to be financed by immediate increases in highly visible income or sales taxes *and* (2) benefits will accrue only a decade hence when the project is completed, the vote-seeking politician may decide to oppose the program. Assume, on the other hand, that a proposed program of Federal aid to municipal police forces is *not* justifiable on the basis of objective benefit-cost analysis. But if costs are concealed and deferred through deficit financing, the program's modest benefits may loom so large that it gains political approval.

NONSELECTIVITY

Public choice theorists also argue that the nature of the political process is such that citizens are forced to be less selective in the choice of public goods and services than they are in the choice of private goods and services. In the market sector, the citizen *as consumer* can reflect personal preferences very precisely by buying certain goods and forgoing others. However, in the public sector the citizen *as voter* is confronted with two or more candidates for office, each of whom represents different "bundles" of programs (public goods and services). The critical point is that in no case is the bundle of public goods represented by any particular candidate likely to fit precisely the wants of the particular voter. For example, voter Smith's favored candidate for office may endorse national health insurance, the development of nuclear energy, subsidies to tobacco farmers, and tariffs on imported automobiles. Citizen Smith votes for this candidate because the bundle of programs she endorses comes closest to matching Smith's preferences, even though Smith may oppose tobacco subsidies and tariffs on foreign cars. The voter, in short, must take the bad with the good; in the public sector, one is forced to "buy" goods and services one does not want. It is as if, in going to a clothing store, you were forced to buy an unwanted pair of slacks to get a wanted pair of shoes. This is clearly a situation where resources are *not* being allocated efficiently so as best to satisfy consumer wants. In this sense, the provision of public goods and services is held to be inherently inefficient.

BUREAUCRACY AND INEFFICIENCY

Finally, it is contended that private businesses are innately more efficient than public agencies. The reason for this is *not* that lazy and incompetent workers somehow end up in the public sector, while the ambitious and capable gravitate to the private sector. Rather, it is held that the market system creates incentives and pressures for internal efficiency which are absent in the public sector. More specifically, the managers of private enterprises have a strong personal incentive—increased profit income—to be efficient in their operation. Whether a private firm is in a competitive or monopolistic environment, lower costs through efficient management contribute to enlarged profits. There is no tangible personal gain—a counterpart to profits—for the government bureau chief who achieves efficiency within his or her domain.

In brief, there is simply less incentive to be cost-conscious in the public sector. Indeed, in a larger sense the market system imposes an explicit test of performance on private firms—the test of profits and losses. A firm which is efficient is profitable and therefore successful; it survives, prospers, and grows. An enterprise which is inefficient is unprofitable and unsuccessful; it declines and in time goes bankrupt and ceases to exist. But there is no similar, clear-cut test by which one can assess the efficiency or inefficiency of public agencies. How can one determine whether TVA, a state university, a local fire department, the Department of Agriculture, or the Bureau of Indian Affairs is operating efficiently?

Cynics argue that, in fact, a public agency which uses its resources inefficiently may be in line for a budget increase! In the private sector, inefficiency and monetary losses lead to the abandonment of certain activities—the discontinuing of

certain products and services. But government, it is contended, is loath to abandon activities in which it has failed. "Indeed, the typical response of government to the failure of an activity is to double its budget and staff."[4] This clearly means that public sector inefficiency may be sustained on a larger scale. Furthermore, returning to our earlier comments regarding special-interest and rent-seeking groups, it has been pointed out that public programs spawn new constituencies of bureaucrats and beneficiaries whose political clout causes programs to be sustained or expanded after they have fulfilled their goals or, alternatively, even if they have failed miserably in their mission. Relevant bureaucrats, school administrators, and teachers may band together to become a highly effective special-interest group for sustaining inefficient programs of Federal aid to education or for causing these programs to be expanded beyond the point at which marginal benefits equal marginal costs.

Postscript: Some specific suggestions have been offered recently to deal with the problems of bureaucratic inefficiency. Benefit-cost analysis, of course, is one suggested approach. It has also been proposed that all legislation establishing new programs contain well-defined performance standards so the public can better judge efficiency. Further, the suggestion has been made that expiration dates—so-called "sunset laws"—be written into all new programs, thereby forcing a thorough periodic evaluation which might indicate the need for program abandonment.

IMPERFECT INSTITUTIONS

One might argue that these criticisms of public sector efficiency are overdrawn and too cynical. Perhaps this is so. On the other hand, they are sufficiently persuasive to shake one's faith in a simplistic concept of a benevolent government responding with precision and efficiency to the wants of its citizenry. We have seen that the market system of the private sector is by no means perfectly efficient; indeed, government's economic functions are attempts to correct the market system's shortcomings. But now we find that the public sector

[4] Peter F. Drucker, "The Sickness of Government," *The Public Interest*, Winter 1969, p. 13.

may also be subject to important deficiencies in fulfilling its economic functions. "The relevant comparison is not between perfect markets and imperfect governments, nor between faulty markets and all-knowing, rational, benevolent governments, but between inevitably imperfect institutions."[5]

One of the important implications of the fact that the market system and public agencies are both imperfect institutions is that, in practice, it can be exceedingly difficult to determine whether some particular activity can be performed with greater success in the private or the public sector.[6] It is easy to reach agreement on opposite extremes: National defense must lie in the public sector, whereas wheat production can best be accomplished in the private sector. But what about health insurance? The provision of parks and recreation areas? Fire protection? Garbage collection? Housing? Education? The point is that it is very hard to assess each type of good or service and to say unequivocally that its provision should be assigned to either the public or the private sector. Evidence that this is so is reflected in the fact that all the goods and services mentioned above are provided in part by both private enterprises and public agencies.

The issue of freedom

Finally, let us consider an important, but elusive, question: What is the nature of the relationship between the role and size of the public sector, on the one hand, and freedom, on the other? Although no attempt is made here to explore this issue in depth, it is relevant to indicate the outlines of two divergent views on this question.

THE CONSERVATIVE POSITION

Many conservative economists feel that, in addition to the economic costs involved in any expan-

sion of the public sector, there is also a cost in the form of diminished individual freedom. Several related points constitute this position. First, there is the "power corrupts" argument.[7] "Freedom is a rare and delicate plant. . . . history confirms that the great threat to freedom is the concentration of power. . . . by concentrating power in political hands, [government] is . . . a threat to freedom." Second, one can practice selectivity in the market system of the private sector, using one's income to buy precisely what one chooses and rejecting unwanted commodities. But, as noted earlier, in the public sector—even assuming a high level of political democracy—conformity and coercion are inherent. If the majority decides in favor of certain governmental actions—to build a reservoir, to establish a system of national health insurance, to provide a guaranteed annual income—the minority must conform. Hence, the "use of political channels, while inevitable, tends to strain the social cohesion essential for a stable society."[8] To the extent that decisions can be rendered selectively by individuals through markets, the need for conformity and coercion is lessened and this "strain" reduced. The scope of government should be strictly limited. Finally, the power and activities of government should be dispersed and decentralized.

If government is to exercise power, better in the county than in the state, better in the state than in Washington. If I do not like what my local community does, be it in sewage disposal, or zoning, or schools, I can move to another local community, and though few may take this step, the mere possibility acts as a check. If I do not like what my state does, I can move to another. If I do not like what Washington imposes, I have few alternatives in this world of jealous nations.[9]

THE LIBERAL STANCE

But liberal economists are skeptical of the conservative position. They hold that the conservative view is based upon what we shall call the **fallacy**

---

[5] Otto Eckstein, *Public Finance,* 3d ed. (Englewood Cliffs, N.J.: Prentice-Hall, Inc., 1973), p. 17.

[6] Our survey of the "isms" in Chapter 2 is indicative of the diversity of judgments on this question internationally.

[7] Milton Friedman, *Capitalism and Freedom* (Chicago: The University of Chicago Press, 1962), p. 2.

[8] Ibid., p. 23.

[9] Ibid., p. 3.

of limited decisions. That is, the conservatives implicitly assume that during any particular period of time there is a limited, or fixed, number of decisions to be made in connection with the operation of the economy. Hence, if government makes more of these decisions in performing its stated functions, the private sector of the economy will necessarily have fewer "free" decisions or choices to make. This is held to be fallacious reasoning. By sponsoring the production of public goods, government is, in fact, *extending* the range of free choice by permitting society to enjoy goods and services which would not be available in the absence of governmental provision. One can cogently argue that it is in large measure through the economic functions of government that we have been striving to free ourselves in some measure from ignorance, unemployment, poverty, disease, crime, discrimination, and other ills. Note, too, that in providing most public goods, government does not typically undertake production itself, but rather purchases these goods through private enterprise. When government makes the decision to build an interstate highway, private concerns are given the responsibility of making a myriad of specific decisions and choices in connection with the carrying out of this decision.

Finally, it should be noted that during a depression the number of choices made by private businesses and households is greatly restricted. Why? Because production has been slowed and incomes have been drastically curtailed. The business executive has fewer choices to make concerning, for example, the types of products and combinations of resources he or she may use. Indeed, some firms will have to close down and make no decisions at all. Consumers have fewer decisions to make in disposing of their incomes, because their incomes are now very small or conceivably nonexistent. Now if government, by increased participation and intervention in the economy, can correct or even alleviate a depression, the number of decisions and choices open to both businesses and consumers will increase. That is, government, by making more decisions concerning the operation of the economy, might restore prosperity, permitting the number of private decisions to increase also. Hence, the number of private and public decisions made in the operation of the economy may, *within limits,* vary in the same direction. A larger number of govern-

LAST WORD

Pentagon's anthracite mound

Special-interest legislation forces the Pentagon to buy 300,000 tons of anthracite coal it doesn't want. It plans to spread the coal 20 feet high over 45 acres in Pennsylvania.

WASHINGTON—This year, for the first time since 1962, the Pentagon won't ship American anthracite coal to West Germany, where U.S. bases already own enough to last more than four years.

Instead, the Pentagon will buy 300,000 tons of anthracite that it doesn't need and will spread it 20 feet high over 45 acres of land in eastern Pennsylvania, a monument to Congress and the coal lobby.

"It's difficult to say which is stupider," says Jeffrey A. Jones, the Pentagon's director of energy policy. Or as Sen. Phil Gramm (R., Texas) has put it: "Buying more coal than we are going to use as a compromise to not shipping coal to Newcastle may be an improvement, but it is plain wrong."

Good Guy Here is a case of Pentagon waste in which the Defense Department is the good guy. One of 107 items that President Reagan wants Congress to knock out of the fiscal 1988 budget, this program illustrates one reason the government finds it so tough to cut spending. Every program, no matter how outrageous, has a constituency and a champion somewhere in Washington.

Buried in the spending bill that Congress passed in December is a sentence that requires the Pentagon to buy 300,000 tons of anthracite this year. The provision is the legacy of a Pennsylvania congressman who retired nine years ago and testimony to the persistence of his former aide, now the lobbyist for the slowly dying U.S. anthracite industry. "This is but one of many basic support programs for American industry," says Michael Clark, the lobbyist.

The Pentagon figures it will consume 443,000 tons of anthracite in the next four years, most of it in antiquated boilers that are in use only because congressional restrictions delayed conversion to other fuels. It already has 532,000 tons on hand or on the way—not counting the 300,000 additional tons.

That 300,000 tons, for which the Pentagon expects to pay more than $20 million, represents about 10% of all the anthracite U.S. mines are expected to produce this year. Costly to mine, anthracite has steadily lost ground to cheaper bituminous coal and other fuels. The industry now employs about 2,000 miners. "Wouldn't it be cheaper to somehow pay the miners not to mine the coal?" wonders Mr. Jones, the Pentagon energy chief.

Perhaps. But that's not the way Congress works.

Back in 1962, a congressman from Pennsylvania coal country, Daniel Flood, convinced the Kennedy Administration that a good way to help the struggling American coal industry would be to order U.S. bases abroad to burn U.S. coal. Anthracite turned out to be a good substitute for local German coke.

Gradually, those old coke furnaces were replaced, and the Pentagon's appetite for coal diminished until 1972, when Congress ordered the Pentagon not to convert any more coal furnaces to oil. But as German communities grew increasingly unhappy with coal-generated air pollution, they began offering to heat U.S. bases with steam generated by local utilities. Local utilities already supply the bases with electricity and water. The Pentagon signed as many contracts as it could before Congress put a stop to that in 1984, amid concerns that the Germans were relying too heavily on Soviet natural gas. In fact, says Mr. Jones, Soviet gas generates only a small fraction of the steam supplied by the Germans.

By 1985, the Germans' environmental worries had escalated into a significant diplomatic issue. Finally, Sen. Ted Stevens (R., Alaska), then chairman of the Senate defense appropriations subcommittee, engineered a compromise: Congress would stop forcing the Pentagon to burn coal overseas, and the Pentagon would burn more domestically.

That solved one problem but created another. The natural-gas industry realized that the more coal the Pentagon used, the less natural gas—and its lobbyists leaped into action. "We raised a lot of hell on Capitol Hill and talked with some of our friends," says Michael Baly, vice president of the American Gas Association.

Oil Prices   In 1986, Congress again instructed the Pentagon to plan on burning more coal domestically, but only where coal is the most cost-efficient fuel. With falling oil prices and deregulation of the natural-gas industry, coal isn't an attractive alternative in most places, Mr. Jones says. Where it is, bituminous is cheaper.

Rep. Flood, who pleaded guilty to conspiracy to solicit illegal campaign contributions in 1980, is no longer in Washington. But others—including Pennsylvania's two senators, Republicans Arlen Specter and John Heinz, Rep. Joseph McDade (R., Pa.) and Rep. John Murtha (D., Pa.)—stepped in.

So in the current fiscal year, for the third year in a row, Congress told the Pentagon to buy 300,000 tons of anthracite. Whether the purchase was meant to be part of Sen. Stevens's original compromise or not is in dispute, but it now appears to be.

Last December, Sen. J. Bennett Johnston, a Democrat from the gas-producing state of Louisiana, urged the Senate Appropriations Committee to reduce the mandated purchase to 174,000 tons. It's wasteful, he declared. It isn't, replied Sen. Specter. "It is true that this coal is being stockpiled, but it will be used," he insisted.

Sen. Stevens had the last word. "We made the deal," he said. Sen. Johnston lost, 18–7.

Postscript: The public exposure of this special-interest legislation in newspaper articles such as this one resulted in its repeal by Congress in the fall of 1988.

mental decisions may or may not mean a smaller number of private decisions.

One of America's leading economists has summarized the liberal view in these pointed words:

Traffic lights coerce me and limit my freedom. Yet in the midst of a traffic jam on the unopen road, was I really "free" before there were lights? And has the algebraic total of freedom, for me or the representative motorist or the group as a whole, been increased or decreased by the introduction of well-engineered stop lights? Stop lights, you know, are also go lights. . . . When we introduce the traffic light, we have, although the arch individualist may not like the new order, by cooperation and coercion created by ourselves greater freedom.[10]

CHAPTER SUMMARY

1 Graphically, the collective demand curve for a particular public good can be found by summing *vertically* each of the individual demand curves for that good. The demand curve which results from this process indicates the collective willingness to pay for the last unit of any given amount of the public good.

2 The optimal quantity of a public good occurs where the combined willingness to pay for the last unit—the marginal benefit of the good—equals the good's marginal cost.

3 Benefit-cost analysis can provide useful guidance as to the economic desirability and most efficient scope of public goods output. The major difficulty in applying benefit-cost analysis is that the full costs and benefits of a public good or service are not easily calculated.

4 According to the Coase theorem, private bargaining is capable of solving potential externality problems in situations where **a** the property rights are clearly defined, **b** the number of people involved is small, and **c** bargaining costs are negligible.

5 Creation of a market for pollution rights, in which people could buy and sell the rights to a fixed amount of pollution, would place a price tag on pollution and thereby encourage firms to reduce or eliminate it.

6 Sales and excise taxes affect supply and therefore equilibrium price and quantity. The more inelastic the de-

[10] Paul A. Samuelson, "Personal Freedoms and Economic Freedoms in the Mixed Economy," in Earl F. Cheit (ed.), *The Business Establishment* (New York: John Wiley & Sons, Inc., 1964), p. 219.

mand for a product, the greater is the portion of the tax which is shifted to consumers. The greater the inelasticity of supply, the larger the portion of the tax borne by the seller.

7 Taxation involves the loss of some output whose marginal benefit exceeds it marginal cost. This efficiency loss is called the excess burden of the tax. The more elastic the supply and demand curves, the greater is the excess burden of a particular tax.

8 Majority voting creates a possibility of **a** an underallocation or overallocation of resources to a particular public good, and **b** inconsistent voting outcomes. The median-voter model predicts that, under majority rule, the person holding the middle position on an issue will in a sense determine the election outcome.

9 Public choice theorists cite a number of reasons why government might be inefficient in providing public goods and services. **a** There are strong reasons for politicians to support special-interest legislation. **b** Public choice may be biased in favor of programs with immediate and clear-cut benefits and difficult-to-identify costs *and* against programs with immediate and easily identified costs and vague or deferred benefits. **c** Citizens as voters have less selectivity with respect to public goods and services than they do as consumers in the private sector. **d** Government bureaucracies have less incentive to operate efficiently than do private businesses.

10 There is substantial disagreement as to the relationship between the size of the public sector and individual freedom.

TERMS AND CONCEPTS

public finance	logrolling
public choice theory	paradox of voting
benefit-cost analysis	median-voter model
marginal benefit = marginal cost rule	public sector failure
Coase theorem	special-interest effect
market for externality rights	rent-seeking behavior
excess burden of a tax	fallacy of limited decisions

QUESTIONS AND STUDY SUGGESTIONS

1. Given the following three individual demand schedules for a particular good, and assuming these three people are the only ones in the society, determine **a** the market demand schedule on the assumption that the good is a private good, and **b** the collective demand schedule on the assumption that the good is a public good. Explain the differences, if any, in your schedules.

Individual 1		Individual 2		Individual 3	
P	Q_d	P	Q_d	P	Q_d
$8	0	$8	1	$8	0
7	0	7	2	7	0
6	0	6	3	6	1
5	1	5	4	5	2
4	2	4	5	4	3
3	3	3	6	3	4
2	4	2	7	2	5
1	5	1	8	1	6

2 Use your demand schedule for a public good determined in question 1 and the following supply schedule to ascertain the optimal quantity of this public good. Explan why this is the optimal quantity.

P	Q_s
$19	10
16	8
13	6
10	4
7	2
4	1

3 The following table shows the total costs and total benefits in billions for four different antipollution programs of increasing scope. Which program should be undertaken? Why?

Program	Total cost	Total benefit
A	$ 3	$ 7
B	7	12
C	12	16
D	18	19

4 An apple-grower's orchard provides nectar to a neighbor's bees, while a beekeeper's bees help the apple grower by pollinating the apple blossoms. Use Figure 6-2 to explain why this situation might lead to an underallocation of resources to apple growing and to beekeeping. How might this underallocation get resolved via the means suggested by the Coase theorem?

5 Explain: "In the absence of a market for pollution rights, dumping pollutants into the air or water is costless; in the presence of the right to buy and sell pollution rights, dumping pollution creates an opportunity cost for the polluter." What is the significance of this fact to the search for better technology to reduce pollution?

6 What is the incidence of a sales tax when demand is highly inelastic? Elastic? What effect does the elasticity of supply have upon the incidence of a sales tax?

7 Suppose you are chairperson of a state tax commission that is responsible for establishing a program to raise new revenue through the use of excise taxes. Would elasticity of demand be important to you in determining those products upon which excises should be levied? Explain.

8 Explain the paradox of voting through reference to the accompanying table which shows the ranking of three public goods by voters Larry, Curley, and Moe.

Public good	Larry	Curley	Moe
Courthouse	2d choice	1st choice	3d choice
School	3d choice	2d choice	1st choice
Park	1st choice	3d choice	2d choice

9 Provide a numerical example similar to that in the text to demonstrate how majority voting in a three-person society might result in the production of a public good for which the net benefits are *negative*. Assume there is no logrolling or other activity which might influence the vote.

10 Suppose that there are only five people in a society and that each favors one of the five flood-control options shown in Table 33-2 (include no protection as one of the options). Explain which of these flood-control options will be selected using a majority rule. Will this option be the optimal size of the project from an economic perspective?

11 Carefully evaluate this statement: "The public, as a general rule . . . gets less production in return for a dollar spent by government than from a dollar spent by private enterprise."[11]

12 Carefully evaluate the following statement, and contrast its philosophy with that in question 11.

The admitted functions of government enhance a much wider field that can be easily included within the ring fence of a restrictive definition . . . it is hardly possible to find any ground of justification common to them all, except the comprehensive one of general expediency; nor to limit the interference of government by any universal rule, save the simple and vague one that it should never be admitted but when the case of expediency is strong.[12]

13 "To show that a perfectly functioning government can correct some problem in a free economy is not enough to justify governmental intervention, for government itself does not function perfectly." Discuss in detail.

[11] National Association of Manufacturers, *The American Individual Enterprise System* (New York: McGraw-Hill Book Company, 1946), p. 952.

[12] John Stuart Mill, *Principles of Political Economy* (New York: Appleton-Century-Crofts, Inc., 1878), vol. II, p. 392.

14 How does the problem of nonselectivity in the public sector relate to economic efficiency? Why are public bureaucracies alleged to be less efficient than private enterprises?

15 Explain: "Politicians would make more rational economic decisions if they weren't running for reelection every few years." Do you think this statement has a bearing upon the growth of our public debt?

16 "The market economy is the only system compatible with political freedom. It therefore behooves us to greatly restrain the economic scope of government." Do you agree?

17 *Advanced analysis:* Suppose that the equation for the demand curve for some product X is $P = 8 - .6Q$ and the supply curve is $P = 2 + .4Q$. What is the equilibrium price and quantity? Now suppose that an excise tax is imposed on X such that the new supply equation is $P = 4 + .4Q$. How much tax revenue will this excise tax yield the government? Graph the curves and label the area of the graph which represents the tax collection TC and the area which represents the excess burden of the tax EB. Briefly explain why area EB is the excess burden of the tax.

CHAPTER 34

Antitrust and regulation

In earlier chapters two contrasting points have been made. First, many important American industries—such as those shown in Table 28-1—possess considerable monopoly power. Second, one of the basic economic functions of government is to preserve competition as a key mechanism of control in the economy (Chapter 6). It is therefore imperative that we explore in some detail how government deals with the problem of business monopolies.

The scope of this chapter is as follows. After considering some definitional matters, the debate over the desirability of business monopoly is summarized. Next, we examine government policy toward business monopoly, considering both antitrust legislation and the *economic* regulation of industries which are "natural monopolies." Finally, we discuss the more recent and highly controversial *social* regulation of industry.

Big business and monopoly

Before considering the pros and cons of business monopoly, we must pause to define our terminology.

In Chapter 26 we developed and applied a very strict definition of monopoly. A *pure,* or *absolute,* monopoly, we said, is a one-firm industry—a situation in which a unique product is produced entirely by a single firm, entry to the industry being blocked by certain insurmountable barriers. When a single firm controls an entire market, pure monopoly exists.

In the present chapter we shall find it convenient to use the term *monopoly* in a broader, generic sense. In this context, **business monopoly** *exists whenever a single firm or a small number of firms control the major portion of the output of an important industry.* In other words, one, two, or three firms dominate the particular industry, presumably resulting in higher than competitive prices and economic profits. This definition, which comes closer to the way most people understand monopoly, includes a large number of industries which we have heretofore designated under the category of oligopoly.

What is the difference between business monopoly (as we have just defined it) and big business? The term **big business** may be defined in terms either of a firm's share of the total market for its product or of some absolute measure, such as the volume of its assets, sales, or profits, the number of workers employed, or the number of stockholders. A firm can simultaneously be large *in relation* to the size of the total market but small in an *absolute* sense. The Weeping Water General Store may almost completely dominate the local market for a good many products, yet be exceedingly small by any meaningful absolute standard. Conversely, a firm might be very large in the absolute sense but small in relation to the total market. This is particularly true in markets where there is considerable foreign competition. For example, Zenith—an American maker of television sets—is large by such absolute standards as sales and employment. But compared to Sony and other foreign producers, Zenith is relatively small. However, *in a good many instances, absolute and relative bigness go hand in hand*. A firm which is large in absolute terms very frequently controls a significant portion of the market for its product. Thus, although "big business" and "monopoly" are not necessarily synonymous, they frequently do go together.

In using the term "business monopoly" in this chapter, we refer to those industries in which firms are large in absolute terms *and* in relation to the total market. Examples are the electrical equipment industry, where General Electric and Westinghouse, large by any absolute standard, dominate the market; the automobile industry, where General Motors, Ford, and Chrysler are similarly situated; the chemical industry, dominated by du Pont, Union Carbide, and Allied Chemical; the aluminum industry, where three industrial giants—Alcoa, Reynolds, and Kaiser—reign supreme; and the cigarette industry, where the three giant firms of R. J. Reynolds, Philip Morris, and Brown and Williamson currently command the lion's share of this large market.

Business monopoly: good or evil?

It is not at all clear whether business monopolies are, on balance, advantageous or disadvantageous to the functioning of our economy.

THE CASE AGAINST BUSINESS MONOPOLY

The essence of the case against monopoly and oligopoly was stated in Chapters 26 and 28. Let us summarize and modestly extend those arguments.

1 Inefficient resource allocation Monopolists and oligopolists find it possible and profitable to restrict output and charge higher prices than would be the case if the given industry were organized competitively. Recall that with pure competition production occurs at the point where $P = $ MC (Chapter

25). This equality specifies an efficient allocation of resources because price measures the value or benefit to society of an extra unit of output, while marginal cost reflects the cost or sacrifice of alternative goods. In maximizing profits a business monopolist equates not price, but marginal revenue with marginal cost. At this MR = MC point, price will exceed marginal cost (see Figure 26-3 and footnote 6 in Chapter 26), designating an underallocation of resources to the monopolized product. As a result, the economic well-being of society is less than it would be with pure competition.

2 Unprogressive Critics hold that business monopoly is neither essential for the realization of existing mass-production economies nor is it conducive to technological progress.

Empirical studies suggest that in the vast majority of manufacturing industries, fewness is not essential to the realization of economies of scale. In most industries, firms need only realize a small percentage—in many cases less than 2 or 3 percent—of the total market to achieve low-cost production; monopoly is *not* a prerequisite of productive efficiency.[1] Furthermore, the basic unit for technological efficiency is not the firm, but the individual plant. Thus one can correctly argue that productive efficiency calls for, say, a large-scale, integrated auto-manufacturing plant. But it is perfectly consistent to argue that there is no technological justification for the existence of General Motors, which is essentially a giant business corporation composed of a number of geographically distinct plants. In short, many existing monopolies have attained a size and structure far larger than necessary for the realization of existing economies of scale.

Nor does technological progress depend upon the existence of huge corporations with substantial monopoly power. It is held that the evidence—one might review the closing pages of Chapter 28—does *not* support the view that large size and market power correlate closely with technological progress. Indeed, the sheltered position of the business monopolist is conducive to inefficiency and leth-

[1] F. M. Scherer, Alan Beckenstein, Erich Kaufer, and R. D. Murphy, *The Economics of Multi-Plant Operation: An International Comparisons Study* (Cambridge, Mass.: Harvard University Press, 1975), p. 80.

argy; there is no competitive spur to productive efficiency. Furthermore, business monopolists are inclined to resist or suppress technological advances which may cause the sudden obsolescence of their existing machinery and equipment.

3 Income inequality Monopoly is also criticized as a contributor to income inequality. Because of entry barriers, the monopolist can charge a price above average cost and consistently realize economic profits. These profits are realized by corporate stockholders and executives who are generally among the upper income groups.

4 Political dangers A final criticism is based upon the assumption that economic power and political clout go hand in hand. It is argued that giant corporations exert undue influence over government, and this is reflected in legislation and government policies which are congenial, not to the public interest, but rather, to the preservation and growth of these industrial giants. Big businesses allegedly have exerted political power to become the primary beneficiaries of defense contracts, tax loopholes, patent policy, tariff and quota protection, and a variety of other subsidies and privileges. Recall our discussion of rent-seeking activities in Chapter 33.

DEFENSES OF BUSINESS MONOPOLY

Business monopoly is not without significant defenses.

1 Superior products One defense of business monopoly is the contention that monopolists and oligopolists have gained their positions of market dominance by offering superior products. Business monopolists do not coerce consumers to buy, say, Colgate or Crest toothpaste, soft drinks from Coca-Cola and Pepsi, mainframe computers from IBM, ketchup from Heinz, or soup from Campbell. Consumers have collectively decided that these products are more desirable than those offered by other producers. Hence, it is alleged that monopoly profits and large market shares have been "earned" through superior performance.

2 Underestimating competition A second defense of business monopoly is that economists may view competition too narrowly. For example, while there may be only a few firms producing a given product, those firms may be faced with severe **interindustry competition.** That is, firms may face competition from other firms producing distinct but highly substitutable products. The fact that a handful of firms are responsible for the nation's output of aluminum belies the competition which aluminum faces in specific markets from steel, copper, wood, plastics, and a host of other products. **Foreign competition** must also be taken into account. While General Motors dominates domestic automobile production, growing import competition constrains its pricing and output decisions. Furthermore, the large profits resulting from the full exploitation of a monopolist's market power is an inducement to potential competitors to enter the industry. Stated differently, **potential competition** acts as a restraint upon the price and output decisions of firms now possessing market power.

3 Economies of scale Where existing technology is highly advanced, only large producers—firms which are large both absolutely and in relation to the market—can realize low unit costs and therefore sell to consumers at relatively low prices. The traditional antimonopoly contention that monopoly means less output, higher prices, and an inefficient allocation of resources assumes that cost economies would be equally available to firms whether the industry's structure was highly competitive or quite monopolistic. In fact, this is frequently not the case; economies of scale may be accessible only if competition—in the sense of a large number of firms—is absent.

4 Technological progress Recall from Chapter 28 the *Schumpeter-Galbraith view* that monopolistic industries—in particular, three- and four-firm oligopolies—are conducive to a high rate of technological progress. Oligopolistic firms have both the financial resources *and* the incentives to undertake technological research.

The antitrust laws

In view of the sharp conflict of opinion over the relative merits of business monopoly, it is not surprising to find that government policy toward business monopolies has been something less than clear-cut and consistent. While the major thrust of Federal legislation and policy has been to maintain and promote competition, we shall examine later certain policies and acts which have furthered the development of monopoly.

HISTORICAL BACKGROUND

Historically, our economy, steeped in the philosophy of free, competitive markets, has been a fertile ground for the development of a suspicious and fearful public attitude toward business monopolies. Though relatively dormant in the nation's early years, this fundamental distrust of monopoly came into full bloom in the decades following the Civil War. The widening of local markets into national markets as transportation facilities improved, the ever-increasing mechanization of production, and the increasingly widespread adoption of the corporate form of business enterprise were important forces giving rise to the development of "trusts"— that is, business monopolies—in the 1870s and 1880s. Trusts developed in the petroleum, meatpacking, railroad, sugar, lead, coal, whiskey, and tobacco industries, among others, during this era. Not only were questionable tactics employed in monopolizing the various industries, but the resulting market power was almost invariably exerted to the detriment of all who did business with these monopolies. Farmers and small businesses, being particularly vulnerable to the growth and tactics of the giant corporate monopolies, were among the first to censure their development. Consumers and labor unions were not far behind in voicing their disapproval of monopoly power.

Given the development of certain industries in which market forces no longer provided adequate control to ensure socially tolerable behavior, two techniques of control have been adopted as substitutes for, or supplements to, the market. First, in those few markets where economic realities are such as to preclude the effective functioning of the market—that is, where there tends to be a "natural monopoly"—we have established public *regulatory agencies* to control economic behavior. Second, in most other markets in which economic and technological conditions have not made monopoly essential, social control has taken the form of antimo-

nopoly or *antitrust legislation* designed to inhibit or prevent the growth of monopoly. Let us first consider the major pieces of antitrust legislation which, as refined and extended by various amendments, constitute the basic law of the land with respect to corporate size and concentration.

SHERMAN ACT OF 1890

Acute public resentment of the trusts which developed in the 1870s and 1880s culminated in the passage of the **Sherman Act** in 1890. This cornerstone of antitrust legislation is surprisingly brief and, at first glance, directly to the point. The core of the act is embodied in two major provisions:

In Section 1:

Every contract, combination in the form of a trust or otherwise, or conspiracy, in restraint of trade or commerce among the several states, or with foreign nations is hereby declared to be illegal. . . .

In Section 2:

Every person who shall monopolize, or attempt to monopolize, or combine or conspire with any person or persons, to monopolize any part of the trade or commerce among the several states, or with foreign nations, shall be deemed guilty of a misdemeanor. . . .

The act had the effect of making monopoly and "restraints of trade"—for example, collusive price fixing or the dividing up of markets among competitors—criminal offenses against the Federal government. Either the Department of Justice or parties injured by business monopolies could file suits under the Sherman Act. Firms found in violation of the act could be ordered dissolved by the courts, or injunctions could be issued to prohibit practices deemed unlawful under the act. Fines and imprisonment were also possible results of successful prosecution. Further, parties injured by illegal combinations and conspiracies could sue for triple the amount of damages done them. The Sherman Act seemed to provide a sound foundation for positive government action against business monopolies.

However, early court interpretations raised serious questions about the effectiveness of the Sherman Act and it became clear that a more explicit statement of the government's antitrust sentiments was in order. Indeed, the business community itself sought a clearer statement of what was legal and illegal.

CLAYTON ACT OF 1914

This needed elaboration of the Sherman Act took the form of the 1914 **Clayton Act.** The following sections of the Clayton Act were designed to strengthen and make explicit the intent of the Sherman Act:

Section 2 *outlaws price discrimination* between purchasers when such discrimination is not justified on the basis of cost differences.

Section 3 *forbids exclusive,* or **"tying," contracts** whereby a producer would sell a product only on the condition that the buyer acquire other products from the same seller and not from competitors.

Section 7 *prohibits the acquisition of stocks* of competing corporations when the effect is to lessen competition.

Section 8 *prohibits the formation of* **interlocking directorates**—the situation where a director of one firm is also a board member of a competing firm—in large corporations where the effect would be to reduce competition.

Actually, there was little in the Clayton Act which had not already been stated by implication in the Sherman Act. The Clayton Act merely attempted to sharpen and make clear the general provisions of the Sherman Act. Furthermore, the Clayton Act attempted to outlaw the techniques by which monopoly might develop and, in this sense, was a preventive measure. The Sherman Act, by contrast, was aimed more at the punishment of existing monopolies.

FEDERAL TRADE COMMISSION ACT OF 1914

This legislation created the five-member Federal Trade Commission (FTC) and charged it with the responsibility of enforcing the antitrust laws and the Clayton Act in particular. The FTC was given the power to investigate unfair competitive practices on its own initiative or at the request of injured firms. The Commission could hold public hearings on such complaints and, if necessary, issue **cease-and-desist orders** where "unfair methods of competition in commerce" were discovered.

The **Wheeler-Lea Act** of 1938 charged the FTC with the additional responsibility of policing "deceptive acts or practices in commerce" and, as a result, the FTC also undertakes the task of protecting the public against false or misleading advertising and the misrepresentation of products.[2]

The importance of the **Federal Trade Commission Act** is twofold: (1) the act broadened the range of illegal business behavior and (2) it provided an independent antitrust agency with the authority to investigate and to initiate court cases.

CELLER-KEFAUVER ACT OF 1950

This act amended Section 7 of the Clayton Act which, you will recall, prohibits one firm from acquiring the *stock* of competitors when the acquisition would reduce competition. Firms could evade Section 7 by acquiring the physical *assets* (plant and equipment) of competing firms, rather than their stocks. The **Celler-Kefauver Act** plugged this loophole by prohibiting one firm from obtaining the physical assets of another firm when the effect would be to lessen competition.

Antitrust: issues and impact

What major problems arise in interpreting and applying the antitrust laws? And what has been the overall effect or impact of antitrust?

The effectiveness of any law depends upon the vigor with which the government chooses to enforce it and how the law is interpreted by the courts. In fact, the Federal government has varied

[2] For an intriguing discussion of this topic, see Douglas F. Greer, *Industrial Organization and Public Policy,* 2d ed. (New York: Macmillan Publishing Company, Inc., 1984), chap. 16.

considerably in its willingness to apply the acts. Administrations having a laissez-faire philosophy about business monopoly have sometimes emasculated the acts by the simple process of ignoring them or by cutting the budget appropriations of enforcement agencies. Similarly, the courts have run hot and cold in interpreting the antitrust laws. At times, the courts have applied them with vigor, adhering closely to the spirit and objectives of the laws. In other cases, the courts have interpreted the acts in such ways as to render them all but completely innocuous. With this in mind let us examine two of the major issues which arise in interpreting the antitrust laws.

BEHAVIOR OR STRUCTURE?

A comparison of two landmark court decisions reveals the existence of two distinct approaches in the application of antitrust. In the 1920 **U.S. Steel case** the courts applied the **rule of reason** which said in effect that not every monopoly is illegal. Only those which "unreasonably" restrain trade are subject to antitrust action. The court held in this case that mere size was not an offense; although U.S. Steel clearly *possessed* monopoly power, it was innocent because it had not resorted to illegal acts against competitors in obtaining that power, nor had it unreasonably used its monopoly power.

A quarter of a century later in the **Alcoa case** of 1945 the courts did a turnabout. The court held that, even though a firm's behavior might be legal, the mere possession of monopoly power (Alcoa had 90 percent of the aluminum ingot market) was in violation of the antitrust laws.

These two cases point to a continuing controversy in antitrust policy. Should an industry be judged by its *behavior* (as in the U.S. Steel case) or by its *structure* (as in the Alcoa case)? "Structuralists" contend that an industry which has a monopolistic structure will behave like a monopolist. Hence, the economic performance of industries with a monopolistic structure will necessarily be undesirable. Such industries are therefore legitimate targets for antitrust action. On the other hand, the "behavioralists" argue that the relationship between structure and performance is tenuous and unclear. They feel that a monopolistic industry

may be technologically progressive and have an enviable record of providing products of increasing quality at reasonable prices. Therefore, if the industry has served society well and engaged in no anticompetitive practices, it should not be accused of antitrust violation simply because it is highly concentrated. Why use antitrust to penalize efficient, well-managed firms?

Since the Alcoa decision of 1945, the courts have again tended to revert back to the rule of reason. The general sentiment among antitrust economists and those responsible for enforcing the antitrust laws has also swung away from the strict structuralist view. For example, in 1982 the government dropped its 13-year-long monopolization case against IBM on the grounds that IBM had not unreasonably restrained trade.

DEFINING THE MARKET

Court decisions involving existing market power often turn on the issue of the size of the market share of the dominant firm. If the market is defined broadly, then the firm's market share will appear to be small. Conversely, if the market is defined narrowly, the market share will be large. It is the difficult task of the court to determine what is the relevant market for a particular product. For example, in the **du Pont cellophane case** of 1956 the government contended that du Pont, along with a licensee, had 100 percent of the cellophane market. But the Supreme Court defined the market broadly to include all "flexible packaging materials," that is, waxed paper, aluminum foil, and so forth, in addition to cellophane. Hence, despite du Pont's total dominance of the "cellophane market," it only controlled some 20 percent of the "flexible packaging materials" market which the court ruled did not constitute a monopoly.

EFFECTIVENESS

Have the antitrust laws been effective? This is a difficult question, but some insight can be gained by noting how the laws have been applied.

Antitrust is rather strict toward cooperation and mergers, while being largely lenient toward existing concentrations. Thus a firm with a 60 percent market share is permitted to continue untouched, fixing prices pretty much as it pleases over 60 percent of the market. Meanwhile other firms may not merge to acquire as much as 15 percent of the market. Nor may they cooperate to fix prices on *any* part of the market.[3]

It is informative to distinguish in more detail how the antitrust laws have been applied to (1) existing market structures, (2) mergers, and (3) price fixing.

1 Existing market structures As the above quotation indicates, the application of antitrust laws to existing market structures has been lenient. Generally speaking, a firm will be sued if it has more than 60 percent of the relevant market and there is evidence to suggest the firm used abusive conduct to achieve or maintain its market dominance. The most significant recent "victory" against existing market structure has been the 1982 out-of-court settlement between the government and AT&T. AT&T was charged in 1974 with violating the Sherman Act by engaging in a series of anticompetitive actions designed to maintain its domestic telephone communications monopoly. As part of the settlement, AT&T agreed to divest itself of its 22 regional telephone operating companies. In the 1980s, however, the Federal government filed no significant antitrust suits against existing market structure.

2 Mergers The treatment of mergers varies with the type of merger. The government will usually take antitrust action on a **horizontal merger**—that is, a merger between two competitors in the same market such as Ford and Chrysler—provided their combined market share will be above 15 percent. The major exception occurs where one of the merging firms is on the verge of bankruptcy. **Vertical mergers**—the merging of firms at different stages of the production process in the same industry—usually will be challenged if each of the firms has 10 percent or more of its relevant market. The reason is that such mergers foreclose other firms from selling their products to the buying firm. For example, in a 1949 case du Pont had acquired

a controlling interest in General Motors' stock. GM subsequently purchased about two-thirds of the paint and almost half of the fabrics used in its auto manufacturing from du Pont. The impact was to effectively foreclose other paint and fabric manufacturers from selling to GM. The Court ordered du Pont to divest itself of GM stock and sever the tie between the two firms. **Conglomerate mergers**—the acquisition of a firm in one industry by a firm in another unrelated industry—are generally permitted. Hence, if an insurance company acquires a trucking firm, no antitrust action is likely to be taken on the grounds that neither firm has increased the share of its own market as a result of the merger.

3 Price fixing Price fixing is treated strictly. Evidence of price fixing, even by relatively small firms, will elicit antitrust action as will other collusive activities such as schemes to divide up sales in a market. In the parlance of antitrust law, these activities are known as **per se violations,** in that they are *not* subject to the rule of reason. To gain a conviction, the government or other party making the charge need only show that there was a conspiracy to fix prices or divide up sales, not that the conspiracy succeeded or caused serious damage to other parties. There are two major consequences of the government's vigor in prosecuting price fixing. First, price fixing is surrounded by great secrecy; it has been driven underground. Second, collusive action is now much less formal; price leadership and the use of common cost-plus pricing formulas (Chapter 28) have tended to replace formal price-fixing arrangements.

It should be stressed that all the above statements are broad generalizations. Each potential antitrust case entails unique circumstances which may make it an exception. It is also significant to note once again that the strictness with which the antitrust laws are interpreted has varied greatly among various administrations. The Reagan administration, for example, adopted a "lenient" enforcement posture toward existing market structures and mergers, while taking a "strict" position on price fixing. Whether or not these enforcement trends will continue under the Bush administration is difficult to predict. However, it would appear that there is little present sentiment for breaking up

---

[3] William G. Shepherd, *The Economics of Industrial Organization,* 2d ed. (Englewood Cliffs, N.J.: Prentice-Hall, Inc., 1985), p. 347.

existing domestic business monopolies in view of the increasing competition from equally large, or even larger, foreign firms.

RESTRICTING COMPETITION

Our discussion of the antitrust laws and their application must not leave us with the conclusion that government policies are consistently procompetition. It is important to note that (1) there are exemptions from antitrust and (2) a number of public policies have reduced competition.

Labor unions and agricultural cooperatives have been exempt, subject to limitations, from the antitrust laws. We shall see in the next chapter that Federal legislation and policy have attempted to provide some measure of monopolistic power for agriculture and have tended to keep agricultural prices above competitive levels. Similarly, in a subsequent chapter we shall discover that since 1930, Federal legislation on balance has generally promoted the growth of strong labor unions. This federally sponsored growth has resulted, according to some authorities, in the development of union monopolies whose goal is above competitive wage rates. At state and local levels a wide variety of occupational groups has been successful in establishing licensing requirements which arbitrarily restrict entry to certain occupations, thereby keeping wages and earnings above competitive levels (Chapter 30).

American **patent laws**—the first of which was passed in 1790—are aimed at providing sufficient monetary incentive for innovators by granting them exclusive rights to produce and sell a new product or machine for a period of seventeen years. Patent grants have the effect of protecting the innovator from competitors who would otherwise quickly imitate this product and share in the profits, though not the cost and effort, of the research. Few contest the desirability of this particular aspect of our patent laws, particularly when it is recalled that innovation can weaken and undermine existing positions of monopoly power. However, the granting of a patent frequently amounts to the granting of monopoly power in the production of the patented item. Many economists feel that the length of patent protection—seventeen years—is much too long.

The importance of patent laws in the growth of business monopoly must not be underestimated. Such well-known firms as du Pont, General Electric, American Telephone and Telegraph, Eastman Kodak, Alcoa, and innumerable other industrial giants have attained various measures of monopoly power in part through their ownership of certain patent rights.[4]

Although we must postpone any detailed discussion of tariffs until a later chapter, it is relevant at this point to recognize that tariffs and similar trade barriers have the effect of shielding American producers from foreign competition. Protective tariffs are in effect discriminatory taxes against the goods of foreign firms. These taxes make it difficult and often impossible for foreign producers to compete in domestic markets with American firms. The result? A less competitive domestic market and an environment frequently conducive to the growth of domestic business monopolies.

Natural monopolies and their regulation

Antitrust is based upon the assumption that society will benefit by preventing monopoly from evolving or, alternatively, by dissolving monopoly where it already exists. We now consider a special case in which there is an economic rationale for an industry to be organized monopolistically.

NATURAL MONOPOLY

A **natural monopoly** exists when economies of scale are so extensive that a single firm can supply the entire market at lower unit cost than could a number of competing firms. Such conditions exist for the so-called *public utilities*, such as electricity, water, gas, telephone service, and so on (Chapter 26). In these cases the economies of scale in producing and distributing the product are very large

---

[4] For a sophisticated and detailed discussion of this topic, see F. M. Scherer, *Industrial Market Structure and Economic Performance,* 2d ed. (Chicago: Rand McNally & Company, 1980), chap. 16.

so that large-scale operations are necessary if low unit costs—and a low price—are to be realized (see Figure 24-9b). In this situation competition is simply uneconomic. If the market were divided among many producers, economies of scale would not be realized, unit costs would be high, and high prices would be necessary to cover those costs.

Two alternatives present themselves as possible means of ensuring socially acceptable behavior on the part of a natural monopoly. One is public ownership and the other is public regulation. *Public ownership* or some approximation thereof has been established in a few instances; the Postal Service, the Tennessee Valley Authority, and Amtrak come to mind at the national level, while mass transit, the water system, and garbage collection are typically public enterprises at the local level. But *public regulation* has been the option pursued most extensively in the United States. Table 34-1 lists the major Federal regulatory commissions and their areas of jurisdiction. All the states also have such regulatory bodies concerned with intrastate natural monopolies. The regulated sector is quantitatively important; it is estimated that about 10 percent of the GNP is produced by regulated industries.

TABLE 34-1 **The main Federal regulatory commissions**

Commission (year established)	Jurisdiction
Interstate Commerce Commission (1887)	Railroads, trucking, buses, water, shipping, express companies, etc.
Federal Energy Regulatory Commission (1930)*	Electricity, gas, gas pipelines, oil pipelines, water power sites.
Federal Communications Commission (1934)	Telephones, television, cable television, radio, telegraph, CB radios, ham operators, etc.

* Originally called the Federal Power Commission; renamed in 1977.

Source: Adapted from Federal Power Commission, *Federal and State Commission Jurisdiction and Regulation* (Washington: Federal Power Commission, 1973).

The intent of "natural monopoly" legislation is embodied in the **public interest theory of regulation.** This theory envisions that such industries will be regulated for the benefit of the public, to the end that consumers may be assured quality service at reasonable rates. The rationale is this: If competition is inappropriate, *regulated* monopolies should be established to avoid possible abuses of uncontrolled monopoly power. In particular, regulation should guarantee that consumers benefit from the economies of scale—that is, the lower per unit cost—which their natural-monopoly position allows public utilities to achieve. In practice, regulators seek to establish rates which will cover production costs and yield a "fair" or "reasonable" return to the enterprise. More technically, the goal is to set price equal to average total cost. (The reader is urged to review the "Regulated Monopoly" section of Chapter 26 at this point.)

PROBLEMS

While the logic of the theory of regulation rings true, there is considerable disagreement as to the effectiveness of regulation in practice. Let us briefly examine three of the major criticisms of regulation.

1 Costs and efficiency Regulatory experience suggests that there are a number of interrelated problems associated with cost containment and efficiency in the use of resources. First, a major goal of regulation is to establish prices so that the regulated firms will receive a "normal" or "fair" return above their production costs. But this means, in effect, that the firms are operating on the basis of cost-plus pricing and, therefore, have no incentive to contain costs. On the contrary, higher costs will mean larger total profits. Why develop or accept cost-cutting innovations if your "reward" will be a reduction in price? Stated more technically, regulation tends to foster considerable *X-inefficiency* (see Chapter 26). Second, it is also recognized that a regulated firm may resort to accounting skulduggery to overstate its costs and thereby obtain a higher and unjustified profit. Furthermore, in many instances prices are set by the commission so that the firm will receive a stipulated rate of return based upon the value of its real capital. This poses a special problem. In order to increase profits the regulated firm will be inclined to make an uneconomic substitution of capital for labor, thereby contributing to an inefficient allocation of resources within the firm (X-inefficiency).

2 Commission deficiencies Another criticism is that the regulatory commissions function inadequately because they are frequently "captured" or controlled by the industries they are supposed to regulate. Commission members often were executives in these very industries. Hence, regulation is *not* in the public interest, but rather, it protects and nurtures the comfortable position of the natural monopolist. It is alleged that regulation typically becomes a means of guaranteeing profits and protecting the regulated industry from potential new competition which technological change might create.

3 Regulating competitive industries Perhaps the most profound criticism of industrial regulation is that it has sometimes been applied to industries which are *not* natural monopolies and which, in the absence of regulation, would be quite competitive. Specifically, regulation has been used in industries such as trucking and airlines where economies of scale are not great and entry barriers are relatively weak. In such instances it is alleged that regulation itself, by limiting entry, creates the monopoly rather than the conditions portrayed in Figure 26-6. The result is higher prices and less output than would have been the case without regulation. Contrary to the public interest theory of regulation, the beneficiaries of regulation are the regulated firms and their employees. The losers are the public and potential competitors who are barred from entering the industry.

Example: Regulation of the railroads by the Interstate Commerce Commission (ICC) was justifiable in the late 1800s and the early decades of this century. But by the 1930s the nation had developed a network of highways and the trucking industry had seriously undermined the monopoly power of the railroads. At this time it would have been desirable to dismantle the ICC and let the railroads and truckers, along with barges and airlines, compete with one another. Instead, the regulatory net of the ICC was cast wider in the 1930s to include interstate truckers.

LEGAL CARTEL THEORY

The regulation of potentially competitive industries has given rise to the **legal cartel theory of regulation.** In the place of socially minded officials *forcing* regulation upon natural monopolies to protect consumers, this view envisions practical politicians as supplying the "service" of regulation to firms which *want* to be regulated! Regulation is desired because it constitutes, in effect, a kind of legal cartel which can be highly profitable to the regulated firms. Specifically, the regulatory commission performs such functions as dividing up the market (for example, the Civil Aeronautics Board, prior to deregulation, assigning routes to specific airlines) and restricting potential competition by enlarging the cartel (for example, adding the trucking industry to the ICC's domain). While private cartels tend to be unstable and subject to breakdown (Chapter 28), the special attraction of a government-sponsored cartel under the guise of regulation is that it tends to be enduring. In short, the legal cartel theory of regulation suggests that regulation results from rent-seeking activities (Chapter 33).

Proponents of the legal cartel theory of regulation call attention to the fact that the Interstate Commerce Act was supported by the railroads and that the trucking and airline industries both supported the extension of regulation to their industries on the grounds that unregulated competition was severe and destructive. Proponents also point to occupational licensing (Chapter 30) as the labor market manifestation of their theory. Certain occupational groups—barbers, interior designers, or dietitians—demand licensure on the ground that it is necessary to protect the public from charlatans and quacks, but the real reason may be to limit occupational entry so that practitioners may receive monopoly incomes.

Deregulation: the case of the airlines

The legal cartel theory, increasing evidence of waste and inefficiency in regulated industries, and the contention that government was in fact regulating potentially competitive industries, all contributed to the deregulation movement of the 1970s and 1980s. Important legislation has been passed in the past several years which deregulates in varying degrees the airline, trucking, banking, railroad, natural gas, and television broadcasting industries.

CONTROVERSY

Deregulation has been controversial and the nature of the controversy is quite predictable. Basing their arguments on the legal cartel theory, proponents of deregulation contend that it will result in lower prices, more output, and the elimination of bureaucratic inefficiencies. Some critics of deregulation, embracing the public interest theory, argue that deregulation will result in the gradual monopolization of the industry by one or two firms which in turn will lead to higher prices and diminished output or service. Other critics contend that deregulation may lead to excessive competition and industry instability and that vital services (for example, transportation) may be withdrawn from smaller communities. Still others stress that, as increased competition reduces each firm's revenues, firms may lower their standards with respect to safety and risk as they try to reduce costs and remain profitable.

Perhaps the most publicized case of deregulation involves the airlines. The **Airline Deregulation Act** (ADA) was passed in 1978. Prior to ADA the airlines were regulated by the Civil Aeronautics Board (CAB). The CAB controlled airline fares and allocated interstate routes among the airlines. By controlling the allocation of routes the CAB was also able to control industry entry. And, in fact, no new carriers were permitted to enter the major interstate routes from the CAB's creation in 1938 until deregulation began in the late 1970s. All of this changed in the 1980s. The 1978 deregulation act freed airlines to set their own rates and select their own routes. Under the terms of this act, the CAB was abolished in 1985.

EFFECTS OF AIRLINE DEREGULATION

What have been the effects of airline deregulation? Determining the impacts of deregulation has been complicated by such factors as fluctuating airplane fuel costs, the 1981–1982 recession, the dismissal of striking air traffic controllers in 1981, and the significant expansion of national income between 1982 and 1988. Moreover, deregulation is only about a decade old and adjustments are still incomplete. Nevertheless, some of the effects of airline deregulation have become quite clear.

Fares It is evident that deregulation has exerted substantial downward pressure on fares. Air fares overall have risen less than the general price level. Discount air tickets, in particular, have dramatically increased in availability and declined in price. More specifically, in 1976 only 15 percent of passengers enjoyed the use of discount air fares; in 1987, that number had risen to 90 percent. The price of discount tickets for long intercoastal flights (such as from New York to Los Angeles) declined by 35 percent in real terms between 1976 and 1987.[5]

There are two general reasons why deregulation has produced lower air fares. First, competition among air carriers has driven ticket prices downward to a closer proximity of the average cost of service than was the case under the legal cartel form of regulation. Second, competition has greatly pressured firms to reduce their costs. Example: The industry has adopted a "hub and spoke" routing system analogous to a bicycle wheel. Passengers are flown from smaller cities along "spokes" into major "hub" airports where they change planes and then fly to their more distant destinations. This system has reduced unit costs by allowing airlines to use smaller planes on the spoke routes and to make fuller use of the capacity of wide-bodied craft between the major hub airports. Wide-body aircraft cost less to operate per seatmile than smaller aircraft. Second example: The entry of new "nonunion" airlines has forced the major carriers to negotiate wage reductions—often on the order of 10 to 20 percent—with their unions. It has also been common to establish a two-tier wage system whereby new workers are paid substantially less on a given job than are current employees. In many instances union work rules have been made more flexible to increase worker pro-

[5] *Economic Report of the President, 1988* (Washington, D.C.: 1988), p. 203. The ensuing statistical information in this section is from pages 199–229 of this report.

ductivity and reduce wage costs. In short, some of the major cost reductions *and* adjustment problems associated with deregulation have occurred in relevant labor markets.

Service and safety Although critics of airline deregulation predicted that airline service—particularly to smaller communities—would be curtailed or abandoned, this fear has turned out to be exaggerated. While some major airlines have withdrawn from a few smaller cities, commuter airlines have often filled the resulting void. Statistics indicate that the hub and spoke system has increased flight frequencies at the vast majority of airports. It also has reduced the amount of airline switching required of passengers. More concretely, only 12 percent of connecting passengers switched airlines in 1987 compared to 68 percent in 1977. On the negative side, more frequent stopovers now required in hub cities have increased the average travel time between cities. Also, by increasing the volume of air traffic, deregulation has contributed to greater airport congestion which has resulted in more frequent and longer flight delays.

Has deregulation reduced the "safety margin" of air transportation as some critics charge? There is mixed evidence on this question. On the one hand, the increased volume of air traffic has given rise to higher reported instances of near-collisions in midair. On the other hand, the accident and fatal accident rates of airlines are lower today than they were prior to deregulation. Furthermore, because lower air fares have caused people to substitute air travel for more-dangerous automobile travel, deregulation has prevented an estimated 800 deaths annually on the nation's highways.

Industry structure Airline deregulation initially brought with it the entry of numerous new carriers. In the past few years, however, the industry has gone through a "shakeout" in which many firms have failed and others have merged with stronger competitors. Yet, even with this recent consolidation of the industry, the number of carriers operating in the United States is over twice that which existed before deregulation. Because economies of scale appear to be limited in the industry, small- and medium-sized airlines have been able in some instances to compete effectively with the largest

carriers. Thus, it would appear that competition, entry by new firms, and the threat of entry remain sufficient disciplining forces to hold down air fares. Caveat: The lack of further airport capacity—at least in the short term—means that airline markets are clearly *not* perfectly contestable (see the Last Word in Chapter 25). A firm wishing to enter a market because existing carriers are earning above-normal profits will not be able to do so if long-term leases allow existing carriers to control the airline gates at that airport. Some economists have alleged that some gates, in fact, go unused because dominant carriers refuse to release them to competitors. Frequent flyer programs—discounts based on accumulated flight mileage—also may reduce market contestability in that such programs tend to "bind" passengers to existing carriers.

Predictably, evidence suggests that fares are lower relative to cost between cities where competition is brisk and higher where less competition is present. Hence, it is generally agreed that further consolidation of the industry may be detrimental to the very goals of deregulation itself. Strict antitrust enforcement against further mergers and anticompetitive tactics may be required to preserve the substantial gains from deregulation.

Although it is perhaps premature to render a definitive assessment of airline deregulation, it is clear that the overall outcomes to date have been beneficial. The Federal government has estimated that airline deregulation has produced a $100 *billion* net benefit to society during the past decade.

The "new" social regulation[6]

The "old" regulation just discussed has been labeled economic or **industrial regulation.** Here government is concerned with the overall economic

[6] Our discussion of this topic is necessarily cursory. The reader interested in a fuller treatment of this topic should consult H. Craig Petersen, *Business and Government,* 2d ed. (New York: Harper & Row, 1985), pp. 319–387; and Murray L. Weidenbaum, *Business, Government, and the Public,* 3d ed. (Englewood Cliffs, N.J.: Prentice-Hall, 1986).

performance of a few specific industries, and concern focuses upon pricing and service to the public. Beginning largely in the early 1960s, government regulation of a new type evolved and experienced rapid growth. This new **social regulation** is concerned with the conditions under which goods and services are produced, the impact of production upon society, and the physical characteristics of goods themselves. Thus, for example, the Occupational Safety and Health Administration (OSHA) is concerned with protecting workers against occupational injuries and illnesses; the Consumer Products Safety Commission (CPSC) specifies minimum standards for potentially unsafe products; the Environmental Protection Agency (EPA) regulates the amount of pollutants manufacturers can emit; and the Equal Employment Opportunity Commission (EEOC) seeks to ensure that women and minorities have fair access to jobs.

DISTINGUISHING FEATURES

Social regulation differs from economic regulation in several ways. In the first place, social regulation is often applied "across the board" to virtually all industries and thereby directly affects far more people. While the Interstate Commerce Commission (ICC) focuses only upon specific portions of the transport industry, OSHA's rules and regulations apply to every employer. Second, the nature of social regulation entails government involvement in the very details of the production process. For example, rather than simply specifying safety standards for products, CPSC mandates—often in detail—certain characteristics which products must embody. A final distinguishing feature of social regulation is its rapid expansion. For example, between 1970 and 1979 legislation created twenty new Federal regulatory agencies.

The above recitation of the names of a few of the better-known regulatory agencies suggests the basic reason for their creation and growth: Much of our society had achieved a reasonably affluent level of living by the 1960s and attention thus shifted to the realization of improvements in the quality of life. This improvement called for safer and better products, less pollution, better working conditions, and greater equality of opportunity.

COSTS AND CRITICISMS

There is rather widespread agreement that the general objectives of social regulation are laudable. But there is great controversy as to whether the benefits of these regulatory efforts justify the costs. It is generally agreed that social regulation is costly.

Costs The costs of social regulation are of two general types: *administrative costs,* such as salaries paid to employees of the commissions, office expenses, and the like; and *compliance costs,* which are the costs incurred by businesses and state and local governments in meeting the requirements of the regulatory commissions. In 1988 the total administrative costs of social regulation were about $8 billion.[7] Because compliance costs are estimated to be roughly twenty times administrative costs, the total cost of social regulation in 1988 was therefore about $168 billion. In 1988, 79,000 permanent full-time employees worked for Federal regulatory agencies involved in social regulation.[8]

Cost estimates for specific types of regulations are also revealing. The U.S. Council on Environmental Quality has estimated that the cost of pollution control alone for the 1979–1988 period totaled over $700 billion. Federally required safety and antipollution equipment has increased the price of the typical automobile by as much as $2,200.[9] Business firms in the United States spend more than $5 billion annually to meet OSHA requirements.[10]

Criticisms Critics argue that the American economy is now subject to overregulation, that is, regulatory activities have been carried to the point where the marginal costs of regulation exceed the

---

[7] Center for the Study of American Business, Washington University.

[8] Ibid.

[9] Robert W. Crandall, et al., *Regulating the Automobile* (Washington, D.C.: The Brookings Institution, 1986), p. 43.

[10] McGraw-Hill investment survey, cited in Weidenbaum, op. cit., p. 157.

marginal benefits (Chapter 33). Why might this be the case? Why is social regulation allegedly inefficient?

It is contended, in the first place, that many of the social regulation laws are poorly drawn so that regulatory objectives and standards are often stated in legal, political, or engineering terms which result in the pursuit of goals beyond the point at which marginal benefits equal marginal costs. Businesses complain that regulators press for small increments of improvement, unmindful of costs. A requirement to reduce pollution by an incremental 5 percent may cost as much as required to achieve the first 95 percent reduction.

Second, decisions must often be made and rules promulgated on the basis of inadequate and sketchy information. CPSC officials may make sweeping decisions about the use of carcinogens in products upon the basis of very limited experiments with laboratory animals.

Third, it is argued that regulations produce a myriad of unintended side effects which greatly boost the full cost of regulation. Example: A 1988 study concluded that Federal gas mileage standards implemented over the past several years for automobiles would cause 2200 to 3900 traffic deaths in 1989. The reason? Manufacturers have reduced the weight of vehicles as a way to meet the increasingly stringent standards. All else being equal, drivers of lighter cars have a considerably higher fatality rate than drivers of heavier vehicles.

Finally, opponents of social regulation point out that the regulatory agencies may tend to attract overzealous personnel who "believe" in regulation. It is often observed, for example, that the staff of EPA is comprised largely of "environmentalists" who are strongly inclined to punish polluters. "Treating all polluters as sinners is . . . much easier than making quantitative judgments about optimal levels of cleanliness in the air and water, but it leads to inefficient regulations, especially where government statutes imply rigid, national, uniform standards."[11] It is further argued that the bureaucrats of the new regulatory agencies are extremely sensitive to criticism by Congress or some special-

interest group, for example, consumerists, environmentalists, or organized labor. The result is bureaucratic inflexibility and the establishment of extreme or nonsensical regulations so that no watchdog group will question the agency's commitment to its given social goal. OSHA's much-ridiculed specification of the shape of toilet seats and its proposal that farmers and ranchers provide toilet facilities within five minutes walking distance of any point where employees are at work are cases in point. In the words of one critic:

No realistic evaluation of . . . government regulation comfortably fits the notion of benign and wise officials making altogether sensible decisions in the society's greater interests. Instead we find waste, bias, stupidity, concentration on trivia, conflicts among the regulators and, worst of all, arbitrary and uncontrolled power.[12]

ECONOMIC IMPLICATIONS

If overregulation does exist, what are its consequences? First of all, social regulation increases product prices. It does this directly because compliance costs tend to get passed on to consumers. Furthermore, social regulation indirectly contributes to higher product prices to the extent that it reduces labor productivity. Resources invested in antipollution equipment are not available for investment in new machinery to increase output per worker. Where wage rates are inflexible downward, declines in labor productivity increase the marginal and average costs of production. In effect, product supply curves shift leftward, causing product prices to rise. Second, the new regulation may have a negative impact upon the rate of innovation. The fear that a new, technologically superior plant will not meet with EPA approval or that a new product may run into difficulties with CPSC may be sufficient reason to persuade a firm to produce the same old product in the same old way.

Finally, social regulation may have an anticompetitive effect in that it tends to be a relatively greater economic burden for small firms than for large firms. The costs of complying with the new

[11] William Lilley III and James C. Miller III, "The New 'Social Regulation,'" *The Public Interest*, Spring 1977, p. 58.

[12] Murray L. Weidenbaum, "The Cost of Overregulating Business," *Tax Review*, August 1975, p. 33.

regulation are, in effect, fixed costs. Smaller firms produce less output over which to distribute these costs and, hence, their compliance costs per unit of output put them at a competitive disadvantage relative to their larger rivals. Bluntly put, the burden of social regulation is more likely to put small firms out of business and thereby contribute to the increased concentration of industry.

IN SUPPORT OF SOCIAL REGULATION

Social regulation is not without its defenses. The problems with which social regulation contends are serious and substantial in scope. In 1987, 11,100 workers died in job-related accidents in the United States. Particulate and ozone pollution still plagues our major cities, imposing large costs in terms of reduced property values and increased health-care expenses. Thousands of children and adults die each year in accidents which involve poorly designed products. Discrimination against blacks, females, and older workers reduces the earnings of these groups and imposes heavy costs on society as well (Chapter 25).

Proponents of social regulation correctly point out that the relevant economic test of whether social regulation is worthwhile is not whether its costs are high or low, but rather whether benefits *exceed* costs. After years of relative neglect, society cannot expect to cleanse the environment, enhance the safety of the workplace, improve the safety of the automobile, and enhance economic opportunity without incurring substantial costs. Furthermore, cost calculations may paint too dim a picture of social regulation. Benefits tend to be taken for granted, are more difficult to measure than costs, and may accrue to society only after an extended period of time. However, benefits have been substantial. Examples: It is estimated that highway fatalities would be 40 percent greater annually in the absence of the auto safety features mandated through regulation.[13] Compliance with child safety-belt laws has significantly reduced the auto fatality rate for small children. "The motor vehicle fatality rate for the overall population fell 10 per-

cent between 1975 and 1985, but for children under 5 it fell by 32 percent."[14] The National Ambient Air Quality Standards set by law have been reached in nearly all parts of the nation for sulfur dioxide, nitrogen dioxide, and lead. A recent study has found that affirmative action regulations have significantly increased the labor demand for blacks and females.[15] Childproof lids have resulted in a 90 percent decline in child deaths caused by accidental swallowing of poisonous substances.[16]

Although we can expect social regulation to continue to be a matter of considerable controversy, it is generally agreed that the contested "question is not whether (social) regulation should occur, but how and when it should be used; how we can improve the system of regulation; and whether we are fully aware of the costs and benefits involved."[17]

CHAPTER SUMMARY

1 The case against business monopoly centers upon the contentions that business monopoly **a** causes a misallocation of resources; **b** retards the rate of technological advance; **c** promotes income inequality; and **d** poses a threat to political democracy.

2 The defense of business monopoly is built around the following points: **a** firms have obtained their large market shares by offering superior products; **b** interindustry and foreign competition, along with potential competition from new industry entrants, make American industries more competitive than generally believed; **c** some degree of monopoly may be essential to the realization of economies of scale; and **d** business monopolies are technologically progressive.

[13] Crandall, op. cit., p. 155.

[14] *Economic Report of the President, 1987* (Washington, D.C., 1987), p. 188.

[15] Jonathon S. Leonard, "The Impact of Affirmative Action on Employment," *Journal of Labor Economics*, October 1984, pp. 439–463.

[16] U.S. Product Safety Commission estimate.

[17] Testimony of Juanita M. Kreps in *The Cost of Government Regulation* (Washington, D.C., 1978), p. 7.

3 The cornerstone of antitrust policy consists of the Sherman Act of 1890 and the Clayton Act of 1914. The Sherman Act specifies that "Every contract, combination . . . or conspiracy in the restraint of interstate trade . . . is . . . illegal," and that any person who monopolizes or attempts to monopolize interstate trade is guilty of a misdemeanor.

4 The Clayton Act was designed to bolster and make more explicit the provisions of the Sherman Act. To this end the Clayton Act declared that price discrimination, tying contracts, intercorporate stockholdings, and interlocking directorates are illegal when the effect of their use is the lessening of competition.

5 The Federal Trade Commission Act of 1914 created the Federal Trade Commission to investigate antitrust violations and to prevent the use of "unfair methods of competition." Empowered to issue cease-and-desist orders, the Commission also serves as a watchdog agency for the false and deceptive representation of products.

6 The Celler-Kefauver Act of 1950 prohibits one firm from acquiring the assets of another firm where the result is a lessening of competition.

7 Major issues in applying the antitrust laws include **a** the problem of determining whether an industry should be judged by its structure or its behavior and **b** defining the scope and size of the dominant firm's market.

8 Generally speaking, antitrust officials are more likely to challenge price fixing and horizontal mergers among large firms than they are to attempt to break up existing market structures.

9 With respect to agriculture, labor, occupational licensing, patents, and international trade barriers, government policies have tended to restrict competition.

10 The objective of industrial regulation it to protect the public from the market power of natural monopolies by regulating prices and quality of service. Critics contend that industrial regulation is conducive to inefficiency and rising costs and that in many instances it constitutes a legal cartel for the regulated firms. Legislation passed in the late 1970s and in the 1980s has brought about varying degrees of deregulation in the airline, trucking, banking, railroad, and television broadcasting industries.

11 Airline deregulation has lowered fares and increased the efficiency of the industry, producing a sizable net benefit to society.

12 Social regulation is concerned with product safety, safer working conditions, less pollution, and greater economic opportunity. Critics contend that businesses are overregulated in that marginal costs exceed marginal benefits, while defenders dispute that contention.

LAST WORD

Does the United States need an industrial policy?

Should government be more actively involved in determining the structure of industry?

There has been a growing concern in recent years that the United States' industrial preeminence has been seriously eroded. Our domestic markets have been flooded with foreign steel, automobiles, motorcycles, cameras, watches, and stereo equipment, suggesting that our competitive edge has been lost.

Noting apparent Japanese successes, many political, union, and business leaders—but only a limited number of economists—feel that the United States needs an industrial policy to reverse our alleged industrial decline. It is argued that government should undertake a more active and direct role in determining the structure and composition of American industry. Government, it is held, should use low-interest loans, loan guarantees, special tax treatment, research and development subsidies, antitrust immunity, and even foreign trade protection to accelerate the development of "high-tech" industries and to revitalize certain core manufacturing industries such as steel. Conversely, it should hasten the movement of resources out of declining "sunset" industries. Presumably the net result will be that the American economy will enjoy a higher average level of productivity and be more competitive in world markets.

Opponents of industrial policy make a number of points.

1 *Deindustrialization?* Has the United States in fact deindustrialized? Has our manufacturing sector experienced serious decline? Statistics suggest not. While the composition of manufacturing output has changed, manufacturing in the aggregate accounts for virtually the same percentage of national output in 1988 (about 20 percent) as it did in 1950. Similarly, manufacturing's share of the nation's expenditures on new plant and equipment was about the same in 1988 as in 1950. Employment in manufacturing has declined from 34 to 18 percent of total employment in the 1950–1988 period, but that reflects the growth of labor productivity rather than industrial demise. Output and employment in manufacturing suffered in the early and mid-1980s, but the primary cause was a very strong dollar which made foreign imports relatively cheap and American exports relatively expensive.

2 *Foreign experience* Advocates of an industrial policy typically cite Japan as a model. In the post-World War II era Japan has achieved rapid economic growth; it has been highly successful in penetrating world markets; and it has had a much-publicized industrial policy. Yet the overall role of industrial policy as a causal factor in Japanese industrial success is not clear. The picture is mixed.

Japanese industrial policy has had both successes and failures. Some targeted industries, including semiconductor and machine tools, are almost certainly stronger than they would have been without government support and can be claimed as successes for Japanese industrial policy. Other industries, such as shipbuilding and steel, probably grow more quickly because of government aid, but undoubtedly would have developed without any government intervention. However, the Japanese government has also picked losers. Aluminum smelting and petrochemicals were favored industries fifteen years ago, but the public and private investments have paid off very poorly and now their capacity is being reduced. There are also several examples of successful industries that did not receive government assistance, including motorcycles and consumer electronics.*

Industrial policies in Europe have generally been failures. Massive aid to aircraft, computer, and semiconductor industries has simply not paid off.

3 *Markets and politics* While a proposal to create an industrial policy which subsidizes "sunrise" industries and hastens the phasing out of "sunset" industries sounds appealing, critics question the government's ability to identify future industrial "winners" and "losers." The issue here is whether private investors functioning in capital markets have better prescience than public officials in determining industrial winners and losers. Critics argue that private investors have a greater incentive in investing their own funds to obtain accurate information on the future prospects of various industries than might government bureaucrats in investing the *taxpayers'* funds. Furthermore, might not government use its power to allocate investment funds to buy the political support of various industries? Might not the economic goal of enhanced industrial efficiency be subverted to the political goal of getting reelected? It is feared that the creation of a new industrial policy may lead to "lemon socialism," that is, government support or ownership of declining industries and dying companies.

Those who are skeptical of industrial policy contend that government can best stimulate American industry by (1) using monetary and fiscal policy to create a favorable macroeconomic environment (high employment, low inflation, low interest rates) and (2) adjusting tax and regulatory systems to enhance incentives for investment and technological advance.

Economic Report of the President, 1984, p. 98.

Source: Adapted from *Economic Report of the President, 1984.* chap. 3; and Federal Reserve Bank of Kansas City, *Industrial Change and Public Policy* (1983). Updated.

TERMS AND CONCEPTS

business monopoly	rule of reason
big business	Alcoa case
interindustry competition	du Pont cellophane case
foreign competition	horizontal, vertical, and conglomerate mergers
potential competition	per se violations
Sherman Act	patent laws
Clayton Act	natural monopoly
tying contracts	public interest theory of regulation
interlocking directorates	legal cartel theory of regulation
cease-and-desist order	Airline Deregulation Act
Wheeler-Lea Act	industrial regulation
Federal Trade Commission Act	social regulation
Celler-Kefauver Act	
U.S. Steel case	

QUESTIONS AND STUDY SUGGESTIONS

1 "All big firms are monopolistic, but not all monopolistic firms are big." Appraise critically.

2 Suppose you are president of General Motors or Ford. Discuss critically the case against business monopoly. Now suppose you are a representative for a farm organization and are attempting to convince a congressional committee that the presence of business monopolies is a significant factor contributing to the farm problem. Critically evaluate the case for business monopoly.

3 Describe the major provisions of the Sherman and Clayton Acts. Who is responsible for the enforcement of these laws?

4 Briefly indicate the basic issue involved in the U.S. Steel, Alcoa, and du Pont cellophane cases. What issues in antitrust enforcement are implicit in these cases?

5 How would you expect the antitrust authorities to react to *a* a proposed merger of Chrysler and General Motors; *b* evidence of secret meetings by contractors to rig bids for highway construction projects; *c* a proposed merger of a large shoe manufacturer and a chain of retail shoe stores; and *d* a proposed merger of a small life insurance company and a regional candy manufacturer.

6 Suppose a proposed merger of firms will simultaneously lessen competition and reduce unit costs through the greater realization of economies of scale. Do you feel such a merger should be allowed?

7 In 1986 PepsiCo Inc., which currently had 28 percent of the soft drink market, proposed to acquire the Seven-Up Co. Shortly thereafter the Coca-Cola Company, with 39 percent of the market, indicated it wished to acquire the Dr. Pepper Company. Seven-Up and Dr. Pepper each controlled about 7 percent of the market. In your judgment, was the government's decision to block these mergers appropriate?

8 "The antitrust laws serve to penalize efficiently managed firms." Do you agree?

9 "The social desirability of any given business enterprise should be judged not on the basis of the structure of the industry in which it finds itself, but rather on the basis of the market performance and behavior of that firm." Analyze critically.

10 What types of industries should be subjected to industrial regulation? What specific problems does industrial regulation entail? Why might an inefficient combination of capital and labor be employed by a regulated natural monopoly?

11 Given some of the problems involved in regulating natural monopolies, compare socially optimal (marginal-cost) pricing and fair-return pricing by referring again to Figure 26-6. Assuming a government subsidy might be used to cover any loss entailed by marginal-cost pricing, which pricing policy would you favor? What problems might the subsidy entail?

12 How does social regulation differ from industrial regulation? What types of costs and benefits are associated with social regulation?

13 The following are research estimates of the average cost per life saved of three specific social regulations: 1967 automobile steering column protection rule costs $100,000 per life saved; 1979 FDA ban on DES (a suspected carcinogen) in cattle feed costs $132 million per life saved; the EPA's proposed restrictions on the disposal of dioxins and solvents on land costs $3.5 billion per life saved.[18] Based on this information, do you favor each of these social regulations? If not, why not? Discuss: "Implicit within the setting of safety standards for products is the valuation of human life."

---

[18] *Economic Report of the President, 1987* (Washington, D.C., 1987), p. 183.

CHAPTER 35

Rural economics: the farm problem

T his chapter is essentially a case study of the agricultural sector of our economy and the problems it faces. A case study of this type is justified on several grounds. First, agriculture is the nation's largest industry. Consumers spend almost a fifth of their incomes on food and other farm products (Table 7-3). Agriculture contributed about $170 billion to the GNP in 1988 and employed about 2 percent of the labor force. Agriculture is also a major source of American export trade; some $36 billion of farm products were exported in 1988, providing over 10 percent of America's export revenues. Second, agriculture provides us with a real-world case study of an industry which, in the absence of government farm programs, approximates Chapter 25's purely competitive market model. Finally, American agriculture embodies a paradox which calls out for explanation. Characterized by a rate of productivity growth substantially in excess of any other major sector of the economy, our agricultural abundance has been the envy of the world. But, ironically, farmers have typically received below-average incomes for their remarkable production feats.

More specifically, the major objectives of this chapter are: (1) to describe "the farm problem" and outline its causes and (2) to discuss public policy toward agriculture and comment upon its effectiveness.

History of the farm problem

The two decades prior to World War I were exceedingly prosperous ones for agriculture; indeed, this period has been dubbed "the golden age of American agriculture." The demand for farm products, farm prices, and farm incomes all rose. World War I intensified these good times. Foreign demand for the output of American farmers skyrocketed during, and immediately following, the war. Foreign countries, diverting resources from agriculture to war goods production, turned to American agriculture for food and fiber. High prices and an almost insatiable demand were the happy lot of American farmers during this period.

These highly favorable conditions were not to last. A sharp postwar depression in 1920 was a sudden and severe shock to agriculture. In particular, the large volume of mortgage indebtedness incurred during the previous years of prosperity proved a heavy burden. The economy as a whole quickly recovered from this downturn, however, and by 1921 the booming twenties were upon us. But agriculture failed to share in this prosperity to the extent that other segments of the economy did.

The reasons for this were several. European agriculture not only recovered from the war but also began to expand rapidly under the impetus of new technological advances. Hence, foreign demand for American farm goods began to level off and then to decline. American foreign trade policies also contributed to this deterioration in foreign demand. High tariffs on goods imported to the United States helped undermine foreign demand for American farm products. To the extent that foreigners could not sell to us because of trade restrictions, they were unable to earn the funds they needed to buy from American producers. Furthermore, the domestic demand for farm products did not rise very much in the twenties. Most American stomachs were full, and as a result, income increases were used to buy automobiles, refrigerators, and a host of other new products of industry. Finally, on the supply side of the picture, technological advances boosted farm output markedly. The net result of a lagging, inelastic demand and a sharply increasing supply of farm products was low farm prices and incomes.

The Great Depression of the 1930s was a particularly acute blow to American agriculture. The highly competitive nature of agriculture makes it especially vulnerable to bad times. Unlike sellers who possess a modicum of monopoly power, farmers are unable to influence their prices. They are "price takers" at the mercy of the market. Therefore, when market demand declines as it did during the Depression, farm prices and farm incomes fall sharply. Ironically, farmers buy in markets in which prices are relatively inflexible downward. Hence, while their incomes fell by very large amounts, the prices of farmers' purchases declined very modestly. Farmers in the 1920s and 1930s found themselves in a harsh price-cost squeeze.

World War II provided welcome but temporary relief for the farmer. Both domestic and foreign demand for agricultural products boomed during the war, and prosperity returned to agriculture. Except for the 1948–49 slump, the middle and the late forties were peak years for American farmers. Then in the 1950s a slow but certain relapse became evident, and agriculture was once again encountering difficulty.

But in the 1970s farm prices and incomes rose quite dramatically. The basic reason for this was a sharp increase in exports. A number of factors underlay this export boom. On a worldwide basis—and especially in western Europe and Japan—incomes had been expanding rapidly. But most countries had little or no excess capacity in agriculture; indeed, many countries were already large importers of food. Hence, much of their increased food and fiber demand was for American output. Also, poor harvests in a number of countries boosted their demand for American foodstuffs. Finally, American agricultural exports received a further stimulus from the depreciation of the dollar in international trade. That is, dollars became less expensive in terms of other currencies, making American products—including farm products—cheaper for foreigners to buy. In short, all these factors, coupled with a rather strong expansion of

incomes domestically, sharply boosted agricultural demand, farm prices, and receipts.

In the early 1980s this picture changed quite abruptly. Many of the forces which produced the export boom of the 1970s essentially reversed themselves to create a "harvest of despair." First, many other industrially advanced countries undertook policies to boost their agricultural outputs and many became self-sufficient in farm products. For example, the Common Market nations of Western Europe changed from large importers to large exporters of grains between the mid-1970s and the mid-1980s. Second, many of the less developed countries were forced to limit their purchases of American farm products in order to make interest and principal payments on large external debts. Third, the dollar's international value appreciated, making our farm products more expensive to foreigners and causing their purchases to decline. Domestically, restrictive macroeconomic policies designed to halt inflation resulted in very high real rates of interest which made it difficult for many farmers to finance their operations and remain profitable. Although these highly adverse circumstances abated by the late 1980s, the economic prospects for the agricultural sector remain problematic.

Farm incomes and their diversity

A comparison of the incomes of farmers and nonfarmers reveals several significant points.

1 Historically, relatively low incomes have been the most obvious symptom of the farm problem. In the past, farm incomes have typically been significantly less than nonfarm incomes. For example, in the early 1960s farm incomes were only about three-quarters of those of nonfarmers. Again, in the early 1980s the ratio of farm to nonfarm incomes hovered around 80 percent.

2 The farm–nonfarm income gap has narrowed in recent years. Indeed, in the agricultural "boom" years of the mid-1970s the incomes of farm households actually exceeded those of nonfarm households. This has also been true in recent years. For example, in 1985 the average income of farm households was $29,436 as compared to the overall

national average of $29,066. Comparable 1986 figures were $34,305 for farmers and $30,759 for the economy as a whole. It should be noted, however, that a significant percentage of farm incomes are derived from government subsidies.

3 As the above comments and our earlier discussion of the history of the farm problem both suggest, farm incomes are much more variable than nonfarm incomes.

4 Although farm and nonfarm incomes have been quite comparable in recent years, the distribution of farm income is highly unequal. Thus we find that in 1986 some 20 percent of farm people lived in poverty as compared to less than 14 percent for the economy as a whole.

5 Much of the historical improvement in the incomes of farm households vis-à-vis nonfarm households reflects the increase in the off-farm incomes of farm families. That is, many farm families—particularly those with low earnings from farming—also earn considerable income from off-farm work. If you will glance below to the bottom of columns 5 and 6 in Table 35-1, you will note that in 1987 the average income per farm from farming was $21,545

(below the national average), but that average income from all sources (farm plus nonfarm production) was $43,037. This latter figure was above the national average. Columns 5 and 6 of Table 35-1 also reveal that most of the income from the four lowest income classes (all farms with annual gross sales of less than $40,000) came from off-farm productive activities.

Let us examine Table 35-1 more carefully to grasp the great income diversity existing within agriculture. In fact, there are three quite different groups within the farm sector.

Group 1 Of the nation's 2.2 million farms the 14 percent with annual gross sales of $100,000 or more accounted for about 71 percent of total output. These large commercial farms realize long-run average incomes far above those of nonfarm families as column 6 of Table 35-1 makes evident.

Group 2 At the other extreme are those 1.6 million farms with gross annual sales of less than $40,000. Although they comprise about 73 percent of all farms, they account for only less than 15 percent of

TABLE 35-1 **The structure of American agriculture, 1987**

(1) Farm size, by annual gross sales (in dollars)	(2) Number of farms	(3) Percent of all farms	(4) Percent of gross farm income	(5) Average net farm income per farm (in dollars)	(6) Average income per farm from all sources (in dollars)
500,000 and over	29,000	1.3	32.2	738,132	767,495
250,000 to 499,999	71,000	3.2	16.9	128,678	144,760
100,000 to 249,999	201,000	9.2	22.1	51,749	66,132
40,000 to 99,999	286,000	13.2	14.3	18,713	33,334
20,000 to 39,999	209,000	9.6	5.0	6,058	27,980
10,000 to 19,999	241,000	11.1	3.2	2,038	25,886
5,000 to 9,999	302,000	13.9	2.6	930	20,326
Less than 5,000	837,000	38.5	3.6	−1,455	24,251
Total or all-farm average	2,176,000	100.0	100.0	21,545	43,037

Source: U.S. Department of Agriculture, *Economic Indicators of the Farm Sector: National Financial Summary, 1987.*

total farm output. These farms are essentially rural residences or so-called "hobby farms" and are too small to provide an adequate family income. These families rely mainly upon off-farm employment for their incomes. As column 5 of Table 35-1 indicates, most of these farms realize negligible or even negative incomes from farming. The median income of this group is well below that for the economy as a whole.

Group 3   Some 286,000 farms fall in the $40,000 to $100,000 gross sales category. These account for about 13 percent of all farms and earn about 14 percent of gross farm income. Although these are generally full-time farms, they are too small to yield incomes comparable to nonfarm incomes. The median income of Group 3 farms from farming was $18,713 in 1987 as compared to $30,853 for the economy as a whole.

At the risk of getting ahead of ourselves, we should note that this diversity greatly complicates farm policy. It makes little or no sense to formulate farm programs to meet the perceived needs of a "typical" farm family. The large farms of Group 1 do not need income subsidies in the long run, but as we shall see, they do face serious problems of income instability. The small farms of Group 2 are not greatly aided by existing farm policy because farm income subsidies vary proportionately with output and the output of these farms is very small. In fact, the existence of this group suggests that a substantial amount of human and property resources could leave agriculture without causing a very significant decline in total farm output.

It is interesting to note in Table 35-1 that almost 40 percent of all farms have annual gross sales of less than $5000 and their output is only 3.6 percent of total farm production! Job training and overall macroeconomic prosperity are perhaps more important than farm policy in raising the relatively low incomes of this group. The intermediate-sized farms of Group 3 face both the twin problems of low incomes and income instability.

Causes of the farm problem: short run and long run

It is a bit misleading to talk of "the" farm problem. Actually, the changes which have occurred in farm incomes suggest the presence of both a long-run problem and a short-run problem. The long-run problem concerns those forces which have tended to cause farm prices and incomes to lag behind the trends of prices and incomes for the economy as a whole. The short-run problem has to do with the often extreme year-to-year instability of farm incomes.

LONG-RUN PROBLEM: LOW INCOMES

Complex problems can rarely be stated accurately in brief terms. This is certainly true of the **long-run problem** which plagues American agriculture. Nevertheless, a workable picture of the problem can be portrayed through the economic tools of demand and supply. In these terms, we may say that the causes of the long-run farm problem are embodied in

1 The *price inelasticity* of the demand for agricultural products
2 The *shifts* which have occurred over time in the demand and supply curves for farm products
3 The relative *immobility* of agricultural resources

This combination of forces has generated a tendency for farm prices (and incomes) to fall relative to other prices (Figure 35-4, page 693).

Inelastic demand for agricultural products   In most developed societies, the price elasticity of demand for agricultural products is low. For farm products in the aggregate, the elasticity coefficient is estimated to be from .20 to .25.[1] These figures suggest that the prices of agricultural products would have to fall by 40 to 50 percent in order for consumers to increase their purchases by a mere 10 percent. Consumers apparently put a low value on additional agricultural output as compared with alternative goods. Why is this so? You will recall that the basic determinant of elasticity of demand is substitutability. That is, when the price of a product falls, the consumer will tend to substitute *that* product for other products whose prices presuma-

---

[1] Dale E. Hathaway, *Problems of Progress in the Agricultural Economy* (Chicago: Scott, Foresman and Company, 1964), p. 10.

bly have not fallen. But in wealthy societies this "substitution effect" (Chapter 23) is very modest for food. People simply do not switch from three to five or six meals each day in response to declines in the relative prices of agricultural products. An individual's capacity to substitute food for other products is subject to very real biological constraints. The inelasticity of agricultural demand can also be explained in terms of diminishing marginal utility. In a wealthy society, the population by and large is well fed and well clothed, that is, relatively saturated with the food and fiber of agriculture. Therefore, additional agricultural output entails rapidly diminishing marginal utility. Thus it takes very large price cuts to induce small increases in consumption. Curve *D* in Figure 35-2 on page 690 portrays an inelastic demand.

Technological advance and rapid increases in agricultural supply An inelastic demand for farm products is, in and of itself, innocent enough. It is the accompanying fact that the supply of agricultural products has increased in relation to the demand for them that has tended to depress farm incomes.

On the supply side of the picture, a rapid rate of technological advance, particularly since World War I, has caused significant increases in the supply of agricultural products. This technological progress has many roots: the virtually complete electrification and mechanization of farms; improved techniques of land management and soil conservation; irrigation; the development of hybrid crops; the availability of improved fertilizers and insecticides; improvements in the breeding and care of livestock; and so forth.

How meaningful have these technological advances actually been? Very! For example, the amount of capital used per worker increased fifteen times over the 1930–1980 period, permitting a fivefold increase in the amount of land cultivated per farmer.[2] The simplest general index is the increasing number of people which a single farmer's output will support. In 1820 each farm worker produced enough food and fiber to support four persons. By 1947, about fourteen persons. By 1987 each farmer produced enough to support ninety-six

people! There can be no question but that productivity in agriculture has risen significantly. Since World War II, physical productivity in agriculture has advanced at a rate which is *twice* as fast as that of the nonfarm economy.

Two additional important points must amend this discussion of the increasing productivity in American farming:

1 Most recent technological advances have **not** been initiated by farmers but are, rather, the result of government-sponsored programs of research and education and the work of farm machinery producers. Land-grant colleges, experiment stations, county agents of the Agricultural Extension Service, educational pamphlets issued by the U.S. Department of Agriculture, and the research departments of farm machinery, pesticide, and fertilizer producers are the sources of technological advance in American agriculture.

2 Technological advance has not occurred evenly throughout agriculture. Many farmers are undermechanized, uninformed, and inefficient. It is no surprise that the low-productivity farmers are those on the bottom of Table 35-1's income ladder.

Lagging demand for agricultural products Increases in the demand for agricultural commodities have failed to keep pace with technologically inspired increases in their supply. Why? The answer lies in the two major determinants of agricultural demand—incomes and population.

In less developed countries, consumers must devote the bulk of their meager incomes to the products of agriculture—food and clothing—to sustain themselves. But as income expands beyond the subsistence level and the problem of hunger eventually gives way to one of obesity, consumers will increase their outlays on food at ever-declining rates. Once a consumer's stomach is filled, his or her thoughts turn to the amenities of life which industry, not agriculture, provides. Economic growth in the United States has boosted average per capita income far beyond the level of bare subsistence. As a result, *increases in the incomes of American consumers lead to less than proportionate increases in expenditures on farm products.* In technical terms, the demand for farm products is *income-inelastic;* that is, the demand for most agricultural products is quite insensitive to increases in income. Estimates indicate that a 10 percent increase in real per

---

[2] *Economic Report of the President, 1984,* p. 117.

capita after-tax income entails at the most an increase in the consumption of farm products of only 2 percent.[3] Certain specific farm products—for example, potatoes and lard—may be inferior goods; that is, as incomes increase, purchases of these products may actually *decrease* (Chapter 4).

Population is a somewhat different proposition. Despite the fact that, after a minimum income level is reached, each individual consumer's intake of food and fiber will become relatively fixed, more consumers obviously will mean an increase in the demand for farm products. In most advanced nations the demand for farm products increases at a rate which roughly corresponds to the rate of population growth. But population increases, added to the relatively small increase in the purchase of farm products which occurs as incomes rise, have simply not been great enough to match the concomitant increases in farm output. Indeed, it is pertinent to note that birthrates are down and United States population growth has slowed in recent decades.

Graphic portrayal   When coupled with the inelastic demand for agricultural products, these shifts in supply and demand have tended to reduce farm incomes. This is illustrated in Figure 35-1, where a large increase in supply is shown against a very modest increase in demand. Because of the inelastic demand for farm products, these shifts have resulted in a sharp decline in farm prices accompanied by relatively small increases in sales. Farm incomes therefore tend to decline. Diagrammatically, income before the increase in supply occurs (measured by rectangle $OPAQ$) will exceed farm income after supply increases (OP_1BQ_1). The income "loss" of P_1PAC is not fully offset by the income "gain" of $QCBQ_1$. In summary, *given an inelastic demand for farm products, an increase in the supply of farm products relative to the demand for them has created persistent tendencies for farm incomes to fall.* This is not to say that farm incomes have necessarily fallen absolutely, but rather, that farm incomes have tended to lag behind the nonfarm sector of the economy. Furthermore, the prices which farmers have received for their output

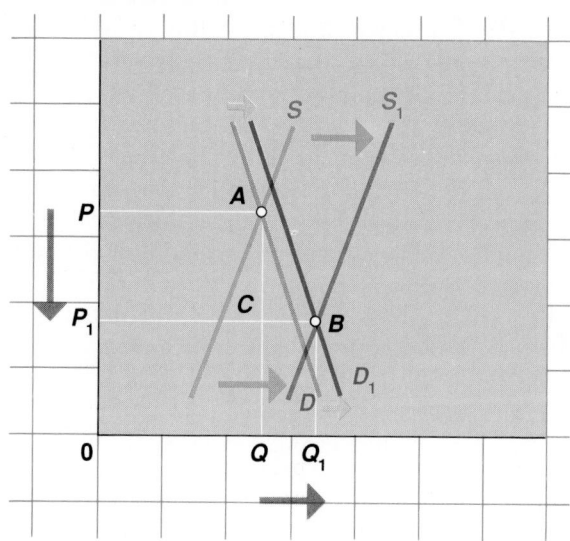

FIGURE 35-I

A graphic summary of the long-run farm problem

In the long run, increases in the demand for agricultural products (D to D_1) have not kept pace with the increases in supply (S to S_1) which technological advances have permitted. Coupled with the fact that agricultural demand is inelastic, these shifts have tended to depress farm prices (as from P to P_1) and income (as from $OPAQ$ to OP_1BQ_1).

have declined relative to the prices farmers have had to pay for all the inputs used in farm production; that is, farmers have faced a chronic price-cost squeeze (Figure 35-4).

Relative immobility of resources   Our previous discussions of the workings of the market system would certainly suggest an obvious and automatic solution to the long-run problem faced by agriculture. As noted earlier, agriculture is a highly competitive industry, characterized by large numbers of independent firms, each of which produces a minute fraction of the overall output of quite highly standardized products. One would expect declining farm prices and incomes to signal an exodus of resources from agriculture. Prices and incomes which are low in relation to the rest of the economy would seemingly prompt farmers to leave their farms in favor of more lucrative occupations. The adjustments of a competitive industry, as outlined in Chapters 5 and 25, indicate that this exodus of

[3] Joint Economic Committee, *Staff Report on Employment, Growth, and Price Levels* (Washington, 1960), p. 190.

farmers would reduce industry supply in relation to demand, thereby boosting farm prices and incomes. This reallocation of resources away from agriculture and toward industry, one can assume, would bring farm incomes into rough accord with those of the rest of the economy.

Human resources *have* shifted out of agriculture in large numbers as the competitive market model would predict. But, except for the minute portion of total farmland which borders on metropolitan areas, most farmland has no real alternative uses. Farmers leave, but the land they leave is acquired by other farmers and remains in production. Furthermore, we must recognize that the farm–nonfarm disequilibrium is not the result of a single, one-shot imbalance. Hence, even as labor leaves agriculture in the pursuit of higher incomes in nonfarm sectors of the economy, the components of the long-run farm problem *continue* to depress farm incomes and to set the stage for a further exodus. Despite the remarkable secular decline in the farm population displayed in Table 35-2, agricultural economists still talk of surplus labor in the agricultural sector and the prospect of additional farmers being forced off the land.

It is correct to say that, historically, the relative slowness of the reallocation of farmers from agriculture to industry is the crux of the farm problem. Ironically enough, in an industry long associated with the word "surplus," we find that the biggest and most fundamental farm surplus of all has been the number of farmers. Indeed, the farm problem can be correctly envisioned as a problem of resource misallocation. It is the fact that too many farmers are sharing agriculture's shrinking slice of the national income pie that makes income per farmer small.

SHORT-RUN PROBLEM: INCOME INSTABILITY

The tendency of farm incomes to lag behind the rest of the economy is evidence of the long-run agricultural problem. Substantial year-to-year fluctuations in farm prices and therefore in incomes reflect a **short-run problem.** This short-run instability is the result of the inelastic demand for agricultural products coupled with (1) fluctuations in farm output and (2) shifts in the demand curve itself.

TABLE 35-2 **The declining farm population, selected years, 1910–1987**

Year	Farm population, millions	Percentage of the total population
1910	32.1	35
1920	31.9	30
1930	30.5	25
1935	32.2	25
1940	30.5	23
1945	24.4	18
1950	23.0	15
1955	19.1	12
1960	15.6	9
1965	12.4	6
1970	9.7	5
1975	8.9	4
1980	7.2	3
1985	5.4	2
1987	5.0	2

Source: *Statistical Abstract of the United States; Economic Report of the President.*

Fluctuations in output On the production side of the picture, the inelastic demand for farm products causes small changes in agricultural production to be magnified into relatively larger changes in farm prices and incomes. To understand this point, we must first note that farmers possess only limited control over their production. In the first place, floods, droughts, an unexpected frost, insect damage, and similar disasters can mean poor crops. Conversely, an excellent growing season may mean bumper crops. Weather factors are beyond the control of farmers, yet they exert an important influence upon production. Second, the highly competitive nature of agriculture makes it virtually impossible for farmers to form a huge combination to control their production. If all the millions of widely scattered and independent producers should by chance plant an unusually large or abnormally small portion of their land, extra large or small outputs would result even if the growing season were normal.

Now, putting the instability of farm production together with an inelastic demand for farm products, we can readily discover why farm prices and incomes are highly unstable. Figure 35-2 is pertinent. Even if we assume that the market demand for agriculture products is stable at D, the inelastic nature of demand will magnify small changes in output into relatively large changes in farm prices and income. For example, assume that a "normal" crop of Q_n results in a "normal" price of P_n and a "normal" farm income of OP_nNQ_n. But a bumper crop or a poor crop will cause large deviations from these normal prices and incomes; these results stem from the inelasticity of demand for farm products.

If an unusually good growing season occurs, the resulting bumper crop of Q_b will cause farm incomes to *fall* from OP_nNQ_n to OP_bBQ_b. Why? Because when demand is inelastic, an increase in the quantity sold will be accompanied by a *more than* proportionate decline in price. The net result is that total revenue, that is, total farm income, will decline. Similarly, for farmers as a group, a poor crop caused by, say, drought may boost farm in-

comes. A poor crop of Q_p will raise total farm income from OP_nNQ_n to OP_pPQ_p. Why? Because a decline in output will cause a *more than* proportionate increase in price when demand is inelastic. Ironically, for farmers as a group, a poor crop may be a blessing and a bumper crop a hardship. Our conclusion is this: Given a stable market demand for farm products, the inelasticity of that demand will turn relatively small changes in output into relatively larger changes in farm prices and incomes.

Fluctuations in domestic demand   The other aspect of the short-run instability of farm incomes has to do with shifts in the demand curve for agricultural products. Let us suppose that somehow agricultural output is stabilized at the "normal" level of Q_n in Figure 35-3. Now, because of the inelasticity of the demand for farm products, short-run fluctuations in the demand for these products—prompted perhaps by cyclical changes in the economy—will

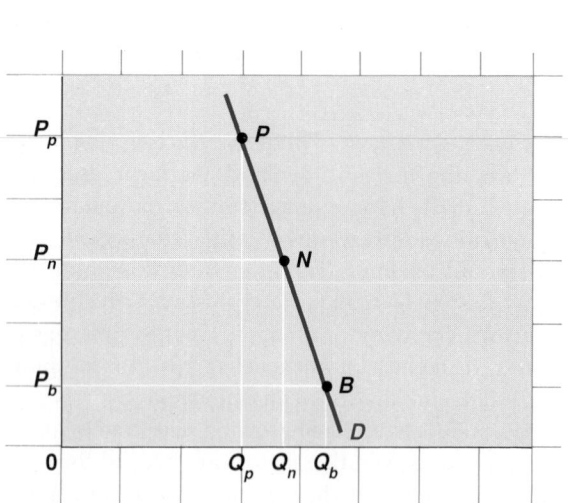

FIGURE 35-2

The effect of output changes on farm prices and incomes

Because of the inelasticity of demand for farm products, a relatively small change in output (Q_n to Q_p or Q_b) will cause relatively large changes in farm prices (P_n to P_p or P_b) and incomes (OP_nNQ_n to OP_pPQ_p or OP_bBQ_b).

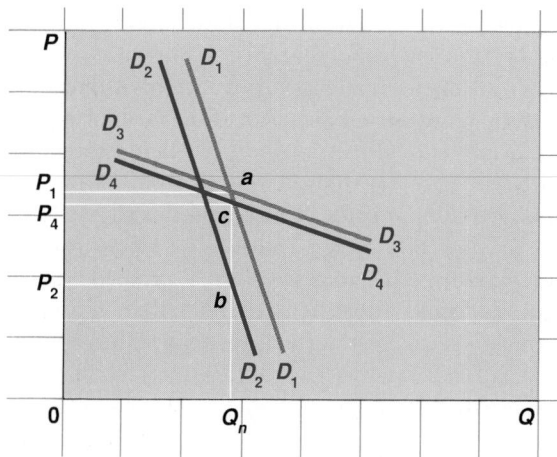

FIGURE 35-3

The effect of demand changes on farm prices and incomes

Because of the highly inelastic demand for agricultural products, a small shift in demand (D_1D_1 to D_2D_2) will cause drastically different levels of farm prices (P_1 to P_2) and farm incomes (OP_1aQ_n to OP_2bQ_n) to be associated with a given level of production Q_n. Note that equal changes in a more elastic demand curve (D_3D_3 to D_4D_4) will be accompanied by much smaller price (P_1 to P_4) and income (OP_1aQ_n to OP_4cQ_n) alterations.

cause markedly different prices and incomes to be associated with this level of production that we assume to be constant. That is, a slight drop in demand from D_1D_1 to D_2D_2 will cause farm incomes to fall from OP_1aQ_n to OP_2bQ_n. A relatively small decline in demand gives farmers a drastically reduced money reward for the same amount of production. Conversely, a slight increase in demand will bring an equally sharp increase in farm incomes for the same volume of output. These large price-income changes are linked to the fact that demand is inelastic. This relationship can be grasped by observing the much smaller price-income changes which accompany an equal shift in demand from the more elastic demand curve D_3D_3.[4] If demand drops from D_3D_3 to D_4D_4, price will fall very modestly from P_1 to P_4 and income will fall only from OP_1aQ_n to OP_4cQ_n.

It is tempting to argue that the sharp declines in farm prices which accompany a decrease in demand will cause many farmers to close down in the short run, thereby reducing total output and alleviating these price-income declines. But farm production is relatively insensitive to price changes, because farmers' fixed costs are high compared with their variable costs. Interest, rental, tax, and mortgage payments on buildings and equipment are the major costs faced by the farmer. These are clearly fixed charges. Furthermore, the labor supply of farmers and their families can also be regarded as a fixed cost. So long as they stay on their farms, farmers cannot reduce their costs by firing themselves! This means that their variable costs are for the small amounts of hired help they may employ, plus expenditures for seed, fertilizer, and fuel. As a result of this high volume of fixed costs, farmers are almost invariably better off when working their land than when sitting idle and attempting to pay their fixed costs out of pocket. The other factors, noted previously, which contribute to the relative immobility of farmers are also pertinent. In particular, if a decline in the demand for farm output is part of an overall recession, there will be no real incentive for farmers to stop produc-

tion in order to seek nonexistent jobs in industry. In fact, a migration in the opposite direction—from the city to the farm—often accompanies a full-scale depression. Note in Table 35-2 the absolute *increase* in the farm population which occurred between 1930 and 1935. Note, too, in Figure 10-3 that between 1929 and 1933, farm prices fell by 63 percent and farm output by a mere 6 percent.

Unstable foreign demand In our historical overview of the farm problem we noted that the essential cause of farm prosperity in the 1970s was booming agricultural exports, while the collapse of export markets was a major cause of the farm crisis of the early 1980s. This dramatic turnabout correctly suggests that American agriculture's dependence upon world markets is a source of demand volatility. The incomes of American farmers are now sensitive to changes in weather and crop production *in other countries*. Similarly, cyclical fluctuations in incomes in Europe or Japan, for example, can shift the demand for American farm products. So can changes in foreign economic policies. For example, if the nations of western Europe decide to provide their farmers with greater protection from foreign (American) competition, American farmers will have less access to those markets and export demand will fall. International politics can also add to demand instability. Changing U.S.–U.S.S.R. political relations boosted American grain sales in the early 1970s and reduced them at the end of the decade. Changes in the international value of the dollar can be critical. Recall that the depreciation of the dollar in the 1970s increased the demand for American farm products, while appreciation of the dollar decreased foreign demand in the early 1980s. To summarize: The increasing relative importance of exports has increased the instability of the demand for American farm products. Farm exports are affected, not only by weather, income fluctuations, and economic policies abroad, but also by international politics and fluctuations in the international value of the dollar.

A RESTATEMENT

Let us pause at this point to bring our knowledge of the causes of the long- and short-run farm problems into sharper focus. The *long-run* problem is

[4] Though they may not appear so graphically, these two shifts in demand are equal in the sense that in each instance buyers want to purchase the same amount less at each possible price.

the result of the unhappy combination of four factors.

1 The demand for agricultural commodities is inelastic.

2 Rapid technological advance has given rise to significant increases in the supply of farm products.

3 The demand for agricultural commodities has increased very modestly. This consideration, combined with factors 1 and 2, has therefore resulted in a tendency for farm prices and incomes to fall or to grow only modestly.

4 The relatively fixed nature of agricultural resources—land, capital, and farmers themselves—has caused low prices and incomes to persist; resources have not been reallocated from agriculture rapidly enough to offset the tendency for agricultural prices and incomes to decline.

In the *short run,* the extreme volatility of farm prices and incomes is based upon the inelastic demand for agricultural products which transforms small changes in farm output and demand into much larger changes in farm prices and incomes.

AGRICULTURE AND GROWTH

A slightly different perspective on our explanation of the long-run farm problem correctly puts emphasis upon resource misallocation and couches the problem in terms of a growing economy. Of necessity, primitive or underdeveloped countries have essentially agrarian economies. The total population of such a nation must devote its efforts to agricultural endeavors to provide enough food and fiber to sustain itself. But, as technological advance increases productivity per farmer, the economy can maintain or even increase its consumption of food and clothing and simultaneously transfer a portion of its population into nonagricultural pursuits. This is the path which any expanding, progressive economy follows. Indeed, the shift of resources from agricultural to industrial pursuits is the earmark of a growing economy. The experience of the United States is illustrative. About 90 percent of our population was devoted to agriculture in the eighteenth century. At present about 2 percent of the population is in farming, the remaining 98 percent being free to produce personal computers, furniture, automobiles, and the thousands of other goods and services which make up a high

standard of living. But, in our economy, the actual shift of resources to nonagricultural employments has not kept pace with the rate of reallocation which rapid technological advance permits. The result has been persistent downward pressure on farm prices and incomes.

Rationale for public policy

Historically, many arguments have been used in seeking and rationalizing public aid to agriculture. It has been contended, for example, that farming, and particularly the family farm, is a fundamental American institution and should be nurtured as "a way of life." Furthermore, farmers are subject to certain extraordinary hazards—floods, droughts, and invasion by hordes of insects—to which other industries are not exposed and which cannot be fully insured. It has been held, too, that agriculture is a major cog in the American economy, and therefore prosperity for farmers is a prerequisite for prosperity in the economy as a whole.

Perhaps a more substantial argument is that, while agriculture has made great contributions to the nation's economic growth, it has had to bear a disproportionately large share of the costs associated with this progress. The rapid rate of physical productivity growth in American agriculture has resulted in substantial and widespread benefits to the economy as a whole. The population has been able to get more and better food and fiber from agriculture in exchange for a smaller proportion of its money income. On the other hand, the peculiar combination of economic circumstances already discussed—an inelastic demand for farm products, rapid technological progress, the slow growth of demand, and the relatively fixed nature of agricultural resources—has caused farm people to bear a large share of the costs of agricultural progress in the form of incomes substantially below those of nonfarm income receivers.

Finally, it has been contended that, while farmers are faced with highly competitive markets for their outputs, they typically buy inputs from industries which have considerable market power. In particular, most of the firms from which farmers buy fertilizer, farm machinery, gasoline, and so forth, have some capacity to control their prices.

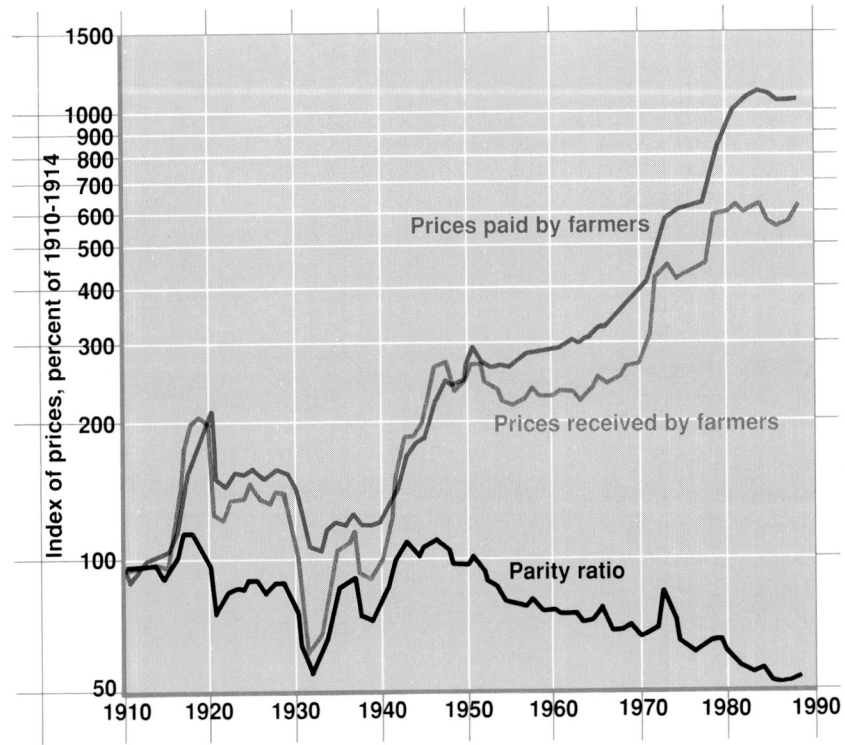

FIGURE 35-4

Prices paid and received by farmers, 1910–1988

In the past four decades the prices paid by farmers have increased ahead of prices received. As a result, the parity ratio—which is simply the ratio of prices received to prices paid—has been less than 100 percent.

Farmers, in contrast, are at the "mercy of the market" in selling their outputs. Stated differently, agriculture is the last stronghold of pure competition in an otherwise imperfectly competitive economy; it warrants public aid to offset the disadvantageous terms of trade which result (see Figure 35-4).

Although the substance and merits of these arguments may be subject to debate, there is no denying that there exists an elaborate and very expensive set of policies designed to subsidize agriculture. The presence and persistence of these programs may well reflect Chapter 33's *special-interest effect*, whereby a small but politically powerful group might promote its own economic interests to the detriment of society as a whole.

Farm policy: parity and price supports

On the basis of these arguments and the strong voice which farmers have historically had in Congress, a detailed "farm program" involving (1) farm prices, incomes, and output; (2) soil and water conservation; (3) agricultural research; (4) farm credit; (5) crop insurance; and other factors has come into being and persisted since the 1930s. However, the typical American farmer and the average politician have both viewed "the farm problem" as essentially a price-income problem. Hence, farm policy has been designed to enhance and stabilize farm prices and incomes.

BACKGROUND: THE PARITY CONCEPT

The **Agricultural Adjustment Act of 1933** established the **parity concept** as a cornerstone of agricultural policy. The simple rationale of the parity concept can be readily envisioned in both real and nominal terms. In real terms, parity says that year after year for a given output of farm products, a farmer should be able to acquire a given total amount of goods and services. A given real output should always result in the same real income. "If a farmer could take a bushel of corn to town in 1912 and sell it and buy himself a shirt, he should be able to take a bushel of corn to town today and buy a shirt." In nominal terms, *the parity concept suggests that the relationship between the prices received by farmers for their output and the prices they must pay for goods and services should remain constant.* The parity concept clearly implies that, if the price of shirts were to triple over some time period, then the price of corn should triple too.

A glance at Figure 35-4 indicates why farmers would benefit from having the prices of their products based upon 100 percent of parity. This graph shows the prices paid and received by farmers from 1910 to 1988 as percentages of the 1910 to 1914 base period. We observe that by 1988 prices paid had increased almost twelvefold and prices received had increased about six times as compared to the base period. The **parity ratio** shown in Figure 35-4 is merely the ratio of prices received relative to prices paid. That is:

$$\frac{\text{Parity}}{\text{ratio}} = \frac{\text{prices received by farmers}}{\text{prices paid by farmers}}$$

In 1988 the parity ratio was about 54 percent ($= 6 \div 12$), indicating that prices received in 1988 were slightly more than one-half as high relative to prices paid as they were in the 1910 to 1914 period. A farm policy calling for 100 percent of parity would entail substantially higher prices for farm products in order to bring the parity ratio up to 100.

PRICE SUPPORTS

The practical importance of the notion of parity prices is that it provides the rationale for government *price floors*—or, as they are commonly called, **price supports**—on farm products. The fact that, in the long run, the market prices received by farmers have not generally kept abreast of prices paid by them means that to achieve parity or some percentage thereof, the government is likely to be required to establish above-equilibrium, or "support," prices on farm products. Although specific price support programs have been many and varied, the following discussion captures the essence of government's attempts to use price floors to stabilize and enhance the incomes of farmers.

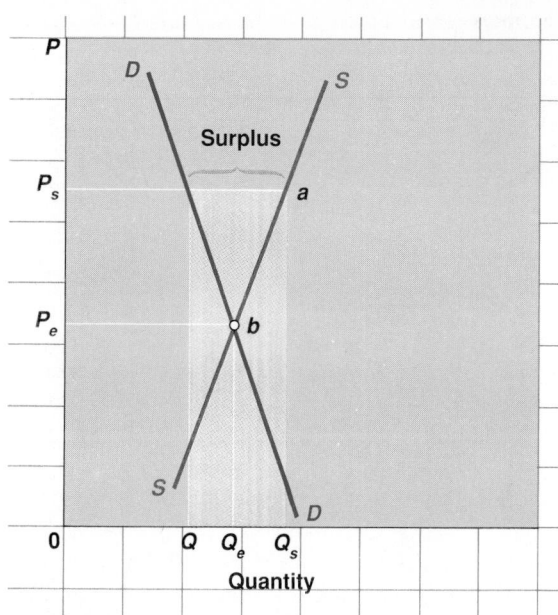

FIGURE 35-5

Effective price supports result in farm surpluses

Application of the parity concept obligates government to support farm prices at above-equilibrium levels. These supported prices result in persistent surpluses of farm products.

Price supports have a number of significant effects. Suppose, in Figure 35-5, that the support price is P_s as compared with the equilibrium price P_e.

I Surplus output The most obvious effect is that product surpluses will result. Private consumers will be willing to purchase only OQ units at the supported price, while farmers will supply OQ_s units. The amount QQ_s is a surplus. What happens to this surplus? The government must buy it in order to make the above-equilibrium support price effective. Huge surpluses of farm commodities accumulated in the 1950s and 1960s and stocks of many farm products remain large. For example, the government holds stocks of wheat and other grains which represent about one year's domestic consumption. As we shall see momentarily, this surplus production is symptomatic of an overallocation of resources to agriculture.

2 Farmers gain Farmers clearly gain from price supports. In Figure 35-5, gross revenues rise from the free-market level of OP_ebQ_e to the supported level of OP_saQ_s.

3 Consumer loss Consumers of farm products lose in that they will be paying a higher price (P_s rather than P_e) and consuming less (Q rather than Q_e) of the product. In some instances the differences between the market price and the supported price can be substantial. For example, the price of a pound of sugar is four times the world market price; a quart of fluid milk is estimated to be twice as high as it would be without government programs.

4 Societal loss Society at large loses in two important ways. First, taxpayers will be paying higher taxes to finance the government's purchase of the surplus. In Figure 35-5, this added tax burden will amount to the surplus output QQ_s, multiplied by its price P_s—as shown by the gray area. Storage costs add to this tax burden.

Society also loses because price supports contribute to economic inefficiency by encouraging an overallocation of resources to agriculture. A price floor or support (P_s) gives rise to a greater commitment of resources to the agricultural sector than would be generated by the free market (P_e). In terms of Chapter 25's purely competitive model, the market supply curve in Figure 35-5 represents the aggregated marginal costs of all farmers producing this product. An efficient allocation of resources occurs where market price, P_e, is equal to marginal cost at point b. The resulting output of Q_e reflects an efficient allocation of resources. In contrast, the Q_s output associated with the P_s price support clearly represents an overallocation of resources; for all units of output in the Q_eQ_s range marginal costs exceed the prices people would be willing to pay for these units. Hence, there is an "efficiency loss" to society.

5 International costs The costs of farm price supports go beyond those implicit in Figure 35-5. In general, price supports generate economic distortions which transcend national boundaries. For example, above-equilibrium price supports make the American market attractive to foreign producers. But inflows of foreign agricultural products would increase supplies in the United States, thereby aggravating our problem of agricultural surpluses. To prevent this from happening the United States is likely to impose import barriers in the form of tariffs or quotas. These barriers often restrict the production of more efficient foreign producers, while simultaneously encouraging more production from less efficient American producers. The result is a less efficient utilization of world agricultural resources. This chapter's Last Word suggests that this is the case for sugar.

Similarly, as the United States and other industrially advanced countries with similar agricultural programs dump surplus farm products on world markets, the prices of such products are depressed. Less developed countries—most of which are heavily dependent upon world commodity markets—are hurt because they find their export earnings are reduced. Thus, United States subsidies for rice production have imposed significant costs on Thailand, a major rice exporter. Similarly, our cotton programs have adversely affected Egypt, Mexico, Bangladesh, and other cotton-exporting nations.

COPING WITH SURPLUSES

By what means might government cope with the surplus farm output which accompanies effective price supports? An elementary knowledge of the tools of supply and demand suggests that programs designed to reduce market supply or increase market demand would help bring the market price up to the desired supported price, thereby reducing or eliminating farm surpluses (Figure 35-5).

Restricting supply On the supply side, public policy has long been aimed at restricting farm output. In particular, "set aside" or **acreage allotment programs** have accompanied the application of price supports. In return for the privilege of getting price supports on their crops, farmers must agree to limit the number of acres planted. Attempting to bring quantity supplied and quantity demanded into balance, the Department of Agriculture estimates the amount of each product which private buyers will take at the supported price. This amount is then translated into the number of acres of planting which will produce this amount. The total acreage figure is apportioned among states, counties, and ultimately individual farmers. Similarly, various programs have been employed whereby the Department of Agriculture makes direct payments to farmers for removing land entirely from crop production. For example, under the *soil bank* program, the government in effect rented land from farmers. Such idle land was to be planted in cover crops or timber, not in cash crops.

Have these supply-restricting programs been successful? It is difficult to give an unqualified answer. Certainly they have not eliminated surplus farm production. The basic reason is that acreage reduction invariably results in less than proportionate declines in production. Why? Farmers retire their worst land and keep their best in production. Those acres which are tilled are cultivated more intensively. The use of better seed, more and better fertilizer and insecticides, and more labor will enhance output per acre. Nonparticipating farmers may expand their acreage in anticipation of higher prices. However, without these output controls, there is no doubt that accumulated farm surpluses and their associated costs would have been much greater than has actually been the case.

Bolstering demand Government has followed a number of paths in seeking to augment the demand for agricultural products.

I NEW USES Both government and private industry have spent considerable sums for research to uncover new uses for agricultural commodities. The production of "gasohol"—a blend of gasoline and alcohol made from grain—is a current and controversial attempt to create a new demand for agricultural output. Most experts conclude that we have only been modestly successful in such endeavors.

2 DOMESTIC AND FOREIGN DEMAND A variety of programs has been invoked to augment the domestic consumption of farm products. For example, the *food-stamp program* is designed to bolster low-income families' demand for food. Similarly, our **Food for Peace program** under Public Law 480 has permitted the less developed countries to buy our surplus farm products with their own currencies, rather than with dollars. Furthermore, in international trade bargaining, our negotiators have pressed hard to persuade foreign nations to reduce protective tariffs and other barriers against our farm products.

Although the government's supply-restricting and demand-increasing efforts undoubtedly helped to reduce the amount of surplus production, they have not been successful in eliminating surpluses. Hence, in the 1960s it was not at all uncommon for government to spend $2 to $4 billion per year for surplus farm commodities. Outlays have risen sharply in the 1980s. Price support payments alone were about $17 billion in 1987.

Farm policy at the crossroads?

After more than a half century of experience with government policies designed to stabilize and enhance farm incomes, there is considerable evidence to suggest that these programs are not working well. Hence, there is a growing feeling among economists and political leaders that the traditional goals and techniques of farm policy must be reexamined and revised.

SOME CRITICISMS

Let us review some of the more important criticisms of agricultural policy.

I Symptoms and causes Our farm programs have failed to get at the causes of the farm problem. Public policy toward agriculture is designed to treat symptoms and not causes. The root *cause* of the farm problem has been a misallocation of resources between agriculture and the rest of the economy. Historically, the problem has been one of too many farmers. The effect or symptom of this misallocation of resources is low farm incomes. *For the most part, public policy in agriculture has been oriented toward supporting farm prices and incomes rather than toward alleviating the resource allocation problem, which is the fundamental cause of these sagging farm incomes.*

Some critics go further and argue that price-income supports have encouraged people to stay in agriculture when they otherwise would have migrated to some nonfarm occupation. That is, the price-income orientation of the farm program has deterred the very reallocation of resources which is necessary to resolve the long-run farm problem.

2 Misguided subsidies A related criticism is that price-income support programs have most benefited those farmers who least need government assistance. Assuming the goal of our farm program is the bolstering of low farm incomes, it follows that any program of government aid should be aimed at farmers at the bottom of the farm income distribution. But the poor, small-output farmer simply does not produce and sell enough in the market to get much aid from price supports. It is the large corporate farm which reaps the benefits by virtue of its large output. In 1987, for example, the 14 percent of all farms with sales of $100,000 or more received over 55 percent of all direct government subsidies. The poorest 52 percent of all farmers—those in Table 35-1 who earned $9,999 or less from farming in 1987—received only 5 percent of all direct subsidy payments.[5] If public policy must be designed to supplement farm incomes, a strong case can certainly be made for making those benefits vary inversely, rather than directly, with one's position in the income distribution. An income-support program should be geared to *people*, not *commodities*. Many economists contend that, on equity grounds, direct income subsidies to poor farmers are highly preferable to indirect price support subsidies which go primarily to large and prosperous farmers.

A related point has to do with land values. The price and income benefits which the various farm programs provide are eventually capitalized into higher farmland values. By making crops more valuable, price supports have made the land itself more valuable. Sometimes this is helpful to farmers, but often it is not. Farmers rent about 40 percent of their farmland, mostly from relatively well-to-do nonfarm landlords. In this fashion price supports become a subsidy to people who are *not* actively engaged in farming.

3 Policy contradictions The complexity and multiple objectives embedded in farm policy yield a number of conflicts and contradictions. We observe but a few. Subsidized research is aimed at increasing farm productivity and increasing the supply of farm products, while acreage reserve and "set

aside" programs pay farmers to take land out of production in order to reduce supply. Price supports for crops mean increased feed costs for ranchers and high prices for animal products to consumers. Finally, in recent years the prosperity of American farmers has depended increasingly upon their ability to sell their outputs in world markets. Because the United States is the major exporter of many farm products, price supports have had the effect of putting a floor under world farm prices. These above-equilibrium prices simultaneously discourage foreigners from buying our farm products and encourage foreign farmers to produce more. The result is a loss of income to American farmers.[6]

4 Declining effectiveness There is also reason to believe that, waiving all other problems, farm policy has simply become less effective in accomplishing its goals. In the 1930s most farms were relatively small, semi-isolated units which employed relatively modest amounts of machinery and equipment and provided most of their own inputs. Currently, however, farms are larger, highly capital-intensive, and closely integrated with both the domestic and international economies. Farmers now depend on others for such inputs as seed, fertilizers, insecticides, and so forth. American agriculture uses more than twice as much physical capital (machinery and buildings) per worker than does the economy as a whole. This means that farmers now need to borrow large amounts of money to finance the purchases of capital equipment and land *and* for operating capital. Hence, despite a well-conceived farm policy designed to enhance farm incomes, high interest rates can easily precipitate losses or bankruptcy for many farmers. Dependence upon export markets can also undermine farm policy. A fall in foreign incomes or an increase in the international value of the dollar (which makes American farm products more expensive to foreigners) can cause an unexpected

---

[5] U.S. Department of Agriculture, *Economic Indicators of the Farm Sector: National Financial Summary, 1987*, p. 43.

[6] Export demand tends to be more responsive to price changes—that is, more elastic—than domestic demand. This means that, in comparison to the situation portrayed in Figure 35-2, an increase in the world price of a farm commodity will *reduce* the total revenue of American farmers because the decline in the amount sold is larger proportionately than the increase in price.

decline in American farm exports and easily wipe out any positive effects of agricultural programs upon farm incomes. In short, a much wider range of variables may now alter farm incomes and thereby diminish the impact of farm programs.

5 Program costs In recent years the cost of our various farm programs has increased significantly. For example, in the 1981–1985 period Federal expenditures on farm price and income support programs were approximately $60 billion. As noted earlier, price support payments in 1987 totaled some $17 billion.

The difficult issue being brought into focus by these and similar criticisms is whether an increasingly expensive farm program is economically justifiable. Farm programs entail huge and increasing budgetary costs. The subsidies involved do not benefit the most needy farmers. Farm price supports distort economic incentives, causing overproduction to persist. Farm programs impose substantial costs on consumers and complicate our international economic policies. Against this web of criticism, a number of economists feel that our farm policy is an example of public sector failure. They suggest that public policy has not resolved the problems of American agriculture, but rather has become a part of those problems.

MARKET-ORIENTED INCOME STABILIZATION

Given the various criticisms of farm policy, it is no surprise that economists and politicians have been seeking new approaches to agricultural policy. One frequently mentioned view is that policy should shift from the goal of enhancing to that of stabilizing farm incomes. The goal of *stabilization* is to reduce the sharp year-to-year fluctuations in farm incomes and prices, but to accept the long-run average of farm prices and incomes which free markets would provide. This is in contrast to income *enhancement* which seeks to provide farmers with commodity prices and incomes above those which free markets would yield. How might government moderate the boom and bust character of agricultural markets? The proposed answer is that government would support prices and accumulate surplus stocks when prices fell significantly below the

long-run trend of prices. Conversely, government would augment supply by selling from these stocks when prices rose significantly above the long-run trend.

Proponents feel that the **market-oriented income stabilization policy** has a number of advantages. First, government involvement in agriculture would be diminished in that programs of supply management through acreage reduction would be abandoned. Second, prices would reflect long-run equilibrium levels and therefore be conducive to an efficient allocation of resources between agriculture and the rest of the economy. Stated differently, by providing farmers with incomes consistent with market-clearing prices, the market system would provide the needed signals to accelerate the movement of farmers to nonfarm jobs. Third, taxpayer costs would be significantly reduced. And, finally, the lower average level of farm prices would help to stimulate agricultural exports.

IMPORTANCE OF NONFARM POLICIES

It was suggested above that farm policy may be of diminished effectiveness because other events might swamp the impact of such policy upon farm incomes. This implies that *favorable nonfarm policies are critical to agriculture's well-being.* As noted, agriculture is much more highly integrated into the national and world economies than it was a scant 40 or 50 years ago. If monetary and fiscal policy—specifically, tight money and large Federal deficits—result in high interest rates as they have in recent years, the chances for profitable farming are considerably diminished. Farmers are heavily dependent upon borrowing, both to finance current operations and to buy machinery and land. The ability of farmers to carry some $143 billion of current farm sector debt clearly depends upon the level of interest rates.

Given agriculture's great dependence upon world markets, it is also evident that American farmers have a great stake in a policy of free and unrestricted international trade which makes foreign markets increasingly accessible. Similarly, we observed earlier that fluctuations in the international value of the dollar can have substantial effects upon American farm exports.

Global view: feast or famine?

The American farm problem—supply outrunning demand and farm policies which foster surplus production—is not common to most other nations. Many of the less developed nations, not to mention the Soviet Union, must persistently import foodstuffs. We frequently read of malnutrition, chronic food shortages, and famine in Africa and elsewhere. Can we expect at some future date—say, four or five decades from now—that the world will be unable to feed itself?

While there is no simple response to this question, it is of interest to summarize some of the pros and cons pertinent to the issue. Pessimists, envisioning impending famine as demand increases ahead of supply, make these arguments. First, the quantity of arable land is finite and its quality is being seriously impaired by wind and water erosion. Second, urban sprawl and industrial expansion continue to convert prime land from agriculture to nonagricultural uses. Third, our underground water system upon which farmers depend for irrigation is being mined at such a rapid rate that farmlands in some areas will have to be abandoned. Fourth, world population continues to grow; every day there are thousands of new mouths to feed. Finally, some environmentalists suggest that unfavorable long-run climatic changes will undermine future agricultural production.

Optimists offer counterarguments such as the following. First, the number of acres planted to crops has been increasing and the world is far from bringing all its arable land into production. Second, agricultural productivity continues to rise and the possibility of dramatic productivity breakthroughs lies ahead as we enter the age of genetic engineering. There is also room for very substantial productivity increases in the agricultural sectors of the less developed countries. For example, improved economic incentives for farm workers in China were instrumental in expanding agricultural output by about one-third between 1980 and 1985. Third, the rate of growth of world population has in fact been diminishing. Finally, we must reckon with the adjustment processes elicited by the market system. If food shortages were to develop, food prices would rise. Higher prices would induce more production and simultaneously constrain the amount demanded, thereby tending to head off the shortages.

Admittedly, the "feast or famine" debate is highly speculative; a clear picture of the world's future production capabilities and consumption needs is not easily discerned. Perhaps the main point to be made is that American agricultural policies should take global considerations into account.

CHAPTER SUMMARY

1 American agriculture has had a "boom" and "bust" history.

2 Rapid technological advance, coupled with a highly inelastic and relatively constant demand for agricultural output, has caused farm incomes to be relatively low. Because of the relatively fixed nature of both property and human resources, the market system has failed to correct the farm problem by reallocating sufficient amounts of resources out of agriculture.

3 In the short run, the highly inelastic nature of agricultural demand translates small changes in output and small shifts in domestic or foreign demand into large fluctuations in prices and incomes.

4 Historically, agricultural policy has been price-centered and based upon the parity concept which suggests that the relationship between the prices received and paid by farmers should remain constant.

5 The use of price floors or supports has a number of economic effects: *a* surplus production occurs; *b* the incomes of farmers are increased; *c* consumers pay higher prices for farm products; *d* society at large pays higher taxes to purchase and store surplus output, and also bears the cost of an overallocation of resources to agriculture; and *e* other nations bear the costs associated with import barriers and depressed world farm commodity prices.

6 Government has pursued with limited success a variety of programs to reduce the supply of, and increase the demand for, agricultural products in order to reduce the surpluses associated with price supports.

7 Farm policy has been criticized for *a* confusing symptoms (low farm incomes) with causes (excess capacity); *b* providing the largest subsidies to high-income farmers; *c* contradictions among specific farm programs; *d* declining effectiveness; and *e* increasing costs.

8 A number of economists advocate a program of stabilizing, but not enhancing, farm incomes.

9 Nonfarm policies—particularly macro and international trade policies—are critical to agriculture's prosperity.

TERMS AND CONCEPTS

long-run problem

short-run problem

Agricultural Adjustment Act of 1933

parity concept

parity ratio

price supports

acreage allotment programs

Food for Peace program

market-oriented income stabilization policy

QUESTIONS AND STUDY SUGGESTIONS

1 Explain how each of the following contributes to the farm problem: *a* the inelasticity of the demand for farm products, *b* rapid technological progress in farming, *c* the modest long-run growth in the demand for farm commodities, *d* the competitiveness of agriculture, and *e* the relative fixity or immobility of agricultural resources. Do exports increase or reduce the instability of demand for farm products?

2 What relationship, if any, can you detect between the fact that the farmer's fixed costs of production are large and the fact that the supply of most agricultural products is generally inelastic? Be specific in your answer.

3 "The supply and demand for agricultural products are such that small changes in agricultural supply will result in drastic changes in prices. However, large changes in farm prices have modest effect on agricultural output." Carefully evaluate. *Hint:* A brief review of the distinction between *supply* and *quantity supplied* may be of assistance.

4 "The whole process of economic growth is one of making agriculture less fundamental in the economic system."[7] Evaluate this statement.

5 The key to efficient resource allocation is the shifting of resources from low-productivity to high-productivity uses. Given the high and expanding physical productivity of agricultural resources, explain why many economists want to get more resources out of farming in the interest of greater allocative efficiency.

[7] Lauren Soth, *Farm Trouble* (Princeton, N.J.: Princeton University Press, 1957), p. 40.

LAST WORD

International implications of the domestic sugar program

Domestic agricultural programs frequently have significant international ramifications.

The United States' program of price supports for sugar has entailed significant costs both domestically and internationally. Recent price supports for some 19,000 American producers have maintained domestic sugar prices at three to four times the world price. As a consequence, foreign sugar producers have had a very strong incentive to sell their outputs in the United States. But an influx of much cheaper foreign sugar into our domestic market would undermine domestic price supports. Hence, our government has imposed import quotas upon foreign sugar. As the difference between United States-supported prices and world prices has increased, import quotas have become more restrictive with the result that imported sugar has become a declining proportion of our consumption of sweeteners (see figure). High domestic sugar prices have also prompted a consumer shift from sugar to corn syrup and other sweeteners. Perhaps the crucial point to note here is that our agricultural policy in the domestic sugar industry largely dictates our international trade policy with respect to that product.

The loss of the American market has had a number of very harmful effects upon many of the less developed sugar-exporting countries such as the Philippines, Brazil, and a number of Central American countries. First and most obviously, exclusion

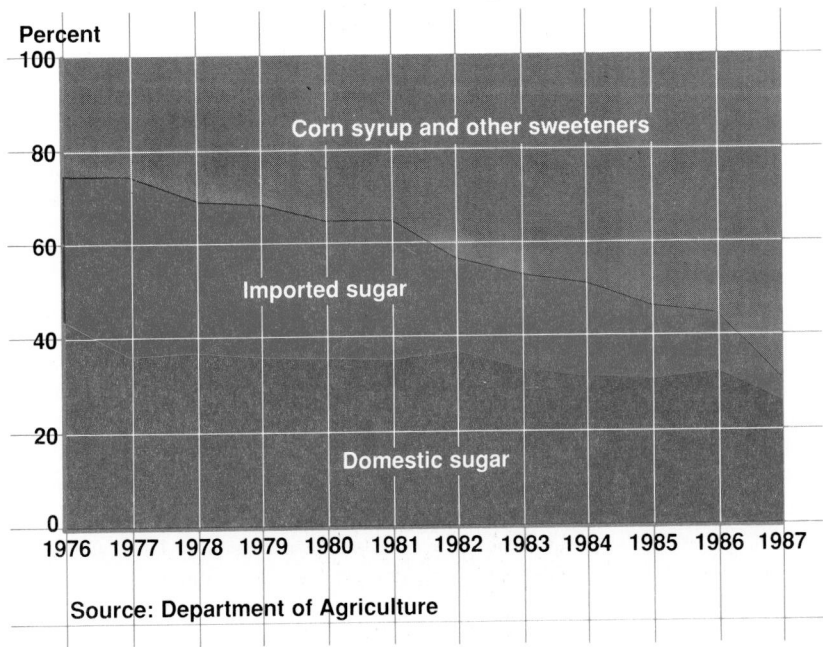

Percent

Corn syrup and other sweeteners

Imported sugar

Domestic sugar

1976 1977 1978 1979 1980 1981 1982 1983 1984 1985 1986 1987

Source: Department of Agriculture

from the American market has significantly reduced their export earnings and national incomes. The decline in export revenues is particularly important because many of the sugar-producing countries are highly dependent upon such revenues to pay interest and principal on massive external debts owed to the United States and other industrially advanced nations. Second, barred by quotas from selling in the United States market, the sugar produced by the less developed countries has been added to world markets, where the increased supply has depressed the world price of sugar. Third, under the impetus of domestic price supports, American sugar production has increased to the extent that the United States may soon change from a sugar-importing to a sugar-exporting nation. That is, our sugar program may soon be a source of new competition for the sugar producers of the less devel-

oped countries. Sugar price supports in the European Common Market have already turned that group of nations into sugar exporters. Finally, from both a domestic and a global perspective, the sugar price support programs of the United States and other industrially advanced economies have distorted the worldwide allocation of agricultural resources. Price supports have signaled an overallocation of resources to sugar production by relatively less efficient American producers. American import quotas and consequent low world sugar prices have signaled more efficient foreign producers to restrict their production. In short, high-cost producers are producing more and low-cost producers are producing less sugar with the result being an inefficient allocation of the world's agricultural resources.

Based upon *Economic Report of the President, 1987* (Washington, D.C., 1987), pp. 165–169.

6 "Industry complains of the higher taxes it must pay to finance subsidies to agriculture. Yet the fact that the trend of agricultural prices has been downward while industrial prices have been moving upward suggests that on balance agriculture is actually subsidizing industry." Explain and evaluate.

7 "Because consumers as a whole must ultimately pay the total incomes received by farmers, it makes no real difference whether this income is paid through free farm markets or through supported prices supplemented by subsidies financed out of tax revenues." Do you agree?

8 Suppose you are the president of a local chapter of one of the major farm organizations. You are directed by the chapter's membership to formulate policy statements for the chapter which cover the following topics: **a** antitrust policy, **b** monetary policy, **c** fiscal policy, and **d** tariff policy. Briefly outline the policy statements which will best serve the interest of farmers. What is the rationale underlying each statement? Do you see any conflicts or inconsistencies in your policy statements?

9 Carefully demonstrate the economic effects of price supports. On what grounds do economists contend that price supports cause a misallocation of resources?

10 If in a given year the indexes of prices received and paid by farmers were 120 and 165 respectively, what would the parity ratio be? Explain the meaning of this ratio.

11 Explain and evaluate the following statements:
a "Price supports intensify rather than resolve the farm problem."
b "The best farm program is the Employment Act of 1946."
c "The trouble with parity prices in agriculture is that they strip the price mechanism of its ability to allocate resources."
d "The problem for current farm policy is that not all farmers are poor."

12 Reconcile these two statements: "The farm problem is one of overproduction." "Despite the tremendous productive capacity of American agriculture, plenty of Americans are going hungry." What assumptions about the market system are implied in your answer?

13 How do you reconcile increasingly large aggregate subsidies to agriculture with a declining farm population?

14 What are the major criticisms of farm policy? Do you feel that government should attempt to enhance farm incomes, stabilize farm incomes, or allow farm incomes to be determined by free markets? Justify your position.

CHAPTER 36

Urban economics: the problems of the cities

america's cities are a curious paradox. They are the depositories of great wealth and the source of abundant incomes; they are the nucleus of economic activity and opportunity. Yet these same cities simultaneously embody blighted neighborhoods, homeless "street people," faltering school systems, street drugs and high crime rates, an acutely deteriorating physical environment, a sense of social unrest and alienation, and perhaps the evolution of a social "underclass."

Fly over Manhattan or Nob Hill or the Chicago Loop and the breathtaking skyline will excite your pride with the very grandeur of the American achievement. These towering symbols give dramatic character to the core of our giant cities. But their shadows cannot hide the disgrace at their feet.

There we find the decayed and decaying center cities, traffic-clogged, smoke-polluted, crime-ridden, recreationally barren. It is there we find the segregated slum with its crumbling tenement house, waiting to crush the hope of the black and the displaced farmer who has pursued his dream into the city. There too we find the suburbs ringing the cities in their rapid, undisciplined growth with ugly, congested webs of ticky-tacky houses and macadam-burst shopping centers. . . .

How have we built, or let build, this somewhat lacking, somehow defective, maculate home for man?[1]

[1] Terry Sanford, "The States and the Cities: The Unfinished Agenda," in Brian J. L. Berry and Jack Meltzer (eds.)., *Goals for Urban America* (Englewood Cliffs, N.J.: Prentice-Hall, Inc., 1967), pp. 52–53.

This chapter will explore a number of the paradoxes and problems posed by the dominant role of the city in American life. First, what is the economic rationale for the evolution of cities? Why have cities developed and grown? A second and closely related objective is to explain the more recent phenomenon of suburban growth. What economic considerations underlie urban sprawl? Next, we will consider some problems which have been spawned by the dynamics of urban growth. These include central-city poverty, transportation problems, and environmental pollution. Finally, we will consider some possible solutions to the problems of the cities.

As a prelude to these questions and issues, we must first determine the extent to which the United States is urbanized. Today the United States is clearly an urban nation. But, as Table 36-1 indicates, this has not always been so. Musty records reveal that in 1790 some 95 percent of our population lived in rural areas, mostly on farms. But by 1920 a majority of the population had become urban. Currently, about three-fourths of our population is located in urban areas. While future demographic changes are difficult to forecast, there is no question that the United States is—and will continue to be—a nation of city dwellers.

Why cities develop

There are substantial economic reasons why modern cities have evolved and grown. Let us look at these reasons—the economic rationale for cities—in both general and specific terms. Consider first the production or supply aspect of this rationale.

TABLE 36-1 **Urban population growth in the United States**

Year	Urban population (millions)	Rural population (millions)	Urban as a percent of total population
1790	.2	3.7	5
1810	.5	6.7	7
1830	1.1	11.7	9
1850	3.5	19.6	15
1870	9.9	28.7	25
1890	22.1	40.8	35
1910	42.0	50.0	46
1930	69.0	53.8	56
1950	96.5	54.2	64
1970	149.8	53.9	73
1975	155.9	57.3	73
1980	170.5	56.1	74
1986	177.7	63.4	74

Source: U.S. Bureau of the Census. "Urban areas" are defined by the Census Bureau as cities and other incorporated places which have 2500 or more inhabitants.

IN GENERAL: WHERE TO PRODUCE?

The very important question of business location was hidden in Chapter 5's discussion of the Five Fundamental Questions. In fact, the question of organizing production—*how* to produce?—implies the problem of location, or *where* to produce. Our analysis of the firm (particularly in Chapter 25) implicitly assumed that all production took place at some fixed geographic point. In effect, we supposed that the market for inputs was located at the firm's back door, and the market for outputs at its front door. This is clearly unrealistic; transportation or transfer costs are involved both in getting raw materials and other inputs to the plant and in delivering the finished product to buyers. Production decisions have a spatial or locational aspect.

Stated differently, one of the important costs in organizing resources for production is the cost of overcoming geographic space, that is, the amounts of time and resources necessary for transportation and communication. If producers locate close to those from whom they purchase inputs and also near to those to whom they sell their outputs, transportation and communication costs will be reduced. Crudely put, there are economic advantages accruing to firms which agglomerate, that is, locate in proximity to one another and to their markets. These spatial advantages are fundamental to the economic rationale of urban growth.

IN PARTICULAR: ECONOMIES OF AGGLOMERATION

But let us back up and explain the economic reasons for the evolution of cities in more detail. In the first place, the necessary condition for the development of cities is the capacity of a nation's agriculture to produce surplus food and fiber. The rapidly expanding productivity of American agriculture, detailed in Chapter 35, has freed the vast majority of our population from farming so that this labor might turn to the production of nonagricultural goods and services. Because we are social animals and because specialized industrial production demands large numbers of workers, it was only natural that labor, when released from an increasingly efficient agriculture, would cluster in villages, towns, and cities.

Although an increasingly efficient agricultural sector has "pushed" labor out of farming, it has been **economies of agglomeration** which have "pulled" population and industry to the villages, towns, and cities. What are agglomeration economies? Generally speaking, agglomeration economies refer to the "cheapening" of production or marketing which results from the fact that firms locate relatively close to one another. The economies which result from such agglomeration are of several interrelated and admittedly overlapping types.

Internal economies of scale Perhaps the simplest basis for spatial concentration is the economies of large-scale production. Recall that where economies of scale are substantial, reasonably efficient production will be possible only with a few producers relative to the total market. This suggests that one large producer can serve a number of market areas more cheaply than can many small, decentralized producers. Cities have large populations

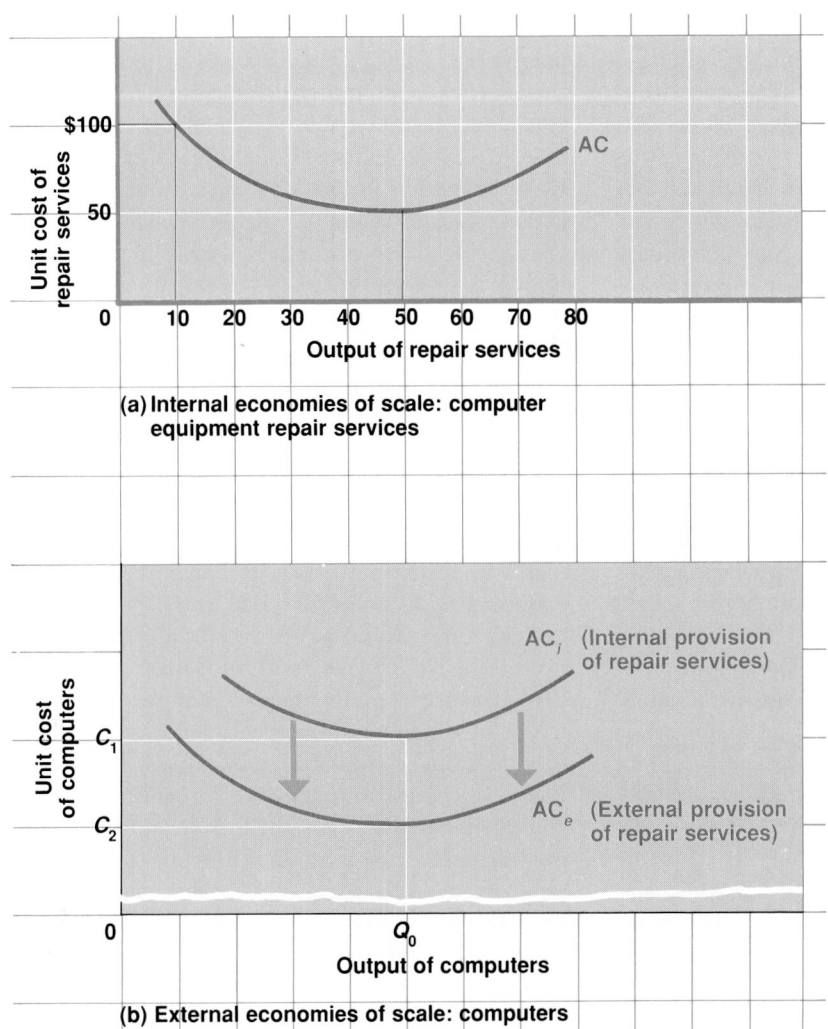

FIGURE 36-1

Internal and external economies of scale

(a) Internal economics of scale. The large markets provided by cities typically allow firms to move down their long-run average cost curves and realize low unit costs as the result of *internal* economies of scale.
(b) External economies of scale. If firms require relatively small amounts of certain inputs, they will be unable to realize economies of scale by producing them internally for themselves. For example, in (a), unit cost will be $100 if the firm requires only 10 units of input and produces them internally. But if, say, five firms requiring this input locate in proximity to one another, then a separate firm specializing in the input can realize efficient production of 50 units at a cost of $50 per unit. As shown in (b), this lowers the price of the input to users and shifts their average-cost curves downward as from AC_i to AC_e. This phenomenon is known as *external* economies of scale.

and therefore large potential markets which give producers the opportunity to move down their long-run average-cost curves and achieve low unit costs as shown in Figure 36-1a. Such economies are labeled **internal economies of scale** because their

realization depends upon the level of production within the firm itself.

Locational (transport) economies The location of business enterprise is strongly influenced by the availability of transportation facilities. Transport costs will be higher for a firm if required inputs and markets for outputs are not readily accessible. Hence, at any given time the locational choice of a firm will be strongly influenced by the existing transportation network. It is no accident that our major cities historically have grown around low-cost natural or human-made transportation nodes, that is, along seaboards (New York, San Francisco), on major rivers (St. Louis), or around railroad terminals (Chicago).

Perhaps less obvious as an incentive to agglomeration is the matter of "industrial linkages." Technological progress has caused the chain of goods production and assembly to become longer and more complex. The outputs of a growing number of firms and industries constitute the inputs of still other firms and industries. This growing specialization in production means that industrially linked firms can realize substantial economies in transportation and communication by locating in proximity. It is not difficult to see why the attraction of industry and therefore of population to the cities tends to be a self-perpetuating process. For evident reasons, the location of an automobile assembly plant in a given city may induce tire and glass producers, for example, to locate plants in the same area. In turn, the existence of the glass and tire plants may induce still another automobile manufacturer to establish an assembly plant in the area. And so it goes.

External economies of scale The foregoing discussion of internal economies of scale and locational economies is not sufficient to explain fully the phenomenon of urban growth. A more complete explanation involves *external economies of scale* and the *infrastructure* of urban areas.

Recall that in the case of *internal* economies of scale, lower unit costs are achievable because of the size of the firm's own output. In other words, technology confronts the firm with a *given* long-run average-cost curve which declines over a very substantial range, such as in Figure 36-1a, and it is entirely up to the firm to achieve the high levels of production prerequisite to low unit costs. Now we must consider scale economies of a different type. Specifically, there may exist certain economies which cause the long-run average-cost curves of firms to *shift downward* as indicated in Figure

36-1b. These downward shifts of the long-run average-cost curves of individual firms depend upon the expansion of the entire *industry* or group of firms, not of the single *firm*. Therefore, such economies are called **external economies of scale,** for their realization lies beyond, or is external to, the actions and decisions of any single firm.

Specifically, as a number of firms agglomerate, they may *as a group* be able to realize lower input prices and therefore lower cost curves than if they were geographically dispersed. That is, as firms agglomerate, it tends to become profitable for specialized firms to perform certain functions for the industry on a larger scale—and therefore more cheaply—than can each firm internally.

Consider, for example, the computer industry. Computer manufacturers periodically require highly specialized workers to repair their capital equipment. A geographically isolated computer manufacturer would have two options. One would be to employ its own full-time repair specialists. But, because the amount of repair work is relatively small, these specialists would be underutilized and this would be a costly option. In terms of Figure 36-1a, the amount of repair work would not be large enough to allow the firm to achieve potential internal economies of scale by "producing" repair services for itself. The second option would be to bring in repair specialists from some distance as needed. This, too, would be costly in terms of time and money.

But when firms cluster together, a third and less costly option arises. When a number of computer manufacturers locate in the same area, the combined *industry* demand is sufficient to support one or more separate firms which specialize in repair services in that same geographic area. The specialist does a sufficient volume of business to realize internal economies of scale. It can therefore provide repair services at a lower unit cost than can a computer manufacturer requiring this service. In terms of Figure 36-1a, an individual computer manufacturer needs only, say, 10 units of repair service per week, which costs $100 per unit when self-provided. But an independent firm specializing in repair services provides, say, 50 units of this service to the entire group of, say, five computer manufacturers which have clustered together. This larger output of repair services allows the specialist to exhaust all economies of scale and thus provide the service at a cost of, say, $50 per unit. Simply put, each firm in the computer manufacturing industry may be able to purchase repair services from a firm specializing in this service more cheaply than each manufacturer can provide the service for itself. The resulting lower input price for repair services has the effect of shifting downward the long-run cost curves of computer manufacturers. This is illustrated in Figure 36-1b where the "provided internally" long-run average cost curve, AC_i, of computers lies above the "purchased externally" long-run curve, AC_ϵ. At the optimal scale of output of computers—shown by Q_o in Figure 36-1b—the average cost of computers falls from C_1 to C_2. This example potentially could be extended to component parts, technological and market research, financial services, and a host of other inputs. In any event, it is such external economies of scale which help explain the concentration of the computer manufacturing industry in such places as California's Silicon Valley, Route 128 near Boston, and North Carolina's Research Triangle.[2]

Such specialization leads to an increased interdependence among various types of manufacturing and service establishments. Thus, the location of the individual establishments which are highly interdependent is, in a sense, determined simultaneously. Broadly speaking, producers of final goods must have easy access both to the intermediate goods and services needed as inputs and to the markets for their final product. Similarly, the suppliers of intermediate goods and services must have easy access to markets sufficient in scale to realize internal economies of large-scale production. It follows that the solution for both groups is the same—to cluster in cities that alone can provide both inputs and markets in sufficient scale and variety to meet their total needs. Thus, it is not difficult to see why the attraction of industry and therefore of population to the cities tends to be a self-perpetuating, cumulative process.

Infrastructure The **infrastructure** of an urban area is a source of economies or cost advantages

not entirely unlike external economies of scale. Specifically, a city provides its firms with important services and facilities upon which producers rely and which would be costly for each firm to provide in the small amounts it alone needs. This infrastructure comprises such obvious things as ample water, electric power, waste treatment facilities, transportation facilities, research and engineering facilities, financial and banking institutions, management and public relations consultants, specialized legal services, and so forth.

A rich and varied infrastructure may be the strongest agglomerative force explaining the continuing and persistent growth of our largest urban areas. For example, one of the conclusions of a study of the New York metropolitan area is that even though the New York metropolitan area has lost nearly every industry it has ever had—flour mills, foundries, meat-packing plants, textile mills, and tanneries—the area continues to grow and earn above-average income. The report states that New York's propensity for growth and above-average income can be attributed to its rich infrastructure which attracts new enterprises that require highly specialized and sophisticated services.

DEMAND CONSIDERATIONS

Aside from the importance of market demand as a requisite for firms and industries to realize both internal and external economies of scale, market demand plays another role in explaining urban growth. The large populations of the cities mean that a wider variety of products and services are available. Put bluntly, while the populations of Chicago and Philadelphia will generate a market demand sufficient to support various ethnic restaurants and shops with exotic imports, the demand for such products in Grand Mound, Iowa, or Eureka, Montana, is insufficient to make such enterprises profitable. Similarly, the live theater, symphony orchestras, highly specialized medical and professional facilities, and professional athletics are commercially feasible only in larger cities.[3] In gen-

---

[2] This example is based upon Gerald A. Carlino, "Productivity In Cities: Does City Size Matter?" *Business Review* (Federal Reserve Bank of Philadelphia), December 1987, pp. 3–12.

[3] For a good discussion of art and culture in urban areas, see Werner Z. Hirsch, *Urban Economics* (New York: The Macmillan Publishing Company, 1984), chap. 6.

eral, many of the refinements and amenities of modern life are urban-based because of adequate demand. This means that cities are places not only where goods and services can be produced more cheaply, but also where consumers can attain a higher level of satisfaction because of a finer matching of their wants with the wider variety of available goods and services.

DEGLOMERATIVE FORCES

The advantages of agglomeration cannot be reaped indefinitely. Beyond some critical and difficult-to-specify point—a point which some of our larger cities have apparently passed—continued city growth and geographic concentration of industry will tend to create counterforces which give rise to higher production costs. That is, continued efforts to realize the economies of agglomeration may create certain offsetting diseconomies, or what are termed **deglomerative forces.**

Certain costs associated with geographic concentration are internal to, and therefore must be borne by, the producers themselves. For example, a growing concentration of industry in a given geographic area will mean higher land values and rents. (Figure 31-1 reminds us that a rising demand for a perfectly inelastic supply of centrally located sites will have a large price effect.) In turn, rising land values will make it increasingly costly for new firms to locate in an area or for existing firms to expand facilities. Furthermore, the intensified demand for labor which accompanies industrial agglomeration may be reflected in increased bargaining power for workers and rising wage costs. It is no accident that approximately one-half of all unionized workers reside in just six heavily urbanized states.

But many of the disadvantages and problems associated with urbanization stem from externalities or spillovers. That is, within the context of the city the marketplace simply fails to correctly charge or reward individuals and businesses for their decisions. Consider spillover costs. As producers agglomerate in an urban area, air and water pollution may become so severe as to make the city a decidedly less attractive place for additional firms and households to locate. Similarly, beyond some point traffic congestion (also an externality problem) slows deliveries of both inputs and finished products, making the city a more costly environment in which to operate. Urban blight is largely a problem of spillover costs. Landlords who decide it is in their own self-interest to permit their properties to fall into disrepair are allowing the quality of the entire neighborhood to deteriorate, making it a less attractive place for households and businesses to locate. Run-down properties "pollute" a neighborhood in the same general way as do factory smokestacks.

Have deglomerative forces become sufficiently important in recent years so that they offset some of the advantages of agglomeration? Recent changes in urbanization patterns seem to indicate that this is the case. The growth of suburbia at the expense of the central cities is consistent with the notion that deglomerative forces are at work.

The flight to the suburbs: urban sprawl

This brief introduction to the economies and diseconomies of agglomeration helps explain the paradox stated at the outset of this chapter. The cities are centers of great wealth and income. They are centers of economic activity and for many people a magnet of economic opportunity. But the very growth and maturation of the modern city spawn spillover costs, not to mention the inevitable social tensions which characterize areas of high population density. These latter features of the cities tend to make urban life less attractive. Hence, actual or potential urban residents—both businesses and households—ask themselves this question: How can the advantages and opportunities of the metropolitan area be realized without also incurring the disadvantages? How can one tap the economic activity of the city and realize a higher income *and* at the same time enjoy fresh air, space, privacy, and tranquillity?

The answer for millions of more affluent Americans has been a move to the suburbs. It is significant that the percentage of our population living in the central city has actually been declining since the turn of the century; virtually all our metropolitan population growth has been in the suburbs.

Many factors have contributed to this rapid growth. Rising real incomes, abetted by governmentally guaranteed mortgage credit, have made suburban living accessible to more and more families. Automobile ownership, as a convenient means of commuting, has been an important permissive factor.

Suburban growth has resulted not merely in the relocation of people, but also in the movement of businesses. The reasons for this are complex and diverse. In the first place, it is easy to see why many of the retail and personal service industries—groceries, hardware and furniture stores, laundries and cleaners, barber and beauty shops—have moved to the suburbs. Such establishments must be close to people; in particular, to people who have money. But many manufacturing firms have also fled the central city. We have already hit upon a couple of reasons for such shifts. Rising land costs make plant expansion very costly in the central city. And spillover costs make downtown locations less attractive. Firms which have their own truck transportation encounter costly problems of traffic congestion, loading and parking, and so forth. In addition, technological changes have encouraged many manufacturers to migrate to the suburbs. The rapid development of truck transportation has freed many firms from the need to locate near downtown railroad terminals and harbor facilities. Perhaps more important is the great emphasis that modern production technology has put upon highly integrated, continuous processes which assume an extensive one-story plant layout. Space for the utilization of this technology is not available—or only available at prohibitive cost—in the central city.

This is not to suggest that *all* major businesses have fled to the suburbs. Certain kinds of businesses have remained—and prospered—in the central cities:

These are the highly specialized areas of finance, business services, and central office administration, whose inputs are skill or knowledge or information, whose outputs are not goods but service or advice or decisions. It is these establishments—banks and law offices, advertising agencies and central administrative offices, consulting firms and government agencies—which are filling more and more of the central cities of most urban areas, and are becoming the primary function of . . . the city's central business district.[4]

Overall, however, the trend has been to the suburbs.

POLITICAL FRAGMENTATION

This dramatic flight to the suburbs has been accompanied by the **political fragmentation** of our large cities. That is, the central cities have become encircled with a large number of new suburbs, each of which is a separate political entity. Figure 36-2 shows the case of St. Louis. The St. Louis urban area is served by 474 local governments which are almost equally divided between Illinois and Missouri. These 474 governmental units include over 100 separate municipalities. St. Louis is hardly an exceptional case. There are over 1400 separate units of government in the New York City metropolitan area and almost 1000 in the San Francisco Bay area.

ECONOMIC IMBALANCE AND CUMULATIVE DECLINE

Political balkanization is the source of many urban problems. But it is particularly troublesome because the process of urban decentralization or suburban growth has brought about a highly unequal distribution of wealth and incomes geographically. The more prosperous people and many of the newer and more profitable industries have fled the central city in favor of the suburbs. By and large, the poorer people and many of the less profitable industries have been left behind in the central city.

This dramatic process of change in the structure of metropolitan areas has been self-reinforcing and cumulative. The migration of both the wealthier people and businesses to new political entities in the suburbs seriously erodes the property-tax base of the central cities.[5] New plants and new housing are built in the suburban ring, not in the central cities. To maintain public services, property-tax

[4] Benjamin Chinitz (ed.), *City and Suburb* (Englewood Cliffs, N.J.: Prentice-Hall, Inc., 1964), p. 26.

[5] Recall from Table 8-4 that property taxes are the main source of revenue for local units of government.

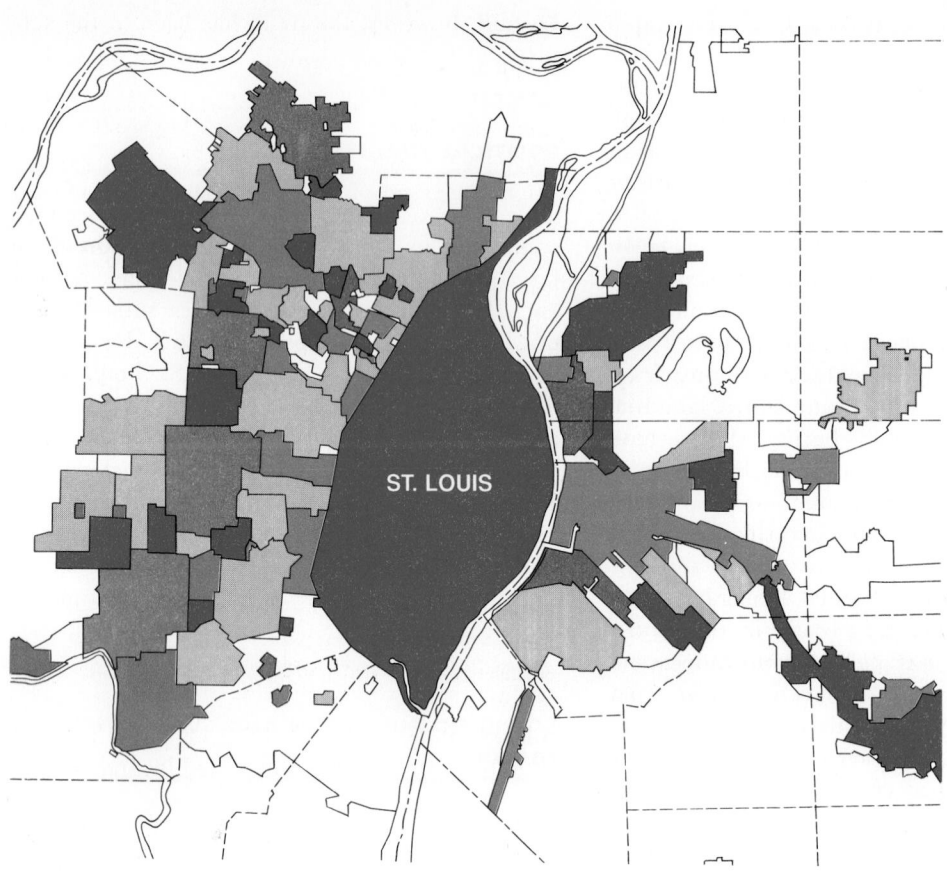

FIGURE 36-2

Political fragmentation: the case of St. Louis

The dynamics of urban expansion has given rise to the growth of numerous politically distinct subdivisions around the central city. The 474 units of local government which comprise the St. Louis metropolitan area are quite typical of this political balkanization. (Advisory Commission on Intergovernmental Relations, *Urban America and the Federal System,* Washington, 1969, p. 85.)

rates must be increased in the central city. But these rising rates further motivate households and businesses to flee to the suburbs.

Furthermore, the poor, predominantly black families who by virtue of their poverty and because of discrimination are left behind in the central cities are "high cost" citizens. An unusually high percentage is on welfare. Children are numerous, and education costs are high. High population densities—New York City has over 24,000 people per square mile—mean that the costs of governing, of collecting garbage, and of maintaining law and order are high.

All this is complicated and given further impetus by the fact that central-city decay, or urban blight, tends to be a cumulative process.

The older structures concentrated near the city center lose their economic usefulness as the functions of the downtown areas change. Extensive conversion, rehabilitation, and reconstruction are needed. If a few buildings need to be replaced or renovated in an otherwise prosperous area, the market provides private developers and builders with sufficient incentives to undertake the work. However, when a pattern of decay permeates a large area, the dilapidation of neighboring buildings reduces the profitability of improving a particular property. A large area must then be improved as a single unit, and the cost and difficulties of acquiring and redeveloping a large tract of central city land are likely to deter private investors from the undertaking.[6]

To summarize: The basic consequence of the dynamics of urban growth and the accompanying political fragmentation has been "to forge a white, middle- and high-income noose around the increasingly black and poor inner city. . . . " The losers in the flight to politically splintered suburbs have been the central cities, saddled with an inadequate and shrinking tax base and the burgeoning expenditure demands "incident to the governing, educating, and 'welfaring' of an increasing proportion of relatively poor [and usually] black families."[7] The winners, on the other hand, have been the more wealthy white suburban localities where income and wealth have been sufficient to underwrite viable public services with relatively modest tax efforts.

The dynamics of urban growth and the crazy quilt of political entities which has accompanied this growth have spawned a host of acute and interrelated problems. Let us now briefly survey some of these problems and sketch possible avenues for their resolution. Although the problems of the cities are manifold and not subject to simple classification, we will concentrate on three main problem areas: the ghettos and central-city poverty, urban transportation, and pollution.

The central-city ghettos[8]

The poverty and debased conditions of life which are pervasive in the ghettos are well known. The oldest, most deteriorated, and most crowded housing is in the central-city ghetto. In general, schools are grossly inadequate, and, as a result, ghetto students fall further behind nonghetto students with each level of school completed. Mortality rates are high, the result of inadequate nutrition, high incidence of disease, drug use, insufficient medical care, deplorable levels of sanitation, and so forth. Social disintegration is acute and crime rates are high. And, perhaps most important, ghetto income levels are abysmally low; in 1986 the central city poverty rate was 18.6 percent as compared to 13.5 percent for the nation as a whole.

We have just discussed many of the basic causes of the development of urban ghettos. In the first place, the whole process of urban decentralization is very much involved. Historically, the better-educated, better-trained, more prosperous whites have moved in large numbers from the central city to the suburbs, leaving behind obsolete housing in decaying neighborhoods. Their places have been taken by poorly educated, unskilled, low-income blacks migrating largely from the rural South, by Puerto Ricans, by Hispanics, and by Indians. Second, the dynamics of urban growth have shifted: "The activities which have been the traditional points of labor force entry for the urban unskilled—manufacturing, wholesale and retail trade, construction—are precisely those that have been suburbanizing most rapidly, making entry for the central-city poor difficult indeed."[9] And this movement of jobs to the suburbs is particularly adverse because it is both difficult and costly for central-city residents to get to the suburbs for jobs.

But, from a long-run viewpoint, discrimination is perhaps the most important force underlying the black ghettos. It has been asserted that past and present policies of discrimination have divided the nation into two societies, one largely black and poor, located in the central cities; the other, predominantly white and affluent, located in the suburbs and outlying areas. Discrimination has taken many forms: Blacks have been denied adequate education; they have been denied entry to certain occupations; they have been paid lower wages than whites on given jobs; and they have been the last hired and the first fired (Chapter 38).

[6] *Economic Report of the President, 1965*, pp. 149–150.

[7] Advisory Commission on Intergovernmental Relations, *Urban America and the Federal System* (Washington, 1969), pp. 2, 8.

[8] The organization of this section follows Dick Netzer, *Economics and Urban Problems*, 2d ed. (New York: Basic Books, Inc., Publishers, 1974), chaps. 3 and 4. Netzer's book, which is both readable and perceptive, is recommended reading.

[9] Ibid., p. 29.

Given the complexity of the problems of the ghettos, our discussion of potential remedies will necessarily be brief and incomplete. To facilitate matters we will treat the human (poverty) and the physical (housing) aspects of the ghetto problem separately; in fact, they are very closely interrelated.

THE HUMAN ASPECT: ALLEVIATING GHETTO POVERTY

How can the poverty which is endemic to the black ghetto be alleviated? At the outset we must acknowledge that experts disagree as to the tractability of the problem. In particular, a disturbing and controversial debate has come to the fore in recent years. Some observers contend that the city ghettos are spawning a "black underclass" which is trapped in a permanent cycle of unemployment, broken homes, welfare, and, frequently, drugs and crime. Relevant statistics are alarming: 1 out of 2 black youths lives in poverty; 1 out of 2 black youths grows up without a father; nearly 40 percent of black teenagers are unemployed; 1 out of 4 births is to a teenager; more than 80 percent of children born to black teenagers are illegitimate; and 1 of every 21 young black men is a homocide victim. It is argued that in the social and economic isolation of the urban ghetto a new culture—a culture of poverty and dependency—has evolved where attitudes, values, and morality are substantially different from those of mainstream America. Welfare programs—Aid to Families with Dependent Children (AFDC), food stamps, housing subsidies, and the rest—have allegedly undermined incentives to work and have created welfare-dependent families. Furthermore, the historical exodus from the central city of middle-class blacks has left drug dealers, prostitutes, hustlers, and small-time criminals as role models for youngsters. Low-quality schools grossly underprepare minority youth for the job market, while a lenient legal system increases the attractiveness of crime as an alternative to work.

At the level of policy, the black underclass view asserts that, although there has been a significant diminution in discrimination over the past several decades and although hundreds of billions have been expended on antipoverty programs, the poverty problem persists. The implication is that the responsibility for poverty rests largely upon the poor themselves and that self-help is essential to the alleviation of poverty.

Critics of the black underclass view contend that it is a simplistic and callous position which incorrectly implies that the blame for poverty rests with its victims and not with larger social and economic considerations. Critics of the underclass view also contend that central-city poverty is heterogeneous and has a multitude of causes. Furthermore, it is argued that the "culture of poverty," if it exists, can be effectively countered by a variety of means.

1 More and better jobs Unemployment among central-city blacks is notoriously high and a major cause of poverty. The unemployment rate for nonwhites is generally twice that for whites. Black teenagers face a chronic depression; their unemployment rates are typically 35 to 40 percent or more. Given the present education and qualifications of the ghetto labor force, how can the unemployment situation be improved?

Two complementary approaches present themselves: Bring ghetto residents to existing jobs in the suburbs, **and** bring new jobs to the ghettos. Consider the first approach. Mobility in terms of residence is extremely difficult for ghetto dwellers. On the one hand, the incomes of most central-city blacks are so low that they simply cannot afford to move to the suburbs. On the other hand, those who can afford suburban housing are confronted with problems of discrimination. Real estate agencies and landlords have used a variety of both crude and subtle techniques for prohibiting or restricting these moves. Many suburban areas have purposely zoned for large minimum lot sizes and have enacted strict building and housing codes which push up housing prices to prohibit any influx of lower-income (black) families from the central city.

The second approach is to create new job opportunities in the ghettos. **Black capitalism** is a generic term which refers to the creation of new businesses, owned and operated by blacks, in ghetto areas. A variety of proposals—a few of which have become operational—have been made in support of black capitalism. These proposals advocate governmentally sponsored programs to provide liberal credit, tax incentives and subsidies, managerial assistance and training, and so forth, to present or potential black entrepreneurs. Related proposals urge governmental subsidies to major corporations which are willing to build plants in the ghettos and to train black workers to staff them.

It must be added that the overall state of the economy is critical for black employment. For example, in the recession year of 1983 the overall unemployment rate was 9.6 percent, while the rate for blacks was 19.5 percent. As the economy approached full employment with a 5.4 percent rate in 1988, the black unemployment rate fell very sharply to 11.7 percent.

2 Income maintenance A second means of alleviating ghetto poverty is the welfare system, which provides minimum incomes to the aged, the disabled, and mothers with dependent children. The characteristics of existing welfare programs and associated problems will be discussed at some length in Chapter 37. We simply reemphasize at this point that a major criticism of the welfare system is that it dampens incentives to work for many who are capable of holding jobs. The proposed solutions to this problem include job training, subsidized child care, and "workfare," a concept which obligates welfare recipients to perform some sort of work in return for their benefits.

3 Improved education and training Many ghetto residents who are fully employed nevertheless live in poverty. The reason? They have not had access to sufficient education and training to qualify for jobs which pay higher wages. The major piece of Federal legislation in this area was the Comprehensive Employment and Training Act of 1973 which expired in 1982. CETA provided grants to state and local governments, but allowed state and municipal governments to develop training programs appropriate to their needs and to spend the Federal funds accordingly. CETA entailed both job training and public sector employment opportunities. Program enrollees were overwhelmingly from low-income families. Young workers who had not completed high school dominated the programs and minorities were heavily represented. The 1982 Job Partnership Training Act which replaced CETA provides vocational training opportunities, but not public sector jobs.

THE PHYSICAL ASPECT: HOUSING AND URBAN RENEWAL

The urban ghetto is not only a visible and potentially explosive concentration of poverty. It is also characterized by extensive deterioration of the physical environment; much of the housing and many commercial buildings are substandard and dilapidated. Many buildings have simply been abandoned by their owners.

Why has urban blight occurred? The reasons are manifold and include the following:

1 Exodus and externalities The physical decay of the central cities is a legacy of the flight to the suburbs. As the more prosperous households and businesses leave, so do the financial resources required for the maintenance of housing and commercial buildings. And as physical deterioration begins, the problem of external or spillover costs arises to reinforce the process. When landlord X allows his property to fall into disrepair, this decision contributes to the overall deterioration of the neighborhood and imposes costs upon other landlords in that neighborhood. Because of X's decision, there will be a smaller economic payoff to landlords Y and Z in maintaining their properties. Hence, a neighborhood can fall into a cumulative cycle of deterioration and decline. It is this externality problem, incidentally, which provides an economic rationale for government action in the area of urban renewal.

2 Property-tax spiral Historically, the process of urban blight was often reinforced by rising property-tax rates. As properties deteriorated and were abandoned, the central-city property-tax base would shrink. At the same time, the poor central-city areas became increasingly costly to govern. Welfare costs, the costs of police and fire protection, the costs of public hospitals and clinics, all tended to rise. Given the dependence of municipalities upon the property tax, the inevitable result was higher property-tax rates which provided a further inducement for landlords to neglect or abandon properties. In contrast, property owners in the more affluent suburbs usually enjoyed better-quality schools and other public services *while paying lower tax rates*. This is the case because the value of suburban property is so much higher. A 5 percent tax on a $200,000 home in a relatively wealthy suburb will generate $10,000 of tax revenue. A 10 percent tax on a $40,000 home in a deteriorating central-city area will only generate $4000 of revenue.

3 Discrimination Discrimination in housing has been a basic consideration in restricting blacks and other minorities to the decaying ghettos of the central cities. It is true that the incomes of most central-city residents are so low that they cannot afford to move to the suburbs. But some could and would if housing were more readily available to them.

One need merely recall the simple tools of supply and demand to grasp the impact of discrimination upon housing prices and rents. The immediate effect is to make available a disproportionately small supply of housing to blacks. This restricted supply means higher housing prices and rents. One result is that blacks are forced to use a very large proportion of their income for housing. But even so, the housing is likely to be of inferior quality. High rents induce ghetto families to "double up" on available housing. Landlords respond on the supply side by subdividing apartments. And, needless to say, a captive market provides little incentive for owners to repair or improve their property. The overall consequence is typically high rents for crowded and dilapidated housing.

4 Rent controls The fixing of rents by government at below-equilibrium levels has also contributed to urban blight. Once a New York phenomenon, rent controls have been adopted by Los Angeles, Boston, San Francisco, Washington, D.C., and dozens of more modest-sized cities. Many other cities are considering such controls. At first glance the objective of rent controls—to protect tenants from the skyrocketing increases in rents caused by demand increasing faster than supply—seems laudable. But there is rather overwhelming evidence that the actual long-run consequences tend to be much different.

As a direct consequence of rent controls, landlords receive a below-normal return on their housing investments. This prompts them to shift their financial capital to other kinds of investments or into geographic areas where controls do not exist. The amount of new housing constructed in rent-controlled cities will thereby decline. Similarly, the low return on rental housing makes it unprofitable to maintain existing structures and so the existing stock of housing will deteriorate. Rather than resolve the housing scarcity, rent controls tend to aggravate that problem. Housing is now even scarcer; at the controlled—below-equilibrium—price, quantity demanded exceeds quantity supplied so that a true shortage now exists. It is a useful exercise for the reader to construct a simple supply and demand diagram for housing units to verify these points.

If rent controls have such counterproductive effects, why have they persisted and tended to spread? The answer is that tenants outnumber landlords and builders. Current tenants who benefit from controls constitute a sizable and effective special-interest group (Chapter 33).

Policy failures Since the late 1930s the Federal government has heavily subsidized the efforts of state and local governments to provide low-rent public housing for the poor. Urban renewal programs—again, subsidized with Federal funds—have attempted to reverse the spread of urban blight by rebuilding central-city areas.

Ironically, on balance, urban renewal programs have *reduced* the supply of housing available to low-income families. Some urban renewal efforts have not been primarily concerned with housing, but rather, the strategy has been to shore up the vitality of the central city by replacing slum neighborhoods with new office buildings to house both public services and private enterprises. This tendency helps explain the paradox that many ghetto dwellers are opposed to urban renewal. Witness the slogan: "Urban renewal is black removal." Furthermore, some families have been uprooted several times by public housing projects which have in fact increased the supply of housing available to middle-income families, but reduced it for low-income families.[10]

---

[10] For more on urban housing problems and policies, see John M. Levy, *Urban and Metropolitan Economics* (New York: McGraw-Hill Book Company, 1985), chaps. 7 and 8.

The transportation problem

We have seen that one fundamental characteristic of urban growth is the direct relationship one finds between distance from the central city and income and wealth. Generally speaking, those living furthest from "downtown" are the professional, technical, and white-collar workers. A large proportion of these higher-income people work downtown; that is, they are employed in the banking and financial firms, the legal and consulting firms, and the advertising agencies which have remained in the central city. On the other hand, we have seen that many kinds of manufacturing, wholesale, retail, and personal service industries—industries which require blue-collar and less skilled workers—have moved to suburbia. The result is a significant locational mismatch of jobs and labor force between suburbs and central city. This mismatch creates the need for an effective transportation system to negotiate the required cross-hauling of the population.

But the need for efficient transportation is even more pervasive. Accessibility is the *sine qua non* of effective participation in urban life. Most of the cultural and social advantages of city life can only be efficiently realized through a viable transportation system. Museums, art galleries, professional sports stadiums, and concert halls are indivisible, or "lumpy," goods; since they cannot be divided and taken home by consumers, the consumer must go to them. Similarly, comparative shopping in the city assumes adequate transportation.

Given the convenience of private automobile travel, most suburbanites have chosen this form of transportation. Transportation by private cars has soared, while the use of public transportation has declined. Indeed, large Federal subsidies to highway construction have created a substantial financial bias in favor of the automobile. The greatly expanded use of auto transportation has given rise to increasingly acute problems of traffic congestion, not to mention the automobile's substantial contribution to air pollution. The response to traffic congestion, of course, has been to construct more highways. But the additional highways permit the growth of still more distant suburbs and elicit more traffic. So mammoth highway construction programs usually have been accompanied by more—not less—traffic congestion and parking problems. We have witnessed a vicious cycle of more autos, more highways which induce more autos, and the construction of still more highways.

The other side of the coin has been the general deterioration of the mass-transit system of the cities. The vast geographic dispersion of population throughout the suburbs has made it difficult for mass-transit systems to realize the heavy trunk-line operations requisite to their prosperity or survival. Again, we encounter a cumulative process. As patronage declines, unit costs rise and commuter fares must be increased, on the one hand, and the quality of both equipment and service deteriorates, on the other. So more people choose to drive their cars to work, and the process repeats itself.

It is worth remembering from Chapter 22 that the determination of fares for mass transit is complicated by evidence that, while the short-run demand for commuter transportation may be inelastic, the long-run demand is likely to be elastic. Thus, the immediate or short-run impact of a fare increase is to increase total revenue and relieve the financial problems of a troubled transit system. But in the long run—that is, over a period of several years, when commuters have had time to make additional decisions concerning car purchases, car pooling, or changing residences and places of employment—the demand for commuter transportation is price-elastic, and higher fares will mean a *decrease* in total revenue. In the case of commuter rail transportation in the Philadelphia area it was estimated that a $.25 or 9 percent increase in the price of a one-way ticket would *increase* the system's total revenue by $8,000 per day in the short run, but *decrease* it by over $19,000 per day in the long run. A fare increase which is helpful to a mass-transit system in the short run may merely compound its financial difficulties in the long run.[11]

Unfortunately, not all people have the option of using either mass transit or their automobile. The poor and less skilled of the central city must rely upon mass transit. Shrinkage and service deterioration of the transit system, accompanied by the shift of blue-collar jobs to the suburbs, unfortu-

[11] Richard Voith, "Commuter Rail Ridership: The Long and the Short Haul," *Business Review* (Federal Reserve Bank of Philadelphia), November–December 1987, pp. 13–23.

nately leave many of the central-city residents isolated from the economic opportunities of the metropolitan area.

Improving urban transportation

In considering possible solutions, it is both convenient and meaningful to consider the urban transport problem in two parts: the short-run problem and the long-run problem.

THE SHORT RUN: USER CHARGES AND PEAK PRICING

First, there is a short-run problem: *Given existing transportation facilities and technology,* how can this transportation "plant" be used most efficiently? What is the best way of utilizing *existing* freeway, street, parking, and mass-transit facilities? We have already noted that, historically, governmental subsidies have been heavily biased in favor of automobile transportation. Specifically, urban freeway and street construction has been heavily subsidized by Federal grants; financing also comes from state gasoline-tax revenues. A number of urban economists feel that a system of **user charges** on drivers would be very useful in achieving a better balance in the use of mass transit and auto transportation and, in particular, in alleviating the problem of traffic congestion. They contend that the city's streets and highways are overused and congested because drivers do not bear the full cost of driving; they are in fact subsidized by society (taxpayers) at large. More specifically, it is argued that automobile drivers should be confronted "as near as possible in time and place to the act of making the decision to drive" with a price—a user charge—which covers the full cost of driving. By "full cost" is meant not only the cost of highway construction and repair but also the cost of traffic control devices and traffic police and even automobile pollution costs. Price, after all, is a rationing device or disciplining mechanism, and traffic congestion is a symptom of quantity demanded in excess of quantity supplied at the going price. "Surely, we would have traffic jams in the aisles of food stores and 'shortages' of food if we tried to

administer free food stores supported by general taxation. The food shortages would be analogous to the shortages of street space per automobile (traffic jams) and the shortages of parking places that characterize our underpriced and tax-supported urban transportation industry."[12] In short, the purpose of user charges is to relieve traffic congestion by rationing some people out of the "driving market"; that is, they will use the public transportation system or, if they have the option, will make fewer trips downtown.

Recognizing that the morning and evening rush hours are the focal points of the urban transportation problem, many advocates of user charges also contend that the pricing of both auto and mass-transit facilities should vary according to the time of day. That is, **peak pricing** should be used; charges should be higher during the peak or rush hours and lower during off-peak hours. The purpose, of course, is to "ration out" travelers whose need to travel during rush hours is less pressing or less necessary. For example, shoppers might be induced by a system of peak prices to alter the timing of their trips to and from downtown so that they do not coincide with the travel times of commuting workers.

At a more pragmatic level, some cities have encouraged car pools in the hope of reducing both traffic congestion and air pollution. For example, larger firms in the Los Angeles area have been directed to draw up plans to encourage ride-sharing among their employees. Similarly, a number of cities have experimented with "car pool lanes," which can only be used by autos with, say, three or more occupants, on their freeways.

THE LONG RUN: MASS TRANSIT

This brings us to the long-run aspect of the urban transportation problem: What should be the character of future public investments in urban transportation facilities? There has been a revival of interest in the revitalization and development of public mass-transit systems—commuter railroads, subways, buses, monorails, and so forth. First,

[12] Wilbur R. Thompson, *A Preface to Urban Economics* (Baltimore: The Johns Hopkins Press, 1965), pp. 340–341.

given projections of suburban population growth and the consequent possibility that the volume of urban automobile traffic may double in the next twenty years, many city planners and public officials feel that effective alternatives to auto transportation are imperative. This is particularly so in view of the previously noted point that increased investment in streets and freeways often seems to induce a higher volume of traffic, rather than relieve congestion. Despite the existence of an elaborate system of supposedly high-speed freeways, the average rate of travel on Los Angeles' freeways is only 37 miles per hour and this figure is expected to fall to 17 miles per hour by the turn of the century. In fact, Los Angeles freeway drivers now spend 10 percent of their time stopped! Second, it is felt that an expanded and improved mass-transit system can yield substantial social benefits in terms of (1) a viable and revitalized central city with an expanding property-tax base, (2) greater accessibility to suburban jobs for the central-city poor, and (3) avoidance of an increasingly acute pollution problem which an expansion of automobile transportation is likely to entail. In fact, after mass-transit ridership hit bottom in the early 1970s, some of the larger systems began to make a comeback.

The pollution problem: the effluent society?

Cities do not have a monopoly on the pollution problem. Yet, the high population densities and high levels of industrial concentration and automobile use which are the earmarks of urban life make pollution problems most acute in the cities.

DIMENSIONS OF THE PROBLEM

The seriousness of water, air, and solid-waste pollution has been well documented in the popular press and needs only brief review here. We know that rivers and lakes have been turned into municipal and industrial sewers. Almost half our population drinks water of dubious quality. Air pollution contributes to lung cancer, emphysema, pneumonia, and other respiratory diseases. Solid waste (garbage) disposal has become an acute problem for many cities as the most readily available dump sites have been filled and citizens resist the establishment of dumps or incinerators near them.

Possible longer-run consequences of environmental pollution are even more disturbing. Some scientists contend that the concentrations of industry, people, structures, and cement which constitute cities might create air and heat pollution sufficient to cause irreversible and potentially disastrous changes in the earth's climate and weather patterns through the so-called greenhouse effect.

CAUSES: MATERIALS BALANCE APPROACH

The roots of the pollution problem can best be envisioned through the **materials balance approach,** which is the simple notion that the weight of the inputs (fuels, raw materials, water, and so forth) used in the economy's production processes will ultimately result in a roughly equivalent residual of wastes.

Fortunately, the ecological system—Nature, if you are over forty—has the self-regenerating capacity which allows it, within limits, to absorb or recycle such wastes. But the volume of such residuals has tended to outrun this absorptive capacity.

Why has this happened? Why do we have a pollution problem? Causes are manifold, but perhaps four are paramount.

1 **Population density** There is the simple matter of population growth. An ecological system which may accommodate 50 or 100 million people may begin to break down under the pressures of 200 or 300 million.

2 **Rising incomes** Economic growth means that each person consumes and disposes of more output. Paradoxically, the affluent society helps to spawn the effluent society. A rising GNP (gross national product) means a rising GNG (gross national garbage). Thus a high standard of living permits Americans to own over 176 million motor vehicles. But autos and trucks are a primary source of air pollution and, concomitantly, give rise to the hard problem of disposing of some 10 or 11 million junked vehicles each year.

3 Technology Technological change is another contributor to pollution. For example, the addition of lead to gasoline posed a serious threat to human health, leading to the government requirement of unleaded fuel. The development and widespread use of "throw-away" containers made of virtually indestructible aluminum or plastic add substantially to the solid-waste crisis. Some detergent soap products have been highly resistant to sanitary treatment and recycling.

4 Incentives Profit-seeking manufacturers will choose the least-cost combination of inputs and will find it advantageous to bear only unavoidable costs. If they can dump waste chemicals into rivers and lakes rather than pay for expensive treatment and proper disposal, businesses will be inclined to do so. If manufacturers can discharge smoke and the hot water used to cool machinery rather than purchase expensive abatement and cooling facilities, they will tend to do so. The result is air and water pollution—both chemical and thermal—and, in the economist's jargon, the shifting of certain costs to the community at large as external or spillover costs. Enjoying lower "internal" costs than if they had not polluted the environment, the producers can sell their products more cheaply, expand their production, and realize larger profits. The supply curve of a polluting firm or industry lies too far to the right because it omits the cost which society bears in the form of a debased environment. The result is an overallocation of resources to the polluter's commodity.

But it is neither just nor accurate to lay the entire blame for pollution at the door of industry. On the one hand, a well-intentioned firm which wants to operate in a socially responsible way with respect to pollution may find itself in an untenable position. If an individual firm "internalizes" all its external or spillover costs by installing, say, water-treatment and smoke-abatement equipment, the firm will find itself at a cost disadvantage in comparison to its polluting competitors. The socially responsible firm will have higher costs and will be forced to raise its product price. The "reward" for the pollution-conscious firm is a declining market for its product, diminished profits, and, in the extreme, the prospect of bankruptcy. This correctly suggests that effective action to combat pollution must be undertaken collectively through govern-

ment. On the other hand, given that an important function of government is to correct the misallocation of resources which accompanies spillover costs, it is ironic that most major cities are heavy contributors to the pollution problem. Municipal power plants are frequently major contributors to air pollution; many cities discharge inadequately treated sewage into rivers or lakes because it is cheap and convenient to do so. Similarly, individuals avoid the costs of proper refuse pickup and disposal by burning their garbage. We also find it easier to use throw-away containers rather than recycle "return" containers.

ANTIPOLLUTION POLICIES

Because environmental pollution is a problem in spillover or external costs,[13] the task of antipollution policy is to devise ways of "internalizing" the external costs of pollution. The objective is to make the polluter pay *all* the costs associated with its activities.

We have earlier indicated a variety of possible remedies for pollution. First, in Chapter 6 we found that legislated standards and specific taxes—sometimes called **emission fees**—could be used to internalize the external costs which pollution entails. In terms of Figure 6-1, legislation and emission fees can be used to eliminate the discrepancy between the costs borne by the producer and total costs by shifting S to, or at least toward, S_t. Second, in Chapter 33 it was noted that under certain conditions, private negotiation would be used to resolve a pollution problem. More specifically, the *Coase theorem* suggests that, if property rights are clearly defined, the number of people involved is small, and bargaining costs are negligible, external cost problems can be corrected through private bargaining. In Chapter 33 we were also introduced to a more novel policy option in which the environment would be treated as a scarce resource and pollution rights would be sold within the capacity of the environment to recycle or absorb industrial wastes. Recall that such a market would directly confront potential polluters with a monetary incentive not to pollute. Furthermore, the increase in

[13] Rereading the section entitled "Spillovers or Externalities" in Chapter 6 may be useful at this point.

demand for pollution rights which accompanies economic growth would increase the price of those rights and thereby stimulate the search for pollution-abating technologies. Finally, with respect to solid waste disposal, the diminishing number of acceptable dump sites has accelerated interest in recycling. Ten states have thus far passed laws requiring some form of recycling and an estimated 10 percent of the nation's garbage is recycled.

Problems The problems involved in establishing and administering these antipollution proposals are both numerous and substantial. First, pollution standards are difficult to establish because of incomplete and disputed technological and biological information. We simply do not know with certainty the effects—the economic and human costs—of certain pollutants. This lack of information is important because it is not economically rational to prohibit or flatly eliminate pollution, but rather to use benefit-cost analysis (Chapter 33) to determine the optimal extent to which antipollution programs should be pursued. This entails the very difficult problem of calculating the marginal benefits and marginal costs of such programs. Second, the administration and enforcement of legislated controls or standards can be both difficult and costly. Finally, governmental units—the very institutions we would expect to create and enforce antipollution policies—are themselves major polluters.[14]

Solving urban problems: the prerequisites

We have outlined the general character of certain problems of the cities and have indicated specific remedies. We must now recognize that there exist certain institutional and financial prerequisites to the resolution or amelioration of urban problems.

[14] If you are inclined to pursue the economics of pollution, you will find Thomas D. Crocker and A. J. Rogers, III, *Environmental Economics* (Hinsdale, Ill.: The Dryden Press, Inc., 1971), to be entertaining reading. For a more comprehensive treatment, see Thomas H. Tietenberg, *Environmental and Natural Resource Economics* (Glenview, Ill.: Scott, Foresman and Company, 1984).

POLITICAL CONSOLIDATION

Most urbanologists agree that one of the basic prerequisites to resolving urban problems is political consolidation. In particular, the design of efficient and equitable solutions to the problems of the cities depends in good measure on overcoming the political fragmentation which now exists in most cities.

Urban areas are in fact highly integrated and highly interdependent economic units. Most urban problems—transportation; discrimination in housing, employment, and education; pollution; land use—are clearly areawide in character. The individual, fragmented political units of the cities do not have effective jurisdiction over these problems; in our large cities, the local units of government have been losing the capacity to govern effectively. The realization of efficient and equitable—as opposed to politically feasible—solutions to urban problems depends upon coordinated areawide action, that is, upon political consolidation.

Efficiency Looked at from the economist's point of view, political consolidation can stimulate more efficient decision making in dealing with urban problems for several reasons.

I SCALE ECONOMIES Small political subdivisions will frequently be unable to realize economies of scale in providing certain public facilities, such as water and sewage systems. Levels of output will be low and these facilities will operate at points high on their unit-cost curves (Figure 36-1a).

2 PLANNING AND COORDINATION A closely related point is that in such endeavors as police and fire protection, street construction, and public transit, political fragmentation results in the loss of certain qualitative advantages which would stem from the planning and coordination of these public services at the metropolitan level. "The case for bigness in public services probably rests more on quality than on cost; an areawide police force is better coordinated for traffic control and hot pursuit, and big enough to afford scientific crime detection facilities and specialists in juvenile and race problems.[15] Similarly, although the actual unit cost (per mile)

[15] Thompson, op. cit., pp. 267–268.

of producing streets may be roughly the same whether provided by many small, independent municipalities or by a large metropolitan government, there are obvious advantages in having an overall plan to coordinate a given volume of street construction in the interest of maximum effectiveness.

3 CAPTURING EXTERNALITIES Still another reason why most urban economists favor political consolidation is that, because of the small geographic size of many existing urban political units, many of the benefits associated with the provision of needed public facilities in such areas as, say, education, recreation, and environmental improvement will accrue to individuals and businesses residing in other political units. For example, a small urban political unit which builds an excellent school system, provides for the treatment of sewage and industrial wastes, and constructs ample reacreational facilities will be providing benefits which in part spill over its political boundaries, that is, are external to it in that they are realized by the residents of other political units. Graduates of its school system may take jobs in adjacent political subdivisions. And those living in other political subdivisions will use its parks and playgrounds and benefit from its antipollution activities. The crucial point is that, when spillover benefits are large, a good or service will tend to be underproduced (Figure 6-2). More specifically, the voters in each small political entity will not be anxious to tax themselves heavily to provide services and facilities whose benefits accrue in significant amounts to others.

Equity The case for political consolidation also rests on grounds of equity. We have emphasized that political fragmentation has created serious fiscal disparities within the urban areas. Resources and needs have become separated in the political jungle of the cities. As we have seen, the problems are largely concentrated in the central city while the resources are located in the suburbs. Political consolidation would have the desirable effect of putting resources and needs within the same political jurisdiction.

Avenues of consolidation Political consolidation can be achieved in a variety of ways: the annexation of surrounding suburban areas by the city; the con-

solidation of city and county governments; the establishment of special regional authorities to deal with such particular problems as transportation or pollution.

But it would be unrealistic to expect that consolidation will be easily and quickly achieved. The "haves" of the wealthier suburbs have shown little inclination to assume the moral and financial responsibility for the glaring problems of the "have nots" in the central city. Nor can we expect the officials of local governmental units to be eager to give up their power and functions. More positively, one can make counterarguments in favor of the present fragmented system. First, small local government is likely to be more conducive to personal political participation and more responsive to the needs and aspirations of its constituents than is a metropolitanwide government. A specific example: Some blacks feel that with fragmentation they at least can gain political control of those geographic areas where they are numerically dominant, whereas with consolidation they are destined to be a largely ignored minority. Second, wasteful bureaucracy—inefficiencies in public administration—may tend to offset assumed cost economies in the provision and coordination of public goods and services by a consolidated urban government (Chapter 33). Finally, some would argue that small local governments contribute to the heterogeneity of urban living areas in that they provide residents with a variety of choices as to levels of local taxes and amounts and quality of public services. Thus, although most urbanologists endorse political consolidation, the case for it is not as clear-cut as one might at first suppose.

THE LARGER FISCAL PROBLEM

The second prerequisite to the resolving of urban problems is adequate financing. In the past decade or so a number of large cities have experienced much-publicized financial difficulties. Even with political consolidation, it is questionable that the tax resources of the urban areas will be sufficient to meet the rising costs of urban governments. Consider some specific factors which have made urban government very costly. Most big cities are old and, as a result, their physical plant—public buildings, sewer and electrical systems, streets, and so forth—is costly to maintain. Given the central city's dense concentrations of very low-income populations, it is no surprise that crime rates—and consequently law-enforcement costs—are high. Welfare costs are very high and the public provision of many basic services (for example, medical care) is extensive. Financially troubled mass-transit systems require subsidies. More recently, strong government employee unions have evolved and have aggressively pushed up wages and fringe benefits, including ofttimes-generous pension systems. The sheer size of big city bureaucracies may lead to inefficiencies which would not arise in smaller cities and towns. Empirical data show that the number of municipal workers per 1000 of population grows steadily as city size increases. It may also be that the kinds of services provided by cities are simply not susceptible to large productivity increases. For example, social workers, correctional officials, teachers, and public health physicians are all involved in direct person-to-person contact. In comparison to the mass production of air conditioners or automobiles, there is relatively little opportunity to save labor costs through mechanization and technological progress. This means in turn that there is little or no productivity increase to offset the increases in the money wages and salaries of municipal workers. In brief, a significant part of the rapid rise in the cost of municipal services may stem from the fact that these services are inherently characterized by small and sporadic productivity increases.

There are a number of proposed solutions to the revenue crisis faced by local governments: (1) Federal revenue sharing, (2) the shifting of certain fiscal burdens to the Federal government, and (3) the restructuring of the property tax.[16]

Federal revenue sharing Recall from Chapter 8 that a system of intergovernmental transfer payments exists in the United States. In this system the Federal government is the donor and state and local governments are the recipients. The large excess of expenditures over receipts for local governments

shown in Table 8-4 is largely offset by Federal grants. The fiscal crunch faced by the cities has been greatly eased by transfers from the Federal government.

Shifting financial responsibility Another recommendation is to have the Federal or state governments assume the financial responsibility for meeting certain urban problems and obligations. For example, some economists advocate that the Federal government establish and finance an income-maintenance program to relieve poverty, thereby reducing the heavy welfare costs now borne by the cities (Chapter 37). Also, the shifting of all local costs of elementary and secondary education to the states or the Federal government would not only relieve the fiscal crisis of the cities, but might also help to ensure greater equality of educational opportunity.

But there is little reason to be optimistic with respect to municipal finance. During the Reagan administration, for example, the growth of Federal aid to state and local governments was constrained. Furthermore, the large Federal budget deficits of the 1980s (Chapter 20) have generated great pressures for the realization of a balanced budget. The reduction of transfers to state and local governments is likely to be a part of any program to reduce Federal deficits.

Overhauling the tax system Like sin, everyone deplores the property tax. It is regressive because low-income people spend a larger proportion of their incomes for rental housing than do high-income people. It is difficult and costly to administer. Equitable assessment of property is difficult. Furthermore, we have seen that rising property-tax rates have been a part of the self-reinforcing process by which wealthy people and prosperous businesses have fled to the suburbs. Yet the property tax is clearly the main source of revenue for local governments (Table 8-4) and is likely to remain so. It is therefore relevant to ask: Is it possible to restructure and revitalize the property tax so as to provide more revenue, on the one hand, and to reduce its harmful economic effects, on the other?

The basic proposal here is to shift the property-tax emphasis from buildings to land. Interest in land-value taxation has both an equity and an efficiency aspect. The *equity* argument is that much of the value of urban land reflects public decisions

---

[16] For a thorough discussion of the fiscal problems of the cities, see James Heilbrun, *Urban Economics and Public Policy*, 2d ed. (New York: St. Martin's Press, 1981), chaps. 14 and 15.

with respect to zoning and the provision of roads, schools, and utilities. Most of the dramatic increases in urban land values are windfall gains in the sense that they are not the consequence of the efforts or expenditures of landowners. It would seem fair for society to tax away much of the increase in land value which society's decisions and expenditures have provided. The *efficiency* argument is that a tax on land has a neutral effect upon the use or allocation of land; a land-value tax does not contribute to a misallocation of land (Chapter 31).

In the cities the present arrangement of relatively high property taxes on buildings and relatively low taxes on land tends to have perverse effects upon incentives. Specifically, heavy taxes on buildings harm the incentives of builders and property owners to construct new buildings and improve existing ones. This fact helps to explain central-city decay and blight. The relatively light taxes on land mean that landowners find the tax costs involved in holding vacant land to be comparatively small, and so they are encouraged to withhold land from productive uses in order to speculate on increases in its value. Such action—or inaction—prevents growth of the property-tax base and contributes to the fiscal problems of the cities. By raising taxes on land and lowering taxes on buildings the land speculator who impedes development will be penalized and the investor in new and better buildings will be rewarded.

CHAPTER SUMMARY

1 The economies of agglomeration are significant in explaining the growth of cities. Similarly, deglomerative forces account for the shift of population and economic activity from the central city to the suburbs. Political fragmentation and pronounced economic imbalances have accompanied urban sprawl.

2 The central-city ghettos are heavily populated by blacks and other minorities who, because of low incomes and discrimination, cannot escape to suburban areas. Enlarged job opportunities, income-maintenance programs, and improved education and training are potential ways of reducing ghetto poverty. Urban renewal and public housing programs have met with limited success in revitalizing the central-city areas and generally have done little to increase the supply of low-income housing.

LAST WORD

The economics of crime

Crime is a pervasive problem in our society. However, like pollution, the problem is particularly pronounced in our urban areas. Crime rates are higher in urban than in nonurban areas, and higher in central cities than in suburbs.

Let us consider two questions. First, why are crime rates high in urban areas? Second, how do economists analyze the problem of crime?

There are several interrelated reasons why crime is concentrated in cities. First, there is the matter of crowding or high population density. In a small town the local police know residents from strangers and can, if necessary, keep an eye on the latter. Such a personalized approach to crime prevention is clearly impossible in large cities. Second, as the introduction to this chapter makes clear, our cities are repositories of great wealth. This wealth provides the "loot" which attracts criminals. Third, we have seen that poverty is concentrated in cities and, in particular, in the central cities. Empirical data show that a large proportion of criminals come from poor families. Hence, the concentration of the poor in urban areas generates a large potential supply of criminals.

How do economists approach the study of crime? While economic analysis is not particularly relevant in explaining crimes of passion and violence (for example, murder and rape), it does provide interesting insights with regard to crimes of property, such as robbery, burglary, and auto theft. More specifically, economists view crime as a subset of the negative externality problem discussed in Chapters 6 and 33. In a sense, society defines crime as specific activities which impose large external costs on others—costs which are not reimbursed. Example: You can remove a textbook from the campus bookstore either by buying or stealing it. If you *buy* the book, your action is legal; you have fully compensated the bookstore for its product. If you *steal* the book, you have broken the law. Society has enacted laws against stealing because theft imposes high uncompensated costs on others. In this case, your action reduces the bookstore's revenue and may force it to charge higher prices to cover its loss.

Why might someone engage in criminal activity such as stealing? At this point in your study of economics, you are well aware that economists assume individuals act rationally and in so doing compare the expected costs and the expected benefits of their actions. If the expected benefits (to them) exceed the expected costs (also to them), the individual undertakes this activity, be it legitimate production and consumption or some illegal pursuit which transfers external costs to others.

Most people do *not* steal things from others. Why not? The answer is that they perceive the expected cost of theft to be greater than the expected benefit. That is, the value of the stolen good is not as great as the perceived costs of the illegal activity. Costs of illegal actions are of two general types. First, there are "guilt costs," which for many people are quite high. Such individuals would not steal from others even if there were no penalties for doing so. Their moral sense of right and wrong simply would entail too great a guilt cost relative to the benefit of having the stolen good.

But society knows from experience that guilt costs alone are *not* sufficient to deter some people from stealing. Hence, society imposes a second type of cost—fines and imprisonment—on law breakers. Given these penalties, the potential criminal must estimate the expected cost of getting caught. For example, if there is a $300 fine for stealing a $40 textbook and a 10 percent chance of being caught, the expected cost of stealing the textbook is $30 ($=300 \times .10$). Someone who has guilt costs of zero will choose to steal the book; the expected benefit of $40 will exceed the expected cost of $30. On the other hand, someone having a guilt cost of, say, $20 will not steal the book. The expected benefit of $40 will not be as great as the expected cost of $50 ($=$30 of penalty cost $+ $20 of guilt cost). Note that society can reduce property crimes by nourishing guilt costs, imposing greater penalties, or taking crime prevention measures which increase the probability of being caught.

How much crime prevention should society undertake? To what extent should the bookstore in our example undertake measures to deter theft? Chapter 33's application of benefit-cost analysis to a flood-control project (Table 33-2) is relevant. Each individual, business, and unit of government must compare marginal benefits and marginal costs in determining the extent to which it is economically rational to pursue crime prevention. Should a retail store such as the campus bookstore do nothing to prevent crime? Should it install an alarm system? Should it hire a store detective? A night security guard? Should it purchase sensitized price tags to reduce shoplifting? As the store considers successively more sophisticated and more costly crime-prevention techniques, it must compare marginal benefits (reduced losses from shoplifting and robbery) with marginal costs. The rational solution for a store and for society is to seek the optimal level of crime prevention where marginal benefits equal marginal costs.

3 The short-run urban transportation problem is concerned with the most efficient use of existing transportation facilities. Although administrative problems are substantial, user charges and peak pricing are advocated by many economists. The long-run problem is concerned with the character of future investment in transportation facilities. For a variety of reasons, city planners and public officials tend to favor expanded and improved mass-transit systems.

4 Pollution is a problem of spillover or external costs. Most proposed solutions—such as legislated controls and standards, emission fees, and markets for pollution rights—seek to internalize these spillover costs to offending firms.

5 Because of the areawide character of urban problems and the unequal distribution of income and wealth between central city and suburbs, political consolidation would be very helpful in resolving many of the problems of the cities.

6 Even if political consolidation is realized, fiscal assistance in such forms as Federal revenue sharing and the shifting of fiscal responsibility for certain specific urban problems and obligations to the state or Federal governments may be necessary. The cities may reduce the harmful effects of property taxation and simultaneously obtain more revenue by shifting the relative burden of the property tax away from buildings and toward land.

TERMS AND CONCEPTS

economies of agglomeration

internal and external economies of scale

infrastructure

deglomerative forces

political fragmentation

black capitalism

user charges

peak pricing

materials balance approach

emission fees

QUESTIONS AND STUDY SUGGESTIONS

1 Explain: "To agglomerate is to economize." What, specifically, are the economies of agglomeration? Use graphic analysis to distinguish between internal and external economies of scale. What is the urban infrastructure? Discuss the demand aspects of urban growth.

2 What socioeconomic forces underlie urban sprawl? Explain in detail why the process of urban sprawl has

been to the economic and fiscal disadvantage of the central city. Of what significance is the fact that suburbs are typically separate political entities? What arguments can be made for and against political consolidation?

3 "If cities are too large to be efficient or are poorly organized, the problem can be traced in large part to a failure to charge people for all the costs they impose or to reward them fully for the benefits of their actions." Do you agree? Explain.

4 What is the nature of the urban transportation problem? Explain: "Although improved transportation has been a necessary condition for decentralization and urban sprawl, this decentralization has also created acute transportation problems."

5 What are the main causes of environmental pollution? Explain: "Clean air and water have become increasingly scarce and valuable resources precisely because they have been treated in the past as if they were free and unlimited in supply." What methods might be used to internalize spillover costs?

6 What is the role of racial discrimination in explaining the poverty of central cities? Analyze the economics of the ghetto housing market. Explain: "Urban blight—the cumulative deterioration of entire neighborhoods or areas—occurs because individual owners have little or no economic incentive to improve their property."

7 Explain: "The great density of people and businesses in the cities heightens the publicness of decisions because it is probable that the decisions of one economic unit will affect the well-being of others." Can you apply this statement to urban blight, pollution, and transportation problems?

8 "We can go far to solve the central-city housing crisis by simply changing tax policy. First, tax unused land at higher rates than land with buildings on it. Second, tax new and improved housing at low rates and dilapidated and old housing at high rates." Do you think these policies would have the indicated results? Explain.

9 "Increases in the value of land in cities are the consequence of public decisions about zoning and investment in public utilities and facilities, not the result of individual efforts by owners. Therefore, the city should recapture the unearned incomes from rising land values by taxation and use these revenues for public purposes." Do you agree?

10 Analyze the fiscal problems of the cities. What solutions do you recommend?

11 "The purpose of user charges is to confront decision makers with the external or spillover costs of their decisions and in so doing cause them to alter their decisions." Explain and illustrate this statement in terms of the urban transportation and pollution problems.

CHAPTER 37

Income distribution: inequality and poverty

The question of how income should be distributed has a long and controversial history in both economics and philosophy. Should our national income and wealth be more or less equally distributed than is now the case? Or, in terms of Chapter 5, is society making the proper response to the "For whom" question? The egalitarian debate has produced a wide spectrum of responses and positions. At one extreme we are urged to believe that greater equality is the basic prerequisite of capitalism's survival. At the other, we are warned that a "rush toward equality" will undermine the system and lead to its demise.

In this chapter we begin by surveying some basic facts concerning the distribution of income in the United States. Next, the major causes of income inequality are considered. Third, we examine the debate over income inequality and the tradeoff between equality and efficiency implied by this debate. Fourth, we will look at the poverty problem. Finally, we consider public policy; existing income-security programs are outlined and alternative approaches to welfare reform are discussed.

Income inequality: the facts

How equally—or unequally—is income distributed in the United States? How wide is the gulf between rich and poor? Has the degree of income inequality increased or lessened over time?

PERSONAL INCOME DISTRIBUTION

Average income in the United States is among the highest in the world. The average income for all families was $34,924 in 1986. But now we must envision how income is distributed around the average. Table 37-1 is instructive. At the low end of the scale we find that 12 percent of all families receive about 2 percent of total personal income. Only 6 percent of the total income went to the 22 percent of the families receiving under $15,000 per year in 1986. At the top of the income pyramid we find that 7 percent of the families received incomes of $75,000 or more per year; this group received about 21 percent of total personal income. These figures suggest *there is considerable* **income inequality** *in the United States.*

TRENDS IN INCOME INEQUALITY

We know from Chapter 21 that economic growth has raised incomes: *Absolutely,* the entire distribution of income has been moving upward over time. Has this changed the *relative* distribution of income? Incomes can move up absolutely, and the degree of inequality may or may not be affected. Table 37-2 is instructive on the relative distribution of income. In the table we divide the total number of income receivers into five numerically equal groups, or *quintiles,* and show the percentage of total personal (before-tax) income received by each in selected years. It is useful to examine the data in

TABLE 37-1 **The distribution of personal income by families, 1986**

(1) Personal income class	(2) Percentage of all families in this class	(3) Percentage of total personal income received by families in this class	(4) Percentage of all families in this class and all lower classes	(5) Percentage of income received by this class and all lower classes
Under $10,000	12	2	12	2
$10,000–$14,999	10	4	22	6
$15,000–$24,999	19	11	41	17
$25,000–$34,999	18	16	59	33
$35,000–$49,999	20	22	79	55
$50,000–$74,999	14	24	93	79
$75,000 and over	7	21	100	100
	100	100		

Source: Bureau of the Census, *Money Income of Households, Families, and Persons in the United States: 1986,* Current Population Reports, Series P-60, No. 159, 1988.

Table 37-2 over three periods: 1929–1947, 1947–1969, and 1969–1987.

The 1929–1947 period Comparison of the income distribution data for 1929 and 1947 suggests that a significant reduction in income inequality occurred between these years. Note in Table 37-2 the declining percentage of personal income going to the top quintile and the increasing percentage received by the other four quintiles during this period. Many of the forces at work during World War II undoubtedly contributed to this decline in inequality. War-born prosperity eliminated the many low incomes caused by the severe unemployment of the 1930s, brought a reduction of wage and salary differentials, boosted depressed farm incomes through

TABLE 37-2 **Percentage of total before-tax income received by each one-fifth, and by the top 5 percent, of families, selected years**

Quintile	1929	1935–1936	1947	1955	1969	1979	1987
Lowest 20 percent	12.5	4.1	5.0	4.8	5.6	5.3	4.6
Second 20 percent		9.2	11.8	12.2	12.4	11.6	10.8
Third 20 percent	13.8	14.1	17.0	17.7	17.7	17.5	16.9
Fourth 20 percent	19.3	20.9	23.1	23.7	23.7	24.1	24.1
Highest 20 percent	54.4	51.7	43.0	41.6	40.6	41.6	43.7
Total	100.0	100.0	100.0	100.0	100.0	100.0	100.0
Top 5 percent	30.0	26.5	17.2	16.8	15.6	15.7	16.9

Source: U.S. Bureau of the Census data. Details may not add up to totals because of rounding.

sharp increases in farm prices, temporarily diminished discrimination in employment, was accompanied by a decline in property incomes as a share of the national income, and so forth.

The 1947–1969 period Many of the forces making for greater equality during World War II ceased to be of great importance after the war. During the period between 1947 and 1969, the quintile distribution continued its previous trend toward less inequality, but at a far slower pace. Observe that the income share of the lowest income group rose by .6 of a percentage point between 1947 and 1969, while that of the wealthiest quintile fell by 2.4 percentage points.

The 1969–1987 period The distribution of income by quintiles has become more unequal since 1969. In 1987 the lowest 20 percent of families received only 4.6 percent of the total before-tax income, compared to 5.6 percent in 1969. Meanwhile, the income share received by the highest 20 percent rose from 40.6 percent to 43.7 percent. The reasons for this latest trend in income inequality are not as yet fully understood. The most often cited explanations are the many inexperienced baby-boom workers who have entered the labor force and the increase in the number of families headed by low-wage-earning females.

Recapitulation and conclusion: Income inequality fell significantly between 1929 and 1947. Since then, it has moved slightly toward increased equality and more recently toward less equality. But, as a direct comparison of the data for 1947 and 1987 in Table 37-2 reveals, the relative distribution in 1987 was very similar to what it was forty years earlier. *It is fair to generalize that the distribution of income has been relatively stable since World War II.*

THE LORENZ CURVE

The degree of income inequality can be envisioned through a **Lorenz curve** as shown in Figure 37-1. Here we *cumulate* the "percent of families" on the horizontal axis and the "percent of income" on the vertical axis. The theoretical possibility of a com-

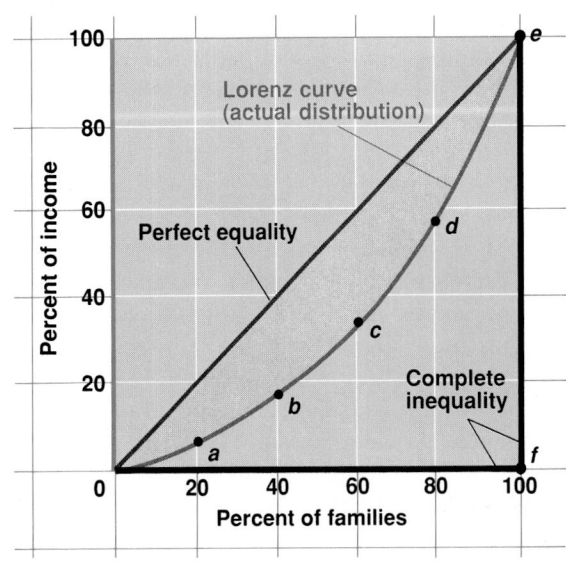

FIGURE 37-1

The Lorenz curve

The Lorenz curve is a convenient means of visualizing the degree of income inequality. Specifically, the orange area between the line of perfect equality and the Lorenz curve reflects the degree of income inequality.

pletely equal distribution of income is represented by a diagonal line because such a line indicates that any given percentage of families receives that same percentage of income. That is, if 20 percent of all families receive 20 percent of total income, 40 percent receive 40 percent, 60 percent receive 60 percent, and so on, all these points will fall on the diagonal line.

By plotting the 1987 data from Table 37-2 we locate the Lorenz curve to visualize the actual distribution of income. We find that the bottom 20 percent of all families received about 4.6 percent of the income as shown by point *a*; the bottom 40 percent received 15.4 percent (= 4.6 + 10.8) as shown by point *b*; and so forth. The orange area, determined by the extent to which the resulting Lorenz curve sags away from the line of perfect equality, indicates the degree of income inequality. The larger this area or gap, the greater the degree of income inequality. If the actual income distribution were perfectly equal, the Lorenz curve and the diagonal would coincide and the gap would disappear. At the opposite extreme is the situation of complete inequality where 1 percent of the families have 100 percent of the income and the rest have none. In this case the Lorenz curve would coincide with the horizontal and right vertical axes of the graph, forming a right angle at point *f* as indicated by the heavy black lines. This extreme degree of inequality would be indicated by the entire area southeast of the diagonal.

The Lorenz curve can be used to contrast the distribution of income at different points in time, among different groups (for example, blacks and whites), before and after taxes and transfer payments are taken into account, or among different countries. As previously observed, the data in Table 37-2 tells us that the Lorenz curve shifted slightly toward the diagonal between 1947 and 1969 and then back away from the diagonal between 1969 and 1987. Comparisons with other nations suggest that the distribution of income in the United States is somewhat less equal than in most other industrially advanced countries.

Alternative interpretations

There has been substantial controversy in recent years as to whether the Bureau of Census data of Tables 37-1 and 37-2 provide an accurate portrayal of the degree of income inequality. Some scholars feel that the yearly census figures are inadequate. To understand the nature of these alleged deficiencies, we must first reiterate the nature of these data. The census figures of Tables 37-1 and 37-2 show the distribution of *nominal* income and include not only wages, salaries, dividends, and interest, but also all *cash transfer payments* such as social security and unemployment compensation benefits. The data are *before taxes* in that they do not exclude personal income and payroll (social security) taxes which are levied directly upon income receivers.

Let us consider two major criticisms of the census data. First, the income concept employed is too narrow. Second, the income accounting period of one year is too short.

BROADENED INCOME CONCEPT

Edgar K. Browning[1] has made a number of adjustments in the Census Bureau data which result in a quite different picture of income distribution. Among other adjustments, Browning estimates the market value and distribution of *in-kind transfers,* that is, transfers of goods and services which take place under such programs as Medicare, Medicaid, housing subsidies, and food stamps. Similarly, he takes into account the value and distribution of governmentally provided education. Next, he adds capital gains such as increases in the value of stocks, bonds, and real estate. Finally, he subtracts Federal personal income taxes and payroll taxes. The picture which emerges from these adjustments not only is a much more equal distribution of income in each year, but also indicates a trend toward greater equality over time. The movement toward greater equality is primarily a reflection of the rapid growth of in-kind transfers in the past twenty years or so.

It should be noted that Browning has been criticized for overadjusting the census data and thereby concluding that there is greater income equality than actually exists. Indeed, our basic point is that income distribution data are subject to a variety of interpretations. In this regard, a recent study by the Census Bureau has confirmed that a broader definition of income translates into reduced inequality in the distribution of income. The Census Bureau has found, however, that its broader income concept tightens the "official" income distribution by only 4 percent.[2]

LIFETIME INCOME

Another objection to the census data is that they portray the distribution of income in a single year

[1] Edgar K. Browning, "The Trend Toward Equality in the Distribution of Net Income," *Southern Economic Journal,* July 1976, pp. 912–923; and Browning, "How Much More Equality Can We Afford?" *The Public Interest,* Spring 1976, pp. 90–110.

[2] Bureau of the Census, *Measuring the Effect of Benefits and Taxes on Income and Poverty: 1986,* Current Population Report, Series P-60, No. 164-RD-1, 1988, p. 7.

and thereby conceal the possibility that the *lifetime earnings* of families might be more equal. Suppose Ben earns $1000 in year 1 and $100,000 in year 2, while Holly earns $100,000 in year 1 and only $1000 in year 2. Do we have income inequality? The answer depends upon the period of measurement. Annual data would reveal great income inequality; but for the two-year period we have complete equality. This is important because there is some evidence to suggest that there is a considerable amount of "churning around" in the distribution of income over time. In fact, most income receivers follow an age-earnings profile whereby their income starts at relatively low levels, reaches a peak during middle age, and then declines. A glance back at Figure 30-9 reveals this general pattern. It follows that, even if everyone received the same stream of income over his or her lifetime, there would still be considerable income inequality in any given year because of age differences. In any year the young and old would receive low incomes while the middle-aged received high incomes. This would occur despite complete equality of lifetime incomes. Morton Paglin[3] has attempted to adjust the quintile data of Table 37-2 for age differences. He found that (1) there is greater income equality when the time factor is taken into account and (2) there was a trend toward greater income equality during the period studied: 1947–1972. The latter conclusion is attributed to the expansion of postsecondary education.

Government and redistribution

You will recall from Chapter 6 that one of the basic functions of government is to redistribute income. As Figure 37-2 and the accompanying table reveal, the distribution of household income *before* taxes and transfers are taken into account is substantially less equal than is the distribution *after* taxes and transfers are included.[4] *Government's tax system and transfer programs do reduce significantly the degree of inequality in the distribution of income.*

[3] Morton Paglin, "The Measurement and Trend of Inequality: A Basic Revision," *American Economic Review*, September 1975, pp. 598–609.

Most of the reduction in income inequality—roughly 80 percent of it—is attributable to transfer payments. Recall from Chapter 8 that our tax system (Federal, state, and local taxes combined) is not highly progressive and, hence, the before-tax and after-tax distributions of income do not differ greatly. But transfers are vital in contributing to greater income equality. More specifically, government transfer payments account for over 75 percent of the income of the lowest quintile and have clearly been the most important means of alleviating poverty in the United States.

Income inequality: causes

Why does the United States have the degree of income inequality evidenced in Tables 37-1 and 37-2? In general, we note that the market system is an impersonal mechanism. It has no conscience, and it does not cater to any set of ethical standards concerning what is an "equitable," or "just," distribution of income. In fact, the basically individualistic environment of the capitalist economy is more than permissive of a high degree of income inequality. Some of the more specific factors contributing to income inequality include:

I **Ability differences** People have different mental, physical, and aesthetic talents. Some individuals have had the good fortune to inherit the exceptional mental qualities essential to entering the relatively high-paying fields of medicine, dentistry, and law. Others, rated as "dull normals" or "mentally retarded," are assigned to the most menial and low-paying occupations or are incapable of earning income at all. Some are blessed with the physical capacity and coordination to become

[4] The "before" data in this table differ from the data of Table 37-2 because the latter includes cash transfers. Also, the data in Table 37-2 are for families (a group of two persons or more related by birth, marriage, or adoption and residing together), whereas the data in Figure 37-2 are for all households (one or more persons occupying a housing unit). Finally, the data in Figure 37-2 are based on a broader concept of income than the data in Table 37-2.

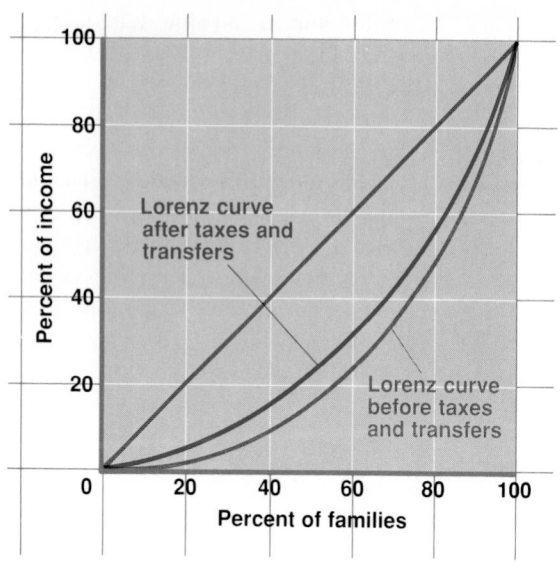

	Percent of income received, 1986	
Quintile	Before taxes and transfers	After taxes and transfers
Lowest 20 percent	1.0	4.7
Second 20 percent	7.6	10.6
Third 20 percent	15.0	16.1
Fourth 20 percent	24.1	23.0
Highest 20 percent	52.4	45.7

Source: Bureau of the Census, *Measuring the Effect of Benefits and Taxes on Income and Poverty: 1986*, Current Population Report, Series P-60, No. 164-RD-1, 1988, p. 5. The data include all money income from private sources, including realized capital gains and employer-provided health insurance. The "after taxes and transfers" data include the value of noncash transfers as well as cash transfers.

FIGURE 37-2

The impact of government taxes and transfers upon income inequality

The distribution of personal income is significantly more equal after taxes and transfer payments are taken into account. Transfers account for most of the lessening of inequality and provide most of the income received by the lowest quintile of families.

highly paid professional athletes. A few have the aesthetic qualities prerequisite to becoming great artists or musicians. In brief, native talents put some individuals in a position to make contributions to total output which command very high incomes. Others are in much less fortunate circumstances.

2 Education and training In Chapter 30 we discussed investment in human capital, that is, expenditures on education and training. The point to be made here is that individuals differ significantly in the amounts of education and training they have obtained and, hence, in their capacities to earn income. In part, these differences are a matter of voluntary choice. Smith chooses to enter the labor force upon high school graduation, while Jones decides to attend college. On the other hand, such differences may be involuntary: Smith's family may simply be unable to finance a college education.

3 Job tastes and risks Incomes differ because of differences in "job tastes." Individuals who are will-

ing to take arduous, unpleasant jobs—for example, underground mining and garbage collecting—and to work long hours with great intensity will tend to earn more. Some individuals boost their incomes by "moonlighting," that is, by holding two jobs. Individuals also differ in their willingness to assume risk. We refer here not only to the steeplejack, but to entrepreneurial risk. Though most fail, the fortunate few who gamble successfully on the introduction of a new product or service may realize very substantial incomes.

4 Property ownership The ownership of property resources, and hence the receipt of property incomes, is very unequal. The vast majority of households own little or no property resources, while the remaining few supply very great quantities of machinery, real estate, farmland, and so forth. A government study shows that in 1983 the top 10 percent of income receivers in the United States (those with annual incomes of $50,000 or more) owned 72 percent of all stocks, 86 percent of all tax-free bonds, 70 percent of all taxable bonds, and 50 percent of all real estate. The top 2 percent of American income receivers (with annual incomes of $100,000 or more) owned 50 percent of all stocks, 71 percent of all tax-free bonds, 39 percent of all taxable bonds, and 20 percent of all real estate.[5] Asset holdings are much more highly concentrated than are family incomes. Basically, property incomes account for the position of those households at the very pinnacle of the income pyramid. The right of inheritance and the fact that "wealth begets wealth" reinforce the role played by unequal ownership of property resources in determining income inequality.

5 Market power Ability to "rig the market" on one's own behalf is undoubtedly a major factor in accounting for income inequality. Certain unions and professional groups have adopted policies which limit the supplies of their productive services, thereby boosting the incomes of those "on the inside." Legislation which provides for occupational licensing for barbers, beauticians, taxi drivers, and so forth, can also be a basis for exerting market power in favor of the licensed group. The same holds true in the product market; profit receivers in particular stand to benefit when their firm develops some degree of monopoly power.

6 Luck, connections, misfortune, and discrimination There are other important forces which play a part in explaining income inequality. Luck, chance, and "being in the right place at the right time" have all caused individuals to stumble into fortunes. Discovering oil on a run-down farm or meeting the right press agent have accounted for some high incomes. Nor can personal contacts and political influence be discounted as means of attaining the higher income brackets. On the other hand, a host of economic misfortunes in such forms as prolonged illness, serious accident, death of the family breadwinner, and unemployment may plunge a family into relative poverty. The burden of such misfortunes is borne very unevenly by the population and hence contributes to the degree of income inequality. Discrimination is such a significant

cause of inequality that we treat it in some detail in Chapter 38.

Equality versus efficiency

The critical policy issue concerning income inequality is: What is the optimal amount? While there is no generally accepted answer to this question, much can be learned by exploring the cases for and against greater equality.

THE CASE FOR EQUALITY: MAXIMIZING UTILITY

The basic argument in the case for an equal distribution of income is that income equality is necessary if consumer satisfaction or utility is to be maximized. The rationale for this argument can be seen in terms of Figure 37-3 where it is assumed that the money incomes of two individuals, Anderson and Brooks, are subject to diminishing marginal utility (Chapter 23). In any time period income receivers spend the first dollars received on those products which they value most, that is, on products whose marginal utility is high. As their most pressing wants become satisfied, consumers then will spend additional dollars of income on less important, lower marginal utility, goods. The identical diminishing "marginal utility from income" curves reflect the assumption that Anderson and Brooks have the same capacity to derive utility from income.

Now suppose there is, say, $10,000 worth of income (output) to be distributed between Anderson and Brooks. What is the best or optimal distribution? The answer: An equal distribution which causes the marginal utility of the last dollar to be the same for both persons. We can prove this by demonstrating that, for an initially unequal distribution of income, the combined total utility of two individuals can be increased by moving toward equality. For example, suppose that initially the $10,000 of income is distributed unequally so that Anderson gets only $2500 and Brooks receives $7500. We observe that the marginal utility from the last dollar received by Anderson is high ($0a$) and the marginal utility from Brooks' last dollar of

[5] "Survey of Consumer Finances, 1983," *Federal Reserve Bulletin*, September 1984, pp. 679–692. Also see "Financial Characteristics of High-Income Families," *Federal Reserve Bulletin*, March 1986, pp. 163–177.

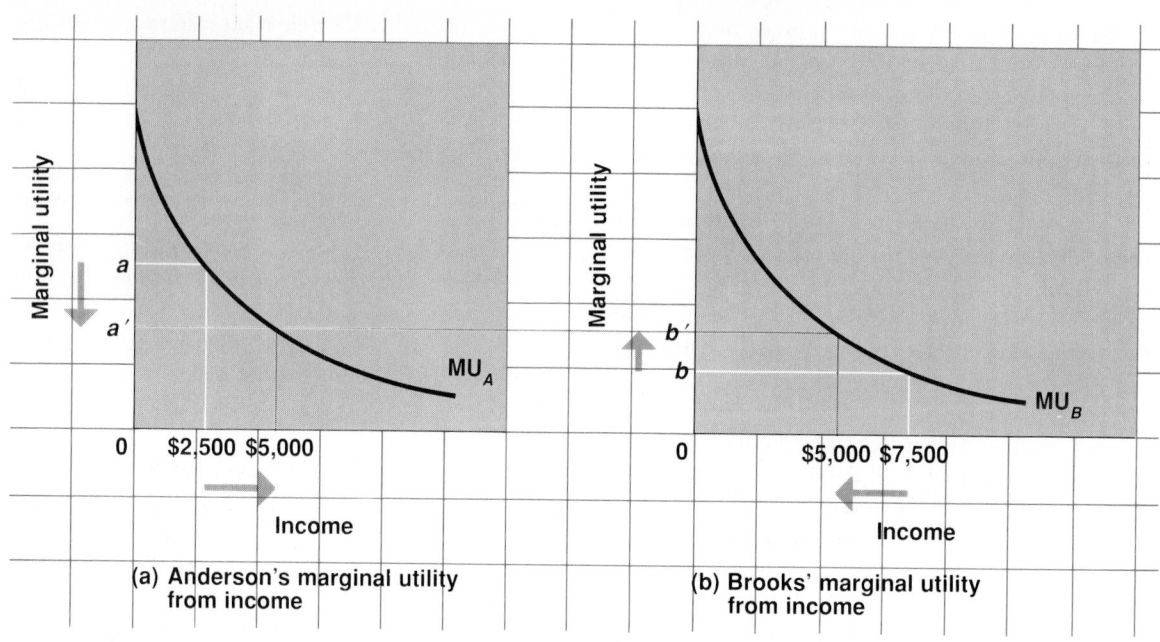

FIGURE 37-3

The utility-maximizing distribution of a given income

Proponents of income equality argue that, given identical "marginal utility from income" curves, Anderson and Brooks will maximize their combined utility when any given income (say, $10,000) is equally distributed. If income is unequally distributed ($2500 to Anderson and $7500 to Brooks), the marginal utility derived from the last dollar will be greater for Anderson (0*a*) than for Brooks (0*b*) and, hence, a redistribution toward equality will result in a net increase in total utility. When equality is achieved, the marginal utility derived from the last dollar of income will be equal for both consumers (0*a'* = 0*b'*) and, therefore, there is no further redistribution of income which will increase total utility.

income is low (0*b*). Clearly the redistribution of a dollar's worth of income from Brooks to Anderson—that is, toward greater equality—would increase (by 0*a* − 0*b*) the combined total utility of the two consumers. Anderson's utility gain exceeds Brooks' loss. This will continue to be the case until income is equally distributed with each person receiving $5000. At this point the marginal utility of the last dollar is identical for Anderson and Brooks (0*a'* = 0*b'*) and, hence, further redistribution cannot increase total utility.

THE CASE FOR INEQUALITY: INCENTIVES AND EFFICIENCY

Although the logic of the argument for equality is impeccable, critics attack its fundamental assumption that there exists some fixed amount of income

to be distributed.[6] Critics of income equality argue that *the way in which income is distributed is an important determinant of the amount of income produced and available for distribution.* Suppose in Figure 37-3 that Anderson earns $2500 and Brooks earns $7500. In moving toward equality, society (government) must *tax* away some of Brooks' income and *transfer* it to Anderson. This tax-transfer process will diminish the income rewards of high-

[6] Incidentally, the case for income equality does *not* rest upon the assumption of identical "marginal utility from income" curves. If these curves are different for Anderson and Brooks, it can be argued on probability grounds that an equal distribution of income is most likely to maximize consumer satisfactions. See Abba Lerner, *The Economics of Control* (New York: The Macmillan Company, 1944), chap. 3.

income Brooks and raise the income rewards of low-income Anderson and in so doing reduce the incentives of both to *earn* high incomes. Why should Brooks work hard, save and invest, or undertake entrepreneurial risks, when the rewards from such activities will be reduced by taxation? And why should Anderson be motivated to increase his income through market activities when government stands ready to transfer income to him? In the extreme, argue the defenders of income inequality, imagine a situation in which government levies a 100 percent tax on income and distributes the tax revenue equally to its citizenry. Why work hard? Indeed, why work at all? Why assume business risks? Why save—that is, forgo current consumption—in order to invest? The economic incentives to "get ahead" will have been removed and we can expect the productive efficiency of the economy—and hence the amount of income to be distributed—to diminish. The way the income pie is distributed affects the size of that pie! *The basic argument for income inequality is that it is essential to maintain incentives to produce output and income.*

THE EQUALITY–EFFICIENCY TRADEOFF[7]

The essence of the income (in)equality debate is that there exists a fundamental **tradeoff between equality and efficiency.**

The contrasts among American families in living standards and in material wealth reflect a system of rewards and penalties that is intended to encourage effort and channel it into socially productive activity. To the extent that the system succeeds, it generates an efficient economy. But that pursuit of efficiency necessarily creates inequalities. And hence society faces a tradeoff between equality and efficiency.[8]

Thus the problem for a society inclined toward egalitarianism is how to achieve a given redistribution of income in such a way as to minimize the

adverse effects upon economic efficiency. Consider this *leaky-bucket analogy.* Assume society agrees to shift income from the rich to the poor. But the money must be transferred from affluent to indigent in a leaky bucket. How much leakage will society accept and continue to endorse the redistribution? In other words, if cutting the income pie in more equal slices tends to shrink the pie, what amount of shrinkage will society tolerate? Is a loss of one cent on each redistributed dollar acceptable? Five cents? Twenty-five cents? Fifty cents? This is clearly a critical, value-laden question which will permeate future political debates over extensions and contractions of our income-maintenance programs.

Fueling this debate over the equality–efficiency tradeoff are relatively recent studies which suggest that the loss from the redistribution bucket may be far higher than generally thought.

Edgar Browning and William Johnson . . . concluded that the upper-income groups bearing the costs of the taxes would sacrifice $350 for every $100 that the poor gained—a net efficiency loss of $250. In Arthur Okun's terms, the leaks in the redistribution bucket are enormous—starting out with a bucket of $350 raised from the nonpoor, $250 is lost on the way to delivering it to the poor. For several reasons, critics of this study have found the estimate to be substantially too high. However, even if cut in half, this loss would be troublesome. Would our society be willing to accept a loss of economic efficiency of $125—or even $100—in order to equalize the distribution of income be transferring $100 to the poor? The answer is by no means clear.[9]

The dismal economics of poverty

Many people are less concerned with the larger question of income distribution than they are with the more specific issue of income inadequacy. Therefore, armed with some background informa-

[7] This section is based directly upon Arthur M. Okun, *Equality and Efficiency: The Big Tradeoff* (Washington, D.C.: The Brookings Institution, 1975).

[8] Ibid., p. 1.

[9] Robert H. Haveman, "New Policy for the New Poverty," *Challenge,* September/October 1988, p. 32.

tion on income inequality, let us now turn to the poverty problem. How extensive is poverty in the United States? What are the characteristics of the poor? And what is the best strategy to take to lessen poverty?

DEFINING POVERTY

Poverty does not lend itself to precise definition. But, as a broad generalization, we might say that a family lives in poverty when its basic needs exceed its available means of satisfying them. A family's needs have many determinants: its size, its health, the ages of its members, and so forth. Its means include currently earned income, transfer payments, past savings, property owned, and so on. The definitions of poverty accepted by concerned government agencies are based on family size. Hence, in 1987 an unattached individual receiving less than $5778 per year was living in poverty. For a family of four the poverty line was $11,611. For a family of six, it was $15,509. Applying these definitions to income data for the United States, it is found that *about 13.5 percent of the nation—about 33 million people—lives in poverty.*

WHO ARE THE POOR?

Who are these 33 million or so individuals who live in poverty? Unfortunately for purposes of public policy, the poor are heterogeneous; they can be found in all geographic regions, they are whites and nonwhites, they include large numbers of both rural and urban people, they are both old and young. Yet, as Table 37-3 clearly indicates, poverty is far from randomly distributed. While the total poverty rate for the entire population was 13.5 percent, blacks and Hispanics bore a disproportionate share as compared to whites. The incidence of poverty is extremely high among female-headed families and it is particularly alarming that a full one-fifth of all children under 18 years of age live in poverty. The poverty rate among black children was 46 percent in 1987. On the other hand, thanks to a quite generous social security system, the incidence of poverty among the elderly is less than that for the population as a whole.

TABLE 37-3 **The distribution of poverty, 1987**

Population group	Percent in poverty
Total population	13.5
Whites	10.5
Blacks	33.1
Hispanics	28.2
Families headed by women	34.3
Children under 18	20.0
Elderly (65 or older)	12.2

Source: Bureau of the Census, *Money Income and Poverty Status in the United States: 1987,* Current Population Reports, series P-60, no. 161, 1988.

POVERTY TRENDS

Not revealed in Table 37-3 is the fact that the percentage of the population living in poverty was higher in 1987 than it was a decade or so ago. This disturbing reality is revealed in Figure 37-4, which traces out the percentage of people in poverty—or the **poverty rate**—for each year since 1960. Observe that the poverty rate fell significantly between 1960 and 1968, remained relatively unchanged from 1969–1978, and then increased sharply during the early 1980s. This recent increase in the poverty rate resulted from sluggish economic growth, high unemployment rates, and lower real levels of transfer payments. Beginning in 1984, the poverty rate began a gradual decline as the economy vigorously expanded toward full employment. As has been observed, the poverty rate in 1987 was a relatively high 13.5 percent.

Qualification: Although the income levels used to compute the poverty rates shown in Figure 37-4 include cash transfer payments, they do *not* include the monetary value of such noncash transfers as medical care, housing assistance, and food stamps which the poor receive. These noncash transfers are similar to income in that they enable the poor to purchase needed goods and services. Recently, the Census Bureau began estimating an alternative poverty rate which includes the value of noncash transfers. The poverty rate for 1987 was 8.5 percent

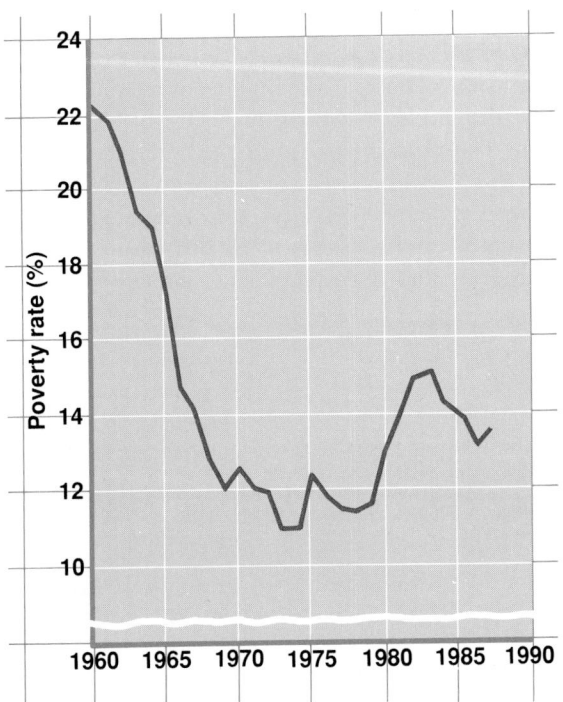

FIGURE 37-4

The U.S. poverty rate, 1960–1987

The percentage of the population living in poverty fell dramatically between 1960 and 1968, remained relatively constant for the next decade, and then climbed between 1978 and 1983. Beginning in 1984, the poverty rate once again began to decline but remained higher in 1987 than it was in the 1970s.

using this expanded definition of income. But, irrespective of definitions of income, the basic point remains: poverty continues to be a persistent and difficult problem.

THE "INVISIBLE" POOR

These facts and figures on the extent and character of poverty may be a bit difficult to accept. After all, ours is presumably the affluent society. How does one square the depressing statistics on poverty with everyday observations of abundance? The answer lies in good measure in the fact that much American poverty is hidden; it is largely invisible. There

are three major reasons for this invisibility. First, a sizable proportion of the people in the poverty pool change from year to year. Research has shown that as many as one-half of those in poverty are poor for only one or two years before successfully climbing out of poverty.[10] Hence, many of these people are not visible to us as being permanently downtrodden and needy. Second, the "permanently poor" are increasingly isolated in large cities, because the middle and upper classes have migrated away from them to suburbia. Poverty persists in the slums and ghettos, and is not readily visible from the freeway or commuter train. Similarly, rural poverty and the chronically depressed areas of Appalachia, the South, and the Southwest are also off the beaten path. Third, and perhaps most important,

The poor are politically invisible. . . . [They] do not, by far and large, belong to unions, to fraternal organizations, or to political parties. They are without lobbies of their own; they put forward no legislative program. As a group they are atomized. They have no face; they have no voice.[11]

Indeed, the American poor have been labeled "the world's least revolutionary proletariat."

DISCRIMINATION AND POVERTY

Noting that blacks, Hispanics, and women bear a disproportionately large burden of poverty, it is important to recognize that discrimination is an important factor in understanding poverty. We will defer discussion of discrimination to Chapter 38, which examines labor market issues. But as a glance ahead at Table 38-1 will reveal, there is casual evidence which suggests the presence of racial discrimination. Quite similar data imply discrimination on the basis of gender. It is generally acknowledged that programs which successfully reduce discrimination also reduce poverty.

[10] Greg J. Duncan, *Years of Poverty, Years of Plenty* (Ann Arbor, Mich.: University of Michigan Press, 1984).

[11] Michael Harrington, *The Other America: Poverty in the United States,* rev. ed. (New York: The Macmillan Company, 1970), p. 14.

The income maintenance system

The existence of a wide variety of income-maintenance programs (Table 37-4) is evidence that the alleviation of poverty has been accepted as a legitimate goal of public policy. Despite cutbacks in many programs in recent years, income-mainte- nance programs involve very substantial monetary outlays and large numbers of beneficiaries.

Basically, our income-maintenance system consists of two kinds of programs. On the one hand, *social insurance programs* partially replace earnings lost due to retirement and temporary unemployment. "Social security" (technically Old Age, Survivors, and Disability Health Insurance or OASDHI) and unemployment compensation, the

TABLE 37-4 **Characteristics of major income-maintenance programs**

Program	Basis of eligibility	Source of funds	Form of aid	Fiscal 1987 Expenditures* (billions of dollars)	Beneficiaries (millions)
Social Insurance Programs					
Old Age, Survivors, and Disability Health Insurance (OASDHI)	Age, disability, or death of parent or spouse; individual earnings	Federal payroll taxes on employers and employees	Cash	$204	38
Medicare	Age or disability	Federal payroll tax on employers and employees	Subsidized health insurance	80	32
Unemployment compensation	Unemployment	State and Federal payroll taxes on employers	Cash	7	14
Public Assistance Programs					
Supplemental Security Income (SSI)	Age or disability; income	Federal revenues	Cash	13	4
Aid to Families with Dependent Children (AFDC)	Certain families with children; income	Federal-state-local revenues	Cash and services	16	11
Food stamps	Income	Federal revenues	Vouchers	11	18
Medicaid	Persons eligible for AFDC or SSI and medically indigent	Federal-state-local revenues	Subsidized medical services	45	23

*Expenditures by Federal, state, and local governments; excludes administrative expenses.

Source: *Statistical Abstract of the United States, 1989.*

main social insurance programs, are financed out of earmarked payroll taxes. Benefits are viewed as earned rights and do not carry the stigma of public charity. On the other hand, *public assistance,* or *welfare, programs* provide benefits for those who are unable to earn income because of permanent handicaps or dependent children. These programs are financed out of general tax revenues and are regarded as public charity. Individuals and families must demonstrate low incomes in order to qualify for aid.

Total spending for income maintenance has expanded from about 4 percent of GNP in 1940 to about 18 percent of GNP currently. The Federal government finances virtually all the social insurance programs and about two-thirds of the welfare program expenditures.

OASDHI AND MEDICARE

OASDHI—Old Age, Survivors, and Disability Health Insurance—is essentially a gigantic social insurance program financed by compulsory payroll taxes levied upon both employers and employees. Generically known as "social security," the program is designed to replace earnings lost because of a worker's retirement, disability, or death. A payroll tax of 7.51 percent is levied on both worker and employer and applies to the first $48,000 of wage income. Workers may retire at 65 with full benefits or at 62 with reduced benefits. When the worker dies, benefits accrue to the survivors. Special provisions provide benefits for disabled workers. Currently, social insurance covers over 90 percent of all employed persons in the United States. In 1987 some 38 million people were receiving OASDHI checks averaging about $513 per month. **Medicare** was appended to OASDHI in 1965. The hospital insurance it provides for the elderly and disabled is financed out of the payroll tax. Medicare also makes available a low-cost voluntary insurance program which helps pay doctor fees.

UNEMPLOYMENT COMPENSATION

All fifty states sponsor unemployment insurance programs. **Unemployment compensation** is fi-

nanced by a $3\frac{1}{2}$ percent tax which employers pay on average on the first $7000 of earnings of each covered worker. Any insured worker who becomes unemployed can, after a short waiting period (usually a week), become eligible for benefit payments. Almost 90 percent of all civilian workers are covered by the program. Size of payments and the number of weeks they may be received vary considerably from state to state. Generally speaking, benefits approximate one-half of a worker's after-tax wages up to a certain maximum payment. Benefits averaged $140 weekly in 1987. Obviously, the number of beneficiaries and the level of total disbursements vary greatly over the business cycle. It is to be recalled that unemployment compensation benefits are one of our important built-in stabilizers.

THE WELFARE PROGRAMS

Many needy persons who do not qualify for social insurance programs are assisted through other programs. Beginning in 1972 Federal grants to states for public assistance to the aged, the blind, and the disabled were terminated and a new Federally financed and administered **Supplemental Security Income (SSI) program** was created. The purpose of SSI is to establish a uniform, nationwide minimum income for these three categories of people who are unable to work. Over half the states provide additional income supplements to the aged, blind, and disabled.

The **Aid to Families with Dependent Children (AFDC) program** is state-administered, but is partly financed with Federal grants. The purpose is to provide aid to families in which dependent children do not have the financial support of a parent, usually the father, because of death, disability, divorce, or desertion.

The **food stamp program** is designed to provide all low-income Americans with a "nutritionally adequate diet." Under the program eligible households receive monthly allotments of coupons which are redeemable for food. The amount of food stamps received varies inversely with a family's earned income.

Medicaid helps finance medical expenses of individuals participating in both the SSI and the AFDC programs.

"THE WELFARE MESS"

There can be no doubt that the income maintainence system—not to mention local relief, housing subsidies, minimum-wage legislation, agricultural subsidies, veterans' benefits, private transfers through charities, pensions, supplementary unemployment benefits, and so forth—provides important means of alleviating poverty. On the other hand, the system has been subject to a wide variety of criticisms in recent years.

1 Administrative inefficiencies Critics charge that the willy-nilly growth of our welfare programs has created a clumsy and inefficient system, characterized by red tape and dependent upon a huge bureaucracy for its administration. Administrative costs account for relatively large portions of the total budget of many programs.

The amount necessary to lift every man, woman, and child in America above the poverty line has been calculated, and it is *one-third* of what is in fact spent on poverty programs. Clearly, much of the transfer ends up in the pockets of highly paid administrators, consultants, and staff as well as higher income recipients of benefits from programs advertised as anti-poverty efforts.[12]

2 Inequities Serious inequities arise in welfare programs in that people with similar needs may be treated much differently.

Benefit levels vary widely among States and among different demographic and family groups. Geographic differentials arise primarily because benefits under the two major public assistance programs—AFDC and Medicaid—are essentially controlled by the States. As a result, sharp disparities in benefit levels exist between the poorer, rural States and the wealthier, more urban areas. . . . [13]

Hence, a family in New York City might receive welfare benefits two times as great as the same family in Mississippi. Furthermore, control of the system is fragmented and some low-income families "fall between the slats" while other families collect benefits to which they are not entitled.

3 Work incentives A major criticism is that most of our income-maintenance programs impair incentives to work. This is the case because all welfare programs are constructed so that a dollar's worth of earned income yields less than a dollar of net income. As earned income increases, program benefits are reduced. An individual or family participating in several welfare programs may find that, when the loss of program benefits and the effect of payroll taxes on earnings are taken into account, the individual or family is absolutely worse off by working. In effect, the marginal tax rate on earned income exceeds 100 percent!

There are other criticisms. Noncash transfers interfere with freedom of consumer choice. Public assistance programs sap initiative and encourage dependency. AFDC regulations in some states promote family breakup by encouraging unemployed fathers to abandon their families so that the spouse and children can qualify for benefits. AFDC benefits subsidize birth outside of marriage; nearly one-half of the mothers in the AFDC program have illegitimate children. Various welfare programs foster social divisiveness between workers and welfare recipients. For example, working mothers with small children may wonder out loud why poor mothers should not also work for their money.

Reform proposals

Emerging from this array of criticism have been calls to reform the public assistance system. Although reform proposals have taken numerous forms, two broad approaches have dominated: negative income tax schemes and "workfare" plans.

NEGATIVE INCOME TAX

One contention is that the entire patchwork of existing welfare programs should be replaced by a **negative income tax** (NIT). The term NIT sug-

---

[12] Thomas Sowell, *Markets and Minorities* (New York: Basic Books, Inc., Publishers, 1981), p. 122.

[13] *Economic Report of the President, 1978,* pp. 225–226.

gests that, just as the present (positive) income tax calls for families to "subsidize" the government through taxes when their incomes rise *above* a certain level, the government should subsidize households with NIT payments when household incomes fall *below* a certain level.

Comparing plans Let us examine the two critical elements of any NIT plan. First, a NIT plan specifies a **guaranteed annual income** below which family incomes would not be allowed to fall. Second, the plan embodies a **benefit-loss rate** which indicates the rate at which subsidy benefits are reduced or "lost" as a consequence of earned income. Consider Plan One of the three illustrative plans shown in Table 37-5. In Plan One the guaranteed annual income is assumed to be $8000 and the benefit-loss rate is 50 percent. Hence, if the family earns no income, it will receive a NIT subsidy of $8000. If it earns $4000, it will lose $2000 ($4000 of earnings *times* the 50 percent benefit-loss rate) of subsidy benefits and total income will be $10,000 (= $4000 of earnings *plus* $6000 of subsidy). If $8000 is earned, the subsidy will fall to $4000, and so on. Note that at $16,000 the NIT subsidy becomes zero. The level of earned income at which

the subsidy disappears and at which normal (positive) income taxes apply to further increases in earned income is called the **break-even income.**

But one might criticize Plan One on the grounds that a 50 percent benefit-loss rate is too high and therefore does not provide sufficient incentives to work. Hence, in Plan Two the $8000 guaranteed income is retained, but the benefit-loss rate is reduced to 25 percent. We observe, however, that the break-even level of income increases to $32,000 and many more families would now qualify for NIT subsidies. Furthermore, a family with any given earned income will now receive a larger NIT subsidy. For both of these reasons, a reduction of the benefit-loss rate to enhance work incentives will raise the cost of a NIT plan.

Examining Plans One and Two, still another critic might argue that the guaranteed annual income is too low in that it does not get families out of poverty. Plan Three raises the guaranteed annual income to $12,000 and retains the 50 percent benefit-loss rate of Plan One. While Plan Three obviously does a better job of raising the incomes of the poor, it too yields a higher break-even income than Plan One and would therefore be more costly. Furthermore, if the $12,000 income guarantee of Plan

TABLE 37-5 **The negative income tax: three plans (*hypothetical data for a family of four*)**

Plan One ($8,000 guaranteed income and 50% benefit-loss rate)			Plan Two ($8,000 guaranteed income and 25% benefit-loss rate)			Plan Three ($12,000 guaranteed income and 50% benefit-loss rate)		
Earned income	NIT subsidy	Total income	Earned income	NIT subsidy	Total income	Earned income	NIT subsidy	Total income
$ 0	$8,000	$ 8,000	$ 0	$8,000	$ 8,000	$ 0	$12,000	$12,000
4,000	6,000	10,000	8,000	6,000	14,000	8,000	8,000	16,000
8,000	4,000	12,000	16,000	4,000	20,000	16,000	4,000	20,000
12,000	2,000	14,000	24,000	2,000	26,000	24,000*	0	24,000
16,000*	0	16,000	32,000*	0	32,000			

*Indicates break-even income. Determined by dividing the guaranteed income by the benefit-loss rate.

Three were coupled with Plan Two's 25 percent benefit-loss rate to strengthen work incentives, the break-even income level would shoot up to $48,000 and add even more to NIT costs.[14]

Goals and conflicts The point to be derived by comparing these three plans is that there are conflicts or tradeoffs among the goals of an "ideal" income-maintenance plan. First, a plan should be effective in getting families out of poverty. Second, it should provide adequate incentives to work. Third, the plan's costs should be reasonable. Table 37-5 tells us that these three objectives conflict with one another and that compromises or tradeoffs are necessary. Plan One, with a low guaranteed income and a high benefit-loss rate, keeps costs down. But the low-income guarantee means it is not very effective in eliminating poverty and the high benefit-loss rate weakens work incentives. In comparison, Plan Two has a lower benefit-loss rate and therefore stronger work incentives. But it is more costly because it involves a higher break-even income and therefore pays benefits to more families. Compared to Plan One, Plan Three entails a higher guaranteed income and is clearly more effective in eliminating poverty. While work incentives are the same as with Plan One, the higher guaranteed income makes the plan more costly. The problem is to find the magic numbers which will provide a "decent" guaranteed income, maintain "reasonable" incentives to work, and entail "acceptable" costs. While abolishing most of our current public assistance programs in favor of the NIT might be an improvement, the NIT is fraught with internal tradeoffs and should not be regarded as a panacea. In fact, reform efforts have moved away from the NIT in recent years.

[14] The alert reader may have sensed the generalization that, given the guaranteed income, the break-even level of income varies *inversely* with the benefit-loss rate. Specifically, the break-even income can be found by dividing the guaranteed income by the benefit-loss rate. Hence, for Plan One, $8000/.50 = $16,000. Can you also demonstrate that, given the benefit-loss rate, the break-even level of income varies *directly* with the guaranteed income?

LAST WORD

Welfare reform: The Family Support Act of 1988

The Federal government has recently reformed the Aid to Families with Dependent Children program (AFDC) to give welfare families a comprehensive package of training, child care, and health services designed to move them from welfare to work. What are the major provisions of the law? What do proponents and critics of the law have to say about it?

The Family Support Act of 1988, hereafter designated as FSA, is the most extensive reform of America's welfare system during the past two decades. FSA is complex and detailed, but its more important features are as follows.*

1 *Job Opportunities and Basic Skills program* Each state must establish a Job Opportunities and Basic Skills program (JOBS) through which AFDC parents will be offered basic and remedial education, literacy classes, job skills training, job readiness activities, and job placement. States must assure that child care and transportation are available to the welfare participants in the JOBS program.

2 *Exemptions* AFDC mothers with children under 3 years of age, or under 1 year of age at the option of each state, are exempt from the provisions of the act. Also exempt are women who are in their fourth week or more of pregnancy, stu-

* This summary is based upon newspaper and magazine synopses of the new legislation.

dents under the age of 16, and parents who are needed at home to take care of sick or disabled family members.

3 *Federal grants to states* The Federal government will provide payments to states on a matching basis to help cover the expenses of the JOBS programs.

4 *Other state services* States must provide a minimum of two other services from the following list: help with job search, on-the-job training, community work experience, or subsidization of private wages paid to those moving from welfare to work.

5 *Completion of high school* Welfare parents under the age of 20 must earn a high school diploma or its equivalent.

6 *Transitional child care and Medicaid* Beginning in April 1990, states must provide child care and Medicaid coverage for 12 months to welfare families switching from welfare rolls to employment. The purpose is to reduce the costs of moving from welfare to work and thus to lessen the incentives to stay on welfare.

7 *Welfare benefits for two-parent welfare families* Beginning in October of 1990, all states must begin offering welfare benefits to qualified two-parent families when the main wage earner is unemployed. The purpose of this provision is to reduce the incidence of family break-up associated with the AFDC program. At the time of passage of FSA, twenty-four states provided AFDC benefits only to single-parent families.

8 *Workfare* Beginning in 1994, one member of a two-parent welfare family will have to participate in 16 hours of unpaid, state-organized work per week.

9 *Withholding of child-support payments* FSA tightens the enforcement of child-support payments by absent parents. Starting in 1994, employers will be forced to withhold child support payments from paychecks of absent parents.

10 *Cost* The measure will cost the Federal government an estimated $3.3 billion dollars over the first five years. Because the most costly provisions are phased in gradually, the costs over the first seven years are expected to reach $6.8 billion.

Supporters of FSA point out that this law transforms the AFDC program from a direct transfer program into a program which more aggressively provides skills, support services, and work incentives to welfare parents. FSA, say its proponents, will help people extract themselves and their families from the culture of poverty and welfare. Supporters of FSA also contend that the act will strengthen families by eliminating the incentive for unemployed fathers to abandon their families to qualify their families for welfare benefits.

Some critics of the new law argue that the additional Federal spending associated with the program could more beneficially be spent by simply boosting existing AFDC cash welfare benefits. They also object to the training and workfare requirements of the law, arguing that the training programs will remove mothers from their children during their children's formative years and that the workfare requirements in the law are punitive and mean-spirited.

Charles Murray—a conservative critic of FSA—argues that FSA will *increase* the welfare rolls. Upon losing jobs, some single mothers with children will now have an incentive to go on welfare rather than immediately take a new job which might be available. This action will allow these people to qualify for transitional child care and Medicaid benefits when a new job is found. Additionally, some workers may decide to conveniently "lose" their jobs once their transitional child care and Medicaid benefits expire. Hence, they will fall back on the welfare rolls, which will again qualify them for child care and Medicaid benefits for a year once a new job is found.[†]

But these criticisms aside, the consensus view of Congress at the time FSA was enacted was that the law will yield beneficial outcomes to people needing welfare and will bolster public support for the nation's basic welfare program.

[†] Charles Murray, "New Welfare Bill, New Welfare Cheats," *The Wall Street Journal*, October 13, 1988.

WORKFARE PLANS

However desirable the establishment of a NIT might be, political realities are such that piecemeal changes to the income supplement system are more likely. In fact, most critical attention has focused upon AFDC. The reasons for this are manifold. First, as noted earlier, AFDC may encourage family dissolution. Second, it is contended that the program encourages—or at least subsidizes—illegitimate births. Third, some critics contend that AFDC is conducive to a "culture of poverty" whereby poverty becomes a way of life and is passed from generation to generation. Also, according to government studies, many recipients of AFDC receive benefits fraudulently. Fifth, as more middle-class mothers with children join the labor force, a consensus is emerging that poor mothers receiving AFDC should also work for their incomes. Finally, the public's false perception is that a disproportionate number of welfare recipients are black, and, as a result, most of the (white) population does not identify with their problems and circumstances.

These criticisms have given rise to a variety of **workfare proposals**—also called "welfare-to-work" plans—which would alter the AFDC program by providing an array of work, training, and education activities to help, and eventually require, welfare recipients to move from public assistance to employment. People on welfare who are undertaking training or entering the labor force would also receive child care and transportation subsidies. As an additional aspect of this overall approach, earnings of absentee parents—whether married or unmarried—would be taken directly from workers' paychecks to pay child support.

Several states have had some success in their experiments with the "welfare-to-work" approach to poverty. The success of these state programs helped generate support for an overhaul of the AFDC program nationally. In late 1988 Congress passed and the President signed into law the **Family Support Act of 1988,** more commonly called the *Welfare Reform Act of 1988*. This important law embraces the workfare approach and is the subject of this chapter's Last Word. Supporters of the law believe that it can play an important role in helping end a "culture of welfare" in which dropping out of school, having a child, and going on welfare have allegedly become a normal way of life for a portion of the welfare population.

CHAPTER SUMMARY

1 The distribution of personal income in the United States reflects considerable inequality. The Lorenz curve shows the degree of income inequality graphically.

2 Income inequality lessened quite significantly between 1929 and the end of World War II. Census data show that the income distributions in 1987 and 1947 are nearly identical. But inequality has increased since 1969.

3 Critics contend that *a* the use of a broadened concept of income and *b* recognition that the positions of individual families in the distribution of income change over time would reveal less income inequality than do census data.

4 Government taxes and transfers—particularly the latter—lessen the degree of income inequality significantly.

5 Causes of income inequality include differences in abilities, education and training, job tastes, property ownership, and market power.

6 The basic argument for income equality is that it maximizes consumer satisfaction from a given income. The main argument against income equality is that equality undermines incentives to work, invest, and assume risks, thereby tending to reduce the amount of income available for distribution.

7 Current statistics suggest that 13.5 percent of the nation lives in poverty. Although the poor are a heterogeneous group, poverty is concentrated among blacks, Hispanics, female-headed families, and young children.

8 After falling dramatically between 1960 and 1969, the poverty rate remained relatively unchanged over the next decade. The rate rose sharply between 1978 and 1983, but has slowly declined since then.

9 Our present income-maintenance system is comprised of social insurance programs (OASDHI, Medicare, and unemployment compensation) and public assistance programs (SSI, AFDC, food stamps, and Medicaid).

10 The present welfare programs have been severely criticized as being administratively inefficient, fraught with inequities, and detrimental to work incentives. Reform proposals have been of two basic types: negative income tax proposals and "workfare" plans. In 1988

Congress passed the Family Support Act, which overhauls the AFDC program and incorporates workfare provisions.

TERMS AND CONCEPTS

income inequality	food stamp program
Lorenz curve	Medicaid
tradeoff between equality and efficiency	negative income tax
poverty rate	guaranteed annual income
OASDHI	benefit-loss rate
Medicare	break-even income
unemployment compensation	workfare proposals
Supplemental Security Income (SSI)	Family Support Act of 1988
Aid to Families with Dependent Children (AFDC)	

QUESTIONS AND STUDY SUGGESTIONS

1 What criticisms have been made of Census Bureau data on income inequality? How and to what extent does government contribute to income equality?

2 Assume Al, Beth, Carol, David, and Ed receive incomes of $500, $250, $125, $75, and $50 respectively. Construct and interpret a Lorenz curve for this five-person economy.

3 Briefly discuss the major causes of income inequality. With respect to income inequality, is there any difference between inheriting property and inheriting a high IQ? Explain.

4 Use the "leaky-bucket analogy" to discuss the equality–efficiency tradeoff. As compared to our present income-maintenance system, do you feel that a negative income tax would reduce the leak?

5 Should a nation's income be distributed to its members according to their contributions to the production of that total income or to the members' needs? Should society attempt to equalize income *or* economic opportunities? Are the issues of "equity" and "equality" in the distribution of income synonymous? To what degree, if any, is income inequality equitable?

6 Analyze in detail: "There need be no tradeoff between equality and efficiency. An 'efficient' economy which yields an income distribution which many regard as unfair may cause those with meager income rewards to become discouraged and stop trying. Hence, efficiency is undermined. A fairer distribution of rewards may generate a higher average productive effort on the part of the population, thereby enhancing efficiency. If people think they are playing a fair economic game and this belief causes them to try harder, an economy with an equitable income distribution may be efficient as well."[15]

7 Comment upon or explain:
   a "To endow everyone with equal income will certainly make for very unequal enjoyment and satisfaction."
   b "Equality is a 'superior good'; the richer we become, the more of it we can afford."
   c "The mob goes in search of bread, and the means it employs is generally to wreck the bakeries."
   d "Under our welfare system we have foolishly clung to the notion that employment and receipt of assistance must be mutually exclusive."
   e "Some freedoms may be more important in the long run than freedom from want on the part of every individual."
   f "Capitalism and democracy are really a most improbable mixture. Maybe that is why they need each other—to put some rationality into equality and some humanity into efficiency."

8 What are the essential differences between social insurance and public assistance programs? What are the major criticisms of our present income-maintenance system?

9 The table at the top of page 744 contains three illustrative negative income tax (NIT) plans.
   a Determine the basic benefit, the benefit-loss rate, and the break-even income for each plan.
   b Which plan is the most costly? The least costly? Which plan is most effective in reducing poverty? The least effective? Which plan embodies the strongest disincentive to work? The weakest disincentive to work?
   c Use your answers in part *b* to explain the following statement: "The dilemma of the negative income tax is that you cannot bring families up to the poverty level on the one hand, and simultaneously preserve work incentives and minimize program costs on the other."

[15] Paraphrased from Andrew Schotter, *Free Market Economics* (New York: St. Martin's Press, 1985), pp. 30–31.

Plan One			Plan Two			Plan Three		
Earned income	NIT subsidy	Total income	Earned income	NIT subsidy	Total income	Earned income	NIT subsidy	Total income
$ 0	$4,000	$4,000	$ 0	$4,000	$ 4,000	$ 0	$8,000	$ 8,000
2,000	3,000	5,000	4,000	3,000	7,000	4,000	6,000	10,000
4,000	2,000	6,000	8,000	2,000	10,000	8,000	4,000	12,000
6,000	1,000	7,000	12,000	1,000	13,000	12,000	2,000	14,000

10 "The father of a child has a responsibility to help support that child, irrespective of whether or not he is married to the mother. In addition, the able-bodied single mother has a responsibility to help support her child by working." Do you agree? How might these "principles" be incorporated into a welfare program? What problems might arise in implementing this program in the real world?

CHAPTER 38

Labor-market issues: unionism, discrimination, and immigration*

In this chapter we turn our attention to three important labor market issues: unionism, discrimination, and immigration. Although largely unrelated to each other, each issue is significant in its own right. Much of the chapter consists of a rather detailed look at organized labor, collective bargaining, and the economic effects of unionism. What are the reasons for the historical growth and the recent decline of unionism? What impact do unions have on wages, efficiency and productivity, the distribution of earnings, and inflation? Turning to a second important aspect of the labor market, we next discuss discrimination. What are the dimensions of discrimination? And the costs? Finally, we consider the much publicized issue of immigration of foreign labor to the United States. How many people enter the United States legally and illegally each year? What are the economic ramifications of this inflow of people?

* Instructors may choose to treat the three topics in this chapter selectively.

Brief history of American unionism

Some 17 million workers—about 14.5 percent of the labor force—now belong to labor unions. Bare statistics, however, may understate the importance of unions. The wage rates, hours, and working conditions of nonunionized firms and industries are influenced by those determined in organized industries. Unions are clearly important institutions of American capitalism.

Let us consider how the labor movement evolved in the United States. Attainment of this objective necessarily involves a discussion of government policy toward organized labor, because labor legislation and union growth are intimately related. In terms of national labor policy, the American labor movement has gone through three phases: repression (1790 to 1930), encouragement (1930 to 1947), and intervention (1947 to date). Though the dates are somewhat arbitrary, these three phases serve as an excellent guide for our discussion.

REPRESSION PHASE: 1790 TO 1930

Labor unions have existed in the United States for almost 200 years. The shoemakers, carpenters, printers, and other skilled craftsmen formed unions of some permanence in the early 1790s. As Figure 38-1 indicates, despite this early start, union growth was relatively slow and sporadic until the 1930s. Two considerations go far to account for this meager progress: (1) the hostility of the courts toward labor unions, and (2) the extreme reluctance of American businesses to recognize and bargain with unions.

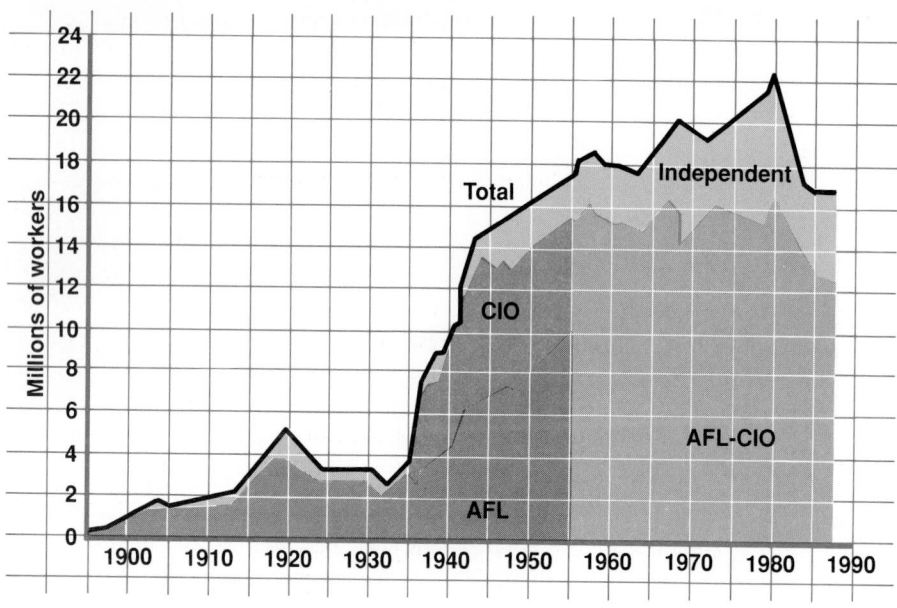

FIGURE 38-1

The growth and
decline of union
membership

**Most of the absolute
growth in organized
labor has occurred
since 1935. However,
organized labor has
been declining as a per-
centage of the labor
force for some time
and, in recent years,
the absolute number of
union members has also
diminished. (U.S. Bureau
of the Census and Bu-
reau of Labor Statis-
tics.)**

Unions and the courts It was not until the 1930s
that legislation spelled out the Federal government's policy toward labor unions. In the absence
of a national labor policy, it was up to the courts to
decide upon specific union-management conflicts.
And, much to the dismay of organized labor, the
courts were generally hostile toward unions. Their
hostility had two sources. First, most judges had
propertied-class backgrounds. Second, the courts
are inherently conservative institutions charged
with the responsibility of protecting *established*
property rights. Unions, throughout the 1800s and
the early decades of the 1900s, were in the unenviable position of seeking rights for labor at the expense of the *existing* rights of management.

The hostility of the courts was first given vent
in the **criminal conspiracy doctrine.** This doctrine, "imported" by the American courts from
English common law at the turn of the nineteenth
century, flatly concluded that combinations of
workers to raise wages were criminal conspiracies
and hence illegal. Although unions, as such, were
later recognized by the courts as legal organizations, the techniques employed by unions to press
their demands—strikes, picketing, and boycotting
—were generally held to be illegal. And, in the latter part of the 1800s, the courts employed both an-

titrust laws and injunctions in such a way as to
impede the labor movement significantly.

Although Congress passed the Sherman Act of
1890 (Chapter 34) for the expressed purpose of
thwarting the growth of business monopolies, the
courts interpreted the loose wording of the act to
include labor unions as conspiracies in restraint of
trade and frequently so applied the act.

A simpler and equally effective antiunion device was the **injunction.** An injunction, or restraining order, is a court order directing that some
act not be carried out, on the ground that irreparable damage will be done to those affected by the
action. The attitude of the courts toward unions
was such that it was extremely easy for employers
to obtain injunctions from the courts, prohibiting
unions from enforcing their demands by striking,
picketing, and boycotting. Stripped of these weapons, unions were relatively powerless to obtain the
status and rights they sought.

To summarize: The courts employed the criminal conspiracy doctrine, the Sherman Act, and injunctions, to the end that union growth was greatly
retarded during the 1790–1930 period.

Antiunion techniques of management The business
community, hostile to unions from their inception,

developed a group of techniques to undermine unions. A startlingly simple antiunion technique was that of ferreting out and firing prounion workers. Too, many employers felt it their duty to inform fellow employers that the discharged workers were "troublemakers" and "labor agitators" and not fit to be hired. This combination of **discriminatory discharge** and **blacklisting** made it extremely risky for workers even to think in terms of organizing a union. One's present and future employment opportunities were at stake.

Another potent weapon in management's struggle to keep unions down was the **lockout,** management's counterpart of the strike. By closing up shop for a few weeks, employers were frequently able to bring their employees to terms and to destroy any notions they might have about organizing a union. Remember: Workers of the late 1800s and early 1900s were not blessed with savings accounts or multimillion-dollar strike funds to draw upon in such emergencies.

Where workers were determined to organize, pitched battles often ensued. Rocks, clubs, shotguns, and an occasional stick of dynamite were the shadowy ancestors of collective bargaining. Some of the darkest pages of American labor history concern the violent clashes between workers and company-hired *strikebreakers*. The Homestead strike of 1892, the Pullman strike of 1894, and the Ludlow Massacre of 1914 are cases in point. Less dramatic skirmishes erupt down to the present time.

But management tactics were often more subtle than a cracked skull. The **yellow-dog contract** was one of the more ingenious antiunion devices fostered by management. In such contracts workers agreed to remain nonunion as a condition of employment. They often had little choice but to sign such contracts—no contract, no job. Violation of a yellow-dog contract exposed a worker to a lawsuit by his employer, the result of which might be a court-imposed fine or even imprisonment.

As a last resort, an employer might shower his work force with such amenities as group insurance and pension programs and stock ownership and profit-sharing schemes to convince them that employers would look after the interests of the workers as effectively as would unions established by "outsiders." The next step beyond such *paternalism* was employee-representation schemes or **company unions,** that is, employer-dominated "dummy"

unions which, it was hoped, would discourage the establishment of genuine unions. Paternalism and company unions were decidedly effective in retarding union growth as late as the 1920s.[1]

Evolution of business unionism The growth which occurred in the labor movement during the 1800s not only was modest, but it also embodied a variety of union philosophies. The mid-1800s were in effect a laboratory in which American labor experimented with alternative forms of unionism—Marxism, utopianism, reformism, and other isms. But such unions usually floundered in the span of a few short years because of the internal conflict between the workers' interest in short-run practical goals (higher wages and shorter hours) and the long-run utopian goals (producer cooperatives, creation of a labor party) of the union leaders.

Then, in 1886, a new labor organization—the **American Federation of Labor (AFL)**—which was to dominate the labor movement for the next fifty years was formed. Under the leadership of Samuel Gompers, labor charted a conservative course which has been very influential down to the present date.[2] Appropriately honored as "the father of the American labor movement," Gompers preached three fundamental ideas: (1) practical business unionism, (2) political neutrality for labor, and (3) the autonomy of each trade or craft.

I BUSINESS UNIONISM Gompers was firmly convinced that "safe and sane" **business unionism**

---

[1] During a prolonged strike in the bituminous coal industry in 1902, a spokesman for the mine operators, George F. Baer, issued the classic statement of business paternalism: "The rights and interests of the laboring man will be protected and cared for—not by the labor agitators, but by the Christian men to whom God in His infinite wisdom has given the control of the property interests of this country."

[2] This is not to say that all unions have followed conservative paths since Gompers first espoused the virtues of business unionism. The Industrial Workers of the World, founded in 1905, advocated a decidedly revolutionary brand of left-wing unionism. And in the late thirties and early forties, Communists infiltrated a number of CIO unions. In 1949 and 1950, the CIO expelled eleven affiliated unions whose leadership had come to be dominated by Communists.

was the only course for American labor to follow. Gompers flatly rejected long-run idealistic schemes entailing the overthrow of the capitalistic system. He spurned intellectuals and theorizers and emphasized that unions should be concerned with practical short-run economic objectives—higher pay, shorter hours, and improved working conditions. In the words of one scholar, Gompers felt that "you must offer the American working man bread and butter in the here and now instead of pie in the sky in the sweet by and by."[3]

2 POLITICAL NEUTRALITY Insofar as politics was concerned, Gompers was convinced that government should keep its nose out of labor-management relations and collective bargaining. Although he recognized that governmental interference on behalf of labor might be a boon to union growth, Gompers was equally certain that antiunion government policies could stifle the progress of the entire labor movement. In pursuing the idea of political neutrality, Gompers cautioned organized labor not to align itself with any political party. Preoccupation with long-run political goals, he argued, merely causes labor to lose sight of the short-run economic objectives it ought to seek. Gompers admonished organized labor to follow one simple principle in the political arena: Reward labor's friends and punish its enemies at the polls without regard to political affiliation.

3 TRADE AUTONOMY Finally, Gompers was firmly convinced that "autonomy of the trade," that is, unions organized on the basis of specific crafts, was the only permanent foundation for the labor movement. Unions composed of many different crafts lack the cohesiveness, he argued, that is essential to strong, hard-hitting, business unionism. These craft unions should then be affiliated in a national federation. "One union to each trade, affiliated for one labor movement."

This philosophy—conservative business unionism, political "neutrality," and the craft principle of union organization—was destined to dominate

[3] Charles C. Killingsworth, "Organized Labor in a Free Enterprise Economy," in Walter Adams (ed.), *The Structure of American Industry,* 3d ed. (New York: The Macmillan Company, 1961), p. 570.

the AFL and the entire labor movement for the next half-century. Indeed, the AFL, operating under Gompers's leadership, met with considerable success—at least for a time. AFL membership hit a high-water mark of about 4 million members by the end of World War I. Then a combination of circumstances arose in the 1920s which forced the AFL into an eclipse (see Figure 38-1). One factor was a strong antiunion drive by employers. Spearheaded by the National Association of Manufacturers, businesses waged a last-ditch effort to stem the rising tide of organized labor. Then, too, many firms introduced employee representation plans, company unions, and a host of paternalistic schemes to convince workers that employers were better prepared to look out for their employees' interests than were labor leaders. Finally, the AFL clung tenaciously to the craft principle of union organization, thereby ignoring the ever-increasing number of unskilled workers employed by the rapidly expanding mass-production industries—the automobile and steel industries in particular.

ENCOURAGEMENT PHASE: 1930 TO 1947

Two significant events occurred in the 1930s which revived the labor movement and inaugurated a period of rapid growth. Most important, the attitude of the Federal government toward unions changed from one of indifference, not to say hostility, to one of encouragement. Also, a major structural change in the labor movement accompanied the founding of the Committee (later the Congress) of Industrial Organizations in 1936. Both events, coupled with the wartime prosperity of the 1940s, greatly swelled the ranks of organized labor.

Prolabor legislation of the 1930s Against the background of the depressed thirties, the Federal government enacted two decidedly prolabor acts. In part, the passage of these acts reflected the strong opposition of organized labor to the previously described weapons employed by the courts and by management to suppress unions. In part, they reflected a Democratic administration replacing a Republican administration. In part, they echoed the widely held opinion that strong unions, by achieving higher wages through collective bargaining, would increase aggregate demand—or at least prevent it from falling—and help alleviate the Great Depression.

NORRIS–LA GUARDIA ACT OF 1932 The **Norris–La Guardia Act of 1932** did much to clear the path for union growth by outlawing two of the more effective antiunion weapons. Specifically, the act

1 Made it decidedly more difficult for employers to obtain injunctions against unions

2 Declared that yellow-dog contracts were unenforceable

WAGNER ACT OF 1935 Three years later, in 1935, the Federal government took more positive steps to encourage union growth. The **Wagner Act of 1935** (officially the National Labor Relations Act) guaranteed the "twin rights" of labor: the right of self-organization and the right to bargain collectively with employers. The act listed a number of "unfair labor practices" on the part of management. Specifically it

1 Forbade employers from interfering with the right of workers to form unions

2 Outlawed company unions

3 Prohibited antiunion discrimination by employers in hiring, firing, and promoting

4 Outlawed discrimination against any worker who files charges or gives testimony under the act

5 Obligated employers to bargain in good faith with a union duly established by their employees

The Wagner Act was clearly "labor's Magna Charta."

A **National Labor Relations Board (NLRB)** was established by the act and charged with the authority to investigate unfair labor practices occurring under the act, to issue cease-and-desist orders in the event of violations, and to conduct worker elections in deciding which specific union, if any, workers might want to represent them.

The Wagner Act was tailored to accelerate union growth. It was extremely successful in achieving this goal. The protective umbrella provided to unions by this act in conjunction with the Norris–La Guardia Act played a major role in causing the ranks of organized labor to mushroom from about 4 million in 1935 to 15 million in 1947.

Industrial unionism: the CIO We have already noted that one of the causes of stagnation in the AFL during the 1920s was its unwillingness to organize the growing masses of unskilled assembly-line workers. Though the majority of AFL leaders chose to ignore the unskilled workers, a vocal minority under the leadership of John L. Lewis contended that craft unionism would be ineffective as a means of organizing the hundreds of thousands of workers in the growing mass-production industries. According to Lewis and his followers, the basis for organization should be shifted from **craft unionism** to **industrial unionism,** that is, away from unions which only encompass a specific type of skilled workers to unions which include all workers—both skilled and unskilled—in a given industry or group of related industries.[4] This conflict came to a head, and in 1936 Lewis and his sympathizers withdrew their unions (and were simultaneously expelled) from the AFL.

The withdrawing unions established themselves as the **Congress of Industrial Organizations (CIO).** The CIO met with startling success in organizing the automobile and steel industries. So great was this success that the AFL also moved in the direction of organizing on an industrial basis. By 1940, total union membership approximated 9 million workers.

INTERVENTION PHASE: 1947 TO DATE

The prolabor legislation of the 1930s, the birth of industrial unionism, and the booming prosperity of the war years brought rapid union growth (see Figure 38-1). As unions gathered strength—both numerical and financial—it became increasingly evident that labor unions could no longer be regarded as the weak sister or underdog in their negotiations with management. Just as the growing power of business monopolies brought a clamor for public control in the 1870s and 1880s, the upsurge of union power in the 1930s and 1940s brought a similar outcry for regulation. This pressure for union control came to a head in the years immediately following World War II and culminated in the passage of the **Taft-Hartley Act of 1947.**

[4] Figures 30-6 and 30-7 compare the techniques employed by craft and industrial unions in attempting to raise wages.

Taft-Hartley Act of 1947   Officially called the Labor-Management Relations Act, the provisions of this detailed piece of legislation generally fall under four headings: (1) provisions which designate and outlaw certain "unfair union practices," (2) provisions which regulate the internal administration of unions, (3) provisions which specify collective bargaining procedures and regulate the actual contents of bargaining agreements, and (4) provisions for the handling of strikes imperiling the health and safety of the nation.

1 UNFAIR UNION PRACTICES   You will recall that the Wagner Act outlined a number of "unfair labor practices" on the part of management. A new and crucial feature of the Taft-Hartley Act was that it listed a number of "unfair labor practices" on the part of unions. These unfair practices, which constitute some of the most controversial sections of the act, are as follows: *(a)* Unions are prohibited from coercing employees to become union members. *(b)* **Jurisdictional strikes** (disputes between unions over the question of which has the authority to perform a specific job) are forbidden, as are **secondary boycotts** (refusing to buy or handle products produced by another union or group of workers) and certain **sympathy strikes** (strikes designed to assist some other union in gaining employer recognition or some other objective). *(c)* Unions are prohibited from charging excessive or discriminatory initiation fees or dues. *(d)* **Featherbedding,** a mild form of extortion wherein the union or its members receive payment for work not actually performed, is specifically outlawed. *(e)* Unions cannot refuse to bargain in good faith with management.

2 UNION ADMINISTRATION   Taft-Hartley also imposed controls on the internal processes of labor unions: *(a)* Unions are obligated to make detailed financial reports to the National Labor Relations Board and to make such information available to its members. *(b)* Unions are prohibited from making political contributions in elections, primaries, or conventions which involve Federal offices. *(c)* Originally, union officials were required to sign non-Communist affidavits.

3 CONTRACT CONTENTS   Other Taft-Hartley provisions are designed to control the actual collective bargaining process and the contents of the work agreement resulting therefrom: *(a)* The **closed shop** (which requires that a firm hire only workers who are already union members) is specifically outlawed for workers engaged in interstate commerce; that is, a closed-shop arrangement cannot be written into a collective bargaining agreement. *(b)* Collective bargaining agreements must provide that, where they exist, welfare and pension funds are kept separate from other union funds and jointly administered by the union and management. *(c)* Bargaining agreements must contain termination or *reopening clauses* whereby both labor and management must give the other party 60 days' notice of the intent to modify or terminate the existing work agreement.

4 "HEALTH AND SAFETY" STRIKES   Finally, the Taft-Hartley Act outlines a procedure for avoiding major strikes which might disrupt the entire economy and thereby imperil the health or safety of the nation. According to this procedure, the President may obtain an injunction to delay such strikes for an 80-day "cooling off" period. Within this period the involved workers are polled by the NLRB as to the acceptability of the last offer of the employer. If the last offer is rejected, the union can then strike. The government's only recourse—one of questionable legality—is seizure of the industry.

Landrum-Griffin Act of 1959   Government regulation of the internal processes of labor unions was extended by passage of the **Landrum-Griffin Act** (officially the Labor-Management Reporting and Disclosure Act) in 1959. The act regulates union elections by requiring regularly scheduled elections of officers and the use of secret ballots; restrictions are placed upon ex-convicts and Communists in holding union offices. Furthermore, union officials are now held strictly accountable for union funds and property. Officers handling union funds must be bonded; the embezzlement of union funds is made a Federal offense; and close restrictions are placed upon a union's loans to its officers and members. The act is also aimed at preventing autocratic union leaders from infringing upon the individual worker's rights to attend and participate in union meetings, to vote in union proceedings, and to nominate officers. The act permits a worker to sue his union if it denies him these rights. Under the act the Secretary of Labor is given broad powers in investigating violations of the act.

Unionism's decline

In 1955 unity was formally reestablished in the American labor movement with the merger of the AFL and CIO. Two factors were especially important in closing the breach which had existed for almost two decades. First, the political and legislative setbacks which labor had encountered since the prolabor era of the 1930s convinced labor leaders that unity in the labor movement was a necessary first step toward bolstering the political influence of organized labor. Second and perhaps more important, failure to achieve the desired rate of growth in the ranks of organized labor in the post-World War II years made it evident to organized labor that a concerted, unified effort was needed to organize currently nonunion firms and industries.

In fact, however, the period since the AFL-CIO merger has *not* been characterized by a resurgence of organized labor. The growth of union membership has failed to keep pace with the growth of the labor force. While 25 percent of the labor force was organized in the mid-1950s, currently less than 15 percent are members. Indeed, in recent years the absolute number of union members has declined significantly. Over 22 million workers were unionized in 1980; that figure had fallen to only about 17 million in 1988.

Why has this happened? There is no consensus on this issue, but it is revealing to consider two possible explanations. These explanations are complementary in the sense that each might explain some portion of the relative membership decline.

1 Structural changes The traditional view, which we shall dub the **structural-change hypothesis,** is that many structural changes have occurred both in our economy and in the labor force which have been unfavorable to the expansion of union membership. This view embraces a number of interrelated observations. First, consumer demand and therefore employment patterns have shifted away from traditional union strongholds. Generally speaking, the industry-mix of national output has been shifting relatively away from manufactured goods (where unions have been strong) to services (where unions have been weak). This change in industry-mix may be reinforced by increased competition from imports in highly unionized sectors such as automobiles and steel. Growing import competition in these industries has curtailed domestic employment and therefore union membership. Second, an unusually large proportion of the increase in employment in recent years has been concentrated among women, youths, and part-time workers, groups which are allegedly difficult to organize because of their less firm attachment to the labor force. Third, spurred by rising energy costs, the long-run trend for industry to shift from the Northeast and the Midwest where unionism is "a way of life" to "hard to organize" areas of the South and Southwest may have impeded the expansion of union membership.

A fourth and ironic possibility is that the relative decline of unionism may be in part a reflection of the success unions have had in gaining a sizable wage advantage over nonunion workers in the United States and abroad. Confronted with high union wages, we would expect union employers to substitute machinery for workers, subcontract more work to nonunion suppliers, open nonunion plants in less industrialized areas, or have components produced in low-wage nations. These actions reduce the growth of employment opportunities in the union sector as compared to the nonunion sector. Perhaps more important, we would also expect output and employment in low-cost nonunion firms and industries to increase at the expense of output and employment in higher-cost union firms and industries. In short, union success in raising wages may have changed the composition of industry to the disadvantage of union employment and membership.

2 Managerial-opposition hypothesis A more recent view is that intensified **managerial opposition** to unions has been a major deterrent to union growth. It is argued that in the past decade or so unions have increased the union wage advantage which they enjoy vis-à-vis nonunion workers and, as a result, union firms have become less profitable than nonunion firms. As a reaction, managerial opposition to unions has crystalized and become more aggressive. One managerial strategy has been to employ labor-management consultants who specialize in the mounting of aggressive antiunion drives to dissuade workers from unionizing or, alternatively, to persuade union workers to decertify their union. In this regard, an organization called Executive Enterprises, Inc., boasted in a 1984 brochure that over 20,000 management representatives had attended its seminars on "How to Maintain Nonunion Status" and "The Process of Decertification."

It is also alleged that there has been a dramatic increase in the use of illegal antiunion tactics. In particular, it has become increasingly common to identify and dismiss leading prounion workers even though this is prohibited by the Wagner Act. Coupling these antiunion strategies with evidence that unions are devoting fewer resources to organizing the unorganized and that NLRB rulings have become increasingly antilabor, the labor movement has gone into relative and absolute eclipse.

Collective bargaining

Despite the decline of unionism, collective bargaining remains an important feature of labor-management relations. It is estimated that almost 200,000 collective bargaining agreements are now in force in the United States.

THE BARGAINING PROCESS

To the outsider, collective bargaining is a dramatic clash every two or three years between labor and management. And it is easy to get the impression from the newspapers that labor and management settle their differences only with strikes, picketing, and not infrequent acts of violence.

These impressions are largely inaccurate. Collective bargaining is a somewhat less colorful process than most people believe. In negotiating important contracts, the union is represented by top local and national officials, duly supplemented with lawyers and research economists. Management representatives include top policy-making executives, plant managers, personnel and labor relations specialists, lawyers, and staff economists. The union usually assumes the initiative, outlining its demands. These take the form of specific adjust-

ments in the current work agreement. The merits and demerits of these demands are then debated. Typically, a compromise solution is reached and written into a new work agreement. Strikes, picketing, and violence are clearly the exception and not the rule. About 95 percent of all bargaining contracts are negotiated without resort to work stoppages. In recent years it has generally held true that less than one-fifth of 1 percent of all working time has been lost each year as a result of work stoppages resulting from labor-management disputes. *Labor and management display a marked capacity for compromise and agreement.* We must keep in mind that strikes and labor-management violence are newsworthy, whereas the peaceful renewal of a work agreement hardly rates a page-5 column.

THE WORK AGREEMENT

Collective bargaining agreements assume a variety of forms. Some agreements are amazingly brief, covering two or three typewritten pages; others are highly detailed, involving 200 or 300 pages of fine print. Some agreements involve only a local union and a single plant; others set wages, hours, and working conditions for entire industries. There is no such thing as an "average" or "typical" collective bargaining agreement.

At the risk of oversimplification, collective bargaining agreements usually cover four basic areas: (1) the degree of recognition and status accorded the union and the prerogatives of management, (2) wages and hours, (3) seniority and job opportunities, and (4) a procedure for settling grievances.

Union status and managerial prerogatives Unions enjoy differing degrees of recognition from management. Listed in order of the union's preference are (1) the closed shop, (2) the union shop, and (3) the open shop.

Prior to being outlawed by the Taft-Hartley Act, the closed shop afforded the greatest security to a union. Under a closed shop a worker must be a member of the union before being hired. A **union shop,** on the other hand, permits the employer to hire nonunion workers but provides that these workers must join the union in a specified period—say, thirty days—or relinquish their jobs. Some twenty states now have so-called **right-to-work laws** which make compulsory union membership, and therefore the union shop, illegal. Under the **open shop,** management may hire union or non-union workers. Those who are nonunion are not obligated to join the union; they may continue on their jobs indefinitely as nonunion workers. Finally, we must also mention the **nonunion shop.** Here no union exists, and the employer makes a conscious effort to hire those workers who are least inclined to form or join a union.

The other side of the union-status coin is the issue of *managerial prerogatives.* Many business executives fear that in time the expansion of the scope of collective bargaining may reach the point where certain fundamental management decisions will become matters to be decided jointly by management and labor. It is felt by business that such an eventuality will "tie the hands" of management to the extent that efficient business operation may be jeopardized. For this reason, at the insistence of management most work agreements contain clauses outlining certain decisions which are to be made solely by management. These managerial prerogatives usually cover such matters as the size and location of plants, products to be manufactured, types of equipment and materials used in production, and the scheduling of production. Frequently the hiring, transfer, discipline, discharge, and promotion of workers are decisions made solely by management but are subject to the general principle of seniority and to challenge by the union through the grievance procedure.

Wages and hours The focal point of any bargaining agreement is wages and hours. Both labor and management tend to be highly pragmatic and opportunistic in wage bargaining. The criteria, or "talking points," most frequently invoked by labor in demanding (and by management in resisting) wage boosts are (1) "what others are getting," (2) ability to pay, (3) cost of living, and (4) productivity. If a given firm has basic rates below those of comparable firms, the union is likely to stress that wages should be increased to bring them into line with what workers employed by other firms are getting. Similarly, if the firm has had a very profitable year, the union is likely to demand high wages on the ground that the company has ample ability to grant such increments. In recent years unions

have achieved considerable success in tying wages to the cost of living. It is estimated that about 40 percent of all union workers are covered by some kind of *cost-of-living adjustment* (COLA). Finally, unions bargain for their "fair share" of the additional revenues associated with increases in productivity.

The four wage criteria are clearly two-edged propositions. For example, the cost-of-living criterion is invoked by the union only when prices are hurrying upward; unions conveniently ignore this criterion when prices are stable or declining. Similarly, the union considers the ability-to-pay argument to be of importance only when profits are large. Management is equally opportunistic in the evaluation it places on the various wage-bargaining standards.

Hours of work, overtime pay, holiday and vacation provisions, and **fringe benefits**—health plans and pension benefits—are other important "economic" issues which must be addressed in the bargaining process.

Seniority and the control of job opportunities The uncertainty of employment in a capitalistic economy, coupled with the fear of antiunion discrimination on the part of employers, has made workers and their unions decidedly "job-conscious." The explicit and detailed provisions covering job opportunities which most work agreements contain reflect this concern. Unions stress **seniority** as the basis for worker promotion and for layoff and recall. The worker with the longest continuous service has the first chance at relevant promotions, is the last to be laid off, and the first to be recalled from a layoff.

Grievance procedure It is unthinkable that even the most detailed and comprehensive work agreement can anticipate all the issues and problems which might occur during its life. What if workers show up for work on a Monday morning to find that for some reason—say, a mechanical failure—the plant is closed down? Should they be given "show-up" pay amounting to, say, two or four hours' pay? Or management and the union may disagree as to whether the worker with the most seniority has the ability to perform the job to which he or she wants to be promoted. Such events and disagreements cannot be anticipated by even the most detailed collective bargaining contracts and therefore must be ironed out through a *grievance procedure.* Virtually all bargaining agreements contain an explicit grievance procedure for the handling of disputes which arise during the life of an agreement.

Given the historical and legislative background of the labor movement and some understanding of collective bargaining, let us turn now to a consideration of the economic implications of unions.

The economic effects of unions

Are the economic effects of labor unions positive or negative? We will attempt to respond to this important issue by examining several questions: Do unions raise wages? Do they increase or diminish economic efficiency? Do they make the distribution of earnings more or less equal? Do unions contribute to inflation? The reader should be forewarned that there is considerable uncertainty and debate with regard to the answers to these questions.

THE UNION WAGE ADVANTAGE

The three union models of Chapter 30 (see Figures 30-5, 30-6, and 30-7 and the accompanying discussions) all imply that unions have the capacity to raise wages. Has unionization in fact caused wage rates to be higher than otherwise? On the face of it, this might seem to be a naïve question, the answer to which must be an unqualified "Yes." Despite the much-publicized "give-backs" of the autoworkers, steelworkers, airline employees, and others in the early 1980s, don't we usually read of specific unions successfully bargaining for substantial wage gains? And doesn't casual observation suggest that the average wage for organized workers is higher than for unorganized workers? Indeed, Department of Labor data show that the median weekly earnings of union members was $480 in 1988 as compared to $385 for nonunion workers.

Yet, one may have second thoughts. For example, we know that the long-run trend of real wages in the United States has been upward (Figure 30-2). So the real question is not solely whether unions successfully bargain for wage increases, but rather whether these increases are larger than, smaller than, or about the same as those which the subtle, undramatic workings of the market would have brought about. Wages rose in the automobile industry long before it was organized in 1938–1941 and undoubtedly would have risen substantially in the past several decades had the industry remained unorganized. Furthermore, there is the historical fact that unions have been most successful in organizing the more prosperous industries. Many of the now-unionized high-wage industries were also high-wage industries *before* they were organized. Again the automobile industry is a good illustration. Thus one may legitimately ask if the fact that unionized industries pay higher wages than unorganized industries is the result of unionization or, alternatively, if unions are getting credit for wage increases attributable to favorable market forces.

Despite these questions, empirical research quite overwhelmingly suggests that *unions do raise the wages of their members relative to comparable nonunion workers,* although the size of the union wage advantage varies according to occupation, industry, race, and sex.[5] There is also evidence to suggest that the union wage advantage increased in the 1970s. Hence, early research suggests that over the 1923–1958 period the average union–nonunion pay difference was on the order of 10 to 15 percent. More recent studies indicate that the difference widened to 20 to 30 percent in the 1970s.[6] It is to be reemphasized that these are average differentials and that there is considerable variation among industries and occupations. Furthermore, the wage freezes and pay cuts ("wage give-backs") suffered by organized labor in the early and mid-1980s most likely have significantly diminished the 20 to 30 percent union wage advantage. Labor economists have speculated that the union wage advantage may have returned to the 10 to 15 percent range by the end of the 1980s.

[5] See C. J. Parsley, "Labor Union Effects on Wage Gains: A Survey of Recent Literature," *Journal of Economic Literature,* March 1980, pp. 1–31.

[6] Daniel J. B. Mitchell, *Unions, Wages, and Inflation* (Washington, D.C.: The Brookings Institution, 1980). See also Richard B. Freeman and James L. Medoff, *What Do Unions Do?* (New York: Basic Books, Inc., Publishers, 1984), chap. 14.

These estimates of the union wage advantage tend to be understated because union workers enjoy substantially larger *fringe benefits* than do nonunion workers. That is, union workers are more likely to have private pensions, medical and dental insurance, paid vacations and sick leaves, and so forth, than are nonunion workers. Where such benefits are available to both union and nonunion workers, their magnitude is greater for the union workers. Thus the total compensation (wage rates plus fringe benefits) advantage of union workers is greater than the previously indicated 10 to 15 percent.

Economists are also in general agreement that *unions have probably had little or no impact upon the average level of real wages received by labor—both organized and unorganized—taken as a whole.* At first glance these two conclusions—that unions gain a wage advantage but do not affect the average level of real wages—may seem inconsistent. But they need not be if the wage gains of organized workers are at the expense of unorganized workers. As we shall see momentarily (Figure 38-2), higher wages in unionized labor markets may cause employers to move back up their labor demand curves and hire fewer workers. These unemployed workers may seek employment in nonunion labor markets. The resulting increase in the supply of labor will tend to depress wage rates in these nonunion markets. The net result may well be no change in the average level of wages. Indeed, the tight relationship between productivity and the average level of real wages shown in Figure 30-1 correctly suggests that unions have little power to raise real wage rates for labor as a whole. But Figure 30-1 is an average relationship and is therefore compatible with certain groups of (union) workers getting higher relative wages if other (nonunion) workers are simultaneously getting lower real wages.

EFFICIENCY AND PRODUCTIVITY

Are unions a positive or a negative force insofar as economic efficiency and productivity are concerned? How do unions affect the allocation of resources? While there is a great deal of disagreement as to the efficiency aspects of unionism, it is instructive to consider some of the avenues through which unions might affect efficiency both negatively and positively. We will consider the negative view first.

Negative view There are essentially three basic means by which unions might exert a negative impact upon efficiency.

I FEATHERBEDDING AND WORK RULES Some unions have undoubtedly diminished productivity growth by engaging in "make-work" or "featherbedding" practices and resisting the introduction of output-increasing machinery and equipment. These productivity-reducing practices often come into being against a backdrop of technological change. That is, labor and management may agree to a crew size which is reasonable and appropriate at the time the agreement is concluded. But labor-saving technology may then emerge which renders the crew too large. The union is likely to resist the potential loss of jobs. For example, for many years the Brotherhood of Locomotive Firemen and Engineers was able to retain a fireman on train crews, even though his function was eliminated by the shift from steam to diesel engines. Similarly, union painters sometimes eschewed the use of spray guns and in some instances limited the width of paint brushes. In more recent years, the typographer unions resisted the introduction of computers in setting type. Historically, the musicians' union insisted upon oversized orchestras for musical shows and required that a union standby orchestra be paid by employers using nonunion orchestras.

More generally, one can argue that unions are responsible for the establishment of work rules and practices which are inimical to efficient production. For example, under seniority rules workers may be promoted in accordance with their employment tenure, rather than in terms of who can perform the available job with the greatest efficiency. Also, unions may impose jurisdictional restrictions upon the kinds of jobs which workers may perform. For example, sheet-metal workers or bricklayers may be prohibited from performing the simple carpentry work which is often associated with their jobs. Observance of such rules means, in this instance, that unneeded and underutilized carpenters must be available. Finally, it is often contended that unions constrain managerial prerogatives to establish work schedules, determine production targets, and to make freely the myriad decisions which contribute to productive efficiency.

2 STRIKES A second means by which unions may adversely affect efficiency is through strikes. If union and management reach an impasse in their negotiations, a strike will result and the firm's production will cease for the strike's duration. The firm will forgo sales and profits and workers will sacrifice income.

Simple statistics on strike activity suggest that strikes are relatively rare and the associated aggregate economic losses are relatively minimal. While currently an estimated 80,000 collective bargaining agreements are negotiated each year, the number of strikes is typically on the order of 5000. Furthermore, most of these strikes last only a few days. As indicated earlier, the average amount of work-time lost each year because of strikes is only about one-fifth of 1 percent of total work-time. This loss is the equivalent of 4 hours per worker per year, which is less than 5 minutes per worker per week![7]

It should be added that the economic costs associated with strikes may be greater or less than suggested by the amount of work-time lost. The costs may be greater if the production of nonstruck firms is disrupted. For example, an extended strike in the steel or rail transportation industries could have serious adverse repercussions for production and employment in many other industries and sectors of the economy. On the other hand, costs may be less than implied by workdays lost by strikers in that nonstruck firms may increase their output to offset the loss of production by struck firms. For example, while the output of General Motors will fall when its workers strike, car buyers may shift their demand to Ford and Chrysler which respond by increasing their employment and outputs. While GM and its employees are hurt by a strike, society as a whole may experience little or no decline in employment, real output, and income.

3 LABOR MISALLOCATION A third and more subtle avenue through which unions might adversely affect efficiency is the union wage advantage itself. Figure 38-2 is instructive. Here we have drawn (for

simplicity's sake) identical labor demand curves for the unionized and nonunion sectors of the labor market for some particular kind of labor.[8] If there were no union present initially, then the wage rate which would result from the competitive hire of labor would be, say, W_n. We now assume a union comes into being in sector 1 and succeeds in increasing the wage rate from W_n to W_u. As a consequence, N_1N_2 workers lose their jobs in the union sector. Let us assume that they all move to nonunion sector 2 where they secure employment. This increase in labor supply in the nonunion sector depresses the wage rate from W_n to W_s.

Recall that the labor demand curves reflect the marginal revenue products (MRPs) of workers or, in other words, the contributions which workers make to the national output. This means that the shaded area $A + B + C$ in the union sector represents the **decrease** in national output caused by the N_1N_2 employment decline in that sector. This $A + B + C$ area is simply the sum of the MRPs—the total contribution to national output—of the workers displaced by the W_n to W_u wage increase achieved by the union. Similarly, the reemployment of these workers in nonunion sector 2 results in an **increase** in national output indicated by the shaded area $D + E$. Because area $A + B + C$ exceeds area $D + E$, there is a net loss of national output. More precisely, because $A = D$ and $C = E$, the **net** loss attributable to the union wage advantage is equal to area B. Since the same amount of employed labor is now producing a smaller output, labor is clearly being misallocated and inefficiently used.

Viewed from a slightly different perspective, **after** the shift of N_1N_2 workers from the union to the nonunion sector has occurred, workers will be paid a wage rate equal to their MRPs in both sectors. But the MRPs of the union workers will be higher than the MRPs of the nonunion workers. The economy will always benefit from a larger national output when any given type of labor is reallocated from a relatively low MRP use to a relatively high MRP use. But, given the union's presence and its ability to maintain the W_u wage rate in its sector, this reallocation from sector 2 to 1 will **not** occur.

[7] Marten Estey, *The Unions*, 3d ed. (New York: Harcourt Brace Jovanovich, Inc., 1981), p. 140.

[8] Technical note: Our discussion assumes pure competition in both product and resource markets.

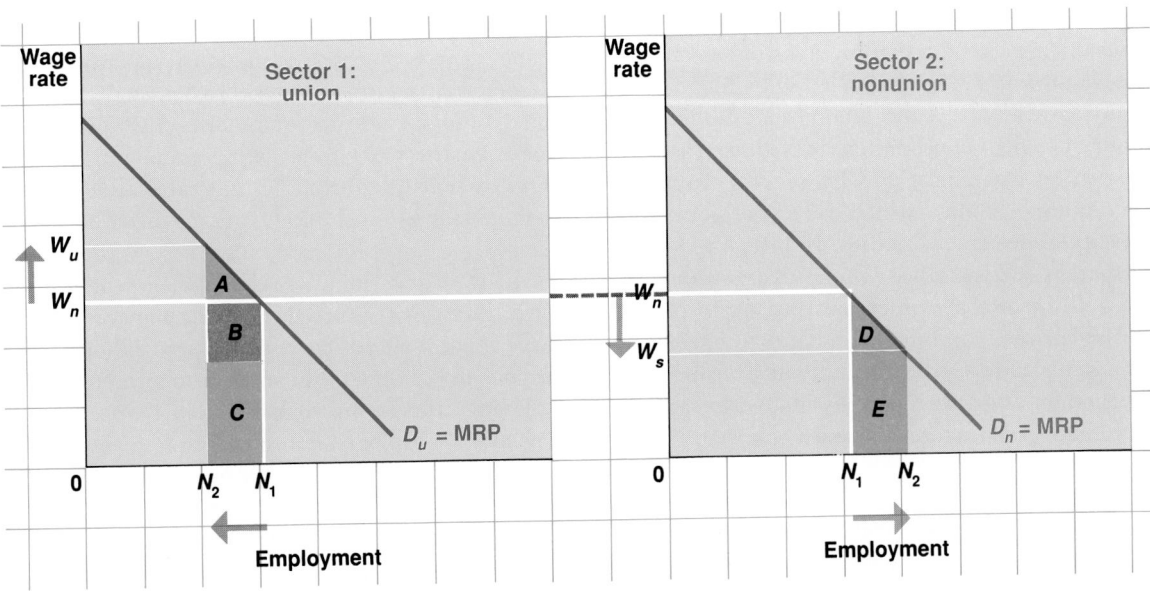

FIGURE 38-2

The effect of the union wage advantage on the allocation of labor

The higher wage W_u, which the union achieves in sector I causes the displacement of $N_1 N_2$ workers. The re-employment of these workers in nonunion sector 2 reduces the wage rate there from W_n to W_s. The associated loss of output in the union sector is area $A + B + C$, while the gain in the nonunion sector is only area $D + E$. Hence, the net loss of output is equal to area B. This suggests that the union wage advantage has resulted in the misallocation of labor and a decline in economic efficiency.

Attempts by economists to estimate the output loss due to the allocative inefficiency associated with union wage gains suggest that the loss is relatively small. In a pioneering study Albert Rees assumed a 15 percent union wage advantage and estimated that approximately 0.14 percent—only about one-seventh of 1 percent—of the national output was lost![9] Similarly, an estimate by Freeman and Medoff indicates that "union monopoly wage gains cost the economy 0.2 to 0.4 percent of gross national product."[10] In 1988 this cost would

amount to about $10 to $20 billion or $40.00 to $80.00 per person.

Positive view   Other economists take the position that on balance unions make a positive contribution to productivity and efficiency.

I MANAGERIAL PERFORMANCE: THE SHOCK EFFECT   You may recall in Chapter 30's discussion of the minimum wage the notion of a shock effect was introduced. The **shock effect** is the idea that a wage increase, imposed by a union in this instance, may induce affected firms to adopt improved production and personnel methods and thereby become more efficient. One may carry Figure 38-2's analysis of labor misallocation one step further and argue that the union wage advantage will prompt union firms to **accelerate** the substitution of capital

[9] Albert Rees, "The Effects of Unions on Resource Allocation," *The Journal of Law and Economics,* October 1963, pp. 69–78. More recently Robert H. DeFina has estimated that a 15 percent union wage advantage would result in only a 0.08 to 0.09 percentage loss of output. See his "Unions, Relative Wages, and Economic Efficiency," *Journal of Labor Economics,* October 1983, pp. 408–429.

[10] Freeman and Medoff, op. cit., p. 57.

for labor (Chapter 29) and *hasten* the search for cost-reducing (productivity-increasing) technologies. That is to say, when faced with higher production costs due to the union wage advantage, employers will be prompted to reduce costs by using more machinery and by seeking improved production techniques which use less of both labor and capital per unit of output. In fact, if the product market is reasonably competitive, a unionized firm with labor costs which are, say, 10 to 15 percent higher than nonunion competitors will simply not survive unless productivity can be raised. In short, union wage pressure may inadvertently generate managerial actions which increase national productivity.

2 REDUCED WORKER TURNOVER Freeman and Medoff[11] have recently stressed the view that on balance unions contribute to rising productivity within firms through their effects upon worker turnover and worker security. In their view the positive impact of unions upon productivity occurs in part because unions function as a **collective voice** for its members in resolving disputes, improving working conditions, and so forth. That is, if a group of workers is dissatisfied with its conditions of employment, it has two potential means of response. These are the "exit mechanism" and the "voice mechanism." The **exit mechanism** simply refers to the use of the labor market—leave or exit your present job in search of a better one—as a means of reacting to "bad" employers and "bad" working conditions. In contrast, the **voice mechanism** entails communication by workers with the employer to improve working conditions and resolve worker grievances. It may well be risky for *individual* workers to express their dissatisfaction to employers because employers may retaliate by firing such workers as "troublemakers." But unions can provide workers with a *collective* voice to communicate problems and grievances to management and to press for their satisfactory resolution.

More specifically, unions may help reduce worker turnover in two ways. First, unions provide the voice mechanism as a substitute for the exit mechanism. Unions are effective in correcting job dissatisfactions which would otherwise be "re-

solved" by workers through the exit mechanism of changing jobs. Second, the union wage advantage is a deterrent to job changes. Higher wages tend to make unionized firms more attractive places to work. A variety of studies by Freeman and Medoff suggests that the decline in quit rates attributable to unionism is substantial, ranging from 31 to 65 percent.[12]

A lower quit rate increases efficiency in several ways. First, lower turnover means a more experienced and, hence, more productive labor force. Second, fewer quits reduce the firm's recruitment, screening, and hiring costs. Finally, reduced turnover makes employers more willing to invest in the training (and therefore the productivity) of their workers. If a worker quits or "exits" at the end of, say, a year's training, the employer will get no return from the higher worker productivity attributable to that training. Lower turnover increases the likelihood that employers will receive a return on any training they provide, thereby making them more willing to upgrade their labor forces.

3 SENIORITY AND INFORMAL TRAINING Much productivity-increasing training is transmitted informally. More-skilled workers may explain their functions to less-skilled workers on the job, during lunch, or during a coffee break. However, a more-skilled senior worker may want to conceal his or her knowledge from less-skilled junior workers *if* the latter can become competitive for the former's job. Because of union insistence upon the primacy of seniority in such matters as promotion and layoff, worker security is enhanced. Given this security, senior workers will be more willing to pass on their job knowledge and skills to new or subordinate workers. This informal training enhances the quality and productivity of the firm's work force.

Mixed research findings A relatively large number of studies have been undertaken to measure the impact of unionization upon productivity. These studies attempt to control for differences in labor quality, the amount of capital equipment used per worker, and other factors aside from unionization which might contribute to productivity differences. Unfortunately, the evidence from these studies is

---

[11] Ibid., chap. 11.

[12] Ibid., chap. 6.

inconclusive. For every study which finds a positive union effect on productivity, another study using different methodology or data concludes that there is a negative effect. Hence, all we can say is that at present there is no generally accepted conclusion regarding the overall impact of unions upon labor productivity.[13]

DISTRIBUTION OF EARNINGS

Labor unions envision themselves as egalitarian forces, that is, as institutions which enhance economic equality. Do unions in fact reduce the inequality with which earnings are distributed? While there is disagreement on this issue, the most convincing evidence suggests that unions reduce earnings inequality.

Increasing inequality Some economists employ Figure 38-2's analysis of labor misallocation to conclude that unions increase earnings inequality. Simply put, they contend that in the absence of the union competition would bring wages into equality at W_n in these two sectors or submarkets. But the higher union wage realized in sector 1 displaces workers who seek reemployment in the nonunion sector. In so doing they depress nonunion wages. Instead of wage equality at W_n, we end up with higher wage rates of W_u for union workers and lower wages of W_s for nonunion workers. The impact of the union is clearly to increase earnings inequality. Furthermore, the fact that unionization is more extensive among the more highly skilled, higher-paid blue-collar workers than it is among less skilled, lower-paid blue-collar workers also suggests that the obtaining of a wage advantage by unions increases the dispersion of earnings.

Promoting equality But there are other aspects of union wage policies which suggest that unionism promotes greater, not less, equality in the distribution of earnings. What are these other ways through which unions tend to equalize wages?

[13] A number of these studies are discussed in Campbell R. McConnell and Stanley L. Brue, *Contemporary Labor Economics* 2d ed. (New York: McGraw-Hill Book Company, 1989), chap. 7.

1 UNIFORM WAGES WITHIN FIRMS In the absence of unions employers are apt to pay different wages to individual workers on the same job. These wage differences are based upon perceived differences in job performance, length of job tenure, and, perhaps, favoritism. Unions, on the other hand, have a tradition of seeking uniform wage rates for all workers performing a particular job. In short, while nonunion firms tend to assign wage rates to *individual workers*, unions—in the interest of worker allegiance and solidarity—seek to assign wage rates to *jobs*. To the extent that unions are successful, wage and earnings differentials based upon supervisory judgments of individual worker performance are eliminated. An important side effect of this standard-wage policy is that wage discrimination against blacks, other minorities, and women is likely to be less when a union is present.

2 UNIFORM WAGES AMONG FIRMS In addition to seeking standard wage rates for given occupational classes *within* firms, unions also seek standard wage rates among firms. The rationale for this policy is almost self-evident. The existence of substantial wage differences among competing firms may undermine the ability of unions to sustain and enhance wage advantages. For example, if one firm in a four-firm oligopoly is allowed to pay significantly lower wages to its union workers, the union is likely to find it difficult to maintain the union wage advantage in the other three firms. In particular, during a recession the high-wage firms are likely to put great pressure on the union to lower wages to the level of the low-wage firm. To avoid this kind of problem unions seek to "take wages out of competition" by standardizing wage rates among firms, thereby tending to reduce the degree of wage dispersion.

What is the *net* effect of unionism upon the distribution of earnings? Although the issue remains controversial, Freeman and Medoff have used statistical studies to conclude that the wage effects indicated in Figure 38-2 *increase* earnings inequality by about 1 percent, but the standardization of wage rates within and among firms *decreases* inequality by about 4 percent. The net result is a 3 percent decline in earnings inequality due to unionism. Noting that only a small proportion of the labor force is unionized, the authors contend that this 3 percent reduction in inequality should be regarded as "substantial."[14]

UNIONS AND INFLATION

Let us now address as best we can the complicated and controversial question of whether unions can increase the average level of money wages and thereby generate cost-push or, more specifically, wage-push inflation.

Two models We have encountered two general models of inflation, namely, the demand-pull and the cost-push models (Figures 11-6b and c and Figure 11-8). The demand-pull model suggests that, given aggregate supply, an increase in aggregate demand will result in a higher price level. The Keynesian version of the model attributes the increase in total demand to any one of its components, that is, to increases in consumption, investment, government spending, or foreign demand. In the monetarist version the increase in aggregate demand is solely the result of an increase in the money supply (Chapter 18). In either case, however, the cause or impetus for inflation arises on the demand side of product markets which then increases the derived demands for labor and pulls up nominal wages. The important point is that in the demand-pull theory of inflation wage increases are an *effect* or symptom of inflation, not a *cause*. Wage increases do *not* cause inflation but are rather the *result* of excess aggregate demand. Wage increases simply transmit inflation, but do not initiate it.

In comparison cost-push models allow for union wage determination to play a causal role in inflation. Specifically, we know from equation (1) in Chapter 19 that if nominal-wage increases exceed increases in labor productivity, then unit labor costs will rise. Given that labor costs comprise about three-fourths of total production costs, we can expect product prices to rise roughly in accord with the increase in unit labor costs. In terms

of Figure 11-8 a decrease in aggregate supply from AS_1 to AS_2 results in a higher price level. Some economists contend that union-inspired money-wage increases in excess of productivity increases can be an important cause of the indicated leftward shift of aggregate supply.

Tentative conclusions Which view is correct? Do nominal wage increases merely accompany and transmit inflation as the demand-pull theory suggests? Or are union wage increases a source of inflation as the cost-push theory suggests? While there is no universally accepted conclusion, most experts downgrade union wage-setting as a causal force in inflation. We know from our experience in the early 1960s that union wage determination can be compatible with price level stability. And one can argue with considerable credibility that the major episodes of rapid inflation in the United States were started either by expansions of aggregate demand or major supply shocks which had little or nothing to do with wage increases. Hence, the "great inflation" of the 1970s was rooted in increases in government military spending in the late 1960s, on the one hand, and supply shocks associated with the OPEC oil cartel and crop shortages, on the other. More important perhaps is the fact that the cost-push model indicates that the leftward shift in aggregate supply which accompanies a union-induced increase in unit labor costs causes declines in output and increases in unemployment which act to restrain union wage demands (Figure 11-8). This suggests that rising unit labor costs could not generate continuing inflation unless accommodating monetary and fiscal policies gave rise to increases in aggregate demand to offset the falling output and rising unemployment which wage inflation would create (Figure 19-7b). Hence, the most reasonable judgment is that unions do *not* appear to be an initiating cause of inflation. Stated differently, unions do *not* seem to cause initial bursts of inflation or major increases in the rate of existing inflation independently of other causes.

[14] Freeman and Medoff, op. cit., pp. 90–93, and additional studies cited therein. See also Nguyen T. Quan, "Unionism and the Size Distribution of Earnings," *Industrial Relations*, Spring 1984, pp. 270–277.

With this survey of unionism and collective bargaining complete, let us now consider two additional factors which affect American labor markets. We first consider the problem of discrimination in labor markets and, second, the controversial immigration issue.

Discrimination

In Chapter 37 we noted that blacks, Hispanics, and women bear a disproportionately large burden of poverty. The low incomes received by these groups are a consequence of the operation of the labor market. Hence, it is important that we consider the labor market aspects of discrimination.

Economic discrimination occurs when female or minority workers, who have the same abilities, education, training, and experience as white male workers, are accorded inferior treatment with respect to hiring, occupational access, promotion, or wage rate.

Discrimination also occurs when females or minorities are denied access to education and training. Table 38-1 provides us with casual evidence which suggests the presence of racial discrimination. Quite similar data imply discrimination on the basis of gender. For example, the weekly earnings of full-time female workers is only about 70 percent that of males.

DIMENSIONS OF DISCRIMINATION

As Table 38-1 and our definition both suggest, discrimination may take several forms. We will couch the ensuing comments in terms of racial discrimination, but keep in mind that these remarks are also generally applicable to sex discrimination.

TABLE 38-1 **Selected measures of discrimination and inequality of opportunity, 1987**

Selected measure	Whites	Blacks
Income		
Median income of families	$32,274	$18,089
Percent of households in poverty	8.2	29.9
Percent of families with incomes of $50,000 or more	24.4	9.5
Unemployment rate (percent of civilian labor force)		
Adult males*	4.8	11.1
Adult females*	4.6	11.6
Teenage† males	15.5	34.4
Teenage† females	13.4	34.9
Education		
Percent of population 25 years and over completing 4 years of high school or more	77.0	63.4
Percent of population 25 years and over completing 4 years of college or more	20.5	10.7
Occupational distribution (percent of total civilian employment)		
Managerial and professional occupations	25.7	15.1
Service occupations	12.2	23.1

* 20 years or older.
† Males and females, 16–19 years old.
Sources: *Statistical Abstract of the United States, 1989, Economic Report of the President, 1989* (Washington), and *Employment and Earnings,* January 1988.

1 **Wage discrimination** occurs when black and other minority workers are paid less than whites for doing the same work. This kind of discrimination is of declining importance because of its explicitness and the fact that it clearly violates Federal law.

2 **Employment discrimination** means that unemployment is concentrated among minorities. Blacks are frequently the last hired and the first fired. Hence, for the past fifteen or twenty years the unemployment rate for blacks has been roughly double that for whites (Table 38-1).

3 **Human-capital discrimination** occurs when investments in education and training are lower for blacks than for whites. The smaller amount (Table 38-1) and inferior quality of the education received by blacks have had the obvious effect of denying them the opportunity to increase their productivity and qualify for better jobs. Unfortunately, a vicious circle seems to exist here. Many blacks are poor because they have acquired little human capital. Being poor, blacks have less financial ability to invest in education and training. They also have less economic motivation to invest in human capital. Facing the very real possibility of wage, employment, and occupational discrimination, blacks tend to receive a lower rate of return on their investments in education and training.

4 **Occupational discrimination** means that minority workers have been arbitrarily restricted or prohibited from entering the more desirable, higher-paying occupations. Black executives and salespeople, not to mention electricians, bricklayers, and plumbers, are relatively few and far between. Historically, many craft unions effectively barred blacks from membership and hence from employment.

OCCUPATIONAL SEGREGATION: THE CROWDING MODEL

This latter form of discrimination—**occupational segregation**—is particularly apparent in our economy. Women are disproportionately concentrated in a limited number of occupations such as nursing, public school teaching, clerical jobs, and retail clerks. Blacks are crowded into a limited number of low-paying jobs such as laundry workers, cleaners and servants, hospital orderlies, and other manual jobs.

The character and income consequences of occupational discrimination can be revealed through a very simple supply and demand model similar to that used to analyze the efficiency consequences of unions. We make the following simplifying assumptions.

1 The labor force is equally divided between males and females (or white and black) workers. Let us say there are 6 million male and 6 million female workers.

2 The economy is comprised of three occupations, each having identical labor demand curves, as shown in Figure 38-3.

Men and women (whites and blacks) are homogeneous with respect to their labor force characteristics; each of the three occupations could be filled equally well by men or women.

Suppose now that, as a consequence of irrational discrimination, the 6 million women are excluded from occupations X and Y and crowded into occupation Z. Men distribute themselves equally among occupations X and Y so there are 3 million male workers in each occupation and the resulting common wage rate for men is $0M$. (Assuming no barriers to mobility, any initially different distribution of males between X and Y would result in a wage differential which would prompt labor shifts from low- to high-wage occupation until wage equality was realized.) Note that women, on the other hand, are crowded into occupation Z and, as a consequence of this occupational segregation, receive a much lower wage rate $0W$. Given the reality of discrimination, this is an "equilibrium" situation. Women *cannot,* because of discrimination, reallocate themselves to occupations X and Y in the pursuit of higher wage rates.

Assume at this point that through legislation or sweeping changes in social attitudes, discrimination disappears. What are the results? Women, attracted by higher wage rates, will shift from Z to X and Y. Specifically, 1 million women will shift into X and another 1 million into Y, leaving 4 million workers in Z. At this point 4 million workers will be in each occupation and wage rates will be equal to $0B$ in all three occupations. Wage equality eliminates the incentive for further reallocations of labor. This new, nondiscriminatory equilibrium is clearly to the advantage of women, who now receive higher wages, and to the disadvantage of men, who now receive lower wages. Women were

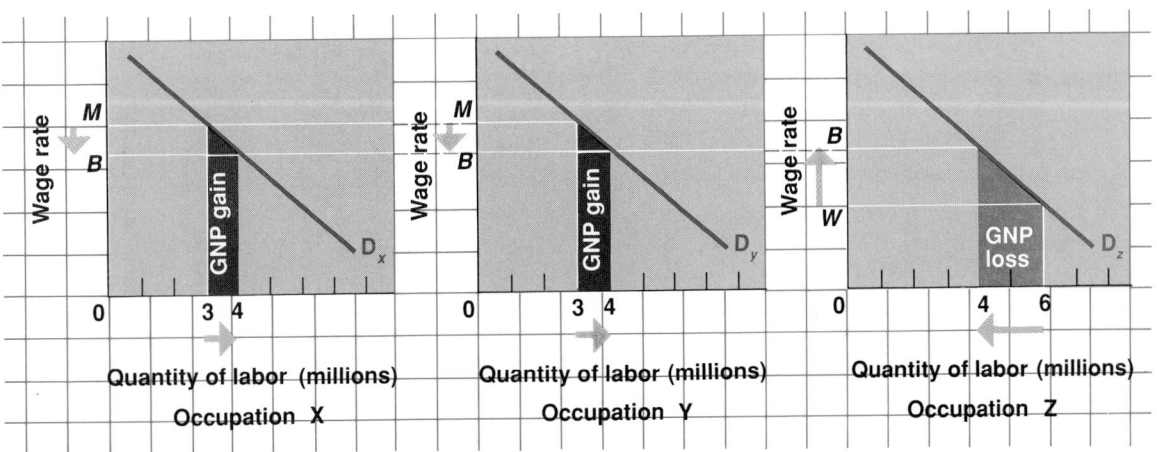

FIGURE 38-3

The simple economics of occupational discrimination

By crowding women into one occupation, men enjoy high wage rates of *OM* in occupations X and Y while women receive low wages of *OW* in occupation Z. The abandonment of discrimination will equalize wage rates at *OB* and result in a net increase in national output.

initially exploited through discrimination to the benefit of men; the termination of discrimination corrects that situation.

But that's not all: There is a net gain to society. Recall that the labor demand curve reflects labor's marginal revenue product (Chapter 29) or, in other words, labor's contribution to the national output.[15] Hence, the gray areas for occupations X and Y show the *increases* in national output—the market value of the marginal or extra output—realized by adding 1 million women workers in each of those two occupations. Similarly, the orange area for occupation Z shows the *decline* in national output caused by the shifting of the 2 million women workers from occupation Z. By inspection we note that the sum of the two additions to national output exceeds the subtraction from national output when discrimination is ended. This is to be expected: After all, women workers are reallocating themselves from occupation Z, where their contribution to national output (their MRP) is relatively low, to alternate employments in X and Y, where their contributions to national output (their MRPs) are relatively high. Conclusion: *Society gains from a more efficient allocation of resources when discrimination is abandoned.* Discrimination influences the distribution of a *diminished* national income. That is, discrimination places the nation on a point inside of its production possibilities curve.

COSTS OF DISCRIMINATION

Given the diverse types of discrimination, the economic costs of discrimination are difficult to estimate. However, one estimate[16] is that if economic and social policies were successful in lowering the black unemployment rate to the level of the white rate, and if education and training opportunities were made available to the black labor force so that the average productivity of black labor became equal to that of white workers, the total output of the economy would rise by about 4 percent. For example, in 1988 the economic cost of racial discrimination alone would be on the order of $181 billion.

[15] Technical note: This assumes pure competition in product and resource markets.

[16] See Joint Economic Committee, *The Cost of Racial Discrimination* (Washington, 1980).

ADDENDA

Two important comments must be appended to our discussion of discrimination.

Comparable worth doctrine The first has to do with public policy. The reality of pervasive occupational segregation has given rise to the issue of comparable worth. Legislation such as the Equal Pay Act of 1963 which forced employers to pay equal wages to men and women performing the same jobs was of no help to many women because occupational segregation limited their access to the jobs held by men. The essence of the **comparable worth doctrine** is that female secretaries, nurses, and clerks should receive the same salaries as male truck drivers or construction workers if the levels of skill, effort, and responsibility in these disparate jobs are comparable.

While the notion of comparable worth has considerable appeal, there are a number of important objections. For example, any comparison of the relative worth of various jobs is necessarily subjective and therefore arbitrary, opening the door to endless controversies and lawsuits. Second, wage setting by administrative or bureaucratic judgment, rather than supply and demand, does not bode well for long-run efficiency. That is, to the extent that the calculated worth of specific jobs varies from their market or equilibrium value, worker shortages or surpluses will develop. Furthermore, might not increasing the wages of women attract even more females to traditionally "women's jobs" and thereby prolong occupational segregation? The comparable worth doctrine promises to be a key issue in antidiscrimination policy in the years ahead.

Nondiscriminatory factors Not all the average income differentials found between blacks and whites *and* males and females are necessarily due to discrimination. Most researchers agree, for example, that some part of the male-female earnings differential is attributable to factors other than discrimination. For example, the work-life cycle of married women who have children historically has involved a continuous period of work until birth of the first child, then a five- to ten-year period of nonparticipation or partial participation in the labor force related to childbearing and child care, followed by a more continuous period of work experience when the mother is in her late thirties or early forties. The net result is that, on the average, married women have accumulated much less labor force experience than men in the same age group. Hence, on the average females are less productive workers and are therefore paid a lower average wage rate. Furthermore, family ties apparently provide married women with less geographical mobility in job choice than is the case with males. In fact, married women may give up good positions to move with husbands who decide to accept jobs located elsewhere. And some married women may put convenience of job location and flexibility of working hours ahead of occupational choice. Again, women may have purposely crowded into such occupations as nursing and elementary school teaching because such occupations have the greatest carryover value for productive activity within the home. Finally, in the past several decades many more women have entered the labor force than have men. This large increase in the supply of female workers has acted as a drag on women's wages and earnings. All this implies that some portion of the male-female earnings differential is due to considerations other than discrimination by gender. It also suggests that the male-female wage gap will narrow in the future, now that a greater number of females are attending college, maintaining employment through their childbearing years, and pursuing higher-paying professional jobs.

Immigration

The immigration issue has long been clouded in controversy and misunderstanding. Should more or fewer people be allowed to migrate to the United States? How should the much-publicized problem of illegal entrants be handled? Let us attempt to throw a bit of light upon this problem by (1) briefly summarizing United States' immigration history and policy, (2) presenting a bare-bones model of the economic effects of immigration, and (3) embellishing this simple model by considering some of the more subtle costs and benefits associated with the international movement of labor.

HISTORY AND POLICY

During the first 140 years of our history as an independent nation, immigration to the United States was virtually unimpeded. And there is little question that the great infusion of foreign labor into our labor-scarce country was a major contributing factor to our nation's economic growth. But the great flood of immigrants which came to the United States in the quarter-century prior to World War I was sharply curtailed by the war itself and by a series of restrictive immigration laws enacted in the 1920s. However, after World War II, immigration policy was liberalized and the annual inflows of **legal immigrants** were roughly 250,000 in the 1950s, 320,000 in the 1960s, and 500,000 or more during most of the 1970s and early 1980s.

These data are very imperfect, however, because they do not include **illegal immigrants.** Estimates suggest that, in recent years, as many as 500,000 illegal aliens may enter the United States each year, most coming from Mexico, the Caribbean, and Latin America. Despite this large annual influx of illegals, the total number of illegal aliens in the United States may only be on the order of $3\frac{1}{2}$ to 5 million (estimates vary from 2 to 12 million). Many illegal aliens come to the United States for a year or so to earn a "grubstake" and then return to their native countries.

Current immigration laws specify that only 270,000 migrants may enter the United States each year, with a ceiling of 20,000 from any one country. In addition, family reunification provisions allow United States' citizens to bring in an unlimited number of immediate relatives—spouses, children, and parents. Furthermore, the law allows an additional 50,000 political refugees to enter each year. The President and Congress can "adjust" this refugee figure upward and have frequently done so. Hence, in 1980, almost 140,000 political refugees entered the United States from Cuba and Haiti. Overall, it is not uncommon in recent years for as many as 500,000 to 600,000 legal immigrants to enter the United States.

Immigration and immigration policy have been highly controversial, focusing largely upon illegal immigrants. The issues are varied. Do foreign workers accept such low wages and poor working conditions that labor markets are debased for American workers? Do illegals put new burdens

upon our educational and income-maintenance systems and therefore impose an avoidable burden on local, state, and national treasuries? While these are critical—and difficult-to-answer—questions, perhaps the main bone of contention concerns competition for jobs. One view is that every job taken by an illegal alien is one less job for an American worker. At the other extreme, it has been argued that illegals take the highly undesirable jobs which Americans are loath to accept and therefore do not contribute to unemployment among native American workers.

ECONOMICS OF IMMIGRATION

We can gain some worthwhile insights as to the economic effects of immigration by employing a modest variation of the crowding model of sex discrimination (Figure 38-3). In Figure 38-4 we portray the demand for labor in the United States as D_u in the left diagram and the demand for labor in Mexico as D_m in the right diagram. The demand for labor is greater in the United States, presumably because of the presence of more capital equipment and more advanced technologies which enhance the productivity of labor. (Recall from Chapter 29 that the labor demand curve is based upon the marginal revenue product of labor.) Conversely, we assume that machinery and equipment are scarce in Mexico and that technology is less sophisticated; hence, labor demand is weak. We also assume that the premigration labor forces of the United States and Mexico are Oc and OC respectively, **and** that full employment exists in both countries.

Now, if we make the further assumptions that (1) migration is costless; (2) it occurs solely in response to wage differentials; and (3) immigration is unimpeded by legislation in either country, workers will migrate from Mexico to the United States until wage rates in the two countries are equal at W_e. In this case some FC ($= fc$) million workers will have migrated from Mexico to the United States before equilibrium is achieved. We observe that, although the average level of wage rates falls from W_u to W_e in the United States, the national output (the sum of the marginal revenue products of the labor force) increases from $Oabc$ to $Oadf$. In Mexico, average wage rates rise from W_m to W_e,

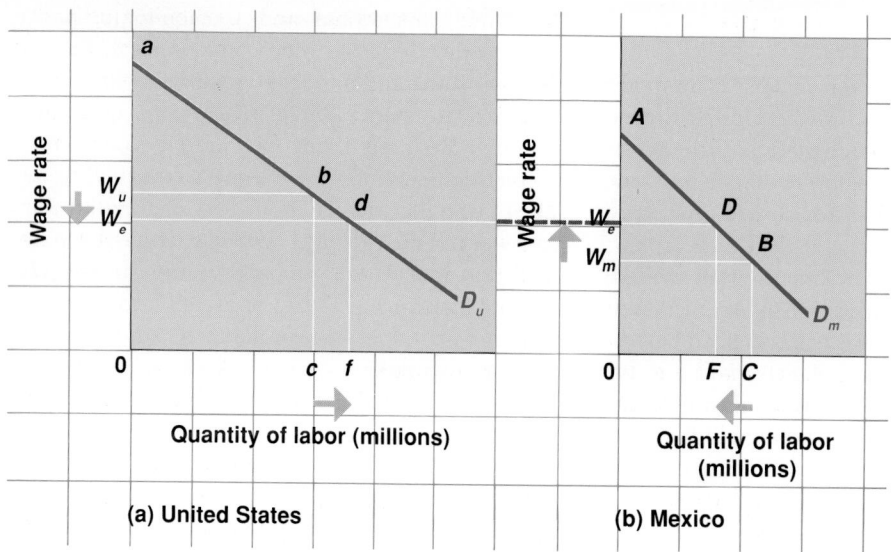

FIGURE 38-4

The simple economics of immigration

The migration of labor to high-income United States (a) from low-income Mexico (b) will increase the national output, reduce the average level of wages, and increase business incomes in the United States, while having the opposite effects in Mexico. The United States' national output gain of *cbdf* exceeds Mexico's national output loss of *FDBC*; hence, there is a net increase in world output.

but national output declines from 0*ABC* to 0*ADF*.[17] Observing that the national output gain of *cbdf* in the United States exceeds the *FDBC* loss in Mexico, we conclude that the world's real output has increased. Just as the elimination of the barrier of sex or racial discrimination enhances economic efficiency within a country, so the elimination of legislative barriers to the international flow of labor increases worldwide economic efficiency. The world gains for the simple reason that freedom to migrate moves people to those countries where they can make a larger contribution to world production. To repeat: Migration involves an effi-

ciency gain. It enables the world to produce a larger real output with a given amount of resources.

Our model also suggests that this flow of immigrants will enhance business or capitalist incomes in the United States and reduce them in Mexico. We have just noted that the before-immigration national output in the United States is 0*abc*. The total wage bill is 0W_u*bc*, that is, the wage rate multiplied by the number of workers. The remaining triangular area W_u*ab* is "business" or capitalist income. The same reasoning applies to Mexico. Our analysis tells us that unimpeded immigration will increase business income from W_u*ab* to W_e*ad* in the United States and reduce it from W_m*AB* to W_e*AD* in Mexico. Business benefits from immigration in the United States; Mexican businesses are hurt by emigration. This is what we would expect intuitively; America is receiving "cheap" labor, Mexico is losing "cheap" labor. This conclusion is consistent with the historical fact that American employers have often actively recruited immigrants.

[17] What happens to the wage bill (wage rate multiplied by the number of workers) in each of the two countries depends upon the elasticity of labor demand. If the demand for labor is elastic in the $W_u W_e$ wage range in the United States, the absolute size of the wage bill will increase. Conversely, if labor demand is inelastic in the $W_u W_e$ wage range, the absolute size of the wage bill will decline. A similar application of the total revenue (earnings) test for elasticity applies to Mexico.

COMPLICATIONS AND MODIFICATIONS

Our model clearly embodies a number of simplifying assumptions and also omits several relevant considerations. Let us therefore release some of the more critical assumptions and introduce omitted factors, observing how our conclusions are affected.

1 Cost of migration The international movement of workers is not costless. Costs entail not only the explicit or out-of-pocket costs of geographically moving oneself and one's possessions, but also the implicit or opportunity cost of lost income during the period of movement and reestablishing oneself in the host country. Still more subtle costs are involved in adapting to a new culture, language, climate, and so forth. All of such *costs* must be estimated by the potential immigrant and weighed against the expected *benefits* of higher wages in the host country. If benefits are estimated to exceed costs, it is rational to migrate. If costs exceed benefits, one should not migrate. In Figure 38-4 the existence of migration costs means that the flow of labor from Mexico to the United States will *not* occur to the extent that wages are equalized. Wages will remain higher in the United States than in Mexico. Furthermore, the world gain from migration will be reduced.

2 Remittances and backflows Many migrants view their moves as temporary. Their plan is to move to a wealthier country, accumulate some desired level of wealth through hard work and frugality, and return home to establish their own enterprises. During their period in the host country, migrants frequently make sizable **remittances** to their families in their home country. This causes a redistribution of the net gain from migration between the countries involved. In Figure 38-4 remittances by Mexican workers in the United States to their relatives would cause the *gain* in United States' national output to be less than that shown and the *loss* of Mexican national output to also be less than that shown.

Actual **backflows**—the return of migrants to their home countries—might also alter gains and losses through time. For example, if some of the Mexican workers who migrated to the United States acquired substantial labor-market or managerial skills and then returned home, their en-

hanced human capital might then make a substantial contribution to economic development in Mexico. Evidence suggests, however, that migrant workers who acquire skills in the receiving country tend *not* to return home. As a matter of fact, in the 1960s the United States was a major beneficiary of a much-publicized "brain drain" as professional and other highly skilled workers left western Europe and other nations in response to higher wages and better job opportunities in the United States.

3 Full employment versus unemployment Our model assumes full employment in both the sending and receiving country. Mexican workers presumably leave low-paying jobs to more-or-less immediately take higher-paying jobs in the United States. However, in many cases the factor that "pushes" immigrants from their homelands is not low wages, but chronic unemployment and underemployment. Many of the less developed countries are characterized by overpopulation and surplus labor; workers are either unemployed or so grossly underemployed that their marginal revenue product is zero. Again, allowance for this possibility affects our discussion of gains and losses. Specifically, Mexico would *gain* (not lose!) by having such workers emigrate. These unemployed workers are making no contribution to Mexico's national output and must be sustained by transfers from the rest of the labor force. The remaining Mexican labor force will be better off by the amount of the transfers after the unemployed workers have migrated to the United States. Conversely, if the Mexican immigrant workers are unable to find jobs in the United States and are sustained through transfers from employed American workers, then the real income of native American workers will decline.

4 Fiscal aspects What impacts do immigrants have upon the tax revenues and government spending of the receiving country? Although evidence is scanty and subject to dispute, the consensus seems to be that immigrants are probably net contributors to the fiscal system of the host country. Immigrants are disproportionately comprised of younger people—frequently, unattached young males—who are in the prime of life and who have received some amount of schooling in their native country. Certainly, highly skilled migrants who already speak the host country's language are likely to be heavy net taxpayers. Less skilled workers—for example, political refugees from Haiti or Central America—may require several years of public or philanthropic aid to learn the language and become assimilated. Nevertheless, illegal aliens from, say, Mexico or the Caribbean are likely to be net taxpayers.

Several studies have found that very few illegals collect unemployment compensation, go on welfare, receive food-stamps, or use medicaid. Some do use free public hospitals and send their children to public schools, but the incremental costs involved are probably small. On the tax revenue side, it is clear that most illegals do have social security and federal income taxes withheld from their pay, although a sizable proportion apparently pay less than their legal obligation of the latter.

The very low incidence of social welfare payments to illegals is not a mystery. These payments are usually made only to the unemployed and most illegals are working. When they are not, fear of detection and deportation keeps them from applying to benefit programs. Thus, the direct social welfare costs of illegals are low.[18]

ECONOMICS AND BEYOND

Even our superficial consideration of the economic aspects of immigration makes it clear that the issues involved are complex. Much obviously depends upon the character of the immigrants themselves and economic conditions in the receiving country. One can envision many benefits accruing to the United States from a liberal immigration policy when (1) the immigrants are young, educated, and skilled; and (2) our economy is fully employed and experiencing robust growth. The benefits to Americans are less evident when (1) the immigrants are unskilled and illiterate, and (2) our economy is stagnant and plagued by high unemployment. The "brain drain" of the 1960s and Castro's emptying out of Cuban prisons and mental

[18] Walter Fogel, "Illegal Alien Workers in the United States," *Industrial Relations,* October 1977, p. 255. To the extent that illegal immigrants displace American workers they may impose indirect costs upon our welfare and income-maintenance programs.

LAST WORD

Immigration reform: the Simpson–Rodino Act of 1986

The economic and social issues raised by the large-scale illegal immigration of the late 1970s and 1980s contributed to a public outcry to stem the inflow of illegal migrants. Recognizing this public demand, Congress in 1986 passed the Immigration Reform and Control Act, or the Simpson–Rodino Act.

Among its many provisions, the Simpson–Rodino Act, hereafter called SRA, (1) granted amnesty and eventual citizenship to qualified illegal immigrants already in the United States; (2) imposed sanctions on employers who hired undocumented workers after June 1, 1987; and (3) allowed migrant farm workers who harvest perishable crops to come to the United States to work on a temporary basis.

The provisions of SRA are to be implemented gradually; hence, the full effects on the labor market will not be known for some time. Nevertheless, economists have speculated as to the probable effects of the three major provisions of the law. ***Amnesty*** The amnesty provisions of the Simpson–Rodino law, in essence, transformed illegal workers in the United States into legal workers. Because most of those granted amnesty were already participating in the economy, their new status will

hospitals in 1980 were highly contrasting episodes in American immigration history!

The immigration issue is also complicated by an assortment of essentially noneconomic issues. Do minority immigrants inflame racial problems?

not greatly affect labor supply and therefore is not expected to change wage rates and employment levels. We should note, however, that some detractors argue that the granting of amnesty to present illegal immigrants will encourage other immigrants to cross our borders. That is, future illegal immigrants may migrate in the expectation that Congress will at some future date enact yet another amnesty program.

Employer Sanctions Under provisions of SRA, employers caught *knowingly* hiring illegal immigrants will be fined between $250 and $2000 per worker. The fine will rise to $2000 to $5000 per worker for a second offense, and $3000 to $10,000 for a third offense. Subsequent offenses will land the employer in prison for up to six months. Given these stiff penalties, vigorous enforcement of the employer sanctions can be expected to reduce the flow of illegal aliens into the United States by diminishing or eliminating the demand for their labor services. That is, the threat of large fines, in effect, should reduce the attractiveness of hiring illegal workers, thereby reducing the demand for this type of labor. In this regard, it has been estimated that the employment of illegal migrants eventually will decline by 15 to 25 percent because of the act.

Temporary Farm Labor Many temporary illegal farm workers have opted for the amnesty available under the act. Most of these individuals will probably continue, at least for a time, to offer their services as farm workers. Additionally, the law allows temporary migrants—"guest workers"—to enter the country to harvest perishable crops. Therefore, the future supply of labor in agriculture may not be greatly affected. Once the complex provisions of the new law become better understood, the law's greatest effect on agriculture may come from the added costs to employers of screening for illegal workers and keeping necessary records, rather than from labor shortages and rising wages.

Does the concentration of migrants in urban areas such as New York and Miami generate social tensions and increase crime rates? Would America without fresh inflows of immigrants somehow not be America?

CHAPTER SUMMARY

1 The growth of labor unions was slow and irregular until the 1930s due to court hostility and employer hostility.

2 The AFL dominated the American labor movement from 1886 until the CIO was formed in 1936. Its philosophy was essentially that of Samuel Gompers—business unionism, political neutrality, and craft unionism.

3 Union growth was rapid in the 1930s and 1940s. The shift toward industrial unionism, triggered by the formation of the CIO in 1936, was a significant factor in this growth. Equally important were the prolabor legislation passed by the Federal government in the 1930s and the wartime prosperity of the 1940s.

4 The Norris–La Guardia Act of 1932 rendered yellow-dog contracts unenforceable and sharply limited the use of injunctions in labor disputes. The Wagner Act of 1935—"labor's Magna Charta"—guaranteed labor the rights to organize and to bargain collectively with management.

5 The Taft-Hartley Act of 1947 brought about a shift from government-sponsored to government-regulated collective bargaining. The act **a** specifically outlaws certain "unfair practices" of unions; **b** regulates certain internal operations of unions; **c** controls the content of collective bargaining agreements; and **d** outlines a procedure for handling "national health and welfare" strikes.

6 The Landrum-Griffin Act of 1959 was designed to regulate the internal processes of unions—in particular the handling of union finances and the union's relationships with its members.

7 Unionism has declined relatively in the United States since the mid-1950s. Some labor economists attribute this to changes in the composition of national output and in the demographic structure of the labor force which have been uncongenial to union growth. Others contend that employers, recognizing that unionization results in lower profitability, have more aggressively sought to dissuade workers from being union members.

8 Labor and management "live together" under the terms of collective bargaining agreements. These work agreements cover four major topics: **a** union status and managerial prerogatives; **b** wages and hours; **c** seniority and job control; and **d** a grievance procedure.

9 Union workers currently enjoy wages which are 10 to 15 percent higher than comparable nonunion workers. There is little evidence to suggest that unions have been able to raise the average level of real wages for labor as a whole.

10 There is disagreement as to whether the net effect of unions upon allocative efficiency and productivity is positive or negative. The negative view cites *a* the inefficiencies associated with featherbedding and union-imposed work rules; *b* the loss of output through strikes; and *c* the misallocation of labor to which the union wage advantage gives rise. The positive view holds that *a* through the shock effect union wage pressure spurs technological advance and mechanization of the production process; *b* as collective voice institutions unions contribute to rising productivity by reducing labor turnover; and *c* the enhanced security of union workers increases their willingness to make their skills known to less experienced workers.

11 Those who contend that unions increase earnings inequality argue that *a* unionization increases the wages of union workers but lowers the wages of nonunion workers and *b* unions are strongest among highly paid, skilled blue-collar workers but relatively weak among low-paid, unskilled blue-collar workers. But other economists contend that unions contribute to greater earnings equality because unions *a* seek uniform wages for given jobs within firms and *b* seek uniform wages among firms.

12 The demand-pull model of inflation suggests that wage increases transmit, but do not cause, inflation. In contrast union wage increases can cause the price level to rise in the context of the cost-push theory of inflation. Most economists, however, do not regard union wage-setting as a fundamental cause of inflation.

13 The incomes of blacks and other racial minorities are below those of whites, while the incomes of females are below those of males. In part, these differences arise because of wage, employment, human-capital, and occupational discrimination.

14 The crowding model of occupational segregation indicates how white males may gain higher earnings at the expense of blacks and women. The model also shows that discrimination involves a net loss of national output.

15 Simple supply and demand analysis suggests that the movement of migrants from a poor to a rich country will *a* increase the national income, *b* reduce the average level of wages, and *c* increase business incomes in the receiving country. The opposite effects will occur in the sending country, but the world as a whole can be expected to realize a larger total output.

TERMS AND CONCEPTS

criminal conspiracy doctrine

American Federation of Labor (AFL)

injunction

discriminatory discharge

blacklisting

lockout

yellow-dog contract

company unions

Landrum-Griffin Act of 1959

business unionism

Norris–La Guardia Act of 1932

Wagner Act of 1935

National Labor Relations Board (NLRB)

craft and industrial unionism

Congress of Industrial Organizations (CIO)

Taft-Hartley Act of 1947

jurisdictional strikes

secondary boycotts

sympathy strikes

featherbedding

closed shop

structural-change and managerial-opposition hypotheses

union shop

right-to-work laws

open shop

nonunion shop

fringe benefits

seniority

collective voice

exit and voice mechanisms

wage, employment, occupational, and human-capital discrimination

occupational segregation

comparable worth doctrine

legal and illegal immigrants

remittances

backflows

QUESTIONS AND STUDY SUGGESTIONS

1 Briefly describe the repression, encouragement, and intervention phases of the American labor movement.

2 It has been said that the Taft-Hartley Act was passed to achieve three major goals: *a* to reestablish an equality of bargaining power between labor and management to maintain industrial peace; *b* to protect "neutrals," that is, third parties who are not directly concerned with a given labor-management dispute; and *c* to protect the rights of individual workers in their relations with unions. Review the Taft-Hartley provisions as outlined in this chapter, and relate each to these three major goals.

3 Use the structural-change and managerial-opposition hypotheses to explain the relative decline of organized labor in the United States. In your opinion which explanation is more convincing?

4 Suppose you are the president of a newly established local union which is about to bargain with an employer for the first time. Make a list of those points which you would want to be covered explicitly in the work agreement. Assuming the economic climate which exists at this moment, what criteria would you use in backing your wage demands? Explain.

5 "There are legislative, executive, and judicial aspects to collective bargaining." Explain.

6 What is the estimated size of the union wage advantage? Explain: "Although unions get higher wages than nonunion workers, unions have not been successful in raising the average real wage of the American labor force."

7 Comment on each of the following statements:
  a "By constraining the decisions of management, unions inhibit efficiency and productivity growth."
  b "As collective voice institutions unions increase productivity by reducing worker turnover, inducing managerial efficiency, and enhancing worker security."

8 "There is an inherent cost to society that accompanies any union wage gain. That cost is the diminished efficiency with which labor resources are allocated." Explain this contention. Are you in agreement?

9 Describe the various avenues through which unions might alter the distribution of earnings. Evaluate: "Unions purport to be egalitarian institutions, but their effect is to increase earnings inequality among American workers."

10 Use both the demand-pull and the cost-push theories of inflation to discuss union wage-setting as a potential cause of inflation. Evaluate: "Union wage determination transmits and perpetuates, but does not cause, inflation." Use Figure 19-7b to explain the following statement: "Unionism can only be a cause of inflation if government is strongly committed to maintaining full employment."

11 Compare and account for differences in the economic status of whites and nonwhites. Distinguish between the various kinds of economic discrimination. Do you believe on balance that the distribution of education and training in our society alleviates, or contributes to, income inequality? Explain.

12 Use simple supply and demand analysis to explain the impact of occupational segregation or "crowding" upon the relative wage rates and earnings of men and women. Who gains and who loses as a consequence of eliminating occupational segregation? Is there a net gain or loss to society as a whole? "Wage differences between men and women do not reflect discrimination, but rather differences in job continuity and rational decisions with respect to education and training." Do you agree?

13 Use a simple demand and supply model to determine the gains and losses associated with the migration of population from low- to high-income countries. Explain how your conclusions are affected by **a** unemployment, **b** remittances from the host country, **c** backflows of migrants to their home countries, and **d** the personal characteristics of the migrants. If the migrants are highly skilled workers, is there any justification for the sending country to levy a "brain drain" tax on emigrants?

14 If one favors the free movement of labor within the United States, is one being inconsistent in favoring restrictions upon the international movement of labor?

15 Evaluate: "If we deported 1 million illegal aliens who are in America, our total national unemployment would decline by 1 million."

PART 7

GOSPLAN
GOSPLAN
GOSPLAN
GOSPLAN
GOSPLAN
GOSPLAN
GOSPLAN
GOSPLAN
GOSPLAN
GOSPLAN
GOSPLAN
GOSPLAN
GOSPLAN

LESS DEVELOPED COUNTRIES
LESS DEVELOPED COUNTRIES
LESS DEVELOPED COUNTRIES
LESS DEVELOPED COUNTRIES
LESS DEVELOPED COUNTRIES
LESS DEVELOPED COUNTRIES
LESS DEVELOPED COUNTRIES
LESS DEVELOPED COUNTRIES
LESS DEVELOPED COUNTRIES
LESS DEVELOPED COUNTRIES
LESS DEVELOPED COUNTRIES

PROTECTIONISM
PROTECTIONISM
PROTECTIONISM
PROTECTIONISM
PROTECTIONISM
PROTECTIONISM
PROTECTIONISM
PROTECTIONISM
PROTECTIONISM
PROTECTIONISM
PROTECTIONISM
PROTECTIONISM
PROTECTIONISM

GORBACHEV REFORMS
GORBACHEV REFORMS
GORBACHEV REFORMS
GORBACHEV REFORMS
GORBACHEV REFORMS
GORBACHEV REFORMS
GORBACHEV REFORMS
GORBACHEV REFORMS
GORBACHEV REFORMS
GORBACHEV REFORMS

International Economics and the World Economy

TARIFFS
TARIFFS

BALANCE OF PAYMENTS
BALANCE OF PAYMENTS
BALANCE OF PAYMENTS
BALANCE OF PAYMENTS
BALANCE OF PAYMENTS
BALANCE OF PAYMENTS
BALANCE OF PAYMENTS
BALANCE OF PAYMENTS
BALANCE OF PAYMENTS
BALANCE OF PAYMENTS
BALANCE OF PAYMENTS

TURNOVER TAX
TURNOVER TAX
TURNOVER TAX
TURNOVER TAX
TURNOVER TAX
TURNOVER TAX
TURNOVER TAX
TURNOVER TAX
TURNOVER TAX
TURNOVER TAX
TURNOVER TAX
TURNOVER TAX

TARIFFS
TARIFFS
TARIFFS
TARIFFS
TARIFFS
TARIFFS

WORLD BANK
WORLD BANK
WORLD BANK
WORLD BANK
WORLD BANK
WORLD BANK
WORLD BANK
WORLD BANK
WORLD BANK
WORLD BANK
WORLD BANK
WORLD BANK
WORLD BANK

TARIFFS
TARIFFS
TARIFFS
TARIFFS

FLOATING EXCHANGE RATES
FLOATING EXCHANGE RATES
FLOATING EXCHANGE RATES
FLOATING EXCHANGE RATES
FLOATING EXCHANGE RATES
FLOATING EXCHANGE RATES
FLOATING EXCHANGE RATES
FLOATING EXCHANGE RATES
FLOATING EXCHANGE RATES
FLOATING EXCHANGE RATES
FLOATING EXCHANGE RATES
FLOATING EXCHANGE RATES
FLOATING EXCHANGE RATES
FLOATING EXCHANGE RATES

GOLD STANDARD
GOLD STANDARD
GOLD STANDARD
GOLD STANDARD
GOLD STANDARD
GOLD STANDARD
GOLD STANDARD
GOLD STANDARD
GOLD STANDARD
GOLD STANDARD
GOLD STANDARD
GOLD STANDARD

PERESTROIKA
PERESTROIKA
PERESTROIKA
PERESTROIKA
PERESTROIKA
PERESTROIKA
PERESTROIKA
PERESTROIKA
PERESTROIKA
PERESTROIKA
PERESTROIKA
PERESTROIKA
PERESTROIKA
PERESTROIKA

COMPARATIVE ADVANTAGE
COMPARATIVE ADVANTAGE
COMPARATIVE ADVANTAGE
COMPARATIVE ADVANTAGE
COMPARATIVE ADVANTAGE
COMPARATIVE ADVANTAGE
COMPARATIVE ADVANTAGE
COMPARATIVE ADVANTAGE
COMPARATIVE ADVANTAGE
COMPARATIVE ADVANTAGE
COMPARATIVE ADVANTAGE
COMPARATIVE ADVANTAGE

CHAPTER 39

International trade: comparative advantage and protectionism

I n previous discussions we have emphasized that ours is an "open economy" which is linked to other nations of the world through a complex network of international trade and financial relationships. Now in Part 7 we will describe and analyze these relationships in more detail and assess both the advantages and the problems associated with them. Additionally, we will discuss the special difficulties facing the less developed nations of the world and take a close look at the economy of the Soviet Union.

The goals of the present chapter are modest in number, but of fundamental importance. First, we will look briefly at the volume and unique characteristics of international trade. Second, the principle of comparative advantage is introduced to explain how international specialization and trade can be mutually beneficial to participating nations. Third, we examine the economic impact of trade barriers such as tariffs and import quotas. Next, we set forth and evaluate critically the arguments for protectionism. The evolution of international trade policies is then summarized. Finally, we examine the recent resurgence of protectionism, noting causes, examples, and associated costs.

Importance of world trade

Is the volume of world trade sufficiently great, or are its characteristics so unique, as to merit special consideration?

VOLUME AND PATTERN

Table 39-1 provides us with a rough index of the importance of world trade for a number of representative countries. Many nations which have restricted resource bases and limited domestic markets simply cannot produce with reasonable efficiency the variety of goods they want to consume. For such countries, exports are the route for obtaining goods they desire and therefore exports

TABLE 39-1 **Merchandise exports as a percentage of gross national product, selected countries, 1986**

Country	Exports	
	Percentage of GNP	Total volume (billions of dollars)
The Netherlands	45	$ 79
Canada	28	90
West Germany	27	243
United Kingdom	23	107
New Zealand	22	6
Italy	16	98
France	17	125
Japan	11	211

Source: The World Bank, *World Development Report, 1988.*

may run from 25 to 35 percent or more of their GNP. Other countries—the United States and the Soviet Union, for example—have rich and highly diversified resource bases and vast internal markets and are therefore less dependent upon world trade.

1 Volume In the case of the United States the volume of international trade has been increasing both absolutely and relatively. Table 39-2 reflects the substantial growth in the dollar volume of both exports and imports over the past three decades. Observe that since 1960 United States' exports and imports of goods and services have more than doubled as a percentage of our GNP. Exports and imports currently are each about 11 to 13 percent of GNP. Curiously, however, the United States accounts for a diminishing percentage of total world trade. Thus in 1947 we supplied about one-third of the world's total exports as compared to about one-tenth today. World trade has increased even more rapidly for other nations than it has for the United States. *But in terms of absolute volumes of imports and exports the United States is the world's leading trading nation.*

2 Dependence There can be no question as to the United States' dependence upon the world economy. We are almost entirely dependent upon other countries for such products as bananas, cocoa, coffee, spices, tea, raw silk, nickel, tin, natural rubber, and diamonds. Casual observation suggests that imported goods compete strongly in many of our domestic markets: Japanese cameras and video recorders, French and Italian wines, English bicycles, and Japanese motorcycles and autos are a few cases in point. Foreign cars have made persistent gains in American markets and now account for about 25 percent of total sales in the United States. Even the great American pastime—baseball—relies heavily upon imported gloves!

But world trade is a two-way street, and a host of American industries are highly dependent upon foreign markets. Almost all segments of agriculture rely heavily upon foreign markets—rice, wheat, cotton, and tobacco exports vary from one-fourth to more than one-half of total output. The chemical, aircraft, automobile, machine tool, coal, and computer industries are only a few of many American industries which sell significant portions of their output in international markets. Table 39-3 shows some of the major commodity exports and imports of the United States.

3 Trade patterns We provided an overall picture of the pattern of United States merchandise trade in Table 7-6. A quick review of that table provides the basis for several observations. First, in 1988 our imports of goods from abroad were substantially in excess of our exports of goods. Second, the bulk of our export and import trade is with other developed nations, not with the less developed nations or the socialist countries of eastern Europe. Third, Canada is our most important trading partner quantitatively. Observe that 23 percent of our exports are sold to Canadians, who in turn provide us with 19 percent of our imports. Fourth, there is a sizable imbalance in our trade with Japan; our

TABLE 39-2 **Trade in the U.S. economy, 1960–1988*** *(dollars in billions)*

	1960		1970		1988	
	Amount	Percent of GNP	Amount	Percent of GNP	Amount	Percent of GNP
Exports of goods and services	$29.9	5.8	$68.9	6.8	$518.7	10.7
Imports of goods and services	24.0	4.7	60.5	6.0	611.9	12.6
Net exports	5.9	1.1	8.5	0.8	−93.2	1.9

* Data are on a national income accounts basis.

Source: Department of Commerce.

TABLE 39-3 **Principal commodity exports and imports of the United States, 1988** *(in billions)*

Exports	Amount	Imports	Amount
Chemicals	$20.5	Automobiles	$47.9
Computers	17.4	Petroleum	42.9
Grains	10.5	Clothing	20.5
Generating equipment	8.4	Household appliances	16.1
Automobiles	7.5	Computers	14.9
Aircraft	7.5	Iron and steel	11.0
Consumer durables	6.6	Chemicals	9.9
Nonferrous metals	6.4	Telecommunications	8.1
Paper	6.0	Semiconductors	7.8
Semiconductors	5.4	Toys and sporting goods	7.2

Source: U.S. Department of Commerce.

imports greatly exceed our exports. Finally, our dependence upon foreign oil is reflected in the excess of imports over exports in our trade with the OPEC nations.

4 Level of output Changes in net exports, that is, in the difference between the value of a nation's exports and that of its imports, have multiple effects upon the level of national income in roughly the same fashion as do fluctuations in the various types of domestic spending. A small change in the volume of American imports and exports can have magnified repercussions upon the domestic levels of income, employment, and prices.

With these points in mind, we need not belabor the significance of international trade for such nations as the Netherlands, Japan, Australia, and Great Britain, whose volumes of international trade constitute substantially larger fractions of their national incomes.

UNIQUE ASPECTS

Aside from essentially quantitative considerations, world trade has certain unique characteristics which require us to devote special attention to it.

1 Mobility differences Though the difference is a matter of degree, the mobility of resources is considerably less among nations than it is within nations. American workers, for example, are free to move from Iowa to California or from Maine to Texas. If workers want to move, they can do so. Crossing international boundaries is a different story.

Immigration laws, not to mention language and cultural barriers, put severe restrictions upon the migration of labor between nations. Different tax laws, different governmental regulations, different business practices, and a host of other institutional barriers limit the migration of real capital over international boundaries.

International trade is a substitute for the international mobility of resources. If human and property resources do not move readily among nations, the movement of goods and services can provide an effective substitute.

2 Currency differences Each nation uses a different currency. Hence, an American firm distributing Hondas or Jaguars in the United States must buy yen or pounds to pay the Japanese or British automobile manufacturers. The possible complications which may accompany this exchange of currencies will be pursued in Chapter 40.

3 Politics As we will note shortly, international trade is subject to political interferences and controls which differ markedly in degree and kind from those applying to domestic trade.

The economic basis for trade

But why do nations trade? What is the basis for trade between nations? Stated most generally, *international trade is a means by which nations can specialize, increase the productivity of their resources, and thereby realize a larger total output than otherwise.* Sovereign nations, like individuals and regions of a nation, can gain by specializing in those products which they can produce with greatest relative efficiency and by trading for those goods they cannot produce efficiently.

While the above rationale for world trade is quite correct, it in a sense begs the question. A more sophisticated answer to the question "Why do nations trade?" hinges upon two points. First, the distribution of economic resources—natural, human, and capital goods—among the nations of the world is quite uneven; nations are substantially different in their endowments of economic resources. Second, the efficient production of various goods requires different technologies or combinations of resources.

The character and interaction of these two points can be readily illustrated. Japan, for example, has a large and well-educated labor force; skilled labor is abundant and therefore cheap. Hence, Japan can produce efficiently (at low cost) a variety of goods whose production requires much skilled labor; cameras, transistor radios, and video recorders are some examples of such **labor-intensive** commodities. In contrast, Australia has vast amounts of land in comparison with its human and capital resources and hence can cheaply produce such **land-intensive** commodities as wheat, wool, and meat. Brazil possesses the soil, tropical climate, rainfall, and ample supplies of unskilled labor requisite to the efficient low-cost production of coffee. Industrially advanced nations are in a strategic position to produce cheaply a variety of **capital-intensive** goods, for example, automobiles, agricultural equipment, machinery, and chemicals.

It is important to emphasize that the economic efficiency with which nations can produce various goods can and does change over time. Both the distribution of resources and technology can change so as to alter the relative efficiency with which goods can be produced by various countries. For example, in the past fifty years the Soviet Union has substantially upgraded the quality of its labor force and has greatly expanded its stock of capital. Hence, although Russia was primarily an exporter of agricultural products and raw materials a half-century ago, it now exports large quantities of manufactured goods. Similarly, the new technologies which gave rise to synthetic fibers and synthetic rubber drastically altered the resource-mix needed to produce these goods and thereby changed the relative efficiency of nations in manufacturing them. In short, as national economies evolve, the size and quality of their labor forces may change, the volume and composition of their capital stocks may shift, new technologies will develop, and even the quantity and quality of land and natural resources may be altered. As these changes occur, the relative efficiency with which a nation can produce various goods will also change.

Specialization and comparative advantage

Let us now introduce the concept of comparative advantage and employ it in analyzing the basis for international specialization and trade.

THE BASIC PRINCIPLE

The central idea underlying the concept of comparative advantage is illustrated in Chapter 3's Last Word, which you should review at this point. In that example we found that an accountant could lower his cost of getting his house painted by specializing in accounting and using some of the proceeds to hire a house painter. Similarly, the house painter could reduce the costs of getting his tax returns completed by specializing in painting and employing the accountant to complete his returns. The gains from specialization and exchange occurred because the accountant had a relative or comparative advantage in accounting, while the painter had a relative or comparative advantage in painting houses. Although the accountant was better than the professional painter at both accounting and painting, specialization by comparative advantage yielded advantages to each. The illustration makes clear that specialization and trade can lower the cost of obtaining valuable products and services.

With this simple example in mind, let us turn to an international trade model to acquire an understanding of the gains from international specialization and trade.

TWO ISOLATED NATIONS

Suppose the world economy is composed of just two nations, say, the United States and Brazil. Assume further that each is capable of producing both wheat and coffee, but at differing levels of economic efficiency. To be specific, let us suppose that

the United States' and Brazilian domestic production possibilities curves for coffee and wheat are as shown in Figure 39-1a and b. Two characteristics of these production possibilities curves must be stressed.

I Constant costs We have purposely drawn the "curves" as straight lines, in contrast to the concave-from-the-origin type of production possibilities boundaries introduced in Chapter 2. This means we have in effect replaced the law of increasing costs with the assumption of constant costs. This simplification will greatly facilitate our discussion. With increasing costs, the comparative costs of the two nations in producing coffee and wheat would vary with the amounts produced, and comparative advantages might even change. The assumption of constant costs permits us to complete our entire analysis without having to shift to different comparative-cost ratios with every variation in output. The constant-cost assumption will not impair the validity of our analysis and conclu-

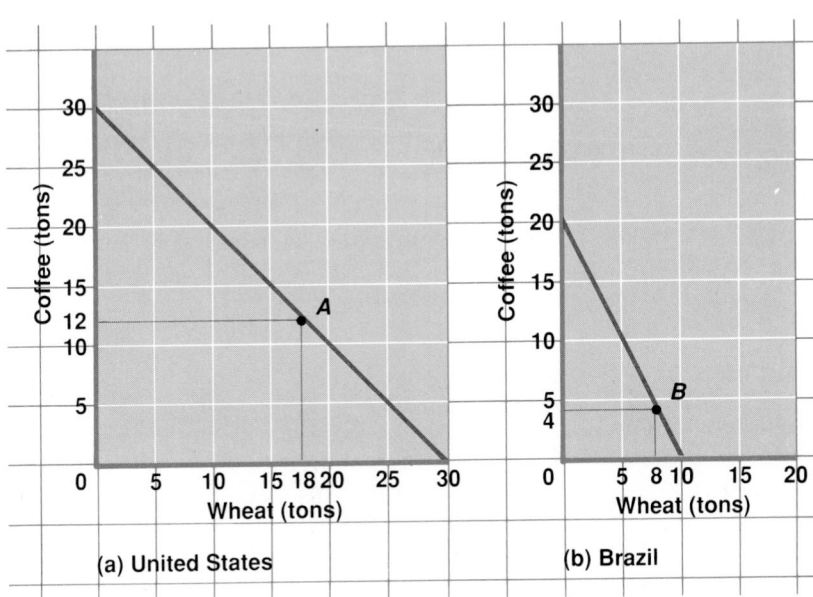

FIGURE 39-1

Production possibilities for the United States and Brazil

The two production possibilities lines show the amounts of coffee and wheat the United States (a) and Brazil (b) can produce domestically. The production possibilities for both countries are straight lines because we are assuming constant costs. The different cost ratios—1W = 1C for the United States and 1W = 2C for Brazil—are reflected in the different slopes of the two lines.

sions. We shall consider later in our discussion the effect of the more realistic assumption of increasing costs.

2 Different costs   The production possibilities lines of the United States and Brazil are drawn differently, reflecting different resource mixes and differing levels of technological progress. More specifically, the opportunity costs of producing wheat and coffee differ between the two nations. We note in Figure 39-1a that under conditions of full employment, the United States can increase its output of wheat 30 tons by forgoing 30 tons of coffee output. In other words, the slope of the production possibilities curve is -1 $(= -1/1)$, which implies that 1 ton of wheat can be obtained for every 1 ton of coffee sacrificed. That is to say, in the United States the domestic exchange ratio or **cost ratio** for the two products is 1 ton of wheat for 1 ton of coffee, or simply $1W = 1C$. The United States, in effect, can "exchange" a ton of wheat for a ton of coffee domestically by shifting resources from wheat to coffee. Our constant-cost assumption means that this exchange or cost ratio prevails for all possible shifts from one point to another along the United States' production possibilities curve.

Brazil's production possibilities line in Figure 39-1b reveals a different exchange or cost ratio. In Brazil 20 tons of coffee must be given up to get 10 tons of wheat. Hence, the slope of the production possibilities curve is $-2(= -2/1)$. This means that in Brazil the domestic cost ratio for the two goods is 1 ton of wheat for 2 tons of coffee, or $1W = 2C$.

Self-sufficiency   If the United States and Brazil are isolated and therefore self-sufficient, each must choose some output-mix on its production possibilities line. Let us assume that point *A* in Figure 39-1a is regarded as the optimal output-mix in the United States. The choice of this combination of 18 tons of wheat and 12 tons of coffee is presumably rendered through the market system, as described in Chapters 5 and 32. Suppose Brazil's optimal product-mix is 8 tons of wheat and 4 tons of coffee, as indicated by point *B* in Figure 39-1b. These choices are also reflected in column 1 of Table 39-4.

SPECIALIZING ACCORDING TO COMPARATIVE ADVANTAGE

Given these different cost ratios, is there any rule or guideline which will tell us the products in which the United States and Brazil should specialize? Yes, there is: The **principle of comparative advantage** says that *total output will be greatest when each good is produced by that nation which has the lower opportunity cost.* For our illustration, the United States' opportunity cost is lower for wheat, that is, the United States need only forgo 1 ton of coffee to produce 1 ton of wheat, whereas Brazil must forgo 2 tons of coffee for 1 ton of wheat. *The United States, therefore, has a comparative (cost) advantage in wheat, and it should specialize in wheat production.* The "world" (the United States and

TABLE 39-4 **International specialization according to comparative advantage and the gains from trade** *(hypothetical data; in tons)*

Country	(1) Outputs before specialization	(2) Outputs after specialization	(3) Amounts exported (−) and imported (+)	(4) Outputs available after trade	(5) = (4) − (1) Gains from specialization and trade
United States	18 wheat 12 coffee	30 wheat 0 coffee	−10 wheat +15 coffee	20 wheat 15 coffee	2 wheat 3 coffee
Brazil	8 wheat 4 coffee	0 wheat 20 coffee	+10 wheat −15 coffee	10 wheat 5 coffee	2 wheat 1 coffee

Brazil) clearly is *not* economizing in the use of its resources if a given product (wheat) is produced by a high-cost producer (Brazil) when it could have been produced by a low-cost producer (the United States). To have Brazil produce wheat would mean that the world economy would have to give up more coffee than is necessary to obtain a ton of wheat.

Conversely, Brazil's opportunity cost is lower for coffee, that is, Brazil must sacrifice only $\frac{1}{2}$ ton of wheat in producing 1 ton of coffee, whereas the United States must forgo 1 ton of wheat in producing a ton of coffee. *Brazil has a comparative advantage in coffee, and therefore it should specialize in coffee production.* Again, the world would *not* be employing its resources economically if coffee were produced by a high-cost producer (the United States) rather than a low-cost producer (Brazil). If the United States produced coffee, the world would be giving up more wheat than would be necessary to obtain each ton of coffee. *Economizing—using given quantities of scarce resources so as to obtain the greatest total output—requires that any particular good be produced by that nation which has the lower opportunity cost or, in other words, which has the comparative advantage.* In our illustration, the United States should produce wheat and Brazil should produce coffee.

By looking at column 2 of Table 39-4, we can quickly verify that specialized production in accordance with the principle of comparative advantage does, indeed, allow the world to get more output from its fixed amount of resources. By specializing completely in wheat, the United States can produce 30 tons of wheat and no coffee. Similarly, by specializing completely in coffee, Brazil produces 20 tons of coffee and no wheat. We note that the world has more wheat—30 tons as compared with 26 (= 18 + 8) tons—*and* more coffee—20 tons as compared with 16 (= 12 + 4) tons—than in the case of self-sufficiency or unspecialized production.

TERMS OF TRADE

But the consumers of each nation will want *both* wheat and coffee. Specialization implies the need to trade or exchange the two products. What will be the **terms of trade?** At what exchange ratio will

the United States and Brazil trade wheat and coffee? We know that because $1W = 1C$ in the United States, the United States must get *more than* 1 ton of coffee for each ton of wheat exported or it will not pay the United States to export wheat in exchange for Brazilian coffee. Stated differently, the United States must get a better price (more coffee) for its wheat in the world market than it can get domestically, or else trade will not be advantageous. Similarly, because $1W = 2C$ in Brazil, we know that Brazil must be able to get 1 ton of wheat by exporting some amount *less than* 2 tons of coffee. Brazil must be able to pay a lower "price" for wheat in the world market than it must pay domestically, or it will not wish to engage in international trade. Thus we can be certain that the international exchange ratio or **terms of trade** must lie somewhere between

$$1W = 1C$$

and

$$1W = 2C$$

But where will the actual world exchange ratio fall between the $1W = 1C$ limit (established by cost conditions in the United States) and the $1W = 2C$ limit (determined by cost conditions in Brazil)? This question is very important, because the exchange ratio or terms of trade determine how the gains from international specialization and trade are divided among the two nations. Of course, the United States will prefer a rate close to $1W = 2C$, say, $1W = 1\frac{3}{4}C$. Americans want to get a great deal of coffee for each ton of wheat they export. Similarly, Brazil desires a rate approximating $1W = 1C$, say, $1W = 1\frac{1}{4}C$. Brazil wants to export as little coffee as possible for each ton of wheat it receives in exchange.

The actual exchange ratio that will materialize between the two limits depends upon world supply and demand conditions for the two products. If the overall world demand for coffee is weak relative to its supply and the demand for wheat is strong relative to its supply, the price of coffee will be low and that of wheat high. The exchange ratio will settle near the $1W = 2C$ figure preferred by the United States. Under the opposite world supply and demand conditions, the ratio will settle near the $1W = 1C$ level most favorable to Brazil.

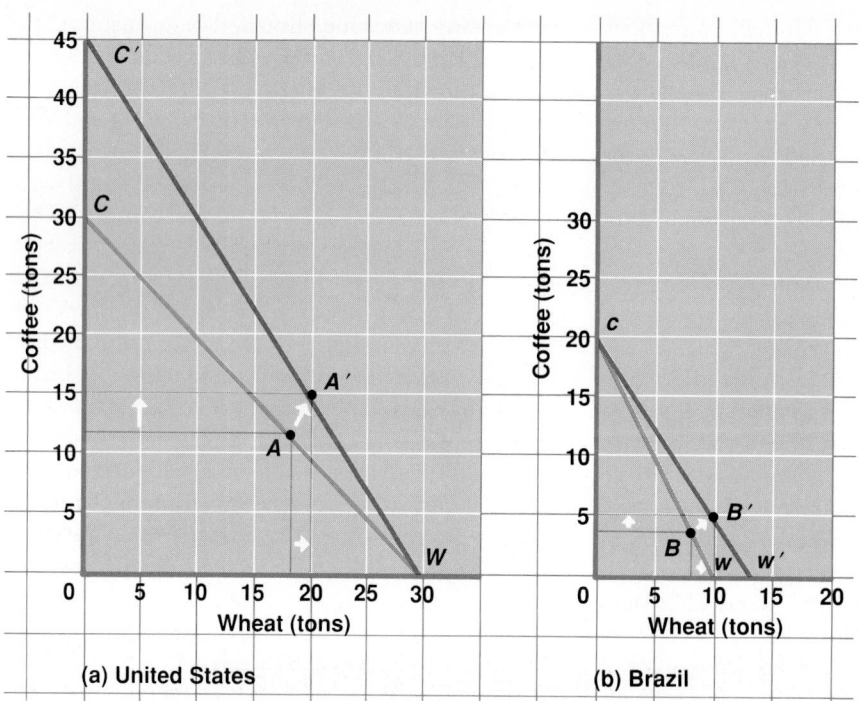

FIGURE 39-2

Trading possibilities lines and the gains from trade

As a result of international specialization and trade, the United States and Brazil can both realize levels of output superior to those attainable on their domestic production possibilities curves. For example, the United States in (a) can move from point *A* on its domestic production possibilities line to point *A′* on its trading possibilities line; similarly, Brazil in (b) can move from *B* to *B′*.

THE GAINS FROM TRADE

Let us arbitrarily suppose that the international exchange ratio or terms of trade are actually $1W = 1\frac{1}{2}C$. The possibility of trading on these terms permits each nation to supplement its domestic production possibilities line with a **trading possibilities line.** This can be seen in Figure 39-2a and b. Just as a production possibilities line shows the options that a full-employment economy has in obtaining one product by shifting resources from the production of another, so a trading possibilities line shows the options that a nation has by specializing in one product and trading (exporting) its speciality to obtain the other product. The trading possibilities lines in Figure 39-2 are drawn on the assumption that both nations specialize in accordance with comparative advantage and therefore that the United States specializes completely in wheat (point *W* in Figure 39-2a) and Brazil completely in coffee (point *c* in Figure 39-2b).

Now, instead of being constrained by its domestic production possibilities line and having to give up 1 ton of wheat for every ton of coffee it wants as it moves up its domestic production possibilities

line from point *W*, the United States, through trade with Brazil, can get $1\frac{1}{2}$ tons of coffee for every ton of wheat it exports to Brazil as it moves up the trading line *WC′*.

Similarly, we can think of Brazil as starting at point *c*, and instead of having to move down its domestic production possibilities line and thereby having to give up 2 tons of coffee for each ton of wheat it wants, it can now export just $1\frac{1}{2}$ tons of coffee for each ton of wheat it wants by moving down its *cw′* trading possibilities line.

Specialization and trade give rise to a new exchange ratio between wheat and coffee which is reflected in a nation's trading possibilities line. This new exchange ratio is superior for both nations to the self-sufficiency exchange ratio embodied in the production possibilities line of each. By specializing in wheat and trading for Brazil's coffee, the United States can obtain *more than* 1 ton of coffee for 1 ton of wheat. Similarly, by specializing in coffee and trading for the United States' wheat, Brazil can get 1 ton of wheat for *less than* 2 tons of coffee.

The crucial fact to note is that by specializing according to comparative advantage and trading for those goods produced with the least relative efficiency domestically, both the United States and Brazil can realize combinations of wheat and coffee which lie beyond their production possibilities boundaries. *Specialization according to comparative advantage results in a more efficient allocation of world resources, and larger outputs of both wheat and coffee are therefore available to the United States and Brazil.* To be more specific, suppose that at the $1W = 1\frac{1}{2}C$ terms of trade, the United States exports 10 tons of wheat to Brazil and Brazil in return exports 15 tons of coffee to the United States.

How do the new quantities of wheat and coffee available to the two nations compare with the optimal product-mixes that existed before specialization and trade? Point *A* in Figure 39-2a reminds us that the United States chose 18 tons of wheat and 12 tons of coffee originally. But, by producing 30 tons of wheat and no coffee, and by trading 10 tons of wheat for 15 tons of coffee, the United States can enjoy 20 tons of wheat and 15 tons of coffee. This new, superior combination of wheat and coffee is shown by point *A'* in Figure 39-2a. Compared with the nontrading figures of 18 tons of wheat and 12 tons of coffee, the United States' **gains from trade** are 2 tons of wheat and 3 tons of coffee. Similarly, we assumed Brazil's optimal product-mix was 4 tons of coffee and 8 tons of wheat (point *B*) before specialization and trade. Now, by specializing in coffee and thereby producing 20 tons of coffee and no wheat, Brazil can realize a combination of 5 tons of coffee and 10 tons of wheat by exporting 15 tons of its coffee in exchange for 10 tons of American wheat. This new position is shown by point *B'* in Figure 39-2b. Brazil's gains from trade are 1 ton of coffee and 2 tons of wheat.

As a result of specialization and trade, both countries have more of both products. Table 39-4 is a summary statement of all these figures and merits careful study by the reader.

The fact that points *A'* and *B'* are economic positions superior to *A* and *B* is extremely important. You will recall from Chapter 2 that a given nation can expand its production possibilities boundary by (1) expanding the quantity and improving the quality of its resources or (2) realizing technological progress. We have now discovered another means—international trade—by which a nation can circumvent the output constraint imposed by its production possibilities curve. The effects of international specialization and trade are tantamount to having more and better resources or discovering improved production techniques.

INCREASING COSTS

In formulating a straightforward statement of the principles underlying international trade, we have invoked a number of simplifying assumptions. Our discussion was purposely limited to two products and two nations in order to minimize verbiage; multination and multiproduct examples yield similar conclusions. The assumption of constant costs, on the other hand, is a more substantive simplification. Let us therefore pause to consider the significance of increasing costs (concave-from-the-origin production possibility curves) for our analysis.

Suppose, as in our previous constant-cost illustration, that the United States and Brazil are at positions on their production possibilities curves where their cost ratios are initially $1W = 1C$ and $1W = 2C$ respectively. As before, comparative advantage indicates that the United States should specialize in wheat and Brazil in coffee. But now, as the United States begins to expand its wheat production, its $1W = 1C$ cost ratio will *fall*; that is, it will have to sacrifice *more than* 1 ton of coffee to get 1 additional ton of wheat. Resources are no longer perfectly shiftable between alternative uses, as the constant-cost assumption implied. Resources less and less suitable to wheat production must be allocated to the American wheat industry in expanding wheat output, and this means increasing costs—the sacrifice of larger and larger amounts of coffee for each additional ton of wheat. Similarly, Brazil, starting from its $1W = 2C$ cost ratio position, expands coffee production. But as it does, it will find that its $1W = 2C$ cost ratio begins to *rise*. Sacrificing a ton of wheat will free resources which are only capable of producing something *less than* 2 tons of coffee, because these transferred resources are less suitable to coffee production.

Hence, as the American cost ratio falls from $1W = 1C$ and Brazil's rises from $1W = 2C$, a point will be reached at which the cost ratios are equal in the two nations, for example, at $1W = 1\frac{1}{2}C$. At this point the underlying basis for further specialization and trade—differing cost ratios—has disappeared, and further specialization is therefore uneconomic. And most important, this point of equal cost ratio may be realized where the United States is still producing some coffee along with its wheat and Brazil is producing some wheat along with its coffee. *The primary effect of increasing costs is to make specialization less than complete.* For this reason we often find domestically produced products competing directly against identical or similar imported products within a particular economy.

THE CASE FOR FREE TRADE RESTATED

The compelling logic of the case for free trade is hardly new. Indeed, in 1776 Adam Smith got to the heart of the matter by asserting:

It is the maxim of every prudent master of a family, never to attempt to make at home what it will cost him more to make than to buy. The taylor does not attempt to make his own shoes, but buys them of the shoemaker. The shoemaker does not attempt to make his own clothes but employs a taylor. The farmer attempts to make neither the one nor the other, but employs those different artificers. All of them find it for their interest to employ their whole industry in a way in which they have some advantage over their neighbors, and to purchase with a part of its produce, or what is the same thing, with the price of a part of it, whatever else they have occasion for.[1]

In modern jargon, the case for free trade comes down to this one potent argument. *Through free trade based upon the principle of comparative advantage, the world economy can achieve a more efficient allocation of resources and a higher level of material well-being.* The resource mixes and technological knowledge of each country are different. Therefore, each nation can produce particular commodities at different real costs. Each nation should produce goods for which its costs are low relative to those of other nations and exchange these specialities for products for which its costs are high relative to those of other nations. If each nation does this, the world can realize fully the advantages of geographic and human specialization. That is, the world—and each free-trading nation—can realize a larger real income from the given supplies of resources available to it. Protection—barriers to free trade—lessens or eliminates the gains from specialization. If nations cannot freely trade, they must shift resources from efficient (low-cost) to inefficient (high-cost) uses in order to satisfy their diverse wants.

A side benefit of free trade is that it promotes competition and deters monopoly. The increased competition afforded by foreign firms forces domestic firms to adopt the lowest-cost production techniques. It also compels them to be innovative and progressive with respect to both product quality and production methods, thereby contributing to economic growth. And free trade provides consumers with a wider range of products from which to choose. The reasons to favor free trade are essentially the same reasons which endorse competition. Therefore, it is not surprising that the vast majority of economists embrace the case for free trade as an economically valid position.

Trade barriers

No matter how compelling the logic of the case for free trade, in fact a wide variety of barriers to free trade do exist.

1 Tariffs are excise taxes on imported goods; they may be imposed for purposes of revenue or protection. **Revenue tariffs** are usually applied to products which are not produced domestically, for example, tin, coffee, and bananas in the case of the United States. Rates on revenue tariffs are typically modest and their purpose is to provide the Federal government with tax revenues. **Protective tariffs,** on the other hand, are designed to shield domestic producers from foreign competition. Although protective tariffs are usually not high enough to prohibit the importation of foreign goods, they put foreign producers at a competitive disadvantage in selling in domestic markets.

2 Import quotas specify the maximum amounts of commodities which may be imported in any period of time. Frequently, import quotas are more effective in retarding international commerce than are tariffs. A given product might be imported in relatively large quantities despite high tariffs; low import quotas, on the other hand, completely prohibit imports once the quotas are filled. We will empha-

[1] Adam Smith, *The Wealth of Nations* (New York: Modern Library, Inc., 1937), p. 424.

size protective tariffs in the following discussion of protectionism.

3 Nontariff barriers (NTBs) refer to licensing requirements, unreasonable standards pertaining to product quality and safety, or simply unnecessary bureaucratic red tape in customs procedures. To illustrate: Japan and the European countries frequently require their domestic importers of foreign goods to obtain licenses. By restricting the issuance of licenses, imports can be effectively restricted. Great Britain bars the importation of coal in this way.

4 Voluntary export restrictions (VERs) are a relatively new trade barrier by which foreign firms "voluntarily" limit the amount of their exports to a particular country. VERs, which have the effect of import quotas, are agreed to by exporters in the hope of avoiding more stringent trade barriers. Thus Japanese auto manufacturers agreed to a VER on exports to the United States under the threat of higher U.S. tariffs or the imposition of low import quotas.

MOTIVATIONS: SPECIAL-INTEREST EFFECT

If tariffs and quotas impede free trade and thereby diminish economic efficiency, why do we have them? While nations as a whole gain from free international trade, particular industries and groups of resource suppliers can be hurt. In our comparative advantage example, specialization and trade adversely affected the American coffee industry and the Brazilian wheat industry. It is easy to see why such groups may seek to preserve or improve their economic positions by persuading the government to impose tariffs or quotas to protect them from the detrimental effects of free trade. Chapter 33's special-interest effect—or concept of rent-seeking activity—is highly relevant.

The direct beneficiaries of import relief or export subsidy are usually few in number, but each has a large individual stake in the outcome. Thus, their incentive for vigorous political activity is strong.

But the costs of such policies may far exceed the benefits. It may cost the public $40,000–$50,000 a year to protect a domestic job that might otherwise pay an employee only half that amount in wages and benefits. Furthermore, the costs of protection are widely dif-

fused—in the United States, among 50 States and [240] million citizens. Since the cost borne by any one citizen is likely to be quite small, and may even go unnoticed, resistance at the grass-roots level to protectionist measures often is considerably less than pressures for their adoption.[2]

It should also be added that the costs of protectionism are hidden because tariffs and quotas are embedded in the prices of goods. Thus policy makers face fewer political restraints in responding positively to demands for protectionism.

Later in this chapter we will consider the specific arguments and appeals which are made to justify protection.

ECONOMIC IMPACT OF TARIFFS

Let us now employ simple supply and demand analysis to examine the economic effects of the most widely used trade barrier—protective tariffs. The D_d and S_d curves in Figure 39-3 show domestic demand and supply for a product in which the United States has a comparative *dis*advantage, for example, cassette recorders. In the absence of world trade, the domestic price and output would be OP_d and Oq, respectively.

Assume now that the domestic economy is opened to world trade, and that the Japanese, who have a comparative advantage in cassette recorders and dominate the world market, begin to sell their recorders in the United States. We assume that with free trade the domestic price cannot differ from the lower world price, which here is OP_w. We observe at OP_w that domestic consumption is Od, domestic production is Oa, and the difference between the two, ad, reflects imports.

Direct effects Suppose now that the United States imposes a tariff of P_wP_t per unit on the imported recorders. This will raise the domestic price from OP_w to OP_t and will have a variety of effects.

First, the consumption of recorders in the United States will decline from Od to Oc as the higher price moves buyers up their demand curve. American consumers are clearly injured by the tariff. Because of the tariff, they pay P_wP_t more for

[2] *Economic Report of the President, 1982*, p. 177.

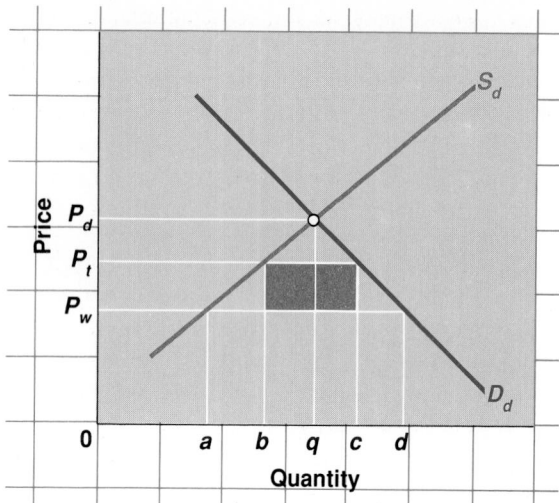

FIGURE 39-3

The economic effects of a protective tariff

A tariff of P_wP_t will reduce domestic consumption from Od to Oc. Domestic producers will be able to sell more output (Ob rather than Oa) at a higher price (OP_t rather than OP_w). Foreign exporters are injured because they are able to sell less output (bc rather than ad) in the United States. The orange area indicates the amount of tariffs paid by American consumers.

each of the Oc units which they now buy at price P_t. Additionally, the tariff prompts consumers to buy fewer recorders; that is, to reallocate a portion of their expenditures to less desired substitute products.

Second, American producers—who are *not* subject to the tariff—will receive a higher price of OP_t per unit. Because this new price is higher than the pretariff or world price of OP_w, the domestic recorder industry will move up its supply curve S_d, increasing domestic output from Oa to Ob. Domestic producers will enjoy both a higher price and expanded sales. These effects explain the interest of domestic producers in lobbying for protective tariffs. From a social point of view, however, the expanded domestic production of ab reflects the fact that the tariff permits domestic producers of recorders to bid resources away from other, more efficient, industries.

Third, Japanese producers will be hurt. Although the sales price of recorders is higher by P_wP_t, that increase accrues to the United States

government and not to Japanese producers. The after-tariff world price, and thus the per unit revenue to Japanese producers, remains at OP_w, while the volume of United States imports (Japanese exports) falls from ad to bc.

Finally, note that the orange rectangle indicates the amount of revenue which the tariff yields. Specifically, total revenue from the tariff is determined by multiplying the tariff of P_tP_w per unit by the number of imported recorders, bc. This tariff revenue is essentially a transfer of income from consumers to government and does not represent any net change in the nation's economic well-being. The result is that government gains a portion of what consumers lose.

Indirect effects   There are more subtle effects of tariffs which go beyond our simple supply and demand diagram. Because of diminished sales of recorders in the United States, Japan will now earn fewer dollars with which to buy American exports. That is, American export industries—industries in which the United States has a comparative advantage—will cut production and release resources. These are highly efficient industries, as is evidenced by their comparative advantage and their ability to sell goods in world markets. In short, *tariffs directly promote the expansion of relatively inefficient industries which do not have a comparative advantage and indirectly cause the contraction of relatively efficient industries which do have a comparative advantage.* This means that tariffs cause resources to be shifted in the wrong direction. This is not surprising. We know that specialization and unfettered world trade based on comparative advantage would lead to the efficient use of world resources and an expansion of the world's real output. The purpose and effect of protective tariffs are to reduce world trade. Therefore, aside from their specific effects upon consumers and foreign and domestic producers, tariffs diminish the world's real output.

The case for protection: a critical review

Although free-trade advocates tend to prevail in the classroom, protectionists sometimes dominate the halls of Congress. What arguments do protectionists make to justify trade barriers? Of what validity are these arguments?

MILITARY SELF-SUFFICIENCY ARGUMENT

The argument here is not economic, but rather, it is of a political-military nature: Protective tariffs are needed to preserve or strengthen industries producing strategic goods and materials essential for defense or war. It very plausibly contends that in an uncertain world, political-military objectives (self-sufficiency) must take precedence over economic goals (efficiency in the allocation of world resources).

Unfortunately, there is no objective criterion for weighing the relative worth of the increase in national security on the one hand, and the decrease in productive efficiency on the other, which accompany the reallocation of resources toward strategic industries when such tariffs are imposed. The economist can only call attention to the fact that certain economic costs are involved when tariffs are levied to enhance military self-sufficiency.

Although we might all agree that it is probably not a good idea to import our missile guidance systems from the Soviet Union, the self-sufficiency argument is nevertheless open to serious abuse. Virtually every industry can directly or indirectly claim a contribution to national security. Can you name an industry which did *not* contribute in some small way to the execution of World War II? Aside from abuses, are there not means superior to tariffs which will provide for needed strength in strategic industries? When achieved through tariffs, self-sufficiency gives rise to costs in the form of higher domestic prices on the output of the shielded industry. The cost of enhanced military security is apportioned arbitrarily among those consumers who buy the industry's product. Virtually all economists agree that a direct subsidy to strategic industries, financed out of general tax revenues, would entail a more equitable distribution of these costs.

INCREASE DOMESTIC EMPLOYMENT

This "save American jobs" argument for tariffs becomes increasingly fashionable as an economy encounters a recession. It is rooted in macro analysis. Aggregate expenditures in an open economy are comprised of consumption expenditures (C) plus investment expenditures (I) plus government expenditures (G) plus net export expenditures (X_n). Net export expenditures consist of exports (X) minus imports (M). By reducing imports, M, aggregate expenditures will rise, stimulating the domestic economy by boosting income and employment. But there are important shortcomings associated with this policy.

1 While imports may eliminate some American jobs, they create others. Imports may have eliminated the jobs of American steel and textile workers in recent years, but others have gained jobs selling Hondas and imported electronics equipment. Thus, while import restrictions alter the composition of employment, they may actually have little or no effect on the volume of employment.

2 It is apparent that all nations cannot simultaneously succeed in import restriction. The exports of one nation must be the imports of another. To the extent that one country is able to stimulate its economy through an excess of exports over imports, some other economy's unemployment problem is worsened by the resulting excess of imports over exports. It is no wonder that tariff boosts and the imposition of import quotas for the purposes of achieving domestic full employment are termed "beggar my neighbor" policies. They achieve domestic goals by making trading partners poorer.

3 Nations adversely affected by tariffs and quotas are likely to retaliate, causing a competitive raising of trade barriers which will choke off trade to the end that all nations are worse off. It is not surprising that the **Smoot-Hawley Tariff Act of 1930,** which imposed the highest tariffs ever enacted in the United States, backfired miserably. Rather than stimulate the American economy, this tariff act only induced a series of retaliatory restrictions by adversely affected nations. This caused a further contraction of international trade and tended to lower the income and employment levels of all nations.

4 Lastly, in the long run an excess of exports over imports is doomed to failure as a device for stimulating domestic employment. Remember: It is through American imports that foreign nations earn dollars with which to purchase American exports. In the long run a nation must import in

order to export. Hence, the long-run impact of tariffs is not to increase domestic employment but at best to reallocate workers away from export industries and toward protected domestic industries. This shift implies a less efficient allocation of resources. Tariffs divert resources away from those industries in which production is so efficient as to provide a comparative advantage. There is little doubt that intelligent, well-timed monetary and fiscal policies are preferable to tariff and quota adjustments as anticyclical techniques.

In summary, the argument that tariffs increase net exports and therefore create jobs is misleading:

Overall employment in an economy is determined by internal conditions and macroeconomic policies, not by the existence of trade barriers and the level of trade flows. The United States created nearly 15 million payroll jobs over the course of the current economic expansion, a period of U.S. trade deficits and relatively open U.S. markets. During the same period the European Community (EC) created virtually no net new jobs, even though they experienced trade surpluses. The same level of employment can be obtained in the total absence of free trade as when trade is completely free. But without foreign trade a nation will be worse off economically because, in effect, it will throw away part of its productive capability—the ability to convert surplus goods into other goods through foreign trade.[3]

DIVERSIFICATION FOR STABILITY

Closely related to the increase-domestic-employment argument for tariff protection is the diversification-for-stability argument. The point here is that highly specialized economies—for example, Kuwait's oil economy or Cuba's sugar economy—are highly dependent upon international markets for their incomes. Wars, cyclical fluctuations, and adverse changes in the structure of industry will force large and frequently painful readjustments upon such economies. It is therefore alleged that tariff and quota protection is needed in such nations to promote greater industrial diversification and consequently less dependence upon world markets for just one or two products. This will help

[3] *Economic Report of the President, 1988,* p. 131.

insulate the domestic economy from international political developments, depressions abroad, and from random fluctuations in world supply and demand for one or two particular commodities, thereby providing greater domestic stability.

There is some truth in this argument. There are also serious qualifications and shortcomings. First, the argument has little or no relevance to the United States and other advanced economies. Second, the economic costs of diversification may be great; for example, one-crop economies may be highly inefficient in manufacturing.

INFANT-INDUSTRY ARGUMENT

The infant-industry argument contends that protective tariffs are needed for the purpose of allowing new domestic industries to establish themselves. Temporarily shielding young domestic firms from the severe competition afforded by more mature and therefore currently more efficient foreign firms will give the infant industries a chance to develop and become efficient producers. This argument for protection rests upon an alleged exception to the case for free trade. The exception is that all industries have not had, and in the presence of mature foreign competition, will never have, the chance to make long-run adjustments in the direction of larger scale and greater efficiency in production. The provision of tariff protection for infant industries will therefore correct a current misallocation of world resources now perpetuated by historically different levels of economic development between domestic and foreign industries.

Counterarguments Though the infant-industry argument has logical validity, these qualifying points must be noted. First, this argument is not particularly pertinent to industrially advanced nations such as the United States. Second, in the less developed nations it is very difficult to determine which industries are the infants capable of achieving economic maturity and therefore deserving of protection. Third, unlike old soldiers, protective tariffs may not fade away, but rather, persist even after industrial maturity has been realized. Finally, most economists feel that if infant industries are to be subsidized, there are better means than tariffs for doing it. Direct subsidies, for example, have the advantage of making explicit which industries are being aided and to what degree.

"Breathing spell" variant In recent years the infant-industry argument has taken a somewhat modified form. Suddenly confronted with foreign competition, an American industry may argue that it needs protection to provide a "breathing spell" so that it may modernize and become more competitive. The problem with this argument is that, while protection may enhance profits and therefore provide the means for modernization, it also reduces the pressures for adjustment. Instead of improving an industry's efficiency, protection may cause it to further deteriorate. Moreover, this type of protection may send a message to other industries that they also can expect similar protection in the event they encounter strong import competition in the future. Hence, these other industries may become lax in their efforts to improve product quality and minimize production costs.

PROTECTION AGAINST "DUMPING"

The protection-against-dumping argument for tariffs contends that tariffs are needed to protect American firms from foreign producers which "dump" their excess goods onto the American market at less than cost. Two reasons have been suggested as to why foreign firms might wish to sell in America at below cost. First, these firms may use **dumping** to drive out American competitors, obtain monopoly power, and then raise prices. The long-term economic profits resulting from this strategy may more than offset the earlier losses which accompany the dumping. Second, dumping may be a complex form of price discrimination—charging different prices to different customers. The foreign seller may find that it can maximize its profits by charging a high price in its monopolized domestic market while unloading its surplus output at a lower price in the United States. The surplus output may be needed to obtain the overall per unit cost saving associated with large-scale production.

Because dumping is a legitimate concern, it is prohibited under American trade law. Where dumping occurs and is shown to injure American firms, the Federal government imposes tariffs

called "antidumping duties" on the dumped goods. But relative to the number of goods exported to the United States, documented cases of dumping are few. Dumping therefore does *not* justify widespread, permanent tariffs. Moreover, allegations of dumping require careful investigation to determine their validity. Foreign producers often allege that dumping allegations and antidumping duties are an American method of restricting legitimate trade. The fact is that some foreign firms can produce certain goods at substantially less cost than can American competitors. Hence, what on the surface may seem to be dumping often is simply the principle of comparative advantage at work. If abused, the antidumping law can increase the price of imports and restrict competition in the American market. This reduced competition allows American firms to raise prices at consumers' expense. And even where true dumping does occur, American consumers gain from the lower-priced product—at least in the short term—much as they gain from a price war among American producers.

CHEAP FOREIGN LABOR

The cheap-foreign-labor argument holds that domestic firms and workers must be shielded from the ruinous competition of countries where wages are low. If protection is not provided, cheap imports will flood American markets and the prices of American goods—along with the wages of American workers—will be pulled down and our domestic living standards reduced.

This argument can be rebutted at several levels. First, the logic of the argument would suggest that it is *not* mutually beneficial for rich and poor persons to trade with one another. However, that is not the case. A low-income farm worker may pick lettuce or tomatoes for a rich landowner and both may benefit from the transaction. And don't American consumers gain when they buy a Taiwanese vest pocket radio priced at $12 as opposed to a qualitatively similar American-made radio selling for $20?

Second, recall that the gains from trade are based upon comparative advantage. For example, looking back at Figure 39-1, let us suppose that the United States and Brazil have labor forces of exactly the same size. Noting the positions of the production possibilities curves, we observe that American labor is absolutely more productive because our labor force can produce more of either good. Because of this greater productivity, we can expect wages and living standards to be higher for American labor. Conversely, Brazil's less-productive labor will receive lower wages. Now the cheap-foreign-labor argument would suggest that, to maintain our standard of living, America should not trade with low-wage Brazil. Suppose we don't trade with Brazil. Will wages and living standards rise in the United States as a result? The answer is a resounding "No." To obtain coffee America will now have to reallocate a portion of its labor from its relatively efficient wheat industry to its relatively inefficient coffee industry. As a result, the average productivity of American labor will fall as will real wages and living standards. In fact, the labor forces of *both* countries will have diminished standards of living because without specialization and trade they will simply have less output available to them. Compare column 4 with column 1 in Table 39-4 or points A' and B' with A and B in Figure 39-2 to confirm this point.

A SUMMING UP

The arguments for protection are numerous, but they are not weighty. Under proper conditions, the infant-industry argument stands as a valid exception, justifiable on economic grounds. And on political-military grounds, the self-sufficiency argument can be used to validate protection. Both arguments, however, are susceptible to severe abuses, and both neglect alternative means of fostering industrial development and military self-sufficiency. Most other arguments are semi-emotional appeals in the form of half-truths and outright fallacies. These arguments note only the immediate and direct consequences of protective tariffs. They ignore the plain truth that in the long run a nation must import in order to export.

There is also compelling historical evidence which suggests that free trade has been conducive to prosperity and growth and that protectionism has had the opposite effects. Several examples follow.

1 The United States Constitution forbids individual states from levying tariffs, making America a huge free-trade area. Economic historians acknowledge this to be an important positive factor in the economic development of our nation.

2 Great Britain's movement toward freer international trade in the mid-nineteenth century was instrumental in its industrialization and growth in that century.

3 As we shall see shortly, the creation of the Common Market in Europe after World War II has largely eliminated tariffs among the member nations. Economists agree that the creation of this free-trade area has been an important ingredient in the western European prosperity of recent decades.

4 More generally, the trend toward tariff reduction since the mid-1930s has been a stimulus to post-World War II expansion of the world economy.

5 We have already noted that the high tariffs imposed by our Smoot-Hawley Act of 1930 and the retaliation which it engendered worsened the Great Depression of the 1930s.

6 Studies of the less developed countries overwhelmingly suggest that those which have relied upon import restrictions to protect their domestic industries have realized slow growth in comparison to those pursuing more open economic policies.[4]

International trade policies

As Figure 39-4 makes clear, tariffs in the United States have had their ups and downs.[5] Generally speaking, the United States tended to be a high-tariff nation over much of its history. Note that the Smoot-Hawley Tariff Act enacted in 1930 embodied some of the highest tariff rates ever imposed by the United States.

---

[4] Examples are from *Economic Report of the President 1985*, pp. 115–117.

[5] Technical footnote: Average tariff-rate figures understate the importance of tariffs by not accounting for the fact that some goods are *excluded* from American markets because of existing tariffs. Then, too, average figures conceal the high tariffs on particular items: watches, china, hats, textiles, scissors, wine, jewelry, glassware, wood products, and so forth.

Given the case for free trade, this high-tariff heritage may be a bit surprising. If tariffs are economically undesirable, why has Congress been so willing to employ them? As suggested earlier in this chapter, the answer lies in the political realities of tariff making and, more specifically, in the special-interest effect. A small group of domestic producers who will receive large economic gains from tariffs and quotas will press vigorously for protection through well-financed and well-informed political lobbyists. The large number of consumers who individually will have small losses imposed upon them will be generally uninformed and indifferent. Indeed, the public may be won over, not only by

the vigor, but also by the apparent plausibility ("Cut imports and prevent domestic unemployment") and the patriotic ring ("Buy American!") of the protectionists. Alleged tariff benefits seem immediate and clear-cut to the public. The adverse effects cited by economists appear ever so obscure and widely dispersed over the economy. Then, too, the public is likely to stumble on the fallacy of composition: "If a quota on Japanese automobiles will preserve profits and employment in the American automobile industry, how can it be detrimental to the economy as a whole?" When political logrolling (Chapter 33) is added in—"You back tariffs for industry X in my state and I'll do the same for

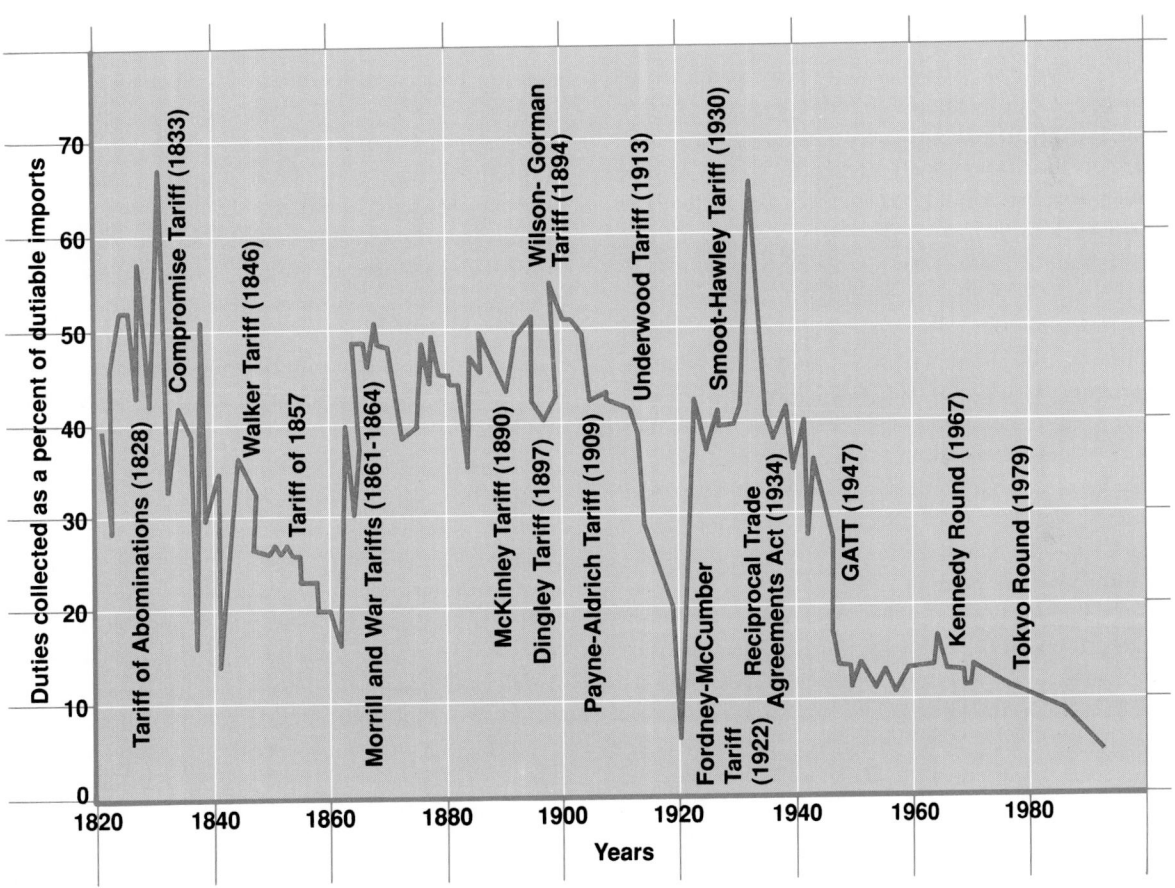

FIGURE 39-4

United States' tariff rates, 1820–1988

American tariff rates have fluctuated historically. But beginning with the Reciprocal Trade Agreements Act of 1934, the trend has been downward. (U.S. Department of Commerce data.)

industry Y in your state"—the sum can be protective tariffs and import quotas.

RECIPROCAL TRADE ACT AND GATT

The downward trend of tariffs since Smoot-Hawley was inaugurated with the **Reciprocal Trade Agreements Act of 1934.** Specifically aimed at tariff reduction, the act had two main features:

1 Negotiating authority It authorized the President to negotiate agreements with foreign nations which would reduce American tariffs up to 50 percent of the existing rates. Tariff reductions were to hinge upon the willingness of other nations to reciprocate by lowering tariffs on American exports.

2 Generalized reductions By incorporating **most-favored-nation clauses** in these agreements, the resulting tariff reductions not only would apply to the specific nation negotiating with the United States, but they would be *generalized* so as to apply to all nations.

But the Reciprocal Trade Act gave rise to only bilateral (two-nation) negotiations. This approach was broadened in 1947 when twenty-three nations, including the United States, signed a **General Agreement on Tariffs and Trade (GATT).** GATT is based on three cardinal principles: (1) equal, nondiscriminatory treatment for all member nations; (2) the reduction of tariffs by *multilateral* negotiations; and (3) the elimination of import quotas. Basically, GATT is a forum for the negotiation of reductions in tariff barriers on a multilateral basis. Almost one hundred nations now belong to GATT, and there is little doubt but that it has been an important force in the trend toward liberalized trade. Under its sponsorship, seven "rounds" of negotiations to reduce trade barriers have been completed in the post-World War II period.

In 1986, the eighth "round" of GATT negotiations began in Uruguay. Proposals now being discussed at the "Uruguay Round" include (1) eliminating trade barriers and domestic subsidies in agriculture, (2) removing barriers to trade in services (which now account for 20 percent of international trade), (3) ending restrictions on foreign economic investments, and (4) establishing and enforcing patent, copyright, and trademark rights on an international basis.

ECONOMIC INTEGRATION

Another crucial development in trade liberalization has taken the form of **economic integration**—the joining of the markets of two or more nations into a free-trade zone. Two illustrations of economic integration are the European Economic Community (EEC) and the U.S.–Canadian Free-Trade Agreement.

The Common Market The most dramatic example of economic integration is the **European Economic Community** (EEC), or the **Common Market,** as it is popularly known. Begun in 1958, the EEC now comprises thirteen western European nations.

GOALS The Common Market calls for (1) the gradual abolition of tariffs and import quotas on all products traded among the thirteen participating nations; (2) the establishment of a common system of tariffs applicable to all goods received from nations outside the Common Market; (3) the eventual free movement of capital and labor within the Market; and (4) the creation of common policies with respect to a number of other economic matters of joint concern, for example, agriculture, transportation, and restrictive business practices. These goals are set to be fully achieved in 1992.

RESULTS Motives for creating the Common Market were both political and economic. The primary economic motive, of course, was to gain the advantages of freer trade for members. While it is difficult to determine the extent to which EEC prosperity and growth has been due to economic integration, it is clear that integration creates the mass markets which are essential to Common Market industries if economies of large-scale production are to be realized. More efficient production for a large-scale market permits European industries to realize the lower costs which small, localized markets have historically denied them.

The effects upon nonmember nations, such as the United States, are less certain. On the one hand, a peaceful and increasingly prosperous Common Market makes member nations better potential customers for American exports. On the other hand, American firms encounter tariffs which make it difficult to compete in EEC markets. For example, *before* the establishment of the Common Market, American, German, and French automobile manufacturers all faced the same tariff in selling their products to, say, Belgium. However, with the establishment of internal free trade among EEC members, Belgian tariffs on German Volkswagens and French Renaults fell to zero, but an external tariff still applies to American Chevrolets and Fords. This clearly puts American firms and those of other nonmember nations at a serious competitive disadvantage.

The elimination of this disadvantage has been one of the United States' motivations for promoting freer trade through GATT. And, in fact, the so-called "Kennedy Round" of negotiations completed in 1967 and the "Tokyo Round" which ended in 1979 have been quite successful in reducing tariffs. Specifically, in 1988 import tariffs among major industrialized countries averaged below 5 percent on industrial products, compared to averages of more than 50 percent in the 1930s.

U.S.–Canadian Free-Trade Agreement A second and very recent example of economic integration is the **U.S.–Canadian Free-Trade Agreement** signed by President Reagan and Prime Minister Mulroney in 1988. Although three-fourths of the trade between the United States and Canada was already duty-free in 1988, the U.S.–Canadian accord is highly significant: It will create the largest free-trade area in the world. Under terms of the agreement, all trade restrictions such as tariffs, quotas, and nontariff barriers will be eliminated within a ten-year period. Canadian producers will gain increased access to a market ten times the size of Canada, while U.S. consumers will gain the advantage of lower-priced Canadian goods. In return, Canada will cut its tariffs by more than the United States because Canadian tariffs are higher than those in the United States. These reduced Canadian tariffs will help American producers and Canadian consumers.

We know from Table 7-6 that Canada is the United State's most significant trade partner quantitatively. Similarly, the United States is the main buyer of Canadian exports. Hence, the potential gain to each country from the U.S.–Canadian ac-

cord is large. It has been estimated that the free-trade agreement will generate $1 billion to $3 billion of annual gains for each nation when it is fully implemented.[6]

The U.S.–Canadian accord has global significance. For example, it is expected to prod multilateral tariff reductions through GATT negotiations. Put simply, nations which are not party to the free-trade agreement do not wish to be disadvantaged in a relative sense in selling their goods in the United States and Canada. In this respect, the U.S.–Canadian pact also places the two nations in a powerful position to negotiate reductions in trade barriers with Common Market nations. Access to the vast North American market is as important to Common Market countries as is access to the European market by the United States and Canada. Finally, the agreement with Canada has stimulated the United States and Mexico to begin serious discussion of how trade barriers between Mexico and the United States might be reduced or eliminated.

PROTECTIONISM REBORN

Despite marked progress in reducing and eliminating tariffs, much remains to be done. The previously mentioned "Uruguay Round" agenda is a case in point. In the past, GATT negotiations have tended to focus upon manufactured goods to the end that other aspects of international trade and finance have received little or no attention. These neglected areas include agriculture, services (for example, transportation, insurance, and banking), international investment, and patents and copyrights. There is also the problem of integrating the many nonmember less developed countries into the GATT framework. More ominously, there has occured in the 1980s a vigorous resurgence of protectionist pressures. Nontariff barriers continue to be a serious problem; import quotas and voluntary export restrictions have been on the rise.

Causes A number of factors explain the new pressures for protection. In the first place, the pressures for protection are in part a backlash to past reductions in trade barriers. Industries and workers whose profits and jobs have been adversely affected

[6] *Economic Report of the President, 1988*, p. 131.

by freer trade have sought the restoration of protection. A closely related point is that the American economy is much more "internationalized" than it was a decade or so ago (Table 39-2) and therefore there are simply more firms and workers upon whom increased foreign competition might have an adverse effect. Third, other nations have in fact become increasingly competitive with American producers. In the late 1970s and 1980s rates of labor productivity growth in Japan and much of western Europe exceeded those of the United States. The result was lower unit labor costs and lower relative prices for imported goods. Competition from a number of the so-called "newly industrialized countries" such as Korea, Taiwan, Hong Kong, and Singapore is also asserting itself. Finally, in the past several years American imports have greatly exceeded American exports. Rising imports tend to have a negative impact upon production and employment in those domestic industries which directly compete with imported products. The industries and workers adversely affected seek government help in the form of trade barriers. Our persistent trade deficit has, in effect, provided a convenient rationale for the enactment of protectionist measures to help injured industries. Furthermore, the trade deficit has rallied public support for proposals to retaliate against trading partners which restrict the sale of our products in their countries.

Examples While the United States is formally committed to work for the reduction of trade barriers through GATT, we have in fact invoked a number of trade-restricting measures during the last decade. Example: In 1981 a "voluntary" agreement was reached with Japan to limit the number of Japanese automobiles imported to the United States. This agreement expired in 1985. Example: In 1982 import quotas were imposed on sugar, causing potentially severe problems for Central American and Caribbean nations which are heavily dependent upon sugar exports to the United States. Example: In 1982 the United States negotiated a "voluntary" agreement with the Common Market nations which imposed a quota upon their steel exports to the United States. Example: The industrially advanced nations have revised the international textile agreement to tighten restrictions

LAST WORD

Petition of the candlemakers, 1845

The French economist Frédéric Bastiat (1801–1850) devastated the proponents of protectionism by satirically extending their reasoning to its logical and absurd conclusions.

Petition of the Manufacturers of Candles, Waxlights, Lamps, Candlesticks, Street Lamps, Snuffers, Extinguishers, and of the Producers of Oil Tallow, Rosin, Alcohol, and, Generally, of Everything Connected with Lighting.

**TO MESSIEURS THE MEMBERS
OF THE CHAMBER
OF DEPUTIES.**

Gentlemen—You are on the right road. You reject abstract theories, and have little consideration for cheapness and plenty. Your chief care is the interest of the producer. You desire to emancipate him from external competition, and reserve the *national market* for *national industry*.

We are about to offer you an admirable opportunity of applying your—what shall we call it? your theory? No; nothing is more deceptive than theory; your doctrine? your system? your principle? but you dislike doctrines, you abhor systems, and as for principles, you deny that there are any in social economy: we shall say, then, your practice, your practice without theory and without principle.

We are suffering from the intolerable competition of a foreign rival, placed, it would seem, in a condition so far superior to ours for the production of light, that he absolutely *inundates* our *national market* with it at a price fabulously reduced. The moment he shows himself, our trade leaves us—all consumers apply to him; and a branch of native industry, having countless ramifications, is all at once rendered completely stagnant. This rival . . . is no other than the Sun.

What we pray for is, that it may please you to pass a law ordering the shutting up of all windows, sky-lights, dormerwindows, outside and inside shutters, curtains, blinds, bull's-eyes; in a word, of all openings, holes, chinks, clefts, and fissures, by or through which the light of the sun has been in use to enter houses, to the prejudice of the meritorious manufactures with which we flatter ourselves we have accommodated our country,—a country which, in gratitude, ought not to abandon us now to a strife so unequal.

If you shut up as much as possible all access to natural light, and create a demand for artificial light, which of our French manufactures will not be encouraged by it?

If more tallow is consumed, then there must be more oxen and sheep; and, consequently, we shall behold the multiplication of artificial meadows, meat, wool, hides, and, above all, manure, which is the basis and foundation of all agricultural wealth.

The same remark apples to navigation. Thousands of vessels will proceed to the whale fishery; and, in a short time, we shall possess a navy capable of maintaining the honour of France, and gratifying the patriotic aspirations of your petitioners, the undersigned candlemakers and others.

Only have the goodness to reflect, Gentlemen, and you will be convinced that there is, perhaps, no Frenchman, from the wealthy coalmaster to the humblest vender of lucifer matches, whose lot will not be ameliorated by the success of this our petition.

Source: Frédéric Bastiat, *Economic Sophisms* (Edinburgh: Oliver and Boyd, Tweeddale Court, 1873), pp. 49–53, abridged.

upon textile imports from the less developed countries.

Protectionist sentiment is also evidenced in recent trade proposals and laws. Example: In 1987, legislation was introduced to require tariff retaliation against trading partners having "excessive and unwarranted" trade surpluses with the United States. Under threat of Presidential veto, Congress ultimately rejected this proposal. However, the Comprehensive Trade Act of 1988 did contain provisions which ease the procedures for initiating unfair-trade investigations of countries with consistent patterns of unfair-trade practices (tariffs, quotas, nontariff barriers, dumping). Discretion, however, is given to the administration whether and how to retaliate against such practices. Final example: The Textile and Apparel Trade Bill of 1988 passed both houses of Congress before being vetoed by the President in 1988. The legislation would have limited the growth of textile imports to 1 percent a year. Ironically, the U.S. textile industry imports one-half of its machinery!

We should also note that, although overall American tariffs are low, the United States does have very high tariffs on some goods and imposes quantitative restrictions (quotas) upon a small but important list of products. Dairy and meat products, tobacco, fruit juices, motorcycles, and cookware are all subject to significant restrictions. In addition, the footwear, machine tool, copper, shipbuilding, wine, costume jewelry, and shrimp and tuna industries, among others, have all recently sought additional protection.

Costs How costly is U.S. trade protection to American consumers? The consumer cost of trade restrictions can be calculated by determining the effect they have upon the prices of protected goods. Specifically, protection will raise the price of a product in three ways. First, the price of the imported product goes up (Figure 39-3). Second, the higher price of imports will cause some consumers to shift their purchases to higher-priced domestically produced goods. Finally, the prices of domestically produced goods may rise because import competition has declined.

Several research studies indicate that the costs to consumers of protected products is strikingly high. One study examined thirty-one classes of protected products and found that the total annual consumer losses from protection on these goods was about $82.6 billion.[7] Annual consumer losses from trade restrictions were particularly large for clothing ($27 billion), petroleum products ($6.9 billion), carbon steel ($6.8 billion), automobiles ($5.8 billion), and dairy products ($5.5 billion). These large costs indicate that trade barriers are a very expensive means of saving jobs. More specifically, the estimated cost of trade restrictions per job saved is $750,000 in the carbon steel industry; $550,000 in the bolt, nuts, and large screws industry; $220,000 in the dairy industry; $240,000 in the orange juice industry; and $200,000 in the glassware industry. Because wages per job in these industries are only a fraction of these amounts, protectionism can hardly be called a bargain.

Other studies show that import restrictions affect low-income families proportionately more than high-income families.[8] Given that tariffs and quotas are much like sales taxes, it is no surprise that these trade restrictions are highly regressive. For example, the cost of protection was found to be seven times as large for the lowest-income group (incomes under $10,000 per year) as for the highest-income group (incomes over $60,000 per year).

But might not the gains to American producers together with the tariff revenues received by the U.S. government outweigh the high consumer costs of trade protection? The answer is a definite "No." Research studies indicate that the gains from trade restrictions are substantially exceeded by the costs which trade restrictions impose on consumers.[9] Furthermore, the net losses from trade barriers tend to be greater than the losses estimated by the statistical studies. The reasons are twofold. First, tariffs and quotas produce a myriad of costly, difficult-to-quantify secondary effects.

---

[7] Cletus C. Coughlin et al., "Protectionist Trade Policies: A Survey of Theory, Evidence and Rationale," *Review* (Federal Reserve Bank of St. Louis), January/February 1988), pp. 17–18.

[8] "The Consumer Cost of U.S. Trade Restraints," *Quarterly Review* (Federal Reserve Bank of New York), Summer 1985, pp. 1–12.

[9] Coughlin et al., op. cit., p. 19.

For example, import restraints on foreign steel drive up the price of steel to all American buyers of steel—such as American automakers. Therefore American automakers have higher costs and are less competitive in world markets. Second, industries employ large amounts of economic resources for the purpose of influencing Congress to pass and retain protectionist laws. To the extent that these efforts divert resources away from more socially desirable purposes, society bears an added cost of trade restrictions. To repeat: *Authoritative observers conclude that the gains which trade barriers create for protected industries come at the expense of much greater losses for the economy as a whole.*

CHAPTER SUMMARY

1 International trade is important, quantitatively and otherwise, to most nations. World trade is vital to the United States in several respects. **a** The absolute volumes of American imports and exports exceed those of any other single nation. **b** The United States is completely dependent upon trade for certain commodities and materials which cannot be obtained domestically. **c** Changes in the volume of net exports can have magnified effects upon the domestic levels of output and income.

2 International and domestic trade differ in that **a** resources are less mobile internationally than domestically: **b** each nation uses a different currency; and **c** international trade is subject to more political controls.

3 World trade is ultimately based upon two considerations: the uneven distribution of economic resources among nations, and the fact that the efficient production of various goods requires particular techniques or combinations of resources.

4 Mutually advantageous specialization and trade are possible between any two nations so long as the domestic cost ratios for any two products differ. By specializing according to comparative advantage, nations can realize larger real incomes with fixed amounts of resources. The terms of trade determine how this increase in world output is shared by the trading nations. Increasing costs impose limits upon the gains from specialization and trade.

5 Trade barriers take the form of protective tariffs, quotas, nontariff barriers, and "voluntary" export restrictions. Supply and demand analysis reveals that protective tariffs increase the prices and reduce the quantities demanded of affected goods. Foreign exporters find their sales diminish. Domestic producers, however, enjoy higher prices and enlarged sales. Tariffs promote a less efficient allocation of domestic and world resources.

6 When applicable, the strongest arguments for protection are the infant-industry and military self-sufficiency arguments. Most of the other arguments for protection are half-truths, emotional appeals, or fallacies which typically emphasize the immediate effects of trade barriers while ignoring long-run consequences. There are numerous historical examples which suggest that free trade promotes economic growth and protectionism does not.

7 The Reciprocal Trade Agreements Act of 1934 was the beginning of a trend toward lower American tariffs. In 1947 the General Agreement on Tariffs and Trade (GATT) was formed **a** to encourage nondiscriminatory treatment for all trading nations, **b** to achieve tariff reduction, and **c** to eliminate import quotas.

8 Economic integration is an important means of liberalizing trade. The outstanding illustration is the European Common Market wherein internal trade barriers are abolished, a common system of tariffs is applied to nonmembers, and the free internal movement of labor and capital is perceived. The 1988 U.S.–Canadian Free-trade Agreement is another example of economic integration.

9 In recent years there has been a resurgence of protectionist pressures, but empirical evidence indicates that the costs of protectionist policies outweigh the benefits.

TERMS AND CONCEPTS

labor- (land-, capital-) intensive commodity	**Smoot-Hawley Tariff Act of 1930**
cost ratio	**dumping**
principle of comparative advantage	**Reciprocal Trade Agreements Act of 1934**
terms of trade	**most-favored-nation clauses**
trading possibilities line	**General Agreement on Tariffs and Trade (GATT)**
gains from trade	
revenue and protective tariffs	**economic integration**
import quotas	**European Economic Community (Common Market)**
nontariff barriers	
voluntary export restrictions	**U.S.–Canadian Free-Trade Agreement**

QUESTIONS AND STUDY SUGGESTIONS

1 In what ways are domestic and foreign trade similar? In what ways do they differ?

2 Assume that by using all its resources to produce X, nation A can produce 80 units of X; by devoting all its resources to Y, it can produce 40 Y. Comparable figures for nation B are 60 X and 60 Y. Assuming constant costs, in which product should each nation specialize? Why? Indicate the limits of the terms of trade.

3 "The United States can produce product X more efficiently than can Great Britain. Yet we import X from Great Britain." Explain.

4 State the economist's case for free trade. Given this case, how do you explain the existence of artificial barriers to international trade?

5 Draw a domestic supply and demand diagram for a product in which the United States does not have a comparative advantage. Indicate the impact of foreign imports upon domestic price and quantity. Now show a protective tariff which eliminates approximately one-half the assumed imports. Indicate the price-quantity effects of this tariff to **a** domestic consumers, **b** domestic producers, and **c** foreign exporters.

6 "The most valid arguments for tariff protection are also the most easily abused." What are these arguments? Why are they susceptible to abuse? Carefully evaluate the use of artificial trade barriers, such as tariffs and import quotas, as a means of achieving and maintaining full employment.

7 The following are production possibilities tables for Japan and Hawaii. Assume that prior to specialization and trade, the optimal product-mix for Japan is alternative B and for Hawaii alternative D.

Product	Japan's production alternatives					
	A	B	C	D	E	F
Radios (in thousands)	30	24	18	12	6	0
Pineapples (in tons)	0	6	12	18	24	30

Product	Hawaii's production alternatives					
	A	B	C	D	E	F
Radios (in thousands)	10	8	6	4	2	0
Pineapples (in tons)	0	4	8	12	16	20

a Are comparative-cost conditions such that the two nations should specialize? If so, what product should each produce?

b What is the total gain in radio and pineapple output which results from this specialization?

c What are the limits of the terms of trade? Suppose that actual terms of trade are 1 unit of radios for 1½ units of pineapples and the 4 units of radios are exchanged for 6 units of pineapples. What are the gains from specialization and trade for each nation?

d Can you conclude from this illustration that specialization according to comparative advantage results in the more efficient use of world resources? Explain.

8 Carefully evaluate the following statements:

a "Protective tariffs limit both the imports and the exports of the nation levying tariffs."

b "The extensive application of protective tariffs destroys the ability of the international market system to allocate resources efficiently."

c "Apparent unemployment can often be reduced through tariff protection, but by the same token disguised unemployment typically increases."

d "Foreign firms which 'dump' their products onto the American market are in effect presenting the American people with gifts."

e "Given the rapidity with which technological advance is dispersed around the world, free trade will inevitably yield structural maladjustments, unemployment, and balance of payments problems for industrially advanced nations."

f "Free trade can improve the composition and efficiency of domestic output. Only the Volkswagen forced Detroit to make a compact car, and only foreign success with the oxygen process forced American steel firms to modernize."

g "In the long run foreign trade is neutral with respect to total employment."

9 In the 1981–1985 period the Japanese agreed to a voluntary export restriction which reduced American imports of Japanese automobiles by about 10 percent. What would you expect the short-run effects to have been upon the American and Japanese automobile industries? If this restriction were made permanent, what would be its long-run effects upon *a* the allocation of resources, *b* the volume of employment, *c* the price level, and *d* the standard of living in the two nations?

10 Use the "economies of scale" analysis of Chapter 24 to explain why the Common Market has enabled many European industries to compete more effectively in international markets. Explain: "Economic integration leads a double life: It can promote free trade among members, but pose serious trade obstacles for nonmembers."

11 What are the benefits and the costs of protectionist policies? Compare the two.

12 Explain the following findings from a 1987 research study on the effects of the 1984 imports restraints which limited the level of steel imports to the United States: increased employment in the steel industry, 14,000; increased employment in the industries producing inputs for steel, 2,800; job losses by American steel-using firms, 52,400.[10]

---

[10] Arthur T. Denzau, "How Import Restraints Reduce Employment" (Washington University Center for the Study of American Business, Formal Publication #80, June 1987), as reported in Coughlin, op. cit., p. 6.

CHAPTER 40

Exchange rates, the balance of payments, and the trade "crisis"

I n Chapter 39 we examined comparative advantage as the underlying economic basis of world trade and discussed the effects of barriers to free trade. The goals of the present chapter are several. First, we want to introduce explicitly the monetary or financial aspects of international trade. How are the currencies of different nations exchanged for one another when import and export transactions occur? Second, we seek to analyze and interpret a nation's international balance of payments. What is meant, for example, by a "favorable" or "unfavorable" balance of trade? What is the meaning and significance of a balance of payments deficit or surplus? Third, we explain and evaluate the various kinds of exchange rate systems which trading nations have used. To accomplish this goal we first examine the polar extremes of freely flexible and fixed exchange rates and then survey the actual systems which have been employed historically. Finally, we will examine the balance of trade "crisis" which the United States has encountered over the past several years. Why has this "crisis" happened? What are the economic implications and the possible solutions?

Financing international trade

Recall from Chapters 4 and 39 that a basic feature which distinguishes international from domestic payments is that two different national currencies are involved. Thus, for instance, when American firms export goods to British firms, the American exporter will want to be paid in dollars. But the British importers have pounds sterling. The problem, then, is to exchange pounds for dollars to permit the American export transaction to occur.

We discovered in Chapter 4 that this problem is resolved by the existence of *foreign exchange markets* in which dollars can be used to purchase British pounds, Japanese yen, German marks, Italian lira, and so forth, and vice versa. Sponsored by major banks in New York, London, Zurich, and elsewhere, foreign exchange markets facilitate American exports and imports.

AMERICAN EXPORT TRANSACTION

Suppose an American exporter agrees to sell $30,000 worth of computers to a British firm. Assume that the *rate of exchange*—that is, the rate or price at which pounds can be exchanged for, or converted into, dollars, and vice versa—is $2 for £1.[1] This means that the British importer must pay £15,000 to the American exporter. Let us summarize what occurs in terms of simple bank balance sheets (Figure 40-1) such as those employed in Part 3.

---

[1] We explained briefly in Chapter 4 how exchange rates are determined.

LONDON BANK		NEW YORK BANK	
Assets	**Liabilities and net worth**	**Assets**	**Liabilities and net worth**
	Demand deposit of British importer −£15,000(a) Deposit of New York bank +£15,000(c)	Deposit in London bank +£15,000(c) ($30,000)	Demand deposit of American exporter +$30,000(b)

FIGURE 40-1

Financing a U.S. export transaction

American export transactions create a foreign demand for dollars. The satisfaction of this demand increases the supplies of foreign monies held by American banks.

a To pay for the American computers, the British buyer draws a check on its demand deposit in a London bank for £15,000. This fact is denoted by the −£15,000 demand deposit entry in the right-hand side of the balance sheet of the London bank.

b The British firm then sends this £15,000 check to the American exporter. But the rub is that the American exporting firm must pay its employees and materials suppliers, as well as its taxes, in dollars, not pounds. So the exporter sells the £15,000 check or draft on the London bank to some large American bank, probably located in New York City, which is a dealer in foreign exchange. The American firm is given a $30,000 demand deposit in the New York bank in exchange for the £15,000 check. In this regard, observe the new demand deposit entry of +$30,000 in the New York bank.

c And what does the New York bank do with the £15,000? It in turn deposits it in a correspondent London bank for future sale. Hence, we see that +£15,000 of demand deposits appear in the liabilities column of the balance sheet of the London bank. This +£15,000 ($30,000) is an asset as viewed by the New York bank. To simplify, we assume that the correspondent bank in London is the same bank from which the British importer obtained the £15,000 draft.

Note these salient points. First, *American exports create a foreign demand for dollars, and the satisfaction of this demand generates a supply of for-* *eign monies—pounds, in this case—held by American banks and available to American buyers.* Second, the financing of an American export (British import) reduces the supply of money (demand deposits) in Britain and increases the supply of money in the United States by the amount of the purchase.

AMERICAN IMPORT TRANSACTION

But a question persists: Why would the New York bank be willing to give up dollars for pounds sterling? As just indicated, the New York bank is a dealer in foreign exchange; it is in the business of buying—for a fee—and, conversely, in selling—also for a fee—pounds for dollars. Having just explained that the New York bank would buy pounds with dollars in connection with an American export transaction, we shall now examine how it would sell pounds for dollars in helping to finance an American import (British export) transaction. Specifically, suppose that an American retail concern wants to import £15,000 worth of woolens from a British mill. Again we rely on simple commercial bank balance sheets to summarize our discussion (Figure 40-2).

a Because the British exporting firm must pay its obligations in pounds rather than dollars, the American importer must somehow exchange dollars for pounds. It can do this by going to the New

LONDON BANK		NEW YORK BANK	
Assets	**Liabilities and net worth**	**Assets**	**Liabilities and net worth**
	Demand deposit of British exporter $+£15,000(b)$	Deposit in London bank $-£15,000(a)$ $(\$30,000)$	Demand deposit of American importer $-\$30,000(a)$
	Deposit of New York bank $-£15,000(a)$		

FIGURE 40-2

Financing a U.S. import transaction

American import transactions create an American demand for foreign monies. The satisfaction of that demand reduces the supplies of foreign monies held by American banks.

York bank and purchasing £15,000 for $30,000—perhaps the American importer purchases the very same £15,000 which the New York bank acquired in the previous American export transaction. As shown in Figure 40-2, this purchase reduces the American importer's demand deposit in the New York bank by $30,000 and, of course, the New York bank gives up its £15,000 deposit in the London bank.

b The American importer sends its newly purchased check for £15,000 to the British firm, which deposits it in the London bank. Note the +£15,000 deposit in the liabilities and net worth column of Figure 40-2.

We find that American imports create a domestic demand for foreign monies (pounds sterling, in this case) and that the fulfillment of this demand reduces the supplies of foreign monies held by American banks. Moreover, an American import transaction increases the supply of money in Britain and reduces the supply of money in the United States.

By putting these two transactions together, a further point comes into focus. American exports (in this case, computers) make available, or "earn," a supply of foreign monies for American banks, and American imports (British woolens, in this instance) create a demand for these monies. That is, in a broad sense, *any nation's exports finance or "pay for" its imports.* Exports provide the foreign currencies needed to pay for imports. From

Britain's point of view, we note that its exports of woolens earn a supply of dollars, which are then used to meet the demand for dollars associated with Britain's imports of computers.

Postscript: Although our examples are confined to the exporting and importing of goods, we shall find momentarily that demands for and supplies of pounds also arise from transactions involving services and the payment of interest and dividends on foreign investments. Thus Americans demand pounds not only to finance imports, but also to purchase insurance and transportation services from the British, to vacation in London, to pay dividends and interest upon British investments in the United States, and to make new financial and real investments in Britain.

The international balance of payments

We now want to gain a fuller understanding of the wide variety of international transactions which create a demand for and generate a supply of a given currency. This spectrum of international trade and financial transactions is reflected in the United States' international **balance of payments.** A nation's balance of payments statement attempts to record *all* the transactions which take place between its residents (including individuals,

TABLE 40-1 **The United States balance of payments, 1987** *(in billions)*

Current account

(1) U.S. merchandise exports	$+251	
(2) U.S. merchandise imports	−410	
(3)　　Balance of trade		$−159
(4) U.S. exports of services	+70	
(5) U.S. imports of services	−72	
(6)　　Balance on goods and services		−161
(7) Net investment income	+14	
(8) Net transfers	−14	
(9)　　Balance on current account		−161

Capital account

(10) Capital inflows to the U.S.	+180*	
(11) Capital outflows from the U.S.	−74	
(12)　　Balance on capital account		+106
(13)　　Current and capital account balance		−55
(14)　　Official reserves		+55
		$　0

* Includes a $22 billion statistical discrepancy which is believed to be comprised primarily of unaccounted capital inflows.

Source: *Survey of Current Business,* March 1988, p. 41.

businesses, and governmental units) and the residents of all foreign nations. These transactions include merchandise exports and imports, tourist expenditures, purchases and sales of shipping and insurance services, interest and dividends received or paid abroad, purchases and sales of financial or real assets abroad, and so forth. Stated differently, the United States' balance of payments shows the balance between all the payments the United States receives from foreign countries and all the payments which we make to them. A simplified balance of payments for the United States in 1987 is shown in Table 40-1. Let us analyze this accounting statement to see what it reveals about our international trade and finance.

CURRENT ACCOUNT

The top portion of Table 40-1 summarizes the United States' trade in currently produced goods and services and is therefore called the **current account.** Items 1 and 2 show American exports and imports of merchandise (goods) respectively in 1987. Note that we have designated American exports with a *plus* sign and our imports with a *minus* sign. The reason for this is that American merchandise exports (and other export-type transactions) are **credits** in that they create or earn supplies of foreign exchange. As we saw in our discussion of how international trade is financed, any export-type transaction which obligates foreigners to make "inpayments" to the United States generates supplies of foreign monies in American banks. Conversely, American imports (and other import-type transactions) are **debits** in that they use up foreign exchange. Again, our earlier discussion of trade financing indicated to us that American imports obligate Americans to make "outpayments" to the rest of the world which draw down available supplies of foreign currencies held by American banks.

Trade balance Observing items 1 and 2 in Table 40-1 we find that in 1987 our merchandise exports of $251 billion did *not* earn the United States enough foreign monies to finance our merchandise imports of $410 billion. Specifically, the merchandise balance of trade or, more simply, the **trade balance** refers to the difference between a country's merchandise exports and merchandise imports. If exports exceed imports, then a *trade surplus* or "favorable balance of trade" is being realized. If imports exceed exports, then a *trade deficit* or "unfavorable balance of trade" is occurring. In 1987 we note in item 3 that the United States incurred a trade deficit of $159 billion.

Balance on goods and services Item 4 tells us that the United States not only exports autos and computers, but also sells transportation services, insurance, and tourist and brokerage services to residents of foreign countries. These service sales or "exports" amounted to $70 billion in 1987. Item 5 merely indicates that Americans buy or "import" similar services from foreigners. These service imports amounted to $72 billion in 1987.

The **balance on goods and services,** shown in Table 40-1 as item 6, refers to the difference between our exports of goods and services (items 1 and 4) and our imports of goods and services (items 2 and 5). In 1987 our exports of goods and services fell short of our imports of goods and services by $161 billion.

Balance on current account Item 7 reflects the fact that historically the United States has been a net international lender. Over time we have invested more abroad than foreigners have invested in the United States. Thus net investment income represents the excess of interest and dividend payments which foreigners have paid us for the services of our exported capital over what we paid in 1987 in interest and dividends for their capital invested in the United States. Table 40-1 tells us that, on balance, our net investment income earned us $14 billion worth of foreign currencies for "exporting" the services of American money capital invested abroad.

Item 8 reflects net transfers, both public and private, from the United States to the rest of the world. Included here is American foreign aid, pensions paid to Americans living abroad, and remittances of immigrants to relatives abroad. Note that

these $14 billion of transfers are "outpayments" and exhaust available supplies of foreign exchange. As it has been facetiously put, net transfers entail the importing of "goodwill" or "thank-you notes."

By taking all the transactions in the current account into consideration we obtain the **balance on current account** shown by item 9 in Table 40-1. In 1987 the United States realized a current account deficit of $161 billion. This means that our current account import transactions (items 2, 5, and 8) created a demand for a larger quantity of foreign currencies than our export transactions (items 1, 4, and 7) supplied.

CAPITAL ACCOUNT

The **capital account** reflects capital flows involving the purchase or sale of real and financial assets which occurred in 1987. For example, Honda or Nissan might acquire an automobile assembly plant in the United States. Or, alternatively, the investments may be of a financial nature, for example, a rich Arabian oil sheik might purchase GM stock or Treasury bonds. In either event such transactions generate supplies of foreign currencies for the United States. They are therefore credit or inpayment items and so are designated with a plus sign. The United States is exporting stocks and bonds and thereby earning foreign exchange. Item 10 in Table 40-1 indicates that such transactions amounted to $180 billion in 1987.

Conversely, Americans invest abroad. Zenith might purchase a plant in Hong Kong or Singapore to assemble pocket radios or video recorders. Or a well-to-do American might buy stock in an Italian shoe factory. Or an American bank might finance the construction of a meat processing plant in Argentina. These transactions have a common feature; they all use up or exhaust supplies of foreign currencies. We therefore attach a minus sign to remind us that these are debit or outpayment transactions. The United States is importing stocks, bonds, and IOUs from abroad. Item 11 in Table 40-1 reveals that $74 billion of such transactions occurred in 1987. We also see that, when items 7 and 8 are combined, the **balance on the capital account** was a *plus* $106 billion. In other words, the United States enjoyed a capital account surplus of $106 billion in 1987.

INTERRELATIONSHIPS

The current and capital accounts are interrelated; they are essentially reflections of one another. The current account *deficit* tells us that American exports of goods and services were not sufficient to pay for our imports of goods and services.[2] How did we finance the difference? The answer is that the United States must either borrow from abroad or give up ownership of some of its assets to foreigners as reflected in the capital account. A simple analogy is useful in explaining this notion. Suppose in a given year your expenditures exceed your earnings. How will you finance your "deficit"? The answer is by selling off some of your assets or by borrowing. You might sell some real assets (your car or stereo) or perhaps some financial assets (stocks or bonds) which you own. Or you might obtain a loan from your family or a bank. Similarly, when a nation incurs a deficit in its current account, this means that its expenditures for foreign goods and services (its imports) exceed the income received from the international sales of its own goods and services (its exports). It must somehow finance that current account deficit. But how? The answer is by selling off assets and by borrowing, that is, by going into debt. And that is what is reflected in the capital account surplus. Our capital account surplus of $106 billion (item 12) indicates that in 1987 the United States "sold off" real assets (buildings, farmland) and received loans from the rest of the world in that amount to help finance our current account deficit of $161 billion. Recap: A nation's current account deficit will be financed essentially by a net capital inflow in its capital account. Conversely, a nation's current account *surplus* would be accompanied by a net capital *outflow* in its capital account. In this latter instance the excess earnings from its current account surplus will be used to purchase the real assets of, and to make loans to, other nations of the world.

OFFICIAL RESERVES

The central banks of the various nations hold quantities of foreign currencies called **official re-**

[2] We ignore transfer payments (item 8) in making this statement.

serves which are added to or drawn upon to settle any *net* differences in current and capital account balances. For example, in 1987 the surplus in our capital account was considerably less than the deficit in our current account so we had a $55 billion net deficit on the combined accounts (item 13). Stated differently, the United States earned less foreign monies in all of its international trade and financial transactions than it used. This deficiency of earnings of foreign currencies was subtracted from the existing balances of foreign monies held by our central banks. In particular, the *plus* $55 billion of official reserves shown by item 14 in Table 40-1 represents this reduction of our stocks of foreign currencies. Why the plus sign? Because this is a credit or "export-type" transaction in that it represents a supply of foreign exchange.

Frequently the relationship between the current and capital account is just opposite that shown in Table 40-1. That is, the current account deficit is less than the capital account surplus. Hence, our central banks would experience an increase in their holdings of foreign currencies. This would show as a *minus* item in the balance of payments; it is a debit or "import-type" transaction because it represents a use of foreign exchange.

The important point for immediate purposes is that the three components of the balance of payments statement—the current account, the capital account, and the official reserves account—must sum to zero. Every unit of foreign exchange used (as reflected in our "minus" outpayment or debit transactions) in our international transactions must have a source (our "plus" inpayment or credit transactions).

PAYMENTS DEFICITS AND SURPLUSES

Although the balance of payments must always balance or sum to zero, economists and political officials frequently speak of **balance of payments deficits and surpluses.** In doing so they are referring to the "current and capital account balance" shown as item 13 in Table 40-1. If this is a negative item, a balance of payments deficit is being realized as was the case for the United States in 1987. This means that in 1987 the United States earned less foreign monies from all of its trade and financial transactions than it used. The United States did not "pay its way" in world trade and finance and therefore depleted its official reserves of foreign monies. If the current and capital account balance were positive, then the United States would be faced with a balance of payments surplus. The United States would have earned sufficient foreign exchange from its export-type transactions to pay for its import-type transactions. As we saw a moment ago, it would add to its stocks of foreign monies—that is, increase its official reserve holdings.

More simply put, *a decrease in official reserves (shown by a positive official reserves item in Table 40-1) measures a nation's balance of payments deficit; an increase in official reserves (shown by a negative official reserves item) measures its balance of payments surplus.*

DEFICITS AND SURPLUSES: BAD OR GOOD?

We have defined a variety of deficits and surpluses in discussing the balance of payments. We must now inquire as to their desirability. Are deficits bad, as the term itself implies? Is a surplus desirable, as that term suggests? The answer to both questions is "not necessarily." For example, a large merchandise trade deficit such as the United States has been incurring in recent years is regarded by many as "unfavorable" or "adverse" in that it suggests American producers are perhaps losing their competitiveness in world markets. Our industries seem to be having trouble selling their goods abroad and are simultaneously facing strong competition from imported goods. On the other hand, a trade deficit is clearly *not* unfavorable from the vantage point of American consumers who are currently receiving more goods as imports than they are forgoing as exports.

Similarly, the desirability of a balance of payments deficit or surplus depends upon (1) the events causing them and (2) their persistence through time. For example, the large payments deficits imposed upon the United States and other oil-importing nations by OPEC's dramatic runup of oil prices in 1973–1974 and 1979–1980 were very disruptive in that they forced the United States to invoke a variety of policies to curtail oil imports. Similarly, any nation's official reserves are limited. Therefore, persistent or long-term pay-

ments deficits, which must be financed by drawing down those reserves, would ultimately cause reserves to be depleted. In this case that nation would have to undertake specific policies to correct its balance of payments. These policies might entail painful macroeconomic adjustments, the use of trade barriers and similar restrictions, or changing the international value of its currency.

Exchange rate systems and balance of payments adjustments

Both the size and persistence of a nation's balance of payments deficits and surpluses and the kind of adjustments it would be obligated to make in correcting these imbalances depend upon the system of exchange rates being used. There are two polar options: (1) a system of **flexible** or **floating exchange rates** where the rates at which national currencies exchange for one another are determined by demand and supply; and (2) a system of rigidly **fixed exchange rates** wherein governmental intervention in foreign exchange markets or some other mechanism offsets the changes in exchange rates which fluctuations in demand and supply would otherwise cause.

FREELY FLOATING EXCHANGE RATES

Freely floating exchange rates are determined by the unimpeded forces of demand and supply. Let us examine the rate, or price, at which American dollars might be exchanged for, say, British pounds sterling. As indicated in Figure 40-3, the demand for pounds will be downsloping, and the supply of pounds will be upsloping. Why?

The downsloping *demand for pounds* shown by *DD* indicates that, if pounds become less expensive to Americans, British goods will become cheaper to Americans. This fact causes Americans to demand larger quantities of British goods and therefore larger amounts of pounds with which to buy those goods.

The *supply of pounds* is upsloping, as *SS*, because, as the dollar price of pounds *rises* (that is,

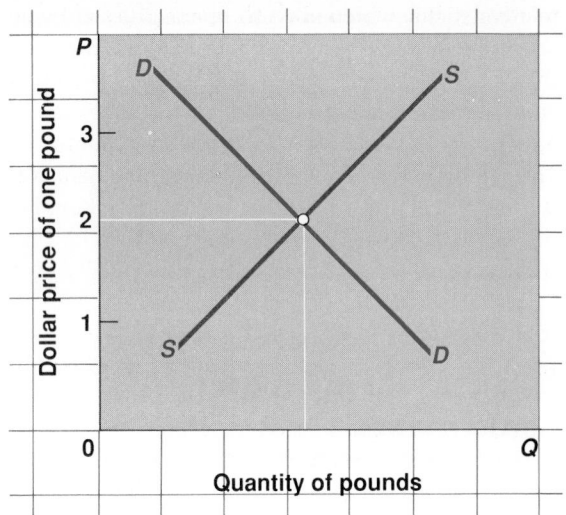

FIGURE 40-3

The market for foreign exchange

The American demand for pounds is downsloping because, as pounds become less expensive, all British goods and services become cheaper to Americans. The supply of pounds to Americans is upsloping because at higher dollar prices for pounds the British will want to purchase larger quantities of American goods and services. The intersection of the demand and supply curves will determine the equilibrium rate of exchange.

the pound price of dollars *falls*), the British will be inclined to purchase more American goods. The reason, of course, is that at higher and higher dollar prices for pounds, the British can get more American dollars and therefore more American goods per pound. Thus, American goods become cheaper to the British, inducing the British to buy more of these goods. When the British buy American goods, they supply pounds to the foreign exchange market because they must exchange pounds for dollars to purchase our goods.

The intersection of the supply and demand for pounds will determine the dollar price of pounds. In this instance the equilibrium rate of exchange is $2 to £1.

Depreciation and appreciation An exchange rate which is determined by free-market forces can and does change frequently. When the dollar price of

pounds increases, for example, goes from $2 for £1 to $3 for £1, we say that the value of the dollar has **depreciated** relative to the pound. More generally, currency depreciation means that it takes more units of a country's currency (dollars) to buy a single unit of some foreign currency (pounds). Conversely, when the dollar price of pounds decreases—goes from $2 for £1 to $1 for £1—the value of the dollar has **appreciated** relative to the pound. In general terms, currency appreciation means that it takes fewer units of a country's currency (dollars) to buy a single unit of some foreign currency (pounds).

Observe in our American-British illustrations that when the dollar depreciates the pound necessarily appreciates and vice versa. When the exchange rate between dollars and pounds changes from $2 = £1 to $3 = £1, it now takes *more* dollars to buy £1 and the dollar has depreciated. But it now takes *fewer* pounds to buy a dollar. That is, at the initial rate it took £$\frac{1}{2}$ to buy $1; at the new rate it only takes £$\frac{1}{3}$ to buy $1. Therefore, the pound has appreciated relative to the dollar. *If the dollar depreciates vis-à-vis the pound, the pound appreciates vis-à-vis the dollar. Conversely, if the dollar appreciates vis-à-vis the pound, the pound depreciates vis-à-vis the dollar.* We summarize and generalize these relationships in Figure 40-4.

Determinants of exchange rates Why are the demand for and the supply of pounds located as they are in Figure 40-3? Stated differently, what forces will cause the demand and supply curves for pounds to change and thereby cause the dollar to appreciate or depreciate? Consider briefly some of the more important factors.

CHANGES IN TASTES Any change in consumer tastes or preferences for the products of a foreign country will alter the demand for, or supply of, that nation's currency and change its exchange rate. For example, if American technological advances in computers make them more attractive to British consumers and businesses, then they will supply more pounds in exchange markets in purchasing more American computers and the dollar will appreciate. Conversely, if British tweeds become more fashionable in the United States, our demand for pounds will increase and the dollar will depreciate.

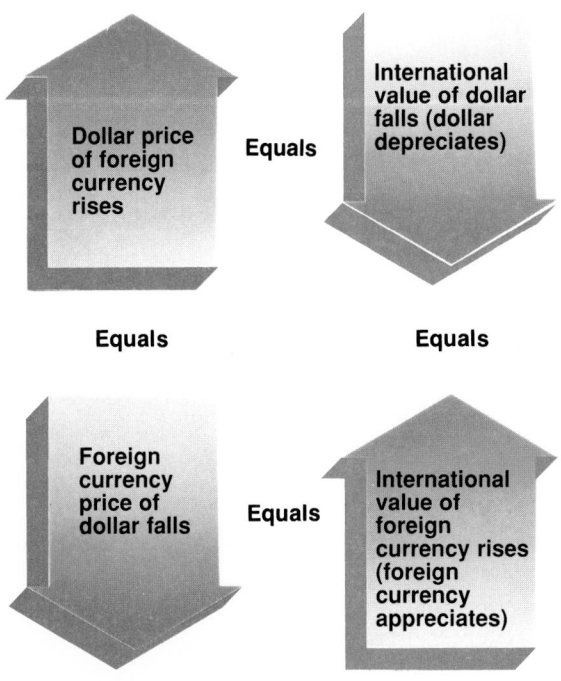

FIGURE 40-4

Currency appreciation and depreciation

An increase in the dollar price of foreign currency is equivalent to a decline in the international value of the dollar (dollar depreciates). An increase in the dollar price of foreign currency also implies a decline in the foreign currency price of dollars. That is, the international value of foreign currency rises relative to the dollar (foreign currency appreciates).

RELATIVE INCOME CHANGES If the growth of a nation's national income is more rapid than other countries, its currency is likely to depreciate. A country's imports vary directly with its level of income. For example, as incomes rise in the United States, American consumers will buy more domestically produced goods *and* also more foreign goods. If the United States' economy is expanding rapidly and the British economy is stagnant, American imports of British goods—and therefore U.S. demand for pounds—will increase. The dollar price of pounds will rise and this means the dollar has depreciated.

RELATIVE PRICE CHANGES If the domestic price level rises rapidly in the United States and remains constant in Britain, American consumers will seek out relatively low-priced British goods, thereby increasing the demand for pounds. Conversely, the British will be less inclined to purchase American goods, reducing the supply of pounds. This combination of an increase in the demand for, and a reduction in the supply of, pounds will cause the dollar to depreciate.

RELATIVE REAL INTEREST RATES Suppose the United States restricts the growth of its money supply (tight money policy), as was the case in the late 1970s and early 1980s, in order to control inflation. As a result, *real* interest rates—money interest rates adjusted for the rate of inflation—were high in the United States in comparison to most other nations. Consequently, British individuals and firms found the United States to be a very attractive place in which to make financial investments. This increase in the demand for American financial assets meant an increase in the supply of British pounds and the dollar therefore appreciated in value.

SPECULATION Suppose it is widely anticipated that the American economy will **(a)** grow faster than the British economy, **(b)** experience more rapid inflation than the British economy, and **(c)** have lower future real interest rates than in Britain. All these expectations would lead one to believe that in the future the dollar will depreciate and, conversely, the pound will appreciate. Hence, holders of dollars will attempt to convert them into pounds, increasing the demand for pounds. This conversion, of course, causes the dollar to depreciate and the pound to appreciate. We have, in effect, a self-fulfilling prophecy: The dollar depreciates and the pound appreciates because speculators act on the supposition that these changes in currency values will in fact happen.

Flexible rates and the balance of payments Proponents of flexible exchange rates argue that such rates embody a compelling virtue: *Flexible rates automatically adjust so as eventually to eliminate balance of payments deficits or surpluses.* We can explain this by looking at *SS* and *DD* in Figure 40-5 which merely restate the demand for, and supply of, pounds curves from Figure 40-3. The resulting equilibrium exchange rate of $2 = £1 correctly suggests that there is no balance of payments deficit or surplus. At the $2 = £1 exchange rate the quantity of pounds demanded by Americans in order to import British goods, buy British transportation and insurance services, and to pay interest and dividends on British investments in the United States is equal to the amount of pounds supplied by the British in buying American exports, purchasing services from Americans, and making interest and dividend payments on American investments in Britain. More succinctly, there would be no change in official reserves in Table 40-1.

Now let us suppose there is a change of tastes such that Americans decide to buy more British automobiles. Or we might assume that the American price level has increased relative to Britain or that interest rates have fallen in the United States as compared to Britain. Any or all of these changes

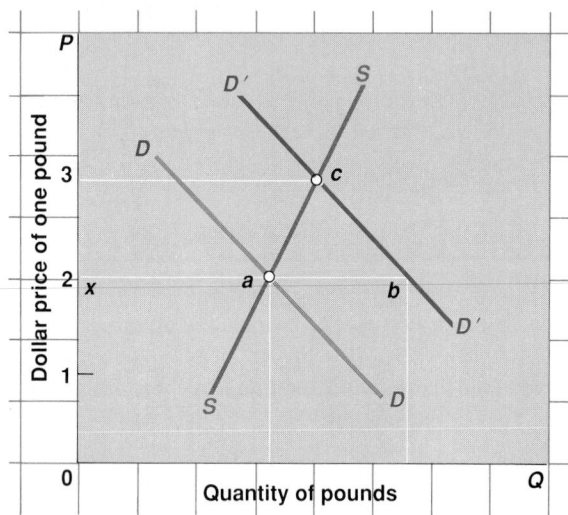

FIGURE 40-5

Adjustments under flexible exchange rates, fixed exchange rates, and the gold standard

Under flexible rates an American trade deficit at the $2-for-£1 rate would be corrected by an increase in the rate to $3 for £1. Under fixed rates the *ab* shortage of pounds would be met out of international monetary reserves. Under the gold standard the deficit would cause changes in domestic price and income levels which would shift the demand for pounds (*D′D′*) to the left and the supply (*SS*) to the right, sustaining equilibrium at the $2-for-£1 rate.

will cause the American demand for British pounds to increase from *DD* to, say, *D′D′* in Figure 40-5. We observe that *at the initial $2 = £1 exchange rate* an American balance of payments deficit has been created in the amount *ab*. That is, at the $2 = £1 rate there is a shortage of pounds in the amount *ab* to Americans. American export-type transactions will earn *xa* pounds, but Americans will want *xb* pounds to finance import-type transactions. Because this is a free competitive market, the shortage will change the exchange rate (the dollar price of pounds) from $2 = £1 to, say, $3 = £1; that is, the dollar has *depreciated*.

At this point it must be emphasized that *the exchange rate is a very special price which links all domestic (United States') prices with all foreign (British) prices.* A change in the exchange rate therefore alters the prices of all British goods to Americans and all American goods to potential British buyers. Specifically, this particular change in the exchange rate will alter the relative attractiveness of American imports and exports in such a way as to restore equilibrium in the balance of payments of the United States. From the American point of view, as the dollar price of pounds changes from $2 to $3, the Triumph automobile priced at £9000, which formerly cost an American $18,000, now costs $27,000. Other British goods will also be more expensive to Americans. Hence, American imports of British goods and services will tend to decline. Graphically, this is shown as a move from point *b* toward point *c* in Figure 40-5.

Conversely, from Britain's standpoint the exchange rate, that is, the pound price of dollars, has fallen (from £$\frac{1}{2}$ to £$\frac{1}{3}$ for $1). The international value of the pound has *appreciated*. The British previously got only $2 for £1; now they get $3 for £1. American goods are therefore cheaper to the British, and as a result American exports to Great Britain tend to rise. In Figure 40-5 this is indicated by the move from point *a* toward point *c*. The two adjustments described—a decrease in American imports from Great Britain and an increase in American exports to Great Britain—are precisely those needed to correct the American balance of payments deficit. (The reader should reason through the operation of freely fluctuating exchange rates in correcting an initial American balance of payments surplus in its trade with Great

Britain.) In short, the free fluctuation of exchange rates in response to shifts in the supply of, and demand for, foreign monies automatically corrects balance of payments deficits and surpluses.

Disadvantages Though freely fluctuating exchange rates automatically tend to eliminate payments imbalances, they may entail several significant problems:

1 UNCERTAINTY AND DIMINISHED TRADE The risks and uncertainties associated with flexible exchange rates may discourage the flow of trade. To illustrate: Suppose an American automobile dealer contracts to purchase ten Triumph cars for £90,000. At the current exchange rate of, say, $2 for £1, the American importer expects to pay $180,000 for these automobiles. But if in the three-month delivery period the rate of exchange shifts to $3 for £1, the £90,000 payment contracted by the American importer will now amount to $270,000. This unheralded increase in the dollar price of pounds may easily turn the potential American importer's anticipated profits into substantial losses. Aware at the outset of the possibility of an adverse change in the exchange rate, the American importer may simply not be willing to assume the risks involved. The American firm therefore confines its operations to domestic automobiles, with the result that international trade does not occur in this item.

The same rationale applies to investment. Assume that, when the exchange rate is $3 to £1, an American firm invests $30,000 (or £10,000) in a British enterprise. It estimates a return of 10 percent, that is, it anticipates earnings of $3000 or £1000. Suppose these expectations prove correct in the sense that the British firm earns £1000 the first year on the £10,000 investment. But suppose that during the year, the value of the dollar *appreciates* to $2 = £1. The absolute return is now only $2000 (rather than $3000) and the rate of return falls from the anticipated 10 percent to only $6\frac{2}{3}$ percent (= $2000/$30,000). Investment is inherently risky. The added risk posed by adverse changes in exchange rates may persuade the potential American investor to shy away from overseas ventures.[3]

2 TERMS OF TRADE A nation's terms of trade will tend to be worsened by a decline in the interna-

tional value of its currency. For example, an increase in the dollar price of pounds will mean that the United States must export a larger volume of goods and services to finance a given level of imports from Britain.

3 INSTABILITY Freely fluctuating exchange rates may also have destabilizing effects upon the domestic economy as wide fluctuations stimulate and then depress those industries producing internationally traded goods. If the American economy is operating at full employment and the international value of its currency depreciates as in our illustration, the results will be inflationary. This is so for two reasons. First, foreign demand for American goods will increase, that is, the net exports component of aggregate expenditures will increase and cause demand-pull inflation. Second, the prices of all American imports will increase. Conversely, appreciation of the dollar would lower exports and increase imports, tending to cause unemployment. Looked at from the vantage point of policy, acceptance of floating exchange rates may complicate the use of domestic fiscal and monetary policies in seeking full employment and price stability. This is especially so for those nations whose exports and imports may amount to 20 to 30 percent of their GNPs (Table 39-1).

FIXED EXCHANGE RATES

At the other extreme nations have often fixed or "pegged" their exchange rates in an effort to cir-

---

[3] At some cost and inconvenience a *trader* can circumvent a portion of the risk of unfavorable exchange rate fluctuations by "hedging" in the "futures market" for foreign exchange. For example, our American auto importer can purchase the needed pounds at the current $2 for £1 exchange rate to be made available three months in the future when the British cars are delivered. Unfortunately, this does not eliminate entirely exchange rate risks. Suppose the dollar price of pounds *falls* (the dollar appreciates) in the three-month delivery period and a competing importing firm did not hedge its foreign exchange purchase. This means the competitor will obtain its shipment of Triumphs at a lower price and will be able to undersell our original importer.

cumvent the disadvantages associated with floating rates. To analyze the implications and problems associated with fixed rates, let us assume that the United States and Britain agree to maintain a $2 = £1 exchange rate.

The basic problem, of course, is that a governmental proclamation that a dollar will be worth so many pounds does **not** mandate stability with respect to the demand for, and the supply of, pounds. As demand and supply shift over time, government must intervene directly or indirectly in the foreign exchange market if the exchange rate is to be stabilized. Consider Figure 40-5 once again. We assume that the American demand for pounds increases from **DD** to **D'D'** and an American payments deficit of **ab** arises. This means that the American government is committed to an exchange rate ($2 = £1) which is below the equilibrium rate ($3 = £1). How can the United States prevent the shortage of pounds—reflecting an American balance of payments deficit—from driving the exchange rate up to the equilibrium level? The answer clearly is to alter market demand or supply or both so that they continue to intersect at the $2 = £1 rate of exchange. There are several means by which this can be achieved.

1 Use of reserves   The most desirable means of pegging an exchange rate is to manipulate the market through the use of official reserves. We know that international monetary **reserves** are simply stocks for foreign monies owned by a particular government. How do reserves originate? Let us conveniently assume that in the past the opposite market condition prevailed wherein there was a surplus, rather than a shortage, of pounds, and the United States government had acquired that surplus. That is, at some earlier time the United States government spent dollars to buy surplus pounds which were threatening to reduce the $2 = £1 exchange rate to, say, $1 = £1. By now selling a part of its reserve of pounds, the United States government could shift the supply of pounds curve to the right so that it intersects **D'D'** at **b** in Figure 40-5, thereby maintaining the exchange rate at $2 = £1.

Historically nations have used gold as "international money" or, in other words, as reserves. Hence, in our example the United States govern-

ment might sell some of the gold which it owns to Britain for pounds. The pounds thus acquired could be used to augment the supply earned through American trade and financial transactions to shift the supply of pounds to the right in order to maintain the $2 = £1 exchange rate.

Note that it is critical that the amount of reserves be enough to accomplish the required increase in the supply of pounds. This is **not** a problem if deficits and surpluses occur more or less randomly and are of approximately equivalent size. That is, last year's balance of payments surplus with Britain will increase the United States' reserve of pounds and this reserve can be used to "finance" this year's deficit. But if the United States encounters persistent and sizable deficits for an extended period of time, the reserves problem can become critical and force the abandonment of a system of fixed exchange rates. Or, at least, a nation whose reserves are inadequate must resort to less appealing options if it hopes to maintain exchange rate stability. Let us consider these other options.

2 Trade policies   One set of policy options entails measures designed to control directly the flows of trade and finance. The United States might undertake to maintain the $2 = £1 exchange rate in the face of a shortage of pounds by discouraging imports (thereby reducing the demand for pounds) and by encouraging exports (thereby increasing the supply of pounds). Specifically, imports can be reduced by imposing tariffs or import quotas (Chapter 39). Similarly, special taxes may be levied on the interest and dividends which Americans receive for foreign investments. On the other hand, the United States government might subsidize certain American exports and thus increase the supply of pounds.

The fundamental problem with these policies is that they reduce the volume of world trade and distort its composition or pattern away from that which is economically desirable. That is, tariffs, quotas, and the like can be imposed only at the sacrifice of some portion of the economic gains or benefits attainable from a free flow of world trade based upon the principle of comparative advantage. These effects should not be underestimated; remember that the imposition of trade barriers can elicit retaliatory responses from other nations which are adversely affected.

3 Exchange controls: rationing Another option is exchange controls or rationing. Under exchange controls the United States government would handle the problem of a pound shortage by requiring that all pounds obtained by American exporters be sold to it. Then, in turn, the government allocates or rations this short supply of pounds (*xa* in Figure 40-5) among various American importers who demand the quantity *xb*. In this way the American government would be restricting American imports to the amount of foreign exchange earned by American exports. American demand for British pounds in the amount *ab* would simply be unfulfilled. Government eliminates a balance of payments deficit by restricting imports to the value of exports.

There are many objections to exchange controls. First, like trade controls—tariffs, quotas, and export subsidies—exchange controls distort the pattern of international trade away from that based upon comparative advantage. Second, the process of rationing scarce foreign exchange necessarily involves discrimination among importers. Serious problems of equity and favoritism are implicit in the rationing process. Third, controls impinge upon freedom of consumer choice. Americans who prefer Scotch may be forced to buy bourbon. The business opportunities of some American importers will necessarily be impaired because imports are being constrained by government. Finally, there are likely to be enforcement problems. The market forces of demand and supply indicate there are American importers who want foreign exchange badly enough to pay *more* than the $2 = £1 official rate; this sets the stage for extralegal or "black market" foreign exchange dealings.

4 Domestic macro adjustments A final means of maintaining a stable exchange rate is to use domestic fiscal and monetary policies in such a way as to eliminate the shortage of pounds. In particular, restrictive fiscal and monetary measures will reduce the United States' national income relative to Britain's. Because American imports vary directly with our national income, our demand for British goods, and therefore for pounds, will be restrained.

To the extent that these contractionary policies cause our price level to decline relative to Britain's, American buyers of consumption and investment goods will divert their demands from British to American goods, also restricting the demand for pounds. Finally, a restrictive (tight) money policy will increase United States' interest rates as compared to Britain and, hence, reduce American demand for pounds to make financial investments in Britain. From Britain's standpoint lower prices on American goods and higher American interest rates will increase British imports of American goods and stimulate British financial investment in the United States. Both developments will increase the supply of pounds. The combination of a decrease in the demand for and an increase in the supply of pounds will tend to eliminate the initial American payments deficit. In terms of the curves shown in Figure 40-5 the new supply and demand curves will intersect at some new equilibrium point on the white *ab* line where the exchange rate persists at $2 = £1.

This means of maintaining pegged exchange rates is hardly appealing. The "price" of exchange rate stability for the United States is falling output, employment, and price levels—in other words, a recession. Achieving a balance of payments equilibrium and realizing domestic stability are both important national economic objectives; but to sacrifice the latter for the former is to let the tail wag the dog.

Recapitulation: Proponents of fixed exchange rates contend that such rates lessen the risks and uncertainties associated with international trade and finance. Fixed rates are thereby said to be conducive to a large and expanding volume of mutually advantageous trade and financial transactions. However, the viability of a fixed-rate system hinges upon two interrelated conditions: (1) the availability of adequate amounts of reserves and (2) the random occurrence of payments deficits and surpluses which are of modest size. Large and persistent deficits may deplete a nation's reserves. A nation with inadequate reserves is confronted with less desirable options. On the one hand, it may have to submit to painful and politically unpopular macroeconomic adjustments in the form of inflation or recession. On the other hand, that nation may have to resort to protectionist trade policies or exchange controls, both of which inhibit the volume of international trade and finance.

International exchange rate systems

Given this survey of the functioning of flexible and fixed exchange rates, we now want to discuss briefly the three different exchange rate systems which the nations of the world have employed in recent history. Over the 1879–1934 period—with the exception of the World War I years—an international monetary system known as the *gold standard* prevailed. From the end of World War II in the mid-1940s until 1971 the so-called *Bretton Woods system* prevailed. These two systems both stressed fixed exchange rates, although the latter allowed for periodic rate adjustments. Since 1971 a system of essentially freely flexible or floating rates has been in operation. This system has been dubbed *managed floating exchange rates,* however, because governments often intervene in exchange markets to alter the international value of their currency. Let us examine these three systems in the order stated.

THE GOLD STANDARD: FIXED EXCHANGE RATES

The **gold standard** system provided for fixed exchange rates and a backward glance at its operation and ultimate downfall is instructive with respect to the functioning and some of the advantages and problems associated with fixed-rate systems. It is to be emphasized that currently a number of economists advocate fixed exchange rates and a few even call for a return to the international gold standard.[4]

Conditions   A nation is on the gold standard when it fulfills three conditions:
1 It must define its monetary unit in terms of a certain quantity of gold.

[4] At this point you may want to reread Chapter 17's Last Word which summarizes the pros and cons of the gold standard.

2 It must maintain a fixed relationship between its stock of gold and its domestic money supply.
3 It must allow gold to be freely exported and imported.

If each nation defines its monetary unit in terms of gold, the various national currencies will have a fixed relationship to one another. For example, suppose the United States defines a dollar as being worth, say, 25 grains of gold and Britain defines its pound sterling as being worth 50 grains of gold. This means that a British pound is worth $\frac{50}{25}$ dollars or, simply, £1 equals $2.

Gold flows   Now, if we momentarily ignore the costs of packing, insuring, and shipping gold between countries, under the gold standard the rate of exchange would not vary from this $2-for-£1 rate. And the reason is clear: No one in the United States would pay more than $2 for £1, because one could always buy 50 grains of gold for $2 in the United States, ship it to Britain, and sell it for £1. Nor would the English pay more than £1 for $2. Why should you, when you could buy 50 grains of gold in England for £1, send it to the United States, and sell it for $2?

Of course, in practice the costs of packing, insuring, and shipping gold must be taken into account. But these costs would only amount to a few cents per 50 grains of gold. For example, if these costs were 3 cents for 50 grains of gold, Americans wanting pounds would pay up to $2.03 for a pound rather than buy and export 50 grains of gold to get the pound. Why? Because it would cost them $2 for the 50 grains of gold plus 3 cents to send it to England to be exchanged for £1. This $2.03 exchange rate, above which gold would begin to flow out of the United States, is called the **gold export point.** Conversely, the exchange rate would fall to $1.97 before gold would flow into the United States. The English, wanting dollars, would accept as little as $1.97 in exchange for £1, because from the $2 which they could get by buying 50 grains of gold in England and reselling it in the United States, 3 cents must be subtracted to pay shipping and related costs. This $1.97 exchange rate, below which gold would flow into the United States, is called the **gold import point.** Our basic conclusion is that *under the gold standard the flow of gold between nations would result in exchange rates which for all practical purposes are fixed.*

Domestic macro adjustments Figure 40-5 is useful in explaining the kinds of adjustments which the gold standard would entail. Here we assume that initially the demand for and the supply of pounds are *DD* and *SS* respectively and the resulting intersection point at *a* coincides with the fixed exchange rate which results from the "in gold" definitions of the pound and the dollar. That is, the United States has defined the dollar to be 25 grains of gold and Britain has defined the pound to be 50 grains of gold so the resulting gold standard exchange rate is $2 for £1. Let us now suppose that for some reason American tastes or preferences for British goods increase, shifting the demand for pounds to *D'D'*. We now find in Figure 40-5 that there is a shortage of pounds equal to *ab*, implying an American balance of payments deficit.

What will happen? Remember that the rules of the gold standard game prohibit the exchange rate from moving from the fixed $2 = £1 relationship; the rate can *not* move up to a new equilibrium of $3 = £1 at point *c* as it would under freely floating rates. What would happen is that the exchange rate would rise by a few cents to the American gold export point at which gold would flow from the United States to Britain. Recall that the gold standard requires participants to maintain a fixed relationship between their domestic money supplies and their quantities of gold. Therefore, the flow of gold from the United States to Britain would bring about a contraction of the money supply in America and an expansion of the money supply in Britain. Other things being equal, this will bring about a decline in aggregate demand and, therefore, in real national output, employment, and the price level in the United States. Also, the reduced money supply will boost American interest rates. The opposite occurs in Britain. The inflow of gold increases the money supply, causing aggregate demand, national income, employment, and the price level to all increase. The increased money supply will also lower interest rates in Britain.

How will all these macroeconomic adjustments impact upon Figure 40-5? Declining American incomes and prices will reduce our demand for British goods and services and therefore reduce the American demand for pounds. Lower relative interest rates in Britain will make it less attractive for Americans to invest there, also reducing the demand for pounds. For all these reasons the *D'D'*

curve will shift to the left. Similarly, increased incomes and prices in Britain will increase British demand for American goods and services and higher American interest rates will encourage the British to invest more in the United States. These developments all increase the supply of pounds available to Americans, shifting the *SS* curve of Figure 40-5 to the right. In short, domestic macroeconomic adjustments in America and Britain, triggered by the international flow of gold, will give rise to new demand and supply for pound curves which intersect at some point on the white horizontal line between points *a* and *b*.

Take note of the critical difference in the adjustment mechanisms associated with freely floating exchange rates and the fixed rates of the gold standard. With floating rates the burden of the adjustment is upon the exchange rate itself. In contrast the gold standard entails changes in the domestic money supplies of participating nations which in turn precipitate changes in price levels, real national output and employment, and interest rates.

Evaluation The gold standard entails these advantages:

1 The stable exchange rates the gold standard fosters reduce uncertainty and risk and thereby stimulate the volume of international trade.
2 The gold standard *automatically* corrects balance of payments deficits or surpluses. If an American payments deficit occurs as is implied by the shift of the American demand curve for pounds from *DD* to *D'D'* in Figure 40-5, inevitable gold flows will cause shifts in the supply and demand curves for pounds until they intersect once again at the fixed $2 = £1 exchange rate. The payments deficit implied by the initial *ab* shortage of pounds will have been eliminated. Note that the rules of the gold standard make these adjustments automatic; no discretionary policy actions have been taken. It is not surprising that economists who advocate the gold standard are generally those who are distrustful of discretionary governmental policies.

The gold standard also has two salient shortcomings:

1 The basic drawback of the gold standard is apparent from our discussion of the adjustment processes it entails. Nations on the gold standard must accept domestic adjustments in such distasteful forms as unemployment and falling incomes, on the one hand, or inflation, on the other. In playing the gold standard (fixed exchange rate) game nations must be willing to submit their domestic economies to painful macroeconomic adjustments. As our example makes clear, under the gold standard a nation's monetary policy would be determined largely by changes in the demand for and supply of foreign exchange. If the United States, for example, was already tending toward recession, the loss of gold under the gold standard would reduce its money supply and intensify the problem. Under the international gold standard nations would have to forgo independent monetary policies.

2 The gold standard can only function so long as no participants run out of gold. Thus, if the United States were not a gold producer and it experienced persistent gold outflows, it would be forced at some point to abandon the gold standard. Stated differently, gold constitutes the official reserves of this system and nations can only meet the requirement of keeping their exchange rate fixed when such reserves are available to them.

Demise The worldwide Great Depression of the 1930s signaled the end of the gold standard. As national outputs and employment plummeted worldwide, the restoration of prosperity became the primary goal of afflicted nations. You will recall from Chapter 39 that protectionist measures—for example, the United States' Smoot-Hawley Tariff—were enacted as the various nations sought to increase net exports and thereby stimulate their domestic economies. And each nation was fearful that its economic recovery would be aborted by a balance of payments deficit which would lead to an outflow of gold and consequent contractionary effects. Indeed, the various gold standard nations attempted to devalue their currencies in terms of gold so as to make their exports more attractive and imports less attractive. These devaluations undermined a basic condition of the gold standard and the system simply broke down.

THE BRETTON WOODS SYSTEM

We have just noted that the Great Depression of the 1930s led to the downfall of the gold standard. It also prompted the erection of trade barriers

which greatly impaired international trade. World War II was similarly disruptive to world trade and finance. Hence, it is fair to say that as World War II drew to a close the world trading and monetary systems were in a shambles.

In order to lay the groundwork for a new international monetary system, an international conference of Allied nations was held at Bretton Woods, New Hampshire, in 1944. Out of this conference evolved a commitment to an *adjustable-peg system* of exchange rates, sometimes called the **Bretton Woods system.** The new system sought to capture the advantages of the old gold standard (fixed exchange rates), while avoiding its disadvantages (painful domestic macroeconomic adjustments). Furthermore, the conference created the **International Monetary Fund** (IMF) to make the new exchange rate system feasible and workable. This international monetary system, emphasizing relatively fixed exchange rates and managed through the IMF, prevailed with modifications until 1971. The IMF continues to play a basic role in international finance and in recent years the IMF has performed a major role in ameliorating the debt problems of the less developed countries (Chapter 41).

IMF and pegged exchange rates What was the Bretton Woods adjustable-peg system? Why was it evolved? What caused its demise? Consider the second question first. We have noted that during the depressed 1930s, various countries resorted to the practice of **devaluation**—devaluing[5] their currencies in the hope of stimulating domestic employment. For example, if the United States was faced with growing unemployment, it might devalue the dollar by *increasing* the dollar price of pounds from $2.50 for £1 to, say, $3 for £1. This action would make American goods cheaper to the British and British goods dearer to Americans, increasing American exports and reducing American imports.

---

[5] A note on terminology is in order. We noted earlier in this chapter that the dollar has *appreciated (depreciated)* when its international value has increased (decreased) as the result of changes in the demand for, or supply of, dollars in foreign exchange markets. The terms *devalue* and *revalue* are used to describe an increase or decrease, respectively, in the international value of a currency which occurs as the result of governmental action.

The resulting increase in net exports, abetted by the multiplier effect, would stimulate output and employment in the United States. But the problem was that every nation can play the devaluation game, and most gave it a whirl. The resulting rounds of competitive devaluations benefited no one; on the contrary, they actually contributed to the further demoralization of world trade. Nations at Bretton Woods therefore agreed that the postwar monetary system must provide for overall exchange rate stability whereby disruptive currency devaluations could be avoided.

What was the adjustable-peg system of exchange rates like? First, reminiscent of the gold standard, each member of the IMF was obligated to define its monetary unit in terms of gold (or dollars), thereby establishing par rates of exchange between its currency and the currencies of all other members. Each nation was further obligated to keep its exchange rate stable vis-à-vis any other currency.

But how was this obligation to be fulfilled? The answer, as we discovered in our earlier discussion of fixed exchange rates, is that governments must use international monetary reserves to intervene in foreign exchange markets. Assume, for example, that under the Bretton Woods system the dollar was "pegged" to the British pound at $2 = £1. Now suppose in Figure 40-5 that the American demand for pounds temporarily increases from *DD* to *D'D'* so that a shortage of pounds of *ab* arises at the pegged rate. How can the United States keep its pledge to maintain a $2 = £1 rate when the new market or equilibrium rate would be at $3 = £1? The answer is that the United States could supply additional pounds in the exchange market, shifting the supply of pounds curve to the right so that it intersects *D'D'* at *b* and thereby maintains the $2 = £1 rate of exchange.

Where would the United States obtain the needed pounds? Under the Bretton Woods system there were three main sources. First, the United States might currently possess pounds in a "stabilization fund" as the result of the opposite exchange market condition existing in the past. That is, at some earlier time the United States government may have spent dollars to purchase surplus pounds which were threatening to reduce the $2 = £1 exchange rate to, say, $1 = £1. Or, secondly, the United States government might sell some of the gold it holds to Britain for pounds. The proceeds would then be offered in the exchange market to augment the supply of pounds. Finally, the needed pounds might be borrowed from the IMF. Nations participating in the Bretton Woods system were required to make contributions to the IMF on the basis of the size of their national income, population, and volume of trade. Thus, if necessary, the United States could borrow pounds on a short-term basis from the IMF by supplying its own currency as collateral.

Fundamental imbalances: adjusting the peg A fixed-rate system such as Bretton Woods functions well so long as a nation's payments deficits and surpluses occur more or less randomly and are approximately equal in size. If a nation's payments surplus last year allows it to add a sufficient amount to its international monetary reserves to finance this year's payments deficit, no problems will arise. But what if the United States, for example, were to encounter a "fundamental imbalance" in its international trade and finance so that it was confronted with persistent and sizable payments deficits? In this case it is evident that the United States will eventually run out of reserves and hence be unable to maintain its fixed exchange rate.

The option provided by the Bretton Woods system was to correct a fundamental payments deficit by devaluation, that is, by an "orderly" reduction in the nation's pegged exchange rate. Under the Bretton Woods system, the IMF allowed each member nation to alter the value of its currency by 10 percent without explicit permission from the Fund in order to correct a deeply rooted or "fundamental" balance of payments deficit. Larger exchange rate changes required the sanction of the Fund's board of directors. By requiring approval of significant rate changes, the Fund attempted to guard against arbitrary and competitive currency devaluation prompted by nations seeking a temporary stimulus to their domestic economies. In our illustration the devaluing of the dollar would increase American exports and lower American imports, thereby tending to correct its persistent payments deficits.

The objective of the adjustable-peg system was to realize a world monetary system which embraced the best features of both a fixed exchange rate system (such as the old international gold standard) and a system of freely fluctuating exchange rates. By reducing risk and uncertainty, short-term exchange rate stability—pegged exchange rates—would presumably stimulate trade and be conducive to the efficient use of world resources. Periodic exchange rate adjustments—adjustment of the pegs—made in an orderly fashion through the IMF, and on the basis of permanent or long-run changes in a country's payments position, provided a mechanism by which persistent international payments imbalances could be resolved by means other than painful changes in domestic levels of output and prices.

Demise of the Bretton Woods system Under the Bretton Woods system gold and the dollar came to be accepted as international reserves. The acceptability of gold as an international medium of exchange was derived from its role under the international gold standard of an earlier era. The dollar became acceptable as international money for two reasons. First, the United States emerged from World War II as the free world's strongest economy. Second, the United States had accumulated large quantities of gold and between 1934 and 1971 maintained a policy of buying gold from, and selling gold to, foreign monetary authorities at a fixed price of $35 per ounce. Thus the dollar was convertible into gold on demand; the dollar came to be regarded as a substitute for gold and therefore "as good as gold."

But the role of the dollar as a component of international monetary reserves contained the seeds of a dilemma. Consider the situation as it developed in the 1950s and 1960s. The problem with gold as international money was a quantitative one. The growth of the world's money stock depends upon the amount of newly mined gold, less any amounts hoarded for speculative purposes or used for industrial and artistic purposes. Unfortunately, the growth of the gold stock lagged behind the rapidly expanding volume of international trade and finance. Thus the dollar came to occupy an increasingly important role as an international monetary reserve. Question: How do economies of the world acquire dollars as reserves? Answer: As the result of United States' balance of payments deficits. With the exception of some three or four years, the United States incurred persistent payments deficits throughout the 1950s and 1960s.

These deficits were financed in part by drawing down American gold reserves. But for the most part United States' deficits were financed by growing foreign holdings of American dollars which, remember, were "as good as gold" until 1971.

As the amount of dollars held by foreigners soared and as our gold reserves dwindled, other nations inevitably began to question whether the dollar was really "as good as gold." The ability of the United States to maintain the convertibility of the dollar into gold became increasingly doubtful, and, therefore, so did the role of the dollar as generally accepted international monetary reserves. Hence, the dilemma: ". . . to preserve the status of the dollar as a reserve medium, the payments deficit of the United States had to be eliminated; but elimination of the deficit would mean a drying up of the source of additional dollar reserves for the system."[6] The United States had to reduce or eliminate its payments deficits to preserve the dollar's status as an international medium of exchange. But success in this endeavor would limit the expansion of international reserves or liquidity and therefore tend to restrict the growth of international trade and finance.

This problem came to a head in the early 1970s. Faced with persistent and growing United States payments deficits, President Nixon suspended the dollar's convertibility into gold on August 15, 1971. This suspension abrogated the policy to exchange gold for dollars at $35 per ounce, which had existed for thirty-seven years. This new policy severed the link between gold and the international value of the dollar, thereby "floating" the dollar and allowing its value to be determined by market forces. The floating of the dollar withdrew American support from the old Bretton Woods system of fixed exchange rates and sounded the death knell for that system.

THE MANAGED FLOAT

The system of exchange rates which has since evolved is not easily described; it can probably best

[6] Delbert A. Snider, *Introduction to International Economics*, 7th ed. (Homewood, Ill.: Richard D. Irwin, Inc., 1979), p. 352.

be labeled a system of **managed floating exchange rates.** On the one hand, it is recognized that changing economic conditions among nations require continuing changes in exchange rates to avoid persistent payments deficits or surpluses; exchange rates must be allowed to float. On the other hand, short-term changes in exchange rates—perhaps accentuated by purchases and sales by speculators—tend to disrupt and discourage the flow of trade and finance. Hence, it is generally agreed that the central banks of the various nations should buy and sell foreign exchange to smooth out such fluctuations in rates. In other words, central banks should "manage" or stabilize short-term speculative variations in their exchange rates. These characteristics were formalized by a leading group of IMF nations in 1976. Thus, ideally, the new system will entail not only the needed long-term exchange rate flexibility to correct fundamental payments imbalances, but also sufficient short-term stability of rates to sustain and encourage international trade and finance.

Actually, the current exchange rate system is a bit more complicated than the previous paragraph suggests. While the major currencies—such as American and Canadian dollars, Japanese yen, and the British pound—fluctuate or float in response to changing demand and supply conditions, most of the European Common Market nations are attempting to peg their currencies to one another. Furthermore, many less developed nations peg their currencies to that of a major industrial country and fluctuate with it. Thus, for example, some forty less developed countries have pegged their currencies to the dollar. Finally, some nations peg the value of their currencies to a "basket" or group of other currencies.

How well has the managed floating system worked? Although our experience with this system is historically too short for a definitive assessment, the system has both proponents and critics.

Pros Proponents argue that the system has functioned well—far better than anticipated—during its relatively brief existence.

1 TRADE GROWTH In the first place, fluctuating exchange rates did not give rise to the diminution of world trade and finance that skeptics had predicted. In fact, in real terms world trade has grown at approximately the same rate under the managed float as it did during the decade of the 1960s under the fixed exchange rates of the Bretton Woods system.

2 MANAGING TURBULENCE Proponents argue that the managed float has weathered severe economic turbulence which, in the view of one authority, might well have caused a fixed exchange regime to have broken down several times over.[7] More specifically, such dramatic events as worldwide agricultural shortfalls in 1972–1974, extraordinary oil-price increases in 1973–1974 and again in 1979–1980, worldwide stagflation in 1974–1976 and 1981–1983, and large U.S. budget deficits in the 1980s, all tended to generate substantial international trade and financial imbalances. It is contended that flexible rates facilitated international adjustments to these developments, whereas the same events would have put unbearable pressures upon a fixed-rate system.

Cons But there is still considerable sentiment in favor of a system characterized by greater exchange rate stability. Those favoring stable rates envision problems with the current system.

1 VOLATILITY AND ADJUSTMENT Critics argue that exchange rates have been excessively volatile under the managed float. This volatility, it is argued, has occurred even when the underlying economic and financial conditions of particular nations have been quite stable. Perhaps more importantly, it is contended that the managed float has not readily resolved balance of payments imbalances as flexible rates are presumably capable of doing. Thus the United States has run persistent trade deficits in recent years, while Germany and Japan have had persistent surpluses. Changes in the international values of the dollar, mark, and yen have not yet corrected these imbalances.

2 A "NONSYSTEM"? Skeptics feel that the managed float is basically a "nonsystem"; that is, the rules and guidelines circumscribing the behavior of each

---

[7] Mordechai E. Kreinin, "U.S. Foreign Economic Policy: An Overview," *Journal of Economic Issues*, September 1980, p. 715.

nation vis-à-vis its exchange rate are not sufficiently clear or constraining to make the system viable in the long run. Bluntly put, the various nations will inevitably be tempted to intervene in foreign exchange markets, not merely to smooth out short-term or speculative fluctuations in the value of their currencies, but to prop up their currency if it is chronically weak or to purposely manipulate the value of their currency to achieve domestic stabilization goals. In short, there is fear that in time there may be more "managing" and less "floating" of exchange rates, and this may be fatal to the present loosely defined system.

Illustration: Japan has been accused of intervening in exchange markets in 1976 to keep the value of the yen down. The alleged purpose was to gain a competitive advantage in trade by making its exports cheap to the rest of the world. The stimulus to Japanese exports from an undervalued yen was designed to reduce unemployment and stimulate growth in Japan, whose economy was sluggish at the time.

A second example of more "managing" and less "floating" of exchange rates occurred in February 1987 when the "Group of Seven" industrial nations (**G-7 nations**)—the United States, West Germany, Japan, Britain, France, Italy, and Canada—agreed to take actions to stabilize the value of the dollar. In the previous two years the dollar had declined rapidly because of a sizable U.S. trade deficit. Although the U.S. trade deficit remained large, it was felt that a further depreciation of the dollar might be disruptive to economic growth in several of the G-7 economies. Hence, the G-7 nations bought large quantities of dollars to prop up the dollar's value in foreign exchange markets. Since 1987 the G-7 nations have periodically intervened in the foreign exchange markets to keep the value of the dollar relatively stable. Do these actions represent an admission by the industrial economies that the system of flexible exchange rates is seriously flawed?

The jury is still out on the managed float and no clear assessment has been reached: "Flexible rates have neither attained their proponents' wildest hopes nor confirmed their opponents' worst fears. But they have seen the major industrial economies through [two decades] mined with major disturbances to the international economy."[8]

A "crisis" in foreign trade?

The 1980s experienced a pronounced acceleration in American imports relative to the growth of American exports. Figure 40-6 reflects this trend and indicates the resultant growth in our merchandise trade deficit. Specifically, our merchandise trade deficit jumped from about $25 billion in 1980 to about $160 billion in 1987. Our current account balance shows a similar sharp decline. In 1980 the United States had a current account *surplus* of $2 billion; by 1987 this had changed to a $160 billion *deficit.*

What are the causes of these large trade deficits? What are their effects? And what policies might end this so-called **foreign trade crisis?**

CAUSES OF THE TRADE DEFICITS

It is generally agreed that there are three major causes of our persistent trade deficits. First, between 1980 and 1985 the dollar rose rapidly in value relative to the currencies of our major trading partners. Moreover, the sharp decline in the value of the dollar in 1985 and 1986 did not bring forth an immediate improvement in the trade deficit. Second, our economy has been growing faster than other major industrialized countries with whom we trade. Finally, heavily indebted less developed countries have curtailed their purchases of American exports.

The dance of the dollar As Figure 40-7 indicates, there was a pronounced rise in the international value of the dollar between 1980 and 1985. Here the value of the dollar is compared to ten other major currencies (weighted by the amount of trade we carry on with each country). By the end of 1984 the dollar was about 65 percent above its 1980 average value and at the highest level since floating exchange rates were adopted in 1973. As you will recall from Figure 40-4, a strong or appreciated

[8] Richard E. Caves and Ronald W. Jones, *World Trade and Payments*, 3d ed. (Boston: Little, Brown and Company, 1981), p. 471.

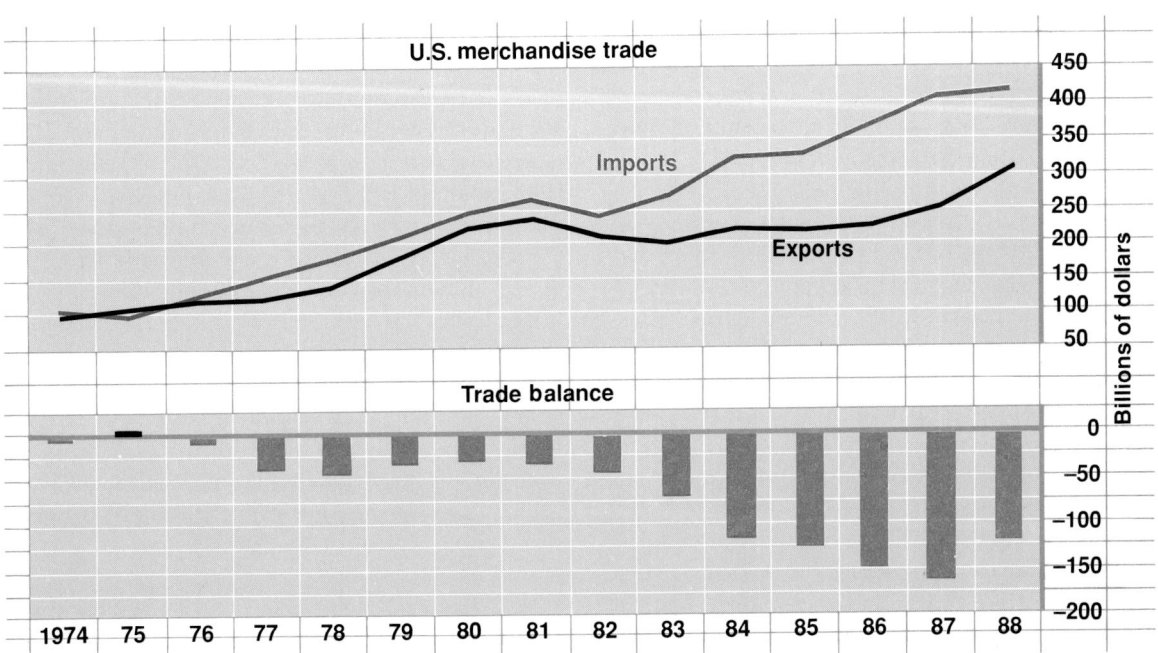

FIGURE 40-6

United States merchandise exports and imports and the trade balance

In recent years there has been a dramatic increase in American trade deficits.

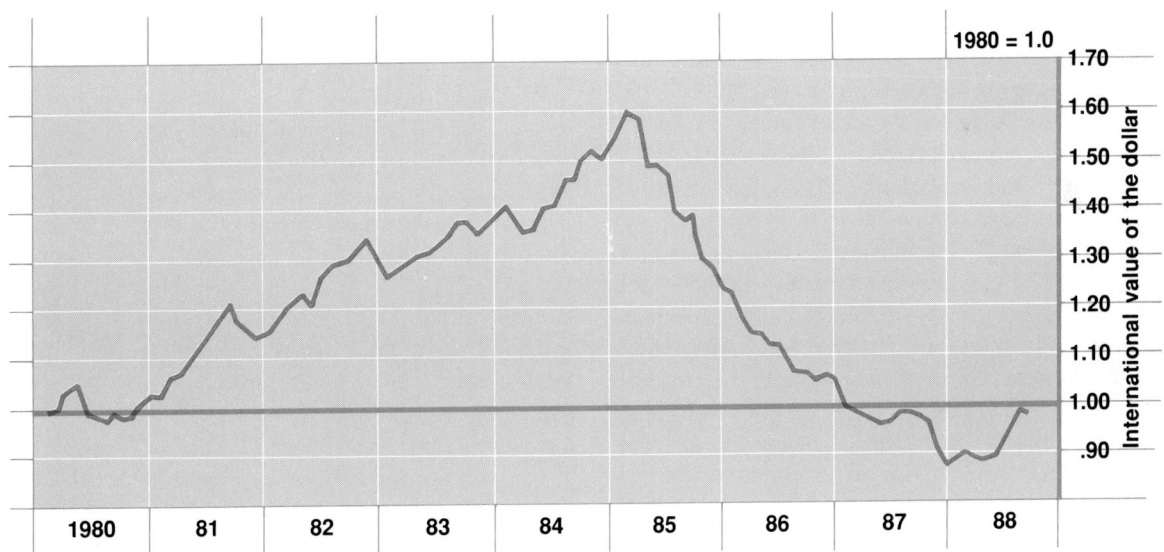

FIGURE 40-7

The international value of the dollar

Between 1980 and 1985 the value of the dollar increased greatly relative to other major currencies, tending to increase our imports and decrease our exports. The dollar fell sharply between 1985 and 1987, but the trade deficits persisted.

dollar means that foreign monies are cheaper to Americans and, conversely, dollars are more expensive to foreigners. As a result, foreign goods are cheap to Americans and, hence, our imports rise. Conversely, American goods are expensive to foreigners and our exports fall.

But why did the value of the dollar increase between 1980 and 1985? The basic answer is that real interest rates in the United States—money interest rates less the rate of inflation—rose in the United States in comparison to foreign countries. High real interest rates made the United States a very attractive place for foreigners to invest. As a result, the demand for dollars to make such investments increased, causing the dollar to appreciate in value.

Now we must ask why real interest rates were relatively high in America. The answer to this query has several parts. First, the large Federal budget deficits of the 1980s (Chapter 20) are cited by many economists as a basic cause of high interest rates. Simply put, government borrowing to finance its deficits increased the demand for money and boosted interest rates. Second, in 1979 the United States shifted to a tighter money policy in its efforts to control inflation. This action increased interest rates directly by reducing the supply of money relative to its demand. Indirectly the lower rate of inflation tended to keep the demand of foreign investors for dollars high because lower inflation means a higher *real* rate of return on investments in the United States.

By 1985 the U.S. budget deficit had reached $122 billion. Two factors then began to interact to reduce the dollar's value sharply over the ensuing two years. First, five industrial nations—the United States, West Germany, Great Britain, France, and Japan—collectively decided to nudge the dollar downward to help correct the massive U.S. trade deficit and the trade surpluses in Japan and other nations. Specifically, these five nations agreed to increase the supply of dollars in foreign exchange markets to reduce the dollar's value. Second, the demand for foreign currency in the United States rose sharply because more foreign money was needed to pay for the expanding volume of imports. This increase in the demand for yen, franc, and other foreign currencies in turn increased the value of these currencies relative to the dollar. As shown in Figure 40-7, the value of the

dollar declined sharply relative to other currencies over the 1985–1988 period.

Despite the sharp decline in the dollar between 1985 and 1987, the American trade imbalance stubbornly persisted. Why? The major reason was that Japanese and other foreign importers did not immediately increase their dollar prices of products by as much as the decline in the international value of the dollar. Instead of increasing their prices, major importers accepted lower per unit profits on their goods. Therefore, imports to the United States for a time continued to rise, offsetting increases in American exports. Also, recall that in 1987 the G-7 nations agreed to halt the decline in the value of the dollar. Only in the second half of 1988 did the American trade deficit finally begin to shrink.

Rapid American growth　A second cause of the trade deficit is that the United States has experienced a more rapid recovery from the 1980–1982 world recession than has its major trading partners. For example, American growth was about double that of Europe in 1983 and nearly triple the European rate in 1984. Although the gap in growth rates narrowed, the American growth rate continued to outpace the European rate over the 1985–1988 period. This is significant because, like domestic consumption, a nation's purchases of foreign goods (its imports) vary directly with the level of domestic income. Because our national income has been expanding relatively rapidly, our imports have also been expanding rapidly. The slower growth of foreign national incomes has meant that their imports (our exports) have grown slowly.

Exports to less developed countries　A third factor contributing to our large trade deficits is a falloff in our exports to the less developed countries (LDCs). An important source of the LDCs' external debt problem has been their need to finance large international trade deficits by borrowing from the industrially advanced nations. As a part of rescheduling and restructuring their debts in the 1980s, the less developed countries had to agree to lessen their trade deficits. Thus they have reduced their imports by invoking more restrictive monetary and fiscal policies to restrain the growth of their national incomes. In so doing their demands for imported goods have declined. A portion of those import reductions has entailed American goods, that is, United States exports. Many LDCs have also *devalued* their currencies or, in other words, lowered the exchange rate value of their currencies by governmental decree. Devaluation restricts their imports and stimulates their exports. Thus the LDCs buy less from, and sell more to, the United States.

EFFECTS OF U.S. TRADE DEFICITS

What are the effects or consequences of our foreign trade crisis? A trade deficit entails both costs and benefits to the nation incurring it.

Dampened aggregate demand A trade deficit—more specifically, negative net exports—reduces aggregate demand and therefore tends to diminish the levels of real national output and employment via the multiplier effect. While this was a factor in keeping our level of employment below the full-employment rate for much of the 1980s, it also helped to restrain inflation. A strong, appreciated dollar also lowers the prices of all imported goods. Furthermore, a surging volume of imports exerts downward pressure on the prices of domestic goods that compete with those imports.

The constraining effect of a trade deficit will be concentrated upon industries which are highly dependent upon export markets or which are most competitive with imports. Some of the problems faced by American farmers, automobile manufacturers, and steel producers in the past decade, for example, were related to the strong dollar and the associated trade deficits. These difficulties in turn contributed greatly to the upsurge in political pressure for protectionist policies which we discussed in Chapter 39. They also generated interest in industrial policies (see Chapter 34's Last Word) designed to provide special help for allegedly "key" industries which are deemed critical to American industrial preeminence.

Increased American indebtedness A trade deficit is also considered "unfavorable" because it must be financed by increased American indebtedness to foreigners. A trade deficit—the fact that our exports of goods and services do not pay for our imports of goods and services—means that we must borrow from the rest of the world to finance that

deficit. This failure to "pay our way" in international trade is usually interpreted as a sign of domestic economic weakness and, hence, undesirable. However, economists point out that, at the time a trade or current account deficit is occurring, it is clearly beneficial to American consumers. After all, a trade deficit means that Americans are currently receiving more goods and services as imports from the rest of the world than we are sending to the rest of the world as exports. Trade deficits augment our domestic living standards during the period in which they occur.

A related consequence of our recent trade deficits is that in 1985 the United States' status changed from that of a net creditor to that of a *net debtor* for the first time since 1914. This simply means that the United States now owes foreigners more than they owe this country. Recall that current account deficits are financed primarily by net capital inflows to the United States. Bluntly stated, when our exports are insufficient to pay for our imports, we finance the difference by borrowing from foreigners or, in other words, by going into debt. The financing of our recent large trade deficits has caused foreigners to accumulate a larger volume of claims against American assets than we have accumulated against foreign assets. The U.S. foreign debt burden climbed to $368 billion in 1987, making us the largest debtor nation in the world. One implication of net debtor status is that we can no longer look forward to a net inflow of dividend and interest payments (see item 7 in Table 40-1's balance of payments) to help cover deficits in our merchandise and services trade. A second implication is that more of our corporations are becoming foreign-owned.

Generally speaking, the above comments on the economic effects of our trade deficit for the United States economy can be thrown into reverse as far as our industrialized trading partners are concerned. The current accounts of Japan, West Germany, and Great Britain, for example, will tend to move toward surplus. These countries will experience an expansionary-inflationary stimulus and unusual growth in their export-dependent industries. They will also increase their holdings of American debt.

The appreciated dollar of the mid-1980s posed additional problems for those less developed countries which had large outstanding dollar-denominated debts. Given that both principal and interest had to be paid in dollars, the appreciated dollar meant that the real burden of their debts increased. The problem was compounded for oil-importing countries because OPEC oil prices are set in dollar terms. Therefore, a rise in the exchange value of the dollar is tantamount to an increase in oil prices. These difficulties were alleviated but not ended by the slide in the value of the dollar between 1985 and 1987.

POLICIES FOR REDUCING U.S. TRADE DEFICITS

What policies might reduce the American trade deficit? Two kinds of policies are most often cited: reduction of the Federal budget deficit and measures to accelerate economic growth abroad.

Reduction of the budget deficit   Many economists are in agreement that the most critical causal factor in our continuing trade deficits has been our large annual Federal budget deficits. It is argued that a reduction in the size of our Federal budget deficit will lower the real interest rate in the United States in comparison to other nations. In other words, a reduction in the government's demand for funds to finance its deficits will lower domestic interest rates and thus make financial investments in the United States less attractive to foreigners. The demand for dollars by foreigners therefore will decline and the dollar will depreciate. Given a depreciated dollar, our exports will increase and imports will fall, tending to correct our trade deficit. You may recognize that this scenario is exactly opposite the one which we traced out earlier in Figure 20-2. In fact, we recommend that you review this figure at this time.

Would not a "managed" depreciation of the dollar by the G-7 nations produce a decline in the U.S. trade deficit, even without a reduction in our budget deficit? Perhaps so, but this point may be moot. Our trading partners have not been interested in allowing the dollar to fall below its 1988 level, unless we reduce our budget deficit. In effect, these nations contend that the United States must "get its fiscal house in order" to achieve a better balance of international trade. Moreover, American policy makers have feared that a substantial decline in the value of the dollar—independent of a decline in the budget deficit—might precipitate

LAST WORD

$150 takes you for a ride in Tokyo

A dollar would buy 262 yen in 1985; in 1988 it would buy only 123 yen. Thus, the dollar price of goods in Japan has soared.

TOKYO—The Japanese call it *endaka:* the almighty yen. USA translation: highway robbery.

Charles Anderson of San Francisco spent $450 for dinner for two at a French restaurant one night in the resort town of Hakone. Jill Martin of Evanston, Ill., paid $30 in Kyoto for a $10.50 bottle of Chanel nail polish.

Keith Sanders of Honolulu shelled out $15 in Tokyo for one shot of his beloved cognac. "Damn," says Sanders, 25. "It almost makes me want to quit."

The strong yen has so weakened the dollar's buying power here in the last year that finding a USA tourist is as rare as snagging a bargain at a Ginza department store. With the dollar now at 123 yen, compared with a high of 262 in 1985, business travel remains strong, but tourism is suffering.

"We see businessmen, but no tourists," says Dorothy Guzzwell, 45, a United Airlines flight attendant on the Seattle–Tokyo route. "There aren't the little old ladies coming over on shopping sprees. There are no bargains here."

rapid inflation. At the beginning of 1989, the American economy was nearing full employment. Therefore there was concern that additional spending on American goods caused by a rise in net exports would tend to be inflationary.

Indeed, that first brush with Japanese prices can be a shocker: $154 for a one-hour cab ride from Narita Airport to downtown Tokyo; $80-a-person for dinner in a traditional Japanese restaurant; $4.06 for a cup of coffee in the deluxe Okura Hotel.

The gut reaction from most tourists: "Ouch," says Linda Babcock, 30, of Tallahassee, Fla., who has been living in Tokyo for a year with husband Bruce, who researches economic trends for a USA stock brokerage.

Maxine Moore, 70, of Danbury, Conn., also has felt the pinch. She arrived about a month ago to visit her friend Malee Sladek, 26, whose husband works here for IBM. Moore has spent more than $1,000 and has only "trinkets"—key chains, saki sets and trays—to take home.

"I don't have a lot to show for it," says Moore.

No wonder, then, that so many of the USA citizens you still see here are people on expense accounts.

"Wanna see our empty wallets? We're too poor to be tourists," says Art Skantz, of Highland Park, Ill., taking a break with a business colleague on the gourmet food floor of Matsuya department store. Skantz, who works for Quaker Oats, marvels at the price his product fetches here. "It's tripled over a 15-year period—$7 a box," he says.

Shops catering to foreigners are feeling effects of the tourism malaise. At Hiyashi Kimono in Tokyo, business has dropped 10 percent from last year, even though kimono prices have been kept deliberately low to encourage more USA business. "American tourists, unfortunately, not so many as before," says manager Iyuzi Sawaguchi.

Tokyo, in fact, is now the most expensive city in the world to visit, according to *Consumer Reports Travel Letter*. A day in this city for two people, including a moderately priced double hotel room,

three meals, transportation and incidentals costs $460, $91 more than the runner-up for the world's most pricey destination—Paris—and $202 more than New York.

At Tokyo's deluxe Imperial Hotel, a double room costs $269.10; suite, $583.33. A double at Tokyo's moderately priced Hilltop Hotel was $60 in 1984; today it's $191.

"When you look at the prices, they knock you silly," says Margaret Egan, 82, here from New York to visit a friend.

A sampling:

The cover charge for a nightclub in Roppongi, a popular night-life district in Tokyo: $156.

One beer at the Hard Rock Cafe in Tokyo: $8.

One kilogram (2.2 pounds) of high-grade beef: $243.90. A bottle of Cutty Sark whisky: $40.66. A half-pound of Brie cheese: $12.07. One box of Cocoa Puffs cereal: $7.32. A 2-pound box of Velveeta cheese, $10.81.

Much has been made of the high cost of fruit in Japan. At the Kinokuniya Supermarket in Tokyo, you can buy a little over a pound of cherries for $120.95; a box of five peaches for $40.65; or two perfect musk melons for $165.85. But if you're a USA tourist, you probably wouldn't.

These items are products of labor-intensive agriculture, intended for purchase by Japanese as gifts on special occasions.

But the ultimate survival tip for Tokyo-bound tourists comes from David Scott, 27, here 1½ years working for a USA economic consulting firm: "I stopped thinking in dollars a long time ago. If you do, it makes your head hurt."

Economic growth abroad   The American trade deficit can also be reduced if nations abroad undertake policies to speed up their rates of economic growth. Higher levels of national income abroad increase the demand for American exports. The G-7 group of industrial nations has recognized the importance of economic growth in the nations which have trade surpluses as a way to reduce these surpluses and improve the American trade deficit. In particular, the governments of Japan and West Germany have recently established expansionary fiscal and monetary policies to bolster national income and thereby increase the demand for goods produced in America.

Other "solutions" There are several other possible "solutions" to the trade crisis. Let us examine five of them.

EASY MONEY POLICY Under appropriate circumstances, an easy money policy reduces real interest rates and reduces a trade deficit. The process works as follows. The decline in interest rates reduces the international demand for dollars, which results in a depreciation of the dollar. Dollar depreciation, we have noted, raises our exports and lowers our imports (Table 17-4). But if the economy is at or near full employment, as it was at the beginning of 1989, an easy money policy runs the risk of promoting domestic inflation.

PROTECTIVE TARIFFS Protective tariffs can be used to reduce imports. But we have noted that this strategy results in the loss of the gains from specialization and international trade. Furthermore, this strategy may not be successful: Tariffs which reduce our *imports* tend to foster retaliatory tariffs abroad which reduce our *exports*. Trade deficits do not disappear in this circumstance; instead, all trading partners suffer declines in their living standards.

RECESSION A major recession in the United States could be expected to reduce imports, thus trimming our trade deficit. Our imports tend to fall as our national income declines. But, economists agree that recession is an undesirable "solution" to the trade deficit in that recession imposes higher economic costs (lost output) on society than the costs associated with the trade deficit itself.

INCREASED U.S. COMPETITIVENESS The U.S. trade deficits can be reduced by lowering the costs of, and improving the quality of, American goods and services relative to foreign goods. The use of cost-saving production technologies, the development of improved products, and the use of more efficient management techniques each can contribute to a decline in the trade deficit by lowering U.S. de-

mand for imported goods and increasing foreign demand for U.S. goods.

DIRECT FOREIGN INVESTMENT Ironically, our persistent trade deficit has set off a chain of events which has begun to feed back to reduce the trade deficit itself. The vast accumulation of American dollars in foreign hands has enabled foreign individuals and firms to buy American factories or to build new plants in the United States. Furthermore, the fall in the value of the dollar has provided an incentive for foreign firms to produce in the United States rather than in their own nations. In short, the trade deficit has given rise to an increase in *direct foreign investment* in the form of plant and equipment. Foreign-owned factories are beginning to turn out increasing volumes of goods that otherwise would have had to be imported. For example, Hondas and Mazdas, produced in American factories, have replaced Hondas and Mazdas formerly imported from Japan. Other examples abound. The upshot is that the American trade deficit may shrink as imports are replaced with goods produced in foreign-owned factories in the United States.

CHAPTER SUMMARY

1 American exports create a foreign demand for dollars and make a supply of foreign exchange available to Americans. Conversely, American imports simultaneously create a demand for foreign exchange and make a supply of dollars available to foreigners. Generally speaking, a nation's exports earn the foreign currencies needed to pay for its imports.

2 The balance of payments records all of the international trade and financial transactions which take place between a given nation and the rest of the world. The trade balance compares merchandise exports and imports. The balance on goods and services compares exports and imports of both goods and services. The current account balance considers not only goods and services transactions, but also net investment income and net transfers.

3 A deficit on the current account will be largely offset by a surplus on the capital account. Conversely, a surplus on the current account will be largely offset by a deficit on the capital account. A balance of payments deficit occurs when the sum of the current and capital accounts is in deficit. A payments deficit is financed by drawing down official reserves. A balance of payments surplus occurs when the sum of the current and capital accounts is in surplus. A payments surplus results in an increase in official reserves. The desirability of a balance of payments deficit or surplus depends upon its causes and its persistence over time.

4 Flexible or floating exchange rates are determined by the demand for and supply of foreign currencies. Under floating rates a currency will depreciate or appreciate as a result of changes in tastes, relative income changes, relative price changes, relative changes in real interest rates, and because of speculation.

5 Maintenance of fixed exchange rates requires adequate reserves to accommodate periodic payments deficits. If reserves are inadequate, nations must invoke protectionist trade policies, engage in exchange controls, or endure undesirable domestic macroeconomic adjustments.

6 Historically, the gold standard provided exchange rate stability until its disintegration during the 1930s. Under this system, gold flows between nations precipitated sometimes painful changes in price, income, and employment levels in bringing about international equilibrium.

7 Under the Bretton Woods system exchange rates were pegged to one another and were stable. Participating nations were obligated to maintain these rates by using stabilization funds, gold, or borrowings from the IMF. Persistent or "fundamental" payments deficits could be met by IMF-sanctioned currency devaluations.

8 Since 1971 a system of managed floating exchange rates has been in use. Rates are generally set by market forces, although governments intervene with varying frequency to alter their exchange rates.

9 Between 1980 and 1988 the United States experienced a rapidly growing international trade deficit. Causes include *a* a rapidly appreciating dollar between 1980 and 1985; *b* relatively rapid expansion of the American economy; and *c* curtailed purchases of our exports by the less developed countries.

10 The effects of this large trade deficit have been manifold. It has had a contractionary, anti-inflationary effect upon our domestic economy. American export-dependent industries have experienced declines in output, employment, and profits, thereby generating political pressures for protection. The United States has become the world's largest debtor nation. However, the trade deficit has meant a current increase in the living standards of American consumers.

11 The appreciated dollar of the mid-1980s posed special problems for less developed nations with large external dollar-denominated debts and for oil-importing nations.

12 Two solutions to the trade deficit are *a* reduction of budget deficit and *b* faster economic growth abroad. Other "solutions" are an easy money policy, protective tariffs, recession, improved U.S. competitiveness, and direct foreign investment.

TERMS AND CONCEPTS

balance of payments

current account

credits

debits

trade balance

balance on goods and services

balance on current account

capital account

balance on the capital account

official reserves

balance of payments deficits and surpluses

flexible or floating exchange rates

fixed exchange rates

depreciation and appreciation

gold standard

gold import and export points

Bretton Woods system

International Monetary Fund

devaluation

managed floating exchange rates

G-7 nations

foreign trade crisis

QUESTIONS AND STUDY SUGGESTIONS

1 Explain how an American automobile importer might finance a shipment of Renaults from France. Demonstrate how an American export of machinery to Italy might be financed. Explain: "American exports earn supplies of foreign monies which Americans can use to finance imports."

2 "A rise in the dollar price of yen necessarily means a fall in the yen price of dollars." Do you agree? Illustrate and elaborate: "The critical thing about exchange rates is that they provide a direct link between the prices of goods and services produced in all trading nations of the world."

3 Indicate whether each of the following creates a demand for, or a supply of, French francs in foreign exchange markets:

a An American importer purchases a shipload of Bordeaux wine

b A French automobile firm decides to build an assembly plant in Los Angeles

c An American college student decides to spend a year studying at the Sorbonne

d A French manufacturer exports machinery to Morocco on an American freighter

e The United States incurs a balance of payments deficit in its transactions with France

f A United States government bond held by a French citizen matures

g It is widely believed that the international value of the franc will fall in the near future

4 Explain why the American demand for Mexican pesos is downsloping and the supply of pesos to Americans is upsloping. Assuming a system of floating exchange rates between Mexico and the United States, indicate whether each of the following would cause the Mexican peso to appreciate or depreciate:

a The United States unilaterally reduces tariffs on Mexican products

b Mexico encounters severe inflation

c Deteriorating political relations reduce American tourism in Mexico

d The United States' economy moves into a severe recession

e The Board of Governors embarks upon a tight money policy

f Mexican products become more fashionable to Americans

g The Mexican government invites American firms to invest in Mexican oil fields

h The rate of productivity growth in the United States diminishes sharply

5 Explain whether or not you agree with the following statements:

a "A country which grows faster than its major trading partners can expect the international value of its currency to depreciate."

b "A nation whose interest rate is rising more rapidly than in other nations can expect the international value of its currency to appreciate."

c "A country's currency will appreciate if its inflation rate is less than the rest of the world."

6 "Exports pay for imports. Yet in 1987 the rest of the world exported about $160 billion more worth of goods and services to the United States than were imported from the United States." Resolve the apparent inconsistency of these two statements.

7 Answer the following questions on the basis of Scorpio's balance of payments for 1990 as shown below. All figures are in billions of dollars. What is the balance of trade? The balance on goods and services? The balance on current account? The balance on capital account? Does Scorpio have a balance of payments deficit or surplus? Would you surmise that Scorpio is participating in a system of fixed or flexible exchange rates? Are Scorpio's international transactions having a contractionary or expansionary effect on its domestic economy?

Merchandise exports	+$40	Net transfers	+$10
Merchandise imports	− 30	Capital inflows	+ 10
Service exports	+ 15	Capital outflows	− 40
Service imports	− 10	Official reserves	+ 10
Net investment income	− 5		

8 Explain in detail how a balance of payments deficit would be resolved under **a** the gold standard, **b** the Bretton Woods system, and **c** freely floating exchange rates. What are the advantages and shortcomings of each system?

9 Outline the major costs and benefits associated with a large trade or current account deficit. Explain: "A current account deficit means we are receiving more goods and services from abroad than we are sending abroad. How can that be called 'unfavorable'?"

10 What is meant when it is asserted that the United States is facing a foreign trade "crisis"? What are the major causes of this crisis?

11 Why did the dollar's record high international value in the mid-1980s pose problems for the less developed countries? For oil-importing nations?

12 Cite and explain two reasons for the decline in the international value of the dollar between 1985 and 1987. Why did the U.S. trade deficit remain high, even though the dollar fell in value?

13 Explain how a reduction in the Federal budget deficit could conceivably contribute to a decline in the U.S. trade deficit.

CHAPTER 41

Growth and the less developed countries

It is exceedingly difficult for the typical American family, whose 1987 average income was $30,853, to grasp the hard fact that some two-thirds of the world's population persistently lives at, or perilously close to, the subsistence level. Ironically, most Americans are too preoccupied with problems associated with affluence—pollution, urban growth, the monotony and alienation which often accompany employment in large-scale enterprises—to acknowledge the abject poverty which characterizes much of our planet. But, in fact, hunger, squalor, and disease are commonplace in many nations of the world.

The purposes of this chapter are as follows. First, we want to identify the poor or less developed nations of the world. Second, we seek to determine why they are poor. What are the obstacles to growth? Third, the potential role of government in the process of economic development is considered. Fourth, the use of international trade, private capital flows, and foreign aid are examined as vehicles of growth. Fifth, the external debt problems faced by many of the poor nations are analyzed. Finally, we present the demands of the poor nations to establish a "new international economic order."

The rich and the poor

Just as there is considerable income disparity among individual families within a nation (Chapter 37), so there also is great economic inequality among the family of nations. It is instructive to use Table 41-1 to identify the following groups of nations.

First, there are the **industrially advanced countries (IACs),** which include the United States, Canada, Australia, New Zealand, Japan, and most of the nations of western Europe. These nations have developed market economies based upon large stocks of capital goods, advanced production technologies, and well-educated labor forces. As column 1 of Table 41-1 indicates, the salient feature of these nineteen economies is a high per capita (per person) GNP.

Second, there is a small group of oil-exporting countries (for example, Saudi Arabia and Kuwait) which, as indicated in column 1 of Table 41-1, also enjoy quite impressive per capita GNPs due to their oil exports. However, these nations are not highly industrialized.

Third, most of the remaining nations of the world[1]—located in Africa, Asia, and Latin America—are underdeveloped or **less developed countries (LDCs).** These ninety-seven nations are unindustrialized and their labor forces are heavily committed to agriculture. Literacy rates are low, unemployment is high, population growth is rapid, and exports consist largely of agricultural commodities (cocoa, bananas, sugar, raw cotton) and raw materials (copper, iron ore, natural rubber). Capital equipment is scarce, production technologies are typically primitive, and labor force productivity is low. About three-fourths of the world's

---

[1] We omit here the Soviet Union and the communist bloc nations which do not report their economic data.

TABLE 41-1 **GNP per capita, population, and growth rates**

	GNP per capita		Population	
	(1) Dollars, 1986	(2) Annual growth rate, 1965–1986	(3) Millions, 1986	(4) Annual growth rate, 1980–1986
Industrially advanced countries:				
IACs (19 nations)	$12,960	2.3%	742	0.6%
High-income oil exporters (4 nations)	6,740	1.8	19	4.2
Less developed countries:				
LDCs (97 nations)	610	2.9	3,761	2.0
Middle-income LDCs (58 nations)	1,270	2.6	1,268	2.3
Low-income LDCs (39 nations)	270	3.1	2,493	1.9

Source: World Bank, *World Development Report, 1988* (New York: Oxford University Press).

population lives in these nations, which share the characteristic of widespread poverty.

In Table 41-1 we have divided the poor nations into two groups.

The first group comprises fifty-eight "middle-income" LDCs with an average annual per capita GNP of $1270. The range of per capita GNPs of this rather diverse group is from $450 to $7410. The other group is made up of thirty-nine "low-income" LDCs with per capita GNPs ranging from $120 to $450 and averaging only $270. This unfortunate group is dominated by India, China, and the sub-Saharan nations of Africa.

Several simple comparisons may be helpful in bringing global income disparities into even sharper focus. Example: The United States' 1986 GNP was approximately $4.2 trillion; the combined GNPs of the ninety-seven LDCs in that year was only $2.4 trillion. Example: The United States with only about 5 percent of the world's population produces approximately one-fourth of the world's output. Example: The annual sales of many large U.S. corporations exceed the GNPs of many of the LDCs. General Motors—America's largest corporation in 1986—had sales of $103 billion in that year. This volume of sales was greater than the GNP of all but 22 or so nations of the world. Example: Per capita GNP in the United States is 146 times greater than in Ethiopia, the world's poorest nation.

GROWTH, DECLINE, AND INCOME GAPS

It is important to append two other points to our discussion of Table 41-1. In the first place, there have been considerable differences in the ability of the various LDCs to improve their circumstances over time. On the one hand, a group of so-called newly industrialized economies—consisting of Singapore, Hong Kong, Taiwan, and South Korea—have achieved very high annual growth rates of real GNP of 8 to 9 percent over the 1960–1987 period. As a consequence, real per capita GNPs rose fivefold in these nations. In vivid contrast, many of the highly indebted LDCs and the very poor sub-Saharan nations of Africa have experienced *declining* real per capita GNPs in the 1980s.

The second point is implicit in column 2 of Table 41-1. We observe there that the average annual growth rates of per capita GNP were quite similar for the LDCs and the IACs over the 1965–1986 period. Despite this similarity, the income gap between rich and poor nations has been widening. Let us simplify and assume that the per capita GNPs of the advanced and less developed countries have both been growing at about 2 percent per year. The fact that the income base in the advanced countries is initially much higher causes the income gap to increase. For example, if per capita income is $400 a year, a 2 percent growth rate means an $8 increase in income. Where per capita income is $4000 per year, the same 2 percent growth rate translates into an $80 increase in income. Thus, the absolute income gap will have increased from $3600 (= $4000 − $400) to $3672 (= $4080 − $408).

IMPLICATIONS

Mere statistics conceal the human implications of the extreme poverty which characterizes so much of our planet:

Let us examine a typical "extended" family in rural Asia. The Asian household is likely to comprise ten or more people, including parents, five to seven children, two grandparents, and some aunts and uncles. They have a combined annual income, both in money and in "kind" (i.e., they consume a share of the food they grow), of from $150 to $200. Together they live in a one-room poorly constructed house as tenant farmers on a large agricultural estate owned by an absentee landlord who lives in the nearby city. The father, mother, uncle, and the older children must work all day on the land. None of the adults can read or write, and of the five school-age children only one attends school regularly; and he cannot expect to proceed beyond three or four years of primary education. There is only one meal a day; it rarely changes and it is rarely sufficent to alleviate the constant hunger pains experienced by the children. The house has no electricity, sanitation, or fresh water supply. There is much sickness, but qualified doctors and medical practitioners are far away in the cities attending to the needs of wealthier families. The work is hard, the sun is hot, and aspirations for a better life are constantly being snuffed out. In this part of the world the only relief from the daily struggle for physical survival lies in the spiritual traditions of the people.[2]

In Table 41-2 various socioeconomic indicators for selected LDCs are contrasted with those for the United States and Japan. These data clearly confirm the major points stressed in the above quotation.

[2] Michael P. Todaro, *Economic Development in the Third World,* 3d ed. (New York: Longman, 1985), p. 4.

TABLE 41-2 **Selected socioeconomic indicators of development**

Country	(1) Per capita GNP, 1986	(2) Life expectancy at birth, 1988	(3) Infant mortality per 1000 live births, 1988	(4) Adult literacy rate, 1985	(5) Daily per capita calorie supply, 1985	(6) Per capita energy consumption, 1986*
United States	$17,480	75 years	11	99%	3,682	7,193
Japan	12,840	78	6	99	2,695	3,186
Brazil	1,810	67	60	78	2,657	830
Mauritania	420	47	127	17	2,071	114
Haiti	330	55	94	5	1,784	50
India	290	57	94	43	2,126	208
Bangladesh	160	51	135	33	1,804	46
Ethiopia	120	51	116	5	1,704	21

*Kilograms of oil equivalent.

Source: *World Development Report,* 1988, and *Statistical Abstract of the United States.*

Breaking the poverty barrier

The avenues of economic growth are essentially the same for both industrially advanced and less developed nations:

1 Existing supplies of resources must be used more efficiently. This entails not only the elimination of unemployment but also the achievement of greater efficiency in the allocation of resources.

2 The supplies of productive resources must be altered—typically, increased. By expanding the supplies of raw materials, capital equipment, effective labor, and technological knowledge, a nation can push its production possibilities curve to the right (Chapter 21).

Why have some nations been successful in pursuing these avenues of growth while other countries have lagged far behind? The answer lies in differences in the physical and sociocultural environments of the various nations. Our plan of attack is to examine the obstacles in the LDCs to altering the quantities and improving efficiency in the use of (1) natural resources, (2) human resources, (3) capital goods, and (4) technological knowledge. Emphasis here will be upon the private sector of the economy. In addition, social, institutional, and cultural impediments to growth will be illustrated. And finally, the roles of government and foreign aid in the development process will be analyzed.

NATURAL RESOURCES

There is no simple generalization with respect to the role of natural resources in the economic development of the LDCs. This is true mainly because the distribution of natural resources among these nations is very uneven. Some less developed nations encompass valuable deposits of bauxite, tin, copper, tungsten, nitrates, petroleum, and so forth. In a few instances the LDCs have been able to use their natural resource endowments to achieve rapid growth and a significant redistribution of income from the rich to the poor nations. The Organization of Petroleum Exporting Countries (OPEC), of course, is the outstanding example. On the other hand, we must recognize that in many cases natural resources are owned or controlled by the huge multinational corporations of the industrially advanced countries to the end that the economic benefits from these resources are largely diverted abroad. Furthermore, world markets for many of the farm products and raw materials which the LDCs export are subject to great price fluctuations which contribute to instability in their economies.

Other LDCs simply lack mineral deposits, face a paucity of arable land, and have few sources of power. It is important to note that the vast majority of the poor countries are located in Central and South America, Africa, the Indian subcontinent, and Southeast Asia where tropical climates prevail. The hot, humid climate is not conducive to productive labor; human, crop, and livestock diseases are widespread; and weed and insect infestations plague agriculture.

In a very real sense a weak resource base can pose a particularly serious obstacle to growth. Real capital can be accumulated and the quality of the labor force can be improved through education and training. But the natural resource base is largely unaugmentable. Hence, it is probably unrealistic for many of the LDCs to envision an economic destiny comparable with that of the United States, Canada, or the Soviet Union. But, again, we must be careful in generalizing: Switzerland, Israel, and Japan, for example, have achieved relatively high levels of living *despite* restrictive natural resource bases.

HUMAN RESOURCES

Three statements describe many of the LDCs' circumstances with respect to human resources:

1 They are overpopulated.

2 Unemployment and underemployment are widespread.

3 Labor force productivity is low.

Overpopulation As column 3 of Table 41-1 makes clear, many of the LDCs with the most meager natural and capital resources have the largest populations to support. Table 41-3 compares population densities and population growth rates of a few selected nations with those of the United States and the world as a whole. Most important for the long

TABLE 41-3 **Population statistics for selected countries**

Country	Population per square mile, 1988	Annual rate of population increase, 1980–1990
United States	69	0.9%
Pakistan	365	2.8
Bangladesh	2,082	2.7
Venezuela	56	2.7
India	670	2.1
Haiti	608	1.7
Kenya	113	4.2
Philippines	575	2.7
World	101	1.7

Source: *Statistical Abstract of the United States, 1989.*

run is the vivid contrast of population growth rates: The middle- and low-income LDCs of Table 41-1 are now experiencing approximately a 2 percent annual increase in population as compared with a 0.6 percent annual rate for the advanced countries. Recalling the "rule of 70," the current rate suggests that the total population of the LDCs will double in about 35 years. These simple statistics are a significant reason why the per capita income gap between the LDCs and the IACs has tended to widen. In some of the less developed countries rapid population growth actually presses upon the food supply to the extent that per capita food consumption is pulled down perilously close to the subsistence level. In the worst instances, it is only the despicable team of malnutrition and disease and the high death rate they engender which keeps incomes near subsistence.

It would seem at first glance that, since

$$\frac{\text{Per capita}}{\text{standard}} = \frac{\text{consumer goods (food) production}}{\text{population}}$$
$$\text{of living}$$

the standard of living could be raised merely by boosting consumer goods—particularly food—production. But in reality the problem is much more complex than this, because any increase in con-

sumer goods production which initially raises the standard of living is likely to induce a population increase. This increase, if sufficient in size, will dissipate the improvement in living standards, and subsistence living levels will again prevail.

But why does population growth tend to accompany increases in output? First, the nation's *death* or *mortality rate* will decline with initial increases in production. This decline is the result of (1) a higher level of per capita food consumption, and (2) the basic medical and sanitation programs which almost invariably accompany the initial phases of economic development. Second, the *birthrate* will remain high or may even increase, particularly so as the medical and sanitation programs cut the rate of infant mortality. The cliché that "the rich get richer and the poor get children" is uncomfortably accurate for many of the LDCs. In short, an increase in the per capita standard of living may give rise to a population upsurge which will cease only when the standard of living has again been reduced to the level of bare subsistence.

In addition to the fact that rapid population growth can translate an expanding GNP into a stagnant or slow-growing GNP per capita, there are less obvious reasons why population expansion is an obstacle to development. In the first place, large families reduce the capacity of households to save, and this inability restricts the economy's capacity to accumulate capital. Second, as population grows, more investment is required simply to maintain the amount of real capital per person. If investment fails to keep pace, each worker will have fewer tools and equipment and that will cause worker productivity (output per worker) to fall. Declining productivity implies stagnating or declining per capita incomes. Third, given that most less developed countries are heavily dependent upon agriculture, rapid population growth may result in the overuse of limited natural resources such as land. The much-publicized African famines are partially the result of past overgrazing and overplanting of land caused by the pressing need to feed a growing population. Finally, rapid population growth in the cities of the LDCs, accompanied by unprecedented flows of rural migrants, are generating massive urban problems (Chapter 36). Substandard housing in impoverished slums, deteriorating public services, congestion, pollution, and crime are all problems which are seriously exacerbated by rapid population growth. The resolution or amelioration of these difficulties necessitates a diversion of resources from growth-oriented uses.

Most authorities advocate birth control as the obvious and most effective means for breaking out of this dilemma. And breakthroughs in contraceptive technology in the past three or four decades have made this solution increasingly relevant. But the obstacles to population control are great. Low literacy rates make it difficult to disseminate information on the use of contraceptive devices. In peasant agriculture, large families are a major source of labor. Furthermore, adults may look upon having many children as a kind of informal social security system; the more children one has, the greater the probability of having a relative to care for one during old age. Finally, many nations which stand to gain the most through birth control are often the least willing, for religious and sociocultural reasons, to embrace contraception programs. Population growth in Latin America, for example, is among the most rapid in the world. There are a few success stories, however. China's "one-child program" begun in the late 1970s has reduced its population growth from 2.7 percent per year in 1965–1973 to 1.3 percent in the 1980–1990 period. Coupled with a large increase in food production, China has significantly improved the dietary standards of its people.

Caution: Not all less developed nations suffer from overpopulation, nor may one conclude that a large population necessarily means underdevelopment. The points to note are: (1) A large and rapidly growing population may pose a special obstacle to economic development; and (2) many of the LDCs are so burdened.

Unemployment and underemployment Reliable unemployment statistics for the LDCs are not readily available. But it is felt that unemployment and underemployment are both quite high in most LDCs. **Unemployment** occurs when someone who is willing and able to work cannot find a job. In contrast, **underemployment** occurs when workers are employed fewer hours or days per week than they desire, or work at jobs in which they are less productive than they would be if their skills were being fully used.

Many economists contend that unemployment is high—perhaps as much as 15 to 20 percent—in the rapidly growing urban areas of the LDCs. Most less developed countries have experienced a substantial migration of population from rural to urban areas. This migration is motivated by the *expectation* of finding jobs with higher wage rates than are available in agricultural and other rural employments. But this huge migration makes it very unlikely that a migrant will in fact obtain a job. Stated differently, migration to the cities has greatly exceeded the growth of urban job opportunities, resulting in very high urban unemployment rates. Thus, rapid rural-urban migration has given rise to urban unemployment rates which are two or three times as great as rural rates.

It is also felt that underemployment is widespread and endemic to most LDCs. For example, in many LDCs rural agricultural labor may be so abundant relative to capital and natural resources that a significant percentage of this labor contributes little or nothing to agricultural output. Similarly, many LDC workers are self-employed as proprietors of small shops, in handicrafts, or as street vendors. A lack of demand means that small shop owners or vendors spend more time in idleness in the shop or on the street. While they are not without jobs, they are underemployed.

Low labor productivity Labor productivity tends to be very low in most LDCs. As we shall see momentarily, the LDCs have found it difficult to invest in *physical capital*. As a result, their workers are underequipped with machinery and tools and are destined to be relatively unproductive. In addition, most of the poor countries have not been able to invest sufficiently in their *human capital* (Table 41-2, columns 4 and 5); that is, expenditures on health and education have been meager. Low levels of literacy, malnutrition, the absence of proper medical care, and insufficient educational facilities all contribute to populations ill equipped for economic development and industrialization. Particularly vital is the absence of a vigorous entrepreneurial class willing to bear risks, accumulate capital, and provide the organizational requisites essential to economic growth. Closely related is the dearth of labor that is prepared to handle the routine supervisory functions basic to any program of development.

One special irony is that, while migration from the LDCs has provided a modest offset to rapid population growth, it has also deprived some LDCs of highly productive workers. It is often the best-trained and most highly motivated workers—physicians, engineers, teachers, and nurses—who leave the LDCs to seek their fortunes in the IACs. This so-called **brain drain** contributes to the deterioration in the overall skill level and productivity of the labor force.

CAPITAL ACCUMULATION

Most economists feel that an important focal point of economic development is the accumulation of capital goods. There are several reasons for this emphasis upon capital formation:

1 All LDCs do suffer from a critical shortage of capital goods—factories, machinery and equipment, public utilities, and so forth. There can be no doubt that better-equipped labor forces would greatly enhance the productivity of the LDCs and help to boost the per capita standard of living. As we found in Chapter 21, there is a close relationship between output per worker (labor productivity) and real income per worker. A nation must produce more goods and services per worker to enjoy more goods and services per worker as income. One basic means of increasing labor productivity is to provide each worker with more tools and equipment. Indeed, empirical studies for the LDCs confirm a significant positive relationship between investment and the growth of GNP. On the average a 1 percentage point increase in the ratio of investment to GNP tends to raise the overall growth rate by about one-tenth of 1 percentage point. Thus, for example, an increase in the investment-to-GNP ratio from 10 to 15 percent would increase the growth of real GNP by one-half of 1 percentage point.[3]

2 Increasing the stock of capital goods is crucial because of the very limited possibility of increasing the supply of arable land. If there is little likelihood of increasing agricultural output by increasing the supply of land, an alternative is to use more and better capital equipment with the available agricultural work force.

3 Once initiated, the process of capital accumulation *may* be cumulative. If capital accumulation can increase output ahead of population growth, a margin of saving may arise which permits further capital formation. In a sense, capital accumulation can feed upon itself.

Let us first consider the prospects for less developed nations to accumulate capital domestically. Then later we shall examine the possibility of foreign capital flowing into them.

Domestic capital formation How does a less developed nation—or any nation for that matter—accumulate capital? The answer: through the processes of saving and investing. A nation must save or, in other words, refrain from consumption, to release resources from consumer goods production. Investment spending must then occur to absorb these released resources in the production of capital goods. But the impediments to saving and investing are much greater in a low-income nation than in an advanced economy.

SAVINGS POTENTIAL Consider first the savings side of the picture. The situation here is mixed and varies greatly between countries. Some of the very poor countries such as Ethiopia, Bangladesh, Uganda, Haiti, and Madagascar save only from 2 to 5 percent of their national outputs. They simply are too poor to save a significant portion of their incomes. Interestingly, however, other less developed countries save as large a percentage of their national outputs as do the advanced industrial countries. For example, in 1986 India and China saved 21 and 36 percent of their national outputs, respectively, as compared to 32 percent for Japan, 24 percent for West Germany, and 15 percent for the United States. The problem is that the national outputs of the LDCs are so low that, even when saving rates are comparable to the advanced nations, the total absolute volume of saving is not large. As we shall see momentarily, foreign capital inflows and foreign aid are means of supplementing domestic saving.

CAPITAL FLIGHT There is substantial evidence to suggest that many of the LDCs have experienced a substantial **capital flight.** That is, citizens of the LDCs have transferred their savings to, or invested their savings in, the IACs. Why might this happen?

[3] International Monetary Fund, *World Economic Outlook* (Washington, D.C., 1988), p. 76.

The primary reason is that the citizens of many LDCs regard the risks of investing at home to be high as compared to the industrially advanced nations. These risks include the loss of savings or real capital due to government expropriation, taxation, or higher rates of inflation. If an LDC's political climate is volatile, savers may shift their funds overseas to a "safe haven" in fear that a new government might confiscate their wealth. Likewise, rapid or galloping inflation in an LDC would have similar confiscatory effects (Chapter 10). The transfer of savings overseas may also be a means of evading domestic taxes on interest income or capital gains. Finally, financial capital may flow to the IACs because of higher interest rates or simply because of the greater variety of investment opportunities available in the industrialized countries.

Whatever the motivation, research studies suggest that capital flight from the LDCs is quantitatively significant. For example, between 1974 and 1982 Argentina borrowed almost $33 billion from other nations, while its level of capital flight has been estimated to range from $15 to over $27 billion over the same period. And while the inflow of capital to Mexico was $79 billion in the 1976–1984 period, the outflow has been estimated at between $26 and $54 billion for the same period.[4] The basic point is that a significant portion of the lending by the IACs to the LDCs finds its way into the hands of LDC savers who in turn invest it in the industrially advanced nations. As a result, the flow of money capital to the LDCs results in comparatively little productivity-increasing investment in physical capital in the LDCs.

INVESTMENT OBSTACLES The investment side of the capital formation process abounds with equally serious obstacles. These obstacles undermine the rate of capital formation even when a sufficient volume of saving is available to finance the needed investment. *The major obstacles to investment fall into two categories: the lack of investors and the lack of incentives to invest.*

Oddly enough, in some less developed countries the major obstacle to investment is basically the lack of business executives who are willing to assume the risks associated with investment. This, of course, is a special case of qualitative deficiencies of the labor force previously discussed.

But even if substantial savings and a vigorous entrepreneurial class are present, an essential ingredient in capital formation—the incentive to invest—may be weak. And clearly a host of factors may combine in an LDC to cripple investment incentives. Indeed, we have just mentioned such factors as political instability and higher rates of inflation in our discussion of capital flight. Similarly, very low incomes mean a limited domestic market—a lack of demand—for most nonagricultural goods. This factor is especially crucial when one recognizes that the chances of successfully competing with the mature industries of the advanced nations in international markets are meager. Then, too, the previously cited lack of trained administrative and operating personnel may be a vital factor in retarding investment. Finally, many of the LDCs simply do not have an adequate **infrastructure,** that is, the public capital goods, which are prerequisite to private investment of a productive nature. Poor roads and bridges, inadequate railways, little gas and electricity production, antiquated communications, unsatisfactory housing, and meager educational and public health facilities scarcely provide an inviting environment for investment spending.

The absence of an adequate infrastructure presents more of a problem than one might first surmise. The dearth of public capital goods means that a great deal of investment spending which does not *directly* result in the production of goods and which may not be capable of bearing profits must take place prior to, and simultaneously with, productive investment in manufacturing machinery and equipment. Statistics for the advanced nations indicate that about 60 percent of gross investment goes for housing, public works, and public utilities, leaving about 40 percent for directly productive investment in manufacturing, agriculture, and commerce.[5] These figures probably understate the percentage of total investment which must be devoted to infrastructure in the emerging nations. The volume of investment required to initiate eco-

---

[4] Steven Plaut, "Capital Flight and LDC Debt," *Weekly Letter* (Federal Reserve Bank of San Francisco), Jan. 8, 1988, p. 1.

[5] W. Arthur Lewis, *The Theory of Economic Growth* (Homewood, Ill.: Richard D. Irwin, Inc., 1955), p. 210.

nomic development may be much greater than it first appears.

There is one potential bright spot in this picture: the possibility of accumulating capital through *in-kind* or **nonfinancial investment.** Given the prerequisite leadership and willingness to cooperate, capital can be accumulated by transferring surplus agricultural labor to the improvement of agricultural facilities or the infrastructure. If each agricultural village would allocate its surplus labor to the construction of irrigation canals, wells, schools, sanitary facilities, and roads, significant amounts of capital might be accumulated at no significant sacrifice of consumer goods production. Nonfinancial investment simply bypasses the problems embodied within the financial aspects of the capital accumulation process. Such investment does not require consumers to save portions of their money income, nor does it presume the presence of an entrepreneurial class anxious to invest. In short, provided the leadership and cooperative spirit are present, nonfinancial investment is a promising avenue for the accumulation of basic capital goods.

TECHNOLOGICAL ADVANCE

Technological advance and capital formation are frequently part of the same process. Yet, there are advantages in treating technological advance, or the discovery and application of new ideas concerning methods of producing, and capital formation, or the accumulating of capital goods, as separate processes.

This is particularly so in discussing the LDCs. We view technological advance in the industrially advanced nations as an essentially evolutionary process wherein researchers first inch forward the boundaries of technological knowledge. Then follow the financing and construction of the complex capital equipment which the technological advance demands. But this picture is not accurate for the less developed countries. The rudimentary state of their current technology puts these nations far from the frontiers of technological advance. There already exists an enormous body of technological knowledge accumulated by the advanced nations which the less developed countries *might* adopt and apply without undertaking the expensive task of research. For example, the adoption of modern

crop-rotation practices and the introduction of contour plowing require no additional capital equipment, and they may contribute very significantly to productivity. By raising grain storage bins a few inches above the ground, a large amount of grain spoilage can be avoided. Such changes may sound trivial to people of advanced nations. However, the resulting gains in productivity can mean the difference between subsistence and starvation in some poverty-ridden nations.

In most instances the application of either existing or new technological knowledge entails the use of new and different capital goods. But, within limits, this capital can be obtained without an increase in the rate of capital formation. If the annual flow of replacement investment is rechanneled from technologically inferior to technologically superior capital equipment, productivity can be increased out of a constant level of investment spending. Actually, some technological advances may be **capital-saving** rather than **capital-using.** A new fertilizer, better adapted to a nation's topography and climate, might be cheaper than that currently employed. A seemingly high-priced metal plow which will last ten years may be cheaper in the long run than an inexpensive but technologically inferior wooden plow which requires annual replacement.

But we must be realistic about the transferability of advanced technologies to the less developed countries. In the industrially advanced nations technologies are usually predicated upon relatively scarce, highly skilled labor and relatively abundant capital. Such technologies tend to be capital-using or, alternatively stated, labor-saving. In contrast, the less developed economies require technologies which are appropriate to *their* resource endowments or, in other words, to large quantities of abundant, unskilled labor and very limited quantities of capital goods. Labor-using and capital-saving technologies are typically appropriate to the LDCs. This means that much of the highly advanced technology of the advanced nations is inappropriate in the less developed countries and therefore they must develop their own technologies. Recall, too, that many of the less developed nations have "traditional economies" (Chapter 2) and are not highly receptive to change. This is particularly true in peasant agriculture which dominates the economies of most LDCs. A potential technological advance which fails can mean hunger and malnutrition; therefore, there is a strong propensity to retain traditional production techniques.

SOCIOCULTURAL AND INSTITUTIONAL FACTORS

Purely economic considerations are not sufficient to explain the occurrence or the absence of economic growth. Substantial social and institutional readjustments are usually an integral part of the growth process. Economic development entails not only changes in a nation's physical environment (that is, new transportation and communications facilities, new schools, new housing, new plants and equipment), but also drastic changes in the ways in which people think, behave, and associate with one another. Emancipation from custom and tradition is frequently the fundamental prerequisite of economic development. Possibly the most crucial but least tangible ingredient in economic development is **the will to develop.** Economic growth may hinge upon "what individuals and social groups *want,* and *whether they want it badly enough to change their old ways of doing things* and to work hard at installing the new."[6]

Sociocultural obstacles Sociocultural impediments to growth are numerous and varied. Consider a few examples.

l Some of the least developed countries have failed to achieve the preconditions for a national economic unit. Tribal allegiances take precedence over national identity. Warring tribes confine all economic activity within the tribe, eliminating any possibility for production-increasing specialization and trade.

2 Religious beliefs and observances may seriously restrict the length of the workday and divert resources which might otherwise have been used for investment to ceremonial uses. In rural India, for example, total ceremonial expenditures are estimated at about 7 percent of per capita income.[7] More generally, religious and philosophical beliefs

may be dominated by the **capricious universe view,** that is, the notion that there is little or no correlation between an individual's activities and endeavors, on the one hand, and the outcomes or experiences which that person encounters, on the other.

If the universe is deemed capricious, the individual will learn to expect little or no correlation between actions and results. This will result in a fatalistic attitude. . . .

These attitudes impinge on all activities including saving, investment, long-range perspective, supply of effort, and family planning. If a higher standard of living and amassing of wealth is treated as the result of providence rather than springing from hard work and saving, there is little rationale for saving, hard work, innovations, and enterprise.[8]

3 The existence of a caste system—formal or informal—causes labor to be allocated to occupations on the basis of caste or tradition rather than on the basis of skill or merit. The result is clearly a misallocation of human resources.

Institutional obstacles Consider now some growth obstacles of an institutional character. Political corruption and bribery are commonplace in many LDCs. School systems and public service agencies are often ineptly administered and their functioning impaired by petty politics. Tax systems are frequently arbitrary, unjust, cumbersome, and detrimental to incentives to work and invest. Political decisions are often motivated by the desire to enhance the nation's international prestige, rather than to foster development. For example, India's explosion of a nuclear bomb in 1974 created a substantial controversy over societal priorities.

Because of the predominance of farming in the LDCs, the problem of achieving that institutional environment in agriculture which is most conducive to increasing production must be a vital con-

---

[6] Eugene Staley, *The Future of Underdeveloped Countries,* rev. ed. (New York: Frederick A. Praeger, 1961), p. 218.

[7] Inder P. Nijhawan, "Socio-Political Institutions, Cultural Values, and Attitudes: Their Impact on Indian Economic Development," in J. S. Uppal (ed.), *India's Economic Problems* (New Delhi: Tata McGraw-Hill Publishing Company, Ltd., 1975), p. 31.

[8] Ibid., p. 33.

siderátion in any growth program. More specifically, the institutional problem of **land reform**
demands attention in virtually all LDCs. But the
needed reform may vary tremendously between
specific nations. In some LDCs the problem assumes the form of excessive concentration of land
ownership in the hands of a few wealthy families.
This situation is demoralizing for the tenants,
weakening their incentive to produce, and is typically not conducive to capital improvements. At
the other extreme is the absurd arrangement
whereby each and every family owns and farms a
minute fragment of land far too small for the application of modern agricultural technology. An important complication to the problem of land reform
lies in the fact that political considerations sometimes push reform in that direction which is least
defensible on economic grounds. For many nations, land reform may well be the most acute institutional problem to be resolved in initiating the
process of economic development.

The vicious circle: a summing up

It is important to recognize that many of the characteristics of the LDCs just described are simultaneously causes and consequences of their poverty.

These countries are caught in a **vicious circle of
poverty.** They *stay* poor because they *are* poor!
Consider Figure 41-1. The fundamental feature of
an LDC is low per capita income. Being poor, a
family has little ability or incentive to save. Furthermore, low incomes mean low levels of demand.
As a result, there are few available resources, on
the one hand, and no strong incentives, on the
other, for investment in physical or in human capital. This means that labor productivity is low. And,
since output per person is real income per person,
it follows that per capita income is low.

Many experts feel that the key to breaking out
of this vicious circle is to increase the rate of capital
accumulation, to achieve a level of investment of,
say, 10 percent of the national income. But Figure
41-1 reminds us that the real villain for many
LDCs—rapid population growth—may be waiting
in the wings to undo the potentially beneficial effects of this higher rate of capital accumulation.
For example, using hypothetical figures, let us suppose that initially an LDC is realizing no growth in
its real GNP. But now it somehow manages to increase its saving and investment to 10 percent of its
GNP. As a result, its real GNP begins to grow at,
say, 2.5 percent per year. Given a stable population, real GNP per capita will also grow at 2.5 percent per year. If this persists, the standard of living
will *double* in about 28 years. But what if population grows at the Latin American rate of 2.5 per-

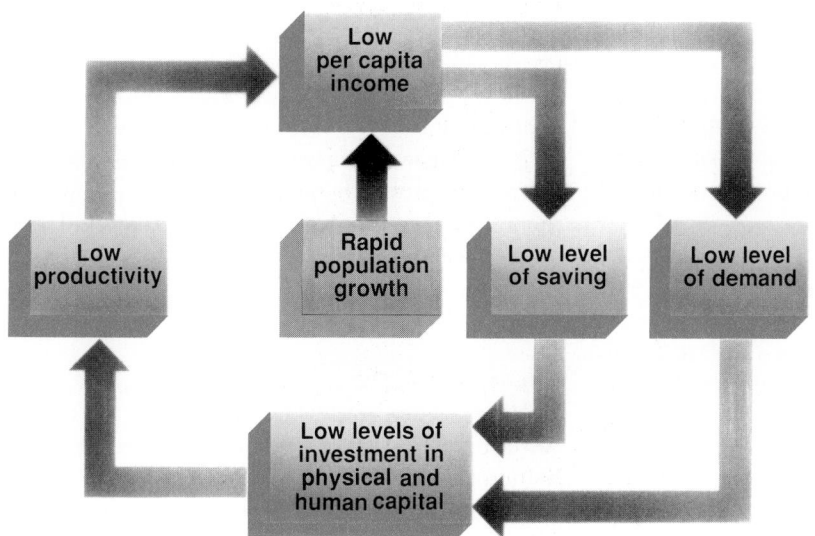

FIGURE 41-1

**The vicious circle of
poverty**

**Low per capita incomes
make it extremely diffi-
cult for poor nations to
save and invest, a con-
dition that perpetuates
low productivity and
low incomes. Further-
more, rapid population
growth may quickly
absorb increases in per
capita real income and
thereby may negate the
possibility of breaking
out of the poverty cir-
cle.**

cent per year? Then real income per person is unchanged and the vicious circle persists.

More optimistically, *if* population can be kept constant or constrained to some growth rate significantly below 2.5 percent, then real income per person will rise. And this implies the possibility of still further enlargement in the flows of saving and investment, continued advances in productivity, and the continued growth of per capita real income. In short, if a process of self-sustaining expansion of income, saving, investment, and productivity can be achieved, the self-perpetuating vicious circle of poverty can be transformed into a self-regenerating, beneficent circle of economic progress. The trick is to make effective those policies and strategies which will accomplish this transition.

Role of government

Economists are not in agreement as to the appropriate role of government in seeking economic growth.

A POSITIVE ROLE

One view is that, at least during the initial stages of development, government needs to play a major role. The reasons for this stem in large part from the character of the obstacles facing the LDCs.

I Law and order Some of the poorest countries are plagued by widespread banditry and intertribal warfare which divert both attention and resources from the task of development. A strong and stable national government is needed to establish domestic law and order and to achieve peace and unity.

2 Lack of entrepreneurship The absence of a sizable and vigorous entrepreneurial class, ready and willing to accumulate capital and initiate production, indicates that in many cases private enterprise is intrinsically not capable of spearheading the growth process.

3 Infrastructure Many obstacles to economic growth center upon deficiencies of public goods and services, or, in other words, an inadequate infrastructure. Sanitation and basic medical programs, education, irrigation and soil conservation projects, and the construction of highways and transportation-communication facilities are all essentially nonmarketable goods and services yielding widespread spillover benefits. Government is the sole institution in a position to provide these goods and services in required quantities.

4 Forced saving and investment Government action may also be required to break through the saving-investment dilemma which impedes capital formation in the LDCs.

It may well be that only governmental fiscal action can provide a solution by forcing the economy to accumulate capital. The alternatives here are essentially twofold. One is to force the economy to save by increasing taxes. These tax revenues can then be channeled into priority investment projects. The problems of honestly and efficiently administering the tax system and achieving a relatively high degree of compliance with tax laws are frequently very great.

The other alternative is to force the economy to save through inflation. Government can finance capital accumulation by creating and spending new money or by selling bonds to banks and spending the proceeds. The resulting inflation, you will recall, is the equivalent of an arbitrary tax upon the economy. There are serious arguments against the advisability of saving through inflation. In the first place, inflation tends to distort the composition of investment away from productive facilities to such items as luxury housing, precious metals and jewels, or foreign securities, which provide a better hedge against rising prices. Furthermore, significant inflation may reduce voluntary private saving as potential savers become less willing to accumulate depreciating money or securities payable in money of declining value. Internationally, inflation may boost the nation's imports and retard its flow of exports, creating balance of payments difficulties.

5 Social-institutional problems Government is in the key position to deal effectively with the social-institutional obstacles to growth. Controlling population growth and land reform are basic problems which call for the broad approach that only government can provide. And government is in an advantageous position to stimulate the will to develop, to change a philosophy of "Heaven and faith will determine the course of events" to one of "God helps those who help themselves."

PUBLIC SECTOR PROBLEMS

But all this must not blind us to certain problems and disadvantages which a governmentally directed development program may entail. If entrepreneurial talent is lacking in the private sector, can we expect leaders of quality to be present in the ranks of government? Is there not a real danger that government bureaucracy will prove an impediment, not a stimulus, to much-needed social and economic change? And, too, what of the tendency of centralized economic planning to favor the spectacular "showpiece" projects at the expense of less showy but more productive programs? Might not political objectives take precedence over the economic goals of a governmentally directed development program?

It is fair to say that development experts are significantly less enthusiastic about the potential role of government in the growth process than they were, say, twenty or twenty-five years ago. Government maladministration and corruption are commonplace in many LDCs. Government officials often line their own pockets with foreign aid funds. Similarly, political leaders frequently confer monopoly privileges upon relatives, friends, and political supporters. For example, a political leader may grant exclusive rights upon relatives or friends to produce, import, or export certain products. These monopoly privileges are conducive to higher domestic prices for the relevant products and diminished ability for the LDC to compete in world markets. In a similar fashion, the managers of state-owned enterprises are often appointed on the basis of cronyism rather than competence. In recent years the perception of government has shifted from that of catalyst and promoter of growth to that of a potential impediment to development.

We might also note that the Soviet central planning model, in which government is the primary engine of economic growth, has been widely discounted as an effective means of development. Many of the LDCs—most notably China—have come to recognize that competition and individual economic incentives are important ingredients in the development process. The LDCs increasingly have recognized that their citizens need to see direct personal gains from their efforts to motivate them to take actions which will expand production. It is relevant that the Soviet Union itself has recently embarked upon a potentially far-reaching reform program designed to enhance economic incentives and competition (Chapter 42).

Role of the advanced nations

What are the ways by which the industrially advanced nations can help the less developed countries in their quest for growth? To what degree have these avenues of assistance been pursued?

Generally speaking, less developed nations can benefit from (1) an expanding volume of trade with advanced nations; (2) foreign aid in the form of grants and loans from the governments of advanced nations; and (3) flows of private capital from the more affluent nations. Let us consider these possibilities in the order stated.

EXPANDING TRADE

Some authorities maintain that the simplest and most effective means by which the United States and other industrially advanced nations can aid the less developed nations is by lowering international trade barriers, thereby enabling the LDCs to expand their national incomes through an increased volume of trade.

Though there is undoubtedly some truth in this view, lowered trade barriers are not a panacea. It is true that some of the poor nations need only large foreign markets for their raw materials to achieve growth. But the problem for many is not that of obtaining markets for the utilization of existing productive capacity or the sale of relatively abundant raw materials, but rather, the more fundamental one of getting the capital and technical assistance needed to produce something for export.

Furthermore, it must be recognized that close trade ties with advanced nations is not without disadvantages. The old quip, "When Uncle Sam gets his feet wet, the rest of the world gets pneumonia," contains considerable truth for many less developed nations. In particular, a recession among the IACs can have disastrous consequences for the prices of raw materials and the export earnings of the LDCs. For example, in mid-1974 copper was $1.52 per pound; by the end of 1975 it had fallen to $.53 per pound! Stability and growth in the industrially advanced nations are clearly important to progress in the less developed countries.

FOREIGN AID: PUBLIC LOANS AND GRANTS

Our vicious circle of poverty emphasizes the importance of capital accumulation in achieving economic growth. Foreign capital—both public and private—can be used to supplement an emerging country's saving and investment efforts and play a crucial role in breaking the circle of poverty.

As noted earlier, most of the LDCs have inadequate infrastructures. That is, they are sadly lacking in basic public goods—irrigation and public health programs and educational, transportation, and communications systems—prerequisites to the attraction of either domestic or foreign private capital. Foreign public aid is needed to tear down this major roadblock to the flow of private capital to the LDCs.

Direct aid The United States has assisted the LDCs directly through a variety of programs and through participation in international institutions designed to stimulate economic development. Over the 1976–1985 period, American aid to the LDCs—including both loans and grants—has averaged $9.4 billion per year. In 1987 American aid was over $10 billion. The bulk of this aid is administered by our Agency for International Development (AID). Some, however, takes the form of grants of surplus food under the Food for Peace program. Other advanced nations have also embarked upon substantial foreign aid programs. In 1986 foreign aid from all advanced noncommunist nations was over $36 billion. In addition, the OPEC nations donated almost $5 billion and the Soviet bloc another $4 billion.

The World Bank group The United States is a major participant in the **World Bank,** the major objective of which is to assist the LDCs in achieving growth. Supported by some 151 member nations, the World Bank not only lends out of its capital funds, but also (1) sells bonds and lends the proceeds, and (2) guarantees and insures private loans.

Several characteristics of the World Bank merit comment.
1 The World Bank is in a sense a "last resort" lending agency; its loans are limited to productive projects for which private funds are not readily available.
2 Because many World Bank loans have been for basic development projects—multipurpose dams, irrigation projects, health and sanitation programs, communications and transportation facilities—it has been hoped that the Bank's activities will provide the infrastructure prerequisite to substantial flows of private capital.
3 The Bank has played a significant role in providing technical assistance to the LDCs by helping them discover what avenues of growth seem most appropriate for their economic development.

Two World Bank affiliates function in areas where the World Bank has been weak. The ***International Finance Corporation (IFC)*** has the primary function of investing in ***private*** enterprises in the LDCs. The ***International Development Association (IDA)*** makes "soft loans"—loans which may not be self-liquidating—to the poorest on the LDCs on more liberal terms than does the World Bank.

PRIVATE CAPITAL FLOWS

The LDCs have also received substantial flows of private capital from the IACs. Who, specifically, are these private investors? For the most part they are large corporations and commercial banks. For example, General Motors or Chrysler might finance the construction of a plant in Mexico or Brazil to assemble autos or produce auto parts. Or Citicorp or Bank of America may make loans to the governments of Argentina or the Philippines.

Although these private capital flows were relatively modest in the 1950s and 1960s—ranging from $2 to $4 billion per year—they grew dramatically in the 1970s. Specifically, average annual private flows of capital to the LDCs in the decade of the 1970s was $28 billion. Then in the early 1980s an LDC debt crisis developed and since then private capital flows to the poor nations have fallen precipitously.

The LDC debt crisis

Let us now consider the much-publicized LDC debt crisis. What is the magnitude of LDC debt? What are its causes? And effects? What, if anything, might be done to resolve the debt problem?

THE DEBT AND ITS GROWTH

The external debt (that is, debts owed to foreign governments and foreign financial institutions) of the LDCs has grown tremendously in the past two decades. Figure 41-2 gives us an overall picture of how the long-term debts of the LDCs to both foreign governments (shown in blue) and to foreign private lenders (shown in orange) have expanded since 1970. If short-term external debts were included, we would find the total external debt of the LDCs to be considerably larger. For example, total LDC debt grew from $842 billion in 1982 to $1217 billion in 1987. This latter figure is equal to about

TABLE 41-4 Selected heavily indebted LDCs, 1986

Country	Total external debt (billions of dollars)	External debt as a percentage of GNP
Brazil	$111	32%
Mexico	102	63
Argentina	49	46
Venezuela	34	51
Philippines	28	66
Indonesia	24	44
Nigeria	22	44
Chile	21	101
Thailand	18	27
Colombia	15	37

Source: The World Bank, *World Development Report, 1988* (New York: Oxford University Press, 1988), pp. 252–253 and 256–257.

39 percent of the aggregated gross national products of the LDCs. Table 41-4 lists some of the heavily indebted LDCs and indicates both the absolute amount of their external debts and the size of these debts in comparison to their GNPs.

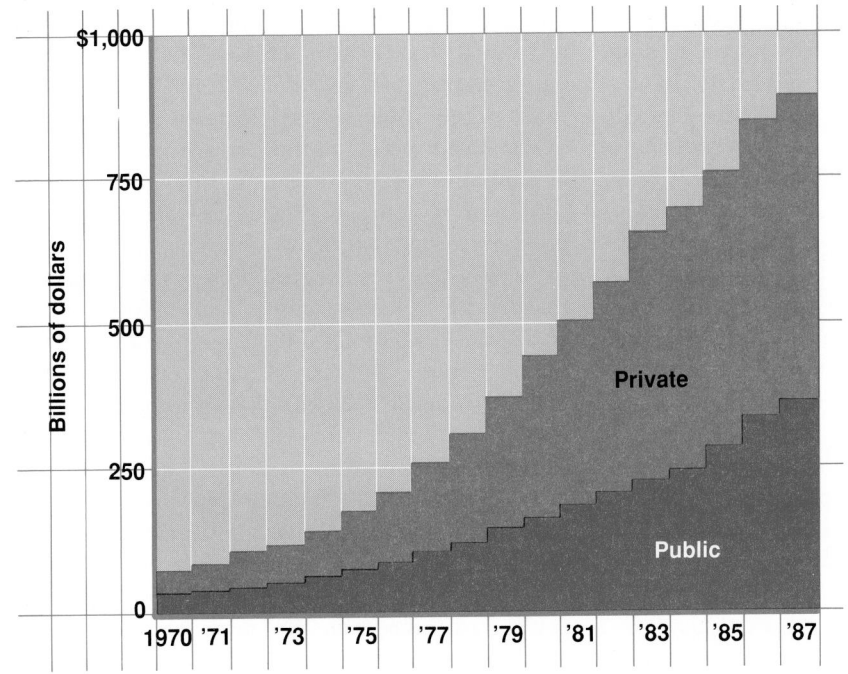

FIGURE 41-2

Growth of long-term external debt of the LDCs, 1970–1987

The long-term external debt of the LDCs to both foreign governments (in blue) and to foreign financial institutions (in orange) has grown sharply since 1980. [*Source: The World Bank,* World Development Report, 1988 *(New York: Oxford University Press, 1988), p. 29.*]

To repeat: LDC external debt has grown very substantially in recent years and for many of the LDCs this debt is now large both absolutely and in relation to GNP.

CAUSES OF THE CRISIS

We have noted that private capital flows—particularly from large IAC commercial banks—increased greatly in the 1970s. But in the 1970s and early 1980s a series of converging world economic events had serious adverse effects upon the LDCs and precipitated a debt crisis.

First, the dramatic runup of oil prices by OPEC in 1973–1974 and again in 1979–1980 (raising the price of a barrel of oil from about $2.50 to $35) greatly increased the energy bills of the oil-importing LDCs. More specifically, the oil-importing LDCs were faced with growing current account deficits in their balance of payments which were financed largely by increased borrowing. Hence, the external debt of the oil-importing LDCs grew from $130 billion in 1973 to $700 billion by 1982. Borrowed funds which could have been used for development were instead used to pay higher energy costs.

Second, in the early 1980s the IACs—and the United States in particular—invoked strong anti-inflationary monetary policies. These tight money policies triggered two adverse effects for the LDCs. On the one hand, the growth of IAC national incomes slowed; indeed, in 1980–1982 the United States suffered its most serious postwar recession. As a result, IAC demands for the raw material and farm product exports of the LDCs declined. This meant sharp reductions in the export earnings which the LDCs needed to pay interest and principal on their debts. On the other hand, tight money policies in the IACs resulted in substantially higher interest rates. This, of course, greatly increased the cost to the LDCs in servicing their debts.

Third, the burden of LDC debt rose for still another reason. Over the 1981–1984 period the international value of the dollar appreciated in value. This meant that the LDCs now had to pay more for their imports of American manufactured goods. And, because much LDC debt is denominated in dollars, it also meant that the LDCs would have to export a larger amount of goods to acquire each dollar needed to pay interest and principal on their debts.

Finally, in 1982 Mexico was on the verge of defaulting on its debt and creditors were forced to reschedule that debt and make further loans to Mexico. This Mexican debt crisis precipitated an abrupt loss of confidence in the creditworthiness of many of the highly indebted LDCs. As a result, private voluntary lending to the LDCs declined sharply. This was complicated by the fact that the United States was incurring very large Federal budget deficits during the 1980s (Chapter 20). The sale of United States government bonds to finance these deficits absorbed a significant portion of the world's financial capital which might otherwise have been available to the LDCs.

In short, higher prices on imported oil, declines in LDC export earnings, higher interest rates, appreciation of the dollar, and declines in recent private lending to the LDCs all combined to create a debt crisis. By 1982 and 1983 many of the LDCs found themselves unable to make scheduled payments on their external debts.

ECONOMIC CONSEQUENCES

There has followed a period of "muddling through" during which the creditor nations in cooperation with the International Monetary Fund attempted to deal with the LDC debt crisis on a nation-by-nation basis. For example, the debts of many of the LDCs were rescheduled (stretched out over a longer period of time) to reduce the burden of annual interest and principal payments. In return for these concessions the LDCs had to agree to domestic austerity programs to improve their prospects for debt repayment. This typically meant that the LDCs had to reduce their imports and increase their exports in order to realize more international trade earnings for debt repayment. But increased exports and reduced imports clearly imply a further impairment of living standards in the LDCs. Similarly, with net export earnings being used primarily for debt retirement, there is little or nothing left to invest in development projects. It is not by chance that, while the growth of real GNP for the LDCs as a group was 3.9 percent per year over the 1980–1987 period, the rate for the highly indebted LDCs was only 1.1 percent. Indeed, the per capita real GNPs of the highly in-debted nations actually *declined* over this time pe-riod.

The debt crisis has also had adverse repercus-sions in the IACs. IAC commercial banks have been forced to write off some of the LDC debt as uncollectible. Thus in mid-1987 Citicorp increased its bad-debt reserves by $3 billion in recognition that as much as 25 percent of its loans to the LDCs would not be repaid. Some experts have expressed the fear that the LDC debt is a potential threat to the banking and financial systems of the IACs.

SOLUTIONS?

What, if anything, can be done to alleviate or cor-rect the lingering LDC debt crisis? Fortunately, some of the economic developments which contrib-uted to the crisis have tended to alleviate the prob-lem. For example, oil prices and interest rates have both fallen; the dollar has depreciated in value; and the economic stagnation which characterized the IACs in the early 1980s has generally given way to growth. On the other hand, LDC debt clearly re-mains a serious problem.

There seem to be two general routes to follow in seeking a solution. One is to continue the piece-meal, country-by-country approach which has been followed since 1982. The problem with this approach is that it may go on for decades, and, as it does, continue to thwart the possibilities that the LDCs will achieve significant growth. The other option is debt relief. That is, the IACs might sim-ply forgive some significant portion of outstanding LDC debt. There are several problems with this solution. First and most obviously, the forgiving of private debt imposes costs upon the lending com-mercial banks and their stockholders. The forgiv-ing of public debt imposes costs upon American and other IAC taxpayers. Second, any significant "write-down" of the debt will undoubtedly have a highly adverse effect on new private lending to the LDCs. It is unrealistic to expect creditors to take large losses and then turn around and extend new loans. On the borrowing side, the problem is that debt forgiveness may be an invitation for the LDCs to default on debts incurred in the future. It is evi-dent that no easy solution to the debt issue presents itself.

Toward a "new international economic order"?[9]

Despite flows of private investment and foreign aid, the LDCs are far from content with their relation-ships vis-à-vis the industrially advanced nations. As noted earlier, the absolute income gap between the IACs and the LDCs has widened over time. Furthermore, despite achieving political indepen-dence, the LDCs feel that an economic-based **neo-colonialism** persists. Both private investment and public aid, it is contended, have tended to exploit the LDCs and keep them dependent upon, and subservient to, the rich nations. It is no surprise that in the past decade or so the LDCs have pressed more aggressively for basic changes in the international economic order which would acceler-ate their growth and redistribute world income to their benefit. In arguing for the creation of a **New International Economic Order (NIEO)**[10] spokesmen for the LDCs make the following argu-ments and proposals.

1 Rules of the game Although they represent the vast majority of the world's population, the LDCs have less than one-third of the total votes in the key international institutions which formulate the over-all character of the world economy. Indeed, the LDCs were simply not involved in the creation of the post-World War II institutions and programs which establish the rules and regulations by which international trade, finance, and investment are conducted. For example, the industrially advanced nations control the International Monetary Fund which provides monetary reserves for the financing of international trade. The LDCs question the eq-

[9] This section draws upon Edwin P. Reubens, ed., *The Challenge of the New International Economic Order* (Boulder, Colo.: Westview Press, 1981), chap. 1; and Todaro, op. cit., pp. 559–565. For a detailed statement on the NIEO, see Mahbub ul Haq, *The Third World and the International Economic Order* (Washington: Overseas Development Council, 1976).

[10] The term "New International Economic Order" arose from a 1974 United Nations declaration on the problem of economic development.

uity and legitimacy of these rules and argue that the institutions and programs of the existing economic order are stacked against them.

2 Trade barriers The poor nations contend that, rhetoric to the contrary, the advanced nations have retarded their development by using a variety of trade barriers—for example, tariffs and import quotas—to deprive them of export markets. The LDCs feel they are in a "Catch-22" situation. If they effectively utilize the financial and technical aid provided by the advanced nations to create efficient low-cost manufacturing industries, the LDCs then become competitive with industries in the advanced nations. The IACs respond to this situation by using trade barriers to protect their domestic industries from the new competition. The LDCs have argued for **preferential tariff treatment**—that is, lower tariffs than those paid by developed countries—to stimulate their industrial growth.

3 Exploitation and dependence The LDCs also contend that most of the contracts, leases, and concessions which the multinational corporations of the advanced countries have negotiated with them have benefited the multinationals at the expense of the host country. The poor countries argue that the major portion of the benefits from the exploitation of their natural resources accrues to others. Furthermore, the LDCs seek to achieve greater diversification and therefore greater stability in their economies. Foreign private capital, however, seeks out those industries which are currently the most profitable, that is, the ones which are now producing for the export market. In brief, while the LDCs strive for less dependence on world markets, flows of foreign private capital often tend to enhance that dependence. Exxon, Alcoa, United Fruit, and the rest are after profits and they allegedly have no particular interest in either the economic independence, diversification, or overall progress of the LDCs.

4 Terms of trade As exporters of raw materials (bauxite, tin, copper, manganese) and basic farm products (cocoa, coffee, cotton, rubber, tea, timber), the LDCs are greatly affected by the extreme price fluctuations which characterize these highly competitive markets. In particular, the high variability of their import earnings makes it very diffi-

LAST WORD

Famine in Africa

The roots of Africa's persistent famines include both natural and human causes.

Famine in Africa is not uncommon. The much-publicized 1984 famine in Ethiopia accounted for 1 million deaths. In 1987 Ethiopia again appealed to the world for drought relief. Angola—burdened by a civil war of twelve years' duration—also requested emergency food aid in 1987. The World Food Program reported in late 1987 that Ethiopia, Mozambique, Malawi, Angola, Somalia, and the Sudan needed 2.3 million tons of food in 1988, approximately twice as much as has been pledged by food-surplus countries. In a wide band of sub-Saharan nations some tens of millions of people are confronted with hunger, malnutrition, and starvation. This tragic situation is especially ironic because most African countries were self-sufficient in food at the time they became independent nations; they are now heavily dependent upon imported foodstuffs for survival.

The immediate and much-publicized cause of this catastrophe is drought. But the ultimate causes of Africa's declining ability to feed itself are more complex and multifaceted, an interplay of natural and human conditions. In addition to a lack of rainfall, these include rapid population growth, widespread soil erosion, and counterproductive public policies.

The hard fact is that in Africa population is growing more rapidly than is food production. Specifically, population is increasing at about 3 percent per year while food output is growing at only 2 percent per year. This grim arithmetic suggests declining living standards, hunger, and malnutrition. The World Bank reports that during the 1980s the per capita incomes of the sub-Saharan nations fell to about three-quarters of the level reached by the end of the 1970s.

But apart from the simple numbers involved, population growth has apparently contributed to the ecological degradation of Africa. Given population pressures and the increasing need for food, marginal land has been deforested and put into crop production. In many cases trees which have served as a barrier to the encroachment of the desert have been cut for fuel, allowing the fragile topsoil to be blown away by desert winds. The ultimate scarcity of wood which has accompanied deforestation has forced the use of animal dung for fuel, thereby denying its traditional use as fertilizer. Furthermore, traditional fallow periods have been shortened, resulting in overplanting and overgrazing and, in simple terms, a wearing out of the soil. Deforestation and land overuse have reduced the capacity of the land to absorb moisture, diminishing its productivity and its ability to resist drought. Some authorities feel that the diminished ability of the land to absorb water reduces the amount of moisture which evaporates into the clouds to return ultimately as rainfall. All of this is complicated by the fact that there are few facilities for crop storage. Thus, even when crops are good, it is difficult to accumulate a surplus for future lean years. A large percentage of domestic farm output in some parts of Africa is lost to rats, insects, and spoilage.

It is generally agreed that ill-advised public policies have contributed to Africa's famine. In the first place, African governments have generally neglected investment in agriculture in favor of industrial development and military strength. It is estimated that African governments on the average spend four times as much on armaments as they do on agriculture. Over 40 percent of Ethiopia's budget is for the support of an oppressive military. Second, many African governments have followed the policy of establishing the prices of agricultural commodities at low levels to provide cheap food for growing urban populations. This low-price policy has diminished the incentives of farmers to increase productivity. While foreign aid has helped to ease the effects of Africa's food-population problems, most experts reject aid as a long-term solution. Indeed, experience suggests that aid in the form of foodstuffs can only provide temporary relief and may undermine the realization of long-run local self-sufficiency. Foreign food aid, it is contended, merely treats symptoms and not causes.

All of this is made more complex by the fact that the sub-Saharan nations are burdened with relatively large and growing external debts. The IMF reports that the aggregate debt of these nations rose from $21 billion in 1976 to $138 billion in 1987. As a condition of further aid, these nations have had to invoke austerity programs which have contributed to the declines in their per capita incomes. One tragic consequence is that many of these nations have cut back on social service programs for children. A UNICEF spokesman has indicated that 3 million children died in 1987 worldwide "because they didn't have 50 cents worth of vaccine in them."

To summarize: The famine confronting much of Africa is partly a phenomenon of nature and in part self-inflicted. Drought, overpopulation, ecological deterioration, and errant public policies have all been contributing factors. This complex of causes implies that hunger and malnutrition in Africa may persist long after the rains return.

cult for LDCs to plan and finance development programs. Worse yet, the long-run price trend of LDC commodity exports has been downward. On the other hand, the LDCs import manufactured goods produced by the corporate giants of the advanced nations which have the market power to charge high prices. Thus the LDCs argue that over time the **terms of trade** have shifted against them; the prices of their exports tend to be depressed while the prices of their imports tend to rise. Hence, it takes more of the LDCs' exports to purchase a given quantity of imports.

The poor countries have pushed two proposals designed to relieve this alleged inequity. First, they seek establishment of a **stabilization fund** for some twenty basic food and raw material exports of major importance to them. The fund would be used to buy each of these various products when its world price fell and, conversely, to sell those products when world prices rose. Therefore, prices would tend to be stabilized. The second proposal involves *indexing*. That is, the LDCs want to tie the prices of their commodity exports to the prices they must pay for their imports from the IACs in order to maintain the purchasing power of their exports.

5 Debt relief The LDCs have also sought debt relief. Their view is that the present debt is so large that it constitutes a severe obstacle to LDC growth. Arguing that the prosperity of the IACs depends upon the prosperity of the LDCs, the LDCs feel that forgiving some portion of the debt would be mutually beneficial. Thus, in the fall of 1987 some twenty-four LDC governments sought both debt relief and additional loans at the annual joint meeting of the World Bank and the International Monetary Fund.

6 Aid and redistribution The LDCs take the position that past foreign aid has been insufficient and ineffective. It has been insufficient in that, as a group the advanced nations have only made annual aid contributions equal to about one-third of 1 percent of their GNPs. (Although the United States is the largest contributor in absolute terms, giving over $10 billion in 1987, that figure is only one-fourth of one percent of our GNP). Aid has been relatively ineffective for several reasons. First, much of it is "tied" to the donor country; for exam-

ple, American aid must be spent on American goods and services. This means that the LDCs are denied the opportunity to "shop around" in world markets for potentially better buys on capital goods and technological assistance. Second, inflation has greatly eroded the real value of aid dollars to recipient nations. Third, as already noted, a large portion of aid must be used to pay interest on the external debts of the LDCs and, hence, is not available for development.

One of the objectives of the NIEO is to have each of the IACs progressively increase its aid to 0.7 percent of its GNP as recommended by the United Nations over a decade ago. This aid should have "no strings attached" and should be provided on a long-term and automatic basis. The influential Brandt Commission[11] has endorsed this 0.7 percent goal. This implies a doubling of the current level of developmental aid.

The NIEO agenda is very controversial. While the poor countries feel the NIEO proposals are egalitarian and just, many of the advanced nations envision them as a demand for a massive redistribution of world income and wealth which is simply not in the cards. Many of the industrialized nations feel that there is no "quick fix" for underdevelopment and that the LDCs must undergo the same process of patient hard work and gradual capital formation as did the advanced nations over the past two centuries. Needless to say, the stagflation and sluggish growth which have periodically plagued the advanced economies in recent years hardly provide an environment conducive to greater generosity and understanding of LDC problems.[12]

---

[11] *North-South: A Program for Survival* (Cambridge, Mass.: MIT Press, 1980). This commission, which studied a far-ranging agenda of international economic issues, was chaired by Willy Brandt, former Chancellor of West Germany.

[12] A few economists take the position that, on balance, the contribution of foreign aid to Third World development "cannot be significant, and is much more likely to be negative." See Peter Bauer and Basil Yamey, "The Political Economy of Foreign Aid," *Lloyds Bank Review*, October 1981, pp. 1–14.

CHAPTER SUMMARY

1 Most of the nations of the world are less developed (low per capita income) nations. While some LDCs have been achieving quite rapid growth rates in recent years, others have realized little or no growth at all.

2 Initial scarcities of natural resources and the limited possibility of augmenting existing supplies may impose a serious limitation upon a nation's capacity to develop.

3 The presence of large and rapidly growing populations in less developed countries contributes to low per capita incomes. In particular, increases in per capita incomes frequently induce rapid population growth, to the end that per capita incomes again deteriorate to near subsistence levels.

4 Most LDCs suffer from both unemployment and underemployment. Labor productivity is low because of insufficient investment in physical and human capital.

5 In many LDCs both the saving and investment aspects of capital formation are impeded by formidable obstacles. In some of the poorest LDCs the savings potential is very low. Many LDC savers have chosen to transfer their funds to the IACs rather than invest domestically. The absence of a vigorous entrepreneurial class and the weakness of investment incentives are also serious impediments to capital accumulation.

6 Appropriate social and institutional changes and, in particular, the presence of "the will to develop" are essential ingredients in economic development.

7 The vicious circle of poverty brings together many of the obstacles to growth and says in effect that "poor countries stay poor because of their poverty." Low incomes inhibit saving and the accumulation of physical and human capital, making it difficult to increase productivity and incomes. Rapid population growth can offset otherwise promising attempts to break the vicious circle.

8 The nature of the obstacles to growth—the absence of an entrepreneurial class, the dearth of infrastructure, the saving-investment dilemma, and the presence of social-institutional obstacles to growth—suggests the need for government action in initiating the growth process. However, the corruption and maladministration which are quite common to the public sectors of the LDCs suggest that government may be relatively ineffective as an instigator of growth.

9 The advanced nations can assist in development by reducing trade barriers and by providing both public and private capital.

10 Rising energy prices, declining export prices, depre-

ciation of the dollar, and concern about LDCs' creditworthiness combined to create an LDC debt crisis in the early 1980s. External debt problems of LDCs remain serious and inhibit their growth.

11 The LDCs are calling for a New International Economic Order (NIEO) which will give them *a* a greater voice in the policies of international financial institutions, *b* preferential tariff treatment, *c* a greater share of the income derived from contracts and leases negotiated with multinational corporations, *d* improved terms of trade, *e* the cancellation or rescheduling of their external debts, and *f* a larger and automatic inflow of foreign aid.

TERMS AND CONCEPTS

industrially advanced countries (IACs)	**the will to develop**
less developed countries (LDCs)	**capricious universe view**
unemployment and underemployment	**land reform**
brain drain	**vicious circle of poverty**
capital flight	**World Bank**
infrastructure	**neocolonialism**
nonfinancial investment	**New International Economic Order (NIEO)**
capital-saving and capital-using technological advance	**preferential tariff treatment**
	terms of trade
	stabilization fund

QUESTIONS AND STUDY SUGGESTIONS

1 What are the major characteristics of an LDC? List the major avenues of economic development available to such a nation. State and explain the obstacles which face the LDCs in breaking the poverty barrier. Use the "vicious circle of poverty" to outline in detail the steps which an LDC might take to initiate economic development.

2 Explain how the absolute per capita income gap between rich and poor nations might increase, even though per capita GNP is growing faster in the LDCs than it is in the IACs.

3 Discuss and evaluate:

   a "The path to economic development has been clearly blazed by American capitalism. It is only for the LDCs to follow this trail."

b "Economic inequality is conducive to saving, and saving is the prerequisite of investment. Therefore, greater inequality in the income distribution of the LDCs would be a spur to capital accumulation and growth."

c "The IACs fear the complications which stem from oversaving; the LDCs bear the yoke of undersaving."

d "The core of the development process involves changing human beings more than it does altering a nation's physical environment."

e "America's 'foreign aid' program is a sham. In reality it represents neocolonialism—a means by which the LDCs can be nominally free in a political sense but remain totally subservient in an economic sense."

f "Poverty and freedom cannot persist side by side; one must triumph over the other."

g "The biggest obstacle facing poor nations in their quest for development is the lack of capital goods."

h "A high per capita GNP does not necessarily identify an industrially advanced nation."

4 Explain how population growth might be an impediment to economic growth. How would you define the optimal population of a country? Some experts argue that children are "net assets" in poor countries, but "net liabilities" in rich countries. Can you provide a rationale for this assertion? If the statement is true, does it imply that a rising per capita income is the prerequisite for population control?

5 Much of the initial investment in an LDC must be devoted to infrastructure which does not directly or immediately lead to a greater production of goods and services. What bearing might this have upon the degree of inflation which results as government finances capital accumulation through the creating and spending of new money?

6 "The nature of the problems faced by the LDCs creates a bias in favor of a governmentally directed as opposed to a decentralized development process." Do you agree? Substantiate your position.

7 What is the LDC debt crisis? How did it come about? What solutions can you offer?

8 What types of products do the LDCs export? Can you use Chapter 39's law of comparative advantage to explain the character of these exports?

9 Outline the main components of the New International Economic Order proposed by the LDCs. Which of these demands do you feel are most justified?

10 What would be the implications of a worldwide policy of unrestricted immigration between nations for economic efficiency and the global distribution of income?

CHAPTER 42

The economy of the Soviet Union

Mikhail Gorbachev came to power in the Soviet Union in March of 1985 and almost immediately launched a campaign to restructure the Soviet economy in the hope of improving its performance. His proposals are potentially radical and have caused political leaders, academicians, and interested citizens to focus their attention upon this rival economy.

Hence, in this final chapter we find it highly relevant to gain a rudimentary understanding of the Soviet economy. Our specific objectives are as follows. First, we examine the underlying ideology and institutions of the economy. Next, we pursue a rather detailed discussion of Soviet central planning. How are Soviet Five-year Plans constructed and implemented? What is the role of prices in the planned economy? Our next goal is to consider the performance of the Soviet economy and the reasons for General Secretary Gorbachev's proposed reforms. Then, finally, we want to obtain an overview of the Gorbachev program to restructure the Soviet economy. An important by-product of our endeavor is that, by examining an economy at the opposite end of the ideological spectrum, we cannot help but enhance our understanding of our own economy.

The command economy: ideology and institutions

To understand the Soviet economy one must understand its ideology and institutions.

MARXIAN IDEOLOGY

The Soviet government—which we can safely identify with the Communist Party—views itself as a dictatorship of the proletariat or working class. Based upon Marxism-Leninism, the Soviet leadership envisions its system as the inevitable successor to capitalism, the latter being plagued by internal contradictions stemming from the exploitation, injustice, and insecurity which it allegedly embodies. Especially important for our purposes is the Marxian notion of a **labor theory of value,** that is, the idea that the economic or exchange value of any commodity is determined solely by the amount of labor time required for its production. Thanks to the capitalistic institution of private property, capitalists own the machinery and equipment necessary for production in an industrial society. The propertyless working class is therefore dependent upon the capitalists for employment and for its livelihood. Given the worker's inferior bargaining position and the capitalist's pursuit of profits, the capitalist will exploit labor by paying a daily wage which is much less than the value of the worker's daily production. The capitalist can and will pay workers a subsistence wage and expropriate the remaining fruits of their labor as profits or what Marx termed **surplus value.** The function of the Communist Party is to overthrow this system and to replace it with a classless society within which human exploitation is absent. The Soviet government thus views itself as the vanguard of the working class; its actions are held to be in keeping with the legitimate goals of the proletariat.

INSTITUTIONS

There are two outstanding institutional characteristics of the Soviet economy: (1) state ownership of property resources, and (2) authoritarian central economic planning.

State ownership   The Soviet constitution of 1977 makes the pervasiveness of public ownership of property resources quite clear.

Socialist ownership of the means of production in the form of **state ownership** (that of all the people) . . . is the foundation of the USSR's economic system. . . . The land, its mineral wealth, the waters and the forests are the exclusive property of the state. The principal means of production in industry, construction and agriculture, means of transport and communication, banks, the property of trade, municipal-service and other enterprises organized by the state and the bulk of the urban housing stock, as well as other property necessary to carry out the state's tasks, belong to the state.

The Soviet state owns all land, natural resources, transportation and communication facilities, the banking system, and virtually all industry. Most retail and wholesale enterprises and most urban housing are governmentally owned. In agriculture many farms are state-owned; most, however, are government-organized collective farms, that is, essentially cooperatives to which the state assigns land "for free use for an unlimited time." A near exception to state ownership is the small plot of land which each collective farm family has set aside for its personal use: "Citizens may have the use of plots of land . . . for auxiliary farming operations (including the keeping of livestock and poultry), the growing of fruit and vegetables, and also for individual housing construction." And, of course, clothing, household furnishings, and small tools and implements used by craftsmen are privately owned. About one-half of the total Soviet population, and about one-fourth of the urban population, reside in privately owned housing.

Central economic planning   Despite a highly democratic constitution, in practice the government of the Soviet Union is a strong dictatorship. Many westerners characterize the Soviet government as a dictatorship *over* the proletariat, rather than *of* the proletariat. In any event the Communist Party, although limited in membership to the most dedicated 4 or 5 percent of the total population, stands unchallenged. Indeed, the party and the government can be regarded as virtually synonymous.

As the constitution makes clear, the Soviet economy is based upon **central economic planning:**

The economy of the USSR is a single national-economic complex embracing all elements of social production, distribution, and exchange. . . . Management of the economy is carried out on the basis of state plans of economic and social development. . . .

In contrast with the decentralized market economy of the United States, that of the Soviet Union is a centralized "command" economy functioning in terms of a detailed economic plan. The Soviet economy is government-directed rather than market-directed.

Circumscribed freedom   The dominant roles of state ownership and central planning correctly imply that it is not the free decisions of consumers and business owners which determine the allocation of resources and the composition of total output in the Soviet Union. Yet, subject to the restraints imposed by the central planners, consumers and laborers have a degree of free choice.

CONSUMERS   The concept of consumer sovereignty as we know it does not exist in the Soviet Union. The preferences of individual consumers, as reflected in the size and structure of consumer demand, do *not* determine the volume and composition of consumer goods production in the Soviet Union; this determination is made by the government and implemented through the plan. However, consumers are free to spend their money incomes as they see fit on those consumer goods for which the central plan provides.

WORKERS   Although the Soviet Union has a history of compulsory job assignment, harsh labor codes, and, in the extreme, slave labor, much greater reliance has been put upon free occupational choice in recent years. Workers in the U.S.S.R. are generally free to be mobile, to quit one job in favor of another, and to move geographically. If central direction and coercion are *not* dominant mechanisms for allocating labor, how do planners achieve an occupational, industrial, and geographic allocation of labor reasonably consistent with the production goals specified in the central plan? The basic answer is that the composition and allocation of labor is strongly influenced by (1) state control over the educational system, and (2) state determination and manipulation of wages.

The Soviet government has virtually total control over the educational system and exerts considerable pressures, directly and indirectly, upon students to choose those curricula and careers which are consistent with the output goals of the plans. If, for example, the perceived need of the national economy is for more oil, then the number of openings for geology students in higher education will be expanded and the stipends paid to such students will be increased by state directives. In general, the Soviet government is actively and deeply involved in determining the quantity and the composition of education and training acquired by the labor force so that planned production goals can be achieved.

Planners also design the structure of wages to achieve an industrial and geographic allocation of labor consistent with planned production goals. Thus, if the state wants to increase output in, say, the steel and hydroelectric industries, then it will raise wage rates to attract more workers to these industries. If it desires to increase oil exploration or timber production in Siberia, it attempts to establish an equalizing wage differential (Chapter 30) to induce the required number of workers to bear the harsh climate and general lack of amenities in the area. Similarly, if consumer goods production and distribution are assigned a low priority in the plan, the wages of workers in these sectors will be set at relatively low levels. In short, education and training programs *and* wage differentials are structured to provide the kinds and amounts of labor which "fit" the plan.

Central planning

Perhaps the most dramatic feature of the Soviet economy is its use of central planning. In the Soviet Union the means of answering the Five Fundamental Questions is central planning. Choices made primarily through the market in our United States' economy must be consciously made by bureaucratic decision in the U.S.S.R. The overall character of the Soviet Five-year Plans has been succinctly described in these words:

The Soviet economic plan is a gigantic, comprehensive blueprint that attempts to govern the economic activities and interrelations of all persons and institutions in the U.S.S.R., as well as the economic relations of the U.S.S.R. with other countries. To the extent that the plan actually controls the development of events, all the manifold activities of the Soviet economy are coordinated as if they were parts of one incredibly enormous enterprise directed from the central headquarters in Moscow.[1]

Now let us probe below the surface. What are the goals of the plans? How are the plans constructed and implemented? What problems does central planning entail?

FIVE- AND ONE-YEAR PLANS

In practice, the Soviet economy is guided by a variety of plans, the most important of which are the Five-year and the One-year Plans. The **Five-year Plan** is a general statement of the country's basic strategy for economic development and resource allocation. It indicates overall target growth rates for the economy as a whole and for its major sectors. For example, the Five-year Plan will specify growth targets for GNP, for industrial output, for investment, for agricultural products and consumer goods, and so forth. Special projects—the construction of a hydroelectric plant or an oil pipeline from Siberia to western Russia—are included in such plans. The Five-year Plan also provides a general portrayal of the composition of output. For example, the overall investment target may indicate general goals for the production of, say, machine tools and agricultural equipment.

It is to be stressed that, while the State Planning Commission or **Gosplan** has the task of constructing the Five-year Plan, it is the Soviet government—more precisely, the Communist Party—

[1] Harry Schwartz, *Russia's Soviet Economy,* 2d ed. (Englewood Cliffs, N.J.: Prentice-Hall, Inc., 1954), p. 146.

which determines the basic goals embodied in the plan. Historically, great emphasis has been placed upon (1) rapid economic growth through the development of heavy industry, and (2) military strength.

The **One-year Plans** are the operational plans in that they translate the aggregative goals of the Five-year Plans into a detailed product-mix and into specific directives for enterprise managers. Thus, while the Five-year Plan may call for a 3 percent increase in the aggregate production of agricultural machinery, it is in the One-year Plan that Gosplan specifies the number and kinds of tractors, combines, cultivators, and milking machines that will be produced. And it is through the One-year Plan that each enterprise is provided with specific detailed directives telling it how much output to produce and to what other enterprises their output is to be delivered.

BASIC PLANNING PROBLEM: COORDINATION

It is no simple matter to sweep away the guiding function of the market system, as the Soviet Union has done, and replace it with an effective central plan. After all, we have found that the market system is a powerful organizing force which coordinates millions upon millions of individual decisions by consumers, entrepreneurs, and resource suppliers and fosters a reasonably efficient allocation of resources. Is central planning a satisfactory substitute for the market?

The core of the planning problem is revealed by the input-output table (Table 32-1). Input-output analysis, you will recall, demonstrates the highly interdependent character of the various industries or sectors of the economy. Each industry employs the outputs of other industries as its inputs; in turn its outputs are inputs to still other firms. This means that a planning decision to increase the production of machinery by, say, 10 percent is not a single, isolated directive, but rather a decision which implies a myriad of related decisions for fulfillment. For example, in terms of Table 32-1, if planners do not make the related decisions to increase metal output by 6.5 units, fuel by 0.5 units, agricultural products by 1 unit, and to provide an extra 20 units of labor (not to mention additional second-round increases in all these inputs because

2.5 more inputs of machinery are also needed to increase machinery output!), bottlenecks will develop, and the planned increase in machinery output cannot be realized.

Let us look at the matter from a slightly different vantage point: Even if an internally consistent set of decisions—a perfectly coordinated plan—could be constructed by the central planners, the failure of any single industry to fulfill its output target would cause an almost endless chain of adverse repercussions. If iron mines—for want of machinery or labor or transportation inputs—fail to supply the steel industry with the required inputs of iron ore, the steel industry in turn will be unable to fulfill the input needs of the myriad industries dependent upon steel. All these steel-using industries will therefore be unable to fulfill their planned production goals. And so the bottleneck chain reaction goes on to all those firms which use steel parts or components as inputs.

It must be emphasized that our illustrative input-output table (Table 32-1) is a gross oversimplification of the problem of coordinating a command economy. There are now some 200,000 industrial enterprises producing goods in the Soviet Union. The central planners must see to it that all the resources needed by these enterprises to fulfill their assigned production targets are somehow allocated to them.

The literally billions of planning decisions that must be made to achieve consistency result in a complex and complete interlocking of macro- and micromanagement. . . . The number of planned interconnections increases more rapidly than the size of the economy. . . . Even with the most sophisticated mathematical techniques and electronic computers, the task of interrelating demands and factor inputs for every possible item by every possible subcategory becomes impossible for the central planners alone.[2]

COORDINATION TECHNIQUES

Although Soviet central planning has encountered increasingly severe problems in the past fifteen or twenty years, Soviet planning has worked and his-

[2] Barry M. Richman, *Soviet Management* (Englewood Cliffs, N.J.: Prentice-Hall, Inc., 1965), p. 17.

torically has functioned reasonably well. It is certainly legitimate to inquire: Why? What techniques have Soviet planners employed to achieve the level of coordination sufficient to make central planning workable? The answers lie substantially in the way the plans are constructed and implemented.

1 Achieving "material balances" To begin with, Gosplan attempts to make the plans realistic and internally consistent by establishing **material balances.** Hence, in the Five-year Plan material balances are constructed for some 300 inputs. By establishing material balances we simply mean that Gosplan tries to determine whether the quantities supplied will match the quantities demanded for each basic input. Thus for, say, cement, all available sources of supply (domestic output, imports, stocks on hand) are compared with planned requirements (factory and housing construction, exports, additions to stocks) to determine whether the two "match." If they do not, the plan will be adjusted to achieve a match. In the One-year Plans, Gosplan and its subsidiary planning agencies attempt to work out material balances for an estimated 20,000 commodity groups.

2 Planning by negotiation In formulating a plan, the Gosplan collects voluminous amounts of statistical data from a host of subordinate ministries, each of which is concerned with the operation of certain industries. From these data, a tentative plan is constructed. In advance of its finalization, each One-year Plan is submitted to the various units of the Soviet administrative hierarchy for study, evaluation, and criticism. This criticism, it must be noted, concerns the specific details of the economic plan and anticipated problems in its fulfillment, not the overall goals which the plan seeks.

Let us illustrate the procedure. A tentative One-year Plan will be made available to the various ministries in charge of individual industries or sectors (for example, the Ministry of Coal Industries), to the various regional planning and administrative authorities, and ultimately to the individual enterprises. At each level the plan is analyzed, suggestions are made for revision, and perhaps alterations are proposed in production goals or planned allocations of inputs. These evaluations are passed back up the planning hierarchy to Gosplan. Taking into account those suggestions and

criticisms which it feels are worthy, Gosplan then draws up a final plan. When rubber-stamped by the party and the government, this becomes the official One-year Plan.

The point to be emphasized is this: By breaking the overall plan into its component parts and subjecting these detailed segments to considerable critical examination by the various levels of the hierarchy, Gosplan hopes to establish a final plan which is more realistic and workable than would otherwise be the case. Soviet planners apparently recognize their limitations in obtaining and digesting masses of detailed information. The "down-and-up" evaluation of the tentative plan by the administrative hierarchy and its subsequent revision is aimed at obtaining on-the-spot knowledge and an understanding of immediate, detailed facts and circumstances which a relatively small group of planners could not otherwise grasp. To the extent that the resulting plan is more realistic and feasible, the chance is less that problems of coordination—in particular, bottlenecks—will arise to jeopardize plan fulfillment.

But "planning by negotiation" is not without problems. Enterprise managers and their work forces receive substantial bonuses for fulfilling or overfulfilling assigned production targets. It is therefore in the interest of the enterprise to conceal production capacity and to bargain for reduced production targets or, alternatively, for larger allocations of material inputs and labor. The planners in Gosplan, however, are well aware of such tactics and tend to impose "taut" plans on the enterprises as an offset. Depending upon the outcome of this negotiating "game," a particular enterprise might be assigned an unrealistically high production target which is necessarily underfulfilled and a source of production bottlenecks to other enterprises. Or an "easy" target may be assigned which allows for underemployed productive capacity within the enterprise. Neither outcome is in the interest of economic efficiency.

3 Priority principle A third means of making central planning workable is embodied in the **priority principle** of resource allocation. Not all production goals established by Gosplan are held to be of equal importance. The goals of certain "leading links" sectors or industries (machinery, chemicals, steel) are given high priority; other industries (clothing, automobiles) are assigned low priorities. Thus, when bottlenecks arise in the actual operation of the national plan, resources or inputs are shifted from low-priority to high-priority sectors of the economy. Coordination and plan fulfillment are sacrificed in low-priority production in order to maintain coordination and fulfill production targets in high-priority sectors. This accounts for the unevenness with which the goals of the various central plans have been fulfilled. Traditionally, planned increases in housing and consumer goods have been sacrificed to realize the planned increases in industrial and military goods production.

4 Reserve stocks To some extent, coordination problems—bottlenecks and the chain reactions they precipitate—can be avoided by drawing upon reserve stocks of various inputs. Inventories, in other words, are used as a cushion or buffer to resolve specific bottlenecks or input deficiencies before they can trigger a chain of production shortfalls.

5 "The second economy" Besides the official, socialist, centrally directed economy, the Soviet Union also has a **second economy** which consists of a wide spectrum of semilegal and illegal markets or activities. The second economy includes, for example, the paying of bribes to retail store clerks for access to scarce consumer goods, the peasant who steals collective farm fertilizer for use on his "private" plot of ground, the worker who "borrows" state tools and materials to ply his trade "on the side," the physician who steals medicine for his or her "unofficial" practice, and so forth. Relevant for present purposes is the fact that state enterprises may engage in extralegal operations in seeking to fulfill their plans.

Put yourself in the shoes of a Soviet plant manager. You are under pressure to fulfill an ambitious production target assigned by Gosplan. You and your subordinates will receive substantial bonuses by fulfilling or overfulfilling the plan. But you know from past experience that the supplies of required inputs from other plants are sporadic and unreliable. To enhance the possibility of obtaining sufficient inputs to meet your output target you surreptitiously employ an "expediter" or "pusher" to scour the economy for needed supplies. The expediter may pay bribes or engage in barter activities ("we will swap some of the machine tools our enterprise has hoarded for some of your fabricated steel") to obtain needed inputs. Despite the illegality of such activities, they play a significant role in making Soviet central planning workable.

. . . the second economy, grafted onto the present institutional setup in the USSR, is a kind of spontaneous surrogate economic reform that imparts a necessary modicum of flexibility, adaptability, and responsiveness to a formal setup that is too often paralyzing in its rigidity, slowness, and inefficiency. It represents a de facto decentralization, with overtones of the market. It keeps the wheels of production turning.[3]

Although all these techniques contribute in varying degrees to the workability of Soviet central planning, they by no means ensure a high degree of efficiency. There is a great amount of evidence gathered from Soviet sources to indicate that bottlenecks do occur with rather alarming regularity. The result is frequent production stoppages and underfulfillment of production plans.[4]

EXECUTING THE PLAN: CONTROL AGENCIES

The Soviet government is not inclined to sit back after each industrial plant and farm has been assigned its production targets and hope for favorable results. On the contrary, an abundance of control agencies supervises the carrying out of each plan. Most obvious, of course, is the Gosplan and the various subordinate planning groups affiliated with it. These administrative units keep a running check on the progress of the plan. The Central Committee of the Communist Party and a variety of subordinate party organizations function as watchdog agencies by uncovering, reporting, and

---

[3] Gregory Grossman, "The 'Second Economy' of the USSR," in Morris Bornstein (ed.), *The Soviet Economy: Continuity and Change* (Boulder, Colo.: Westview Press, 1981), p. 88.

[4] Ibid., p. 123. For an authoritative discussion of the processes and problems of Soviet planning, see Alec Nove, *The Soviet Economic System*, 3d ed. (Boston: Allen & Unwin, Inc., 1986), chaps. 1–4.

helping to correct deviations from the plan. The control functions of the infamous secret police are well known. And, too, a less formal type of control is exercised through a much-publicized program of "criticism and self-criticism," whereby the Soviet citizenry is encouraged to register complaints concerning deviations from, and violations of, the plan.

Perhaps the most vital enforcement agency is the state banking system, or **Gosbank.** The Gosbank, with its thousands of branches, supervises the financial aspects of each plant's production activities and in this manner has a running account of each plant's performance. More precisely, this supervision—called **control by the ruble**—works something like this: The government establishes prices on all resources and finished products. As a greatly simplified example, the Leningrad Machine Tool Plant may require 1000 tons of steel and 100 workers to produce 5000 units of output per year. If steel costs 60 rubles per ton and each worker is paid 1000 rubles per year, the total cost of the 5000 units of output will be 160,000 rubles. Gosplan then directs the Gosbank to make this amount of credit available to the plant over the course of the year. Now, because all the plant's financial transactions—both receipts and expenditures—must be completed through the use of checks, the Gosbank will have an accurate record (in effect, a running audit) of the plant's progress, or lack thereof, in fulfilling the production targets assigned by the One-year Plan. Should the plant achieve its assigned output at an expense less than 160,000 rubles, it will have overfulfilled its production goal. Inefficient, wasteful production will cause the plant to exhaust its bank credit before its production goal is reached. Either eventuality will be reflected in the plant's account with the Gosbank.

INCENTIVES

How are the various economic units motivated toward fulfillment of the One-year Plan?

Monetary incentives The Soviet government relies quite heavily upon monetary incentives to obtain the maximum productive effort from labor. In particular, wages are geared to skill and productivity.

The resulting wage differentials are considerable. Great emphasis is put upon piecework, more so than in the United States. Probably as much as four-fifths of the Soviet labor force works under a piecework plan of one sort or another. Elaborate systems of bonuses and premiums induce workers to exceed normal production rates. On the other hand, there is evidence to suggest that the economic incentives of workers may be blunted by the relatively low priority assigned to consumption goods in the Five-year Plans. In particular, the Soviet worker-consumer only has a limited array of relatively low-quality goods and services available for purchase. This means that it is difficult to translate differences in *nominal* incomes into differences in *real* incomes.

Nonmonetary incentives A variety of nonmonetary inducements also exist to stimulate labor to greater productivity. A rather comprehensive system of awards and decorations exists to cite exemplary workers. These are closely correlated with material rewards. For example, a "Hero of Socialist Labor" is likely to be accorded certain tax exemptions, monthly bonuses, low rental on state housing, free use of transportation facilities, government-supplied vacations at a Crimean resort, and so forth. The real standard of living of the average Soviet citizen is roughly one-third that of an American counterpart, so that the value of such benefits is considerable. Much publicity accompanies these awards. A member of the "Order of Lenin" may enjoy fame and prestige comparable to that of a professional baseball player or movie star in the United States. In addition, "socialist competitions" are encouraged by the party, pitting the productive capacities of various groups of workers against one another.

The labor unions to which virtually all Soviet workers belong bear little or no resemblance to their American counterparts. In effect, Russian labor unions are essentially functionaries of the state; their basic goals are to encourage a high level of productivity among their members in carrying out the economic plan, to train new workers, to aid in the solution of labor discipline problems, and to administer the social security system. Wage rates are set by the government; collective bargaining as we know it does not exist. Although strikes are not illegal as such, they are strongly discouraged and pose considerable risk to participants. Soviet ideology views strikes as meaningless and counterrevolutionary because in theory state enterprises are owned by, and operated in the interest of, workers. Therefore, it is reasoned that it makes no sense for workers to strike because they are in fact striking against themselves! Reliable statistics on strikes do not exist because the Soviet government suppresses such information. But there is ample anecdotal evidence to indicate that worker protests—reflected in either strikes or slowdowns—do occur with some frequency. Worker strikes may reflect worker concerns with unsafe working conditions, managerial corruption, the boosting of work norms, and so forth. In other cases strikes may reflect tensions arising from broader economic problems, for example, food shortages and price increases. Soviet labor unions do prevent undue exploitation of their members by plant managers eager to fulfill their assigned production quotas. They also play an active role in providing recreational and cultural programs for workers.

Admonitions to work The choice of an able-bodied adult to be a nonworker is also constrained in the U.S.S.R. Soviet workers are not only guaranteed the "right" to work, but also have a positive obligation to do so. Indeed, the old Soviet constitution of 1936 flatly stated that "Work in the U.S.S.R. is a duty and a matter of honor for every able-bodied citizen, in accordance with the principle 'He who does not work, neither shall he eat.'" It is pertinent to note that the Soviet Union does *not* have a system of unemployment insurance; an unemployed worker is therefore exposed to more severe financial exigencies than is his or her American counterpart. Furthermore, a Soviet "parasitism" law specifies that any able-bodied individual who is unemployed for more than four months a year may be liable for two years imprisonment. Given these pressures to work, it is not surprising that participation rates in the Soviet Union are higher than any other industrialized nation in the world. For all men between the ages of 16 to 60 the Soviet labor force participation rate is 87 percent; the comparable figure for women is 79 percent. We shall see later, however, that labor discipline in the Soviet Union has often been poor and one consequence is a low and falling rate of labor productivity growth.

Comparable monetary and nonmonetary in-

ducements bear upon plant managers. High salaries, bonuses, awards, and promotion await those who fulfill their production targets. Failure exposes the plant manager to investigation and reassignment to a less palatable position. A good many plant managers are members of the party and therefore inspired by party doctrines.

PLANNING AND PRICES

To say that the Soviet system is a command economy rather than a market economy is not to say that prices have no role to play in the centrally planned system. Although Soviet prices are not employed as a guiding mechanism in determining the structure of output, they are used in *implementing* the production objectives established by the state. *Soviet prices are government-determined and manipulated to aid in the achievement of state-established goals.*

Actually, the function of prices in the Soviet Union differs considerably between the production process, on the one hand, and the sale of final products to consumers, on the other. In the first instance, prices are merely accounting devices which facilitate checking the efficiency with which products are manufactured. In the latter case, prices are employed as rationing devices to distribute products to consumers without the use of government rationing.

Producer prices In producing, say, a television set, a Soviet plant will be faced with certain governmentally established prices for component parts, labor, and other needed resources. And, similarly, the government will determine the price of the final product. Generally speaking, the basic principle in establishing these prices is that a plant or an industry of average efficiency would realize total receipts from its production which will cover its total costs and yield a "planned profit" of 5 to 10 percent. If production is less efficient than that deemed average by the plan, planned profits will not be achieved and losses may result. Greater-than-average efficiency will result in unplanned profits.[5] In short, the prices of resources and components are used as accounting costs to assess the efficiency with which various plants and industries operate. Except for the fact that capitalistic prices are essentially market-determined rather than government-determined, this role of the Soviet price system parallels that of its capitalistic counterpart. But here—for two reasons—the similarity ends.

1 In a capitalistic economy, losses call for a contraction of output and a release of resources by the affected industry; profits signal industry expansion and the absorption of resources (Chapters 5 and 25). Not so in the Soviet Union. Expansion and contraction of industry are determined by the government, not by consumer sovereignty functioning through the price system. Therefore, a relatively inefficient industry which is considered vital by the state may be expanded despite losses. Similarly, a highly efficient, profit-realizing industry may be purposely contracted by state planning.

2 Despite market imperfections, input prices in a capitalistic system reflect with some reasonable degree of accuracy the relative scarcity of resources and their value in alternative uses. Thus, to minimize money costs in the production of a product is to minimize real costs, that is, to get a given good produced with a minimum sacrifice of alternative goods (Chapter 25). But in the Soviet Union prices are governmentally determined and therefore do not accurately reflect the relative scarcity of resources. Hence, the minimization of money costs in a Soviet enterprise does not mean that real costs of production are being minimized. This is a fundamental source of inefficiency in the Soviet economy.

Consumer prices Whereas prices in the production process are essentially accounting devices used to gauge plan fulfillment, the prices of finished goods are established to serve as rationing devices. Planners attempt to set consumer goods prices at levels which will clear the market so there will be no persistent shortages or surpluses. As a result, the price of television sets which is used for accounting purposes may vary considerably from the price which is charged consumers who purchase them. The difference typically takes the form of what the Rus-

sians call a **turnover tax,** which is similar to an excise tax.

To illustrate: Suppose the accounting price of a finished television set is 200 rubles. This price is used by the Gosplan in judging the efficiency of the assembly plant. But because of the low priority traditionally assigned to consumer goods, consumer demand in the Soviet Union has persistently exceeded the available supply of many consumer goods. This means that, if shortages and government rationing are to be avoided, the price charged by the state in selling television sets to consumers must be higher than the accounting price. Suppose the government estimates that the consumer price of television sets must be 400 rubles to bring the quantity demanded into balance with the quantity available. This is accomplished by adding a 100 percent (200 ruble) turnover tax to TV sets. At this price the market will be cleared and government rationing avoided.

Turnover taxes—which, incidentally, are the major source of tax revenue in Russia—vary widely among various products. High turnover taxes on particularly scarce goods greatly discourage their consumption and attempt to force the amounts demanded into accord with the modest quantities allowed by the plan. Lower rates on abundantly available consumer staples—for example, potatoes and certain other vegetables—encourage their consumption. In general, the greater the relative scarcity of a product, the higher the turnover tax placed upon it. The total prices of such products will necessarily be higher and purchases discouraged. Lower tax rates on more abundant products give them lower relative prices and encourage their consumption. In this way inflation-causing income is taxed away, and the pattern of consumer spending is forced into rough accord with the planned composition of consumer goods output. Furthermore, the use of differential turnover tax rates tends to make *real* income differentials less than *nominal* income differentials. That is, turnover taxes tend to be higher on "luxury goods" than on "necessities." Evidence suggests that consumer prices function very imperfectly in balancing quantities demanded and supplied. On the one hand, frequent lines of consumers in front of retail stores attest to persistent shortages. On the other hand, articles in the Soviet press complain of unwanted and unsold goods rotting in warehouses!

---

[5] For the most part, these profits will accrue to the government as revenue from state-owned enterprises. A part may be used to expand the industry, if such expansion is consistent with the objectives of the plan. Another portion may be shared by the plant's workers and executives as a bonus for their efficiency.

Economic performance

How effectively has the Soviet economy performed under central planning? From an historical perspective the picture is mixed. In the early years of planning, economic growth was rapid, exceeding that realized by the market-oriented economies. There can be no question that, since the revolution in 1917, the Soviet Union has been transformed from a less developed, quasi-feudalistic society into an important industrial power. As Table 42-1 indicates, the Soviet growth rate exceeded that of the United States until the mid-1970s. But in the past two decades Soviet growth has diminished significantly and currently is less than that of the United States. There is also widespread agreement that the Soviet system has not served consumers well.

SOURCES OF ECONOMIC GROWTH

Let us first pinpoint certain factors which have contributed to the Soviet Union's historically high growth rates.

I Natural resource base The Soviet Union has a generous and varied natural resource base. Although they differ significantly in composition, it is not inaccurate to say that the natural resource endowments of the U.S.S.R. are roughly comparable with those of the United States. There is a major exception to this generalization. U.S. agricultural resources are much superior to those of the U.S.S.R. Much of the Soviet Union's most fertile soil lies in regions susceptible to drought and short growing seasons. The Soviets are much more vulnerable to substantial fluctuations in agricultural output.

2 Totalitarianism and investment Because the Soviet Union is a totalitarian state, the government can and does exercise tight political control over the allocation of resources. The Soviet Union has used central planning to pursue with great vigor the goal of rapid growth and the political-military strength derived therefrom. Indeed, the Soviet economy has aptly been described as "totalitarianism harnessed to the task of rapid industrialization and economic

TABLE 42-1 **Real GNP growth in the Soviet Union and the United States, 1961–1988 (average annual rates)**

Period	Soviet Union	United States
1961–1965	4.8%	4.6%
1966–1970	5.0	3.0
1971–1975	3.1	2.2
1976–1982	2.1	2.3
1983–1988	2.0	4.0

Source: *Economic Report of the President, 1989,* p. 434.

growth."[6] This effort is reflected in Figure 42-1 where we find that the Soviet Union devotes about 33 percent of its total output to investment, compared to 14 percent for the United States. Furthermore, the composition of Soviet investment has put great emphasis upon those industries most crucial to the growth process. Retail and wholesale distributional facilities, for example, have been largely ignored in favor of steel, petroleum, chemicals, and machine tools.

3 Surplus farm labor At the time of the revolution Soviet agriculture was characterized by sizable quantities of underemployed or surplus labor. Under central planning, much of this low-productivity farm labor was shifted to newly created industries, where its productivity was substantially higher. In 1925, 84 percent of the Soviet labor force was in agriculture; currently, about 30 percent is so employed. This reallocation has resulted in significant increases in the Soviet GNP.

4 Full employment The Soviet economy's growth rate, unlike those of the United States and other capitalistic nations, has benefited in that, since about 1930, Soviet economic planning has virtually eliminated cyclical unemployment. Unemployment in the Soviet Union is estimated to be as low as 1 to 2 percent of the labor force. Unlike the

[6] Robert W. Campbell, *The Soviet-type Economies,* 3d ed. (Boston: Houghton Mifflin Company, 1974), p. 3.

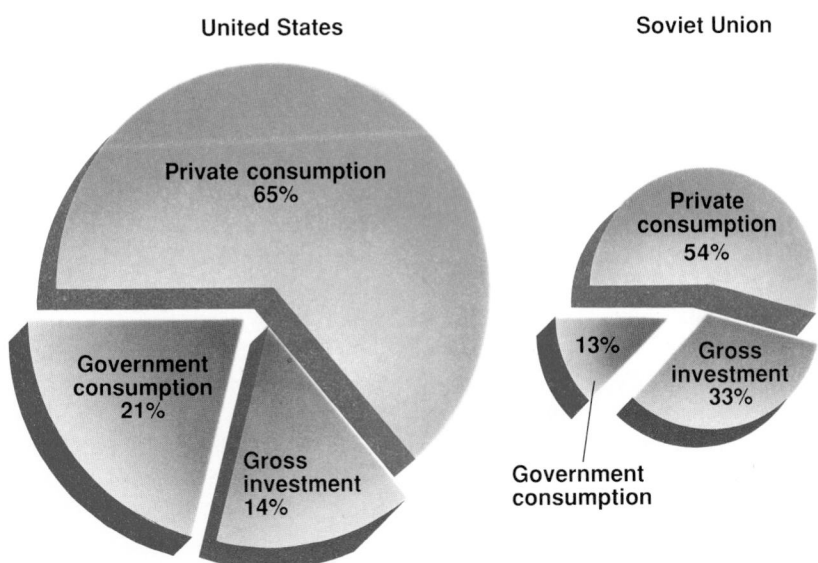

United States

Soviet Union

FIGURE 42-1

Size and composition of GNP in the United States and the Soviet Union

The Soviet Union's GNP is about 50 percent the size of the United States' GNP. As compared with the United States, the Soviet Union puts relatively greater emphasis on investment goods than on consumer goods. [Joint Economic Committee, *USSR: Measures of Economic Growth and Development, 1950–1980* (Washington, 1982), p. 67, and *Economic Report of the President.*]

United States, the Soviet Union has *not* had to count years of zero or negative growth due to recession in calculating its long-term rate of growth.

RECENT GROWTH SLOWDOWN

The Soviet Union's impressive growth performance of the 1950s and 1960s has waned significantly in the past fifteen or twenty years (Table 42-1). Why has this happened? What growth-retarding forces have come into play in the past two decades?

1 The military burden The Soviet Union, with a GNP of about 50 percent that of the United States, has a roughly comparable military establishment. Large Soviet military expenditures in recent years have diverted resources from more growth-effective uses. In particular, growing defense outlays have caused declines in both the quantity and quality of industrial investment. Furthermore, the "policy of channeling superior management and the best sci-

entists and engineers into defense research and production denies prime innovative resources to civilian oriented investment"[7] and has adversely affected technological progress and quality (productivity) of investment in the civilian sector.

2 Labor shortage Whereas much of the Soviet Union's earlier growth was attributable to shifts of surplus labor from agriculture to industry, the Soviet Union is finding it increasingly difficult to make additional labor shifts without significantly imperiling the output of an already troubled agricultural sector. More importantly, the Soviet Union is faced with a significant slowing down of labor force growth. While the annual average increase in the labor force was 1.5 percent in the 1971–1981 decade, it is predicted to be only 0.6 percent in the 1981–1991 period. Anticipated in-

[7] Stanley H. Cohn, "General Growth Performance of the Soviet Economy," in Joint Economic Committee, *Economic Performance and the Military Burden in the Soviet Union* (Washington, 1970), p. 12.

creases in the 1990–2000 period are likely to be near zero. These declines are the consequence of two demographic developments: (1) fewer young people are reaching working age and (2) more adults will be retiring from the labor force. The former development is a reflection of a rather dramatic decline in birthrates during the 1960s. The latter is complicated by a rising mortality rate among Soviet males, attributable to increasing incidence of alcoholism, industrial accidents, and cardiovascular disease.[8] The problem of greatly diminished labor force growth is a particularly acute one for the Soviet Union because past growth of the national output has been much more dependent upon labor force growth than it has been upon productivity growth. Stated differently, historical growth of Soviet GNP has been largely attributable to more inputs of labor as opposed to realizing more output per worker.

3 Agricultural drag By western standards Soviet agriculture is something of a monument to inefficiency and now constitutes a drag upon economic growth, engulfing as it does some 30 percent of the labor force and roughly one-third of annual investment. Furthermore, output per worker is only 10 to 25 percent of the United States' level![9] The low productivity of Soviet agriculture is attributable to many factors: the relative scarcity of good land; vagaries in rainfall and length of growing season; the limited use of chemical fertilizers; serious errors in planning and administration; and perhaps most important, the failure to construct an effective incentive system. Once a major exporter of grain and other agricultural products, the Soviet Union has recently become one of the world's largest importers of agricultural commodities. Indeed, agricultural imports have been a serious drain upon Soviet foreign currency reserves which its leadership

would prefer to use in financing imports of western capital goods and technology.

4 Productivity slowdown The productivity of Soviet labor is significantly lower than in most other industrialized nations. Soviet workers are only about two-fifths as productive as American workers, three-fifths as productive as Japanese workers, and approximately half as productive as West German and Italian workers.[10] More pertinent to the present discussion is the fact that, as in the western nations, Soviet productivity growth has been falling. Soviet labor productivity, which increased by 3.2 percent per year in the 1966–1970 period, declined to 2.0 percent per year in 1971–1975 and then to about 1.2 percent in 1976–1982.[11] Let us comment upon a few of the factors which have contributed to the productivity slowdown.

NATURAL RESOURCE DEPLETION While the Soviet Union has a generous resource base, it is also true that it is having to resort to increasingly inferior and less accessible natural resources. In particular, ores, petroleum, electric power, and timber are all becoming increasingly costly because reserves in the industrialized western Soviet Union are being depleted, and it is very costly to extract and transport such resources from Siberia and other remote areas.

LACK OF INNOVATION It is well known that Soviet central planning and its incentive system are not conducive to innovation and technological advance.

The bureaucratic immobility of the Soviet decision-making mechanism smothers a great deal of the volatility present in a normal market economy. Established procedures regularly grind out standard forms of output, while conventional methods enlarge capital stocks embodying orthodox technology. This stability has, of course, its advantages, but it also means that unfavorable conditions and unsatisfactory performance

---

[8] Ann Goodman and Goeffrey Schleifer, "The Soviet Labor Market in the 1980s," in Joint Economic Committee, *Soviet Economy in the 1980s: Problems and Prospects, Part 2* (Washington, D.C., 1982), pp. 326–327. See also David E. Powell, "The Soviet Labor Force," *Current History,* October 1984, pp. 327–330, 342–344.

[9] Carl W. Ek, "Overview," in Joint Economic Committee, *Gorbachev's Economic Plans,* vol. 2 (Washington, D.C., 1987), p. 3.

[10] Gertrude E. Schroeder, "The Soviet Economy," *Current History,* October 1985, p. 312.

[11] Stanley H. Cohn, "Soviet Intensive Economic Development Strategy in Perspective," in Joint Economic Committee, *Gorbachev's Economic Plans,* vol. 1 (Washington, D.C., 1987), p. 15.

are hard to remedy. Where new procedures are required in order to produce new forms of output involving altered capital stocks embodying unfamiliar technology, the Soviet system responds poorly. The rewards and penalties that motivate Soviet managers and workers serve admirably to replicate and enlarge the existing economy. These same rewards and penalties act negatively, however, with the effect of protecting the system against changes—even if the needed changes are improvements.[12]

Because enterprise bonuses are tied to the fulfillment of monthly and annual production targets, managements are reluctant to jeopardize plan fulfillment by trying new production techniques. The penalties for failure are considerable, while the rewards for success are small. Furthermore, because markets are guaranteed and competitors are absent, the inducements to innovate are weak. Thus Soviet technology lags well behind western technology and the gap has *not* narrowed in the past fifteen or twenty years.[13]

WORKER DISCIPLINE There is persistent evidence in the Soviet press that the Soviet work force lacks discipline. Drunkenness, poor work habits, absenteeism, and a high rate of turnover are common. This lack of discipline may be due in part to weak material incentives. As noted earlier, the fact that consumer goods are of poor quality and available in limited quantities makes it difficult for Soviet workers to translate increases in *nominal* incomes into proportionate increases in *real* incomes. As a Soviet worker once remarked to a western journalist: "The government pretends to pay us and we pretend to work."

OBSOLETE PLANNING MECHANISM? A final and more general consideration which may be contributing to the slowing of Soviet growth is the planning mechanism itself. Early planning under Stalin was not unlike the wartime planning of western nations: A limited number of key production goals

were established, and resources were centrally directed toward the fulfillment of these goals regardless of costs or consumer welfare. But the past success of such "campaign planning" has resulted in a complex, industrially advanced economy. The planning techniques which were more-or-less adequate for the Stalinist era of the 1930s and 1940s are much less efficient in the more sophisticated economy of the 1980s and 1990s. To state the situation quite simply, the Soviet economy has tended to outgrow its planning mechanisms. This fact has posed serious questions concerning the efficiency of the system and its capacity to sustain its growth rate.

CONSUMPTION AND LIVING STANDARDS

The assertion that Soviet consumers have fared badly is no surprise. A full-employment economy which devotes relatively large proportions of its GNP to investment and to the military will necessarily have a relatively small share for consumers (Figure 42-1). Simply put, the costs of past rapid industrialization and growth have been borne largely by consumers. Overall real per capita consumption in the Soviet Union is only about *one-third* of that in the United States.

The Soviet lag is massive (less than 20 percent of the US level) in consumer durables and household services. In terms of housing services, for example, the Soviet level is only one-seventh of that in the United States. In contrast, the Soviets exceed the United States in per capita consumption of alcoholic beverages (especially hard liquor) and in provision of public transportation. Education and health services, which the USSR supplies mainly without direct charge, are at about half the US level, with a considerably better showing in education (77 percent) than in health (33 percent).[14]

Unfavorable as they are, these comparisons are probably biased in favor of the Soviet Union. The reasons are that Soviet consumer goods are of "notoriously poor quality and narrow assortment." Shortages, queues, black markets, and corruption

[12] Holland Hunter, M. Mark Earle, Jr., and Richard B. Foster, "Assessment of Alternative Long-Range Soviet Growth Strategies," in Joint Economic Committee, *Soviet Economic Prospects for the Seventies,* (Washington, D.C., 1973), p. 212.

[13] Schroeder, op. cit., p. 312.

[14] Joint Economic Committee, *Consumption in the USSR: An International Comparison* (Washington: Government Printing Office, 1981), pp. v–vii.

in the distribution of consumer goods are all characteristic of the Soviet consumer sector.[15] As far as the consumer is concerned, the Soviet Union is far from a society of abundance. While the Communist Party boasted some twenty years ago that the Soviet people would have "the highest living standard in the world by 1980," the actual course of events has been quite different!

The low Soviet standard of living is only partly the consequence of planning priorities. It also reflects microeconomic inefficiencies associated with Soviet central planning. On the one hand, lacking a genuine market system to communicate the wants of consumers and producers, central planners have frequently directed enterprises to produce consumer goods for which there is little or no demand. The result is unwanted inventories of unsalable goods. On the other hand, the major "success indicator" for Soviet enterprise managers has been the quantity of output; the enterprise's main goal is to fulfill or overfulfill its assigned production target. Product quality and variety are secondary considerations at best. Indeed, planners have found it very difficult to state a quantitative production target without unintentionally eliciting ridiculous "distortions" in output. Example: If an enterprise manufacturing nails has its production target stated in terms of weight (tons of nails), it will tend to produce all large nails. But if its target is a numerical one (thousands of nails), it will be motivated to produce all small nails! The problem for consumers is that they want *both* large and small nails. The Soviet press persistently denounces the poor quality of both consumer goods and many producer goods.

Gorbachev's economic program[16]

The Soviet economy of the 1980s is fraught with problems. As noted, the economy's growth record has deteriorated significantly in the past two dec-

ades. The economy's industrial base has become relatively antiquated. The technological gap between the Soviet Union and the western industrial nations has been widening. For example, in such vital manufacturing sectors as computers and machine tools it is estimated that Soviet technology lags some seven to twelve years behind the United States. Furthermore, the quality of most Soviet manufactured goods simply does not meet world standards. Finally, the Soviet government has had an implicit "social contract" with its citizenry to the effect that, by enduring the sacrifices associated with the high rates of saving and investment prerequisite to industrialization and growth, the population would be rewarded with economic abundance in the future. This promised consumer cornucopia has simply not been realized.

Since coming to power in 1985 Mikhail Gorbachev has moved aggressively to meet this array of problems by attempting to revitalize the Soviet economy. It should be stressed at the outset that a number of the Gorbachev proposals go back to reform efforts of the 1950s and 1960s. What distinguishes **Gorbachev's economic program** is its comprehensiveness and the vigor with which it is being pursued. In Gorbachev's words, his program calls for "radical reform" and a profound "restructuring" *(perestroika)* of the economy. This hoped-for restructuring is to be accompanied by a campaign for greater "openness" *(glasnost)* which will presumably provide greater opportunity for workers, consumers, enterprise managers, political leaders, and others to voice complaints and make suggestions for improving the functioning of the economy.

At the risk of oversimplification, the Gorbachev strategy embodies six interrelated elements: (1) the modernization of industry; (2) greater decentralization of decision making; (3) modest expansion of the private sector; (4) improved worker discipline and incentives; (5) a more rational price system; and (6) an enlarged role in the international economy.

---

[15] For an intriguing account of corruption in the Soviet economy, see Hedrick Smith, *The Russians* (New York: Quadrangle/The New York Times Book Co., 1976), chap. 3.

[16] This section draws largely upon Joint Economic Committee, *Gorbachev's Economic Plans*, vols. 1 and 2 (Washington, D.C., 1987). The interested reader may want to consult Mikhail Gorbachev, *Perestroika: New Thinking for Our Country and the World* (New York: Harper & Row, Publishers, 1987).

MODERNIZATION: THE RESTRUCTURING OF INVESTMENT

The Gorbachev program stresses the increasing of investment relative to consumption *and,* more importantly, the reallocation of investment toward research and development and toward high technology industries. A strong effort is being made to modernize the Soviet Union's rather antiquated capital stock through heavy investment in the machine-building industry. It is intended that up to one-third of the nation's plant and equipment will be replaced by the early 1990s. Emphasis is to be placed upon the updating of productive facilities through the renovation of existing plants, rather than the construction of new factory buildings. As noted earlier, the Soviet system has been resistant to innovation and technological progress; the Gorbachev program specifically recognizes that problem and seeks to overcome it. The goal is computer-driven machines and automated assembly lines comparable to those of the western industrialized nations.

DECENTRALIZATION AND SELF-FINANCING

The Gorbachev reforms also seek to improve the planning mechanism by decentralizing decision making and increasing the autonomy of individual enterprises. More specifically, Gosplan will now shift its attention from current day-to-day problems and issues to long-run planning and major allocational issues. In particular, Gorbachev wants to keep the planning hierarchy from interfering with the detailed internal activities and decisions of individual enterprises.

The other side of the coin is that enterprise managers will have greater autonomy and responsibility in decision making. More importantly, the primary incentive for enterprises will now be profitability rather than the fulfillment of an assigned quantitative output target. While some portion of an enterprise's output must be sold to the state, the remaining output can be sold to buyers at contracted prices. The proceeds from such sales will be used by the enterprise to "self-finance" its production costs and its own investment. Perhaps the basic point is that the introduction of "profitability" as a success or performance indicator means

that greater attention must be paid to the salability and therefore the quality of products. In this regard it is relevant to note that an ambitious new quality control program has been instigated at some 1500 key enterprises which account for about 15 percent of all industrial production. Independent inspectors have the authority to reject qualitatively inferior units of output, and such units will not be counted in determining an enterprise's production performance. This chapter's Last Word provides some insight as to the adjustments workers and managers are making in order to achieve self-financing.

State control over enterprises will also entail a substitution of "normatives" for "directives," which also will enhance enterprise independence.

. . . when a ministry controls wage expenditures by a directive, it says to the enterprise: given your output plan, you may spend 1 million rubles on wages. When it controls wages by a normative, it says you may spend 20 rubles on wages for every 100 rubles of output. Direct control is more centralized; if the enterprise intends to overfulfill its output plan, it must first apply for authorization to overspend its wage limit. Under normative control it can spend however much it needs to, without requiring authorization, as long as it stays within its normative of 20 rubles per 100 rubles of output. Thus control by normatives does transfer a certain degree of authority from ministry to enterprise.[17]

ENLARGED PRIVATE SECTOR

The Gorbachev proposals also encourage a *limited* expansion of private enterprise with respect to consumer goods and services. Private production activities—such as the production of clothing, furniture, and rugs, and the provision of services such as taxi transport, hairdressing, appliance repair, and small-scale construction—are to be encouraged. However, there are important constraints upon such activities. Full-time participation in such work is restricted to those who would not typically hold public-sector (state enterprise) jobs, such as housewives or pensioners. However, those holding full-time state jobs may engage in private activities in their free time. Permits are required for private

[17] Joseph S. Berliner, "Organizational Restructuring of the Soviet Economy," in *Gorbachev's Economic Plans,* p. 77.

economic activities; financial records must be kept; and income taxes must be paid. In agriculture it is proposed that collective farmland be leased to small groups and families who will be able to decide what to plant and retain most of the profits they realize from their output. The intent is to increase productivity in a sector of the economy which has been notoriously inefficient. Middleman activities—wholesaling and retailing activities where a product is bought at one price and sold at a higher price—are prohibited. Furthermore, the hiring of someone else's labor is forbidden in keeping with Marxism-Leninism. This latter restriction virtually guarantees that the private sector will largely be limited to very small-scale family enterprises. The use of cooperatives circumvents the prohibition on hiring workers and therefore their importance may increase.

The government's hope is that the modest expansion of private economic activity will help alleviate persistent shortages of consumer goods and services. More generally, the encouragement of private production has the advantage of making legal many of the previously noted "second economy" activities which have helped to make the Soviet system workable.

DISCIPLINE AND INCENTIVES

Gorbachev's proposed reforms are also directed at improving the "human factors" in the production process. In general, a number of actions have been taken to dismiss incompetent planning officials and enterprise managers, to trim the size of the planning bureaucracies, and to improve worker attitudes and behavior. Campaigns against corruption and alcoholism are intended to reduce inefficiency resulting from theft, absenteeism, industrial accidents, and high rates of labor turnover.

The salaries and bonuses of scientific workers and engineers are to be increased to encourage the creation and use of new technologies. The overall wage-bonus system of pay is to be more closely tied to worker productivity and firm profitability. The previously noted shift from "directives" to "normatives" is important with respect to incentives. Under the "directives" system the overfulfillment of a production plan by an enterprise would often prompt the central planners to "ratchet up" the

LAST WORD

Self-financing in a Soviet tractor factory

Soviet economic reforms are imposing substantial changes on both workers and managers.

It's the morning shift at the A.A. Zhdanov Vladimir Tractor Works, and workers are hustling around the dreary plant. Fenders dangle from hooks on 1940s-vintage assembly lines. From a poster on the wall, Lenin looks down, proclaiming the "inevitable victory of communism." As deputy manager Josef A. Bakaleynek tours the line, a worker shares her view of *perestroika:* "Dengee, dengee, dengee," she says. "Money, money, money."

That's just what Bakaleynek wants to hear. It means that incentives introduced in the past two years are encouraging Zhdanov's employees—or at least some of them—to push harder and produce more. That's important because Zhdanov, located 130 miles east of Moscow in Vladimir, faces a crucial test on January 1, when it and many of the Soviet Union's 48,000 enterprises become "self-financing."

For the first time, Zhdanov will have to cover all of its costs and earn enough to finance investments, after turning over half its profits to the Soviet Tractor & Agricultural Machinery Ministry. To ease the adjustment, the state will continue to buy about 70% of its output for the next three years. **Crash Course** Not every Soviet manager or

production target. But under the new program normatives are to be stable for a specified period of time—for example, the duration of a given five-year plan—so that workers and managers can in-worker approves of this new market-oriented thinking. Many do not yet understand it. But reluctant or not, all of Soviet industry is gearing up. Government officials and top managers are taking crash courses at Moscow think tanks on Mikhail S. Gorbachev's new economic mechanism.

At the Zhdanov plant, the entire work force of 16,000 is immersed in a 52-hour classroom course. Posters on self-financing, complete with flow charts, festoon the plant. Workers are coming to understand the ideas of *perestroika,* says Bakaleynek, "but it is very hard to put it in life."

Indeed, the Zhdanov plant has seen both the pluses and minuses of *perestroika.* Workers say they like the brigade system, which allows them to group in teams of about 10 that earn bonuses for good performance. The typical worker makes 210 rubles, or $336, a month, but that jumps up by 40% if the team exceeds its quota and makes high-quality tractors.

However, some brigades have run into trouble with *gospriemka,* or quality control, a key part of Gorbachev's program. When state inspectors arrived earlier this year, they rejected 15% to 20% of Zhdanov's tractors. As a result, the plant won't meet its 1987 production quota, and both managers and workers face smaller bonuses. It's a widespread problem: The crackdown is expected to trim nearly a percentage point from the 4.4% growth projected for Soviet industrial output this year.

To improve the quality and competitiveness of its tractors, Zhdanov is undertaking a five-year, $387 million renovation of its 43-year-old plant. It also plans to install as many as 100 computer workstations. These will give managers instant access to production schedules, deliveries, and data to make more customized tractors. If the Soviets can persuade the West to ease export controls, says Bakaleynek, Zhdanov will buy International Business Machines Corp. personal computers.

Until now, the Tractor Ministry has bought the plant's yearly output of 36,500, 30-horsepower tractors and distributed them domestically and in 52 foreign markets—including the U.S., where they sell for about $5,000. But by 1992, says Bakaleynek, the state is likely to buy just 25% of sales. Through its new foreign trade firm, Vladimiretz, the factory will aim to export half its output. The remaining 25% will go directly to Soviet enterprises and individuals, Bakaleynek says.

At Odds   Preparing to become self-financing has sparked divisions between old-style managers and a new breed of institute-educated executives. At Zhdanov, Bakaleynek and factory director Anatoli V. Grishin often disagree. With a doctorate in economics, Bakaleynek, 35, talks of letting sales—not production quotas—determine success. Grishin sticks to socialist principles. He spent 33 of his 56 years working his way to the top.

While Bakaleynek sees bonuses as an effective incentive, Grishin considers them a capitalist intrusion. Says Grishin: "Some workers think their job is [only to earn] wages and bonuses," rather than to strive for the good of all. He predicts that freeing up wholesale trade will create "economic chaos." Bakaleynek retorts that it will weed out inefficient enterprises.

The pressure to cut costs, find customers, and seek the best sources of supplies will place the Zhdanov factory—and the rest of Soviet industry—in a new and trying position. Many Soviets predict confusion as industry and the bureaucracy struggle to adapt to self-financing. But after 50 years of Stalinist central planning, the economy needs such a jolt to begin to change.

Source: "A Tractor Factory Tries to Pull Its Own Weight," *Business Week,* Dec. 7, 1987, p. 79. Reprinted from December 7, 1987 issue of *Business Week* by special permission, copyright © 1987 by McGraw-Hill, Inc.

crease their incomes significantly by overfulfilling their plans. Hence, in effect there will be no limit on a worker's earnings; a worker who doubles his production will double his earnings.

MORE RATIONAL PRICING

It is clearly recognized in the Gorbachev proposals that efficient production requires that prices reflect the relative scarcities of both inputs and outputs. For example, the underpricing of energy partly explains why the Soviet Union—which is the world's largest producer of energy—uses two to three times as much energy per unit of output as the leading industrial countries. Hence, the proposals call for a comprehensive reform of the price system so that prices will more accurately reflect supply and demand. The number of prices fixed by the central planners is to be reduced sharply over time and ultimately such prices will apply only to the most essential producer and consumer goods. More specifically, it is intended that by the early 1990s there will be a shift toward market pricing at the wholesale level. Producing and purchasing enterprises will presumably negotiate sales contracts in the same general fashion as might capitalistic firms.

WORLD ECONOMY INITIATIVES

The Soviet Union has undertaken a rather broad campaign in recent years to increase its role in world economic affairs. This initiative entails the exploration of a closer relationship with the European Common Market and other western industrial nations *and* some modest interest in international economic institutions such as the General Agreement on Tariffs and Trade, the World Bank, and the International Monetary Fund. Association with such institutions could be expected to enhance Soviet world trade opportunities, especially through tariff reductions.

A second major effort has been to encourage joint ventures in the Soviet Union with western firms in a wide range of activities ranging from fast-food restaurants to the construction and operation of petrochemical plants. It may be surmised that such ventures are viewed by the Soviets as a relatively inexpensive means of acquiring western technologies and management skills.

Whether the Soviet Union's role in the world economy will increase in the future is problematic. In this regard it should be noted that declines in oil and gold prices which began in the early 1980s have caused significant declines in Soviet earnings of foreign exchange and thereby restricted the U.S.S.R.'s ability to purchase goods and services from the industrialized capitalistic nations. An

expanded role for the Soviet Union in the world economy may depend in good measure upon the overall success of the Gorbachev program in revitalizing the domestic economy itself.

OBSTACLES AND RESISTANCE

It is to be emphasized that much of the Gorbachev program has not as yet been implemented; it is a set of goals or options and the intention is to have some significant portion of the program embodied in the 1991–1995 Five-year Plan. Given that previous reforms which contained elements of the Gorbachev program have failed, it is relevant to note some of the major obstacles which face the current reforms.

First, the proposals threaten the jobs and status of many party members and bureaucrats. These individuals now have positions of power and prestige and therefore have a strong interest in maintaining the status quo.

Second, the program is asking workers and managers to be more disciplined and to work harder and more productively. Such admonitions are difficult to accept in an economy which historically has served consumer-workers poorly. Money wage increases do not provide incentives without corresponding improvements in the quantity and quality of housing, food, and other consumer goods and services. Recall that the program's stress on investment to modernize industry suggests that at least in the short run the production of consumer goods will continue to be assigned a low priority.

Third, the capitalistic orientation of the reforms may engender resistance and suspicion. The reforms may generate the specter of unemployment, inflation, and greater inequality in the distribution of income, all of which conflict with what Soviet citizens and leaders consider to be among the major advantages of socialism. Similarly, the Soviet Union's last experience with a market system occurred in the 1920s. Hence, any significant rationalization of prices will entail a significant and perhaps difficult learning process for Soviet workers, managers, and planners. And the move to scarcity prices will necessitate the phasing out of a vast array of government subsidies which at least in the short run will be unwelcome to Soviet consumer-workers.

Finally, there is the possibility that a restructuring of the economy will pose a threat to the existing political system. It is difficult to separate economic and political freedom. There are obvious problems in telling workers and enterprise managers to think more freely and innovatively about the production of computers or machine-tools, but not to think openly about political issues. Gorbachev has encouraged openness *(glasnost)* in debating economic issues; the problem for the Soviet leadership is to prevent an unwanted application of *glasnost* to political issues. In fact, under *glasnost* the Baltic republics are currently pressing for greater autonomy from the Kremlin.

The extent to which the Gorbachev proposals will be instituted and their relative success is unclear at this point. While there may be broad agreement among the Soviet leadership as to the need for change, there is less consensus as to the character and extent of reform. The forces of conservatism are strong in the Soviet Union, but change is clearly on the agenda.

CHAPTER SUMMARY

1 The vivid contrast which the Soviet economy provides to American capitalism, the economic challenge it presents to the western world, and the rapid economic growth achieved historically in the Soviet Union are important reasons for studying the Soviet economic system.

2 Virtually complete state ownership of property resources and authoritarian central planning are the outstanding institutional features of the Soviet economy. The major goals of the Five-year Plans, as determined by the government, have been rapid industrialization, growth, and military strength.

3 The basic problem of central planners is to achieve coordination or internal consistency in their plans so as to avoid bottlenecks and the chain reaction of production failures which they cause. The use of "material balances," evaluation of preliminary plans by the administrative hierarchy, the assignment of priorities to planned goals, reserve stocks, and the existence of the "second economy" all help to prevent or alleviate coordination problems in the U.S.S.R.

4 Many agencies check upon the actual execution of the Five-year Plans—the planning hierarchy, the Communist Party and its numerous officials, and the secret police. The most important of these agencies is the Gosbank, which exerts "control by the ruble."

5 In the production process, governmentally determined prices on resources and components and on finished products serve as accounting devices to evaluate the efficiency of production. In consumer goods markets, prices are adjusted through the turnover tax to ration products to consumers, that is, to balance the amounts demanded with available supplies.

6 A generous natural resource base, great emphasis upon capital formation, the transfer of surplus agricultural labor to industry, and the planning away of cyclical unemployment are factors which contributed to high historical growth rates in the Soviet Union.

7 A number of factors have brought about the recent decline in the Soviet growth rate: the burden of a large military establishment, a growing shortage of labor, the stagnation of agriculture, and declining productivity growth.

8 The Soviet Union's emphasis upon investment and military strength has resulted in relatively low living standards. Soviet per capita consumption is only about one-third that of the United States.

9 The Gorbachev program to revitalize the Soviet economy entails: *a* the modernization of productive facilities; *b* greater autonomy at the enterprise level; *c* some expansion of private economic activity; *d* efforts to improve worker discipline and productivity; *e* a shift from state- to market-determined prices; and *f* a more prominent role in the world economy.

TERMS AND CONCEPTS

labor theory of value	material balances
surplus value	priority principle
state ownership	"second economy"
central economic planning	Gosbank
Five-year Plan	control by the ruble
Gosplan	turnover tax
One-year Plan	Gorbachev's economic program

QUESTIONS AND STUDY SUGGESTIONS

1 Compare the institutional framework of the Soviet economy with that of American capitalism. Contrast the manner in which production is motivated in these two economic systems.

2 "So long as a central planning board, as opposed to society as a whole, sets the economic goals, there can be no freedom of occupational or consumer choice." Do you agree? Explain.

3 Compare the sources of insecurity which face an American and a Soviet steelworker. What incentives do each have to be productive workers?

4 "It has become increasingly difficult for thoughtful men to find meaningful alternatives posed in the traditional choices between socialism and capitalism, planning and the free market, regulation and laissez faire, for they find their actual choices neither simple nor so grand." [18] Explain and evaluate.

5 How does Soviet planning attempt to cope with the Five Fundamental Questions which all economies must face? Discuss the problem of coordination. What mechanisms do Soviet planners use to avoid and correct problems of coordination? Explain: "Soviet planning problems mainly arise from the fact that the command economy is rooted in the logic of haste."

[18] Robert A. Dahl and Charles E. Lindblom, *Politics, Economics and Welfare* (New York: Harper & Row, Publishers, Incorporated, 1953), p. 1.

6 "The very nature of Soviet planning precludes the efficient allocation of scarce resources." Do you agree? Explain.

7 Carefully contrast the role of the market system in the Soviet Union and the United States, distinguishing between resource and product markets. Explain the use of turnover taxes. How is the number of automobiles to be produced determined in American capitalism? In the Soviet Union? How are these decisions implemented in the two economies?

8 Compare the size, composition, and rate of growth of the GNPs of the United States and the Soviet Union. What have been the major sources of Soviet economic growth? Why did Soviet growth diminish in the 1970s and 1980s?

9 Assume you are the chief central planner in a socialist nation. Assuming profits are unacceptable on ideological grounds, what success indicators would you impose to judge the performance of enterprises? Would these indicators ensure efficient resource use? Explain.

10 What are the major elements of Gorbachev's reform program? What obstacles might impede the achievement of each goal? Are the elements of the program consistent with each other or are they in conflict? It has been said that the Soviet economy is destined by its own ideology to be inefficient. Do you agree?

Glossary

Ability-to-pay principle The belief that those who have the greater income (or wealth) should be taxed absolutely and relatively more than those who have less.

Abstraction Elimination of irrelevant and noneconomic facts to obtain an economic principle.

Acreage-allotment program The program which determines the total number of acres that are to be used to produce various agricultural products and allocates these acres among individual farmers who are required to limit their plantings to the number of acres allotted to them if they wished to obtain the Support price for their crops.

Actual budget The amount spent by the Federal government (to purchase goods and services and for transfer payments) less the amount of tax revenue collected by it in any (fiscal) year; and which can *not* reliably be used to determine whether it is pursuing an expansionary or contractionary fiscal policy. Compare *(see)* the Full-employment budget.

Actual deficit The size of the Federal government's Budget deficit *(see)* or surplus actually measured or recorded in any given year.

Actual investment The amount which business Firms do invest; equal to Planned investment plus Unplanned investment.

Actual reserves The amount of funds which a Member bank has on deposit at the Federal Reserve bank of its district (plus its Vault cash).

Adaptive expectations theory The idea that people determine their expectations about future events (for example, inflation) on the basis of past and present events (rates of inflation) and only change their expectations as events unfold.

Adjustable pegs The device utilized in the Bretton Woods system *(see)* to change Exchange rates in an orderly way to eliminate persistent Payments deficits and surpluses: each nation defined its monetary unit in terms of (pegged it to) gold or the dollar, kept the Rate of exchange for its money stable in the short run, and changed (adjusted) it in the long run when faced with international disequilibrium.

AFDC *(See* Aid to families with dependent children.)

Aggregate demand A schedule or curve which shows the total quantity of goods and services that will be demanded (purchased) at different price levels.

Aggregate demand–aggregate supply model The macroeconomic model which uses Aggregate demand and Aggregate supply *(see* both) to determine and explain the Price level and the real National output.

Aggregate expenditures The total amount spent for final goods and services in the economy.

Aggregate expenditures–national output approach Determination of the Equilibrium net national product *(see)* by finding the real NNP at which Aggregate expenditures are equal to the National output.

Aggregate expenditures schedule A schedule or curve which shows the total amount spent for final goods and services at different levels of real NNP.

Aggregate supply A schedule or curve which shows the total quantity of goods and services that will be supplied (produced) at different price levels.

Aggregation Combining individual units or data into one unit or number. For example, all prices of individual goods and services are combined into a Price level, or all units of output are aggregated into Real net national product.

Agricultural Adjustment Act The Federal act of 1933 which established the Parity concept *(see)* as the cornerstone of American agricultural policy and provided Price supports for farm products, restriction of agricultural production, and the disposal of surplus output.

Aid to families with dependent children A state-administered and partly Federally funded program in the United States which provides aid to families in which dependent children do not have the support of a parent because of his or her death, disability, or desertion.

Alcoa case The case decided by the Federal courts in 1945 in which the courts ruled that the possession of monopoly power, no matter how reasonably that power had been used, was a violation of the antitrust laws; and which overturned the Rule of reason *(see)* applied in the U.S. Steel case *(see)*.

Allocative efficiency The apportionment of resources among firms and industries to obtain the production of the products most wanted by society (consumers); the output of each product at which its Marginal cost and Price are equal.

Allocative factor The ability of an economy to reallocate resources to achieve the Economic growth which the Supply factors *(see)* make possible.

American Federation of Labor The organization of affiliated Craft unions formed in 1886.

Annually balanced budget The equality of government expenditures and tax collections during a year.

Anticipated inflation Inflation *(see)* at a rate which was equal to the rate expected in that period of time.

Anticompetitive view of advertising Position that advertising persuades consumers that Product differentiation *(see)* is extensive, which in turn increases the market power of advertisers; views advertising as a Barrier to entry *(see)*.

Applied economics *(See* Policy economics.)

Appreciation of the dollar An increase in the value of the dollar relative to the currency of another nation; a dollar now buys a larger amount of the foreign currency. For example, if the dollar price of a British pound changes from $3 to $2, the dollar has appreciated.

Asset Anything with a monetary value owned by a firm or individual.

Asset demand for money The amount of money people want to hold as a Store of value (the amount of their financial assets they wish to have in the form of Money); and which varies inversely with the Rate of interest.

ATS account Automatic transfer services account *(see)*.

Authoritarian capitalism An economic system (method of organization) in which property resources are privately owned and government extensively directs and controls the economy.

Authoritarian socialism *(See* Command economy.)

Automatic transfer services account The combination of a Checking account and an interest-bearing Savings account at a Commercial bank that automatically transfers funds from the latter to the former account when checks are written against it.

Average fixed costs The total Fixed cost *(see)* of a Firm divided by its output (the quantity of product produced).

Average product The total output produced per unit of a resource employed (total product divided by the quantity of a resource employed).

Average propensity to consume Fraction of Disposable income which households spend for consumer goods and services; consumption divided by Disposable income.

Average propensity to save Fraction of Disposable income which households save; Saving divided by Disposable income.

Average revenue Total revenue from the sale of a product divided by the quantity of the product sold (demanded); equal to the price at which the product is sold so long as all units of the product are sold at the same price.

Average tax rate Total tax paid divided by total (taxable) income; the tax rate on total (taxable) income.

Average (total) cost The Total cost of a Firm divided by its output (the quantity of product produced); equal to Average fixed cost *(see)* plus Average variable cost *(see)*.

Average variable cost The total Variable cost *(see)* of a Firm divided by its output (the quantity of product produced).

Backflows The return of workers to the countries from which they originally migrated.

Balanced budget multiplier The effect of equal increases (decreases) in government spending for goods and services and in taxes is to increase (decrease) the Equilibrium net national product by the amount of the equal increases (decreases).

Balance of payments deficit The sum of the Balance on current account *(see)* and the Balance on the capital account *(see)* is negative.

Balance of payments surplus The sum of the Balance on current account *(see)* and the Balance on the capital account *(see)* is positive.

Balance on current account The exports of goods (merchandise) and services of a nation less its imports of goods (merchandise) and services plus its Net investment income and Net transfers.

Balance on goods and services The exports of goods (merchandise) and services of a nation less its imports of goods (merchandise) and services.

Balance on the capital account The Capital inflows *(see)* of a nation less its Capital outflows *(see)*.

Balance sheet A statement of the Assets *(see)*, Liabilities *(see)*, and Net worth *(see)* of a firm or individual at some given time.

Balanced-budget amendment Proposed constitutional amendment which would require Congress to balance the Federal budget annually.

Bankers' bank A bank which accepts the deposits of and makes loans to Depository institutions; a Federal Reserve Bank.

Barrier to entry Anything that artificially prevents the entry of Firms into an industry.

Barter The exchange of one good or service for another good or service.

Base year The year with which prices in other years are compared when a Price index *(see)* is constructed.

Benefit-cost analysis Deciding whether to employ resources and the quantity of resources to employ for a project or program (for the production of a good or service) by comparing the benefit with the cost.

Benefit-loss rate The percentage by which subsidy benefits in a Negative income tax plan *(see)* are reduced as earned income rises.

Benefits-received principle The belief that those who receive the benefits of goods and services provided by government should pay the taxes required to finance them.

Big business A business Firm which either produces a large percentage of the total output of an industry, is large (in terms of number of employees or stockholders, sales, assets, or profits) compared with other Firms in the economy, or both.

Bilateral monopoly A market in which there is a single seller (Monopoly) and a single buyer (Monopsony).

Black capitalism The creation of new business Firms owned and operated by blacks.

Blacklisting The passing from one employer to another of the names of workers who favor the formation of labor unions and who ought not to be hired.

Board of Governors The seven-member group that supervises and controls the money and banking system of the United States; formally, the Board of Governors of the Federal Reserve System; the Federal Reserve Board.

Brain drain The emigration of highly educated, highly skilled workers from a country.

Break-even income The level of Disposable income at which Households plan to consume (spend) all of their income (for consumer goods and services) and to save none of it; also denotes that level of earned income at which subsidy payments become zero in an income maintenance program.

Break-even point Any output which a (competitive) Firm might produce at which its Total cost and Total revenue would be equal; an output at which it has neither an Economic profit nor a loss.

Bretton Woods system The international monetary system developed after World War II in which Adjustable pegs *(see)* were employed, the International Monetary Fund *(see)* helped to stabilize Foreign exchange rates, and gold and the dollar *(see)* were used as International monetary reserves *(see)*.

Budget deficit The amount by which the expenditures of the Federal government exceed its revenues in any year.

Budget line A line which shows the different combinations of two products a consumer can purchase with a given money income.

Budget restraint The limit the size of the consumer's income (and the prices that must be paid for the goods and services) imposes upon the ability of an individual consumer to obtain goods and services.

Built-in stability The effect of Nondiscretionary fiscal policy *(see)* upon the economy; when Net taxes vary directly with the Net national product, the fall (rise) in Net taxes during a recession (inflation) helps to eliminate unemployment (inflationary pressures).

Business cycle Recurrent ups and downs over a period of years in the level of economic activity.

Business monopoly A market situation in which a single firm or small number of firms dominate the output of an industry.

Business unionism The belief that the labor union should concern itself with such practical and short-run objectives as higher wages, shorter hours, and improved working conditions and should not concern itself with long-run and idealistic changes in the capitalistic system.

Capital Human-made resources used to produce goods and services; goods which do not directly satisfy human wants; capital goods.

Capital account The section in a nation's International balance of payments *(see)* in which are recorded the Capital inflows *(see)* and the Capital outflows *(see)* of that nation.

Capital account deficit A negative Balance on the capital account *(see)*.

Capital account surplus A positive Balance on the capital account *(see)*.

Capital consumption allowances Estimate of the amount of Capital worn out or used up (consumed) in producing the Gross national product; depreciation.

Capital flight The transfer of savings from less developed to industrially advanced countries to avoid government expropriation, taxation, and high rates of inflation or to realize better investment opportunities.

Capital gain The gain realized when securities or properties are sold for a price greater than the price paid for them.

Capital goods *(See* Capital.)

Capital inflow The expenditures made by the residents of foreign nations to purchase real and financial capital from the residents of a nation.

Capital-intensive commodity A product which requires a relatively large amount of Capital to produce.

Capital outflow The expenditures made by the residents of a nation to purchase real and financial capital from the residents of foreign nations.

Capital-saving technological advance An improvement in technology that permits a greater quantity of a product to be produced with a given amount of Capital (or the same amount of the product to be produced with a smaller amount of Capital).

Capital-using technological advance An improvement in technology that requires the use of a greater amount of Capital to produce a given quantity of a product.

Cartel A formal written or oral agreement among Firms to set the price of the product and the outputs of the individual firms or to divide the market for the product geographically.

Causation A cause-and-effect relationship; one or several events bring about or result in another event.

CEA (*See* Council of Economic Advisers.)

Cease-and-desist order An order from a court or government agency (commission or board) to a corporation or individual to stop engaging in a specified practice.

Ceiling price (*See* Price ceiling.)

Celler-Kefauver Act The Federal act of 1950 which amended the Clayton Act *(see)* by prohibiting the acquisition of the assets of one firm by another firm when the effect would be to lessen competition.

Central bank A bank whose chief function is the control of the nation's money supply.

Central economic planning Government determination of the objectives of the economy and the direction of its resources to the attainment of these objectives.

Ceteris paribus assumption (*See* "other things being equal" assumption.)

Change in amount consumed Increase or decrease in consumption spending that results from an increase or decrease in Disposable income, the Consumption schedule (curve) remaining unchanged; movement from one row (point) to another on the same Consumption schedule (curve).

Change in amount saved Increase or decrease in Saving that results from an increase or decrease in Disposable income, the Saving schedule (curve) remaining unchanged; movement from one row (point) to another on the same Saving schedule (curve).

Change in the consumption schedule An increase or decrease in consumption at each level of Disposable income caused by changes in the Nonincome determinants of consumption and saving *(see)*; an upward or downward movement of the Consumption schedule.

Change in the saving schedule An increase or decrease in Saving at each level of Disposable income caused by changes in the Nonincome determinants of consumption and saving *(see)*; an upward or downward movement of the Saving schedule.

Checkable deposit Any deposit in a commercial bank or Thrift institution against which a check may be written; includes Demand deposits and NOW, ATS, and Share draft accounts.

Checking account A Checkable deposit *(see)* in a Commercial bank or Thrift institution.

Circuit velocity of money (*See* Velocity of money.)

Circular flow of income The flow of resources from Households to Firms and of products from Firms to Households accompanied in an economy using money by flows of money from Households to Firms and from Firms to Households.

Classical range The vertical segment of the Aggregate supply curve along which the economy is at Full employment.

Classical theory The Classical theory of employment *(see)*.

Classical theory of employment The Macroeconomic generalizations which were accepted by most economists prior to the 1930s and which led to the conclusion that a capitalistic economy would tend to employ its resources fully.

Clayton Act The Federal antitrust act of 1914 which strengthened the Sherman Act *(see)* by making it illegal for business firms to engage in certain specified practices.

Closed economy An economy which neither exports nor imports goods and services.

Close-down case The circumstance in which a Firm would experience a loss greater than its total Fixed cost if it were to produce any output greater than zero; alternatively, a situation in which a firm would cease to operate when the price at which it can sell its product is less than its Average variable cost.

Closed shop A place of employment at which only workers who are already members of a labor union may be hired.

Coase theorem The idea that Externality problems may be resolved through private negotiations of the affected parties.

Coincidence of wants The item (good or service) which one trader wishes to obtain is the same item which another trader desires to give up and the item which the second trader wishes to acquire is the same item the first trader desires to surrender.

COLA (*See* Cost-of-living adjustment.)

Collection of checks The process by which funds are transferred from the checking accounts of the writers of checks to the checking accounts of the recipients of the checks; also called the "clearing" of checks.

Collective voice The function a union performs for its members as a group when it communicates their problems and grievances to management and presses management for a satisfactory resolution to them.

Collusion A situation in which Firms act together and in agreement (collude) to set the price of the product and the output each firm will produce or to determine the geographic area in which each firm will sell.

Command economy An economic system (method of organization) in which property resources are publicly owned and Central economic planning *(see)* is used to direct and coordinate economic activities.

Commercial bank Firm which has a charter from either a state government or the Federal government to engage in the business of banking.

Commercial banking system All Commercial banks and Thrift institutions as a group.

Communism (*See* Command economy.)

Company union An organization of employees which is dominated by the employer (the company) and does not engage in genuine collective bargaining with the employer.

Comparable worth doctrine The belief that women should receive the same salaries (wages) as men when the levels of skill, effort, and responsibility in their different jobs are the same.

Comparative advantage A lower relative or Comparative cost *(see)* than another producer.

Comparative cost The amount the production of one product must be reduced to increase the production of another product; Opportunity cost *(see)*.

Compensation to employees Wages and salaries paid by employers to workers plus Wage and salary supplements *(see)*.

Competing goods (*See* Substitute goods.)

Competition The presence in a market of a large number of independent buyers and sellers and the freedom of buyers and sellers to enter and to leave the market.

Competitive industry's short-run supply curve The horizontal summation of the short-run supply curves of the Firms in a purely competitive industry (*See* Pure competition); a curve which shows the total quantities that will be offered for sale at various prices by the Firms in an industry in the Short run *(see)*.

Competitive industry's short-run supply schedule The summation of the short-run supply schedules of the Firms in a purely competitive industry (*See* Pure competition); a schedule which shows the total quantities that will be offered for sale at various prices by the Firms in an industry in the Short run *(see)*.

Competitive labor market A market in which a large number of (noncolluding) firms demand a particular type of labor from a large number of nonunionized workers.

Complementary goods Goods or services for which there is an inverse relationship between the price of one and the demand for the other; when the price of one falls (rises) the demand for the other increases (decreases).

Complex multiplier The Multiplier *(see)* when changes in the Net national product change Net taxes and Imports, as well as Saving.

Concentration ratio The percentage of the total sales of an industry made by the four (or some other number) largest sellers (Firms) in the industry.

Conglomerate combination A group of Plants *(see)* owned by a single Firm and engaged at one or more stages in the production of different products (of products which do not compete with each other).

Conglomerate merger The merger of a Firm in one Industry with a Firm in another Industry (with a Firm that is neither supplier, customer, nor competitor).

Congress of Industrial Organizations The organization of affiliated Industrial unions formed in 1936.

Constant-cost industry An industry in which the expansion of the Industry by the entry of new Firms has no effect upon the prices the Firms in the industry pay for resources and no effect, therefore, upon their cost schedules (curves).

Consumer goods Goods and services which satisfy human wants directly.

Consumer sovereignty Determination by consumers of the types and quantities of goods and services that are produced from the scarce resources of the economy.

Consumption schedule Schedule which shows the amounts Households plan to spend for Consumer goods at different levels of Disposable income.

Contractionary fiscal policy A decrease in Aggregate demand brought about by a decrease in Government expenditures for goods and services, an increase in Net taxes, or some combination of the two.

"Control by the ruble" The requirement in the U.S.S.R. that each plant's receipts and expenditures be completed through the use of checks drawn on *Gosbank (see)* which enables *Gosbank* to record the performance and progress of each plant toward the fulfillment of the production targets assigned it by *Gosplan*.

Corporate income tax A tax levied on the net income (profit) of Corporations.

Corporation A legal entity ("person") chartered by a state or the Federal government, and distinct and separate from the individuals who own it.

Correlation Systematic and dependable association between two sets of data (two kinds of events).

Cost-of-living adjustment An increase in the incomes (wages) of workers which is automatically received by them when there is inflation in the economy and guaranteed by a clause in their labor contracts with their employer.

Cost-plus pricing A procedure used by (oligopolistic) Firms to determine the price they will charge for a product and in which a percentage markup is added to the estimated average cost of producing the product.

Cost-push inflation Inflation that results from a decrease in Aggregate supply (from higher wage rates and raw material prices) and which is accompanied by decreases in real output and employment (by increases in the Unemployment rate).

Cost ratio The ratio of the decrease in the production of one product to the increase in the production of another product when resources are shifted from the production of the first to the production of the second product; the amount the production of one product decreases when the production of a second product increases by one unit.

Council of Economic Advisers A group of three persons which advises and assists the President of the United States on economic matters (including the preparation of the economic report of the President to Congress).

Craft union A labor union which limits its membership to workers with a particular skill (craft).

Credit An accounting notation that the value of an asset (such as the foreign money owned by the residents of a nation) has increased.

Credit union An association of persons who have a common tie (such as being employees of the same Firm or members of the same Labor union) which sells shares to (accepts deposits from) its members and makes loans to them.

Criminal-conspiracy doctrine The (now outdated) legal doctrine that combinations of workers (Labor unions) to raise wages were criminal conspiracies and, therefore, illegal.

Crowding model of occupational discrimination A model of labor markets that assumes Occupational discrimination *(see)* against women and blacks has kept them out of many occupations and forced them into a limited number of other occupations in which the large Supply of labor (relative to the Demand) results in lower wages and incomes.

Crowding-out effect The rise in interest rates and the resulting decrease in planned net investment spending in the economy caused by increased borrowing in the money market by the Federal government.

Currency Coins and Paper money.

Currency appreciation (*See* Exchange rate appreciation.)

Currency depreciation (*See* Exchange rate depreciation.)

Current account The section in a nation's International balance of payments *(see)* in which are recorded its exports and imports of goods (merchandise) and services, its net investment income, and its net transfers.

Current account deficit A negative Balance on current account *(see)*.

Current account surplus A positive Balance on current account *(see)*.

Customary economy (*See* Traditional economy.)

Cyclical deficit A Federal Budget deficit which is caused by a recession and the consequent decline in tax revenues.

Cyclical unemployment Unemployment caused by insufficient Aggregate expenditures.

Cyclically balanced budget The equality of Government expenditures for goods and services and Net tax collections over the course of a Business cycle; deficits incurred during periods of recession are offset by surpluses obtained during periods of prosperity (inflation).

Debit An accounting notation that the value of an asset (such as the foreign money owned by the residents of a nation) has decreased.

Declining economy An economy in which Net private domestic investment *(see)* is less than zero (Gross private domestic investment is less than Depreciation).

Declining industry An industry in which Economic profits are negative (losses are incurred) and which will, therefore, decrease its output as Firms leave the industry.

Decrease in demand A decrease in the Quantity demanded of a good or service at every price; a shift of the Demand curve to the left.

Decrease in supply A decrease in the Quantity supplied of a good or service at every price; a shift of the Supply curve to the left.

Deduction Reasoning from assumptions to conclusions; a method of reasoning that tests a hypothesis (an assumption) by comparing the conclusions to which it leads with economic facts.

Deflating Finding the Real gross national product *(see)* by decreasing the dollar value of the Gross national product produced in a year in which prices were higher than in the Base year *(see)*.

Deflation A fall in the general (average) level of prices in the economy.

Deglomerative forces Increases in the cost of producing and marketing that result from the growth of cities and the concentration of firms and industries within a geographic area.

Demand A Demand schedule or a Demand curve *(see both)*.

Demand curve A curve which shows the amounts of a good or service buyers wish to purchase at various prices during some period of time.

Demand deposit A deposit in a Commercial bank against which checks may be written; a Checking account or checking-account money.

Demand-deposit multiplier (*See* Monetary multiplier.)

Demand factor The increase in the level of Aggregate demand which brings about the Economic growth made possible by an increase in the productive potential of the economy.

Demand management The use of Fiscal policy *(see)* and Monetary policy *(see)* to increase or decrease Aggregate demand.

Demand-pull inflation Inflation which is the result of an increase in Aggregate demand.

Demand schedule A schedule which shows the amounts of a good or service buyers wish to purchase at various prices during some period of time.

Dependent variable A variable which changes as a consequence of a change in some other (independent) variable; the "effect" or outcome.

Depository institution A Firm that accepts the deposits of Money of the public (businesses and persons); Commercial banks, Savings and loan associations, Mutual savings banks, and Credit unions.

Depository Institutions Deregulation and Monetary Control Act Federal legislation of 1980 which, among other things, allowed Thrift institutions to accept Checkable deposits and to use the check-clearing facilities of the Federal Reserve and to borrow from the Federal Reserve Banks; subjected the Thrifts to the reserve requirements of the Fed; and provided for the gradual elimination of the maximum interest rates that could be paid by Depository institutions on Savings and Time deposits.

Depreciation (*See* Capital consumption allowances.)

Depreciation of the dollar A decrease in the value of the dollar relative to another currency; a dollar now buys a smaller amount of the foreign currency. For example, if the dollar price of a British pound changes from $2 to $3, the dollar has depreciated.

Derived demand The demand for a good or service which is dependent upon or related to the demand for some other good or service; the demand for a resource which depends upon the demand for the products it can be used to produce.

Descriptive economics The gathering or collection of relevant economic facts (data).

Devaluation A decrease in the defined value of a currency.

DI (*See* Disposable income.)

DIDMCA (*See* Depository Institutions Deregulation and Monetary Control Act.)

Differentiated oligopoly An Oligopoly in which the firms produce a Differentiated product *(see)*.

Differentiated product A product which differs physically or in some other way from the similar products produced by other Firms; a product which is similar to but not identical with and, therefore, not a perfect substitute for other products; a product such that buyers are not indifferent to the seller from whom they purchase it so long as the price charged by all sellers is the same.

Dilemma of regulation When a Regulatory agency *(see)* must establish the maximum legal price a monopolist may charge, it finds that if it sets the price at the Socially optimal price *(see)* this price is below Average cost (and either bankrupts the Firm or requires that it be subsidized) and if it sets the price at the Fair-return price *(see)* it has failed to eliminate fully the underallocation of resources that is the consequence of unregulated monopoly.

Directing function of prices (*See* Guiding function of prices.)

Directly related Two sets of economic data that change in the same direction; when one variable increases (decreases) the other increases (decreases).

Direct relationship The relationship between two variables which change in the same direction, for example, product price and quantity supplied.

Discount rate The interest rate which the Federal Reserve Banks charge on the loans they make to Depository institutions.

Discouraged workers Workers who have left the Labor force *(see)* because they have not been able to find employment.

Discretionary fiscal policy Deliberate changes in taxes (tax rates) and government spending (spending for goods and services and transfer payment programs) by Congress for the purpose of achieving a full-employment noninflationary Net national product and economic growth.

Discriminatory discharge The firing of workers who favor the formation of labor unions.

Diseconomies of scale The forces which increase the Average cost of producing a product as the Firm expands the size of its Plant (its output) in the Long run *(see)*.

Disinflation A reduction in the rate of Inflation *(see)*.

Disposable income Personal income *(see)* less Personal taxes *(see)*; income available for Personal consumption expenditures *(see)* and Personal saving *(see)*.

Dissaving Spending for consumer goods and services in excess of Disposable income; the amount by which Personal consumption expenditures *(see)* exceed Disposable income.

Division of labor Dividing the work required to produce a product into a number of different tasks which are performed by different workers; Specialization *(see)* of workers.

Dollar votes The "votes" which consumers and entrepreneurs in effect cast for the production of the different kinds of consumer and capital goods, respectively, when they purchase them in the markets of the economy.

Domestic capital formation Adding to a nation's stock of Capital by saving a part of its own national output.

Domestic economic goal Assumed to be full employment with little or no inflation.

Double counting Including the value of intermediate goods *(see)* in the Gross national product; counting the same good or service more than once.

Double taxation Taxation of both corporate net income (profits) and the dividends paid from this net income when they become the Personal income of households.

Dumping The sale of products below cost in a foreign country.

Du Pont cellophane case The antitrust case brought against du Pont in which the U.S. Supreme Court ruled (in 1956) that while du Pont (and one licensee) had a monopoly in the narrowly defined market for cellophane it did not monopolize the more broadly defined market for flexible packaging materials, and was not guilty, therefore, of violating the Sherman Act.

Durable good A consumer good with an expected life (use) of one year or more.

Dynamic progress The development over time of more efficient (less costly) techniques of producing existing products and of improved products; technological progress.

Earnings The money income received by a worker; equal to the Wage (rate) multiplied by the quantity of labor supplied (the amount of time worked) by the worker.

Easy money policy Expanding the Money supply.

Economic analysis Deriving Economic principles *(see)* from relevant economic facts.

Economic cost A payment that must be made to obtain and retain the services of a resource; the income a Firm must provide to a resource supplier to attract the resource away from an alternative use; equal to the quantity of other products that cannot be produced when resources are employed to produce a particular product.

Economic efficiency The relationship between the input of scarce resources and the resulting output of a good or service; production of an output with a given dollar-and-cents value with the smallest total expendi-

ture for resources; obtaining the largest total production of a good or service with resources of a given dollar-and-cents value.

Economic growth (1) An increase in the Production possibilities schedule or curve that results from an increase in resource supplies or an improvement in Technology; (2) an increase either in real output (Gross national product) or in real output per capita.

Economic integration Cooperation among and the complete or partial unification of the economies of different nations; the elimination of the barriers to trade among these nations; the bringing together of the markets in each of the separate economies to form one large (a common) market.

Economic law *(See* Economic principle.)

Economic model A simplified picture of reality; an abstract generalization.

Economic perspective A viewpoint which envisions individuals and institutions making rational or purposeful decisions based upon a consideration of the benefits and costs associated with their actions.

Economic policy Course of action that will correct or avoid a problem.

Economic principle Generalization of the economic behavior of individuals and institutions.

Economic profit The Total revenue of a firm less all its Economic costs; also called "pure profit" and "above normal profit."

Economic Recovery Tax Act The Federal act of 1981 which reduced personal income tax rates, lowered Capital gains tax rates, allowed a more rapid writeoff against taxes of business expenditures for new plants and equipment, lowered the rates at which corporate incomes are taxed, and provided for the adjustment of tax brackets for inflation.

Economic regulation *(See* Industrial regulation.)

Economic rent The price paid for the use of land and other natural resources, the supply of which is fixed (perfectly inelastic).

Economics Social science concerned with using scarce resources to obtain the maximum satisfaction of the unlimited material wants of society.

Economic theory Deriving Economic principles *(see)* from relevant economic facts; an Economic principle *(see)*.

Economies of agglomeration The reduction in the cost of producing or marketing that results from the location of Firms relatively close to each other.

Economies of scale The forces which reduce the Average cost of producing a product as the Firm expands the size of its Plant (its output) in the Long run *(see)*; the economies of mass production.

Economizing problem Society's material wants are unlimited but the resources available to produce the goods and services that satisfy wants are limited (scarce); the inability of any economy to produce unlimited quantities of goods and services.

EEC European Economic Community; *(See* European Common Market).

Efficient allocation of resources That allocation of the resources of an economy among the production of different products which leads to the maximum satisfaction of the wants of consumers.

Elastic demand The Elasticity coefficient *(see)* is greater than one; the percentage change in Quantity demanded is greater than the percentage change in price.

Elasticity coefficient The number obtained when the percentage change in quantity demanded (or supplied) is divided by the percentage change in the price of the commodity.

Elasticity formula The price elasticity of demand (supply) is equal to

$$\frac{\text{percentage change in quantity}}{\text{percentage change in price}}$$

which is equal to

$$\frac{\text{change in quantity demanded (supplied)}}{\text{original quantity demanded (supplied)}}$$

$$\text{divided by } \frac{\text{change in price}}{\text{original price}}$$

Elastic supply The Elasticity coefficient *(see)* is greater than one; the percentage change in Quantity supplied is greater than the percentage change in price.

Emission fees Special fees that might be levied against those who discharge pollutants into the environment.

Employment Act of 1946 Federal legislation which committed the Federal government to the maintenance of economic stability (Full employment, stable prices, and Economic growth); established the Council of Economic Advisers *(see)*; and the Joint Economic Committee *(see)*; and provided for the annual economic report of the President to Congress.

Employment discrimination The employment of whites before blacks (and other minority groups) are employed and the discharge of blacks (and other minority groups) before whites are discharged.

Employment rate The percentage of the Labor force *(see)* employed at any time.

Entrepreneurial ability The human resource which combines the other resources to produce a product, makes nonroutine decisions, innovates, and bears risks.

Equality vs. efficiency tradeoff The decrease in Economic efficiency *(see)* that appears to accompany a decrease in income inequality *(see)*; the presumption that an increase in Income inequality is required to increase Economic efficiency.

Equalizing differences The differences in the Wages received by workers in different jobs which compensate for nonmonetary differences in the jobs.

Equation of exchange $MV = PQ$; in which M is the Money supply *(see)*, V is the Income velocity of money *(see)*, P is the Price level, and Q is the physical volume of final goods and services produced.

Equilibrium national output The real National output at which the Aggregate demand curve intersects the Aggregate supply curve.

Equilibrium NNP The Net national product at which the total quantity of final goods and services produced (the National output) is equal to the total quantity of final goods and services purchased (Aggregate expenditures).

Equilibrium position The point at which the Budget line *(see)* is tangent to an Indifference curve *(see)* in the indifference curve approach to the theory of consumer behavior.

Equilibrium price The price in a competitive market at which the Quantity demanded *(see)* and the Quantity supplied *(see)* are equal; at which there is neither a shortage nor a surplus; and at which there is no tendency for price to rise or fall.

Equilibrium price level The price level at which the Aggregate demand curve intersects the Aggregate supply curve.

Equilibrium quantity The Quantity demanded *(see)* and Quantity supplied *(see)* at the Equilibrium price *(see)* in a competitive market.

Equilibrium real national output The real national output which is determined by the equality (intersection) of Aggregate demand and Aggregate supply.

ERTA *(See* Economic Recovery Tax Act.)

European Common Market The association of thirteen European nations initiated in 1958 to abolish gradually the tariffs and Import quotas that exist among them, to establish common Tariffs for goods imported from outside the member nations, to allow the eventual free movement of labor and capital among them, and to create other common economic policies.

European Economic Community *(See* European Common Market.)

Excess burden of a tax The loss of net benefits to society because the imposition of a tax reduces the production and consumption of a good below the optimal level.

Excess reserves The amount by which a Member bank's Actual reserves *(see)* exceeds its required reserves *(see)*; Actual reserves minus required reserves.

Exchange control (*See* Foreign exchange control.)

Exchange rate The Rate of exchange *(see)*.

Exchange rate appreciation An increase in the value of a nation's money in foreign exchange markets; an increase in the Rates of exchange for foreign monies.

Exchange rate depreciation A decrease in the value of a nation's money in foreign exchange markets; a decrease in the Rates of exchange for foreign monies.

Exchange rate determinant Any factor other than the Rate of exchange *(see)* that determines the demand for and the supply of a currency in the Foreign exchange market *(see)*.

Excise tax A tax levied on the expenditure for a specific product or on the quantity of the product purchased.

Exclusion principle The exclusion of those who do not pay for a product from the benefits of the product.

Exclusive unionism The policies employed by a Labor union to restrict the supply of labor by excluding potential members in order to increase the Wages received by its members; the Policies typically employed by a Craft union *(see)*.

Exhaustive expenditure An expenditure by government that results directly in the employment of economic resources and in the absorption by government of the goods and services these resources produce; Government purchase *(see)*.

Exit mechanism Leaving a job and searching for another one in order to improve the conditions under which a worker is employed.

Expanding economy An economy in which Net private domestic investment *(see)* is greater than zero (Gross private domestic investment is greater than Depreciation).

Expanding industry An industry in which Economic profits are obtained by the firms in the industry and which will, therefore, increase its output as new firms enter the industry.

Expansionary fiscal policy An increase in Aggregate demand brought about by an increase in Government expenditures for goods and services, a decrease in Net taxes, or some combination of the two.

Expectations What consumers, business Firms, and others believe will happen or what conditions will be in the future.

Expected rate of net profits Annual profits which a firm anticipates it will obtain by purchasing Capital (by investing) expressed as a percentage of the price (cost) of the Capital.

Expenditures approach The method which adds all the expenditures made for Final goods and services to measure the Gross national product.

Expenditures-output · approach (*See* Aggregate expenditures–national output approach.)

Explicit cost The monetary payment a Firm must make to an outsider to obtain a resource.

Exports Goods and services produced in a given nation and sold to customers in other nations.

Export transactions A sale of a good or service which increases the amount of foreign money held by the citizens, firms, and governments of a nation.

External benefit (*See* Spillover benefit.)

External cost (*See* Spillover cost.)

External debt Public debt *(see)* owed to foreign citizens, firms, and institutions.

External economic goal (*See* International economic goal.)

External economies of scale The reduction in a Firm's cost of producing and marketing that results from the expansion of (the output or the number of Firms in) the Industry of which the Firm is a member.

Externality (*See* Spillover.)

Face value The dollar or cents value stamped on a coin.

Factors of production Economic resources: Land, Capital, Labor, and Entrepreneurial ability.

Fair-return price The price of a product which enables its producer to obtain a Normal profit *(see)* and which is equal to the Average cost of producing it.

Fallacy of composition Incorrectly reasoning that what is true for the individual (or part) is therefore necessarily true for the group (or whole).

Fallacy of limited decisions The false notion that there are a limited number of economic decisions to be made so that, if government makes more decisions, there will be fewer private decisions to render.

Farm problem The relatively low income of many farmers (compared with incomes in the nonagricultural sectors of the economy) and the tendency for farm income to fluctuate sharply from year to year.

FDIC (*See* Federal Deposit Insurance Corporation.)

Featherbedding Payment by an employer to a worker for work not actually performed.

Federal Advisory Committee The group of twelve commercial bankers which advises the Board of Governors *(see)* on banking policy.

Federal Deposit Insurance Corporation The Federally chartered corporation which insures the deposit liabilities of Commercial banks (Member and qualified nonmember banks).

Federal Open Market Committee (*See* Open Market Committee.)

Federal Reserve Bank Any one of the twelve banks chartered by the United States government to control the Money supply and perform other functions; (*See* Central bank, Quasi-public bank, *and* Banker's bank.)

Federal Reserve Note Paper money issued by the Federal Reserve Banks.

Federal Savings and Loan Insurance Corporation The federally chartered corporation which insures the deposit liabilities of Savings and loan associations.

Federal Trade Commission The commission of five members established by the Federal Trade Commission Act of 1914 to investigate unfair competitive practices of business Firms, to hold hearings of the complaints of such practices, and to issue Cease-and-desist orders *(see)* when Firms were found to engage in such practices.

Federal Trade Commission Act The Federal act of 1914 which established the Federal Trade Commission *(see)*.

Feedback effects The effects which a change in the money supply will have (because it affects the interest rate, planned investment, and the equilibrium NNP) on the demand for money which is itself directly related to the NNP.

Female labor force participation rate The percentage of the female population of working age in the Labor force *(see)*.

Fewness A relatively small number of sellers (or buyers) of a good or service.

Fiat money Anything that is Money because government has decreed it to be Money.

Final goods Goods which have been purchased for final use and not for resale or further processing or manufacturing (during the year).

Financial capital (*See* Money capital.)

Financing exports and imports The use of Foreign exchange markets by exporters and importers to receive and make payments for goods and services they sell and buy in foreign nations.

Firm An organization that employs resources to produce a good or service for profit and owns and operates one or more Plants *(see)*.

(The) firm's short-run supply curve A curve which shows the quantities of a product a Firm in a purely competitive industry (*see* Pure competition) will offer to sell at various prices in the Short run *(see)*; the portion of the Firm's short-run Marginal cost *(see)* curve which lies above its Average variable cost curve.

(The) firm's short-run supply schedule A schedule which shows the quantities of a product a Firm in a purely competitive industry (*see* Pure competition) will offer to sell at various prices in the Short run *(see)*; the portion of the Firm's short-run marginal cost *(see)* schedule in which Marginal cost is equal to or greater than Average variable cost.

Fiscal federalism The system of transfers (grants) by which the Federal government shares its revenues with state and local governments.

Fiscal policy Changes in government spending and tax collections for the purpose of achieving a full-employment and noninflationary national output.

Five fundamental economic questions The five questions which every economy must answer: what to produce, how to produce, how to divide the total output, how to maintain Full employment, and how to assure economic flexibility.

Five-year Plan A statement of the basic strategy for economic development and resource allocation which is prepared by *Gosplan (see)* and which includes target rates of growth for the Soviet economy and its major sectors and the general composition of the national output for a five-year period.

Fixed cost Any cost which in total does not change when the Firm changes its output; the cost of Fixed resources *(see)*.

Fixed exchange rate A Rate of exchange that is prevented from rising or falling.

Fixed resource Any resource employed by a Firm the quantity of which the firm cannot change.

Flexible exchange rate A rate of exchange that is determined by the demand for and supply of the foreign money and is free to rise or fall.

Floating exchange rate (*See* Flexible exchange rate.)

Food for peace program The program established under the provisions of Public Law 480 which permits less developed nations to buy surplus American agricultural products and pay for them with their own monies (instead of dollars).

Food stamp program A program in the United States which permits low-income persons to purchase for less than their retail value, or to obtain without cost, coupons that can be exchanged for food items at retail stores.

Foreign competition (*see* Import competition.)

Foreign exchange control The control a government may exercise over the quantity of foreign money demanded by its citizens and business firms and over the Rates of exchange in order to limit its outpayments to its inpayments (to eliminate a Payments deficit, *see*).

Foreign exchange system A market in which the money (currency) used by one nation is used to purchase (is exchanged for) the money used by another nation.

Foreign exchange rate (*see* Rate of exchange.)

Foreign purchases effect The inverse relationship between the Net exports (*see*) of an economy and its Price level (*see*) relative to foreign Price levels.

Foreign-trade crisis The large and expanding trade (merchandise and current-account) deficits of the United States during the 1980s.

45-degree line A line along which the value of the NNP (measured horizontally) is equal to the value of Aggregate expenditures (measured vertically).

Fractional reserve A Reserve ratio (*see*) that is less than 100 percent of the deposit liabilities of a Commercial bank.

Freedom of choice Freedom of owners of property resources and money to employ or dispose of these resources as they see fit, of workers to enter any line of work for which they are qualified, and of consumers to spend their incomes in a manner which they deem to be appropriate (best for them).

Freedom of enterprise Freedom of business Firms to employ economic resources, to use these resources to produce products of the firm's own choosing, and to sell these products in markets of their choice.

Freely floating exchange rates Rates of exchange (*see*) which are not controlled and which may, therefore, rise and fall; and which are determined by the demand for and the supply of foreign monies.

Free-rider problem The inability of those who might provide the economy with an economically desirable and indivisible good or service to obtain payment from those who benefit from the good or service because the Exclusion principle (*see*) cannot be applied to it.

Free trade The absence of artificial (government imposed) barriers to trade among individuals and firms in different nations.

Frictional unemployment Unemployment caused by workers voluntarily changing jobs and by temporary layoffs; unemployed workers between jobs.

Fringe benefits The rewards other than Wages that employees receive from their employers and which include pensions, medical and dental insurance, paid vacations, and sick leaves.

FSLIC (*See* Federal Savings and Loan Insurance Corporation.)

Full employment (1) Using all available resources to produce goods and services; (2) when the Unemployment rate is equal to the Full-employment unemployment rate and there is Frictional and Structural but no Cyclical unemployment (and the Real output of the economy is equal to its Potential real output).

Full Employment and Balanced Growth Act of 1978 The Federal Act which supplements the Employment Act of 1946 (*see*), and requires the Federal government to establish five-year goals for the economy and to make plans to achieve these goals.

Full-employment budget What the government expenditures and revenues and its surplus or deficit would be if the economy were to operate at Full employment throughout the year.

Full-employment unemployment rate The Unemployment rate (*see*) at which there is no Cyclical unemployment (*see*) of the Labor force (*see*); and because some Frictional and Structural unemployment is unavoidable, equal to about 5 or 6 percent.

Full production The maximum amount of goods and services that can be produced from the employed resources of an economy; the absence of Underemployment (*see*).

Functional distribution of income The manner in which the economy's (the national) income is divided among those who perform different functions (provide the economy with different kinds of resources); the division of National income (*see*) into wages and salaries, proprietors' income, corporate profits, interest, and rent.

Functional finance Use of Fiscal policy to achieve a full-employment noninflationary Net national product without regard to the effect on the Public debt (*see*).

GATT (*See* General agreement on Tariffs and Trade.)

General Agreement on Tariffs and Trade The international agreement reached in 1947 by twenty-three nations (including the United States) in which each nation agreed to give equal and nondiscriminatory treatment to the other nations, to reduce tariff rates by multinational negotiations, and to eliminate Import quotas.

General equilibrium analysis A study of the Market system as a whole; of the interrelations among equilibrium prices, outputs, and employments in all the different markets of the economy.

Generalization Statistical or probability statement; statement of the nature of the relation between two or more sets of facts.

Gentleman's agreement An informal understanding

on the price to be charged among the firm in an Oligopoly.

GNP (*See* Gross national product.)

GNP deflator The Price index *(see)* for all final goods and services used to adjust the money (or nominal) GNP to measure the real GNP.

GNP gap Potential Real gross national product less actual Real gross national product.

Gold export point The rate of exchange for a foreign money above which—when nations participate in the International gold standard *(see)*—the foreign money will not be purchased and gold will be sent (exported) to the foreign country to make payments there.

Gold flow The movement of gold into or out of a nation.

Gold import point The Rate of exchange for a foreign money below which—when nations participate in the International gold standard *(see)*—a nation's own money will not be purchased and gold will be sent (imported) into that country by foreigners to make payments there.

Gorbachev's economic program A recent series of reforms designed to revitalize the Soviet economy. The reforms stress the modernization of productive facilities, less centralized control, improved worker discipline and productivity, more emphasis upon market prices, and an expansion of private economic activity.

Gosbank The state owned and operated (and the only) bank in the U.S.S.R.

Gosplan The State Planning Commission in the U.S.S.R.

Government purchase Disbursement of money by government for which government receives a currently produced good or service in return.

Government purchases of goods and services The expenditures of all governments in the economy for Final goods *(see)* and services.

Government transfer payment The disbursement of money (or goods and services) by government for which government receives no currently produced good or service in return.

Grain reserve program A program in which grain is put into a reserve to reduce market supply when prices are low and sold from the reserve when prices are unusually high in order to increase the market supply.

Gramm-Rudman-Hollings Act Legislation enacted in 1985 by the Federal government requiring annual reductions in Federal budget deficits and, as amended, a balanced budget by 1993; and mandating an automatic decrease in expenditures when Congress and the President cannot agree on how to meet the targeted reductions in the budget deficit.

Grievance procedure The methods used by a Labor union and the Firm to settle disputes that arise during the life of the collective bargaining agreement between them.

Gross national product The total market value of all Final goods *(see)* and services produced in the economy during a year.

Gross private domestic investment Expenditures for newly produced Capital goods *(see)*—machinery, equipment, tools, and buildings—and for additions to inventories.

Guaranteed income The minimum income a family (or individual) would receive if a Negative income tax *(see)* were to be adopted.

Guiding function of prices The ability of price changes to bring about changes in the quantities of products and resources demanded and supplied (*See* Incentive function of price.)

Homogeneous oligopoly An Oligopoly in which the firms produce a Standardized product *(see)*.

Horizontal axis The "left–right" or "west–east" axis on a graph or grid.

Horizontal combination A group of Plants *(see)* in the same stage of production and owned by a single Firm *(see)*.

Horizontal merger The merger of one or more Firms producing the same product into a single Firm.

Household An economic unit (of one or more persons) which provides the economy with resources and uses the money paid to it for these resources to purchase goods and services that satisfy material wants.

Human-capital discrimination The denial to blacks (and other minority groups) of the same quality and quantity of education and training received by whites.

Human-capital investment Any action taken to increase the productivity (by improving the skills and abilities) of workers; expenditures made to improve the education, health, or mobility of workers.

Humphrey-Hawkins Act (*See* Full Employment and Balanced Growth Act of 1978.)

Hyperinflation A very rapid rise in the price level.

Illegal immigrant A person who unlawfully enters a country.

IMF (*See* International Monetary Fund.)

Immobility The inability or unwillingness of a worker or another resource to move from one geographic area or occupation to another or from a lower-paying to a higher-paying job.

Imperfect competition All markets except Pure competition *(see)*; Monopoly, Monopsony, Monopolistic competition, Oligopoly, and Oligopsony *(see all)*.

Implicit cost The monetary income a Firm sacrifices when it employs a resource it owns to produce a product rather than supplying the resource in the market; equal to what the resource could have earned in the best-paying alternative employment.

Import competition Competition which domestic firms encounter from the products and services of foreign suppliers.

Import quota A limit imposed by a nation on the quantity of a good that may be imported from abroad during some period of time.

Imports Spending by individuals, Firms, and governments of an economy for goods and services produced in foreign nations.

Import transaction The purchase of a good or service which decreases the amount of foreign money held by citizens, firms, and governments of a nation.

Incentive function The inducement which an increase (a decrease) in the price of a commodity offers to sellers of the commodity to make more (less) of it available; and the inducement which an increase (decrease) in price offers to buyers to purchase smaller (larger) quantities; the Guiding function of prices *(see)*.

Inclusive unionism The policies employed by a Labor union that does not limit the number of workers in the union in order to increase the Wage (rate); the policies of an Industrial union *(see)*.

Income approach The method which adds all the incomes generated by the production of Final goods and services to measure the Gross national product.

Income effect The effect which a change in the price of a product has upon the Real income (purchasing power) of a consumer and the resulting effect upon the quantity of that product the consumer would purchase after the consequences of the Substitution effect *(see)* have been taken into account (eliminated).

Income inequality The unequal distribution of an economy's total income among persons or families in the economy.

Income-maintenance system The programs designed to eliminate poverty and to reduce inequality in the distribution of income.

Incomes policy Government policy that affects the Money incomes of individuals (the wages workers receive) and the prices they pay for goods and services and thereby affects their Real incomes; *(see* Wage-price policy).

Income velocity of money *(See* Velocity of money.)

Increase in demand An increase in the Quantity demanded of a good or service at every price; a shift in the Demand curve to the right.

Increase in supply An increase in the Quantity supplied of a good or service at every price; a shift in the Supply curve to the right.

Increasing-cost industry An Industry in which the expansion of the Industry through the entry of new firms increases the prices the Firms in the Industry must pay for resources and, therefore, increases their cost schedules (moves their cost curves upward).

Increasing returns An increase in the Marginal product *(see)* of a resource as successive units of the resource are employed.

Independent goods Goods or services such that there is no relationship between the price of one and the demand for the other; when the price of one rises or falls the demand for the other remains constant.

Independent variable The variable which causes a change in some other (dependent) variable.

Indifference curve A curve which shows the different combinations of two products which give a consumer the same satisfaction or Utility *(see)*.

Indifference map A series of indifference curves *(see)*, each of which represents a different level of Utility; and which together show the preferences of the consumer.

Indirect business taxes Such taxes as Sales, Excise, and business Property taxes *(see all)*, license fees, and Tariffs *(see)* which Firms treat as costs of producing a product and pass on (in whole or in part) to buyers of the product by charging them higher prices.

Individual demand The Demand schedule *(see)* or Demand curve *(see)* of a single buyer of a good or service.

Individual supply The Supply schedule *(see)* or Supply curve *(see)* of a single seller of a good or service.

Induction A method of reasoning that proceeds from facts to Generalization *(see)*.

Industrial policy Any policy in which government takes a direct and active role in shaping the structure and composition of industry to promote economic growth.

Industrial regulation The older and more traditional type of regulation in which government is concerned with the prices charged and the services provided the public in specific industries; in contrast to Social regulation *(see)*.

Industrially advanced countries (IACs) Countries such as the United States, Canada, Japan, and the nations of western Europe which have developed Market economies based upon large stocks of technologically advanced capital goods and skilled labor forces.

Industrial union A Labor union which accepts as members all workers employed in a particular industry (or by a particular firm) and which contains largely unskilled or semiskilled workers.

Industry The group of (one or more) Firms that produce identical or similar products.

Inelastic demand The Elasticity coefficient *(see)* is less than one; the percentage change in price is greater than the percentage change in Quantity demanded.

Inelastic supply The Elasticity coefficient *(see)* is less than one; the percentage change in price is greater than the percentage change in Quantity supplied.

Inferior good A good or service of which consumers purchase less (more) at every price when their incomes increase (decrease).

Inflating Finding the Real gross national product *(see)* by increasing the dollar value of the Gross national product produced in a year in which prices are lower than they were in the Base year *(see)*.

Inflation A rise in the general (average) level of prices in the economy.

Inflationary expectations The belief of workers, business Firms, and consumers that there will be substantial inflation in the future.

Inflationary gap The amount by which the Aggregate-expenditures schedule (curve) must decrease (shift downward) to decrease the nominal NNP to the full-employment noninflationary level.

Inflationary recession *(See* Stagflation.)

Infrastructure For the economy, the capital goods usually provided by the Public sector for the use of its citizens and Firms (e.g., highways, bridges, transit systems, waste-water treatment facilities, municipal water systems, and airports). For the Firm, the services and facilities which it must have to produce its products, which would be too costly for it to provide for itself, and which are provided by governments or other Firms (e.g., water, electricity, waste treatment, transportation, research, engineering, finance, and banking).

Injection An addition of spending to the income-expenditure stream: Investment, Government purchases of goods and services, and Exports.

Injunction An order from a court of law that directs a person or organization not to perform a certain act because the act would do irreparable damage to some other person or persons; a restraining order.

In-kind investment Nonfinancial investment *(see)*.

In-kind transfer The distribution by government of goods and services to individuals and for which the government receives no currently produced good or service in return; a Government transfer payment *(see)* made in goods or services rather than in money.

Innovation The introduction of a new product, the use of a new method of production, or the employment of a new form of business organization.

Inpayments The receipts of (its own or foreign) money which the individuals, Firms, and governments of one nation obtain from the sale of goods and services, investment income, Remittances, and Capital inflows from abroad.

Input-output analysis Using an Input-output table *(see)* to examine interdependence among different parts (sectors and industries) of the economy and to make economic forecasts and plans.

Input-output table A table which lists (along the left side) the producing sectors and (along the top) the consuming or using sectors of the economy and which shows quantitatively in each of its rows how the output of a producing sector was distributed among consuming sectors and quantitatively in each of its columns the producing sectors from which a consuming sector obtained its inputs during some period of time (a year).

Insurable risk An event, the average occurrence of which can be estimated with considerable accuracy, which would result in a loss that can be avoided by purchasing insurance.

Interest The payment made for the use of money (of borrowed funds).

Interest income Income of those who supply the economy with Capital *(see)*.

Interest rate The Rate of interest *(see)*.

Interest-rate effect The tendency for increases (decreases) in the Price level to increase (decrease) the demand for money; raise (lower) interest rates; and, as a result, to reduce (expand) total spending in the economy.

Interindustry competition Competition or rivalry between the products produced by Firms in one Industry *(see)* and the products produced by Firms in another industry (or in other industries).

Interlocking directorate A situation in which one or more of the members of the board of directors of one Corporation are also on the board of directors of another Corporation; and which is illegal when it tends to reduce competition among the Corporations.

Intermediate goods Goods which are purchased for resale or further processing or manufacturing during the year.

Intermediate range The upsloping segment of the Aggregate supply curve that lies between the Keynesian range and the Classical range *(see both)*.

Internal economic goal (*See* Domestic economic goal.)

Internal economies The reduction in the cost of producing or marketing a product that results from an increase in output of the Firm; [*see* Economies of (large) scale].

Internally held public debt Public debt *(see)* owed to (United States government securities owned by) American citizens, Firms, and institutions.

International balance of payments Summary statement of the transactions which took place between the individuals, Firms, and governments of one nation and those in all other nations during the year.

International balance of payments deficit (*See* Balance of payments deficit.)

International balance of payments surplus (*See* Balance of payments surplus.)

International Bank for Reconstruction and Development (*See* World Bank.)

International economic goal Assumed to be a current-account balance of zero.

International gold standard An international monetary system employed in the nineteenth and early twentieth centuries in which each nation defined its money in terms of a quantity of gold, maintained a fixed relationship between its gold stock and money supply, and allowed the free importation and exportation of gold.

International Monetary Fund The international association of nations which was formed after World War II to make loans of foreign monies to nations with temporary Payments deficits *(see)* and to administer the Adjustable pegs *(see)*.

International monetary reserves The foreign monies and such assets as gold a nation may use to settle a Payments deficit. *(see)*.

International value of the dollar The price that must be paid in foreign currency (money) to obtain one American dollar.

Interstate Commerce Commission The commission established in 1887 to regulate the rates and monitor the services of the railroads in the United States.

Interstate Commerce Commission Act The Federal legislation of 1887 which established the Interstate Commerce Commission *(see)*.

Intrinsic value The value in the market of the metal in a coin.

Inverse relationship The relationship between two variables which change in opposite directions, for example, product price and quantity demanded.

Investment Spending for (the production and accumulation of) Capital goods *(see)* and additions to inventories.

Investment curve A curve which shows the amounts firms plan to invest (along the vertical axis) at different income (Net national product) levels (along the horizontal axis).

Investment-demand curve A curve which shows Rates of interest (along the vertical axis) and the amount of Investment (along the horizontal axis) at each Rate of interest.

Investment-demand schedule Schedule which shows Rates of interest and the amount of Investment at each Rate of interest.

Investment in human capital (*See* Human capital investment.)

Investment schedule A schedule which shows the amounts Firms plan to invest at different income (Net national product) levels.

Invisible hand The tendency of Firms and resource suppliers seeking to further their self-interests in competitive markets to further the best interest of society as a whole (the maximum satisfaction of wants).

JEC (*See* Joint Economic Committee.)

Joint Economic Committee Committee of Senators and Congressmen which investigates economic problems of national interest.

Jurisdictional strike Withholding from an employer the labor services of its members by a Labor union that is engaged in a dispute with another Labor union over which is to perform a specific kind of work for the employer.

Keynesian economics The macroeconomic generalizations which are today accepted by most (but not all) economists and which lead to the conclusion that a capitalistic economy does not always employ its resources fully and that Fiscal policy *(see)* and Monetary policy *(see)* can be used to promote Full employment *(see)*.

Keynesianism The philosophical, ideological, and analytical views of the prevailing majority of American economists; and their employment theory and stabilization policies.

Keynesian range The horizontal segment of the Aggregate-supply curve along which the price level is constant as real national output changes.

Kinked demand curve The demand curve which a noncollusive oligopolist sees for its output and which is based on the assumption that rivals will follow a price decrease and will not follow a price increase.

Labor The physical and mental talents (efforts) of people which can be used to produce goods and services.

Labor force Persons sixteen years of age and older who are not in institutions and who are employed or are unemployed and seeking work.

Labor-intensive commodity A product which requires a relatively large amount of Labor to produce.

Labor-Management Relations Act (*See* Taft-Hartley Act.)

Labor-Management Reporting and Disclosure Act (*See* Landrum-Griffin Act.)

Labor productivity Total output divided by the quantity of labor employed to produce the output; the Average product *(see)* of labor or output per worker per hour.

Labor theory of value The Marxian notion that the economic value of any commodity is determined solely by the amount of labor required to produce it.

Labor union A group of workers organized to advance the interests of the group (to increase wages, shorten the hours worked, improve working conditions, etc.).

Laffer Curve A curve which shows the relationship between tax rates and the tax revenues of government and on which there is a tax rate (between zero and 100 percent) at which tax revenues are a maximum.

Laissez faire capitalism (*See* Pure capitalism.)

Land Natural resources ("free gifts of nature") which can be used to produce goods and services.

Land-intensive commodity A product which requires a relatively large amount of Land to produce.

Landrum-Griffin Act The Federal act of 1959 which regulates the elections and finances of Labor unions and guarantees certain rights to their members.

Law of demand The inverse relationship between the price and the Quantity demanded *(see)* of a good or service during some period of time.

Law of diminishing marginal utility As a consumer increases the consumption of a good or service, the Marginal utility *(see)* obtained from each additional unit of the good or service decreases.

Law of diminishing returns When successive equal increments of a Variable resource *(see)* are added to the Fixed resources *(see)*, beyond some level of employment, the Marginal product *(see)* of the Variable resource will decrease.

Law of increasing opportunity cost As the amount of a product produced is increased, the Opportunity cost *(see)*—Marginal cost *(see)*—of producing an additional unit of the product increases.

Law of supply The direct relationship between the price and the Quantity supplied *(see)* of a good or service during some period of time.

Leakage (1) a withdrawal of potential spending from the income-expenditures stream: Saving *(see)*, tax payments, and Imports *(see)*; (2) a withdrawal which reduces the lending potential of the Commercial banking system.

Leakages-injections approach Determination of the Equilibrium net national product *(see)* by finding the Net national product at which Leakages *(see)* are equal to Injections *(see)*.

Least-cost combination rule (of resources) The quantity of each resource a Firm must employ if it is to produce any output at the lowest total cost; the combination on which the ratio of the Marginal product *(see)* of a resource to its Marginal resource cost *(see)* (to its price if the resource is employed in a competitive market) is the same for all resources employed.

Legal cartel theory of regulation The hypothesis that industries want to be regulated so that they may form legal Cartels *(see)* and that government officials (the government) provide the regulation in return for their political and financial support.

Legal immigrant A person who lawfully enters a country.

Legal reserves (deposit) The minimum amount which a Depository institution *(see)* must keep on deposit with the Federal Reserve Bank in its district, or in Vault cash *(see)*.

Legal tender Anything that government has decreed must be accepted in payment of a debt.

Lending potential of an individual commercial bank The amount by which a single Commercial bank can safely increase the Money supply by making new loans to (or buying securities from) the public; equal to the Commercial bank's Excess reserves *(see)*.

Lending potential of the banking system The amount by which the Commercial banking system *(see)* can increase the Money supply by making new loans to (or buying securities from) the public; equal to the Excess reserves *(see)* of the Commercial banking system multiplied by the Monetary multiplier *(see)*.

Less developed countries (LDCs) Many countries of Africa, Asia, and Latin America which are characterized by a lack of capital goods, primitive production technologies, low literacy rates, high unemployment, rapid population growth, and labor forces heavily committed to agriculture.

Liability A debt with a monetary value; an amount owed by a Firm or an individual.

Limited liability Restriction of the maximum that may be lost to a predetermined amount; the maximum amount that may be lost by the owners (stockholders) of a Corporation is the amount they paid for their shares of stock.

Line-item veto A proposal to give the President the power to delete specific expenditure items from spending legislation passed by Congress.

Liquidity Money or things which can be quickly and easily converted into Money with little or no loss of purchasing power.

Liquidity preference theory of interest The theory in which the demand for Liquidity (the quantity of Money firms and households wish to possess) and the supply of Liquidity (the quantity of Money available) determine the equilibrium Rate of interest in the economy.

Loaded terminology Terms which arouse emotions and elicit approval or disapproval.

Loanable funds theory of interest The concept that the supply of and demand for loanable funds determines the equilibrium rate of interest.

Lockout The temporary closing of a place of employment and the halting of production by an employer in order to discourage the formation of a Labor union or to compel a Labor union to modify its demands.

Logrolling The trading of votes by legislators to secure favorable outcomes on decisions to provide public goods and services.

Long run A period of time long enough to enable producers of a product to change the quantities of all the resources they employ; in which all resources and costs are variable and no resources or costs are fixed.

Long-run aggregate supply curve The aggregate supply curve associated with a time period in which input prices (especially nominal wages) are fully responsive to changes in the price level.

Long-run competitive equilibrium The price at which Firms in Pure competition *(see)* neither obtain Economic profit nor suffer losses in the Long run and the total quantity demanded and supplied at that price are equal; a price equal to the minimum long-run average cost of producing the product.

Long-run farm problem The tendency for the incomes of many farmers to decline relative to incomes in the rest of the economy.

Long-run supply A schedule or curve which shows the prices at which a Purely competitive industry will make various quantities of the product available in the Long run.

Lorenz curve A curve which can be used to show the distribution of income in an economy; and when used for this purpose the cumulated percentage of families (income receivers) is measured along the horizontal axis and the cumulated percentage of income is measured along the vertical axis.

Loss-minimizing case The circumstances which result in a loss which is less than its Total fixed cost when a competitive Firm produces the output at which total profit is a maximum (or total loss is a minimum): when the price at which the firm can sell its product is less than Average total but greater than Average variable cost.

M1 The narrowly defined Money supply; the Currency and Checkable deposits *(see)* not owned by the Federal government, Federal Reserve Banks, or Depository institutions.

M2 A more broadly defined Money supply; equal to *M*1 *(see)* plus Noncheckable savings deposits and small Time deposits (deposits of less than $100,000).

M3 A still more broadly defined Money supply; equal to *M*2 *(see)* plus large Time deposits (deposits of $100,000 or more).

Macroeconomics The part of economics concerned with the economy as a whole; with such major aggregates as the household, business, and governmental sectors and with totals for the economy.

Managed floating exchange rate An Exchange rate that is allowed to change (float) to eliminate persistent Payments deficit and surpluses and is controlled (managed) to reduce day-to-day fluctuations.

Managerial-opposition hypothesis The explanation that attributes the relative decline of unionism in the United States to the increased and more aggressive opposition of management to unions.

Managerial prerogatives The decisions, often enumerated in the contract between a Labor union and a business Firm, that the management of the Firm has the sole right to make.

Marginal cost The extra (additional) cost of producing one more unit of output; equal to the change in Total cost divided by the change in output (and in the short run to the change in total Variable cost divided by the change in output).

Marginal labor cost The amount by which the total cost of employing Labor increases when a Firm employs one additional unit of Labor (the quantity of other resources employed remaining constant); equal to the change in the total cost of Labor divided by the change in the quantity of Labor employed.

Marginal product The additional output produced when one additional unit of a resource is employed (the quantity of all other resources employed remaining constant); equal to the change in total product divided by the change in the quantity of a resource employed.

Marginal productivity theory of income distribution The contention that the distribution of income is equitable when each unit of each resource receives a money payment equal to its marginal contribution to the firm's revenue (its Marginal revenue product).

Marginal propensity to consume Fraction of any change in Disposable income which is spent for Consumer goods; equal to the change in consumption divided by the change in Disposable income.

Marginal propensity to save Fraction of any change in Disposable income which households save; equal to change in Saving *(see)* divided by the change in Disposable income.

Marginal rate of substitution The rate (at the margin) at which a consumer is prepared to substitute one good or service for another and remain equally satisfied (have the same total Utility); and equal to the slope of an Indifference curve *(see)*.

Marginal resource cost The amount by which the total cost of employing a resource increases when a Firm employs one additional unit of the resource (the quantity of all other resources employed remaining constant); equal to the change in the Total cost of the resource divided by the change in the quantity of the resource employed.

Marginal revenue The change in the Total revenue of the Firm that results from the sale of one additional unit of its product; equal to the change in Total revenue divided by the change in the quantity of the product sold (demanded).

Marginal-revenue–marginal-cost approach The method which finds the total output at which Economic profit *(see)* is a maximum (or losses a minimum) by comparing the Marginal revenue *(see)* and the Marginal cost *(see)* of additional units of output.

Marginal revenue product The change in the Total revenue of the Firm when it employs one additional unit of a resource (the quantity of all other resources employed remaining constant); equal to the change in Total revenue divided by the change in the quantity of the resource employed.

Marginal tax rate The fraction of additional (taxable) income that must be paid in taxes.

Marginal utility The extra Utility *(see)* a consumer obtains from the consumption of one additional unit of a good or service; equal to the change in total Utility divided by the change in the quantity consumed.

Margin requirement The minimum percentage down payment which purchasers of shares of stock must make.

Market Any institution or mechanism that brings together the buyers (demanders) and sellers (suppliers) of a particular good or service.

Market demand (*See* Total demand.)

Market economy An economy in which only the private decisions of consumers, resource suppliers, and business Firms determine how resources are allocated; the Market system.

Market failure The failure of a market to bring about the allocation of resources that best satisfies the wants of society (that maximizes the satisfaction of wants). In particular, the over- or underallocation of resources to the production of a particular good or service (because of Spillovers) and no allocation of resources to the production of Public goods *(see)*.

Market for externality rights A market in which the Perfectly inelastic supply *(see)* of the right to pollute the environment and the demand for the right to pollute would determine the price which a polluter would have to pay for the right.

Market-oriented income stabilization The proposal to shift the goal of farm policy from the enhancement to the stabilization of farm prices and incomes; allow farm prices and incomes to move toward their free-market levels in the long run; and have government stabilize farm prices and incomes from year to year by purchasing farm products when their prices fell below and by selling surplus farm products when their prices rose above their long-run trend of prices.

Market period A period of time in which producers of a product are unable to change the quantity produced in response to a change in its price; in which there is Perfect inelasticity of supply *(see)*; and in which all resources are Fixed resources *(see)*.

Market policies Government policies designed to reduce the market power of labor unions and large business firms and to reduce or eliminate imbalances and bottlenecks in labor markets.

Market socialism An economic system (method of organization) in which property resources are publicly owned and markets and prices are used to direct and coordinate economic activities.

Market system All the product and resource markets of the economy and the relationships among them; a method which allows the prices determined in these markets to allocate the economy's scarce resources and to communicate and coordinate the decisions made by consumers, business firms, and resource suppliers.

"Material balance" Preparation of the Five- and One-year Plans *(see each)* by *Gosplan (see)* so that the planned requirements and the available supplies of each input and commodity are equal.

Materials balance approach A method of dealing with pollution problems which compares the production of waste materials with the capacity of the environment to absorb these materials.

Median-voter model The view that under majority

rule the median (middle) voter will be in the dominant position to determine the outcome of an election.

Medicaid A Federal program in the United States which helps to finance the medical expenses of individuals covered by the Supplemental security income *(see)* and the Aid to families with dependent children *(see)* programs.

Medicare A Federal program which is financed by Payroll taxes *(see)* and provides for (1) compulsory hospital insurance for senior citizens and (2) low-cost voluntary insurance to help older Americans pay physicians' fees.

Medium of exchange Money *(see)*; a convenient means of exchanging goods and services without engaging in Barter *(see)*; what sellers generally accept and buyers generally use to pay for a good or service.

Member bank A Commercial bank *(see)* which is a member of the Federal Reserve system; all National banks *(see)* and the State banks *(see)* which have chosen to join the system.

Member bank deposits The deposits which Member banks *(see)* have at the Federal Reserve Banks *(see)*.

Member bank reserves Member bank deposits *(see)* plus their Vault cash *(see)*.

Microeconomics The part of economics concerned with such individual units within the economy as Industries, firms, and Households; and with individual markets, particular prices, and specific goods and services.

Minimum wage The lowest Wage (rate) employers may legally pay for an hour of Labor.

Mixed capitalism An economy in which both government and private decisions determine how resources are allocated.

Monetarism An alternative to Keynesianism *(see)*; the philosophical, ideological, and analytical view of a minority of American economists; and their employment theory and stabilization policy which stress the role of money.

Monetary multiplier The multiple of its Excess reserves *(see)* by which the Commercial banking system *(see)* can expand the Money supply and Demand deposits by making new loans (or buying securities); and equal to one divided by the Required reserve ratio *(see)*.

Monetary policy Changing the Money supply *(see)* in order to assist the economy to achieve a full-employment, noninflationary level of total output.

Monetary rule The rule suggested by Monetarism *(see)*; the Money supply should be expanded each year at the same annual rate as the potential rate of growth of the Real gross national product; the supply of money should be increased steadily at from 3 to 5 percent.

Money Any item which is generally acceptable to sellers in exchange for goods and services.

Money capital Money available to purchase Capital goods *(see)*.

Money income *(See* Nominal income.)

Money interest rate The Nominal interest rate *(see)*.

Money market The market in which the demand for and the supply of money determine the Interest rate (or the level of interest rates) in the economy.

Money supply Narrowly defined *(see)* $M1$, more broadly defined *(see)* $M2$ and $M3$.

Money wage The amount of money received by a worker per unit of time (hour, day, etc.); nominal wage.

Money wage rate *(See* Money wage.)

Monopolistic competition A market in which many Firms sell a Differentiated product *(see)*, into which entry is relatively easy, in which the Firm has some control over the price at which the product it produces is sold, and in which there is considerable Nonprice competition *(see)*.

Monopoly (1) A market in which the number of sellers is so few that each seller is able to influence the total supply and the price of the good or service; (2) a major industry in which a small number of Firms control all or a large portion of its output (Business monopoly).

Monopsony A market in which there is only one buyer of the good, service, or resource.

Moral suasion The statements, pronouncements, and appeals made by the Federal Reserve Banks which are intended to influence the lending policies of Commercial banks.

Most-favored-nation clause A clause in a trade agreement between the United States and another nation which provides that the other nation's Imports into the United States will be subjected to the lowest tariff levied then or later on any other nation's Imports into the United States.

MR = MC rule A Firm will maximize its Economic profit (or minimize its losses) by producing the output at which Marginal revenue *(see)* and Marginal cost *(see)* are equal—provided the price at which it can sell its products is equal to or greater than Average variable cost *(see)*.

MRP = MRC rule To maximize Economic profit (or minimize losses) a Firm should employ the quantity of a resource at which its Marginal revenue product *(see)* is equal to its Marginal resource cost *(see)*.

Multiplier The ratio of the change in the Equilibrium NNP to the change in Investment *(see)*, or to the change in any other component of the Aggregate expenditures schedule or to the change in Net taxes; the number by which a change in any component in the Aggregate expenditures schedule or in Net taxes must be multiplied to find the resulting change in the Equilibrium NNP.

Multiplier effect The effect upon the Equilibrium net national product of a change in the Aggregate expenditures schedule (caused by a change in the Consumption schedule, Investment, Net taxes, Government expenditures for goods and services, or Exports).

Mutual interdependence Situation in which a change in price (or in some other policy) by one Firm will affect the sales and profits of another Firm (or other Firms) and any Firm which makes such a change can expect the other Firm(s) to react in an unpredictable (uncertain) way.

Mutually exclusive goals Goals which conflict and cannot be achieved simultaneously.

Mutual savings bank A Firm without stockholders which accepts deposits primarily from small individual savers and which lends primarily to individuals to finance the purchases of residences.

National bank A Commercial bank *(see)* chartered by the United States government.

National income Total income earned by resource suppliers for their contributions to the production of the Gross national product *(see)*; equal to the Gross national product minus the Nonincome charges *(see)*.

National income accounting The techniques employed to measure (estimate) the overall production of the economy and other related totals for the nation as a whole.

National Labor Relations Act *(See* Wagner Act.)

National Labor Relations Board The board established by the Wagner (National Labor Relations) Act *(see)* of 1935 to investigate unfair labor practices, issue Cease-and-desist orders *(see)*, and to conduct elections among employees to determine if they wish to be represented by a Labor union and which union they wish to represent them.

National output The Net (or gross) national product; the total output of final goods and services produced in the economy.

Natural monopoly An industry in which the Economies of scale *(see)* are so great that the product can be produced by one Firm at an average cost which is lower than it would be if it were produced by more than one Firm.

Natural rate hypothesis Contends that the economy is stable in the long run at the natural rate of unemployment; views the long-run Phillips Curve *(see)* as being vertical at the natural rate of unemployment.

Natural rate of unemployment *(See* Full-employment unemployment rate.)

Near-money Financial assets, the most important of which are Noncheckable savings accounts, Time deposits, and U.S. short-term securities and savings bonds, that are not a medium of exchange but can be readily converted into Money.

Negative income tax The proposal to subsidize families and individuals with money payments when their incomes fall below a Guaranteed income *(see)*; the negative tax would decrease as earned income increases *(See* Benefits-loss rate.)

Negative relationship *(See* Inverse relationship.)

Negotiable order of withdrawal account An account (deposit) in a Savings and loan association *(see)* or Mutual savings bank *(see)* against which a check may be written and which pays interest to the depositor.

Net capital movement The difference between the real and financial investments and loans made by individuals and Firms of one nation in the other nations of the world and the investments and loans made by individuals and Firms from other nations in a nation; Capital inflows less Capital outflows.

Net export effect The notion that the impact of a change in Monetary policy (Fiscal policy) will be strengthened (weakened) by the consequent change in Net exports *(see)*. For example, a tight (easy) money policy will increase (decrease) domestic interest rates, thereby increasing (decreasing) the foreign demand for dollars. As a result, the dollar appreciates (depreciates) and causes American net exports to decrease (increase).

Net exports Exports *(see)* minus Imports *(see)*.

Net investment income The interest and dividend income received by the residents of a nation from residents of other nations less the interest and dividend payments made by the residents of that nation to the residents of other nations.

Net national product Gross national product *(see)* less that part of the output needed to replace the Capital goods worn out in producing the output (Capital consumption allowances, *see)*.

Net private domestic investment Gross private domestic investment *(see)* less Capital consumption allowances *(see)*; the addition to the nation's stock of Capital during a year.

Net taxes The taxes collected by government less Government transfer payments *(see)*.

Net transfers The personal and government transfer payments made to residents of foreign nations less the personal and government transfer payments received from residents of foreign nations.

Net worth The total Assets *(see)* less the total Liabilities *(see)* of a Firm or an individual; the claims of the owners of a firm against its total Assets.

New classical economics The theory that, although unanticipated price level changes may create macroeconomic instability in the short run, the economy is stable at the full-employment level of national output in the long run because of price and wage flexibility.

New International Economic Order A series of proposals made by the Less developed countries (LDCs) *(see)* for basic changes in its relationships with the advanced industrialized nations that would accelerate the growth of and redistribute world income to the LDCs.

NIEO New International Economic Order *(see).*

NIT *(See* Negative income tax.)

NLRB *(See* National Labor Relations Board.)

NNP *(See* Net national product.)

Nominal income The number of dollars received by an individual or group during some period of time.

Nominal interest rate The rate of interest expressed in dollars of current value (not adjusted for inflation).

Nominal national output (NNP) The NNP *(see)* measured in terms of the price level at the time of measurement (unadjusted for changes on the price level).

Nominal wage rate The Money wage *(see).*

Noncheckable savings account A Savings account *(see)* against which a check may not be written; a Savings account which is not a NOW, ATS, or share draft account.

Noncollusive oligopoly An Oligopoly *(see)* in which the Firms do not act together and in agreement to determine the price of the product and the output each Firm will produce or to determine the geographic area in which each Firm will sell.

Noncompeting groups Groups of workers in the economy that do not compete with each other for employment because the skill and training of the workers in one group are substantially different from those of the workers in other groups.

Nondiscretionary fiscal policy The increases (decreases) in Net taxes *(see)* which occur without Congressional action when the Net national product rises (falls) and which tend to stabilize the economy.

Nondurable good A Consumer good *(see)* with an expected life (use) of less than one year.

Nonexhaustive expenditure An expenditure by government that does not result directly in the employment of economic resources or the production of goods and services; *see* Government transfer payment.

Nonfinancial investment An investment which does not require households to save a part of their money incomes; but which uses surplus (unproductive) labor to build Capital goods.

Nonincome charges Capital consumption allowances *(see)* and Indirect business taxes *(see).*

Nonincome determinants of consumption and saving All influences on consumption spending and saving other than the level of Disposable income.

Noninterest determinants of investment All influences on the level of investment spending other than the rate of interest.

Noninvestment transaction An expenditure for stocks, bonds, or second-hand Capital goods.

Nonmarket transactions The production of goods and services not included in the measurement of the Gross national product because the goods and services are not bought and sold.

Nonprice competition The means other than decreasing the prices of their products which Firms employ to attempt to increase the sale of their products; and which includes Product differentiation *(see)*, advertising, and sales promotion activities.

Nonprice determinant of demand Factors other than its price which determine the quantities demanded of a good or service.

Nonprice determinant of supply Factors other than its price which determine the quantities supplied of a good or service.

Nonprice-level-determinants of aggregate demand Factors such as consumption, investment, government, and net export spending which, if they change, will shift the aggregate demand curve.

Nonprice-level-determinants of aggregate supply Factors such as input prices, productivity, and the legal-institutional environment which, if they change, will shift the aggregate supply curve.

Nonproductive transaction The purchase and sale of any item that is not a currently produced good or service.

Nontariff barriers All barriers other than Tariffs *(see)* which nations erect to impede trade among nations: Import quotas *(see)*, licensing requirements, unreasonable product-quality standards, unnecessary red tape in customs procedures, etc.

Nonunion shop A place of employment at which none of the employees are members of a Labor union (and at which the employer attempts to hire only workers who are not apt to join a union).

Normal good A good or service of which consumers will purchase more (less) at every price when their incomes increase (decrease).

Normal profit Payment that must be made by a Firm to obtain and retain Entrepreneurial ability *(see)*; the minimum payment (income) Entrepreneurial ability must (expect to) receive to induce it to perform the entrepreneurial functions for a Firm; an Implicit cost *(see)*.

Normative economics That part of economics which pertains to value judgments about what the economy should be like; concerned with economic goals and policies.

Norris-LaGuardia Act The Federal act of 1932 which made it more difficult for employers to obtain Injunctions *(see)* against Labor unions in Federal courts and which declared that Yellow-dog contracts *(see)* were unenforceable.

NOW account Negotiable order of withdrawal account *(see)*.

NTBs *(See* Nontariff barriers.)

OASDHI *(See* Old age, survivors, and disability health insurance.)

Occupational discrimination The arbitrary restrictions which prevent blacks (and other minority groups) or women from entering the more desirable and higher-paying occupations.

Occupational licensure The laws of state or local governments which require a worker to obtain a license from a licensing board (by satisfying certain specified requirements) before engaging in a particular occupation.

Official reserves The foreign monies (currencies) owned by the central bank of a nation.

Okun's law The generalization that any one percentage point rise in the Unemployment rate above the Full-employment unemployment rate will increase the GNP gap by 2.5 percent of the Potential output (GNP) of the economy.

Old age, survivors, and disability health insurance The social program in the United States which is financed by Federal Payroll taxes *(see)* on employers and employees and which is designed to replace the Earnings lost when workers retire, die, or become unable to work.

Oligopoly A market in which a few Firms sell either a Standardized or Differentiated product, into which entry is difficult, in which the Firm's control over the price at which it sells its product is limited by Mutual interdependence *(see)* (except when there is collusion among firms), and in which there is typically a great deal of Nonprice competition *(see)*.

Oligopsony A market in which there are a few buyers.

One-year Plan A detailed operational plan which is prepared by *Gosplan (see)* and which specifies the inputs and outputs of each enterprise in the U.S.S.R. for a one-year period.

OPEC An acronym for the Organization of Petroleum Exporting Countries *(see)*.

Open economy An economy which both exports and imports goods and services.

Open Market Committee The twelve-member group that determines the purchase-and-sale policies of the Federal Reserve Banks in the market for United States government securities.

Open-market operations The buying and selling of United States government securities by the Federal Reserve Banks.

Open shop A place of employment at which the employer may hire either Labor union members or workers who are not (and need not become) members of the union.

Opportunity cost The amount of other products that must be forgone or sacrificed to produce a unit of a product.

Organization of Petroleum Exporting Countries The cartel formed in 1970 by thirteen oil-producing countries to control the price at which they sell crude oil to foreign importers and the quantity of oil exported by its members and which accounts for a large proportion of the world's export of oil.

"Other things being equal" assumption Assuming that factors other than those being considered are constant.

Outpayments The expenditures of (its own or foreign) money which the individuals, Firms, and governments of one nation make to purchase goods and services, for Remittances, as investment income, and Capital outflows abroad.

Output effect The impact which a change in the price of a resource has upon the output a Firm finds it most profitable to produce and the resulting effect upon the quantity of the resource (and the quantities of other resources) employed by the Firm after the consequences of the Substitution effect *(see)* have been taken into account (eliminated).

Paper money Pieces of paper used as a Medium of exchange *(see)*; in the United States, Federal Reserve Notes *(see)*.

Paradox of thrift The attempt of society to save more results in the same amount of, or less, Saving.

Paradox of voting A situation wherein voting by majority rule fails to provide a consistent ranking of society's preferences for public goods or services.

Parity concept The notion that year after year a given output of a farm product should enable a farmer to acquire a constant amount of nonagricultural goods and services.

Parity price The price at which a given amount of an agricultural product would have to be sold to enable a farmer to obtain year after year money income needed to purchase a constant total quantity of nonagricultural goods and services.

Parity ratio The ratio (index) of the price received by farmers from the sale of an agricultural commodity to the (index of the) prices paid by them; used as a rationale for Price supports *(see)*.

Partial equilibrium analysis The study of equilibrium prices and equilibrium outputs or employments in a particular market which assumes prices, outputs, and employments in the other markets of the economy remain unchanged.

Partnership An unincorporated business Firm owned and operated by two or more persons.

Patent laws The Federal laws which grant to inventors and innovators the exclusive right to produce and sell a new product or machine for a period of seventeen years.

Payments deficit (*See* Balance of payments deficit.)

Payments surplus (*See* Balance of payments surplus.)

Payroll tax A tax levied on employers of Labor equal to a percentage of all or part of the wages and salaries paid by them; and on employees equal to a percentage of all or part of the wages and salaries received by them.

Peak pricing Setting the price charged for the use of a facility (the User charge, *see*) or for a good or service at a higher level when the demand for the use of the facility or for the good or service is greater and at a lower level when the demand for it is less.

Perfect elasticity of demand A change in the Quantity demanded requires no change in the price of the commodity; buyers will purchase as much of a commodity as is available at a constant price.

Perfect elasticity of supply A change in the Quantity supplied requires no change in the price of the commodity; sellers will make available as much of the commodity as buyers will purchase at a constant price.

Perfect inelasticity of demand A change in price results in no change in the Quantity demanded of a commodity; the Quantity demanded is the same at all prices.

Perfect inelasticity of supply A change in price results in no change in the Quantity supplied of a commodity; The Quantity supplied is the same at all prices.

Per se violations Collusive actions, such as attempts to fix prices or divide a market, which are violations of the antitrust laws even though the actions are unsuccessful.

Personal consumption expenditures The expenditures of Households for Durable and Nondurable consumer goods and services.

Personal distribution of income The manner in which the economy's Personal or Disposable income is divided among different income classes or different households.

Personal income The income, part of which is earned and the remainder of which is unearned, available to resource suppliers and others before the payment of Personal taxes *(see)*.

Personal income tax A tax levied on the taxable income of individuals (households and unincorporated firms).

Personal saving The Personal income of households less Personal taxes *(see)* and Personal consumption expenditures *(see)*; Disposable income not spent for Consumer goods *(see)*.

Phillips Curve A curve which shows the relationship between the Unemployment rate *(see)* (on the horizontal axis) and the annual rate of increase in the Price level (on the vertical axis).

Planned economy An economy in which only government determines how resources are allocated.

Planned investment The amount which business firms plan or intend to invest.

Plant A physical establishment (Land and Capital) which performs one or more of the functions in the production (fabrication and distribution) of goods and services.

P = MC rule A firm in Pure competition *(see)* will maximize its Economic profit *(see)* or minimize its losses by producing the output at which the price of the product is equal to Marginal cost *(see)*, provided that price is equal to or greater than Average variable cost *(see)* in the short run and equal to or greater than Average (total) cost *(see)* in the long run.

Policy economics The formulation of courses of action to bring about desired results or to prevent undesired occurrences (to control economic events).

Political business cycle The tendency of Congress to destabilize the economy by reducing taxes and increasing government expenditures before elections and to raise taxes and lower expenditures after the elections.

Political fragmentation The existence within the larger urban (metropolitan) areas of a great number of separate political entities (states, counties, cities, etc.) which have their own governments.

Positive economics The analysis of facts or data for the purpose of establishing scientific generalizations about economic behavior; compare Normative economics.

Positive relationship The relationship between two

variables which change in the same direction, for example, product price and quantity supplied.

Post hoc, ergo propter hoc **fallacy** Incorrectly reasoning that when one event precedes another the first event is the cause of the second.

Potential competition The possibility that new competitors will be induced to enter an industry if firms presently in that industry are realizing large economic profits.

Potential output The real output (GNP) an economy is able to produce when it fully employs its available resources.

Poverty An existence in which the basic needs of an individual or family exceed the means to satisfy them.

Poverty rate The percentage of the population with incomes below the official poverty income levels established by the Federal government.

Preferential hiring A practice (often required by the provisions of a contract between a Labor union and an employer) which requires the employer to hire union members so long as they are available and to hire nonunion workers only when union members are not available.

Preferential tariff treatment Setting Tariffs lower for one nation (or group of nations) than for others.

Premature inflation Inflation *(see)* which occurs before the economy has reached Full employment *(see)*.

Price The quantity of money (or of other goods and services) paid and received for a unit of a good or service.

Price ceiling A legally established maximum price for a good or service.

Price-decreasing effect The effect in a competitive market of a decrease in Demand or an increase in Supply upon the Equilibrium price *(see)*.

Price discrimination The selling of a product (at a given time) to different buyers at different prices when the price differences are not justified by differences in the cost of producing the product for the different buyers; and a practice made illegal by the Clayton Act *(see)* when it reduces competition.

Price elasticity of demand The ratio of the percentage change in Quantity demanded of a commodity to the percentage change in its price; the responsiveness or sensitivity of the quantity of a commodity buyers demand to a change in the price of a commodity.

Price elasticity of supply The ratio of the percentage change in Quantity supplied of a commodity to the percentage change in its price; the responsiveness or sensitivity of the quantity of a commodity supplied to a change in the price of a commodity.

Price floor A legally determined price which is above the Equilibrium price.

Price guidepost The price charged by an industry for its product should increase by no more than the increase in the Unit labor cost *(see)* of producing the product.

Price increasing effect The effect in a competitive market of an increase in Demand or a decrease in Supply upon the Equilibrium price .

Price index An index number which shows how the average price of a "market basket" of goods changes through time. A price index is used to change nominal output (income) into real output (income).

Price leadership An informal method which the Firms in an Oligopoly *(see)* may employ to set the price of the product they produce: one firm (the leader) is the first to announce a change in price and the other firms (the followers) quickly announce identical (or similar) changes in price.

Price level The weighted average of the Prices paid for the final goods and services produced in the economy.

Price level surprises Unanticipated changes in the price level.

Price maker A seller (or buyer) of a commodity that is able to affect the price at which the commodity sells by changing the amount it sells (buys).

Price support The minimum price which government allows sellers to receive for a good or service; a price which is a legally established or maintained minimum price.

Price taker A seller (or buyer) of a commodity that is unable to affect the price at which a commodity sells by changing the amount it sells (or buys).

Price-wage flexibility Changes in the prices of products and in the Wages paid to workers; the ability of prices and Wages to rise or to fall.

Price war Successive and continued decreases in the prices charged by the firms in an oligopolistic industry by which each firm hopes to increase its sales and revenues and from which firms seldom benefit.

Priority principle The assignment of priorities to the planned outputs of the various sectors and industries in the economy of the U.S.S.R. and the shifting of resources, when bottlenecks develop, from low- to high-priority sectors and industries to assure the fulfillment of the production targets of the latter sectors and industries.

Private good A good or service to which the Exclusion principle *(see)* is applicable and which is provided by privately owned firms to those who are willing to pay for it.

Private property The right of private persons and Firms to obtain, own, control, employ, dispose of, and bequeath Land, Capital, and other Assets.

Private sector The Households and business firms of the economy.

Procompetition view of advertising Envisions advertising as a means of informing consumers that various products are substitutable, thereby reducing the market power of firms; advertising is a mechanism by which new products become established in markets.

Product differentiation Physical or other differences between the products produced by different Firms which result in individual buyers preferring (so long as the price changed by all sellers is the same) the product of one Firm to the Products of the other Firms.

Production possibilities curve A curve which shows the different combinations of two goods or services that can be produced in a Full-employment *(see)*, Full-production *(see)* economy in which the available supplies of resources and technology are constant.

Production possibilities table A table which shows the different combinations of two goods or services that can be produced in a Full-employment *(see)*, Full-production *(see)* economy in which the available supplies of resources and technology are constant.

Productive efficiency The production of a good in the least-costly way: employing the minimum quantity of resources needed to produce a given output and producing the output at which Average total cost is a minimum.

Productivity A measure of average output or real output per unit of input. For example, the productivity of labor may be determined by dividing hours of work into real output.

Productivity slowdown The recent decline in the rate at which Labor productivity *(see)* in the United States has increased.

Product market A market in which Households buy and Firms sell the products they have produced.

Profit *(See)* Economic profit and Normal profit; without an adjective preceding it, the income of those who supply the economy with Entrepreneurial ability *(see)* or Normal profit.

Profit-maximizing case The circumstances which result in an Economic profit *(see)* for a (competitive) Firm when it produces the output at which Economic profit is a maximum or losses a minimum: when the price at which the Firm can sell its product is greater than the Average (total) cost of producing it.

Profit-maximizing rule (combination of resources) The quantity of each resource a Firm must employ if its Economic profit *(see)* is to be a maximum or its losses a minimum; the combination in which the Marginal revenue product *(see)* of each resource is equal to its Marginal resource cost *(see)* (to its price if the resource is employed in a competitive market).

Progressive tax A tax such that the Average tax rate increases as the taxpayer's income increases and decreases as income decreases.

Property tax A tax on the value of property (Capital, Land, stocks and bonds, and other Assets) owned by Firms and Households.

Proportional tax A tax such that the Average tax rate remains constant as the taxpayer's income increases and decreases.

Proprietors' income The net income of the owners of unincorporated Firms (proprietorships and partnerships).

Prosperous industry (*See* Expanding industry.)

Protective tariff A Tariff *(see)* designed to protect domestic producers of a good from the competition of foreign producers.

Public assistance programs Programs which pay benefits to those who are unable to earn income (because of permanent handicaps or because they are dependent children) which are financed by general tax revenues, and which are viewed as public charity (rather than earned rights).

Public choice theory Generalizations that describe how government (the Public sector) makes decisions for the use of economic resources.

Public debt The total amount owed by the Federal government (to the owners of government securities) and equal to the sum of its past Budget deficits (less its budget surpluses).

Public finance The branch of economics which analyzes government revenues and expenditures.

Public good A good or service to which the Exclusion principle *(see)* is not applicable; and which is provided by government if it yields substantial benefits to society.

Public interest theory of regulation The presumption that the purpose of the regulation of an Industry is to protect the public (consumers) from the abuse of the power possessed by Natural monopolies *(see)*.

Public sector The part of the economy that contains all its governments; government.

Public-sector failure The failure of the Public sector (government) to resolve socioeconomic problems because it performs its functions in an economically inefficient fashion.

Public utility A Firm which produces an essential good or service, has obtained from a government the right to be the sole supplier of the good or service in the area, and is regulated by that government to prevent the abuse of its monopoly power.

Pure capitalism An economic system (method of organization) in which property resources are privately owned and markets and prices are used to direct and coordinate economic activities.

Pure competition (1) A market in which a very large number of Firms sells a Standardized product *(see)*, into which entry is very easy, in which the individual seller has no control over the price at which the product sells, and in which there is no Nonprice competition *(see)*; (2) a market in which there is a very large number of buyers.

Pure monopoly A market in which one Firm sells a unique product (one for which there are no close substitutes), into which entry is blocked, in which the Firm has considerable control over the price at which the product sells, and in which Nonprice competition *(see)* may or may not be found.

Pure profit *(See* Economic profit.)

Pure rate of interest *(See The* rate of interest.)

Pursuit and escape theory An explanation of the stability of labor's relative share of the National income *(see)* in which Labor tries to obtain (pursues) higher money wages by decreasing the Economic profits of capitalists and capitalists avoid (escape) a reduction in their profits by increasing the productivity of labor or the prices they charge for products.

Quantity-decreasing effect The effect in a competitive market of a decrease in Demand or a decrease in Supply upon the Equilibrium quantity *(see)*.

Quantity demanded The amount of a good or service buyers wish (or a buyer wishes) to purchase at a particular price during some period of time.

Quantity-increasing effect The effect in a competitive market of an increase in Demand or an increase in Supply upon the Equilibrium quantity *(see)*.

Quantity supplied The amount of a good or service sellers offer (or a seller offers) to sell at a particular price during some period of time.

Quasi-public bank A bank which is privately owned but governmentally (publicly) controlled; each of the Federal Reserve banks.

Quasi-public good A good or service to which the Exclusion principle *(see)* could be applied, but which has such a large Spillover benefit *(see)* that government sponsors its production to prevent an underallocation of resources.

R&D Research and development; activities undertaken to bring about Technological progress.

Ratchet effect The tendency for the Price level to rise when Aggregate demand increases, but not fall when Aggregate demand declines.

Rate of exchange The price paid in one's own money to acquire one unit of a foreign money; the rate at which the money of one nation is exchanged for the money of another nation.

Rate of interest Price paid for the use of Money or for the use of Capital; interest rate.

Rational An adjective that describes the behavior of any individual who consistently does those things that will enable him or her to achieve the declared objective of the individual; and that describes the behavior of a consumer who uses money income to buy the collection of goods and services that yields the maximum amount of Utility *(see)*.

Rational expectations theory The hypothesis that business firms and households expect monetary and fiscal policies to have certain effects on the economy and take, in pursuit of their own self-interests, actions which make these policies ineffective.

Rationing function of price The ability of a price in a competitive market to equalize Quantity demanded and Quantity supplied and to eliminate shortages and surpluses by rising or falling.

Reaganomics The policies of the Reagan administration based on Supply-side economics *(see)* and intended to reduce inflation and the Unemployment rate (Stagflation).

Real-balances effect The tendency for increases (decreases) in the price level to lower (raise) the real value (or purchasing power) of financial assets with fixed money values; and, as a result, to reduce (expand) total spending in the economy.

Real capital *(See* Capital.)

Real gross national product Gross national product *(see)* adjusted for changes in the price level; Gross national product in a year divided by the GNP deflator *(see)* for that year.

Real income The amount of goods and services an individual or group can purchase with his, her, or its Nominal income during some period of time; Nominal income adjusted for changes in the Price level.

Real interest rate The rate of interest expressed in dollars of constant value (adjusted for inflation); and equal to the Nominal interest rate *(see)* less the rate of inflation.

Real net national product (NNP) The NNP *(see)* measured in terms of a constant price level (adjusted for changes in the price level).

Real rate of interest The Real interest rate *(see)*.

Real wage The amount of goods and services a worker can purchase with his or her Money wage *(see)*; the purchasing power of the Money wage; the Money wage adjusted for changes in the Price level.

Real wage rate (*See* Real wage.)

Recessionary gap The amount by which the Aggregate expenditures schedule (curve) must increase (shift upward) to increase the real NNP to the full-employment noninflationary level.

Reciprocal Trade Agreements Act of 1934 The Federal act which gave the President the authority to negotiate agreements with foreign nations and lower American tariff rates by up to 50 percent if the foreign nations would reduce tariff rates on American goods and which incorporated Most-favored-nation clauses *(see)* in the agreements reached with these nations.

Refinancing the public debt Paying owners of maturing United States government securities with money obtained by selling new securities or with new securities.

Regressive tax A tax such that the Average tax rate decreases (increases) as the taxpayer's income increases (decreases).

Regulatory agency An agency (commission or board) established by the Federal or a state government to control for the benefit of the public the prices charged and the services offered (output produced) by a Natural monopoly *(see)*.

Remittance A gift or grant; a payment for which no good or service is received in return; the funds sent by workers who have legally or illegally entered a foreign nation to their families in the nations from which they have migrated.

Rental income Income received by those who supply the economy with Land *(see)*.

Rent-seeking behavior The pursuit through government of a transfer of income or wealth to a resource supplier, business, or consumer at someone else's or society's expense.

Required reserve ratio (*See* Reserve ratio.)

Required reserves (*See* Legal reserves.)

Reserve ratio The specified minimum percentage of its deposit liabilities which a Member bank *(see)* must keep on deposit at the Federal Reserve Bank in its district, or in Vault cash *(see)*.

Resource market A market in which Households sell and Firms buy the services of resources.

Retiring the public debt Reducing the size of the Public debt by paying money to owners of maturing United States government securities.

Revaluation An increase in the defined value of a currency.

Revenue tariff A Tariff *(see)* designed to produce income for the (Federal) government.

Right-to-work law A law which has been enacted in twenty states that makes it illegal in those states to require a worker to join a Labor union in order to retain his or her job with an employer.

Roundabout production The construction and use of Capital *(see)* to aid in the production of Consumer goods *(see)*.

Rule of reason The rule stated and applied in the U.S. Steel case *(see)* that only combinations and contracts that unreasonably restrain trade are subject to actions under the antitrust laws and that size and the possession of monopoly were not themselves illegal.

Rule of 70 A method by which the number of years it will take for the Price level to double can be calculated; divide 70 by the annual rate of inflation.

Sales tax A tax levied on expenditures for a broad group of products.

Saving Disposable income not spent for Consumer goods *(see)*; not spending for consumption; equal to Disposable income minus Personal consumption expenditures *(see)*.

Savings account A deposit in a Depository institution *(see)* which is interest-earning and which can normally be withdrawn by the depositor at any time (though the institution may legally require fourteen days' notice for withdrawal).

Savings and loan association A Firm which accepts deposits primarily from small individual savers, and lends primarily to individuals to finance purchases of residences.

Saving schedule Schedule which shows the amounts Households plan to save (plan not to spend for Consumer goods, *see*) at different levels of Disposable income.

Savings institution A Thrift institution *(see)*.

Say's Law The (discredited) macroeconomic generalization that the production of goods and services (supply) creates an equal Aggregate demand for these goods and services.

Scarce resources The fixed (limited) quantities of Land, Capital, Labor, and Entrepreneurial ability *(see all)* which are never sufficient to satisfy the material wants of humans because their wants are unlimited.

Schumpeter-Galbraith view (of oligopoly) The belief shared by these two economists that large oligopolistic firms are necessary if there is to be a rapid rate of technological progress (because only this kind of firm has both the means and the incentive to introduce technological changes).

Seasonal variation An increase or decrease during a single year in the level of economic activity caused by a change in the season.

Secondary boycott The refusal of a Labor union to buy or to work with the products produced by another union or a group of nonunion workers.

"Second economy" The semilegal and illegal markets and activities which exist side by side with the legal and official markets and activities in the U.S.S.R.

Secular trend The expansion or contraction in the level of economic activity over a long period of years.

Selective controls The techniques the Federal Reserve Banks employ to change the availability of certain specific types of credit.

Self-interest What each Firm, property owner, worker, and consumer believes is best for itself and seeks to obtain.

Seniority The length of time a worker has been employed by an employer relative to the lengths of time the employer's other workers have been employed; the principle which is used to determine which workers will be laid off when there is insufficient work for them all and who will be rehired when more work becomes available.

Separation of ownership and control Difference between the group that owns the Corporation (the stockholders) and the group that manages it (the directors and officers) and between the interests (goals) of the two groups.

Service That which is intangible (invisible) and for which a consumer, firm, or government is willing to exchange something of value.

Share draft account A deposit in a Credit union *(see)* against which a check may be written and which earns interest for the depositor (member).

Sherman Act The Federal antitrust act of 1890 which made monopoly, restraint of trade, and attempts, combinations, and conspiracies to monopolize or to restrain trade criminal offenses; and allowed the Federal government or injured parties to take legal action against those committing these offenses.

Short run A period of time in which producers of a product are able to change the quantity of some but not all of the resources they employ; in which some resources—the Plant *(see)*—are Fixed resources *(see)* and some are Variable resources *(see)*; in which some costs are Fixed costs *(see)* and some are Variable costs *(see)*; a period of time too brief to allow a Firm to vary its plant capacity but long enough to permit it to change the level at which the plant capacity is utilized; a period of time not long enough to enable Firms to enter or to leave an Industry *(see)*.

Short-run aggregate supply curve The aggregate supply curve relevant to a time period wherein input prices (particularly nominal wages) remain constant when the price level changes.

Short-run competitive equilibrium The price at which the total quantity of a product supplied in the Short run *(see)* by a purely competitive industry and the total quantity of the product demanded are equal and which is equal to or greater than the Average variable cost *(see)* of producing the product; and the quantity of the product demanded and supplied at this price.

Short-run farm problem The sharp year-to-year changes in the prices of agricultural products and in the incomes of farmers.

Simple multiplier The Multiplier *(see)* in an economy in which government collects no Net taxes *(see)*, there are no Imports *(see)*, and Investment *(see)* is independent of the level of income (Net national product); equal to one divided by the Marginal propensity to save *(see)*.

Single-tax movement The attempt of a group which followed the teachings of Henry George to eliminate all taxes except one which would tax all Rental income *(see)* at a rate of 100 percent.

Slope of a line The ratio of the vertical change (the rise or fall) to the horizontal change (the run) in moving between two points on a line. The slope of an upward sloping line is positive, reflecting a direct relationship between two variables; the slope of a downward sloping line is negative, reflecting an inverse relationship between two variables.

Smoot-Hawley Tariff Act Passed in 1930, this legislation established some of the highest tariffs in United States history. Its objective was to reduce imports and stimulate the domestic economy.

Social accounting *(See* National income accounting.)

Socially optimal price The price of a product which results in the most efficient allocation of an economy's resources and which is equal to the Marginal cost *(see)* of the last unit of the product produced.

Social regulation The newer and different type of regulation in which government is concerned with the conditions under which goods and services are produced, their physical characteristics, and the impact of their production upon society; in contrast to Industrial regulation *(see)*.

Social security programs The programs which replace the earnings lost when people retire or are temporarily unemployed, which are financed by Payroll taxes *(see)*, and which are viewed as earned rights (rather than charity).

Sole proprietorship An unincorporated business firm owned and operated by a single person.

Special-interest effect Effect on public decision making and the allocation of resources in the economy when government promotes the interests (goals) of small groups to the detriment of society as a whole.

Specialization The use of the resources of an individual, a Firm, a region, or a nation to produce one or a few goods and services.

Spillover A benefit or cost associated with the consumption or production of a good or service which is obtained by or inflicted without compensation upon a party other than the buyer or seller of the good or service; (*see* Spillover benefit and Spillover cost).

Spillover benefit The benefit obtained neither by producers nor by consumers of a product but without compensation by a third party (society as a whole).

Spillover cost The cost of producing a product borne neither by producers nor by consumers of the product but without compensation by a third party (society as a whole).

SSI (*See* Supplemental security income.)

Stabilization fund A stock of money and of a commodity that is used to prevent the price of the commodity from changing by buying (selling) the commodity when its price decreases (increases).

Stabilization policy dilemma The use of monetary and fiscal policy to decrease the Unemployment rate increases the rate of inflation, and the use of monetary and fiscal policy to decrease the rate of inflation increases the Unemployment rate.

Stagflation Inflation accompanied by stagnation in the rate of growth of output and a high unemployment rate in the economy; simultaneous increases in both the Price level and the Unemployment rate.

Standardized product A product such that buyers are indifferent to the seller from whom they purchase it so long as the price charged by all sellers is the same; a product such that all units of the product are perfect substitutes for each other (are identical).

State bank A Commercial bank chartered to engage in the business of banking by a state government.

State ownership The ownership of property (Land and Capital) by government (the state); in the U.S.S.R. by the central government (the nation).

Static economy (1) An economy in which Net private domestic investment *(see)* is equal to zero—Gross private domestic investment *(see)* is equal to the Capital consumption allowances *(see)*; (2) an economy in which the supplies of resources, technology, and the tastes of consumers do not change and in which, therefore, the economic future is perfectly predictable and there is no uncertainty.

Store of value Any Asset *(see)* or wealth set aside for future use.

Strike The withholding of their labor services by an organized group of workers (a Labor union).

Strikebreaker A person employed by a Firm when its employees are engaged in a strike against the firm.

Structural-change hypothesis The explanation that attributes the relative decline of unionism in the United States to changes in the structure of the economy and of the labor force.

Structural deficit The difference between Federal tax revenues and expenditures when the economy is at full employment.

Structural unemployment Unemployment caused by changes in the structure of demand for Consumer goods and in technology; workers who are unemployed either because their skills are not demanded by employers or because they lack sufficient skills to obtain employment.

Subsidy A payment of funds (or goods and services) by a government, business firm, or household for which it receives no good or service in return. When made by a government, it is a Government transfer payment *(see)*.

Substitute goods Goods or services such that there is a direct relationship between the price of one and the Demand for the other; when the price of one falls (rises) the Demand for the other decreases (increases).

Substitution effect (1) The effect which a change in the price of a Consumer good would have upon the relative expensiveness of that good and the resulting effect upon the quantity of the good a consumer would purchase if the consumer's Real income *(see)* remained constant; (2) the effect which a change in the price of a resource would have upon the quantity of the resource employed by a firm if the firm did not change its output.

Superior good (*See* Normal good.)

Supplemental security income A program Federally financed and administered which provides a uniform nationwide minimum income for the aged, blind, and disabled who do not qualify for benefits under the Old age, survivors, and disability health insurance *(see)* or Unemployment insurance *(see)* programs in the United States.

Supply A Supply schedule or a Supply curve *(see both)*.

Supply curve A curve which shows the amounts of a good or service sellers (a seller) will offer to sell at various prices during some period of time.

Supply factor An increase in the available quantity of a resource, an improvement in its quality, or an expansion of technological knowledge which makes it possible for an economy to produce a greater output of goods and services.

Supply schedule A schedule which shows the amounts of a good or service sellers (or seller) will offer to sell at various prices during some period of time.

Supply shock One of several events of the 1970s and early 1980s which increased production costs, decreased Aggregate supply, and generated Stagflation in the United States.

Supply-side economics The part of modern macroeconomics that emphasizes the role of costs and Aggregate supply in its explanation of Inflation and unemployed labor.

Supply-side view The view of fiscal policy held by the advocates of Supply-side economics which emphasizes increasing Aggregate supply *(see)* as a means of reducing the Unemployment rate and Inflation and encouraging Economic Growth.

Support price *(See* Price support.)

Sympathy strike Withholding from an employer the labor services of its members by a Labor union that does not have a disagreement with the employer but wishes to assist another Labor union that does have a disagreement with the employer.

Tacit collusion Any method utilized in a Collusive oligopoly *(see)* to set prices and outputs or the market area of each firm that does not involve outright (or overt) collusion (formal agreements or secret meetings); and of which Price leadership *(see)* is a frequent example.

Taft-Hartley Act The Federal act of 1947 which marked the shift from government sponsorship to government regulation of Labor unions.

Tangent The point at which a line touches, but does not intersect, a curve.

Target dilemma A problem which arises because monetary authorities cannot simultaneously stabilize both the money supply and the level of interest rates.

Tariff A tax imposed (only by the Federal government in the United States) on an imported good.

Tax A nonvoluntary payment of money (or goods and services) to a government by a Household or Firm for which the Household or Firm receives no good or service directly in return and which is not a fine imposed by a court for an illegal act.

Tax incidence The income or purchasing power which different persons and groups lose as a result of the imposition of a tax after Tax shifting *(see)* has occurred.

Tax Reform Act of 1986 Federal legislation which broadened the personal income tax base, but also lowered both tax rates and the number of tax brackets.

Tax shifting The transfer to others of all or part of a tax by charging them a higher price or by paying them a lower price for a good or service.

Tax-transfer disincentives Decreases in the incentives to work, save, invest, innovate, and take risks that allegedly result from high Marginal tax rates and Transfer-payment programs.

Tax "wedge" Such taxes as Indirect business taxes *(see)* and Payroll taxes *(see)* which are treated as a cost by business firms and reflected in the prices of the products produced by them; equal to the price of the product less the cost of the resources required to produce it.

Technology The body of knowledge that can be used to produce goods and services from Economic resources.

Terms of trade The rate at which units of one product can be exchanged for units of another product; the Price *(see)* of a good or service; the amount of one good or service that must be given up to obtain one unit of another good or service.

Theory of human capital Generalization that Wage differentials *(see)* are the result of differences in the amount of Human capital investment *(see)*; and that the incomes of lower-paid workers are increased by increasing the amount of such investment.

The **rate of interest** The Rate of interest *(see)* which is paid solely for the use of Money over an extended period of time and which excludes the charges made for the riskiness of the loan and its administrative costs; and which is approximately equal to the rate of interest paid on the long-term and virtually riskless bonds of the United States government.

Thrift institution A Savings and loan association, Mutual savings bank, or Credit union *(see all)*.

Tight money policy Contracting, or restricting the growth of, the nation's Money supply *(see)*.

Till money *(See* Vault cash.)

Time deposit An interest-earning deposit in a Depository institution *(see)* which may be withdrawn by the depositor without a loss of interest on or after a specific date or at the end of a specific period of time.

Token money Coins which have a Face value *(see)* greater than their Intrinsic value *(see)*.

Total cost The sum of Fixed cost *(see)* and Variable cost *(see)*.

Total demand The Demand schedule *(see)* or the Demand curve *(see)* of all buyers of a good or service.

Total demand for money The sum of the Transactions demand for money *(see)* and Asset demand for money *(see)*; the relationship between the total amount of money demanded, nominal GNP, and the Rate of Interest.

Total product The total output of a particular good or service produced by a firm (a group of firms or the entire economy).

Total revenue The total number of dollars received by a Firm (or Firms) from the sale of a product; equal to the total expenditures for the product produced by the Firm (or Firms); equal to the quantity sold (demanded) multiplied by the price at which it is sold—by the Average revenue *(see)* from its sale.

Total-revenue–total-cost approach The method which finds the output at which Economic profit *(see)* is a maximum or losses a minimum by comparing the Total revenue and the Total costs of a Firm at different outputs.

Total-revenue test A test to determine whether Demand is Elastic *(see)*, Inelastic *(see)*, or of Unitary elasticity *(see)* between any two prices: Demand is elastic (inelastic, unit elastic) if the Total revenue *(see)* of sellers of the commodity increases (decreases, remains constant) when the price of the commodity falls; or Total revenue decreases (increases, remains constant) when its price rises.

Total spending The total amount buyers of goods and services spend or plan to spend.

Total supply The Supply schedule *(see)* or the Supply curve *(see)* of all sellers of a good or service.

Trade balance The export of merchandise (goods) of a nation less its imports of merchandise (goods).

Trade controls Tariffs *(see)*, export subsidies, Import quotas *(see)*, and other means a nation may employ to reduce Imports *(see)* and expand Exports *(see)* in order to eliminate a Balance of payments deficit *(see)*.

Trade deficit The amount by which a nation's imports of merchandise (goods) exceed its exports of merchandise (goods).

Trade surplus The amount by which a nation's exports of merchandise (goods) exceed its imports of merchandise (goods).

Trading possibilities line A line which shows the different combinations of two products an economy is able to obtain (consume) when it specializes in the production of one product and trades (exports) this product to obtain the other product.

Traditional economy An economic system (method of organization) in which traditions and customs determine how the economy will use its scarce resources.

Traditional view (of oligopoly) The belief that oligopoly (because it is similar to Monopoly) will result in smaller outputs, higher prices and profits, and slower technological progress.

Transactions demand for money The amount of money people want to hold to use as a Medium of exchange (to make payments); and which varies directly with the nominal GNP.

Transfer payment A payment of money (or goods and services) by a government or a Firm to a Household or Firm for which the payer receives no good or service directly in return.

Truth in Lending Act Federal law enacted in 1968 that is designed to protect consumers who borrow; and that requires the lender to state in concise and uniform language the costs and terms of the credit (the finance charges and the annual percentage rate of interest).

Turnover tax The tax added to the accounting price of a good in the U.S.S.R. to determine the price at which the quantity of the good demanded will equal the quantity of the good it has been decided to produce, the rate of taxation being higher on relatively scarce and lower on relatively abundant goods.

Tying agreement A promise made by a buyer when allowed to purchase a patented product from a seller that it will make all of its purchases of certain other products from the same seller; and a practice forbidden by the Clayton Act *(see)*.

Unanticipated inflation Inflation *(see)* at a rate which was greater than the rate expected in that period of time.

Underemployment Failure to produce the maximum amount of goods and services that can be produced from the resources employed; failure to achieve Full production *(see)*.

Undistributed corporate profits The after-tax profits of corporations not distributed as dividends to stockholders; corporate or business saving.

Unemployment Failure to use all available Economic resources to produce goods and services; failure of the economy to employ fully its Labor force *(see)*.

Unemployment compensation (*See* Unemployment insurance.)

Unemployment insurance The insurance program which in the United States is financed by state Payroll taxes *(see)* on employers and makes income available to workers who are unable to find jobs.

Unemployment rate The percentage of the Labor force *(see)* that is unemployed at any time.

Unfair competition Any practice which is employed by a Firm either to eliminate a rival or to block the entry of a new Firm into an Industry and which society (or a rival) believes to be an unacceptable method of achieving these ends.

Uninsurable risk An event, the occurrence of which is uncontrollable and unpredictable, which would result in a loss that cannot be avoided by purchasing insurance and must be assumed by an entrepreneur (*See* Entrepreneurial ability); sometimes called "uncertainty."

Union shop A place of employment at which the employer may hire either labor union members or workers who are not members of the union but who must become members within a specified period of time or lose their jobs.

Unitary elasticity The Elasticity coefficient *(see)* is equal to one; the percentage change in the quantity (demanded or supplied) is equal to the percentage change in price.

United States–Canadian Free-Trade Agreement An accord signed in 1988 to eliminate all trade barriers between the two nations over a 10-year period

Unit labor cost Labor costs per unit of output; equal to the Money wage rate *(see)* divided by the Average product *(see)* of labor.

Unlimited liability Absence of any limit on the maximum amount that may be lost by an individual and that the individual may become legally required to pay; the amount that may be lost and that a sole proprietor or partner may be required to pay.

Unlimited wants The insatiable desire of consumers (people) for goods and services that will give them pleasure or satisfaction.

Unplanned investment Actual investment less Planned investment; increases or decreases in the inventories of business firms that result from production greater than sales.

Unprosperous industry (*See* Declining industry.)

Urban sprawl The movement of people and firms from the central city and into the suburbs of a metropolitan area and the resulting expansion of the geographic size of the metropolitan area.

User charge A price paid by those who use a facility which covers the full cost of using the facility.

U.S. Steel case The antitrust action brought by the Federal government against the U.S. Steel Corporation in which the courts ruled (in 1920) that only unreasonable restraints of trade were illegal and size and the possession of monopoly power were not violations of the antitrust laws.

Utility The want-satisfying power of a good or service; the satisfaction or pleasure a consumer obtains from the consumption of a good or service (or from the consumption of a collection of goods and services).

Utility-maximizing rule To obtain the greatest Utility *(see)* the consumer should allocate his Money income so that the last dollar spent on each good or service yields the same Marginal utility *(see)*; so that the Marginal util-

ity of each good or service divided by its price is the same for all goods and services.

Value added The value of the product sold by a Firm less the value of the goods (materials) purchased and used by the Firm to produce the product; and equal to the revenue which can be used for Wages, rent, interest, and profits.

Value-added tax A tax imposed upon the difference between the value of the goods sold by a firm and the value of the goods purchased by the firm from other firms.

Value judgment Opinion of what is desirable or undesirable; belief regarding what ought or ought not to be (regarding what is right or just and wrong or unjust).

Value of money The quantity of goods and services for which a unit of money (a dollar) can be exchanged; the purchasing power of a unit of money; the reciprocal of the Price level.

Variable cost A cost which in total increases (decreases) when the firm increases (decreases) its output; the cost of Variable resources *(see)*.

Variable resource Any resource employed by a firm the quantity of which can be increased or decreased (varied).

VAT Value-added tax *(see)*.

Vault cash The Currency *(see)* a bank has in its safe (vault) and cash drawers.

Velocity of money The number of times per year the average dollar in the Money supply *(see)* is spent for Final goods *(see)*.

VERs (*See* Voluntary export restrictions.)

Vertical axis The "up–down" or "north–south" axis on a graph or grid.

Vertical combination A group of Plants *(see)* engaged in different stages of the production of a final product and owned by a single Firm *(see)*.

Vertical intercept The point at which a line meets the vertical axis of a graph.

Vertical merger The merger of one or more Firms engaged in different stages of the production of a final product into a single Firm.

Vicious circle of poverty A problem common to the less developed countries wherein their low per capita incomes are an obstacle to realizing the levels of saving and investment requisite to acceptable rates of economic growth.

Voice mechanism Communication by workers through their union to resolve grievances with an employer.

Voluntary export restrictions The limitation by firms of their exports to particular foreign nations in order to avoid the erection of other trade barriers by the foreign nations.

Wage The price paid for Labor (for the use or services of Labor, *see*) per unit of time (per hour, per day, etc.).

Wage and salary supplements Payments made by employers of Labor into social insurance and private pension, health, and welfare funds for workers; and a part of the employer's cost of obtaining Labor.

Wage differential The difference between the Wage *(see)* received by one worker or group of workers and that received by another worker or group of workers.

Wage discrimination The payments to blacks (or other minority groups) of a wage lower than that paid to whites for doing the same work.

Wage guidepost Wages *(see)* in all industries in the economy should increase at an annual rate equal to the rate of increase in the Average product *(see)* of Labor in the economy.

Wage-price controls A Wage-price policy *(see)* that legally fixes the maximum amounts by which Wages *(see)* and prices may be increased in any period of time.

Wage-price guideposts A Wage-price policy *(see)* that depends upon the voluntary cooperation of Labor unions and business firms.

Wage-price inflationary spiral Increases in wage rates which bring about increases in prices which in turn result in further increases in wage rates and in prices.

Wage-price policy Government policy that attempts to alter the behavior of Labor unions and business firms in order to make their Wage and price decisions more nearly compatible with the goals of Full employment and a stable price level.

Wage rate (*See* Wage.)

Wages The income of those who supply the economy with Labor *(see)*.

Wagner Act The Federal act of 1938 which established the National Labor Relations Board *(see)*, guaranteed the rights of Labor unions to organize and to bargain collectively with employers, and listed and prohibited a number of unfair labor practices by employers.

Wastes of monopolistic competition The waste of economic resources that is the result of producing an output at which price is less than marginal cost and average cost is less than the minimum average cost.

Wealth effect (*See* Real balances effect.)

Welfare programs (*See* Public assistance programs.)

Wheeler-Lea Act The Federal act of 1938 which amended the Federal Trade Commission Act *(see)* by prohibiting and giving the commission power to investigate unfair and deceptive acts or practices on commerce (false and misleading advertising and the misrepresentation of products).

(The) "will to develop" Wanting economic growth strongly enough to change from old to new ways of doing things.

Workfare plans Reforms of the welfare system, particularly AFDC, designed to provide education and training for recipients so that they may move from public assistance to gainful employment.

World bank A bank supported by 151 nations which lends (and guarantees loans) to less developed nations to assist them to grow; formally, the International Bank for Reconstruction and Development.

X-inefficiency Failure to produce any given output at the lowest average (and total) cost possible.

Yellow-dog contract The (now illegal) contract in which an employee agrees when he or she accepts employment with a Firm that he or she will not become a member of a Labor union while employed by the Firm.

Index

National income and related statistics for years, 1965–1988

National income statistics are in billions of current dollars. Details may not add to totals because of rounding.

			1965	1966	1967	1968	1969	1970	1971	1972	1973	1974
THE SUM OF	1	Personal consumption expenditures	440.7	477.3	503.6	552.5	597.9	640.0	691.6	757.6	837.2	916.5
	2	Gross private domestic investment	116.2	128.6	125.7	137.0	153.2	148.8	172.5	202.0	238.8	240.8
	3	Government purchases of goods and services	138.6	158.6	179.7	197.7	207.3	218.2	232.4	250.0	266.5	299.1
	4	Net exports	9.7	7.5	7.4	5.5	5.6	8.5	6.3	3.2	16.8	16.3
EQUALS	5	Gross national product	705.1	772.0	816.4	892.7	963.9	1,015.5	1,102.7	1,212.8	1,359.3	1,472.8
LESS	6	Capital consumption allowance	57.4	62.1	67.4	73.9	81.4	88.8	97.5	107.9	118.1	137.5
EQUALS	7	Net national product	647.7	709.9	749.0	818.7	882.5	926.6	1,005.1	1,104.8	1,241.2	1,335.4
LESS	8	Indirect business taxes	62.5	67.9	71.3	79.6	84.4	94.0	107.0	110.7	118.5	131.9
EQUALS	9	National income	585.2	642.0	677.7	739.1	798.1	832.6	898.1	994.1	1,122.7	1,203.5
LESS	10	Social security contributions	31.6	40.6	45.5	50.4	57.9	62.2	68.9	79.0	97.6	110.5
	11	Corporate income taxes	30.9	33.7	32.7	39.4	39.7	34.4	37.7	41.9	49.3	51.8
	12	Undistributed corporate profits	31.3	33.5	31.2	29.3	25.2	17.8	26.5	34.4	37.0	20.2
PLUS	13	Transfer payments	60.6	66.6	76.2	87.2	97.6	113.6	129.0	142.8	162.9	189.1
EQUALS	14	Personal income	552.0	600.8	644.5	707.2	772.9	831.8	894.0	981.6	1,101.7	1,210.1
LESS	15	Personal taxes	65.2	74.9	82.4	97.7	116.3	116.2	117.3	142.0	152.0	171.8
EQUALS	16	Disposable income	486.8	525.9	562.1	609.6	656.7	715.6	776.8	839.6	949.8	1,038.4
	17	Real gross national product (1982 dollars)	2,087.6	2,208.3	2,271.4	2,365.6	2,423.3	2,416.2	2,484.8	2,608.5	2,744.1	2,729.3
	18	Percent change in real GNP	5.8	5.8	2.9	4.1	2.4	−.3	2.8	5.0	5.2	−.5
	19	Real disposable income per capita (in 1982 dollars)	1,365.7	1,431.3	1,493.2	1,551.3	1,599.8	1,668.1	1,728.4	1,797.4	1,916.3	1,896.6

RELATED STATISTICS			1965	1966	1967	1968	1969	1970	1971	1972	1973	1974
	20	Consumer price index (1982–84 = 100)	31.5	32.4	33.4	34.8	36.7	38.8	40.5	41.8	44.4	49.3
	21	Rate of inflation (%)	1.6	2.9	3.1	4.2	5.5	5.7	4.4	3.2	6.2	11.0
	22	Index of industrial production (1977 = 100)	66.1	72.0	73.5	77.6	81.2	78.5	79.6	87.3	94.4	93.0
	23	Supply of money, M1 (in billions of dollars)	169.5	173.7	185.1	199.4	205.8	216.6	230.8	252.0	265.9	277.5
	24	Population (in millions)	194.3	196.6	198.7	200.7	202.7	205.1	207.7	209.9	211.9	213.8
	25	Civilian labor force (in millions)	74.5	75.8	77.3	78.7	80.7	82.8	84.4	87.0	89.4	91.9
	26	Unemployment (in millions)	3.4	2.9	3.0	2.8	2.8	4.1	5.0	4.9	4.4	5.2
	27	Unemployment as a % of civilian labor force	4.5	3.8	3.8	3.6	3.5	4.9	5.9	5.6	4.9	5.6
	28	Index of productivity (1977 = 100)	81.0	83.2	85.5	87.8	87.8	88.4	91.3	94.1	95.9	93.9
	29	Annual change in productivity (%)	3.0	2.8	2.7	2.7	.1	.7	3.2	3.0	2.0	−2.1